They enhance the **learning of critical thinking, problem solving, and performance skills** of individuals with ELN, and increase their self-awareness, self-management, self-control, self-reliance, and self-esteem. Moreover, special educators emphasize the **development, maintenance, and generalization** of knowledge and skills across environments, settings, and the lifespan.

## Special Education Content Standard 5:
## LEARNING ENVIRONMENTS AND SOCIAL INTERACTIONS

Special educators actively **create learning environments** for individuals with ELN that foster cultural understanding, safety and emotional well-being, positive social interactions, and **active engagement** of individuals with ELN. In addition, special educators **foster environments in which diversity is valued** and individuals are taught to live harmoniously and productively in a culturally diverse world. Special educators shape **environments to encourage the independence,** self-motivation, self-direction, personal empowerment, and self-advocacy of individuals with ELN. Special educators **help their general education colleagues integrate individuals** with ELN in regular environments and engage them in meaningful learning activities and interactions. Special educators use **direct motivational and instructional interventions** with individuals with ELN to teach them to respond effectively to current expectations. When necessary, special educators can safely **intervene with individuals with ELN in crisis.** Special educators coordinate all these efforts and provide **guidance and direction to paraeducators and others,** such as classroom volunteers and tutors.

## Special Education Content Standard 6:
## COMMUNICATION

Special educators understand **typical and atypical language development** and the ways in which exceptional conditions can interact with an individual's experience with and use of language. Special educators use individualized strategies to **enhance language development** and **teach communication skills** to individuals with ELN. Special educators are familiar with **augmentative, alternative, and assis-**tive technologies to support and enhance communication of individuals with exceptional needs. Special educators match their communication methods to an individual's language proficiency and cultural and linguistic differences. Special educators provide **effective language models** and they use communication strategies and resources to **facilitate understanding of subject matter for individuals with ELN whose primary language is not English.**

## Special Education Content Standard 7:
## INSTRUCTIONAL PLANNING

Individualized decision-making and instruction is at the center of special education practice. Special educators develop **long-range individualized instructional plans** anchored in both general and special curricula. In addition, special educators systematically translate these individualized plans into carefully selected **shorter-range goals and objectives,** taking into consideration an individual's abilities and needs, the learning environment, and a myriad of cultural and linguistic factors. Individualized instructional plans emphasize **explicit modeling** and **efficient guided practice** to assure acquisition and fluency through maintenance and generalization. Understanding of these factors, as well as the implications of an individual's exceptional condition, guides the special educator's selection, adaptation, and creation of materials, and the use of powerful instructional variables. Instructional plans are **modified based on ongoing analysis of the individual's learning progress.** Moreover, special educators facilitate this instructional planning in a **collaborative context** including the individuals with exceptionalities, families, professional colleagues, and personnel from other agencies as appropriate. Special educators also develop a variety of **individualized transition plans,** such as transitions from preschool to elementary school and from secondary settings to a variety of postsecondary work and learning contexts. Special educators are comfortable using **appropriate technologies** to support instructional planning and individualized instruction.

## Special Education Content Standard 8:
## ASSESSMENT

Assessment is integral to the decision-making and teaching of special educators, and special educators use **multiple types of assessment information** for a variety of educational decisions. Special educators use the results of assessments to help identify exceptional learning needs and to develop and implement individualized instructional programs, as well as to adjust instruction in response to ongoing learning progress. Special educators understand the **legal policies and ethical principles of measurement and assessment** related to referral, eligibility, program planning, instruction, and placement for individuals with ELN, including those from culturally and linguistically diverse backgrounds. Special educators understand **measurement theory and practices** for addressing issues of validity, reliability, norms, bias, and interpretation of assessment results. In addition, special educators understand the appropriate **use and limitations** of various types of assessments. Special educators collaborate with families and other colleagues to assure **non-biased, meaningful assessments and decision-making.** Special educators conduct **formal and informal assessments** of behavior, learning, achievement, and environments to design learning experiences that support the growth and development of individuals with ELN. Special educators use assessment information to **identify supports and adaptations** required for individuals with ELN to access the general curriculum and to participate in school-, system-, and statewide assessment programs. Special educators **regularly monitor the progress** of individuals with ELN in general and special curricula. Special educators use **appropriate technologies** to support their assessments.

## Special Education Content Standard 9:
## PROFESSIONAL AND ETHICAL PRACTICE

Special educators are guided by the profession's ethical and professional practice standards. Special educators practice in multiple roles and complex situations across wide age and developmental ranges. Their practice requires ongoing attention to **legal matters** along with serious professional and **ethical considerations.** Special educators engage in **professional activities** and participate in learning communities that benefit individuals with ELN, their families, colleagues, and their own professional growth. Special educators view themselves as **life-long learners** and regularly reflect on and adjust their practice. Special educators are aware of how their own and others' attitudes, behaviors, and ways of communicating can influence their practice. Special educators understand that culture and language can interact with exceptionalities, and [they] are **sensitive to the many aspects of diversity** of individuals with ELN and their families. Special educators actively plan and engage in activities that foster their professional growth and keep them **current with evidence-based best practices.** Special educators know their own limits of practice and practice within them.

## Special Education Content Standard 10:
## COLLABORATION

Special educators routinely and effectively **collaborate with families, other educators, related service providers, and personnel from community agencies in culturally responsive ways.** This collaboration assures that the needs of individuals with ELN are addressed throughout schooling. Moreover, special educators embrace their special role as advocates for individuals with ELN. Special educators promote and advocate the learning and well-being of individuals with ELN across a wide range of settings and a range of different learning experiences. Special educators are viewed as specialists by a myriad of people who actively seek their collaboration to effectively include and teach individuals with ELN. Special educators are a **resource to their colleagues** in understanding the laws and policies relevant to individuals with ELN. Special educators use collaboration to **facilitate the successful transitions** of individuals with ELN across settings and services.

## IDEA 2004 Update Edition

# Human Exceptionality

## School, Community, and Family

**EIGHTH EDITION**

**Michael L. Hardman**
University of Utah

**Clifford J. Drew**
University of Utah

**M. Winston Egan**
Brigham Young University

**ALLYN AND BACON**

Boston    New York    San Francisco
Mexico City    Montreal    Toronto    London    Madrid    Munich    Paris
Hong Kong    Singapore    Tokyo    Cape Town    Sydney

Executive Editor:  Virginia Lanigan

Development Editor:  Sonny Regelman

Executive Marketing Manager:  Amy Cronin Jordan

Associate Editor:  Tom Jefferies

Editorial Assistant:  Scott Blaszak

Senior Production Editor:  Annette Pagliaro

Editorial-Production Service:  Barbara Gracia

Manufacturing Buyer:  Andrew Turso

Text Designer:  Geri Davis

Electronic Composition:  Modern Graphics, Inc.

Text Illustrations:  Schneck-DePippo Graphics

Photo Research:  Katharine S. Cook

Cover Administrator:  Linda Knowles

Printed in the United States of America

10 9 8 7 6 5 4 3 2 1—VHP—08 07 06 05

Photo credits appear on page 638, which constitutes a continuation of the copyright page.

# What is an IDEA 2004 Update Edition?

*Human Exceptionality: School, Community, and Family,* Eighth Edition, has been updated to reflect this long-anticipated legislation in two ways . . .

- **Relevant discussion throughout the book has been revised to reflect IDEA '04.** These revisions have been made while still preserving the original pagination of the text, so no changes to lecture notes or reading assignments are necessary, and all supplementary materials (and page references therein) remain accurate. An "IDEA 2004" icon appears in the margins adjacent to the updates.

- **A guide to IDEA 2004 has been included as an appendix.** This clear, comprehensive, jargon-free appendix gives a brief side-by-side comparison of IDEA '04 versus the previous '97 legislation for each of the statutes. When a little friendly "background" would help the reader better understand the practical implications of the law, an additional note is provided.

---

more of the following areas: oral expression, listening comprehension, written expression, basic reading skill, reading comprehension, mathematical calculation, or mathematical reasoning.

The meaning of the term *severe discrepancy* is debated among professionals (e.g., Van den Broeck, 2002; Willson, & Reynolds, 2002). Although it is often stipulated as a classification parameter, there is no broadly accepted way to measure it. What is an "acceptable" discrepancy between a child's achievement and what is expected at his or her grade level—25 percent? 35 percent? 50 percent? Recent research on discrepancy classifications, particularly in reading, have found that the discrepancy concept is not strongly supported by data (Stuebing et al., 2002).

In recognizing the controversy surrounding the use of a "discrepancy formula" as the only criteria for determining eligibility for special education services, IDEA 2004 no longer required that school districts must take into consideration whether a child has a severe discrepancy between intellectual ability and achievement. In using evaluation procedures to determine whether a child has a specific learning disability, schools now have the option of using a process that determines a child's **response to intervention (RTI)** that is scientific and research-based. (IDEA 2004, PL 108-446, Sec.614(b))

Lack of agreement about concepts basic to the field has caused difficulties in both research and treatment. Nonetheless, many people who display the challenging characteristics of learning disabilities are successful in life and have become leaders in their fields (an example is Charles "Pete" Conrad Jr., who became an astronaut).

## Prevalence

Problems in determining the numbers of people with learning disabilities are amplified by differing definitions, theoretical views, and assessment procedures. Prevalence estimates are highly variable, ranging from 2.7% to 30% of the school-age population (Gettinger & Koscik, 2001; Lerner, 2003). Within the total school-age population, the most reasonable estimates range from 5% to 10%, as shown in Figure 7.1.

**Response to Intervention**
A term that describes how a student responds to instructional interventions that have been determined to be effective through scientifically based research.

**FOCUS 3**
Give two current estimated ranges for the prevalence of learning disabilities.

**FIGURE 7.1**

**The Prevalence of Learning Disabilities for Students 6–21 Years of Age**

4.45% Learning disabilities

50% All other disabilities | 50% Learning disabilities

Total School-Age Population

School-Age Population with Disabilities

SOURCE: U.S. Department of Education, 2000a.

www.ablongman.com/hardman8e          PREVALENCE  171

---

### IDEA '97 (P.L. 105-17)

*Sec. 612(a)(15). Personnel Standards.*

1. States must establish and maintain standards to ensure that personnel are appropriately and adequately prepared and trained. Standards must be consistent with any State-approved or recognized certification or licensure or other comparable requirements.

2. To the extent those standards are not based on the highest State requirements applicable to a specific profession or discipline, the State is taking steps to retrain or hire personnel that meet the highest requirements.

3. State standards shall allow appropriately trained and supervised paraprofessionals and assistants to assist in provision of services.

4. States may require LEAs to make ongoing good faith efforts to recruit and hire appropriately and adequately trained personnel, including where there are shortages, individuals who will meet the highest standard within three years.

### IDEA '04 (P.L. 108-446)

*Sec. 612(a)(14). Personnel Qualifications.* Throughout the law, the word *standards* has been replaced by the word *qualifications* in regard to personnel issues. The "highest requirement" language has been eliminated. Other changes include:

1. Qualifications established for related services personnel must ensure that those individuals meet any State-approved or State-recognized certification, licensure, registration, or other comparable requirements. Licensure or certification may not have been waived on an emergency, temporary, or provisional basis.

2. Special education teachers must be highly qualified by the NCLB deadline (not later than the end of the 2005–06 school year).

3. Language regarding three-year waiver to meet highest standard has been eliminated. Instead, the State must adopt a policy that requires LEAs to take "measurable steps to recruit, hire, train, and retain highly qualified personnel."

4. This provision does not create a right of action for the failure of a staff person to be highly qualified. However, parents may file a State complaint about staff qualifications.

**Personnel Qualifications.** In the conference report, the Conference Committee states its intention that SEAs establish "rigorous qualifications" (p. 192) for related services personnel. The Committee felt that SEAs needed greater flexibility and should consult with other State agencies, LEAs, and the professional organizations representing the service providers in establishing these standards.

*Sec. 612(a)(16). Performance Goals and Indicators.* States must establish performance goals consistent with standards for students without disabilities. States must have performance indicators to assess progress toward meeting performance goals that, at a minimum, address performance on assessments and dropout and graduation rates.

*Sec. 612(a)(15). Performance Goals and Indictors.* Additions include:

1. Performance goals must be the same as the State's definition of adequate yearly progress, including the State's objectives for progress by children with disabilities, as required under NCLB.

2. States report annually on progress toward meeting goals, which may include elements of the reports required under NCLB.

**Performance Goals and Indicators.** Performance goals for students with disabilities must conform to the State's definition of "adequate yearly progress" (AYP) under NCLB. AYP is a measure established by each State to demonstrate students' progress in meeting proficiency on assessments keyed to the State's academic achievement standards. Students with disabilities constitute a specific subgroup under NCLB, and data on those students' progress must be disaggregated and publicly reported.

*Sec. 612(a)(17). Participation in Assessments.* Children with disabilities will be included in general State- and district-wide assessments, with appropriate accommodations.

1. State or LEA, as appropriate, develops guidelines for participation and develops and conducts alternate assessments.

2. State must report, with the same frequency as for children without disabilities, on the number of children with disabilities taking regular and alternate assessments and on the performance on those assessments.

*Sec. 612(a)(16) Participation in Assessments.* Adds the following:

1. *All* children with disabilities participate in *all* assessments, with accommodations and alternate assessments as indicated on the IEP.

2. State, or, for district-wide assessments, the LEA guidelines must provide for alternate assessments aligned with the State's academic content and achievement standards. If the State has adopted alternate achievement standards, students working under those standards are assessed on those standards.

www.ablongman.com/hardman8e          APPENDIX: WHAT EVERY TEACHER SHOULD KNOW ABOUT IDEA 2004   557

This book is dedicated to people with differences everywhere, who have risen to the challenge of living in a society that is sometimes nurturing, but all too often ambivalent.

To our families, a loving and appreciative thank you for being so patient and caring during the more than 25 years of writing, rewriting, and revising this text.

MLH
CJD
MWE

# Brief Contents

# Contents

# 3 Inclusion and Collaboration in the Early Childhood and Elementary School Years        57

# 4 Transition and Adult Life    91

## 7 Learning Disabilities    165

# Attention-Deficit/Hyperactivity Disorder 207

# Emotional/Behavioral Disorders 231

## 10   Mental Retardation (Intellectual Disabilities)   271

# Comunication Disorders   303

# Severe and Multiple Disabilities   335

# 16 Vision Loss 441

# 17 Physical Disabilities and Health Disorders 471

# Gifted, Creative, and Talented     513

# Selected Features

# DEBATE FORUM

# INCLUSION THROUGH THE LIFESPAN

# REFLECT ON THIS

# About the Authors

**Michael L. Hardman** is the Associate Dean for Research in the College of Education, as well as department chair and professor in Special Education at the University of Utah. He is also the Chief Education Advisor to the Joseph P. Kennedy, Jr. Foundation in Washington, DC. Dr. Hardman, who completed his doctorate in educational administration with an emphasis in special education, has published in national journals throughout the field of education and has authored ten college textbooks. This textbook, *Human Exceptionality*, has been adopted by universities and colleges throughout the United States. Other recent books include *Lifespan Perspective on the Family and Disability, Mental Retardation: A Lifespan Approach to People with Intellectual Disabilities (eighth edition),* and *Introduction to Persons with Moderate and Severe Disabilities (second edition).*

As a researcher, Dr. Hardman has contributed to numerous professional journals and has directed international and national demonstration projects in the areas of intellectual/developmental disabilities, school reform and professional development, inclusive education, transition from school to adult life, the future of the Individuals with Disabilities Education Act, and training future leaders in special education. Dr. Hardman is the recipient of the 2000 National Distinguished Service Award from the Council for Exceptional Children, Division on Teacher Education.

**Clifford J. Drew** is Associate Vice President for Instructional Technology and Outreach in the Office of the Sr. Vice President for Academic Affairs at the University of Utah. He is also a professor in the Special Education and Educational Psychology departments. Dr. Drew came to the University of Utah in 1971 after serving on the faculties of the University of Texas at Austin and Kent State University. He received his master's degree from the University of Illinois and his Ph.D. from the University of Oregon. He has published numerous articles on topics in education and related areas, including mental retardation, research design, statistics, diagnostic assessment, cognition, evaluation related to the law, and information technology. His most recent book, *Mental Retardation: A Lifespan Approach to People with Intellectual Disabilities,* is Dr. Drew's 26th text. His professional interests include research methods in education and psychology, human development and disabilities, applications of information technology, and outreach and continuing education in higher education.

**M. Winston Egan**, chair of the Teacher Education Department in the David O. McKay School of Education at Brigham Young University, has taught children of all ages, preschool through high school. He began his special education career at Utah Boys Ranch. His writings appear in *Behavior Disorders, Journal of Teacher Education, Teacher Education and Special Education, Journal of Technology and Teacher Education, American Journal of Distance Education, Journal of Special Education, Rural Special Education Quarterly,* and *Teaching and Teacher Education.* He has been honored with several univeristy teaching awards, including Professor of the Year; Blue Key National Honor Society at Brigham Young University; and Excellence in Teaching Award, Graduate School of Education, University of Utah. He has also been an associate of the National Network of Education Renewal (NNER). His interests include youth development, video-anchored instruction, teacher socialization and development, and emotional/behavior disorders.

# Preface

> *I have walked with people whose eyes are full of light but who see nothing in sea or sky, nothing in city streets, nothing in books. It were far better to sail forever in the night of blindness with sense, and feeling, and mind, than to be content with the mere act of seeing. The only lightless dark is the night of darkness in ignorance and insensibility.*
>
> —HELEN KELLER

Welcome to the eighth edition of *Human Exceptionality: School, Community, and Family!* We would like to launch your exploration into the lives of people who are exceptional by providing some perspective on those features of the seventh edition that we have retained, as well as on those that are new and different in the eighth. It is important to remember that this text is about people—people with diverse needs, characteristics, and lifestyles—people who for one reason or another are considered "exceptional." What does the word *exceptional* mean to you? For that matter, what do the words *disordered, deviant, disabled, challenged, different,* and *handicapped* mean to you? Who or what influenced your knowledge and attitudes about these terms and the people they have been used to describe? Up to this point in your life, you have probably been most influenced by life experiences and not by any formal training. You may have a family member, friend, or casual acquaintance who is exceptional in some way. It may be that you are a person with an exceptional condition. Then again, you may be approaching the study of human exceptionality with little or no background. You will find that the study of human exceptionality is the study of being human. Perhaps you will come to understand yourself better in the process. As suggested by the novelist Louis Bromfield,

> *There is a rhythm in life, a certain beauty which operates by a variation of lights and shadows, happiness alternating with sorrow, content with discontent, distilling in this process of contrast a sense of satisfaction, of richness that can be captured and pinned down only by those who possess the gift of awareness.*

## New in This Edition

- The eighth edition of *Human Exceptionality* contains over 1,000 citations from sources published since the year 2000. Additionally, we have changed the subtitle of this edition to *School, Community, and Family* in order to better reflect our emphasis on exceptionalities in *education,* as well as in the community and family. You'll see this increased emphasis on education throughout the book, especially in the completely revised Chapters 1, 2, and 3—"Understanding Exceptionality," "Education for All," and "Inclusion and Collaboration in the Early Childhood and Elementary School Years." Enhanced education topics include assessment and accountability for all students, collaboration among general and special educators, effective practices in special education, and a single system of educational services and supports.
- The first six chapters of the book have been reorganized to present the fundamental topics of exceptionality first, followed by chapters dealing with exceptionality throughout the lifespan and then multicultural and family topics.

## Organization, Pedagogy, and Special Features in This Edition

In addition to providing you with current and informative content, we are committed to making your first formal experience with exceptionality interesting, enjoyable, and productive. To this end, the features incorporated into the eighth edition should greatly enhance your desire to learn more about human exceptionality.

## FOCUS PEDAGOGY

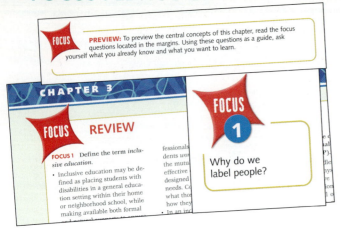

At the beginning of the chapter and throughout, we've provided tools to help you understand the key topics within each section. The **Focus Preview** at the beginning of each chapter sets the stage for upcoming chapter content. The margins of each chapter contain a series of **Focus Questions** that highlight the most important information within the chapter. Each chapter concludes with a **Focus Review** that repeats the Focus Questions and answers them on the basis of chapter material.

## TO BEGIN WITH . . .

*To Begin With . . .* excerpts, found at the beginning of each chapter, are designed to introduce and stimulate interest in the chapter topic. They offer a variety of fascinating and current personal anecdotes, facts, and figures.

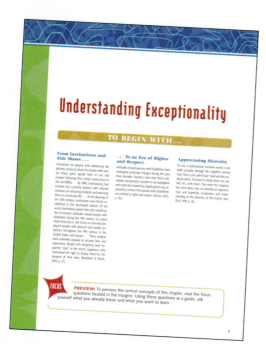

## SNAPSHOT

*Snapshot* features are personal insights that focus on the lives of people with differences. These insights may come from teachers, family members, friends, peers, and professionals, as well as from the person who is exceptional. We believe you will find the *Snapshots* to be one of the most enriching aspects of your introduction to human exceptionality.

## INCLUSION THROUGH THE LIFESPAN

*Inclusion Through the Lifespan* (formerly called *Interacting in Natural Settings*) is intended to provide some brief tips on ways to interact with, communicate with, or teach people who are exceptional across a variety of settings (home, school, and community) and across age spans (early childhood through the adult years). The tips should stimulate further thinking on how to include these individuals as family members, school peers, friends, or neighbors.

## REFLECT ON THIS

The *Reflect on This* features highlight interesting and relevant information about exceptionality to enhance your learning and enjoyment of the chapter.

## ASSISTIVE TECHNOLOGY

The eighth edition offers much information on the expanding use of technology for people who are exceptional. *Assistive Technology* features (formerly called *Today's Technology*) highlight some of the innovations in areas such as computers, biomedical engineering, and instructional systems.

## DEBATE FORUM

Every chapter in the eighth edition includes a *Debate Forum* to broaden your view of various issues that affect people with differences. For each issue discussed, a position taken (*point*) and an alternative to that position (*counterpoint*) are given. The purpose of the Debate Forum is to help you better understand the range of issues concerning exceptional individuals.

## CASE STUDY

Each chapter includes a *Case Study*, an in-depth look at a personal story of exceptionality. Each *Case Study* is followed by Application Questions to extend your knowledge and give you an opportunity to apply what you have learned from each vignette.

# NEW! CHAPTER-CLOSING RESOURCES

At the end of each chapter, you will find several new resources to help you understand exceptionalities and expand what you have learned in that chapter. The Further Readings section lists selected books and journals that provide additional information about each chapter topic. The Web Resources section discusses important websites that you can visit to learn more about exceptionalities. Building Your Portfolio is a resource for preservice teachers of general and special education. It explains which CEC (Council for Exceptional Children) standards the chapter covers, and it offers tips on collecting the materials you prepare for this class in order to build a professional portfolio correlated with those standards. Themes of the Times points you to the Companion Website, where you will find a link to articles from the *New York Times* about exceptionalities in school, the family, and the community.

# A Comprehensive Teaching and Learning Package

Allyn and Bacon is committed to preparing the best possible supplements for its textbooks, and the supplements for the eighth edition of *Human Exceptionality* reflect this commitment. The following supplements provide an outstanding array of resources that facilitate learning about students with disabilities and their families. For more information about the instructor and student supplements that accompany and support the text, ask your local Allyn and Bacon representative or contact the Allyn and Bacon Sales Support Department (1-800-852-8024).

# OUTSTANDING MEDIA RESOURCES

- **mylabschool** *MyLabSchool™* Discover where the classroom comes to life! From video clips of teachers and students interacting to sample lessons, portfolio templates, and standards integration, Allyn & Bacon brings your students the tools they'll need to succeed in the classroom—with content easily integrated into your existing course.

  Delivered within Course Compass, Allyn & Bacon's course management system, this program gives your students powerful insights into how real classrooms work and a rich array of tools that will support them on their journey from their first class to their first classroom.

- *VideoWorkshop for Special Education CD-ROM* Available free when packaged with the textbook, the CD-ROM contains ten modules of 3- to 5-minute digitized video clips featuring snapshots of teachers and students in real classroom settings. The VideoWorkshop CD comes with a Student Study Guide, which contains a wide variety of materials to help students get the most out of this exciting media product. With questions for reflection before, during, and after viewing, this guide extends classroom discussion and makes it possible to spend more in-class time on analysis of material. An Instructor's Teaching Guide is also available. It provides ideas and exercises to help teachers incorporate this convenient supplement into course assignments and assessments. (Visit www.ablongman.com/videoworkshop for more details.)

- **"What's Best for Matthew?" Interactive CD-ROM Case Study for Learning to Develop IEPs, Version 2.0**  This CD-ROM helps preservice and in-service teachers develop their IEP-writing skills through the case study of Matthew, a 9-year-old boy with autism. The CD is sold separately and it is also available free *only* when packaged with *Human Exceptionality*, eighth edition, as a "value package."

- **Research Navigator™ (with Content-Select Research Database)**  (Access Code Required) Using Research Navigator™ (researchnavigator.com) is the easiest way for students to start a research assignment or research paper. Complete with extensive help on the research process and three exclusive online databases of credible and reliable source material, including EBSCO's ContentSelect™ Academic Journal Database, *New York Times* Search by Subject Archive, and "Best of the Web" Link Library, Research Navigator™ helps students quickly and efficiently make the most of their research time. Research Navigator™ is free when packaged with the textbook and requires an Access Code.

## INSTRUCTOR SUPPLEMENTS: A COMPLETE INSTRUCTIONAL PACKAGE

A variety of teaching tools are available to assist instructors in organizing lectures, planning evaluations, and ensuring student comprehension.

- **Instructor's Resource Manual and Test Bank.**  Prepared by Matt Jameson, University of Utah, the Instructor's Resource Manual includes a wealth of interesting ideas and activities designed to help instructors teach the course. Each chapter of the Manual includes at-a-glance grids, a chapter outline, notes on introducing the chapter, a lecture outline, related discussion/activities, case study feedback, related media, and handout masters. Prepared by the textbook authors, the Test Bank has been significantly improved to include more challenging essay, multiple-choice, true/false, short answer, and case study questions for every chapter. Page number references, suggested answers, and skill level have been added to each question to help instructors create and evaluate student tests.

- **Computerized Test Bank.**  The printed Test Bank is also available electronically through our computerized testing system, TestGen EQ. Instructors can use TestGen EQ to create exams in just minutes by selecting from the existing database of questions, editing questions, and/or writing original questions.

- **Digital Media Archive for Special Education.**  This CD-ROM contains a variety of media elements that instructors can use to create electronic presentations in the classroom. It includes hundreds of original images, as well as art selected from Allyn and Bacon special education texts, providing instructors with a broad selection of graphs, charts, and tables. For classrooms with full multimedia capability, it also contains video segments and web links.

- **PowerPoint™ Presentation.**  Ideal for lecture presentations or student handouts, the PowerPoint™ presentation created for this text provides dozens of ready-to-use graphical and text images, including illustrations from the text (available for download from Supplement Central at www.suppscentral.ablongman.com).

- **The "Snapshots" Video Series for Special Education**

  - **Snapshots: Inclusion Video**  (©1995, 22 minutes long) profiles three students of differing ages and with various levels of disability in inclusive class settings. In each case, parents, classroom teachers, special education teachers, and school administrators talk about the steps they have taken to help the students succeed in inclusive settings.

  - **Snapshots 2: Video for Special Education**  (categorical organization) (©1995, 20–25 minutes long) is a two-video set of six segments (traumatic brain injury, behavior disorders, learning disabilities, mental retardation, hearing impairments, and visual impairments) designed specifically for use in college classrooms. Each segment profiles three individuals and their families, teachers, and experiences. These programs are of high interest to students; instructors who have used the tapes in their courses have found that they help in disabusing students of stereotypical viewpoints and put a "human face" on the course material.

- **Professionals in Action Videotape: Teaching Students with Special Needs**  (©2000, 120 minutes long) This *Professionals in Action* video consists of five 15–30-minute modules presenting viewpoints on and approaches to teaching students with various disabilities, in general education classrooms, separate education settings, and various combinations of the two. Each module explores its topic via actual classroom footage and through interviews with general and special education teachers, parents, and the students themselves.

- *Allyn and Bacon Transparencies for Special Education 2005* This revised package includes 100 acetates, most in full color.
- *Online Course Management System for Introduction to Special Education and Inclusion.* Available in CourseCompass, WebCT and Blackboard formats and hosted nationally, Allyn and Bacon's own course management system helps you manage all aspects of teaching your course, and provides preloaded premium content to support Introduction to Special Education and Inclusion courses using Allyn & Bacon texts. For the Instructor, the course cartridge includes instructor's manuals, testbanks and PowerPoint slides for our texts in these two course areas, as well as convenient teaching resources such as the Digital Media Archive for Special Education. For the student, the premium content includes: text-specfic practice tests and learning objectives, topical "Suggested Readings" lists, Flashcards, and VideoWorkshop clips, and links to *New York Times* articles and *ResearchNavigator.* Go to www.coursecompass.com to register and preview this premium online course.

## STUDENT SUPPLEMENTS: AN INTEGRATED LEARNING SYSTEM

Building on the study aids found in the text, Allyn and Bacon offers a number of supplements for students.

- *Student Study Guide* Prepared by Christine K. Ormsbee, University of Oklahoma. Completely rewritten, the Student Study Guide that accompanies the text features numerous ways of helping students apply and practice what they have learned in the text, including
  - **Guided Review**—guides students through the key concepts in each chapter, using a KWL process model.
  - **Best Practices**—websites, videos, books, and models with suggestions on how best to serve children with disabilities.
  - **Community Activities**—activities that help students understand how IDEA is implemented in their local system.
  - **Case Study**—case studies with multiple-choice and critical thinking questions that ask students to apply what they have learned in each chapter.
  - **Getting Involved**—a list of contacts to help students identify ways of becoming involved.
  - **Practice Test**—up to 20 questions per chapter.

- *Companion Website* This website was Prepared by Jeff Bakken, Illinois State University. Students who visit the companion website that accompanies the text (www.ablongman.com/hardman8e) will find many features and activities to help them in their studies: web links, learning activities, practice tests, video and audio clips, text correlations to national and state professional standards and the Praxis II exams, and vocabulary flash cards. The website also features an interactive Special Education Timeline that highlights the people and events that have shaped special education through history.
- *ResearchNavigator™ Guide for Special Education* This free reference guide includes tips, resources, activities, and URLs to help students use the Internet for their research projects. Part 1 of the guide introduces students to the resources on Research Navigator™. Part 2 includes information on how to conduct online research correctly. Part 3 suggests many net activities related to the content of the text. Part 4 lists hundreds of special education Internet resources. Includes Access Code for Research Navigator™.

# Acknowledgments

We begin with a very big "thank you" to our colleagues from around the country who provided indepth and constructive feedback on the eighth edition of *Human Exceptionality:*

Ron Alexander, The University of Texas at San Antonio

Ellyn Arwood, University of Portland

Dan Baker, University of Oregon

Jeffrey P. Bakken, Illinois State University

Nancy Brawner-Jones, Portland State University

Rhonda Collins Morton, Auburn University–Montgomery

William Drakeford, University of Maryland

Dan Glasgow, Northeastern State University

Thomas Grayson, University of Illinois

Michelle Hosp, University of Utah

Donna Kearns, University of Central Oklahoma

Adrian F. Moriarty, Morehead State University

Mark O'Dekirk, Meredith College

Rob O'Neill, University of Utah

Christine Ormsbee, University of Oklahoma

Marianne C. Reynolds, Mercer County Community College

Loline J. Saras, Kutztown University
Randy Seevers, University of Houston–
Clear Lake

Special thanks to the people with disabilities and their families who participated in the snapshots and case studies for this text. These are the people who make up the heart of what this book is all about. Throughout the writing and production of this book, they made us keenly aware that this book is first and foremost about people.

For a job exceptionally well done, we extend our gratitude to Matt Jameson at the University of Utah for his first-rate effort in taking the lead in revising the instructor's manual and test bank for this text. Matt spent untold hours developing and editing lecture notes, creating related activities, and locating the most current and informative media available in the area of exceptionality. Matt was always on time with a high quality product. We also extend our thanks to the faculty and students at the University of Utah and Brigham Young University who continue to teach us a great deal about writing textbooks. Many of the changes incorporated into this eight edition are a direct result of critiques from university colleagues and students in our classes.

As authors, we are certainly grateful for the continuing strong commitment of the Allyn and Bacon editorial and production team in bringing to fruition the highest quality text possible. As is true with other editions, the team has sought to consistently improve the readability, utility, and appearance of this book. We want to especially thank our Executive Editor, Virginia Lanigan. Virginia has worked closely with us, providing leadership and invaluable advice throughout the revision of this book. Virginia's knowledge of the needs and interests of professors and students in the field of education helped us to cast this edition into a comprehensive text for the new century and beyond. Our Associate Editor, Tom Jefferies, has been a wonderful addition to the editorial team. He worked closely with the authors to ensure quality supplements, including the instructor's manual and test bank, student study guide, companion website, transparencies package, and PowerPoint slides.

We genuinely appreciated the opportunity to work with Sonny Regelman as our developmental editor. Sonny defines professional. She has been terrific to work with from the very beginning, attending not only to the quality of the content but also ensuring that the book maintains its strong user-friendly approach to instruction. Her careful and in-depth editing of the manuscript has been crucial in presenting a product of which we are all very proud. We will miss her regular e-mails alerting us to what was working, what we missed, and what was next in the development process. We sincerely thank Connie Day, copyeditor, for her unwavering attention to the important details related to text figures, tables, sentence and paragraph structure, typographical errors, and APA style that can make or break a text. As was true in the last two editions, Barbara Gracia, Editorial Production Service, showed considerable patience as we all sought perfection in the galleys and final page proofs. The photo researcher for this book was Katharine Cook, who did an outstanding job of locating photos that brought to life the text's printed word. Under her direction, we have included the most recent photographs from photo shoots in general education classes, including school systems that work with the inclusion model around the country. This photo resource also contains families with children and/or adults with disabilities. We are also especially pleased to have had the opportunity to work with Allyn and Bacon Executive Marketing Manager, Amy Cronin Jordan, our text designer Geri Davis, the work of Modern Graphics in completing electronic composition, and our excellent Cover Administrator, Linda Knowles. At last, but certainly not least, we thank Annette Pagliaro, Senior Production Editor, for her leadership in bringing this eighth edition home. It continues to amaze us how production quality, which is so good to begin with, can continue to get better and better with each new edition. From where we sit, Annette's leadership is a big reason why we keep improving.

To Kristin Smith and Marti Hoge at the University of Utah, we express our appreciation for the painstaking proofing, copying, and mailing of the manuscript.

To those professors who have chosen this book for adoption, and to those students who will be using this book as their first information source on people with differences, we hope our eighth edition of *Human Exceptionality* meets your expectations.

A loving thank you to our families who have always been there during the past 25 years of writing and rewriting this text. We have strived oh so hard to produce a product of which you can be proud.

Michael L. Hardman
Clifford J. Drew
M. Winston Egan

# Human Exceptionality
## School, Community, and Family

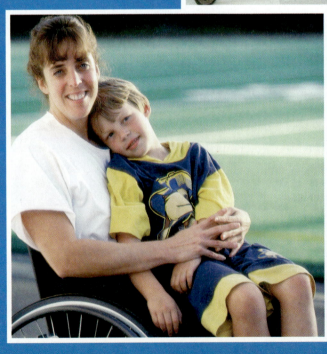

# Understanding Exceptionality

### From Institutions and Side Shows . . .

Institutions for people with intellectual disabilities, similar to those for people with mental illness, grew rapidly both in size and number following their initial construction in the mid-1800s. . . . By 1880, [institutions] had evolved into custodial asylums with reduced emphasis on educating residents and returning them to community life. . . . At the dawning of the 20th century, institutions were firmly established in the developed nations of the world. Institutions weren't the only manifestation of society's attitudes toward people with disabilities during the 19th century. So-called freak shows [a.k.a. side shows or carnivals] displayed people with physical and mental disabilities throughout the 19th century in the United States and Europe. . . . These exhibits were extremely popular at circuses, fairs, and expositions. People with disabilities were frequently "sold" to the shows' organizers, who maintained the right to display them for the duration of their lives. (Braddock & Parish, 2002, p. 27)

### . . . To an Era of Rights and Respect

Attitudes toward persons with disabilities have undergone profound changes during the past three decades. Society's view that these individuals represented a burden to be segregated and medically treated has largely given way, replaced by notions that people with disabilities are entitled to rights and respect. (Parish, 2002, p. 353)

### Appreciating Diversity

For me, a multicultural, inclusive world is not really possible through the cognitive avenue only. That is, you cannot just "read and discuss" about others. You have to study, work, live, eat, talk, etc., with them. The more this happens, the more likely one can develop an appreciation, and hopefully, acceptance and understanding of the diversity of the human race. (Paul, 1998, p. 16)

**FOCUS**

**PREVIEW:** To preview the central concepts of this chapter, read the focus questions located in the margins. Using these questions as a guide, ask yourself what you already know and what you want to learn.

# Franklin Delano Roosevelt

This snapshot was adapted from the remarks of Senator Robert Dole to his colleagues in the United States Senate on April 14, 1995. Senator Dole, disabled himself following a serious injury in World War II, remembers President Franklin Roosevelt as a master politician; an energetic and inspiring leader during the dark days of the Depression; a tough, single-minded commander-in-chief during World War II; a statesman; the first elected leader in history with a disability; and a disability hero.

## FDR'S Splendid Deception

In 1921, at age 39, Franklin Roosevelt was a young man in a hurry. He was following the same political path that took his cousin Theodore Roosevelt to the White House. He was elected to the New York State Senate in 1910 and later was appointed assistant secretary of the Navy. In 1920, he was the Democratic candidate for vice president. Then, on the evening of August 10, while on vacation, he felt ill and went to bed early. Within three days he was paralyzed from the chest down. Although the muscles of his upper body soon recovered, he remained paralyzed below the waist. His political career screeched to a halt. He spent the next seven years in rehabilitation, determined to walk again. He never did. He mostly used a wheelchair. Sometimes he was carried by his sons or aides. Other times he crawled on the floor. But he did perfect the illusion of walking—believing that otherwise his political ambitions were dead. He could stand upright only with his lower body painfully wrapped in steel braces. He moved forward by swinging his hips, leaning on the arm of a family member or aide. It worked for only a few feet at a time. It was dangerous. But it was enough to convince people that FDR was not a "cripple." FDR biographer Hugh Gallagher has called this effort, and other tricks used to hide his disability, "FDR's splendid deception." This deception was aided and abetted by many others. The press were co-conspirators. No reporter wrote that FDR could not walk, and no photographer took a picture of him in his wheelchair. For that matter, thousands saw him struggle when he "walked." Maybe they didn't believe or understand what they saw. In 1928, FDR ended his political exile and was elected governor of New York. Four years later, he was president. On March 4, 1933, standing at the East Front of this Capitol, he said, "The only thing we have to fear is fear itself." He was 35 feet from his wheelchair. Few people knew from what deep personal experiences he spoke. Perhaps the only occasion where FDR fully acknowledged the extent of his disability in public was a visit to a military hospital in Hawaii. He toured the amputee wards in his wheelchair. He went by each bed, letting the men see him exactly as he was. He didn't need to give any pep talks—his example said it all.

## FDR: A Disability Hero

Earlier I called FDR a "disability hero." But it was not for the reasons some might think. It would be easy to cite his courage and grit. But FDR would not want that. "No sob stuff," he told the press in 1928 when he started his comeback. Even within his own family, he did not discuss his disability. It was simply a fact of life. In my view, FDR is a hero for his efforts on behalf of others with a disability. In 1926, he purchased a run-down resort in Warm Springs, Georgia and, over the next 20 years, turned it into a unique, first-class rehabilitation center. It was based on a new philosophy of treatment—one where psychological recovery was as important as medical treatment. FDR believed in an independent life for people with disabilities—at a time when society thought they belonged at home or in institutions. Warm Springs was run by people with polio, for people with polio. In that spirit, FDR is the father of the modern independent living movement, which puts people with disabilities in control of their own lives. He also founded the National Foundation for Infantile Paralysis—known as the "March of Dimes"—and raised millions of dollars to help others with polio and find a cure. In public policy, FDR understood that government help in rehabilitating people with disabilities is "good business"—often returning more in taxes and savings than it costs. It is unfortunately a philosophy that we often pay more lip service than practice.

## Disability Today and Tomorrow

Our nation has come a long way in its understanding of disability since the days of President Roosevelt. For example, we recognize that disability is a natural part of life. We have begun to build a world that is accessible. No longer do we accept that buildings—through either design or indifference—be inaccessible, which is a "Keep Out" sign for the disabled. We have come a long way in another respect—in attitudes. Fifty years ago, we had a president who could not walk and believed it was necessary to disguise that fact from the American people. Today, I trust that Americans would have no problem in electing as president a man or woman with a disability. (Dole, 1995)

**FOCUS 1**

Why do we label people?

Franklin Delano Roosevelt (FDR) has been hailed as one of the greatest U.S. presidents in history. *Time* magazine (December 31, 1999, www.Time.com) named FDR as one of the three finalists for "most important person of the 20th century," describing him as a statesman who helped define the political and social fabric of our time. What *Time* didn't talk about was FDR's life as a person with a disability and why he was forced to hide the fact that he had had polio and couldn't walk. In our opening snapshot, we learn of Roosevelt's deception and why he is considered by many to be a disability hero even though he publicly denied his physical differences. Throughout his life, FDR did everything possible to avoid being "labeled" as a person with a disability. In Roosevelt's time, *disability* meant "weakness," and he believed that revealing his paralysis would jeopardize his standing as a national leader. Fortunately, we have a much better understanding of human diversity in today's society—that is, most people realize that everyone is unique in some way. In fact, a 1995 Lou Harris survey found that in that year, more than 80% of Americans knew FDR was paralyzed. Of those who knew of his disability, 75% favored the depiction of him in a wheelchair at the new FDR national monument in Washington, DC. (National Organization on Disability [N.O.D.]/Harris & Associates, 1995).

# Describing People with Differences

To address differences, society creates descriptors to identify people who vary significantly from the norm. This process is called *labeling*. Sociologists use labels to describe people who do not follow society's expectations; educators and psychologists use labels to identify and provide services for students with learning, physical, and behavioral differences; and physicians use labels to distinguish the sick from the healthy.

## Common Terminology

Common descriptors used to describe people with differences include *disorder, disability*, and *handicap*. These terms are not synonymous. **Disorder,** the broadest of the three terms, refers to a general disturbance in mental, physical, or psychological functioning. A **disability** is more specific than a disorder and results from a loss of physical functioning (e.g., loss of sight, hearing, or mobility) or from difficulty in learning and social adjustment that significantly interferes with typical growth and development. A **handicap** is a limitation imposed on the individual by the demands in the environment and is related to the individual's ability to adapt or adjust to those demands. For example, Franklin Roosevelt used a wheelchair because of a physical disability—the inability to walk. He was dependent on the wheelchair to move from place to place. When the environment didn't accommodate his wheelchair (e.g., when he encountered a building without ramps, accessible only by stairs), his disability became a handicap.

When applied as an educational label, *handicapped* has a narrow focus and a negative meaning. The word *handicapped* literally means "cap in hand"; its application derives from a time when people with disabilities were forced to beg in the streets merely to survive.

**Exceptional** is a much more comprehensive term. It may be used to describe an individual whose physical, intellectual, or behavioral performance differs substantially from the norm, either higher or lower. People described as exceptional include those with extraordinary abilities (such as **gifts and talents**) and/or disabilities (such as **learning disabilities** or **mental retardation**). People who are exceptional, whether gifted or disabled, often benefit from individualized assistance, supports, or accommodations in school and society.

Labels are only rough approximations of characteristics. Some labels, such as **deaf,** might describe a permanent characteristic—loss of hearing; others, such as *overweight*, might describe a temporary characteristic. Some labels are positive, and others are negative. Labels communicate whether a person meets the expectations of the culture. A society establishes criteria that are easily exceeded by some but are far beyond the reach of others. For example, a society may value creativity, innovation, and imagination and may reward those who have such attributes with positive labels, such as *bright, intelligent,* or *gifted.* That same society, however, may brand anyone whose ideas drastically exceed the limits of conformity with negative labels, such as *radical, extremist,* or *rebel.*

Moreover, the same label may have different meanings for different groups, depending on each group's viewpoint. For example, Ellen is labeled by her high school

**Disorder**

A disturbance in normal functioning (mental, physical, or psychological).

**Disability**

A condition resulting from a loss of physical functioning; or, difficulties in learning and social adjustment that significantly interfere with normal growth and development. A person with a disability has a physical or mental impairment that substantially limits the person in some major life activity.

**Handicap**

A limitation imposed on an individual by the environment and the person's capacity to cope with that limitation.

**Exceptional**

A term describing any individual whose physical, mental, or behavioral performance deviates so substantially from the average (higher or lower) that additional support is required to meet the individual's needs.

**Gifts and talents**

Extraordinary abilities in one or more areas.

**Learning disabilities**

A condition in which one or more of an individual's basic psychological processes in understanding or using language are deficient.

**Mental retardation**

Substantial limitations in functioning, characterized by significantly subaverage intellectual functioning concurrent with related limitations into two or more adaptive skills. Mental retardation manifests itself prior to age 18.

**Deaf**

A term used to describe individuals who have hearing losses greater than 75 to 80 dB, have vision as their primary input, and cannot understand speech through the ear.

*Labels have been the basis for developing and providing services to people with disabilities. Can they also promote stereotyping, discrimination, and exclusion?*

teachers as a *conformist* because she always follows the rules. From the teacher's point of view, this is a positive characteristic, but to the student's peer group, it may have more negative connotations. Ellen may be described by her high school classmates as a "brown noser" or "teacher's pet."

What are the ramifications of using labels to describe people? Labels are based on ideas, not facts. "When we create or construct [labels], we do so within particular cultural contexts. That is, someone observes particular behaviors or ways of being and then describes these . . . with a label" (Kliewer & Biklen, 1996, pp. 83–84). Thus, even though labels have been the basis for developing and providing services to people, they can also promote stereotyping, discrimination, and exclusion. Some professionals believe that the practice of labeling people has perpetuated and reinforced both the label and the behaviors it implies (Cook, 2001; Forts, 1998; Lipsky & Gartner, 1999; National Council on Disability, 2000).

If the use of labels may have negative consequences, why is labeling used so extensively? One reason is that many social services and educational programs for people who are exceptional require the use of labels to distinguish those who are eligible for services from those who are not. Kauffman (1998), discussing the need to label students who have learning and behavior differences, argued that "either all students are treated the same or some are treated differently. Any student who is treated differently is inevitably labeled. . . . Labeling a problem clearly is the first step in dealing productively with it" (p. 12). Funding may even be contingent on the numbers and types of individuals who are deemed eligible. To illustrate, Maria, a child with a hearing loss, must be assessed in her local school district and labeled as having a hearing loss before specialized educational or social services can be made available to her. Another reason for the continued use of labels is that they help professionals communicate effectively with one another and provide a common ground for evaluating research findings. A third reason is that labeling helps identify the specific needs of a particular group of people. Labeling can help planners determine degrees of needs and set priorities for services when societal resources are limited.

## When Someone Doesn't Conform to the Norm

Significant physical, behavioral, and learning differences are found in every society but occur infrequently. Most people in any given culture conform to its established standards. Conformity—doing what we are supposed to do—is the rule for most of us, most of the time (Baron & Byrne, 2003). Usually, we look the way we are expected to look, behave the way we are expected to behave, and learn the way we are expected to learn. When someone differs substantially from the norm, three approaches may be used to describe the nature and extent of these differences (see Figure 1.1).

**A DEVELOPMENTAL APPROACH.** To understand human differences, which result from an interaction of biological and environmental factors, we must first establish what is "normal" or typical development. According to the developmental view, typical development can be described statistically, by observing in large numbers of individuals those characteristics that occur most frequently at a specific age. For example, consider the statement that the average 3-month-old infant is able to follow a moving object visually. Here *average* is a statistical term based on observations of the behavior of 3-month-old infants. When professionals compare an individual

**FOCUS 2**

Identify three approaches to describing human differences.

child's growth pattern to that group average, they label differences in development (either advanced or delayed) accordingly.

**A CULTURAL VIEW.**   From a cultural view, "normality" is defined by societal values. Whereas a developmental view invokes only the frequency of behaviors to define differences, a cultural approach suggests that differences can be explained partly by examining the *values* inherent within a culture. What constitutes a significant difference changes over time, from culture to culture, and among the various social classes within a culture. As Kammeyer, Ritzer, and Yetman (1997) suggested, people are considered *deviant* when they do something that is disapproved of by other members within the dominant culture. For example, in some cultures, intelligence is described in terms of how well someone scores on a test measuring a broad range of abilities, and in other cultures, intelligence is assumed to be related to how skillful someone is at hunting or fishing. The idea that human beings are the products of their cultures has received great support from anthropology, which emphasizes the diversity and arbitrary nature of cultural rules about dress, eating habits, sexual habits, politics, and religion.

**SELF-LABELING.**   Everyone engages in a self-labeling process that others may not recognize. Thus, self-imposed labels reflect how we perceive ourselves, not how others see us. Conversely, a person may be labeled by society but not accept that label. Such was the case with Thomas Edison. Although the schools labeled Edison an intellectually incapable child, he eventually recognized that he was an individualist. He proved himself by ignoring the label imposed on him and pursuing his own interests as an inventor. (See the nearby Reflect on This, "A Few Famous People with Disabilities," and take a quiz on other famous people with disabilities.)

**FIGURE 1.1**

**Three Approaches to Describing Human Differences**

Developmental Approach

Cultural View

Self-Labeling

**Reflect on This**

# A FEW FAMOUS PEOPLE WITH DISABILITIES

Match the names to the descriptions:

**1.** He was diagnosed with amyotrophic lateral sclerosis (ALS–Lou Gehrig's disease) at the age of 21. He must use a wheelchair and have round-the-clock nursing care. His speech has been severely affected, and he communicates through a computer by selecting words from a screen that are expressed through a speech synthesizer. Acknowledged as one of the greatest physicists in history, he developed a theory on black holes that provided new insights into the origin of the universe. Currently, he is professor of mathematics at Cambridge University, a post once held by Sir Isaac Newton.

*a. Albert Einstein*

*b. Sarah Bernhardt*

*c. Nelson Rockefeller*

*d. Stephen Hawking*

*e. Whoopi Goldberg*

*f. George S. Patton Jr.*

*g. Walt Disney*

*h. Tom Cruise*

*i. James Earl Jones*

York and was appointed vice president of the United States during the Nixon administration.

**6.** He is the voice of Darth Vader and the most in-demand narrator in Hollywood. Virtually mute as a child, he stuttered throughout most of his youth. With the help of his high school English teacher, he overcame stuttering by reading Shakespeare aloud to himself and then to audiences. He went on to debating and finally to stage and screen acting.

**7.** He was regarded as a slow learner during his school years and never had much success in public education. Later, he became the best-known cartoonist in history, producing the first full-length animated motion picture.

**2.** He did not learn to read at all until he was 12 years old and continued having difficulty reading all his life. He was able to get through school by memorizing his teachers' entire lectures. Acknowledged as one of the greatest strategists in military history, he gained fame as a four-star general in World War II.

**3.** She was disabled by an accident in 1914 and eventually had to have part of her leg amputated. Regarded as one of the greatest French actresses in history, she continued her career on stage until her death in 1923.

**4.** A well-known, tireless humanitarian advocate for children, the homeless, and human rights, also involved in the battles against substance abuse and AIDS, this Oscar-winning actress and Grammy winner is a high school dropout with an acknowledged reading disability.

**5.** He was diagnosed with severe dyslexia, which made reading very difficult for him throughout life. He became a four-term governor of New

**8.** He did not speak until the age of 3. Even as an adult he found that searching for words was laborious. Schoolwork, especially math, was difficult for him, and he was unable to express himself in written language. He was thought to be "simple-minded" (retarded) until he discovered that he could achieve through visualizing rather than the use of oral language. His theory of relativity, which revolutionized modern physics, was developed in his spare time. *Time* magazine named him the most important person of the 20th century.

**9.** He has never learned to read due to severe dyslexia and was unable to finish high school. Today he is regarded as one of most accomplished actors of his time. Although unable to read, he can memorize his lines from an auditory source (cassette tape or someone reading to him).

SOURCE: The source of this quiz is unknown. It was adapted from the *Family Village website (http://www.familyvillage.wisc.edu/index.htmlx)* And from *Take a Walk in My Shoes—A Guide Book for Youth on Diversity Awareness Activities* by Yuri Morita, June 1996, Office of Affirmative Action, Division of Agriculture & National Resources, University of California, 300 Lakeside Drive, 6th Floor, Oakland, CA 94612-3560. Phone 510/987-0096.

Answers: 1(d), 2(f), 3(b), 4(e), 5(c), 6(i), 7(g), 8(a), 9(h)

## The Effects of Being Labeled

Reactions to a label differ greatly from one person to another, but they are often negative (Dajini, 2001; Gustavsson, 1999; Persaud, 2000). In two studies of college students' reactions to various labels used to describe people with mental retardation and learning disabilities, researchers found that older terms, such as *mental subnormality* and *mental handicap,* generate a more negative reaction than newer terms, such as *learning difficulty* and *learning disability* (Hastings & Remington, 1993; Hastings, Sonuga-Barke, & Remington, 1993). However, only one term, *exceptional,* received a positive rating from these college students. The authors attributed this positive reaction to the students defining *exceptional* as "much above average."

**SEPARATING THE PERSON AND THE LABEL.**   Once a label has been affixed to an individual, the two may become inseparable. For example, suppose Becky has been identified as having mental retardation. The tendency is to refer to Becky and her condition as one in the same—to say that Becky is retarded. To describe Becky in terms of this label (retardation) is to lose sight of the fact that she is first and foremost a human being and that her exceptional characteristics (intellectual and social differences) are only a small part of who she is. To treat Becky as a label rather than as a person with special needs is an injustice, not only to Becky but to everyone else as well.

**ENVIRONMENTAL BIAS.**   The environment in which we view someone can influence our perceptions of that person. For example, if you are in a mental hospital, you apparently must be insane. In a classic study, Rosenhan (1973) investigated this premise by having himself and seven other "sane" individuals admitted to a number of state mental hospitals across the United States. Once in the mental hospitals, these subjects behaved normally. The question was whether the staff would perceive them as people who were healthy instead of as patients who were mentally ill. Rosenhan reported that the seven pseudopatients were never detected by the hospital staff, although they were recognized as imposters by several of the real patients. Throughout their hospital stays, the pseudopatients were incorrectly labeled and treated as schizophrenics. Rosenhan's investigation demonstrated that the environment in which the observations are made can bias the perception of whether the observed behavior is normal.

# Including People with Disabilities in Family and Community Settings

## A Brief History

Throughout recorded history, people perceived as disabled have been vulnerable to practices such as infanticide, slavery, physical abuse, and abandonment. These practices reflected a common societal fear that the so-called mentally and morally defective would defile the human race. It was widely believed that most deviance was caused by hereditary factors that, if left unchecked, would result in widespread social problems (Braddock & Parrish, 2002).

In the last half of the 18th century, humanitarian reform ushered in an era of optimism concerning the treatment and eventual cure of people described as deviant. However, when deviance wasn't cured and continued to be a major social problem well into the 19th century, many professionals became convinced that it was necessary to sterilize and segregate large numbers of these "mental and social degenerates." Legal measures were taken to prohibit these people from marrying. Eventually, legislation was expanded to include compulsory **sterilization** of such individuals, and laws were passed in an effort to reduce the numbers of so-called *deviates.* Laws in some countries contained provisions for sterilizing people with mental retardation, individuals with epilepsy, the sexually promiscuous, and criminals. In addition, large

**FOCUS 3**

Describe the services for people with disabilities through most of the 20th century. What was the role of families in bringing about change?

**Sterilization**

The process of making an individual unable to reproduce, usually accomplished surgically.

numbers of individuals were forcibly moved from their local communities to isolated special-care facilities. These facilities became widely known as **institutions** and have gone by many different names, including *school, hospital, colony, prison,* and *asylum.*

The institutions of the early 20th century became preoccupied with social control as they grew in size and as financial resources dwindled. To manage large numbers of individuals on a limited financial base, these facilities had to establish rigid rules and regulations, stripping away individual identities and imposing strict regimentation. For example, individuals could not have personal possessions, were forced to wear institutional clothing, and were given identification tags and numbers. Locked living units, barred windows, and high walls enclosing the grounds characterized institutions. Organized treatment programs declined, and the number of "terminal," uncured patients grew, resulting in institutional expansion and the erection of new buildings. Given the public and professional pessimism concerning the value of treatment programs, this growth meant diminishing funds for mental health care. This alarming situation remained unchanged for nearly five decades and declined even further during the Depression years of the 1930s. By the early 1950s, thousands of people were committed to mental hospitals throughout the United States, and comparable numbers of persons with mental retardation lived in segregated institutions referred to as colonies, hospitals, or training schools. Several attempts to reform institutions were initiated. The American Psychiatric Association led efforts to inspect and rate the nation's mental hospitals and called attention to the lack of therapeutic intervention and the deplorable living conditions. (For more information on the history of institutions in the United States, see Blatt & Kaplan, 1974; Wolfensberger, 1975.)

## Parents and Professionals Organize to Bring About Change

In spite of the growth of segregated institutions in the 20th century, the vast majority of people with disabilities remained at home within their families. For families, choosing to keep the child at home meant going it on their own; they received little or no outside support. Government resources were very limited, and available funding was directed to support services outside of the family, often even beyond the community in which the family lived (Braddock & Parrish, 2002). For the better part of this century, many families who had a child with a disability were unable to get help for basic needs, such as medical and dental care, social services, and education.

In response to the lack of government support—and coinciding with the civil rights movement in the United States—parents of children with disabilities began to organize in about 1950. United Cerebral Palsy (UCP) was founded in 1949, and the National Association for Retarded Children[1] (NARC) began in 1950. The UCP and NARC joined other professional organizations already in existence, such as the National Association for the Deaf, the American Association on Mental Deficiency,[2] the Council for Exceptional Children, and the American Federation for the Blind, to advocate for the rights of persons with disabilities. The purpose of these national organizations was to get accurate information to families with disabilities, professionals, policy makers, and the general public. Each organization focused on the rights of people with disabilities to be included in family and community life and to have access to medical treatment, social services, and education. Other parent groups followed: the National Society for Autistic Children (1961) and the Association for Children with Learning Disabilities[3] (1964). Over the next three decades, litigation ensued on the right of people with disabilities to access services within their own communities. Through the advocacy of parent and professionals organizations, the civil rights of people with disabilities was finally recognized with the passage of the Americans with Disabilities Act (ADA) in 1990. We will now examine the ways in which ADA reaffirmed the rights of people with disabilities to participate as equal members of society.

**Institutions**

Establishments or facilities governed by a collection of fundamental rules.

---

[1]Now the ARC, A National Organization on Mental Retardation.
[2]Now the American Association on Mental Retardation (AAMR).
[3]Now the Learning Disabilities Association (LDA).

# The Americans with Disabilities Act (ADA) ✳

In 1973, the U.S. Congress passed an amendment to the Vocational Rehabilitation Act that included a provision prohibiting discrimination against persons with disabilities in federally assisted programs and activities. **Section 504** of the Act stated that

> No otherwise qualified person with a disability . . . shall, solely on the basis of disability, be denied access to, or the benefits of, or be subjected to discrimination under any program or activity provided by any entity/institution that receives federal financial assistance.

Section 504 has been hailed as the first civil rights law for people with disabilities. It set the stage for passage of the most sweeping civil rights legislation in the United States since the **Civil Rights Act of 1964:** the **Americans with Disabilities Act (ADA)** signed into law in 1990. The purpose of ADA is to prevent discrimination on the basis of disability in employment, programs and services provided by state and local governments, goods and services provided by private companies, and commercial facilities. (See the nearby Reflect on This, "One City's Response to ADA.")

In the past, people with disabilities have had to contend with the reality that learning to live independently did not guarantee access to all that society had to offer in terms of services and jobs. Although several states have long had laws that promised otherwise, access to places such as public restrooms and restaurants and success in mainstream corporate America have often eluded those with disabilities, primarily because of architectural and attitudinal barriers. ADA is intended to change these circumstances, affirming the rights of more than 50 million Americans with disabilities to participate in the life of their community. Much as the Civil Rights Act of 1964 gave clout to the African American struggle for equality, the ADA has promised to do the same for those with disabilities. Whether its effects will include eliminating the fears and prejudices of the general community remains to be seen, but the reasons for such legislation were obvious. First, it was clear that people with disabilities faced discrimination in employment, access to public and private accommodations (such as hotels, theaters, restaurants, and grocery stores), and services offered through state and local governments (N.O.D./Harris & Associates, 1999, 2000). Second, because the historic Civil Rights Act of 1964 did not even mention people with disabilities, they had no federal protection against discrimination except through the somewhat limited provisions in Section 504. As stated by the National Council on Disability,

> ADA is the most comprehensive policy statement ever made in American law about how the nation should address individuals with disabilities. Built on principles of equal opportunity, full participation, independent living and economic self-sufficiency, the law reflects the disability community's convictions and determination to participate as first-class American citizens and to direct their own futures. (1996, p. 23)

In July 2002, the National Organization on Disability (N.O.D.) and Harris and Associates released the results of a survey on how Americans perceived ADA twelve years after its passage. The survey found a strong and sustained public endorsement of this landmark civil rights legislation. Of all respondents, 77% were aware of ADA. Of those who had heard of it, 93% approved of what it was enacted to accomplish.

## The ADA Definition of Disability

Under ADA, a person with a disability is defined as (1) having a physical or mental impairment that substantially limits him or her in some major life activity, and (2) having experienced discrimination resulting from this physical or mental

---

**FOCUS 4**

What is the purpose of the Americans with Disabilities Act?

---

**Section 504**

Provision within the Vocational Rehabilitation Act of 1973 that prohibits discrimination against persons with disabilities in federally assisted programs and activities.

**Civil Rights Act of 1964**

Legislation passed in the United States that prohibits discrimination against individuals on the basis of race, sex, religion, or national origin.

**Americans with Disabilities Act (ADA)**

Civil rights legislation in the United States that provides a mandate to end discrimination against people with disabilities in private sector employment, all public services, public accommodations, transportation, and telecommunications.

---

# ONE CITY'S RESPONSE TO ADA

## Building a Barrier-Free Community for 10-Year-Old Brittany and Her Friends

Fernandina Beach, Florida, a resort community of 8,800 residents on Amelia Island between the Atlantic Ocean and the Amelia River, is Florida's second-oldest city and the state's first resort area. With its 50-block downtown historic district, golf courses, parks and nature areas, beaches, and a resident shrimping fleet, the community welcomes visitors and vacationers from all corners of the country. And recently, Fernandina Beach became an even more welcoming place for people with disabilities.

The city of Fernandina Beach made a decision—and a commitment—to go above and beyond the minimum ADA requirements and to make the city as usable and accessible as possible for everyone. To do this, city officials and residents worked together to find new approaches to accessibility, an experience they found both gratifying and exciting.

The city is working to make all its playgrounds accessible. Each city playground will have new accessible equipment, accessible playground surfaces, and accessible paths to the playground equipment. Cheri Fisher is

thrilled with the changes. She no longer has to lift her daughter onto the play equipment and can happily watch as Brittany and her buddy go down the slide together. "What's really good is that Brittany now can play longer because she's not as tired from trudging to the playground. She also can play on pretty much all the equipment and play together with her friends; she's not being excluded now." Ten-year-old Brittany, who uses crutches and sometimes a wheelchair to get around, agrees. "I like the rope things that go round and round and I like the slide with the bumps and I liked the three of us sliding together!" In addition to creating accessible playgrounds, the city installed an accessible route to the picnic pavilions in each of its city parks and accessible picnic tables in every pavilion.

The city constructed a beach walkover at the Main Beach and constructed an accessible viewing area connected to the accessible beach path, allowing as many as eight people using wheelchairs to sit together on the beach and enjoy an unobstructed view of the surf. The city plans to construct two additional walkovers at opposite ends of the city at the North Park and Seaside Park Beaches to give wheelchair users access to the beach nearest them. The city also purchased two beach wheelchairs for those who wish to join family and friends near the water on the sandy beach. It has plans to buy more.

SOURCE: United States Department of Justice (2003). A resort community improves access to city programs and services for residents and vacationers. Available: http://www.usdoj.gov/crt/ada/fernstor.htm (retrieved February 18, 2003)

---

impairment. Federal ADA regulations define a physical or mental impairment as consisting of

1. Any physiological disorder, or condition, cosmetic disfigurement, or anatomical loss affecting one or more of the following body systems: neurological, musculoskeletal, special sense organs, respiratory (including speech organs), cardiovascular, reproductive, digestive, genito-urinary, hemic and lymphatic, skin, and endocrine; or

2. Any mental or psychological disorder, such as mental retardation, organic brain syndrome, emotional or mental illness, and specific learning disabilities. (29 C.F.R. § 1630.2[h]).

Federal regulations do not establish an exclusive list of specific impairments covered by ADA. Instead, they describe the type of condition that constitutes a physical or mental impairment. ADA does, however, specify certain conditions that are *not* considered impairments. These include homosexuality and bisexuality; environmental, cultural, and economic disadvantages, such as a prison record or a lack of education; and age. (42 U.S.C. § 12211[a]; 29 C.F.R. pt. 1630 app. § 1630.2[h]). A person does not have an impairment simply because he or she is advanced in years.

### Major Provisions of ADA

ADA mandates protections for people with disabilities in public- and private-sector employment, all public services, and public accommodations, transportation, and telecommunications. The U.S. Department of Justice is charged with ensuring that these provisions are enforced on behalf of all people with disabilities. The intent of ADA is to create a "fair and level playing field" for eligible persons with disabilities. To do so, the law specifies that **reasonable accommodations** need to be made that take into account each person's needs resulting from his or her disabilities. As defined in law, the principal test for a reasonable accommodation is its effectiveness: Does the accommodation provide an opportunity for a person with a disability to achieve the same level of performance and to enjoy benefits equal to those of an average, similarly situated person without a disability? (See the nearby Debate Forum, "Leveling the Playing Field or Creating Advantage? Casey's Story.")

The major provisions of the ADA include the following:

- *Employment.* ADA mandates that employers not discriminate in any employment practices, including job application procedures, hiring, firing, advancement, compensation, training, and other terms, conditions, and privileges of employment. It applies to recruitment, advertising, tenure, layoff, leave, fringe benefits, and all other employment-related activities. The law applies to any business with 15 or more employees. (See the nearby Reflect on This, "What Everyone Needs to Know About Employment and the Americans with Disabilities Act.")

- *Transportation.* ADA requires that all new public transit buses, bus and train stations, and rail systems be accessible to people with disabilities. Transit authorities must provide transportation services to individuals with disabilities who cannot use fixed-route bus services. All Amtrak stations must be accessible to people with disabilities by the year 2010. Discrimination by air carriers in areas other than employment is covered not by the ADA but rather by the Air Carrier Access Act (49 U.S.C. 1374 [c]).

- *Public accommodations.* Restaurants, hotels, and retail stores may not discriminate against individuals with disabilities. Physical barriers in existing facilities must be removed if removal is readily achievable. If not, alternative methods of providing the services must be offered. All new construction and alterations of facilities must be accessible.

- *Government.* State and local agencies may not discriminate against qualified individuals with disabilities. All government facilities, services, and communications must be accessible to people with disabilities.

- *Telecommunications.* ADA requires that all companies offering telephone service to the general public must offer telephone relay services to individuals with hearing loss who use telecommunication devices or similar equipment.

# Making the ADA Dream a Reality

Legislating against discrimination is one thing; enforcing compliance with the laws prohibiting it is another. The purpose of ADA was to ensure that comprehensive services (e.g., employment, housing, educational programs, public transportation, restaurant access, and religious activities) would be available to all individuals within or as close as possible to their family and community lives. In 1999 the U.S. Supreme Court ruled, in *L.C. & E.W. v. Olmstead* (now known as *the Olmstead decision*), that it is a violation of ADA to discriminate against people with disabilities by providing services only in institutions when they could be served in a community-based setting. This historic decision encouraged states to reevaluate how they deliver publicly funded long-term care services to people with disabilities. A state can be in compliance with ADA if it has (1) a comprehensive, effective working plan for placing qualified people in less restrictive settings, and (2) a waiting list for community-based services that ensures that people can receive services and be moved off the list at a reasonable pace (Fox-Grage, Folkemer, Straw, & Hansen, 2002).

**Reasonable accommodations**

Requirements within ADA to ensure that a person with a disability has an equal chance of participation. The intent is to create a "fair and level playing field" for the person with a disability. A reasonable accommodation takes into account each person's needs resulting from their disability. Accommodations may be arranged in the areas of employment, transportation, or telecommunications.

## Debate Forum

# LEVELING THE PLAYING FIELD OR CREATING ADVANTAGE? CASEY'S STORY

**C**asey Martin was born on June 2, 1972, with a very rare congenital disorder (Klippel-Trenauny-Weber syndrome), a condition with no known cure. The disorder is degenerative and causes serious blood circulation problems in Casey's right leg and foot. His right leg is about half the size of his left, and when forced to walk on it, Casey experiences excruciating pain and swelling. Casey can only expect these problems to worsen as he grows older, and there is a possibility that leg amputation will be necessary in the future.

Obviously, this condition would be difficult and very painful under any circumstances, but Casey's occupation is professional golf—a career that was fostered early in life and one that he is very good at. During his college years, Casey went to Stanford and played with Tiger Woods on the team that won the 1994 NCAA championship. In 1995, Casey joined the Nike pro tour and was just one step away from the pinnacle of golf, the Professional Golf Association (PGA) tour. However, his condition continued to deteriorate, and the pain in his right leg and foot grew steadily worse. He finally reached the point where he could no longer walk a golf course but had to use a cart to get around. Although the PGA had modified the rules of golf for players with disabilities in recreational settings, the organization did not permit the use of a golf cart during *competitions.* Given the progressive state of his disability, Casey requested an exemption that would allow him to ride rather than walk. The PGA refused his request, and Casey took the matter to court, claiming discrimination on the basis of the

Americans with Disabilities Act. In February of 1998, a U.S. magistrate found in Casey's favor. Casey played the events on the Nike tour throughout 1998 and 1999, qualifying for his first PGA tour event in January 2000. Meanwhile, the PGA appealed the decision to allow Casey to ride a cart, and in a 7-to-2 decision on May 29, 2001, the U.S. Supreme Court ruled that Casey Martin must be allowed to ride a cart during competition. The Court ruled that allowing Casey access to the cart would not "fundamentally alter" the game of golf or give him any advantage over other golfers on the course.

Although the U.S. Supreme Court ruled in Casey's favor, the debate continues over whether he has been given an advantage over his fellow pro golfers by being able to ride a golf cart when others must walk. Is riding a cart an advantage for Casey, or does the golf cart simply allow the "playing field" to be leveled, as intended in the Americans with Disabilities Act? What is your view?

## POINT

The PGA's attempt to disallow Casey Martin's use of a golf cart was an act of discrimination against a person with a disability. The PGA is a public entity, and golf courses are places of public accommodation under the Americans with Disabilities Act. Therefore, the association must provide *reasonable accommodations* for someone with a permanent disability. As the Supreme Court ruling notes, Casey met all the ADA requirements. He has a permanent disability, and without a reasonable accommodation (riding in a golf cart) he could not participate in his chosen profession. The PGA argues that riding in a cart creates an advantage for Casey. Couldn't it be argued that riding is actually a disadvantage? From a sitting position, Casey can't get the same perspective on and feel for the course that his competitors have. The PGA also argued that it should have the right to determine its own rules for competitions. Fine! Change the rules to allow Casey and any other golfer with disabilities to use a cart. In the end, if letting Casey Martin ride means that the PGA must allow every golfer to use a cart, so be it. Isn't the PGA's motto "anything is possible"?

## COUNTERPOINT

One cannot help but express admiration for the grit and determination of Casey Martin. There is no doubt that he is a person with a tragic medical disability. However, with all due respect to the decision of the U.S. Supreme Court, Congress never intended for ADA to require an organization such as the PGA to change its basic rules of operation and thus create an advantage for one golfer over another. Physical requirements, including walking up to five miles on any given day in unfavorable weather, is an *essential element* of golf at its highest level. Any golfer who is allowed to ride in a cart, disabled or not, will have an unfair advantage over other competitors. If the PGA allows this for one player, it will create hardship for others, which is exactly what ADA did not want. The real issue here is that a fundamental rule of golf has stood from its beginning hundreds of years ago: Players in the highest levels of competition must walk the course as part of the test of their skills. One set of rules must apply to all players.

What do you think? To give your opinion, go to Chapter 1 of the companion website (www.ablongman.com/hardman8e), and click on Debate Forum.

## WHAT EVERYONE NEEDS TO KNOW ABOUT EMPLOYMENT AND THE AMERICANS WITH DISABILITIES ACT (ADA)

**What is the Americans with Disabilities Act?**    ADA is a federal law that protects people with a disability against many kinds of discrimination. Discrimination keeps people with a disability from getting a job just because someone says they have a disability. One part of ADA protects them against discrimination at work. ADA can "open doors." It can make it easier for people with a disability to apply for a job. The law can help each individual get a job, learn to do the job, and keep the job. The employer is responsible to help each person work faster and learn the job efficiently.

**Which jobs can people with a disability apply for?**
They can apply for any job for which they can do the important parts of the work, with or without help. ADA refers to the most important parts of a job as the "essential functions." They are the parts that must be done. Here are some examples. A mailroom clerk might have three essential functions: getting mail from a bag, sorting mail, and delivering it. A job that involves putting machine parts together might have four essential functions: getting supplies from a room, choosing the parts needed, putting the parts together, and packing the shipping boxes. These are only examples. Every job has its own essential functions. A person with a disability is qualified for a job if he or she can do the essential functions, with or without help.

**What are "reasonable accommodations"?**    A "reasonable accommodation" is any change or help that makes it easier for a person with a disability to find a job and do the work. Some of the help may come from co-workers. Some may come from job coaches. There are many kinds of "reasonable accommodations" for employment.

   *If help is needed getting a job:*

- Bring a friend or family member along to apply for a job.
- Ask the employer to read the application aloud.
- Ask the employer to write information on the application.
- Ask the employer to let the person with a disability show how he or she would do the job.

   Remember—ADA protects people with disabilities against discrimination. Employers cannot ask whether a person has a disability. They cannot ask whether the person takes certain medicine or has been in an institution. They can ask the person to have a medical exam, but only after offering a job.

**What if the person with a disability can't do some "nonessential" parts of a job?**    Ask the manager for "job restructuring." This means someone else will do the less important parts of the job. The person with a disability will still have to do the most important parts, or essential functions.

**How can a person with a disability get "reasonable accommodations"?**    A person with a disability (with assistance as necessary) can talk to the employer. Together they can decide what reasonable accommodations will help at work. There are many possible reasonable accommodations. They depend on the job and the individual's needs.

**What kind of assistance can people with disabilities ask for?**    They can ask for help applying for a job. They can ask for a reasonable accommodations for learning or doing the job. They can also ask for help with learning the rules at work. If they have trouble getting to work on time, they can ask to change the starting time.

**When can people with disabilities ask for assistance?**
They can ask for reasonable accommodations any time. They can ask when they apply for a job. They can ask when they start a job. They can ask after beginning work. When they start a job, it's important to talk to the employer about the help they might need. They may find that they need more help once they are working. They can ask the employer about a new reasonable accommodation anytime.

**Does the employer have to provide a "reasonable accommodation"?**    Not always. Giving help may cause the employer "undue hardship." The employer doesn't have to give a reasonable accommodation if it costs too much. The employer doesn't have to give a reasonable accommodation if the work won't get done, even with help.

**Can someone come to work to assist people with disabilities?**    Yes. A job coach or counselor can help the individual learn a job. An agency may pay for a job coach or a counselor to help learn the job. Or the employer might let a friend or someone in the family help. The employer does not have to pay for this assistance.

SOURCE:  Adapted from *Opening Doors for You,* The Joseph P. Kennedy Jr. Foundation, n.d., Washington, DC: Author.

What services and supports must be available to ensure that an individual with a disability is able to live and learn successfully in a community setting?

**Barrier-free facility**

A building or other structure that is designed and constructed so that people with mobility disabilities (such as those in wheelchairs) can move freely through all areas without encountering architectural obstructions.

Individuals with disabilities must have access to generic community services, including dental care, medical treatment, life insurance, and so forth. Access to these services gives people the opportunity to be included in community life. Successful inclusion is based on two factors: (1) the individual's ability, with appropriate education and training, to adapt to societal expectations, and (2) the willingness of society to adapt to and accommodate individuals with differences.

Access to adequate housing and a barrier-free environment is essential for people with physical disabilities. A **barrier-free facility** may be created by renovating existing facilities and requiring that new buildings and public transportation incorporate barrier-free designs. People who use wheelchairs or crutches need entrance ramps to and within public buildings; accessibility to public telephones, vending machines, and restrooms; and lifts for public transportation vehicles. Available community living environments could include private homes, specialized boarding homes, supervised apartments, group homes, and foster homes.

Recreation and leisure opportunities within the community vary substantially with the individual's age and the severity of his or her disability, and the availability of such opportunities also varies from community to community. Thus many persons with disabilities may not have access to dance and music lessons, gymnastics training, swimming lessons, and scouting—activities that are generally available to others within the community. Similar problems exist for children, adolescents, and adults with disabilities, many of whom may do little with their leisure time beyond watching television.

Recreational programs must be developed to help individuals take part in worthwhile leisure activities. Therapeutic recreation is a profession concerned specifically with using recreation to help people adapt their physical, emotional, or social characteristics to take advantage of leisure activities more independently in a community setting—and hence to lead more satisfying lives.

Work is essential to the creation of successful lifestyles for all adults, including those with disabilities. Yet many individuals with disabilities are unable to gain employment during their adult years. A poll conducted by the National Organization on Disability and Harris Associates (2000) found significant gaps between the employment rates of people with disabilities and of their peers who were not disabled. Only 32% of people with disabilities (ages 18 to 64) work full-time or part-time, compared to 81% of people who are not disabled. Of the people with disabilities who are not working, two-thirds say that they would prefer to work. A comparison of working and nonworking individuals with disabilities revealed that working individuals were more satisfied with life, had more money, and were less likely to blame their disability for preventing them from reaching their potential. For more insight into the employment of a person with disabilities, see the nearby Case Study, "Sarina."

*The inclusion of children and adults with disabilities in recreation and sports activities recognizes and accepts the range of human diversity. What are some other reasons for people with disabilities to participate in community recreation and sports activities?*

## Case Study

## SARINA

Over the past several years, many changes have occurred in Sarina's life. After spending most of her life in a large institution, Sarina, now in her late 30s, moved into an apartment with two other women, both of whom have a disability. She receives assistance from a local supported-living program in developing skills that will allow her to make her own decisions and become more independent in the community.

Over the years, Sarina has had many labels describing her disability, including mental retardation, epilepsy, autism, physical disability, chronic health problems, and serious emotional disturbance. She is very much challenged both mentally and physically. Medical problems associated with epilepsy necessitate the use of medications that affect Sarina's behavior (motivation, attitude, etc.) and her physical well-being. During her early 20s, while walking up a long flight of stairs, Sarina had a seizure that resulted in a fall and a broken neck. The long-term impact from the fall was a paralyzed right hand and limited use of her left leg.

Sarina's life goal has been to work in a real job, make money, and have choices about how she spends it. For most of her life, the goal has been out of reach. Her only jobs have been in sheltered workshops, where she worked for next to nothing, doing piecemeal work such as sorting envelopes, putting together cardboard boxes, or folding laundry. Whereas most of the focus in the past has been on what Sarina "can't do" (can't read, can't get along with supervisors, can't handle the physical requirements of a job), her family and the professionals on her support team are looking more at her very strong desire to succeed in a community job.

A job has opened up for a stock clerk at a local video store about 3 miles from Sarina's apartment. The store manager is willing to pay minimum wage for someone to work 4 to 6 hours a day stocking the shelves with videos and handling some basic tasks (such as cleaning floors, washing windows, and dusting furniture). Sarina loves movies and is really interested in this job. With the support of family and her professional team, she has applied for the job.

### APPLICATION

1. As Sarina's potential employer, what are some of the issues you would raise about her capability to perform the essential functions of the job?

2. What would you see as the "reasonable accommodations" necessary to help Sarina succeed at this job if she were to be hired?

# Multidisciplinary Perspectives on People with Disabilities

## FOCUS
## 6

How did the work of 19th-century physicians and philosophers contribute to our understanding of people with disabilities?

This chapter concludes with a brief examination of three disciplines concerned with supporting people with disabilities and their families in community settings: medicine, psychology, and sociology. Each discipline is unique in its understanding of, and approach to, people with disabilities. Figure 1.2 lists some terms commonly used in each field.

### Medicine

The **medical model** has two dimensions: normalcy and pathology. *Normalcy* is defined as the absence of a biological problem. **Pathology** consists of alterations caused in an organism by disease and resulting in a state of ill health that interferes with or destroys the integrity of the organism. The medical model, often referred to as the *disease model,* focuses primarily on biological problems and on defining the nature of the disease and its pathological effects on the individual. The model is universal and does not have values that are culturally relative. It is based on the premise that being healthy is better than being sick, regardless of the culture in which one lives.

When diagnosing a problem, a physician carefully follows a definite pattern of procedures that includes questioning the patient to obtain a history of the problem, conducting a physical examination and laboratory studies, and (in some cases) performing surgical exploration. The person who has a biological problem is labeled the *patient,* and the deficits are then described as the *patient's disease.*

We must go back more than 200 years to find the first documented attempts to personalize medical treatment programs to serve the needs of people with differences. In 1799, as a young physician and authority on diseases of the ear and education of those with hearing loss, Jean Marc Itard (1775–1838) believed that the environment,

**Medical model**

Model by which human development is viewed according to two dimensions: normal and pathological. Normal refers to the absence of biological problems; pathological refers to alterations in the organism caused by disease.

**Pathology**

Alterations in an organism that are caused by disease.

FIGURE 1.2

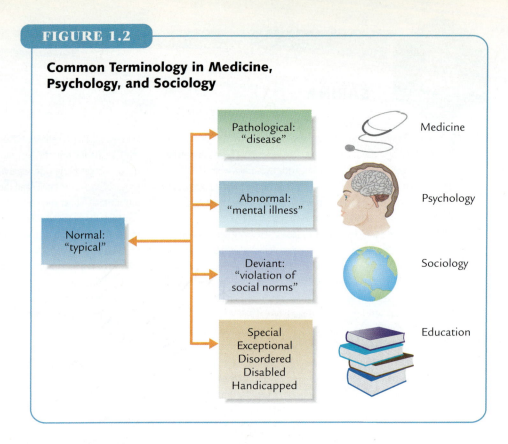

**Common Terminology in Medicine, Psychology, and Sociology**

in conjunction with physiological stimulation, could contribute to the learning potential of any human being. Itard was influenced by the earlier work of Philippe Pinel (1742–1826), a French physician concerned with mental illness, and John Locke (1632–1704), an English philosopher. Pinel argued that people characterized as insane or as idiots needed to be treated humanely, but his teachings also emphasized that they were essentially incurable and that any treatment to remedy their disabilities would be fruitless. Locke, in contrast, described the mind as a "blank slate" that could be opened to all kinds of new stimuli. The positions of Pinel and Locke represent the classic controversy of **nature versus nurture:** What are the roles of heredity and environment in determining a person's capabilities?

Itard tested the theories of Pinel and Locke in his work with Victor, the so-called wild boy of Aveyron. Victor was 12 years old when he was found in the woods by hunters. He had not developed any language, and his behavior was virtually uncontrollable, described as savage or animal-like. Ignoring Pinel's diagnosis that the child was an incurable idiot, Itard took responsibility for Victor and designed a program of sensory stimulation that was intended to cure his condition. After five years, Victor developed some verbal language and became more socialized as he grew accustomed to his new environment. Itard's work with Victor documented for the first time that learning is possible even for individuals described by most professionals as totally helpless.

Medical services for people with disabilities have evolved considerably since Itard's groundbreaking work. The focus today is directly on the individual in family and community settings. In many cases, the physician is the first professional with whom parents have contact about their child's disability, particularly when the child's problem is identifiable immediately after birth or during early childhood. The physician is the family adviser and communicates with the parents regarding the medical prognosis and recommendations for treatment. However, physicians too often assume they are the family's only counseling resource (Drew & Hardman, 2004). Physicians should be aware of additional resources within the community, including other parents, social workers, mental health professionals, and educators.

Medical services are often taken for granted simply because they are readily available to most people. This is not true, however, for many people with disabilities. It is

**Nature versus nurture**

Controversy concerning how much of a person's ability is related to sociocultural influences (nurture) as opposed to genetic factors (nature).

not uncommon for a pediatrician to suggest that parents seek treatment elsewhere for their child with a disability, even when the problem is a common illness such as a cold or a sore throat.

It would be unfair to stereotype medical professionals as unresponsive to the needs of people with disabilities. On the contrary, medical technology has prevented many disabilities from occurring and has enhanced the quality of life for many people. However, to ensure that people with disabilities receive comprehensive medical services in a community setting, several factors must be considered. Physicians in community practice (e.g., general practitioners and pediatricians) must receive more medical training in the medical, psychological, and educational aspects of disability conditions. This training could include instruction regarding developmental milestones; attitudes toward children with disabilities; disabling conditions; prevention; screening, diagnosis, and assessment; interdisciplinary collaboration; effective communication with parents; long-term medical and social treatment programs; and community resources.

*Physicians in community practice must be willing to provide medical care to people with disabilities. What additional training do you think is needed in order for physicians to care for people with disabilities?*

Physicians must also be willing to treat people with disabilities for common illnesses when the patient's disability is irrelevant to the treatment. Physicians need not become disability specialists, but they must have enough knowledge to refer patients to appropriate specialists when necessary. For instance, physicians must be aware of and willing to refer patients to nonmedical community resources, such as social workers, educators, and psychologists. The medical profession must continue to support physician specialists and other allied health personnel who are well equipped to work with people with disabilities. These specialized health professionals include **geneticists** and **genetics counselors, physical therapists** and **occupational therapists,** public health nurses, and nutritional and dietary consultants.

## Psychology

Modern psychology is the science of human and animal behavior—the study of the overt acts and mental events that can be observed in an organism and evaluated. Broadly viewed, psychology is concerned with every detectable action of an individual. Behavior is the focus of psychology, and when the behavior of an individual does not meet the criteria of normalcy, it is labeled *abnormal*.

Psychology, as we know it today, is more than 125 years old. In 1879 Wilhelm Wundt (1832–1920) defined psychology as the science of conscious experience. His definition was based on the *principle of introspection*—looking into oneself to analyze experiences. William James (1842–1910), in his treatise *The Principles of Psychology* (1890), expanded Wundt's conception of conscious experience to include learning, motivation, and emotions. In 1913 John B. Watson (1878–1958) shifted the focus of psychology from conscious experience to observable behavior and mental events.

**Geneticists**

Professionals who specializes in the study of heredity.

**Genetics counselors**

Specially trained professionals who counsel people about their chances of producing a seriously ill infant, in reference to their genetic history.

**Physical therapists**

Professionals who provide services that help restore function, improve mobility, relieve pain, and prevent or limit permanent physical disabilities. They help restore, maintain, and promote overall fitness and health for people of all ages.

**Occupational therapists**

Professionals who specialize in developing self-care, work, and play activities to increase independent function and quality of life, enhance development, and prevent disability.

**FOCUS 7**

Distinguish between abnormal behavior and social deviance.

In 1920 Watson conducted an experiment with an 11-month-old child named Albert. Albert showed no fear of a white rat when he was initially exposed to the animal, seeing it as a toy and playing with it freely. Watson then introduced a loud, terrifying noise directly behind Albert each time the rat was presented. After a period of time, the boy became frightened by the sight of any furry white object, even though the loud noise was no longer presented. Albert had learned to fear rats through **conditioning,** the process in which new objects or situations elicit responses that were previously elicited by other stimuli. Watson thus demonstrated that abnormal behavior could be learned through the interaction of the individual with environmental stimuli (Watson & Rayner, 1920).

In spite of Watson's work, most theorists during the first half of the 20th century considered the medical model the most logical and scientific approach to understanding abnormal behavior. The public was more accepting of the view that people with psychological disturbances were sick and hence were not fully responsible for their problems.

The **ecological approach,** which emerged in the latter half of the 20th century, supported Watson's theories. This approach views abnormal behavior more as a result of an individual's interaction with the environment than as a disease. The approach theorizes that social and environmental stress, in combination with the individual's inability to cope, lead to psychological disturbances.

We cannot live in today's society without encountering the dynamics of abnormal behavior. The media are replete with stories of murder, suicide, sexual aberration, burglary, robbery, embezzlement, child abuse, and other incidents that display abnormal behavior. Each case represents a point on the continuum of personal maladjustment that exists in society. Levels of maladjustment range from behaviors that are slightly deviant or eccentric (but still within the confines of normal human experience) through **neurotic disorders** (partial disorganization characterized by combinations of anxieties, compulsions, obsessions, and phobias) to **psychotic disorders** (severe disorganization resulting in loss of contact with reality and characterized by delusions, hallucinations, and illusions).

In Western culture, the study of abnormal behavior has historically been based in philosophy and religion. Until the Middle Ages, the disturbed or "mad" person was thought to have "made a pact with the devil," and the psychological affliction was believed to be a result of divine punishment or the work of devils, witches, or demons residing within the person. The earliest known treatment for mental disorders, a process called *trephining,* involved drilling holes in the afflicted person's skull to permit evil spirits to leave (Carlson & Buskist, 1997).

Today's psychologists use myriad approaches in the treatment of mental disorders, including behavior therapy, rational-emotive therapy, group psychotherapy, family therapy, and client-centered therapy. According to Carlson and Buskist (1997), the majority of psychologists describe their therapeutic philosophy as eclectic. They choose from many different approaches in determining the best way to work with an individual in need of psychological help.

## Sociology

Whereas psychology focuses primarily on the behavior of the individual, sociology is concerned with modern cultures, group behaviors, societal institutions, and intergroup relationships. Sociology examines individuals in relation to their physical and social environments. When individuals adhere to the social norms of the group, they are considered normal. When individuals are unable to adapt to social roles or to establish appropriate interpersonal relationships, their behaviors are labeled **deviant.** Unlike medical pathology, social deviance cannot be defined in universal terms. Instead, it is defined within the context of the culture, in any way the culture chooses to define it.

Even within the same society, different social groups often define deviance differently. Groups of people who share the same norms and values develop their own rules about what is and what is not deviant behavior. Society at large may not share

**Conditioning**

The process by which new objects or situations elicit responses that were previously elicited by other stimuli.

**Ecological approach**

An approach in psychology that ascribes abnormal behavior more to the interaction of an individual with the environment than to disease.

**Neurotic disorders**

Behavior characterized by combinations of anxieties, compulsions, obsessions, and phobias.

**Psychotic disorders**

A general term referring to a serious behavior disorder resulting in a loss of contact with reality and characterized by delusions, hallucinations, or illusions.

**Deviant**

A term used to describe the behavior of individuals who are unable to adapt to social roles or to establish appropriate interpersonal relationships.

their views, but the group's definitions of deviance still apply to members of the group (Kammeyer et al., 1997).

Four principles serve as guidelines in determining who will be labeled socially deviant:

1. Normal behavior must meet societal, cultural, or group expectations. Deviance is defined as a violation of social norms.

2. Social deviance is not necessarily an illness. Failure to conform to societal norms does not imply that the individual has pathological or biological deficits.

3. Each culture determines the range of behaviors that are defined as normal or deviant and then enforces these norms. Those people with the greatest power within the culture can impose their criteria for normalcy on those who are less powerful.

4. Social deviance may be caused by the interaction of several factors, including genetic makeup and individual experiences within the social environment.

Today, many different kinds of sociologists specialize across more than 50 subfields and specialties. Within each specialty, sociologists undertake a systematic study of the workings and influence of social groups, organizations, cultures, and societies on individual and group behavior. The sociologist accumulates and disseminates information about social behavior (including disability) in the context of the society as a whole (Kammeyer et al., 1997). The following are just a few examples of specialties within sociology that may include an emphasis on disability: deviant behavior and social disorganization, aging, criminology and criminal justice, family and marriage, medicine, and education.

This chapter has examined many different perspectives on people with disabilities, including common terminology used to describe these individuals, bringing about social change and inclusion through the Americans with Disabilities Act, and understanding people with disabilities from the point of view of medicine, psychology, and sociology. In the next chapter, we focus on the education of students with disabilities in America's schools. Chapter 2 examines the origins of special education, the characteristics of effective instruction, the Individuals with Disabilities Education Act, and current trends in educational services and supports.

# FOCUS REVIEW

**FOCUS 1  Why do we label people?**

- Labels are an attempt to describe, identify, and distinguish one person from another.

- Many medical, psychological, social, and educational services require that an individual be labeled in order to determine who is eligible to receive special services.

- Labels help professionals communicate more effectively with one another and provide a common ground for evaluating research findings.

- Labels enable professionals to differentiate more clearly the needs of one group of people from those of another.

**FOCUS 2  Identify three approaches to describing human differences.**

- The developmental approach is based on differences in the course of human development from what is considered normal physical, social, and intellectual growth. Human differences are the result of interaction between biological and environmental factors. Observing large numbers of individuals and looking for the characteristics that occur most frequently at any given age can explain normal growth.

- The cultural approach defines normalcy in terms of established cultural standards. Human differences can be explained by examining the values of any given society. Hence what is considered normal changes over time and differs from culture to culture.

- Self-labeling reflects how we perceive ourselves, although those perceptions may not be consistent with how others see us.

**FOCUS 3** Describe the services for people with disabilities through most of the 20th century. What was the role of families in bringing about change?

- People with disabilities were viewed as being deviant or defective and were considered social problems.
- State laws were passed that prevented people with disabilities from marrying, mandated sterilization, and eventually segregated them into large institutions.
- Many families who had a child with a disability were unable to get help for basic needs, such as medical and dental care, social services, and education.
- In the 1960s, parent and professional organizations were established to fight for recognition of the right of people with disabilities to be included in the community.
- Through the advocacy of parent and professionals organizations,

the civil rights of people with disabilities were finally recognized with the passage of the Americans with Disabilities Act (ADA) in 1990.

**FOCUS 4** What is the purpose of the Americans with Disabilities Act?

- ADA provides a national mandate to end discrimination against individuals with disabilities in private-sector employment, in all public services, and in public accommodations, transportation, and telecommunications.

**FOCUS 5** What services and supports must be available to ensure that an individual with a disability is able to live and learn successfully in a community setting?

- Comprehensive community services must be available, including access to housing, employment, public transportation, recreation, and religious activities.
- The individual should be able to purchase services such as medical and dental care, as well as

adequate life insurance.

**FOCUS 6** How did the work of 19th-century physicians and philosophers contribute to our understanding of people with disabilities?

- Early 19th-century physicians emphasized that people with disabilities should be treated humanely.
- Jean-Marc Itard demonstrated that an individual with a severe disability could learn new skills through physiological stimulation.

**FOCUS 7** Distinguish between abnormal behavior and social deviance.

- Human behavior is the focus of psychology. When the behavior of an individual does not meet the criteria for normalcy, it is labeled *abnormal*.
- Sociology is concerned with modern cultures, group behaviors, societal institutions, and intergroup relationships. When people are unable to adapt to social roles or to establish interpersonal relationships, their behaviors are labeled *deviant*.

## FURTHER READINGS

Braddock, D. (Ed.) (2002). *Disability at the Dawn of the 21st Century and the State of the States*. Washington, DC: The American Association on Mental Retardation.

*This book provides an excellent perspective on the history of programs and services for people with developmental disabilities from the era of institutions to the 21st-century goal of inclusion. The authors also provide interesting facts and figures on state financing of services for people with disabilities.*

Evan Terry Associates (1997). *Pocket Guide to the ADA: Americans with Disabilities Act Accessibility Guidelines for Buildings and Facilities*. Hoboken, NJ: Wiley.

*This book helps businesses and organizations understand the requirements for barrier-free facilities under ADA.*

*The guide is augmented with more than 60 illustrations from the Americans with Disabilities Act Accessibility Guidelines, and it covers special requirements for businesses, restaurants, medical care facilities, libraries, and so on.*

Fleisher, D. J., & Zames, F. (2001). *The Disability Rights Movement: From Charity to Confrontation* (2001). Philadelphia: Temple University Press.

*Based on interviews with almost a hundred activists, this book provides a detailed history of the struggle for disability rights in the United States. It is a complex story of shifts in consciousness and policy and of changing focuses on particular disabilities, such as blindness, deafness, polio, quadriplegia, psychiatric and developmental disabilities, chronic conditions (such as cancer and heart disease), and AIDS.*

## WEB RESOURCES

### Americans with Disabilities Act (ADA)

www.usdoj.gov/crt/ada/adahom1.htm

This website contains up-to-date information on ADA, along with often-asked questions about the law, stories of people with disabilities, and analysis of the law's major provisions.

### The Council for Exceptional Children (CEC)

www.cec.sped.org

The Council for Exceptional Children (CEC) is the largest international professional organization dedicated to improving educational outcomes for individuals with exceptionalities, students with disabilities, and/or the gifted. This site contains information on professional development opportunities, publications and products, and updates on the Individuals with Disabilities Education Act.

### The National Council on Disability (NCD)

www.ncd.gov

This federal agency promotes policies, programs, practices, and procedures that guarantee equal opportunity for those with disabilities. Its goal is to empower individuals with disabilities to achieve economic self-sufficiency, independent living, and inclusion and integration into all aspects of society.

### National Organization on Disability (N.O.D.)

www.nod.org

The mission of the National Organization on Disability (N.O.D.) is to expand the participation and contribution of America's 54 million men, women, and children with disabilities in all aspects of life by raising public awareness of disability. This site contains information on community involvement and economic participation for people with disabilities.

## BUILDING YOUR PORTFOLIO

If you are thinking about a career in special education, you should know that many states use national standards developed by the Council for Exceptional Children (CEC) to assess a teacher candidate's knowledge and skills for working with students with disabilities. See a complete listing of the ten CEC Content Standards on the inside front cover of this text.

### CEC Content Standards Addressed in Chapter 1

1. Foundations
2. Development and Characteristics of Learners
5. Learning Environments and Social Interactions
9. Professional and Ethical Practice

### Assess Your Knowledge of the CEC Standards Addressed in Chapter 1

Some states require that teacher candidates develop a portfolio of products that demonstrate mastery of the CEC content standards. To assist in the development of products for this portfolio, you may wish to complete the following activities.

- Complete a written test of the chapter's content.

  *If your instructor requires a written test of your content knowledge for this chapter, keep a copy for your port-*

*folio. A practice test on the information covered in this chapter is available through the companion website (www.ablongman.com/hardman8e) and the Student Study Guide.*

- Respond to Application Questions for the Case Study "Sarina."

  *Review the Case Study and respond in writing to the application questions. Keep a copy of the Case Study and your written response for your portfolio.*

- Complete the "Take a Stand" activity for the Debate Forum "Leveling the Playing Field or Creating Advantage? Casey's Story."

  *Read the Debate Forum in this chapter and then visit the companion website to complete the activity "Take a Stand." Keep a copy of this activity for your portfolio.*

- Participate in a Community Service Learning Activity.

  *Community service is a valuable way to enhance your learning experience. Visit the companion website for suggested community service learning activities that correspond to the information presented in this chapter. Develop a reflective journal of the service learning experience for your portfolio.*

## THEMES OF THE TIMES

**The New York Times**
nytimes.com

Expand your knowledge of the concepts discussed in this chapter by reading current and historical articles from the *New York Times* by visiting the "Themes of the Times" section of the companion website: **www.ablongman.com/hardman8e.**

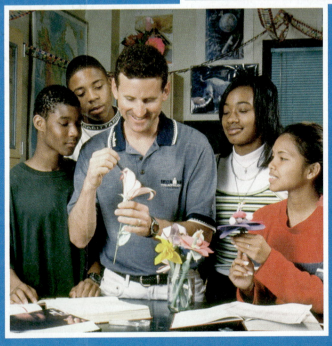

# Education for All

## Much Has Been Accomplished and Much Remains to Be Done

Four decades ago, [the U.S.] Congress began to lend the resources of the federal government to the task of educating children with disabilities. Since then, special education has become one of the most important symbols of American compassion, inclusion, and educational opportunity. Over the years, what has become known as the Individuals with Disabilities Education Act has moved children with disabilities from institutions into classrooms, from the outskirts of society to the center of class instruction. Children who were once ignored are now protected by the law and given unprecedented access to a "free and appropriate public education." But America's special education system presents new and continuing challenges. . . . Hundreds of thousands of parents have seen the benefit of America's inclusive education system. But many more see room for improvement. . . . Although it is true that special education has created a base of civil rights and legal protections, children with disabilities remain those most at risk of being left behind. (President's Commission on Excellence in Special Education, 2002)

## Education for Some, But Not All

In 1970, before the enactment of the federal protections in IDEA, schools in America educated only one in five students with disabilities. More than one million students were excluded from public schools and another 3.5 million did not receive appropriate services. Many states had laws excluding certain students, including those who were blind, deaf, or labeled "emotionally disturbed" or "mentally retarded." Almost 200,000 school-age children with mental retardation and emotional disabilities were institutionalized. The likelihood of exclusion was greater for children with disabilities living in low-income, ethnic and racial minority, or rural communities. (National Council on Disability, 2000, p. 6)

## Ensuring an Education for Every Child

As we chart our personal and collective course for this new millennium, there are some sobering predictions that will cause us to think deeply about who we are as a people and what we value in ourselves. . . . How do we make sense of a world that is so very diverse in so many ways. . . . We will see a rapid growth of ethnic, linguistic, and cultural diversity. Terms such as "minority" and "majority" will lose their current relevance. More persons with exceptionalities will be in the workplace. . . . And so, what relevance does this have . . . for educators, and particularly for special education as a profession? The relevance rests in . . . our appreciation of the gifts, talents, unique characteristics, and needs our students and families bring to our schools and communities. (Bogdan, 2000, p. 4)

**FOCUS**

**PREVIEW:** To preview the central concepts of this chapter, read the focus questions located in the margins. Using these questions as a guide, ask yourself what you already know and what you want to learn.

# Educating Reed

I was just a mom who wanted a program for my son. That really is the whole story. Eleven years ago we adopted a little boy with Down syndrome. We were excited and nervous and overwhelmed. He was our sixth child, the fourth one we adopted, and the only one with disabilities. . . . [Our local neighborhood] school wasn't ready to have Reed in a regular classroom, but they got ready. . . . Reed has been in the neighborhood school for five years now. We've had our ups and downs but we've worked things out. The [special education] resource teacher was wonderful at working with the regular education teachers. For instance, Reed's second-grade teacher did creative writing for part of the day. But Reed wasn't at the point where he could sit down and compose something on his own. So his resource teacher had Reed dictate something to her in the morning. (She found out all our family secrets!) Then in the afternoon, when his regular class did creative writing, he would take what she had written down and copy it. They adapted the curriculum like that throughout the year.

One day that year, I overheard Reed talking to one of his friends. His friend said, "I did really good on my test today." Reed said, "I didn't. I don't do good on tests." So I went back to talk to his teacher. Apparently, every Thursday they had a multiple-choice and fill-in-the-blank history test that was about six pages long. I told the teacher that Reed didn't do very well with that format. The process of reading and understanding the questions and filling in the bubbles and blanks just took him longer. I also told his teacher that I was really concerned about Reed's self-esteem because he feels he doesn't do well on tests. "I know what we can do," the teacher said. "We can send the test home on Wednesday night and he can do it at home." I thought, "Oh, great! One more thing to do with everything else." But I wanted it to work, so I said, "Let's try it." Reed started bringing home his history tests. Often when we were in the car going somewhere, he would read the test aloud and fill in the blanks and the bubbles. It blew me away how much of the stuff he knew! I knew that he wasn't just guessing because he got so many of the questions right. He had successes in science that year too. His teachers told me, "I'm delighted with what he knows. He raises his hand to answer just about every question, and even if he doesn't know the right answer, he knows the context. He knows how to make the experiments work. He figures things out faster than some of the other kids."

His homeroom teacher called me after a few weeks and said, "I figured out what you want."

"What's that?" I said.

"You want me to have him in the regular class as much as I can, and just have him be part of the class with the rest of the kids. You don't want me to overwhelm him, or frustrate him, but you don't want me to underestimate him either."

I said, "That's it. You've just spelled out inclusion. That's exactly what my dream is." (Hahne, K., 2000, p. 105, 109–111)

Access to education is a basic American value, reflecting the belief that each individual should have an opportunity to learn and develop to the best of his or her ability. Schools are responsible for every student, from the most academically capable to those in need of specialized services and supports, such as Reed from our opening Snapshot. All Karen wanted for her son was the opportunity for him to learn the skills that would facilitate his success in school, family, and community. Karen's dream for Reed was no different from what all parents want from their child's education: literacy, personal autonomy, economic self-sufficiency, personal fulfillment, and citizenship. She believed that the dream could best be accomplished in an educational setting where general and special education teachers work together to understand and meet Reed's educational needs.

**FOCUS 1**

What educational services were available for students with disabilities during most of the 20th century?

# Origins of Special Education

The goal of education is full participation for everyone, regardless of race, cultural background, socioeconomic status, physical disability, or mental limitation. Unfortunately, it wasn't until 1975 that this value was put into practice for all students with disabilities in the United States. This section discusses early special education programs, the period when education was viewed as a privilege and not a right for students with disabilities, and the expanding role of the federal government in the 1960s.

## Early Special Education Programs

Throughout most of the last three centuries, many families who had a child with a disability were unable to get help with that child's most basic needs, such as medical and dental care, social services, and education. In the eighteenth and nineteenth centuries, educational services for children with disabilities were largely confined to residential schools for students with physical disabilities and those who were deaf and blind. In the early 1900s, educational programs for children with disabilities gained some momentum through the efforts of many dedicated professionals. Most such programs were separate from the public schools and were established mainly for children who were described as "slow learners" or had hearing or sight loss. These students were usually placed in segregated classrooms in a public school building or in separate schools. Special education meant segregated education. Moreover, students with substantial differences were excluded from public education entirely.

## Education as a Privilege but Not a Right

From 1920 to 1960, the availability of public school programs for children with disabilities continued to be sporadic and selective. Most states merely allowed for special education; they did not mandate it. Services to children with mild emotional disorders (discipline problems) were initiated in the early 1930s, but mental hospitals continued to be the only alternative for most individuals with severe emotional problems. Special classes for children with physical disabilities expanded in the 1930s, primarily for those with "crippling" conditions, heart defects, and other health-related problems that interfered with participation in general education programs. Separate schools for these children, which were very popular during the late 1950s, were equipped with elevators, ramps, and modified doors, toilets, and desks.

During the 1940s, special school versus general school placement for students with disabilities emerged as an important policy issue. Educators became more aware of the need for these students to be educated in an environment that would promote "normal" social interaction.

By the 1950s, many countries around the world began to expand educational opportunities for students with disabilities in special schools and classes funded through public education. Two separate events had a significant impact on the evolution of educational programs for students with disabilities. First, in many countries, parents of children with disabilities organized in order to lobby policy makers for more appropriate social and educational services for their children. Second, professionals from both the behavioral and the medical sciences became more interested in services for individuals with disabilities. Their research enriched the available knowledge, which could then be integrated into effective practice.

The number of public school classes for students with mild mental retardation and those with behavior disorders increased in the late 1950s. For the most part, these children continued to be educated in an environment that isolated them from peers without disabilities. Whether segregation was a valid approach continued to be an important issue. Several studies in the 1950s and 1960s (e.g., Cassidy & Stanton, 1959; Johnson, 1961; Jordan & deCharms, 1959; Thurstone, 1959) examined the efficacy of special classes for children with mild mental retardation. Summarizing this research, Johnson (1962) suggested that the academic achievement of learners with mental retardation did not depend on whether they were placed in special or general education classes and that the child's social adjustment was not harmed by the special program. Although numerous criticisms regarding the design of efficacy studies have been made over the years, they did result in a movement toward expanding services beyond special classes in public schools. An example of this outcome was the development of a model whereby a child could remain in the general class program for the majority, if not all, of the school day, receiving special education when and where it was needed.

## Expanding the Role of the Federal Government

The 1960s brought major changes in the education of students with disabilities. President John F. Kennedy expanded the role of the federal government, providing financial support to university programs for the preparation of special education teachers. The Bureau of Education for the Handicapped (BEH) in the Office of Education (presently the Office of Special Education and Rehabilitative Services in the U.S. Department of Education) was created as a clearinghouse for information at the federal level. Demonstration projects were funded nationwide to establish a research base for the education of students with disabilities in the public schools.

**FOCUS 2**

Identify the principal issues in the right-to-education cases that led to eventual passage of the national mandate to educate students with disabilities.

# The Right to Education

The right of children with disabilities to education came to the public forum as a part of a larger social issue in the United States: the civil rights of people from differing ethnic and racial backgrounds. The civil rights movement of the 1950s and 1960s awakened the public to the issues of discrimination in employment, housing, access to public facilities (such as restaurants and transportation), and public education.

Education was reaffirmed as a right and not a privilege by the U.S. Supreme Court in the landmark case of *Brown v. Topeka, Kansas, Board of Education* (1954). In its decision, the court ruled that education must be made available to everyone on an equal basis. A unanimous Supreme Court stated, "In these days, it is doubtful that any child may reasonably be expected to succeed in life if he is denied the opportunity of an education. Such an opportunity, where the state has undertaken to provide it, is a right which must be made available to all on equal terms" (*Brown v. Topeka, Kansas, Board of Education,* 1954).

Although usually heralded for striking down racial segregation, this decision also set a major precedent for the education of students with disabilities. Unfortunately, it was nearly 20 years before federal courts were confronted with the issue of a free and appropriate education for these students.

The 1970s have often been described as a decade of revolution in the field of special education. Many of the landmark cases addressing the right to education for students with disabilities were brought before the courts during this period. In addition, major pieces of state and federal legislation were enacted to reaffirm the right of students with disabilities to a free public education.

In 1971 the Pennsylvania Association for Retarded Citizens filed a class-action suit on behalf of children with mental retardation who were excluded from public education on the basis of intellectual deficiency (*Pennsylvania Association for Retarded Citizens v. Commonwealth of Pennsylvania,* 1971). The suit charged that these children were being denied their right to a free public education. The plaintiffs claimed that children with mental retardation can learn if the educational program is adjusted to meet their individual needs. The issue was whether public school programs should be required to accommodate children with intellectual differences. The court ordered Pennsylvania schools to provide a free public education to all children with mental retardation between the ages of 6 and 21, commensurate with their individual learning needs. In addition, preschool education was to be provided for children with mental retardation if the local school district provided it for children who were not disabled.

The case of *Mills v. District of Columbia Board of Education* (1972) expanded the Pennsylvania decision to include all children with disabilities. District of Columbia schools were ordered to provide a free and appropriate education to every school-age child with a disability. The court further ordered that when general public school assignment was not appropriate, alternative educational services had to be made available. Thus the right of students with disabilities to an education was reaffirmed. The *Pennsylvania* and *Mills* cases served as catalysts for several court cases and pieces of legislation in the years that followed. Table 2.1 summarizes precedents regarding the right to education for students with disabilities.

**Education for All Handicapped Children Act (Public Law 94-142)**

Passed in 1975, this federal law made a free and appropriate public education available to all eligible students, regardless of the extent or type of handicap (disability). Eligible students must receive special education and related services necessary to meet their individual needs.

**TABLE 2.1**

### Major Court Cases and Federal Legislation Focusing on the Right to Education for Individuals with Disabilities (1954–2005)

IDEA 2004

| COURT CASES AND FEDERAL LEGISLATION | PRECEDENTS ESTABLISHED |
|---|---|
| *Brown v. Topeka, Kansas, Board of Education* (1954) | Segregation of students by race is held unconstitutional. |
| | Education is a right that must be available to all on equal terms. |
| *Hobsen v. Hansen* (1969) | The doctrine of equal educational opportunity is a part of the law of due process, and denying an equal educational opportunity is a violation of the Constitution. |
| | Placement of children in educational tracks based on performance on standardized tests is unconstitutional and discriminates against poor and minority children. |
| *Diana v. California State Board of Education* (1970) | Children tested for potential placement in a special education program must be assessed in their native or primary language. |
| | Children cannot be placed in special classes on the basis of culturally biased tests. |
| *Pennsylvania Association for Retarded Citizens v. Commonwealth of Pennsylvania* (1971) | Pennsylvania schools must provide a free public education to all school-age children with mental retardation. |
| *Mills v. Board of Education of the District of Columbia* (1972) | Exclusion of individuals with disabilities from free, appropriate public education is a violation of the due-process and equal protection clauses of the Fourteenth Amendment to the Constitution. |
| | Public schools in the District of Columbia must provide a free education to all children with disabilities regardless of their functional level or ability to adapt to the present educational system. |
| Public Law 93-112, Vocational Rehabilitation Act of 1973, Section 504 (1973) | Individuals with disabilities cannot be excluded from participation in, denied benefits of, or subjected to discrimination under any program or activity receiving federal financial assistance. |
| Public Law 94-142, Part B of the Education of the Handicapped Act (1975) | A free and appropriate public education must be provided for all children with disabilities in the United States. (Those up through 5 years old may be excluded in some states.) |
| *Hendrick Hudson District Board of Education v. Rowley* (1982) | The U.S. Supreme Court held that in order for special education and related services to be appropriate, they must be reasonably calculated to enable the student to receive educational benefits. |
| Public Law 99-457, Education of the Handicapped Act amendments (1986) | A new authority extends free and appropriate education to all children with disabilities ages 3 through 5 and provides a new early intervention program for infants and toddlers. |
| Public Law 99-372, Handicapped Children's Protection Act (1986) | Reimbursement of attorneys' fees and expenses is given to parents who prevail in administrative proceedings or court actions. |
| Public Law 101-336, Americans with Disabilities Act (1990) | Civil rights protections are provided for people with disabilities in private-sector employment, all public services, and public accommodations, transportation, and telecommunications. |
| Public Law 101-476, Individuals with Disabilities Education Act (1990) | The Education of the Handicapped Act amendments are renamed the Individuals with Disabilities Education Act (IDEA). Two new categories of disability are added: autism and traumatic brain injury. IDEA requires that an individualized transition plan be developed no later than age 16 as a component of the IEP process. |
| | Rehabilitation and social work services are included as related services. |
| Public Law 105-17, Amendments to the Individuals with Disabilities Education Act (1997) (Commonly referred to as IDEA 97) | IDEA 97 expands the emphasis for students with disabilities from public school access to improving individual outcomes (results). The 1997 amendments modify eligibility requirements, IEP requirements, public and private placements, disciplining of students, and procedural safeguards. |
| Public Law 108-446, Individuals with Disabilities Education Improvement Act of 2004 | IDEA 2004 eliminates IEP short-term objectives for most students; new state pilot programs for multi-year IEPs and paperwork reduction; establishes qualifications to become a highly qualified special education teacher |

# The Individuals with Disabilities Education Act (IDEA)

In 1975 the U.S. Congress brought together various pieces of state and federal legislation into one comprehensive national law. The **Education for All Handicapped Children Act** (Public Law 94-142) made available a free and appropriate public

Legislation that extended the rights and protections of Public Law 94-142 to preschool-age children (ages 3 through 5). The law also established an optional state program for infants and toddlers with disabilities.

**Individualized family service plan (IFSP)**

A plan of services for infants and toddlers and their families. Such a plan includes statements regarding the child's present development level, the family's strengths and needs, the major outcomes of the plan, specific interventions and delivery systems to accomplish outcomes, dates of initiation and duration of services, and a plan for transition into public schools.

**Individuals with Disabilities Education Act (IDEA—Public Law 101-476)**

The new name for the Education for All Handicapped Children Act (Public Law 94-142) in accordance with the 1990 amendments to the law.

**Zero-exclusion principle**

The principle that no person with a disability can be rejected for a service, regardless of the nature, type, or extent of the disabling condition.

**Special education**

Specially designed instruction provided to children, at no cost to parents, in all settings (such as the classroom, physical education facilities, the home, and hospitals or institutions).

**Related services**

Those services necessary to ensure that students with disabilities benefit from their educational experience. Related services may include special transportation, speech and language services, psychological services, physical and occupational therapy, recreation, rehabilitation counseling, social work, and medical services.

**Orthopedic impairments**

Bodily impairments that interfere with an individual's mobility, coordination, communication, learning, and/or personal adjustment.

education to nearly four million school-age students with disabilities in the United States between the ages of 6 and 21. The law included provisions for an individualized education program, procedural safeguards to protect the rights of students and their parents, nondiscriminatory and multidisciplinary assessment, and an education in the least restrictive environment consistent with each student's needs. Each of these provisions is discussed in detail later in this chapter.

In 1986 Congress amended the Education for All Handicapped Children Act to make available a free and appropriate public education for preschool-age students. **Public Law 99-457** extended all the rights and protections of school-age children (ages 6 through 21) to preschoolers ages 3 through 5. PL 99-457 also established a state grant program for infants and toddlers up through 2 years old. Infants and toddlers with developmental delays, as defined by each state, became eligible for services that included a multidisciplinary assessment and an **individualized family service plan (IFSP).** Although this provision did not mandate that states provide services to all infants and toddlers with developmental delays, it did establish financial incentives for state participation. (The IFSP and other provisions of PL 99-457 are discussed in more depth in Chapter 3.)

In 1990, the same year that ADA was signed into law, Congress renamed the Education for All Handicapped Children Act. It is now known as the **Individuals with Disabilities Education Act (IDEA),** reflecting "people first" language and national use of the term *disabilities.*

## What Is Special Education?

Referred to as the **zero-exclusion principle,** IDEA requires that public schools provide special education and related services to meet the individual needs of all eligible students, regardless of the extent or type of their disability. **Special education** means specially designed instruction provided at no cost to parents in all settings (such as the classroom, physical education facilities, the home, and hospitals or institutions). IDEA also stipulates that students with disabilities must receive any related services necessary to ensure that they benefit from their educational experience. **Related services** include

- transportation, and such developmental, corrective, and other supportive services (including speech-language pathology and audiology services, psychological services, physical and occupational therapy, recreation, including therapeutic recreation, social work services, counseling services, including rehabilitation counseling, orientation and mobility services, and medical services, except that such medical services shall be for diagnostic and evaluation purposes only) as may be required to assist a child with a disability to benefit from special education, and . . . the early identification and assessment of disabling conditions in children. (2004 Amendments to IDEA, PL 108-446, Sec. 602[26])

## Who Is Eligible for Special Education?

In order for a student to receive the specialized services available under IDEA, two criteria must be met. First, the student must be identified as having one of the disability conditions cited in federal law or a corresponding condition defined in a state's special education rules and regulations. These conditions include mental retardation, specific learning disabilities, serious emotional disturbances (behavior disorders), speech or language impairments, vision loss (including blindness), hearing loss (including deafness), **orthopedic impairments,** other health impairments, deafness-blindness, multiple disabilities, **autism,** and **traumatic brain injury.** Each disability will be defined and described in depth in subsequent chapters of this text.

The 2004 amendments to IDEA gives states and local education agencies (LEAs) the option of eliminating categories of disability (such as mental retardation or specific learning disabilities) for children ages 3 through 9. For this age group, a state or

LEA may define a child with a disability as a child

(i) experiencing developmental delays, as defined by the State and as measured by appropriate diagnostic instruments and procedures, in one or more of the following areas: physical development, cognitive development, communication development, social or emotional development, or adaptive development; and (ii) who, by reason thereof, needs special education and related services. (IDEA 2004, PL 108-446, Sec. 602[3][B])

*IDEA mandates a free and appropriate public education for students with disabilities ages 3 to 21. What are the major provisions of IDEA?*

FOCUS 3

Identify five major provisions of the Individuals with Disabilities Education Act.

The second criterion for eligibility is the student's demonstrated need for specialized instruction and related services in order to receive an appropriate education. This need is determined by a team of professionals and parents. Both criteria for eligibility must be met. If this is not the case, it is possible for a student to be identified as disabled but not to be eligible to receive special education services. These students may still be entitled to accommodations or modifications in their educational program. (See "Providing Reasonable Accommodations Under Section 504/ADA" on page 48.)

## Major Provisions of IDEA

The five major provisions of IDEA are as follows:

1. All students with disabilities are entitled to a free and appropriate public education designed to meet their unique needs and prepare them for employment and independent living.

2. Schools must use nondiscriminatory and multidisciplinary assessments in determining a student's educational needs.

3. Parents have the right to be involved in decisions regarding their son or daughter's special education program.

4. Every student must have an individualized education program (IEP).

5. Every student has the right to receive her or his education with nondisabled peers to the maximum extent appropriate.

**A FREE AND APPROPRIATE PUBLIC EDUCATION (FAPE).** IDEA is based on the principle that every student can learn. Accordingly, all students with disabilities are entitled to a **free and appropriate public education (FAPE)** designed to meet their unique needs. Schools must provide special education and related services at no cost to parents. The IDEA provisions related to FAPE are based on the Fourteenth Amendment to the U.S. Constitution guaranteeing equal protection of the law. No student can be excluded from a public education because of a disability (the zero-exclusion principle). A major interpretation of FAPE was handed down by the U.S. Supreme Court in *Hendrick Hudson District Board of Education v. Rowley* (1982). The Supreme Court declared that an appropriate education consists of "specially designed instruction and related services" that are "individually designed" to provide "educational benefit." Often referred to as the "some educational benefit" standard, the ruling mandates not that a state provide an ideal education, but that it provide a beneficial one for students with disabilities.

### Autism

A childhood disorder with onset prior to 36 months of age. It is characterized by extreme withdrawal, self-stimulation, intellectual deficits, and language disorders.

### Traumatic brain injury

Direct injuries to the brain, such as tearing of nerve fibers, bruising of the brain tissue against the skull, brain stem trauma, and swelling.

### Free and appropriate public education (FAPE)

Provision within IDEA requiring that every eligible student with a disability be included in public education. The Supreme Court declared that an appropriate education consists of "specially designed instruction and related services" that are "individually designed" to provide "educational benefit."

**NONDISCRIMINATORY AND MULTIDISCIPLINARY ASSESSMENT.** IDEA incorporated several provisions related to the use of nondiscriminatory testing procedures in labeling and placement of students for special education services. Among those provisions are the following:

- The testing of students in their native or primary language, whenever possible
- The use of evaluation procedures selected and administered in such a way as to prevent cultural or racial discrimination
- Validation of assessment tools for the purpose for which they are being used
- Assessment by a team of school professionals, utilizing several pieces of information to formulate a placement decision.

Students with disabilities have too often been placed in special education programs on the basis of inadequate or invalid assessment information. One result of such oversights was the placement of a disproportionate number of ethnic minority children and children from low socioeconomic backgrounds in special education programs.

**PARENTAL SAFEGUARDS AND INVOLVEMENT.** IDEA granted parents the following rights in the education of their children:

- To give consent in writing before the child is initially evaluated
- To give consent in writing before the child is initially placed in a special education program
- To request an independent education evaluation if they feel the school's evaluation is inappropriate
- To request an evaluation at public expense if the parent disagrees with the school's evaluation
- To participate on the committee that considers the evaluation of, placement of, and programming for the child
- To inspect and review educational records and challenge information believed to be inaccurate, misleading, or in violation of the privacy or other rights of the child
- To request a copy of information from the child's educational record
- To request a hearing concerning the school's proposal or refusal to initiate or change the identification, evaluation, or placement of the child or the provision of a free and appropriate public education.

The intent of these safeguards is twofold: first, to create an opportunity for parents to be more involved in decisions regarding their child's education program; and second, to protect the student and family from decisions that could adversely affect their lives. Families thus can be secure in the knowledge that every reasonable attempt is being made to educate their child appropriately.

Some professionals and parents have argued that IDEA's goal of creating a partnership between parent and professional has never been fully realized. A recent survey found that the vast majority of parents of children receiving special education were convinced that their child needed special education but that they had to fight an uphill battle to secure

The development of the IEP is a collaborative process, involving parents, educators, and students. Why is it important for parents to participate in the development of the IEP?

services (Johnson, Duffett, Farkas, & Wilson, 2002). At the same time, parents reported they could not "envision what their children's lives would be like without the special services their school offers" (p. 10).

Powell and Graham (1996) suggested that many barriers exist between the school and the home, such as "a lack of understanding, mistrust, a decrease in services as the child ages, and limited coordination of services" (p. 603). These authors further indicated a need to prevent the adversarial relationships that often result from due-process hearings. Such hearings may lead to mistrust and long-term problems. IDEA responds to the need for a mediation process to resolve any conflict between parents and school personnel and to prevent long-term adversarial relationships. The law requires states to establish a mediation system in which parents and schools voluntarily participate. In such a system, an impartial individual would listen to parents and school personnel and attempt to work out a mutually agreeable arrangement in the best interest of the student with a disability. Although mediation is intended to facilitate the partnership between parents and professionals, it must not be used to deny or delay the parents' right to a due-process hearing.

**THE INDIVIDUALIZED EDUCATION PROGRAM (IEP).** The vehicle for delivering a free and appropriate public education to every eligible student with a disability is a written statement referred to as an **individualized education program (IEP).** The IEP provides an opportunity for parents and professionals to join together in developing and delivering specially designed instruction to meet student needs.

The team responsible for developing the IEP should consist of the student's parents; at least one special education teacher; at least one general education teacher if the child is, or may be, participating in the general education environment; and a LEA (school district) representative. The LEA representative must be qualified to provide, or supervise the provision of, specially designed instruction to meet the unique needs of children with disabilities. This individual must also be knowledgeable about the **general curriculum** and the availability of resources within the LEA.

The IEP team must also include an individual who can interpret the instructional implications of evaluation results. Other individuals who have knowledge or special expertise regarding the child (including related services personnel as appropriate and, whenever appropriate, the student with a disability) may be included at the discretion of the parents or LEA.

The intended result of the IEP process is more continuity in the delivery of educational services for students on a daily as well as an annual basis. The IEP also promotes more effective communication between school personnel and the home. IDEA requires that each child's IEP include

- A statement of the child's present levels of academic achievement and functional performance, including how the child's disability affects the child's involvement and progress in the general education curriculum. For preschool children, as appropriate, how the disability affects the child's participation in appropriate activities.

- A statement of measurable annual goals, including academic and functional goals, designed to meet the child's needs that result from the child's disability to enable the child to be involved in and make progress in the general education curriculum; and meet each of the child's other educational needs that result from the child's disability. For children with disabilities who take alternate assessments aligned to alternate achievement standards, a description of benchmarks or short-term objectives.

- Description of how the child's progress toward meeting the annual goals described will be measured and when periodic reports on the progress the child is making toward meeting the annual goals will be provided.

- A statement of the special education and related services and supplementary aids and services, based on peer-reviewed research to the extent practicable, to

**Individualized education program (IEP)**

A program devised to satisfy IDEA's requirement that students with disabilities must receive an educational program based on multidisciplinary assessment and designed to meet their individual needs. The IEP must include consideration of the student's present level of performance, annual goals, special education and related services, time in general education, timeline for special education services, and an annual evaluation.

**General curriculum**

Instructional content that all students are expected to learn as they progress through school and earn a high school diploma. The specific content and performance standards for student achievement are set by each individual state or local school district.

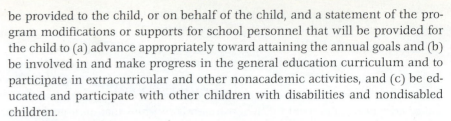

be provided to the child, or on behalf of the child, and a statement of the program modifications or supports for school personnel that will be provided for the child to (a) advance appropriately toward attaining the annual goals and (b) be involved in and make progress in the general education curriculum and to participate in extracurricular and other nonacademic activities, and (c) be educated and participate with other children with disabilities and nondisabled children.

- An explanation of the extent, if any, to which the child will not participate with nondisabled children in the regular [general education] class.

- A statement of any individual appropriate accommodations that are necessary to measure the academic achievement and functional performance of the child on State and districtwide assessments, or if the IEP Team determines that the child shall take an alternate assessment of student achievement, a statement of why the child cannot participate in the regular assessment; and the particular alternate assessment selected is appropriate for the child. (IDEA 2004, P.L. 108-446, Sec. 614[d])

**EDUCATION IN THE LEAST RESTRICTIVE ENVIRONMENT.** All students with disabilities have the right to learn in an environment consistent with their academic, social, and physical needs. Such a setting constitutes the **least restrictive environment (LRE)** suitable for an appropriate education. IDEA mandated ensuring that

> To the maximum extent appropriate, children with disabilities, including children in public or private institutions or other care facilities, are educated with children who are not disabled, and that special classes, separate schooling, or other removal of children with disabilities from the regular education environment occurs only when the nature or severity of the disability is such that education in regular classes with the use of supplementary aids and services cannot be achieved satisfactorily. (IDEA, 20 U.S.C. 1412 [5](B))

To be certain that schools meet this mandate, federal regulations required the development of a continuum of placements, ranging from general classrooms with support services to homebound and hospital programs. Placement in a setting along this continuum is based on the premise that this is the most appropriate environment to implement a student's individualized program as developed by the IEP team. Figure 2.1 presents an educational services model depicting seven levels on the continuum of placements.

Some parents and professionals have criticized the concept of "a continuum of placements" in recent years. The concern is that, despite IDEA's strong preference for students with disabilities to be educated with their peers who are not disabled, the continuum has legitimized and supported the need for more restrictive, segregated settings. Additionally, the continuum has created the perception that students with disabilities must "go to" services, rather than those services coming to them. In other words, as students move farther from the general education class, the resources available to meet their needs increase concomitantly. A recent examination of the placement of students with disabilities in America's schools suggests that about 4.0% of all students with disabilities between the ages of 6 and 21 receive their education in separate schools and residential facilities (U.S. Department of Education, 2002). For a closer look at who is being served in special education programs, and where, see Figure 2.2.

## The Special Education Referral, Planning, and Placement Process

The special education referral, planning, and placement process, as mandated in IDEA, is intended to ensure that all eligible students with disabilities have the opportunity to receive a free and appropriate public education. The process involves four sequential phases: (1) initiating the referral, (2) assessing student eligibility and

**FOCUS 4**

Identify the four phases of the special education referral, planning, and placement process.

**Least restrictive environment (LRE)**

The principle that, to the maximum extent appropriate, students with disabilities are to be educated with their peers who are not disabled.

**FIGURE 2.1**

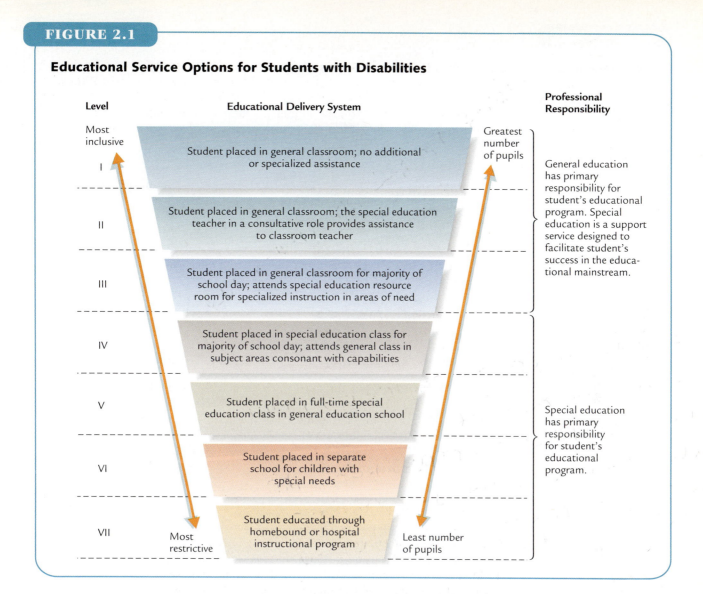

**Educational Service Options for Students with Disabilities**

| Level | Educational Delivery System | Professional Responsibility |
|---|---|---|

Most inclusive

I — Student placed in general classroom; no additional or specialized assistance — Greatest number of pupils

II — Student placed in general classroom; the special education teacher in a consultative role provides assistance to classroom teacher

III — Student placed in general classroom for majority of school day; attends special education resource room for specialized instruction in areas of need

*General education has primary responsibility for student's educational program. Special education is a support service designed to facilitate student's success in the educational mainstream.*

IV — Student placed in special education class for majority of school day; attends general class in subject areas consonant with capabilities

V — Student placed in full-time special education class in general education school

VI — Student placed in separate school for children with special needs

VII — Student educated through homebound or hospital instructional program — Least number of pupils

Most restrictive

*Special education has primary responsibility for student's educational program.*

educational need, (3) developing the individualized education program (IEP), and (4) determining the least restrictive environment. (See Table 2.2.)

**PHASE I: INITIATING THE REFERRAL.** Referral for special education can occur at different times for different students, depending on the type and severity of the need. Students with more severe disabilities are likely to be referred prior to elementary school and to receive early intervention and preschool services. For children with milder disabilities, referral could be initiated at any time during elementary school when they appear to have difficulty in academic learning, in exhibiting appropriate behavior, or in overall development. For these children, the general education teacher is the most likely referral source.

The referral begins with a request to the school's prereferral team (also known as a *special services committee* or *child-study team*) for an assessment to determine whether the student qualifies for special education services. Once the team receives the referral, it may either (1) attempt to modify or adapt current instruction in the general education class, or (2) conduct a formal evaluation to determine the student's eligibility for special education services.

The first step, **prereferral intervention,** involves instructional adaptations or accommodations designed to provide additional support to children who are at risk for educational failure prior to referring them for special education services. Parents are notified that the child is having difficulty and are asked to meet with the

**Prereferral intervention**

Instructional adaptations or accommodations designed to provide additional support to children who are at risk for educational failure and implemented before the children are referred for special education services. If the student does not progress satisfactorily, a referral process for special education may be initiated.

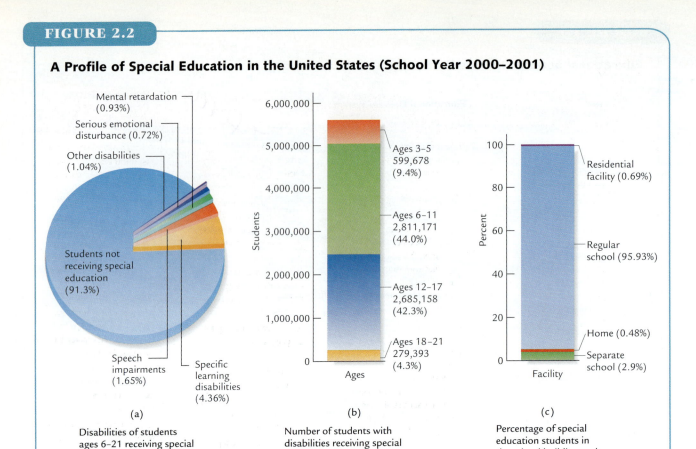

## FIGURE 2.2

### A Profile of Special Education in the United States (School Year 2000–2001)

**(a)**
- Mental retardation (0.93%)
- Serious emotional disturbance (0.72%)
- Other disabilities (1.04%)
- Students not receiving special education (91.3%)
- Speech impairments (1.65%)
- Specific learning disabilities (4.36%)

Disabilities of students ages 6–21 receiving special education as a percentage of all students ages 6–21

**(b)**
- Ages 3–5 599,678 (9.4%)
- Ages 6–11 2,811,171 (44.0%)
- Ages 12–17 2,685,158 (42.3%)
- Ages 18–21 279,393 (4.3%)

Number of students with disabilities receiving special education services by age under IDEA (6,375,400 children served)

**(c)**
- Residential facility (0.69%)
- Regular school (95.93%)
- Home (0.48%)
- Separate school (2.9%)

Percentage of special education students in the school building and other sites

SOURCE: *The 24th Annual Report to Congress on the Implementation of the Individuals with Disabilities Education Act,* 2002, Washington, DC: U.S. Government Printing Office.

school team. The team and the parents discuss the student's needs and recommend possible changes. Adaptations vary according to student need but most often involve modifying the curriculum, changing a seating arrangement, adjusting the length and difficulty of homework or classroom assignments, using peer tutors or volunteer parents to assist with instructional programs, or implementing a behavior management program. It is the responsibility of the general education teacher to implement the modified instruction and to assess the student's progress over a predetermined period of time. If the modifications are successful, there will be no further need to make a referral for special education. However, if the team determines that the student's educational progress is not satisfactory, the referral process for special education may be initiated.

If a formal referral for special education services is determined to be appropriate, the team reviews the information documented by the classroom teacher and other education professionals, describing the child's needs. Documentation may include results from achievement tests, classroom performance tests, samples of student work, behavioral observations, and/or anecdotal notes (such as teacher journal entries). The team decides whether additional assessment information is needed in order to determine eligibility for special education. At this time a written notice, indicating that the school proposes to initiate or change the identification, evaluation, or educational placement of the child, must be provided to parents. The content of the notice must include

- A full explanation of the procedural safeguards available to the parents

TABLE 2.2

## The Four-Phase Special Education, Referral Planning, and Placement Process

| PHASE 1 INITIATING THE REFERRAL | PHASE 2 ASSESSING STUDENT ELIGIBILITY AND EDUCATIONAL NEED | PHASE 3 DEVELOPING THE INDIVIDUALIZED EDUCATION PROGRAM (IEP) | PHASE 4 DETERMINING THE LEAST RESTRICTIVE ENVIRONMENT (LRE) |
|---|---|---|---|
| • School personnel or parents indicate concern about student's learning, behavior, or overall development.<br><br>• If referral is made by school personnel, parents are notified of concerns.<br><br>• Child-study team decides to provide additional support services and adapt student's instructional program prior to initiating formal assessment for eligibility. (This step may be bypassed, and team may choose to immediately seek parental permission to evaluate the student's eligibility for special education.)<br><br>• School seeks and receives parents' permission to evaluate student's eligibility for special education services. (This will occur if the additional support services and adaptive instruction are unsuccessful OR if the team has chosen to move directly to a formal evaluation to determine student eligibility.) | • Multidisciplinary and nondiscriminatory assessment tools and strategies are used to evaluate student's eligibility for special education services.<br><br>• Child-study team reviews assessment information to determine (1) whether student meets eligibility requirements for special education services under 1 of 12 disability classifications or meets the definition of developmentally delayed (for students between ages 3 and 9), and (2) whether student requires special education services.<br><br>• If team agrees that the student is eligible for and needs special education services, then the process moves to phase 3: developing the IEP. | • Appropriate professionals to serve on an IEP team are identified. A team coordinator is appointed.<br><br>• Parents (and student when appropriate) participate as equal members of the team and are provided with written copies of all assessment information.<br><br>• Team meets and agrees upon the essential elements of the student's individualized education program plan:<br>— Measurable annual goals<br>— Skill areas needing special education and related services<br>— Persons responsible for providing services and supports to meet student's identified needs<br>— Criteria/evaluation procedures to assess progress<br>— Student's access to the general education curriculum<br>— Student's participation in state-wide or school district assessments<br>— Beginning and end dates for special education services<br>— A process for reporting to parents on student's progress toward annual goals<br>— Positive behavioral intervention plan if needed | • Identify potential educational placements based on student's annual goals and special education services to be provided.<br><br>• Adhering to the principle that students with disabilities are to be educated with their nondisabled peers to the maximum extent appropriate, justify any removal of the child from the general education classroom.<br><br>• With parents involved in the decision-making process, determine student's appropriate educational placement.<br><br>• Document, on the student's IEP, justification for any removal from the general education classroom.<br><br>• Team members agree in writing to the essential elements of the IEP and to the educational placement where special education and related services are to be provided.<br><br>• As members of the IEP team, parents must consent in writing to the agreed-upon educational placement for their child. |

- A description of the action proposed or refused by the school, why the school proposes or refuses to take the action, and a description of any options the school considered and the reasons why those options were rejected

- A description of each evaluation procedure, test, record, or report that the school used as a basis for the proposal or refusal

- A description of any other factors relevant to the school's proposal or refusal to take action.

Following such written notice, the school must seek consent in writing from the parents in order to move ahead with the evaluation process. Informed consent means that parents

- have been fully informed of all information relevant to the activity for which consent is sought, in their native language or other mode of communication.

- understand and agree in writing to the carrying out of the activity for which their consent is sought (the consent describes that activity and lists any record that will be released and to whom).

- understand that their consent is voluntary and that they may revoke it at any time.

### PHASE 2: ASSESSING STUDENT ELIGIBILITY AND EDUCATIONAL NEED.

Once written consent to evaluate has been obtained from parents, the school team moves ahead to assess the student's educational need. The purpose of this assessment is to evaluate whether the student meets eligibility criteria under IDEA and to determine the need for special education services. The assessment should include the student's performance in both school and home environments. When the assessment process is complete, a decision is made regarding the student's eligibility for special education and his or her disability classification.

Presently, the most common way to classify students for special education is to categorize them into one of the disability areas (such as specific learning disabilities, autism, and so on). IDEA also gives states or LEAs the option of classifying students with disabilities between the ages of 3 through 9 as developmentally delayed. Developmental delays may be in one or more of the following areas: physical development, cognitive development, communication development, social or emotional development, and adaptive development.

### PHASE 3: DEVELOPING THE INDIVIDUALIZED EDUCATION PROGRAM (IEP).

The IEP is the cornerstone of a free and appropriate public education (National Information Center for Children and Youth with Disabilities, 2003). Once it has been determined that the student is eligible for special education services under IDEA, the next step is to establish an IEP team as determined by the evaluation of the student's educational needs. At a minimum this team consists of the student's parents, the student (when appropriate), a special education teacher, a general education teacher (if the student is participating in the general education environment), and a representative of the LEA. As stated in IDEA, the LEA representative must be qualified to "provide, or supervise the provision of, specially designed instruction to meet the unique needs of children with disabilities" (20 U.S.C. 1414[d]). This person must also be knowledgeable about the general curriculum and the availability of resources within the district or agency. IDEA requires that someone (either a current team member or someone from outside the team, such as a school psychologist) be available to interpret the results of the student evaluations. At the discretion of the parents or district/agency, other individuals with knowledge or special expertise, including related services specialists, may also be invited to participate on the IEP team.

Each IEP team should have a coordinator (such as the special education teacher, school psychologist, or school principal) who serves as liaison between the school and the family. The coordinator has the responsibility to (1) inform parents and respond to any

*Prereferral intervention involves adapting instruction to the need of the student before initiating a referral for special education services. What are some prereferral strategies that teachers can use in their classrooms?*

concerns they may have regarding the IEP process, (2) assist parents in developing specific goals they would like to see their child achieve, (3) schedule IEP meetings that are mutually convenient for both school personnel and parents, and (4) lead the IEP meetings. Prior to the initial IEP meeting, parents should be provided with written copies of all assessment information on their child. Individual conferences with members of the IEP team or a full team meeting may be necessary prior to developing the IEP. This will further assist parents in understanding and interpreting evaluation information. Analysis of the assessment information should include a summary of the child's strengths as well as of areas in which the child may require special education or related services beyond his or her current program.

Once there is agreement between educators and parents on the interpretation of the assessment results, the team coordinator organizes and leads the IEP meeting(s). Such meeting(s) are meant to achieve the following purposes:

- Document each student's present levels of performance.
- Agree on measurable annual goals.
- Identify skill areas where special education (including physical education) and related services are needed, who will be responsible for delivering these services, and what criteria/evaluation procedures will be applied to assess progress.
- Document student access to the general curriculum.
- Document student participation in state- and district-wide assessment programs with individual modifications or adaptations made, as necessary, in how the tests are administered. For children who cannot participate in regular assessments, the team must document the use of state-developed **alternate assessments.**
- Establish beginning and end dates for special education services.
- Determine a process for reporting to parents on student progress toward annual goals.

See Figure 2.3, a sample individualized education program for Diane, an elementary school-age student with disabilities.

**PHASE 4: DETERMINING THE LEAST RESTRICTIVE ENVIRONMENT.**  A student's educational placement is determined only after educators and parents have agreed on annual goals. The decision regarding placement rests upon the answers to two questions: First, what is the appropriate placement for the student, given his or her annual goals? Second, which of the placement alternatives under consideration is consistent with the least restrictive environment? As stated in IDEA, to the maximum extent appropriate, the student is to be educated with peers who are not disabled. To ensure that this principle is applied in making placement decisions, IDEA begins with the premise that the general education classroom is where all children belong. Thus any movement away from the general education class must be justified and documented on the student's IEP.

Finally, the implementation of decisions about the appropriate placement for a student is most successful when parents are viewed as valued and equal participants in the process. Parents must be fully involved in and eventually consent to the educational placement for their child. Parents should be encouraged not only to share their expectations for the child, but also to express approval for or concerns about the goals, objectives, resources, or timelines that are being proposed by educators. The IEP must be the result of a collaborative process that reflects the views of both the school and the family. For more insight into the important issues that must be considered by professionals, parents, and students in developing IEP goals and determining the most appropriate educational placement, see the Case Study, "Jerald," on page 43.

**Alternate assessments**

Assessments mandated in IDEA 2004 for students who are unable to participate in required state- or district-wide assessments. They ensure that all students, regardless of the severity of their disabilities, are included in the state's accountability system.

# FIGURE 2.3

# A Sample Individualized Education Program (IEP)

**Student's Primary Classification:** Serious Emotional Disturbance

**Secondary Classification:** None

---

Student Name _Diane_

Date of Birth _5-3-93_

Primary Language:

HOME _English_   Student _English_

Date of IEP Meeting _April 27, 2004_

Entry Date to Program _April 27, 2004_

Projected Duration of Services _One school year_

Services Required _Specify amount of time in educational and/or related services per day or week_

General Education Class _4–5 hours p/day_

Resource Room _1–2 hours p/day_

Special Ed Consultation in General Ed Classroom _Co-teaching and consultation with general education teacher in the areas of academic and adaptive skills as indicated in annual goals and short-term objectives._

Self-Contained _none_

Related Services _Group counseling sessions twice weekly with guidance counselor. Counseling to focus on adaptive skill development as described in annual goals and short-term objectives_

P.E. Program _45 min. daily in general ed PE class with support from adapted PE teacher as necessary_

Assessment

Intellectual _WISC-R_

Educational _Key Math Woodcock Reading_

Behavioral/Adaptive _Burks_

Speech/Language

Other

Vision _Within normal limits_

Hearing _Within normal limits_

---

Classroom Observation Done

Dates _1/15–2/25/2004_

Personnel Conducting Observation _School Psychologist, Special Education Teacher, General Education Teacher_

Present Level of Performance Strengths

1) _Polite to teachers and peers_

2) _Helpful and cooperative in the classroom_

3) _Good grooming skills_

4) _Good in sports activities_

Access to General Education Curriculum

_Diane will participate in all content areas within the general education curriculum. Special education supports and services will be provided in the areas of math, reading, and social skills development._

Effect of Disability on Access to General Education Curriculum

_Emotional disabilities make it difficult for Diane to achieve at expected grade level performance in general education curriculum in the areas of reading and math. It is expected that this will further impact her access to the general education curriculum in other content areas (such as history, biology, English) as she enters junior high school._

Participation in Statewide or District Assessments

_Diane will participate in all state and districtwide assessments of achievement. No adaptations or modifications required for participation._

Justification for Removal from General Education Classroom

_Diane's objectives require that she be placed in a general education classroom with support from a special education teacher for the majority of the school day. Based on adaptive behavior assessment and observations, Diane will receive instruction in a resource room for approximately one to two hours per day in the areas of social skills development._

Reports to Parents on Progress toward Annual Goals

_Parents will be informed of Diane's progress through weekly reports of progress on short-term goals, monthly phone calls from general ed teachers, special education teachers, and school psychologist, as well as regularly scheduled report cards at the end of each term._

**FIGURE 2.3** *(continued)*

Areas Needing Specialized Instruction and Support

1. Adaptive Skills
   - Limited interaction skills with peers and adults
   - Excessive facial tics and grimaces
   - Difficulty staying on task in content subjects, especially reading and math
   - Difficulty expressing feelings, needs, and interests
2. Academic Skills
   - Significantly below grade level in math—3.9
   - Significantly below grade level in reading—4.3

Annual Review: _____ Date: _____

Comments/Recommendations _____

Team Signatures     IEP Review Date _____

LEA Rep. _____

Parent _____

Sp Ed Teacher _____

Gen Ed Teacher _____

School Psych _____

Student (as appropriate) _____

Related Services Personnel (as appropriate) _____

Objective Criteria and Evaluation Procedures _____

| IEP—Annual Goals | Persons Responsible | Objective Criteria and Evaluation Procedures |
| --- | --- | --- |
| #1 ANNUAL GOAL: *Diane will improve her interaction skills with peers and adults.* | *General education teacher and special ed teacher (resource room)* <br> *School psychologist consultation* | *Classroom observations and documented data on target behavior* |

**FIGURE 2.3**

*(continued)*

| IEP—Annual Goals | Persons Responsible | Objective Criteria and Evaluation Procedures |
|---|---|---|
| #2 ANNUAL GOAL: *Diane will increase her ability to control hand and facial movements.* | *General education teacher and special ed teacher (resource room)*<br><br>*School psychologist consultation* | *Classroom observations and documented data on target behavior* |
| #3 ANNUAL GOAL: *Diane will improve her ability to remain on task during academic work.* | *General education teacher and special ed teacher (resource room)*<br><br>*School psychologist consultation* | *Classroom observations and documented data on target behavior* |
| #4 ANNUAL GOAL: *Diane will improve her ability to express her feelings.* | *General education teacher and special ed teacher (resource room)*<br><br>*School psychologist consultation* | *Classroom observations and documented data on target behavior* |
| #5 ANNUAL GOAL: *Diane will improve math skills by one grade level.* | *Collaboration of general education teacher and special education teacher through co-teaching and consultation* | *Precision teaching*<br><br>*Addison Wesley Math Program Scope and Sequence*<br><br>*Districtwide Assessment of Academic Achievement* |
| #6 ANNUAL GOAL: *Diane will improve reading skills by one grade level.* | *Collaboration of general education teacher and special education teacher through co-teaching and consultation* | *Precision teaching Barnell & Loft Scope and Sequence*<br><br>*Districtwide Assessment of Academic Achievement* |

## Case Study

# JERALD

Jerald is finishing up his last two months in a second-grade classroom at Robert F. Kennedy Elementary School. Kennedy is a large urban school with a number of students from low economic and culturally diverse backgrounds. Many of its students are described as "disadvantaged" and at significant risk of school failure.

Next year, Jerald will move to third grade, and his parents and teachers have expressed some concerns. "Jerry is an outgoing kid who loves to talk about anything to anyone at any time," says his mother. His current second grade teacher, Miss Robins, complains that he is "hyperactive, inattentive, and a behavior problem." His mom, his dad, and his teacher agree that Jerald has a great deal of difficulty with controlling his emotions.

MOTHER: I just wish he wasn't so easily frustrated at home when things aren't going his way.

MISS ROBINS: He's always in a state of fight or flight. When he is in a fighting mode, he hits, teases, and screams at me or the other students. When in a state of "flight," he withdraws and refuses to comply with any requests. He may even put his head on his desk and openly cry to vent his frustrations.

During second grade, his "fight" behavior has increased considerably. Miss Robins reported that "he has made very little progress and is uncontrollable—a very disruptive influence on the other children in the class." With permission from Jerald's parents, she initiated a referral to the school's child-study team to assess his eligibility for special education services. His overall assessment indicated that he was falling further behind in reading (word decoding skills at grade level 1.5; reading comprehension at grade level 1.0) and math (grade level 1.9). Behaviorally, he has difficulty expressing his feelings in an appropriate manner. He is impulsive, easily distracted, and not well liked by his peers. After determining his eligibility for special education services, the school IEP team developed Jerald's third-grade annual goals. The focus will be on

1. improving Jerald's reading and math achievement by ensuring access to general curriculum with specialized academic instruction and support—Jerald is to be included in the district and state testing program.

2. teaching Jerald the skills to (a) manage his own behavior when faced with difficult or frustrating situations and (b) improve daily interactions with teachers and peers—the activities for these goals will be included on the IEP as components of Jerald's *behavioral intervention plan.*

Once the team had agreed on annual goals for Jerald, they discussed various classroom and school settings that would be appropriate to his needs as described in the IEP. Miss Robins and the school principal are concerned that his disruptive behavior will be too difficult to control in a general education classroom. They would like to see him placed in a special self-contained class for students who are emotionally disturbed. They are concerned not only for Jerald's education but also about the negative effect he has on his classroom peers. Miss Robins reported that she had to spend a disproportionate amount of her time dealing with Jerald's inappropriate behavior.

Taking into account the views of Jerald's teachers and the school principal, the team is considering placement in a special education class for students with serious behavior problems. Such a class is not available at his home school, so Jerald would have to be transported to a special education program in another location. Ms. Beckman, the special education consulting teacher, has an alternative point of view. She proposes that Jerald stay at Kennedy Elementary and that his behavioral intervention plan and specialized academic instruction be implemented in next year's third-grade classroom. Working in collaboration with Jerald's general education teacher and other members of the school's assistance team, Ms. Beckman suggests using cooperative learning techniques, co-teaching among the general and special education teachers, and ongoing support from the school psychologist.

Jerald's parents, although they recognize that his disruptive behavior is increasing and that he is falling further behind academically, are reluctant to have him transferred to another school. They feel it would remove him from his family and neighborhood supports. His brother, who will be in the fifth grade, also goes to Kennedy Elementary.

### APPLICATION

1. What do you see as the important issues for the team to consider in deciding what educational setting would be most appropriate to meet Jerald's needs?

2. In addition to the recommendations made by Ms. Beckman, the special education resource room teacher, what suggestions would you have to adapt Jerald's academic and behavioral program if he were to remain in his third-grade class at Kennedy Elementary?

3. Should he remain in his third-grade class at Kennedy Elementary?

# Current Trends in the Education of Students with Disabilities

The education of students with disabilities has gone through many changes during the past three decades. In this section, we take a close look at four trends in today's schools that directly affect each student's opportunity to get an appropriate education:

**FOCUS 5**

Identify three characteristics of effective special education that enhance learning opportunities for students with disabilities.

(1) effective special education practice; (2) access to the general curriculum and greater accountability for student learning; (3) reasonable accommodations in assessment and instruction; and (4) establishing safe schools.

## Characteristics of Effective Special Education

Ensuring an appropriate educational experience for students with disabilities depends on providing effective special education services. The characteristics of special education that enhance learning opportunities for students of all ages and across multiple settings include the following:

- *Individualization:* A student-centered approach to instructional decision making
- *Intensive instruction:* Frequent instructional experiences of significant duration
- *The explicit teaching of academic, adaptive, and/or functional life skills* (McLaughlin, 2002; McLaughlin, Fuchs, & Hardman, 1999; National Research Council, 1997).

**INDIVIDUALIZATION.** The hallmark of special education is **individualization**—developing and implementing an appropriate educational experience based on the individual needs of each student. Research indicates that fundamental differences characterize the ways in which special educators approach instruction and distinguish them from their general education colleagues. Hocutt (1996) suggested that instruction in general education is most often oriented to the masses and centered on the curriculum:

> Undifferentiated large-group instruction appears to be the norm in general education. Individual assignments, small-group work, and student pairing occur, but much less frequently than whole-class instruction. Teachers typically follow the sequence of lessons outlined in teachers' manuals and focus on content coverage. . . . When surveyed, teachers do not perceive themselves as having the skills for adapting instruction in ways that facilitate individual or small-group instruction. (p. 81)

Special education, on the other hand, is designed to meet the unique needs of every student, no matter what the student's educational need or ability. Using an individually referenced approach to decision making, special education teachers must continually plan and adjust curriculum and instruction in response to the student. Teachers must have at their disposal multiple ways to adapt the curriculum, modify their instructional approaches, and motivate their students to learn (Nevin, 1998; Peterson & Hittie, 2003; Vaughn, Bos, & Schumm, 2003). Hardman, McDonnell, and Welch (1998) suggested that the vast majority of teachers, whether in general or special education, do not have expertise both in the subject matter being taught and in adapting curriculum and instruction. Thus general and special educators need to (1) acquire a core of knowledge and skills that facilitates their ability to teach all students, and (2) work collaboratively in meeting the instructional needs of students with disabilities.

**INTENSIVE INSTRUCTION.** **Intensive instruction** involves (1) actively engaging students in their learning by requiring high rates of appropriate response to the material presented, (2) carefully matching instruction to student ability and skill level, (3) providing instructional cues and prompts to support learning and then fading them when appropriate, and (4) providing detailed feedback that is directly focused on the task the student is expected to complete (McLaughlin et al., 1999). Intensive instruction may involve both group and one-to-one learning. Research suggests that intensive instruction can significantly improve the academic achievement and functional skill levels of students with disabilities (Billingsley, Liberty, & White, 1994; Elbaum, Vaughn, Huges, & Moody, 2000; O'Connor, 2000; Torgesen, 1996). Lyon (1996) reported that for students with learning disabilities, "intensive instruction of appropriate duration provided by trained teachers can

**Individualization**

A student-centered approach to instructional decision making.

**Intensive instruction**

An instructional approach that involves (1) actively engaging students in their learning by requiring high rates of appropriate response, (2) carefully matching instruction to student ability and skill level, (3) providing instructional cues and prompts to support learning and then fading them when appropriate, and (4) providing detailed feedback directly focused on the task the student is expected to complete.

remediate the deficient reading skills of many children" (p. 70). For students with severe disabilities, Billingsley et al. (1994) found that one-to-one intensive instruction resulted in significant gains in functional skills (such as dressing, money management, and sexual behavior).

**THE EXPLICIT TEACHING OF ACADEMIC, ADAPTIVE, AND FUNCTIONAL LIFE SKILLS.** In addition to needing individualized and intensive instruction, students with disabilities require more structured and teacher-directed approaches to learning than do students who are not disabled (Peterson & Hittie, 2003; Tarver, 1996). Learning is a continual process of adaptation for students with disabilities as they attempt to meet the demands of school. These students do not learn as quickly or as efficiently as their classmates and are constantly battling time and failure. They must somehow learn to deal with a system that is often rigid and allows little room for differences in learning or behavior. Students with disabilities must also adapt to a teaching process that may be oriented toward the majority of students within a general classroom and not based on individualized assessment of needs or personalized instruction. Despite these obstacles, however, students with disabilities can learn social and academic skills that will orient them toward striving for success rather than fighting against failure. Success can be achieved only when educators remain flexible, constantly adjusting to meet the needs of these students.

The teaching of explicit skills to students with disabilities includes instruction in core academic areas, adaptive skills, and **functional life skills.** Instruction in core academic areas (such as reading, math, and science) stresses that the student must learn a specified set of sequenced skills, each a prerequisite to the next. This process, which is sometimes referred to as the developmental approach, can be illustrated by briefly analyzing the teaching of reading. When learning to read, the student must acquire many individual skills and then be able to link them together as a whole. The student is then able to decode abstract information and turn it into meaningful content. When one of the separate skills required for reading is not learned, the entire process may break down. Teaching core academic skills, whether in reading or any other content area, lays the groundwork for further development and higher levels of functioning. Vaughn et al. (2003) suggested that reading instruction is *appropriate* and *intensive* when

- Students have a clear understanding of teacher expectations and the goals of instruction.
- The instruction provided matches the reader's instructional reading level and needs.
- Instruction is *explicit* and direct in the skills and strategies the reader needs to become more proficient and more independent.
- Students are grouped appropriately, which includes ability-level grouping.
- Instruction includes frequent opportunities for responding with feedback and ongoing monitoring of progress.
- Teachers and peers support the students when necessary. (pp. 352–353)

Not all children are able to learn core academic skills within the timeframe dictated by schools. The degree to which a student is able to cope with the requirements of a school setting and the extent to which the school recognizes and accommodates individual diversity are known as **adaptive fit.** This fit is dynamic and constantly changes in the negotiations between the individual and the environment.

For the student with a disability, adaptive fit may involve learning and applying various strategies that will facilitate the student's ability to meet the expectations of a learning environment. Such a student may find that the requirements for success within a general education classroom are beyond his or her adaptive capabilities and that the system is unwilling to accommodate academic, behavioral, physical, sensory, or communicative differences. As a result, the student develops negative

**Functional Life Skills**

Practical skills that facilitate a person's participation and involvement in family, school, and community life.

**Adaptive fit**

Compatibility between demands of a task or setting and a person's needs and abilities.

attitudes toward school. Imagine yourself in a setting that constantly disapproves of how you act and what you do, a place in which activities are difficult and overwhelming, a setting in which your least desirable qualities are emphasized. What would you think about spending more than 1,000 hours a year in such a place?

Over the years, educators have responded in several ways to mismatches between the needs of the student and the demands of the learning environment. The more traditional approach was to leave the student in the negative situation and do nothing until the inevitable failure occurred. This changed with the advent of special education and the continuum of placements, whereby students are pulled out of settings where they do not thrive and are moved to a classroom or school more conducive to meeting their individual needs. In this approach, no attempt is made to modify the student's current environment. A third alternative has been to seek ways of creating a better adaptive fit between the student and the learning environment through a process known as **adaptive instruction.** Adaptive instruction seeks to enhance student performance in a given content area (such as reading) by modifying the way in which instruction is delivered and by changing the environment where the learning takes place. This approach exploits a variety of instructional procedures, materials, and alternative learning sequences in the classroom setting to help students master content consistent with their needs, abilities, and interests (Bradley & King-Sears, 1997; Friend & Bursuck, 2001; Peterson, 2000; Wood, 1997). For example, a student who is unable to memorize multiplication tables may be taught to use a calculator to complete the task. Learning to use the calculator would probably take place not in a large-group setting but in a one-to-one or small-group situation. The task's degree of difficulty is modified to fit with the conceptual ability of the student, and the alteration within the learning environment allows the student to be taught an explicit skill through intensive instruction.

For some time, the general classroom teacher had to work with students who have disabilities without the benefit of any effective support. This is no longer the case in many of today's schools. The emergence of inclusive education programs in elementary schools throughout the United States has strengthened collaborative efforts between the general education classroom teacher and the network of supports available in the schools. When student need and ability make it appropriate, instruction in functional life skills can be implemented. Students are taught only those skills that will help them succeed in accessing and participating in a natural setting, whether it be the classroom, family, or neighborhood. Functional life skills may include daily living (such as self-help, personal finances, and community travel), personal-social development (such as learning **self-determination** and socially responsible behaviors), communication skills, recreational and leisure activities, and employment skills.

The functional life skills approach is based on the premise that if these practical skills are not taught through formal instruction, they will not be learned. (Most students do not need to be taught functional skills, because they have already learned them through everyday experience.) This does not mean that students being taught through a functional approach are not also learning core academic skills. Instruction may occur in academic content areas, but not in the same sequence. For example, a functional life skills reading approach would initially teach frequently used words that are necessary for survival within the environment (examples include danger, exit, and rest room signs) and then pair them directly with an environmental cue.

## Access to the General Curriculum and Greater Accountability for Student Learning

The rallying cry in today's schools is "higher expectations for all students." This call for more accountability for student progress culminated in the passage of the *No Child Left Behind Act of 2001* (NCLB). NCLB espouses a **standards-based approach** to reforming schools: Set high standards for what should be taught and how student performance should be measured. Four principles that characterize school accountability under NCLB are

**FOCUS 6**

Identify four principles for school accountability as required in No Child Left Behind. Under IDEA, what must a student's IEP include relative to accessing the general curriculum?

**Adaptive instruction**

Modifies the way in which instruction is delivered and the environment where the learning takes place in order to accommodate unique learner characteristics.

**Self-determination**

The ability of a person to consider options and make appropriate choices.

**Standards-based approach**

Instruction that emphasizes challenging academic standards specifying knowledge and skills and the levels at which students should demonstrate mastery of them.

1. A focus on student achievement as the primary measure of school success.

2. An emphasis on challenging academic standards that specify the knowledge and skills students should acquire and the levels at which they should demonstrate mastery.

3. A desire to extend the standards to all students, including those for whom expectations have been traditionally low.

4. Heavy reliance on achievement testing to spur the reforms and to monitor their impact. (National Research Council, 1997; U.S. Department of Education, 2003)

Students with disabilities must have access to the general curriculum and be included in statewide testing programs when appropriate. Do you think participation in the general curriculum results in higher academic achievement for students with disabilities?

Advocates for standards-based reform have strongly emphasized the importance of acknowledging the inclusion of students with disabilities in a state and school district accountability system. Yet, in spite of the call to include all students in school reform initiatives, concerns have arisen that students with disabilities and other students at a disadvantage have been left out. Research suggests that the participation of students with disabilities in the general curriculum and in state-wide assessments of student performance have varied considerably from state to state and district to district (Erickson, 1998; Erickson, Thurlow, & Thor, 1995; McLaughlin, 1998). Hehir (2002) suggests that "one of the reasons students with disabilities are not performing better is that they have not had sufficient access to the general curriculum" (p. 6). The National Research Council (1997) cited anecdotal evidence that states and local school districts are keeping students with disabilities out of their accountability systems because of fear that they pull down scores.

In response to these concerns, IDEA required that a student's IEP describe how the disability affects the child's involvement and progress in the general curriculum. In addition, the IEP goals must enable the child to access the general curriculum when appropriate. The law requires an explanation of any individual modifications in the administration of state- or district-wide assessment of student achievement that are needed in order for the child to participate.

As the movement to a standards-based system under NCLB moves forward and students with disabilities gain more access to the general curriculum, several questions are yet to be answered:

- How will the standards-based system deal with the diverse needs and functioning levels of students with disabilities?

- Will participation of students with disabilities in a standards-based general curriculum result in higher academic achievement?

- Are the knowledge and skills learned in the general curriculum the same ones that are necessary for the successful transition out of school and access to valued postschool outcomes during adult life?

- Will a variety of student performance measures be used, or will criteria be based solely on standardized achievement tests?

## Providing Reasonable Accommodations Under Section 504/ADA

**FOCUS 7**

Distinguish between students with disabilities who are eligible for services under Section 504/ADA and those eligible under IDEA.

Today's schools must provide supports and services to two groups of students with disabilities. One group qualifies for special education services under IDEA because their disability limits their access to an appropriate education. Another group, although they are not viewed as educationally limited by their disability and are therefore ineligible for special education, are protected against discrimination under Section 504 of the Vocational Rehabilitation Act and the Americans with Disabilities Act (ADA).[1] These two laws are comparable in focus, but ADA includes conditions such as HIV infections, heart disease, drug addiction, and alcoholism under the definition of disability. For its part, Section 504 has more specific information on "what it would mean not to discriminate on the basis of disability in various educational settings" (Jarrow, 1999, p. 3). Together, Section 504 and ADA address issues of nondiscrimination and equal opportunity for students with disabilities.

Students eligible under Section 504/ADA are entitled to have a *written plan* that ensures their access to an education comparable to that of students who are not disabled. A **504/ADA plan** is different from an IEP in scope and intent. Whereas an IEP is concerned with ensuring access to a free and appropriate education designed to provide educational benefit, a 504 plan provides for reasonable accommodations or modifications as a means to "create a fair and level playing field" for the student. For example, a student who uses a wheelchair but does not require special education services may still need a written 504/ADA plan in order to gain access to adapted transportation or physical therapy (Jarrow, 1999). A comparison of IDEA and 504/ADA provisions is found in Table 2.3.

Numerous accommodations or modifications can be made for students, depending on identified need. Examples include untimed tests, extra time to complete assignments, changes in seating arrangements to accommodate vision or hearing loss or distractibility, the opportunity to respond orally on assignments and tests, taped textbooks, access to peer tutoring, access to a study carrel for independent work, the availability of supplementary materials such as visual or auditory aids, and so on.

## Safe Schools: Zero-Tolerance Versus Zero-Exclusion

**FOCUS 8**

Distinguish between the principles of zero tolerance and zero exclusion in America's schools.

In the past several years, maintaining a safe school environment for America's children has become a critical priority for parents, school personnel, policy makers, and government officials. Today, 1 out of every 620 school-age children in America is killed by gunfire before the age of 20—about 13 children every day (Children's Defense Fund, 2003). About 8% of America's children are victims of crimes at school each year (National Center for Education Statistics, 2002). In 1994 the U.S. Congress passed the Gun-Free Schools Act. This federal legislation mandated that every state receiving federal education funds enact a law requiring all local educational agencies (school districts) to expel for at least a year any student who brings a firearm to school. In 1999, 7% of students in grades 9 through 12 reported carrying a weapon such as a gun or knife to school. (National Center for Education Statistics, 2002).

The Gun-Free School Act and the corresponding state legislation employ the principle of **zero-tolerance.** This principle states that the consequences of a student's misbehavior are predetermined (a 1-year expulsion) and that no individual reasons or circumstances are to be considered. The National Center for Education Statistics (1998) reported that the proportion of public schools with zero-tolerance policies ranged from 79% for violence and tobacco to 94% for firearms.

**504/ADA plan**

A written plan that provides for reasonable accommodations or modifications in assessment and instruction as a means to "create a fair and level playing field" for students who qualify as disabled under Section 504 of the Vocational Rehabilitation Act and the Americans with Disabilities Act.

**Zero-tolerance**

An approach whereby the consequences for a student's misbehavior are predetermined, and no individual reasons or circumstances are considered.

---

[1]See Chapter 1 for a more detailed description of Section 504 and ADA.

TABLE 2.3

## A Comparison of the Purposes and Provisions of IDEA and Section 504/ADA

| | IDEA | SECTION 504/ADA |
|---|---|---|
| **GENERAL PURPOSE** | This federal funding statute provides financial aid to states in their efforts to ensure adequate and appropriate services for children and youth with disabilities. | This broad civil rights law prevents discrimination on the basis of disability in employment, programs and services provided by state and local governments, goods and services provided by private companies, and commercial facilities. |
| **DEFINITION OF DISABILITY** | IDEA identifies 12 categories of disability conditions. However, the law also allows states and school districts the option of eliminating categories for children ages 3 through 9 and defining them as developmentally delayed. | 504/ADA identifies students as disabled if they meet the definition of a qualified handicapped [disabled] person (i.e., student has or has had a physical or mental impairment that substantially limits a major life activity, or student is regarded as disabled by others). |
| **RESPONSIBILITY TO PROVIDE A FREE AND APPROPRIATE PUBLIC EDUCATION (FAPE)** | Both require the provision of a free and appropriate education, including individually designed instruction, to students covered under specific eligibility criteria. | |
| | IDEA requires a written IEP document. | 504/ADA does not require a written IEP document but does require a written plan. |
| | "Appropriate education" means a program designed to provide "educational benefit." | "Appropriate" means an education comparable to the education provided to students who are not disabled. |
| **SPECIAL EDUCATION OR GENERAL EDUCATION** | A student is eligible to receive IDEA services only if the child-study team determines that the student is disabled under 1 of the 12 qualifying conditions and requires special education. Eligible students receive special education and related services. | An eligible student meets the definition of qualified person with a disability: one who currently has or has had a physical or mental impairment that substantially limits a major life activity or who is regarded as disabled by others. The student is not required to need special education in order to be protected. |
| **FUNDING** | IDEA provides additional funding if a student is eligible. | 504/ADA does not provide additional funds. |
| **ACCESSIBILITY** | IDEA requires that modifications be made, if necessary, to provide access to a free and appropriate education. | 504/ADA includes regulations regarding building and program accessibility. |
| **NOTICE SAFEGUARDS** | Both require notice to the parent or guardian with respect to identification, evaluation, and/or placement. | |
| | IDEA requires written notice. | 504/ADA does not require written notice, but a district would be wise to provide it. |
| | It delineates required components of written notice. | Particular components are not delineated. |
| | It requires written notices prior to *any* change in placement. | It requires notice only before a "significant change" in placement. |
| **EVALUATIONS** | IDEA requires consent before an initial evaluation is conducted. | 504/ADA does not require consent but does require notice. |
| | It requires reevaluations at least every 3 years. | It requires periodic reevaluations. |
| | It requires an update and/or review before *any* change in placement. | Reevaluation is required before a significant change in placement. |
| | It provides for independent educational evaluations. | Independent educational evaluations are not mentioned. |
| **DUE PROCESS** | Both statutes require districts to provide impartial hearings for parents or guardians who disagree with the identification, evaluation, or placement of a student with disabilities. | |
| | Specific requirements are detailed in IDEA. | 504/ADA requires that the parent have an opportunity to participate and be represented by counsel. Other details are left to the discretion of the local school district. These should be covered in school district policy. |
| **ENFORCEMENT** | IDEA is enforced by the Office of Special Education Programs in the Department of Education. | 504/ADA is enforced by the Office for Civil Rights in the Department of Justice. |

*One out of ten children are victims of crime in America's schools. Thirteen children are killed everyday by gunfire in America. This child is participating in a drill to prepare children for a potential terrorist attack. What else can society do to make America's school safe?*

The principle of zero tolerance has both supporters and detractors, but it has posed a particularly serious problem for students with disabilities receiving services under the provisions of IDEA. IDEA employs a principle of zero-rejection: An eligible student with a disability cannot be denied access to a free and appropriate public education (FAPE). How, then, can a student with a disability be expelled from school under any circumstances?

Many professionals and parents of students with disabilities are concerned that if schools allow a cessation of services, it will undermine IDEA's zero-exclusion principle. Others argue that students with disabilities should be treated no differently than students without disabilities when the individual is likely to cause injury to others and themselves. For more insight into the debate on safe schools and the zero-exclusion principle, see the nearby Debate Forum, "What Should We Do with Lance?"

**Debate Forum**

## WHAT SHOULD WE DO WITH LANCE?

The following is an interview from a segment from the TV newsmagazine *60 Minutes*. CBS newsman Morley Safer is interviewing David Whetstone, the Baldwin County, Alabama, district attorney, and Ms. Ann Vinson, a special education teacher, regarding Lance Landers, an Alabama student with a disability who is prone to violence and verbal abuse. The program was aired by CBS television in 2000.

MORLEY SAFER.  Sixteen-year-old Lance Landers looks like a typical American kid, but everyone who knows him, including his mother, says he's a very troubled American kid. At school in Gulf Shores, Alabama, he picked fights with students, he spit in their food, he threatened to kill his teacher and his classmates, and he addressed the principal in the most offensive language. When [the events at] Columbine [High School] happened and Baldwin County's district attorney, David Whetstone, heard about Lance, he decided to act.

MR. DAVID WHETSTONE.  I looked at Columbine and I was shocked, like the rest of the country, and then I found something in my school I thought could be the same thing. And we had to take a stand. I think in Columbine, if you could have removed those kids before the acts took place, that would have been a preferable act to do.

SAFER.  What you're saying, in effect, is that—that Lance will probably kill somebody if left in the school system.

WHETSTONE.  I think there's a chance that he will act violently, because that has been his situation throughout his life.

SAFER.  The final straw came on a school bus full of children. When Lance erupted and threatened to cause a crash, a teacher's aide had to restrain him. Lance hit and kicked the aide. The district attorney went to court and asked a judge to throw Lance not just out of the school, but out of the entire state school system.

WHETSTONE.  I wanted to ask the question "Do the other children and the teachers have the right to go to school in safety and not be disturbed? And can a court of law protect that in the state of Alabama?" The answer to that was yes.

MS. ANN VINSON. There was no call for him to have been pulled out of all the schools in Alabama.

SAFER. If any other student had done the things Lance did, the principal could have expelled him. But Lance was special, considered disabled, and the school had to find a way to continue to educate him. It consulted his mother, and together they agreed to send Lance to a treatment program that offered psychiatric help. He wouldn't cooperate, so doctors sent him back to public school, which felt it had no choice but to take him. The behavior continued. The school assigned Lance his own private teacher. That didn't work out. His mother tried home-schooling him, but he was violent there, too. She called the police a number of times. He assaulted her.

SAFER. The school finally recommended that Lance go to a special public school for at risk children. The closest one was an hour and a half away. His mother refused, saying her son could not handle the daily commute, so he was put back into his regular classroom.

WHETSTONE. Because of his status—his special protected status—he was allowed to continue and continue to do the acts and get worse and worse and worse.

SAFER. Is Lance himself aware that he's got this, what you would call, I guess, a free pass?

WHETSTONE. Yeah. Lance has said, "You can't touch me. I'm d—, I'm special." Well, I wanted to touch him. I wanted to let him know that somebody could touch him, and we did.

SAFER. What District Attorney Whetstone did was to take Lance to state court, which flew in the face of federal law and banned the boy from public school. Just describe how this federal law works.

WHETSTONE. If you fall under a certain type of disabilities set by Congress, then you cannot be disciplined as other children. For example, if you threaten to hurt someone at school, you are—you are protected more than all the other children.

SAFER. That's because the lawmakers felt that disabled children needed more protection. Until the mid-1970s . . . schools were allowed to exclude children they considered too difficult to educate. That changed in 1975 when Congress passed a law forcing public schools to accept the disabled and to protect them. Lance had the same rights as any student in a wheelchair. There are mechanisms in the law for schools to keep potentially dangerous students out of class, but they can involve long, drawn-out legal proceedings, and many schools fear the consequences.

WHETSTONE. We have schools so afraid they're going to be personally sued because they have not given someone all the rights under this disability act, that they're afraid to do anything.

VINSON. Let me ask you a question. Which is more dangerous: a child who is in a classroom learning, or someone who's out on the streets not learning, becoming angry?

SAFER. For Lance, it's neither the street nor his classroom. As punishment for the bus incident, a state agency sent him to Glenwood, a tough, private institution for troubled kids. He's getting an education and treatment, and his mother says he's making progress.

VINSON. We have not given up on Lance, and we won't give up on Lance. He's part of our family; he's part of us. And I think that he deserves a public, appropriate education. And I truly believe that when he finishes this program, he'll be able to attend a school—a regular public school—and do well.

SAFER. That's if he wins the right to. When he's released, probably this summer, he'll still be banned from all schools in the state, if David Whetstone has his way.

WHETSTONE. I—I hope he gets a good education, and I hope he becomes a good person. But as long as he's going to act the way he is, he's not welcome in the public schools of Alabama.*

---

## POINT

Students with behavior disorders, particularly those served in general education settings, should be treated like other students in schools. If they come with weapons, distribute drugs, or engage in behaviors dangerous to others, they should be treated like other students guilty of similar offenses. They should experience the same disciplinary consequences as students without disabilities. When students with behavior disorders violate school rules and state and national laws, they should forfeit their rights just as other students do.

## COUNTERPOINT

On both legal and ethical grounds, students with behavior disorders should not be suspended or expelled from school. Removing students with behavior disorders from the school setting without giving them appropriate services as determined in their IEPs merely exacerbates their problems. They need the interventions and services that are targeted to their particular problems and needs. Without these services, they are likely to create even more serious problems for their neighborhoods and communities. Suspending or expelling students with behavior disorders without providing appropriate, ongoing education services is equivalent to refusing a child with a serious illness appropriate medical care precisely because the child is sick.

What do you think? To give your opinion, go to Chapter 2 of the companion website **(www. ablongman.com/hardman8e)**, and click on Debate Forum.

---

*SOURCE: Adapted from *60 Minutes: The Columbine Effect,* produced by C. Olian of MM CBS. New York: CBS News, 2000.

In dealing with this controversial issue, IDEA reiterated that a free and appropriate public education must be available to all students with disabilities and that there should be no cessation of services. Schools must seek to employ instructional alternatives to expulsion—that is, helping children to learn decision-making and problem-solving skills that promote acceptable behavior. Hartwig and Ruesch (2000) suggested that it is important to have a balanced approach to discipline that includes "both proactive strategies to prevent problem behavior and well-specified, procedurally sound responses to problem behavior" (p. 246).

This chapter has briefly discussed the history of special education services in the United States, the movement to reaffirm the rights of students with disabilities to a free and appropriate public education, the basic tenets of the Individuals with Disabilities Education Act, and current trends in the field of special education. Chapter 3 focuses on effective practices for inclusion and collaboration in the early childhood and elementary school years.

# FOCUS REVIEW

**FOCUS 1** What educational services were available for students with disabilities during most of the 20th century?

- At the beginning of the 20th century, such educational programs were provided primarily in separate, special schools.
- For the first 75 years of the 20th century, the availability of educational programs for students with disabilities was sporadic and selective. Special education was allowed in many states but required in only a few.
- Research on the efficacy of special classes for students with mild disabilities suggested that there was little or no benefit in removing students from general education classrooms.

**FOCUS 2** Identify the principal issues in the right-to-education cases that led to eventual passage of the national mandate to educate students with disabilities.

- The U.S. Supreme Court reaffirmed education as a right and not a privilege.
- In Pennsylvania, the courts ordered the schools to provide a free public education to all children with mental retardation between the ages of 6 and 21.
- The *Mills* case extended the right to a free public education to all school-age children with disabilities.

**FOCUS 3** Identify five major provisions of the Individuals with Disabilities Education Act.

- Nondiscriminatory and multi-

disciplinary assessment is required for the identification of students with disabilities and their placement in educational programs.
- Parental safeguards and involvement in the educational process include consent for testing and placement and parental participation as a team member in the development of an IEP.
- Procedural safeguards (such as due-process) protect the child and family from decisions that could adversely affect their lives.
- Every student with a disability is entitled to a free and appropriate public education.
- The delivery of an appropriate education occurs through an individualized education program (IEP).

- All children have the right to learn in an environment consistent with their academic, social, and physical needs. The law mandated that, to the greatest extent appropriate, children with disabilities receive their education with peers who are not disabled.

**FOCUS 4** Identify the four phases of the special education referral, planning, and placement process.

- Initiating the referral
- Assessing student eligibility and educational need
- Developing the individualized education program (IEP)
- Determining the least restrictive environment

**FOCUS 5** Identify three characteristics of effective special education that enhance learning opportunities for students with disabilities.

- Individualization: A student-centered approach to instructional decision making
- Intensive instruction: Frequent instructional experiences of significant duration
- The explicit teaching of academic, adaptive, and/or functional life skills

**FOCUS 6** Identify four principles for school accountability

as required in No Child Left Behind. Under IDEA, what must a student's IEP include relative to accessing the general curriculum?

- The four principles are
  1. A focus on student achievement as the primary measure of school success.
  2. An emphasis on challenging academic standards that specify the knowledge and skills students should acquire and the levels at which they should demonstrate mastery.
  3. A desire to extend the standards to all students, including those for whom expectations have traditionally been low.
  4. Heavy reliance on achievement testing to spur the reforms and to monitor their impact.

- IDEA requires that a student's IEP describe how the disability affects the individual's involvement and progress in the general curriculum. IEP goals must enable the student to access the general curriculum when appropriate.

**FOCUS 7** Distinguish between students with disabilities who are eligible for services under Section 504/ADA and those eligible under IDEA.

- Students eligible under ADA are entitled to accommodations and/or modifications to their educational program that will ensure that they receive an appropriate education comparable to that of their peers without disabilities.
- Students eligible under IDEA are entitled to special education and related services to ensure that they receive a free and appropriate education.

**FOCUS 8** Distinguish between the principles of zero tolerance and zero exclusion in America's schools.

- The principle of zero tolerance states that the consequences for a student's misbehavior are predetermined and that no individual reasons or circumstances may be considered.
- The principle of zero exclusion states that no student with a disability can be denied a free and appropriate public education, regardless of the nature, type, or extent of his or her disabling condition. Thus a student with a disability cannot be expelled from school for misbehavior.

## FURTHER READINGS

Council for Exceptional Children (1999). *The IEP team guide*. Ballston, VA: Author.

*This book guides IEP team members through the development and revision of an IEP. Emphasis is on the importance of each team member, including the student and parents. Strategies for ensuring active participation of each team member are presented.*

Edelman, M. W. (2003). *The State of America's Children Yearbook*. Washington, DC: The Children's Defense Fund.

*The book provides comprehensive and state-by-state data on family income, child health, children and families in crisis, the relationship between child care and early childhood development, child nutrition, education, adolescent pregnancy, and violence. It features information on national trends in child poverty, birth to teens, mothers in the work force, and youth unemployment.*

**Huefner, D. (2000).** *Getting Comfortable with Special Education Law: A Framework for Working with Children with Disabilities.* **Norwood, MA: Christopher-Gordon Publishers.**

*This book is a guide to understanding the needs of children with disabilities; the complex legal relationship between federal and state governments; the contributions being made by legislation, regulations, and court deci-*

*sions; and the ultimate responsibilities of parents and teachers to make appropriate education a reality for all children with disabilities.*

**Pitaski, V. M. (2002).** *What Do I Do When . . . The Answer Book on Placement Under the IDEA and Section 504.* **Alexandria, VA: LRP Publications.**

*In a question-and-answer format, this book provides solutions to educational placement under IDEA and Section 504/ADA. The legal obligations of schools and agencies are described, including cross-references to judicial decisions and administrative rulings.*

# WEB RESOURCES

### The Office of Special Education Programs (OSEP)

www.ed.gov/about/offices/list/OSERS/OSEP/Resources/index.html

This office is dedicated to improving results for infants, toddlers, children, and youth with disabilities from birth through age 21 by providing leadership and financial support to assist states and local districts. This website offers information on IDEA grants to states and discretionary grants to universities/colleges and other not-for-profit organizations to support research, demonstra-tions, technical assistance and dissemination, technology and personnel development, and parent-training and information centers.

### IDEA Practices

www.ideapractices.org

This website provides up-to-date news on IDEA, information and questions and answers on the provisions of the law and federal regulations, and professional development resources.

### National Dissemination Center for Children with Disabilities (NICHCY)

www.nichcy.org

This site provides information on disabilities and disability-related issues. NICHCY's website has information on specific disabilities; special education and related services for children in school; individualized education programs; parent materials; disability-related organizations; professional associations; education rights and what the law requires; early intervention services for infants and toddlers; and transition to adult life.

# BUILDING YOUR PORTFOLIO

If you are thinking about a career in special education, you should know that many states use national standards developed by the Council for Exceptional Children (CEC) to assess a teacher candidate's knowledge about and skills for working with students with disabilities. See a complete listing of the ten CEC Content Standards on the inside front cover of this text.

### CEC Content Standards Addressed in Chapter 2

1. Foundations
2. Development and Characteristics of Learners
3. Individual Learning Differences

7. Instructional Planning
8. Assessment
9. Professional and Ethical Practice

### Assess Your Knowledge of the CEC Standards Addressed in Chapter 2

Some states require that teacher candidates develop a portfolio of products that demonstrate mastery of the CEC content standards. To assist in the development of products for this portfolio, you may wish to complete the following activities.

- Complete a written test of the chapter's content.

  *If your instructor requires a written test of your content knowledge for this chapter, keep a copy for your portfolio. A practice test on the information covered in this chapter is available through the companion website (www.ablongman.com/hardman8e) and the Student Study Guide.*

- Respond to Application Questions for the Case Study "Jerald."

  *Review the Case Study and respond in writing to the application questions. Keep a copy of the case study and your written response for your portfolio.*

- Complete the "Take a Stand" activity for the Debate Forum "What Should We Do with Lance?"

  *Read the Debate Forum in this chapter and then visit our companion website to complete the activity "Take a Stand." Keep a copy of this activity for your portfolio.*

- Participate in a Community Service Learning Activity.

  *Community service is a valuable way to enhance your learning experience. Visit our companion website for suggested community service learning activities that correspond to the information presented in this chapter. Develop a reflective journal of the service learning experience for your portfolio.*

## THEMES OF THE TIMES

Expand your knowledge of the concepts discussed in this chapter by reading current and historical articles from the *New York Times* by visiting the "Themes of the Times" section of the companion website: **www.ablongman.com/hardman8e.**

# Inclusion and Collaboration in the Early Childhood and Elementary School Years

## TO BEGIN WITH...

### Meeting the Challenge of Inclusive Education

Representatives from 92 governments came together in Salamanca, Spain to promote inclusive education, namely enabling schools to serve all children, particularly those with special educational needs. The conference adopted the United Nations Salamanca Statement:

- Every child has a fundamental right to education, and must be given the opportunity to achieve and maintain an acceptable level of learning.
  Every child has unique characteristics, interests, abilities and learning needs.

- Education systems should be designed and educational programs implemented to take into account the wide diversity of these characteristics and needs.

- Those with special educational needs must have access to regular schools which should accommodate them within a child-centered pedagogy capable of meeting these needs.

- Regular schools with this inclusive orientation are the most effective means of combating discriminatory attitudes, creating welcoming communities, building an inclusive society and achieving education for all; moreover, they provide an effective education to the majority of children and improve the efficiency and ultimately the cost-effectiveness of the entire education system. (United Nations Educational, Scientific, and Cultural Organization, 2003)

### Special Education Works!

John, 23, has a severe reading disability. Despite his disability, he graduated from high school and received training as an electrician. After working for a national company for two years, he now runs his own company. . . . Alfie, 25, has Down syndrome. Though the "medical experts" said there was "no hope" and that he would never even speak, Alfie is bilingual, reads at a 6th grade level, and is in a job training program. Lindsay, 11, has severe cerebral palsy. Though she is unable to use her hands, she maintains an A/B average and also keeps up with her classmates in written work—she types with her feet. The stories of John, . . . Alfie, and Lindsay are not atypical. Every special educator can look at the students he or she has taught and mark their progress—and the often remarkable success—students with disabilities achieve with the support of special education. (Council for Exceptional Children, 1999)

### Sharing the Responsibility

The most recent descriptor for the effort to create greater integration of children with disabilities into school programs is the term *inclusion*. For many educators, the term is viewed as a more positive description of efforts to include children with disabilities in genuine and comprehensive ways in the total life of schools. . . . The most effective and needed services that special education can provide must be preserved. At the same time, the education of children with disabilities must be viewed by all educators as a shared responsibility and privilege. Most important, every child must have a place and be made welcome in a regular classroom. (Smith, 1998, pp. 17, 18)

**FOCUS**

**PREVIEW:** To preview the central concepts of this chapter, read the focus questions located in the margins. Using these questions as a guide, ask yourself what you already know and what you want to learn.

## Supporting Bill, the New Kid At School

Bill lived in an institution until he was 12. When his new foster parents brought him home, they enrolled him in the local elementary school. Bill's first IEP meeting included his foster parents, teachers, specialists, some schoolmates, and Bill. First they discussed Bill's strengths. Though they had just met, and Bill didn't talk, his classmates thought he was very friendly and nice to be around. "Great smile" went up on his list of strengths. His foster parents added, "Loves music." His teacher, Mr. Lewis, noted that Bill seemed to be enjoying the meeting and added, "Likes to be involved." The listing continued.

Bill's goals were discussed. He needed to work on "tracking"—visually following and focusing on key people and things in his environment. Bill was assigned to work with a sixth grade math teacher who was famous for his animated teaching and for pacing around the classroom. Bill would have lots of opportunity to "track" this teacher while he also worked on responding vocally and helping to pass out materials to classmates. In PE, classmates decided "being cool" was a goal they thought Bill would want, so they cued his foster parents in on clothes that Bill would need and on the latest in backpack styles. They also arranged to meet Bill at his bus, taking him with them to hang out with friends before school each day. Other goals were discussed. Learning to operate a switch so that he might eventually operate an electric wheelchair was one. Another goal was improving the coordination of his movements and broadening the range of motion of his stiffened joints by helping to reshelve books in the library.

After a while, his teachers and classmates worked on their own creative-thinking goals by beginning each lesson by brainstorming about how Bill could be included in the lesson. The day frogs were dissected in a biology lesson, Bill's group decided to dissect theirs on his wheelchair tray. Bill squealed like everyone else when the frog parts were held up for inspection. His goal of "vocalizing" was easily met that day! Another student had Bill help him color the frog anatomy handout with marker pens: practice in coordinated movement.

When Bill's homeroom teacher told the class they could listen to music for ten minutes each day, it took them exactly two days to teach him to operate the switch that turned on the music for everyone. In Home Skills class, he was the only one allowed to operate the switch on the mixer that made the cookies that the class eventually named "Bill's Cool Cookies" and sold as a fundraiser for their field trip. In PE, Bill's classmates put the bat in his hands, helped him hit the ball, and raced the wheelchair around the bases with Bill laughing all the way. The next year Bill died unexpectedly in his sleep. Hundreds of kids from his school went to the funeral. (Adapted from National Institute for Urban School Development, 2003, p. 11)

This chapter explores inclusive education, collaboration, and programs and services in the early childhood and elementary school years. For infants, toddlers, and preschool-age children, the world is defined primarily through family and a small group of same-age peers. As the child progresses in age and development, the world expands to include the neighborhood, the school, and eventually the community. Bill, in our opening Snapshot, spent the first 12 years of his life confined to an institution. Here he had few personal possessions, wore clothing designed more for utility than fashion, and lived under a regimented set of rules that controlled when he ate, when he played, and when he slept. Bill's life was dramatically changed when he left the institution and his new foster parents enrolled him in the neighborhood elementary school. Bill became the new kid on the block. Inclusion for Bill meant hanging out with friends, learning new skills side-by-side with peers, and racing around the bases in his wheelchair during PE class.

# Inclusive Education

The history of education has seen an evolution of terms used to describe the concept of educating students with disabilities in a general education setting, side-by-side with their peers without disabilities. The most common such terms are *mainstreaming, least restrictive environment,* and *inclusive education.* We discussed the least restrictive environment in the context of IDEA in Chapter 2. The expression *mainstreaming* dates back to the very beginnings of the field of special education. It didn't come into widespread use until the 1960s, however, with the growth of classes for children with disabilities in the public schools, most of which separated students with disabilities from their peers without disabilities.

At that time, some professionals called into question the validity of separate programs. Dunn (1968) charged that classes for children with mild retardation could not be justified: "Let us stop being pressured into continuing and expanding a special education program that we know now to be undesirable for many of the children we are dedicated to serve" (p. 5). Dunn, among others, called for a placement model whereby students with disabilities could remain in the general education class program for at least some portion of the school day and receive special education when and where it was needed. This model became widely known as **mainstreaming.**

Although mainstreaming implied that students with disabilities would receive individual planning and support from both general and special educators, this did not always happen in actual practice. In fact, the term *mainstreaming* fell from favor when it became associated with placing students with disabilities in general education classes without providing additional support, as a means to save money and limit the number of students who could receive additional specialized services. Such practices gave rise to the term *maindumping* as an alternative to mainstreaming. However, the term *mainstreaming* remains in some use today as one way to describe educating students with disabilities in general education settings.

## What Is Inclusive Education?

*Mainstreaming* and *inclusive education,* although often used interchangeably, are not synonymous. Whereas *mainstreaming* implies the physical placement of students with disabilities in the same school or classroom as students without disabilities, inclusive education suggests that mere placement is not enough. **Inclusive education** *means students with disabilities receive the services and supports appropriate to their individual needs within the general education setting.* Peterson and Hittie (2003) described this paradigm as "push-in services" (p. 21). Whereas the traditional model for special education has been "pulling the student out" of the general education class to receive support, inclusive education focuses on "pushing services and supports into" the general education setting for both students and teachers.

Inclusive education may also be defined by the extent of the student's access to, and participation in, the general education classroom. **Full inclusion** is an approach whereby students with disabilities receive all instruction in a general education classroom; support services come to the student. **Partial inclusion** involves students with disabilities receiving some of their instruction in a general education classroom, with *"pull out"* to another instructional setting when appropriate to their individual needs. The success of full-inclusion and partial-inclusion programs depends on several factors, including a strong belief in the value of inclusion on the part of professionals and parents, the availability of a support network of general and special education professionals, and access to a curriculum that meets the needs of each student.

A number of educators have argued that in spite of certain accomplishments, pull-out programs have had negative effects or acted as obstacles to the appropriate education of students with disabilities (Lipsky & Gartner, 1999; Paul, 1998; Sailor, Gee, & Karasoff, 2000). On the other hand, proponents of pull-out programs have argued that the available research doesn't support the premise that full-time placement in a general education classroom is superior to special education classes for all students with disabilities (Dupre, 1997; Fox & Ysseldyke, 1997; Mills, Cole, Jenkins, & Day 1998). For a more in-depth look at the differing perspectives on full inclusion, see the nearby Debate Forum.

## Characteristics of Effective Inclusive Schools

The passage of the *No Child Left Behind Act* in 2001 launched a great deal of discussion about which characteristics, taken together, constitute an effective school for all students. There seems to be considerable agreement that schools are most

**FOCUS 1**

Define the term *inclusive education.*

**Mainstreaming**

Placing students with disabilities in general education classrooms for some or all of the school day.

**Inclusive education**

Approach in which students with disabilities receive the services and supports appropriate to their individual needs within the general education setting.

**Full inclusion**

Type of inclusive education in which students with disabilities receive all instruction in a general education classroom; support services come to the student.

**Partial inclusion**

Type of inclusive education in which students with disabilities receive some of their instruction in a general education classroom, with "pull out" to another instructional setting when appropriate to their individual needs.

FOCUS 2

List the characteristics of effective inclusive schools.

successful in promoting student achievement and valued postschool outcomes when they

- establish high expectations for learning that are linked with a clear and focused mission.
- establish strong instructional leadership with frequent monitoring of student progress.
- promote the values of diversity, acceptance, and belonging.
- ensure the availability of formal and natural supports within the general education setting.
- provide services and supports in age-appropriate classrooms in neighborhood schools.
- ensure access to the general curriculum while meeting the individualized needs of each student.
- provide a schoolwide support system to meet the needs of all students.

Debate Forum

## PERSPECTIVES ON FULL INCLUSION OF STUDENTS WITH DISABILITIES

Full inclusion: Students are placed in a general education classroom for the entire school day. The supports and services necessary to ensure an appropriate education come to the student in the general education class; the student is *not* "pulled out" into a special education classroom for instruction.

### POINT

The goal behind full inclusion is to educate students with disabilities with their nondisabled peers in a general education class setting, as a way to increase their access to, and participation in, all natural settings. The general education classroom is a microcosm of the larger society. For the preschool-age child, the world is defined primarily through family and a small same-age peer group. As the child gets older, the world expands to the neighborhood, to the school, and eventually to the larger, heterogeneous community. As educators, we must ask how we can educate the child with a disability to foster full participation as the life space of the individual is expanded. What are the barriers to full participation, and how do we work to break them down? A partnership between general and special education is a good beginning to breaking down barriers. Each professional brings his or her knowledge and resources into a single setting in the development of an instructional program that is directly oriented to student need. This unified approach to instruction will give teachers the opportunity to work across disciplines and gain a broader understanding of the diversity in all children. Pull-out programs result in a fragmented approach to instruction with little cooperation between general and special education.

Finally, students in pull-out programs are much more likely to be stigmatized. Separate education on the basis of a child's learning or behavioral characteristics is inherently unequal.

### COUNTERPOINT

Full inclusion is a laudable goal but nevertheless a misguided one, because it is neither achievable nor even desirable for some students with disabilities. The reality is that specialized academic and social instruction can best be provided, at least for some students, in a pull-out setting. These more restricted settings are the least restrictive environment for some students. Pull-out programs will more effectively prepare the student to return to less restricted settings, such as the general education class. A move to full inclusion will result in the loss of special education personnel who have been trained to work with students who have diverse needs. In spite of the rhetoric about collaboration between general and special education, responsibility for the student's education in a full-inclusion classroom will move to the general education class teacher with little or no support. The result will be that these students have been dumped into an environment that does not meet their needs.

## POINT

We must rethink our current approach to the educational placement of students with disabilities. Pulling these students out of general education classrooms and placing them in separate settings does not make sense from the standpoint either of values or of "what works." As a moral imperative, inclusion is the right thing to do. Putnam (1998a) (pp. 7–8) put it as follows:

> The most compelling rationale for inclusive education is based on cultural and human rights. The civil rights movement used the legislative mandate of the Brown v. Board of Education (1954) decision in the fight to eliminate the negative effects of political, social, and educational segregation. [Today], advocates are fighting against another insidious form of segregation—the denial of equal opportunities to students who have disabilities. . . . According to the 14th Amendment to the U.S. Constitution, people are equal under the law and, thus, deserve equal opportunities in U.S. public schools.

## COUNTERPOINT

No one is questioning the value of children belonging and being a part of society. However, it is not necessarily true that placing a child with a disability in a general education classroom is a denial of human rights. Is it a denial of human rights to remove a student with a disability from a setting where that child receives inadequate academic support to meet his or her instructional needs? Is it a denial of human rights to remove a child from a classroom where she or he is socially isolated? How do you translate the moral imperative into action when the social and academic needs of these students are beyond the expertise of a general education teacher? We must separate the vision from the reality. General education does not have the inclination or the expertise to meet the diverse needs of all students with disabilities. General education is already overburdened with the increasing number of at risk students, large class sizes, and an inadequate support system.

## POINT

Let's indeed separate reality from vision. The reality is that traditional special education has failed; it does not work (Lipsky & Gartner, 1999; Meyer, 2001; Peterson & Hittie, 2003). Setting the values inherent in the inclusion of all students aside, let's look at the reality (Wagner & Blackorby, 1996):

- Only 56% of students in special education graduate with a diploma.
- Some 38% percent drop out of school.
- About 31% receive failing grades in school.
- Only 55% of special education graduates and 40% of the dropouts are employed following their exit from school.
- Only 21% of special education graduates and 5% of the dropouts pursue any type of postsecondary training.

Wagner and Blackorby (1996) also pointed out that having positive experiences in school, including interactions with nondisabled peers, puts students with disabilities on a better trajectory toward successful transition into adult life. Several other authors (Lipsky & Gartner, 1999; Drew & Hardman, 2004; Stainback, Stainback, & Ayres, 1996; Vaughn, Moody, & Schumm, 1998) have noted that there is no evidence that pulling them out of general education classrooms benefits students with disabilities.

## COUNTERPOINT

There is always a flip side to the research coin. What about the following research findings?

- Research doesn't support the premise that full-time placement in a general education classroom is superior to special education pull-out programs for all students with disabilities (Fox & Ysseldyke, 1997; Mills et al., 1998).
- General education teachers have little expertise in assisting students with learning and behavioral difficulties and are already overburdened with large class size and inadequate support services (Kavale & Forness, 2000; Scruggs & Mastropieri, 1996).
- Special educators have been specifically trained to individualize instruction, develop instructional strategies, and use proven techniques that facilitate learning for students with disabilities (National Research Council, 1997).
- In general, both parents and professionals are quite satisfied with the special education continuum of placements (Johnson & Duffett, 2002).

Additionally, on what basis do you attach blame to special education for low graduation and high dropout rates or for the lack of access to postsecondary education? Given that 94% of all students with disabilities are spending at least a portion of their day in general classes, shouldn't we be looking at the system as a whole, not just at special education, in trying to deal with student failure? Concerning the high unemployment rate for people with disabilities, shouldn't we look at the failure of adult services to expand opportunities for individuals to receive the training and support they need to find a job and succeed in community employment settings?

The conclusions of researchers who believe that special education has failed can be countered by other investigators who offer a very different interpretation (Dupre, 1997; Hocutt, 1996; Kauffman & Hallahan, 1997). These researchers, although they call for improvements in special education, don't support its abolition.

What do you think? To give your opinion, go to Chapter 3 of the companion website (www.ablongman.com/hardman8e), and click on Debate Forum.

*Effective inclusive classrooms promote diversity, acceptance, and belonging for all children. What are the responsibilities of professionals to ensure a successful inclusive program?*

**DIVERSITY, ACCEPTANCE, AND BELONGING.** An effective inclusive school promotes both acceptance and belonging within a diverse culture. Wade and Zone (2000) described this value as "building community and affirming diversity. . . . Struggling learners can be actively involved, socially accepted, and motivated to achieve the best of their individual and multiple abilities" (p. 22). Landers and Weaver (1997) indicated that "inclusion is an attitude of unqualified acceptance and the fostering of student growth, at any level, on the part of all adults involved in a student's education" (p. 7). These authors further suggested that the responsibility for ensuring a successful inclusive program lies with adults. "Adults must be able to design appropriate educational opportunities that foster the individual student's growth within the context of the student's talents and interests among age-appropriate peers" (p. 7). (See the nearby Reflect on This, "Including Ross.")

**FORMAL AND NATURAL SUPPORTS.** Within an effective inclusive school, students with disabilities must have access to both formal and natural support networks. **Formal supports** are those provided by, and funded through, the public school system. They include qualified teachers, paraprofessionals, and access to instructional materials designed for, or adapted to, individual need. **Natural supports** consist of the student's family and classmates. These individuals constitute a support network of mutual caring that promotes greater inclusion within the classroom and school, access to effective instruction, and the development of social relationships (friendships). The importance of formal and natural support networks cannot be overstated. Through these networks, students with disabilities achieve success in an inclusive school. High-quality formal supports, including teachers and paraprofessionals, are the source for learning valued instructional content. Through the natural support network, students are able to bond with others who will listen, understand, and support them as they attempt to cope with the challenges of being in an inclusive setting.

**AGE-APPROPRIATE CLASSROOMS IN A NEIGHBORHOOD SCHOOL.** Effective inclusive schools provide services and support to students with disabilities in age-appropriate classrooms within a neighborhood school. The National Association of School Psychologists (2003) defines inclusive education as the opportunity for students with disabilities, no matter how severe, to attend the same school they would attend if they were not disabled.

**ACCESS TO THE GENERAL CURRICULUM.** Access to the general curriculum for students with disabilities is a critical provision of IDEA. As suggested within the law, "almost 30 years of research and experience has demonstrated that the education of children with disabilities can be made more effective by having high expectations for such children and ensuring their access in the general curriculum to the maximum extent possible" (IDEA 2004, PL 108-446, Sec. 682[C][5]). A student's IEP must describe how the disability affects the child's involvement and progress in the general curriculum. An effective inclusive school promotes meaningful participation for each student within the subject matter content areas identified in the general curriculum (reading, mathematics, science, and so on). Meaningful participation in the general curriculum will necessitate the development and use of effective strategies, such as universally designed curriculum, instructional adaptations, multilevel instruction, assistive technology, and cooperative learning. Each of these strategies is discussed in detail later in this chapter.

**Formal supports**

Educational supports provided by, and funded through, the public school system. They include qualified teachers, paraprofessionals, and access to instructional materials designed for, or adapted to, individual needs.

**Natural supports**

The student's family and classmates. These individuals make up a support network of mutual caring that promotes greater inclusion within the classroom and school, access to effective instruction, and the development of social relationships (friendships).

## INCLUDING ROSS

**R**oss, age 11, has achdroplasia, a skeletal disorder that causes short limbs and other orthopedic problems. The bones of his head and face do not develop normally, and this has left him with a small amount of permanent hearing loss necessitating the use of hearing aids. Ross, who also has a learning disability, attends Public School 234 in Lower Manhattan. His mother, Tracey, reflects on how easy it is for his classmates to include him.

*Standing outside the school yard at recess on a warm winter day, I watch Ross at the center of a swirl of children playing blackboard, which looks like tag on steroids. He is smaller than the others, with legs that are again starting to look short and bowed because they do not grow at the same rate as his torso. Still, I am amazed to see him playing like this. Best of all, the other children instinctively adapt their games so he can participate, including him as a matter of course, changing the rules slightly. If only the adults at school were this flexible, I tell myself. That has been another story entirely.*

SOURCE: From The "Disabilities You Can See May Be Easier to Deal With Than the Ones You Can't," by T. Harden, 2003, *New York Times,* April 13, Section 4a, p. 2.

**SCHOOLWIDE SUPPORT FOR ALL STUDENTS.** Effective inclusive schools are characterized by a schoolwide support system that uses both general and special education resources in combination to benefit all students in the school (Ainscow, 1999; Peterson & Hittie, 2003; Wade & Zone, 2000). The leadership of the school principal is vital. The principal should openly support the inclusion of all students in the activities of the school, advocate for the necessary resources to meet student needs, and strongly encourage cooperative learning and peer support programs (Friend & Cook, 2003; Gee, 1996). Inclusive classrooms are characterized by a philosophy that celebrates diversity, rewards collaboration among professionals, and teaches students how to help and support one another. In the next section, we discuss the essential elements of schoolwide collaboration, why it is an important concept within an inclusive school, and who must be involved for it to be effective.

# Collaboration

**Collaboration** is defined as professionals, parents, and students *working together* to achieve the mutual goal of delivering an effective educational program designed to meet individual needs. It should always be viewed as a cooperative, not a competitive, endeavor. As suggested by Friend and Bursuck (2002), collaboration is not *what* those involved do, it is *how* they do it. This process can be described as a *collaborative ethic,* in which everyone works together to meet the needs of all students, including those with disabilities. The team focuses on mastering the process of collaboration as well as the professional values and skills necessary to work effectively as part of a team.

> No one teacher can be skillful at teaching so many different students. She [or he] needs a little help from . . . colleagues. When teachers with different areas of expertise and skill work together, they can individually tailor learning better for all their students. (National Institute for Urban School Improvement, 2003, p. 9)

In an inclusive school, effective collaboration has several key characteristics:

- Parents are viewed as active partners in the education of their children.
- Team members share responsibility; individual roles are clearly understood and valued.
- Team members promote peer support and cooperative learning.

FOCUS 3

Define *collaboration* and identify its key characteristics.

**Collaboration**

Professionals, parents, and students *working together* to create an effective educational program designed to meet individual needs.

## Parents as Valued Partners

Inclusive schools are most successful when they value families and establish positive and frequent relationships with parents. A strong home-school relationship is characterized by a clear understanding of the philosophical and practical approaches to meeting the needs of the student with a disability within the general education setting. Collaboration among parents and educators is most effective when everyone:

- acknowledges and respects each other's differences in values and culture.
- listens openly and attentively to the other's concerns.
- values opinions and ideas.
- discusses issues openly and in an atmosphere of trust.
- shares in the responsibility and consequences for making a decision. (Berry & Hardman, 1998, p. 198)

When parents feel valued as equal members of the team, they are more likely to develop a positive attitude toward school professionals. Consequently, educators are able to work more closely with parents to understand each student's needs and functioning level. Home–school collaboration will only work if communication is a two-way process where everyone feels respected.

## Sharing the Responsibility

An inclusive school cannot be effective if professionals work in isolation from one another. Unfortunately, professional isolation was the norm for teachers of students with disabilities for more than a century. Special education meant separate education. However, in the late 1980s, some parents and professionals questioned whether it was in the best interest of students with disabilities to be taught solely by special education teachers in separate classrooms or schools. A merger of general and special education was proposed to ensure that these students would have access to qualified professionals from both disciplines. The proposed merger became known as the **regular education initiative** (REI). The goal of REI was for general and special education teachers to share responsibility in ensuring an appropriate educational experience for students with disabilities. Ultimately, the separate special education system would be eliminated. Although REI was viewed by some as an attempt on the part of the federal government to reduce the number of students with mild disabilities receiving special education, and thus ultimately to reduce the cost of special education, it did result in a re-examination of the roles of general and special educators within the inclusive school. "Shared responsibility" became the means by which students with disabilities could receive both the formal and the natural supports necessary for them to participate in the general curriculum and in the inclusive classroom.

**SCHOOLWIDE ASSISTANCE TEAMS.** To meet the needs of a diverse group of students, including those with disabilities, schools have developed sup-

---

**Regular education initiative**

A merger of general and special education proposed in the late 1980s so that all educators would share responsibility for ensuring that students with disabilities receive an appropriate educational experience.

*When parents feel valued as members of the IEP team, they are likely to have positive attitudes toward teachers and school administrators. What are some strategies that professionals could use to develop an effective home-school partnership?*

port networks that facilitate collaboration among professionals. **Schoolwide assistance teams** (SWATs), sometimes referred to as *teacher assistance teams* (TATs), involve groups of professionals, students, and/or parents working together to solve problems, develop instructional strategies, and support classroom teachers. SWATs use a variety of strategies to help teachers make appropriate referrals for students who may need specialized services, adapt instruction or develop accommodations consistent with individual student needs, involve parents in planning and instruction, and coordinate services across the various team members. (See the nearby Reflect on This, "What's My Role on the Schoolwide Assistance Team?")

**Schoolwide assistance teams (SWATS)**

Groups of professionals, students, and/or parents working together to solve problems, develop instructional strategies, and support classroom teachers.

**Reflect on This**

## SCHOOLWIDE ASSISTANCE AND SUPPORT: WHAT'S MY ROLE AS A TEAM MEMBER?

A team is a group of professionals, parents, and/or students who join together to plan and implement an appropriate educational program for a student at risk or with a disability. Team members may be trained in different areas of study, including education, health services, speech and language, school administration, and so on. In the team approach, these individuals sit down together and coordinate their efforts to help the student, regardless of where or how they were trained. For this approach to work, each team member must clearly understand his or her role and responsibilities as a member of the team. Let's visit with some team members and their role in working with a student.

### Special Education Teacher

It's my responsibility to coordinate the student's individualized education program. I work with each member of the team to assist in selecting, administering, and interpreting appropriate assessment information. I maintain ongoing communication with each team member to ensure that we are all working together to help the student. It's my responsibility to compile, organize, and maintain good, accurate records on each student. I propose instructional alternatives for the student and work with others in the implementation of the recommended instruction. To carry this out, I locate or develop the necessary materials to meet each student's specific needs. I work directly with the student's parents to ensure that they are familiar with what is being taught at school and can reinforce school learning experiences at home.

### Parents

We work with each team member to ensure that our child is involved in an appropriate educational program. We give the team information about our child's life outside school and suggest experiences that might be relevant to the home and the community. We also work with our child at home to reinforce what is learned in school. As members of the team, we give our written consent for any evaluations of our child and any changes in our child's educational placement.

### School Psychologist

I select, administer, and interpret appropriate psychological, educational, and behavioral assessment instruments. I consult directly with team members regarding the student's overall educational development. It is also my responsibility to directly observe the student's performance in the classroom and assist in the design of appropriate behavioral management programs in the school and at home.

### School Administrator

As the school district's representative, I work with the team to ensure that the resources of my school and district are used appropriately in providing services to the student. I am ultimately responsible for ensuring that the team's decisions are implemented properly.

### General Education Classroom Teacher

I work with the team to develop and implement appropriate educational experiences for the student during the time that he or she spends in my classroom. I ensure that the student's experiences outside my classroom are consistent with the instruction he or she receives from me. In carrying out my responsibilities, I keep an accurate and continuous record of the student's progress. I am also responsible for referring any other students in my classroom who are at risk and may need specialized services to the school district for an evaluation of their needs.

### Adapted Physical Education Teacher

I am an adapted physical education specialist who works with the team to determine whether the student needs adapted physical education services as a component of his or her individualized education program.

### Related-Services Specialist

I may be a speech and language specialist, social worker, school counselor, school nurse, occupational or physical therapist, juvenile court authority, physician, or school technology coordinator. I provide any additional services necessary to ensure that the student receives an appropriate educational experience.

**TRANSDISCIPLINARY TEAMING.** Students with disabilities have very diverse needs, ranging from academic and behavioral support to functional life skills, communication, and motor development. These needs require that students have access to many different education and related-services specialists who work together in delivering instruction and providing appropriate resources (McDonnell, Hardman, & McDonnell, 2003). Examples of these specialists include general and special education teachers, speech and language specialists, physical therapists, and behavior specialists. Three models of professional collaboration have been used to teach and support students with disabilities: multidisciplinary, interdisciplinary, and transdisciplinary models (see Table 3.1).

Each model has a role in the education of students with disabilities, but the use of transdisciplinary teaming is critical to meeting students' needs effectively and efficiently in an inclusive setting. As suggested in Table 3.1, **transdisciplinary teaming** involves bringing key specialists together to develop an instructional program that views the student from a holistic perspective. The members of the team work together to integrate instructional strategies and therapy concurrently within the classroom, as well as to evaluate the effectiveness of their individual roles in meeting the needs of each student.

As advantageous as transdisciplinary teaming is in an inclusive setting, it may be difficult to implement because team members may have different philosophical orientations. If a professional believes that only he or she is qualified to provide instruction or support in particular area of need (such as communication or motor development), then efforts to share successful strategies are inhibited (McDonnell et al., 2003; Vaughn, Bos, & Schumm, 2003). To overcome this barrier, several strategies can be used to facilitate successful transdisciplinary teaming:

- Always focus on the needs of the student first, rather than on the individual philosophy or expertise of each professional.

- View team members as collaborators rather than as experts. Understand what each professional has to offer in planning, implementing, integrating, and evaluating instructional strategies in an inclusive setting.

- Openly communicate the value of each professional's role in meeting student needs. Maintain an open and positive attitude toward other professionals' philosophy and practices.

- Meet regularly and consult one another on how the student is progressing. Identify what is working, barriers to progress, and next steps in furthering the student's learning and development. (Giangreco, 1997; Orelove & Sobsey, 1996)

### Transdisciplinary teaming

Professionals from various disciplines coming together to develop an instructional program that views the student from a holistic perspective. All members of the team work together to integrate instructional strategies and therapy concurrently within the classroom, and to evaluate the effectiveness of their individual roles in meeting the needs of each student.

## Peer Support and Cooperative Learning

Peers may serve as powerful natural supports for students with disabilities in both academic and social areas (Maheady, Harper, & Mallette, 2001). They often have more influence on their classmates' behavior than the teacher does. Peer support programs may range from the simple creation of opportunities for students with disabilities to interact socially with peers without disabilities to highly structured pro-

### TABLE 3.1

### Models of Professional Collaboration

| MODEL | DESCRIPTION |
|---|---|
| Multidisciplinary | Professional staff members recognize the important contribution that other specialties make to the educational program of each child. However, assessment, IEP development, design and implementations of instruction/therapy, and evaluation are completed independently by each professional. |
| Interdisciplinary | Professional staff members not only recognize the contributions of other staff members but also acknowledge the impact that other specialties may have on his or her area of service delivery. Assessment and IEP development are usually completed jointly by all staff members. In addition, specialists share information with one another in order to integrate services for the student more fully. However, they deliver services independently. |
| Transdisciplinary | Professional staff members are committed to working collaboratively across disciplinary lines. All aspects of students' educational programs are implemented jointly. Specialists train each other to integrate instructional and therapy strategies into their practice. |

SOURCE: *Introduction to Persons with Moderate and Severe Disabilities*, (p. 299), by J. McDonnell, M. Hardman, & A. P. McDonnell, 2003, Boston: Allyn and Bacon.

grams of peer-mediated instruction. **Peer-mediated instruction** involves a structured interaction between two or more students under the direct supervision of a classroom teacher. The instruction may use peer and cross-age tutoring and/or cooperative learning. **Peer tutoring** and **cross-age tutoring** emphasize individual student learning, whereas **cooperative learning** emphasizes the simultaneous learning of students as they seek to achieve group goals. Although

*In addition to being effective teaching strategies, peer support and cooperative learning build self-esteem and increase the acceptance of students with disabilities in inclusive classrooms. Why do you think these strategies are often underutilized in general education classrooms?*

they are often an underrated and underused resource in general education, peers are very reliable and effective in implementing both academic and social programs with students who have disabilities (Gillies & Ashman, 2000; Graves & Bradley, 1997; Putnam, 1998b). In addition, cooperative learning is beneficial to all students, from the highest achievers to those at risk of school failure. It builds self-esteem, strengthens peer relationships, and increases the acceptance of students with disabilities in inclusive classrooms. The effectiveness of peers, however, is dependent on carefully managing the program so that students both with and without disabilities benefit. It is important for teachers to select, train, and monitor the performance of students working as peer tutors. Cooperative learning appears to be most effective when it includes goals for the group as a whole, as well as for individual members (Eggen & Kauchak, 2001; McDonnell et al., 2003; Vaughn, et al., 2003).

# The Early Childhood Years

The past two decades have seen a growing recognition of the educational, social, and health needs of young children with disabilities. This is certainly true for Yvonne from the nearby Snapshot. Yvonne was born with cerebral palsy, requiring immediate services and supports from many different professionals. Yvonne's early learning experiences provided a foundation for her future learning, growth, and development. Early intervention was also crucial to the family's understanding of Yvonne's needs and to the forging of a strong parent/professional partnership.

The first years of life are critical to the overall development of children, including those defined as at risk for disabilities. Moreover, classic studies in the behavioral sciences from the 1960s and 1970s indicated that early stimulation is critical to the later development of language, intelligence, personality, and a sense of self-worth (Bloom, 1964; Hunt, 1961; Piaget, 1970; White, 1975).

Advocates of **early intervention** for children at risk for disabilities believe that intervention should begin as early as possible in an environment free of traditional disability labels (such as "mentally retarded" or "emotionally disturbed"). Carefully selected services and supports can reduce the long-term impact of the disability and counteract any negative effects of waiting to intervene. The postponement of services may, in fact, undermine a child's overall development as well as his or her acquisition of specific skills (Burchinal, Campbell, Bryant, Wasik, & Ramey, 1997; Guralnick, 2001; Ramey & Ramey, 1999).

## Bringing About Change for Young Children with Disabilities

For the better part of the 20th century, comprehensive educational and social services for young children with disabilities were nonexistent or were provided sporadically at best. For families of children with more severe disabilities, often the only option was

**Peer-mediated instruction**

A structured interaction between two or more students under the direct supervision of a classroom teacher. Peers assist in teaching skills to other students.

**Peer tutoring**

An instructional method to facilitate learning of students with disabilities in a general education class. One student provides instruction and/or support to another student or group of students.

**Cross-age tutoring**

An instructional method that pairs older students with younger students to facilitate learning.

**Cooperative learning**

An instructional method that emphasizes the simultaneous learning of students as they work together to achieve group goals.

**Early intervention**

Comprehensive services for infants and toddlers who are disabled or at risk of acquiring a disability. Services may include education, health care, and/or social or psychological assistance.

# Yvonne

## The Early Childhood Years

Anita was elated. She had just learned during an ultrascan that she was going to have twin girls. As the delivery date neared, she thought about how much fun it would be to take them on long summer walks in the new double stroller. Two weeks after her estimated delivery date, she was in the hospital, giving birth to her twins. The first little girl arrived without a problem. Unfortunately, this was not the case for the second.

There was something different about her; it became obvious almost immediately after the birth. Yvonne just didn't seem to have the same body tone as her sister. Within a couple of days, Yvonne was diagnosed as having cerebral palsy. Her head and the left side of her body seemed to be affected most seriously. The pediatrician calmly told the family that Yvonne would undoubtedly have learning and physical problems throughout her life. She referred the parents to a division of the state health agency responsible for assisting families with children who have disabilities. Further testing was done, and Yvonne was placed in an early intervention program for infants with developmental disabilities. When she reached the age of 3, Yvonne's parents enrolled her in a preschool program where she would have the opportunity to learn communication and social skills, while interacting with children of her own age with and without disabilities. Because neither of the parents had any direct experience with a child with disabilities, they were uncertain how to help Yvonne. Would this program really help her that much, or should they work with her at home only? It was hard for them to see this little girl go to school so very early in her life.

## FOCUS 4

Why is it so important to provide early intervention services as soon as possible to young children at risk?

institutionalization. As recently as the 1950s, many parents were advised to institutionalize a child immediately after birth if he or she had a recognizable physical condition associated with a disability (such as Down syndrome). The objective was for the family not to become attached to the child in the hospital or after returning home.

The efforts of parents and professionals to gain national support to develop and implement community services for young children at risk began in 1968 with the passage of Public Law (PL) 90-538, the Handicapped Children's Early Education Program (HCEEP). A primary purpose of HCEEP was to fund model demonstration programs focused on experimental practices for young children with disabilities. Many of the best approaches that emerged from these experimental projects were transferred to other early intervention programs via outreach efforts funded through HCEEP. The documented success of HCEEP eventually culminated in the passage of PL 99-457, in the form of amendments to the Education for All Handicapped Children Act (now known as IDEA), in 1986. The most important piece of legislation ever enacted on behalf of infants and preschool-age children with disabilities, this act opened up a new era of services for young children with disabilities. It required that all states ensure a free and appropriate public education to every eligible child with a disability between 3 and 5 years of age. For infants and toddlers (birth to 2 years of age), a new program, Part H (changed to Part C in the 1997 Amendments to IDEA), was established to help states develop and implement programs for early intervention services. Part C has several purposes:

1. Enhance the development of infants and toddlers with disabilities, to minimize their potential for developmental delay, and to recognize the significant brain development that occurs during a child's first 3 years of life;

2. Reduce the educational costs to our society, including our nation's schools, by minimizing the need for special education and related services after infants and toddlers with disabilities reach school age;

3. Maximize the potential for individuals with disabilities to live independently in society;

4. Enhance the capacity of families to meet the special needs of their infants and toddlers with disabilities; and

5. Enhance the capacity of State and local agencies and service providers to identify, evaluate, and meet the needs of all children, particularly minority, low-income, inner city, and rural children, and infants and toddlers in foster care. (IDEA 2004, P.L. 108-446, Part C Sec. 631[a])

Although states are not *required* to participate, every state provides at least some services under Part C of IDEA.

## Early Intervention Under Part C of IDEA

Early intervention focuses on the identification and provision of education, health care, and social services as a means to enhance learning and development, reduce the effects of a disability, and prevent the occurrence of future difficulties for young children. IDEA defines eligible infants and toddlers as those under 3 years of age who need early intervention services for one of two reasons: (1) there is a developmental delay in one or more of the areas of cognitive development, physical development, communication development, social or emotional development, and adaptive development; or (2) there is a diagnosis of a physical or mental condition that has a high probability of resulting in a developmental delay (IDEA 2004, PL 108—446, Part C Sec. 632[5]).

Timing is critical in the delivery of early intervention services. The maxim "the earlier, the better" is very true. Moreover, early intervention may be less costly and more effective than providing services later in the individual's life (Guralnick, 1997, 1998; Liaw & Brooks-Gunn 1994; Young, 1996). Effective early intervention services are directed not only to the young child with a disability but to family members as well (McDonnell et al., 2003). Berry and Hardman (1998) suggested that all early intervention services must be designed and delivered within the framework of informing and empowering family members. Comprehensive early intervention is broad in scope, as illustrated in the list of IDEA, Part C services found in Table 3.2.

The services under Part C of IDEA that are needed for a particular child and the child's family are identified through the development of an **individualized family service plan (IFSP).** The IFSP is structured much like the individualized education program (IEP), but it broadens the focus to include all members of the family. Table 3.3 lists the required components of the IFSP. The nearby Reflect on This, "It Takes a Whole Village to Develop an IFSP," describes how each component is incorporated into the development and implementation of the IFSP.

## Effective Early Intervention

This section takes a closer look at effective models for delivering services and supports to infants and toddlers, including developmentally supportive care in hospitals and in center-based and home-based programs. In order for these models to be effective, services should focus on individualization, intense interventions, and a comprehensive approach to meeting the needs of each child and family.

**SERVICE DELIVERY.** Advancements in health care have increased the number of infants at risk who survive birth. **Intensive care specialists,** working with sophisticated medical technologies in newborn intensive care units and providing developmentally supportive care, are able to save the lives of infants who years ago would have died in the first days or weeks of life. **Developmentally supportive care** views the infant as "an active collaborator" in determining what services are necessary to enhance her or his survival. In this approach, infant behavior is carefully observed to determine what strategies (such as responding to light, noise, or touch) the infant is using to try to survive. Specially trained developmental specialists then focus on understanding the infant's "developmental agenda," in

**FOCUS 5**

Identify the components of the individualized family service plan (IFSP).

### Individualized family service plan (IFSP)

Service plan intended to ensure that infants and toddlers receive appropriate services under Part C of IDEA. The IFSP is structured much like the individualized education program (IEP), but it broadens the focus to include all members of the family.

### Intensive care specialists

Health care professionals (such as physicians and nurses) trained specifically to provide medical care to newborns who are seriously ill, disabled, or at risk of serious medical problems; also referred to as *neonatal specialists.*

### Developmentally supportive care

An approach to care that views the infant as "an active collaborator" in determining what services are necessary to enhance survival.

---

| TABLE 3.2 |
| --- |

### Services Provided to Infants and Toddlers Under Part C of IDEA

| | |
| --- | --- |
| • Special instruction | • Assistive technology devices and services |
| • Speech and language instruction | • Family training, counseling, and home visits |
| • Occupational and physical therapy | • Early identification, screening, and assessment |
| • Psychological testing and counseling | • Health services necessary to enable the infant or toddler to benefit from the other early intervention services |
| • Service coordination | |
| • Diagnostic and evaluative medical services | |
| • Social work services | • Transportation and related costs as necessary to ensure that the infant or toddler and the family receive appropriate services |
| • Sign language and cued speech services | |

TABLE 3.3

**Required Components of the IFSP**

1. Infant's or toddler's present levels of physical development, cognitive development, communication development, social or emotional development, and adaptive development, based on objective criteria;

2. Family's resources, priorities, and concerns relating to enhancing the development of the family's infant or toddler with a disability;

3. Measurable results or outcomes expected to be achieved for the infant or toddler and the family, including pre-literacy and language skills, as developmentally appropriate for the child, and the criteria, procedures, and timelines used to determine the degree to which progress toward achieving the results or outcomes is being made and whether modifications or revisions of the results or outcomes or services are necessary;

4. Specific early intervention services based on peer-reviewed research, to the extent practicable, necessary to meet the unique needs of the infant or toddler and the family, including the frequency, intensity, and method of delivering services;

5. Natural environments in which early intervention services will appropriately be provided, including a justification of the extent, if any, to which the services will not be provided in a natural environment;

6. Projected dates for initiation of services and the anticipated length, duration, and frequency of the services;

7. Identification of the service coordinator from the profession most immediately relevant to the infant's or toddler's or family's needs who will be responsible for the implementation of the plan and coordination with other agencies and persons, including transition services; and

8. Steps to be taken to support the transition of the toddler with a disability to preschool or other appropriate services. (IDEA 2004, PL 108-446, Sec. 636[d])

order to provide appropriate supports and services to enhance the infant's further growth and development (Als & Gilkerson, 1995).

In addition to the intensive services provided in hospital newborn intensive care units, early intervention may be delivered through center-based and home-based programs or through a combination of the two (Bruder, 2001; McDonnell et al., 2003). The center-based model requires families to take their child from the home to a setting where comprehensive services are provided. These sites may be hospitals, churches, schools, or other community facilities. The centers use various instructional approaches, including both developmental and therapeutic models, to meet the needs of infants and toddlers. Center-based programs tend to look like hospitals or health care facilities in which the primary orientation is therapy.

In contrast to the center-based model, a home-based program provides services to the child and family in their natural living environment. Using the natural resources of the home, professionals address the needs of the child in terms of individual fam-

**Reflect on This**

## IT TAKES A WHOLE VILLAGE TO DEVELOP AN IFSP

The African saying "It takes a whole village to raise a child," best illustrates the individualized family service plan (IFSP). No one person can accurately decide what is the best treatment or care for a child with special needs. That's why Part C of IDEA stipulates that infants and toddlers with disabilities must have an IFSP. The IFSP is an ongoing written service plan for children from birth to age 3 until they transition into preschool. Anything of concern to a family is outlined and highlighted in the IFSP:

- *Medical history/developmental information:* Includes diagnosis, medications, strengths, concerns such as a breakdown of the child's fine and gross motor skills, communication, social-emotional issues, and self-help as well as play and cognitive skills.

- *Family interest and concerns:* Everything from housing, transportation, health, and financial issues to employment, social service programs, legal services, early intervention programs, and therapy.

*The IFSP is a team effort involving families and professionals.*

- *Timeline:* A breakdown in months detailing when the family would like to see events occur in a child's development; includes a plan of action, a service provider, cost, and outcome.

- *Preschool transition plan:* Includes what school district the child resides in, the district contact person, and a plan of action for how and when the transition to preschool services will take place.

An assigned person, known as a service coordinator, generally initiates an IFSP and works with the family to complete it as the child approaches preschool age. The service coordinator works with a variety of people and agencies to ensure that the child's and family's needs are met. A family's priorities can easily change, and for that reason, the IFSP is a working, flexible document. Its focus is to help provide families with support and encourage them to seek community resources.

SOURCE: *The Individualized Family Service Plan,* by Resources for Young Children and Families, 2000, Colorado Springs, CO. Author. Available: *http://www.rycf.org/ifsp.html*

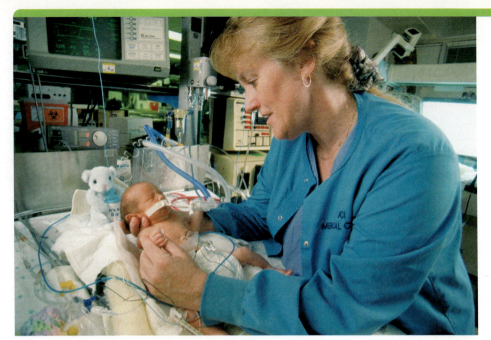

ily values and lifestyles. As suggested by Bruder (2001), the focus on natural environments

> has created multiple opportunities for children with disabilities to participate in a variety of home and community activities as environments for learning. Home activities are events that occur on either a regular or periodic basis in a child's primary living setting (e.g., getting dressed, taking a bath), and community activities include a wide range of informal (e.g., visits to the park, taking a walk) and formal (e.g., storytime at the library) experiences. . . . (p. 210)

Finally, early intervention may be provided through a combination of services at both a center and the home. Infants or toddlers may spend some time in a center-based program, receiving instruction and therapy in individual or group settings, and also receive in-home services to promote learning and generalization in their natural environment.

**INDIVIDUALIZED, INTENSIVE, AND COMPREHENSIVE SERVICES.**  Early intervention programs for infants and toddlers should be based on individual need, and they should be intensive over time and comprehensive. Intensity reflects the frequency and amount of time that an infant or child is engaged in intervention activities. An intensive approach requires that the child participate in intervention activities that involve two to three hours of contact each day, at least four or five times a week. Until the 1980s, this child-centered model of service delivery placed parents in the role of trainers who provided direct instruction to the child and helped him or her transfer the learning activities from the therapeutic setting to the home environment. The model of parents as trainers, however, came to be questioned by many professionals and family members. Families were dropping out of programs, and many parents either did not use the intervention techniques effectively with their children or simply preferred to be parents, not trainers (McDonnell et al., 2003). With the passage of PL 99-457 in 1986 (now IDEA), early intervention evolved into a more family-centered approach in which individual family needs and strengths are the basis for determining program goals, supports needed, and services to be provided.

Providing the breadth of services necessary to meet the individual needs of an infant or toddler within the family constellation requires a cross-disciplinary intervention team. It should include professionals with varied experiential backgrounds—such as speech and language therapy, physical therapy, nursing, and education—and also at least one of the child's parents or his or her guardian. The team should review the IFSP at least annually and should issue progress updates to the parents every six months. Coordination of early intervention services across disciplines and with the family is crucial if the goals of the program are to be realized.

The traditional academic-year programming (lasting approximately nine months) common to many public school programs is not in the best interests of infants and toddlers who are at risk or have disabilities. Continuity is essential. Services and support must be provided throughout the early years without lengthy interruptions.

## Preschool Services: Referral, Assessment, and IEP Development

Four-year-old Matt from the nearby Snapshot began receiving preschool services as soon as he came out of the coma that resulted from his being hit by a car. Although he suffered a severe head trauma and still has to wear a helmet and use a walker, Matt is doing well in his kindergarten class. Preschool services for Matt began with a referral to his local school in order to assess the type and extent of his perceived delays relative to same-age peers without disabilities. Once Matt's needs were identified and the educational team determined his eligibility for preschool special education services, the indicated developmental and age-appropriate instructional strategies were implemented in a school-based classroom.

**REFERRAL.** Programs for preschool-age children with disabilities have several important components. First, a **child-find system** is set up in each state to locate preschool-age (ages 3 to 5) children at risk and make referrals to the local education agency. Referrals may come from parents, the family physician, health or social service agencies, or the child's day care or preschool teacher. Referrals for preschool services may be based on a child's perceived delays in physical development (such as not walking by age 2), speech and language delays (such as still being nonverbal by age 3), excessive inappropriate behavior (such as frequent temper tantrums, violent behavior, extreme shyness, or excessive crying), or sensory difficulties (such as being unresponsive to sounds or unable to visually track objects in the environment).

**FOCUS**

**6**

Identify effective instructional approaches for preschool-age children with disabilities.

**Child-find system**

A system within a state or local area that attempts to identify all children who are disabled or at risk in order to refer them for appropriate support services.

# SNAPSHOT

## Matt

One day, 4-year-old Matt was playing across the street from his house. As he crossed the street to return home, he was hit by a car. Matt suffered a severe trauma as a result of the accident and was in a coma for more than 2 months. Now he's in school and is doing well.

Matt wears a helmet to protect his head, and he uses a walker in his general education kindergarten class in the morning and special education class in the afternoon. The general education kindergarten children sing songs together and work on handwriting, before they work at centers in the classroom. Matt's favorite center is the block area. He spends most of his time there. Recently, however, he has become interested in the computer and math centers.

He is working on his fine motor skills and speech skills so he can learn to write and use a pencil again. The focus of his academic learning is mastering the alphabet, learning how to count,

and recognizing numbers. He also receives regular speech therapy. He speaks in sentences, but it is very difficult for others to understand what he is saying.

Matt is well liked by his classmates. His teacher enjoys seeing his progress. "Well, it's our hope that he'll be integrated with the other kids eventually, and through the activities we do in the classroom here (in special education) and in the kindergarten, we hope the kids will get to know him and interact with him and that this will help pull up his skills to the level where he can go back to the general education classroom for all his schoolwork."

**ASSESSMENT.** Following a referral, a child-study team initiates an assessment to determine whether the child is eligible for preschool special education services under IDEA. A preschool-age child with disabilities is eligible if he or she meets both of the following requirements. First, developmental delays are evident as measured by appropriate diagnostic instruments and procedures, in one or more of the following areas: physical development, cognitive development, communication development, social or emotional development, or adaptive development. Second, as a result of these delays, the child needs special education and related services (IDEA 2004, P.L. 108–446, Sec. 602[3]).

**DEVELOPING AN IEP FOR THE PRESCHOOL-AGE CHILD.** If the child is eligible, an individualized education program (IEP) is developed. Specialists from several disciplines—including physical therapy, occupational therapy, speech and language therapy, pediatrics, social work, and special education—participate in the development and implementation of IEPs for preschool-age children. The purpose of preschool programs for young children with disabilities is to assist them in living in and adapting to a variety of environmental settings, including home, neighborhood, and school. Depending on individual needs, preschool programs may focus on developing skills in communication, social and emotional learning, physical well-being, self-care, and/or coping (Davis, Kilgo, & Gamel-McCormick, 1998; McLean, Wolery & Bailey, 1996; Odom & Bailey, 2001). The decision regarding which skill areas are to be taught should be based on a functional assessment of the child and the setting where he or she spends time. **Functional assessments** determine the child's skills, the characteristics of the setting, and the family's needs, resources, expectations, and aspirations (Horner, Albin, Sprague, & Todd, 2000). Through a functional assessment, professionals and parents come together to plan a program that supports the preschool-age child in meeting the demands of the home, school, or community setting. (See Table 3.4.)

## Effective Practices In Preschool Education

This section reviews the concept of developmentally appropriate practice (DAP) for preschool-age children and explains how it serves as a foundation to meet the individual needs of young children with disabilities in age-appropriate placements. We also examine the importance of teaching functional skills in inclusive preschool settings.

**DEVELOPMENTALLY APPROPRIATE PRACTICE.** Early child educators share the conviction that programs for young children should be based on **developmentally appropriate practice (DAP).** DAP is grounded in the belief that too much emphasis has been placed on preparing preschool-age children for academic learning and not enough on activities that are initiated by the child such as play, exploration, social interaction, and inquiry. Child-initiated activities are based on the assumption that "young children are intrinsically motivated to learn by their desire to understand their environment" (Udell, Peters, & Templeman, 1998, p. 44). DAP is viewed as culturally sensitive because it emphasizes interaction between children and adults. Adults become "guides" for student learning rather than controlling what, where, and how students acquire knowledge.

DAP is strongly advocated by the National Association for the Education of Young Children (NAEYC), the nation's largest national organization for professionals in early childhood education. NAEYC has developed several guiding principles for DAP:

- *Create a caring community of learners.* Developmentally appropriate practices occur within a context that supports the development of relationships between adults and children, among children, among teachers, and between teachers and families.

- *Teach to enhance development and learning.* Adults are responsible for ensuring children's healthy development and learning. From birth, relationships with adults are critical to children's healthy social and emotional development and also serve as mediators of language and intellectual development.

**Functional assessment**

Assessment to determine the child's skills, the characteristics of the setting, and the family's needs, resources, expectations, and aspirations.

**Developmentally appropriate practice (DAP)**

Instructional approach that uses curriculum and learning environments consistent with the child's developmental level. Such practices provide young children with opportunities to explore, discover, choose, and acquire skills that are sensitive and responsive for their ages and abilities.

TABLE 3.4

## Information Needed to Plan Programs for Young Children with Disabilities

**GOALS FOR THE CHILD**

- What is the child's current level of developmental functioning in communication, social, physical, cognitive, and self-care areas?
- What does the child need to be independent in the classroom, home, and community?
- What are the effects of adaptations and assistance on the child's performance?
- What usual patterns of responding and what relationships with environmental variables appear to influence the child's performance?
- What are the child's most important behaviors, skills, abilities, and patterns of responding?

**CHILD'S ENVIRONMENTS**

- In what environments (home, classroom, etc.) does the child spend time?
- How much time is spent in each environment?
- Who cares for and interacts with the child in those environments?

**PHYSICAL DIMENSIONS AND ORGANIZATION OF ENVIRONMENT**

- What materials and toys are in each environment?
- How are those toys and materials organized and placed about the room?
- Can the child access all areas and materials and, if so, how?
- How much space is available, and how many children and adults are in it?
- What adaptations of equipment and materials are needed?

**TEMPORAL DIMENSIONS AND ORGANIZATION OF ROUTINES**

- What is the child's typical daily schedule (from awakening to bedtime)?
- How are activities within the classroom sequenced?
- How long do activities last?
- What routines (e.g., meals, toileting) happen every day?

**ADULTS' USUAL ROLES IN ACTIVITIES**

- For each part of the day, what do adults do in relation to the child?
- When do adults observe children, interact with them, and take care of organizational tasks (prepare materials)?
- When, if ever, do adults lead activities?
- How do adults interact with children (e.g., direct a child, respond to a child)?
- What types of verbal interactions (e.g., questions, commands, comments) do adults use, and when?

**ACTIVITY STRUCTURES**

- How is each activity in the classroom organized?
- How does the child get into and out of each activity?
- How does the child know what is expected in each activity?
- What is the child expected to do in each activity?
- How are expectations communicated to the child?

SOURCE: From "Implementing Instruction for Young Children with Special Needs in Early Childhood Classrooms," by M. Wolery. *Including Children with Special Needs in Early Childhood Programs,* edited by M. Wolery and J. S. Wilbers, 1994, pp. 151–166. Washington, DC: National Association for the Education of Young Children.

- *Construct an appropriate curriculum.* The content of the early childhood curriculum is determined by many factors, including the subject matter of the disciplines, social or cultural values, and parental input. In developmentally appropriate programs, decisions about curriculum content also take into consideration the age and experience of the learners.

- *Assess children's learning and development.* Assessment of individual children's development and learning is essential for planning and implementing an appropriate curriculum. In developmentally appropriate programs, assessment and curriculum are integrated, with teachers continually engaging in observational assessment for the purpose of improving teaching and learning.

- *Establish reciprocal relationships with families.* Developmentally appropriate practices derive from deep knowledge of individual children and the context within which they develop and learn. The younger the child, the more important it is for professionals to acquire this knowledge through relationships with the child's family. (National Association for the Education of Young Children Position Statement, 1997)

**AGE-APPROPRIATE PLACEMENT.** As we have noted, DAP is widely accepted throughout the early childhood community, but many special educators see DAP as a base or foundation to build on in order to meet the individual needs of young children with disabilities. Early childhood programs for students with disabilities must also take into account age-appropriate placements and functional skill learning.

**Age-appropriate placement** emphasizes the child's chronological age over her or his developmental level. Thus a 2-year-old with developmental delays is first and foremost a 2-year-old, regardless of whether he or she has disabilities. In other words, a young child with disabilities should be exposed to the same instructional settings as a peer without disabilities of the same chronological age. Age-appropriate learning prepares the child to live and learn in inclusive environments with same-age peers. Arguing that DAP and age-appropriate practice are compatible, McDonnell and colleagues (2003) suggested that there are many ways to create learning experiences for young children that are both developmentally appropriate and age-appropriate. The following is one example:

> Mark is a 5-year-old with limited gross and fine motor movement and control. His cognitive development is similar to a typically developing 11-month-old. Mark is learning to use adaptive switches to activate toys and a radio or [CD] player. Mark enjoys listening to music and toys that make noise and move simultaneously. Mark would also enjoy the lullabies and battery-operated lamb and giraffe toys that might usually be purchased for an 11-month-old. However, he also enjoys Raffi songs and songs from Disney movies, as well as automated race tracks and battery-operated dinosaurs and robots. The latter selection of music and toys would also interest other children of his age . . . and could provide some familiar and pleasurable experiences for Mark to enjoy in classroom and play settings with typical peers. (p. 239)

**TEACHING FUNCTIONAL SKILLS.** As is consistent with its focus on the individualized needs of the child and the expectations of the family, teaching functional skills facilitates the young child's learning in the natural setting (such as home and family). Functional skill development helps the child adapt to the demands of a given environment—that is, it creates an adaptive fit between the child and the setting in which he or she must learn to function. Udell and colleagues (1998) indicated that in early childhood settings, functional skills are important because in acquiring them, the child learns to be more independent and to interact positively with others in his or her immediate environment. "For example, it is probably more functional for a child to be able to carry out his or her own toileting functions independently than to be able to name 10 farm animals" (p. 46).

**INCLUSIVE PRESCHOOL CLASSROOMS.** In the inclusive classroom, young children with disabilities receive their educational program alongside peers without disabilities in a regular preschool or day care program. Effective programs are staffed by both child care providers and paraprofessionals, with a special education preschool teacher in a co-teaching or consultant role. Table 3.5 presents several indicators of quality for an inclusive preschool program.

In a study of child care providers, Devore & Hanley-Maxwell (2000) identified five critical factors that contributed to their successfully serving young children with disabilities in inclusive, community-based child care settings: (1) a willingness on the part of the child care provider to make inclusion work; (2) a realistic balance between the resources available in the program and the needs of the student; (3) continual problem solving with parents; (4) access to emotional support and technical assistance from special educators and early intervention therapists; and (5) access to other supports, such as other child care providers, respite care providers, and houses of worship.

Age-appropriate placement

A child's educational placement in an instructional program consistent with chronological age rather than developmental level.

*Effective inclusive preschool classrooms are staffed by highly trained professionals in both childcare and special education. What other indicators of quality should we look for in an inclusive preschool classroom?*

**TABLE 3.5**

## Indicators of Quality in an Inclusive Preschool Program

- *A holistic view of child development.* Teachers must enter the classroom with a thorough understanding of child development to support the inclusion of diverse learners.

- *Class as community.* Educators provide students with opportunities to enhance feelings of self-worth, social responsibility, and belonging.

- *Collaboration.* Critical to the success of collaboration is that colleagues view each other as equals. They must share a common body of knowledge and repertoire of skills.

- *Authentic assessment.* Authentic assessment procedures consist of a variety of performance-based assessments that require children to demonstrate a response in a real-life context.

- *Heterogeneous grouping.* All children should have opportunities throughout the day to work and play in diverse and heterogeneous groups that are responsive to individual strengths and needs.

- *Range of individualized supports and services.* Successful inclusion is dependent on the belief that all children can learn, participate in, and benefit from all areas of the curriculum.

- *Engagement and active learning.* "Actively engage" is a concept from classic child development theories that emphasize the importance of learning by doing in meaningful contexts.

- *Reflective teaching.* Teachers must become good observers of their own behavior, as well as the behavior of their children. This type of thoughtful inquiry allows teachers to study individual child behavior within the context of the learning environment.

- *Multiple ways of teaching and learning.* Teachers who support diverse learners are more likely to use a variety of teaching and learning strategies that challenge the strengths and support the needs of their students. Children in these classrooms are encouraged to use multiple methods to solve problems.

SOURCE: I. S. Schwartz & L. H. Meyer (1997, April). Blending best practices for young children. *TASH Newsletter,* p. 8–10.

There are many reasons for the increasing number of inclusive classrooms for preschool students with disabilities. Inclusive classrooms create opportunities for social interaction and the development of friendships among children with disabilities and same-age peers without disabilities. The social development skills learned in inclusive settings are applied at home and community as well as in future educational and social settings. Preschool-age children without disabilities learn to accept and value diversity (Drew & Hardman, 2004; Schwartz, Billingsley, & McBride, 1998).

## Head Start

**Head Start** is the nation's largest federally funded early childhood program. It was enacted into law in 1965 and has served over 16 million children. The program was developed around a strong research base suggesting that early enrichment experiences for children with economic disadvantages would better prepare them for elementary school (Davis et al., 1998). Although the original legislation did not include children with disabilities, the law was expanded in 1992 to require that at least 10% of Head Start enrollment be reserved for these children. The U.S. Department of Health and Human Services (2003) reported that of the estimated 915,000 children in Head Start programs, children with disabilities accounted for 13% of this population. Head Start has been hailed through the years as a major breakthrough in federal support for early childhood education.

Federal regulations under Head Start have been expanded to ensure that a disabilities service plan is developed to meet the needs of each child with disabilities and his or her family, that the programs designate a coordinator of services for children with disabilities, and that the necessary special education and related services be provided for children who are designated as disabled under IDEA.

## Transition from Preschool to Elementary School

Transitions, although a natural and ongoing part of everyone's life, are often difficult under the best of circumstances. For preschool-age children with disabilities and their families, the transition from early childhood programs to kindergarten can be very stressful. Early childhood programs for preschool-age children with disabilities commonly employ many adults (both professional and paraprofessional). In contrast, kindergarten programs are often not able to offer the same level of staff support, particularly in more inclusive educational settings. Additionally, children in kindergarten programs are expected to "work more independently, follow group directions, and attend to their own needs" (Rous & Hallam, 1998, p. 17). Thus it is important for preschool professionals responsible for transition planning to attend not only to the needs and skills of the individual student, but also to how he or she can meet the performance demands of the elementary school and classroom setting. Sainato and Morrison (2001) indicated that successful transition from preschool to

**Head start**

A federally funded preschool program for children from a background of economic disadvantage. Gives each child "a head start" prior to elementary school.

elementary programs is a critical factor in inclusion. These authors make several suggestions for professionals engaged in the transition process:

- The child's skill level is viewed as the predictor of the potential for success.
- Kindergarten teachers identify functional, social, and behavioral skills as more important for successful transition than academic skills.
- Readiness skills, language competence, self-care skills, appropriate social behavior, and independent performance during group activities are identified as prerequisites to inclusive placements in elementary school programs.
- Focusing on the prerequisite skills that are likely to increase the child's success in inclusive elementary settings is important, but it must not be used to prevent young children from participating in inclusive placements.

In order to identify the skills needed in the elementary school environment, a preschool transition plan should begin at least one to two years prior to the child's actual move. This move is facilitated when the early intervention specialist, the child's future kindergarten teacher, and the parents engage in a careful planning process that recognizes the significant changes that the child and the family will go through as they enter a new and unfamiliar situation (Udell et al., 1998).

In summary, early childhood programs for children with disabilities focus on teaching skills that will improve a child's opportunities for living a rich life and on preparing the child to function successfully in family, school, and neighborhood environments. Young children with disabilities are prepared as early as possible to share meaningful experiences with same-age peers. Additionally, early childhood programs lessen the impact of conditions that may deteriorate or become more severe without timely and adequate intervention, and they may prevent children from developing other, secondary disabling conditions. The intended outcomes of these programs will not, however, be accomplished without consistent family participation and professional collaboration.

# The Elementary School Years

**FOCUS 7**

Describe the roles of special education teachers and general education teachers in an inclusive classroom setting.

In the elementary school years, the focus is on supporting children as they try to meet the expectations of the general education curriculum. The degree to which a child is able to cope with these expectations depends to a great extent on how effectively the school will accommodate individual needs. For Ricardo in the nearby Case Study, the school's expectations were difficult to meet, and he fell significantly behind his classmates in reading and language. His third grade teacher initiated a referral to evaluate Ricardo's eligibility for special education services. Once it was determined that Ricardo qualified as a student with a learning disability, a team made up of special educators, general educators, and his parents worked together to develop his individualized education program (IEP) and meet his reading and language needs.

## Building the General Education/Special Education Partnership

Today's teachers face the challenge of preparing the next generation for a changing world and of responding to an increasingly diverse group of students. The growing student diversity includes increasing numbers from ethnically diverse backgrounds, those with disabilities, and children at risk of educational failure. Each of these factors contributes to the critical need for both general and special education teachers to work together in preparing all students for the many challenges of the next century, while at the same time not losing sight of individual learning needs, styles, and preferences.

The current wave of reform in America's schools, as played out in federal law through the No Child Left Behind Act and IDEA, is centered on finding new and

## Case Study

# RICARDO

Ricardo, a third grader at Bloomington Hill Elementary School, has recently been referred by his teacher, Ms. Thompson, to the school's prereferral team for an evaluation. During the first four months of school, Ricardo has continued to fall further behind in reading and language. He entered third grade with some skills in letter and sound recognition but had difficulty reading and comprehending material beyond a first grade level. It was also clear to Ms. Thompson that Ricardo's language development was delayed as well. He had a very limited expressive vocabulary and had some difficulty following directions if more than one or two steps were involved.

Ricardo's mother, Maria Galleghos (a single parent), was contacted by Ms. Thompson to inform her that she would like to refer Ricardo for an in-depth evaluation of his reading and language skills. A representative from the school would be calling her to explain what the evaluation meant and to get her approval for the necessary testing. The school psychologist, Jean Andreas, made the call to Ms. Galleghos. During the phone conversation Ms. Galleghos reminded the school psychologist that the primary language spoken in the home was Spanish, even though Ricardo, his parents, and his siblings spoke English too. Ms. Andreas indicated that the assessment would be conducted in both Spanish and English in order to determine whether Ricardo's problems were related to a disability in reading or perhaps to problems with English as a second language.

Having received written approval from Ricardo's mother, the school's prereferral team conducted an evaluation of Ricardo's academic performance. The formal evaluation included achievement tests, classroom performance tests, samples of Ricardo's work, behavioral observations, and anecdotal notes from Ms. Thompson. An interview with Mrs. Galleghos was conducted as part of the process to gain her perceptions of Ricardo's

strengths and problem areas and to give her an opportunity to relate pertinent family history.

The evaluation confirmed his teacher's concerns. Ricardo was more than two years below what was expected for a child his age in both reading and language development. Ricardo's difficulties in these areas did not seem to be related to his being bilingual, but the issue of English as a second language would need to be taken into careful consideration in developing an appropriate learning experience.

The team determined that Ricardo qualified for special education services as a student with a specific learning disability. Once again, Ms. Andreas contacted Mrs. Galleghos with the results, indicating that Ricardo qualified for special education services in reading and language. Ms. Andreas pointed out that as a parent of a student with an identified disability, she had some specific legal rights that would be further explained to her both in writing and orally.

One of those rights is the right to participate as a partner in the development of Ricardo's individualized education program (IEP). Ms. Andreas further explained that a meeting would be set up at a mutually convenient time to develop a plan to assist Ricardo over the next year.

### APPLICATION

1. Prior to the meeting, what could Ricardo's teachers do to help his parents feel valued as a member of the IEP team and to better understand their role in developing the IEP?

2. What additional information could Ricardo's parents provide that would help the team better understand his needs and interests, particularly in the areas of reading and language development?

3. What do you see as important for Ricardo to learn in school?

---

more effective ways to increase student learning by establishing high standards for *what* should be taught and *how* performance will be measured. Accountability for meeting high standards rests at several levels, but the ultimate test of success is what happens between teacher and student in the day-to-day classroom.

Growing student diversity in the schools will require general educators to teach students whose needs exceed those of what has traditionally been defined as the "typical child." Thus special education teachers must have the specialized skills to meet the needs of students with disabilities and will also be called upon to apply this expertise to a much broader group of "high-risk students" in a collaborative educational environment. The combination of all these factors makes a very strong case for a partnership between general and special education.

**THE MANY ROLES OF THE SPECIAL EDUCATION TEACHER.** In an inclusive school, special educators are called upon to fill multiple roles, including the "three Cs": collaborator, consultant, and coordinator. In the role of *collaborator,* special educators

- work with school personnel (such as general educators, the school principal, and related-services personnel) and parents to identify the educational needs of students with disabilities.

- link student assessment information to the development of the IEP and access to the general curriculum.
- determine appropriate student accommodations and instructional adaptations.
- deliver intensive instruction using specialized teaching methods.

Special educators provide instruction and support in academic, behavioral, and/or adaptive/functional areas, as well as fostering student self-determination and self-management skills. As collaborators, special education teachers use effective problem-solving strategies to facilitate student learning, co-teach with general educators, and apply effective accountability measures to evaluate individual students' progress and long-term results.

In the role of *consultant,* the special education teacher must be able to serve as a resource to general educators and parents on effective instructional practices for students with disabilities. Expertise may be provided in content areas (such as effective approaches to teaching reading to students with special needs) and/or problem-solving skills (such as strategies to motivate students to participate in class activities).

In the role of *coordinator,* the special education teacher takes primary responsibility for organizing the activities of the school team in developing, implementing, and evaluating student IEPs. He or she may also be responsible for organizing school resources to meet the needs of students with disabilities; may initiate professional development activities for school team members; may supervise paraprofessionals, peer support, and volunteers; and may facilitate positive communication with parents.

**THE GENERAL EDUCATION TEACHER: MEETING THE CHALLENGE OF "LEAVING NO CHILD BEHIND."** General education teachers must meet the challenges of achieving increased academic excellence as mandated in the No Child Left Behind Act as well as responding to students with many different needs coming together in a common environment. The inclusion of students with disabilities in general education classes need not be met with teacher frustration, anger, or refusal. These reactions are merely symptomatic of the confusion surrounding inclusive education. Huefner (2000) suggested that the IDEA requirement that general educators be members of the IEP team provides a "new leverage to obtain the supports they need to be effective with special education students" (p. 203). As members of the IEP team, general educators are in a better position to share their knowledge and insight on individual students and to provide important information on how the student will fare in the general education curriculum and classroom setting.

Specific roles for general educators in working collaboratively with special education and related-services personnel include

- identifying and referring students who may be in need of some additional support in order to succeed in an inclusive setting.

- understanding each student's individual strengths and limitations and the effects of these characteristics on learning.

*General education teachers face the challenges of working with students from different ethnic backgrounds and students with disabilities. What training and support do general education teachers need to successfully implement an inclusive education program?*

- implementing an appropriate individualized instructional program that is focused on supporting student success in the general education curriculum.
- initiating and maintaining ongoing communication with parents.

Inclusive education must not be synonymous with dumping a student with disabilities into a general education class without the necessary supports to the teacher or to the student, and at the expense of others in the class. In a survey (Hobbs, 1997), general education teachers identified four major problem areas in their attempts to meet the needs of students with disabilities:

- disruptive students who lacked the social and behavioral skills necessary to succeed in a general education setting.
- lack of specialized assistance from a special education teacher or other school personnel.
- lack of information regarding the appropriate instructional adaptations necessary to meet the needs of any given student with a disability.
- concerns regarding the social acceptance of students with disabilities (peers sometimes isolate, tease, or bully these students).

To address these concerns, general educators must receive more training during their initial university preparation and as a component of their ongoing professional development. Unfortunately, general and special education teachers are often prepared in separate programs. Consequently, many newly prepared general education teachers lack the skills necessary to meet the diverse needs of students in their classrooms and to work effectively with their special education colleagues. (See the Reflect on This, "Perspectives from General Education Teachers on What Is Needed to Implement an Inclusive Education Program.")

The role of the general education teacher extends not only to working with students with mild disabilities, but also to involvement with those who have more severe disabilities. Success in a general education class for students with severe

## Reflect on This

## PERSPECTIVES FROM GENERAL EDUCATION TEACHERS ON WHAT IS NEEDED TO IMPLEMENT AN INCLUSIVE EDUCATION PROGRAM

- *Time.* Teachers need 1 hour or more per day to plan for students with disabilities.
- *Training.* Teachers need systematic, intensive training, either as part of their certification programs (i.e., as intensive and well-planned in-services) or as an ongoing process with consultants.
- *Personal resources.* Teachers report a need for additional personnel assistance to carry out inclusion objectives. This could include a part-time aide and daily contact with special education teachers.
- *Material resources.* Teachers need adequate curriculum materials and other classroom equipment appropriate to the needs of students with disabilities.

- *Class size.* Teachers agree that their class size should be reduced to fewer than 20 students if students with disabilities are included in their general classrooms.
- *Consideration of severity of disability.* Teachers are more willing to include students with mild disabilities than students with more severe disabilities, apparently because of teachers' perceived ability to carry on their teaching mission for the entire classroom. By implication, the more severe the disabilities represented in the inclusive setting, the more the previously mentioned sources of support would be needed.

SOURCE: From "Teacher Perceptions of Mainstreaming/Inclusion, 1958–1995: A Research Synthesis," by T. E. Scruggs and M. A. Mastropieri, 1996, *Exceptional Children, 63* (1), p. 17.

disabilities depends critically on the cooperative relationship among the general ed-ucation teacher, special education teacher, and the school support team. The general educator works with the team to create opportunities to include students with more severe disabilities. Inclusion may be achieved by having the general education class serve as a homeroom for the student; by developing opportunities for students with severe disabilities to be with their peers without disabilities as often as possible both within the general education class and in school activities such as recess, lunch, and assemblies; by developing a peer support program; and by using effective practices such as multilevel instruction, universal design, direct instruction, assistive technol-ogy, and curriculum-based measurement.

**FOCUS**
**8**

Why are multilevel instruction, universal design for learning, direct instruction, assistive technology, and curriculum-based assessment con-sidered effective practice in an inclusive classroom?

## Effective Practices in Inclusive Elementary School Programs

As discussed throughout this chapter, we are seeing a greater emphasis on access to the general curriculum and accountability for student learning in the United States. What does access to the general curriculum mean for students with disabilities? How can schools make the curriculum accessible to all students in an inclusive setting? What approaches are needed to measure student progress effectively? In this section, we take a closer look at instructional approaches that have proved effective in creat-ing access to the general education curriculum and facilitating student learning in an inclusive setting.

**MULTILEVEL INSTRUCTION.** Today's classrooms include children with many dif-ferent abilities. Tomlinson (1995) describes what it is like for a teacher to face the challenge of a mixed-ability class:

> Each September, many first graders arrive already able to read third grade books with comprehension, while their peers grapple for months with the idea of left-to-right print progression or the difference between short and long vowels. Some third graders make an independent leap from multiplication to division before any explanation has been offered. Many of these same children, when they reach middle school, also make connections between themes in social studies and literature, or apply advanced mathematical tools to solving science problems before others students in their classes grasp the main idea of a chapter in the textbook. . . . Acknowledging that students learn at different speeds and that they differ widely in their ability to think abstractly or understand complex ideas is like acknowledging that students at any given age aren't all the same height: It is not a statement of worth, but of reality. (p. 1)

Students of the same age are clearly not alike in how they learn or their rate of learning. Therefore, teachers must use multilevel instruction (also referred to as *dif-ferentiated instruction*), in which multiple teaching approaches within the same cur-riculum are *adapted* to individual need and functioning level. **Multilevel instruction** provides students with many different ways to access and learn content within the general education curriculum. Peterson and Hittie (2003) describe multi-level instruction as "designing for diversity" and suggest several strategies for imple-mentation:

- Design lessons at multiple levels.
- Challenge students at their own level.
- Provide support to push children ahead to their next level of learning.
- Engage children in learning via activities that relate to the real world—to their lives at home and in the community.
- Engage the **multiple intelligences** and learning styles of children so that many pathways for learning and demonstrating achievement are available.
- Involve students in collaborative pair or group work in which children draw on each other's strengths. (p. 46)

**Multilevel instruction**

Differing levels of instruction that provide students with many different ways to access and learn content within the general education curriculum.

**Multiple intelligences**

The theory that people have intelligence across several domains, including linguistic, logical-mathematical, spatial, musical, bodily-kinesthetic, interpersonal (responds to the needs of others), intrapersonal (self-knowledge), and naturalistic (knowledge of the natural world).

To be effective, multilevel instruction requires that teachers accept individual goals, within the curriculum, for each child. They use many different instructional strategies that are consistent with a student's level and rate of learning. Finally, students are able to demonstrate progress in multiple ways.

**UNIVERSAL DESIGN FOR LEARNING.** Universal design for learning (UDL) goes one step beyond multilevel instruction, creating instructional programs and environments that work for all students, to the greatest extent possible, *without the need for adaptation*. The concept was adapted from architecture, where buildings are created from the beginning with diverse users in mind as a way to avoid costly retrofitting of features such as the curb cuts, ramps, and automatic doors that accommodate the needs of people with disabilities.

The basic premise of universal design for learning is to make the curriculum accessible and applicable to all students, regardless of their abilities or learning styles. A range of options are available to each student that support access to, and engagement with, the learning materials (Rose & Meyer, 2002). Table 3.6 describes the basic principles of the universal design curriculum and offers an example of its application in the teaching of mathematics.

**DIRECT INSTRUCTION.** A primary characteristic of special education is the *explicit teaching* of academic, adaptive, and functional skills. (See Chapter 2 for more information on the characteristics of effective special education). Research suggests that students with learning difficulties, particularly those with cognitive disabilities, learn more efficiently through the structured, teacher-directed approach often referred to as **direct instruction** (Carnine, 2000; Stein, Carnine, & Dixon, 1998). Direct instruction has several key elements (Friend & Bursuck, 2002):

- The teacher presents new content or skills in small steps, incorporating illustrations and concrete examples.
- Under direct guidance and questioning from the teacher, the student practices on new content or skills.
- Students receive immediate feedback on all correct or incorrect responses, correction, and re-teaching as necessary.
- Student practice independently on skills that have been presented until they reach a high rate of correct responses.
- Learned material is reviewed systematically through homework or exams.
- Re-teaching takes place when material is missed in homework assignments or exams.

**Universal design for learning (UDL)**

Instructional programs and environments that work for all students, to the greatest extent possible, without the need for adaptation. Such a curriculum must be accessible and applicable to students, teachers, and parents with different backgrounds, learning styles, abilities, and disabilities in widely varied learning contexts.

**Direct instruction**

Instruction that focuses on the explicit teaching of academic, adaptive, and functional skills. A structured, teacher-directed approach is used to teach children new skills.

**Assistive technology**

Any item, piece of equipment, or product system, whether acquired commercially off the shelf, modified, or customized, that is used to increase, maintain, or improve the functional capabilities of a child with disabilities.

Universal design for learning helps make the curriculum accessible and applicable to every student, regardless of their abilities or learning styles. Here the students are using a digital talking textbook. What are some other ways universal design for learning can help students with disabilities in an inclusive classroom?

**ASSISTIVE TECHNOLOGY.** Have you ever watched a program with closed-captioning or a foreign movie with subtitles? Do you turn on your television and open your garage door with a remote control device? Do you use speed dial or a digital address book on your cell phone? If so, you use assistive technology. **Assistive technology** is "any item, piece of equipment, or product system, whether acquired commercially off the shelf, modified, or customized, that is used to increase, maintain, or improve the functional capabilities of a

## Principles of the Universal Design Curriculum and Their Application to Teaching Mathematics

**IN A UDL CURRICULUM . . .**

- *Goals* provide an appropriate challenge for all students.
- *Materials* have a flexible format, supporting transformation between media and multiple representations of content to support all students' learning.
- *Methods* are flexible and diverse enough to provide appropriate learning experiences, challenges, and supports for all students.
- *Assessment* is sufficiently flexible to provide accurate, ongoing information that helps teachers adjust instruction and maximize learning.

**TEACHING MATH USING UDL**

Suppose a math teacher uses the UDL approach to convey the critical features of a right triangle. With software that supports graphics and hyperlinks, a document is prepared that shows:

- Multiple examples of right triangles in different orientations and sizes, with the right angle and the three points highlighted.
- An animation of the right triangle morphing into an isosceles triangle or into a rectangle, with voice and on-screen text to highlight the differences.
- Links to reviews on the characteristics of triangles and of right angles.
- Links to examples of right triangles in various real-world contexts.
- Links to pages that students can go to on their own for review or enrichment on the subject.
- The teacher could then project the documentation onto a large screen in front of the class. Thus the teacher would present the concept not simply by explaining it verbally or by assigning a textbook chapter or workbook page, but by using many modalities and with options for extra support or extra enrichment.

SOURCE: From "Providing New Access to the General Curriculum: Universal Design for Learning, *Teaching Exceptional Children*," by C. Hitchcock, A. Meyer, D. Rose, & R. Jackson, 2002, November/December, pp. 8, 13.

---

child with disabilities" (Technology-Related Assistance for Individuals with Disabilities Act, 20 U.S.C. 1401[1]).

Assistive technology can take many forms (high-tech or low-tech) and can be helpful to students with disabilities in several different ways. A high-tech digital textbook could help students with reading problems decode and comprehend text. Students who have difficulty in verbally communicating with others might use a low-tech language board on which they point to pictures cut from magazines to indicate what they would like for lunch. Students with motor difficulties could learn to operate a joystick so that they can move their power wheelchair in any direction. For more information on what assistive technology looks like and how it can be used, see the nearby Assistive Technology, "What It Looks Like and How It Can Be Used."

**CURRICULUM-BASED ASSESSMENT.** In this era of accountability, developing assessments that will reliably monitor student learning is an essential component of instruction. As described by Howell and Nolet (2000), "Assessment is the process of collecting information by reviewing the products of student work, interviewing, observing, or testing" (p. 3). Educators assess students for the purpose of deciding whether the students are making adequate progress and, if not, what additional or different services and supports they need.

The hallmarks of any good assessment are its accuracy, fairness, and utility. (For a more in-depth discussion of nondiscriminatory and multidisciplinary assessment, see Chapter 2). Traditional standardized tests (such as intelligence [IQ] or achievement tests) compare one student to another in order to determine how each individual compares to the overall average. For example, an average score on the Stanford-Binet IQ test is 100. Any score (higher or lower) would be described as deviating from the average. Significantly higher scores may lead to the use of such

## WHAT IT LOOKS LIKE AND HOW IT CAN BE USED

Young children with significant cognitive delays may use a single switch (see Figure A), instead of a standard computer keyboard, to interact with software that helps them to identify letters, numbers, and colors.

Middle school students with a learning disability may use software such as the CAST eReader (www.cast.org) (see Figure B) to complete an assignment to search the Internet for a report. The student can highlight portions of the text and use the built-in text-to-speech features to have the information read to them.

Although the term *assistive technology* is often associated with computers and other electronic devices (high-tech), it also applies to a whole array of other devices. Examples of low-tech assistive technologies include adaptive eating utensils (see Figure C), ramps, and seating and positioning aids.

**FIGURE A**

*The Big Red ® Switch is a commonly used switch for controlling electronic toys as well as computers. Reprinted with permission of AbleNet, Inc.*

**FIGURE B**

*CAST eReader software supports reading and research. Used with permission of CAST.*

**FIGURE C**

*An example of an adaptive eating utensil. Used with permission. Simmons Preston Rolyan, 800/523-5547.*

SOURCE: From *What Every Teacher Should Know About Assistive Technology,* by D. L. Edyburn, 2003, Boston: Allyn and Bacon.

---

descriptors as *gifted* or *talented.* Significantly lower scores may result in the label of *mental retardation* (*intellectual disabilities*).

Although traditional standardized assessments may be useful in determining a student's eligibility for special education (comparing the student to the average performance of peers), many educators question their use in planning for instruction and measuring day-to-day student learning. An alternative approach to traditional tests is the use of **curriculum-based assessment (CBA).** As King-Sears, Burges, and Lawson (1999) express it, CBA consists of

> Direct and frequent measurement of observable student behaviors toward progress within the curriculum. . . . Curriculum-based assessment features brief measurements—or probes—during instructional units. . . . The premise of CBA is not to measure all skills students acquire with an [instructional] unit, but to select critical skills that serve as indicators, or benchmarks, of student progress. (p. 32)

The steps in the effective use of CBA are described in the nearby Reflect on This, "Steps to an Effective Curriculum-Based Assessment."

As we conclude this section on the elementary years, it is important to review some of the factors associated with an effective inclusive education program. First, teachers must work together to develop and use effective instructional practices that promote access to the general curriculum and increase student learning and achievement. Effective practices include the use of multilevel instruction, universal design for learning, direct instruction, assistive technology, and curriculum-based measurement.

**Curriculum-based assessment (CBA)**

The direct and frequent measurement of observable student behaviors to track students' progress within the curriculum.

## STEPS TO AN EFFECTIVE CURRICULUM-BASED ASSESSMENT

What's a teacher to do when the 30 students in her class have 30 greatly differing achievement, performance, and interest levels, to say nothing of different learning styles, family backgrounds and language preferences? One strategy is to find ways to discover—early, often, and at the end of every unit or semester—what the students know and can do. And these tests must be efficient and fast. Here's where curriculum-based assessment (CBA) can help.

### Apply: The Steps to Effective CBA

**1.** *Analyze the curriculum.* Educators select critical skills on the basis of students' IEP goals and objectives or general education curriculum competencies.

**2.** *Prepare items to meet the curriculum objectives.* Critical skills that

educators target during curriculum analysis drive the items used on a CBA probe. Probes can take many formats. (For example, given a brief passage to read, the student answers five questions that include recall, inferential, and prediction responses.)

**3.** *Probe frequently.* By administering the CBA on several occasions across days during an instructional unit, educators can make timely decisions about how well students are learning and the effectiveness of the instruction.

**4.** *Load data using a graph format.* Quantifiable information provided by a student's performance on a CBA probe is transferred to a graph.

**5.** *Yield to results—Revisions and decisions.* Student data on CBA graphs represent their progress within the instructional unit.

SOURCE: From "Applying Curriculum-Based Assessment in Inclusive Settings," by M. E. King-Sears, M. Burges, & T. L. Lawson, 1999, *Teaching Exceptional Children*, September/October pp. 30–38.

## FOCUS REVIEW

**FOCUS 1** Define the term *inclusive education.*

- Inclusive education may be defined as placing students with disabilities in a general education setting within their home or neighborhood school, while making available both formal and natural supports to ensure an appropriate educational experience.
- In full inclusion, the student with a disability receives all instruction and support within the general education classroom. In partial inclusion, the student with a disability receives most instruction within the general education classroom but is "pulled out" for spe-

cialized services during part of the school day.

**FOCUS 2** Cite the characteristics of effective inclusive schools.

Effective inclusive schools
- promote the values of diversity, acceptance, and belonging.
- ensure the availability of formal and natural supports within the general education setting.
- provide services and supports in age-appropriate classrooms in neighborhood schools.
- ensure access to the general curriculum while meeting the individualized needs of each student.

- provide a schoolwide support system to meet the needs of all students.

**FOCUS 3** Define *collaboration* and identify its key characteristics.

- Collaboration occurs when professionals, parents, and students *work together* to achieve the mutual goal of delivering an effective educational program designed to meet individual needs. Collaboration is not what those involved do; it is how they do it.
- In an inclusive school, effective collaboration has several key characteristics:

1. Parents are viewed as active partners in the education of their children.
2. Team members share responsibility.
3. Individual roles are clearly understood and valued.
4. Team members promote peer support and cooperative learning.

**FOCUS 4** Why is it so important to provide early intervention services as soon as possible to young children at risk?

- The first years of life are critical to the overall development of all children—those without special challenges, those at risk, and those who have disabilities.
- Early stimulation is crucial to the later development of language, intelligence, personality, and self-worth.
- Early intervention may prevent and lessen the overall impact of disabilities, as well as counteracting the negative effects of delayed intervention.
- Early intervention may in the long run be less costly and more effective than providing services later in the individual's life.

**FOCUS 5** Identify the components of the individualized family service plan (IFSP).

- The infant's or toddler's present levels of physical development, cognitive development, communication development, social or emotional development, and adaptive development.
- The family's resources, priorities, and concerns related to enhancing the development of the young child with a disability.

- The major results to be achieved for the infant or toddler and the family, and the criteria, procedures, and timelines used to determine progress toward achieving those outcomes.
- Specific early intervention services necessary to meet the unique needs of the infant or toddler and the family.
- The natural environments in which early intervention services are to be provided, including a justification of the extent, if any, to which the services will not be provided in a natural environment.
- The projected dates for initiation of services and the anticipated duration of the services.
- Identification of the service coordinator.
- The steps to be taken to support the transition of the toddler with a disability to preschool or other appropriate services.

**FOCUS 6** Identify effective instructional approaches for preschool-age children with disabilities.

- A child-find system in each state to locate young children at risk and make referrals to appropriate agencies for preschool services.
- An individualized education program plan that involves specialists across several disciplines.
- Instruction that reflects developmentally appropriate practice, age-appropriate practice, and the teaching of functional skills.
- Inclusive preschool classrooms where young children with disabilities are educated alongside peers without disabilities.

**FOCUS 7** Describe the roles of special education teachers and general education teachers in an inclusive classroom setting.

- Special education teachers have multiple roles that may be referred to as the "three Cs": They function as collaborator, consultant, and coordinator.
- In the role of *collaborator,* special educators work with school to assess student needs, develop the IEP, determine appropriate accommodations and instructional adaptations, and deliver intensive instruction in academic, behavioral, and/or adaptive functional areas. Special education teachers use effective problem-solving strategies to facilitate student learning, co-teach with general educators, and apply effective accountability measures to evaluate individual student progress and long-term results.
- In the role of *consultant,* the special education teacher serves as a resource to general educators and parents on effective instructional practices for students with disabilities.
- In the role of *coordinator,* the special education teacher takes the lead in organizing the activities of the school team in developing, implementing, and evaluating student IEPs. She or he may also be responsible for organizing school resources; for planning professional development activities; for supervising paraprofessionals, peer support, and volunteers; and for facilitating positive communication with parents.
- General educators must be able to identify and refer students who may be in need of additional support; to understand each student's individual

strengths and limitations, and their effects on learning; implement an appropriate individualized instructional program that is focused on supporting student success in the general education curriculum; and to initiate and maintain ongoing communication with parents.

**FOCUS 8** Why are multilevel instruction, universal design for learning, direct instruction, assistive technology, and curriculum-based assessment considered effective practice in an inclusive classroom?

- Students of the same age are clearly not alike in how they learn or their rate of learning. Accordingly, teachers must use multilevel instruction (also re-

ferred to as *differentiated instruction*), in which multiple teaching approaches within the same curriculum are *adapted* to individual needs and functioning level.

- Universal design goes one step beyond multilevel instruction, creating instructional programs and environments that work for all students, to the greatest extent possible, without the need for adaptation.
- A primary characteristic of special education is the *explicit teaching* of academic, adaptive, and functional skills. Research suggests that students with disabilities learn more efficiently in a structured, teacher-directed approach. This approach is often referred to as *direct instruction*.

- Assistive technology can take many forms and can be helpful to students with disabilities in several different ways (examples include high-tech digital textbooks, low-tech language boards, and a joystick to guide a power wheelchair).
- Traditional standardized assessments may be useful in determining a student's eligibility for special education, but many educators question their use in planning for instruction and measuring day-to-day student learning. An alternative approach to traditional tests is the use of curriculum-based assessments (CBAs). CBAs provide direct and frequent measurement of observable student progress within the curriculum.

## FURTHER READINGS

Friend, M., & Cook, L. (2002). *Interactions: Collaboration Skills for School Professionals* (4th ed.). Boston: Allyn and Bacon.

*This book looks at how teams of school professionals—classroom teachers, special education teachers, and counselors—can work together effectively to provide an essential range of services to students with special needs. Future teachers learn how to collaborate with school professionals and families to help special education students who are more and more often being placed in general classroom settings.*

Lerner, J. W., Lowenthal, B., & Egan, R. W. (2002). *Preschool Children with Special Needs: Children at Risk, Children with Disabilities* (2nd ed.). Boston: Allyn and Bacon.

*This book examines issues in early childhood general and special education, emphasizing the needs of preschoolers*

*age 3 to 5. It provides information for teachers and others who work with young children in all settings. Current models of curricula, which incorporate research and practical experiences with children who have special needs, are described and discussed.*

Peterson, M. J. (2003). *Inclusive Teaching: Creating Effective Schools for All Learners.* Boston: Allyn and Bacon.

*A comprehensive book designed to help educators meet the needs of all students in inclusive settings. Topics include celebrating difference, a vision for inclusive schools, parent and community partnerships, planning for instruction with diverse learners, collaboration, and strategies for inclusive teaching.*

# WEB RESOURCES

### Center for Applied Special Technology (CAST)

www.cast.org

CAST is a not-for-profit organization that uses technology to expand opportunities for all people, especially those with disabilities. This website contains information on how technology can help students with disabilities by improving their access to and progress and participation in the general education curriculum.

### The Division for Early Childhood (DEC) of the Council for Exceptional Children

www.dec-sped.org

The Division for Early Childhood (DEC) of the Council for Exceptional Children advocates for individuals who work with or on behalf of children with special needs, birth through age 8, and their families. This website contains information on early childhood conferences, publications, government services, and jobs.

### Inclusive Education Website: The "Whats" and "How Tos" of Inclusive Education

www.uni.edu/coe/inclusion/

Whether you're familiar with inclusive education or have little idea what the term means, this website is designed to help you learn more about it. It answers some of the most frequently asked questions on inclusion and offers basic guidelines for teaching in an inclusive classroom. Resources for learning more about inclusive education are also included.

### Special Education Resources on the Internet

seriweb.com

Special Education Resources on the Internet (SERI) is a collection of Internet-accessible information resources of interest to those involved in the education of students with disabilities. This collection exists in order to make on-line special education resources more readily available in one location.

# BUILDING YOUR PORTFOLIO

If you are thinking about a career in special education, you should know that many states use national standards developed by the Council for Exceptional Children (CEC) to assess a teacher candidate's knowledge about and skills for working with students with disabilities. See a complete listing of the ten CEC Content Standards on the inside front cover of this text.

### CEC Content Standards Addressed in Chapter 3

1. Foundations
2. Development and Characteristics of Learners
3. Individual Learning Differences
4. Instructional Strategies
5. Learning Environments and Social Interactions
7. Instructional Planning
9. Professional and Ethical Practice
10. Collaboration

### Assess Your Knowledge of the CEC Standards Addressed in Chapter 3

Some states require that teacher candidates develop a portfolio of products that demonstrate mastery of the CEC content standards. To assist in the development of products for this portfolio, you may wish to complete the following activities.

- Complete a written test of the chapter's content.

  *If your instructor requires a written test of your content knowledge for this chapter, keep a copy for your portfolio. A practice test on the information covered in this chapter is available through the companion website (www.ablongman.com/hardman8e) and the Student Study Guide.*

- Respond to Application Questions for the Case Study "Ricardo."

  *Review the Case Study and respond in writing to the application questions. Keep a copy of the case study and your written response for your portfolio.*

- Complete the "Take a Stand" activity for the Debate Forum "Perspectives on Full Inclusion of Students with Disabilities."

  *Read the Debate Forum in this chapter and then visit the Companion Website to complete the activity "Take a Stand." Keep a copy of this activity for your portfolio.*

- Participate in a Community Service Learning Activity.

  *Community service is a valuable way to enhance your learning experience. Visit our companion website for suggested community service learning activities that correspond to the information presented in this chapter. Develop a reflective journal of the service learning experience for your portfolio.*

## THEMES OF THE TIMES

The New York Times
expect the world®
nytimes.com

Expand your knowledge of the concepts discussed in this chapter by reading current and historical articles from the *New York Times* by visiting the "Themes of the Times" section of the companion website: **www.ablongman.com/hardman8e.**

CHAPTER

4

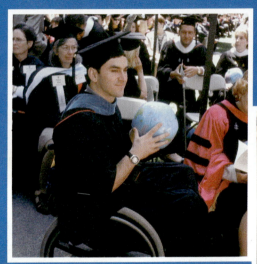

# Transition and Adult Life

### Different Students, Different Needs

A successful schooling experience will provide the student with the tools and skills necessary to make the transition effectively to the next stage of life. For some, this means going on to college or another educational experience. For others, it means entering the workforce. For students with severe disabilities . . . long-term outcomes (e.g., degree of independence, employment) are designated through the IEP process; instruction then focuses on building skills that will lead to these outcomes in age-appropriate natural settings. . . . For students with mild disabilities, a combination of academic, vocational, and functional outcomes is often selected with the specific mix of components dependent on individual student goals and needs. (National Research Council, 1997, pp. 119, 120)

### The Challenges of Secondary Education

As more educators and parents experience the benefits of inclusion in elementary schools, methods to promote inclusion at a secondary level have increased. . . . In secondary settings, however, special educators face challenges in collaborating with general educators, handling the logistics of scheduling, and providing staff and peer support. . . . Educators at the secondary level encounter challenging tasks related to inclusion: selecting general education classes; infusing student goals across subject areas; and establishing teaching partnerships and curricular adaptations. (Siegel-Causey, McMorris, McGowen, & Sands-Buss, 1998, p. 66)

### College-Bound Students with Disabilities

Today, there are more students with documented disabilities in higher education than ever before—over 9.5% of all freshmen as compared with only 2.6% in 1978. Although the process has been slow, colleges and universities have made their programs more and more accessible, sometimes in good faith, sometimes due to coercion made by federal agencies and courts. Only modest progress was made between 1973 and 1990; however, once the ADA [Americans with Disabilities Act] was passed . . . [universities and colleges] that had made little or no progress in making their buildings and programs accessible increased their efforts. . . . Of particular significance in recent years has been the growth in the number of students with learning disabilities. Over 35% of the freshmen in 1996 who reported having a disability were purported to have a learning disability. . . . The growth in the number of students with learning disabilities has created a new challenge to professors and colleges. . . . Many professors prefer that all students meet the same set of requirements, within the same time period . . . and in the same way, and are ill-prepared to adapt their instruction to address the individual needs of students or to identify appropriate, fair, and reasonable accommodations. (Thomas, 2000, p. 248)

**FOCUS**

**PREVIEW:** To preview the central concepts of this chapter, read the focus questions located in the margins. Using these questions as a guide, ask yourself what you already know and what you want to learn.

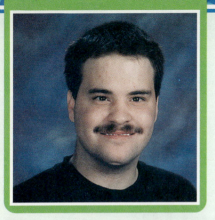

# Lee

**L**ee is a high school student with a part-time job stocking shelves at a local store. Lee walks from his high school to catch the bus to work. On his way to the bus, everyone says hello to Lee. He's a great friend to everybody. Everyone makes it a point to stop and ask how he's doing.

At work, his employer gives him a checklist indicating how many cases of each item Lee needs to bring from the backroom to stock on the shelves. Lee can't read, but he can associate the item with the cases in the backroom. Most of Lee's education occurs in the community with the assistance of peer tutors who help him learn to purchase foods, bank, use the bus, and perform various work functions.

In his high school classes, Lee also has access to peer tutors who work with him. They may provide one-on-one tutoring or participate with him in a weight-lifting class. They are invaluable to him and his teachers.

Lee has become much more independent because of the skills he has learned in school and practiced in the community. Eventually, he plans to live independently.

What are society's expectations of an individual who is leaving school and moving into adult life? Early adulthood marks a time of transition from relative dependence on the family to increasing responsibility for one's own life. Young adults are concerned with furthering their education, earning a living, establishing their independence, and creating social networks. As an adolescent leaves high school, decisions need to be made. A person may reflect on many questions: What kind of career or job do I want? Should I further my education to increase my career choices? Where shall I live and with whom shall I live? How shall I spend my money? With whom do I choose to spend time? Who will be my friends?

Most adolescents face these choices as a natural part of growing into adult life, but the issues confronting individuals with disabilities and their families may be very different. For many, the choice may be to disappear into the fabric of society and try to make it on their own without the supports and services that were so much a part of their public school experience. Others may choose to go to college, seeking the accommodations they need (such as more time to take tests, large-print books, or interpreters) to have a fighting chance to succeed in an academic world. Still others will need ongoing supports to find and keep a job and to live successfully in the community.

Given these expectations of adult life, the school's responsibility is to teach the critical skills that will facilitate access to valued postschool outcomes for students with disabilities. For Lee, in the opening Snapshot, instruction focused on increasing his independence by teaching him how to ride the bus, work in the community, take care of his personal needs (such as shopping and using a checking account), and enjoy his free-time lifting weights. Although much as been done to improve the quality of life for adults with disabilities, many individuals are still unable to access the services or supports necessary for success after graduation. The next section presents information on the lives of adults with disabilities.

**FOCUS 1**

What do we know about access to community living and employment for people with disabilities after they leave school?

# Research on the Lives of Adults with Disabilities

One measure of an educational program's effectiveness is the success of its graduates. Although 2005 marks the 30th anniversary of the passage of Public Law 94-142), now the Individuals with Disabilities Education Act (IDEA), the educational opportunities afforded by this landmark legislation have not yet led to full participation of special education graduates in the social and economic mainstream of their local communities (National Organization on Disability [N.O.D.]/Harris, 2000). Results of several follow-up studies of special education graduates have suggested that they were unable to participate fully in community activities and were socially isolated in comparison to people who were not disabled. The majority of these adults were not employed (Hasazi, Furney, & Destefano, 1999; Wagner & Blackorby, 1996). The nearby Reflect on This highlights some aspects of life as an adult with disabilities nearly three decades since the passage of IDEA and more than a decade after the passage of ADA.

## High School Completion and Access to Valued Postschool Outcomes

The increasing emphasis on the transition from school to adult life by policy makers, professionals, and parents has altered many perceptions about individuals with disabilities. Without question, the potential of adults with disabilities has been significantly underestimated. In recent years, professionals and parents have begun to address some of the crucial issues facing students with disabilities as they prepare to leave school and face life as adults in their local communities. Nearly half a million students with disabilities exit school each year. Since the passage of IDEA, schools have taken significant strides in preparing youth with disabilities for adult life, but much remains to be done. Of the students with disabilities age 14 and older exiting school, only 56% leave with a standard high school diploma, compared to 90% of their peers without disabilities (U.S. Department of Education, 2002). Many of the current graduates from special education programs are not adequately prepared for employment and are unable to access further education. They are also unable to locate the critical programs and services necessary for success as adults in their local communities (Chadsey-Rusch & Heal, 1998; N.O.D./Harris, 2000; Wehman, 2001). For people with more severe disabilities, long waiting lists for employment and housing services prove frustrating (McDonnell, Hardman, & McDonnell, 2003). Prouty, Smith, and Lakin (2001) reported that nearly 72,000 adults with severe disabilities were on waiting lists for residential, day treatment, or family support services. Furthermore, individuals with disabilities who enroll in postsecondary education often find that the supports and services necessary for them to achieve success in college are also not available (Gartin, Rumrill, & Serebreni, 1996; Thomas, 2000).

## Employment

The U.S. Department of Education's National Longitudinal Transition Study (Wagner & Blackorby, 1996) reported that paid employment during high school had become more common; 42% of students with disabilities were being placed in community vocational or employment programs. However, 25% of these students worked fewer than 10 hours per week and were paid below minimum wage. Additionally, most students were in service positions or doing manual labor. Five years out of high school, only 57% of these students were in competitive employment positions, and only 43% were working full-time. These numbers indicate that the employment rate for people with disabilities was far below that of peers without disabilities. Worse yet, the employment rate as reported by Wagner and Blackorby in 1996 is significantly higher than that found in the 2000 N.O.D./Harris poll, in which only 32% of the people with disabilities indicated that they were working full- or part-time.

# Closing the Gap: Transition Planning and Services

The transition from school to adult life is a complex and dynamic process. Transition planning should culminate with the transfer of support from the school to an adult service agency, access to postsecondary education, or life as an independent adult. The

# A DECADE AFTER THE PASSAGE OF ADA, ADULTS WITH DISABILITIES STILL FACE SHARP GAPS IN EMPLOYMENT, EDUCATION, AND DAILY LIVING

A 2000 poll by the National Organization on Disability/Harris found that Americans with disabilities ages 18 to 64 were still lagging far behind nondisabled adults in overall satisfaction with life, employment and income levels, education, health care, civic participation, and access to transportation and recreation.

## Satisfaction With Life

• Only about one in three (33%) adults with disabilities is very satisfied with life in general, compared to fully seven out of ten (67%) adults without disabilities.

## Employment

• Only 32% of adults with disabilities work full- or part-time, compared to 81% of those who are not disabled—a gap of nearly 50 percentage points.
• Of those with disabilities who are of working age but are not working, 67% say that they would prefer to work.
• Forty-three percent of adults say that their disability has prevented their getting, or made it more difficult for them to get, the kind of job they would like to have.

## Income

• One out of three (29%) adults with disabilities lives in a household with an annual income of less than $15,000, compared to only 12% of those without disabilities.

## Education

• One out of five (22%) adults with disabilities has not graduated from high school, compared to only one out of ten (9%) of nondisabled adults.
• Approximately one out of ten people with disabilities graduates from college, compared to slightly more than two out of ten nondisabled people.

## Health Care

• One out of five (19%) adults with a disability did not get the medical care that he or she needed on at least one occasion during the past year, compared to only 6% of people of nondisabled adults.
• One in four (28%) adults with disabilities postponed getting health care they thought they needed in the past year because they couldn't afford it.

• Although nine out of ten (90%) adults with disabilities are covered by health insurance, they are more likely than nondisabled adults (28% versus 7%) not to have their special needs covered.

## Voting

• People with disabilities are less likely to be registered to vote than people without disabilities (62% versus 78%, respectively).

## Access to Transportation

• Inadequate transportation is considered a problem by 30% of adults with disabilities but by only 10% of nondisabled adults.

## Frequency of Socializing

• Seven out of ten (70%) adults with disabilities socialize with close friends, relatives, or neighbors at least once a week, compared to more than eight out of ten (85%) of nondisabled adults.

## Entertainment/Going Out

• One in four (40%) of adults with disabilities go to a restaurant at least once a week, compared to six out of ten (59%) of those without disabilities.

## Other Key Findings

• Over the past 14 years, education has shown signs of improvement for all people with disabilities, and employment has shown signs of improvement for people who say they are able to work.
• Among people with disabilities who say they are able to work despite their disability or health problem, 56% are working today, compared to only 46% in 1986. These improvements probably stem from multiple causes, including the Americans with Disabilities Act and the Individuals with Disabilities Education Act.
• Over 70% of people with disabilities agree that access to public facilities such as restaurants, theaters, stores, and museums has gotten better over the past four years.
• In an era of economic expansion, it appears that people with disabilities have been less likely to benefit. They are more likely to have lower incomes than people without disabilities, and lower-income individuals are less likely to benefit from increases in the stock market or an overall economic surge.

SOURCE: From *National Organization on Disability/Harris Survey of Americans with Disabilities (Executive Summary),* by N.O.D./L. Harris and Associates, 2000, pp. 14–20. New York: Author.

planning process involves a series of choices about which experiences would best prepare students with disabilities in their remaining school years for what lies ahead in the adult world. A successful transition from school to the adult years requires both formal (government-funded) and natural supports (Ferguson & Ferguson, 2000; Tymchuk, Lakin, & Luckasson, 2001). Historically, providing formal supports, such as health care, employment preparation, and supported living, has been emphasized. Only recently has society begun to understand the importance of the family and other natural support networks in preparing the adolescent with disabilities for adult life. Research suggests that the family unit may be the single most powerful force in preparing the adolescent with disabilities for the adult years (Berry & Hardman, 1998).

The principal components of an effective transition system are as follows:

- Effective middle and high school programs that link instruction to further education (such as college or trade schools) and to valued postschool outcomes (such as employment, independent living, and recreation/leisure activities).

- A cooperative system of transition planning that involves public education, adult services, and an array of natural supports (family and friends) in order to ensure access to valued postschool outcomes.

- The availability of formal government-funded programs following school that are capable of meeting the unique educational, employment, housing, and leisure needs of people with disabilities in a community setting.

## IDEA Transition Planning Requirements

IDEA requires that every student with a disability receive transition services. **Transition services** for a student with a disability are a coordinated set of activities with the following attributes:

- Designed to be within a results-oriented process that is focused on improving the academic and functional achievement of the child with a disability to facilitate the child's movement from school to post-school activities, including post-secondary education, vocational education, integrated employment (including supported employment), continuing and adult education, adult services, independent living, or community participation.

- Based on the individual child's needs, taking into account the child's strengths, preferences, and interests.

- Includes instruction, related services, community experiences, the development of employment and other post-school adult living objectives, and, when appropriate, acquisition of daily living skills and functional vocational evaluation. (IDEA 2004, PL 108-446, Sec. 602[34])

IDEA requires that, beginning at age 16 and updated annually, a student's individualized program should include appropriate measurable postsecondary goals based upon age appropriate transition assessments related to training, education, employment, and, where appropriate, independent living skills. The IEP must include a statement of transition services that relate to various courses of study (such as participation in advanced placement courses or a vocational education program) that will assist the student in reaching their goals. (IDEA 2004, PL 108-446, Sec. 614[d])

## Other Federal Laws Linked to IDEA and Transition Planning

Five other pieces of federal legislation that are directly linked to the IDEA transition requirements also help facilitate an effective transition planning process. They are: Vocational Rehabilitation Act, the Carl Perkins Vocational and Applied Technology Education Act, the Americans with Disabilities Act (ADA), the School-to-Work Opportunities Act, and the Work Incentives Improvement Act. The Vocational Rehabilitation Act provides services through rehabilitation counselors in several areas (such as guidance and counseling, vocational evaluation, vocational training and job placement, transportation, family services, interpreter services, and telecommuni-

**IDEA 2004**

**FOCUS 2**

What are the requirements for transition planning in IDEA?

**Transition services**

A coordinated set of activities for students with disabilities that are designed to facilitate the move from school to employment, further education, vocational training, independent living, and community participation.

cation aids and devices). Recent amendments to the act encourage stronger collaboration and outreach between the schools and the rehabilitation counselors in transition planning.

Greater connections between education and vocational rehabilitation are expected to help students with disabilities in moving on to postsecondary education or in obtaining employment. The Carl Perkins Vocational and Technical Education Act provides students with disabilities greater access to vocational education services. ADA addresses equal access to public accommodations, employment, transportation, and telecommunication services following the school transition years. (See Chapter 1.) Such services are often directly targeted as a part of the student's transition plan.

The School-to-Work Opportunities Act provides all students in the public schools with education and training to prepare them for first jobs in high-skill, high-wage careers and for further education following high school. Students with disabilities are specifically identified as a target population of the act. The Ticket to Work and Work Incentives Improvement Act provides greater opportunities for the employment of people with disabilities by allowing them to work and still keep critical health care coverage. Prior to the passage of this act, many people with disabilities were not able to work because federal Social Security laws put them at risk of losing Medicaid and Medicare coverage if they accrued any significant earnings. Thus there was little incentive for people with disabilities to work because they could not access health insurance. The Work Incentives Improvement Act made health insurance available and affordable when a person with a disability goes to work or develops a significant disability while working.

# Developing the Individualized Transition Plan (ITP)

FOCUS
3

Identify the purpose of an ITP and the basic steps in its formulation.

Transition involves much more than the mere transfer of administrative responsibility from the school to an adult service agency. An individualized transition plan, based on an evaluation of student needs and preferences, must be developed and implemented. The plan should include access to the general education curriculum and/or a focus on the adaptive and functional skills that will facilitate life in the community following school (Alberto, Taber, Brozovic, & Elliot, 1997; deFur, 1999, 2000).

The **individualized transition plan (ITP)** is a statement within each student's IEP describing needed transition services. See Figure 4.1 for an illustration of an ITP in the area of employment preparation. The purpose of the transition statement is to (1) identify the type and range of transitional services and supports, and (2) establish timelines and personnel responsible for completing the plan. Wehman, Everson, and Reid (2001) identify six basic steps in the formulation of a student's ITP. They are shown in Table 4.1.

## Facilitating Student and Parent Involvement

In the transition from school to adult life, many students and parents receive quite a shock. Once they leave school, students may not receive any further assistance from government programs, or, at the least, they may be placed on long waiting lists for employment training, housing, or education assistance. As a consequence, the person with a disability may experience a significant loss in services at a crucial time. Many students and their parents know little, if anything, about what life during the adult years may bring for individuals with disabilities.

To prepare fully for the transition from school, students and parents must be educated about critical components of adult service systems, including the characteristics of service agencies and what constitutes a good program, as well as current and

**Individualized transition plan (ITP)**

A statement about transition services within each student's IEP. It identifies the range of services needed, the high school activities that will facilitate the individual's access to adult programs if necessary, timelines, and responsibilities for completion of these activities.

potential opportunities for employment, independent living, or further education (deFur, 2000). McDonnell, Mathot-Buckner, and Ferguson (1996) suggested three strategies that schools can use to facilitate family involvement in the transition process:

- *Adopt a person-centered approach to transition planning.* The student should be at the center of the planning process, and his or her specific needs, preferences, and values should come first.

- *Assist parents in identifying their daughter's or son's preferences.* Families have the most comprehensive understanding of the student with a disability. Schools must work with the family to help the student to understand and verbalize, as much as possible, his or her values, wants, and needs prior to entering adult life.

- *Help parents explore and identify their own expectations.* Parents will differ in their individual expectations. Some will have difficulty letting go and giving their daughter or son more responsibility and freedom as an adult. Others view greater independence from the family as an important part of their son or daughter's transition to adult life.

---

### FIGURE 4.1

## Illustrative Transition Planning Form in the Area of Employment

Student: *Robert Brown*

Meeting Date: *January 20, 2003*

Graduation Date: *June, 2004*

IEP/Transition Planning Team Members: *Robert Brown (student), Mrs. Brown (parent), Jill Green (teacher), Mike Weatherby (Vocational Education), Dick Rose (Rehabilitation), Susan Marr (Developmental Disabilities Agency)*

---

TRANSITION PLANNING AREA: *Employment*

Student Preferences and
Desired Postschool Goals: *Robert would like to work in a grocery store as a produce stocker.*

Present Levels of Performance: *Robert has held several work experience placements in local grocery stores (see attached placement summaries). He requires a self-management checklist using symbols to complete assigned work tasks. His rate of task completion is below the expected employer levels.*

Need Transition Services: *Robert will require job placement, training, and follow-along services from an employment specialist. In addition, he needs bus training to get to his job.*

---

ANNUAL GOAL: *Robert will work Monday through Friday from 1:00 to 4:00 p.m. at Smith's Food Center as a produce stocker, completing all assigned tasks without assistance from the employment specialist on ten consecutive weekly performance probes.*

| Activities | Person | Completion Date |
|---|---|---|
| 1. Place Robert on the state supported employment waiting list. | Susan Marr | May 1, 2003 |
| 2. Obtain a monthly bus pass. | Mrs. Brown | February 1, 2003 |
| 3. Schedule Robert for employee orientation training. | | February 16, 2003 |

SOURCE: *Introduction to persons with moderate and severe disabilities* (p. 321), by J.M. McDonnell, M.L. Hardman & A.P. McDonnell, 2003, Boston: Allyn and Bacon.

---

## Working with Adult Services

In addition to the student, parents, and school personnel, professionals from adult service agencies (such as vocational rehabilitation counselors, representatives from university or college centers for students with disabilities, the state developmental disability agency, etc.) may be involved in transition planning. **Adult service agencies** assist individuals with disabilities in accessing postsecondary education, employment, supported living, or leisure activities. Agencies may provide support in vocational rehabilitation, social services, and mental health. Examples of supports

**Adult Service Agencies**

Agencies with a major focus on providing services and supports to help people with disabilities become more independent as adults. Adult service agencies include rehabilitation services, social services, mental health services, and the like.

**TABLE 4.1**

### Basic Steps in the Formulation of an ITP

1. Convene IEP teams, individualized around the wants and needs of each transition-age student.
   - Identify all transition-age students
   - Identify appropriate school service personnel
   - Identify appropriate adult service agencies
   - Identify appropriate members of the student's networks
2. Review assessment data and conduct additional assessment activities.
   - Meet with transition-age student and small circle of friends, family members, coworkers, neighbors, church members, and/or staff to establish individual needs and preferences for adult life.
3. Teams develop ITPs.
   - Schedule the IEP meeting
   - Conduct the IEP meeting
   - Develop the ITP
4. Implement the ITP.
   - Operate according to guidelines defined in interagency agreements
   - Use a transdisciplinary model and cross-agency approach to delivering services
5. Update the ITP annually during IEP meetings and implement follow-up procedures.
   - Phase out involvement of school personnel while increasing involvement of adult service agencies
   - Contact persons responsible for completion of ITP goals to monitor progress
6. Hold an exit meeting.
   - Ensure most appropriate employment outcome or access to further education
   - Ensure most appropriate community living and recreation outcome
   - Ensure referrals to all appropriate adult agencies and support services

SOURCE: *Life beyond the classroom: Transition strategies for young people with disabilities (3rd ed.),* by P. Wehman, J. M. Everson, & D. H. Reid, 2001, Baltimore: Paul H. Brookes, pp. 99–121.

include career, education, or mental health counseling, job training and support (such as a job coach), further education (college or trade school), attendant services, and interpreter services. Adult service agencies should become involved early in transition planning to begin targeting the services that will be necessary once the student leaves school. Adult service professionals should collaborate with the school in establishing transition goals and identifying appropriate activities for the student during the final school years. Additionally, adult service professionals must be involved in developing information systems that can effectively track students as they leave school and can monitor the availability and appropriateness of services to be provided during adulthood (Wehman, 2001).

# Preparing Students for Adult Life: The Role of Secondary Schools

*Schools have many roles in the transition planning process. What do you think are a school's most important responsibilities in facilitating a successful transition from school to adult life?*

Successful transition begins with a solid foundation—the school. Secondary schools have many roles in the transition process: assessing individual needs, helping each student develop a transition plan, coordinating transition planning with adult service agencies, participating with parents and students in the planning process, and providing experiences to facilitate access to community services and employment. For Lee, in the opening Snapshot, these experiences included learning to shop in a neighborhood grocery store and training for a job in the community. For another student with a disability who has different needs and abilities, the activities may be more academically oriented, with college preparation as the immediate goal.

Several outcomes are expected for students with disabilities as they enter adulthood. First, they should be able to function as independently as possible in their daily lives; their reliance on others to meet their needs should be minimized. As students with disabilities leave school, they should be able to make choices about where they will live, how they will spend their free time, and whether they will be employed in the community or go on to college. For students with disabilities who are considering college, Gartin, Rumrill, and Srebreni (1996) identify guidelines for facilitating the transition to higher education. (See Table 4.2)

Secondary schools are in the unique position of being able to coordinate activities that enhance student participation in the community and link students, such as Lee, with needed programs and services. The next section discusses the school's role in teaching self-determination, academic skills, adaptive and functional life skills, and employment preparation.

## TABLE 4.2

### Higher Education Transition Model

| ESSENTIAL CURRICULAR ELEMENTS | INSTRUCTIONAL OBJECTIVES |
|---|---|
| Psychosocial adjustment | 1. Self-advocacy skill development |
| | 2. Handling frustration |
| | 3. Social problem-solving |
| | 4. College-level social skills |
| | 5. Mentor relationships |
| Academic development | 1. College entrance exam preparation |
| | 2. Test-taking strategies/accommodations |
| | 3. Career awareness |
| | 4. Goal setting |
| | 5. Academic remediation |
| | 6. Career preparation |
| | 7. Learning strategies/study skills |
| | 8. College services |
| | 9. Transition to college |
| College/community orientation | 1. College-level linkage |
| | 2. Buddy systems |
| | 3. College choices |
| | 4. College resources/activities |
| | 5. College orientation program |
| | 6. Campus support groups |
| | 7. Community services assessment |

SOURCE: From "The Higher Education Transition Model: Guidelines for Facilitating College Transition Among College-Bound Students with Disabilities," by B. C. Gartin, P. Rumrill, and R. Serebreni, 1996, *Teaching Exceptional Children, 29*(1), p. 31. Copyright 1996 by the Council for Exceptional Children. Reprinted with permission.

## Teaching Self-Determination

Self-determination plays a critical role in the successful transition from school to adult life. (Bremer, Kachgal, & Schoeller, 2003; Field & Hoffman, 1999; Morgan, Ellerd, Gerity, & Blair, 2000). Definitions of self-determination focus on a person's ability to consider options and make appropriate decisions and to exercise free will, independence, and individual responsibility (University of Illinois at Chicago National Research and Training Center, 2003). The need for secondary schools to teach self-determination skills is evident from research related to positive transition outcomes. In one study, Wehmeyer and Schwartz (1997) found that youth characterized as "self-determined" experienced a greater number of positive adult outcomes, including employment, than those who were not self-determined.

Teaching self-determination skills to students with disabilities helps them become more efficient in acquiring knowledge and solving problems (Browder & Bambara, 2000). Students who have learned such skills will be better able to achieve goals that will facilitate their transition out of school and be more aware of the specific challenges they will face in the adult years. Ultimately, such a student leaves school with a better developed sense of personal worth, social responsibility, and problem-solving skills (Agran & Wehmeyer, 1999). Benjamin (1996) recommended a four-step problem-solving process in which schools and

**FOCUS 4**

Why is it important for students with disabilities to receive instruction in self-determination, academics, adaptive and functional life skills, and employment preparation during the secondary school years?

parents can support the development of self-determination for students with disabilities:

1. Through role playing and simulated activities, teach students to observe and analyze a situation by identifying a problem in the situation and giving it a name.

2. Ask students to think about possible options that might solve the problem. If they are unable to do so, teach them how to access resources, such as libraries and knowledgeable people, that will help them generate possible solutions.

3. Once a student has identified possible solutions and selected one, encourage him or her to see if any problem still exists. If yes, ask the student what he or she might do to change the plan and solve the problem.

4. Ask students to think about how to use strategies to solve similar problems in other situations.

Creating opportunities for individual choice and decision making is an important element in the transition from school to adult life. Each individual must be able to consider options and make appropriate choices. This means less problem solving and decision making on the part of service providers and family members and a greater focus on teaching and promoting choice. The planning process associated with the development of a student's IEP is an excellent opportunity to promote self-determination. Unfortunately, very few adolescents with disabilities attend their IEP meetings, and fewer yet actively participate (Wehman, et al., 2001).

Although we have discussed self-determination in the context of the secondary school years, instruction in this area must begin early in a child's life. As suggested by Abery (1994), "striving to attain self-determination doesn't begin (or end) during adolescence or early adulthood. Rather it is initiated shortly after birth and continues until we have breathed our last breath" (p. 2). See Table 4.3, Promoting Self-Determination in Youth With Disabilities: Tips for Families and Professionals.

## Teaching Academic Skills and Access to the General Curriculum

Evidence indicates that students with disabilities are not faring well in the academic content of high school programs or in postsecondary education (U.S. Department of Education, 2002). These students have high dropout rates and low academic achievement. However, the research also suggests that students with mild disabilities, particularly those with learning disabilities, can achieve in academic content beyond their current performance (Friend & Bursuck, 2002; National Research Council, 1997). Getzel and Gugerty (2001) suggest that high school programs for students with mild disabilities must

- develop teaching strategies based on the unique learning characteristics of each student.
- take into account the cultural background of the student and its effect on learning.
- determine the student's strongest learning modes (visual, auditory, and/or tactile) and adapt instruction accordingly.
- use assistive technology (such as laptop computers, personal data managers, pocket-size spellcheckers, and the like) to help students capitalize on their strengths.
- create positive learning environments to enable students to feel motivated and build their self-esteem.

For students with moderate to severe disabilities, the purpose of academic learning may be more functional and compensatory—to teach skills that have immediate and frequent use in the student's environment (Browder & Snell, 2000). Instruction concentrates on skills that occur as part of the student's daily living routine. For example, safety skills may include reading street signs, railroad crossings, entrance/exit signs,

TABLE 4.3

## Promoting Self-Determination in Youth with Disabilities: Tips for Families and Professionals

**PROMOTE CHOICE MAKING**

- Identify strengths, interests, and learning styles.
- Provide choices about clothing, social activities, family events, and methods of learning new information.
- Hold high expectations for youth.
- Teach youth about their disability.
- Involve children and youth in self-determination/self-advocacy; opportunities in school, home and community.
- Prepare children and youth for school meetings.
- Speak directly to children and youth.
- Involve children and youth in educational, medical, and family decisions.
- Allow for mistakes and natural consequences.
- Listen often to children and youth.

**ENCOURAGE EXPLORATION OF POSSIBILITIES**

- Promote exploration of the world every day.
- Use personal, tactile, visual, and auditory methods for exploration.
- Identify young adult mentors with similar disabilities.
- Talk about future jobs, hobbies, and family lifestyles.
- Develop personal collages/scrap books based on interests and goals.
- Involve children and youth in service learning (4H, Ameri-Corps, local volunteering).

**PROMOTE REASONABLE RISK TAKING**

- Make choice maps listing risks, benefits, and consequences of choice.
- Build safety nets through family members, friends, schools, and others.
- Develop skills in problem solving.
- Develop skills in evaluating consequences.

**ENCOURAGE PROBLEM SOLVING**

- Teach problem solving skills.
- Allow ownership of challenges and problems.
- Accept problems as part of healthy development.
- Hold family meetings to identify problems at home and in the community.
- Hold class meetings to identify problems in school.
- Allow children and youth to develop a list of self-identified consequences.

**PROMOTE SELF-ADVOCACY**

- Encourage communication and self-representation.

- Praise all efforts of assertiveness and problem solving.
- Develop opportunities at home and in school for self-advocacy.
- Provide opportunities for leadership roles at home and in school.
- Encourage self-advocates to speak in class.
- Teach about appropriate accommodation needs.
- Practice ways to disclose disability and accommodation needs.
- Create opportunities to speak about the disability in school, home, church, business and community.

**FACILITATE DEVELOPMENT OF SELF-ESTEEM**

- Create a sense of belonging within schools and communities.
- Provide experiences for children and youth to use their talents.
- Provide opportunities to youth for contributing to their families, schools, and communities.
- Provide opportunities for individuality and independence.
- Identify caring adult mentors at home, school, church, or in the community.
- Model a sense of self-esteem and self-confidence.

**DEVELOP GOAL SETTING AND PLANNING**

- Teach children and youth family values, priorities, and goals.
- Make posters that reflect values and are age-appropriate.
- Define what a goal is and demonstrate the steps to reach a goal.
- Make a road map to mark the short-term identifiers as they work toward a goal.
- Support children and youth in developing values and goals.
- Discuss family history and culture—make a family tree.
- Be flexible in supporting youth to reach their goals; some days they may need much motivation and help; other days they may want to try alone.

**HELP YOUTH UNDERSTAND THEIR DISABILITIES**

- Develop a process that is directed by youth for self-identity: Who are you? What do you want? What are your challenges and barriers? What supports do you need?
- Direct children and youth to write an autobiography.
- Talk about the youth's disability.
- Talk about the youth's abilities.
- Involve children and youth in their IEP.
- Use good learning style inventories and transition assessments.
- Identify and utilize support systems for all people.

SOURCE: Self-determination: Supporting successful transition by C. D., Bremer, M. Kachgal, & K. Schoeller, 2003, April, *Research to Practice Brief of the National Center on Secondary Education and Transition, 2* (1), p. 3.

and product labels. Information skills may include reading job application forms, classified ads, maps, telephone directories, and catalogs.

With the job market's increasing emphasis on academics, there is a growing concern about students with disabilities having the opportunity to earn a high school diploma. Since employers views the high school diploma as a minimum requirement signaling competence, what does this mean for students with disabilities who are unable to meet academic criteria? Many students with disabilities do not receive the same high school diploma as their peers without disabilities. Some states and

In many school districts, students with disabilities must meet the same requirements as their peers without disabilities in order to receive a high school diploma. Do you think students with disabilities should be held to the same standards as those who are not disabled?

local school districts have adopted graduation criteria that include successful completion of a certain number of credits. Students with disabilities must meet the same requirements as their peers in order to receive a "regular" high school diploma. If a student with a disability fails to meet graduation requirements, he or she may be awarded an "IEP diploma," marking progress toward annual goals, or a certificate of high school completion (or attendance). IEP diplomas and certificates of completion communicate that a student was unable to meet the requirements to obtain a standard diploma.

Other states award students with disabilities the standard high school diploma on the basis of modified criteria that are individually referenced, reflecting the successful completion of IEP goals and objectives as determined by a multidisciplinary team of professionals and the student's parents. For more insight into the controversy surrounding this issue, see the nearby Debate Forum, "Students with Disabilities and the Meaning of a High School Diploma."

## Teaching Adaptive and Functional Life Skills

Students with disabilities need access to social activities in the secondary school years. Adaptive and functional life skills training may include accessing socialization activities in and out of school and learning to manage one's personal affairs. It may be important to provide basic instruction on how to develop positive interpersonal relationships and the behaviors that are conducive to participating successfully in community settings (Agran & Wehmeyer, 1999; McDonnell et al., 2003; Wehmeyer, 2001). Instruction may include co-teaching among general and special education teachers, as well as the use of peer tutors to both model and teach appropriate social skills in community settings such as restaurants, theaters, and shopping malls. See nearby Reflect on This, "Co-Teaching in a High School Life Skills Class."

## Preparation for Employment

People with disabilities are often characterized as consumers of society's resources rather than as contributors, but employment goes a long way toward dispelling this idea. Paid employment means earning wages through which individuals can buy goods and enhance their quality of life; it also contributes to personal identity and status (Drew & Hardman, 2004).

In the past, high schools have been somewhat passive in their approach to employment training, focusing primarily on teaching vocational readiness through simulations in a classroom setting. More recently, high schools have begun to emphasize employment preparation for students with disabilities through work experience, career education, and community-referenced instruction. In a work experience program, the student spends a portion of the school day in classroom settings (which may emphasize academic and/or vocational skills) and the remainder at an off-campus site receiving on-the-job training. The responsibility for the training may be shared among the high school special education teacher, vocational rehabilitation counselor, and vocational education teacher.

## Debate Forum

# STUDENTS WITH DISABILITIES AND THE MEANING OF A HIGH SCHOOL DIPLOMA

Should students with disabilities be required to demonstrate the same academic competence as their peers without disabilities in order to receive a high school diploma? Or, if they are unable to meet graduation requirements, should they receive an IEP diploma or certificate of completion?

### POINT

The purpose of a high school diploma is to communicate to employers, colleges, and society in general that an individual has acquired a specified set of knowledge and skills that prepares him or her to leave school and enter postsecondary education or the world of work. All students must be held to the same standards, or the diploma will have no meaning as a "signal" of competence and will make no impression on employers or colleges. For those students with disabilities who cannot meet graduation requirements, there is certainly a need to signal what the individual has achieved during high school, even though it is not to the same performance level as those who are awarded the diploma. This can be accomplished through a certificate of completion with modified criteria for graduation. What is most important is not to devalue the high school diploma by lowering the requirements for earning it. Otherwise, employers and colleges will continue to lose faith in public education as a credible system for preparing students for the future.

### COUNTERPOINT

Although the move to hold all students to specific requirements (or standards) is to be applauded, it is discriminatory to expect all students to meet the same standards in order to receive a high school diploma. The purpose of a high school diploma is to communicate that the individual has demonstrated a "personal best" while in school, thus acquiring knowledge and a set of skills consistent with his or her ability. I would also support the viewpoint that students with disabilities can achieve at much higher levels than they do now, and expectations should be raised. However, some will never be able to satisfy the graduation requirements now in place in many states and school districts. Students with disabilities who cannot perform at the level mandated in graduation requirements should still be awarded a standard diploma based on their having met requirements consistent with their individual needs and abilities. This is the basis of a free and appropriate public education for students with disabilities. If a standard diploma is not awarded, students with disabilities will be immediately singled out as incompetent and will be at a major disadvantage with employers, regardless of the skills they possess.

What do you think? To give your opinion, go to Chapter 4 of the companion website (ablongman.com/hardman8e), and click on Debate Forum.

---

Career education includes training in social skills development as well as general occupational skills. Career education programs usually concentrate on becoming aware of various career choices, exploring occupational opportunities, and developing appropriate attitudes, social skills, and work habits.

Whereas career education is geared to developing an awareness of various occupations, community-referenced instruction involves direct training and ongoing support in a community employment site. The demands of the work setting and the functioning level, interests, and wishes of each individual determine the goals and objectives of the training. The most notable difference between community-referenced instruction and work experience programs is that the former focuses on the activities to be accomplished at the work site rather than on the development of isolated skills in the classroom. An employment training program based on a community-referenced approach includes the following elements:

- A primary focus on student and family needs and preferences
- A balance between time spent in inclusive general education classrooms and placement and employment preparation at least until age 18
- A curriculum that reflects the job opportunities available in the local community
- An employment training program that takes place at actual job sites

## CO-TEACHING IN A HIGH SCHOOL LIFE SKILLS CLASS

A general education teacher and a special education teacher co-teach the "Survival Skills" class at Ralston High School in Nebraska. General education course offerings at Ralston include a full array of college preparatory and basic academic classes, elective courses, and honors classes. Special education services within the building provided a continuum of resource classes, strategy instruction, self-contained subject classes, life skills instruction, community-based instruction, and community job placements with job coaching. Concurrently, academic departments reduced the number of basic track classes, and the special education department minimized the use of self-contained classes, while retaining the continuum of special services on a much smaller scale.

### Meet the Co-Teachers

A special education teacher who was certified to teach students with mild disabilities and the home economics teacher agreed to redesign "Survival Skills." The home economics teacher had no previous experience with co-teaching but wanted to address the needs of students with mild and moderate disabilities who frequently enrolled in her classes. The special education teacher was well informed about co-teaching from reading, research, and her prior teaching experiences with a social studies teacher and a math teacher. Both teachers were experienced in their respective areas of certification, and both had taught students with a variety of disabilities.

Together the co-teachers restructured the curriculum with community experiences and simulations and modifications for reading, writing, mathematics, and oral language. The general education teacher selected most curriculum topics and materials, and the special education teacher introduced ideas for modifications based on the disabilities of students likely to enroll in the class.

- The special education co-teacher communicated with resource teachers to obtain information from students' individualized education programs (IEPs), to inform resource teachers of progress or concerns, to arrange support for assignments outside of class, and to arrange consultation services for students with hearing impairments or cognitive disabilities.
- The co-teachers shared many responsibilities: lesson planning, responding to phone inquiries, arranging field trips, grading papers, obtaining guest presenters, and applying for a corporate mini-grant.

SOURCE: From "Co-teaching: An Inclusive Curriculum for Transition," by E. Fennick, 2001, *Teaching Exceptional Children,* July/August, pp. 60–62.

---

- Training designed to sample the student's performance across a variety of economically viable alternatives
- Ongoing opportunities for students to interact with peers without disabilities in a work setting
- Training that culminates in employment placement
- Job placement linked to comprehensive transition planning, which focuses on establishing interagency agreements that support the student's full participation in the community. (Drew & Hardman, 2004; Moon & Inge, 2000).

For more insight into employment preparation during the high school years, see the nearby Case Study, "Maria."

# The Adult Years

In the past, much of the attention paid to people with disabilities focused on children and youth. More recently, professionals and parents have begun to address the challenges encountered by adults, altering our overall perspective of disability and broadening the views across the disciplines. Would Adolphe's life in the nearby Snapshot have been better if intervention had occurred when he was younger? What can be done now to ensure that Adolphe has the supports he needs to participate actively in the life of his community?

When we reach adulthood, we leave home, go to college or get a job, and become more self-reliant. For adults with disabilities, living situations and lifestyles vary greatly. Many people with disabilities lead a somewhat typical existence, living and working in their community, perhaps marrying, and for the most part supporting themselves financially. These adults may still need support, however, as may people

## MARIA

Maria is 19 years old and leaving high school to begin her adult life. For most of her high school years, she was in special education classes for reading and math, because she was about three grade levels behind her peers without disabilities. During the last term of high school, she attended a class on exploring possible careers and finding and keeping a job. The class was required for graduation, but it didn't make much sense to Maria because she had never had any experience with this area before. It just didn't seem to be related to her other schoolwork.

Although Maria wants to get a job in a retail store (such as stocking clothing or shoes), she isn't having much success. She doesn't have a driver's license, and her parents don't have time to run her around to apply for various jobs. The businesses she approached are close by her home and know her well, but they keep telling her she isn't *qualified* for the jobs available. She has never had any on-the-job training in the community.

Maria's parents are not very enthusiastic about her finding employment because they are afraid she might lose some of her government-funded medical benefits.

### APPLICATION

1. In retrospect, what transition planning services would you have recommended for Maria during her last years of high school?

2. How would you help Maria now? Do you see the Americans with Disabilities Act playing a role in Maria's story?

3. Whose responsibility is it to work with potential employers to explore "the reasonable accommodations" that would facilitate the opportunity for Maria to succeed in a community job?

---

who are not disabled. That support is most often "time-limited" (such as vocational rehabilitation services) or informal (attention from family members and friends). Those with more severe disabilities reach adulthood still in need of a formal support system that facilitates their opportunities for access to paid employment, housing in the community, and recreation and leisure experiences.

The next section examines some of the decisions that individuals with disabilities and their families face during the adult years. This chapter concludes with a discussion about what it takes to build a support network for adults with disabilities.

## Making Choices

For people with disabilities and their families, adult life is often paradoxical. On the one hand, many parents struggle with their son or daughter's "right to grow up." On the other hand, some families must face the realities of a continuing need for support, further complicated by the issues surrounding what legally or practically constitutes adult status. Just as there is a great deal of variability in the needs and functioning level of people with disabilities, there is also considerable variability in lifestyle during the adult years. Some adults with mild disabilities go on to college and become self-supporting, eventually working and becoming quite independent of their immediate family. As is true for people without disabilities, however, some of these adults may still need assistance, whether it be government-funded or from family, friends, and neighbors. For adults with more severe disabilities, ongoing formal and natural supports are critical in order to ensure their access to and participation in employment, supported residential living, and recreation in their local community. Parents and family members of people with severe disabilities often face the stark reality that their caregiving role may not diminish during the adult years of the family member with disabilities and could well extend through his or her lifetime. About 60% of adults with more severe disabilities of all ages live at home with their parents and/or siblings (Heller, 2000). One in four of the family caregivers is over the age of 60 years (Braddock, 1999).

Whereas most people face many choices as a natural part of the transition into adult life, the questions facing a person with disabilities and his or her family may be quite different. Issues concerning the competence of the person with a disability to make decisions in his or her best interest, as well as the role of formal and informal support networks to assist in such decision making, may also arise.

# Adolphe

Adolphe was 31 when he came to what may have been the most startling realization of his life: he was learning disabled! Adolphe was uncertain what this label meant, but at least he now had a term for what had mostly been a difficult life. The label came from a clinical psychologist who had administered a number of tests after Adolphe had been referred by his counselor, whom he had been seeing since his divorce a year ago. The past year had been particularly rough, although most of Adolphe's life had been troublesome.

As a young child, Adolphe was often left out of group activities. He was not very adept at sports, was uncoordinated, and could not catch or hit a baseball no matter how hard he tried. School was worse. Adolphe had a difficult time completing assignments and often forgot instructions. Paying attention in class was difficult, and it often seemed as though there were more interesting activities than the assignments. Adolphe finally gave up on school when he was a junior and took a job in a local service station. That employment did not last long, for he was terminated because of frequent billing errors. The owners said they could not afford to lose so much money because of "stupid mistakes on credit card invoices."

The loss of that job did not bother Adolphe much. An enterprising young man, he had already found employment in the post office, which paid much more and seemed to have greater respectability. Sorting letters presented a problem, however, and loss of that job did trouble Adolphe. He began to doubt his mental ability further and sought comfort in his girlfriend, whom he had met recently at a YMCA dance. They married quickly when she became pregnant, but things did not become easier. After 12 years of marriage, two children, a divorce, and five jobs, Adolphe is finally gaining some understanding of why he has been so challenged throughout his life.

**FOCUS 5**

Describe government-funded and natural supports for people with disabilities.

**Income support**

A government-sponsored program whereby the individual receives cash payments to support living needs.

**Medicaid**

A government-sponsored health care program for eligible people with disabilities and others that pays for hospital services, laboratory services, and early screening, diagnosis, treatment, and immunization for children.

## Building a Support Network

Adults with disabilities and their families must not only come to terms with planning for the future but must also deal with the maze of options of government-funded programs. Over the past 30 years, adult services have gone through major reform. The system has evolved from a narrow focus on protecting, managing, and caring for persons with disabilities in segregated settings to a broadened focus on providing what is necessary for the person to participate in family and community life. As we move through the 21st century, adult services will continue adapting to the changing needs and preferences of the person with a disability and his or her network of family and friends. However, as suggested by a recent survey of Americans with disabilities (N.O.D./Harris, 2000), there is still a long way to go.

**GOVERNMENT-FUNDED PROGRAMS.** Federal and state governments fund several different programs for people with disabilities. These include income support, health care, Medicare, supported residential living, and employment.

**Income Support.** Government **income support** programs, enacted through Social Security legislation (Supplemental Security Income [SSI] and Social Security Disability Insurance [SSDI]), provide direct cash payments to people with disabilities, thus providing basic economic assistance. Income support programs have been both praised and criticized. They have been praised because money is provided to people in need who otherwise would have no means to support themselves. They have been criticized because such support programs can make it economically advantageous for people with disabilities to remain unemployed and dependent on society. For many years, individuals who went to work at even 50% of minimum wage could lose income support and medical benefits whose value far exceeded the amount they would earn on the job. This disincentive to work has been significantly reduced with passage of the Work Incentives Improvement Act. Many people with disabilities can now go to work and not worry about losing critical health care coverage.

**Health Care.** Government-sponsored health care for people with disabilities comes under two programs: Medicaid and Medicare. **Medicaid,** established in 1965, pays for health care services for individuals receiving SSI cash payments, as well as for families receiving welfare payments. Medicaid is an example of a federal–state partnership program that requires participating states to provide funds to match available federal dollars. The state match can be as low as 22% and as high as 50%, depending on state per capita income.

The Medicaid program can pay for inpatient and outpatient hospital services, laboratory services, and early screening, diagnosis, treatment, and immunization for children. Working within federal regulations, states design their own plans for the delivery of Medicaid services. Thus a service provided in one state may not be provided in another.

**Medicare** is a national insurance program for individuals over the age of 65 and for eligible people with disabilities. Medicare has two parts: hospital insurance and supplementary medical insurance. The Hospital Insurance Program pays for short-term hospitalization, related care in skilled nursing facilities, and some home care. The Supplementary Medical Insurance Program covers physician services, outpatient services, ambulance services, some medical supplies, and medical equipment.

**Supported Residential Living.**   For most of the 20th century, federal government support for residential living was directed to large congregate care settings (institutions and nursing homes). In the 21st century, however, people with disabilities, their families, and professionals are advocating for smaller community-based residences within local neighborhoods and communities. In the past 20 years, spending for smaller community residences increased sevenfold (Braddock, Hemp, Rizzolo, Parish, & Pomeranz, 2002). People with disabilities and their families are also advocating for choice, individualization, and a focus on people's abilities, rather than on their disabilities, in making decisions about community living.

Three of the most widely used models for residential living are group homes, semi-independent homes and apartments, and foster family care. **Group homes** may be large (as many as fifteen or more people) or small (four or fewer people). In the group home model, professionals provide ongoing training and support to people with disabilities, aiming to make daily living experiences as similar as possible to those of people who are not disabled. The **semi-independent apartment or home** provides housing for people with disabilities who may require less supervision and support. This model for residential living may include apartment clusters (several apartments located close together), a single co-residence home or apartment in which a staff member shares the dwelling, or a single home or apartment occupied by a person with a disability who may or may not receive assistance from a professional.

**Foster family care** provides a surrogate family for persons with a disability. The goal of foster care is to integrate individuals with disabilities into a family setting where they will learn adaptive skills and work in the community. Foster family care settings may accommodate up to six adults with disabilities.

**Employment.**   Sustained competitive employment for people with disabilities is important for many reasons (such as monetary rewards, adult identity, social contacts, and inclusion in a community setting). Yet adults with disabilities are significantly underemployed and unemployed when compared to their peers without disabilities (N.O.D./Harris, 2000).

In spite of discouraging data on the unemployment rates of people with disabilities, there is good reason to be optimistic about their future employment opportunities. A greater emphasis is being placed on employment opportunities for these people than ever before (Braddock et al., 2002; Ryan, 2000). Competitive employment can now be described in terms of three alternatives: employment with no support services, employment with time-limited support services, and employment with ongoing support services.

An adult with a disability may be able to locate and maintain employment without support from government-funded programs. Many find jobs through contacts with family and friends, a local job service, want ads, and the like. For people with mild disabilities, the potential for locating and maintaining a job is enhanced greatly if the individual has received employment training and experience during the school years.

**Medicare**

A government-sponsored national insurance program for people over 65 years of age and eligible people with disabilities. Medicare may pay for hospital and physician-related costs.

**Group home**

A supported living arrangement for people with disabilities, in which professionals provide ongoing training and support in a community home setting.

**Semi-independent apartment or home**

A model for providing housing for persons with disabilities who may require less supervision and support.

**Foster family care**

A supported living arrangement for persons with disabilities, whereby an individual(s) lives in a family setting, learns adaptive skills, and works in a community job.

*Vocational rehabilitation services include intensive short-term training and support for people with disabilities who are seeking gainful employment. What are some other community employment and support living services available to people with disabilities?*

An adult with a disability may also have access to several employment services on a time-limited, short-term basis; these services may include vocational rehabilitation, vocational education, and on-the-job training. Time-limited employment services provide intensive, short-term support to people with disabilities who have the potential to make it on their own after receiving government assistance. **Vocational rehabilitation,** for example provides services to enable people with disabilities, including those with the most severe disabilities, to pursue meaningful careers by securing gainful employment commensurate with their preferences and abilities. Through the vocational rehabilitation program, federal funds pass to the states to provide services in counseling, training, and job placement. Vocational rehabilitation services may also include short-term job training for those who are in a supported employment program.

**Supported employment** is work in an integrated setting provided for people with disabilities who need some type of continuing support and for whom competitive employment has traditionally not been possible. The criteria for supported employment programs require that the job provide at least 20 hours of work per week in a real job setting.

Over the past two decades, supported employment has become a viable employment program for people with disabilities who need long-term support. In the United States, federal and state funding for supported employment programs increased by 33% from 1996 to 2000. The number of people with disabilities participating in supported employment increased by 22%. The efficacy of supported employment has been documented through a variety of research studies (Mank, Cioffi, & Yovanoff, 1998; Morgan, Ellerd, Jensen, & Taylor, 2000).

Supported employment consists of four main features: wages, social integration with peers who are not disabled, ongoing support provided as necessary by a job coach or through natural supports (co-workers), and application of a zero-exclusion principle. A zero-exclusion principle veers from the more traditional approach of "getting individuals with disabilities ready for work" to a principle of placing the individual on a job and providing the necessary supports to ensure success. The essential element of a successful supported employment program is establishing a match between the needs and abilities of the individual and the demands of a particular job.

**NATURAL SUPPORTS.** The importance of natural supports for adults with disabilities, including family, friends, neighbors, and co-workers, cannot be overstated. As is true for all of us, adults with disabilities need a support network that extends beyond government-funded programs. Some adults with disabilities may never move away from their primary family. Parents, and in some cases siblings, assume the major responsibilities of ongoing support for a lifetime (Freedman, Krauss, & Seltzer, 1997). It is estimated that eight out of ten adults with more severe disabilities live with their parents for most of their lives (Braddock et al., 2002; Seltzer & Krauss, 1994). This "perpetual parenthood" results from a son or daughter's continuing dependence through the adult years, either because of a lack of formal resources for the family or because the family simply chooses to care for the individual at home.

### Vocational rehabilitation

A government-sponsored program to help people with disabilities find employment consistent with their needs and abilities.

### Supported employment

Employment in an integrated setting provided for people with disabilities who need some type of continuing support and for whom competitive employment has traditionally not been possible.

Siblings appear to have attitudes similar to those of their parents. A study by Griffiths and Unger (1994) suggested that many siblings believe that families should be responsible for the care of members who are disabled. Most indicated that they were "willing to assume future caregiving responsibilities for their brothers/sisters" (p. 225). In a longitudinal study of 140 families who had adults with mental retardation still living at home, Krauss, Seltzer, Gordon, and Friedman (1996) found that many siblings remained very actively involved with their brother or sister well into the adult years. These siblings had frequent contact with their brother or sister and were knowledgeable about the life of their sibling with a disability. In addition, they played a major role in their parents' support network. Interestingly, about one in three of these siblings reported planning to reside with their brother or sister at some point during the latter's adult life.

Extended family members (grandparents, aunts, uncles, and so on) often remain important sources of support as well. Extended family members may help with transportation, meals, housecleaning, or just "being there" for the individual. Similar support may also come from friends, neighbors, and co-workers. The nature and type of support provided by individuals outside of the family will be unique to the individuals involved and will depend on a mutual level of comfort in both seeking and providing assistance. Clear communication regarding what friends or neighbors are willing to do, and how that matches with the needs and preferences of each individual, is essential.

From the high school transition years through adult life, the issues surrounding quality services and supports for people with disabilities are ever-changing, varied, and complex. With the information in Chapters 1 through 4 as a foundation, we will now move on to a discussion of multicultural and diversity issues in the education of students with disabilities.

# FOCUS REVIEW

**FOCUS 1** **What do we know about access to community living and employment for people with disabilities after they leave school?**

- Special education graduates are often unable to participate fully in community activities and are socially isolated in comparison to people without disabilities.
- Many current graduates are not adequately prepared for employment and are unable to get help to enroll in higher education. The majority of adults with disabilities are unemployed.
- Adult service systems do not have the resources to meet the needs of students with disabilities after the school years.

- The capabilities of adults with disabilities are often underestimated.

**FOCUS 2** **What are the requirements for transition planning in IDEA?**

- IDEA requires that every student with a disability receive transition services.
- Transition services must be designed within an outcome-oriented process, which promotes movement from school to postschool activities.
- Transition services must be based on the individual student's needs, taking into account the student's preferences and interests.

- Transition services must include instruction, related services, community experiences, the development of employment, and other postschool adult living objectives.
- IDEA requires that, beginning at age 16 and updated annually, a student's IEP should include appropriate measurable postsecondary goals related to training, education, employment, and, where appropriate, independent living skills.
- The IEP must include a statement of transition services that relate to various courses of study that will assist the student in reaching their goals.

**FOCUS 3** Identify the purpose of an ITP and the basic steps in its formulation.

- An ITP is developed to ensure each student's access to the general education curriculum and/or a focus on the adaptive and functional skills that will facilitate life in the community following school. The ITP identifies the type and range of transitional services that are needed and establishes timelines and personnel responsible.

- The basic steps in the formulation of the ITP include convening an IEP team individualized in terms of the wants and needs of each transition-age student, reviewing assessment data and conducting additional assessment activities, developing and implementing the ITP, updating the ITP annually during IEP meetings and implementing follow-up procedures, and holding an exit meeting.

**FOCUS 4** Why is it important for students with disabilities to receive instruction in self-determination, academics, adaptive and functional life skills, and employment preparation during the secondary school years?

- Self-determination skills help students to solve problems, consider options, and make appropriate choices as they negotiate the transition into adult life.

- Academic skills are essential in meeting high school graduation requirements and preparing students with disabilities for college. A functional academic program helps students learn applied skills in daily living, leisure activities, and employment preparation.

- Adaptive and functional life skills help students learn how to socialize with others, maintain their personal appearance, and make choices about how to spend free time.

- Employment preparation during high school increases the probability of success on the job during the adult years and places the person with a disability in the role of a contributor to society.

**FOCUS 5** Describe government-funded and natural supports for people with disabilities.

- Income support programs are direct cash payments to people with disabilities, providing basic economic assistance.

- Medicaid and Medicare are government-supported health care programs. The Medicaid program can pay for inpatient and outpatient hospital services, laboratory services, and early screening, diagnosis, treatment, and immunization for children. Medicare is a national insurance program with two parts: hospital insurance and supplementary medical insurance.

- Residential services indicate a trend toward smaller, community-based residences located within local neighborhoods and communities. These residences may include group homes, semi-independent homes and apartments, and/or foster family care. The purpose of residential services is to give persons with disabilities a variety of options for living in the community.

- There are essentially three approaches to competitive employment for people with disabilities: employment with no support services, employment with time-limited support services, and employment with ongoing support services. The purpose of all three approaches is to assist people with disabilities in obtaining a job and maintaining it over time.

- Natural supports include family, friends, neighbors, and coworkers.

## FURTHER READINGS

Agran, M., Wehmeyer, M., Hughes, C., & Wehman, P. (1997). *Teaching Self-Determination to Students with Disabilities: Basic Skills for Successful Transition.* Baltimore: Paul H. Brookes.

*This book presents strategies for promoting autonomous and self-regulated behavior for people with disabilities. The authors discuss the development of self-advocacy and leadership skills, assertiveness and effective communication, self-realization, and empowerment.*

Brinckerhoff, L. C., McGuire, J. M., & Shaw, S. F. (2001). *Transition to Postsecondary Education: Strategies for Students with Learning Disabilities* (2nd ed.). Austin, TX: ProEd.

*This book provides in-depth information on transition planning from high school to college, determining eligibility for services and testing accommodations, policy development, provision of accommodations, service delivery options for college students with learning disabilities and attention deficit hyperactive disorder (ADHD), advances in assistive technology, and approaches to professional development and program evaluation.*

Wehman, P. (2001). *Life Beyond the Classroom: Transition Strategies for Young People with Disabilities* (3rd ed.). Baltimore: Paul H. Brookes.

*This book provides comprehensive coverage of transition issues, including defining and planning transition, facilitation and support of transition, and ways of customizing delivery of transition services to people with specific types of disabilities. Information is also provided on person-centered planning and* *consumer choice, control, and satisfaction, as well as on independent living, mobility, and assistive technology.*

## WEB RESOURCES

### National Center on Secondary Education and Transition

www.ncset.org

The National Center on Secondary Education and Transition (NCSET) at the University of Minnesota coordinates national resources, offers technical assistance, and disseminates information related to secondary education and transition for youth with disabilities in order to create opportunities for them to achieve successful futures. This website contains information on transition issues, publications, other links, and state resources.

### Transition Research Institute at the University of Illinois at Urbana-Champaign

www.ed.uiuc.edu/SPED/tri/institute.html

The Transition Research Institute at the University of Illinois at Urbana-Champaign (TRI) identifies effective prac-

tices, conducts intervention and evaluation research, and provides technical assistance activities that promote the successful transition of youth with disabilities from school to adult life. This website contains resources (such as recent publications, videos, and curricula) for teachers, service providers, and researchers on transition.

### Association for Persons in Supported Employment

www.apse.org

The Association for Persons in Supported Employment provides information on improving and expanding integrated employment opportunities, services, and outcomes for persons with disabilities. This website provides information on supported employment resources and education for professionals, consumers, family members, and employers.

## BUILDING YOUR PORTFOLIO

If you are thinking about a career in special education, you should know that many states use national standards developed by the Council for Exceptional Children (CEC) to assess a teacher candidate's knowledge about and skills for working with students with disabilities. See a complete listing of the ten CEC Content Standards on the inside front cover of this text.

### CEC Content Standards Addressed in Chapter 4

1. Foundations
2. Development and Characteristics of Learners
3. Individual Learning Differences
4. Instructional Strategies
5. Learning Environments and Social Interactions
7. Instructional Planning
9. Professional and Ethical Practice

### Assess Your Knowledge of the CEC Standards Addressed in Chapter 4

Some states require that teacher candidates develop a portfolio of products that demonstrate mastery of the CEC content standards. To assist in the development of products for this portfolio, you may wish to complete the following activities.

- Complete a written test of the chapter's content.

  *If your instructor requires a written test of your content knowledge for this chapter, keep a copy for your portfolio. A practice test on the information covered in this chapter is available through the companion website (www. ablongman .com/hardman8e) and the Student Study Guide.*

- Respond to Application Questions for the Case Study "Maria."

  *Review the Case Study and respond in writing to the application questions. Keep a copy of the case study and your written response for your portfolio.*

- Complete the "Take a Stand" activity for the Debate Forum "Students with Disabilities and the Meaning of a High School Diploma."

  *Read the Debate Forum in this chapter and then visit the Companion Website to complete the activity "Take a Stand." Keep a copy of this activity for your portfolio.*

- Participate in a Community Service Learning Activity.

  *Community service is a valuable way to enhance your learning experience. Visit our Companion Website for suggested community service learning activities that correspond to the information presented in this chapter. Develop a reflective journal of the service learning experience for your portfolio.*

## THEMES OF THE TIMES

Expand your knowledge of the concepts discussed in this chapter by reading current and historical articles from the *New York Times* by visiting the "Themes of the Times" section of the companion website:
www.ablongman.com/hardman8e.

# Multicultural and Diversity Issues

## Potential Bias in Testing Minority Children

Youngsters from minority backgrounds do appear more frequently in disability categories than would be expected on the basis of the proportion of culturally different people in the population. This high rate of identification often involves assessment using psychoeducational instruments, which suggests that the assessment and uses of test information may include serious bias. (e.g., Bondurant-Utz, 2002; Spinelli, 2002)

## Poverty More Often Found in Some Minority Groups

Proportionally, almost three times as many African Americans and Hispanics as non-Hispanic whites live in poverty. (U.S. Bureau of the Census, 2000)

## Early Learning May Account for Some Cultural Differences

Learning during the early years plays a vitally important role in later behavior. The content of what is learned during this period may produce sociocultural differences that set minority youngsters apart from their peers in the cultural majority. (Capage, Bennet, & McNeil, 2001; Harrison-Hale, 2002)

## Multicultural Education Aimed at All Students

Multicultural education is intended to teach all students about different cultures. It teaches all students about cultural diversity, shows them how to function in a multicultural society, and has the goal of enhancing equity for marginalized groups of children. (Banks, 2003; Seidl & Friend, 2002)

**FOCUS**

**PREVIEW:** To preview the central concepts of this chapter, read the focus questions located in the margins. Using these questions as a guide, ask yourself what you already know and what you want to learn.

# Denise

"Denise is a 9-year-old African American girl in the fourth grade. Her elementary school is in a midsize city in the south-eastern United States. Denise lives with her parents and two older brothers in an apartment complex in a working-class African American neighborhood. Because of recent redistricting, Denise is being bused from an all-black school in her neighborhood to a predominantly middle-class white elementary school across town. This is her first year in the school, and Denise is one of only five African American girls in the fourth grade.

"Denise has always been a good student with no social problems. This had been the case when she started the year at her new school. Recently, however, Denise has gotten into fights with several of her classmates. She has also been failing to complete her classwork and has been talking back to her teacher."[1]

# Raphael

Ten-year-old Raphael lives with his adoptive parents. He is proud of his deafness—he accepts it and is comfortable with it. His mother is very conscientious about using sign language whenever Raphael is in the room, even if she is speaking to someone else. "If Raphael is watching, then I will sign. He deserves it."

Raphael does very well integrating with his hearing peers at recess. There are a group of guys—little boys—10 or 11 years old who are always coming around, "Can Raphael come out? Can Raphael do this? . . . Just ask him if he'll play with me." A lot of them are picking up the basic signs. So there's a lot of interaction going on.

"He's one of the most popular kids in the neighborhood, and he can play with anybody. He knows how to get his point of view across to the others, and the others—they make up their own little signs that are not really sign language or anything, but they know what they're talking about. When we first moved to this neighborhood, the responses we got from our neighbors, that we have a deaf kid is, 'Wow. That's neat,' and then they'd kind of go, 'All right, now let's hold back.'

Denise's situation presents a significant challenge for the education system and raises a number of questions. Should someone in the school system be fighting to keep Denise from being labeled? Or should she be classified as having disabilities so that she can receive specialized help? Should she be considered as having disabilities because of her behavioral and academic difficulties? Do her problems reflect stress related to the change in school or cultural stressors? In this chapter, we will examine many such complicated issues related to cultural and ethnic diversity and their impact on public education.

Our complex culture reflects an enormous array of needs because a wide variety of individuals take part in our society. Meeting those needs seriously tests the capacities of service organizations such as the education system and of many other private and governmental agencies. Because so many groups require special attention, advocacy groups have emerged to champion certain causes. In some of these cases, a particular group's educational needs have not been adequately met by school systems that are structured to serve the majority.

**Multicultural education** arose from a belief that the needs of certain children—children whose cultural backgrounds differ from those of the majority—were not being appropriately met. Broad societal unrest related to racial discrimination fueled and augmented this belief. Similarly, **special education** evolved from the failure of general education to meet the needs of youngsters who were not learning as rapidly or in the same way as their peers. Reformers believed that two particular groups of students were being mistreated—in one case, because of their cultural or racial background, and in the other, because of their disabilities.

To explore multiculturalism and diversity, we will first discuss the basic purpose of general education and the conventional approaches used to achieve this purpose. We will also compare the underlying purposes and approaches of special education and multicultural education and discuss the connections between the two. After building this foundation, we will examine multicultural and diversity issues in the context of this book's focus: human exceptionality in society, school,

**Multicultural education**

Education that promotes learning about multiple cultures and their values.

**Special education**

As defined in IDEA, specially designed instruction provided to students with disabilities in all settings, including the workplace and training centers.

But when he goes out there, they see that he can play basketball with any kid in his neighborhood, that he can play street hockey, he can rollerblade, he can ride bikes, and he's not a problem to anybody. In fact, he's the most popular kid in the neighborhood.

"I see Raphael's future as . . . I'm really not sure yet. He's really getting involved in his computers at school. And I'd like to see him continue that way. His working with computers has made a whole new person out of him."

## Daniel

"Daniel is an 8-year-old second-grader. He and his family arrived in the United States from Mexico two years ago. Daniel has a 14-year-old brother, Julian, who is in middle school. Julian fills a role that is common for children in recently immigrated families, serving as the family's link to the English-speaking world through his ability to translate. Three additional siblings born between Daniel and his brother are still in Mexico. The family's support system includes the father's brothers and their wives, all recent immigrants from Mexico. Daniel's father is a construction worker, and his mother is a housewife.

"Daniel's academic performance has been average. He has consistently submitted required assignments, he has perfect attendance, and his interactions with teachers and peers have been good. Recently, Daniel's academic performance has declined, and he has become withdrawn. His teacher, Mrs. Strickland, noted that Daniel has failed several tests, that he has not had his parents sign the required school folder (which includes the tests he failed), and that he has not had his parents sign permission slips needed for planned field trips. As a result, Daniel has lost recess privileges, has had to eat by himself at lunch time, and has not been allowed to participate in two field trips. (Although he had earned the right to participate in the field trips, the fact that he did not have written parental permission prevented him from doing so.)

"Mrs. Strickland wrote the parents a note on Daniel's folder, explaining that they needed to sign his folder and that Daniel needed to study for his tests. She also telephoned Daniel's home and talked to 'someone' there about the situation who said, 'OK.' Mrs. Strickland had become extremely frustrated because there had been no change. Every morning, she reprimanded Daniel for not bringing the required signed folder and demanded an explanation. Daniel did not respond."[2]

[1]SOURCE: Excerpted from "Counseling Interventions with African American Youth," by D. C. Locke. In *Counseling for Diversity*, edited by C. C. Lee, 1995, pp. 26–27. Boston: Allyn & Bacon, Inc. Reprinted by permission.

[2]SOURCE: Excerpted from "Counseling Hispanic Children and Youth," by J. T. Zapata. In *Counseling for Diversity*, edited by C. C. Lee, 1995, pp. 103–104. Boston: Allyn & Bacon. Reprinted by permission.

and family. This process will highlight an interesting twist on one of the major themes of the book: collaboration among general and special educators. In the context of multicultural and diversity issues, this notion of collaboration becomes more complex, as we shall see. Professionals and advocates in multicultural education face a troubling reality: Not all children from multicultural backgrounds need special education, but specialized instruction and services may fill important needs for many of them.

# Purposes of and Approaches to Education

The fundamental purpose of education in the United States is to produce literate citizens. According to this perspective, education is presumably intended for everyone; all children should have access to public education through the level of high school. In general terms, this goal is implemented by grouping and teaching students according to chronological age and evaluating their performance on the basis of what society expects children of each age to achieve. Society uses what youngsters of each age typically can learn as its yardstick for assessing their progress. Thus American education is aimed at the masses, and performance is judged in terms of an average. Through this system, schools attempt to bring most students to a similar, or at least a minimal, level of knowledge.

## Cultural Pluralism and the Role of Education

Understanding diverse cultures and the impact of collective culture on individuals is an ongoing challenge for research in social science (Bond, 2002; Fiske, 2002; Oyserman, Coon, & Kemmelmeir, 2002). Multicultural education values and promotes

**FOCUS 1**

Identify three ways in which the purposes of and approaches to general education in the United States sometimes differ from those of special education and multicultural education.

**cultural pluralism.** It teaches all students about cultural diversity and how to function in a multicultural society and is not aimed only at students of cultural or racial minorities (Mirel, 2002; Seidl & Friend, 2002). Gollnick and Chinn (2002), asserting that multicultural education is a concept that addresses cultural diversity, cited six beliefs and assumptions on which it is based:

1. Cultural differences have strength and value.
2. Schools should be models for the expression of human rights and respect for cultural differences.
3. Social justice and equality for all people should be of paramount importance in the design and delivery of curricula.
4. Attitudes and values necessary for the continuation of a democratic society can be promoted in schools.
5. Schooling can provide the knowledge, dispositions, and skills for the redistribution of power and income among cultural groups.
6. Educators working with families and communities can create an environment that is supportive of multiculturalism. (p. 30)

Rather than seeking to homogenize the population, current multicultural education promotes the notion that schools should encourage students to gain information about multiple cultures and competence in understanding both those present in our society and those existing throughout the world (Grant & Gomez, 2001). This perspective opposes the once-prevalent view that schools should minimize cultural differences.

Multicultural education is intended to teach all students about different cultures. Yet despite some progress, we still largely lack an awareness of how members of different cultural groups have contributed to major developments in our country's history. To illustrate, the 1990s PBS series on the Civil War, produced by Kenneth Burns, highlighted significant roles played by African Americans that many of us did not learn about in school. Also, during World War II, Native Americans known as "Code Talkers" served in critical communications roles by transmitting messages in their native language, which could not be decoded by Axis forces. And despite the degrading abuse that they received from many sources, Japanese Americans volunteered for critical assignments and served the United States with distinction during World War II. Such stories need to be told.

Young people develop many of their enduring attitudes and a significant knowledge base at school. Their thoughts and feelings about diverse cultures are at least partially shaped by what they learn in the classroom. Incomplete information and stereotypical presentations about different cultures detract from students' understanding of the variety of people that characterizes our world (e.g., Cohen & Steele, 2002; Gordijn, Koomen, & Stapel, 2001; Rueda De Leon, 2001). Careless treatment of this important topic perpetuates two problems: a lack of factual information about numerous cultures and a lack of skill in relating to those of different backgrounds. A complete education must include recognition of the roles of many peoples in shaping our country and our world and must foster respect and appreciation.

General education, special education, and multicultural education have some very important differences in their fundamental purposes. From the outset, the primary purpose of general education runs counter to those of the other two. Aimed

**Cultural pluralism**

Arrangement in which multiple cultural subgroups live together in a manner that preserves group differences, thereby maintaining each group's cultural or ethnic traditions.

*A goal of many educators is to promote an understanding of the world's diverse cultures.*

at serving the masses, general education attempts to create a leveling effect by bringing everyone to more or less the same level, teaching similar topics in groups, and evaluating achievement on the basis of a norm, or average. Special education, in contrast, tends to focus on the individual. Special education professionals would agree that the basic purpose of special education is to provide an opportunity for each child with a disability to learn and develop to his or her individual potential. Current special education efforts focus on individual needs, strengths, and preferences. This individualized approach is important because many students in special education seem unable to learn well through instruction that is broadly directed at large groups. Thus special education tends to emphasize individuals and specific skill levels. Evaluation is based, at least in part, on individual attainment of a specified mastery level, not entirely on **norm-based averages** (average performance scores of peers).

At a certain level, the overarching goal of multicultural education is also somewhat at odds with general education's goal of achieving consistency (bringing the population to a comparable level of performance in similar areas of knowledge). Further, general education largely reflects a societal self-portrait of the United States as a "melting pot" for peoples of all backgrounds, emphasizing similarities and downplaying differences. Contemporary multicultural education, on the other hand, sees the school as a powerful tool for appreciating and promoting diversity.

The differences among the goals and approaches of general, special, and multicultural education can create considerable difficulty within school systems and among educators. As one faction (multicultural education) attempts to make inroads into the broader domain of another (general education), an adversarial or competitive situation may result. Yet such misunderstandings can be diminished through thoughtful discussion and examination of the issues.

# Multiculturalism/Diversity and Special Education

Connections between multicultural education and special education have not always been comfortable. They have often involved issues of racial discrimination and inappropriate educational programming. For example, one connection between multicultural and special education surfaces in special education's role of serving children who are failing in the general education system. Unfortunately, a disproportionately large number of students placed in special education are from minority backgrounds (Coutinho, & Oswald, 2000). This issue continues to surface (Bondurant-Utz, 2002; Meyer, Bevan-Brown, Harry, & Sapon-Shevin, 2003; Spinelli, 2002), fueling suspicion that special education has been used as a tool of discrimination or as a means of separating racial and ethnic minorities from the majority. Still, certain instructional approaches common to both special and multicultural education can meet a student's academic needs.

Our discussion of special and multicultural education will focus on the prevalence of culturally diverse students in special education, along with four major elements of the Individuals with Disabilities Education Act (IDEA, presented in Chapter 1): nondiscriminatory and multidisciplinary assessment, parental involvement in developing each child's educational program, a free and appropriate public education delivered through an individualized education plan (IEP), and education in the least restrictive environment.

## Prevalence and Overrepresentation of Culturally Diverse Students in Special Education

The term *prevalence* generally refers to the number of people in a given population who exhibit a condition, problem, or particular status (those who have a hearing loss, for example, or who have red hair). In general terms, a phenomenon's prevalence is determined by counting how often it occurs. In this section, we will examine

**FOCUS 2**

Describe population trends among culturally diverse groups in the United States. How do these changes affect the educational system?

**Norm-based averages**

Comparison of a person's performance with the average performance scores of age-mates.

prevalence in a somewhat different sense, discussing certain factors relevant to the relationship between human exceptionality and multicultural issues, and examine the proportion of students from culturally diverse backgrounds in special education.

There are several factors associated with students at risk for academic failure. They include diverse cultural background, limited background in speaking English, and poverty. It is important to emphasize that these factors only indicate *risk* for difficulties in school; they do not necessarily destine a student for a special education placement. Yet a disproportionate number of special education students are from nonmainstream cultural backgrounds (Coutinho & Oswald, 2000; Grossman, 2002; Jones & Menchetti, 2001). The overrepresentation of students of color in groups labeled as having disabilities is cause for concern. African American children, for instance, appear more frequently than expected in classes for students with serious emotional disturbance and mental retardation, and Latinos also represent a large and rapidly growing group in special education (Drew & Hardman, 2004). At the other end of the spectrum, disproportionately few ethnic minority students are found in academically rigorous and gifted programs (Gollnick & Chinn, 2002). The Case Study illustrates a tangled web of issues, pertaining to school funding, assessment, and misdiagnosis/discrimination, that contribute to the overrepresentation of nonmainstream students in special education.

These are issues concerning school placement, and the result from assessments that are heavily influenced by the academic context (Bondurant-Utz, 2002; Spinelli, 2002). Some contend that in these circumstances, social factors play a significant role in shaping definitions, diagnoses, and resulting intervention or treatment (Becker & Luthar, 2002; Capage, Bennett, & McNeil, 2001; Harrison-Hale, 2002). Practically speaking, this means that the mainstream culture largely determines the definitions, diagnoses, and treatments that result in more nonmainstream children than expected being identified as needing specialized education. Even so, however, the evidence is mixed. Some results indicate that people of color and some other ethnicities actually exhibit a lower prevalence than their Caucasian counterparts in disability categories such as mood and anxiety disorders (Holzer & Copeland, 2000; Husaini et al., 2002).

Furthermore, cultural minority students do not complete school in the same proportions as their peers from the cultural majority. School dropout figures are about 13% for African American youngsters and between 28.6% and 38.2% for Latinos, depending on the sample (Banks, 2002). This compares with just over 7% for whites in the same age range. Dropout rates also correlate closely with family income and vary across income groups (Alexander, Entwisle, & Kabbani, 2001; Battin-Pearson et al., 2000; Grant & Sleeter, 2003). In an outcome related to these circumstances, Caucasian children from more privileged neighborhoods tend to have higher educational and occupational expectations than their minority counterparts (Barnett & Camilli, 2002; Buckner, Bassuk, & Weinreb, 2002). Accordingly, some researchers see poverty as a threat to academic performance (Mitchell, 2000; Sanders, 2000). However, poverty does not exert a simple, singular influence; rather, it is accompanied by a complex set of other influences, including detrimental physical elements of the environment (such as limited or substandard health care, increased risks related to health and development), the children's assessment of their own abilities, teachers' judg-

*Some culturally diverse students may be inappropriately placed into special education classes, resulting in overrepresentation.*

## Case Study

# A CASE OF OVERREPRESENTATION, FINANCES, AND SCHOOL REFORM

An associate dean of education, who happens to be African American, was labeled as having mental retardation and placed in special education for a significant portion of his school life. This is just one example of egregious misdiagnoses and possible discrimination in special education placement. Although IDEA is aimed at integrating youngsters with disabilities into the educational mainstream and guarding against ethnic discrimination, overrepresentation still occurs at the beginning of the 21st century. In fact, a 1993 report by *U.S. News & World Report* suggests that placement of disproportionately high numbers of minorities in special education programs continues at a level far beyond what would be expected on the basis of population demographics. This report indicates that nearly 80% of the states have an overrepresentation of African American students in special education. This information is based on Department of Education survey data provided by the states themselves.

Overrepresentation of students of color in special education has been a continuing concern, as indicated throughout this chapter. Concerns regarding misdiagnosis (which occurred in the case of the associate dean) and discriminatory practices have always surfaced in examinations of this problem; sociocultural issues are raised as well as the personal implications for individual children and their families. Other matters that also seem notable are related to serious and broad-based school reform.

Cost factors, for example, cannot be overlooked. The national price tag for special education services has risen *thirtyfold,* to over $30 billion, since 1977. And there is considerable inducement for school districts to expand special education (even in separate rather than integrated programs). First, districts often receive additional funding for special education students over those not receiving such labels. Texas, for example, pays local districts 10 times the normal per-student rate for teaching a youngster in a special education class (the national average is 3 times the normal per-student rate). Second, many states exclude special education scores in the statistical analysis of statewide competency exams. Consequently, their average scores are higher and these districts receive more favorable publicity and have more supportive boards of education. Such circumstances may translate into a better budget once again, to say nothing of enhancing the reputation of the administrator.

So this is a multihorned dilemma. An administrator can increase his or her budget and enhance the prestige of a district by channeling low-achieving students into special education. Such pragmatism, however, runs counter to the fundamental concepts of IDEA and contributes to overrepresentation of minorities in special education. In addition to these serious moral issues, litigation has become an increasing significant alternative for remedying educational problems. Lawsuits can be very disruptive to the operation of a school district, as well as to an administrator's personal life. Of five district administrators at a meeting in August 1994 (a meeting unrelated to any administrative problems), the one with the *fewest* crises had *"only one half-million-dollar lawsuit pending."*

### APPLICATION

1. How can we balance the various facets of cultural diversity, integrated special services to students with disabilities, and a large public educational system within the context of our general society?

2. How should school finances and other incentives be coordinated with public policy and federal and state legislation?

    Some vocal critics claim that the educational system should be discarded and a new approach developed "from scratch." However, there is no clear evidence that financial savings would result or that reforming our existing system would not be an equally effective alternative.

3. What would you do as an administrator?

4. What would you suggest as the parent of a minority child?

---

ments of the children's performance, and other environmental influences (Franklin, 2000; Hout, 2002; Li, 2003). Impoverished environmental effects surface as topics of serious concern in most discussions of educational problems, related reforms, and early intervention efforts. Research evidence does indicate that thoughtfully developed early intervention programs have beneficial effects on poor children's academic performance, cognitive development, and general health (Barnett & Camilli, 2002; Halfon & McLearn, 2002; Li, 2003). Family assistance generally has very positive outcomes; examples include home visitation programs, nutrition assistance and guidance, and the availability of family health care and guidance in accessing it (Zigler, Finn-Stevenson, & Hall, 2002).

Several culturally or ethnically diverse populations are growing rapidly because of increasing birthrates and immigration levels. For example, African Americans represented approximately 13% of the total population in the United States in 2002, a modest increase from 2000 but one that continues many years of growth (McKinnon, 2001; McKinnon, 2003). Figure 5.1 graphically portrays the U.S.

population by ethnic background, with growth projections through 2050. The increase of culturally and ethnically diverse groups will have a profound impact on education, presenting diverse needs that demand a broad a spectrum of additional educational services.

Language differences also often contribute to academic difficulties for students from diverse backgrounds who are educated in a system designed by the cultural majority (Chiappe, Siegel, & Gottardo, 2002; Law et al., 2002). Census data indicate that over 21 million people 5 years of age or older speak English less than "very well" (U.S. Bureau of the Census, 2000). This represents nearly 18 percent of the total population in this age range and has an enormous impact on schools in general. Particular challenges surface in circumstances where youngsters have a disability and also have limited English skills.

For example, people from Southeast Asia constitute a rapidly growing sector of the U.S. population. This influx has had a major impact on school systems; the number of youngsters speaking Asian languages in many schools has significantly increased recently (Choi & Harachi, 2002; Fernandez, 2000). Such growth places a heavy demand on U.S. school systems to provide linguistically appropriate instruction and to exercise vigilance and caution in assessment (e.g., Beekmans et al., 2001; Craig & Washington, 2000; Reynolds, 2001). And this trend continues—it is anticipated that the number of students with limited English proficiency (LEP) will continue to grow more rapidly than other groups of students.

Such figures only broadly reflect students who are either bilingual or linguistically diverse. Certainly, many come from backgrounds that permit them to achieve academically in a school system based primarily on the English language. Not all students accounted for here will need special supports or programs. Also, estimates and actual census data are always subject to a certain level of error. However, analyses thus far suggest that such error is relatively small and that, if anything, these data are likely to underestimate the problem somewhat. The importance of linguistically appropriate instruction is magnified considerably when we consider other multicultural factors, such as the need for a careful examination of educational goals and the methods of achieving them (Heredia & Altarriba, 2002). However, these issues become politicized and complex as legislators enact laws that dictate matters of language. (See the nearby Debate Forum, "English-Only or Bilingual Education?")

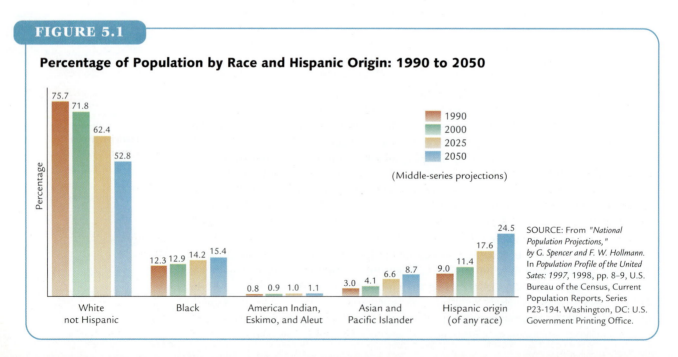

## FIGURE 5.1

**Percentage of Population by Race and Hispanic Origin: 1990 to 2050**

Legend:
- 1990
- 2000
- 2025
- 2050

(Middle-series projections)

White not Hispanic: 75.7, 71.8, 62.4, 52.8
Black: 12.3, 12.9, 14.2, 15.4
American Indian, Eskimo, and Aleut: 0.8, 0.9, 1.0, 1.1
Asian and Pacific Islander: 3.0, 4.1, 6.6, 8.7
Hispanic origin (of any race): 9.0, 11.4, 17.6, 24.5

SOURCE: From "National Population Projections," by G. Spencer and F. W. Hollmann. In *Population Profile of the United Sates: 1997*, 1998, pp. 8–9, U.S. Bureau of the Census, Current Population Reports, Series P23-194. Washington, DC: U.S. Government Printing Office.

# ENGLISH-ONLY OR BILINGUAL EDUCATION?

**D**eclaring English as the official language has had a certain level of support by lawmakers at several levels during the past few years, as recently as 2000. Initiatives to promote such legislation have been evident in nearly 75% of the states as recently as 1987. Yet English is not the primary language for many Americans. Students from culturally diverse backgrounds represent a very large portion of the school enrollment across the country. Critics claim that bilingual education places an unacceptable burden on the educational system, compromising its ability to provide specialized educational services to meet students' needs.

## POINT

Children from different cultures must have certain skills to survive in the world of the cultural majority. They should be taught in English and taught the knowledge base of the cultural majority for their own good. This knowledge will prepare them for success and will more efficiently utilize the limited funds available, since specialized culturally sensitive services will not be required.

## COUNTERPOINT

Children from cultures different from that of the majority must have an equal opportunity to learn in the most effective manner possible. This may mean teaching them in their native language, at least for some of the time. To do otherwise is a waste of talent, which can ultimately affect the overall progress of our country. To force students who are culturally diverse to use English is also an example of discrimination by the cultural majority.

What do you think? To give your opinion, go to Chapter 5 of the companion website **(www.ablongman.com/hardman8e)**, and click on Debate Forum.

# Nondiscriminatory and Multidisciplinary Assessment

Assessment and accountability are receiving increased public attention as politicians require evidence of the impact of tax support for education. Substantiation of such an impact has been sought for all students in education and is a theme that weaves its way through all of human exceptionality. This theme is also present as we consider multicultural and diversity issues. In this latter context, the history of assessment and accountability raises serious issues of accuracy, fairness, and our ability to provide appropriate services to children. Many of these challenges remain before us, even though a great deal of progress has occurred.

Perhaps nowhere is the link between special and multicultural education more obvious than in issues of **nondiscriminatory assessment.** As mentioned earlier, disproportionate numbers of minority students are found in special education classes (Coutinho, & Oswald, 2000; Jones & Menchetti, 2001). Decisions regarding referral and placement in these classes are based on psychological assessment, which typically is based on standardized evaluations of intellectual and social functioning. Such assessments often discriminate or are biased against children from ethnically and culturally diverse backgrounds (Grossman, 2002; Linn & Gronlund, 2000; Venn, 2000).

In several early cases, courts determined that reliance on such evaluations did indeed discriminate against Latino students (*Diana v. State Board of Education,* 1970, 1973) and African American students (*Larry P. v. Riles,* 1972, 1979). Assessment and instruction for Asian American children were addressed in the case of *Lau v. Nichols* (1974). These California cases had a national impact and greatly influenced the drafting of IDEA. Two prominent precedents in IDEA, for example, were established in the case of *Diana v. State Board of Education:* (1) children tested for potential placement in

**Nondiscriminatory assessment**

One of the provisions of IDEA, which requires that testing be done in a child's native or primary language. Procedures to prevent cultural or racial discrimination are also stipulated, as is the use of validated assessment tools. Assessment must be conducted by a multidisciplinary team using several kinds or sources of information to make a placement decision.

special education must be assessed in their native or primary language, and (2) children cannot be placed in special classes on the basis of culturally biased tests. Finally, IDEA also mandates that evaluation involve a multidisciplinary team using several sources of information to make a placement decision. To put these safeguards in context, it is necessary to examine the assessment process and how cultural bias can occur.

## Cultural Bias and Assessment Error

Because assessment for special education must avoid cultural bias, it is a source of major controversy. **Measurement bias** produces error during testing, leading to unfair or inaccurate test results that do not reflect the student's actual mental abilities or skills (Manly & Jacobs, 2002). In many cases, cultural bias taints both the construction and development of assessment instruments and their use (Beekmans et al., 2001; Pawlik et al., 2000; Reynolds, 2001). Standardized, norm-referenced instruments have been particularly criticized because the performances of children from different cultures are often compared with norms developed on the basis of other populations. Under these testing conditions, children from nonmainstream backgrounds often appear disadvantaged by cultural differences (Bondurant-Utz, 2002; Pierangelo & Giuliana, 2001; Spinelli, 2002).

Bias in psychological assessment has been recognized as a problem for many years and continues to concern professionals (Cohen, 2002; Linn & Gronlund, 2000; Teresi et al., 2001). Some assessment procedures simply fail to document the same level of performance by individuals from diverse cultural backgrounds, even if they have similar abilities. This phenomenon is referred to as **test bias.**

Considerable effort has been expended to develop tests that are culture-free or culture-fair (e.g., using test items that do not ask for information available primarily in the majority culture). This effort was rooted in the belief that the test itself was the major element contributing to bias or unfairness. But this simplistic perspective was flawed, because it focused solely on the test instrument itself and did not adequately address bias in the use of an instrument or the interpretation of data (in other words, administration and interpretation should include adjustment for cultural differences). Over the years, however, this effort did lead to some improvements in areas where cultural bias was involved in instrument construction or procedural adaptations. Revision minimized the most glaring problems by reducing both the amount of culture-specific content (e.g., naming items more familiar to middle-class Caucasians than to others) and the culture-specific language proficiency required to perform test tasks (e.g., using language more commonly heard in middle-class, English-speaking homes than in others).

However, refinements to test instruments have limited effectiveness when the use of the test and the interpretation of results are not appropriate and conceptually sound. Although concern about administration and interpretation is not new, recent attention has led to a more balanced focus on procedures as well as on the test instrument itself (Dana, 2000; Linn, 2002; Willingham, 2002). One of the best ways to ensure fair testing is to prepare those who give tests and interpret the results so that they understand cultural issues in assessment. Adjustments may entail interpersonal interaction during test sessions that may be unfamiliar or offensive to a child from a different culture. Professionals need explicit and focused training to help them see how easily bias can creep in (Merrell, 2002). Personal preferences, such as racial biases, may substantially influence evaluation and, in turn, result in the incorrect assessment of a student.

## Language Diversity

A significant challenge in assessing students with diverse cultural backgrounds has always been language differences. Assessment of non-English-speaking children has often been biased, providing an inaccurate reflection of those children's abilities (Beekmans et al., 2001; Pawlik et al., 2000; Reynolds, 2001). If language diversity is

**FOCUS 3**

Identify two ways in which assessment may contribute to the overrepresentation of culturally diverse students in special education programs.

**Measurement bias**

An unfairness or inaccuracy of test results that is related to cultural background, sex, or race.

**Test bias**

An unfairness of a testing procedure or test instrument, which gives one group a particular advantage or another a disadvantage as a consequence of factors unrelated to ability, such as culture, sex, or race.

not considered during assessment and educational planning, a child may receive an inappropriate special education placement (Pena, Iglesias, & Lidz, 2001; Ukrainetz, Harpell, Walsh, & Coyle, 2000).

A particularly difficult situation exists for students with limited English proficiency and a language disorder, such as delayed language development (Battle, 2002; Puckett, 2001; Trawick-Smith, 2000). Determining the degree to which each factor contributes to aca-demic deficiency is difficult. In fact, it may not be important to apportion a certain amount of performance deficit to language differences versus intellectual or academic ability. What may be vitally important, however, is identifying students with language differences and finding appropriate educational services, other than special education, to help them. Such services may include intensive language assistance or other tutorial help, but not placement in special education classes or the special education system. It may be hard to decide whether such a child should be placed in special education. Special education placement will surely raise questions about whether such placement is occurring because the child is linguistically diverse as a consequence of his or her cultural background or is linguistically deficient for developmental reasons. Although these questions are not easily answered, the field is enormously strengthened because they are at last being asked and addressed (e.g., Dana, 2000; Hernandez, 2001; Scheffner-Hammer, Pennock-Roman, Rzasa, & Tomblin, 2002).

As indicated earlier, census data show a substantially increasing number of children in the American educational system who speak languages other than English (Choi & Harachi, 2002; Fernandez, 2000). Therefore, all teachers, related education personnel, social workers, psychologists, and administrators must become aware of the challenges to making appropriate educational assessments of students with language diversity (Beekmans et al., 2001; Hernandez, 2001; Reynolds, 2001). In many cases this means that specific, focused training must be included in professional preparation programs.

One of the seemingly positive safeguards in IDEA, requiring assessment of a child in his or her native language, also raises new questions. Although this law represents a positive step toward fair treatment of students with linguistically diverse backgrounds, some difficulties have emerged in its implementation. Specifically, the legislation defines *native language* as that used in the home, yet a regulation implementing IDEA defined it as that which is normally used by the youngster in school. This latter definition may present problems for a bilingual student who has achieved a conversational fluency in English, yet whose proficiency may not be adequate to sustain academic work. For this child, testing in English is likely to be biased, even though it is considered a proper procedure according to regulations.

*Educators must avoid test bias in assessing children for potential special education placement.*

**FOCUS**

**4**

Identify three ways in which language diversity may contribute to assessment difficulties with students who are from a variety of cultures.

## Assessment and the Preparation of Professionals

Proper training of assessment professionals working with children from diverse backgrounds is particularly important to obtain accurate data and minimize interpretations that may lead to bias (Merrell, 2002). Additionally, professionals must be constantly alert to potential bias due to language differences as well as other factors that may mask students' true abilities. In many cases, information about the child's home life and other environmental matters can provide valuable insight to aid evaluators in both administering assessment and interpreting results. That information includes what languages are spoken in the household and by whom, who the child's caregivers are (parents and others), how much time the child spends with caregivers, and the child's out-of-school activities. Uninformed assumptions about family and circumstances can lead to inaccurate assessment, so the evaluator must obtain as much information as possible about the child and her or his life.

It is vitally important to understand the child in the context of his or her family (Lopez, 2001; Sheldon, 2002). Such understanding includes the child and her or his family, as well as interaction patterns between family members and professionals such as teachers and social workers. This understanding is not readily available and often is not included in professional preparation programs. Professional training challenges are often addressed unsuccessfully in programs in psychology, teacher education, and a number of related areas (e.g., Causey, Thomas, & Armento, 2000; Guadarrama, 2000).

Assessment is a very important tool in education, particularly in special and multicultural education. Effective, unbiased assessment requires that instruments be correctly constructed and used. To that end, the purposes of assessment, and of education itself, must be considered from the outset: Are we attempting to bring the bulk of citizenry to a similar point in education or knowledge? Are we creating a leveling effect, trying to make all people alike to some degree? Or are we promoting individual growth and development and encouraging cultural diversity and individual differences?

# Parents from Different Cultures and Involvement in Special Education

**FOCUS 5**

Identify three ways in which differing sociocultural customs may affect the manner in which parents become involved in the educational process.

Parental involvement in the education of students with disabilities is required by IDEA. Parent rights, however, are based on certain assumptions. One fundamental assumption is that parents are consistently proactive and will challenge the school if their child is not being treated properly. Although true of some parents of children in special education, this assumption is not true for all. Some parents are reluctant or afraid to interact with the educational system (Sheldon, 2002). The manner in which parents are involved, their goals for such involvement, and evaluation of the outcomes of family participation are important to achieving maximum benefit (Bailey, 2001; McConnell, 2001; Schwartz & Rodriguez, 2001).

The acceptance of a child's disability is not easy for any parent, and a family's attitude toward exceptionality can influence how a child's intervention proceeds. People of diverse cultural backgrounds have perspectives and beliefs regarding illness, disability, and specialized services that may differ from those of the majority culture (Drew & Hardman, 2004; Littlewood, 2001). For example, some cultures have great difficulty accepting disabilities because of religious beliefs and values. Views about the family also can affect treatment of children with disabilities. The extended family structures common in African American and Latin cultures can cause hesitation about accepting care from outside the family and anxieties about special education. Parents of children with disabilities who are from lower socioeconomic levels, have a minority background, and speak a primary language other than English face enormous disadvantages in interacting with the special education system.

Sensitivity in interpersonal communication is very important when professionals deliver services to children of families who are culturally diverse (Sheldon, 2002). The meaning and interpretation of certain facial expressions, the expression of emotions, manners, and behaviors denoting respect and interpersonal matters vary greatly among cultures (e.g., Elfenbein & Ambady, 2002, Matsumoto, 2002). Such connotations affect the interactions between minority family members, between

*Families can support multicultural education by working with children on school projects that are focused on their cultural heritage.*

these individuals and those of the cultural majority, and certainly with educational professionals. Some families from nonmainstream cultures may be reluctant to receive assistance from outside the family for a variety of reasons. For example, some parents may feel shame that their child has been identified as having disabilities, and this response is likely to influence their acceptance of the situation (Drew & Hardman, 2004). Moreover, professionals should keep in mind that the immigration status of some families may affect the manner in which they react to attempts to provide services for their children. Although this constitutes a pragmatic consideration rather than a cultural difference, a family that is residing in the United States illegally or feels uncertain about its residency status may avoid interacting with an educational system.

U.S. public education predominantly reflects the philosophy of the cultural majority. This is not surprising, since social institutions—in this case, formal schooling—are typically founded on such mainstream views. Yet the social customs of the minority subcultures may continue to flourish in private and often emerge in individual interactions and behaviors (Dika & Singh, 2002; Lam, Yim, & Lam, 2002; O'Connor, 2002). Such differences surface in discussions of disabilities. For example, although mental retardation is recognized by all cultures, its conceptualization, social interpretation, and treatment are cultural-specific (Drew & Hardman, 2004). The condition may be considered as negative (being viewed as a punishment visited on the family, for example) or may be viewed favorably (as the blessing of knowing an unusual, rare person, for instance) depending on the cultural context. Similarly, certain behaviors that a professional of the majority culture might view as a learning problem may in fact be a product of the acculturation process or be considered normal within a child's cultural background. For example, a Native American child may not respond to some questions in a testing situation because his or her cultural custom is to not speak of such matters. The white test administrator, however, interprets this lack of response as meaning that the child does not know the answer and therefore classifies it as an error on the test. Some level of cultural bias and insensitivity is present in many aspects of professional work, including the research reports we read. This is important to remember as we attempt to understand cultural differences and provide services in a society characterized by cultural pluralism (e.g., Grant & Sleeter, 2003; Mirel, 2002, Mueller & Pope, 2001).

**FOCUS 6**

Identify two areas that require particular attention in the development of an individualized education plan (IEP) for a student from a culturally diverse background.

# Education for Culturally Diverse Students

## Individualized Education

Developing an individualized education plan (IEP) for each student with a disability is required by IDEA. Most school districts have considerable experience in this process, but they must also meet further requirements when addressing the needs of a child with cultural and/or linguistic differences (Hendrick, 2001; Morrison, 2001). Depending on her or his background and capabilities, such a student may need remediation for a specific disability, catch-up work in academic subjects, and instruction in English as a second language. The IEP must consider cultural factors, such as language differences, as well as learning and behavior disabilities and may have to provide for specialized instruction from different professionals for each facet of education. Rarely will a single professional have the training and background in culture, language, and the specialized skills needed to remediate disabilities. Rather, effective educational programming for culturally diverse students requires a team effort (Craig, Hull, Haggart, & Perez-Selles, 2000).

When developing an IEP for a student from a culturally diverse background, education professionals should avoid making stereotypical assumptions about ethnic and cultural background. These may involve well-intentioned but misguided efforts to integrate into instruction culturally relevant foods, activities, or holidays. The utmost care should be taken to make sure that such content is specifically correct (not just an uninformed generalization about a religious celebration or folk dance) and is actually related to the student's experience—some foods typical to an ethnic group may not be eaten in a particular child's family or neighborhood. Insensitive use of such material may do more to perpetuate an unfortunate stereotype than to enrich a child's understanding of his or her heritage. Selection of culturally appropriate instructional materials requires a knowledge base that is beyond that of many educational professionals and requires a thorough analysis (Santos, Fowler, Corso, & Bruns, 2000; Taylor, 2000). IEPs written for children from culturally diverse backgrounds must truly be developed in an individualized fashion, perhaps even more so than for children with disabilities who come from the cultural majority.

## The Least Restrictive Environment

**FOCUS 7**

Identify two considerations that represent particular difficulties in serving children from culturally diverse backgrounds in the least restrictive environment.

Education in the least restrictive environment (LRE) involves a wide variety of placement options (see Chapter 2). The guiding principle is that instruction for students with disabilities should take place in an environment as similar to that of the educational mainstream as possible and alongside peers without disabilities to the greatest extent appropriate. The same is true for a child from a culturally diverse background who is receiving appropriate special education services, although some unique circumstances require additional attention (e.g., attention to a developmental language delay as well as limited English skill). In all cases such inclusive settings must also be sensitive to family and cultural differences (e.g., a family that speaks primarily a language other than English in the home). If possible, such cultural differences may be used as instructional tools or enhancements. For example, the teacher might ask the youngster to help teach part of a lesson on Spanish culture. What may seem like a subtle nuance can become an important positive lesson in cultural difference and respect.

Children with exceptionalities who have language differences may also receive assistance from bilingual education staff. In some cases, the language instruction may be incorporated into other teaching (Dong, 2002). In situations where the disability is more severe or the language difference is extreme (perhaps the child has little or no English proficiency), the student may be placed in a separate setting for a portion of instructional time.

Children from culturally diverse backgrounds receiving special education services must be taught in settings with nondisabled peers to the maximum extent appropriate.

Cultural and language instruction may vary as the child grows older, according to the model used in a given school district. Figure 5.2 illustrates how various approaches might be structured into a daily or weekly educational schedule as a student moves from kindergarten to the twelfth grade. Each approach differs somewhat in the degree of integration recommended. Part I, the transition model, moves the student into the instructional mainstream as rapidly as possible while addressing issues of linguistic performance and disability remediation. Parts III and IV involve instruction that takes place while the student remains in an integrated setting as much as possible. Part II represents what has long been known as a **pull-out program** and does not reflect integrated instruction. Although some students may require placement in such a setting, pull-out programs have not been viewed favorably in recent years. Collier noted that "there is still considerable debate concerning how and where the bilingual exceptional child should be served" (1998, p. 295).

# Other Diversity Considerations

Many influences come into play as we consider multicultural and diversity issues in education. In some cases, societal problems contribute to a child's development of learning difficulties; an example is parental neglect for extensive periods of time, resulting in little language and cognitive development occurring in a very young child. In other cases, the complications involved in educating people from a variety of cultures who also have differing abilities produce a host of challenges in assessment and instruction. It is important to note that the study of culture and associated variables, such as poverty and migrancy, is seldom well served by attempts to identify simplistic causal relationships. For example, findings of differences in self-esteem between people of differing ethnic backgrounds may be due to racial differences, differences in economic status, or a combination of influences (Twenge & Crocker, 2002). Research on race and culture involves complex and interacting variables that defy simple conclusions (Li, 2003).

## Children Living in Poverty

One important example of how social and cultural factors are interrelated is found in the conditions associated with poverty. A child from an impoverished environment may be destined for special education even before birth. Increased health risks

**Pull-out programs**

Programs that move the student with a disability from the general education classroom to a separate class for at least part of the school day.

www.ablongman.com/hardman8e

OTHER DIVERSITY CONSIDERATIONS    127

FIGURE 5.2

## Bilingual–Bicultural Inclusion Models: Teacher Competencies for Mainstreaming Bilingual Exceptional Children

**I. Transition Model**

*Daily/weekly schedule*

English language

Regular curriculum in both languages, increasing in English over time

Native language

K — 12

**II. Pull-Out Model**

*Daily/weekly schedule*

Instruction in English as second language

K — 12

**III. Restoration/Maintenance Model**

*Daily/weekly schedule*

Regular curriculum in English

Instruction in native language and ethnic heritage

K — 12

**IV. Restoration/Maintenance Model**

*Daily/weekly schedule*

Regular curriculum primarily in English

Native language and heritage continued throughout schooling process

Various curriculum areas primarily in native language

K — 12

SOURCE: From "Including Bilingual Exceptional Children in the General Education Classroom," by C. Collier. In *The Bilingual Special Education Interface* (3rd ed.), edited by L. M. Baca and H. T. Cervantes, 1998, p. 297. Columbus, OH: Merrill/Macmillan.

**FOCUS 8**

Identify two ways in which poverty may contribute to the academic difficulties of children from culturally diverse backgrounds, often resulting in their referral to special education.

during pregnancy arise from more limited prenatal health care, poorer maternal nutrition, and potential exposure to other risk factors that are associated with birth complications (Gelfand & Drew, 2003). Children who begin their lives facing such challenges are more likely to have difficulty later than those who do not. Children who live in poverty may be more frail, be sick more often, experience greater stress, and exhibit more neurological problems that later contribute to academic difficulties (Drew & Hardman, 2004; Ewart & Suchday, 2002; Gallo & Matthews, 2003). These conditions are more prevalent in the lives of cultural and ethnic minorities (e.g., Buckner et al., 2002; Hout, 2002; Torres, 2002). Census data published in 2000 indicated that 22.1% of all African Americans and 21.2% of Latinos lived below the poverty level, compared to 7.5% of the non-Hispanic white population. Other census data present an even more disturbing picture for children: 20.8% of all children were considered to be living below the poverty level (U.S. Bureau of the Census, 2000).

The effects of impoverished environments continue to cast the shadow of health risk beyond childhood and often over a lifetime. These influences often include shortened life expectancy, relatively poorer physical health, and more chronic health problems (Abernathy, Webster, & Vermeulen, 2002; Dancy & Ralston, 2002; Seccombe, 2002). Poverty is found more often in populations having multicultural education needs than in populations without such needs and is also associated with homelessness and academic risk (Barnett & Camilli, 2002; Gelfand & Drew, 2003;

Torres, 2002), contributing to the link between special and multicultural education. Figure 5.3 summarizes poverty rates across several characteristics.

## Children in Migrant Families

Although migrancy is often associated with minority status and poverty, this is not always the case. Frequent mobility sometimes characterizes affluent families, such as those who move from a summer home to a winter home or take extended trips when it suits parents, rather than school schedules. Similarly, children of military personnel may change schools frequently on a schedule that does not coincide with the academic year.

Forces that interrupt the continuity of schooling have an impact on learning, teacher and peer relationships, and general academic progress (Nakagawa, Stafford, Fisher, & Matthews, 2002). Often this is a detrimental influence. The mobility of wealthy people and others subject to frequent reassignment also has an impact, but it is frequently offset by other circumstances that contribute to a child's general education (such as the opportunity for travel and the assistance of tutors). These children are not subject to the same risks as children from families who migrate as a way of life without the financial resources to offset negative impacts. Unlike military personnel, for example, migrant workers are not assured of employment, housing, or a welcoming sponsor.

In many cases, the circumstances of migrancy are associated with ethnic or cultural diversity as well as economic disadvantage, language differences, and social and physical isolation from much of the larger community. Often the proportion of migrant workers from minority backgrounds is extremely high, and it varies

**FOCUS 9**

Identify two ways in which migrancy among culturally diverse populations may contribute to academic difficulties.

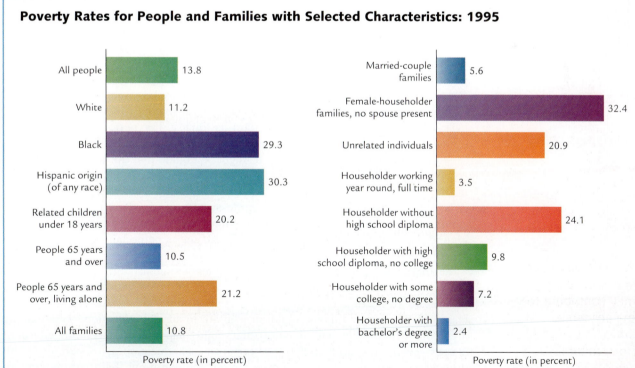

**FIGURE 5.3**

**Poverty Rates for People and Families with Selected Characteristics: 1995**

| Characteristic | Poverty rate (in percent) |
| --- | --- |
| All people | 13.8 |
| White | 11.2 |
| Black | 29.3 |
| Hispanic origin (of any race) | 30.3 |
| Related children under 18 years | 20.2 |
| People 65 years and over | 10.5 |
| People 65 years and over, living alone | 21.2 |
| All families | 10.8 |

| Characteristic | Poverty rate (in percent) |
| --- | --- |
| Married-couple families | 5.6 |
| Female-householder families, no spouse present | 32.4 |
| Unrelated individuals | 20.9 |
| Householder working year round, full time | 3.5 |
| Householder without high school diploma | 24.1 |
| Householder with high school diploma, no college | 9.8 |
| Householder with some college, no degree | 7.2 |
| Householder with bachelor's degree or more | 2.4 |

SOURCE: From "Poverty," by B. D. Proctor. In *Population Profile of the United States:* 1997, 1998, pp. 40–41. U.S. Bureau of the Census, Current Population Reports, Series P23-194. Washington, DC: U.S. Government Printing Office.

geographically. For example, evidence indicates that over 80% of the farm laborers employed in California and other western states are recent immigrants from Mexico. Although reliable data are not available for other regions, migrancy is rather widespread and involves seasonal or migrant workers throughout the nation (Buckner et al., 2002; Drew & Hardman, 2004; Tighe, 2001).

The issues created by poverty and language diversity are even more difficult to address when a child moves three or four times each year. Children experience limited continuity and considerable inconsistency in educational programming. These children may begin the school year in one reading program and finish only a lesson or two before they are moved to another school in a different location that uses a totally different program and approach to the topic. They often have little access to services because of short-term enrollment or a school's limited service capabilities. It is quite possible for these children to be in each school for such a short time that they are never identified or referred as needing specialized instructional assistance. It is difficult to pinpoint the exact effects of mobility on children's academic progress, but the problem is significant. Even using a consistent tracking system that could move with the child would be helpful to the receiving school or district.

## Other Factors

A number of other factors link special and multicultural education. Some of them raise serious concerns about the placement of minority children in special education, and others pertain to how such placements might best occur.

Special education focuses on differences. If a young girl has academic difficulty, perhaps failing in reading and math, she is singled out as different. She is different in that her math and reading performances are far below those of her peers, and so she may receive special help in these subjects. Several questions emerge as we consider this example: How do we determine that the student is doing poorly in reading and math? Is the student a candidate for special education? What is the primary reason why the student might be a candidate for special education?

What if the student comes from a culturally different background, as does Denise in the opening Snapshot? Is Denise considered disabled because of her academic performance or because of her culturally different background? This question may not have a clear answer, for contributing factors may be so intertwined that they cannot be separated and weighed in a meaningful manner. Denise may be appropriately considered for special education as long as her performance is not preeminently a cultural matter (attributable merely to her being from a background different from that of the majority). It might be argued that the reason for Denise's receiving special help is irrelevant as long as she gets extra instruction and assistance with behavioral problems. This perspective may have intuitive appeal, but it is not a satisfactory position for professionals involved in multicultural education. If Denise is receiving special education because of her cultural background, not primarily because she is disabled, she is being labeled and placed inappropriately.

Furthermore, special education often carries a stigma. Many people infer that children in special education are somehow inferior to those who do not require such instruction. Unfortunately, this view persists despite efforts by professionals to change it. Peers may ridicule children who are in special education. Some parents are more comfortable with having their child placed in the general education classes—even if the child might do better in special education. Even parents of children who are gifted and talented are often quick to point out that their children are in an accelerated class so that no one assumes that they are attending a special education class.

This negative perspective on special education is especially harmful to children like Denise if their placement stems from mislabeling or flawed assessment. Multi-

**FOCUS 10**

Identify three conceptual factors that have contributed to heightened attention and concern regarding the placement of children from ethnic and cultural groups in special education.

cultural advocates may correctly claim that placing students in special education because of cultural differences is an example of discrimination and perhaps oppression by the cultural majority. This view explains why the advocates of multicultural education become concerned, even angry, when children with culturally diverse backgrounds appear to be overrepresented in special education.

An additional problem may occur if a child's special education placement is not multiculturally sensitive and appropriate. The wrong special education intervention can do more harm than good. For instance, even the best instruction will be ineffective if it is provided in English and the student does not comprehend or speak it fluently. As noted earlier, designing appropriate instructional programs for children from culturally different backgrounds is complex and is likely to involve a number of different specialists operating in a team (Craig et al., 2000; Morrison, 2001). Such instruction may also require some changes or adaptations in the organization of the educational system so that these children may progress satisfactorily through the academic material (Boudah et al., 2000).

Denise's placement in special education may impede her academic progress to the extent that her failure becomes a self-fulfilling prophecy. In short, Denise may *become* what she has been *labeled*. Her poor academic and social performance may be due to cultural differences, not to disability. If the initial assessment inaccurately construes her cultural differences as indicating a low level of ability, Denise may be turned into a poor student by the system itself. The concept of the self-fulfilling prophecy has been discussed for many years and continues to receive attention in a variety of contexts from management to education (Conlon, Devaraj, & Matta, 2001; Drew & Hardman, 2004; Edwards, 2001). This factor warrants particular attention as we study multicultural issues and specialized instruction.

# Multicultural Issues and Specialized Instruction

Specialized instruction for students with disabilities who come from culturally diverse backgrounds must be based on individual need. The IEP must include specific cultural considerations that are relevant for a particular child, addressing language dominance and language proficiency in terms of both conversational and academic skills. The IEP may need to address the type of language intervention needed, which might include enrichment (either in a native language or in English) or language development intervention, which also may be either in a native language or in English. Instruction may target language enhancement through a strategy integrated with existing curriculum material, such as children's literature.

These are only examples of the considerations that may need attention, and they are issues related primarily to language diversity. Environmental conditions, such as extreme poverty and developmental deprivation, may dictate that services and supports focus on environmental stimulation that was lacking in the child's early learning (Barnett & Camilli, 2002; Hendrick, 2001; Li, 2003). The possible individual strategies are as varied as the factors that make up a child's background.

It is also important to note that most children from culturally diverse backgrounds do not require special education. Although the factors discussed here may place such students at risk for special education referral, general instruction may meet their needs without special education services. When this is possible, it is a mistake to label such students as disabled. Table 5.1 outlines points that educators should consider as they address various elements of the referral process for children from diverse backgrounds.

**TABLE 5.1**

## Process Checklist for Serving Children from Diverse Backgrounds

This checklist provides professionals with points to consider in the process of educating children from culturally diverse backgrounds. These matters should be considered during each of the following: referral and testing or diagnostic assessment; classification, labeling, or class assignment change; teacher conferences or home communication.

| PROCESS | ISSUES | QUESTION TO BE ASKED |
|---|---|---|
| Referral, testing, or diagnostic assessment | Language issues | Is the native language different from the language in which the child is being taught, and should this be considered in the assessment process? What is the home language? What is the normal conversational language? In what language can the student be successfully taught or assessed (academic language)? |
| | Cultural issues | What are the views toward schooling of the culture from which the child comes? Do differences exist in expectations between the school and family for the child's schooling goals? What are the cultural views toward illness or disability? |
| | Home issues | What is the family constellation, and who are the family members? What is the family's economic status? |
| Classification, labeling, or class assignment change | Language issues | Does the proposed placement change account for any language differences that are relevant, particularly academic language? |
| | Cultural issues | Does the proposed placement change consider any unique cultural views regarding schooling? |
| | Home issues | Does the proposed change consider pertinent family matters? |
| Teacher conferences or home communication | Language issues | Is the communication to parents or other family members in a language they understand? |
| | Cultural issues | Do cultural views influence communication between family members and the schools as a formal governmental organization? Is there a cultural reluctance of family members to come to the school? Are home visits a desirable alternative? Is communication from teachers viewed positively? |
| | Home issues | Is the family constellation such that communication with the schools is possible and positive? Are family members positioned economically and otherwise to respond to communication from the schools in a productive manner? If the family is of low SES, is transportation a problem for conferences? |

# FOCUS REVIEW

**FOCUS 1** Identify three ways in which the purposes of and approaches to general education in the United States sometimes differ from those of special education and multicultural education.

- A major purpose of general education is to provide education for everyone and to bring all students to a similar level of performance.
- Special education focuses on individual differences and often evaluates performance in terms of an individually set or prescribed performance level.
- Multicultural education promotes cultural pluralism and, therefore, promotes differences.

**FOCUS 2** Describe population trends among culturally diverse groups in the United States. How do these changes affect the educational system?

- Ethnically and culturally diverse groups, such as Latinos, African Americans, and others, represent substantial portions of the U.S. population.
- Population growth in ethnically and culturally diverse groups is increasing at a phenomenal rate—in some cases, at twice the rate of growth in the Caucasian population. Both immigration and birthrates contribute to this growth.
- Increased demands for services will be placed on the educational system as growth rates continue among culturally diverse populations.

**FOCUS 3** Identify two ways in which assessment may contribute to the overrepresentation of culturally diverse students in special education programs.

- Using assessment instruments that are designed and constructed with specific language and content that "favors" the cultural majority.
- Using assessment procedures that are biased, either implicitly or explicitly, against people from culturally different backgrounds.

**FOCUS 4** Identify three ways in which language diversity may contribute to assessment difficulties with students who are from a variety of cultures.

- Students with limited or no English proficiency may be thought to have speech or language disorders and hence may be referred and tested for special education placement.
- A child's native language may appear to be English because of conversational fluency at school, but he or she may not be proficient enough to engage in academic work or assessment in English.
- A child's academic or psychological assessment may inaccurately portray his or her ability because of his or her language differences.

**FOCUS 5** Identify three ways in which differing sociocultural customs may affect the manner in which parents become involved in the educational process.

- Parents from some cultural backgrounds may view special assistance differently than educational institutions do.

- Parents from some cultural backgrounds may be reluctant to take an active role in interacting with the educational system.
- Certain behaviors that may suggest a disabling condition that calls for special education assistance are viewed as normal in some cultures, and parents from those cultures may not see them as problematic.

**FOCUS 6** Identify two areas that require particular attention in the development of an individualized education plan (IEP) for a student from a culturally diverse background.

- Coordination of different services and professional personnel becomes crucial.
- Cultural stereotypes should not be perpetuated by assumptions that are inappropriate for an IEP or otherwise improper for education.

**FOCUS 7** Identify two considerations that represent particular difficulties in serving children from culturally diverse backgrounds in the least restrictive environment.

- Cultural or language instruction may be needed in addition to other teaching that focuses on remediation of a learning problem, making integration into the educational mainstream more difficult.
- Training limitations of school staff, rather than the child's needs, may influence placement decisions.

**FOCUS 8** Identify two ways in which poverty may contribute to the academic difficulties of children from culturally diverse backgrounds, often resulting in their referral to special education.

- Circumstances resulting in disadvantaged prenatal development and birth complications occur much more frequently among those of low socioeconomic status and nonmainstream populations.
- Environmental circumstances, such as malnutrition and the presence of toxic agents, that place children at risk are found most frequently in impoverished households, and poverty often afflicts ethnic minority populations.

**FOCUS 9** Identify two ways in which migrancy among culturally diverse populations may contribute to academic difficulties.

- In many cases, migrant families are characterized by economic disadvantages and language differences.
- Children in migrant households may move and change educational placements several times a year, limiting continuity and contributing to inconsistent educational programming.

**FOCUS 10:** Identify three conceptual factors that have contributed to heightened attention and concern regarding the placement of children from ethnic and cultural groups in special education.

- A stigma is attached to special education.
- Special education placement for children from culturally and ethnically diverse groups may not be educationally effective in meeting their academic needs.
- A self-fulfilling prophecy may occur, resulting in youngsters becoming what they are labeled.

# FURTHER READINGS

Anderson, J., Anderson, A., Lynch, J., & Shapiro, J. (2003). "Storybook reading in a multicultural society: Critical perspectives." In *On Reading Books to Children: Parents and Teachers,* ed. A. Van Kleeck, S. Stahl, and E. Bauer. Mahwah, NJ: Erlbaum.

*This chapter discusses storybook reading from a multicultural perspective and within the context of literacy.*

Jewel, P. (2002). "Multicultural counseling research: An evaluation with proposals for future research." In *Multicultural Counseling: A Reader,* ed. S. Palmer. Thousand Oaks, CA: Sage Publications.

*This chapter attempts to overcome the frequent criticism that traditional counseling lacks relevance for multicultural circumstances.*

Nieto, S. (2002). *Language, Culture, and Teaching: Critical Perspectives for a New Century.* Mahwah, NJ: Erlbaum.

*This book presents realistic examples of dilemmas about diversity faced by teachers in their classrooms.*

Utley, C., Obiakor, F., & Ford, B. (2002). "Professional Development: An Essential Component for Educating Teachers as Lifelong Learners." In *Educating All Learners: Refocusing the Comprehensive Support Model,* ed. F. Obiakor and P. Grant. Springfield, IL: Charles C Thomas.

*This chapter examines the crucial aspects of professional development for teachers and describes key elements of a multicultural professional development training program.*

# WEB RESOURCES

## National Association for Multicultural Education

www.nameorg.org

The National Association for Multicultural Education was founded to bring together individuals and groups with an interest in multicultural education from all levels of education, different disciplines, and diverse professions and organizations. This website provides information about the organization, its activities, and a variety of other resources pertaining to multicultural education.

## Electronic Magazine of Multicultural Education

www.eastern.edu/publications/emme

This is an on-line magazine for scholars, practitioners, and students of multicultural education. EMME includes material for both the general public and professionals working in multicultural education. Content is compiled as theme-based issues that contain articles, teaching ideas, and reviews of juvenile and professional books.

## Center for Multilingual, Multicultural Research (CMMR)

www.usc.edu/dept/education/cmmr

This website provides a rich source of bilingual, ESL, and multicultural education resources. The visitor will find articles and links to websites that include full text presentations and a broad array of other resources. The full spectrum of age ranges may be seen in the material available.

## Center for Multicultural Education at the University of Washington

depts.washington.edu/centerme/home.htm

This website reports on research and activities aimed at improving practice related to equity issues, intergroup relations, and achievement by students of color. This site includes information about the center's research and teaching missions, successful K–12 programs, and events that are scheduled at the center.

# BUILDING YOUR PORTFOLIO

If you are thinking about a career in special education, you should know that many states use national standards developed by the Council for Exceptional Children (CEC) to assess a teacher candidate's knowledge about and skills for working with students with disabilities. See a complete listing of the ten CEC Content Standards on the inside front cover of this text.

## CEC Content Standards Addressed in Chapter 5

1. Foundations
2. Development and Characteristics of Learners
3. Individual Learning Differences
5. Learning Environments and Social Interactions
9. Professional and Ethical Practice

**Assess Your Knowledge of the CEC Standards Addressed in Chapter 5**

Some states require that teacher candidates develop a portfolio of products that demonstrate mastery of the CEC content standards. To assist in the development of products for this portfolio, you may wish to complete the following activities.

- Complete a written test of the chapter's content.

  *If your instructor requires a written test of your content knowledge for this chapter, keep a copy for your portfolio. A practice test on the information covered in this chapter is available through the companion website (www.ablongman.com/hardman8e) and the Student Study Guide.*

- Respond to Application Questions for the Case Study, "A Case of Overrepresentation, Finances, and School Reform."

  *Review the Case Study and respond in writing to the application questions. Keep a copy of the Case Study and your written response for your portfolio.*

- Complete the "Take a Stand" activity for the Debate Forum "English-Only or Bilingual Education?"

  *Read the Debate Forum in this chapter and then visit the companion website to complete the activity "Take a Stand." Keep a copy of this activity for your portfolio.*

- Participate in a Community Service Learning Activity.

  *Community service is a valuable way to enhance your learning experience. Visit our companion website for suggested community service learning activities that correspond to the information presented in this chapter. Develop a reflective journal of the service learning experience for your portfolio.*

## THEMES OF THE TIMES

The New York Times
nytimes.com
expect the world®

Expand your knowledge of the concepts discussed in this chapter by reading current and historical articles from the *New York Times* by visiting the "Themes of the Times" section of the companion website: **www.ablongman.com/hardman8e.**

# Exceptionality and the Family

## She May Not Be Normal

I was admitted to the hospital the night before for an induction because of a low level of amniotic fluid. Things happened fast and I knew something was wrong. It was too late for a caesarean section and Sarah was born ... face sideways instead of face down. ... I had no idea at the time how dangerous this was, nor were these dangers conveyed to me. ... There was no way of knowing that the damage was already done.

There have been lots of tears and sleepless nights, uncertainties and immeasurable heartache. Yet nothing can equal the joy that Sarah has brought to my life. Her smile speaks volumes and her eyes lead my heart. I can honestly say that she touches the lives of everyone she meets. To know her is to love her. Although she may not be "normal," she is certainly perfect, and worthy of every effort to improve her quality of life. When I tire of the endless rounds of doctors, therapists, hospitals, schools and tests, I remember that Sarah and I are not alone. There are thousands of children with special needs all over the world and each one of them is worthy of the efforts that parents, caregivers, doctors, researchers, therapists, schools, hospitals and legislatures can make to improve their lives. (Frost, 2002, p. 71)

## Just Make It Go Away!

It wasn't until I took the children to visit my family in Atlanta when Alison was seven weeks old that everything came crashing down. Fast. Hard. Unexpected.

"Just make it go away." At first, we thought it was allergies—that the little pollens wafting around in the humid Southern air had caused her respiratory attack. But the moment my sister's pediatrician saw Alison, he sent her to the emergency room and she was immediately admitted.

A parade of specialists examined her, took copious notes, huddled in the hallway. Radiologists scanned her brain and made X-rays of her body. Lab technicians took samples of everything—her blood, her urine, her mucus, her sweat—to run diagnostic tests.

No one could tell us what, exactly, was wrong with Alison.

My mother says she vividly remembers finding me sitting cross-legged in the guest room, putting her arms around me and saying, "Is there anything I can do?"

"Just make it go away," I whispered.

I cried the whole way home. I had never in my life felt such a deep, painful depression. For the first time since the crisis began, I started thinking about the future. Would Alison live? If she did, what would her life be like? And, to be honest, would taking care of a child with chronic medical and developmental problems destroy our lives?

These thoughts seemed so selfish. I felt guilty. (Anton, 2002, pp. 28–32)

## Am I Insane?

Am I insane? I hang up the phone. Yup, definitely lost my mind. I have just informed my mother that we will be coming for a visit. For 10 days. Call the looney bin—I'm on my way!

I can call back and renege. But she was so thrilled. How naïve of her. Had she forgotten the last visit? The disastrous long weekend last year, the first time he had been home with me since his diagnosis? Did she really not remember the birthday party where he had screamed at the top of his lungs when everyone sang, pressing his head between my knees, then raced over to the table and knocked the entire chocolate fudge cheesecake—my sister's favorite—to the floor? Or the next day, when one of his young cousins unwittingly got too close and my son put his hands around his neck?

I remember. The emotional roller coaster. The frustration and embarrassment about his strange behavior. The pain at seeing his autism outlined so hard and cold against the warm background of my "normal" family. Catching those glimpses of pity in my siblings' eyes. All weekend, I fought the impulse to run into my mother's arms. I was afraid that if I gave in, I would never stop crying. (Overton, 2000, p. 222)

**FOCUS**

**PREVIEW:** To preview the central concepts of this chapter, read the focus questions located in the margins. Using these questions as a guide, ask yourself what you already know and what you want to learn.

## Carlyn

Carlyn is 3 years old. Her brother, Parker, and sister, Rachel, love to laugh and play with Carlyn. They take her sledding; her brother enjoys wrestling with her. They just love being together. In fact, Parker tells his mother that Carlyn is his favorite person in the whole world.

When Carlyn was first born, she wasn't breathing. Then, after the doctors got her breathing, they found other physical difficulties and diagnosed her as having mental retardation. Her mother, Janna, explains, "It was heartbreaking. I can't ex-plain how you feel inside when you know there's something wrong with your baby."

Carlyn's father is very involved with Carlyn. "Janna and I have had a lot of conversations about Carlyn. One of the things that we have noticed is that sometimes people tend to treat Carlyn a little differently when they interact with her. You know, they feel good about it, which is okay and right, but we want Carlyn to have the same experiences that our other children have. We want people to know that it's normal to talk and interact with children with disabilities—that it should just be an everyday occurrence. I have a lot of faith and hope that Carlyn will have a bright future to look forward to. And I'm very grateful—I think all of us are—that we have Carlyn. That really sustains us at times, because some times are stressful, and they're very difficult, but nevertheless we're very grateful for Carlyn. That gives us a lot of joy."

When Carlyn first went to the elementary school, she was in preschool. The school seemed quite large and was probably frightening for her. At first she just observed; she didn't interact with the children. But now she loves to play cars with the boys and dolls with the girls. She's learning and enjoys being with the others. She uses all the children around her to learn; she has good role models.

At school, Carlyn works on her feeding and drinking. Academically, she practices fine motor skills. Her teacher sends notes home when Carlyn passes a milestone—when she walked 10 feet, when she took 5 swallows of a liquid, when she put a puzzle together. Carlyn's teacher hopes that when Carlyn turns 5, she will go to an integrated kindergarten class that will provide any of the services she may need.

According to Carlyn's teacher, "Carlyn's growing by leaps and bounds. She's benefiting from us as much as we are from her."

**FOCUS 1**

Identify five factors that influence the ways in which families respond to infants with birth defects or disabilities.

### Social/ecological system

An organization that provides structure for human interactions, for defining individual and group roles, for establishing expectations about behavior, and for specifying individual and group responsibilities in a social environment. Also called a social system. The system is ecological; changes in one individual or element in the environment often spell changes for other individuals within the system.

Nowhere is the impact of an individual who is exceptional felt so strongly as in the family (Fine & Simpson, 2000; Turnbull & Turnbull, 1997). The birth of an infant with disabilities may alter the family as a social unit in a variety of ways (Fuller & Olsen, 1998). Parents and siblings may react with shock, disappointment, anger, depression, guilt, and confusion. Over time, many parents and siblings develop coping skills that enhance their sense of well-being and their capacity to deal with the stressful demands of caring for a child, youth, or adult with a disability (Gray, 2002; Hauser-Cram, Warfield, Shonkoff, & Krauss, 2001; Pipp-Siegel, Sedey, & Yoshinaga-Itano, 2002). Many family members become resilient (Blacher, 2002), and many adapt well to having a child with a disability (Hastings & Taunt, 2002).

A child with physical, intellectual, or behavioral disabilities presents unique and diverse challenges to the family unit (Cuskelly, Chant, & Hayes, 1998). In one instance, the child may hurl the family into crisis, precipitating major conflicts among its members. Family relationships may be weakened by the added and unexpected physical, emotional, and financial stress. In another instance, this child may be a source of unity that bonds family members together and strengthens their relationships (Ferguson, 2002). Many factors influence the reactions of the family, including the emotional stability of each individual, religious values and beliefs, socioeconomic status, time constraints, and the severity and type of the child's disability (Kellegrew, 2000; Turnbull & Turnbull, 2002). Twenty-eight percent of the children with disabilities in the United States live in poverty. They and their families experience hunger, greatly diminished access to health care, often overcrowded and unclean housing, unsafe neighborhoods and schools, and a host of other, equally challenging circumstances (Park, Turnbull, & Turnbull, 2002).

This chapter discusses how raising children with disabilities affects parents, siblings, grandparents, and other extended family members. We will examine an array of issues directly related to families with children who are disabled. Additionally, this chapter examines the family as a **social/ecological system** defined by a set of purposes, cultural beliefs, parent and child roles, expectations, and family socio-economic conditions (Fine & Simpson, 2000; Kellegrew, 2000; Lambie, 2000a; Turn-bull & Turnbull, 2002; Zhang & Bennett, 2001). A social/ecological system approach looks at how each family member fulfills roles consistent with expectations established by discussion, traditions, beliefs, or other means. In the process, each member functions in an interdependent manner with other members to pursue family goals and to achieve various expectations (Danseco, 1997; Howie, 1999). This approach also examines the **ecocultural** and socioeconomic factors that impinge on the children with disabilities and their families (Turnbull & Turnbull, 2002). For example, a family who has experienced substantial income loss because of layoffs or a family whose parents are drug abusers may not be as effective, resilient, or resourceful in responding to a child or youth with a disability. A social/ecological framework makes it easy to see how changes in one family member can affect every other member and consequently the entire family system (Ferguson, 2002; Fox, Vaughan, Wyatte, & Dunlap, 2002; Hauser-Cram et al., 2001; Kellegrew, 2000).

# Understanding Families

## Reacting to Crisis

The birth of an infant with significant disabilities has a profound impact on the family (Fox et al., 2002). The expected or fantasized child whom the parents and other family members have anticipated does not arrive, and the parents are thrown into a state of emotional shock.

Some conditions, such as **spina bifida** and **Down syndrome,** are readily apparent at birth, whereas others, such as hearing impairments and learning disabilities, are not detectable until later. Even if attending physicians suspect the presence of a disabling condition, they may be unable to give a confirmed diagnosis without the passage of some time and further testing. When the parents also suspect that something is wrong, waiting for a diagnosis can be agonizing (Derer & D'Alonzo, 2000; Frost, 2002; Fox et al., 2002).

The most immediate and predictable reaction to the birth of a child with a disability is shock, characterized by feelings of disappointment, sadness or depression, loneliness, fear, anger, frustration, devastation, numbness, uncertainty, and a sense of being trapped. Both mothers and fathers report having these or similar feelings intermittently during the lifespan of their child (Blaska, 1998; Fuller & Olsen, 1998). Another reaction is depression, often exhibited in the form of grief or mourning. Some parents describe such emotions as very much like those suffered after the death of a loved one. Many mothers whose babies with abnormalities survive suffer more acute feelings of grief than mothers whose infants with defects die. Recurrent sorrow and frequent feelings of inadequacy are persistent emotions that many parents experience as they gradually adjust to having an infant with a disability (Lee et al., 2001). These ongoing feelings of grief may be

**Ecocultural**

A term referring to cultural and environmental factors that influence family functioning, such as unemployment, the primary language spoken in the home, the country-of-origin traditions, parental illness, number of children in the family, and educational background.

**Spina bifida**

A developmental defect of the spinal column.

**Down syndrome**

A condition caused by a chromosomal abnormality that results in unique physical characteristics and varying degrees of mental retardation. This condition was once described as "mongolism," a term that is no longer acceptable.

*Receiving the news that your child might have a disability produces powerful emotions.*

**FOCUS**

**2**

What three statements can be made about the stages parents may experience in responding to infants or young children with disabilities?

triggered by health or behavior challenges presented by the child, unusual child care demands, lack of achievement of developmental milestones in the child, and insensitivity of extended family and community members (Gray, 2002; Lee, et al., 2001).

Although the parents of children with disabilities experience many of the same feelings and reactions, their intensity, their relationship to specific stages, and the eventual adjustments made individually and collectively by family members vary from one person to another (Lee et al., 2001; Turnbull & Turnbull, 2002). Stages associated with various kinds of emotions may overlap one another (see Figure 6.1) and resurface during another period. Some parents may go through distinct periods of adjustment, whereas others may adjust without passing through any identifiable sequence of stages. The process of adjustment for parents is continuous and distinc-

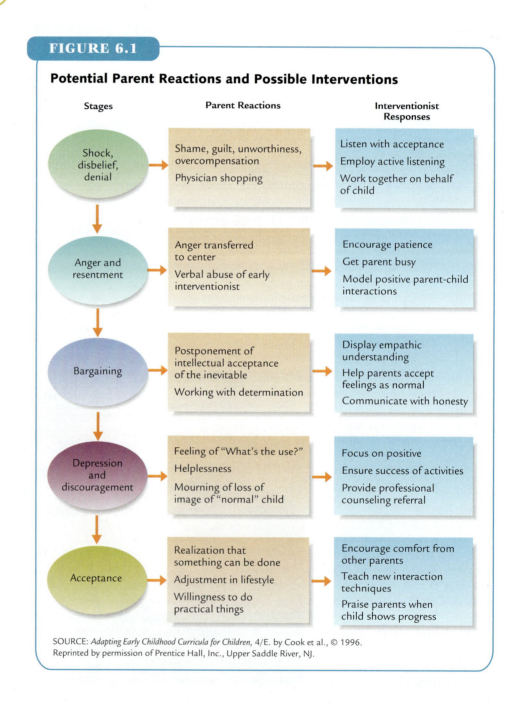

**FIGURE 6.1**

**Potential Parent Reactions and Possible Interventions**

| Stages | Parent Reactions | Interventionist Responses |
|---|---|---|
| Shock, disbelief, denial | Shame, guilt, unworthiness, overcompensation; Physician shopping | Listen with acceptance; Employ active listening; Work together on behalf of child |
| Anger and resentment | Anger transferred to center; Verbal abuse of early interventionist | Encourage patience; Get parent busy; Model positive parent-child interactions |
| Bargaining | Postponement of intellectual acceptance of the inevitable; Working with determination | Display empathic understanding; Help parents accept feelings as normal; Communicate with honesty |
| Depression and discouragement | Feeling of "What's the use?"; Helplessness; Mourning of loss of image of "normal" child | Focus on positive; Ensure success of activities; Provide professional counseling referral |
| Acceptance | Realization that something can be done; Adjustment in lifestyle; Willingness to do practical things | Encourage comfort from other parents; Teach new interaction techniques; Praise parents when child shows progress |

SOURCE: *Adapting Early Childhood Curricula for Children,* 4/E. by Cook et al., © 1996. Reprinted by permission of Prentice Hall, Inc., Upper Saddle River, NJ.

tively individual (Baxter, Cummins, & Yiolitis, 2000; Fine & Nissenbaum, 2000; Lee et al., 2001). Consider the following:

> When our son was born, my husband and I were told that the parents of a child [with a disability] move through certain stages of reaction: shock, guilt, . . . and anger, all terminating in the final, blissful stage of adjustment. I do not believe in this pattern. I now know too many parents of children [with disabilities] to be a believer in any set pattern.
>
> I feel we do move through these emotions, and just because we have come to adjustment (which I prefer to call "acceptance" because we spend our whole lives adjusting, although we may at one point accept the situation), that does not mean we never return to other emotions. We may continue to feel any of these emotions at any time, in any order. (West, 1981, p. S10)

Some parents, siblings, and even relatives of children with disabilities employ a kind of cognitive coping that enables them to think about the child, sibling, or grandchild with disabilities in ways that enhance their sense of well-being and capacity for responding positively (Beach Center, 1998c; Turnbull & Turnbull, 1993). For example, read the following account of one mother and her response to the birth of a child with a disability:

> Something like this could tear a marriage apart . . . but instead it has brought us closer.
>
> Right after she was born, I remember this revelation. She was teaching us something . . . how to keep things in perspective . . . to realize what's important. I've learned that everything is tentative and that you never know what life will bring.
>
> I've learned that I'm a much stronger person than I had thought. I look back, see how far I've come, and feel very pleased.
>
> The good that's come from this is that I marvel at what a miracle she is . . . it is a miracle that she's alive and that we are going to take her home. (Affleck & Tennen, 1993, p. 136)

This mother was able to interpret the birth and subsequent events in a positive manner. Her thinking or cognitive coping helped her reduce or successfully manage feelings of shock, distress, and depression. Additionally, her positive interpretation of this event aided her adjustment and contributed to her capacity to respond effectively to her child's needs.

**SHOCK.** The initial response to the birth of an infant with a disability is generally shock, distinguished variously by feelings of anxiety, guilt, numbness, confusion, helplessness, anger, disbelief, denial, and despair (Friend & Cook, 2003; Gray, 2002). Parents sometimes also have feelings of grief, detachment, bewilderment, or bereavement. At this time, when many parents are most in need of assistance, the least amount of help may be available. Physicians, nurses, and other care providers may not adequately sense the profound feelings that parents are experiencing. Furthermore, they may not know what to say or how to respond in a supportive manner. The ways in which parents react during this period depend on their psychological makeup, the types of assistance rendered, and the nature and severity of the disability (Turnbull & Turnbull, 2002). Over time, many parents move from being victims to being survivors of the trauma (Gray, 2002).

> I'll guarantee that every parent, at some point between the thrill of conception and the anxiety of the delivery room, has experienced the same fear, "What if something is wrong with my baby?"
>
> Most of us like to think we would do anything, make any sacrifice, for our children. But when the vague fear you have tried to stifle becomes a reality, when your child is born with a severe physical or mental disability that threatens your own freedom and lifestyle, that commitment is put to the test.

After you have experienced the shock, the denial, the grief, it slowly begins to dawn on you. Your life has changed forever, in ways you never expected, never wanted, never dared to imagine.

I know. It happened to me. (Anton, 2002, p. 28)

During the initial period of shock, parents may be unable to process or comprehend information provided by medical and other health-related personnel. For this reason, information may need to be communicated to parents several times until they have fully grasped the important concepts. Parents may experience the greatest assaults on their self-worth and value systems during this time. They may blame themselves for their child's disabilities and may seriously question their positive self-perceptions. Likewise, they may be forced to reassess the meaning of life and the reasons for their present challenges. Blacher (1984) has referred to this stage as the *period of emotional disorganization*.

**REALIZATION.** The stage of realization is characterized by several types of parental behavior. Parents may be anxious or fearful about their ability to cope with the demands of caring for a child with unique needs. They may be easily irritated or upset and spend considerable time in self-accusation, self-pity, or self-hate. They may continue to reject or deny information provided by health care professionals (Powell-Smith & Stollar, 1997). During this stage, however, parents do come to understand the actual demands and constraints that will come with raising a child with a disability (Lee et al., 2001). For example, one parent wrote,

"It's probably Cerebral Palsy," said the Early Intervention therapist. Rachel was only four months old during this initial evaluation. She couldn't hold her head up, roll over, sit up, or crawl. She couldn't even lift her arms or legs. She had no eye contact, cried constantly, and never slept. I knew something was wrong and feared she would never bond with me.

I remember starting to cry. The grandmothers looked on, tried to hold back their tears, but they couldn't. My perfect child was officially not perfect. After collecting my thoughts and trying to shed the feeling of devastation, I tried to think of the positives. As long as it's CP, I thought, this diagnosis meant that she would be physically disabled, but her mental faculties would be intact. We called to make an appointment with a neurologist within 10 minutes of the initial CP diagnosis. Unfortunately, two months passed before we could get an appointment (Epstein & Bessell, 2002, p. 56).

When Rachel was six months old the neurologist ordered an MRI. He informed us that "She has 'white matter disorder' and it is probably degenerative," although he wasn't at all certain exactly what it was. Now I was wishing it was "only CP." More tests were ordered and we didn't get an affirmative diagnosis until Rachel was eight months old. We now know Rachel has Canavan Disease, a genetic disorder she inherited from both [of us. Both] Ken and I . . . carry a mutated gene that caused Rachel to be born without an enzyme in her brain to neutralize the brain fluid. Because the fluid is so acidic, the myelin in Rachel's brain is deteriorating. (Epstein & Bessell, 2002, p. 56)

**DEFENSIVE RETREAT.** During the stage of defensive retreat, parents attempt to avoid dealing with the anxiety-producing realities of their child's condition. Some try to solve their dilemma by seeking placement for the child in a clinic, institution, or residential setting. Other parents disappear for a while or retreat to a safer and less demanding environment. One mother, on returning home from the hospital with her infant with Down syndrome, quickly packed her suitcase and left with the infant in the family car, not knowing what her destination would be. She simply did not want to face her immediate family or relatives. After driving around for several hours, she decided to return home. Within several months, she adapted very well to her daughter's needs and began to provide the stimulation necessary for gradual, persistent growth. Her daughter is now married and works full time in a day care center for young children.

**ACKNOWLEDGMENT.** Acknowledgment is the stage in which parents mobilize their strengths to confront the conditions created by having a child with a disability. At this time, parents begin to involve themselves in the intervention and treatment process. They are also better able to comprehend information or directions provided by a specialist concerning their child's condition and treatment. Some parents become interested in joining an advocacy organization that is suited to their child's condition and the needs of the family (Fuller & Olsen, 1998). Parents begin to accept the child with the disability (Friend & Cook, 2003). It is during this stage that parents can direct their energies to challenges external to themselves. An excellent example of a mother who found a positive outlet for her experiences and those of her son is found in the nearby Reflect on This, *"Sesame Street."*

**Reflect on This**

## SESAME STREET: MODELING A WORLD THAT RESPECTS EVERY CHILD

In 1970, *Sesame Street* was a very young television program, only in its second season. And I was the show's newest, youngest writer. . . .

I became pregnant. In June 1974, my son, Jason, was born—with Down syndrome. Overnight, my academic interest in disability issues became intensely personal. Suddenly, I was struck by the absolute and total *absence* of children like mine in the media. Everyone on television looked so "perfect," so very—the word still catches in my throat—"normal." I looked at television programming, advertising, catalogs, illustrations in magazines; the media was not depicting *my* experience at all!

It was as if my child and I had instantaneously fallen off the face of the earth. We had, in fact, just joined America's largest minority group, but as far as the media was concerned, we were insignificant to the point of invisibility. It was a terrible feeling—a feeling of isolation, of alienation, of hurt and pain at society's total disregard for the integrity and value of my precious son.

Suddenly, the inclusion of children with disabilities—children like *my* child—on *Sesame Street* was an issue of profound personal importance. Fortunately, all the people at *Sesame Street* were being sensitized at the same time.

I am extremely proud to have written many of the "disability segments" for *Sesame Street* during the past 26 years. But it is the real and sincere commitment to those principles shared by all the other writers and, in fact, every member of the show's staff and

*Jason Kingsley, who was born with Down syndrome, as he appeared at age 3 on Sesame Street demonstrating his letter identification skills.*

*Living independently, Jason proudly opens the door of his new apartment.*

crew that makes me so grateful and proud to have been associated with *Sesame Street* and Children's Television Workshop for all these years. I am confident that as long as *Sesame Street* exists, it will continue to model a world in which *all* children are understood, accepted, cherished, and respected.[1]

As a young boy, Jason Kingsley, who has Down syndrome, made several appearances on *Sesame Street, All My Children,* and other television programs. In 1994, Jason and his friend, Mitchell Levitz, published their book *Count Us In: Growing Up with Down Syndrome.* The book, published by Harcourt Brace & Company, is currently in its fourth printing.

Jason lived in Chappaqua, New York, where he graduated from high school with a full academic diploma in June 1994. He attended the Maplebrook School in Armenia, New York, a postsecondary program for students with learning disabilities. He was the school's first student with Down syndrome and was voted dorm representative.

Kingsley, now 24, enjoys some of the benefits of adulthood—like a nice cold beer in the shade. Jason's dreams for the future include getting a job, living in his own place, getting married, and maybe even being a father.

Currently, Jason is working full time as assistant cultural arts program coordinator for Westchester Arc. He is living independently in his own apartment like Mitchell. Jason explains, "He is a good inspiration for me."[2]

[1]SOURCE: From "Sesame Street: Modeling a World That Respects Every Child," by E. P. Kingsley, 1996, *Exceptional Parent, 26*(6), pp. 74–76.

[2]SOURCE: From "25 Role Models for the Next 25 Years," 1996, *Exceptional Parent, 26*(6), p. 54.

**FOCUS**

**3**

Identify three ways in which a newborn child with disabilities influences the family social/ecological system.

## Family Characteristics and Interactions

The birth of a child with disabilities and the continued presence of that child strongly influence how family members respond to one another, particularly if the child is severely disabled or has multiple disabilities. In many families, the mother experiences the greatest amount of trauma and strain. In caring for such a child, she may no longer be able to handle many of the tasks she once performed, and her attention to other family members may be greatly reduced.

When the mother is drawn away from the tasks she used to perform, other family members often must assume more responsibility. Adjusting to the new roles and routines may be difficult, and family members may need to alter their personal routines in order to assist the mother. Responses of family and extended family members may vary according to their cultural backgrounds and related beliefs about children with disabilities. In this regard, we are just beginning to understand the influence of various cultures on the ways in which children with disabilities are viewed and treated within these cultures (Beach Center, 1998d; Linan-Thompson & Jean, 1997; Skinner, Bailey, Correa, & Rodriguez, 1999). Teachers and other treatment providers need to be sensitive to child-rearing practices, roles of family members, as well parents' religious beliefs and views about the role of education (Rivers, 2000; Zhang & Bennett, 2001). Professionals also need to be aware of the different meanings that parents assign to their children with disabilities. Furthermore, greater efforts must be directed at finding appropriate interpreters for IFSP and IEP meetings, becoming adept in

**Reflect on This**

## AMERICAN INDIANS AND DISABILITY

**How do traditional teachings about the causes of disability differ from current medical understanding?**

Overall, American Indians historically have linked the source of disability to natural causes or the consequence of breaking sacred laws and taboos.

**How does the concept of spirit influence disability belief?**

A common traditional belief among American Indians is that humans have these elements: body, mind, and spirit. Most tribes believe the spirit chooses its earthly body, which may be a disabled body. In terms of value, the body is less important than the spirit. A family may reject medical efforts to save a person with critical injuries or with severe deformities, because to save a body may thwart the spirit's attempt to leave the body. The spirit is not "trapped" within a body; it makes the choice. When a spirit chooses to live in a body with a disability, this act reflects a strong spirit. This belief in choice extends to all of life—choice of who and what a person is.

**How do American Indian beliefs on health and disability affect medical practices?**

American Indians tend to believe that modern medicine treats only the body, a method that does not address the spiritual component. Family-centered medical service providers understand this and encourage necessary ceremonial practices (e.g., marking a hospitalized baby with significant religious symbols and adorning a crib with eagle feathers) to restore harmony.

**How does American Indian language reflect disability beliefs?**

Generally speaking, no tribe has a word similar to "disability." However, Indian languages commonly have words or phrases for specific circumstances, such as "crooked back" or "no-eyes."

**Are there any phrases to avoid when talking about disability?**

Virtually all American Indian cultures believe thoughts and words have power: Thinking or speaking about something can make it happen. If a person says someone will die or never walk again, and that statement proves true, then the originator of the words bears responsibility. Service providers should refrain from comments such as "will not be able" and other limiting phrases.

SOURCE: Adapted from *What You Should Know About American Indians and Disability*, by the Beach Center on Families and Disability, University of Kansas, 1998. Available: *http://www.lsi.ukans.edu/beach/html/m6.htm*

cross-cultural communication, learning how to do home visits, and becoming skilled in connecting with diverse families and communities.

As the child with disabilities grows older, the mother frequently faces a unique dilemma: how to strike a balance between the nurturing activities she associates with her role as caregiver and the activities associated with fostering independence. Seeing her child struggle with new tasks and suffer some of the natural consequences of trying new behaviors can be difficult. For many mothers, conquering overprotectiveness is extremely difficult, but it can be accomplished with help from those who have already experienced and surmounted this problem (Beach, 1998g). If the mother or other care providers continue to be overprotective, the results can be problematic, especially when the child reaches late adolescence and is unprepared for entry into adulthood or semi-independent living (Kellegrew, 2000).

Mothers often develop strong **dyadic relationships** with their children with a disability (Fuller & Olsen, 1998: Kellegrew, 2000). Dyadic relationships are evidenced by very close ties between these children and their mothers. Rather than communicating with all members of the family, a child may use his or her mother as the exclusive conduit for communicating needs and making requests. Dyadic relationships may also develop between other members of the family. Certain siblings may turn to each other for support and nurturing. Older siblings may take on the role of parent substitutes as a result of their new caregiving responsibilities, and their younger siblings, who come to depend on older siblings for care, then tend to develop strong relationships with them.

Every family has a unique power structure. In some families the father holds most of the power or control, and in others the governance of the family lies with the mother or the family at large. Power, in the context of this discussion, is defined as the amount of con rol or influence one or more family members exert in managing family decisions, assigning family tasks, and implementing family activities. Just as families vary greatly in their membership and their organization, the power structure within each family varies with the characteristics of the members. That power structure is often altered substantially by the arrival of an infant with disabilities. Siblings, for example, assume greater power as they assume more responsibility.

Many children with disabilities are being raised by foster parents, single parents, parents of blended families, and gay couples. Furthermore, about half a million children are cared for through various state social services organizations and agencies (Fish, 2000). It is clear that all child care professionals need to work effectively and respectfully with all families, learning about their unique needs and responding with family-sensitive programs and interventions. A number of organizations provide support to these families, including the Single Parent Resource Center, Single Parents, Family Pride Coalition, SafeTPlace, the Single Parents Association Online, Parents Without Partners, and the Single Parent Network.

The nature of such families may vary, but one common factor is the presence of a child with a disability. This child deserves the attention and support of school personnel and other professionals—no matter what type of family unit the child is part of. The people who serve as primary caregivers or legal guardians of the child should be invited to participate fully in any programs and support services (Fish, 2000).

## Spousal Relationships

The following statement illustrates the interactions and outcomes that a couple may experience in living with a child with a disability.

> When I think about having another child, I panic. In fact, I have consumed hours of psychological time thinking about my little boy and our response to him. Actually, my husband and I really haven't dealt successfully with our feelings. Two years ago, I gave birth to a little boy who is severely disabled. I was about 26 years old and my husband was 27.

**FOCUS 4**

Identify three aspects of raising a child with a disability that contribute to spousal stress.

**Dyadic relationships**

Relationships involving two individuals who develop and maintain a significant affiliation over time.

*Parents of children with disabilities need time to be together. This is often made possible through respite care.*

We didn't know much about children, let alone children with disabilities, nor did we ever think that we would have a child who would be seriously disabled. When the pediatrician suggested institutionalization for the child, we just nodded our heads. Believe it or not, I had merely looked at him through the observation windows once or twice.

Recently, my husband gave me an ultimatum: "Either you decide to have some children, or I'm going to find someone who will." (There are, of course, other things that are bothering him.) Since the birth of this child, I have been absolutely terrified of becoming pregnant again. As a result, my responses to my husband's needs for physical affection have been practically absent—or should I say, nonexistent. I guess you could say we really need some help.

An infant with a chronic health condition or disability may require more immediate and prolonged attention from the mother for feeding, treatment, and general care, and her attention may become riveted on the life of the child. The balance that once existed between being a mother and being a partner no longer exists. The mother may become so involved with caring for the child that other relationships lose their quality and intensity. The following statements express the feelings that may surface as a result:

> Angela spends so much time with Juan that she has little energy left for me. It is as if she has become consumed with his care.
>
> You ask me to pay attention to Juan, but you rarely spend any time with me. When am I going to be a part of your life again?
>
> I am developing a resentment toward you and Juan. Who wants to come home when all your time is spent waiting on him?

Although these feelings are typical of some fathers, other fathers have the opposite reaction. Some may become excessively involved with their disabled children's lives, causing their partners to feel neglected. Mothers deeply involved in caregiving may feel overworked, overwhelmed, and in need of a break or reprieve. They may wonder why their spouses are not more helpful and understanding. However, fathers who assist with the burdens of caring serve as a buffer, contributing to their partner's well-being and resilience. Day-to-day physical and psychological support provided by fathers is invaluable to mothers of children with disabilities (Simmerman, Blacher, & Baker, 2001). This support is also predictive of couple satisfaction and contentment (Simmerman et al., 2001; Willoughby & Glidden, 1995).

Fear, anger, guilt, and resentment often interfere with a couple's capacity to communicate and seek realistic solutions. Fatigue itself profoundly affects how couples function and communicate. As a result, some parents of children with disabilities join together to create **respite care** programs, which give them a chance to get away from the demands of childrearing and to relax and renew their relationship (Chan & Sigafoos, 2000).

Other factors may also contribute to spousal stress: unusually heavy financial burdens for medical treatment or therapy; frequent visits to treatment facilities; forgone time in couple-related activities; lost sleep and fatigue, particularly in the early years of the child's life; and social isolation from relatives and friends.

**Respite care**

Assistance provided by individuals outside of the immediate family to give parents and other children within the family time away from the child with a disability for a recreational event, a vacation, and so on. Some states provide funding to families to secure this kind of care.

Research related to spousal stress and instability is often contradictory (Powell-Smith & Stollar, 1997; Seligman & Darling, 1989; Turbiville, 1997; Turnbull & Turnbull, 1997). Some families appear to experience extreme spousal turmoil, often culminating in separation and eventually divorce, yet others "report no more frequent problems than comparison families" (Seligman & Darling, 1989, p. 93). Still other families report an improvement in relationships following diagnosis of a child with a disability (Turnbull & Turnbull, 1997).

## Parent-Child Relationships

The relationships between parents and children with disabilities are a function of many factors. Some of the most crucial factors include the child's age and gender; the family's socioeconomic status, coping strength, and composition (one-parent family, two-parent family, or blended family); and the nature and seriousness of the disability. Families go through a developmental sequence in responding to the needs and nuances of caring for children with disabilities:

1. The time at which parents learn about or suspect a disability in their child

2. The period in which the parents make plans regarding the child's education

3. The point at which the individual with a disability has completed his or her education

4. The period when the parents are older and may be unable to care for their adult offspring (Turner, 2000)

The nature and severity of the disability and the willingness of the parents to adapt and to educate themselves regarding their role in helping the child have an appreciable influence on the parent-child relationship that eventually emerges.

Many mothers of children with severe disabilities or serious illnesses face the dilemma of finding a baby-sitter. The challenge is far greater than one might imagine:

> Marcia's a very mature girl for her age, but she becomes almost terrified when she thinks that she might have to hold our new son, Jeremy. He has multiple disabilities.
>
> I don't dare leave him with our other two children, Amy and Mary Ann. They're much too young to handle Jeremy. But I need to get away from the demands that seem to be ever present in caring for Jeremy. If I could just find one person who could help us, even just once a month, things would be a lot better for me and my family.

Locating a youth or adult who is willing and able to provide quality care for an evening or weekend is extremely difficult. In some areas of the country, however, enterprising teenagers have developed baby-sitting businesses that specialize in tending children with disabilities. Frequently, local disability associations and parent-to-parent programs help families find qualified baby-sitters or other respite care providers (Beach Center, 1998h).

Time away from the child with a disability or serious illness gives parents and siblings a chance to meet some of their own needs (Chan & Sigafoos, 2000). Parents can recharge themselves for their demanding regimens, and siblings can use the exclusive attention of their parents to reaffirm their importance in the family and their value as individuals (Beach Center, 1998e; Powell-Smith & Stollar, 1997).

**MOTHER-CHILD RELATIONSHIPS.** If a child's impairment is congenital and readily apparent at birth, the mother often becomes primarily responsible for relating to the child and his or her needs. If the infant is born prematurely or needs extensive, early medical assistance, that relationship may be slow to emerge, for many reasons. The mother may be prevented from engaging in the feeding and caregiving activities, because the child may need to spend many weeks in an isolette supported by sophisticated medical equipment. As a consequence of the remoteness they experience in interacting with their infants in a personally satisfying manner, some mothers even come to question whether they really had a baby. For all these reasons the

**FOCUS 5**

Identify four general phases that parents may experience in rearing a child with a disability.

**FOCUS 6**

Identify four factors that influence the relationship that develops between infants with disabilities and their mothers.

UNDERSTANDING FAMILIES

Mothers who have appropriately high expectations for their children contribute a great deal to their development over time.

process of mother-child attachment may be impeded.

In other cases, a mother may be virtually forced into a close physical and emotional relationship with her child with a disability or injury (Hauser-Cram et al., 2001). The bond that develops between mother and child is one that cannot be severed. She assumes primary responsibility for fostering the child's emotional adjustment and developing the child's initial skills, and she acts as the child's personal representative or interpreter. In this role, the mother becomes responsible for communicating the child's needs and desires to other family members.

Because of the sheer weight of these responsibilities, other relationships often wane or even disappear. The mother who assumes this role and develops a very close relationship with her offspring with a disability often walks a variety of tightropes (Larsen, 2000). In her desire to protect her child, she may become overprotective and thus deny the child opportunities to practice the skills and participate in the activities that ultimately lead to independence. The mother may also underestimate her child's capacities and may be reluctant to allow her child to engage in challenging or risky ventures. In contrast, other mothers may neglect their children with disabilities and not provide the stimulation so critical to their optimal development. The mother's long-term vision for her child with a disability dramatically influences her behavior in preparing her son or daughter for adulthood and appropriate independence.

**FOCUS**

**7**

Identify three ways in which fathers may respond to their children with disabilities.

**FATHER-CHILD RELATIONSHIPS.** Information about fathers of children with disabilities is primarily anecdotal in nature or appears in case studies, websites, magazine articles, and books (Beach Center, 1998h; Dollahite, 2001; Meyer, 1995). Some research suggests that the child care involvement of fathers with children with disabilities is not significantly different from that of fathers of other children (Turbiville, 1997; Young & Roopnarine, 1994). Moreover, fathers are generally more reserved and guarded in expressing their feelings than other family members (Lamb & Meyer, 1991). Fathers are more likely to internalize their feelings and may respond with coping mechanisms such as withdrawal, sublimation, and intellectualization. Fathers of children with mental retardation are typically more concerned than mothers about their children's social development and eventual educational status, particularly if the children are boys (Turbiville, 1997). Likewise, they are more affected than mothers by the visibility and severity of their children's condition (Lamb & Meyer, 1991; Turbiville, 1997). Often, fathers of children with severe disabilities spend less time interacting with them, playing with them, and engaging in school-related tasks. Also, fathers are more likely to be involved with their children with disabilities if the children are able to speak or interact with words and phrases.

The relationships that emerge between fathers and children with disabilities are affected by the same factors as mother-child relationships. One important factor may be the gender of the child (Turbiville, 1997). If the child is male and the father had idealized the role he would eventually assume in interacting with a son, the adjustment for the father can be very difficult. The father may have had hopes of playing football with the child, of his eventually becoming a business partner, or of participating with his son in a variety of recreational activities. Many of these hopes will not be realized with a son who has a severe disability. When fathers withdraw or remain uninvolved with the child, other family members, particularly mothers, shoulder the caregiving responsibilities (Lamb & Meyer, 1991; Turbiville, 1997). This withdrawal often creates significant stress for mothers and other family members.

Fathers of children with disabilities prefer events and learning activities that are directed at the whole family, not just themselves (Turbiville & Marquis, 2001). They want to learn with other family members and other families how to encourage learning, language development, and so on (Johnson, 2000). Service providers often neglect fathers, not realizing what important contributions they are capable of making (Beach Center, 1998a, Hauser-Cram, Warfield, Shonkoff, & Krauss, 2001). Fathers prefer programs that clearly address their preferences and priorities—programs that focus on their needs (Carpenter, 2000; Turbiville & Marquis, 2001). Children whose fathers are involved in their education perform better in school, evidence better social skills, are more highly motivated to succeed in school, and are less likely to exhibit violent or delinquent behavior (Johnson, 2000; Beach Center, 1998a; Turbiville, 1997).

## Sibling Relationships

The responses of siblings to a sister or brother with a disability vary (Harland & Cuskelly, 2000; Masson, Kruse, Farabaugh, Gershberg, & Kohler, 2000; Meyers, 1997). Upon learning that a brother or sister has a disability, siblings are frequently encumbered with different kinds of concerns. A number of questions are commonly asked: "Why did this happen?" "Is my brother contagious? Can I catch what he has?" "What am I going to say to my friends?" "I can't baby-sit him!" "Am I going to have to take care of him all of my life?" "Will I have children who are disabled too?" "How will I later meet my responsibilities to my brother with a disability and also meet the needs of my future wife and children?"

Like their parents, siblings want to know and understand as much as they can about the disability of their sibling. They want to know how they should respond and how their lives might be different as a result of this event. If these concerns can be adequately addressed, the prognosis for positive sibling involvement with the brother or sister with a disability is much better (Darley, Porter, Werner, & Eberly, 2002).

Parents' attitudes and behaviors significantly affect those of their children toward siblings with disabilities. If parents are optimistic and realistic in their views toward the child with a disability, then siblings are likely to mirror these attitudes. Generally, siblings have positive feelings about having a sister or brother with a disability and believe that their experiences with these siblings with disabilities made them better individuals (Beach Center, 1998d;

**FOCUS 8**

Identify four ways in which siblings respond to a brother or sister with a disability.

*Supportive fathers contribute to the happiness of their children and their spouses by being available for child care and other home-centered support.*

Siblings may play many roles in nurturing and supporting a brother or sister with a disaiblity.

Fuller & Olsen, 1998; Harland & Cuskelly, 2000; McHugh, 1999). Siblings who are kindly disposed toward assisting the child with a disability can be a real source of support (Harland & Cuskelly, 2000). One mother of an 11-year-old son put it this way: "In the past he has said, 'I wish I had a regular brother, I wish I had someone to play with.' And there are really some hard, sad things like that. But over the years, he has been such a support, and he will help in any way that we ask. I'm pleased with the qualities that I see in him" (Darley et al., 2002). Many siblings play a crucial role in fostering the intellectual, social, and affective development of a brother or sister with a disability.

However, negative feelings do exist among siblings of children with disabilities (Cuskelly et al., 1998; Fine & Nissenbaum, 2000; Gray 2002; Masson et al., 2000). Loneliness, anxiety, guilt, and envy are common. Feelings of loneliness may surface in children who wanted a brother or sister with whom they could play. Anxiety may be present in a youth who wonders who will care for the sibling with a disability when the parents are no longer able to do so or are no longer alive. Guilt may arise for many reasons. Siblings, believing they are obligated to care for the sibling with a disability, believe that failing to provide such care would make them bad or immoral. Similarly, they may feel guilty about the thoughts and feelings they have about their sibling, such as anger, frustration, resentment, and even hate. Realizing that many parents would not respond positively to the expression of such feelings, some siblings carry them inside for a long time. One sibling put it this way:

The more I learn about sibling relationships, the more impressed I am with what ambivalent relationships they are—even when there is no disability. It seems that when disabilities are present, the ambivalence only gets stronger—the highs are higher. (For example, "Donny has brought me unending joy and laughter, and probably increased my sensitivity a hundredfold." Would many of us make such a comment about a sibling who wasn't disabled?) And the lows are lower. ("On the other hand, sometimes I can't help but feel frustrated and cheated.") The challenge, I suppose, is to celebrate the insights and sensitivity one gains as a result of the relationship, learn sometimes painful lessons from the frustrations, and then—somehow—move on. (Parent Project for Muscular Dystrophy Research, Inc., 2000, p.1)

With increased inclusion of students with disabilities in neighborhood schools and other general education settings (Berry & Hardman, 1998), siblings are often "called into action." They may be asked to explain their brother or sister's behavior, to give ongoing support, and respond to questions teachers and others might ask. Furthermore, they may be subject to teasing and related behaviors. Because of these and other factors, some siblings experience a greater risk for behavior problems (Lobato, Faust, & Spirito, 1988).

Many siblings resent the time and attention that parents devote to their sister or brother with a disability. This resentment may also take the form of jealousy. Some siblings feel emotionally neglected, convinced that their parents are not responsive to their needs for attention and emotional support (McHugh, 1999). For some siblings, the predominant feeling is one of bitter resentment or even rage. For others, the predominant attitude toward the family experience of growing up with a brother or sister with a disability is a feeling of deprivation—the sense that their social, educational, and recreational pursuits have been seriously limited.

*Support groups play an integral role in helping families understand and plan for their children with disabilities.*

The following statements are examples of such feelings: "We never went on a family vacation because of my brother, Steven." "How could I invite a friend over? I never knew how my autistic brother would behave." "How do you explain to a date that you have a sister who is retarded?" "Many of my friends stopped coming to my house because they didn't know how to handle my brother, Mike, who is deaf. They simply could not understand him." "I was always shackled with the responsibilities of tending my little sister. I didn't have time to have fun with my friends." "I want a real brother, not a retarded one."

Siblings of children with disabilities may also believe they must compensate for their parents' disappointment about having a child with a disability (McHugh, 1999). They may feel an undue amount of pressure to excel or to be successful in a particular academic or artistic pursuit. Such perceived pressure can have a profound effect on siblings' physical and mental health, as can the expressed expectations of parents: "Why do I always feel as if I have to be the perfect child or the one who always does things right? I'm getting tired of constantly having to win my parents' admiration. Why can't I just be average for once?"

Support groups for siblings of children with disabilities are emerging and can be particularly helpful to adolescents. These groups introduce children and youth to the important aspects of having such a sibling in the family. They establish appropriate expectations and discuss questions that children may be hesitant to ask in a family context. These groups also provide a therapeutic means by which these individuals analyze family needs and identify practical solutions (McHugh, 1999).

The best way to help siblings of children with disabilities is to support their parents and families (Berry & Hardman, 1998; Powell-Smith & Stollar, 1997). Participating in programs that encourage them to share information, to express feelings, and to learn how to be meaningfully involved with their sister or brother with a disability contributes much to their well-being.

## Extended Family Relationships

The term **extended family** is frequently used to describe a household in which an immediate (nuclear) family lives with relatives. For the purposes of this section, we use this term to refer to close relatives with whom the immediate family has regular and frequent contact, even though they do not necessarily live in the same household. These individuals may include grandparents, uncles, aunts, cousins, close neighbors, or friends.

When a grandchild with a disability is born, the joy of the occasion may dissipate. Like parents, grandparents are hurled into a crisis that necessitates reevaluation and reorientation (Scherman, Gardner, & Brown, 1995; Seligman & Darling, 1989). They must decide not only how they will respond to their child, who is now a parent, but also how they will relate to the new grandchild. Many grandparents, having grown up in a time when deviation from the norm was barely tolerated, much less under-

**FOCUS 9**

Identify three types of support that grandparents and other extended family members may render to families with children who have disabilities.

**Extended family**

Close relatives who visit or interact with a family on a regular basis.

*Grandparents or other close relatives may be very helpful in providing respite care.*

stood, enter the process of weathering this crisis without much understanding. In their day such a birth may have signified the presence of "bad blood" within a family, so the mother or father of the newborn child may be selected as the scapegoat. Blaming provides only temporary relief. It does little to promote the optimal family functioning that will be essential in the weeks and months to come.

Often, the initial response of grandparents to the newly born child with a disability may be to provide evidence that they are "pure and not responsible for the present suffering" (McPhee, 1982, p. 14). This is, of course, very counterproductive to the well-being of the mother and father of the newborn child. Research indicates that grandparents, particularly during the diagnostic phase, play an influential role in how their children—the new parents—respond to the child with a disability. If the grandparents are understanding and emotionally supportive and provide good role models of effective coping, they may have a positive impact on their own children, the mother and father. If the grandparents are critical or not accepting, they may add to the parents' burden and complicate it even further (Beach Center, 1998b; Seligman & Darling, 1989).

Grandparents and other family members may contribute a great deal to the primary family unit (Darley et al., 2002; Fox et al., 2002). The correlation between grandparent support and positive paternal adjustment is significant (Sandler, Warren, & Raver, 1995). If grandparents live near the family, they may become an integral part of the resource network and, as such, may be able to provide support before the energies of their children are so severely depleted that they require additional, costly help. To be of assistance, grandparents must be prepared and informed, which can be achieved in a variety of ways. They must have an opportunity to voice their questions, feelings, and concerns about the disability and its complications, and they must have means by which they can become informed. Parents can aid in this process by sharing, with their own parents and siblings, the pamphlets, materials, and books suggested by health and educational personnel. They may also encourage their families to become involved in parent and grandparent support groups (Bell & Smith, 1996; Fuller & Olsen, 1998; Kroth & Edge, 1997).

Grandparents may be helpful in several other ways, providing much-needed respite care and sometimes financial assistance in the form of a "special needs" trust for long-term support of the grandchild (Carpenter, 2000). Furthermore, they may be able to give parents a weekend reprieve from the pressures of maintaining the household and assist with transportation or baby-sitting. Grandparents may often serve as third-party evaluators, providing solutions to seemingly unresolvable problems. The child with a disability profits from the unique attention that only grandparents can provide. This attention can be a natural part of special occasions such as birthdays, vacations, fishing trips, and other traditional family activities.

## Family-Centered Support

Family-centered services and programs encourage families to take the lead in establishing and pursuing their priorities (Carpenter, 2000; Dunst, 2002; Nassar-McMillan & Algozzine, 2001). Teachers, medical personnel, and other professionals who embrace a family-centered philosophy focuses on the strengths and capabilities of families, not their deficits (Muscott, 2002). Furthermore, family-centered services are directed at

## LEARNING TO COPE. . .

I joined a support group soon after I found out about Garrett's hearing impairment. Boy, what a lifesaver that turned out to be. Support groups not only provide support, they also offer advice, encouragement, and helpful information about testing and resources. That old saying "been there, done that" holds a lot of water when you feel as though no one else knows what you're going through.

The leader of my support group, Mary, gave me good advice. The first thing she told me was that from time to time I might get depressed about my son's having a disability but that I should try not to beat myself up over it. She was right. A long time may go by without my getting upset about Garrett's deafness, but when it happens, I know that it's normal, and it's okay.

Mary also told us that a lot of people will tell us we have to accept the hand we were dealt, that there's something wrong with us if we don't. Mary told us to substitute the word "cope" for the word "accept." She said that learning to cope with a new situation is the only thing anyone can do. (Stebelton, 2001, p. 74)

---

the entire family, not just the mother and the child or youth with a disability (Cantu, 2002; Hauser-Cram et al., 2001; Turnbull & Turnbull, 2002). "The pivotal element of family-centered care is the recognition that the family is constant and the intervention setting is temporary. . . . Family members are the hour-to-hour, day-to-day therapists and teachers" (Cantu, 2002, p. 48). Unfortunately, family-centered support is primarily an early childhood phenomenon. The term "family-centered" and its variants are rarely found in the elementary research literature (Dunst, 2002, p. 142). The picture is even more appalling in secondary schools whose structural and organizational features do not promote effective collaboration with parents and families (Dunst, 2002). These structural and organizational barriers include large student-to-teacher ratios often as high as 180 students per general education teacher, large administrative bureaucracies, and diminished commitments to working with parents and families.

Patterns of family-centered support vary as a function of the life cycle of the family, in parallel with the changing needs of parents, children with disabilities, and their siblings (Dunst, 2002; Turnbull & Turnbull, 2002; Vacca & Feinberg, 2000). Family support during the early childhood years focuses on delivering appropriate services in natural environments and on helping family members develop an understanding of the child's disability, deal with child-related behavior problems, become knowledgeable about their legal rights, learn how to deal with the stress in their lives, and learn how to communicate and work effectively with caregivers (Bruder, 2000; Derer & D'Alonzo, 2000; Devore & Hanley-Maxwell, 2000; Hauser-Cram et al., 2001; Shelden & Rush, 2001).

Family-centered, home-based services delivered by educational and social services workers are directed at fostering appropriate motor development, promoting speech and language development, assisting with toilet training, and stimulating cognitive development. Other assistance may be targeted at helping parents address specific physical or health conditions that may require special diets, medications, or therapy regimens.

During the elementary school years, parents become increasingly concerned about their children's academic achievement and social relationships. With the movement in many school systems to more inclusionary programs, parents may be particularly

*Many children with disabilities attend their own neighborhood schools and are fully included in most every activity.*

## FAMILY VOICES ARE HEARD

Garret Frey, a Cedar Rapids, Iowa, high school student was paralyzed in a childhood accident. Currently, he uses a power wheelchair, has a tracheotomy, needs a ventilator, and is catheterized daily. His equipment and health status require monitoring 24 hours a day.

When he started school, Garret had a specially trained attendant. Later, the Cedar Rapids school district insisted that he have the assistance of a licensed practical nurse (LPN), paid for through his family's insurance. Once his family's insurance cap was reached, Garret was ineligible for private insurance. The school district claimed that because they believed that Garret's condition required "medical treatment" by a registered nurse during school hours, it was not obliged to pay for the care. It suggested the Frey family

1. pay for a nurse at school, or

2. have Garret tutored at home one hour per day.

The Freys believed that IDEA (Individuals with Disabilities Education Act) obligates school districts to pay for related school health services. Earlier federal court decisions agreed. Unable to reach a compromise with the school district, the Frey family sought a legal solution.

Garret's case won at several court levels, finally reaching the United States Supreme Court. In August 1998, Family Voices, the American Academy of Pediatrics, and the National Association of School Nurses filed an amicus brief on Garret's behalf.

On March 3, 1999, in a 7-to-2 ruling, the U.S. Supreme Court said that IDEA requires schools to provide health supports for students who need them. This support should be provided, as long as it is not medical in nature and performed by doctors, "to help guarantee that students like Garret are integrated into the public school." This means that all students, whatever their health condition, have a right to safely attend school, with necessary services paid [for] by the school district. In most cases a well-trained attendant, backed up by a regular school nurse, is sufficient.

Cedar Rapids says Garret's nurse will cost $30,000 to $40,000 annually, and his attendant will cost an additional $12,000. Garret's lawyer says the two positions can be combined for $18,000. The National School Board Association argues that with 17,000 students like Garret, federal dollars are inadequate for school districts' obligations. How many students need such support or what those services cost is really unknown. Institutional care can run $80,000 per year. And the ultimate price Garret and society will pay if he does not attend school is impossible to calculate. (*Exceptional Parent,* 1999a, p. 31)

### APPLICATION

1. What are the key issues in this dispute?

2. What steps need to be taken to resolve the financial issues associated with Garret's placement in an integrated school setting?

3. What should a school district do to address funding issues such as this one?

4. What should state boards of education do to provide assistance for students like these?

5. On what basis would you seek funding for Garret from a philanthropical agency?

---

anxious about their children's social acceptance by peers without disabilities and about the intensity and appropriateness of instructional programs delivered in general education settings. Overall, parents seem to be pleased with the possibilities associated with inclusion, particularly its social aspects. Intervention efforts during this period are based on the individualized education program (IEP). Consistent collaboration between parents and various multidisciplinary team members is crucial to the actual achievement of IEP goals and objectives. Interestingly, little is known from a research perspective about the actual achievement outcomes of the IEP process (Turnbull & Turnbull, 2002).

The secondary school years frequently pose significant challenges for adolescents with disabilities, their parents, and their families. Like their peers, adolescents with disabilities confront significant physical and psychological issues, including learning how to deal with their emergent sexuality, developing satisfactory relationships with individuals outside of the home environment, and becoming appropriately independent. Parents of adolescents with disabilities agree that academic achievement is vitally important; nevertheless, they want their sons and daughters to develop solid social skills and other behaviors associated with empathy, perseverance, and character (Geisthardt, Brotherson, & Cook, 2002; Kolb & Hanley-Maxwell, 2003). Other issues must also be addressed during these years, including preparation for employment, learning how to access adult services, and developing community living skills.

During their children's adolescence, parents often experience less compliance with their requests and greater resistance to their authority. Parents who are attuned to the unique challenges and opportunities of this developmental phase work closely with education and other personnel to develop IEPs that address these issues and prepare the adolescent with disabilities for entry into adulthood. Parents may also benefit from training that is directly related to dealing with teenage behavior and the challenges it presents.

During adolescence, parents are taught how to "let go," how to access adult services, and how to further their son or daughter's independence. Parents need information about the steps necessary to develop trusts and other legal documents for the welfare of all of their children.

The movement from high school to community and adult life can be achieved successfully by adolescents with disabilities if parents and other support personnel have consistently planned for this transition (Levinson, McKee, & DeMatteo, 2000). Transition planning is mandated by IDEA and is achieved primarily through the IEP planning process. IEP goals during this period are directed at providing instruction that is specifically related to succeeding in the community and functioning as an adult. The challenge for parents and care providers is to help adolescents with disabilities achieve as much independence as possible, given their strengths and challenges.

## Collaboration with Professionals

The interaction between professionals and parents is too often marked by confusion, dissatisfaction, disappointment, and anger (Caprenter, 2000). Consider this father's expressed concern:

> When the physician walked in to deliver the message he looked squarely into my wife's eyes. Even though we were sitting side by side on a chair turned hospital bed, his eyes never made contact with mine. I can surely empathize with the physician, who no doubt recognized the pain in my beautiful wife's eyes. The fact remained however that I, the father, was also in a state of complete emotional collapse. The failure of this particular physician to even make eye contact with me seemed to send the message that either I was not hurting, or I was to simply "take it like a man." I have to believe that this extremely capable physician did not do this with any degree of premeditation. Rather, he avoided eye contact with me, much less a dialogue, out of conditioning. While the mother-child bond is undeniably powerful, . . . our health care providers [must recognize] the equally powerful father-child bond. . . . Countless nights spent with grieving fathers over late night coffee has made me realize that many of my brothers are hurting and have minimal outlets for emotional expression. (Fischer, 2003, p. 1)

Available research and other new developments have led many observers to believe that relationships between parents and professionals can be significantly improved (Carpenter, 2000; Fine & Nissenbaum, 2000; Johnson, 2000; Lake & Billingsley, 2000; McKay, 2000). One parent described the emotional support she received in this way: ". . . there was no time that I didn't think I could call Dr. Tiehl and just cry, or, you know, bring all the boys in and Dr. Tiehl would just scoop up Matthew for me and walk away for a while so that I could talk to Matthew's teacher" (Fox et al., 2002, p. 444).

Another parent, in speaking about a physician, said the following: ". . . every time I talk to him he'll give me words of encouragement. He'll say something like, 'You know you are Devante's primary caretaker and the best thing you can do for him is to love him.' I mean, this is regardless of if I bring him in for a scraped knee or ear infection, it's always something about just loving him and being there for him and understanding" (Fox et al., 2002, p. 444).

Indeed, progress has been made in helping professionals communicate and relate more effectively to parents and others responsible for children and youth with disabilities (Lake & Billingsley, 2000; Simpson & Zurkowski, 2000). This is particularly true in the preparation of special educators and others who serve as direct and indirect service providers in family, school, and community-based programs.

# MANAGED CARE AND CHILDREN WITH CHRONIC ILLNESSES OR DISABILITIES

## REAL LIVES–REAL CONCERNS

Joanne Kocourek is one of these warriors. A registered nurse who manages clinical research for a large hospital in Chicago, Illinois, she is exhausted, frustrated, "financially drained," at wit's end—but persevering. The family's former health plan denied vital services and constantly threatened to reduce others for Kristen, the Kocoureks' 9-year-old daughter, who is adopted. Kristen has congenital central hypoventilation syndrome, which causes breathing problems, and mitochondrial cytopathy, an inherited metabolic disorder in which the body cannot generate enough cellular energy. Her sister, Annalies, 13, also has mitochondrial cytopathy.

Of the two, Kristen requires more care. A private nurse spends week nights at the family's home so Joanne and her husband, Tom, can sleep. On weekends, Joanne provides most of the care for Kristen, including intermittent ventilation. The fourth-grader also needs megadose vitamin supplements.

About four years ago, their former health plan pressured the Kocoureks to reduce in-home nursing care to just three nights a week—an effort they successfully fought with the help of their doctors. Their current health plan has pushed for institutional care, which the family maintains would be just as expensive, if not more so, than in-home care: $7,000 to $9,000 per month. The Kocoureks also believe that institutional care would not be the best arrangement in terms of Kristen's quality of life.

Moreover, says Joanne Kocourek, the health plan won't pay for the costly vitamin supplements because lower dose—and less expensive—supplements are available over the counter. It also will not pay for the physical or occupational therapy that clinicians believe would help develop both Kristen's and Annalies's delayed motor skills, arguing that the children's parents are responsible for such therapy.

There are other snags that the family has run into. One is the insurer's refusal to commit itself in writing when denying or granting coverage. The other is the family's financial status—it is "too well off" to qualify for public aid, but [does] not have enough money to pay many medical bills out of pocket. "It has been a battle all the way," Joanne Kocourek says with a sigh.

## PUTTING CHILDREN'S NEEDS FIRST

Recent media reports have focused on the misdeeds of health maintenance organizations (HMOs) among the general population. They tend to overlook how managed care has affected treatment for kids with a chronic illness or disability.

About 20% of all children have a chronic physical or mental condition requiring services that typically extend well beyond the services most healthy children receive, according to national data. These difficult and expensive-to-treat conditions run the gamut—from asthma and attention deficit disorder to sickle cell disease, cerebral palsy, cystic fibrosis, spina bifida, craniofacial abnormalities, and adolescent depression.

Around 5% of all children with special needs account for about 90% of all pediatric health care spending. Particularly pricey are treatments by specialists, physical and speech therapy, medical supplies and equipment, and long-term care.

And there is the rub in this age of cost-conscious managed care. To keep a lid on spending, managed care organizations—HMOs, preferred-provider organizations, or medical groups with managed care contracts—have strong incentives for enrollees to obtain health care from a selected pool of physicians, therapists, and hospitals.

They also impose preauthorization and other techniques to limit hospitalizations, prescription-drug and medical-gear purchases, and access to specialty care, diagnostic tests, and the like. Managed care physicians receive a per-person, or capitated, fee. They do not bill for the actual cost of their services, so there is a financial incentive for them not to provide what they deem to be unnecessary care.

As of late 1998, about 85% of all workers were covered by some type of managed care plan, up 50% since 1994. Some of these health plans simply don't have the capacity to care for children with special health needs. Their panels of physicians and ancillary providers may not include all of the pediatric specialists, therapists, and others who are best qualified to treat these young patients.

**FOCUS 10**

Describe five behaviors that skilled professionals exhibit when interacting with and relating to families that include children with disabilities.

One such collaborative approach of working with families and other care providers is Positive Behavior Support (PBS) (Fox & Dunlap, 2002; Frankland, Edmonson, & Turnbull, 2001). This approach focuses on changing disruptive behaviors and supporting behaviors that are needed and valued by parents, neighbors, teachers, and other community members. In effect, all important players in the child's or youth's life become interveners, working together to achieve well-defined outcomes. These may include skills related to making and keeping friends, replacing loud vocalizations with more appropriately toned speech and language, and developing new ways of responding to events that normally produce aggression or property destruction (Fox et al., 2002). The intent of PBS is to develop behaviors that are useful and highly valued at home, at school, and in the community.

Effective collaborators establish rapport with the families, create supportive environments, demonstrate sensitive to family issues, affirm the positive features of the child with a disability, share valuable information, contribute to the parent's confidence, clarify expectations, and listen well (Worthington, Hernandez, Friedman, &

Furthermore, the needs of children with chronic illnesses or disabilities—even those with the same condition—can vary tremendously, a situation that health plans may overlook. As Peter D. Rappo, M.D., a pediatrician, wrote in 1997 in *Medical Economics* magazine: "Even within one diagnosis code, there's a range of severity. Some of my spina bifida patients can kick a soccer ball, while others are confined to a wheelchair."

My own research indicates that some health plans may not have the necessary experience or knowledge to adequately oversee the care of children with chronic illnesses or disabilities, and sometimes they don't reimburse for critical aspects of preventive care. For example, one of the leading causes of death among kids with spina bifida is renal failure. Yet some plans routinely don't cover urological tests with the frequency that could lead to early detection and treatment of urological complications of the disease.

## POINT

Families with children with disabilities should have access to health insurance that covers reasonable health care for all family members. Insurance companies currently base their coverage on "experience ratings" rather than "community ratings." Using experience ratings, they identify groups of individuals with whom they can make significant profits, given their past health care requirements. They should use community ratings that consider the health needs of all individuals in a given area or location and base their pricing and potential profit structures on these community ratings. As a society, we should be willing to share the expense of providing basic medical care to all families and their members. Present insurance policies are patently discriminatory.

## COUNTERPOINT

Insurance companies are private entities and for-profit businesses. As such, they must operate in ways that allow them to make profits as well as fund the expenses incurred in paying for health care delivered to families and individuals. If insurance companies were to alter their current underwriting standards, their expenses would exceed their incomes and they would not be able to provide health insurance for anyone.

What do you think? To give your opinion, go to Chapter 6 of the companion website **(www.ablongman.com/hardman8e)**, and click on Debate Forum.

SOURCE: From "Managed Care and Children with Chronic Illnesses or Disabilities," by E. J. Jameson, 1999, *Exceptional Parent, 29* (9), pp. 104–105.

Uzzell, 2001). Care providers seek to understand the family, its ecology, and its culture, taking the time to listen and to build relationships (Fox et al., 2002; Rivers, 2000; Zhang & Bennett, 2001). Professionals who take a sincere interest in families and effectively collaborate with them contribute significantly to their success, their feelings of adequacy, and their capacity to cope with the demands of caring for their children with disabilities (Lucyshyn, Blumberg, & Kayser, 2000; Peterson, Derby, Berg, & Horner, 2002). Superb family support programs help keep families together, enhancing their capacity to meet the needs of the individual with a disability, reducing the need for out-of-home placement, and giving families access to typical social and recreational activities (Beach Center, 1998i). The following statement expresses a parent's wonderment at the effectiveness of family-centered support: "They never give up. I am just astounded by the many creative ways they keep coming up with to help him. Oftentimes they do not understand him, but they never give up. At one point I had to ask myself: Are these people for real? . . . I cannot believe how genuine and real they really are" (Worthington et al., 2001, p. 77).

**FOCUS**

**11**

What are the five goals of family support systems?

## Strengthening Family Supports

The primacy of the family in contributing to the well-being of all children is obvious. Research indicates that family members provide one another with the most lasting, and often the most meaningful, support (Cantu, 2002; Turnbull & Turnbull, 2002). Much of what has been done to assist children with disabilities, however, has supplanted rather than supported families in their efforts to care and provide for their children. Monies and resources have been directed historically at services and supports outside the family environment or even beyond the neighborhood or community in which the family lives.

Increasingly, policy makers and program providers are realizing the importance of the family and its crucial role in the development and ongoing care of a child with a disability. Services are now being directed at the family as a whole, rather than just at the child with the disability. This support is particularly evident in the individualized family service plan (IFSP), as discussed earlier in this chapter and in Chapter 3. Such an orientation honors the distinctive and essential role of parents, siblings, and other extended family members as primary caregivers, nurturers, and teachers. Additionally, these services provide parents and siblings with opportunities to engage in other activities that are important to their physical, emotional, and social well-being.

Family supports are directed at several goals. These include enhancing the caregiving capacity of the family; giving parents and other family members respite from the often tedious and sometimes unrelenting demands of caring for a child with a serious disability; assisting the family with persistent financial demands related to the disability; providing valuable training to families, extended family members, concerned neighbors, and caring friends; and improving the quality of life for all family members.

Research suggests that family support services, particularly parent-to-parent programs, have reduced family stress, increased the capacity of family members to maintain arduous care routines, improved the actual care delivered by family members, and reduced out-of-home placements (Beach Center, 1998j). Parent-to-parent programs carefully match a parent in a one-to-one relationship with a trained and experienced supporting parent. The supporting parent is a volunteer who has attended a training program and is open to listening, sharing, and being available when a parent needs support (Herbert, Klemm, & Schimanski, 1999, p. 58).

Because of these family support services and parent-to-parent programs, many children and youth enjoy the relationships and activities that are a natural part of living in their own homes, neighborhoods, and communities (Beach Center, 1998f, 1998h). These services allow children and youth with disabilities to be truly a part of their families, neighborhoods, and communities.

## Training for Parents, Professionals, and Families

**PARENT TRAINING.** Parent training is an essential part of most early intervention programs for children with disabilities. As part of IDEA, the thrust of parent training is directed at helping parents acquire the essential skills that will assist them in implementing their child's IEP or IFSP (Tyunan and Wornian, 2002). No longer is the child viewed as the primary recipient of services; instead, services and training are directed at the complex and varied needs of each family and its members (Adams, 2001). Much of the training is conducted by experienced and skilled parents of children with disabilities, who volunteer their time as part of their affiliation with an advocacy or support group. These support groups play an invaluable role in helping parents, other family members, neighbors, and friends respond effectively to the child or youth with a disability. In describing her experiences with parent training, one mother made the following comments:

> Oh yes, she [the parent trainer] was excellent. Our third child was a 29 weeker. We didn't know any of that stuff. . . . I enjoyed finding out what was going on and knowing the signals, because if he's going to throw up a red flag to me, I

want to know how to react. . . . I couldn't believe all the stuff that she told me that I didn't know. . . . she related to all members of the family. . . . I appreciated what she did. (Ward, Cronin, Renfro, Loman, & Copper, 2000)

Training may be focused on feeding techniques, language development activities, toilet training programs, behavior management approaches, motor development activities, or other related issues important to parents (Tynan & Wornian, 2002). For parents of youth or adults with disabilities, the training may be directed at understanding adult services, accessing recreational programs, finding postsecondary vocational programs, or locating appropriate housing. In some instances, the training centers on giving parents meaningful information about their legal rights, preparing them to participate effectively in IEP meetings, helping them understand the nature of their child's disability, making them aware of recreational programs in their communities, or alerting them to specific funding opportunities (Amlund & Kardash, 1994). Through these training programs, parents learn how to engage effectively in problem solving and conflict resolution and thus are empowered and prepared to advocate for their children and themselves. Parent involvement with the schooling of their children with disabilities significantly benefits the children's learning and overall school performance.

**TRAINING FOR PROFESSIONALS.** Training for professionals—educators, social workers, psychologists, medical professionals—focuses primarily on relationship building, communication, collaboration skills, and cross-cultural understanding (Correa & Jones, 2000; Santarelli, Koegel, Casas, & Koegel, 2001; Taylor & Baglin, 2000; Zhang & Bennett, 2001). Such training is also aimed at helping professionals understand the complex nature of family cultures, structures, functions, and interactions, as well as at encouraging them to take a close look at their own attitudes, feelings, values, and perceptions about families that include children, youth, and adults with disabilities (Correa & Jones, 2000; Lee et al., 2001; Turnbull & Turnbull, 2002). Unfortunately, some professionals see parents as part of the child's problem rather than as partners on a team (Powell-Smith & Stollar, 1997). Moreover, they may be insensitive to the daily demands inherent in living with a child, youth, or adult who presents persistent challenges. As a consequence, they may use vocabulary that is unfamiliar to parents, may speak a language that is foreign to parents, may not give parents enough time to express their feelings and perceptions, and may be insensitive to cultural variations in ways of relating and communicating (Lambie, 2000b). Hence the communication and collaboration skills that are stressed in training for professionals include effective communication, problem-solving strategies, negotiation, and conflict resolution.

**TRAINING FOR FAMILIES.** The training of families is directed at siblings, grandparents, and other relatives. It may even involve close neighbors or caring friends who wish to contribute to the well-being of the family. Often these are individuals who are tied to the family through religious affiliations or long-standing friendships (Kroth & Edge, 1997). Some families use a process referred to as GAP (group action planning) (Beach Center, 1998b). In this process, family members meet with service providers (case workers, speech clinicians, and other professionals) on a regular basis to learn together, to plan, and to make adjustments in the interventions currently in place.

Siblings of children with disabilities need information about the nature and possible

> ### FOCUS
> ### 12
> What are five potential thrusts of parent training?

*Training provides parents with skills for promoting cognitive development, for dealing with challenging behaviors, and for setting appropriate expectations.*

## Reflect on This

# I HAVE LEARNED. . .

The birth of our third child was supposed to be a scheduled cesarean section, performed at the hospital where I practice. However, several days before the appointed date, my wife began labor, and her scheduled section turned into an urgent one. Not long after the procedure began, our new baby, our Corrie, was handed to me with the pediatrician's pronouncement, "Here's your perfect baby girl."

Not more than five minutes later, I felt a hand, gentle yet insistent, on my left shoulder. One of the nurses was there, whispering to me that the pediatrician needed to speak to me. I thought to myself that he was simply being a polite colleague, wanting to wish us luck. Nothing could be wrong, I reasoned, because he had used the words "perfect baby girl." But the look on his face when I saw him waiting in the hallway told me that something had changed.

"I can't be sure," he began haltingly, "but I'm concerned that Corrie may have Down syndrome."

I shook his hand and thanked him for his thoroughness. I then felt a real physical pain, the likes of which I had never experienced in my life. It began in my gut, went up through my chest, and terminated in a wave of nausea and tremulousness that seized my entire being. I was helped to a chair and given a cup of water while I waited for the obstetrician to complete his work.

It is now a year since Corrie's birth, and our lives truly have been changed—changed in ways I could not have imagined twelve months ago.

No longer do I think of words like "horror" and "fear" when I describe our situation or Corrie's life. I think of the beautiful images I have seen: the joyful expression on my wife's face that has replaced her dread, the sheer delight our older children get when Corrie responds to their play, the look Corrie gets when her daddy holds her (a look I'm convinced she reserves for me), and the incredible joy we all feel as she attains each milestone. I think of the progress she has made and of the staff of teachers and therapists who have cared for her, people who have, for me, defined the word "dedication."

And, yes, Corrie has changed the way I live, and so has changed the way I practice medicine. I have a new sense of appreciation for my truly ill patients and maybe a little less patience for those with trivial complaints.

But mostly I think I have learned about myself, and about love. And while we don't know what the future will hold for Corrie, I realize that we can't predict this for anyone, even for ourselves. I realize that I have made certain foolish assumptions in my life. I took it as a given that my children would all go to school, would all attain some stature in the world that I used to know and took for granted. But that world is very different to me now, and I realize just how arrogant such assumptions really are. And because of that, I have learned to try to appreciate all that surrounds me, as often as I can, for there is truly so much to be amazed by and to be thankful for. (Last, 2001, pp. 56–60)

course of disabilities affecting their brother or sister. Furthermore, they need social and emotional support and acknowledgment of their own needs for nurturing, attention, and affirmation (Powell-Smith & Stollar, 1997). Some research suggests that many siblings know very little about their brother's or sister's disability, its manifestations, and its consequences (Seligman, 1991). Siblings need to understand that they are not responsible for a particular condition or disability. Other questions also need addressing. These questions deal with the heritability of the disability, the siblings' future role in providing care, the ways in which siblings might explain the disability to their friends, and how the presence of the brother or sister with a disability will affect their family and themselves.

In most instances, the training of siblings occurs through support groups that are specifically designed for a particular age group. In these groups, siblings can express feelings, vent frustrations, and learn from others. They may also pick up pointers on how to deal with predictable situations—that is, what to say or how to respond. They may learn sign language, how to complete simple medical procedures, how to manage misbehavior, or how to use certain incentive systems. In some cases, they may become prepared for the eventual death of a brother or sister who has a life-threatening condition.

Training of grandparents, other relatives, neighbors, and friends is also crucial. They, like the siblings of children with disabilities, must be informed, must have opportunities to express feelings, must be able to ask pertinent questions, and must receive training that is tailored to their needs. If informed and well trained, they often provide the only consistent respite care that is available to families. Also, they may contribute invaluable transportation, recreational activities, baby-sitting, critical emotional support, and/or short-term and long-term financial assistance (Harmon, 1999).

# FOCUS REVIEW

**FOCUS 1**   Identify five factors that influence the ways in which families respond to infants with birth defects or disabilities.

- The emotional stability of each family member
- Religious values and beliefs
- Socioeconomic status
- The severity of the disability
- The type of disability

**FOCUS 2**   What three statements can be made about the stages parents may experience in responding to infants or young children with disabilities?

- The stage approach needs further refinement and validation before it can be used accurately to understand, predict, or help parents deal with young infants and children with disabilities.
- Parental responses are highly variable.
- The adjustment process, for most parents, is continuous and distinctively individual.

**FOCUS 3**   Identify three ways in which a newborn child with disabilities influences the family social/ecological system.

- The communication patterns within the family may change.
- The power structure within the family may be altered.
- The roles and responsibilities assumed by various family members may be modified.

**FOCUS 4**   Identify three aspects of raising a child with a disability that contribute to spousal stress.

- A decrease in the amount of time available for the couple's activities
- Heavy financial burdens
- Fatigue

**FOCUS 5**   Identify four general phases that parents may experience in rearing a child with a disability.

- The diagnostic period: Does the child truly have a disability?
- The school period (elementary and secondary, with their inherent challenges: dealing with teasing and other peer-related behaviors, as well as learning academic, social, and vocational skills): Included in this period are the challenges of adolescence.
- The postschool period: The child makes the transition from school to other educational or vocational activities.
- The period when the parents are no longer able to provide direct care and guidance for their son or daughter.

**FOCUS 6**   Identify four factors that influence the relationship that develops between infants with disabilities and their mothers.

- The mother may be unable to engage in typical feeding and caregiving activities because of the intensive medical care being provided.
- Some mothers may have difficulty bonding to children with whom they have little physical and social interaction.
- Some mothers are given little direction in becoming involved with their children. Without minimal involvement, some mothers become estranged from their children and find it difficult to begin the caring and bonding process.
- The expectations that mothers have about their children and their own functions in nurturing them play a significant role

in the relationship that develops.

**FOCUS 7**   Identify three ways in which fathers may respond to their children with disabilities.

- Fathers are more likely to internalize their feelings than are mothers.
- Fathers often respond to sons with disabilities differently from the way they respond to daughters.
- Fathers may resent the time their wives spend in caring for their children with disabilities.

**FOCUS 8**   Identify four ways in which siblings respond to a brother or sister with a disability.

- Siblings tend to mirror the attitudes and behaviors of their parents toward a child with disabilities.
- Siblings may play a crucial role in fostering the intellectual, social, and affective development of the child with a disability.
- Some siblings may attempt to compensate for their parents' disappointment by excelling in an academic or artistic pursuit.
- Some siblings respond with feelings of resentment or deprivation.

**FOCUS 9**   Identify three types of support that grandparents and other extended family members may render to families with children who have disabilities.

- They may provide their own children with weekend respite from the pressures of the home environment.
- They may assist occasionally with baby-sitting or transportation.
- They may support their children in times of crisis by

listening and helping them deal with seemingly unresolvable problems and by providing short-term and long-term financial assistance.

**FOCUS 10** Describe five behaviors that skilled professionals exhibit when interacting with and relating to families that include children with disabilities.

- They establish rapport.
- They create supportive environments.
- The demonstrate sensitivity to the needs of these families and seek to understand the culture and ecology of each family.
- They share valuable information.
- They listen well.

**FOCUS 11** What are the five goals of family support systems?

- Enhancing the caregiving capacity of the family
- Giving parents and other family members respite from the demands of caring for a child with a disability
- Assisting the family with persistent financial demands related to the child's disability
- Providing valuable training to families, extended family members, concerned neighbors, and caring friends
- Improving the quality of life for all family members

**FOCUS 12** What are five potential thrusts of parent training?

- To help parents with specific activities, such as feeding their children, teaching them language skills, helping them become toilet trained; accessing adult services; finding appropriate housing; and locating appropriate postsecondary vocational training
- To help them understand their legal rights
- To contribute to their understanding of the nature of the disability or disabilities
- To make them aware of services in the community
- To alert them to financial assistance that is available

## FURTHER READINGS

*Exceptional Parent (EP) Magazine.*

*For years, the editors and writers of* Exceptional Parent (EP) Magazine *have provided parents, families, and professionals with insightful information related to children, youth, and adults with disabilities. Many of the articles are written by parents or siblings of children with disabilities. This magazine is published in River Edge, New Jersey. Its website is http://www.exceptionalparent.com.*

Fine, M. J., and Simpson, R. L. (Eds.) (2000). *Collaboration with Parents and Families of Children and Youth with Disabilities.* Austin, TX: PRO-ED.

*This book provides information on a broad array of topics, including nontraditional families, multicultural issues, sexuality, and disability, along with disability-specific information for parents about autism, chronic illnesses, learning disabilities, and giftedness.*

Klein, S. D., and Shive, K. (Eds.) (2001). *You Will Dream New Dreams.* New York: New York: Kensington Books.

*This is a wonderful compendium of inspirational stories, personal experiences, and reflections written by parents of children with disabilities. Many of the stories are drawn from articles published in EP Magazine.*

Meyer, D. J. (Ed.) (1995). *Uncommon Fathers: Reflections on Raising a Child with a Disability.* Bethesda, MD: Woodbine House.

*This book provides a very helpful, in-depth look at fathers and their experiences with sons and daughters with disabilities.*

McHugh, M. (1999). *Special Siblings: Growing Up with Someone with a Disability.* New York: Hyperion.

*Mary McHugh offers a sensitive and compelling account of her own experiences as a sibling of a brother with a disability. The book is packed with interesting and emotion-filled stories about her years growing up with her brother, Jack.*

## WEB RESOURCES

**The Fathers Network**

www.fathersnetwork.org

The Fathers Network offers resources and information for fathers, family members, and care providers. The

network provides news, press releases, and recent articles about children and youth with disabilities and their families.

### Beach Center on Disability

www.beachcenter.org

This website is designed for parents and other family members who are interested in children, youth, and adults with disabilities. The Beach Center provides meaningful materials, training, and other services to families that include children with disabilities.

### Children with Disabilities

www.childrenwithdisabilities.ncjrs.org

This website gives service providers, other professionals, and families pertinent information about education, employment, advocacy, housing, health, recreation, and transportation. It also provides in-depth information about specific disabilities.

### Families and Advocates Partnership for Education (FAPE)

www.fape.org

This project is funded by the federal government. The website links families, disability advocates, and other care providers who are interested in and committed to IDEA. Specifically, the project is designed to improve the outcomes of special education services.

### National Dissemination Center for Children with Disabilities (NICHCY)

www.nichcy.org

This center funded by the federal government provides up-to-date information about disabilities and special education issues.

## BUILDING YOUR PORTFOLIO

If you are thinking about a career in special education, you should know that many states use national standards developed by the Council for Exceptional Children (CEC) to assess a teacher candidate's knowledge about and skills for working with students with disabilities. See a complete listing of the ten CEC Content Standards on the inside front cover of this text.

### CEC Content Standards Addressed in Chapter 6

1. Foundations
3. Individual Differences
5. Learning Environments and Social Interactions
9. Professional and Ethical Practice
10. Collaboration

### Assess Your Knowledge of the CEC Standards Addressed in Chapter 6

Some states require that teacher candidates develop a portfolio of products that demonstrate mastery of the CEC content standards. To assist in the development of products for this portfolio, you may wish to complete the following activities.

• Complete a written test of the chapter's content.

*If your instructor requires a written test of your content knowledge for this chapter, keep a copy for your portfo-*lio. *A practice test on the information covered in this chapter is available through the companion website (www.ablongman.com/hardman8e) and the Student Study Guide.*

• Respond to Application Questions for Case Study "Family Voices Are Heard."

*Review the Case Study and respond in writing to the application questions. Keep a copy of the Case Study and your written response for your portfolio.*

• Complete the "Take a Stand" activity for the Debate Forum "Managed Care and Children with Chronic Illnesses or Disabilities."

*Read the Debate Forum and then visit the companion website to complete the activity "Take a Stand." Keep a copy of this activity for your portfolio.*

• Participate in a Community Service Learning Activity.

*Community service is a valuable way to enhance your learning experience. Visit our companion website for suggested community service learning activities that correspond to the information presented in this chapter. Develop a reflective journal of the service learning experience for your portfolio.*

## THEMES OF THE TIMES

Expand your knowledge of the concepts discussed in this chapter and reading current and historical articles from the *New York Times* by visiting the "Themes of the Times" section of the companion website:

**www.ablongman.com/hardman8e.**

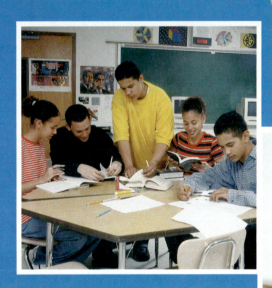

# Learning Disabilities

## Learning Disabilities on the Increase

Specific learning disabilities continued to make up the most prevalent kind of disability in the United States. In 2000–2001, nearly 2.9 million children with learning disabilities were served under IDEA. (U.S. Department of Education, 2002)

## Boys with Learning Disabilities Outnumber Girls—Maybe

Conventional wisdom has suggested that boys identified with learning disabilities substantially outnumber girls, although some recent research calls into question the levels cited in the past. (Lerner, 2003)

## Learning Disability Accommodations on SAT Increasing

The number of students requesting accommodations on SAT tests—the great majority involving claims for a learning disability—has increased, although questions have been raised regarding the benefits and validity of this procedure. (Ungerleider & Maslow, 2001)

## Direct Instruction Effective with Those Having Learning Disabilities

A review of direct instruction by the Division of Learning Disabilities of the Council for Exceptional Children leads to the conclusion that "it is an effective and reliably implementable instructional approach for students with LD in those skill and content domains studied to date." (Division of Learning Disabilities, 1999, p. 3)

## FOCUS

**PREVIEW:** To preview the central concepts of this chapter, read the focus questions located in the margins. Using these questions as a guide, ask yourself what you already know and what you want to learn.

## Jamaal

**J**amaal's difficulties first became evident in kindergarten, which is somewhat unusual because learning disabilities are more typically identified later in the school years. His parents were frustrated and, like so many parents of children with disabilities, felt that they were not doing something correctly. Jamaal was also aware of some difficulties; he mentioned to the teacher that he sometimes had trouble concentrating.

Jamaal expresses himself well verbally and comes up with great ideas; however, he has particular problems with reading and writing. It appears that he trails his classmates in sight-word vocabulary, which influences both academic areas. His fourth-grade teachers are now working very hard to integrate into his instruction the important skills that he will need in order to succeed as he moves on in school. Although he exhibits some disruptive behaviors, they are relatively minor in the overall context of Jamaal's world. He fundamentally has a positive outlook and already has plans for attending college—rather long-range planning for a fourth grader!

## Mathew

*Note:* The following is an excerpt from a statement prepared by an upper-division psychology undergraduate student who has learning disabilities. Mathew tells his story in his own words, recounting some of his school experiences, his diagnosis, and how his learning disabilities affect his academic efforts.

Imagine having the inability to memorize times tables, not being able to "tell time" until the ninth grade, and taking several days to read a simple chapter from a school textbook.

**Cite four reasons why definitions of learning disabilities have varied.**

The field of learning disabilities was virtually unrecognized prior to the 1960s. These disabilities are often considered mild because people with learning disabilities usually have average or near-average intelligence, although learning disabilities can occur at all intelligence levels. People with learning disabilities achieve at unexpectedly low levels, particularly in reading and mathematics. Recently, the term *learning disabilities* has come to be regarded as a generic label representing a very heterogeneous group of conditions, which range from mild to severe in intensity (Gelfand & Drew, 2003; Smith, 2000). In many cases, people with learning disabilities have been described as having "poor neurological wiring." Individuals with learning disabilities manifest a highly variable and complex set of characteristics and needs. Consequently, they present a substantial challenge to family members and professionals. This set of challenges, however, is repeatedly met with significant success, as evidenced by many stories of outstanding achievement by adults who have histories of learning disabilities in childhood.

## Definitions and Classifications

Confusion, controversy, and polarization have been associated with **learning disabilities** as long as they have been recognized as a family of disabilities. In the past, many children now identified as having specific learning disabilities would have been labeled remedial readers, remedial learners, or emotionally disturbed or even mentally retarded children—if they received any special attention or additional instructional support at all. Impaired academic performance is a major element in most current definitions of learning disabilities (Hallahan, 2002; Stone & May, 2002; Woodward & Morocco, 2002). Today, services related to learning disabilities represent the largest single program for exceptional children in the United States. Although this program is relatively new, its growth rate has been unparalleled by any other area in special education from about 25% of all students with

**Learning disability**

A condition in which one or more of the basic psychological processes involved in understanding or using language are deficient.

In elementary and high school, I was terrified of math classes for several reasons. First, it did not matter how many times I practiced my times tables or other numerical combinations relating to division, subtraction, and addition. I could not remember them. Second, I dreaded the class time itself for inevitably the teacher would call on me for an answer to a "simple" problem. Multiplication was the worst! Since I had to count on my fingers to do multiplication, it would take a lot of time and effort. Do you know how long it takes to calculate $9 \times 7$ or $9 \times 9$ on your fingers? Suffice it to say too long, especially if the teacher and the rest of the class are waiting.

When I was a sophomore at a junior college, I discovered important information about myself.

After two days of clinical cognitive testing, I learned that my brain is wired differently than most individuals. That is, I think, perceive, and process information differently. They discovered several "wiring jobs" which are called learning disabilities. First, I have a problem with processing speed. The ability to bring information from long-term memory to consciousness (into short-term memory) takes me a long time. Second, I have a deficit with my short-term memory. This means that I cannot hold information there very long. When new information is learned, it must be put into long-term memory. This is an arduous process requiring the information to be rehearsed several times. Third, I have a significant problem with fluid reasoning. Fluid reasoning is the ability to go from

A to G without having to go through B, C, D, E, and F. It also includes drawing inferences, coming up with creative solutions to problems, solving unique problems, and the ability to transfer information and generalize. Hence, my math and numerical difficulties. . . .

With all of this knowledge, I was able to use specific strategies that will help me in compensating for these neurological wiring patterns. Now I tape all lectures rather than trying to keep up taking notes. I take tests in a room by myself and they are not timed. Anytime I need to do mathematical calculations I use a calculator. . . .

SOURCE: From *Understanding Child Behavior Disorders* (4th ed., p. 238), by D. M. Gelfand and C. J. Drew, 2003, Belmont, CA: Wadsworth. Used with permission.

disabilities in 1975 to nearly 50% in 2000 (U.S. Department of Education, 2002). Both definition and classification in the field of learning disabilities are still under discussion in forums like that provided by the National Research Center on Learning Disabilities (e.g., Fletcher et al., 2001; Fuchs, Fuchs, Mathes, Lipsey, & Roberts, 2001; Torgeson, 2001).

## Definitions

The definitions of learning disabilities vary considerably. This inconsistency may be due to the field's unique evolution, rapid growth, and strong interdisciplinary nature. The involvement of multiple disciplines (such as medicine, psychology, speech and language, and education) has also contributed to confusing terminology. For example, education coined the phrase *specific learning disabilities;* psychology uses terms such as *perceptual disorders* and *hyperkinetic behavior;* the speech and language field employs the terms *aphasia* and *dyslexia;* and medicine uses the labels *brain damage, minimal brain dysfunction, brain injury,* and *impairment. Brain injury, minimal brain dysfunction,* and *learning disabilities* are the most commonly used terms, though all appear in various disciplines.

A child with a brain injury is described as having an organic impairment resulting in perceptual problems, thinking disorders, and emotional instability. A child with minimal brain dysfunction manifests similar problems but often shows evidence of language, memory, motor, and impulse-control difficulties. Individuals with minimal brain dysfunction are often characterized as average or above average in intelligence, which distinguishes the disorder from mental retardation.

**EARLY HISTORY.**   Samuel Kirk, an educator, introduced the term *specific learning disabilities* in 1963. His original concept remains largely intact today. The concept is defined by delays, deviations, and performance discrepancies in basic academic subjects (e.g., arithmetic, reading, spelling, and writing) and speech and language problems that cannot be attributed to mental retardation, sensory deficits, or emotional disturbance. The common practice in education is to describe individuals with learning disabilities on the basis of what they are not. For example, although they may have a number of problems, they do not have mental retardation, emotional disturbance, or hearing loss. *Learning disabilities* is an umbrella label that includes a variety of conditions and behavioral and performance deficits (Gelfand & Drew, 2003).

**IDEA AND JOINT COMMITTEE DEFINITIONS.** The Individuals with Disabilities Education Act (IDEA) of 2004 stated that

> "Specific learning disability" means a disorder in one or more of the basic psychological processes involved in understanding or in using language, spoken or written, which may manifest itself in an imperfect ability to listen, think, speak, read, write, spell, or to do mathematical calculations. The term includes such conditions as perceptual disabilities, brain injury, minimal brain dysfunction, dyslexia, and developmental aphasia. The term does not include children who have learning problems which are primarily the result of visual, hearing, or motor disabilities, of mental retardation, of emotional disturbance, or of environmental, cultural, or economic disadvantage. (IDEA 2004, PL 108-446, Sec. 602[30])

This definition placed into federal law many of the concepts found earlier in Kirk's description. It also provided a legal focus for the provision of services in the public schools. Providing service guidelines through the IDEA definition matured over the 1990s with criteria from the companion "Rules and Regulations." Table 7.1 summarizes the criteria for identifying a specific learning disability published in the *Federal Register* in 1999. These criteria are consistent with the IDEA definition presented earlier.

The IDEA definition and the guidelines in Table 7.1 primarily describe conditions that are *not* learning disabilities but give little substantive explanation of what *does* constitute a learning disability (i.e., an achievement/ability discrepancy in areas of oral expression, listening, written expression, and so on). This use of exclusionary criteria still surfaces in a variety of circumstances (e.g., Grigorenko & Lockery, 2002; Picton & Karki, 2002). The IDEA definition is also somewhat ambiguous because it

---

**TABLE 7.1**

### Criteria for Identifying a Specific Learning Disability

A team may determine that a child has a specific learning disability if—

1. The child does not achieve commensurate with his or her age and ability levels, that is, demonstrates a severe discrepancy between achievement and intellectual ability, in one or more of the areas listed in items i through vii below, if provided with learning experiences appropriate for the child's age and ability levels.

    i. Oral expression.
    ii. Listening comprehension.
    iii. Written expression.
    iv. Basic reading skill.
    v. Reading comprehension.
    vi. Mathematics calculation.
    vii. Mathematics reasoning.

2. The team may not identify a child as having a specific learning disability if the severe discrepancy between ability and achievement is primarily the result of:

    i. A visual, hearing, or motor impairment
    ii. Mental retardation
    iii. Emotional disturbance, or
    iv. Environmental, cultural, or economic disadvantage.

SOURCE: "Rules and Regulations," March 12, 1999, section 300.541, *Federal Register*, p. 12457.

prescribes no clear way to measure a learning disability. Another definition statement presented by the National Joint Committee for Learning Disabilities (1998) included certain important elements not stated in IDEA:

> *Learning disabilities* is a general term that refers to a heterogeneous group of disorders manifested by significant difficulties in the acquisition and use of listening, speaking, reading, writing, reasoning, or mathematical abilities. These disorders are intrinsic to the individual, [are] presumed to be due to central nervous system dysfunction, and may occur across the lifespan. Problems in self-regulatory behaviors, social perception, and social interaction may exist with learning disabilities but do not by themselves constitute a learning disability. Although learning disabilities may occur concomitantly with other handicapping conditions (e.g., sensory impairment, mental retardation, serious emotional disturbance), or with extrinsic influences (such as cultural differences, insufficient or inappropriate instruction), they are not the result of those conditions or influences. (1998, p. 187)

This definition is important to our discussion for several reasons. First, it describes learning disabilities as a generic term that refers to a heterogeneous group of disorders. Second, a person with learning disabilities must manifest significant difficulties. Use of the word *significant* is an effort to remove the connotation that a learning disability constitutes a mild problem. Finally, this definition highlights learning disabilities as lifelong problems and places them in a context of other disabilities and cultural differences. These are important refinements of earlier definitions.

**OTHER ISSUES IN DEFINING LEARNING DISABILITIES.**  Varying definitions and terminology related to learning disabilities emerged partly because of different theoretical views of the condition. For example, perceptual-motor theories emphasize an interaction between various channels of perception and motor activity. Perceptual-motor theories of learning disabilities focus on contrasts between normal sequential development of motor patterns and the motor development of children with learning disabilities. Children with learning disabilities are seen as having unreliable and unstable perceptual-motor abilities, which present problems when such children encounter activities that require an understanding of time and space.

Language disability theories, on the other hand, concentrate on a child's reception or production of language. Because language is so important in learning, these theories emphasize the relationship between learning disabilities and language deficiencies. Just looking at these two theories, then, makes it clear that very different viewpoints exist regarding these disabilities. This field encompasses many theoretical perspectives on the nature of learning problems, as well as on their causation and treatment.

Still another view of learning disabilities has emerged in the past several years. Some researchers have suggested that many different, specific disorders have been grouped under one term. They see *learning disabilities* as a general umbrella term that includes both academic and behavioral problems, and they have developed terminology to describe particular conditions falling within the broad category of learning disabilities. Some of these terms refer to particular areas of functional academic difficulty (e.g., math, spelling, reading), whereas others reflect difficulties that are behavioral in nature. This perspective was adopted by the American Psychiatric Association in the fourth edition of its *Diagnostic and Statistical Manual of Mental Disorders* (American Psychiatric Association, 2000). This manual uses the term *learning disorders* to refer specifically to disorders in areas such as reading, mathematics, and written expression.

In one sense, this strategy is not surprising. It has long been acknowledged that people with learning disabilities form a very heterogeneous group, yet professionals have continued to describe them as though they were much alike. Such characterizations typically reflect the theoretical or disciplinary perspective of the professional, rather than an objective behavioral description of the individual being evaluated. This has resulted in a tendency to focus on defining a particular *disorder* and then categorizing people according to such definitions, rather than objectively evaluating the *individual* with problems. This approach often leads to error when members of a population that exhibits a wide variety of disorders are evaluated.

Research on learning disabilities also reflects the problems of definition. The wide range of characteristics associated with children who have learning disabilities and various methodological problems (such as poor research design and measurement error) have caused many difficulties in conducting research on learning disabilities (Airasian, 2002; Carnine, 2000; Salkind, 2002). Generalizing research results is hazardous, and replication of studies is very difficult. Efforts to standardize and clarify definitions continue, and they are important for both research and intervention purposes.

The notion of severity has largely been ignored in earlier definitions and concepts related to learning disabilities. Although this has changed somewhat, severity still receives only limited attention (see Henry, 2001; Kerr, 2001; Richman & Wood, 2002). Learning disabilities have probably been defined in more ways by more disciplines and professional groups than any other type of disability (Mastropieri & Scruggs, 2000). We describe the behavioral characteristics of learning disabilities from different theoretical viewpoints, because it is important to know how a person might be classified as having a learning disability according to different perspectives.

Identify three classification schemes that have been used with people who have learning disabilities.

## Classification

*Learning disabilities* is a term applied to a complex constellation of behaviors and symptoms. Many of these symptoms or characteristics have been used for classification purposes at one time or another. Fletcher and his colleagues note that three major elements have a substantial history of being employed in classifying learning disabilities: discrepancy, heterogeneity, and exclusion—all points that we noted earlier (Fletcher et al., 2001). Discrepancy approaches to classification are based on the notion that there is an identifiable gap between intelligence and achievement in particular areas, such as reading, math, language, and other areas. Heterogeneity classification addresses the differing array of academic domains where these children often demonstrate performance problems (as in the seven areas noted in Table 7.1). The exclusion approach reflects the idea that the learning disabilities cannot be due to selected other conditions. The evidence supporting the use of discrepancy and exclusion as classification parameters is not strong, whereas heterogeneity seems to be supported. Some of the learning disabilities literature asserts that discrepancy is a worthwhile definition element. Some theorists also contend that the approach to definition should be inclusive, focused on the specific attributes that need attention rather than on what learning disabilities are not (Fletcher et al., 2001, Kavale, 2001).

Reference to severity appears in the literature on learning disabilities fairly often, even though it is not accounted for in most definitions (Gangadharan, Bretherton, & Johnson, 2001; Kerr, 2001; Richman & Wood, 2002). Prior to 2004, IDEA mandated that any criterion for classifying a child as having learning disabilities must be based on a preexisting severe discrepancy between intellectual capacity and achievement. The determination of referral for special services and type of educational placement was related to the following criteria:

1. Whether a child achieves commensurate with his or her age and ability when provided with appropriate educational experiences

2. Whether the child has a severe discrepancy between achievement and intellectual ability in one or more of seven areas relating to communication skills and mathematical abilities

The child's learning disability must be determined on an individual basis, and the severe discrepancy between achievement and intellectual ability must be in one or more of the following areas: oral expression, listening comprehension, written expression, basic reading skill, reading comprehension, mathematical calculation, or mathematical reasoning.

The meaning of the term *severe discrepancy* is debated among professionals (e.g., Van den Broeck, 2002; Willson, & Reynolds, 2002). Although it is often stipulated as a classification parameter, there is no broadly accepted way to measure it. What is an "acceptable" discrepancy between a child's achievement and what is expected at his or her grade level—25 percent? 35 percent? 50 percent? Recent research on discrepancy classifications, particularly in reading, have found that the discrepancy concept is not strongly supported by data (Stuebing et al., 2002).

In recognizing the controversy surrounding the use of a "discrepancy formula" as the only criteria for determining eligibility for special education services, IDEA 2004 no longer required that school districts must take into consideration whether a child has a severe discrepancy between intellectual ability and achievement. In using evaluation procedures to determine whether a child has a specific learning disability, schools now have the option of using a process that determines a child's **response to intervention (RTI)** that is scientific and research-based. (IDEA 2004, PL 108-446, Sec.614[b])

Lack of agreement about concepts basic to the field has caused difficulties in both research and treatment. Nonetheless, many people who display the challenging characteristics of learning disabilities are successful in life and have become leaders in their fields (an example is Charles "Pete" Conrad Jr., who became an astronaut).

# Prevalence

Problems in determining the numbers of people with learning disabilities are amplified by differing definitions, theoretical views, and assessment procedures. Prevalence estimates are highly variable, ranging from 2.7% to 30% of the school-age population (Gettinger & Koscik, 2001; Lerner, 2003). Within the total school-age population, the most reasonable estimates range from 5% to 10%, as shown in Figure 7.1.

**Response to Intervention**

A term that describes how a student responds to instructional interventions that have been determined to be effective through scientifically based research.

Give two current estimated ranges for the prevalence of learning disabilities.

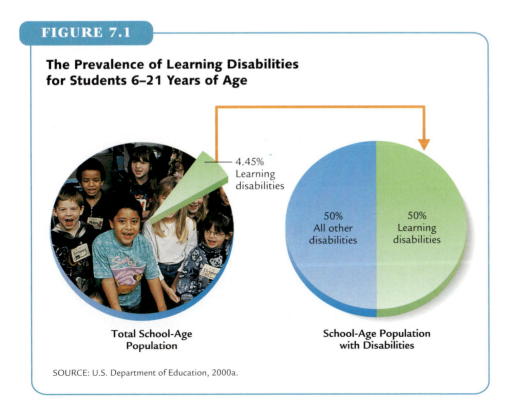

**FIGURE 7.1**

**The Prevalence of Learning Disabilities for Students 6–21 Years of Age**

4.45% Learning disabilities

Total School-Age Population

50% All other disabilities

50% Learning disabilities

School-Age Population with Disabilities

SOURCE: U.S. Department of Education, 2000a.

One of the major recurring themes in this text is that assessment of and accountability for all students are essential, but these are challenges tasks in the area of learning disabilities because of the varying prevalence estimates. Accuracy and reliability are vital cornerstones of assessment and accountability. The variation in prevalence estimates is partially due to changing definition statements, along with the pressing need to provide service to a very large number of children encountering academic problems. Variation in estimates of the prevalence of learning disabilities raises the issue of what is acceptable public and educational policy and is directly related to assessment accuracy.

Since learning disabilities emerged as a category, their prevalence has been high compared to that of other exceptionalities and so has been controversial for many years. Learning disabilities are among the most common of all reported causes of disability. However, it is difficult to find one prevalence figure that is agreed on by all involved in the field. In 2000–2001, over 5.7 million children with disabilities (ages 6–21) were being served under IDEA in the United States. Of that number, nearly 2.9 million were classified as having learning disabilities, a figure that represents nearly 50% of the population with disabilities being served (U.S. Department of Education, 2002).

Professionals and parents involved with other disability groups often question the high prevalence of learning disabilities. In some cases, they simply know they must compete for the limited funds distributed among groups of people with different disabilities. Others, however, are concerned that the learning disabilities category is being overused to avoid the stigma associated with other labels or because of misdiagnosis, which may result in inappropriate treatment. And the heavy use of the learning disabilities label in referrals for services still continues to grow, as illustrated in Table 7.2.

## TABLE 7.2

### Changes in Number of Students Ages 6 Through 21 Served Under IDEA by Disability Category, 1991–1992 and 2000–2001

| DISABILITY | 1991–1992[1] | 2000–2001 | PERCENT CHANGE IN NUMBER |
|---|---|---|---|
| Specific learning disabilities | 2,247,004 | 2,887,217 | 28.5 |
| Speech or language impairments | 998,904 | 1,093,808 | 9.5 |
| Mental retardation | 553,262 | 612,978 | 10.8 |
| Emotional disturbance | 400,211 | 473,663 | 18.4 |
| Multiple disabilities | 98,408 | 122,559 | 24.5 |
| Hearing impairments | 60,727 | 70,767 | 16.5 |
| Orthopedic impairments | 51,389 | 73,057 | 42.2 |
| Other health impairments | 58,749 | 291,850 | 396.8 |
| Visual impairments | 24,083 | 25,975 | 7.9 |
| Autism[2] | 5,415 | 78,749 | 1,354.3 |
| Deaf-blindness | 1,427 | 1,320 | −7.5 |
| Traumatic brain injury[2] | 245 | 14,844 | 5,958.8 |
| Developmental delay | — | 28,935 | — |
| All disabilities | 4,499,824 | 5,775,722 | 28.4 |

[1]Data from 1991–1992 include children with disabilities served under the Chapter 1 Handicapped program.
[2]Reporting on autism and traumatic brain injury was optional in 1991–1992 and required beginning in 1992–1993.
SOURCE: U.S. Department of Education (2002). *Twenty-fourth Annual Report to Congress on the Implementation of the Individuals with Disabilities Act.*

Although discrepancies in prevalence estimates occur in all fields of exceptionality, the area of learning disabilities seems more variable than most. This can be partly attributed to the different procedures used by the agencies, states, and researchers who do the counting and estimating (e.g., Cooper & Bailey, 2001; Morgan et al., 2002). Another source of discrepancy may be differing or vague definitions of learning disabilities. Prevalence figures gathered through various studies are unlikely to match when different definitions determine what is counted. This situation is common in the field of learning disabilities.

Albert Einstein failed math in elementary school and demonstrated little ability or interest in school work. His intellectual genius and capability in science and mathematics was not evident until his early teens. Einstein represents the discrepancy that can exist in an individual student.

# Characteristics

Although specific learning disabilities are often characterized as representing mild disorders, few attempts have been made to validate this premise empirically. Identification of subgroups, subtypes, or severity levels in this heterogeneous population has been largely neglected in the past. However, some attempts have been made in recent years to attend to these issues (Henry, 2001; Kerr, 2001; Richman & Wood, 2002). Subtype and **comorbidity** research are appearing in the current literature at increasing rates (Frank, 2000). Subtype research investigates the characteristics of youngsters to identify distinctive groups within the broad umbrella of learning disabilities. Comorbidity research studies the degree to which youngsters exhibit evidence of multiple disabilities or conditions (e.g., learning disabilities and ADHD, personality disorders) (Forness & Kavale, 2001; Naik, Gangadharan, & Alexander, 2002). In some ways these approaches are exploring similar questions from differing perspectives. Certainly, the learning disabilities category has multiple subgroups, because the definitions have been so broad and the group is so heterogeneous. Likewise, many students who have learning disabilities also exhibit characteristics of other disorders, such as emotional difficulties.

Researchers have investigated a broad array of subgroups ranging from people with reading problems to those with hyperactivity (e.g., Faraone, Biederman, Monuteaux, Doyle, & Seidman, 2001; Richman & Wood, 2002). Attention-deficit/hyperactivity disorder (ADHD) is a condition that is often associated with learning disabilities. Several characteristics of ADHD have long been recognized in many children with learning disabilities, and there is a significant level of comorbidity between the two conditions (some estimates are as high as 25%). However, there is certainly not complete correspondence in characteristics between the two (e.g., Doyle, Faraone, Dupre, & Biederman, 2001; Shapiro, 2002; Westby, 2002). Because of the co-occurrence, distinctions between learning disabilities and ADHD as categories are not always clear. This is not surprising, given the historical overlap in definitions and the very heterogeneous groups of people being considered (Forness & Kavale, 2001; Mayes, Calhoun, & Crowell, 2000; Snider, Frankenberger, & Aspenson, 2000). Chapter 8 examines ADHD in detail.

**FOCUS 4**

Identify seven characteristics attributed to those with learning disabilities, and explain why it is difficult to characterize this group.

**Comorbidity**

A situation in which multiple conditions occur together.

In time, subtype and comorbidity research may lead to more effective intervention, geared precisely to the specific needs of distinctive groups within the large, heterogeneous population with learning disabilities (Bender, 2001; Frank, 2000).

Perceptions of teachers and other professionals have also been investigated in an effort to understand more about learning disabilities (Fuchs, Fuchs, Eaton, Hamlett, & Karns, 2000; Taylor, Anselmo, Foreman, Schatschneider, & Angelopoulos, 2000). Although they too exhibit some error and variability, such ratings are stable enough to support reliable distinctions, in terms of both subtype and severity, among students with learning disabilities. Some research suggests teachers and school psychologists make similar judgments about the nature of a disability and its severity in a particular child (Fuchs et al., 2000; Taylor et al., 2000). Teacher perceptions and knowledge have long been cited as a badly overlooked source of assessment information; their input is vital in designing instructional adaptation for students with learning problems. Also, teachers working with students with learning disabilities quite often encounter youngsters who they firmly believe should not be considered learning disabled. Such reports support the contention that many students currently being served as having learning disabilities may have been inappropriately referred. Over 25 years ago, Larsen (1978) commented on this phenomenon:

> It is . . . likely that the large number of students who are referred for mild to moderate underachievement are simply unmotivated, poorly taught, come from home environments where scholastic success is not highly valued, or are dull [to] normal in intelligence. For all intents and purposes, these students should not automatically be considered as learning disabled, since there is little evidence that placement in special education will improve their academic functioning. (p. 7)

## Academic Achievement

Problems and inconsistencies in academic achievement largely prompted the recognition of learning disabilities as an area of exceptionality. Individuals with learning disabilities, though generally of or above-average or near-average intelligence, seem to have many academic problems. These problems usually persist from the primary

*Many students with learning disabilities have difficulties with word recognition, work knowledge, and the use of context in learning to read.*

grades through the end of formal schooling, including college (Bradshaw, 2001; Gregg, Coleman, Stennett, & Davis, 2002).

**READING.** Reading problems are observed among students with learning disabilities more often than problems in any other area of academic performance. Historically, as the learning disabilities category began to take shape, it was applied to youngsters who had earlier been identified as remedial reading students. Estimates have suggested that as many as 90% of students with learning disabilities have reading difficulties, and even the low estimates are around 60% (Bender, 2001). Clearly, problems with the reading process are very prevalent among students identified as having learning disabilities (Schmidt, Rozendal, & Greenman, 2002). However, the specific problems that they have in reading vary as much as the many components of the reading process.

Both word knowledge and word recognition are vitally important parts of reading skill, and they both cause problems for people with learning disabilities (Calhoon, 2001; Gonzalez, 2002). When most of us encounter a word that we know, we recall its meaning from our "mental dictionary," but for unfamiliar words we must "sound out" the letters and pronounce the words by drawing on our knowledge of typical spelling patterns and pronunciation rules. This ability is very important in reading, both because we cannot memorize all words and because we constantly encountered new ones.

Students must also be able to generalize letter patterns and draw analogies with considerable flexibility. Good readers usually accomplish this task rather easily, fairly quickly, and almost automatically after a little practice (Kamhi & Catts, 2002). Students with reading disabilities, however, experience substantial difficulty with this process, and when they can do it, they seem to manage it only slowly and laboriously. Such students need specific training and practice in strategies that will help them succeed at recognizing words (Lovett et al., 2000).

Another important component of reading involves the use of context to determine meaning. Here again, good readers tend to be rather adept, but poor readers have trouble. Although poor readers encounter substantial problems in using context information to recognize words or infer their meaning, specific instruction improves their performance. Moreover, students with learning disabilities do not use background information effectively. Good and poor readers differ in the degree to which they use background knowledge for reading (Coyne, Kame'enui, & Simmons, 2001; Smith, 2000). Similarly, some students with learning disabilities focus on minor details within a text, without distinguishing the important ideas from those of less significance. A specific focus on learning strategies can help these students. Teaching them skills such as organizing and summarizing, using mnemonics, problem solving, and relational thinking can offset these difficulties and enhance academic performance (Esser, 2002; Taylor, Alber, & Walker, 2002; Vaughn, Gersten, & Chard, 2000).

Reading involves many skills (such as the ability to focus on important, rather than irrelevant, aspects of a task, and the ability to remember) that also affect performance in other subject areas (Jordon, Kaplan, & Hanich, 2002). Some difficulties experienced by people with learning disabilities emerge in more than one area, making the exact deficit difficult to pinpoint and explain. For example, does a child with reading disabilities have attention difficulties or working memory deficits? The problem could be caused by either disability or by a combination of the two. Specific instruction may improve performance, but if the focus of the training is too limited, the student may not generalize it to other relevant areas. Instruction that combines different methods (e.g., using both phonological awareness and instruction in specific skills) may serve students with reading disabilities better than applying only a single method (Bimmel, 2001; Esser, 2002; Fuchs, Fuchs, Thompson et al., 2001). In cases of more severe disability (such as dyslexia), it may be best to teach the person to compensate for the problem by accessing information through other means (see the nearby Reflect on This, "Dyslexia").

## DYSLEXIA: SEARCHING FOR CAUSES

Throughout history there has always been a search for the cause of learning disabilities, particularly the most severe forms, such as dyslexia (a very rare condition). The constant search for [the] single or most prominent cause is jokingly called looking for the "bullet theory" by professionals in the field (who mostly believe that matters are more complicated than singular causation). However, "bullet theory" reports continue to make news in the popular press, perhaps because they are simple enough to report in short accounts (or in sound bites on television) and attribution is simple—the cause is _____ (fill in the blank).

*Time* magazine followed this reporting trend on August 29, 1994, with "Brain Bane," an article reporting that researchers may have found a cause for dyslexia. Beginning with background information on dyslexia, its prevalence and characteristics, this article then moves to the final paragraph,

where barely one-third of the article is devoted to the main object for reporting. Here it is noted that Dr. Albert Galaburda of Harvard and Beth Israel Hospital in Boston has been conducting research on the brains of people with dyslexia who have died. Essentially, the research team sampled brain tissue from people with dyslexia (postmortem) and compared it with brain tissue collected from people who did not have dyslexia. Interestingly enough, these researchers found a difference in the size of nerve cells between the left and right hemispheres in tissue from people with dyslexia, but they found no such difference in the tissue from individuals without dyslexia. The researchers were careful to note that the size differential is only between 10 and 15 percent, but it is enough to capture the attention of *Time*. The public thirst for bullet theories is alive and well.

SOURCE: From "Brain Bane: Researchers May Have Found a Cause for Dyslexia" by C. P. Alexander, 1994, *Time*, 144 (9), p. 61.

**WRITING AND SPELLING.** Children with learning disabilities often exhibit quite different writing performance than do their peers without disabilities. This problem affects their academic achievement and frequently persists into adulthood. Difficulties may occur in handwriting (slow writing, spacing problems, poor formation of letters), spelling skills, and composition (Simner & Eidlitz, 2000; Troia & Graham, 2002). Several such problems are illustrated in Figure 7.2.

Some children are poor at handwriting because they have not mastered the basic developmental skills required for the process, such as grasping a pen or pencil and moving it in a fashion that results in legible writing. In some cases, fine motor development seems delayed in children with learning disabilities, and that of course contributes to physical difficulty in using writing materials. Handwriting also involves an understanding of spatial concepts, such as up, down, top, and bottom. These abilities frequently are less well developed in youngsters with learning disabilities than in their peers without disabilities (Simner & Eidlitz, 2000). The physical actions involved in using pencil or pen, as well as problems in discerning spatial relationships, can make it difficult to form letters and to use spacing between letters, words, and lines. Some children with rather mild handwriting problems may be exhibiting slowness in development, which will improve as they grow older, receive instruction, and practice. However, in more severe cases (e.g., the young adult whose writing sample appears in Figure 7.2), age and practice may not bring about mastery of the handwriting skill.

Some researchers view the handwriting, writing, and composition skills of students with learning disabilities as closely related to their reading ability. For example, research does not clearly indicate that children with learning disabilities write more poorly than their normally achieving peers who are reading at a similar level. Basic transcription processes seem to contribute significantly to writing problems among students with learning disabilities (Dupuy, 2001; MacArthur, 2000). Letter reversals and, in severe cases, **mirror writing** have often been used as illustrations of poor handwriting. Again, however, it is questionable whether children with learning disabilities make these types of errors more often than their peers without disabilities at the same reading level.

**Mirror writing**

Writing backwards from right to left, making letters that look like ordinary writing seen in a mirror.

## FIGURE 7.2

### Writing Samples of a College Freshman with a Learning Disability

As I seT hare Thinking abouT This simiTe I wundr How someone Like Me Cood posblee make iT thou This cors.  BuT some Howl I muse over come my fers and Wrese So I muse Be Calfodn in my sef and be NoT aferad To Trie

3 Reasens I Came To College

Reasen#1   To fofel a Drem that my Parens, Teichers and I hadd — Adrem that I codd some day by come ArchuTeck.

Reasen#2   To pouv rong those who sed I codd NoT make iT.

Reasen#3   Becos I am a bulheded.

**The text of these samples reads as follows:**

As I sit here thinking about this semester, I wonder how someone like me could possibly make it through this course.  But somehow I must overcome my fears and worries.  So I must be confident in myself and be not afraid to try.

Three Reasons I Came To College

Reason #1.   To fulfill a dream that my parents, teachers, and I had—a dream that I could some day become architect.

Reason #2.   To prove wrong those who said I could not make it.

Reason #3.   Because I am bullheaded.

The logic connecting writing and reading abilities has intuitive appeal. Most children write to some degree on their own, prior to receiving instruction in school. In general, children who write spontaneously also seem to read spontaneously and tend to have considerable practice at both before they enter school. Their homes tend to have writing materials readily available for experimentation and practice. Spontaneous writers may often observe their parents writing, and the parents and child may write together. Further research concerning the relationship between reading and handwriting is definitely in order (Vaid, Singh, Sakhuja, & Gupta, 2002). Instruction in writing for children with learning disabilities has historically been somewhat isolated from the act of reading and other content areas, which may have led to another challenge—the lack of skill transfer (Troia & Graham, 2002).

Poor spelling (also evident in Figure 7.2 is often a problem among students with learning disabilities). These children frequently omit letters or add incorrect ones. Their spelling may also show evidence of letter-order confusion and developmentally immature pronunciation (Smith, 2000). Interestingly, relatively little research has been conducted on these spelling difficulties, and teaching methods have been based primarily on individual opinion rather than on proven approaches (Apel, 2001; Scott, 2000). Recent literature suggests that the spelling skills of students with learning disabilities seem to follow developmental patterns similar to those of their peers without disabilities but that they are delayed (Bender, 2001; Lerner, 2003). Characteristics such as visual and auditory processing and memory problems, deficiencies in auditory discrimination, and phonic generalizations have also been implicated in the spelling difficulties that accompany learning disabilities. Data are mixed on these characteristics, and further research on spelling is needed for a clearer understanding of this area (Kujala, 2002).

**MATHEMATICS.**   Arithmetic is another academic area that causes individuals with learning disabilities considerable difficulty. They often have trouble with counting, writing numbers, and mastering other simple math concepts (Cawley, Parmar, Foley, Salmon, & Roy 2001; Geary & Hoard, 2001). Counting objects is perhaps the most fundamental mathematics skill and provides a foundation for the development of the more advanced, yet still basic, skills of addition and subtraction. Some youngsters omit numbers when counting sequences aloud (e.g., 1, 2, 3, 5, 7, 9), and others can count correctly but do not understand the relative values of numbers. Students with arithmetic learning disabilities have additional difficulties when asked to count beyond 9, which requires the use of more than one digit. This skill is somewhat more advanced than single-digit counting and involves knowledge about place value.

Place value is a more complex concept than the counting of objects and is fundamental to understanding addition and subtraction, since it is essential to the processes of carrying and borrowing. Many students with learning disabilities in math have problems understanding place value, particularly the idea that the same digit (e.g., 6) represents different magnitudes when placed in various positions (e.g., 16, 61, 632). Such complexities require strategic problem solving, which presents particular difficulties for students with learning disabilities (Fuchs, Fuchs, Hamlett, & Appleton, 2002).

Some of these basic mathematics difficulties are often major obstacles in the academic paths of students with learning disabilities; they frequently continue to cause problems throughout high school (Faraone et al., 2001). Mastery of fundamental quantitative concepts is vital to learning more abstract and complex mathematics, a requirement for youth with learning disabilities who are seeking to complete high school and attend colleges or universities (Cirino, Morris, & Morris, 2002). These young adults are increasing in number, and it is essential for them to master algebra and geometry during secondary education. These topics have traditionally received minimal or no attention in curricula designed for students with learning disabilities. Such coursework has tended to emphasize computational skills, although change is occurring as parents and educators recognize the need for more advanced instruction in mathematics (Naglieri & Johnson, 2000). Further research on difficulties with mathematics and on effective instruction for students encountering such problems grows more important as such young people seek to achieve more challenging educational goals.

**ACHIEVEMENT DISCREPANCY.** Students with learning disabilities perform below expectations based on their measured potential, in addition to scoring below their peers in overall achievement. This discrepancy between academic achievement and the student's assessed ability and age has prompted considerable research and theorizing. Attempts to quantify the discrepancy between academic achievement and academic potential for students with learning disabilities have appeared in the literature for some time, but the field still lacks a broadly accepted explanation of the phenomenon (Roderiques, 2002; Van-Noord & Prevatt, 2002). Early in the school years, youngsters with learning disabilities may find themselves two to four or more years behind their peers in level of academic achievement, and many fall even further behind as they continue in the educational system. This discouraging pattern often results in students dropping out of high school or graduating without proficiency in basic reading, writing, or math skills (U.S. Department of Education, 2002).

## Intelligence

Certain assumptions about intelligence are being reexamined in research on learning disabilities. Typically, populations with behavior disorders and learning disabilities are thought to include people generally considered above average or near average in intelligence (Van-Noord & Prevatt, 2002; Watkins & Kush, 2002). Differences between students with behavior disorders and those with specific learning disabilities have been defined on the basis of social skill levels and learner characteristics. However, individuals with learning disabilities may also exhibit secondary behavioral disorders, and students with behavior disorders may also have learning difficulties. To further complicate the matter, student classroom performance suggests that behavior problems are not associated with a particular level of intellectual functioning. It is well known that individuals with intellectual deficits and those with learning disabilities may both exhibit a considerable amount of mal-

This teacher is providing several cues to help her students grasp the meaning of the word cytoplasm. She has linked a shaded illustration, the whole word cytoplasm, cytoplasm broken syllable-by-syllable, and the actual writing and visualizing of the word and what it represents. A combination of cues is often important for students with learning disabilities.

adaptive social and interpersonal behavior (Kaukiainen et al., 2002). Problems in social adjustment must be viewed as a shared characteristic.

These insights have affected traditional ideas about the distinctions between learning disabilities and mental retardation. High variability between measured intelligence and academic performance has long been viewed as a defining characteristic of people with learning disabilities (McDonough-Ryan et al., 2002; Van-Noord & Prevatt, 2002). Also, descriptions of learning disabilities have often emphasized great intraindividual differences between skill areas. For example, a youngster may exhibit very low performance in reading but not in arithmetic. Frequently, this variability in aptitude has been used to distinguish populations with learning disabilities from those with mental retardation. A typical view holds that individuals with mental retardation exhibit a consistent profile of abilities (generally, low performance in all areas), in contrast to the pronounced intraindividual variability associated with learning disabilities. However, intraindividual variability is sometimes evident in students with mental retardation and in those with behavior disorders. Furthermore, the widely touted intraindividual variability in students with learning disabilities does not always appear; here again, the research evidence is mixed (Watkins & Worrell, 2000; Mayes, Calhoun, & Crowell, 2000).

## Cognition and Information Processing

People with learning disabilities have certain characteristics related to **cognition,** or **information processing.** Long used in psychology as a model for studying the processes of the mind, theories about cognition focus on the way a person acquires, retains, and manipulates information (e.g., Gettinger & Seibert, 2002). These processes often emerge as problematic for individuals with learning disabilities. For example, teachers have long complained that such children have poor memory. In many cases, these students seem to learn material one day but cannot recall it the next. Research on the memory skills of these children has been relatively scanty, although it is crucial to understanding how information is acquired, stored, selected, and recalled. Memory function is also centrally involved in language skill and development, a challenging area for many children with learning disabilities (Woltz, 2003). Certain evidence has suggested that children with learning disabilities do not perform as well as normal children on some memory tasks, whereas on other tasks,

**Cognition**

The act of thinking, knowing, or processing information.

**Information processing**

A model used to study the way people acquire, remember, and manipulate information.

research results have shown no differences (Dupuy, 2001; Pretorius, Naude, & Becker, 2002).

Research also suggests that children with learning disabilities have differing, rather than uniformly deficient, cognitive abilities (Henry, 2001). This finding has led to the development of specific, highly focused instruction for individuals with learning disabilities to replace generic curricula reflecting the assumption that their cognitive skills are generally poor.

Attention problems have also been associated with learning disabilities. Such problems have often been clinically characterized as **short attention span.** Parents and teachers often note that their children with learning disabilities cannot sustain attention for more than a very short time and that some of them exhibit considerable daydreaming and high distractibility. Some researchers have observed short attention spans in these children, but others have indicated that they have difficulty in *certain types* of attention problems and, in some cases, attend selectively (Bender, 2001). **Selective attention** problems make it difficult to focus on centrally important tasks or information rather than on peripheral or less relevant stimuli. Such problems might emerge when children with learning disabilities are asked to compute simple math problems that are on the chalkboard (which also means they must copy from the board). They may attend to the copying task rather than to the math problems. In this situation, the teacher can easily modify the task (e.g., by using worksheets rather than copying from the board) to facilitate completion of an important lesson. Attention problems remain in the spotlight as the information-processing problems of children with learning disabilities are investigated (e.g., Faraone et al., 2001).

## Learning Characteristics

Although the study of perceptual problems played a significant role early in the history of learning disabilities, interest in this topic has declined. Some researchers, however, continue to view perception difficulties as important. Perception difficulties in people with learning disabilities represent a constellation of behavior anomalies, rather than a single characteristic. Descriptions of these problems have referred to the visual, auditory, and **haptic** sensory systems. Difficulty in visual perception has been closely associated with learning disabilities. It is important to remember that the definitions of learning disabilities exclude impaired vision in the traditional sense; visual perception problems in persons with learning disabilities refer to something distinctly different. This type of abnormality can cause a child to see a visual stimulus as unrelated parts rather than as an integrated pattern; for example, a child may not be able to identify a letter in the alphabet because he or she perceives only unrelated lines, rather than the letter as a meaningful whole. Clearly, such perception would cause severe performance problems in school, particularly during the early years (Smith, 2000).

Visual perception problems may emerge in **figure–ground discrimination,** which is the process of distinguishing an object from its background. Whereas most of us have little difficulty with figure–ground discrimination, certain children labeled as having learning disabilities may have trouble focusing on a word or sentence on the page of a textbook because they cannot distinguish it from the rest of the page. This, of course, results in difficulties with schoolwork. This deficit illustrates one of the problems in research on learning disabilities: It could represent a figure–ground discrimination disorder, but it could also reveal an attention deficit or a memory problem. Thus the same abnormal behavior can be accounted for differently by several theories (e.g., Baum & Olenchak, 2002; Johnson & Slomka, 2000).

Other discrimination problems have also surfaced in descriptions of people with learning disabilities. Individuals with difficulties in **visual discrimination** may be unable to distinguish one visual stimulus from another (e.g., the difference between words such as *sit* and *sat* or letters such as *V* and *W*); they commonly reverse letters such as *b* and *d.* This type of error is common among young children, causing great concern for parents. Yet most youngsters overcome this problem in the course of nor-

**Short attention span**

An inability to focus one's attention on a task for more than a few seconds or minutes.

**Selective attention**

Attending that often does not focus on centrally important tasks or information.

**Haptic**

Related to the sensation of touch and to information transmitted through body movement or position.

**Figure–ground discrimination**

The process of distinguishing an object from its background.

**Visual discrimination**

Distinguishing one visual stimulus from another.

mal development and, by about 7 or 8 years of age, show few reversal or rotation errors with visual images. Children who make frequent errors beyond that age might be viewed as potential problem learners and may need additional instruction specifically aimed at improving such skills.

Auditory perception problems have historically been associated with learning disabilities. Some children have been characterized as unable to distinguish between the sounds of different words or syllables or even to identify certain environmental sounds (e.g., a ringing telephone) and differentiate them from others. Such problems have been termed **auditory discrimination** deficits. People with learning disabilities have also been described as having difficulties in **auditory blending,** auditory memory, and auditory association. Those with auditory blending problems may not be able to blend word parts into an integrated whole as they pronounce the word. **Auditory memory** difficulties may result in an inability to recall information presented orally. **Auditory association** deficiencies may result in an inability to process such information. Difficulties in these areas can obviously create school performance problems for a child. Although some literature related to auditory deficit theories continues to emerge, research attention has diminished in recent years (Erden & Yalin, 2001; Kujala, 2002).

Another area of perceptual difficulty long associated with learning disabilities involves *haptic perception* (touch, body movement, and position sensation). Such difficulties are thought to be relatively uncommon but may be important in some areas of school performance. For example, handwriting requires haptic perception, because tactile information about the grasp of a pen or pencil must be transmitted to the brain. In addition, **kinesthetic** information regarding hand and arm movements is transmitted as one writes. Children with learning disabilities have often been described by teachers as having poor handwriting and difficulties in spacing letters and staying on the lines of the paper. Such problems could also be due to abnormalities in visual perception, however, so definitively attributing some behaviors to a single factor is difficult. Figure 7.2 on page 177 offers an example of writing by a college freshman with learning disabilities. The two samples in this figure were written on consecutive days, each in a 40-minute period. The note below the samples translates what was written.

Not all individuals labeled as having learning disabilities exhibit behaviors that suggest perceptual problems. Patterns of deficiencies vary widely. Also, empirical evidence of perceptual problems in those labeled as having learning disabilities is generally lacking. Overall, the notion of perceptual dysfunction is founded on clinical impressions rather than on rigorous research, but even so, this viewpoint is widespread.

## Hyperactivity

Hyperactivity has commonly been linked to children labeled as having learning disabilities, although current literature more often associates it with attention-deficit/hyperactivity disorder (ADHD) (Gregg et al., 2002; Shapiro, 2002; Westby, 2002). Also termed **hyperkinetic behavior, hyperactivity** is typically defined as a general excess of activity. Professionals working in the area of learning disabilities, particularly teachers, often mention this behavior first in describing their students, depicting them as fidgeting a great deal and as unable to sit still for even a short time (e.g., Brook, Watemberg, & Geva, 2000; Mayes et al., 2000). Most descriptions portray an overly active child with limited ability to self-monitor and attend.

Certain points need to be clarified as we discuss hyperactivity in children with learning disabilities. First, not all children with learning disabilities are hyperactive, and not all hyperactive children have learning disabilities. As many as half the children with learning disabilities may not be hyperactive—certainly it is not a universal characteristic. Mixed research results and confusion currently mark our understanding of how learning disabilities are related to hyperactivity (Bayliss, & Roodenrys, 2000; Nadeau & Quinn, 2002).

**Auditory discrimination**

Distinguishing between the sounds of different words, syllables, or environmental noises.

**Auditory blending**

The act of blending the parts of a word into an integrated whole when speaking.

**Auditory memory**

The ability to recall verbally presented material.

**Auditory association**

The ability to associate verbally presented ideas or information.

**Kinesthetic**

Related to the sensation of body position, presence, or movement, resulting chiefly from stimulation of sensory nerve endings in the muscles, tendons, and joints.

**Hyperkinetic behavior**

An excess of behavior in circumstances where it is not appropriate.

**Hyperactivity**

Perhaps the most frequently mentioned behavior characteristic in the literature on ADHD. In some cases, the term *hyperactivity* refers to too much activity. In others, the term refers to activity inappropriate for a given situation or context.

## Social and Emotional Characteristics

Thus far we have discussed academically related characteristics and behavior of students with learning disabilities. Definitions and labels used for these students tend to focus on the academic perspective. Yet children and adolescents with learning disabilities often have emotional and interpersonal difficulties that are quite serious and highly resistant to treatment (Kaukiainen et al., 2002; Vaughn, Elbaum, & Boardman, 2001). Because of their learning problems, they frequently experience low self-esteem and negative emotional consequences (Cosden, Brown, & Elliott, 2002). They may not be able to interact effectively with others because they misunderstand social cues or cannot discriminate among, or interpret the subtleties of, typical interpersonal associations.

In some cases the social dimensions of life pose greater problems for students with learning disabilities than their specific academic deficits, and yet this trait is essentially ignored in the definitions and labels related to learning disabilities. Some researchers view the broad category of learning disabilities as less functional than specific terminology that more precisely describes particular problems. Many professionals would not support broadening the definition of learning disabilities to incorporate social and emotional dimensions, although it is clear that these are substantial (Hutchinson, Freeman, & Bell, 2002; Vaughn et al., 2001).

# Causation

**FOCUS 5**

List four causes thought to be involved in learning disabilities.

Researchers have theorized about a number of possible causes for learning disabilities. However, despite substantial work related to this field, determining precise causation has been difficult, and the effort to do so still continues. There are probably many different causes of learning disabilities, and in some cases, a specific type of learning disability may have multiple causes (Frank, 2000; Osman, 2000). Also, a single cause may underlie multiple disorders, such as learning disabilities and ADHD, in the same child (Nadeau & Quinn, 2002; Westby, 2002). But because it is imperative to help affected students even though we do not yet fully understand the cause of learning disabilities, the practical issues of assessment and intervention have frequently taken priority in research so that specialized instruction can be offered to such students (Bender, 2002).

## Neurological Factors

For many years, some have viewed the cause of learning disabilities as structural neurological damage, abnormal neurological development, or some type of abnormality in neurological function. A substantial portion of the literature in the field has reflected the interest in this proposition (e.g., Frank, 2000; McCurdy, 2001; Smith, 2000). Neurological factors have been the focus of some research and have been specified as an identification criterion in some literature (Osman, 2000).

Neurological damage associated with learning disabilities can occur in many ways. Damage may be inflicted on the neurological system at birth by conditions such as anoxia (a lack of oxygen) or abnormal fetal positioning during delivery. Infections may also cause neurological damage and learning disabilities, as can certain types of physical injury. In many cases, neurological damage as a cause of learning disability must be largely inferred because direct evidence is not available (Drew & Hardman, 2004; Gelfand & Drew 2003). (Chapter 10 discusses the relationship between the effects of neurological damage and mental retardation). However, advancing technology such as magnetic resonance imaging (MRI) is generating research that supports some unusual neurological functioning in these children (Shaywitz et al., 2002).

## Maturational Delay

Some theories have suggested that a delay in maturation of the neurological system results in the difficulties experienced by some individuals with learning disabilities. In many ways, the behavior and performance of children with learning disabilities resemble those of much younger individuals (Lerner, 2003). They often exhibit delays in skills maturation, such as slower development of language skills, and problems in the visual-motor area and several academic areas, as already noted. Although maturational delay is probably not a causative factor in all types of learning disabilities, it has received considerable support as contributing to some.

## Genetic Factors

Genetic causation has also been implicated in learning disabilities. Genetic abnormalities, which are inherited, are thought to cause or contribute to one or more of the problems categorized as learning disabilities (Johnson & Slomka, 2000; Muir, 2000). This is always a concern for parents, whatever the learning or behavior disorder. Over the years some research, including studies of **identical twins** and **fraternal twins,** has suggested that such disorders may be inherited (Alarcon, Knopik, & DeFries, 2000; Willcutt, Pennington, & DeFries, 2000). These findings must be viewed cautiously because of the well-known problems in separating the influences of heredity and environment, but some evidence supports the idea that some learning disabilities may be inherited (Doyle et al., 2001).

## Environmental Factors

The search for the causes of learning disabilities has also implicated certain environmental influences. Factors such as dietary inadequacies, food additives, radiation stress, fluorescent lighting, unshielded television tubes, drinking, drug consumption, and inappropriate school instruction have all been investigated at one time or another (Riikonen, Salonen, & Verho, 1999; Weinburg, 2001). Some environmental factors, such as irradiation, lead ingestion, maternal smoking, illicit drugs, and family stress, are known to have negative effects on development (Lardieri, Blacher, & Swanson, 2000; Stanton-Chapman, Chapman, & Scott, 2001; U.S. Department of Education, 2002). In some cases, these influences appear to be primarily prenatal concerns; in others, the problems seem limited to the postnatal environment or are attributable to both. Research on environmental causation related specifically to learning disabilities remains inconclusive, but it is the focus of continuing study.

# Assessment

Psychoeducational assessment, or the evaluation of individuals with learning disabilities, has multiple purposes. The ultimate goal is to provide an appropriate intervention, if warranted, for the child or adult being evaluated. Assessment and intervention involve a series of related actions, which include screening, identification, placement, and delivery of specialized assistance. This may mean additional help with academic work, social skills, or support related to any aspect of life and may involve professionals from a number of human service disciplines. Deciding how to meet an individual student's needs requires information obtained through a variety of assessment procedures (Merrell, 2002; Taylor, 2000). This section will examine the purposes and domains of assessment for learning disabilities and will focus on intelligence, adaptive behavior, and academic achievement.

**Identical twins**

Twins that develop from a single fertilized egg in a single placental sac. Such twins are of the same sex and usually resemble one another closely.

**Fraternal twins**

Twins that develop from two fertilized eggs and develop in two placentas. Often such twins do not resemble each other closely.

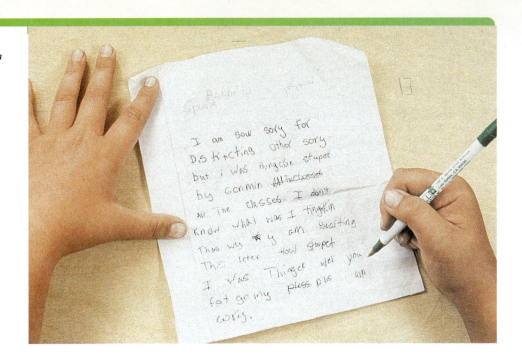

## Formal and Informal Assessment

An individual's status in performance, skills, and ability can be evaluated in a number of ways, either formally or informally. Formal versus informal assessment has grown to mean standardized tests versus teacher-made tests or techniques. Standardized instruments, such as intelligence tests and achievement tests, are published and distributed on a commercial basis. Teacher-made techniques or instruments (or those devised by any professional) are ones that are not commercially available. These may be constructed for specific assessment purposes and are often quite formal, in the sense that great care is taken in the evaluation process (Gronlund, 2003; Nitko, 2001). Both formal and informal assessment techniques are effective ways of evaluating students with learning disabilities and other students as well (Linn & Gronlund, 2001; Oosterhof, 2001). Both are used for evaluation purposes in a number of performance or behavior areas.

Other distinguishing characteristics can be used to describe assessment instruments. **Norm-referenced assessment** compares an individual's skills or performance with that of others, such as peers, usually on the basis of national average scores. Thus a student's counting performance might be compared with that of his or her classmates, with that of others in the school district of the same age, or with state or national average scores. In contrast, **criterion-referenced assessment** compares an individual's skills not with a norm but with a desired level (criterion) of performance or goal. For example, the goal may involve counting to 100 with no errors by the end of the school year. One application of criterion-referenced assessment, **curriculum-based assessment,** has received increasing attention recently. It uses the objectives in a student's curriculum as the criteria against which progress is evaluated (Crawford, Tindal, & Stieber, 2001; Taylor, 2000). The relationship between evaluation and instructional objectives makes instruction planning and assessment more efficient. Other terms (e.g., objectives-referenced measurement) have been used for similar procedures, but they all involve assessment referenced to instruction (Gronlund, 2000).

Both norm- and criterion-referenced assessment are useful for working with students with learning disabilities. Norm-referenced assessment is often used for administrative purposes, such as compiling census data on how many students are achieving at the state or national average. Criterion-referenced assessment is helpful for specific instructional purposes and planning.

**Norm-referenced assessment**

Assessment wherein a person's performance is compared with the average of a larger group.

**Criterion-referenced assessment**

Assessment that compares a person's performance to a specific established level (the criterion). This performance is not compared with that of other people.

**Curriculum-based assessment**

Assessment in which the objectives of a student's curriculum are used as the criteria against which progress is evaluated.

These two types of assessment do not require entirely separate types of assessment instruments or procedures. Depending on how a technique, instrument, or procedure is employed, it may be used in a norm-referenced or a criterion-referenced manner. Some areas, such as intelligence, are more typically evaluated using norm-referenced procedures. However, even a standardized intelligence test can be scored and used in a criterion-referenced fashion (the test would then function as a source of test items, and a student's performance could not be evaluated exactly as the test developer intended). Assessment should always be undertaken with careful attention to the purpose and future use of the evaluation (Drew & Hardman, 2004; Merrell, 2002).

## Screening

**Screening** of students who seem to have learning disabilities has always been an important facet of assessment. Such assessment occurs prior to labeling or treatment of the student, although clinicians or others (often parents) in contact with the child often suspect a problem exists. Some individuals are screened at a rather young age, and their assessment compares them to children of a similar age. But assessment for potential learning disabilities most often takes place during the school years. This is partly because the types of performance that are most problematic for these children are not often required until the child goes to school and partly because one of the important markers for learning disabilities (discrepancy between IQ and achievement) does not seem to show as well very early. However, screening and further assessment steps may be undertaken earlier if a child's difficulties attract attention before school. Such assessment may result in intervention at a very early age, which can be a greatly beneficial step for these children.

The role of screening is to "raise a red flag," or suggest that investigation is needed. Four questions are pertinent at this point of the assessment process:

1. Is there a reason to investigate the abilities of the child more fully?
2. Is there a reason to suspect that the child in any way has disabilities?
3. If the child appears to have disabilities, what are the relevant characteristics, and what sort of intervention is appropriate?
4. How should we plan for the future of the individual?

Answers to these questions might point to a variety of needs: further classification of the disability, planning of such as intervention services psychological treatment or individualized instruction, or ongoing evaluation of progress. For students with learning disabilities, assessment is not a simple, isolated event that results in a single diagnosis but, rather, a complex process involving many different steps (Taylor, 2000). After diagnosis, continuing assessment undergirds all decision making while an individual receives services related to learning disabilities. For our purposes, approaches to assessment focus on intelligence, adaptive skills, and academic achievement.

## Intelligence

For the most part, individuals with learning disabilities are described as having above average or near-average intelligence, although they experience problems in school typical of students with lower intelligence levels. In many cases, measures of intelligence may be inaccurate because of specific visual, auditory, or other limitations that may affect the student's performance (Van-Noord, & Prevatt, 2002). However, intelligence assessment remains an important matter for individuals with learning disabilities and is often carried out with a standardized instrument such as an intelligence test.

Where measured intelligence fits into the definition of learning disabilities is somewhat controversial. Some researchers argue that intelligence is irrelevant to the

**FOCUS 6**

Cite four questions that are addressed by screening assessment in learning disabilities.

**Screening**

A preliminary assessment process that may suggest that further evaluation of a child's needs and functioning level is necessary. The role of screening is to "raise a red flag" if a problem is indicated.

definition of learning disabilities, whereas others see it as important. Still others believe that the traditional way of measuring intelligence is problematic, but not the concept of intelligence per se (Watkins, Kush, & Schaefer, 2002). Such a divergence of opinion is not unusual in the field of learning disabilities.

## Adaptive Skills

People with learning disabilities are frequently described as exhibiting poor adaptive skills—lacking a sense of what constitutes appropriate behavior in a particular environment. Such descriptions have appeared primarily in clinical reports, and evaluation of adaptive skills has not historically been a routine part of assessment of learning disabilities to the same degree as in other areas of exceptionality, such as mental retardation. However, some work has been undertaken to address adaptive and social skills assessment for individuals with learning disabilities (e.g., Gresham, Sugai, & Horner, 2001; Pavri & Monda-Amaya, 2001). Such efforts are based on the assumption that a discrepancy between ability and academic achievement alone is insufficient to fully describe learning disabilities. The study of adaptive skills has contributed to greater understanding of subtypes and severity levels in learning disabilities and is beginning to receive greater attention in the field as researchers focus more on the emotional well-being of students with learning disabilities (see Jefferson-Wilson, 2000; Pavri & Monda-Amaya, 2001).

## Academic Achievement

Academic achievement has always been a major problem for students with learning disabilities. Assessment of academic achievement determines whether there is an overall discrepancy between a student's ability and his or her academic achievement. Such assessment also helps evaluate the student's level of functioning in one or more specific academic areas. Instruments have been developed and used to diagnose specific academic problems. For example, a number of reading tests, including the Woodcock Reading Mastery Tests, the Diagnostic Reading Scales, and the Stanford Diagnostic Reading Test, are used to determine the nature of reading problems. Likewise, mathematics assessment employs instruments such

## SNAPSHOT

## Alice

Alice found herself very frustrated with school. She was in the fourth grade, and her grades were very bad. She had worked very hard, but many of the things that were required just didn't seem to make sense.

History was a perfect example. Alice had looked forward to learning more about history;

it was so interesting when her grandfather told his stories. Alice thought it would have been fun to live back then, when all the kids got to ride horses. But history in school was not fun, and it didn't make any sense at all. Alice had been reading last night, supposedly about a girl who was her age and was moving west with a wagon train. As she looked at the book, Alice read strange

things. One passage said, "Mary pelieveb that things would get detter. What they hab left Missouri they hab enough foob dut now there was darely enough for one meal a bay. Surely the wagon-master woulb finb a wet to solve the brodlem." Alice knew that she would fail the test, and she cried quietly in her room as she dressed for school.

as the Key Math Diagnostic Arithmetic Test and the Stanford Diagnostic Mathematics Test (Gronlund, 2003). All of these assessments may be important for Alice, the young student we met earlier and whom we see again in the nearby Snapshot.

Academic assessment for students with learning disabilities is very important. For the most part, assessment techniques resemble those used in other areas of exceptionality, because deficits in academic achievement are a common problem among students with a variety of disabilities. Diagnosis of deficits in specific skills, however, has a more prominent history in learning disabilities and has prompted the development of focused, skill-oriented assessment of academic achievement in other disability areas as well. As with other exceptionalities, issues of inclusion and collaboration are prominent considerations in choosing the types of assessments employed; they have a significant impact on instructional placement and implementation in the educational program (Bauer & Brown, 2001; Dettmer, Thurston, & Dyck, 2002; Vallecorsa, deBettencourt, & Zigmond, 2000). Assessment with maximum relevance to the setting of application, often termed authentic or alternative assessment, also has attracted growing interest. These methods assess progress or skill using settings and procedures in a context like that in which the student must function, in contrast to the sterile, formal style of test administration used in the past.

# The Elementary School Years

Services and supports for children with learning disabilities have changed over time as professionals have come to view learning disabilities as a constellation of specific individualized needs, rather than as a single generic category. Specific disabilities, such as cognitive learning problems, attention deficit and hyperactivity, social and emotional difficulties, and problems with spoken language, reading, writing, and mathematics, are receiving research attention (e.g., Apel, 2001; Joseph & Hunter, 2001; Vaughn, Levy, Coleman, & Bos, 2002). This approach has resulted in services and supports focused on individual need, rather than on general treatment of learning disabilities. Greater attention is also being paid to social skills instruction for children with learning disabilities and to the effective use of peers as tutors (Gresham, Sugai, & Horner, 2001; Shapiro, 2001). Increasing recognition that these children learn, develop, and live in a broad social context has shifted the focus of services. Rather than intervening in an isolated problem area and ignoring others, professionals attempt to address a broad spectrum of issues. Some services and supports focus on strategic instruction (e.g., teaching the children how to learn), counseling and/or peer and family support (e.g., parent training), and medical treatment, all in the context of a structured educational environment (Heiman, 2002; Miao, Darch, & Rabren, 2002). Early intervention with the most effective instruction possible is viewed as a crucial factor in the child's overall academic success (Graham, Harris, & Larsen, 2001; Mati-Zissi & Zafiropoulou, 2001; Summers & Jenkins, 2001).

Services and supports for adolescents or adults with learning disabilities may differ from those for children. Some changes in approach are due to shifting goals as individuals grow older (e.g., the acquisition of basic counting skills versus math instruction in preparation for college). Educational support requires a broad range of specialized instruction tailored to individual needs that change as the person grows older. See the nearby Inclusion Through the Lifespan for more information about interacting effectively with people with learning disabilities at all ages. Individuals from varied professions must function as a team and also as unique contributors to create a well-balanced program for the student with learning disabilities (Dettmer et al., 2002).

FOCUS
7

Identify three types of interventions or treatments employed with people diagnosed as having learning disabilities.

## Inclusion Through the Lifespan

## PEOPLE WITH LEARNING DISABILITIES

### EARLY YEARS*

#### Tips for the Family

- Play verbal direction games, such as finding certain words or sounds, interspersing those that are difficult with those that are easy for the child with learning disabilities.
- Give the child practice in identifying different sounds (e.g., the doorbell and phone).
- Reinforce the child for paying attention.
- Promote family learning about learning disabilities, their child's specific strengths and limitations, and their respect for their child as a person.

#### Tips for the Preschool Teacher

- Limit verbal instructions to simple sentences, presented briefly, one at a time.
- Determine appropriate content carefully, paying attention to the developmental level of the material.
- Provide multiple examples to clarify points and reinforce meaning.
- Provide more practice than usual, particularly on new material or skills.

#### Tips for Preschool Personnel

- Promote a school environment and attitude that encourage respect for children of all abilities.
- Promote the development of instructional programs focusing on preacademic skills, which may not be necessary for all children but may be very important for young students with learning disabilities.
- Be alert for students who seem to be of average or higher intelligence but, for reasons that may not be evident, are not performing up to ability.

#### Tips for Neighbors and Friends

- Community activities should be arranged to include a broad range of maturational levels so that children with learning disabilities are not shut out and do not experience unnecessary failure at this early age.

*Very young children who may have learning disabilities typically have not been formally diagnosed with the disability, although they may exhibit what appears to be maturational slowness.

### ELEMENTARY SCHOOL YEARS

#### Tips for the Family

- Become involved in the school through parent-teacher organizations and conferences.
- Volunteer as a tutor.
- Learn more about learning disabilities as you begin to understand how they affect your child, perhaps through reading relevant material or enrolling in a short course.

#### Tips for General Education Classroom Teacher

- Keep verbal instructions simple and brief.
- Have the student with learning disabilities repeat directions back to you, to ensure understanding.
- Use mnemonics in instruction to aid memory.
- Intensify instruction by repeating the main points several times to aid memory.
- Provide additional time to learn material, including repetition or reteaching.

#### Tips for School Personnel

- Encourage individual athletic activities (e.g., swimming) rather than competitive team sports.
- Involve the child in appropriate school activities (e.g., chorus or music) where interests are apparent.
- Develop peer tutoring programs, in which older students assist children who are having difficulty.

#### Tips for Neighbors and Friends

- Make contact with advocacy or other groups that can help you learn about and interact with the child with learning disabilities.
- Maintain a relationship with the child's parents, talking with them about the child if and when they feel comfortable doing so.
- As a friend, encourage parents to seek special assistance from agencies that might provide services such as "talking books."
- If you are interested, offer assistance to the child's parents in whatever form they may need, or even volunteer to work with the child as a tutor.

## SECONDARY SCHOOL AND TRANSITION YEARS

### Tips for the Family

- Provide extra support for your youngster in the family setting, encouraging good school performance despite academic problems that may be occurring.
- Encourage your adolescent to talk about and think about future plans as he or she progresses into and through the transition from school to young adult life.
- Try to understand the academic and social difficulties the student may encounter. Encourage impulse control if impulsiveness may be causing some of the problems.
- Do not shy away from the difficult task of encouraging the student to associate with peers who are success-oriented rather than those who may be involved in inappropriate behavior.
- Encourage your adolescent to consider and plan for the years after high school, whether the student wants to go to college or find employment.

### Tips for the General Education Classroom Teacher

- Specifically teach self-recording strategies, such as asking oneself, "Was I paying attention?"
- Relate new material to knowledge the student with learning disabilities already has, making specific connections with familiar information.
- Teach the use of external memory enhancers (e.g., lists and note taking).
- Encourage the use of other devices to improve class performance (e.g., tape recorders).

### Tips for School Personnel

- Promote involvement in social activities and clubs that will enhance interpersonal interaction.
- Where students with learning disabilities have such interests and abilities, encourage participation in athletics or other extracurricular activities.
- Where interests and abilities are present, involve students in support roles to extracurricular activities (e.g., as team equipment manager).
- Promote the development of functional academic programs that are combined with transitional planning and programs.
- Provide information on college for students with learning disabilities, and encourage them to seek counseling about educational options, where appropriate.

### Tips for Neighbors and Friends

- Encourage students to seek assistance from agencies that may provide services (e.g., special newspapers, talking books, and special radio stations).
- Promote involvement in community activities (e.g., scouting, Rotary Club, Chamber of Commerce, or other service organizations for adults).
- Encourage a positive understanding of learning disabilities among neighbors, friends, and community agencies (e.g., law enforcement officials) who may encounter adolescents or adults with disabilities.

## ADULT YEARS

### Tips for the Family

- Interact with your adult family member with learning disabilities on a level that is consistent with his or her adult status. Despite all the difficulties he or she may have experienced in school and while maturing, remember that this person is now an adult.
- While recognizing the person's adult status, also remember that your adult family member with learning disabilities will probably continue to experience specific difficulties related to his or her disability. Help the person to devise ways of compensating.

### Tips for Therapists or Other Professionals

- In adulthood, it is unlikely that basic academic instruction will be the focus of professional intervention. It may be worthwhile to focus on compensatory skills for particularly difficult problem areas.
- Be alert for signs of emotional stress that may require intervention. This person may have a very deep sense of frustration accrued over a lifelong history of difficulties and failure.

### Tips for Neighbors and Friends

- It may be necessary to be more flexible or understanding with adult friends or neighbors with learning disabilities. There may be good explanations for deviations from what is considered normal behavior. However, if certain behaviors are persistent and particularly aggravating to you, you owe it to your friend to discuss the matter rather than letting it interfere with a friendship. You may have numerous friends, but the adult with learning disabilities may have precious few; thus your understanding and honesty are particularly valuable.

## Academic Instruction and Support

A wide variety of instructional approaches has been used over the years for children with learning disabilities. These include strategies to develop cognition, attention, spoken language, and skill in reading, writing, and mathematics (Lerner, 2003; Schmidt et al., 2002). Even within each area, a whole array of instructional procedures has been used to address specific problems. For example, as part of cognitive training, instruction in problem solving, strategies for attacking problems, and social competence has been incorporated (Gresham et al., 2001; Shapiro, 2001).

Various approaches to cognitive instruction are needed to teach the heterogeneous population of children with learning disabilities. Such strategies or tactics are often customized or reconfigured to individualize the program and target a student's specific needs. For example, if a youngster exhibits adaptive skills deficits that interfere with inclusion in general education, such skills may form an instructional focus. Flexible and multiple services or supports may make inclusion possible, providing a well-defined instructional environment, teaching the child important skills, and addressing interpersonal or social-emotional needs (Mastropieri & Scruggs, 2000). Coordinating or orchestrating such an instructional package is not a casual or simple task. Successful inclusion requires determining the intensity and duration of instruction appropriate for the child, choosing supports that will meet the child's needs, and accomplishing this early in the child's life but continuing the strategy through upper grades as well (Bauer & Brown, 2001; Kennedy & Fisher, 2001). Some educators believe that early intervention with a focus on excellent instruction can avoid academic failure for many children who might otherwise be diagnosed as having learning disabilities and thus obviate the need, in their case, for either special education or mainstreaming. Such a program for elementary-level children can build and improve their deficient skills, giving them a more promising prognosis for success in later school programs.

**MATHEMATICS.** Mathematics instruction for students with learning disabilities exemplifies how building a foundation of basic skills can enhance later learning. Earlier, we noted that children with difficulties learning arithmetic may have problems with basic counting and understanding of place value. For these students, counting may be most effectively taught with manipulative objects. Repetitive experience with counting buttons, marbles, or any such objects provides practice in counting, as well as exposure to the concepts of magnitude associated with numbers. Counting and grouping sets of ten objects can help children begin to grasp rudimentary place-value concepts. These activities must often be quite structured for students with learning disabilities.

Commercial programs of instruction in basic math concepts are also available. Cuisenaire Rods, sets of 291 color-coded rods used for manipulative learning experiences, are an example. These rods, whose differing lengths and colors are associated with numbers, can be used to teach basic arithmetic processes to individual students or groups.

Computer technology has also found its way into math skills instruction for students with learning disabilities (Bitter & Pierson, 2002; Parette & Anderson, 2001). Personal computers are particularly appealing for teaching math, because content can be presented in whatever sequence is most helpful. Computers can also provide drill and practice exercises for those who need it, an instructional goal that is often difficult for teaching staff to attain in a classroom with several children. Concern exists, however, regarding the use of computer technology primarily for drill and practice. Although reinforcement of learning is clearly a strength of many math programs, some focus excessively on drill and practice. Some researchers strongly contend that a broad range of instructional applications is needed, extending beyond the development of elementary skills to serve more students (see Bitter & Pierson, 2002). Computer technology has yet to meet the high expectations many have had for its application to instruction. It can provide some effective instruction for some students with learning disabilities, but students for whom the manipulation of objects is helpful in understanding math concepts may find microcomputers less useful. Long-term research is needed to study the effectiveness of computer instruction and to determine its most useful application for these children.

**READING.** It has long been recognized that students with learning disabilities have great difficulty with reading. Because of this, reading instruction has received considerable attention, and many different strategies have been developed to address the problem (Gersten, Fuchs, Williams, & Baker, 2001; Schmidt et al., 2002). Each procedure has succeeded with certain children, but none with all. This result lends credence to the current belief that many different disabilities may affect students who experience problems in the same area. Research on particular types of skill instruction, such as pre-reading activities, guided practice with feedback, and the direct teaching of skills in summarizing, has produced significant improvements for students with learning disabilities (see Lovett, Lacerenza, & Borden, 2000; Mati-Zissi & Zafiropoulou, 2001). Information gained from such research is being incorporated into instructional programs more than ever before and in many different content areas (see the nearby Assistive Technology, ("Software for Writing"). Combined with the realization that one single approach does not fit all students, this trend promises improved instruction and positive outcomes for students with learning disabilities.

Reading programs that base and sequence instruction within a developmental framework often help students with learning disabilities (Smith, 2000). Typically, such programs methodically introduce sight vocabulary based on developmental status, with an emphasis on analytic phonics. Developmental approaches to reading involve basal readers such as Holt Basic Reading; the Ginn 720 Series; Scott, Foresman Reading; and the Macmillan Series E. Such basal readers are most useful for group instruction (they are often designed for three levels), are well sequenced on a developmental basis, and typically provide enough detail to be used effectively by somewhat inexperienced teachers. The orientation toward group instruction, however, is likely to present some limitations for those students with learning disabilities who need a great deal of individual attention. Houghton Mifflin's *Soar to Success* program presents an appealing small-group intervention package that focuses on students performing at a two- to three-grade reading deficit. This program previously focused on grades 3–6, but grades 7 and 8 were added during the spring of 2000. SRA reading programs (e.g., Reading Mastery, Open Court) are considered appropriate for children with learning disabilities in both their scope and sequence; they also incorporate recommended teaching techniques.

Assistive Technology

## SOFTWARE FOR WRITING

Writing has long been recognized as an academic area that presents considerable difficulty for children with learning disabilities. Advances in educational applications of technology, especially the development of new computer software, have the potential to assist children with writing problems (MacArthur, 2000). An example of such software is Write: OutLoud, a talking word processor. Write: OutLoud cues the user with a beep or a flash on the screen in response to an incorrectly spelled word. This program can also speak! It will read back a sentence or a word so the user can check his or her work for accuracy.

Another software package with a speaking component is the Co: Writer, a word prediction program. It lets users write almost as quickly as they can think by predicting words through a program using artificial intelligence. For example, typing in the first letter or two of a word that the user is unsure how to spell will produce a list of possible words from which to choose. It helps those with spelling difficulties and low motor ability; it also helps with grammar and spelling problems.

Many teachers successfully use whole-language strategies to teach reading to students with learning disabilities. This approach tends to deemphasize isolated exercises and drills. Some are concerned, however, that this population needs a balance between a whole-language approach and focused, intensive, direct instruction related to problem areas (e.g., Ernsbarger, 2002; DiCecco & Gleason, 2002; Lerner, 2003). To make significant progress, a student with a serious reading disability often needs individualized reading instruction. A wide variety of materials (e.g., trade books) may be selected to match the student's reading level and cover topics of high interest to the student. The teacher responsible for developing and providing individualized instruction needs to have considerable knowledge of reading skills and the procedures that enhance learning them. Effective individualized instruction also requires evaluation of progress, ongoing monitoring, and detailed record keeping. Increasing the student's responsibility for his or her own learning—by teaching self-monitoring skills, for example—appears to enhance instructional effectiveness for students with learning disabilities (Bender, 2001). This self-directed involvement in learning makes students proactive partners, along with their teachers, in their education. This idea has led to the development of learning strategies packages that teach students effective skills for being better students. One such program is the GET IT strategy, described by its developers as a cognitive learning strategy for reading comprehension (Welch & Sheridan, 1995). (A brief description of the GET IT strategy is presented in the nearby Reflect on This.)

Several commercially available reading programs also provide specific skill-oriented reading instruction that functions in a diagnostic–prescriptive manner. Examples include the Fountain Valley Reading Support System, available from Zweig and Associates, and the Ransom Program from Addison-Wesley. Computer-assisted instruction is employed in some diagnostic–prescriptive reading programs, such as the Harcourt Brace CAI Remedial Reading Program and the Stanford University CAI Project. Individualized instruction is a hallmark of diagnostic–prescriptive reading programs. Such materials let students work at their own pace. These materials teach only those skills that lend themselves to the particular program's format, but

**Reflect on This**

## TEACHING THE MTV GENERATION TO TAKE RESPONSIBILITY FOR LEARNING

The GET IT program is a video-mediated instructional strategy aimed directly at appealing to the student. Emulating television game shows, the program also combines real-life situations of students from their perspectives—their lives as they see them, not as adults conceive them. This program is intended to teach basic learning strategies and responsibility to the student as a learner. The strategy title is a mnemonic provided to help students remember the elements and their tasks:

G: Gather the Objectives (or Get objectives).

E: Execute the search for objectives.

T: Take notes.

I: Inspect the inventory of objectives.

T: Test your comprehension.

The GET IT strategy has been used effectively with a number of student populations in both general and special education settings. The program emphasizes interactive participation of students and does not permit passive viewing. Larsen-Miller (1994) field-tested the program with mainstreamed sixth grade students identified as having learning disabilities. She found that significant gains were made in comprehension, attitude toward reading, and knowledge of the parts of a textbook. This strategy emphasizes students taking responsibility for an increased role in the teaching-learning equation.

SOURCES: *From Educational Partnerships: An Ecological Approach to Serving Students at Risk,* by M. Welch and S. M. Sheridan, 1995, San Francisco, CA: Harcourt; And "An Investigation to Determine the Effects of a Video-Mediated Metacognitive Reading Comprehension Strategy in a Complementary Environment," by L. Larsen-Miller, 1994, unpublished master's thesis, University of Utah.

notwithstanding this limitation, they have considerable strengths. For example, they do not require that the teacher possess the high degree of knowledge and skill that is essential for totally individualized, teacher-generated reading instruction. Additionally, diagnostic–prescriptive programs generally provide ongoing assessment and feedback, and developmental skills are usually well sequenced. Even so, such remedial reading programs are somewhat controversial in terms of both methodology and conceptual arguments about their function and appropriateness (e.g., Lovett et al., 2000; Schmidt et al., 2002).

A variety of other programs and approaches to reading instruction are available, each strategy with its own strengths and limitations for students with learning disabilities. Other developmentally based approaches include synthetic phonics basals, linguistic phonemic programs, and language experience approaches. Some procedures use multisensory techniques to maximize the student's learning. Selection of method and application of instructional technique should be based on a student's particular disability profile and other relevant needs.

Computer software for assessment and instruction in reading can assist students with learning disabilities, and its use will become increasingly common in the future. Computer-presented reading instruction offers some particular advantages. It provides individual instruction, as well as never-ending drill and practice, as mentioned earlier. Programs can also combine feedback with corrective instruction. As computer programs advance, reading instruction software will improve (right now, word-recognition programs seem to be of higher quality than comprehension software) and become more widely available. However, there is continuing concern regarding the appropriate use of software and about the need for long-range planning, faculty training, and other staff development related to applications of technology in instruction (see Bitter & Pierson, 2002). There continues to be a gap between technology developments and their effective broad implementation in education, and many matters require debate and resolution before information technology can realize its full potential in education (Collis & Pals, 2000; Torgerson & Elbourne, 2002).

As children progress into the upper-elementary grades, they may need instruction in compensatory skills or methods to "work around" deficits not yet remedied. This instruction may involve tutoring by an outside agency or an individual specializing in the problem, or it may involve placement in a resource room or even a self-contained class for students with learning disabilities. The approach that is chosen will depend on the severity of the difficulty, the particular area of deficiency, and sometimes (for better or for worse) the resources and attitudes of the decision makers (e.g., families and school districts).

## Behavioral Interventions

Distinctions between behavioral and academic interventions are not always sharp and definitive. Both involve students in learning skills and changing behavior. Behavioral interventions, however, generally use practical applications of learning principles such as reinforcement. Behavioral interventions such as the structured presentation of stimuli (e.g., letters or words), reinforcement for correct responses (e.g., specific praise), and self-monitoring of behavior and performance are used in many instructional approaches (Bredberg & Siegel, 2001; Willner, Jones, Tams, & Green, 2002). In this section, we briefly discuss some behavioral interventions that are used outside of traditional academic areas.

With certain children, instruction may focus on social skills training. Some students with learning disabilities who experience repeated academic failure, despite their great effort, become frustrated and depressed. They may not understand why their classmates without disabilities seem to do little more than they do and yet achieve more success. These students may withdraw or express frustration and anxiety by acting out or becoming aggressive. When this type of behavior emerges, it may be difficult to distinguish individuals with learning difficulties from those with behavior disorders as a primary disability, and therefore, both diagnosis of the problem and treatment may be quite difficult (e.g., Kaukianinen et al., 2002; Vaughn et al., 2001). In fact, these groups of students often exhibit many similar behaviors. The social and behavioral difficulties of students with learning disabilities are receiving increasing attention in the research literature (Bender, 2001; Kaukiainen et al., 2002).

**Behavioral contracts** are one type of intervention often used to change undesirable behavior. Using this approach, a teacher, behavior therapist, or parent establishes a contract with the child that provides him or her with reinforcement for appropriate behavior. Such contracts are either written or spoken, usually focus on a specific behavior (e.g., remaining in his or her seat for a given period of time), and reward the child with something that she or he really likes and considers worth striving for (e.g., going to the library or using the class computer). It is important that the pupil understand clearly what is expected and that the event or consequence be appealing to the child, so that it really does reinforce the appropriate behavior. Behavioral contracts have considerable appeal because they give students some responsibility for their own behavior (Gelfand & Drew, 2003). They can also be used effectively by parents at home. Contracts in various forms can be applied for students at widely differing ages.

Token reinforcement systems represent another behavioral intervention often used with youngsters experiencing learning difficulties. **Token reinforcement systems** allow students to earn tokens for appropriate behavior and eventually to exchange them for a reward of value to them (Gelfand & Drew, 2003). Token systems resemble the work-for-pay lives of most adults and therefore can be generalized to later life experiences. Although token systems require considerable time and effort to plan and implement, they can be truly effective.

Behavioral interventions are based on fundamental principles of learning largely developed from early research in experimental psychology. These principles have been widely applied in many settings for students with learning disabilities as well as other exceptionalities. One of their main strengths is that once the basic theory is understood, behavioral interventions can be modified to suit a wide variety of needs and circumstances.

# The Adolescent Years

Services and supports for adolescents and young adults with learning disabilities differ somewhat from those used for children. Age is an important factor to consider when planning services. Even the services and supports used during childhood vary according to age—appropriate assistance for a child 6 years of age will not typically work for one who is 12. New issues crop up during the teenage years. Adolescents and young adults with learning disabilities may, like their nondisabled peers, become involved in alcohol or drug use and sexual activity (Blum, Kelly, & Ireland, 2001; Molina & Pelham, 2001). Certainly, they are vulnerable to peer pressure and to the temptation of engaging in misconduct. However, adolescents are also influenced by their parents' expectations, which may be an important positive factor in academic achievement. Age-appropriate modifications are essential to effective instruction and services for adolescents with learning disabilities, and most often they must be individually designed.

## Academic Instruction and Support

Academic instruction for adolescents with learning disabilities differs from such programs for younger children. Research suggests that the educational system often fails adolescents with learning disabilities. These students have lower school completion rates than their nondisabled peers, as well as higher unemployment rates (U.S. Department of Education, 2002). The goal of secondary education is to prepare indi-

**FOCUS 8**

How are the services and supports for adolescents and adults with learning disabilities different from those used with children?

**Behavioral contract**

An agreement, written or oral, between people, stating that if one party behaves in a certain manner (for example, the student completes homework), the other (for example, the teacher or parent) will provide a specific reward.

**Token reinforcement system**

A system in which students, by exhibiting positive behavior changes, may earn plastic chips, marbles, or other tangible items that they can exchange for activities, food items, special privileges, or other rewards.

viduals for postschool lives and careers. These findings suggest a serious doubt that youth with learning disabilities are being adequately supported in meeting this goal. Often these adolescents find that they still need to develop basic academic survival skills (and, for some, preparation for college), and they also often lack social skills and comfortable interpersonal relationships (Kaukiainen et al., 2002; Vaughn et al., 2001). Adolescents with learning disabilities are attending college in greater numbers than ever, but they tend to drop out at higher rates than their nondisabled peers (U.S. Department of Education, 2002). Clearly, a comprehensive model, with a variety of components, needs to be developed to address a broad spectrum of needs for adolescents and young adults with learning disabilities.

Relatively speaking, adolescents with learning disabilities have received considerably less attention than their younger counterparts. Academic deficits that first appeared during the younger years tend to grow more marked as students face progressively more challenging work, and by the time many reach secondary school or adolescence, they may be further behind academically than they were in the earlier grades (Bender, 2001). Although academic performance figures prominently in the federal definition of learning disabilities, there still has been relatively little research on factors that influence academic development in adolescents with learning disabilities. Problems in motivation, self-reliance, learning strategies, social competence, and skill generalization all emerge repeatedly in the literature on such adolescents and young adults (e.g., Molina & Pelham, 2001; Swanson & Hoskyn, 2001; Taylor et al., 2002).

Time constraints represent one difficulty that confronts teachers of adolescents with learning disabilities. A limited amount of time is available for instruction, student progress can be slow, and determining what to focus on is difficult. In some areas, high school students may not have progressed beyond fifth grade level academically, and they may have only a rudimentary grasp of some academic topics (Bender, 2001). Yet they are reaching an age at which life grows more complex. A broad array of issues must be addressed, including possible college plans (an increasingly frequent goal for students with learning disabilities), employment goals, and preparation for social and interpersonal life during the adult years. In many areas, instead of building and expanding on a firm foundation of knowledge, many adolescents with learning disabilities are operating on a beginning to intermediate

The goals of adolescents with learning disabilities will vary among individuals. Some students may look forward to employment after high school while others might plan some type of continuing education.

level. They may appear less than fully prepared for the challenges ahead of them, but a well-planned program of supports can do much to smooth the transition to adulthood.

The challenge of time constraints has led researchers to seek alternatives to and supplements for traditional teaching of academic content to students with learning disabilities. Teaching learning strategies to students is one widely used approach that focuses on the learning process. In this approach, students are taught *how to learn* in addition to the content of a given lesson (e.g., Esser, 2002; Taylor et al., 2002). Thus the learning strategies approach promotes self-instruction and frequently emphasizes "thinking about" the act being performed. This *metacognition* process may focus on rather complex academic content such as writing (Klassen, 2002; Woltz, 2003). Learning strategies programs may be employed in the general education classroom, as illustrated in the nearby Reflect on This feature, "Write, P.L.E.A.S.E."

Secondary school instruction for adolescents with learning disabilities may also involve teaching compensatory skills to make up for those not acquired earlier. Compensatory skills often address specific areas of need, such as writing, listening, and social skills. For example, tape recorders may be used in class to offset difficulties in taking notes during lectures and thus compensate for a listening (auditory input) problem. For some individuals, personal problems related to disabilities require counseling or other mental health assistance. And to further complicate matters during adolescence, hormonal changes with strong effects on interpersonal behavior come into play; research results are barely beginning to emerge on such issues for adolescents with learning disabilities (Gutstein & Sheely, 2002; Shapiro, 2001). These students tend to have low social status among nearly all the people around them, including peers, teachers, and even parents. Some may become involved in criminal activities, as mentioned periodically in the literature, although the research evidence linking learning disabilities and juvenile delinquency is mixed (Smith, 2000; Whittel

**Reflect on This**

## WRITE, P.L.E.A.S.E.: A LEARNING STRATEGY TO USE IN THE GENERAL CLASSROOM

Using a bologna sandwich to teach writing skills may seem a bit strange, but it serves a definite purpose. It camouflages the academic overtones of a video-assisted learning strategies program and has been successfully employed with typical students, low-efficiency learners who do not qualify for special education, and students with learning disabilities. This strategy is another in the series developed by M. W. Welch and his colleagues that targets the inclusion of students with learning problems (and low-efficiency students) into the instructional mainstream.

Write, P.L.E.A.S.E. provides students with an easily remembered strategy for planning and executing their written compositions using the mnemonic cues of the title:

Pick: Students pick the topic, the audience, and a textual format appropriate to the topic and audience.

List: Students list information about the topic to be used in generating sentences.

Evaluate: Students evaluate their list and other elements of their writing as they proceed.

Activate: Students activate their paragraph with a topic sentence.

Supply: Students supply supporting sentences, moving from their topic sentence and drawing on their list of ideas.

End: Students end with a concluding sentence and evaluate their work.

Combining mnemonics and the sandwich visual metaphor has given students a means of remembering important elements of writing paragraphs. This uniquely presented learning strategy is effective in the general education classroom as well as in more specialized instructional circumstances.

SOURCE: From "Write, P.L.E.A.S.E.: A Video-Assisted Strategic Intervention to Improve Written Expression of Inefficient Learners," by M. W. Welch and J. Jensen, 1991, *Journal of Remedial and Special Education, 12*, pp. 37–47.

& Ramcharan, 2000). Generally, evidence does not suggest that individuals with learning disabilities are arrested or sentenced to serve jail terms at substantially higher rates than peers without disabilities.

## Transition from School to Adult Life

Some adolescents and adults with learning disabilities have successfully adapted by themselves to a variety of challenges. However, many of the difficulties that adolescents with learning disabilities experience do not disappear as they grow older, and specialized services are often needed throughout adolescence and perhaps into adulthood (Flanagan, Bernier, Keiser, & Ortiz, 2003). The National Research Center on Learning Disabilities emphasized this developmental need, noting that "specific learning disabilities persist across the life span, though manifestations and intensity may vary as a function of developmental stage and environmental demands" (NRCLD, 2002). The importance of this statement is that it explicitly addresses the life span *and* acknowledges the variations that may occur at different ages. We currently do not understand all the factors that contribute to success or lack of it in young adults with learning disabilities. Some ingredients that would seem to contribute to success as a young adult (e.g., verbal intelligence, length of school enrollment) have not proved to be accurate predictors. Perhaps these findings reflect

### Case Study

## ALICE REVISITED

Recall Alice, whom we met in the last Snapshot. When we last saw her, Alice was in the fourth grade and was extremely frustrated with school. Unfortunately, she failed the history test for which she was preparing. She could not obtain enough information from the narrative and consequently could not answer the questions on the test. The exam was a paper-and-pencil test, which, to Alice, looked like the book that she was supposed to read about the family who was moving west with the wagon train. When she received her graded test, Alice broke into tears. This was not the first time she had wept about her schoolwork, but it was the first time that her teacher had observed it.

Alice's teacher, Mr. Dunlap, was worried about her. She was not a troublesome child in class, and she seemed attentive. But she could not do the work. On this occasion, Mr. Dunlap consoled Alice and asked her to stay after school briefly to chat with him about the test. Since it was early in the year, he had no clue what was wrong, except that he knew this charming girl could not answer his test questions. He was astonished when they sat together and he determined that Alice could not even *read* the questions. If she could not read the questions, he thought, then she undoubtedly can't read the book. But he was fairly certain that she was not lacking in basic intelligence—her conversations simply didn't indicate such a problem.

After further consoling Alice regarding her test, Mr. Dunlap sent her home and then contacted her parents. He knew a little about exceptional children and the referral process. He set the process in motion, meeting with the parents, the school psychologist, and the principal, who also sat in on all the team meetings at this school. After a diagnostic evaluation,

the team met again to examine the psychologist's report. Miss Burns, the psychologist, had tested Alice and found that her scores fell in the average range in intelligence (with a full-scale WISC-III score of 114). She had also assessed Alice's abilities with a comprehensive structural analysis of reading skills. This led her to believe that Alice had a rather severe form of dyslexia, which interfered substantially with her ability to read.

Alice's parents expressed a strong desire for her to remain in Mr. Dunlap's class. This was viewed as a desirable choice by each member of the team, and the next step was to determine how an intervention could be undertaken to work with Alice while she remained in her regular class as much as possible. All team members, the parents included, understand that effectively meeting Alice's educational and social needs will be challenging for everyone. However, they are all agreed that they are working toward the same objectives—a very positive first step.

### APPLICATION

Placing yourself in the role of Mr. Dunlap, and given the information that you now have regarding Alice, respond to the following questions.

1. How can you facilitate Alice's social needs, particularly focusing on her relationships with her classmates?

2. Should information about Alice's reading difficulties be shared with classmates, or would this be detrimental to their interactions with her?

3. Who should be a part of this broad educational planning?

4. Should you talk with Alice about it?

difficulties and inaccuracies in measurement as well as challenges in prediction (Lichtenberger, 2001; Smith & Travis, 2001). Accumulating research on the transition years of adolescents with learning disabilities may begin to illuminate some of these methodological problems. We may find that this period of life is characterized by some unique challenges, just as it is for young people with other disabilities (Flanagan et al., 2003; Stacey, 2001).

**TRANSITION SERVICES.** Transition services remain rather sparse for adolescents with learning disabilities. However, this area is beginning to receive increased research attention. We are beginning to learn more about how emotional, interpersonal, and social competence issues affect adults with learning disabilities, and such research will have an impact on transition planning. Research is emerging on factors such as substance abuse; results suggest a possible association between alcohol abuse and learning disabilities (e.g., Blum et al., 2001). Services and supports that address this problem are beginning to be reported (Cummings, Davies, & Campbell, 2002; Wenar & Kerig, 2000). Although the picture remains unclear at this point, some research results suggest that adults with learning disabilities may be at risk of engaging in violence and violent crime (Moore, 2001; Svetaz, Ireland, & Blum, 2000). Research on interpersonal relationships is also under way, and preliminary findings point to a need for transition services for young adults with learning disabilities in areas of emotional well-being, interpersonal intimacy, and sexuality (e.g., Reiff, Hatzes, Bramel, & Gibbon, 2001). Results suggest that the competence of young adults with learning disabilities in these areas is not notably positive.

Those who are planning transition programs for adolescents with learning disabilities must consider that these adolescents' life goals may approximate those of adolescents without disabilities. Some students look forward to employment that will not require education beyond high school. Some plan to continue their schooling in vocational and trade schools (Lerner, 2003). As with other areas of exceptionality, schooling should play a significant role in preparing young adults with learning disabilities for the transition from school to work (Cummings, Maddux, & Casey, 2000; Stacey, 2001). Employment preparation activities such as occupational awareness programs, work experience, career and vocational assessment, development of job-related academic and interpersonal skills, and information about specific employment should be part of transition plans and should benefit these students. In addition, professionals may need to negotiate with employers to secure some accommodations at work for young adults with learning disabilities. Limited data are available on the employment success of young adults with learning disabilities; most reports combine information on people with a number of disabilities. Most authorities agree, however, that the employment years for these individuals usually are not any easier than their school years, and a definite need exists for programs to facilitate the transition from school to work (Gosling & Cotterill, 2000).

**COLLEGE BOUND.** As we have noted, growing numbers of young people with learning disabilities plan to attend a college or university (Mazza, 2002; U.S. Department of Education, 2001). There is little question that they will encounter difficulties and that careful transition planning is essential to their success. Their dropout rates are higher and their academic performance indicators are lower than those of their counterparts without learning disabilities. It is also clear that, with some additional academic assistance, they not only will survive but also can be competitive college students (Hartman-Hall & Haaga, 2002; Rath & Royer, 2002). These students need substantial college preparatory counseling before they leave secondary school. There is a considerable difference between the relatively controlled setting of high school and the more unstructured environment of college. In their preparation for this significant transition, students profit from focused assistance, transition planning, and goal setting, perhaps in conjunction with their high school counselors (e.g., Shapiro, 2002; Trusdell & Horowitz, 2002).

College-bound students with learning disabilities may find that many of their specific needs are related to basic survival skills in higher education. At the college level, it is assumed that students can already take notes and digest lecture information auditorily and that they have adequate writing skills, reading ability, and study habits. Transition programs must strengthen these abilities as much as possible and show the students how to compensate for deficits, using a range of perspectives and strategies to plan the student's pursuit of postsecondary education (Cummings et al., 2000; Stacey, 2001). Taped lectures can be replayed many times to help the student understand the information. Students with reading disabilities can obtain the help of readers who tape-record the content of textbooks so that they can listen to the material, rather than making painfully slow progress if reading is difficult and time-consuming. College students with learning disabilities must also seek out educational support services and social support networks to offset emotional immaturity and personality traits that may impede college achievement (Shapiro, 2002).

Perhaps the most helpful survival technique that can be taught to an adolescent with learning disabilities is actually more than a specific skill; it is a way of thinking about survival—an overall attitude of resourcefulness and a confident approach to solving problems. Recall Mathew, the psychology student in one of this chapter's first Snapshots. Mathew has an amazing array of techniques that he uses to acquire knowledge while compensating for his the specific areas where he has deficits. Students need both proven techniques to deal with problem areas and the ability to generate new ways to tackle the challenges that inevitably arise in college. This positive attitude also includes knowing how to seek help and how to advocate for oneself. Transition programs that can instill such a mind-set in students preparing for college have truly served an important purpose.

Another key transition element involves establishing a support network. Students with learning disabilities should be taught how to establish an interpersonal network of helpers and advocates. An advocate on the faculty can often be more successful than the student in requesting special testing arrangements or other accommodations (at least to begin with). A word of caution is in order, however. Faculty in higher education are bombarded with student complaints and requests, many of which are not based on extreme needs. Consequently, many faculty are wary of granting special considerations such as extra time. However, a request from a faculty colleague may carry more weight. It should also be noted that many faculty are uninformed about learning disabilities, and overtures from a colleague can enhance the credibility of the student's request.

Concern about the accommodations requested by students who claim to have learning disabilities is genuine and is growing. Because these disabilities are "invisible," they are hard to understand, and there is great room for abuse in requests for accommodations. Such requests have increased dramatically, and many faculty are skeptical about their legitimacy. Research suggests that some cynicism is understandable; some claims indeed lack a sound justification, and the diagnostic documentation provided for many college students who claim to need accommodations because of a learning disability is seriously flawed. Although the Americans with Disabilities Act clearly mandates accommodation, college students with learning disabilities should be aware that many higher-education faculty are skeptical about the merits of this mandate and that the process of getting special arrangements approved is not simple (Flanagan et al., 2003; Zuriff, 2000). Some incidents related to this issue have become publicized and politicized, and they may have a detrimental effect on the general higher-education environment for those with learning disabilities. Providing clear diagnostic evidence of a learning disability will enhance the credibility of a request for accommodation. Even faculty in special education have encountered those who have diagnosed themselves and claimed to have a learning disability; this unprofessional approach is counterproductive to improving the experiences of students with learning disabilities in higher education. The accompanying Debate Forum illustrates some elements of these accommodation issues.

Students with learning disabilities can lead productive, even distinguished, adult lives. But some literature suggests that even after they complete a college education, adults with learning disabilities have limited career choices (Bender, 2001). A more comprehensive research base is needed in this area. However, we do know that notable individuals have been identified as having learning disabilities. They include scientist and inventor Thomas Edison, U.S. president Woodrow Wilson, scientist Albert Einstein, and governor of New York and vice president of the United States Nelson Rockefeller. We also know that Mathew graduated from college and entered graduate school and that the young man whose writing we saw in Figure 7.2 became a successful architect. Such achievements are not accomplished without considerable effort, but they show that the outlook for people with learning disabilities is very promising.

## Debate Forum

## REASONABLE ACCOMMODATION VERSUS UNREASONABLE COSTS

No concept seems more likely to be accepted—even embraced—by most people than that of a "fair and level playing field" for all. Yet the notion of reasonable accommodation in providing services for students with disabilities continues to be controversial, especially in institutions of higher education. Sometimes the most vocal participants in the discussions are those with budget responsibilities for education (in some cases, accommodations significantly affect budgets). At other times, strident opposition may be voiced by educators and those who are not requesting accommodation—the classmates of a student with disabilities.

### POINT

Accessing services for students with learning disabilities often involves requests for reasonable accommodations in order to take into account the student's needs resulting from his or her disability. For students with learning disabilities, such requests may involve extensions of time during exams, oral instead of written exams, or modification of homework assignments. In some cases providing accommodations is easily accomplished; in others it is more difficult and creates significant challenges for the teacher and even the educational institution. It is the law, however, and such requests must be honored.

### COUNTERPOINT

Interestingly enough, many educators do not know or have a good grasp of what is involved in reasonable accommodation. As individuals, their sources of information may be rumor and speculation in the teachers' lounge or such faculty gatherings as department meetings in colleges or universities. Sometimes identifying sources of good advice is not that easy. It is probably prudent to consider all requests, but the notion that all requests must be honored is faulty. For example, students in college often make requests of their professors, implying that they have a learning disability but offering no evidence beyond the verbal claim. There needs to be solid evidence, such as a diagnostic review by a campus center for assistance to those with disabilities. Written documentation is required in the protocol negotiated by the institution's legal department. Self-diagnosis is not grounds for accommodations that would, in fact, create a playing field that was far from level.

What do you think? To give your opinion, go to Chapter 7 of the companion website (www.ablongman.com/hardman8e), and click Debate Forum.

# Inclusive Education

Definitions and descriptions of various approaches to inclusive education were introduced in earlier chapters. Much of the impetus for the inclusive education movement emerged from efforts of parents and advocacy organizations; the concept has been known by various terms, such as *mainstreaming, the regular education initiative,* and *integration service models.* A very large proportion of students with learning disabilities receive educational services in settings that are either fully or partially inclusive. In 1999–2000, only 15.7% of students with learning disabilities from 6 to 21 years of age were served outside the regular classroom more than 60% of the time (U.S. Department of Education, 2002).

Inclusive education is an important part of the academic landscape for students with learning disabilities, and a variety of specific instructional strategies are employed to enhance success. Inclusive approaches have received increasing attention in the learning disability literature, which has included thought-provoking debate about appropriate formats and the strengths and limitations of placing students with learning disabilities in fully inclusive educational environments (Bender, 2002; Klinger & Vaughn, 2002). To be successful, inclusive education requires commitment to another of the major themes in this book: collaboration among general and special educators and other team members.

Instructing students with learning disabilities in inclusive settings requires significant advance planning. Increasingly, the education of these students is guided by complex, comprehensive plans incorporating instructional services and supports and multiple approaches. IEPs at this stage have evolved with the student's chronological age and as his or her skills develop. Each student's instructional plan targets specific areas where the individual needs more intense or specialized attention. The academic focus may be on a reading problem or on difficulties in some content area. Social and behavioral issues may emerge in the inclusive environment, and related interventions may form part of the spectrum of services and supports (Schmidt et al., 2002). To be effective, instructional supports must be directly related to the student's needs in the context of a general education classroom.

Several factors affect the success of inclusive education for students with learning disabilities. For example, teacher attitudes are very influential. Some evidence suggests that general education teachers feel unprepared to teach students with disabilities, to collaborate with special educators, and to make academic adaptations. Adequate teacher preparation is a very important factor in effective inclusive education. Such preparation requires a significant collaborative partnership between general education and special education teacher education programs, which has largely been lacking to date. This defect continues to be criticized in teacher education literature and reflects many dilemmas in higher education (Connor, Ferri, Sollis, Valle, & Vopitta, 2002). In addition to teachers' curriculum and instructional skills, their personal attitudes toward inclusive education are vitally important. General education teachers often have less positive attitudes toward and perceptions of inclusive education than special education teachers do, although such attitudes can be changed (Bishop & Jones, 2002; Prochnow, Kearney, & Carroll-Lind, 2000).

Successful inclusion requires much more than merely placing students with learning disabilities in the same classroom with their peers without disabilities. Some researchers have noted that because these students need supports and adaptations, successful inclusion might better be described as supported inclusion simply than as inclusion. Inclusive education must be undertaken only after careful planning of the instructional approach, services, and supports (Bauer & Brown, 2001; Kennedy & Fisher, 2001). Such a program can effectively promote academic support, student motivation, and development of social-emotional skills for students with learning disabilities.

# Medical Services

Medical professionals are sometimes involved in the diagnosis of learning disabilities and in prescribing medications used in treating conditions that may coexist with learning disabilities. The involvement of physicians varies somewhat according to the age of the person with disabilities.

## Childhood

Physicians often diagnose a child's abnormal or delayed development in the areas of language, behavior, and motor functions. It is not uncommon for pediatricians to participate in diagnosing physical disabilities that may significantly affect learning and behavior and then to interpret medical findings to the family and other professionals. Physicians may have early involvement with a child with learning disabilities because of the nature of the problem, such as serious developmental delay or hyperactivity. More often a medical professional sees the young child first because he or she has not entered school yet, and the family physician is a primary adviser for parents (Drew & Hardman, 2004). When other professional expertise is needed, the physician may refer the family to other specialists and then function as a team member in meeting a child's needs.

One example of medical service appropriate for some children with disabilities involves controlling hyperactivity and other challenging behaviors. Many children with learning disabilities receive medication such as Ritalin (generic name, methylphenidate) to control hyperactivity. Although their action is not completely understood, such psychostimulants do appear to result in general improvement for a large proportion of children with ADHD (Pelham et al., 2002; Stein & Batshaw, 2001). Some researchers have expressed caution about such treatment, focusing on matters of effectiveness, overprescription, and side effects (e.g., Putnam, 2001; Rapport & Moffitt, 2002). Concerns have also been expressed about the soundness of research methods used to investigate the effects of medication (e.g., Gelfand, & Drew, 2003).

Too little is known about the effects of medication on hyperactivity, even as evidence continues to accumulate. For example, there are a number of situations where it is not known which drug will be effective until after treatment has begun. Uncertainty regarding dosage level and the fact that high doses may have toxic effects are adding to the confusion. Although there are clear benefits to the use of medication, it may be overprescribed (Pelham et al., 2002; Pozzi, 2000). Continued research is crucial to clarifying many aspects of this treatment.

## Adolescence

As in other treatment areas, medical services for adolescents and young adults with learning disabilities differ somewhat from those for children. The literature directly addressing medical services during adolescence is unfortunately scarce, although some studies have explored specific needs that may require medical attention. For example, stress and serious emotional difficulty, including depression, during the adolescent years are receiving attention (e.g., Grant et al., 2003; Kaukiainen et al., 2002; Vaughn et al., 2001). In some cases, psychiatry may be involved in treatment, either through interactive therapy or prescribing of antidepressant medication. Some efforts are under way to improve the assessment of medical, developmental, functional, and growth variables for individuals with learning difficulties, in a variety of settings (e.g., Martin, Scahill, Klin, & Volkmar, 1999). These efforts too are expanding and may soon systematically address individuals with learning disabilities at various age levels.

Some adolescents receiving medication to control hyperactivity may have been taking it for a number of years, since many such physician assessments and prescriptions are made during childhood. On the other hand, some treatments are of rather short duration and many terminate within two years (Hamilton, 2001). This finding raises serious questions regarding which type of treatment is most suitable.

Other unanswered questions concern problems with side effects and with determining which medications are effective in dealing with particular symptoms (Putnam, 2001; Rapport & Moffitt, 2002). A number of adolescent youth and adults with learning disabilities have struggled through their earlier years and have not received medication until after childhood. In many cases, the medication to assist with behavior and attention problems is again an amphetamine and appears to have the same beneficial results noted earlier (Pelham et al., 2002, Stein & Batshaw, 2001).

The field of learning disabilities and the individuals served within it represent an interesting array of challenges, perhaps the most perplexing among the high-incidence disabilities. In the overall picture of disabilities, these challenges are not trivial, both because they are complex and because they involve such a very large proportion of those who have disabilities. Progress is evident, although it is also clear that intense and systematic research efforts are essential if improvement in service is to continue.

# FOCUS REVIEW

**FOCUS 1** Cite four reasons why definitions of learning disabilities have varied.

- *Learning disabilities* is a broad, generic term that encompasses many different specific problems.
- The study of learning disabilities has been undertaken by a variety of different disciplines.
- The field of learning disabilities per se has existed for only a relatively short period of time and is therefore relatively immature with respect to conceptual development and terminology.
- The field of learning disabilities has grown at a very rapid pace.

**FOCUS 2** Identify three classification schemes that have been used with people who have learning disabilities.

- Discrepancy—based on notion that there is an identifiable gap between intelligence and achievement in particular areas such as math, reading, and language. Discrepancy evaluation

has been controversial, and IDEA 2004 now allows schools to use a "response to intervention" process.
- Heterogeneity—classification based on the differing academic domains where those with learning disabilities experience performance challenges.
- Exclusion—notes what those with learning disabilities are *not*. Might be more useful if it focused on what attributes need attention rather than on what learning disabilities are not.

**FOCUS 3** Give two current estimated ranges for the prevalence of learning disabilities.

- From 2.7% to 30% of the school-age population, depending on the source.
- From 5% to 10% is a reasonable current estimate.

**FOCUS 4** Identify seven characteristics attributed to those with learning disabilities, and explain why it is difficult to characterize this group.

- Typically, of above-average or near-average intelligence
- Uneven skill levels in various areas
- Hyperactivity
- Perceptual problems
- Problems with visual and auditory discrimination
- Cognition deficits, such as in memory
- Attention problems
- The individuals included under the umbrella term *learning disabilities* are so varied that they defy simple characterization in terms of a single concept or label.

**FOCUS 5** List four causes thought to be involved in learning disabilities.

- Neurological damage or malfunction
- Maturational delay of the neurological system
- Genetic abnormality
- Environmental factors

**FOCUS 6** Cite four questions that are addressed by screening assessment in learning disabilities.

- Is there a reason to investigate the abilities of the child more fully?
- Is there a reason to suspect that the child in any way has disabilities?
- If the child appears to have disabilities, what are their characteristics, and what sort of intervention is appropriate?
- How should we plan for the future of the individual?

**FOCUS 7** Identify three types of interventions or treatments employed with people diagnosed as having learning disabilities.

- Medical treatment, in some circumstances involving medication to control hyperactivity
- Academic instruction and support in a wide variety of areas that are specifically aimed at building particular skill
- Behavioral interventions aimed at improving social skills or remediating problems in this area (behavioral procedures may also be a part of academic instruction)

*essay question*

**FOCUS 8** How are the services and supports for adolescents and adults with learning disabilities different from those used with children?

- Services and supports for children focus primarily on building the most basic skills.
- Instruction during adolescence may include skill building but also may involve assistance in compensatory skills to circumvent deficit areas.
- Services during adolescence should include instruction and assistance in transition skills that will prepare students for adulthood, employment, and further education, taking into account the students' own goals.
- Information for adults with learning disabilities should include an awareness of how "invisible" their disability is to others and how requests for accommodation might be viewed with skepticism.

## FURTHER READINGS

Crawford, V. (Ed.) (2002). *Embracing the Monster: Overcoming the Challenges of Hidden Disabilities.* Baltimore, MD: Paul H. Brookes.

*Learning disabilities are often characterized as hidden disabilities. This book provides a first-hand account of Veronica's life with learning disabilities and related challenges. It describes challenges with school, personal relationships, and resulting emotions.*

Nadeau, K. G. and Quinn, P. O. (Eds.) (2000). *Understanding Women with AD/HD.* Silver Spring, MD: Advantage Books.

*This volume includes discussions on both learning disabilities and attention-deficit/hyperactivity disorders. The focus is on women with these disabilities desiring to return to school in order to enhance their self-esteem and personal fulfillment, as well as to increase their career opportunities and earning capacity.*

Sternberg, R. J. (Ed.) (2002). *Why Smart People Can Be So Stupid.* New Haven, CT: Yale University Press.

*This book includes information on people with learning disabilities and describes how some of their behaviors appear different to outside observers. Discussion of the reasoning approaches used by individuals with learning disabilities reveals why others may view them as unusual, may treat them differently, and may even discriminate against them.*

Whittlesey, V. (2001). *Diversity Activities for Psychology.* Boston: Allyn and Bacon.

*This book covers a broad range of activities related to topics that are seldom addressed in the context of learning disabilities and other disabilities. Diversity is a main topic, and issues related to diversity culture, ethnicity, gender, and sexual orientation are included. Activities are included for the topics of emotion, motivation, personality, and human sexuality—discussions that are difficult to find in most sources.*

## WEB RESOURCES

**The Learning Disabilities Council**

www.ldcouncil.org

This site provides a variety of helpful materials for parents of children with learning disabilities and adults with learning disabilities. Includes information on parent guide and workbooks, support groups for adults, and various links to other sites that address useful topics.

## National Center for Learning Disabilities

www.ncld.org

This site includes many resources and fact sheets related to learning disabilities. Topics range from living with learning disabilities to advocacy and lobbying links for those interested in public policy.

## Technical Assistance Alliance for Parent Centers

www.taalliance.org

This site provides a newsline service with information on federal programs and many listings of upcoming events such as conferences. Public law and policy debates are reviewed. Resources include consortia, fundraising opportunities, and a wide array of parent-

related information pertaining to family issues and learning disabilities.

## Learning Disabilities Association of America (LDA)

www.ldanatl.org

This association is a not-for-profit organization of individuals with learning disabilities, professionals working with learning disabilities, and family members. The aim of this organization is to advance the education and welfare of children and adults with learning disabilities. The site links to resources, news and alerts about learning disabilities, and announcements of upcoming events. Legislative action bulletins are also included.

## BUILDING YOUR PORTFOLIO

If you are thinking about a career in special education, you should know that many states use national standards developed by the Council for Exceptional Children (CEC) to assess a teacher candidate's knowledge about and skills for working with students with disabilities. See a complete listing of the ten CEC Content Standards on the inside front cover of this text.

### CEC Content Standards Addressed in Chapter 7

1. Foundations
2. Development and Characteristics of Learners
3. Individual Learning Differences
5. Learning Environments and Social Interaction
7. Instructional Planning
8. Assessment

### Assess Your Knowledge of the CEC Standards Addressed in Chapter 7

Some states require that teacher candidates develop a portfolio of products that demonstrate mastery of the CEC content standards. To assist in the development of products for this portfolio, you may wish to complete the following activities.

• Complete a written test of the chapter's content.

*If your instructor requires a written test of your content knowledge for this chapter, keep a copy for your portfo-*

*lio. A practice test on the information covered in this chapter is available through the companion website (www.ablongman.com/hardman8e) and the Student Study Guide.*

• Respond to Application Questions for the Case Study "Alice Revisited."

*Review the Case Study and respond in writing to the application questions. Keep a copy of the case study and your written response for your portfolio.*

• Complete the "Take a Stand" activity for the Debate Forum "Reasonable Accommodation versus Unreasonable Costs?"

*Read the Debate Forum in this chapter and then visit the companion website to complete the activity "Take a Stand." Keep a copy of this activity for your portfolio.*

• Participate in a Community Service Learning Activity.

*Community service is a valuable way to enhance your learning experience. Visit our companion website for suggested community service learning activities that correspond to the information presented in this chapter. Develop a reflective journal of the service learning experience for your portfolio.*

## THEMES OF THE TIMES

Expand your knowledge of the concepts discussed in this chapter by reading current and historical articles from the *New York Times* by visiting the "Themes of the Times" section of the companion website: www.ablongman.com/hardman8e.

# Attention-Deficit/ Hyperactivity Disorder

## TO BEGIN WITH...

### ADHD: It's Not Just for Kids Anymore

Once considered primarily a childhood condition, ADHD . . . is now known to be a lifelong condition for as many as half of those troubled with its hallmark symptoms of inattention, distractibility, impulsivity and emotional instability starting before age 7. (abcNEWS.com, *Health*, October 28, 2002)

### Diagnosis: ADHD Not Airheads

While the great majority of those diagnosed are boys, experts now believe ADHD may be just as prevalent in girls. . . . The main reason girls are undiagnosed is that the disorder often exhibits itself differently in them, says Dr. Kathleen Nadeau. . . . Boys with ADHD tend to be more disruptive and act out physically, while girls tend to be less rebellious and are written off as airheads. (VanScoy, CBSNEWS.com, "Health News," December 13, 2002)

### Medication of Young Children Increasing

Ritalin, which is commonly used to treat attention-deficit/hyperactivity disorder (ADHD), carries a warning against its use in children under six. . . . [However,] . . . recent studies show a doubling to tripling of the number of children under age 4 taking Ritalin. (Livni, 2000)

### Out of Control: Imperfect Solutions

Wendy Snider and Paul Kirchmeyer asked counselors for help with their son Alex. Dr. William Pelham, who works with Alex and other children [with ADHD] helped them take Alex off the medication patch and start him on a pill: Adderall, another ADHD medication. They tested him on different doses. . . . Dr. Pelham also intensified Alex's behavior program. (CBSNEWS.com. "48 Hours Investigates," September 6, 2002)

**FOCUS**

**PREVIEW:** To preview the central concepts of this chapter, read the focus questions located in the margins. Using these questions as a guide, ask yourself what you already know and what you want to learn.

# James

James has been driving his mother crazy since he was an infant. When he was a baby, he was irritable, colicky, and difficult to predict or manage. His mother recalls that he could run before he could walk, and that he was constantly getting into things. In fact, he was such an active and exploring preschooler [that] he poisoned himself and was well known in the emergency room for a series of accidents.

However, trouble really started to occur for James when he entered school. He had difficulty listening to the teacher and staying on task. He had particular problems with acting before thinking. For example, he would raise his hand even before the teacher finished a question and would invariably not know the answer. He would blurt out comments in the classroom, and he seemed incapable of keeping his hands to himself. He always seemed to be on the move, particularly in structured classrooms. In addition to his classroom and academic problems, James also had social problems. His peers did not like him. They commented that he seemed bossy and uncooperative: "He always had to do things his way."

At first, the teacher thought he was immature, and he was retained for a year. This only made things worse. He did not grow out of his problems, and his peers made fun of him for being stupid. James hated school. He became defiant with the teacher and started fights with the other children on the playground.

Things have improved for James since last year. His doctor has him on a stimulant medication, and he spends part of the school day in a resource room classroom. This classroom is particularly good for James because the teacher has a good program that rewards him for being on task and completing work. The teacher also runs a social skills training group, and James is starting to learn how to cooperate with other children. In addition, James' mother and father have taken a parenting class on how to manage children with ADHD and things have started to improve at home.

SOURCE: From *Understanding Child Behavior Disorders*, (3rd ed., p. 117), by D. M. Gelfand, W. R. Jenson, and C. J. Drew, 1997, Fort Worth: Harcourt.

## FOCUS
## 1

Identify three behavioral symptoms commonly associated with ADHD.

**Attention-deficit/hyperactivity disorder (ADHD)** took center stage as a separate disability during the 1990s. The puzzling characteristics associated with ADHD, descriptions of affected individuals, and collections of symptoms first appeared in historical writings as early as 100 years ago (Matthews, 2002). In the past few decades, ADHD had been viewed as a set of symptoms accompanying other conditions, such as learning disabilities and emotional or behavior disorders. In more recent years, however, ADHD has come increasingly to be treated as a separate and distinct disability, although it is still not viewed as such in IDEA (U.S. Department of Education, 2003).

People with ADHD may exhibit a variety of characteristics, including unusually impulsive behavior, fidgeting or **hyperactivity**, an inability to focus attention, or some combination of these behaviors. In many cases, we define ADHD by what we see—hyperactivity, disruptiveness, and perhaps aggressive behavior. In fact, ADHD is actually a variety of physical processes (such as neurological or chemical malfunctions) interacting with social, psychological, or environmental factors (e.g., frustration, social isolation, poor teaching). In grappling with such behaviors, researchers in ADHD have begun to look beyond these characteristics and to conceptualize the disability as an intense disorder of self-regulation, impulse control, attention span, and activity level. Increasingly, the literature on

*Behaviors of children with ADHD often challenge teachers in both instruction and classroom management.*

ADHD reflects attention to impulse control and thinking about the consequences of one's actions, via studies on concepts such as **executive function**, which is the ability to monitor and regulate one's own behavior (Rucklidge & Tannock, 2002; Sonuga-Barke, Dalen, Daley, & Remington, 2002).

For people with ADHD, their symptoms are often intense enough to interfere with performance and life activities in a number of ways. Children with ADHD often have significant difficulties in school and frequently present a substantial challenge to teachers in terms of both instruction and classroom management. Such children may be in and out of their seats, pestering others, or even exhibiting aggressive behaviors such as hitting or pulling hair. They may be unable to focus on the teacher's instructions and may impulsively start assignments before the directions are complete. In many cases an assignment may not be completed, either because the child did not hear the work objective or because he or she darted to another activity that captured his or her roving attention.

Although much of the attention on ADHD has focused on children and adolescents, this condition may also present major difficulties for adults. Some researchers estimate that ADHD is a lifelong disability for perhaps one-third to one-half of those affected during childhood (O'Donnell, McCann, & Pluth, 2001; Schloesser, Kovacs, & Ferrero, 2002; Shaw, 2000). ADHD during adulthood may make it difficult to focus on specific work responsibilities long enough to see them through to completion. The affected worker may flit from task to task, making a little headway on each but completing none. Such individuals may have difficulty focusing during discussions with their supervisors. They may exhibit well-rehearsed social survival skills such as nodding and looking at the boss, but their thoughts may be far away on a jumble of tasks that are not finished.

# ADHD and Other Disabilities

ADHD has long been associated with learning disabilities. As research evidence has accumulated on both learning disabilities and ADHD, it has become increasingly clear that there is a certain amount of overlap, or comorbidity (conditions occurring together) (Forness & Kavale, 2001). Some researchers describe the co-occurrence as common, and estimates vary from 25% to 70% overlap between learning disabilities and ADHD (Mayes, Calhoun, & Crowell, 2000; Naik, Gangadharan, & Alexander, 2002; Kube, Petersen, & Palmer, 2002).

A number of other conditions appear to have a notable level of comorbidity with ADHD (Nadeau & Quinn, 2002). One is **Tourette's syndrome**, a condition characterized by motor or verbal tics that cause the person to make repetitive movements, emit strange involuntary sounds, and/or say inappropriate words or phrases (sometimes intense swearing). Tourette's does not appear with great frequency among those with ADHD, although about half of the individuals with Tourette's exhibit some ADHD symptoms. There is some evidence that causal culprits in Tourette's may include some of the chemical malfunctions thought to be related to ADHD, although further research is needed in this area (Bradshaw, 2001; Brand et al., 2002).

As indicated in the Case Study, another area of disability that overlaps with ADHD is that of behavior, conduct, and emotional disorders. This covers a very large area, so some level of comorbidity is not surprising. Some of the behaviors exhibited by individuals with ADHD are quite disruptive. In some cases, the level of aggression can easily be interpreted as a conduct or behavior disorder. The literature suggests that such behavior disorders do occur in as many as half of those with ADHD (Burns & Walsh, 2002; Gresham, Lane, & Lambros, 2001; Kube et al., 2002). There are also interesting overlaps between ADHD and certain conditions that might be considered emotional disorders, such as anxiety, depression, obsessive-compulsive disorder, and some levels of neurotic behavior (Barbosa, Tannock, & Manassis, 2002; Chi & Hinshaw, 2002; Kutcher, 2002).

**FOCUS 2**

Identify two ways the behavior of children with ADHD detrimentally affects instructional settings.

**Attention-deficit/ hyperactivity disorder (ADHD)**

A disorder characterized by difficulties in maintaining attention because of a limited ability to concentrate. Children with ADHD exhibit impulsive actions and hyperactive behavior.

**Hyperactivity**

Perhaps the most frequently mentioned behavioral characteristic in the literature on ADHD. In some cases the term *hyperactivity* refers to too much activity, in other cases to activity inappropriate for a given situation or context.

**Executive function**

The ability to monitor and regulate one's own behavior. Executive function reflects an individual's ability to exercise impulse control and to think about and anticipate the consequences of actions.

**Tourette's syndrome**

A condition characterized by motor or verbal tics that cause the person to make repetitive movements, emit strange involuntary sounds, or say words or phrases that are inappropriate for the context.

## COEXISTING CONDITIONS

Jim was a 10-year-old boy enrolled in a mental health day program that treated severely behaviorally disordered children. In this program he was treated for a major fire-setting problem. Jim's developmental history was characterized by deprivation, inadequate parenting, chaotic home life, and a series of foster home placements. He was diagnosed as having both a conduct disorder and attention-deficit disorder. His list of referral problems included stealing, hyperactivity, tantrumming, learning disabilities, aggression, noncompliance, zoophilia, and fire setting. The fire setting had been a problem since Jim was 3, when he burned down the family home. Since his foster placements, Jim had averaged approximately one fire setting every two weeks.

It was assumed that Jim set fires partly because he enjoyed seeing the fires and partly as a reaction to stress. The stress was related to a series of skill deficits in the social and academic areas. In addition, it was assumed that Jim did not fully realize the dangerous consequences of his behavior. His therapy involved a multiple treatment approach. . . .

After treatment, Jim's fire setting dropped from an average of one every two weeks to virtually zero fires at a one-year follow-up. Jim improved his basic social skills and appeared better prepared to handle stressful situations, although some of his inappropriate behaviors, such as stealing and family problems, have continued.

### APPLICATION

1. List the different professionals who may have contact with Jim and his parents as a result of the different types of problems he presents.

2. How important do you believe communication between the various professionals that you listed is? What difficulties are likely to arise if they do not communicate in a coordinated manner?

3. In order to coordinate communication and treatment, who is the best candidate to be the focal point for organizing Jim's case? Should it be his parents or should it be one of the professionals involved in his treatment?

SOURCE: From *Understanding Child Behavior Disorders* (3rd ed., p. 127), by D. M. Gelfand, W. R. Jenson, & C. J. Drew, 1997, Fort Worth: Harcourt Brace & Company.

---

**FOCUS 3**

Identify four other areas of disability that are often found to be comorbid with *ADHD*.

As we examine ADHD, it is important to realize it has many faces. ADHD is not a simple condition that can be defined and categorized easily. The distinctions between ADHD and other conditions are often not clear, in part because certain definitions have historically overlapped and in part because groups of people who have been diagnosed with one condition or another represent very heterogeneous populations (Tervo, Azuma, Fogas, & Fiechtner, 2002). Evidence suggests that a large percentage of those with ADHD demonstrate comorbidity with some other identifiable condition (Gelfand & Drew, 2003; Kube et al., 2002).

# Definitions

**FOCUS 4**

Identify the three major types of ADHD according to the *DSM-IV*.

ADHD characteristics have often been described in the context of other prominent disabilities where there is substantial comorbidity, most frequently learning disabilities and emotional or behavior disorders. The definition of ADHD that is used most often is that provided by the American Psychiatric Association (APA) in the fourth edition of its *Diagnostic and Statistical Manual of Mental Disorders* (DSM-IV) (APA, 2000). The APA definition is presented in Table 8.1.

The APA includes three subcategories of ADHD in its description of diagnostic criteria: (1) ADHD, combined type; (2) ADHD, predominantly inattentive type; and (3) ADHD, predominantly hyperactive–impulsive type (APA, 2000). The diagnostic criteria for these categories, as outlined in DSM-IV, are summarized in Table 8.2. Although many people exhibit symptoms that combine inattention, impulsivity, and hyperactivity, others have a predominant feature that corresponds to one of the other two subtypes.

## TABLE 8.1

### APA Definition of ADHD

| CRITERION | DESCRIPTION |
|---|---|
| Criterion A | The essential feature of attention-deficit/hyperactivity disorder is a persistent pattern of inattention and/or hyperactivity-impulsivity that is more frequent and severe than is typically observed in individuals at a comparable level of development. |
| Criterion B | Some hyperactive-impulsive or inattentive symptoms that cause impairment must have been present before age 7 years, although many individuals are diagnosed after the symptoms have been present for a number of years. |
| Criterion C | Some impairment from the symptoms must be present in at least two settings (e.g., at home and at school work). |
| Criterion D | There must be clear evidence of interference with developmentally appropriate social, academic, or occupational functioning. |
| Criterion E | The disturbance does not occur exclusively during the course of a pervasive developmental disorder, schizophrenia, or other psychotic disorder and is not better accounted for by another mental disorder (e.g., mood disorder, anxiety disorder, dissociative disorder, or personality disorder). |

SOURCE: From *Diagnostic and Statistical Manual of Mental Disorders* (4th ed. Text Revision, p. 85), by the American Psychiatric Association, 2000, Washington, DC: Author.

The American Academy of Pediatrics has issued a set of clinical practice guidelines that build on DSM-IV criteria. These guidelines are intended to provide primary-care clinicians, with further suggestions for making diagnostic decisions for these children. They include the points summarized in Table 8.3.

# Prevalence

Prevalence estimates for ADHD most often suggest that 3% to 7% of all school-aged children may have the disorder, although some researchers believe this is too low (American Psychiatric Association [APA], 2000; Paule et al., 2000). The literature generally indicates that more males are identified with ADHD than females; the average male/female ratio is about 3.5:1 (Gelfand & Drew, 2003). There is wide variation in the gender data, however, with male/female ratios ranging from 2:1 to 10:1, depending on the population sampled (Anastopoulos, Klinger, & Temple, 2001; Solanto, 2001). Young children show higher male/female ratios than older groups. It should be noted that identifying ADHD in children under 4 or 5 years of age is very difficult (APA, 2000). Males and females with ADHD seem to exhibit different symptoms and may have different intervention needs, which could account for differences in identification and incidence. Young males may exhibit more disruptive or aggressive behaviors, which may more readily bring them to the attention of their teachers or parents (Crystal, Ostrander, Chen, & August, 2001; Radford & Ervin, 2002; Theriault & Holmberg, 2001). Young females may exhibit inattentiveness or daydreaming more often. Some questions have been raised about the possibility of gender bias in identification and diagnosis. This assertion suggests that boys may be overidentified, and girls underidentified, partly because of the differing predominant behaviors (Greenberg, Speltz, DeKlyen, & Jones, 2001; McGoey, Eckert, & DuPaul, 2002). The literature remains mixed on this issue, suggesting that although some gender bias may be present, the substantial gender differences probably reflect some actual difference in the prevalence of ADHD in males and females (Jackson, 2002). More recent research shows mixed results on

**FOCUS 5**

Identify two prevalence estimates for ADHD that characterize the difference in occurrence by gender.

## TABLE 8.2

### Diagnostic Criteria for Attention-Deficit/Hyperactivity Disorder

A. Either (1) or (2):

1. Six (or more) of the following symptoms of *inattention* have persisted for at least 6 months to a degree that is maladaptive and inconsistent with developmental level:

   *Inattention*

   a. Often fails to give close attention to details or makes careless mistakes in schoolwork, work, or other activities.

   b. Often has difficulty sustaining attention in tasks or play activities.

   c. Often does not seem to listen when spoken to directly.

   d Often does not follow through on instructions and fails to finish schoolwork, chores, or duties in the workplace (not due to oppositional behavior or failure to understand instructions).

   e. Often has difficulty organizing tasks and activities.

   f. Often avoids, dislikes, or is reluctant to engage in tasks that require sustained mental effort (such as schoolwork or homework).

   g. Often loses things necessary for tasks or activities (e.g., toys, school assignments, pencils, books, or tools).

   h. Is often easily distracted by extraneous stimuli.

   i. Is often forgetful in daily activities.

2. Six (or more) of the following symptoms of *hyperactivity—impulsivity* have persisted for at least 6 months to a degree that is maladaptive and inconsistent with developmental level:

   *Hyperactivity*

   a. Often fidgets with hands or feet or squirms in seat.

   b. Often leaves seat in classroom or in other situations in which remaining seated is expected.

   c. Often runs about or climbs excessively in situations in which it is inappropriate (in adolescents or adults, may be limited to subjective feelings or restlessness).

   d. Often has difficulty playing or engaging in leisure activities quietly.

   e. Is often "on the go" or often acts as if "driven by a motor."

   f. Often talks excessively.

   *Impulsivity*

   g. Often blurts out answers before questions have been completed.

   h. Often has difficulty awaiting turn.

   i. Often interrupts or intrudes on others (e.g., butts into conversations or games).

B. Some hyperactive-impulsive or inattentive symptoms that caused impairment were presented before age 7 years.

C. Some impairment from the symptoms is present in two or more settings (e.g., at school [or work] and at home).

D. There must be clear evidence of clinically significant impairment in social, academic, or occupational functioning.

E. The symptoms do not occur exclusively during the course of a pervasive developmental disorder, schizophrenia, or other psychotic disorder and are not better accounted for by another mental disorder (e.g., mood disorder, anxiety disorder, dissociative disorder, or a personality disorder).

*Code* based on type:

*Attention-Deficit/Hyperactivity Disorder, Combined Type:* if both Criteria A1 and A2 are met for the past 6 months.

*Attention-Deficit/Hyperactivity Disorder, Predominantly Inattentive Type:* if Criterion A1 is met but Criterion A2 is not met for the past 6 months.

*Attention-Deficit/Hyperactivity Disorder, Predominantly Hyperactive—Impulsive Type:* if Criterion A2 is met but Criterion A1 is not met for the past 6 months.

*Coding note:* For individuals (especially adolescents and adults) who currently have symptoms that no longer meet full criteria, "In Partial Remission" should be specified.

SOURCE: Reprinted with permission from the *Diagnostic and Statistical Manual of Mental Disorders,* (4th ed. Text Revision p. 92). Copyright 2000 American Psychiatric Association.

gender prevalence, with some evidence of an increase among young females (Robison, Skaer, Sclar, & Galin, 2002).

There is some evidence that different types of ADHD have differing prevalence levels (inattentive, hyperactive-impulsive, and combined types), although these level vary considerably between studies (Nolan, Gadow, & Sprafkin, 2001). There also appears to be some variation between subgroups by age, gender, and comorbidity with other conditions, although considerably more evidence needs to be accumulated on these issues (Biederman, Mick, & Faraone, 2000; Rowland, Lesesne, & Abramowitz, 2002). Prevalence appears somewhat higher in younger children and in males, although these youngsters may stand out because the disruptive or high-activity symptoms evident in such groups attract attention.

TABLE 8.3

**American Academy of Pediatrics Clinical Practice Guidelines**

1. In a child 6 to 12 years old who presents with inattention, hyperactivity, impulsivity, academic underachievement, or behavior problems, primary care clinicians should initiate an evaluation for ADHD.

2. The diagnoses of ADHD requires that a child meet criteria in *Diagnostic and Statistical Manual of Mental Disorders*, Fourth Edition.

3. The assessment of ADHD requires evidence directly obtained from parents or caregivers regarding the core symptoms of ADHD in various settings, the age of onset, duration of symptoms, and degree of functional impairment.

4. The assessment of ADHD requires evidence directly obtained from the classroom teacher (or other school professional) regarding the core symptom of ADHD, duration of symptoms, degree of functional impairment, and associated conditions.

5. Evaluation of the child with ADHD should include assessment for associated (coexisting) conditions.

6. Other diagnostic tests are not routinely indicated to establish the diagnosis of ADHD but may be used for the assessment of other, coexisting conditions (e.g., learning disabilities and mental retardation).

This clinical practice guideline is not intended as a sole source of guidance in the evaluation of children with ADHD. Rather, it is designed to assist primary care clinicians by providing a framework for diagnostic decision making. It is not intended to replace clinical judgment or to establish a protocol for all children with this condition and may not provide the only appropriate approach to this problem.

SOURCE: From "Diagnosis and Evaluation of the Child with Attention-Deficit/Hyperactivity Disorder (AC0002)," by the American Academy of Pediatrics, 2000, *Pediatrics, 105,* 1158–1170.

There has been substantial growth in services to ADHD students during the last decade, particularly since the U.S. Department of Education stipulated that such students are eligible for services under the IDEA category of Other Health Impairments. Such eligibility is certainly not the only factor affecting the growing number of people in this category, but it is thought to have a substantial impact. (U.S. Department of Education, 2003).

# Assessment and Diagnosis

**FOCUS 6**

Identify the two broad categories of assessment information useful in diagnosing ADHD.

The process of assessing and diagnosing ADHD is a joint venture between multiple disciplines, often including professionals from medicine, psychology, and education (Baum & Olenchak, 2002; Sarampote, Efron, Robb, Pearl, & Stein, 2002). Assessment and diagnostic information for ADHD falls into two broad categories: data that are medical in nature, and data that provide information about educational, behavioral, and contextual circumstances.

Medical data are collected through examinations by pediatricians or other health care professionals. In many cases these health care professionals are family doctors or other referred physicians who are sought out by the parents outside the school system. Clinical interviews and other psychological assessments are undertaken by psychologists who may be on staff in the schools or in private practice. This process is likely to entail compilation of both psychological and environmental data, including information pertaining to family and school matters. Additionally, direct information from parents and teachers is sought and quantified through the completion of rating scales and other such instruments (Krane & Tannock, 2001; Phillips, Greenson, Collett, & Gimpel, 2002; Venn, 2000).

One instrument used to assess ADHD is the Child Behavior Checklist (CBCL) developed by Achenbach (1991, 1992). The CBCL is considered a very useful assessment procedure in child psychopathology (Forbes, 2001; Merrell, 2002). It provides parent data, teacher ratings, and classroom observation protocols to assess academic competence and social problems beginning at age 4 and to evaluate adolescents through age 18. The Snapshot on Doug shows a portion of the CBCL reporting protocol used by parents. The information outlines several challenges facing Doug, as well as the need to use multiple assessment procedures. Other evaluation protocols

## INSURANCE AS A FACTOR IN ASSESSMENT

On the surface, insurance coverage would not seem to play a significant role in assessment and diagnosis of ADHD. However, in many cases it may play more of a role than we might expect. The National Institutes of Health Consensus reported that "The lack of insurance coverage for psychiatric or psychological evaluations, behavior modification programs, school consultation, parent management training, and other specialized programs presents a major barrier to accurate classification, diagnosis, and management of ADHD. Substantial cost barriers exist in that diagnosis results in out-of-pocket costs to families for services not covered by managed care or other health insurance" (1998, p. 10).

Consider the situation of a parent of a child who has just completed a series of tests which have led to a long conversation with the family pediatrician. She has outlined what she believes are the next steps of information gathering, suggested that ADHD may be involved, and discussed how some treatment recommendations may not be covered by insurance. The costs may be significant: several hundred dollars per month for a while and then unknown after that. This is a predicament that is not unknown to parents of ADHD children.

SOURCE: From *Diagnosis and Treatment of Attention-Deficit/Hyperactivity Disorder*, (pp. 1–37), by National Institutes of Health, 1998, NIH Consensus Statement Online, 16(2), November 16–18.

include the Behavior Assessment System for Children—Teacher Rating Scales (BASC–TRS) and the School Situations Questionnaire (SSQ) (Matazow & Kamphaus, 2001). The SSQ uses a different protocol than many rating scales use in that it presents situations where the child being evaluated may encounter problems.

The referral process for evaluating a child typically begins with the educational and psychological data-gathering process outlined in the preceding paragraphs, and information may come from educational professionals or the parents. The initial referral is very important, because it sets in motion a course of action that it is hoped will significantly affect the child's life for the better, in the form of effective treatment (Baum & Olenchak, 2002). As with most referrals, a child with ADHD will enter the process because of some aspect of performance or behavior that sets him or her apart and causes concern for the person or professional who initiates the referral process (such as a classroom teacher or perhaps a parent). Parental concerns may focus on the aggressive and disruptive behavior exhibited by many children with ADHD. Evidence suggests that raising children with such disabilities is likely to contribute to significant parental life stress, which results in a triggering of the referral process (Hankin, Wright, & Gephart, 2001; Johnson & Reader, 2002).

*An important part of the diagnostic evaluation of ADHD is information collected by health care professionals.*

# SNAPSHOT

## Doug

Doug is an 11-year-old, fifth grade male who was referred because of parental and teacher concerns about his school performance. He is suspected of having significant attention problems.

Doug also has significant trouble in peer and other relationships. He often fights and argues with peers, resulting in his often playing by himself.

Doug has a history of significant medical difficulties. He is the product of an at-risk pregnancy. Although he achieved most developmental milestones within normal timeframes, he has a history of motor delays. In second grade he was diagnosed with muscular dystrophy. He also suffers from inflammatory bowel disease, resulting in ongoing treatment for ulcers. He does not tolerate many foods well and consequently his appetite is poor.

In first grade Doug was also diagnosed as learning-disabled, with problems in reading. He is in a resource special education program. He is described by his teacher as "socially inept." He is often disrespectful of teachers and peers. His grades deteriorated significantly toward the end of the last academic year. His teachers consider him to be a capable underachiever with behavior problems such as inattention, excessive talking, fighting, arguing, and poor work completion.

[Doug was evaluated on the CBCL Scales listed below, which indicated a broad range of difficulties for this youngster.]. . .

- Internalizing
- Withdrawn
- Somatic complaints
- Anxious/depressed
- Externalizing
- Social problems
- Thought problems
- Attention problems
- Delinquent behavior
- Aggressive behavior

His mother's report [was] more severe than the majority of the three teacher ratings. His mother's responses to the Parenting Stress Index were also highly significant, revealing stress beyond the 99th percentile on the majority of the PSI scales.

All raters and observations were needed in order to clarify the CBCL results. Aggressive behavior, attention problems, somatic complaints, and depression symptoms were identified by the majority of indices. Enough information was gleaned to make the diagnosis of attention-deficit/hyperactivity disorder and oppositional defiant disorder.

Recommendations for intervention also included treatment for significant sadness, although the criteria for a depressive disorder were not met at the time of the evaluation.

Indications of thought problems were not corroborated by other findings. The clinicians thought that the thought problems scale was elevated for some raters due to interpretation of the items by raters as indicators of hyperactivity or inattention. CBCL Social Problems scores were corroborated by low scores on social skills measures. The social skills measures were used to develop behavioral objectives for Doug's intervention.

This CBCL profile highlights the need, more pressing in a case like this, to complement the CBCL with other measures. In this case, teacher ratings, observations, self-reports, measures of parent stress, history taking, and observations were all needed to clarify diagnostic impressions and identify treatment objectives.

SOURCE: From *Clinical Assessment of Child and Adolescent Personality and Behavior* (p. 131), by R. W. Kamphaus & P. J. Frick, 1996, Needham Heights, MA: Allyn and Bacon. Reprinted by permission.

---

An initial referral is a precursor to a complete evaluation and diagnostic analysis, including a comprehensive clinical interview conducted by a psychologist. At the clinical interview stage, more information is collected on the nature of the child's behavior and the environment in which it occurs (both school and family settings). This stage may also involve the use of behavior checklists, functional assessment, or other protocols that quantify observations in a structured fashion (Radford & Ervin, 2002). One such protocol is the Diagnostic Interview Schedule for Children (DISC-IV) (Shaffer, Fisher, Lucas, Dulcan, & Schwab-Stone, 2000). The DISC is a structured interview designed for use by trained psychologists or lay interviewers.

The final source of diagnostic evaluation is the medical examination. This assessment takes into account all information that has been gathered; its goal is to determine whether other physical conditions may contribute to the behavior observed. The medical examination may also produce the first step in intervention if medication is prescribed.

Much of the referral and diagnostic assessment outlined here involves some professional judgment that might be considered subjective. This is no different from the evaluation process for other disabilities—trained professional judgment is extremely critical. However, for ADHD, some have questioned whether bias affects the accuracy of the assessment process (Kube et al., 2002; Nadder, Silberg, Rutter, Maes, & Eaves, 2001). Such questions also raise concern about how well professionals are prepared to conduct assessments. For example, a teacher may play a very important part in the identification of ADHD. And there is some evidence

## Jordan

Jordan is a 7-year, 3 month-old boy who was referred for a comprehensive psychological evaluation by his parents upon the recommendation of his teachers. His teachers had reported to Jordan's parents that he was having difficulty paying attention and [was] daydreaming, interrupting others, and making careless mistakes in his work. His parents requested a comprehensive evaluation to determine the severity and possible cause for these difficulties and to make recommendations for possible interventions to aid in his school adjustments.

Jordan's background, developmental [history], and medical history were unremarkable. During the testing Jordan had great difficulty concentrating and was easily distracted. He was also very fidgety and restless. Intellectually, Jordan had much better verbal comprehension ability, especially in the area of verbal reasoning, than nonverbal perceptual-organizational abilities. Consistent with his verbal abilities, Jordan scored in the above-average range on measures of reading and math achievement.

Jordan's emotional and behavioral functioning was assessed through the use of structured interviews conducted with Jordan's parents and teachers and through rating scales completed by his parents, teacher, and Jordan himself. The structured interviews were the parent version of the DISC-2.3 and the experimental teacher version used in the DSM-IV field trials (Frick, Silverthorn, & Evans, 1994). The child version was not given to Jordan because he was below the age of 9 and the DISC has not proven to be reliable in this young age group. The following is an excerpt from the report on Jordan's evaluation that illustrates how information from the DISC-2.3 was integrated with other assessment information:

"The only problematic [areas] that emerged from this assessment of Jordan's emotional and behavioral functioning were significant problems of inattention, disorganization, impulsivity, and overactivity that seem to be causing Jordan significant problems in the classroom. Jordan's teachers describe him as being very restless and fidgety, being easily distractible, having very disorganized and messy work habits, having a hard time completing things, and making a lot of careless mistakes. Results from teacher rating scales suggested that these behaviors are more severe than would be typical for children Jordan's age. These behaviors are consistent with a diagnosis of Attention-Deficit Hyperactivity Disorder (ADHD). Also consistent with this diagnosis, his parents reported that many of these behaviors, especially the restless and fidgety behaviors, have been present from very early in life, at least since age 4. These behaviors associated with ADHD seem to be causing significant problems for Jordan in school, affecting the amount and accuracy of schoolwork. A sociometric exercise also suggests that these behaviors may be starting to affect his peer relationships."

SOURCE: *Clinical Assessment of Child and Adolescent Personality and Behavior* (pp. 239–240); by R. W. Kamphaus & P. J. Frick, 1996, Needham Heights, MA: Allyn and Bacon. Reprinted by permission.

that a teacher's decision to refer a student for assessment or identification for ADHD may be influenced considerably by his or her general attitude, style, and beliefs about teaching practices (Hepperlen, Clay, Henly, & Barke, 2002). As illustrated earlier, observations and ratings of children through standardized ADHD protocols are an important part of the evaluation process. Despite the standardized nature of these tools, their accuracy and usefulness depend in large part on the knowledge and experience of those who complete them. Some research suggests that considerable error may occur because the raters' own characteristics influence how they rate a child's behavior problems (Crystal et al., 2001; Volpe & DuPaul, 2001). The Snapshot on Jordan is another example of a comprehensive evaluation process completed on a young boy with ADHD.

If there are significant inaccuracies in the way teachers evaluate children with ADHD, then programs that prepare these professionals need to respond. Some researchers have raised concerns about the way teachers are prepared to work with children who have ADHD. Some evidence suggests that recent graduates from teacher preparation programs are not better prepared than teachers who graduated earlier. Such findings imply that the teacher education curriculum needs to be enhanced with more information and strategies related to ADHD (Brook, Watemberg, & Geva, 2000; Klein, 2002).

**FOCUS 7**

Identify three categories of characteristics that present challenges for individuals with ADHD.

# Characteristics

The opening Snapshot presented James, a child with characteristics associated with ADHD that appeared at a very early age. James's story also illustrates how one type of behavior problem can lead or contribute to another as a child grows older. Discussion of the characteristics of ADHD can clearly become mired in "chicken or egg" issues—which came first, impulsivity and problems with self-regulation, or inattention, hyperactivity, and aggression? This is an important debate to the extent that it helps to identify effective interventions.

James's behavior before he received medication included hyperactivity with disruptive and aggressive tendencies. James seemed not to think ahead about the outcomes or consequences of his actions. He appeared to be impulsive, and an observer could easily infer that he had difficulty regulating his own behavior.

## Self-Regulation, Impulsivity, and Hyperactivity

Difficulty in self-regulation and behavioral inhibition are receiving more attention as theoretical explanations and research models for ADHD (Neef, Bicard, & Endo, 2001; Stevens, Quittner, Zuckerman, & Moore, 2002; Sonuga-Barke, et al., 2002). Some researchers have suggested that this is a very important key to understanding ADHD (e.g., Rucklidge & Tannock, 2002). Discussions include terms such as *behavioral inhibition* and *executive function*, as well as *impulse control*, *self-regulation*, and *self-management*. Problems encountered by the individual under all of these rubrics are quite similar and seem to involve substantial difficulty in thinking through one's actions to see what the effects of certain behaviors might be (Rucklidge & Tannock, 2002; Sonuga-Barke et al., 2002). People with ADHD are not able to consider the following question: "If I behave in a certain manner, what is the probable outcome, and how will it affect those around me?" This was true with James when he raised his hand before the question was asked and without having the answer in mind.

Hyperactivity is a primary characteristic of ADHD, as suggested in the diagnostic criteria summarized in Table 8.2 on page 212. In accordance with these criteria, the hyperactive behavior must persist for at least six months and must be intense enough to create maladaptive problems for the individual. Many parents, teachers, and others describe such youngsters as those who fidget and squirm constantly; are continually running, jumping, and climbing around; and are generally on the move all the time (Niederhofer, Hackenberg, Lanzendorfer, Staffen, & Mair, 2002; Rowland et al., 2002). As most parents will confirm, all children can be characterized in these terms from time to time, but the hyperactive child with ADHD far exceeds the norm. The behaviors are seemingly continuous and occur in inappropriate settings and times.

*Individuals with ADHD have difficulty paying attention. Here is a young woman lost in a daydream during a teacher's lecture.*

Hyperactivity may be the most frequently mentioned characteristic in the literature addressing various facets of ADHD. Being overly active seems to affect about half of the children diagnosed with ADHD. Although the high-activity characteristic appears to diminish as some children get older, for others this is not true. In some cases, the hyperactive behavior begins to surface in adolescence and may be evident through the adult years (Faraone, 2000; Molina, Smith, & Pelham, 2001).

## Social Relationships

Youngsters with ADHD often have difficulties in their social relationships with peers (Kelly, 2001; Mrug, Hoza, & Gerdes, 2001; Yeschin, 2000). Some children encounter difficulty getting along because they exhibit aggressive behavior toward their classmates, and of course this does not promote positive social interactions (McGoey et al., 2002; Radford & Ervin, 2002). Other children with ADHD exhibit seriously antisocial or pathological social behavior, such as cruelty to animals, that may suggest other mental health problems (Hirshfeld-Becker et al., 2002). These behaviors can contribute to low social status among peers, which may persist for years. This pattern may evolve in a variety of ways over time, such as leading to increased risk for criminal activity (Rasmussen, Almvik, & Levander, 2001; Richardson, 2000). Such behavioral patterns present enormous challenges for schools as these children proceed through the system.

The level of severity of ADHD is significant in both males' and females' social relationships, and the outcomes are varied and often serious (Greene et al., 2001). Some youngsters with ADHD grow increasingly frantic as they try to gain friends, which can easily aggravate their already poor self-regulating behavior. They may thereby seem even more of a nuisance to the peers whom they wish to befriend. Accumulated frustration due to low social status and to having few friends may prompt even stranger behaviors aimed at gaining attention from classmates. Some research also suggests that substance abuse may be more likely among those with ADHD (Rosston & Buckingham, 2001; Sullivan & Rudnik-Levin, 2001). Some investigators have claimed that this may be due to the use of psychostimulants as treatment, but there is not enough research evidence to support such an assertion. Some researchers have found that other, comorbid disabilities may be more predictive than ADHD of substance abuse; these conditions include social impairment, conduct disorders, and aggressive behavior (e.g., Klorman, 2000; Kutcher, 2002). Thus research results have so far failed to reveal whether substance abuse is more closely related to ADHD or to other, coexisting conditions, but the combination appears to increase risk substantially.

Individuals with ADHD often feel isolated from others. Social relationships can be a difficult challenge.

## Academic Characteristics

Students with ADHD experience significant challenges in an academic setting. Research suggests that a very large proportion of these children and adolescents experience substantial learning problems in school (Cains, 2000; Dendy, 2000). Such problems increase as the students progress through the educational system and schoolwork demands more and more of the skills with which they have the greatest difficulty: self-management and thinking ahead (De-La-Paz, 2001; Stevens et al., 2002). Although these children may have some specific memory difficulties, their academic performance is more likely to suffer from their being inattentive, impulsive, and less "planful" in addressing their studies (De-La-Paz, 2001; Klingberg, Forssberg, & Westerberg, 2002; Stevens et al., 2002). Failure and poor academic performance also affect other areas, such as self-esteem, creating a repeating cycle of circumstances and symptoms that some researchers believe accumulate dynamically, increasing the likelihood of further problems (Demaray & Elliot, 2001; Knapp & Jongsma, 2002).

Children and adolescents with ADHD are characterized by a lack of academic success compared to their peers without disabilities, and often they do not graduate from high school (Zimmermann, 1999). Poor academic achievement by students with ADHD is usually associated with their disruptive and nonproductive social behaviors, their poor capacity to self-manage, and a reduced social support network that might otherwise help in academic performance (Demaray & Elliot, 2001; Pisecco, Wristers, Swank, Silva, & Baker, 2001). In academic environments that adapt instruction to individual student needs and abilities, students with ADHD can learn, achieve academically, and improve their self-management skills (Davies & Witte, 2000; Nolan & Carr, 2000).

# Causation and Interventions

## Causation

There is considerable difference of opinion regarding the causes of ADHD, and both biological and environmental influences have been identified (e.g., Ravenel, 2002). Speculation has included genetic inheritance, neurological injury during birth complications, and negative impacts of a variety of environmental factors. As we begin to understand ADHD better, we will probably find that multiple causes are associated with this condition.

Neurological causes of ADHD have been suspected for many years, although viewpoints on the nature of such neurological dysfunction have varied considerably. Early investigation on behaviors exhibited by World War I soldiers who had received head injuries focused on a trauma-based or physical cause for brain malfunction. Current theories still include injury-induced brain malfunction, although more current thinking also views chemical imbalances in serotonin and dopamine as possible causes (Oades, 2002; Stefanatos & Wasserstein, 2001).

Documentation of neurological causes for ADHD has progressed enormously through new and developing technology, particularly neuroimaging procedures. Where previously the medical profession speculated about neurological dysfunction on the basis of observed behavior, we are now able to examine the brain directly (see the nearby Assistive Technology). For example, neuroimaging shows that people with ADHD seem to exhibit brain abnormalities in three areas: the **frontal lobes**, selected areas of the **basal ganglia**, and the **cerebellum** (Casey, 2001; Fredericksen et al., 2002; Kim, Lee, Shin, Cho, & Lee, 2002). Figure 8.1 indicates the general areas in the brain that have been identified as having abnormalities associated with ADHD.

In some cases the actual brain structures appear different for individuals with ADHD, whereas in other cases the chemical functioning in the brain may be different from those who do not have the condition (Bradley & Golden, 2001; Rapport, 2001; Stefanatos & Wasserstein, 2001). Such differences in structure and chemical function may have a variety of causes, including physical injury to the brain and developmental factors. It is widely known that environmental influences

FOCUS
8

Identify three possible causes of ADHD.

**Frontal lobes**

The front parts of the brain, which are nearest to the forehead.

**Basal ganglia**

Sections of the brain that are near the stem, close to where the spinal cord meets the bottom of the brain matter.

**Cerebellum**

The part of the brain that coordinates muscle movement. It is located right below the large main sections of the brain.

**FIGURE 8.1**

**Brain Malfunctions in Some Areas of the Brain**
Frontal lobes, basal ganglia, and cerebellum seem to be associated with ADHD.

Caudate nucleus
Putamen
Globus pallidus — Basal ganglia
Lateral medial
Frontal lobes
Cerebellum

during prenatal or neonatal periods can have serious detrimental effects. For example, lead exposure, pregnant mothers' alcohol abuse, and exposure to tobacco smoke place developing embryos and infants at high risk for serious learning and developmental delays. Likewise, low birthweight and delivery complications are high-risk circumstances that may be related to ADHD (Mick, Biederman, Prince, Fischer, & Faraone, 2002; Samuelsson, Finnstroem, Leijon, & Mard, 2000). Emotional and general health status for both the pregnant mother and developing fetus appear to be important predictive factors in ADHD causation (Eshleman, 1999). Serious problems during this critical prenatal period of development can result in a wide variety of undesirable outcomes for the baby that may result in developmental delays or deficiencies in both intellectual and behavioral functioning (Drew & Hardman, 2004; Trawick-Smith, 2000).

Heredity has long been associated with ADHD, which suggests that there may be a genetic transmission of circumstances that result in the condition. Youngsters appear to be at higher risk of being diagnosed with ADHD if parents or siblings have the condition (Sprich, Biederman, Crawford, Mundy, & Faraone, 2000; Wigg et al., 2002). Research on twins also implies a hereditary link in that identical twins (same egg) have a higher coincidence of the condition than fraternal twins (different eggs) (Waldman, Rhee, Levy, & Hay, 2001). Evidence supports the concept that multiple genes may be involved and that they may present a tendency or predisposition in an affected individual that may be triggered by various environmental circumstances (Martin, Scourfield, & McGuffin, 2002; Rhee, Waldman, Hay, & Levy, 2001). Research on the genetic bases of ADHD is ongoing, and results continue to emerge.

### Interventions

ADHD requires multiple interventions that fall into two broad categories: behavioral and medical. As is true in many disability areas, effective treatment involves a multidisciplinary team approach and includes combinations of techniques as determined by individual need (Swanson et al., 2002).

**FOCUS 9**

Identify two approaches to intervention that appear to show positive results with individuals who have ADHD.

## A CAUSE OF HYPERACTIVITY? STUDY SUGGESTS HYPERACTIVE BRAINS GET LESS BLOOD

A new magnetic resonance imaging technique has been used by researchers to investigate certain brain malfunctions in young boys with ADHD. In this case, the team, led by Dr. Martin Teicher, discovered additional evidence for a biological cause of the disability. The researchers found that the MRI indicated a reduced blood flow to a part of the brain known as the putamen. This part of the brain is associated with motor movement and attention, areas often identified as challenging for youngsters with ADHD. The MRI technology also indicated an increase in the blood flow for these young boys when they were given Ritalin. Other young boys with some, but not all, ADHD characteristics showed a decreased blood flow when given Ritalin, as evidenced on the magnetic resonance imaging.

SOURCE: From "A Cause of hyperactivity? Study Suggests Hyper Brains Get Less Blood," ABC News, March 28, 2000. Available: http://abcnews.go.com/sections/living/DailyNews/hyperativebrains000328.html

**THE ELEMENTARY SCHOOL YEARS.**   On a practical level, psychostimulants (e.g., methylphenidate, the generic name for Ritalin) appear to result in behavioral improvement for about 80% of children with ADHD (Pelham et al., 2002; Solanto, Arnsten, & Castellanos, 2001; Wilens, & Spencer, 2000). However, administration of such medication has long presented some perplexing ironies to physicians. Whereas a medication may work well for a child with ADHD, the same medication would make most of us hyperactive. Self-regulation theories tend to approach the problem primarily as a functional deficit in self-regulation or impulse control. Administration of methylphenidate arouses the frontal lobes of the brain, which exert a regulatory influence. This regulatory function affects regions of the nervous system that monitor motor activity and distractibility (Jerome & Segal, 2001).

Controlling hyperactive and impulsive behavior appears to be most effectively accomplished with medication (most often methylphenidate) (Connor, 2002; Paule et al., 2000). Evidence is emerging that pharmacological control of behavioral challenges is more effective than nonmedical interventions, such as behavioral treatment (Pelham et al., 2002; MTA Cooperative Group, 1999a, 1999b). Research supporting the effectiveness of medication is accumulating, but such medical intervention shows no effect, or very limited influence, on academic performance (Evans, et. al., 2001; Northup, Gulley, Edwards, & Fountain, 2001). Current thinking suggests that, although there are clear benefits to the use of medication, it may be overprescribed, and there are side effects and issues of potential abuse that need further research (Bhaumik, Branford, Naik, & Biswas, 2000; Kollins, MacDonald, & Rush, 2001). Some evidence also suggests that medication has positive effects on ADHD combined subtypes, whereas further research is clearly needed on the efficacy of medical intervention for the impulsivity and inattentive types (Tervo et al., 2002).

Some researchers advise caution in the use of psychostimulants for both theoretical and practical reasons. First, there are concerns regarding side effects, as one would expect with any pharmacological treatment that has such widespread use. In some cases, it is difficult to distinguish psychological characteristics that may appear to be side effects (such as increased anxiety) from the symptoms of ADHD itself. Investigators examining these questions are constantly trying to determine whether an increase in anxiety, for example, is due to the use of medication over time or occurs because a child becomes increasingly anxious as a result of negative personality or interpersonal effects of ADHD (e.g., Jensen et al., 2002). Additionally, some researchers express uneasiness about appropriate dosage, overprescription, potential for abuse, and issues related to management planning and implementation for children being treated with medication (Bhaumik et al.,

2000; Kollins et al., 2001). Table 8.4 summarizes a variety of medications, their uses, and some of the side effects observed.

Children who are young when they begin to receive medication may take it over a very long period, and it is unclear what the cumulative effects may be on physical or intellectual development (Kutcher, 2002). For preschoolers, there is some evidence that susceptibility to side effects might be greater (Handen, Feldman, Lurier, & Murray, 1999). Further investigation in both of these areas is certainly warranted. Concerns about medication interventions have been raised in the popular press and continue to arise periodically as the field grapples with the challenges presented by these children (e.g., Bank, 2000). Alternatives to medication have sometimes been proposed, as the Reflect on This "Exploring Other Options" and the nearby Debate Forum indicate.

The hyperactive and impulsive behaviors of many children with ADHD clearly present a significant challenge to parents, teachers, and other school personnel during the elementary school years. Elementary teachers describe these children as fidgety, impulsive, and constantly disruptive. These behaviors are often accompanied by deficits in academic performance (Crystal et al., 2001; Radford & Ervin, 2002; Theriault & Holmberg, 2001). From a teacher's viewpoint, it is difficult for the child to focus on learning if he or she is in constant motion. This point emphasizes two recurring themes in this text: collaboration among general and special educators and focusing on a single system of educational services and supports. The hyperactive

## TABLE 8.4

### Medications, Uses, and Side Effects

#### NEUROLEPTICS

*Medications:* Haloperidol (Haldol), Chlorpromazine (Thorazine), Thioridazine (Mellaril)

*When Prescribed:* Overt psychosis, unmanageable destructive behavior, severe aggression, Tourette's syndrome

*Side Effects:* Sedation, dystonic reactions

#### ANTIDEPRESSANTS

*Medications:* Amitriptyline (ElavilO), Nortriptyline (Aventyl), Imipramine (Tonfranil)

*When Prescribed:* Depression, school refusal with panic, attention-deficit disorder with hyperactivity

*Side Effects:* (Some effects related to dosage level)—dry mouth, blurred vision, constipation, sedation, cardiac toxicity, seizures

#### STIMULANTS

Medications: D-Amphetimine (Dexedrine), Methylphenidate (Ritalin), Pemoline (Cylert)

*When Prescribed:* Attention-deficit disorder with hyperactivity

*Side Effects:* Appetite suppression, insomnia, dysphoric reaction, growth delay

#### TRANQUILIZERS AND SEDATIVES

*Medications:* Diazepam (Valium), Chlordiazepoxide (Librium), Hydroxyzine (Atrax, Vistaril)

*When Prescribed:* Distorted reality perception

*Side Effects:* Sedation, common misuse/abuse

#### LITHIUM CARBONATE

*Medications:* Lithium

*When Prescribed:* Manic depressive or bipolar illness

*Side Effects:* Tremor, nausea, vomiting, weakness

SOURCE: From *Learning Disabilities: Characteristics, Identification, and Teaching Strategies* (4th ed., p. 61), by W. N. Bender, 2001, Boston: Allyn and Bacon.

## EXPLORING OTHER OPTIONS

From time to time, the popular press raises concerns about use of methylphenidate with children. Because of side effects, ongoing worries about overprescription, and other matters, parents are often encouraged to explore other options such as behavioral therapy. Long-term effects of drugs on young developing brains also raise concerns, particularly in view of the frequency of drug treatment for ADHD in children.

Consider the difficult circumstances of a parent with a young child who has ADHD. Research evidence to date shows that the most consistently effective treatment for hyperactivity and other symptoms involves administration of psychostimulant medication. The issues noted above loom large, but you have just "lived through" [a horrible week in which] your young child has been expelled from school for aggressive and disruptive behavior that appears to endanger the health and well-being of other students. You have been told before by your pediatrician that prescription medication is often helpful and she recommended its use. What are you going to do?

SOURCE: From "Misdiagnosing Misbehavior? First Lady Calls for a Closer Look at Psychotropics for Kids, by E. Livini, ABC News, March 20, 2000.

and impulsive behaviors exhibited by many children with ADHD sorely tests their inclusion in general education settings. Because of these behaviors, children with ADHD are often disruptive to the instructional environment and require a great deal of focused time and effort on the part of teachers. It is crucial for these youngsters that the inclusion model not be discarded just because it is difficult to apply for those with ADHD.

Nonmedical, school-based interventions can also be effective in improving the classroom behaviors of elementary-age school children with ADHD, and some are more potent than others. In general, targeted behavior modification strategies appear to be more effective for controlling behavioral problems than those that involve cognitive-behavioral or cognitive interventions. Cognitive-behavioral therapies are based on combining behavioral techniques with efforts to change the way a person thinks about his or her behaviors—that is, attempting to enhance the cognitive control that a person has over his or her actions. Research evidence does not suggest beneficial results from cognitive-behavioral interventions for children with ADHD (Abikoff, 2001; Paoni, 2001). Using behavior modification interventions aimed at controlling a child's behavioral activity and giving structure to the classroom environment both seem to be academically productive. Descriptions of effective instructional settings for children with ADHD consistently include a good deal of structure.

Educators should arrange the classroom setting to enhance the child's ability to respond, attend, and behave in a manner that is conducive to learning. Teachers may have to monitor constantly the directions they give students with ADHD, often cuing them to the fact that a direction or message is about to be delivered. This might be done with a prompt such as "Listen, John" or some other signal that the teacher is comfortable making is and well understood by the student as meaning a directive is to follow. The signal may be accompanied with other signals or procedures that add structure and direct the student's attention to the learning task at hand. Such cues or signals must be designed in a developmentally appropriate manner (Gelfand & Drew, 2003).

Academic instructions must directly target the specific content area wherein the child is experiencing problems. Student learning is enhanced by strategies that involve considerable structure (Lohman, 2002). Instruction, such as writing lessons, may be more effective if reinforcement is combined with modeling and increased practice (De-La-Paz, 2001; Dendy, 2000). With these children, there is a need to demonstrate the learning strategy rather than just describing it. They often require individualized instruction from a teacher or aide, focused on the specific content

## IS MEDICATION BEING APPROPRIATELY USED AS A TREATMENT FOR ADHD?

Concern continues regarding the use of medication, particularly psychostimulants, to treat students with ADHD. The debate becomes increasingly difficult with mounting evidence that medication is the most effective intervention. Some professionals, however, have seriously questioned the administration of medication as currently practiced.

### POINT

Several points must be raised regarding the administration of medication to children with ADHD. The use of medication for treating ADHD is very widespread and may be overprescribed. Some estimates place the number of children receiving psychostimulant treatment near 1 million. In the context of such wide usage, a basic concern emerges about how little we actually know regarding long-term influences and side effects. It is unsettling that we know so little about a treatment that is so widely employed.

### COUNTERPOINT

For some children with ADHD, medication is the only approach that will bring their hyperactivity under control and thereby allow effective instruction to occur. Without such treatment, these students will be unable to attend to their academic work and will be so disruptive in classroom situations that other students will not be effectively taught. Side effects such as insomnia, irritability, and decreased appetite, among others, are relatively minor and temporary for the most part. Research suggests that teachers have reported a substantial proportion of those children receiving medication show an improvement in behavior.

What do you think? To give your opinion, go to Chapter 8 of the companion website (www.ablongman.com/hardman8e) and click on Debate Forum.

area that needs attention, such as reading, math, or spelling. Such individual work is clearly a labor-intensive undertaking. Further research on the practical implementation and effectiveness of such approaches is clearly required.

Multiple treatment approaches—often termed *multimodal treatments* (such as drug and behavior therapies)—are more effective than just one kind of treatment for children with ADHD (Jensen et al., 2002; MTA Cooperative Group, 1999a, 1999b; Swanson et al., 2002). But this approach creates a risk factor that may not emerge with a single treatment. The National Institutes of Health consensus report (1998) noted that communication or coordination among educational (school-based) and health-related (medical) assessments and services is often poor. Diagnosticians and interventionists from both disciplines may have difficulty communicating outside of their field, and this may lead to a worsening of the child's condition or promote additional problems, such as antisocial behaviors. Less than perfect communication and coordination among multiple disciplines have been one of the obstacles that must be overcome in providing services to all people with disabilities (Drew & Hardman, 2004). And this problem is exacerbated in the case of children with ADHD, because such a high proportion are receiving both medical treatment and school-based instruction. The situation can be improved if all parties pay special attention to facilitating communication among attending physicians and others providing treatment. However, this is unlikely to occur unless it is explicitly included in a child's intervention.

**ADOLESCENCE AND ADULTHOOD.** Once viewed as a childhood condition, ADHD is now known to have a significant presence beyond those early years and is accompanied by an array of other behaviors and conditions in adolescence and adulthood (e.g., Nigg et al., 2002; Whalen, Jamner, Henker, Delfino, & Lozano, 2002). Current research suggests that ADHD is far more persistent into adulthood than once was thought and that it often requires continuing adult treatment (Barkley, Fischer, Smallish, & Fletcher, 2002). Interventions appropriate for adolescents and adults with ADHD must be reassessed and, where appropriate, modified in an age-appropriate manner (Wasserstein, Wolf, & LeFever, 2001). However, certain characteristics described for children with ADHD—and certain interventions—seem to apply to adolescents and adults as well. For example, cognitive challenges such as the verbal and nonverbal memory problems found in ADHD children occur in many adults with ADHD as well (Barkley, Edwards, Laneri, Fletcher, & Metevia, 2001; Johnson et al., 2001). The structured environment that is beneficial for school-based instruction appears to facilitate other interventions later in life, such as psychological therapy and self-management (Weiss, Hechtman, & Weiss, 1999). Also reminiscent of treatment at younger ages, instruction for adolescents with ADHD is more effective when the students can employ learning strategies (e.g., mnemonics, conceptual organizers) to assist in the acquisition of academic content (Sealover, 2002). Further, medication remains an effective treatment for the impulsivity and difficulty in focusing on tasks that continue into the adolescent and adult years for many people with ADHD. Stimulant medications, such as methylphenidate, remain effective, although some investigators are exploring alternative medications in order to reduce side effects or lessen the potential for abuse (Connor, 2002; Weiss, et al., 1999). As is the case with other treatments, adaptations and modifications are often required in order to ensure that the treatment is age-appropriate and to achieve the most effective intervention during these years. ADHD may present lifelong symptoms that necessitate intervention or compensatory action by those around the individual, as indicated in the nearby Inclusion Through the Lifespan.

Adolescents and adults with ADHD may not exhibit hyperactivity but may still have considerable difficulty in focusing on tasks and controlling impulses. Again, medication may be an effective treatment for some of these behaviors. However, it is likely that these individuals will also require significantly more structure in their environment than their peers without disabilities. Counseling that emphasizes behavior modification may be enormously helpful. This represents the adult-appropriate remnants of the structured environment that was productive for the individual during childhood. At this point in life, it is probably best to communicate openly with the person about his or her areas of strength and the areas in which ADHD presents the person with the greatest challenges. This type of frank communication will be most effective if used by adult family members, such as spouses, as well as by professional therapists. Such conversations are not always easy, but they become easier over time, especially if they are aimed at a positive enhancement of the lives of all involved.

People with ADHD face significant challenges at every age. Although behaviors of adults with ADHD may look somewhat different from those of children with ADHD, there are some similarities, and adults with ADHD face many significant difficulties. Many mysteries remain to be solved, but there also has been significant progress in treating this disability.

Inclusion Through the Lifespan

# PEOPLE WITH ATTENTION-DEFICIT/ HYPERACTIVITY DISORDER

### Tips for the Family

- Learn about the simple applications of behavior modification in a home environment, perhaps by enrolling in a parent training class.
- Try to structure the home environment in terms of family activities and tasks for the child, perhaps using a similar structure for all family members. This may mean setting a daily routine that is somewhat fixed, or even a fixed routine for portions of the day. Organize activities into groupings so that each is somewhat isolated from the others.
- Learn about ADHD from a practical standpoint that makes sense to family members. Do your best not to focus explicitly on the affected child in a manner that has negative implications for him or her (e.g., direct comments about disability or how difficult life is because . . .). Instead try to arrange the environment and activities in a manner that can best meet the child's needs as a routine approach to family life.
- Maintain communication with the child's physician regarding any medical treatment he or she might be receiving. If questions arise about interventions, they should not hesitate to seek additional opinions.
- Give directions while looking the child in the eyes, thereby gaining attention and building eye contact as a control mechanism.

### Tips for the Preschool Teacher

- Initiate and maintain communication with the child's parents to enhance the information flow and, if possible, to build consistency across environments in rules and reward structures.
- Structure the environment and activities. For instance, divide activities into short sessions, each focusing on a single sub-activity.
- Signal or alert the student when a verbal directive is to be given in order to focus attention. For example, say, "Jim, listen. I want you to. . . ."
- Use a kitchen timer to facilitate time management, and gradually increase periods for activities where attention is focused.
- Monitor stress in the child; exceeding his or her stress thresholds may trigger disruptive behavior or inattention.
- Communicate with other school personnel in order to promote a consistent environment throughout the school regarding appropriate behavior and interactions (e.g., praise, structuring).

### Tips for Preschool Personnel

- Communicate with other preschool staff who are involved in the child's instruction— primarily the teacher.
- Try to communicate with the child in a manner consistent with the teacher's program. The setting may be different (e.g., hallways, playground, or bus), but the contingencies for appropriate behavior should be reasonably consistent.

### Tips for Neighbors and Friends

- These children may be noisier and more active than others in the neighborhood. Try to ignore minor transgressions.
- Communicate with the child's parents to learn what techniques they use for control. Encourage appropriate behavior in a manner that is consistent with what the parents' plan. This may seem awkward at first, but the parents are probably working very hard to provide a good family environment for the child. They will appreciate your help.

### Tips for the Family

- Think about modifying the structured family environment to be appropriate for the developmental level of the child.
- While continuing the overall structure begun during the younger years, gradually lengthen the activity periods.
- Consider varying somewhat the distinctive breaks between activities, and modify rewards for older children.
- Be proactive in communicating with the child's teacher, and facilitate communication between medical and educational professionals.

### Tips for the General Education Classroom Teacher

- Maintain distinctive signals age-appropriate and alerting messages as cues for attention. Minimize drawing the attention of other students to the child's challenges.
- Divide assignments into smaller or shorter segments as necessary.
- Shorten work sessions as needed. Make clear breaks between activities or subjects.
- Give positive rewards for good academic work and appropriate behavior. Such reinforcement is very important for these children.

### Tips for School Personnel

- Participate in ongoing communication with other school staff who are involved with the child including his or her teacher or teachers, the bus driver, counselors, and any extracurricular staff.
- Try to use communication and rules consistent with those employed by the other school team members.

### Tips for Neighbors and Friends

- Recognize that during the elementary years these children may appear more active or noisy than their playmates in the neighborhood.
- Communicate and collaborate with the child's parents in order to provide a reasonably consistent neighborhood environment. For example, if behavior modification is being used in the home to shape other elements of the youngster's behavior, learn the simple components of reinforcement and contingency setting.

## SECONDARY AND TRANSITION YEARS

### Tips for the Family

- Make age-appropriate modifications of the family environment.
- Maintain structuring, but add more adult-like modeling, and demonstrate how to focus attention.
- Continue communication with school personnel, especially the teacher, in order to maintain consistent ways of supporting and challenging the person with ADHD.

### Tips for the General Education Classroom Teacher

- Help the youngster to direct or modify annoying behavior and characteristics to achieve more appropriate and acceptable ways of behaving. Handle this delicately, because the youngster is on the brink of adulthood in some ways yet very immature in many others.
- Initiate communication with other school personnel who are involved in the academic and nonacademic life of the youngster, as well as with the parents. Attempt to collaborate on a plan to provide a relatively consistent environmental structure for the individual.
- Help the youngster to learn strategies for organizing both academic and nonacademic activities. This may involve open acknowledgment of limitations such as a short attention span.

### Tips for School Personnel

- Collaborate and help open lines of communication with all school personnel who are involved with the youngster.
- Depending on your particular role within the school, don't hesitate to visit with the youngster's parents and others in the broader community (e.g., employers, police organizations).
- Help to shape a positive growth environment for the youngster within your realm of responsibility (e.g., coach, etc.). Facilitate this young adult's skill development while acknowledging that her or his daily life may differ from the lives of others.

### Tips for Neighbors and Friends

- Communicate with the youngster's parents about how this period of development is proceeding for the youngster and how you, as a nonfamily adult, can participate with the youngster, if that is a comfortable role.
- Recognize that this young person, who is beginning to look like an adult, still may encounter great difficulty with impulse control and task focus. If you are working with him or her, perhaps as an employer, structure the environment to take advantage of strengths and minimize the effect of limitations.

## ADULT YEARS

### Tips for the Family

- Communicate directly with this family member about his or her personal strengths and limitations. Opening such lines of communication will facilitate adapting the structure of the family environment for this new stage in the individual's life.
- Work with the affected person and other family members to help structure or organize the family environment. The adult with ADHD may not be hyperactive but still may have some challenges with impulse control and task focus.
- Communicate openly with physicians or other health care professionals who are treating the family member with ADHD. This should not be done without the knowledge of the affected individual and will be more productive if all team members work together.

### Tips for Therapists or Other Professionals

- Open lines of communication with other adult family members in order to promote a consistent and productive environment for the client.
- Help your client organize his or her life in order to emphasize personal strengths and lessen the demands in areas where challenges are most evident.

### Tips for Neighbors, Friends, and Employers

- This adult is likely to test your patience. He or she may appear to be a busybody, flitting from task to task without finishing any. If you are an employer, you may find yourself presented with partially completed assignments. Try to be patient.
- Speak directly with the person about his or her strengths, and help the person maintain focus on staying organized.
- Structure the environment in order to take advantage of strengths and minimize the effects of limitations. Limit the areas of responsibility in order to help the individual focus.

## FOCUS REVIEW

**FOCUS 1** Identify three behavioral symptoms commonly associated with ADHD.

- Impulsive behavior
- Fidgeting or hyperactivity
- Inability to focus attention

**FOCUS 2** Identify two ways in which the behavior of children with ADHD detrimentally affects instructional settings.

- Children with ADHD challenge teachers' skills in classroom management, because they are in and out of their seats a lot, pestering their classmates, and perhaps exhibiting aggressive behavior toward other students.
- Children with ADHD challenge teachers' skills in instruction in that they may be unable to focus on instructions, they may impulsively start an assignment before directions are complete, and they may submit incomplete assignments because they did not listen to all the instructions.

**FOCUS 3** Identify four other areas of disability that are often found to be comorbid with ADHD.

- Learning disabilities
- Tourette's syndrome
- Conduct disorders
- Emotional disorders

**FOCUS 4** Identify the three major types of ADHD according to *DSM-IV*.

- Attention-deficit/hyperactivity disorder, combined type
- Attention-deficit/hyperactivity disorder, predominantly inattentive type
- Attention-deficit/hyperactivity disorder, predominantly hyperactive-impulsive type

**FOCUS 5** Identify the range of estimates for the ratio of males with ADHD to females with the disorder, and cite the average ratio.

- Estimates for the ratio of males with ADHD to females with the disorder range from 2:1 to 10:1.
- On the average, the male/female ratio appears to be about 3.5:1.

**FOCUS 6** Identify the two broad categories of assessment information useful in diagnosing ADHD.

- Information about medical status
- Information about educational, behavioral, and contextual circumstances

**FOCUS 7** Identify three categories of characteristics that present challenges for individuals with ADHD.

- Difficulties in self-regulation, impulsivity, and hyperactivity
- Difficulties in social relationships
- Significant challenges in academic performance

**FOCUS 8** Identify three possible causes of ADHD.

- Neurological dysfunction that is trauma-based
- Neurological dysfunction due to differences in brain structure
- Hereditary transmission

**FOCUS 9** Identify two approaches to intervention that appear to show positive results with individuals who have ADHD.

- Medication
- Behavior modification

## FURTHER READINGS

Cimera, R. E. (2002). *Making ADHD a Gift: Teaching Superman How to Fly.* Lanham, MD: Scarecrow Press.

*This book is for parents and beginning teachers who encounter children, teens, or adults with ADHD. The book is aimed at communicating in a nontechnical manner for general audiences. It is written in a personal fashion by an author who has ADHD and offers insights from that perspective.*

Rosenthal, D. and Lovgy, R., (2002). *ADHD: A Survival Guide for Parents and Teachers.* Duarte, CA: Hope Press.

*This book is written for parents and other caretakers of children with ADHD. Practical and easily understood, it presents strategies for working with these children. The style is user-friendly and the volume is a resource that readers will return to repeatedly.*

Nylund, D. (2002). *Treating Huckleberry Finn: A New Narrative Approach to Working with Kids Diagnosed ADD/ADHD.* Hoboken, NJ: John Wiley.

*Could or would Huck Finn be diagnosed with ADHD in today's world? Would he be on Ritalin? This interesting set of questions occurred to the author one night while he was reading to his son. It is a perspective that resonates with issues raised in the popular press about overprescription and the drawbacks of medication.*

# WEB RESOURCES

### ADHD Owner's Manual

www.edutechsbs.com/adhd

This site is a resource that includes information about both learning disabilities and ADHD. It discusses educational and behavioral interventions, medication, and tips for teachers. There is a section entitled "The Feeling of Having ADHD" for those who want to have that perspective as they learn more about this condition.

### Troubled Teen Advisor

troubled-teen-advisor.com/index.php?source=ov&kw=adhd

This site is for parents who are facing the challenges of understanding their teenage children. It places ADHD

in the context of the social world of these teens, along with school challenges, legal issues, substance abuse, runaway behaviors, and depression.

### Diamond Ranch Academy

strugglingteens.us/academic.html

This private commercial website is for an academic program aimed particularly at teens with ADHD and other conditions that result in challenging behaviors. It is representative of the private academic and treatment organizations that some families turn to for assistance with their children or teens who are having difficulty in public school settings.

# BUILDING YOUR PORTFOLIO

If you are thinking about a career in special education, you should know that many states use national standards developed by the Council for Exceptional Children (CEC) to assess a teacher candidate's knowledge and skills for working with students with disabilities. See a complete listing of the ten CEC Content Standards on the inside front cover of this text.

### CEC Content Standards Addressed in Chapter 8

1. Foundations
2. Development and Characteristics of Learners
3. Individual Learning Differences
4. Instructional Strategies
5. Learning Environments and Social Interactions
7. Instructional Planning

### Assess Your Knowledge of the CEC Standards Addressed in Chapter 8

Some states require that teacher candidates develop a portfolio of products that demonstrate mastery of the CEC content standards. To assist in the development of products for this portfolio, you may wish to complete the following activities.

- Complete a written test of the chapter's content.

  *If your instructor requires a written test of your content knowledge for this chapter, keep a copy for your portfo-*

*lio. A practice test on the information covered in this chapter is available through the companion website (www.ablongman.com/hardman8e) and the Student Study Guide.*

- Respond to Application Questions for the Case Study "Coexisting Conditions."

  *Review the Case Study and respond in writing to the application questions. Keep a copy of the case study and your written response for your portfolio.*

- Complete the "Take a Stand" activity for the Debate Forum, "Is Medication an Appropriately Used Treatment for Children with ADHD?"

  *Read the Debate Forum in this chapter and then visit our companion website to complete the activity "Take a Stand." Keep a copy of this activity for your portfolio.*

- Participate in a Community Service Learning Activity.

  *Community service is a valuable way to enhance your learning experience. Visit our companion website for suggested community service learning activities that correspond to the information presented in this chapter. Develop a reflective journal of the service learning experience for your portfolio.*

# THEMES OF THE TIMES

Expand your knowledge of the concepts discussed in this chapter and reading current and historical articles from the *New York Times* by visiting the "Themes of the Times" section of the companion website: www.ablongman.com/hardman8e.

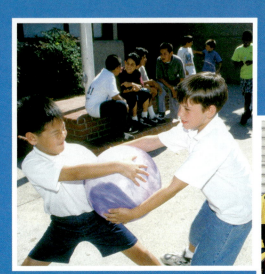

# Emotional/Behavioral Disorders

## TO BEGIN WITH...

### "I want more!"

I'm writing about one of my 4-year-old students, who is displaying a lot of violence toward myself, co-workers, and other children.

Every morning he comes in and demands breakfast, even though he eats at home. When there is no food for him, he begins screaming, "I'm hungry, I'm hungry!" over and over for about half an hour. Sometimes he throws things or hits other children.

Later in the day, he'll begin bothering other children—knocking toys off the table, hitting a child and then saying, "Miss Erin, Danny hit me," when he has been witnessed by teachers and children as being the aggressor. Things go fine until circle time and he doesn't want to clean up. That starts another screaming tantrum of "I don't want to clean up." Nor does he want to sit still or be quiet in circle. Or come in from the playground—in this case, he has to be physically carried from the playground, all the while hitting and kicking at the teacher and screaming, "You're trying to kill me!" Lunchtime is another ordeal. He wants to eat, but he won't sit down at the table. When coaxed to the table, he puts his hands on other children and puts his spoon or fork in their plates. We are not allowed to give children any more than two servings of the main course, and only three of the vegetable or fruit, but when he is cut off, more screaming begins: "I WANT MORE!"

After lunch is nap time, and he will refuse to get on his mat. He will walk around the room, stepping on other children or will take their blankets. He will get toys off the shelves and try to play with them and refuse to put them up. When he is told to put them away, he begins saying things like "You're trying to choke me!" or "You're hurting me!" and "Stop hitting me," even when the teacher is nowhere near him. Sometimes, he'll try to open the door and run down the hall. A teacher has to lean against the door to prevent this from happening. The child will begin kicking at the teacher and hitting, saying, "I'm going to break your arm" and "I'm going to get a gun and shoot you 'til you're dead." (Adapted from "Violent 4-Year Old/Telling Lies" by Becky, *The Behavior Home Page*, Kentucky Department of Education, 2000, p. 1)

### "That *$@%# just doesn't like me!!"

Jamarian sits in the hall beside the classroom door. When asked what happened, he replies, "Nothing!! That *$@%# just doesn't like me!! I hate this school!!" His teacher has a different view: "How do you expect me to teach when students just don't want to learn? Kids like Jamarian should be in special classes so the rest of the class can learn!" (Algozzine & White, 2002, p. 85)

### Hank Is a Lot Happier

I was so afraid that if Hank went on the way he was, he would feel that he couldn't do anything. I felt that way when I was younger and it is not a good feeling. I have noticed that Hank is a lot happier and is making a lot of new friends. Hank doesn't lose his temper at the drop of a hat anymore. I thank this program for that also. I feel that because he is more confident in himself, he don't have to try to prove he is good enough, by fighting. I also think that because of the parent and teacher involvement that this wonderful thing happened. If we were not at it at both ends ... this wouldn't have worked. I feel so good about what Hank has accomplished and I know he does too. (Kay, Fitzgerald, & McConaughy, 2002, p. 104)

**FOCUS**

**PREVIEW:** To preview the central concepts of this chapter, read the focus questions located in the margins. Using these questions as a guide, ask yourself what you already know and what you want to learn.

## Eric

Eric is a preschooler. In his mother's words, "He's busy. He's hyper . . ., but he is very intelligent, very perceptive." Eric spends about 4 hours a day at Children's Center, a day treatment center for young children with serious emotional and behavior problems. Professionals at this center are helping Eric develop a variety of behaviors, one of which is learning how to express himself verbally, rather than physically striking out at others.

Eric was referred to Children's Center because of his persistent fighting, biting, hitting, and screaming. He also had great difficulty in responding to directions and giving sustained attention to various age-appropriate tasks. The center's psychologist described him as being the "most extremely hyperactive child that I have tested." Prior to coming to the center, Eric had been ejected from several day care centers because of his aggressive and noncompliant behaviors.

Eric's mother also experienced great difficulties in managing him. "I feel kind of guilty saying it, but I have to say the truth, I didn't like my son. I couldn't stand him. I couldn't stand being around him for long, I mean I could take about ten minutes. He would, every day, . . . ruin something in the house."

At Children's Center, Eric has the opportunity to interact with some very talented and caring professionals. He spends most of each day with two child therapists who skillfully respond to his negative as well as his positive behaviors. Moreover, each week Eric has a chance to meet one-on-one with Jim, a child therapist, for individual play therapy. At least once a week, his mother meets with Dorothy, a talented social worker who helps Eric's mother with personal concerns and provides suggestions for dealing with Eric at home.

Eric has made significant progress in the past several months. His attention span has increased so significantly that he now can listen to stories and even wait his turn, something that was virtually impossible for him before he came to Children's Center.

## Nick

Nick is a very likable, bright kid. He enjoys athletics and is well above average in his reading performance and other academic skills. During the later part of his fifth-grade year, however, he created significant problems for his teacher, whom he saw as being very rude and always picking on him.

The teacher assistance team in the elementary school attempted a variety of prereferral interventions to bring his behavior under control. However,

---

Individuals with **emotional and behavioral disorders** (E/BD)—such as Eric, Nick, and Amy in the opening snapshots—experience great difficulties in relating appropriately to peers, siblings, parents, and teachers. Students with E/BD also have difficulty responding to academic and social tasks that are essential parts of their schooling. They may be deficient in important academic and social behaviors. For example, Eric's placement in the Children's Center was a function of his excessive, aggressive, or noncompliant behaviors. In other cases, individuals with E/BD may not have learned the essential skills necessary for successful participation in school settings, as demonstrated by Nick. He, for a variety of reasons, had not learned how to relate well with peers or how to accept correction delivered by teachers and others. Amy, as described by her mother, gradually lost her appetite, became suicidal, and dealt with teachers in unacceptable ways. However, she is now making great progress with the assistance of her teachers, vocational trainers, and the dentist with whom she works. Statistically, students with E/BD are more likely to be economically disadvantaged, male, and African American (Kea, Cartledge, & Bowman, 2002).

## Definitions

As you will see, several terms have been developed to describe individuals with E/BD. These terms include *socially maladjusted, emotionally disturbed, conduct disordered,* and *behavior disordered.* In reading this section, think about the words or labels you have used over time to describe peers, relatives, classmates, or other acquaintances who frequently exhibited deviant behaviors and/or unusual emotions.

**Emotional disorders**

Behavior problems that are frequently internal in nature. Persons with these problems may have difficulties in expressing or dealing with emotions evoked in normal family-, school-, or work-related experiences.

**Behavioral disorders**

Conditions in which the emotional or behavioral responses of individuals in various environments significantly differ from those characteristic of their peer and their ethnic and cultural groups. These responses seriously affect social relationships, personal adjustment, schooling, and employment.

he continued to be noncompliant, problematic during recesses, and generally difficult to manage.

In sixth grade he was placed in a self-contained classroom for students with behavior disorders. He did quite well during this entire year, relating well to his special class teacher, Mrs. Backman, and becoming more self-controlled in his responses to peers and most teachers. The next year he moved on to Northwest, an intermediate school in his neighborhood. Again, he was placed in a self-contained, special education setting with some opportunities for involvement in other classes such as physical education and art.

He made significant progress during his first year at Northwest, partly because of his teacher's social skills program and her expertise in dealing with him. He was now more responsive to verbal redirection and much less reactive to criticism. Because of this progress and other changes in his behavior, he was prepared to spend most of his time outside of the special education classroom. In fact, he now participates for several periods a day in a program for students who are gifted.

His mother sums up his future in this fashion, "I think Nick has a very bright future, but he has to want it." His teachers concur.

## Amy

Amy is a very attractive and talented young woman. About midway through the seventh grade, she began to complain about persistent stomachaches, and at the same time, her mother began receiving continual complaints from school personnel about her behavior. In fact, in one year's time, her life went from "beautiful to dismal," as described by her mother. She was not able to eat, was often hostile and suicidal, and did not sleep well. Her behavior at school was "out of control." At this same time, she was prescribed Prozac by one of the physicians with whom her mother was working. Over time, however, her mother took her off this drug, believing that it was not helping her but contributing to her problems in school and at home.

Eventually, Amy was placed in a self-contained classroom at a high school different from the one that she would have attended normally. Her placement in this classroom was based on a number of persistent problems, including a lack of anger control, consistent clashes with authority figures, episodes of inattention, and incomplete school work.

At age 15, after seeing a number of specialists, it was discovered that she had a severe case of endometriosis. She underwent surgery for this condition and gradually things seemed to improve for her.

Amy now spends each morning at a technical training center, where she is learning to become a dental assistant. During the midday hours, she attends several special classes as well as one regular class of biology at her high school. During the afternoon, she works with a dentist who is contributing to her training as a dental assistant. Amy's mother describes her as follows: "Right now Amy's a capable, fairly happy, well-adjusted 17-year-old kid. Two years ago she was withdrawn, hostile . . . she was suicidal—I never knew what was going to come out of her next. She couldn't eat, she couldn't sleep, but she's progressed really, really well . . . I'm so proud of her."

## The IDEA Definition

Emotional disturbance is defined in the Individuals with Disabilities Education Act (IDEA) as . . . :

(I) a condition exhibiting one or more of the following characteristics over a long period of time and to a marked degree, which adversely affects educational performance:

(A) An inability to learn which cannot be explained by intellectual, sensory, or health factors;

(B) An inability to build or maintain satisfactory relationships with peers and teachers;

(C) Inappropriate types of behavior or feelings under normal circumstances;

(D) A general pervasive mood of unhappiness or depression; or

(E) A tendency to develop physical symptoms or fears associated with personal or school problems.

(II) The term does not include children who are socially maladjusted, unless it is determined that they are seriously emotionally disturbed.

Identify six essential parts of the definitions of emotional/ behavioral disorders.

This description of severe emotional disturbance, or E/BD, was adapted from an earlier definition created by Bower (1959). The IDEA definition for E/BD has been criticized for its lack of clarity, for incompleteness, and for its exclusion of individuals described as *socially maladjusted* (Coleman & Webber, 2002; Council for Children with Behavior Disorders, 1987, 1989, 1990; Forness, 1996; Forness & Knitzer, 1990; Webber & Sheuermann, 1997). Furthermore, this definition mandates that assessment personnel demonstrate that the disorder is adversely affecting students' school performance. In many cases, students with serious E/BD—such as eating disorders, depression, suicidal tendencies, and social withdrawal—do not receive appropriate care and treatment, merely because their academic achievement in school appears to be normal or above average. In some cases, these students are gifted (see Chapter 18).

## The Council for Exceptional Children (CEC) Definition

The Council for Exceptional Children has proposed a definition for emotional disturbance that goes beyond the language of IDEA (Council for Exceptional Children, 1991; Forness, 1996; Forness & Knitzer, 1990):

> [The term] *emotional/behavioral disorders* (EBD) refers to a condition in which behavioral or emotional responses of an individual in school are so different from his/her generally accepted, age-appropriate, ethnic, or cultural norms that they adversely affect educational performance in such areas as self-care, social relationships, personal adjustment, academic progress, classroom behavior, or work adjustment. EBD is more than a transient, expected response to stressors in the child's or youth's environment and would persist even with individualized interventions, such as feedback to the individual, consultation with parents or families, and/or modification of the educational environment. The eligibility decision must be based on multiple sources of data about the individual's behavioral or emotional functioning. EBD must be exhibited in at least two different settings, at least one of which must be school related.
>
> EBD can coexist with other disability conditions as defined elsewhere in this law [IDEA].
>
> This category may include children or youth with schizophrenia, affective disorders, or . . . other sustained disturbances of conduct, attention, or adjustment. (Council for Exceptional Children, 1991, p. 10)

Features of this definition represent significant advantages over the IDEA definition: (1) the inclusion of impairments of adaptive behavior as evidenced in emotional, social, or behavioral differences; (2) the use of normative standards of assessment from multiple sources, including consideration of cultural and/or ethnic factors; (3) the examination of prereferral interventions and other efforts to assist children and youth before formally classifying them as disabled; and (4) the potential inclusion of individuals previously labeled as socially maladjusted.

Whether to include children and youth who are considered socially maladjusted in the federal definition of E/BD continues to be sharply debated (Forness & Kavale, 2000; Webber & Scheuerman, 1997). Proponents of the inclusion of the socially maladjusted have argued that both professional practice and current research run counter to the exclusionary clause found in the IDEA definition (Terrasi, Sennett, & Macklin, 1999; Webber & Scheuerman, 1997). Moreover, the clause in the IDEA definition that excludes these children and youth prevents them from receiving appropriate special education services as well as federal protections from disciplinary procedures that might culminate in expulsion from school. We will discuss these protections later in this chapter.

Many professionals believe that greater numbers of young children with E/BD would receive preventive treatment if the more inclusive definitions were adopted by IDEA, thereby decreasing the need for more intensive and expensive services later in these students' lives. Additionally, many clinicians believe that adopting these definitions would lead to greater numbers of children and youth receiving needed special education services directly related to their strengths as well as their challenging behaviors.

### Identifying Normal Behavior

Many factors influence the ways in which we perceive the behaviors of others. Our perceptions of others and their behaviors are significantly influenced by our personal beliefs, standards, and values about what constitutes normal behavior. Our range of tolerance varies greatly, depending on the behavior and the situation. For instance, Eric's aggressive and oppositional behaviors were not tolerated at the various preschools where he was enrolled for very short periods of time. Moreover, what may be viewed as normal by some may be viewed by others as abnormal. For example, parents may have little foundation for determining what is normal behavior, since their perceptions are often limited by their lack of experience with children in general (Newcomer, 2003). They may see their child's behavior as somewhat challenging but not abnormal. Recall the experience that Becky, the preschool teacher in the chapter opener, had with a demanding and aggressive preschooler.

The context in which behaviors occur also dramatically influences our view of their appropriateness. For example, teachers and parents expect children to behave reasonably well in settings where they have interesting things to do or where children are doing things they seem to enjoy. Often children with emotional/behavioral disorders misbehave in these settings. At times, they seem to be oblivious to the environments in which they find themselves. Some have the social skills to act appropriately but choose not to use them. Sometimes the intensity or sheer frequency of some behaviors forces parents and others to ask, "Is this behavior really normal?" For example, Eric's mother was perplexed not only with the intensity of his behaviors but also with their frequency. It seemed that Eric broke or damaged something in their home every day.

Many factors influence the types of behaviors that individuals with E/BD exhibit or suppress: (1) the parents' and teachers' management styles, (2) the school or home environment, (3) the social and cultural values of the family, (4) the social and economic climate of the community, (5) the responses of peers and siblings; and (5) the biological, academic, intellectual, and social-emotional characteristics of the individuals (Coleman & Webber, 2002).

# Classification

We use classification systems to describe various subsets of behaviors. These systems serve several purposes for professionals. First, they provide us with a means for describing various types of behavior problems in children and youth. Second, they provide professionals with a common set of terms for communicating with each other. For example, children who are identified as having Down syndrome, a type of mental retardation, share some rather distinct characteristics (see Chapter 10). Third, physicians and other health care specialists use these characteristics and other information as a basis for diagnosing and treating individuals.

The field of E/BD is broad and includes many different types of problems, so it is not surprising that many approaches have been used to classify these individuals. Some classification systems describe individuals according to statistically derived categories, whereby patterns of strongly related behaviors are identified through sophisticated statistical techniques. Other classification systems are clinically oriented; they are derived from the experiences of physicians and other social scientists who work directly with children, youth, and adults with E/BD. Still other classification systems help us understand emotional/behavioral disorders in terms of their relative severity.

**FOCUS 2**

Identify five factors that influence the ways in which we perceive the behaviors of others.

**FOCUS 3**

List three reasons why classification systems are important to professionals who identify, treat, and educate individuals with E/BD.

FOCUS

4

What differentiates externalizing disorders from internalizing disorders?

## Statistically Derived Classification Systems

For a number of years, researchers have collected information about children with E/BD. Data collected from parent and teacher questionnaires, interviews, and behavior rating scales have been analyzed using advanced statistical techniques. Certain clusters or patterns of related behaviors have emerged from these studies. For example, Peterson (1987) found that the E/BD exhibited by elementary school children could be accounted for by two dimensions: withdrawal and aggression. Similarly, several researchers have intensively studied young psychiatric patients to develop a valid classification system (Achenbach, 1966, 1991a, & 1991b). Statistical analysis of data generated from these studies revealed two broad categories of behavior: externalizing symptoms and internalizing symptoms. The latter category refers to behaviors that seem to be directed more at the self than at others. Withdrawal, depression, shyness, and phobias are examples of internalized behaviors (Coleman & Webber, 2002); some clinicians would describe individuals with these conditions as *emotionally disturbed.*

Children or youth who exhibit externalizing disorders may be described as engaging in behaviors that are directed more at others than at themselves. These behaviors could be characterized as aggressive, noncompliant, defiant, resistive, disruptive, and dangerous. These behaviors significantly affect parents, siblings, classmates, and teachers. Despite the outward differences between internalizing and externalizing behaviors, the distinction between these two categories is not always clear-cut. For example, adolescents who are severely depressed certainly have an impact on their families and others, although the primary locus of their distress is internal or emotional.

Other researchers (Quay, 1975, 1979; Von Isser, Quay, & Love, 1980), using similar methodologies, have reliably identified four distinct categories of E/BD in children:

1. Conduct disorders involve such characteristics as overt aggression, both verbal and physical; disruptiveness; negativism; irresponsibility; and defiance of authority—all of which are at variance with the behavioral expectations of the school and other social institutions.

Youth with E/BD often engage in destructive behaviors directed at themselves or others.

2. Anxiety–withdrawal contrasts sharply with conduct disorders. It involves overanxiety, social withdrawal, seclusiveness, shyness, sensitivity, and other behaviors that imply a retreat from the environment rather than a hostile response to it.

3. Immaturity characteristically involves preoccupation, short attention span, passivity, daydreaming, sluggishness, and other behaviors not consistent with developmental expectations.

4. Socialized aggression typically involves gang activities, cooperative stealing, truancy, and other manifestations of participation in a delinquent subculture. (Von Isser et al., 1980, pp. 272–273)

The fourth category, socialized aggression, is related to social maladjustment. Presently, children and youth identified as socially maladjusted are not eligible for services through IDEA. Socialized aggression is also related to another term we have mentioned very briefly, *conduct disorder*. We will review conduct disorders in greater depth later in this section.

In thinking about these categories, recall the descriptions of Eric, Nick, and Amy in the opening Snapshots. How would they be classified according to these categories? Did Eric have attention-deficit disorder? Was Nick's behavior serious enough to identify him as having a conduct disorder? and what about Amy's behavior? Does she qualify for placement in any of these categories?

## Clinically Derived Classification Systems

Although several clinically derived classification systems have been developed, the system predominantly used by medical and psychological personnel is the American Psychiatric Association's *Diagnostic and Statistical Manual of Mental Disorders* (DSM-IV-TR) (American Psychiatric Association, 2002). It and previous editions were developed and tested by committees of psychiatric, psychological, and health care clinicians—hence the term *clinically derived classifications*. Professionals in each of these groups included people who served or worked closely with children, adolescents, and adults with mental disorders, or, in our terminology, emotional/behavioral disorders (E/BD). The categories and subcategories of DSM-IV-TR (American Psychiatric Association, 2002) were developed after years of investigation and field testing. Unfortunately, these psychiatric categories do not serve educational clinicians well, because they are not generally considered in identifying children or adolescents for special education services.

The current manual, DSM-IV-TR (American Psychiatric Association, 2002), identifies ten major groups of disorders that may be exhibited by infants, children, or adolescents. These include pervasive developmental disorders, attention-deficit and disruptive disorders, feeding and eating disorders, tic disorders, elimination disorders, and other disorders of infancy, childhood, and adolescence. Several of these disorders overlap with other conditions, such as mental retardation and autism.

**PERVASIVE DEVELOPMENTAL DISORDERS.** Children with pervasive developmental disorders exhibit severe deficits in several areas of development. These deficits may include significant problems in relating to parents, siblings, and others; very poor communication skills; and unusual behaviors evidenced in gestures, postures, and facial expressions. Generally these disorders are accompanied by chromosomal abnormalities, structural abnormalities in the nervous system, and congenital infections. Also, these disorders are generally evident at birth or present themselves very early in a child's life. They include autism, Rett's disorder, childhood disintegration disorder, and Asperger's disorder. Autism will be addressed in Chapter 13.

**ATTENTION-DEFICIT AND DISRUPTIVE DISORDERS.** Children with these disorders manifest a variety of symptoms (see Tables 9.1 and 9.2). For example, children with attention deficits have difficulty responding well to typical academic and social tasks and difficulty controlling their level of physical activity. Often their activity appears to be very random or purposeless in nature. See Chapter 8 for information on attention-deficit disorders. Children with disruptive E/BD frequently cause physical harm to other individuals or to animals, often engage in behaviors destructive to others' property, repeatedly participate in theft and deceitful activities, and regularly violate rules and other social conventions. In some instances, children with these disorders are highly oppositional. They exhibit a pattern of recurrent negativism, opposition to authority figures, and loss of temper. Other typical behaviors include disobeying, arguing, blaming others for problems and mistakes, and being spiteful. Most of the students with E/BD who are served in special education through IDEA have a conduct disorder or are oppositionally defiant. Think about Nick, identified in the opening snapshots. How would you classify him?

## TABLE 9.1

### Diagnostic Criteria for Conduct Disorder

A. A repetitive and persistent pattern of behavior in which the basic rights of others or major age-appropriate societal norms or rules are violated, as manifested by the presence of three (or more) of the following criteria in the past 12 months, with at least one criterion present in the past 6 months:

**Aggression to People and Animals**

(1) often bullies, threatens, or intimidates others

(2) often initiates physical fights

(3) has used a weapon that can cause serious physical harm to others (e.g., a bat, brick, broken bottle, knife, gun)

(4) has been physically cruel to people

(5) has been physically cruel to animals

(6) has stolen while confronting a victim (e.g., mugging, purse snatching, extortion, armed robbery)

(7) has forced someone into sexual activity

**Destruction of Property**

(8) has deliberately engaged in fire setting with the intention of causing serious damage

(9) has deliberately destroyed others' property (other than by setting fire)

**Deceitfulness or Theft**

(10) has broken into someone else's house, building, or car

(11) often lies to obtain goods or favors or to avoid obligation (i.e., "cons" others)

(12) has stolen items of nontrivial value without confronting a victim (e.g., shoplifting, but without breaking and entering; forgery)

**Serious Violations of Rules**

(13) often stays out at night despite parental prohibitions, beginning before age of 13 years

(14) has run away from home overnight at least twice while living in parental or parental surrogate home (or once without returning for a lengthy period)

(15) is often truant from school, beginning before age 13 years

B. The disturbance in behavior causes clinically significant impairment in social, academic, or occupational functioning.

C. If the individual is age 18 years or older, criteria are not met for Antisocial Personality Disorder.

SOURCE: Reprinted with permission from the *Diagnostic and Statistical Manual of Mental Disorders*, Fourth Ed., Text Revision (pp. 98–99). Copyright 2002 Amerrican Psychiatric Association

**FEEDING AND EATING DISORDERS.**  The disorder known as pica consists of the persistent eating of nonnutritive materials for at least one month. Materials consumed may be cloth, string, hair, plaster, or even paint. Often children with pervasive developmental disorders manifest pica. Anorexia and bulimia are common eating disorders evidenced by gross disturbances in eating behavior. In the case of anorexia nervosa, the most distinguishing feature is bodyweight that is 15% below the norm. These individuals are intensely afraid of weight gain and exhibit grossly distorted perceptions of their bodies. Bulimia is characterized by repeated episodes of binging, followed by self-induced vomiting or other extreme measures to prevent weight gain. Both of these conditions may result in depressed mood, social with-

*Young people with anorexia nervosa have grossly distorted perceptions about their bodies.*

**TABLE 9.2**

### Diagnostic Criteria for Oppositional Defiant Disorder

A. A pattern of negativistic, hostile, and defiant behavior lasting at least 6 months, during which four (or more) of the following are present:

    (1) often loses temper

    (2) often argues with adults

    (3) often actively defies or refuses to comply with adults' requests or rules

    (4) often deliberately annoys people

    (5) often blames others for his or her mistakes or misbehavior

    (6) is often touchy or easily annoyed by others

    (7) is often angry and resentful

    (8) is often spiteful or vindictive

    Note: Consider a criterion met only if the behavior occurs more frequently than is typically observed in individuals of comparable age and developmental level.

B. The disturbance in behavior causes clinically significant impairment in social, academic, or occupational functioning.

C. The behaviors do not occur exclusively during the course of a Psychotic or mood Disorder.

D. Criteria are not met for Conduct Disorder, and, if the individual is age 18 years or older, criteria are not met for Antisocial Personality Disorder.

SOURCE: Reprinted with permission from the *Diagnostic and Statistical Manual of Mental Disorders*, Fourth Edition, Text Revision (p. 102). Copyright 2002 American Psychiatric Association.

---

drawal, irritability, and other, more serious medical conditions. Rumination disorder is characterized by repeated regurgitation and rechewing of food. This disorder develops after a period of normal feeding and persists for about one month.

**TIC DISORDERS.** Tic disorders involve stereotyped movements or vocalizations that are involuntary, rapid, and recurrent over time. Tics may take the form of eye blinking, facial gestures, sniffing, snorting, repeating certain words or phrases, or grunting. Stress often exacerbates the nature and frequency of tics. These disorders include Tourette syndrome, chronic motor or vocal tic disorder, and transient tic disorder.

**ELIMINATION DISORDERS.** Elimination disorders entail soiling (econpresis) and wetting (enuresis) in older children. Children who continue to have consistent problems with bowel and bladder control past their fourth or fifth birthday may be diagnosed as having an elimination disorder, particularly if the condition is not a function of any physical disorder.

**OTHER DISORDERS OF INFANCY, CHILDHOOD, OR ADOLESCENCE.** The remaining categories in DSM-IV-TR comprise disorders that do not easily fit other categories. Separation anxiety disorder is characterized by inordinate fear of leaving home or being separated from persons to whom the child or adolescent is attached. Behaviors indicative of this disorder include persistent refusal to go to school, excessive worry about personal harm or injury to self or other family members, reluctance to go to sleep, and repeated complaints about headaches, stomachaches, and nausea.

Another condition within this category is elective mutism. It is a persistent refusal to talk in typical social, school, and work environments. This disorder is really quite rare, occurring less than 1% of the time in psychiatric referrals, but it may significantly affect the child's social and educational functioning.

Two other disorders are also classified in this category: reactive attachment disorder of infancy or early childhood and stereotypic movement disorder. The former disorder is represented by noticeably abnormal and developmentally inept social relatedness. Reactive attachment disorders appear as a result of grossly inadequate care. The latter disorder is characterized by recurring, purposeless motor behaviors. These behaviors interfere with the child's functioning and sometimes result in injuries.

The third edition of the *Diagnostic and Statistical Manual of Mental Disorders* included anxiety disorders as a part of infant, childhood, and adolescent disorders. They have subsequently been moved to the adult categories of *generalized anxiety disorder and social phobia.*

Anxiety disorders of childhood or adolescence are very similar to the anxiety–withdrawal category included in the statistically derived classification system. Children and youth with anxiety disorders have difficulty dealing with anxiety-provoking situations and with separating themselves from parents or other attachment figures (e.g., close friends, teachers, coaches). Unrealistic worries about future events, overconcern about achievement, excessive need for reassurance, and somatic complaints are characteristic of young people who exhibit anxiety disorders.

## Prevalence

Estimates of the prevalence of E/BD vary greatly from one source to the next, ranging from 1% to 33% (Coleman & Webber, 2002; Rosenberg, Wilson, Maheady, & Sindelar, 2004). The U.S. Office of Education estimated that 1.2% to 2% of students in the country have E/BD. Other estimates, provided by the Office of Technology Assessment and the National Institute of Medicine, suggest that more than 3% of children and adolescents evidence severe E/BD. During the 2000–2001 school year in the United States, fewer than 1% of children 6 to 21 years of age were identified and served as exhibiting a behavioral disorder (U.S. Department of Education, 2002).

Unfortunately, significant numbers of children and youth with E/BD remain unidentified and do not receive the mental health care or special education they so critically need (Knitzer, Steinberg, & Fleisch, 1990; Ruehl, 1998; Sachs, 1999; Seifert, 2000). Equally distressing is the disproportionate number of young African American males who are identified as having E/BD (Kea et al., 2002).

Some researchers have suggested that the number of students who receive special education is less than one-third of those who actually need this assistance (Brandenburg, Friedman, & Silver, 1990). The low number of students served is due in part to the lack of standardized criteria, varying definitions, and meager research about the

*Youth with E/BD drop out of school at a higher rate than other students with identified disabilities.*

processes related to identifying students as having E/BD (Rosenberg et al., 2004). Also contributing to the problems of identification, classification, and provision of service is the fact that many children and youth with E/BD manifest other disabling conditions (Algozzine, Serna, & Patton, 2001; Forness & Kavale, 2000).

# Characteristics

If you had to describe children and youth with E/BD, what would you say about their intellectual capacity, their behavior, their academic performance, and their long-term prospects for employment and success? This section will give you answers to some of these questions. However, note that the facts and figures introduced here represent averages. Service providers, teachers, and friends must view each child or youth with E/BD individually, focusing on his or her strengths and potential for growth and change.

## Intelligence

Researchers from a variety of disciplines have studied the intellectual capacity of individuals with E/BD. In an early national study of children with E/BD enrolled in public school programs, the majority of these students exhibited above-average intelligence (Morse, Cutler, & Fink, 1964). However, recent research paints a different picture. Children and youth with E/BD tend to have average to below-average IQs compared to their peers without E/BD. (Algozzine et. al., 2001; Coleman & Webber, 2002; Seifert, 2000). Obviously, either the characteristics of students with E/BD have changed or the sampling procedures employed in the earlier study were flawed.

What impact does intelligence have on the educational and social-adaptive performance of children with E/BD? Is the intellectual capacity of a child with E/BD a good predictor of other types of achievement and social behavior? The answer is yes. The IQs of students with E/BD are the best predictors of future academic and social achievement (Kauffman, 1997). The below-average IQs of many of these children contribute significantly to the challenges they experience in mastering academic and social tasks in school and other environments.

**FOCUS 5**

Identify five general characteristics (intellectual, adaptive, social, and achievement) of children and youth with E/BD.

## Social and Adaptive Behavior

Individuals with E/BD exhibit a variety of problems in adapting to their home, school, and community environments (Algozzine et al., 2001; McEvoy & Welker, 2000). Furthermore, they have difficulties in relating socially and responsibly to persons such as peers, parents, teachers, and other authority figures. In one recent study, 89% of the students with E/BD met established criteria for psychiatric disorders (Cassidy, James, & Wiggs, 2001). The two most common diagnoses were ADHD and conduct disorder. In short, students with E/BD are difficult to teach and to parent (Sampers, Anderson, Hartung, & Scambler, 2001). In contrast to their peers who generally follow rules, respond well to their teachers and parents, finish classwork and home chores, and comply promptly with adult requests, children and youth with E/BD often defy their parents and teachers, disturb others, do not complete tasks, and behave in ways that invite rejection by teachers, parents, and peers (Algozzine et al., 2001). These behaviors lead to referral for special education and related services.

Socially, children and youth with E/BD may have difficulty sharing, playing typical age-appropriate games, and apologizing for actions that hurt others. They may be unable to deal appropriately with situations that produce strong feelings, such as anger and frustration. Problem solving, self-control, accepting consequences for misbehavior, negotiating, expressing affection, and reacting appropriately to failure are behaviors that do not come naturally. Because these children have deficits in these social-adaptive behaviors, they frequently experience difficulties in meeting the demands of the classrooms and other social environments in which they live and participate (Algozzine et al., 2001; Seifert, 2000).

A recent study sheds some light on the social difficulties experienced by children with E/BD. Researchers have found that about three out of four children with E/BD show clinically significant language deficits. These include problems related to processing and understanding verbal communication and using language to communicate (Benner, Nelson, & Epstein, 2002). These researchers also found that one out of two children with language deficits is identified as having E/BD. These language deficits may contribute significantly to the social problems experienced by children with E/BD and their care providers.

When we discussed classification earlier in this chapter, we reviewed the statistically derived categories of behaviors that were common to children and adolescents with E/BD. These categories included conduct disorders, anxiety–withdrawal, immaturity, and **socialized aggression**. Children and adolescents with conduct disorders engage in verbal and physical aggression. They may threaten or bully other children, extort money from them, or physically hurt them, often without any provocation. In classrooms, these students often defy authority, refuse to follow the teacher's directions, and frequently engage in power struggles with teachers and administrative personnel (Rosenberg et al., 2004; Seifert, 2000; Wicks-Nelson & Israel, 2003). Students with E/BD are "13.3 times more likely than other students with disabilities to be arrested while in school" (U.S. Department of Education, 1999, p. II-4). Also, 42% of the youth with disabilities in correctional facilities are youngsters with identified E/BD (Burrell & Warboys, 2000; U.S. Department of Education, 1999).

Children and adolescents who are anxious and withdrawn frequently exhibit behaviors such as seclusiveness and shyness. They may find it extremely difficult to interact with others in normal social events. They tend to avoid contact with others and may often be found daydreaming. In the extreme, some of these youth begin to avoid school or refuse to attend. Their school avoidance or refusal is marked by persistent fear of social situations that might arise in school or related settings. These youth fear being humiliated or embarrassed. Their anxiety may be expressed by tantrums, crying, freezing, and other bodily complaints (stomachaches, sickness, etc.). Such children and youth with E/BD, who manifest minimal personal and social skills, are more likely than other youth with disabilities to be victimized during their school years.

Other children and youth with E/BD may struggle with depression (Ialongo, Poduska, Werthamer, & Kellam, 2001). Left untreated, these individuals are at risk for suicide, poor school performance, and relationship problems with peers, siblings, parents, and teachers. Manifestations of depression in children and youth include sleep disturbance (nightmares, night terrors, etc.), fatigue or loss of energy, excessive feelings of guilt or worthlessness, inability to concentrate, and suicidal thoughts.

Youth gang activities, drug abuse, truancy, violence toward others, and other delinquent acts characterize children and adolescents who are identified as "undersocialized aggressive" or "socially maladjusted" or as having a conduct disorder (Burrell & Warboys, 2000; Esbensen, 2000; Howell & Lynch, 2000). These adolescents are often seen as impulsive, hyperactive, irritable, and excessively stubborn. Recent reviews and research studies suggest that as many as 40% to 70% of students with E/BD exhibit attention-deficit/hyperactivity disorder (ADHD) (Place, Wilson, Martin, & Hulsmeier, 1999; Forness & Kavale, 2001). Furthermore, many students with E/BD engage in behaviors that draw attention to themselves, are cruel to others, and are sometimes involved in drug distribution and other illegal activities (Seifert, 2000). It is easy to see how the behaviors associated with these categories are maladaptive and interfere with success in school, family, community, and (eventually) employment.

**Socialized aggression**

Participation in a delinquent subculture that involves activities such as gang behavior, cooperative stealing, and truancy.

## Academic Achievement

As we have noted; students with E/BD experience significant difficulties in academic subject areas (Algozzine et al., 2001; Coleman & Webber, 2002). In contrast to other students with disabilities, students with E/BD are absent more often, fail more classes, are retained more frequently, and are less successful in passing minimum competency examinations (Woodruff et al., 1999). On the high school level, students with E/BD have average GPAs of 1.7, compared with 2.0 for all high school students with disabilities (Osher, Osher, & Smith, 1994; Wagner et al., 1991). The dropout and graduation rates for students with E/BD are staggering (U.S. Department of Education, 2002; Woodruff et al., 1999). About 52% of these students drop out of school, most before they finish the tenth grade (U.S. Department of Education, 2002). A little more than 40% actually graduate from high school (U.S. Department of Education, 2002). About 17% of students with E/BD go on to college. Moreover, the vast majority of students with E/BD receive their services and instruction in settings outside of general education classrooms (U.S. Department of Education, 2002).

Studies dealing with employment rates of students after high school are frankly depressing (Algozzine et al., 2002; Bullis, 2001). Only 41% of students with E/BD who have exited high school are employed two years later, compared with 59% of typical adolescents who have left or completed high school. Three to five years later, the contrasts are even stronger: 69% of students without disabilities are employed, compared with 47% of students with E/BD (Algozzine et al., 2002). Significant challenges persist in preparing young people with E/BD for meaningful employment and involvement in our communities (Bullis, 2001). Later on in this chapter, we will talk about interventions that are designed to address or even prevent these problems.

# Causation

**FOCUS 6**

What can accurately be said about the causes of E/BD?

What causes children and youth to develop E/BD? As you read this section, think about your own patterns of behavior. How would you explain these patterns? What has given rise to them? Also, think about Eric, Nick, and Amy. What factors contributed to their E/BD?

Throughout history, philosophers, physicians, theologians, and others have attempted to explain why people behave as they do. Historically, people who were mentally ill were described as possessed by evil spirits, for which the treatment of choice was religious in nature. Later, Sigmund Freud (1856–1939) and others advanced the notion that behavior could be explained in terms of subconscious phenomena or early traumatic experiences. More recently, some theorists have attributed disordered behaviors to inappropriate learning and complex interactions that take place between individuals and their environments. Others, approaching the issue from a biological perspective, have suggested that aberrant behaviors are caused by certain biochemical substances, brain abnormalities or injuries, and chromosomal irregularities.

With such a wealth of explanations, it is easy to see why practitioners might choose different approaches in identifying, treating, and preventing various behavioral disorders. However, the variety of theoretical frameworks and perspectives provides clinicians with a number of avenues for explaining the presence of certain behaviors (Coleman & Webber, 2002). As you will see, the causes of behavioral disorders are multifaceted and often complex.

## The Biophysical Approach

The biophysical framework explains E/BD as a function of inherited or abnormal biological conditions. Behavior problems are assumed to result from some physiological, biochemical, or genetic abnormality or disease (Coleman & Webber, 2002;

Rosenberg et al., 2004; Wicks-Nelson & Israel, 2003). For example, consider diabetes. This condition is not caused by psychological factors. It has a biophysical basis: a malfunctioning pancreas that does not produce insulin. Another example is schizophrenia, which is far more likely to manifest itself in young adults both of whose parents have been diagnosed as having the disorder. Thus there appears to be a strong genetic basis for the emergence of this serious behavioral disorder. Some individuals with schizophrenia benefit from medications that address some biological factors or deficits that give rise to their challenging behaviors.

## The Psychoanalytic Approach

Subconscious processes, predispositions, and early traumatic experiences explain the presence of E/BD from a psychoanalytic perspective. These internal processes are unobservable events that occur in the mind. As individuals gain insight into their psychic conflicts via psychotherapy, they may be able to eliminate or solve their behavior problems. The return to normalcy may also be aided by a caring therapist or teacher. For children, this process theoretically occurs through play therapy, in which inner conflicts are revealed and subsequently resolved through family therapy and therapeutic play experiences with understanding adults (Coleman & Webber, 2002; Rosenberg et al., 2004; Seifert, 2000; Wicks-Nelson & Israel, 2003). Also, some youth with E/BD may receive various forms of psychotherapy in hospital or other intensive care settings. Few if any school-based intervention programs are centered on principles derived strictly from the psychoanalytic approach.

## The Behavioral Approach

The behavioral approach focuses on aspects of the environment that prompt, reward, diminish, or punish certain behaviors. Through treatment, adults and children are given opportunities to learn new adaptive behaviors by identifying realistic goals, understanding what environmental features trigger both functional and maladaptive behaviors, and receiving positive reinforcement for attaining these goals. Gradually, aberrant behaviors are eliminated or replaced by more appropriate ones (Rosenberg et al., 2004; Wicks-Nelson & Israel, 2003). This approach has had a profound impact on the practices and interventions of special educators and other clinicians. This approach, more than most others, has a significant research base affirming its effectiveness in treating a broad array of disorders and challenging behaviors (Coleman & Webber, 2002; Rosenberg et al., 2004).

## The Phenomenological Approach

From a phenomenological point of view, abnormal behaviors arise from feelings, thoughts, and past events tied to a person's self-perception or self-concept. Faulty perceptions or feelings are thought to cause individuals to behave in ways that are counterproductive to self-fulfillment. Therapy is centered on helping people develop satisfactory perceptions and behaviors that are in agreement with self-selected values.

## The Sociological–Ecological Approach

The sociological–ecological model is by far the most widely encompassing explanation of E/BD. Aberrant behaviors are presumed to be caused by a variety of interactions and transactions with other people. For some theorists, the deviant behaviors are taught as part of the person's culture. For others, the behaviors are a function of labeling. According to this perspective, individuals labeled as juvenile delinquents, gradually adopt the patterns of behavior that are associated with the assigned label. In addition, others who are aware of the label begin to treat the labeled individuals as though they were truly delinquent. Such treatment theoretically promotes the delinquent behavior (Coleman & Webber, 2002; Rosenberg et al., 2004; Wicks-Nelson & Israel, 2003).

This model also specifies another source of aberrant behavior: *differential association*. This concept is closely related to the cultural-transmission explanation of deviance: People exhibit behavior problems in an attempt to conform to the wishes and expectations of a group they want to join or be affiliated with. Finally, the sociological–ecological perspective views the presence of aberrant behavior as a function of a variety of interactions and transactions that are derived from a broad array of environmental settings. For example, a community may sanction or informally support certain aberrant behaviors associated with delinquency, violence, drug abuse, and teen pregnancy.

Each model contributes different explanations for the causes of E/BD. Unfortunately, clinicians are rarely able to isolate the exact cause of a child's E/BD, but they do recognize several factors that contribute to the condition. Many professionals concur with Kauffman (1997) that "Both the disorders of behavior and their causes are usually multidimensional; life seldom refines disorders or their causes into pure unambiguous forms. Children seldom show teachers or researchers a single disorder uncontaminated by elements of other problems, and the cause of a disorder is virtually never found to be a single factor" (p. 159).

Clearly, many factors contribute to the emergence of E/BD. Family and home environments play a critical role. Poverty, involvement of primary caregivers with drugs and alcohol, child abuse and neglect, malnutrition, dysfunctional family environments, family discord, and incompetent parenting have a profound impact on the behaviors observed in children and adolescents (Henry, Tolan, & Gorman-Smith, 2001; Wicks-Nelson & Israel, 2003). For example, "minimal rules in the home, poor monitoring of children, and inconsistent rewards and punishments create an environment in which behavior problems flourish" (Sampers et al., 2001, p. 94). These conclusions are affirmed by several researchers who have examined families intensely over time (Campbell, 1995; Patterson, DeBaryshe, & Ramsey, 1989). In this regard, review the Case Study on page 246. What would you do if you were Karl's mother?

Children reared in low-income families bear increased risks for wide-ranging challenges, including lower intellectual development, deficient school achievement, and high rates of emotional/behavioral problems. Antisocial behaviors often emerge in children whose family poverty is accompanied by other stressors, such as homelessness, the death of a parent, placement in foster care, or persistent child abuse or neglect. Family discord also plays a role in the development of E/BD in some children. Extended marital conflict and distress are associated with several serious child outcomes, including aggressive behavior, difficulty with schoolwork, depression, health problems, and inferior social competence (Wicks-Nelson & Israel, 2003).

Procedures used in child management and discipline also play important roles in the development of E/BD. However, the way in which child management may trigger E/BD is highly complex. Parents who are extremely permissive, who are overly restrictive, or who are aggressive often produce children with conduct disorders. Home environments that are devoid of consistent rules and consequences for child behavior, that lack parental supervision, that reinforce aggressive behavior, and that use aggressive child management practices produce children who are very much at risk for developing conduct disorders (Wicks-Nelson & Israel, 2003).

Child abuse plays a major role in the development of aggression and other problematic behaviors in children and adolescents (Crosson-Tower, 2002; Horton & Cruise, 2001). Effects of child abuse on young children include withdrawal, noncompliance, aggression, enuresis (bed wetting), and physical complaints. Physically abused children exhibit high rates of adjustment problems of all kinds (Wicks-Nelson & Israel, 2003). Neglected children have difficulty in academic subjects and receive below-average grades. Children who have been sexually abused manifest an array of problems, including inappropriate, premature sexual behavior; poor peer relationships; and often serious mental health problems. Similar difficulties are evident in adolescents who have been abused. These include low self-esteem, depression, poor peer relationships and school problems, and self-injurious and suicidal behaviors.

## SHOULD KARL STAY AT HOME OR BE HELPED ELSEWHERE?

Karl is a 7-year-old boy who was referred to the study by a staff member at the mental health clinic where he was receiving weekly outpatient therapy. Though his mother, Ms. S., found their current therapist to be helpful, she felt her family needed more comprehensive assistance. As Karl grew older, his aggressive behaviors were increasingly difficult to manage and residential placement had been discussed. Ms. S. was adamant that "even with all of his problems, he belongs at home." On referral to the study, Karl was randomly assigned to FCICM (Family-Centered Intensive Case Management).

Karl likes to bowl, fish, and play soccer. His mother described him as a very loving and generous child who could be helpful when he wanted to be. Karl liked school but had low-average school achievement and received additional help in reading and math. Karl's teacher reported that he had some behavioral problems in school and difficulty with peer relationships.

At home, Karl behaved aggressively toward his younger sister and mother. Ms. S. reported that he had violent temper tantrums. He was found once putting a pillow over his sister's face, and he had harmed her in other ways. Ms. S. did not feel that she could leave the two children alone for even a few minutes. Karl had purposely injured a pet hamster and animals he found, and he had also set several small fires. His mother was concerned about his increasing withdrawal and "not telling me how he was feeling." He had tried to hang himself with a belt, dashed into busy roads,

and engaged in other risk-taking behaviors. He experienced sleep problems, was diagnosed with depression, and was assessed as functionally impaired in social relationships and self-direction.

Karl's needs contributed to the tension between his mother and stepfather, and the relationship between Karl and his stepfather was difficult. Karl was confused and distressed by the lack of contact with his birth father and imagined his father to be coming for a visit or being able to live with him when there was virtually no contact between them. Karl and his mother had made allegations of psychological abuse and neglect (Evans et al., pp. 563–564).

### APPLICATION

1. With appropriate human and material resources, what would need to be arranged so Karl could remain at home rather than be placed in a residential setting?

2. What family-centered services would help his mother and other family members?

3. What advocacy assistance might the mother profit from in working with Karl's school?

4. On what basis should Karl be removed from his home for other, more intensive treatments or services?

---

As this section shows, the pathways to E/BD are many and varied. However, the more we learn about these pathways, the greater our opportunity to prevent disorders from occurring or to lessen their potential impact. Much can be done for children, at-risk youth, and their families if appropriate preventive measures and interventions are actively pursued and put in place (Eddy, Reid, & Fetrow, 2000; Fishbein, 2000; Kutash, Duchnowski, Sumi, Rudo, & Harris, 2002; Sampers et al., 2001).

# Assessment

## Screening, Prereferral Interventions, and Referral

Screening is the first step in the assessment process to identify children and adolescents most in need of potential treatment and services for E/BD. Screening is based on the belief that early identification leads to early treatment, which may reduce the overall impact of the E/BD on the individual and family. As suggested earlier in this chapter, significant numbers of children and youth with E/BD are *not* identified and thus do not receive appropriate services.

New screening approaches are multiagent, mutimethod, and multigated; that is, they do not rely on one professional, one method, or one observation for assessing a child or youth when E/BD is suspected (Walker & Severson, 1992). Screeners move through successive "gates" in order to identify children or youth for more intensive assessment and prereferral interventions.

One such approach is *Systematic Screening for Behavior Disorders* (SSBD), developed by Walker & Severson (1992). This approach has been very effective in identifying young children who need prereferral interventions and other services. SSBD is a three-stage process, beginning with nominations by a general education teacher. Teachers think about the children in their classes and then group them according to various behavior patterns, some of which mirror the characteristics of children with E/BD, including externalizing and internalizing disorders. Once the children have been grouped, each child is ranked within the group according to the severity and frequency of his or her behavior. The last step is a series of systematic observations conducted in classrooms and in other school environments to see how the children who were ranked most severely affected behave in these environments. As children are progressively and systematically identified through this multiple-gating process, assessment team members determine which children ought to be considered for prereferral interventions or other, more intensive assessments.

Prereferral interventions are designed to address the students' identified behavioral and academic problems and to reduce the likelihood of further, more restrictive actions or placements. Often these interventions are developed, planned, and implemented under the direction of an intervention assistance team. Many states now require prereferral interventions before referrals may be received and processed by school personnel (Rosenberg et al., 2004). Prereferral interventions generally include efforts to remediate the students' difficulties by altering instruction and classroom management procedures, providing additional support for academic and behavioral success, and helping parents and other key individuals respond more effectively to these children.

The actual submission of a referral for a student is generally preceded by several parent-teacher conferences. These conferences help the teacher and parents determine what actions should to be taken. For example, the student's difficulties may be symptomatic of family problems such as a parent's extended illness, marital difficulties, or severe financial challenges. If the parents and teacher continue to be perplexed by a child's behavior, a referral may be initiated. Referrals are generally processed by principals, who review them, consult with parents, and then forward the referrals to a psychologist or other qualified professionals.

Once a referral has been appropriately processed and a parent's or guardian's permission for testing and evaluation has been obtained, assessment team members carefully observe and assess a child's present levels of performance: intellectually, socially, academically, physically, and emotionally. Their task is to determine whether the child has E/BD and whether he or she qualifies for special education services.

## Assessment Factors

As we noted earlier in this chapter, emotional/behavioral disorders have many causes. Likewise, the behaviors of children and youth being assessed for E/BD serve many functions. In other words, behaviors are purposeful. For example, a young child may tantrum in order to avoid schoolwork that is too difficult. Or a youth may engage in destructive behavior to gain attention that he or she does not otherwise get from peers or parents. Behavior is also a function of interactions with environmental factors. Some conditions set off negative behaviors, and other conditions reward or reinforce these same behaviors. Interpersonal factors—such as depression, anxiety, or erroneous interpretations of environment events—may contribute to a child's or youth's problems. If a child or youth is showing behaviors that are highly problematic, teachers and other professionals have an obligation to look at them from a functional point of view—that is, to see what purposes these behaviors serve and what conditions give rise to them (see nearby Reflect on This).

Current IDEA regulations require assessment team members to conduct functional behavioral assessments. Simply defined, "Function assessment is a collection of methods for obtaining information about antecedents (things a child experiences before the behavior of interest), behaviors (what the child does), and consequences (what the child experiences after the behavior of interest). The purpose is to identify the reason

FOCUS
7

What four important outcomes are achieved through a functional behavioral assessment?

**Reflect on This**

## ONE BEHAVIORAL SPECIALIST'S APPROACH TO FUNCTIONAL BEHAVIORAL ASSESSMENT

### What Is Functional Behavioral Assessment?

Functional behavioral assessment (FBA) is a process of gathering information about the things or events that influence a person's problem behaviors. These could be either external events in the person's environment (e.g., interactions with others, work demands) or internal things (e.g., illness, fatigue, depression).

### Why Is FBA Carried Out?

FBA gathers information that is used to guide the development of a treatment or intervention plan. This plan should focus both on reducing or eliminating the problem behaviors and on increasing appropriate, desired behaviors.

### How Is FBA Carried Out?

There are three major strategies for collecting FBA information:

1. **Indirect / informant methods.** This involves collecting information from teachers, parents, or other relevant persons through interviews or the use of checklists, rating scales, or questionnaires.
2. **Systematic observation in typical settings.** This involves conducting structured observations to collect data on the occurrence of the behavior and on things that may be related to it. These observations are usually done during the person's regular activities (e.g., during classroom work periods, on the playground).
3. **Experimental manipulations (functional analysis).** This involves setting up situations in which different events are directly manipulated (i.e., presented and withdrawn) to assess their effects on the person's problem behaviors. Data on the behavior are systematically collected to allow for comparisons of the effects of different manipulations.

### What Should Be the Outcomes of a Good FBA?

- A thorough description of all the problem behaviors of concern, including how often they occur, how long they last, and how intense or potentially damaging they are. Also, it is important to identify behaviors that seem typically to occur together (e.g., the student yells, then throws things).
- Identification of the general and more specific things and events that seem to "set off" the problem behaviors, or predict when and where they are going to occur (e.g., when the student is not getting attention, is asked to do particular activities, or is ill, tired, or hungry).
- Identification of any outcomes or consequences of the behavior that may be reinforcing and maintaining it (e.g., getting attention, getting help with work, avoiding or escaping work demands or activities).
- Summarization of this information into statements or hypotheses about the behavior (e.g., "When Janna gets little sleep the night before and is asked to do math problems that are difficult for her, she will put her head down, refuse, and/or throw or destroy her books to escape having to do the task").
- Some level of systematic observational data that support the statements or hypotheses you've developed. These data could be the systematic observations or experimental manipulations mentioned above.
- The whole purpose of FBA is to guide the development of a plan. Such a plan should include a comprehensive array of strategies, such as changing the curriculum and instruction, teaching alternative skills, and rewarding appropriate behaviors.

SOURCE: From "One Behavioral Specialist's Approach to Functional Behavioral Assessment" by R. O'Neill, in *Getting Comfortable with Special Education Law*, 2000, p. 288, by D. Snow Huefner, Norwood, MA: Christopher-Gordon Publishers.

for the behavior and to use the information to develop strategies that will support positive student performance while reducing the behaviors that interfere with the child's successful functioning" (Witt, Daly, & Noell, 2000, p. 3). Its purpose is to identify the functions of a student's behavior in relationship to various school, home, or community settings (Nelson, Roberts, & Smith, 1998). Assessment team members collect information through interviews, make careful observations (see Assistive Technology on page 250), and examine the effects of probes or experimental manipulations over a period of several days (see nearby Reflect on This, "Amy and Jay," and Table 9.3). Through these procedures, team members and parents discover reliable relationships among specific problem behaviors, the settings or events that give rise to these behaviors, and their consequences.

If the functional behavioral assessment is done well, it gives rise to behavior intervention plans (BIPs) that may be used to assist the child or youth in developing new, more adaptive behaviors. Additionally, the BIP may include new curricular or instructional approaches tailored to the student's learning needs and preferences. The BIP may also identify changes to be implemented in the school or home environment. These might include peer and paraprofessional support, use of conflict resolution specialists, home-based programs, and other carefully selected interventions.

## AMY AND JAY
## Problematic Behaviors

Amy is a third grade student who does well academically but who has some serious social deficits. Specifically, her teacher describes her as "impulsive and aggressive." She has been referred to the principal on several occasions for fighting or otherwise being involved in physical altercations with others. Amy has been suspended four days during the current school year, continues to have difficulty with peers, and is frequently restrained by adults as a consequence.

Jay is a seventh grade student who rarely completes his work and whose teacher describes him as being "bizarre and scattered." Jay exhibits an array of disruptive behaviors in the classroom, including loud and (apparently) purposeful flatulence, sticking pencils up his nose, and licking his desk. He has been sent to the counselor several times during the current year but continues to engage in disruptive behaviors.

Table 9.3 gives the results of a behavioral assessment for Amy and Jay.

SOURCE: From "Using Functional Behavioral Analysis to Develop Effective Intervention Plans," by T. M. Scott and C. M. Nelson, 1999, *Journal of Positive Behavioral Interventions, 1*(4), p. 244.

## Assessment Techniques

Several techniques and procedures are used to identify children with E/BD, all closely paralleling the theoretical framework or philosophical perspective of their evaluators. As we have seen, the identification and classification of a child or youth with E/BD is preceded by a set of screening procedures accompanied by a functional

## TABLE 9.3

### Results of a Functional Behavioral Assessment for Amy and Jay

| EVENT | PROBLEM PATHWAY | REPLACEMENT PATHWAY | POSSIBLE INTERVENTIONS |
|---|---|---|---|
| **AMY** | | | |
| Setting event | Peer altercation ↓ | Peer Altercation ↓ | Teach problem-solving skills |
| Antecedent | Verbal insult ↓ | Verbal insult ↓ | Use prompts and cues |
| Behavior | Physical aggression ↓ | Move away or tell teacher ↓ | Teach anger management skills |
| Consequence | Escape altercation | Escape altercation and access teacher reinforcement | Provide reinforcement for appropriate behavior and response cost for inappropriate behavior |
| **JAY** | | | |
| Setting event | Classroom setting ↓ | Classroom setting ↓ | Use group contingency |
| Antecedent | Peer holds class attention ↓ | Peer holds class attention ↓ | Use prompts and cues |
| Behavior | Disruptive sounds and actions ↓ | Raise hand and make appropriate comment ↓ | Teach student to access peer attention in positive manner |
| Consequence | Peer attention | Peer attention | Provide praise along with student attention and have peers ignore inappropriate behavior under group contingency |

SOURCE: From "Using Functional Behavioral Analysis to Develop Effective Intervention Plans," by T. M. Scott and C. M. Nelson, 1999, *Journal of Positive Behavior Intervention, 1*(4), p. 249.

## USE YOUR PERSONAL DATA ASSISTANT (PDA) TO COLLECT GREAT DATA

!Observe® gives teachers, psychologists, and other professionals a means for recording and processing observational data using any number of hand-held devices. With the !Observe software, one can track up to 24 different behaviors. It also comes with several templates designed for observing various disabling conditions. Additionally, it provides the user with an audio or visual signal indicating the beginning and end of an observational interval. Once the observations have been completed, the data may be easily transferred to a spreadsheet for analysis and graphing.

SOURCE: !Observe®, developed by Dr. Sander Martin for Sopris West, 4093 Specialty Place, Longmont, CO 80504.

behavior assessment, teacher and parent interviews, diagnostic academic assessments, behavior checklists, a variety of sociometric devices (e.g., peer ratings), and the use of teacher rating scales (Rosenberg et al., 2004).

Typically, parents and teachers are asked to respond to a variety of rating-scale items that describe behaviors related to various classifications of E/BD. The number of items marked and the rating given to each item contribute to the behavior profiles generated from the ratings (see Table 9.4). In making their assessments, parents and professionals are asked to consider the child's behavior during the past six months.

A recent development in assessing children and youth for E/BD is **strength-based assessment** (Epstein, 1998; Lyons, 1997). In contrast to deficit-oriented instruments, this approach focuses on the individual's strengths. One such instrument

**Strength-based assessment**

An assessment procedure in which parents, teachers, and other caregivers rate a child's or youth's strengths and use this information to develop strength-centered, rather than deficit-centered, individualized education programs for children and youth with E/BD.

---

### TABLE 9.4

**Representative Items from the Child Behavior Checklist for Ages 4–18**

0 = Not True (as far as you know)

1 = Somewhat or Sometimes True

2 = Very True or Often True

| | | | |
|---|---|---|---|
| 0 | 1 | 2 | 1. Acts too young for his/her age |
| 0 | 1 | 2 | 5. Enjoys very few things |
| 0 | 1 | 2 | 10. Can't sit still, restless, or hyperactive |
| 0 | 1 | 2 | 15. Cruel to animals |
| 0 | 1 | 2 | 20. Destroys his/her own things |
| 0 | 1 | 2 | 25. Doesn't get along with other kids |
| 0 | 1 | 2 | 30. Fears going to school |
| 0 | 1 | 2 | 35. Feels worthless or inferior |
| 0 | 1 | 2 | 40. Hears sounds or voices that aren't there (describe): |
| 0 | 1 | 2 | 45. Nervous, high strung, or tense |
| 0 | 1 | 2 | 50. Too fearful or anxious |

SOURCE: From *Manual for the Child Behavior Checklist/4–18 and 2001 Profile*, by T. M. Achenbach, Burlington, VT: Department of Psychiatry, University of Vermont. Copyright by T. M. Achenbach. Reproduced by permission.

is the *Behavior and Emotional Rating Scale* (BERS) (Epstein & Sharma, 1997). Using this instrument, parents, teachers, and other caregivers rate the child or youth's strengths in several important areas, including interpersonal strength, involvement with family, intrapersonal strength, school functioning, and affective or emotional strength. Skilled clinicians use the BERS and other similar approaches to develop strength-centered, rather than deficit-centered, IEPs for children and youth with E/BD (see Table 9.5).

Once the screening process has been concluded, specialists and/or consultants—including psychologists, special educators, social workers, and psychiatrists—complete in-depth assessments of the child's academic and social-emotional strengths and weaknesses in various settings, such as the classroom, home, and playground. The assessment team may analyze classroom and playground interactions with peers, using functional behavioral assessment techniques; may administer various tests to evaluate personality, achievement, and intellectual factors; and may interview the parents and the child. Additionally, they may observe the child at home, again making use of functional behavioral assessment procedures.

A particularly complex problem for clinicians is the assessment of children and youth who have limited English proficiency and/or are culturally diverse (Council for Children with Behavior Disorders, 1989; Venn, 2000). Unfortunately, many of these children and youth are disproportionately represented in special education settings for students with E/BD. Some progress is being made, especially as practitioners employ functional behavioral assessment and related procedures, prereferral interventions, and positive behavioral support. Both prereferral interventions and positive behavioral support (PBS) hold great promise for helping students from diverse backgrounds remain and succeed in less restrictive settings and in general education classrooms. PBS "is a systems approach for establishing a continuum of proactive, positive discipline procedures for all students and staff members in all types of school settings" (Eber, Sugai, Smith, & Scott, 2002, p. 171). Instead of treating the symptom(s) and ignoring the underlying problems, the thrust of PBS is to address all the features and factors that may be related to a child's or youth's negative behaviors. The primary goals of PBS systems are improved behaviors for all children and youth at home, at school, and in the community; enhanced academic performance; and the prevention of serious violent, aggressive, or destructive behaviors. Schools in which PBS systems are evident define schoolwide expectations and rules; actively and regularly build social competence through active teaching and social skills programming; reward targeted, prosocial behaviors on a regular basis; and

**TABLE 9.5**

### Representative Items from the Behavioral and Emotional Rating Scale (BERS)

| | |
|---|---|
| 0 = Not at all like the child | 2 = Like the child |
| 1 = Not much like the child | 3 = Very much like the child |

| | | | | | |
|---|---|---|---|---|---|
| 0 | 1 | 2 | 3 | 1. | Demonstrates a sense of belonging to family |
| 0 | 1 | 2 | 3 | 3. | Accepts a hug |
| 0 | 1 | 2 | 3 | 6. | Acknowledges painful feelings |
| 0 | 1 | 2 | 3 | 10. | Uses anger management skills |
| 0 | 1 | 2 | 3 | 15. | Interacts positively with parents |
| 0 | 1 | 2 | 3 | 30. | Loses a game gracefully |
| 0 | 1 | 2 | 3 | 34. | Expresses affection for others |
| 0 | 1 | 2 | 3 | 39. | Pays attention in class |

SOURCE: From the BERS (Behavioral and Emotional Rating Scale), by M. H. Epstein and J. Sharma, 1998, Austin, TX: Pro-Ed, Inc.

make decisions on the basis of frequently collected, pertinent data. Individually tailored plans are developed and put into action for students who present chronic, challenging behaviors. These plans evolve from carefully completed functional behavior assessments conducted by key individuals in the child's or youth's school, home, and community settings.

**FOCUS 8**

What five guiding principles are associated with systems of care?

# Interventions

Historically, most children and youth with E/BD received treatments and interventions in isolation from their families, homes, neighborhoods, and communities. These treatments and interventions were based on the assumption that students' problems were exclusively of their own making. Services, if they were delivered at all, were rarely coordinated. Significant changes are beginning to take place, thanks to brave and vocal advocates who chronicled the deplorable plight of children and youth with E/BD (Duchnowski & Friedman, 1990; Knitzer, 1982; Peacock Hill Working Group, 1990; Stroul & Friedman, 1986).

Increasingly, care providers for children and youth with E/BD are establishing systems of care. One very promising practice is the wraparound process (Kendziora, Bruns, Osher, Pacchiano, & Mejia, 2001). "Wraparound is not a service or set of services; it is a planning process. This process is used to build consensus within a team of professionals, family members, and natural support providers to improve the effectiveness, efficiency, and relevance of supports and services developed for children and their families" (Eber et al., 2002, p. 173). We will have more to say about the wraparound process in subsequent sections of this chapter.

Community-based and family-centered systems for delivering services to children and youth with E/BD are also emerging (Eber et al., 2002). In these systems, educational, medical, and community care providers are beginning to pay greater attention to youth with E/BD and their families, as well as to the communities in which they live (Hernandez, Gomez, Lipien, Greenbaum, Armstrong, Gonzalez, 2001; Koyanagi & Feres-Merchant, 2000; Worthington, Hernandez, Friedman, & Uzzell, 2001) (see Figure 9.1). This new approach is based on several core values and guiding principles (see Table 9.6). One of the basic features of the systems-of-care concept is that it does not represent a prescribed structure for assembling a network of services and agencies. Rather, it reflects a philosophy about the way in which services should be delivered to children, youth, and their families. The child and family become the focus of the delivery system, with vital services surrounding them. These services might include home-based services, special class placement, therapeutic foster care, financial assistance, primary health care, outpatient treatment, career education, after-school programs, and family support. An integral part of the systems of care is schoolwide primary prevention (Eber et al., 2002; Greenburg, Domitrovich, & Bumbarger, 2001). Interventions associated with this kind of prevention include teaching conflict resolution, emotional literacy, and anger management to all students in the school—not just to those identified with E/BD. This kind of prevention program can avert 75% to 85% of student adjustment problems (U.S. Department of Education, 1999).

## The Early Childhood Years

The early childhood years are important for all children, particularly those at risk for developing E/BD. Recent research suggests that E/BD can be prevented (Fox, Dunlap,

**FIGURE 9.1**

### The System of Care Framework

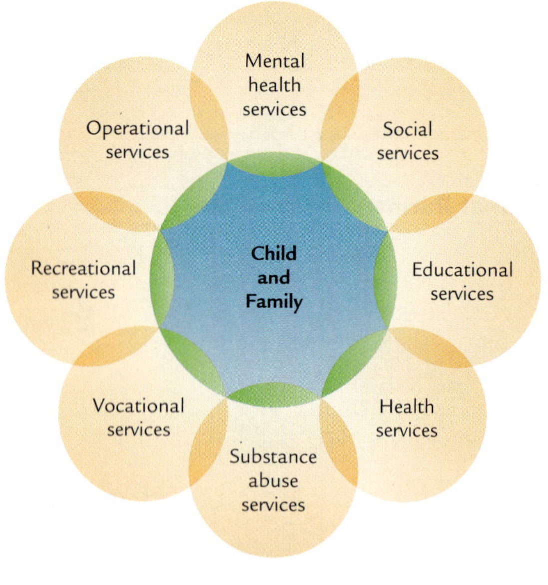

SOURCE: Adapted from *A System of Care for Children and Adolescents with Severe Emotional Disturbances* (p. xxvi), by B. Stroul and R. M. Friedman, 1986 (Rev. ed.), Washington, DC: Georgetown University Child Development Center, National Technical Assistance Center for Children's Mental Health. Copyright 1986 by B. Stroul and R. M. Friedman. Adapted by permission.

## TABLE 9.6

### Core Values and Guiding Principles of Systems of Care

**CORE VALUES**

1. The system of care should be child-centered and family focused, with the needs of the child and family dictating the types and mix of services provided.

2. The system of care should be community-based, with the locus of services as well as management and decision-making responsibility resting at the community level.

3. The system of care should be culturally competent, with agencies, programs, and services that are responsive to the cultural, racial, and ethnic differences of the population they serve.

**GUIDING PRINCIPLES**

1. Children with emotional disturbances should have access to a comprehensive array of services that address physical, emotional, social, and educational needs.

2. Children with emotional disturbances should receive individualized services in accordance with the unique needs and potentials of each child and guided by an individualized service plan.

3. Children with emotional disturbances should receive services within the least restrictive, most normative environment that is clinically appropriate.

4. The families and surrogate families of children with emotional disturbances should be full participants in all aspects of the planning and delivery of services.

5. Children with emotional disturbances should receive services that are integrated, with linkages between child-serving agencies and programs and mechanisms for planning, developing, and coordinating services.

6. Children with emotional disturbances should be provided with case management or similar mechanisms to ensure that multiple services are delivered in a coordinated and therapeutic manner and that they can move through the system of services in accordance with their changing needs.

7. Early identification and intervention for children with emotional disturbances should be promoted by the system of care in order to enhance the likelihood of positive outcomes.

8. Children with emotional disturbances should be ensured smooth transitions to the adult service system as they reach maturity.

9. The rights of children with emotional disturbances should be protected, and effective advocacy efforts for children and youth with emotional disturbances should be promoted.

10. Children with emotional disturbances should receive services without regard to race, religion, national origin, sex, physical disability, or other characteristics, and services should be sensitive and responsive to cultural differences and special needs.

SOURCE: From *A System of Care for Children and Adolescents with Severe Emotional Disturbances* (p. xxiv), by B. Stroul and R. M. Friedman, 1986 (Rev. ed.), Washington, DC: Georgetown University Child Development Center, National Technical Assistance Center for Children's Mental Health. Copyright 1986 by B. Stroul and R. M. Friedman, Reprinted by permission.

& Cushing, 2002; Simpson, Jivanjee, Koroloff, Doerfler, & Garcia, 2001). Many children would not develop serious E/BD if they and their families received early, child-centered, intensive, community-based, and family-focused services and interventions. Moreover, the cost of delivering these prevention services would be far less than that of providing services to these same individuals as teens, young adults, and adults. Society seems unwilling to make investments that would yield remarkable financial, social, and emotional dividends for us, our children, and our communities (Umansky & Hooper, 1998). Key elements of the prevention process include early identification, family-driven needs assessment, home-based and community-based interventions, and collaboration with an array of educational and community agencies (Fox et al., 2002; Serna, Nielsen, Lambros, & Forness, 2000).

Interventions for young children with E/BD are child-, family-, and home-centered. Often they are directed at reducing the effects of the E/BD or even preventing them (Bavolek, 2000; Simpson et al., 2001; Webster-Stratton & Reid, 2002). Thus the goals associated with individualized family service plans (IFSPs) go well beyond the typical educational goals found in individualized education programs (IEPs) for older children. Interventions for young children with E/BD include building positive replacement behaviors for challenging behaviors, promoting appropriate social interactions with peers and others, and creating positive behavioral support across a child's natural environments. Family-centered interventions focus on such things as respite care; parent training directed at managing the young child with E/BD at home and in other community settings; the delivery of family, marital, or drug therapy; and the provision of specialized day care or day treatment (Eddy et al., 2000; Simpson et al., 2001). The nature, intensity, and duration of these services and interventions are determined by the needs of the families and the speed with which they develop new skills and coping strategies. The interventions are delivered in multiple contexts—the places

# PARENTS OF MENTALLY ILL CHILDREN TRADE CUSTODY FOR CARE

F or the parents of some severely mentally ill children, it can come to this: pleading with emergency room psychiatrists who have no good answers. Listening grimly as caseworkers explain their lack of options. Appearing tearfully before family court judges as they take what they regard as a last desperate step in pursuit of medical care.

What these mothers and fathers are being urged to do is agonizing: give up custody of their children and turn them over to New York State's child welfare agencies so that they can get the mental health care that the family cannot otherwise afford or gain access to.

Repeatedly, these parents say, they are told that giving up their children is the only way to get help. Private insurance does not pay for children who may need a year or more of intense treatment, at costs that can exceed $60,000 a year. For the many who cannot afford that, the number of state-financed beds for mental health patients is small and the wait long.

But a child placed in foster care can be sent to facilities that, though not designed to deal with mentally ill children, have many more openings and at least some psychiatric services.

"That was the hardest decision I ever had to make," said Donna O'Clair, who, with her husband Tom, allowed Schenectady County to take custody of their suicidal 11-year-old son when he needed more care than their health insurance would cover.

The state's Office of Children and Family Services, which oversees New York's child welfare agencies, does not keep a record of how many children are turned over to it in need of mental health care. And the state says it discourages the practice by offering alternatives.

But judges, lawyers, social workers, and parents from Brooklyn to Buffalo say it happens regularly.

In New York City, for example, officials at the Administration for Children's Services say about half their intensive-care beds are filled not by abused or neglected youngsters but, rather, by those placed there directly by their parents or through a court program for troubled youths that parents enter voluntarily.

"There are all sorts of [ways in which] folks try . . . to get into the foster care system because they have not been able to get into the mental health system," said Raymond Schimmer, the executive director of the Parsons Child and Family Center in Albany, which runs mental health and foster care facilities. "In extreme cases, you have parents who claim that they've abused or neglected their children."

For parents who resort to giving up a child, eight of whom were interviewed for this article, the experience is fraught with uncertainties. They have the right to ask for their child back but must win the approval of a judge. They receive legal notices warning that after 15 months in custody, their child could be put up for adoption. They have no control over where their child is sent or, in some cases, over what treatments the child receives. Some parents have, for periods, lost track of their children entirely.

"Do you make children with cancer have their parents give up custody so they get the care they need?" asked Tracy Zeltwanger, a county worker in Watertown, New York, who was prodded to relinquish her 9-year-old son, Corey, who doctors say has early-onset bipolar disorder. Ms. Zeltwanger ultimately refused.

New York parents are not alone. At a time when health care costs are soaring and the number of children with complicated disorders is increasing, the quandary of custody versus care is arising throughout the country. Thirteen states have passed laws to prohibit the practice of exchanging custody for care, according to the Bazelon Center for Mental Health Law in Washington.

Such a law might help in New York if mental health resources were not so scarce, said James Dillon, a family court judge in Erie County. "But there are a limited number of beds," he said.

For children who need extensive care, New York offers two basic options. There is the one that was explicitly intended for such children: the state mental health system, which has about 540 residential treatment beds. And there is the one that was not intended for them: the foster care system, which has about 4,000 beds but only limited ability to handle mentally ill children.

where children, family members, and others play, work, learn, and grow (Greenburg et al., 2001).

Often the interventions for young children with E/BD are directed at beginning communication skills; appropriate social interaction with siblings, parents, and peers; beginning social skills; and responding effectively to developmentally appropriate tasks. Also, in keeping with the movement toward inclusion, family intervention and transition specialists will need to pay greater attention to preparing young children for successful participation in less restrictive environments (Kennedy, Long, Jolivette, Cox, Tang, & Thompson, 2001).

## The Elementary School Years

Elementary children with E/BD often present overlapping behavioral problems. Think about Eric and Nick, from the chapter-opening Snapshot. Each child presented behavioral problems related to accepting consequences, interacting successfully with

New York has tried to come up with alternatives that would allow more children to stay at home. The state participates in a Medicaid program that pays for services such as in-home counseling for children who are at risk of being hospitalized, even if they are not eligible for Medicaid. Still, there are only 610 spots, so for parents who say they have tried everything else, giving up custody can seem like the only option.

Some parents, despite the pain of separation, are happy with the services they receive. Other families confront a host of difficulties. They enter a world that is unaccustomed—and, some insist, hostile—to parents who take an acute interest in their children's care. But the biggest frustration, parents say, is that giving up custody does not guarantee that their children will be kept safe or will receive adequate attention.

The money available for providing mental health treatment in foster care is actually very limited. Frequently, said Harriet Mauer, the director of social work for Good Shepherd Services, a foster care provider in New York City, foster care facilities must turn to the same overburdened community mental health clinics that parents do. A determining factor in treatment is often simply the availability of an open bed.

"They push the parents to give up the kids, and I don't understand why, when they don't offer the care that [the kids] need," said Kathryn Strodel, a lawyer at Legal Services of Central New York, in Syracuse, who has represented parents who have relinquished custody.

## POINT

Universal health care should be available to all children. The laws of supply and demand do not provide well for the common good of families who cannot access or pay for needed health care. Children, youth, and families experiencing profound needs for mental health care should not be excluded because they cannot pay, nor should parents or families be encouraged to give the government custody of their children so that the children may receive critical psychiatric or medical care. Access to health care should be considered a basic human right, not a privilege.

## COUNTERPOINT

Government programs are rarely well managed or cost-effective. A universal health system for all children would become nothing more than bloated bureaucracy that would eventually collapse of its own weight. Competition is absolutely essential to the well-being of any health care system. Without competition, the quality, availability, and cost of health care would be severely compromised. Also, billions of dollars that would otherwise go to cost-effective private health providers would be wasted in a universal health care system administered by government bureaucrats.

What do you think? To give your opinion, go to Chapter 9 of the companion website at **www.ablongman.com/hardman8e** and click on Debate Forum.

SOURCE: Adapted from "Parents of Mentally Ill Children Trade Custody for Care," by Shaila K. Dewan, *New York Times*, February 16, 2003. Copyright 2002 The New York Times Company.

others, controlling themselves in various school and family situations, and expressing strong feelings. Such behaviors become the focus of intervention efforts. With the assistance of parents, IEP team members strive to construct a complete picture of each child, determining his or her present levels of intellectual, social, emotional, and academic performance and the contexts that give rise to and support these behaviors. These levels of performance and the outcomes derived from the functional behavioral assessment become the basis for identifying important goals for the child's IEP and for developing behavior intervention plans.

Typically, programs for children with E/BD focus on replacing maladaptive with adaptive behaviors, building appropriate academic skills and dispositions, increasing self-awareness, building self-esteem, and acquiring age-appropriate self-control. Children need these skills and behaviors to succeed in their classrooms, homes, and communities. In the past, many programs for children with E/BD were restrictive, controlling, and punitive in nature (Knitzer et al., 1990). More than on teaching new behaviors, these programs focused on controlling the behaviors of children and youth.

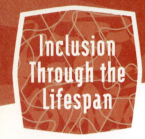

**Inclusion Through the Lifespan**

# PEOPLE WITH EMOTIONAL/ BEHAVIORAL DISORDERS

### Tips for the Family

- Become involved with parent training and other community mental health services.
- Work closely with family support personnel (e.g., social workers, nurses, and parent group volunteers) in developing effective child management strategies.
- Use the same intervention strategies at home that are used effectively in the preschool setting.
- Establish family routines, schedules, and incentive systems that reward positive behaviors.
- Join advocacy or parent support groups.

### Tips for the Preschool Teacher

- Work closely with the support personnel in your preschool (e.g., director, psychologist, social worker, parent trainers, special educators, etc.) to identify effective and realistic strategies.
- Establish clear schedules, class routines, rules, and positive consequences for all children in your classroom.
- Create a learning and social environment that is nurturing and supportive for everyone.
- Teach specific social behaviors (e.g., following directions, greeting other children, sharing toys, using words to express anger, etc.) to all children.
- Do not be reluctant to ask for help from support personnel. Remember, collaboration is the key.

### Tips for Preschool Personnel

- Use older, socially competent children to assist with readiness skills and social skills training.
- Help others (e.g., teaching assistants, aides, volunteers, etc.) know what to do in managing children with behavior disorders.
- Make every effort to involve the children in all schoolwide activities and special performances.
- Orient and teach the other preschool children about disabling conditions and how they should respond and relate to their peers with behavior problems.
- Collaborate with parents in using the same management systems in your preschool classroom that are used in the home and other specialized settings.

### Tips for Neighbors and Friends

- Become familiar with the things you should do as a neighbor or friend in responding to the positive and negative behaviors of a child with behavior disorders.
- Be patient with parents who are attempting to deal with their child's temper tantrum or other challenging behaviors at the grocery store or like environments.
- Offer parents some time away from their preschooler by watching him or her for a couple of hours.
- Involve the child in your family activities.
- Help parents become aware of advocacy or parent support groups.
- Encourage parents to involve their child in neighborhood and community events (e.g., parades, holiday celebrations, and birthday parties).

### Tips for the Family

- Use the effective management techniques that are being used in your child's classroom in your home environment.
- Help your other children (who are not disturbed) to develop an understanding of behavior disorders.
- Establish rules, routines, and consequences that fit your child's developmental age and interests.
- Take advantage of parent training and support groups that are available in your community.
- Obtain counseling when appropriate for yourself, your other children, and your spouse from a community mental health agency or other public or private source.
- Help your other children and their friends understand the things they can do to assist you in rearing your child with behavior disorders.

### Tips for General Education Classroom Teacher

- Provide a structured classroom environment (e.g., clearly stated rules, helpful positive and negative consequences, well-conceived classroom schedules, and carefully taught classroom routines).
- Teach social skills (e.g., dealing with teasing, accepting criticism, etc.) to all of the children with the aid of members of the teacher assistance team.
- Teach self-management skills (e.g., goal selection, self-monitoring, self-reinforcement, etc.) to all children with the aid of members of the teacher assistance team.
- Use cooperative learning strategies to promote the learning of all children and to develop positive relationships among students.
- Do not be reluctant to ask for help from members of your teacher assistance team or the child's parents.

### Tips for School Personnel

- Use same-age or cross-age peers to provide tutoring, coaching, and other kinds of assistance in developing the academic and social skills of children with behavior disorders.
- Develop a schoolwide management program that reinforces individual and group accomplishments.
- Work closely with the teacher assistance team to create a school environment that is positive and caring.
- Use collaborative problem-solving techniques in dealing with difficult or persistent behavior problems.
- Help all children in the school develop an understanding of how they should respond to students with behavior problems.

### Tips for Neighbors and Friends

- Involve the child with behavior problems in appropriate after-school activities (e.g., clubs, specialized tutoring, recreational events, etc.).

- Invite the child to spend time with your family in appropriate recreational events (e.g., swimming, hiking, etc.).
- Teach other children (without behavior problems) how to ignore or support certain behaviors that may occur.
- Catch the child being good rather than looking for "bad" behaviors.
- As a youth leader, coach, or recreational specialist, get to know each child with behavior disorders well so that you can respond with confidence in directing his or her activities.

## SECONDARY AND TRANSITION YEARS

### Tips for the Family

- Continue your efforts to focus on the positive behaviors of your child with behavior disorders.
- Assist your child in selecting appropriate postsecondary training, education, and/or employment.
- Give yourself a regular break from the tedium of being a parent, and engage in a recreational activity that is totally enjoyable for you.
- Ask for help from community mental health services, clergy, or a close friend when you are feeling overwhelmed or stressed.
- Consult regularly with treatment personnel to monitor progress and to obtain ideas for maintaining the behavioral gains made by your child.
- Continue your involvement in advocacy and parent support groups.

### Tips for General Education Classroom Teacher

- Create positive relationships within your classroom with cooperative learning teams and group-oriented assignments.
- Use all students in creating standards for conduct as well as consequences for positive and negative behaviors.
- Focus your efforts on developing a positive relationship with the student with behavior disorders by greeting him or her regularly to your class, informally talking with him or her at appropriate times, attending to improvements in his or her performance, and becoming aware of his or her interests.
- Work closely with the members of the teacher assistance team to be aware of teacher behaviors that may adversely or positively affect the student's performance.
- Realize that changes in behavior often occur very gradually, with periods of regression and sometimes tumult.

### Tips for School Personnel

- Create a school climate that is positive and supportive.
- Provide students with an understanding of their roles and responsibilities in responding to peers who are disabled.
- Use peers in providing social skills training, job coaching, and academic tutoring.
- Use members of the teacher assistance team to help you deal with crisis situations and to provide other supportive therapies and interventions.
- Be sure schoolwide procedures are in place for dealing quickly and efficiently with particularly difficult behaviors.

### Tips for Neighbors, Friends, and Potential Employers

- If you have some expertise in a content area (e.g., math, English, history, etc.), offer to provide regular assistance with homework or other, related school assignments for students with behavior disorders.

- Provide opportunities for students with behavior disorders to be employed in your business.
- Give parents an occasional reprieve by inviting the youth to join your family for a cook-out, video night, or other family-oriented activities.
- Encourage other children (who are not disordered) to volunteer as peer partners, job coaches, and social skills trainers.
- Do not allow others to tease, harass, or ridicule a youth with behavior disorders in your presence.

## ADULT YEARS

### Tips for the Family

- Continue to build on efforts to develop appropriate independence and interdependence.
- Maintain contact with appropriate medical personnel, particularly if the individual is on some form of medication for his or her condition.
- Make use of appropriate adult service agencies that are required by law to assist with your child's employment, housing, and recreation.
- Prepare your other children or other caregivers as appropriate to assume the responsibilities that you may be unable to assume over time.

### Tips for Neighbors, Friends, and Employers

- Be willing to make sensible and reasonable adjustments in the work environments.
- Be aware of adjustments that may need to take place with new medications or treatment regimens.
- Get to know the individual as a person—his or her likes, heroes or heroines, and leisure activities.
- Be willing to involve the individual in appropriate holiday and special-occasion events such as birthdays, athletic activities, and other social gatherings.
- Be aware of what might be irritating or uncomfortable to the individual.
- Make yourself available to communicate with others who may be responsible for the individual's well-being—a job coach, an independent living specialist, and others.

These programs employed the **curriculum of control** (Knitzer et al., 1990) or the *curriculum of noninstruction* (Shores & Wehby, 1999, p. 196). Rather than developing replacement behaviors or new behaviors, children and youth in many of these programs languished or regressed (Knitzer, 1982; Knitzer et al., 1990).

New systems of care for children and youth with E/BD have emerged (Koyanagi & Feres-Merchant, 2000; Worthington et al., 2001; Eber et al., 2002). These systems deliver wraparound services to children and youth with E/BD and their families (see Reflect on This, "Seth: Part One"). As is implied by the word *wraparound*, children, youth, and their families receive the support that they need to address the problems in the family, home, and school that give rise to the E/BD. Services may include in-home child management training, employment assistance, and family therapy—whatever is needed to help families become successful. The essential features of these systems and related programs are as follows:

- The use of clinicians or other providers of student support in the schools. These professionals work with students, their families, and all members of the school community, including teachers and administrators.

- The use of school-based and school-focused wraparound services to support learning and transition.

- The use of school-based case management. Case managers help determine needs; they help identify goals, resources, and activities; they link children and families to other services; they monitor services to ensure that these are delivered appropriately; and they advocate for change when necessary.

- The provision of schoolwide prevention and early intervention programs. Prevention helps those students with or at risk of developing emotional and behavior problems to learn the skills and behaviors that help them to follow school rules and to enjoy positive academic and social outcomes. Early intervention enables schools to provide students with the support and training they need to be more successful in managing their behavior.

- The creation of "centers" within the school. These centers provide support to children and youth with emotional and behavior needs and to their families. Students in the centers interact with caring staff members who can help students and their families connect with the entire system of care.

- The use of family liaisons or advocates. These people strengthen the role and empowerment of family members in their children's education and care. All

**Curriculum of control**

Classroom routine, structures, and instructional strategies focused on controlling children and youth rather than on teaching them new, success-related social and academic behaviors.

## Reflect on This

## SETH: PART ONE

Connie Thomas is a single mother of three children: Sarah, Molly, and Seth, who are now ages 16, 14, and 13. Connie is incredibly open. She is willing to share the most painful details of her life in a way that communicates both genuine acceptance of her family situation and the fatigue of struggle. All of her children have had challenges related to emotional or behavioral problems at one point or another. Connie is quick to note that she herself is a recovering alcoholic and addict. She has been sober for over 20 years now, but until 9 years ago, she was married to a man who abused alcohol and drugs.

When Seth was 7, the Wraparound process began for the Thomas family. Not only was he at imminent risk of removal from his home because of his behavior, but he was also having serious problems in school. Susan, who had been connected to the family as Seth's social worker since he was 4, recalled the school referral that in part began Seth's Wraparound plan of care. "[The principal] called up and said, 'Do something or get this kid out of my school.'" It is at the point when a child has needs across multiple service systems that Stark County's Creative Community Options process kicks in.

SOURCE: Adapted from Kendziora, Bruns, Osher, Pacchiano, & Mejia (2001) *Systems of Care: Promising Practices in Children's Mental Health*, 2001 series, vol. I. Washington, DC: Center for Effective Collaboration and Practice, American Institutes for Research.

three sites studied have harnessed the power that involving family members as equal partners brings to their comprehensive programs (Center for Effective Collaboration and Practice, 1999, pp. 6–7).

At the heart of many new programs is positive behavioral support (PBS) (Bullock & Gable, 2000; Cosmos, 2002). Instead of trying to eliminate or control behaviors, teachers, parents, and clinicians seek to understand the purposes behind children's behaviors. As highlighted in the assessment section of this chapter, professionals use functional behavioral assessment to determine the patterns and functions of certain behaviors. Once these patterns and functions are well understood, teachers and others help children develop positive approaches to achieving their goals and how to deal with their thoughts and feelings in positive ways.

Children who exhibit moderate to severe E/BD may be served in special classes (see Reflect on This, "Seth: Part Two"). In some school systems, special classes are found in elementary schools. They may be grouped in small clusters of two to three classes in selected buildings. Other special classes may be found within hospital units, special schools, residential programs, and specialized treatment facilities.

Most special classes for children with moderate to severe disorders share certain characteristics. The first is a high degree of structure and specialized instruction; in other words, rules are clear and consistently enforced; helpful routines are in place; focused academic and social instruction are provided; and both adult–child relationships and child–child relationships are fostered and developed (Kauffman, Bantz, & McCullough, 2002). Other features include teacher monitoring of student performance, frequent feedback, and reinforcement based on students' academic and social behaviors. Students learn how to express themselves, how to address individual and group problems, and how to deal with very strong feelings and emotions (Kauffman et al., 2002). Often point systems or token economies are used, although some concerns have been raised about them. These systems provide students with a specific number of points or tokens when they maintain certain behaviors or achieve certain goals. The points can be exchanged for various rewards, such as food treats; school supplies, such as pencils, notebooks, and erasers; or activities that students enjoy. Furthermore, all members of special classes are well informed about behavioral expectations (see Figure 9.2).

In addition to behaviorally oriented interventions, students may also receive individual counseling or group and family therapy (Erickson, 1998; Wicks-Nelson &

**Reflect on This**

## SETH: PART TWO

One thing that Connie needed was help at home with Seth. This help was provided in part through an intensive home-based program. Rick was a supervisor and therapist in this program. . . . Rick recalled his early experiences with the Thomas family.

[Seth] was just running crazy around the house—that's the best way to describe it. It was all we could do to try to get him to sit down and participate in some very structured exercises. . . . He was [also] doing some more gross stuff with his sisters, and Sarah and Molly were just not liking it too much—and I don't blame them. So we were going out and trying to do some stabilization in the home.

Since entering middle school, Seth has been placed in a self-contained classroom for children with severe behavioral problems, with five or six students, a teacher, and an aide. Last school year, Seth was not able to stay in this classroom and wound up receiving one-on-one tutoring for half days. . . . After leaving school at about 11:30, Seth would go to his pastor's home, where the pastor's children were home-schooled. Seth would study with them for the remainder of the school day. This combination of formal and informal supports worked well for the Thomas family, and Seth was able to finish out the school year fairly successfully.

SOURCE: Adapted from Kendziora, Bruns, Osher, Pacchiano, & Mejia (2001) *Systems of Care: Promising Practices in Children's Mental Health*, 2001 series, vol. I. Washington, DC: Center for Effective Collaboration and Practice, American Institutes for Research.

FIGURE 9.2

**Point Card for IEP goals**

**Name:** _Mike_      **Date:** _26 November_

1. My IEP goal today is: *Raising my hand to get teacher help, to answer questions, or to participate in class discussions.*

| Goal "Positives" | Goal "Negative" | | Percent "Positives" |
|---|---|---|---|
| T̶H̶L̶ /// | // | | *8/10 = 80%* |

Points Earned on IEP Goal Today ___8___

2. Returned Daily Home Note:   Yes ___✔___ No _____     Points Earned on Daily Home Note ___10___

3. Bus Report:   Poor ___✔___ Good _____ Excellent _____     Points Earned on Bus Report ___3___

| *Positive Classroom Behaviors* | *Appropriate Location* | *On Task, Listened, Worked Consistently, Etc.* | *Appropriate Langauge* | *Respectful of Others and Their Things* | *Appropriate Social Skills* |
|---|---|---|---|---|---|
| **Time** | | | | | |
| 8:30 to 9:00 | *2* | *0* | *2* | *2* | *0* |
| 9:00 to 10:00 | *2* | *2* | *2* | *2* | *2* |
| 11:00 to 12:00 | *2* | *0* | *2* | *2* | *0* |
| 12:00 to 1:00 | *2* | *2* | *2* | *2* | *0* |
| 1:00 to 2:00 | *2* | *0* | *2* | *2* | *0* |
| 2:00 to 3:00 | *2* | *2* | *2* | *2* | *0* |
| 3:00 to 3:30 | *2* | *2* | *2* | *2* | *0* |
| Points Earned | *14* | *8* | *14* | *14* | *2* |

| Total Positive Classroom Points Earned Today | *52* |
|---|---|
| Total Points Earned Today | *73* |
| Total Points Spent Today | *–10* |
| Total Points Banked Today | *63* |

Israel, 2003). Many children with E/BD may take some form of medication (Brown & Sawyer, 1998; Wicks-Nelson & Israel, 2003). These medications may help students who struggle with depression, hyperactivity, impaired attention, and related conditions. These medications may be prescribed by a psychiatrist, pediatrician, or primary-care physician.

## The Adolescent Years

Individually and collectively, adolescents with E/BD pose significant challenges for parents, teachers, and other care providers. These problems include violent exchanges with parents and others, bullying, fighting, withdrawal, substance abuse, and other difficult behaviors. In the past, interventions and programs for adolescents with E/BD, like those created for elementary children, were often punitive, controlling, and negative. As indicated in the previous section, the curriculum of control or of noninstruction predominated (Knitzer et al., 1990; Shores & Wehby, 1999).

Fortunately, perspectives are changing. Professionals in education, medicine, social work, and mental health are developing systems of care. These systems of care are characterized by family-friendly collaboration (Kendziora et al., 2001; Woodruff et al., 1999). Ideally, the care is community-based, family-driven, individualized, based on strengths rather than weaknesses, sensitive to diversity, and team-based. In these systems, the knowledge and views of parents and family members are taken very seriously. These key people help design, shape, and assess intervention programs. If a family needs parent training, family therapy, and employment assistance, the agencies and school work together to provide these services. If the youth needs services beyond those typically delivered in a school, they are provided.

Another approach that is beginning to gather momentum is **individualized care** (IC) (Burchard & Clarke, 1990). IC is linked to the **wraparound approach** (WRAP) (Kendziora et al., 2001). WRAP focuses on improving the outcomes for children and adolescents with E/BD through coordinated, flexible approaches to integrated, family-centered care. Rather than being provided to students only in school settings or at a mental health agency, services are delivered to children and adolescents, their parents, and families where they are needed—frequently in their homes. The case study of Seth provides powerful examples of IC and WRAP in action (see Reflect on This, "Seth: Part Three").

## Gang Membership

As indicated earlier in this chapter, 42% of youth in correctional facilities are young people with identified E/BD (Burrell & Warboys, 2000). Adolescents who are chronically delinquent or are found guilty of felony offenses (e.g., physical assault, armed robbery) present considerable challenges for school and clinical personnel. Addi-

**Individualized care (IC)**

Improving the outcomes for children and adolescents with E/BD through coordinated, flexible approaches to integrated, family-centered care. Services are delivered to children and adolescents, their parents, and families where needed, frequently in their homes.

**Wraparound approach (WRAP)**

Care that provides comprehensive services to youth and their families, addressing individual and family needs through flexible approaches coordinated and orchestrated by a team of caring professionals and paraprofessionals.

## SETH: PART THREE

In the Thomas family's case, there is little question that the Wraparound process helped them "make it work." The element that made the most difference was that their Wraparound plan of care was truly family-driven. Connie said,

> Up until five years ago, when all of [the family advocacy] started taking place, we were in pretty sad shape, but the grant and that whole mindset of letting parents drive their program, and letting them be in the driver's seat, and you just stick in the services—that helped. Ever since then, things have been much easier, much easier. I don't feel like I'm clawing and fighting anymore. Or trying to prove that I haven't done anything wrong that's caused my kid to be this way.

The Wraparound process has helped the Thomas family meet their major life goals—to stay together at home, to keep the children at school, and to get along better with one another. Connie emphasized the progress that Seth has made.

> He has grown from someone I really thought would be institutionalized into—"he's not half bad, is he?" He's not half bad. I think with more work and I'm not sure how much emotionally he'll grow, but each year, I see a little bit more maturity.

SOURCE: Adapted from Kendziora, Bruns, Osher, Pacchiano, & Mejia (2001) *Systems of Care: Promising Practices in Children's Mental Health,* 2001 series, vol. I. Washington, DC: Center for Effective Collaboration and Practice, American Institutes for Research.

---

tionally, the proliferation of gangs in many communities poses serious problems for schools, teachers, community members, and gang members themselves (Esbensen, 2000; Howell & Lynch, 2000). As natural gathering places for gang members, schools provide many opportunities to generate income through extortion, drug sales, and other illegal activities (Howell & Lynch, 2000). With a lack of role models and the widespread decline of family structure and support, young people seek power, friendship, fame, and reputation among their peers through gang membership. Gangs provide these young people with a sense of family, personal identity, and affiliation. All too often, violence and death become everyday realities for gang members, their families, and other innocent bystanders (see Table 9.7).

Programs directed at preventing and treating gang violence are emerging. Generally, these programs center on group support systems, adult mentoring, specific competence training, and the development of healthy relationships with caring adults and other authority figures (Novotney, Mertinko, Lange, & Baker, 2000). Young people are specifically taught how to deal with substance abuse, challenging interpersonal relationships, depression, and situations that may produce uncontrolled anger and violence. They also learn how to assess provocations that lead to aggression, how to analyze and change their self-statements (what they actually say to themselves) in response to these provocations, and how to deal with provocations in healthy and appropriate ways (Wilde, 2002). For youth who have been incarcerated, immediate school placements, appropriate work opportunities, and other targeted transition services greatly reduce their reentry into youth correction facilities or other more restrictive settings (Bullis, 2001; Bullis, Yovanoff, Mueller, & Havel, 2002).

### Inclusive Education

Few issues in recent years have received as much attention in the professional research as inclusion, particularly the **full inclusion** of students with E/BD (Braaten, Kauffman, Braaten, Polsgrove & Nelson, 1988; Bullock & Gable, 1994; Fuchs & Fuchs, 1994; Kauffman & Lloyd, 1995; Lewis, Chard, & Scott, 1994; MacMillan, Gresham, & Forness, 1996). The term *full inclusion* is generally defined as the delivery of appropriate, specialized services to children or adolescents with E/BD or other disabilities in general education settings (Kauffman et al., 2002; Stainback, 2000). These services

**Full inclusion**

The delivery of appropriate, specialized services to children or adolescents with E/BD or other disabilities in general education settings. These services are usually directed at improving students' social skills, developing satisfactory relationships with peers and teachers, building targeted academic skills, and improving the attitudes of peers without disabilities.

are usually directed at improving students' social skills, helping them develop satisfactory relationships with peers and teachers, building targeted academic skills, and improving the attitudes of peers without disabilities (Cheney & Barringer, 1999; Snell, 1990; Stainback & Stainback, 1990; Winzer & Mazurek, 2000).

Another aspect of the full-inclusion movement is that some professionals have recommended elimination of the present delivery systems and variety of placement options (Kauffman et al., 2002; Kavale & Forness, 2000; Stainback & Stainback, 1992). They would be replaced by a model in which all students, regardless of disabling condition, would be educated in their neighborhood schools. These schools would serve all students with disabilities, including those with E/BD; thus special schools, special classes, and other placements associated with the typical continuum of placements would no longer be available. Because of this movement and other factors, many

**FOCUS 9**

What five factors should be considered when placing a child or youth with E/BD in general education settings and related classes?

## TABLE 9.7

### Risk Factors for Youth Gang Membership

| DOMAIN | RISK FACTORS | |
| --- | --- | --- |
| Community | • Social disorganization, including poverty and residential mobility<br>• Underclass communities<br>• Presence of gangs in the neighborhood<br>• Availability of drugs in the neighborhood<br>• Availability of firearms | • Barriers to and lack of social and economic opportunities<br>• Lack of social capital<br>• Cultural norms supporting gang behavior<br>• Feeling unsafe in neighborhood; high crime<br>• Conflict with social control institutions |
| Family | • Family disorganization, including broken homes and parental drug/alcohol abuse<br>• Troubled families, including incest, family violence, and drug addiction<br>• Family members in a gang<br>• Lack of adult male role models | • Lack of parental role models<br>• Low socioeconomic status<br>• Extreme economic deprivation, family management problems, parents with violent attitudes, sibling antisocial behavior |
| School | • Academic failure<br>• Low educational aspirations, especially among females<br>• Negative labeling by teachers<br>• Trouble at school<br>• Few teacher role models | • Educational frustration<br>• Low commitment to school, low school attachment, high levels of antisocial behavior in school, low achievement test scores, and identification as being learning disabled |
| Peer Group | • High commitment to delinquent peers<br>• Low commitment to positive peers<br>• Street socialization<br>• Gang members in class | • Friends who use drugs or who are gang members<br>• Friends who are drug distributors<br>• Interaction with delinquent peers |
| Individual | • Prior delinquency<br>• Deviant attitudes<br>• Street smartness; toughness<br>• Defiant and individualistic character<br>• Fatalistic view of the world<br>• Aggression<br>• Proclivity for excitement and trouble<br>• *Locura* (acting in a daring, courageous, and especially crazy fashion in the face of adversity)<br>• Higher levels of normlessness in the context of family, peer group, and school<br>• Social disabilities | • Illegal gun ownership<br>• Early or precocious sexual activity, especially among females<br>• Alcohol and drug use<br>• Drug trafficking<br>• Desire for group rewards such as status, identity, self-esteem, companionship, and protection<br>• Problem behaviors, hyperactivity, externalizing behaviors, drinking, lack of refusal skills, and early sexual activity<br>• Victimization |

SOURCE: Adapted from "Youth Gangs: An Overview," by J. C. Howell, 1998, *Juvenile Justice Bulletin*, August, pp. 1–19.

services that were once available for students with E/BD have been curtailed or eliminated (Webber & Scheuermann, 1997).

Critics of this movement have expressed strong concerns about its short- and long-term impact on children and adolescents with E/BD and their families. They argue that little research supports elimination of the current placement and service delivery continuum (MacMillan et al., 1996; Sachs & Cheney, 2000). They believe that the current continuum provides a range of options and specialized services in keeping with the unique needs of many students with E/BD and their families. And they believe that many general education teachers and related personnel are not adequately prepared to respond to the needs of children and adolescents with E/BD (Sachs & Cheney, 2000; Winzer, 2000).

Court decisions and the 1997 amendments to the Individuals with Disabilities Act (IDEA) are informative on the topic of full inclusion (Yell, 1998). "The courts have indicated that there are two primary grounds for removing a student from the general education classroom: if the child does not benefit educationally (considering both academic and nonacademic benefits), and if the student disrupts the learning environment or adversely affects the education of other students" (Yell, 1995, p. 188). If a student under consideration for inclusion poses no significant management problems for the teacher, does not interfere with the safety or learning of other classmates, and can benefit from a curriculum parallel or similar to that provided for other students in general classroom settings, he or she will be placed in the general education classroom (Yell, 1998).

Especially relevant to students with E/BD is the fact that IDEA 2004 authorized school personnel to make a change in placement to an appropriate interim alternative educational setting, another setting, or suspension, for no more than 10 school days if the student violates the school's code of conduct. During these 10 days the school must determine if the behavior had a direct relationship to the student's disability. The school must also conduct a functional behavior assessment, if it has not already done so, and must implement a behavioral intervention plan through the IEP process. Any alternative setting for a student must be determined by the IEP team. Furthermore, a hearing officer may order a change in placement to an appropriate interim alternative educational setting for no more than 45 school days, if the hearing officer determines that the current placement is substantially likely to result in injury to the child or others. In making this decision, the hearing officer must consider whether the school has made reasonable efforts to minimize risks of harm in the current placement and whether the interim placement meets the student's needs as described in the IEP.

Despite the emphasis on inclusion, most students with E/BD are served in settings separated from general education classrooms (Knitzer et al., 1990; Stephens & Lakin, 1995; U.S. Department of Education, 2002). In fact, students with E/BD are far more likely to be served in special schools and separate facilities than any other group of students with disabilities. Note also that a fifth of all students served in special day schools and half of all students served in residential facilities are children and youth with E/BD (Koyangi & Gaines, 1993; Stephens & Lakin, 1995).

Inclusion of students with E/BD in general education settings should be determined ultimately by what the child or adolescent with E/BD genuinely needs (Kauffman et al., 2002; Kauffman & Smucker, 1995; Keenan, 1997). These needs are established through the thoughtful deliberations of parents, professionals, and, as appropriate, the child or adolescent, via the IEP process. This process creates the basis for determining the services and supports required to address the child's or adolescent's needs, both present and anticipated. If the identified services and supports can be delivered with appropriate intensity in the general education environment without adversely affecting the learning and safety of other students, placement in this environment should occur. However, if the needs of the student cannot be successfully met in the general education setting, other placement alternatives should be explored and selected (Kauffman et al., 2002). Recent studies suggest that the inclusion of students with E/BD is greatly enhanced when school personnel develop schoolwide structures that support inclusion, when collaborative teaching is fostered, and when general education personnel receive targeted training, timely consultation, and appropriate in-class assistance (Gibb, Allred, Ingram, Young, & Egan 1999; Praisner, 2003; Shapiro, Miller, Sawka, Gardill, & Handler 1999).

# Promising Practices

The National Information Center for Children and Youth with Disabilities (NICHCY) has developed a list of promising practices for chronic behavior problems in children and youth. As you review this list, think about Eric, Nick, and Amy, whom you met at the beginning of this chapter, as well as your own experiences with children and youth with E/BD. Think about how these practices would benefit children and youth with E/BD and their families.

**FOCUS 10**

What are several promising practices for dealing with challenging behavior in children and youth?

1. Assessment of the student's behavior must be linked with interventions that follow the student through whatever placements the student has.

2. Multiple interventions are necessary for improving the behavior of most students. Any positive effect of a single strategy, especially when the intervention is short-term, is likely to be temporary. Just as behavior problems and risk factors come in packages, so too should interventions.

3. To produce lasting effects, interventions must address not only the behavior that led to disciplinary action, but a constellation of related behaviors and contributing factors.

4. Interventions must be sustained and [must] include specific plans for promoting maintenance over time and generalization across settings. Focusing on the student's behavior while [the student is] placed in any short-term setting, such as an interim alternative educational setting, is not sufficient. Interventions need to follow the student to his or her next placement (and elsewhere).

5. A combination of proactive, corrective, and instructive classroom management strategies is needed. Interventions must target specific prosocial and antisocial behaviors and the "thinking skills" that mediate such behaviors. Such a combination provides an atmosphere of warmth, care, support, and necessary structure.

6. Interventions must be developmentally appropriate and [must] address strengths and weaknesses of the individual student and his or her environment.

7. Parent education and family therapy are critical components of effective programs for antisocial children and youth.

8. Interventions are most effective when provided early in life. Devoting resources to prevention reduces the later need for more expensive treatment.

9. Interventions should be guided by schoolwide and districtwide policies that emphasize positive interventions over punitive ones.

10. Interventions should be fair, consistent, culturally and racially nondiscriminatory, and sensitive to cultural diversity.

11. Interventions should be evaluated as to their short-term and long-term effectiveness in improving student behavior. Both the process and the outcome of each intervention should be evaluated.

12. Teachers and support staff need to be well trained with respect to assessment and intervention. Staff working with students who have behavior problems will require ongoing staff development and support services.

13. Effective behavioral interventions require collaborative efforts from the school, home, and community agencies. Helping children and youth must be a shared responsibility (NICHCY 1999, p. 5).

When these practices are consistently and effectively applied, children and youth with E/BD have a greater chance of realizing their full potential, living and succeeding with their families, and making meaningful contributions to their neighborhoods and communities.

# FOCUS REVIEW

**FOCUS 1**  Identify six essential parts of the definitions of emotional/behavioral disorders.

- The behaviors in question must be exhibited to a marked extent.
- Learning problems that are not attributable to intellectual, sensory, or health deficits are common.
- Satisfactory relationships with parents, teachers, siblings, and others are few.
- Behaviors that occur in many settings and under normal circumstances are considered inappropriate.
- Pervasive unhappiness or depression is frequently displayed by children with E/BD.
- Physical symptoms or fears associated with the demands of school are common in some children.

**FOCUS 2**  Identify five factors that influence the ways in which we perceive the behaviors of others.

- Our personal beliefs, standards, and values
- Our tolerance for certain behaviors and our emotional fitness at the time the behaviors are exhibited
- Our perceptions of normalcy, which are often based on personal perspective rather than on an objective standard of nor-

malcy as established by consensus or research
- The context in which a behavior takes place
- The frequency with which the behavior occurs or its intensity

**FOCUS 3**  Cite three reasons why classification systems are important to professionals who identify, treat, and educate individuals with E/BD.

- They provide a means of describing and identifying various types of E/BD.
- They provide a common language for communicating about various types and subtypes of E/BD.
- They sometimes provide a basis for treating a disorder and making predictions about treatment outcomes.

**FOCUS 4**  What differentiates externalizing disorders from internalizing disorders?

- Externalizing disorders involve behaviors that are directed at others (e.g., fighting, assaulting, stealing, vandalizing).
- Internalizing disorders involve behaviors that are directed inwardly, or at oneself, more than at others (e.g., fears, phobias, depression).

**FOCUS 5**  Identify five general characteristics (intellectual, adaptive, social, and achieve-

ment) of children and youth with E/BD.

- Children and youth with E/BD tend to have average to below-average IQs compared to their normal peers.
- Children and youth with E/BD have difficulties in relating socially and responsibly to peers, parents, teachers, and other authority figures.
- Three out of four children with E/BD show clinically significant language deficits.
- More than 40% of the youth with disabilities in correctional facilities are youngsters with identified E/BD.
- Compared to other students with disabilities, students with E/BD are absent more often, fail more classes, are retained more frequently, and are less successful in passing minimum competency examinations.

**FOCUS 6**  What can accurately be said about the causes of E/BD?

- Continuously interacting biological, genetic, cognitive, social, emotional, and cultural variables contribute to E/BD.

**FOCUS 7**  What four important outcomes are achieved through a functional behavioral assessment?

- A complete description of all of the problem behaviors, including their intensity, their length, their frequency, and their impact

- A description of the events that seem to set off the problem behaviors
- One or more predictions regarding when and under what conditions the problem behaviors occur
- Identification of the "purposes" or consequences that the individual achieves by exhibiting the problem behaviors

**FOCUS 8** What five guiding principles are associated with systems of care?

- Children with emotional disturbances have access to services that address physical, emotional, social, and educational needs.
- Children receive individualized services based on unique needs and potentials which are guided by an individualized service plan.
- Children receive services within the least restrictive environment that is appropriate.
- Families are full participants in all aspects of the planning and delivery of services.
- Children receive integrated services with connections between child-serving agencies and programs and mechanisms for planning, developing, and coordinating services.

**FOCUS 9** What five factors should be considered when

placing a child or youth with E/BD in general education settings and related classes?

- Will the child or youth be able to achieve his or her IEP goals and objectives in the general education environment?
- Will the child or youth pose significant management problems for teachers and others in the general education setting?
- Will the behavior(s) of the child or youth pose significant safety problems for other students?
- Will the behavior(s) of the child or youth interfere significantly with the learning of other classmates?
- Will the child or youth benefit from the curriculum delivered in the general education setting?

**FOCUS 10** What are several promising practices for dealing with challenging behavior in children and youth?

- Behavioral assessment must be linked with interventions that follow the student through all placements.
- Multiple interventions are necessary for most students. Any positive effect of a single strategy is likely to be temporary.
- Interventions must address not only the behavior that led to disciplinary action but also a constellation of related behaviors and contributing factors.
- Interventions must promote maintenance over time and

generalization across settings.
- Combined proactive, corrective, and instructive classroom management strategies must target specific prosocial and antisocial behaviors and the "thinking skills" that mediate such behaviors.
- Interventions must be developmentally appropriate and must address strengths and weaknesses of the individual student and his or her environment.
- Parent education and family therapy are critical components of effective programs for children and youth who exhibit antisocial behaviors.
- Interventions are most effective when provided early in life.
- Interventions should be guided by schoolwide and districtwide policies that emphasize positive interventions over punitive ones.
- Interventions should be fair, consistent, culturally and racially nondiscriminatory, and sensitive to cultural diversity.
- Interventions should be evaluated in terms of their short-term and long-term effectiveness.
- Teachers and support staff need to be well trained with respect to assessment and intervention
- The school, home, and community agencies must collaborate to help children and youth.

## FURTHER READINGS

Algozzine, B., & Kay, P. (2002). *Preventing Problem Behaviors.* Thousand Oaks, CA: Corwin Press.

*This book highlights practical tools and interventions that teachers may use in preventing and responding to behavior problems. It also presents proven procedures for establishing positive learning environments.*

Newcomer, P. L. (2003). *Understanding and Teaching Emotionally Disturbed Children and Youth.* Austin, TX: ProEd.

*This book is designed for both special and general educators, as well as for other professional care providers. It offers much information about interventions and about various therapies for children and youth with E/BD.*

Rosenberg, M. S., Wilson, R., Maheady, L., & Sindelar, P. T. (2004). *Educating Students with Behavior Disorders.* Boston, MA: Allyn and Bacon.

This book presents the latest information about best practices for working with children and youth with E/BD. It focuses on definition, assessment, and managing various kinds of challenging behaviors.

Stewart, J. (2002). *Beyond Time Out.* Gorham, ME: Hasting Clinical Associates.

This is a very readable book about understanding and managing aggressive children and youth. The author identifies useful interventions for relating to children and youth with E/BD and responding to their challenging behaviors.

Wicks-Nelson, R., & Israel, A. C. (2003). Behavior disorders of childhood (5th ed.). Upper Saddle River, NJ: Prentice-Hall.

This book presents a comprehensive, in-depth view of behavior disorders in children and youth. It is replete with research findings, interesting case studies, and illustrative materials that are engaging and informative.

## WEB RESOURCES

### Council for Children with Behavior Disorders (CCBD)

www.ccbd.net

CCBD is a division of the Council for Exceptional Children. CCBD, whose members include educators, parents, mental health providers, and other professionals, vigorously pursues quality services and programs for children and youth with E/BD.

### Center for Effective Collaboration and Practice (CECP)

cecp.air.org

CECP improves services for children and youth with E/BD and helps neighborhood and communities create schools that promote emotional well-being, effective instruction, and safe learning. The center is an integral part of the American Institutes for Research and is funded by a cooperative agreement with the Office of Special Education Programs in the U.S. Department of Education.

### The Technical Assistance Center on Positive Behavioral Interventions and Supports (PBIS)

www.pbis.org/english/default.htm

PBIS was established by the Office of Special Education Programs, U.S. Department of Education, to give schools technical assistance for identifying, adapting, and sustaining effective schoolwide disciplinary programs.

### National Mental Health and Education Center for Children and Families

www.naspweb.org/center/

A public service of the National Association of School Psychologists, this network promotes promising and data-driven practices in education and mental health for children, youth, and their families, capitalizing on family strengths, supporting diversity, and sustaining families.

### The National Alliance for the Mentally Ill (NAMI)

www.nami.org

NAMI is an advocacy organization of individuals who are interested in people with severe mental illnesses, such as schizophrenia, major depression, bipolar disorder, obsessive-compulsive disorder, and anxiety disorders.

## BUILDING YOUR PORTFOLIO

If you are thinking about a career in special education, you should know that many states use national standards developed by the Council for Exceptional Children (CEC) to assess a teacher candidate's knowledge and skills for working with students with disabilities. See a complete listing of the ten CEC Content Standards on the inside front cover of this text.

## CEC Standards Addressed in Chapter 9

1. Foundations
2. Development and Characteristics of Learners
3. Individual Learning Differences
4. Instructional Strategies
5. Learning Environments and Social Interactions
7. Instructional Planning
8. Assessment
9. Professional and Ethical Practice
10. Collaboration

## Assess Your Knowledge of CEC Standards Addressed in Chapter 9

Some states require that teacher candidates develop a portfolio of products that demonstrate mastery of the CEC content standards. To assist in the development of products for this portfolio, you may wish to complete the following activities.

- Complete a written test of the chapter's content.

  *If your instructor requires a written test of your content knowledge for this chapter, keep a copy for your portfolio. A practice test on the information covered in this chapter is available through the companion website (www.ablongman.com/hardman8e) and the Student Study Guide.*

- Respond to Application Questions for the Case Study "Should Karl Stay at Home or Be Helped Elsewhere?"

  *Review the Case Study and respond in writing to the application questions. Keep a copy of the case study and your written response for your portfolio.*

- Complete the "Take a Stand" activity for the Debate Forum "Parents of Mentally Ill Children Trade Custody for Care."

  *Read the Debate Forum in this chapter and then visit our companion website to complete the activity "Take a Stand." Keep a copy of this activity for your portfolio.*

- Participate in a Community Service Learning Activity.

  *Community service is a valuable way to enhance your learning experience. Visit our companion website for suggested community service learning activities that correspond to the information presented in this chapter. Develop a reflective journal of the service learning experience for your portfolio.*

## THEMES OF THE TIMES

The New York Times
expect the world®
nytimes.com

Expand your knowledge of the concepts discussed in this chapter by reading current and historical articles from the *New York Times* by visiting the "Themes of the Times" section of the companion website: **www.ablongman.com/hardman8e.**

# Mental Retardation (Intellectual Disabilities)

## TO BEGIN WITH . . .

### I Hear the Music That Is Thomas

Retard! My ninth-grade students toss this word around as if its meaning is clear . . . someone who is slow and stupid. "You retard!" Sometimes I quietly ask them not to call one another names. But some days I feel like making a point, so I just quietly mention that my youngest son, Thomas is retarded. Their faces reveal embarrassment, and I wonder if they know the musical meaning of the word. I hear the music that is Thomas—slow down to a different pace . . . *ritard.* (Corum, 2003, D1)

### Troy Daniel's Class of 2002 Graduation Speech

Troy Daniels, a young man with Down syndrome who uses a wheelchair, was selected to stand before the graduating class at Northfield High School in Vermont and deliver the senior speech. Here is an excerpt:

Not long ago people with disabilities could not go to school with other kids, they had to go to special schools. They could not have real friends; they call people like me "retard." That breaks my heart. . . . The law says that I can come to school but no law can make me have friends. But then some kids started to think that I was okay, first just one or two kids were nice to me. . . . Others started to hang out with me and they found out we could be friends. I cared about them and they cared about me. . . . I want all people to know and see that these students I call my friends are the real teachers of life (T. Daniels, personal communication, May 18, 2003).

### The Keys Are Mine!

When I lived at Lake Owasso State Institution in Minnesota, you had to ask for everything. Can you let me out? Can I have a can of pop? Can I stay up a little longer? When I moved into a group home, I had to follow all of the rules. I had to go to bed at a certain time, and when I was in bed, I had to be asleep; that was that. Two years ago I got married. My wife and I moved into our own apartment. Now that I have my own place, I make my own decisions. I have my own keys. I can let myself out, and let myself back in. Now I can come and go when I want. I can make my own food, and I decide whether I want to have breakfast or lunch. My wife and I decide when the staff come over. They help us with some things but we make our own decisions. (Otley, 2000, p. 24)

**FOCUS**

**PREVIEW:** To preview the central concepts of this chapter, read the focus questions located in the margins. Using these questions as a guide, ask yourself what you already know and what you want to learn.

# Lilly

L illy is an 8-year-old with mental retardation. When she was adopted at the age of 2, her new parents were told she would never talk and might not walk. Through the untiring efforts of her family during the early childhood years, Lilly is able to say some words and use short sentences that are understood by her family and friends. She can now walk without support. Lilly's greatest challenge, according to her mother, is to stay focused. If directed step by step, Lilly is capable of participating in family activities and helping out around the house. Her brother Josh is always there for Lilly, helping her with homework, reading to her, and helping her get dressed in the morning.

At school, Lilly spends part of her day in a classroom with other students who also have mental retardation and part of the day in a general education class with second grade students without disabilities. While in the special education classroom, Lilly works with peer tutors from the sixth grade general education class to help her with schoolwork. Her two peer tutors, Nita and Amy, work with Lilly on using the computer to better develop her communication skills. A computer is a wonderful tool for Lilly because all she has to do is learn to hit the right buttons on the Touch Talker program to communicate with family, friends, and teachers. Lilly's second grade teacher, Mrs. Roberts, describes Lilly as one of the most popular students in her class.

The second grade students love her "neat talking machine." When in the second grade class, Lilly participates in learning centers where she is paired up with students without disabilities working on a variety of activities.

Lilly's mother and teachers are optimistic about her future. The special education teacher hopes that Lilly will be able to go to her neighborhood school next year and spend even more time with "typical" students of her own age. "And from there, with her great social skills and her persistence, I see her as being independent in the future, working in a job setting."

# Roger

Roger is 19 years old and lives at home with his parents. During the day, he attends high school and works in a local toy company on a small work crew with five other individuals who also have disabilities. Roger and his working colleagues are supervised by a job coach. Roger assembles small toys and is learning how to operate power tools for wood- and metal-cutting tasks. His wages are not enough to allow Roger to be financially independent, so he will probably always need some financial support from his family or society.

Roger is capable of caring for his own physical needs. He has learned to dress and feed himself and understands the importance of personal care. He can communicate many of his needs and desires verbally but is limited in his ability to participate in social conversations, such as discussing the weather or what's new at the movies. Roger has never learned to read, and his leisure hours are

spent watching television, listening to the radio, and visiting with friends.

# Becky

Becky is a 6-year-old who has significant delays in intellectual, language, and motor development. These developmental differences have been evident from very early in her life. Her mother experienced a long, unusually difficult labor, and Becky endured severe dips in heart rate; at times, her heart rate was undetectable. During delivery, Becky suffered from birth asphyxiation and epileptic seizures. The attending physician described her as flaccid (soft and limp), with abnormal muscle reflexes. Becky has not yet learned to walk, is not toilet trained, and has no means of communication with others in her environment. She lives at home and attends a local elementary school during the day.

Her education program includes work with therapists to develop her gross motor abilities in order to improve her mobility. Speech and language specialists are examining the possibility of teaching her several alternative forms of communication (e.g., a language board or manual communication system) because Becky has not developed any verbal skills. The special education staff is focusing on decreasing Becky's dependence on others by teaching some basic self-care skills such as eating, toileting, and grooming. The professional staff does not know what the ultimate long-term impact of their intervention will be, but they do know that although Becky is a child with severe mental retardation, *she is learning*.

This chapter discusses people whose intellectual and social capabilities may differ significantly from the average. Their growth and development depend on the educational, social, and medical supports made available throughout life. Lilly from the opening Snapshot is a child with mental retardation who has a wonderful support network of family, friends, and teachers. As she grows older, she may achieve at least partial economical and social independence within her community. Most likely, Lilly will continue to need some assistance from family, friends, and government programs to help her adjust to adult life.

Roger has completed school and is just beginning life as an adult in his community. Roger is a person with moderate mental retardation. Although he will probably require continuing support on his job, he is earning wages that contribute to his success and independence as an adult. Within a few years, Roger is likely to move away from his family and into a supported living arrangement, such as a house or apartment of his own.

Becky has severe mental retardation. Although the long-term prognosis is unknown, she has many opportunities for learning and development that were not available until recently. Through a positive home environment and a school program that supports her learning and applying skills in natural settings, Becky can reach a level of development that was once considered impossible.

Lilly, Roger, and Becky are people with mental retardation, or intellectual disabilities, but they are not necessarily representative of the wide range of people who are characterized as having mental retardation. A 6-year-old described as mildly retarded may be no more than one or two years behind in the development of academic and social skills. Many children with mild mental retardation are not identified until they enter elementary school at age 5 or 6, because they may not exhibit physical or learning delays that are readily identifiable during the early childhood years. As these children enter school, developmental delays become more apparent. During the early primary grades, it is not uncommon for the intellectual and social differences of children with mild mental retardation to be attributed to immaturity. Within a few years, however, educators generally recognize the need for specialized services to support the child's development in the natural settings of school, neighborhood, and home.

People with moderate to severe mental retardation have challenges that transcend the classroom. Some have significant multiple disabling conditions, including sensory, physical, and emotional problems. People with moderate retardation are capable of learning adaptive skills that make possible a degree of independence, with ongoing support. These skills include the ability to dress and feed themselves, to meet their own personal care and health needs, and to develop safety skills that enable them to move without fear wherever they go. These individuals have some means of communication. Most can develop spoken language skills, but some may be able to learn only manual communication (signing). Their social interaction skills are limited, however, making it a challenge for for them to relate spontaneously to others.

People with profound retardation often depend on others to maintain even their most basic life functions, including eating, toileting, and dressing. They may not be capable of self-care and often do not develop functional communication skills. This does not mean that education and treatment beyond routine care and maintenance are not beneficial. The nature of these disabilities is the primary reason why such individuals were excluded from the public schools for so long. Exclusion was often justified on the basis of schools not having the resources, facilities, or trained personnel to deal with the needs of students who functioned at lower levels.

# Definitions and Classification

People with mental retardation have been studied for centuries by a variety of professional disciplines. They are often stereotyped as a homogeneous group of individuals—"the retarded"—who all have similar physical characteristics and learning capabilities. Nothing could be further from the truth. In fact, mental retardation encompasses a broad range of functioning levels and learning capabilities.

## Evolving Terminology

Varying perspectives exist on the use of the term *mental retardation*. In the United States, *mental retardation* has been in widespread use for more than five decades, although usage is changing in some parts of the country. In other regions of the world, *intellectual disabilities* is the more acceptable term.

Recently, many family members and professionals have questioned the continued use of the term *mental retardation*. As suggested by Warren (2002), "it has been attacked as promoting stigma and negative stereotyping" (p. 1). Others point out that although the term is falling out of favor, there is no agreement about what term should be substituted in its place. In this chapter, we use *mental retardation*, while acknowledging that it is likely to be replaced by another term or terms in the years to come. Currently, it remains the term preferred by the major professional association in the field, as well as by many publications throughout the United States.

## Definition

The most widely accepted definition of *mental retardation* is that of the **American Association on Mental Retardation** (AAMR), an organization of professionals of varied backgrounds, such as medicine, law, and education. As defined by AAMR, mental retardation is

> a disability characterized by significant limitations both in intellectual functioning and in adaptive behavior as expressed in conceptual, social and practical adaptive skills. This disability originates before age 18. (AAMR, 2002, p. 1)

The AAMR definition has evolved through years of effort to reflect more clearly the ever-changing perceptions of mental retardation. Historically, definitions of mental retardation were based solely on the measurement of intellect and emphasized routine care and maintenance rather than treatment and education. In recent years, the concept of adaptive behavior has played an increasingly important role in defining and classifying people with mental retardation.

In the next section, we address six major dimensions of the AAMR definition: intellectual abilities; adaptive behavior; participation, interactions, and social roles; health; environmental context; and age of onset.

**INTELLECTUAL ABILITIES.** **Intellectual abilities** include reasoning, planning, solving problems, thinking abstractly, comprehending complex ideas, learning quickly, and learning from experience (AAMR, 2002). They are assessed via a stan-

**FOCUS**

**1**

Identify the major components of the AAMR definition of mental retardation.

**American Association on Mental Retardation (AAMR)**

An organization of professionals from many disciplines involved in the study and treatment of mental retardation.

**Intellectual abilities**

Reasoning, planning, solving problems, thinking abstractly, comprehending complex ideas, learning quickly, and learning from experience.

---

**FIGURE 10.1**

### Examples of Conceptual, Social, and Practical Adaptive Skills

**Conceptual**

Language (receptive and expressive)

Reading and writing

Money concepts

Self-direction

**Social**

Interpersonal skills

Responsibility

Self-esteem

Gullibility

Naiveté

Follows rules

Obeys laws

Avoids victimization

**Practical**

Activities of daily living
- Eating
- Transfer/mobility
- Toileting
- Dressing

Occupational skills

Maintains safe environments

Instrumental activities of daily living
- Meal preparation
- Housekeeping
- Transportation
- Taking medication
- Money management
- Telephone use

SOURCE: Adapted from *Mental Retardation: Definition, Classification, and Systems of Support* (10th ed.) by AAMR Ad Hoc Committee on Terminology and Classification, 2002, Washington, DC: American Association on Mental Retardation.

dardized intelligence test where a person's score is compared to the average of other people who have taken the same test (referred to as a *normative sample*). The statistical average for an intelligence test is generally set at 100. We state this by saying that the person has an intelligence quotient (IQ) of 100. Psychologists use a mathematical procedure called a **standard deviation** to determine the extent to which any given individual's score deviates from this average of 100. An individual who scores more than two standard deviations below 100 on an intelligence test meets AAMR's definition of subaverage general intellectual functioning. This means that people with IQs of approximately 70 to 75 and lower would be considered as having mental retardation.

*on next page → also.*

**ADAPTIVE BEHAVIOR.** AAMR defines **adaptive behavior** as a collection of conceptual, social, and practical skills that "have been learned by people in order to function in their everyday lives" (p. 41). (Figure 10.1 shows several examples of adaptive behavior.) If a person has limitations in these adaptive skills, he or she may need some additional assistance or supports in order to participate more fully in both family and community life. Consider Becky from the chapter-opening Snapshot. She has significant limitations in her adaptive skills. She is unable to walk and take care of her basic needs (practical skills). At 6 years old, she has limited means of communicating with others (conceptual skills).

Like intelligence, adaptive skills can be measured by standardized tests. These tests, most often referred to as *adaptive behavior scales*, generally use structured interviews or direct observations to obtain information. Adaptive behavior scales measure the individual's ability to take care of personal needs (such as hygiene) and to relate appropriately to others in social situations. Adaptive skills may also be assessed through informal appraisal, such as observations by family members or professionals who are familiar with the individual or through anecdotal records.

**PARTICIPATION, INTERACTION, AND SOCIAL ROLES.** AAMR emphasizes the importance of a positive environment for fostering growth, development, and individual well-being. Thus a person's participation and interaction within the environment are an indicator of adaptive functioning. The more an individual engages in valued activities, the more likely that an "adaptive fit" exists between the person and her or his environment. (See Chapter 2 for information about the concept of "adaptive fit.") Valued activities may include an appropriate education, living arrangements, employment settings, and community participation.

The concept of participation in valued activities was introduced by Bengt Nirje from Sweden over three decades ago through the **principle of normalization**. This principle emphasizes the need to make available to the person with mental retardation "the patterns and conditions of everyday life which are as close to the norms and patterns of mainstream society" as possible (Nirje, 1970, p. 181). Normalization goes far beyond the mere physical inclusion of the individual in a community. It also promotes the availability of needed supports, such as training and supervision, without which the individual with

**Standard deviation**

A statistical measure of the amount that an individual score deviates from the average.

**Adaptive behavior**

A collection of conceptual, social, and practical skills that people have learned in order to function in their everyday lives.

**Principle of normalization**

Making the patterns and conditions of everyday life, and of mainstream society, available to persons with mental retardation.

*Learning and applying adaptive skills in a community work setting contributes to the individual's independence and is consistent with the principle of normalization.*

mental retardation may not be prepared to cope with the demands of community life.

**PHYSICAL AND MENTAL HEALTH.** The physical and mental health of an individual influences his or her overall intellectual and adaptive functioning. AAMR indicates that the functioning level for people with mental retardation is significantly affected (facilitated or inhibited) by the effects of physical and mental health. "Some individuals [with mental retardation] enjoy robust good health with no significant activity limitations. . . . On the other hand, some individuals have a variety of significant health limitations, such as epilepsy or cerebral palsy, that greatly impair body functioning and severely restrict personal activities and social participation" (p. 45).

**ENVIRONMENTAL CONTEXT.** As defined by AAMR, *context* is the interrelated conditions in which people live their lives. It is based on an environmental perspective with three different levels: (1) the immediate social setting, which includes the person and his or her family; (2) the broader neighborhood, community, or organizations that provide services and supports (e.g., public education), and (3) the overarching patterns of culture and society. The various levels are important to people with mental retardation because they provide differing opportunities and can foster well-being.

**AGE OF ONSET.** The AAMR defines the age of onset for mental retardation as prior to 18 years. The reason for choosing age 18 as a cutoff point is that mental retardation is part of a family of conditions referred to as **developmental disabilities.** Developmental disabilities are mental and/or physical impairments that are diagnosed at birth or during the childhood and adolescent years. A developmental disability results in substantial functional limitations in at least three areas of major life activity (e.g., self-care, language, learning, mobility, self-direction, capacity for independent living, and economic self-sufficiency).

**PUTTING THE DEFINITION INTO PRACTICE.** Based on the dimensions described AAMR cites five criteria that professionals should apply as they put the definition of mental retardation into practice.

1. Limitations in a person's present functioning must be considered within the context of community environments typical of the individual's age, peers, and culture.

2. Valid assessment considers cultural and linguistic diversity as well as differences in communication, sensory, motor, and behavioral factors.

3. Within an individual, limitations often coexist with strengths.

4. An important purpose of describing limitations is to develop a profile of needed supports.

5. With appropriate personalized supports over a sustained period, the life functioning of the person with mental retardation generally will improve. (AAMR, 2002)

## Classification

Several classification systems have been developed to help us more clearly understand the diversity of people with retardation. Each classification method reflects an attempt by a particular discipline (such as medicine or education) to better understand and respond to the needs of individuals with mental retardation. We will discuss four of these methods.

**SEVERITY OF THE CONDITION.** The extent to which a person's intellectual capabilities and adaptive skills differ from what is considered "normal" can be described by using terms such as *mild, moderate, severe,* and *profound. Mild* describes the highest level of performance; *profound* describes the lowest level. Distinctions between severity levels associated with mental retardation are determined by scores on intelligence tests and limitations in adaptive skills.

**Developmental disabilities**

Mental and/or physical impairments that are diagnosed at birth or during the childhood and adolescent years. For this term to apply, there must be substantial functional limitations in at least three areas of major life activity (e.g., self-care, language, learning, mobility, self-direction, capacity for independent living, or economic self-sufficiency).

A person's adaptive skills can also be categorized in terms of severity. Limitations in adaptive skills can be described in terms of the degree to which an individual's performance differs from what is expected for his or her chronological age. Let's look at Lilly, Roger, and Becky from our opening Snapshot. As an 8-year-old, Lilly has acquired some of the self-care skills expected for a child of her age, and although her socialization and communication skills are below what is expected, she is able to interact successfully with others through the use of **assistive technology**. Roger, at age 19, has developed many skills that enable him to successfully live in his own community with some supervision and support. It took longer for Roger to learn to dress and feed himself than it did for Lilly, but he has learned these skills. Although his verbal communication skills are somewhat rudimentary, he is capable of communicating basic needs and desires. Becky is a child with severe to profound mental retardation. At age 6, her development is significantly delayed in nearly every area. However, it is clear that with appropriate intervention, she is learning.

FOCUS
2

Identify four approaches to classifying people with mental retardation.

**EDUCABILITY EXPECTATIONS.**   To distinguish among the diverse needs of students with mental retardation, the field of education developed its own classification system. As the word *expectations* implies, students with mental retardation have been classified according to how well they are expected to achieve in a classroom situation. The specific descriptors vary greatly from state to state, but most specify an approximate IQ range and a statement of predicted achievement:

- Educable (IQ 55 to about 70). Second to fifth grade achievement in school academic areas. Social adjustment skills will result in independence with intermittent or limited support in the community. Partial or total self-support in a paid community job is a strong possibility.

- Trainable (IQ 40 to 55). Learning primarily in the area of self-care skills; some achievement in functional academics. A range of more extensive support will be needed to help the student adapt to community environments. Opportunities for paid work include supported employment in a community job.

The classification criterion for the expectation of educability was originally developed to determine who would be able to benefit from school and who would not. The term *educable* implied that the child could cope with at least some of the academic demands of the classroom—in other words, that the child could learn basic reading, writing, and arithmetic skills. The term *trainable* indicated that the student was noneducable and capable only of being trained in settings outside of the public school. In fact, until the passage of PL 94-142 in 1975 (now IDEA), many children who were labeled trainable could not get a free public education. In some school systems, the terms *educable* and *trainable* have now been replaced by symptom-severity classifications (mild through severe mental retardation).

**MEDICAL DESCRIPTORS.**   Mental retardation may be classified on the basis of the biological origin of the condition. A classification system that uses the cause of the condition to differentiate people with mental retardation is often referred to as a *medical classification* system, because it emerged primarily from the field of medicine. Common medical descriptors include fetal alcohol syndrome, chromosomal abnormalities (e.g., Down syndrome), metabolic disorders (e.g., phenylketonuria, thyroid dysfunction), and infections (e.g., syphilis, rubella). These medical conditions will be discussed more thoroughly in the section on causation.

**CLASSIFICATION BASED ON NEEDED SUPPORT.**   The AAMR uses a classification system based on the type and extent of the support the individual needs to function in the natural settings of home and community. The AAMR describes four levels of support:

- *Intermittent.* Supports are provided on an "as-needed basis." These supports may be (1) episodic—that is, the person does not always need assistance; or (2) short-term, occurring during lifespan transitions (e.g., job loss or acute medical crisis). Intermittent supports may be of high or low intensity.

**Assistive technology**

Technology devices that help an individual with disabilities adapt to the natural settings of home, school, and family. The technology may include computers, hearing aids, wheelchairs, and so on.

- *Limited.* Supports are characterized by consistency; time required may be limited but not intermittent. Fewer staff may be required, and costs may be lower than those associated with more intensive levels of support (for example, time-limited employment training or supports during transition from school to adulthood).

- *Extensive.* Supports are characterized by regular involvement (e.g., daily) in at least some environments, such as work or home; supports are not time-limited (for example, long-term job and home-living support will be necessary).

- *Pervasive.* Supports must be constant and of high intensity. They have to be provided across multiple environments and may be life-sustaining in nature. Pervasive supports typically involve more staff and are more intrusive than extensive or limited supports.

The AAMR's emphasis on classifying people with mental retardation on the basis of needed support is an important departure from the more restrictive perspectives of the traditional approaches. Supports may be described not only in terms of the level of assistance needed but also by type: formal and natural support systems. Formal supports may be funded through government programs, such as income maintenance, health care, education, housing, and employment. Another type of formal support is the advocacy organization (e.g., **Arc, A National Organization on Mental Retardation**) that lobbies on behalf of people with mental retardation for improved and expanded services and also offers family members a place to interact and support one another. **Natural supports** differ from formal supports in that they are provided not by agencies or organizations but by the nuclear and extended family members, friends, or neighbors. Natural supports are often more effective than formal supports in helping people with mental retardation access and participate in a community setting. Research has suggested that adults with mental retardation who are successfully employed following school find more jobs through their natural support network of friends and family than through formal support systems (Berry & Hardman, 1998).

## Prevalence

The U.S. Department of Education (2002) reported that 612,978 students between the ages of 6 and 21 were labeled in 2000–2001, as having mental retardation and receiving service under IDEA. Approximately 11% of all students with disabilities between the ages of 6 and 21 have mental retardation. Overall, students with mental retardation constitute about 0.93% of the total school population (see Figure 10.2).

The National Health Survey–Disability Supplement (Research and Training Center on Community Living, 1999) found that noninstitutionalized people with mental retardation constitute less than 0.78% of the total population, or about 1.9 million people in the United States. If you add people with mental retardation living in nurs-

## FIGURE 10.2

### Prevalence of Mental Retardation

1% with mental retardation

10% with moderate, severe, and profound mental retardation

90% with mild mental retardation

**Total School-Age Population**

**School Population with Mental Retardation**

SOURCE: From "To Assure the Free Appropriate Public Education of All Children with Disabilities," by the U.S. Department of Education. In *Twenty-fourth Annual Report to Congress on the Implementation of the Individuals with Disabilities Education Act*, 2002, Washington, DC: U.S. Government Printing Office.

ing homes and institutional settings of four or more residents, the prevalence figure increases to 0.83% of the total population, or 2 million people. People with mild mental retardation constitute about 90% of all people with mental retardation, or about 0.75% of the total population. Those with more severe mental retardation constitute a much smaller percentage of the general population (0.25%).

The prevalence figures reported from the National Health Survey are considerably lower than prior estimates of mental retardation. Classified on the basis of an intelligence test score of 70 or lower, people with mental retardation would constitute about 3% of the total population, or about 6.6 million people in the United States (U.S. Census Bureau, 2000). The President's Committee on Mental Retardation (2000) also estimates that between 6.2 and 7.5 million Americans of all ages, or 3% of the general population, experience mental retardation. Note that we can only estimate prevalence, because no one has actually counted the number of people with mental retardation. The closest we can come to actual numbers is through the data from the National Health Survey, which used a random sample of 108,000 people across the United States to make its estimates.

## Characteristics

In this section, we examine the many characteristics of people with mental retardation that can affect their academic learning and their ability to adapt to home, school, and community environments.

### Learning and Memory

Intelligence is the ability to acquire, remember, and use knowledge. A primary characteristic of mental retardation is diminished intellectual ability—a difference, compared to the general population, in the rate and efficiency with which the person acquires, remembers, and uses new knowledge.

The learning and memory capabilities of people with mental retardation are significantly below those of their peers without disabilities. Children with mental retar-

**FOCUS 3**

What is the prevalence of mental retardation?

**FOCUS 4**

Identify the intellectual skills, self-regulation, and adaptive skills characteristics of individuals with mental retardation.

dation, as a group, are less able to grasp abstract concepts. Thus they benefit most from instruction that is meaningful and useful, and they learn more from contact with real objects than from representations or symbols.

Intelligence is also associated with learning how to learn and with the ability to apply what is learned to new experiences. This process is known as establishing learning sets and generalizing them to new situations. Children and adults with mental retardation develop learning sets at a slower rate than nonretarded peers, and they are deficient in relating information to new situations (Beirne-Smith, Ittenbach, & Patton, 2002; Hughes, 1992; Turner, Dofny, & Dutka, 1994). As described by Cipani and Spooner (1994), **generalization** takes place "when a learned response is seen to occur in the presence of 'untaught' stimuli" (p. 157). The greater the severity of intellectual deficit, the greater the difficulties with memory. Memory problems in children with mental retardation have been attributed to several factors. For example, people with mental retardation have difficulty focusing on relevant stimuli in learning and real-life situations, and hence they sometimes attend to the wrong things (Henry & Gudjonsson, 1999; Westling & Fox, 2000).

## Self-Regulation

People with mental retardation do not appear to develop efficient learning strategies, such as the ability to rehearse a task (to practice a new concept, either out loud or to themselves, over and over). The ability to rehearse a task is related to a broad concept known as **self-regulation,** the ability to mediate, or regulate, one's own behavior (Jay, Grote, & Baer, 1999). Whereas most people will rehearse to try to remember, it does not appear that individuals with retardation are able to apply this skill.

Some researchers have begun to focus on **information-processing theories** to better understand learning differences in people with mental retardation. Information-processing theorists study how a person processes information from sensory stimuli to motoric output (Sternberg, 2001; 2002). In information-processing theory, the learning differences in people with mental retardation are seen as the underdevelopment of metacognitive processes. Metacognitive processes help the person plan how to solve a problem. First, the person decides which strategy he or she thinks will solve a problem. Then the strategy is implemented. During implementation, the person monitors whether the strategy is working and makes any changes necessary. Finally, the results of the strategy are evaluated in terms of whether the problem has been solved and how the strategy could be used in other situations (Sternberg, 2002). Even though children with mental retardation may be unable to use the best strategy when confronted with new learning situations, many researchers believe they can be taught to do so (Agran & Hughes, 1997; Mithaug, Wehmeyer, Agran, Martin, & Palmer, 1998; Wehmeyer & Kelchner, 1995).

## Adaptive Skills

The abilities to adapt to the demands of the environment, relate to others, and take care of personal needs are all important aspects of an independent lifestyle. In the school setting, adaptive behavior is defined as the ability to apply skills learned in a classroom to daily activities in natural settings.

The adaptive skills of people with mental retardation are often not comparable to those of their nondisabled peers. A child with mental retardation may have difficulty in both learning and applying skills for a number of reasons, including a higher level of distractibility, inattentiveness, failure to read social cues, and impulsive behavior (Agran & Wehmeyer, 1999; Bergen & Mosley, 1994; Gresham & MacMillan, 1997). These children will need to be taught appropriate reasoning, judgment, and social skills that lead to more positive social relationships and personal competence. Adaptive skill differences in people with mental retardation may also be associated with a lower self-image and a greater expectancy for failure in both academic and social situations. In a study of 764 children in general education classrooms, Siperstein and Leffert (1997) identified the characteristics of 20 socially accepted and 20 socially re-

**Generalization**

The process of applying previously learned information to new settings or situations.

**Self-regulation**

The ability to regulate one's own behavior.

**Information-processing theories**

Theories on how a person processes information from sensory stimuli to motor output.

jected students with mental retardation. The characteristics of socially accepted children included a higher level of social skills. These children were not perceived by their peers without disabilities as aggressive in their behavior. The authors suggested that there is value in recognizing and teaching the skills that directly affect whether these children are accepted by their classmates.

## Academic Achievement

Research on the academic achievement of children with mild to moderate mental retardation suggests that they will experience significant delays in the areas of literacy and mathematics. Reading comprehension is generally considered the weakest area of learning. In general, students with mild retardation are better at decoding words than comprehending their meaning (Drew & Hardman, 2004), and most read below their own mental-age level (Katims, 2000).

Children with mental retardation also perform poorly with mathematical computations, although here their performance may be closer to what is typical for their mental age. These children may be able to learn basic computations but may be unable to apply concepts appropriately in a problem-solving situation (Beirne-Smith et al., 2002).

A growing body of research has indicated that children with moderate and severe mental retardation can be taught functional academics. In a functional reading program, these students are able to develop a useful vocabulary that will facilitate their inclusion in school and community settings (Browder & Snell, 2000). The goal of functional reading is for "students to have enough of a sight word vocabulary to be able to scan printed materials and glean the key information needed in a given activity" (Browder & Snell, p. 526). These children may be able to recognize their names and those of significant others in their lives, as well as common survival words, including *help, hurt, danger,* and *stop.* In a functional math program, students learn such skills as how to tell time, add and subtract small sums to manage finances (such as balancing a checkbook), and appropriately exchange money for products in community settings (e.g., grocery stores, movie theaters, vending machines, etc.).

## Motivation

People with mental retardation are often described as lacking motivation, or outer-directed behavior. They may seem unwilling or unable to complete tasks, take responsibility, and be self-directed. Although people with mental retardation may appear to be less motivated than their peers without disabilities, such behavior may be attributable in part to their having learned to avoid certain situations because of a fear of failure. A child with mental retardation may have a history of failure, particularly in school, and may be afraid to take risks or participate in new situations. The result of failure is often **learned helplessness**— "No matter what I do or how hard I try, I will not succeed." To overcome a child's feelings

**FOCUS 5**

Identify the academic, motivational, speech and language, and physical characteristics of children with mental retardation.

**Learned helplessness**

Refusal or unwillingness to take on new tasks or challenges, resulting from repeated failures or control by others.

*The academic performance of children with mental retardation varies greatly depending on the level of intellectual ability and adaptive skills. Many children with mild mental retardation may learn to read although at a slower rate, while those with moderate mental retardation benefit from a functional academics program.*

of learned helplessness, professionals and family members should focus on providing experiences that have high probabilities for success. The opportunity to strive for success, rather than to avoid failure, is a very important learning experience for these children. Table 10.1 lists several considerations in motivating students with mental retardation.

## Speech and Language

One of the most serious and obvious characteristics of individuals with mental retardation is delayed speech and language development. The most common speech difficulties involve **articulation problems, voice problems,** and **stuttering.** Language problems are generally associated with delays in language development rather than with bizarre use of language (Beirne-Smith et al., 2002; Warren & Yoder, 1997). Kaiser (2000) emphasized that "the overriding goal of language intervention is to increase the functional communication of students" (p. 457).

There is considerable variation in the language skills of people with mental retardation. In general, the severity of the speech and language problems is positively correlated with the cause and severity of the mental retardation: The milder the mental retardation, the less pervasive the language difficulty (Tager-Flusberg & Sullivan, 1998). Speech and language difficulties may range from minor speech defects, such as articulation problems, to the complete absence of expressive language. Speech and language pathologists are able to correct minor speech differences for most students with mental retardation.

Mental retardation may cause speech problems, but some speech difficulties (such as **echolalia**) may also directly contribute to the severity of the mental retardation. Table 10.2 describes the range of speech and language skills for people with moderate to profound mental retardation.

## Physical Development

The physical appearance of most children with mental retardation does not differ from that of same-age children who are not disabled. However, a relationship exists between the severity of the mental retardation and the extent of physical differences (Beirne-Smith et al., 2002; Drew & Hardman, 2004; Horvat, 2000). For the person with severe mental retardation, there is a significant probability of related physical problems; genetic factors probably underlie both disabilities. The individual with mild retardation, in contrast, may exhibit no physical differences because the retardation may be associated with environmental, not genetic, factors. Table 10.3 describes the range of physical characteristics associated with individuals who have moderate to profound mental retardation.

The majority of children with severe and profound retardation have multiple disabilities that affect nearly every aspect of intellectual and physical development (Westling & Fox, 2000). Increasing health problems for children with mental retardation may be associated with genetic or environmental factors. For example, people

**Articulation problems**

Speech problems such as omissions, substitutions, additions, and distortions of words.

**Voice problems**

Abnormal acoustical qualities in a person's speech.

**Stuttering**

A speech problem involving abnormal repetitions, prolongations, and hesitations as one speaks.

**Echolalia**

A meaningless repetition or imitation of words that have been spoken.

## TABLE 10.1

### Motivating Students with Mental Retardation

- Reward the learner for doing what he or she is supposed to do.
- Develop a different activity—one that is more inherently motivating for the learner—to teach the same objective.
- Change the objective.
- Forget about teaching until other considerations are addressed, such as health problems, abuse, or development of rapport.

SOURCE: *Teaching Persons with Mental Retardation* (p. 280), by R. B. Dever & D. R. Knapczyk, 1997, Madison, WI: Brown and Benchmark.

TABLE 10.2

**Speech and Language Skills in Individuals with Moderate to Profound Mental Retardation**

| SEVERITY OF MENTAL RETARDATION | | |
| --- | --- | --- |
| **MODERATE** | **SEVERE** | **PROFOUND** |
| Most individuals have delays or deviations in speech and language skills, but many develop language abilities that make possible some level of communication with others. | Individuals exhibit significant speech and language delays and deviations (such as lack of expressive and receptive language, articulation difficulties, and little, if any, spontaneous interaction). | Individuals do not exhibit spontaneous communication patterns. Echolalic speech, speech out of context, and purposeless speech may be evident. |

with Down syndrome have a higher incidence of congenital heart defects and respiratory problems directly linked to their genetic condition. On the other hand, some children with mental retardation experience health problems because of their living conditions. A significantly higher percentage of children with mental retardation than of their peers without disabilities come from low socioeconomic backgrounds. Children who do not receive proper nutrition and are exposed to inadequate sanitation are more susceptible to infections (Drew & Hardman, 2004). Health services for families in these situations may be minimal or nonexistent, depending on whether they are able to access government medical support. Thus children with mental retardation may become ill more often than those who are not retarded. Consequently, children with retardation may miss more school.

# Causation

Mental retardation is the result of multiple causes, some known, many unknown. For about 30% of all people with mental retardation, the cause of the condition is unknown. This percentage is much higher for people with mild mental retardation, for whom the specific cause cannot be determined in 75% of the cases (The ARC, 2000).

FOCUS
6

Discuss the causes of mental retardation.

TABLE 10.3

**Physical Characteristics of Individuals with Moderate to Profound Mental Retardation**

| SEVERITY OF MENTAL RETARDATION | | |
| --- | --- | --- |
| **MODERATE** | **SEVERE** | **PROFOUND** |
| Gross and fine motor coordination is usually delayed. However, the individual is often ambulatory and capable of independent mobility. Perceptual–motor skills exist (e.g., body awareness, sense of touch, eye–hand coordination) but are often delayed in comparison to the norm. | As many as 80% have significant motor difficulties (i.e., poor or no ambulatory skills). Gross or fine motor skills may be present, but the individual may lack control, resulting in awkward or uncontrolled movement. | Some gross motor development is evident, but fine motor skills are delayed. The individual is usually nonambulatory and not capable of independent mobility within the environment. The individual may lack perceptual–motor skills. |

Possible known causes of mental retardation include sociocultural influences, biomedical factors, behavioral factors, and unknown prenatal influences.

## Sociocultural Influences

For individuals with mild retardation, the cause of the problem is not generally apparent. A significant number of these individuals come from families of low socioeconomic status and diverse cultural backgrounds; their home situations often provide few opportunities for learning, which further contributes to their challenges at school. Moreover, because these high-risk children live in such adverse economic conditions, they generally do not receive proper nutritional care. In addition to poor nutrition, high-risk groups are in greater jeopardy of receiving poor medical care and living in unstable families (Children's Defense Fund, 2003).

An important question to be addressed concerning people who have grown up in adverse sociocultural situations is this: How much of the person's ability is related to sociocultural influences and how much to genetic factors? This issue is referred to as the **nature-versus-nurture controversy.** Numerous studies over the years have focused on the relative contribution of heredity and environment to intelligence. These studies show that although we are reaching a better understanding of the interactive effects of heredity and environment, the exact contribution of each to intellectual growth remains unknown.

The term used to describe mental retardation that may be attributable to both sociocultural and genetic factors is **cultural–familial retardation.** People with this condition are often described as (1) having mild retardation, (2) having no known biological cause for the condition, (3) having at least one parent or sibling who has mild retardation, and (4) having grown up in a low socioeconomic home environment.

## Biomedical Factors

For the majority of people with more severe mental retardation, problems are evident at birth.. As defined by AAMR, **biomedical factors** "relate to biologic processes, such as genetic disorders or nutrition," (AAMR, 2002, p. 126). Many biomedical factors are associated with mental retardation. In this section, we will discuss three major influences: chromosomal abnormalities, metabolism and nutrition, and postnatal brain disease.

**CHROMOSOMAL ABNORMALITIES.** Chromosomes are thread-like bodies that carry the genes that play the critical role in determining inherited characteristics. Defects resulting from **chromosomal abnormalities** are typically severe and accompanied by visually evident abnormalities. Fortunately, genetically caused defects are relatively rare. The vast majority of humans have normal cell structures (46 chromosomes arranged in 23 pairs) and develop without chromosomal mishap. But aberrations in chromosomal arrangement, either before fertilization or during early cell division, can result in a variety of abnormal characteristics.

One of the most widely recognized types of mental retardation, Down syndrome, results from chromosomal abnormality. About 5% to 6% of people with mental retardation have Down syndrome (Beirne-Smith et al., 2002). A person with Down syndrome is characterized by slanting eyes with folds of skin at the inner corners (epicanthal folds); excessive ability to extend the joints; short, broad hands with a single crease across the palm on one or both hands; broad feet with short toes; a flat bridge of the nose; short, low-set ears; a short neck; a small head; a small oral cavity; and/or short, high-pitched cries in infancy.

Down syndrome has received widespread attention in the literature and has been featured in both medical and special education textbooks for many years. Part of this attention is due to the ability to identify a cause with some degree of certainty. The cause of such genetic errors is clearly associated with the age of both the mother and the father. The most common type of Down syndrome is **trisomy 21**. In about 25% of cases of trisomy 21, the age of the father (particularly when he is over 55 years

### Nature-versus-nurture controversy

Controversy over how much of a person's ability is related to sociocultural influences (nurture) and how much to genetic factors (nature).

### Cultural–familial retardation

Mental retardation that may be attributable to both sociocultural and genetic factors.

### Biomedical factors

Biologic processes, such as genetic disorders or malnutrition, that can cause mental retardation or other disabilities.

### Chromosomal abnormalities

Defects or damage in the chromosomes of an individual. Chromosomes are the thread-like bodies that carry the genes and therefore play a central role in inherited characteristics.

### Trisomy 21

Type of Down syndrome in which the chromosomal pairs do not separate properly during the formation of sperm or egg cells, resulting in an extra chromosome on the 21st pair; also called *nondisjunction*.

old), as well as that of the mother, is a factor. For more insight into the myths and truths about Down syndrome, see the nearby Reflect on This.

Other chromosomal abnormalities associated with mental retardation include Williams syndrome and fragile X syndrome. **Williams syndrome** is a rare genetic disease that occurs in about 1 in every 20,000 births and is characterized by an absence of genetic materials on the seventh pair of chromosomes. Most people with Williams syndrome have some degree of mental retardation and associated medical prob-

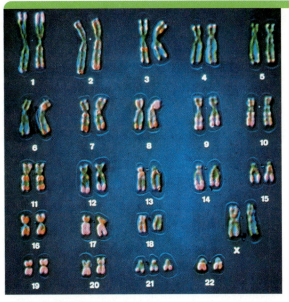

The most common cause of Down syndrome is a chromosomal abnormality known as trisomy 21, in which the twenty-first chromosomal pair carries one extra chromosome.

lems (e.g., heart and blood vessel abnormalities, low weight gain, dental abnormalities, kidney abnormalities, hypersensitive hearing, musculoskeletal problems, and elevated blood calcium levels). Although they have deficits in academic learning and spatial ability typical of people with mental retardation, they are often described as highly personable and verbal, exhibiting unique abilities in spoken language.

**Fragile X syndrome** is a common hereditary cause of mental retardation associated with genetic anomalies in the 23rd pair of chromosomes. Males, with an X and a Y chromosome, are usually more severely affected than females. Females have more protection because they have two X chromosomes; one X contains the normal, functioning version of the gene, and the other is nonfunctioning. The normal gene partially compensates for the nonfunctioning gene. The term *fragile X* refers to the fact that this gene is pinched off in some blood cells. For those affected with fragile X, intellectual differences can range from mild learning disabilities and a normal IQ to severe mental retardation and autism. Physical features may include a large head and flat ears, a long and narrow face with a broad nose, a large forehead, a squared-off chin, prominent testicles, and large hands. People with fragile X are also characterized by speech and language delays or deficiencies and by behavioral problems. Although some people with fragile X are socially engaging and friendly, others have autistic-like characteristics (e.g., poor eye contact, hand flapping, hand biting, and fascination with spinning objects) and may be aggressive. Males may also exhibit hyperactivity.

**METABOLISM AND NUTRITION.** **Metabolic disorders** are characterized by the body's inability to process (metabolize) certain substances that can then become poisonous and damage tissue in the central nervous system. With one such inherited metabolic disorder, **phenylketonuria** (PKU), the baby is not able to process phenylalanine, a substance found in many foods, including the milk ingested by infants. The inability to process phenylalanine results in an accumulation of poisonous substances in the body. If PKU goes untreated or is not treated promptly (mostly through dietary restrictions), it causes from moderate to severe mental retardation. If treatment is promptly instituted, however, damage may be largely prevented or at least reduced. For this reason, states now require screening of all infants for PKU in order to treat the condition as early as possible and prevent lifelong problems.

Milk also presents a problem for infants affected by another metabolic disorder. With **galactosemia**, the child is unable to properly process lactose, which is the primary sugar in milk and is also found in other foods. If galactosemia remains untreated, serious damage results, such as cataracts, heightened susceptibility to infection, and reduced intellectual functioning. Dietary control consists of eliminating milk and other foods that contain lactose.

**Williams syndrome**

A rare genetic disease that occurs in about 1 in every 20,000 births and is characterized by an absence of genetic materials on the seventh pair of chromosomes.

**Fragile X syndrome**

A condition involving damage to the chromosome structure, which appears as a breaking or splitting at the end of the X chromosome.

**Metabolic disorders**

Problems in the body's ability to process (metabolize) substances that can then become poisonous and damage the central nervous system.

**Phenylketonuria (PKU)**

A metabolic disorder that may cause mental retardation if left untreated.

**Galactosemia**

A metabolic disorder that causes an infant to have difficulty in processing lactose. The disorder may cause mental retardation and other problems.

## MYTHS AND TRUTHS ABOUT DOWN SYNDROME

**MYTH:** Down syndrome is a rare genetic disorder.

**TRUTH:** Down syndrome is the most commonly occurring genetic condition. One in every 800 to 1,000 live births is a child with Down syndrome, representing approximately 5,000 births per year in the United States alone. Today, Down syndrome affects more than 350,000 people in the United States.

**MYTH:** Most children with Down syndrome are born to older parents.

**TRUTH:** Eighty percent of children born with Down syndrome are born to women younger than 35 years old. However, the incidence of births of children with Down syndrome increases with the age of the mother.

**MYTH:** People with Down syndrome are severely retarded.

**TRUTH:** Most people with Down syndrome have IQs that fall in the mild to moderate range of retardation. Children with Down syndrome are definitely educable, and educators and researchers are still discovering the full educational potential of people with Down syndrome.

**MYTH:** Most people with Down syndrome are institutionalized.

**TRUTH:** Today people with Down syndrome live at home with their families and are active participants in the educational, vocational, social, and recreational activities of the community. They are integrated into the regular education system and take part in sports, camping, music, art programs, and all the other activities of their communities. In addition, they are socializing with people with and without disabilities and, as adults, are obtaining employment and living in group homes and other independent housing arrangements.

**MYTH:** Parents will not find community support in bringing up their child with Down syndrome.

**TRUTH:** In almost every community of the United States, parent support groups and other community organizations are directly involved in providing services to families of individuals with Down syndrome.

**MYTH:** Children with Down syndrome must be placed in segregated special education programs.

**TRUTH:** Children with Down syndrome have been included in regular academic classrooms in schools across the country. In some instances they are integrated into specific courses, whereas in other situations students are fully included in the regular classroom for all subjects. The degree of mainstreaming is based in the abilities of the individual, but the trend is for full inclusion in the social and educational life of the community.

**MYTH:** Adults with Down syndrome are unemployable.

**TRUTH:** Businesses are seeking young adults with Down syndrome for a variety of positions. They are being employed in small and medium-sized offices: by banks, corporations, nursing homes, hotels, and restaurants. They work in the music and entertainment industry, in clerical positions, and in the computer industry. People with Down syndrome bring to their jobs enthusiasm, reliability, and dedication.

**MYTH:** People with Down syndrome are always happy.

**TRUTH:** People with Down syndrome have feelings just like everyone else in the population. They respond to positive expressions of friendship, and they are hurt and upset by inconsiderate behavior.

**MYTH:** Adults with Down syndrome are unable to form close interpersonal relationships leading to marriage.

**TRUTH:** People with Down syndrome date, socialize and form ongoing relationships. Some are beginning to marry. Women with Down syndrome can and do have children, but there is a 50% chance that their child will have Down syndrome. Men with Down syndrome are believed to be sterile; there is only one documented instance of a male with Down syndrome having fathered a child.

**MYTH:** Down syndrome can never be cured.

**TRUTH:** Research on Down syndrome is making great strides in identifying the genes on chromosome 21 that cause the characteristics of Down syndrome. Scientists now feel strongly that in the future it will be possible to improve, correct, or prevent many of the problems associated with Down syndrome.

SOURCE: From *Down Syndrome: Myths and Truths*, by the National Down Syndrome Society, 2000, New York: Author. [online]. Available: *http://www.ndss.org/aboutds/aboutds.html#Down*

---

**Neurofibromatosis**

An inherited disorder resulting in tumors of the skin and other tissue (such as the brain).

**Tuberous sclerosis**

A birth defect that does not appear until late childhood, is related to mental retardation in about 66% of the cases, and is characterized by tumors on many organs.

**POSTNATAL BRAIN DISEASE.** Some disorders are associated with gross postnatal brain disease. **Neurofibromatosis** is an inherited disorder that results in multiple tumors in the skin, peripheral nerve tissue, and other areas such as the brain. Mental retardation does not occur in all cases, although it may be evident in a small percentage of patients. The severity of mental retardation and other problems resulting from neurofibromatosis seems to be related to the location of the tumors (e.g., in the cerebral tissue) and to their size and pattern of growth. Severe disorders due to postnatal brain disease occur with a variety of other conditions, including **tuberous sclerosis**, which also involves tumors in the central nervous system tissue and degeneration of cerebral white matter.

## Behavioral Factors

Mental retardation may result from behavioral factors that are not genetically based. Behavioral causes of mental retardation include infection and intoxication (such as HIV and **fetal alcohol syndrome**), as well as traumas and physical accidents. As defined by AAMR, **behavioral factors** consist of "potentially causal behaviors, such as dangerous (injurious) activities or maternal substance abuse" (AAMR, 2002, p. 126).

**INFECTION AND INTOXICATION.**   Several types of **maternal infections** may result in difficulties for the unborn child. In some cases, the outcome is spontaneous abortion of the fetus; in others, it may be a severe birth defect. The probability of damage is particularly high if the infection occurs during the first 3 months of pregnancy. **Congenital rubella** (German measles) causes a variety of conditions, including mental retardation, deafness, blindness, cerebral palsy, cardiac problems, seizures, and a variety of other neurological problems. The widespread administration of a rubella vaccine is one major reason why mental retardation as an outcome of rubella has declined significantly in recent years.

Another infection associated with mental retardation is the **human immunodeficiency virus (HIV)**. When transmitted from the mother to the unborn child, HIV can result in significant intellectual deficits. The virus actually crosses the placenta and infects the fetus, damaging the infant's immune system. HIV is a major cause of preventable infectious mental retardation (Kowalski, 2003).

Several prenatal infections can result in other severe disorders. **Toxoplasmosis**, an infection carried by raw meat and fecal material, can cause mental retardation and other problems, such as blindness and convulsions. Toxoplasmosis is primarily a threat if the mother is exposed during pregnancy, whereas infection prior to conception seems to pose minimal danger to the unborn child.

*Intoxication* is cerebral damage due to an excessive level of some toxic agent in the mother–fetus system. Excessive maternal use of alcohol or drugs or exposure to certain environmental hazards (such as x-rays or insecticides) can harm the child. Damage to the fetus from maternal alcohol consumption is characterized by facial abnormalities, heart problems, low birthweight, small brain size, and mental retardation. *Fetal alcohol syndrome (FAS)* and *fetal alcohol effects (FAE)* (a lesser number of the same symptoms associated with FAS) consist of physical and mental birth defects resulting from a woman's drinking alcohol during pregnancy. FAS is recognized as a leading preventable cause of mental retardation. The National Organization on Fetal Alcohol Syndrome (2000) estimated that more than 50,000 babies with alcohol-related problems are born in the United States each year. Similarly, pregnant women who smoke are at greater risk of having a premature baby with complicating developmental problems such as mental retardation (Centers for Disease Control, 2003). The use of drugs during pregnancy has varying effects on the infant, depending on how much drug is used, frequency of use, and drug type. Drugs known to produce serious fetal damage include LSD, heroin, morphine, and cocaine. Prescription drugs such as **anticonvulsants** and antibiotics have also been associated with infant malformations.

Maternal substance abuse is also associated with gestation disorders involving prematurity and low birthweight. The term **prematurity** refers to infants delivered before 35 weeks from the first day of the last menstrual period. **Low birthweight** characterizes babies that weigh 2,500 grams (5.5 pounds) or less at birth. Prematurity and low birthweight significantly increase the risk of serious problems at birth, including mental retardation.

Another factor that can seriously affect the unborn baby is incompatibility between the blood types of mother and fetus. The most widely known form of this problem occurs when the mother's blood is Rh-negative, whereas the fetus has Rh-positive blood. In this situation, the mother's system may become sensitized to the incompatible blood type and produce defensive antibodies that damage the fetus. Medical technology can now prevent this condition through the use of a drug known as Rhogam.

**Fetal alcohol syndrome (FAS)**

Damage caused to the fetus by the mother's consumption of alcohol.

**Behavioral factors**

Behaviors, such as dangerous activities or maternal substance abuse, that can cause mental retardation or other disabilities.

**Maternal infection**

Infection in a mother during pregnancy, sometimes having the potential to injure the unborn child.

**Congenital rubella**

A mother's contracting German measles during pregnancy can cause a variety of conditions, including mental retardation, deafness, blindness, and other neurological problems.

**Human immunodeficiency virus (HIV)**

A virus that reduces immune system function and has been linked to AIDS.

**Toxoplasmosis**

An infection caused by protozoa carried in raw meat and fecal material.

**Anticonvulsants**

Medication prescribed to control seizures (convulsions).

**Prematurity**

Status of infants delivered before 35 weeks from the first day of the mother's last menstrual period.

**Low birthweight**

A weight of 5.5 pounds (2,500 grams) or less at birth.

*Fetal alcohol syndrome is a leading cause of preventable mental retardation.*

Mental retardation can occur as a result of postnatal infections and toxic excess. For example, **encephalitis** may damage the central nervous system following certain types of childhood infections (e.g., measles, mumps). Reactions to certain toxic substances—such as lead, carbon monoxide, and drugs—can also damage the central nervous system.

**TRAUMAS OR PHYSICAL ACCIDENTS.** Traumas or physical accidents can occur prior to birth (e.g., exposure to excessive radiation), during delivery, or after the baby is born. Consider Becky from the chapter-opening Snapshot: The cause of her mental retardation was trauma during delivery. She suffered from birth asphyxiation as well as epileptic seizures. A steady supply of oxygen and nutrients to the baby is a critical factor during delivery. One threat to these processes involves the position of the fetus. Normal fetal position places the baby with the head toward the cervix and the face toward the mother's back. Certain other positions may result in damage to the fetus as delivery proceeds. The baby's oxygen supply may be reduced for a period of time until the head is expelled and the lungs begin to function, and this lack of oxygen may result in damage to the brain. Such a condition is known as **anoxia** (oxygen deprivation).

### Unknown Prenatal Influences

Several conditions associated with unknown prenatal influences can result in severe disorders. One such condition involves malformations of cerebral tissue. The most dramatic of these malformations is known as **anencephaly**, a condition in which the individual has a partial or even complete absence of cerebral tissue. In some cases, portions of the brain appear to develop and then degenerate. In **hydrocephalus**, which also has unknown origins, an excess of cerebrospinal fluid accumulates in the skull and results in potentially damaging pressure on cerebral tissue. Hydrocephalus may involve an enlarged head and result in decreased intellectual functioning. If surgical intervention occurs early, the damage may be slight because the pressure will not have been serious or prolonged.

Although we have presented a number of possible causal factors, the cause of mental retardation is often unknown and is undeterminable in many cases. Additionally, many conditions associated with mental retardation are due to the interaction of both hereditary and environmental factors. Although we are unable to always identify the causes of mental retardation, measures can be taken to prevent its occurrence.

**Encephalitis**

An inflammation of brain tissue that may damage the central nervous system.

**Anoxia**

A lack of oxygen that may result in permanent damage to the brain.

**Anencephaly**

A condition in which the individual has a partial or complete absence of cerebral tissue.

**Hydrocephalus**

An excess of cerebrospinal fluid, often resulting in enlargement of the head and pressure on the brain, which may cause mental retardation.

# Educational Services and Supports

We now turn our attention to educating students with mental retardation from the early childhood years through the transition from school to adult life. For children with mild mental retardation, educational services may not begin until they are in elementary school. However, for those with more severe mental retardation, services and supports will begin at birth and may continue into the adult years.

## The Early Childhood Years

The child with mild retardation may exhibit subtle developmental delays in comparison to age-mates, but parents may not view these discrepancies as significant enough to seek intervention during the preschool years. Even if parents are concerned and seek help for their child prior to elementary school, they are often confronted with professionals who are apathetic toward early childhood education. Some professionals believe that early childhood services can actually create, rather than remedy, problems, because the child may not be mature enough to cope with the pressures of structured learning in an educational environment. Simply stated, the maturation philosophy holds that before entering school, a child should reach a level of growth at which he or she is ready to learn certain skills. Unfortunately, this philosophy has kept many children out of the public schools for years.

The antithesis of the maturation philosophy is the prevention of further learning and behavior problems through intervention. **Head Start**, initially funded as a federal preschool program for students who are disadvantaged, is a prevention program that attempts to identify and instruct at-risk children prior to their entering public school. Although Head Start did not generate the results that were initially anticipated (the virtual elimination of school adjustment problems for students with disadvantages), it has represented a significant move forward and continues to receive widespread support from parents and professionals alike. The rationale for early education is widely accepted in the field of special education and is an important part of the IDEA mandate.

Intervention based on normal patterns of growth is referred to as the *developmental milestones approach* because it seeks to develop, remedy, or adapt learner skills on the basis of the child's variation from what is considered normal. This progression of skills continues as the child ages chronologically; rate of progress depends on the severity of the condition. Some children with profound mental retardation may never exceed a developmental age of 6 months. Those with moderate retardation may develop to a level that will enable them to lead fulfilling lives as adults, with varying levels of support.

The importance of early intervention cannot be overstated. Significant advances in early intervention include better assessment, curricular, and instructional technologies; increasing numbers of children receiving services; and appreciation of the need to individualize services for families as well as children (Guralnick, 2001; Ramey & Ramey, 1999; Young, 1996). Early intervention techniques, such as **infant stimulation** programs, focus on the acquisition of sensorimotor skills and intellectual development. Infant stimulation involves learning simple reflex activity and equilibrium reactions. Subsequent intervention then expands into all areas of human growth and development.

## The Elementary School Years

Public education is a relatively new concept in the education of students with mental retardation, particularly those with more severe characteristics. Historically, many of these students were defined as *noneducable* by the public schools because they did not fit the programs offered by general education. Because such programs were built on a foundation of academic learning that emphasized reading, writing, and arithmetic, students with mental retardation could not meet the academic standards set by the schools and thus were excluded. Public schools were not expected to adapt to the needs of students with retardation; rather, the students were expected to adapt to the schools.

With the passage of Public Law 94-142 (now IDEA), public schools face the challenge of providing an appropriate education for all children with mental

**FOCUS 7**

Why are early intervention services for children with mental retardation so important?

**Head Start**

A federally funded preschool program for students with disadvantages to give them "a head start" prior to elementary school.

**Infant stimulation**

Early intervention procedures that provide an infant with an array of visual, auditory, and physical stimuli to promote development.

*Fine motor skill development and eye-hand coordination are important in fostering independence for the young child with mental retardation.*

**FOCUS 8**

Identify five skill areas that should be addressed in programs for elementary school-age children with mental retardation.

retardation. Education has been redefined in terms of a new set of values. Instruction and support for elementary school-age children with mental retardation focus on decreasing their dependence on others and teaching adaptation to the environment. Therefore, instruction must concentrate on those skills that facilitate the child's interaction with others and emphasize independence in the community. Instruction for children with mental retardation generally includes development of motor skills, self-help skills, social skills, communication skills, and academic skills.

**MOTOR SKILLS.** The acquisition of motor skills is fundamental to the developmental process and a prerequisite to successful learning in other content areas, including self-help and social skills. Gross motor development involves general mobility, including the interaction of the body with the environment. Gross motor skills are developed in a sequence, ranging from movements that make balance possible to higher-order locomotor patterns. Locomotor patterns are intended to move the person freely through the environment. Gross motor skills include controlling the head and neck, rolling, body righting, sitting, creeping, crawling, standing, walking, running, jumping, and skipping.

Fine motor development requires more precision and steadiness than the skills developed in the gross motor area. The development of fine motor skills, including reaching, grasping, and manipulating objects, is initially dependent on the ability of the child to visually fix on an object and visually track a moving target. Coordination of the eye and hand is an integral factor in many skill areas as well as in fine motor development. Eye–hand coordination is the basis of social and leisure activities and is essential to the development of the object-control skills required in employment.

**SELF-HELP SKILLS.** The development of self-help skills is critical to a child's progression toward independence from caregivers. Self-help skills include eating, dressing, and maintaining personal hygiene. Eating skills range from finger feeding and drinking from a cup to using proper table behaviors, such as employing utensils and napkins, serving food, and following etiquette. Dressing skills include buttoning, zipping, buckling, lacing, and tying. Personal hygiene skills are developed in an age-appropriate context. Basic hygiene skills include toileting, face and hand washing, bathing, tooth brushing, hair combing, and shampooing. Skills associated with the adolescent and adult years include skin care, shaving, hair setting, and the use of deodorants and cosmetics.

**SOCIAL SKILLS.** Social skills training emphasizes the importance of learning problem-solving and decision-making skills and of using appropriate communication in a social context. Agran and Wehmeyer (1999) indicated that poor problem-solving and decision-making skills have been barriers to the success of people with mental retardation in community and school settings. These authors further suggested that students with mental retardation will not learn these skills through observation but must be specifically taught how to solve problems. Benjamin (1996) proposed a four-step process:

1. Students learn to observe and analyze a problem situation through role playing and simulation, identify the problem(s) within the situation, and name the problem.

2. Students learn to come up with possible options that could solve the problem. If they are unable to produce options, they learn how to access resources (e.g., talking to other people) that will help generate possible solutions.

3. Once possible options have been identified, students select the most viable option to solve the problem. Once the option is implemented, they check to see whether the problem has been solved. If the problem remains, students decide what can be done to change the plan.

4. Students learn how to use strategies from one problem to solve similar problems in other situations.

In terms of using appropriate communication in a social context, Westling and Fox (2000) suggested several learning outcomes for students. They must be able to initiate and maintain a conversation (whether it be verbal, signed, or pictorial) while using appropriate social conventions and courtesies (e.g., staying on topic, not interrupting the speaker, appropriate body posture). These authors suggested a list of social skills that are important instructional targets for students with mental retardation. (See Table 10.4)

**COMMUNICATION SKILLS.**   The ability to communicate with others is an essential component of growth and development. Without communication, there can be no interaction. Communication systems for children with mental retardation take three general forms: verbal language, augmentative communication (including sign language and language boards), and a combination of the verbal and augmentative approaches. The approach used depends on the child's capability. A child who can develop the requisite skills for spoken language will have greatly enhanced everyday interactive skills. For a child unable to develop verbal skills as an effective means of communication, manual communication must be considered. The child must develop some form of communication that will facilitate inclusion with peers and family members throughout life. The nearby Inclusion Through the Lifespan offers some specific tips.

---

**TABLE 10.4**

### Instructional Targets in Social Skills Training

| | |
|---|---|
| Establish eye contact. | Make requests. |
| Establish appropriate proximity. | Respond to requests. |
| Maintain appropriate body posture during conversation. | Ask for information. |
| Speak with appropriate volume, rate, and expression. | Provide information. |
| | Ask for clarification. |
| Maintain attention during exchange. | Respond to requests for clarification. |
| Initiate greetings. | Extend social invitation. |
| Respond to greetings. | Deliver refusals. |
| Initiate partings. | Respond to refusals. |
| Respond to partings. | Use social courtesies (please, thank you, apology). |
| Discriminate appropriate times to greet or part. | Maintain topic. |
| Answer questions. | Initiate a new topic. |
| Ask questions. | |

SOURCE:  From *Teaching Students with Severe Disabilities* (p. 242), by D. Westling and L. Fox, 2000, Upper Saddle River, NJ: Merrill.

## PEOPLE WITH MENTAL RETARDATION (INTELLECTUAL DISABILITIES)

### EARLY CHILDHOOD YEARS

#### Tips for the Family

- Promote family learning about the diversity of all people in the context of understanding the child with intellectual differences.
- Create opportunities for friendships to develop between your child and children without disabilities, in both family and neighborhood settings.
- Help facilitate your child's opportunities and access to neighborhood preschools by actively participating in the education planning process. Become familiar with the individualized family service plan (IFSP) and how it can serve as a planning tool to support the inclusion of your child in preschool programs that involve students without disabilities.

#### Tips for the General Education Preschool Teacher

- Focus on the child's individual abilities first. Whatever labels have been placed on the child (e.g., "mentally retarded") will have little to do with instructional needs.
- When teaching the child, focus on presenting each component of a task clearly, while reducing outside stimuli that may distract learning.
- Begin with simple tasks, and move to more complex ones as the child masters skills.
- Verbally label stimuli, such as objects or people, as often as possible to provide the child with both auditory and visual input.
- Provide a lot of practice in initial learning phases, using short but frequent sessions to ensure that the child has mastered the skill before moving on to more complex tasks.
- Create success experiences by rewarding correct responses to tasks as well as appropriate behavior with peers who are not disabled.
- It is important for the young child with mental retardation to be able to transfer learning from school to the home and neighborhood. Facilitate such transfer by providing information that is meaningful to the child and noting how the initial and transfer tasks are similar.

#### Tips for Preschool Personnel

- Support the inclusion of young children with mental retardation in classrooms and programs.
- Support teachers, staff, and volunteers as they attempt to create success experiences for the child in the preschool setting.
- Integrate families as well as children into the preschool programs. Offer parents as many opportunities as possible to be part of the program (e.g., advisory boards, volunteer experiences).

#### Tips for Neighbors and Friends

- Look for opportunities for young neighborhood children who are not disabled to interact during play times with the child who is mentally retarded.
- Provide a supportive community environment for the family of a young child who is mentally retarded. Encourage the family, including the child, to participate in neighborhood activities (e.g., outings, barbecues, outdoor yard and street cleanups, crime watches).
- Try to understand how the young child with mental retardation is similar to other children in the neighborhood rather than different. Focus on those similarities in your interactions with other neighbors and children in your community.

### ELEMENTARY YEARS

#### Tips for the Family

- Actively participate in the development of your son or daughter's individualized education program (IEP). Through active participation, fight for those goals that you would like to see on the IEP that will focus on your child's developing social interaction and communication skills in natural settings (e.g., the general education classroom).
- To help facilitate your son or daughter's inclusion in the neighborhood elementary school, help educators and administrators understand the importance of inclusion with peers who are not disabled (e.g., riding on the same school bus, going to recess and lunch at the same time, participating in schoolwide assemblies).
- Participate in as many school functions for parents (e.g., PTA, parent advisory groups, volunteering) as is reasonable, to connect your family to the mainstream of the general education school.
- Create opportunities for your child to make friends with same-age children without disabilities.

#### Tips for the General Education Classroom Teacher

- View children with mental retardation as children, first and foremost. Focus on their similarities with other children rather than on their differences.
- Recognize children with mental retardation for their own accomplishments within the classroom rather than comparing them to those of peers without disabilities.
- Employ cooperative learning strategies wherever possible to promote effective learning by all students. Use peers without disabilities as support for students with mental retardation. This may include establishing peer-buddy programs or peer and cross-age tutoring.
- Consider all members of the classroom when you organize the physical environment. Find ways to meet the individual needs of each child (e.g., establishing aisles that will accommodate a wheelchair and organizing desks to facilitate tutoring on assigned tasks).

#### Tips for School Personnel

- Integrate school resources as well as children.
- Wherever possible, help general classroom teachers access the human and material resources necessary to meet the needs of students with mental retardation. Instructional materials and programs should be made available to whoever needs them, not just to those identified as being in special education.
- Help general and special education teachers to develop nondisabled peer-partner and support networks for students with mental retardation.

- Promote the heterogeneous grouping of students. Try to avoid clustering large numbers of students with mental retardation in a single general education classroom. Integrate no more than one or two in each elementary education classroom.
- Maintain the same schedules for students with mental retardation as for all other students in the building. Recess, lunch, school assemblies, and bus arrival and departure schedules should be identical for all students, with and without disabilities.
- Create opportunities for all school personnel to collaborate in the development and implementation of instructional programs for individual children.

### Tips for Neighbors and Friends

- Support families who are seeking to have their child with mental retardation educated in their local school with children who are not disabled. This will give children with mental retardation more opportunities for interacting with children who are not disabled, both in school and in the local community.

## SECONDARY AND TRANSITION YEARS

### Tips for the Family

- Create opportunities for your son or daughter to participate in activities that are of interest to him or her, beyond the school day, with same-age peers who are not disabled, including high school clubs, sports, or just hanging out in the local mall.
- Promote opportunities for students from your son's or daughter's high school to visit your home. Help arrange get-togethers or parties involving students from the neighborhood and/or school.
- Become actively involved in the development of the individualized education and transition program. Explore with the high school their views on what should be done to assist your son or daughter in the transition from school to adult life.

### Tips for the General Education Classroom Teacher

- Collaborate with special education teachers and other specialists to adapt subject matter in your classroom (e.g., science, math, or physical education) to the individual needs of students with mental retardation.
- Let students without disabilities know that the student with mental retardation belongs in their classroom. The goals and activities of this student may be different from those of other students, but with support, the student with mental retardation will benefit from working with you and the other students in the class.
- Support the student with mental retardation in becoming involved in extracurricular high school activities. If you are the faculty sponsor of a club or organization, explore whether this student is interested and how he or she could get involved.

### Tips for School Personnel

- Advocate for parents of high-school-age students with mental retardation to participate in the activities of the school (e.g., committees and PTA).
- Help facilitate parental involvement in the IEP process during the high school years by valuing parental input that focuses on a desire to include their child in the mainstream of the school. Parents will be more active when school personnel have general and positive contact with the family.
- Provide human and material support to high school special education or vocational teachers seeking to develop community-based instruction programs that focus on students learning and applying skills in actual community settings (e.g., grocery stores, malls, theaters, parks, work sites).

### Tips for Neighbors, Friends, and Potential Employers

- As often as possible, work with the family and school personnel to create opportunities for students with mental retardation to participate in community activities (such as going to the movies, "hanging out" with peers without disabilities in the neighborhood mall, going to high school sports events).
- As a potential employer, work with the high school to locate and establish community-based employment training sites for students with mental retardation.

## ADULT YEARS

### Tips for the Family

- Become aware of what life will be like for your son or daughter in the local community during the adult years. What are the formal (government-funded advocacy organizations) and informal supports available in your community? What are the characteristics of adult service programs? Explore adult support systems in the local community in the areas of supported living, employment, and recreation and leisure.

### Tips for Neighbors, Friends, and Potential Employers

- Seek ways to become part of the community support network for the individual with mental retardation. Be alert to ways in which this individual can become and remain actively involved in community employment, neighborhood recreational activities, and functions at a local house of worship.
- As potential employers in the community, seek information on employment of people with mental retardation. Find out about programs (e.g., supported employment) that focus on establishing work for people with mental retardation while meeting your needs as an employer.

Some students with mental retardation benefit from the use of assistive technology and communication aids. Assistive technology may involve a variety of communication approaches that assist a person with mental retardation who has limited speech ability. These approaches may be low-tech (a language board with pictures) or high-tech (a laptop computer with voice output) Regardless of the approach, a communication aid can be a valuable tool in helping a person with mental retardation communicate with others. For a more in-depth look at assistive technology and communication aids for people with disabilities, see Chapter 3.

**ACADEMIC SKILLS.** Students with mental retardation can benefit from instruction in basic or functional academic programs. In the area of literacy, students with mild mental retardation will require a systematic instructional program that takes into account differences in the rate of learning, but they will learn to read when given "rich, intensive, and extensive literary experiences" (Katims, 2000). In fact, these students may achieve a reading level as high as a fourth or fifth grade. In a 1996 study, Katims found that students with mental retardation made significant progress in literacy programs that emphasized **direct instruction** (the direct teaching of letters, words, and syntactic, phonetic, and semantic analysis) in conjunction with written literature that was meaningful to the student, or from the student's own writings.

A significant relationship exists between measured IQ and reading achievement: Students with mental retardation read well below nondisabled students of the same age. This relationship seems to suggest that reading instruction should be limited to higher-functioning students with mental retardation. A growing body of research, however, indicates that students with more severe mental retardation can learn "useful" academic skills in a functional reading program. Browder and Snell (2000) described functional academics as "simply the most useful parts of the three R's—reading, writing, and arithmetic. . . . Useful must be defined individually by studying each student's current daily routines, predicting future needs, and establishing a set of priorities in basic math and reading" (p. 497). A functional reading program uses materials that are a part of a person's normal routines in work, everyday living, and leisure activities. For example, functional reading involves words that are frequently encountered in the environment, such as those used on labels or signs in public places; words that warn of possible risks; and symbols such as the skull and crossbones to denote poisonous substances.

Students with mental retardation have deficiencies in arithmetic skills, but the majority of those with mild retardation can learn basic addition and subtraction. However, these children will have significant difficulty in mathematical reasoning and problem-solving tasks (Beirne-Smith et al., 2002). Arithmetic skills are taught most efficiently through the use of money concepts. For example, functional math involves activities such as learning to use a checkbook, shop in a grocery store, or operate a vending machine. The immediate practical application motivates the student. Regardless of the approach used, arithmetic instruction must be concrete and practical to compensate for the child's deficiencies in reasoning ability.

For more insight into instruction that facilitates interaction with others and emphasizes independence for elementary school-age students with mental retardation, read the nearby Case Study and respond to the application questions.

## Transition from School to Adult Life

The goals of an educational program for adolescents with mental retardation are to increase personal independence, enhance opportunities for participation in the local community, prepare for employment, and facilitate a successful transition to the adult years.

**PERSONAL INDEPENDENCE AND PARTICIPATION IN THE COMMUNITY.** *Independence* consists of the development and application of skills that lead to greater self-sufficiency in daily personal life, including personal care, self-help, and appro-

**FOCUS 9**

Identify four educational goals for adolescents with mental retardation.

**Direct instruction**

Teaching academic subjects through precisely sequenced lessons involving drill, practice, and immediate feedback. In reading, direct instruction involves the focused teaching of letters and words, as well as syntactic, phonetic, and semantic analysis.

# Case Study

## INCLUDING SCOTT

Scott's parents, Heather and Bill Bonn, discuss their son's educational experiences:

By the time Scott was 10 years old, he had been in five different schools. Because he has Down syndrome, he began his schooling at 18 months, attending the only public special education program in the county once a week. At that time, all children [with mental retardation] were bussed to this central location. Scott stayed at the special education school until he was 3½ years old. He could have stayed there until he was 21, but we wanted something different for him. . . . The transition to Coleridge Elementary School wasn't easy. . . . Scott spent most of the day working on academics in the special education classroom; he was included in the general education classroom for only short periods for art, music, lunch, and show-and-tell. At first, he didn't like going into the general education classroom, but before long it was the reverse: He didn't want to leave. . . . Scott is now fully included. Lately we've noticed that he is more verbal. . . . He is less dependent on an assistant at school and has started to develop independent work skills. (Bonn & Bonn, 2000a, p. 174; Bonn & Bonn, 2000b, pp. 210–211)

### APPLICATION

1. What skills are important for Scott to learn and apply now that he is fully included in a general education classroom?

2. Scott will move to a middle school next year. Can you identify some strategies that teachers might use to help Scott make a successful transition from elementary school to middle school?

---

priate leisure activities. Participation in the community includes access to programs, facilities, and services that people without disabilities often take for granted: grocery stores, shopping malls, restaurants, theaters, and parks. Adolescents with mental retardation need opportunities for interaction with peers without disabilities (other than caregivers), access to community events, sustained social relationships, and involvement in choices that affect their lives. The range of community services and supports that can facilitate the transition of an adolescent with mental retardation into the adult years is shown in Figure 10.3.

**EMPLOYMENT PREPARATION.** Work is a crucial measure of any person's success during adulthood; it offers the primary opportunity for social interaction, a basis for personal identity and status, and a chance to contribute to the community. These needs are basic to adults who have mental retardation, just as they are to their peers without disabilities.

Fortunately, employment training for students with mental retardation is shifting from the isolation and "getting ready" orientation of a **sheltered workshop** to activities accomplished in community employment. Goals and objectives are developed according to the demands of the community work setting and the functioning level of the individual. The focus is on helping each person learn skills and apply them in a job setting while receiving the support she or he needs to succeed. Providing ongoing assistance to the individual on the job is the basis of an approach known as supported employment. **Supported employment** is defined as work

**Sheltered workshop**

A segregated vocational training and employment setting for people with disabilities.

**Supported employment**

Paid work in integrated community settings for individuals with more severe disabilities who are expected to need continuous support services and for whom competitive employment has traditionally not been possible.

*For adolescents with moderate and severe mental retardation, employment preparation during high school is shifting away from segregated sheltered workshops to supported employment in inclusive community settings.*

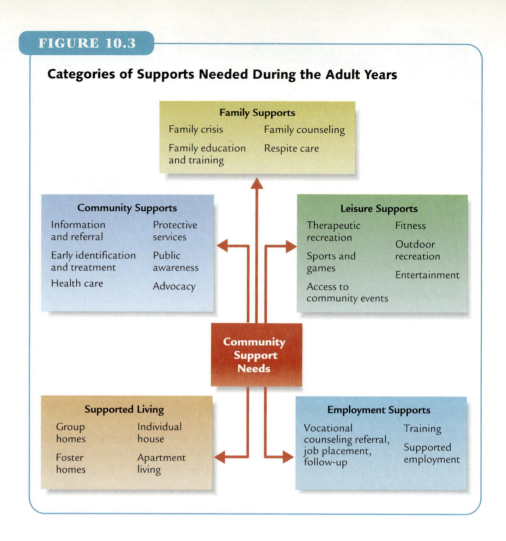

**FIGURE 10.3**

**Categories of Supports Needed During the Adult Years**

**Family Supports**
Family crisis | Family counseling
Family education and training | Respite care

**Community Supports**
Information and referral | Protective services
Early identification and treatment | Public awareness
Health care | Advocacy

**Leisure Supports**
Therapeutic recreation | Fitness
Sports and games | Outdoor recreation
Access to community events | Entertainment

**Community Support Needs**

**Supported Living**
Group homes | Individual house
Foster homes | Apartment living

**Employment Supports**
Vocational counseling referral, job placement, follow-up | Training
Supported employment

in an inclusive setting for individuals with severe disabilities (including those with mental retardation) who are expected to need continuous support services and for whom competitive employment has traditionally not been possible (See Chapter 4 for more information about supported employment).

Research indicates that people with mental retardation can work in community employment if they have adequate training and support (Reiff, Ginsberg, & Gerber, 1997; Wehman, 2001). Below are some guidelines for developing a comprehensive employment-training program for students with mental retardation.

- The student should have the opportunity to make informed choices about what jobs he or she wants to do and where he or she wants to work.

- The student should receive employment training in community settings prior to graduation from high school.

- Employment training should focus on work opportunities present in the local area where the individual currently lives.

- As the student approaches graduation, the employment training should focus on specific job training.

- Collaboration between the school and adult service agencies must be part of the employment-training program. (Drew & Hardman, 2004; Morgan, Ellerd, Gerity, & Blair, 2000)

The nearby Assistive Technology, "Ryan's Story," describes how a high school transition specialist working closely with a local business and using assistive technology developed a successful community-based employment-training program.

## RYAN'S STORY

Ryan is a 20-year-old with mental retardation. Using motion video on CD-ROM, he was able to learn about the complexities of several possible jobs without having to observe any of them in person. Working with a transition specialist at a computer, Ryan was able to learn about and select a list of preferred jobs from a CD-ROM program that distinguished six job domains on the basis of various characteristics (e.g., work location, required physical stamina, level of social activity). Ryan initially identified general work conditions. This screening process then allowed him to select preferences in employment conditions (e.g., inside vs. outside work, heavy vs. light physical involvement, working mostly alone vs. mostly with people). Ryan's story, as told by his transition specialist Becky Blair, follows.

I first met Ryan when he was referred after a series of unsuccessful community-based job placements. The background information I received from his previous service provider described him as unmotivated and sloppy in both appearance and job performance. The professionals who had worked with Ryan in the past recommended that he return to a sheltered day program for "work skills training."

During the intake process, I asked Ryan to name his three most desired jobs. The jobs he identified as most preferred were the same ones from which he had been fired because of extensive absence or poor performance.

Documentation indicated that although Ryan was able to perform the tasks associated with each job, he would lose interest after a short time.

To further assist Ryan in identifying and obtaining employment, staff from a local university project, the *Yes Program,* gave him an opportunity to view a number of jobs on a video. After watching the video, Ryan identified motel housekeeping as a desired job. He seemed really excited about this particular job, so together, he and I began our job search. After a few weeks of job development, we found a rather reluctant employer who was willing to give Ryan a job on a 30-day trial basis. I explained the agreement to Ryan, and again he assured me that this was the job he wanted.

Within 3 weeks, Ryan had become the fastest and most dependable housekeeper on the motel's staff. His employer was so impressed with his work that she asked me if I had other people with disabilities looking for employment. Within 6 weeks of his start date, Ryan was awarded Employee of the Month and was given a cash bonus. Less than 2 months after starting the job, he was promoted to "second floor supervisor" and received a raise. In my last contact with him, Ryan was supervising a crew of employees—adults without disabilities—on an entire motel wing. The once hesitant and skeptical employer now brags about Ryan's performance to anyone who will listen.

SOURCE: Adapted from "That's the Job I Want: How Technology Helps Young People in Transition," by R. L. Morgan, D. A. Ellerd, B. P. Gerity, & R. J. Blair, 2000. *Teaching Exceptional Children, 32*(4), pp. 44–49.

# Inclusive Education

**FOCUS 10**

Why is the inclusion of students with mental retardation in general education settings important to an appropriate educational experience?

Historically, special education for students with mental retardation meant segregated education. Today, however, the focus is on including these students in general education schools and classrooms. Some students with mental retardation are included for only a part of the school day and attend only those general education classes that their individualized education program (IEP) teams consider consistent with their needs and functioning levels (such as physical education, industrial arts, and home economics). Other students with mental retardation attend general education classes for all or the majority of the school day. For these students, special education consists primarily of services and supports intended to facilitate their opportunities and success in the general education classroom. Recent placement information from the U.S. Department of Education (2002) indicated that approximately 94% of students with mental retardation between the ages of 6 and 21 attend general education schools for the entire day. Of these students, about 14% are served in a general education class for at least 80% of the time, and 50% spend more than half of their time outside the general education class.

Another placement option for students with disabilities is the special school. Special schools are facilities exclusively for students with mental retardation or other disabilities. Approximately 4% of students with mental retardation attend public special schools, and less than 10% attend private special schools (U.S. Department of Education). Considerable controversy exists about whether there is any justification for placing students with mental retardation in special schools.. For more insight into this controversy, see the nearby Debate Forum.

## Debate Forum

# CAN SPECIAL SCHOOLS FOR STUDENTS WITH MENTAL RETARDATION BE JUSTIFIED?

### POINT

There will always be a need for special schools. Although inclusion may be appropriate for many students with mental retardation, special schools are the least restrictive environment for a small number of children who require intensive instruction and support that cannot be provided in a general education school or classroom. Special schools provide for greater homogeneity in grouping and programming. Teachers can specialize in particular areas such as art, language, physical education, and music. Teaching materials can be centralized and, thus, used more effectively with larger numbers of students. A special school more efficiently uses available resources. In addition, some parents of students with severe mental retardation believe that their children will be happier in a special school that "protects" them.

### COUNTERPOINT

Research on the efficacy of special schools does not support the contention that such a placement is ever the least restrictive environment (Downing & Eichinger, 1996; Gee, 1996; Sailor, Gee, & Karasoff, 2000). On the contrary, investigations over the past 20 years have strongly indicated that students with mental retardation, regardless of the severity of their condition, benefit from placement in general education environments where opportunities for interaction with students who are not disabled are systematically planned and implemented (Hunt, Staub, Alwell, & Goetz, 1994; Meyer, Peck, & Brown, 1991; Sailor et al., 2000). Inclusion for students with mental retardation embodies a variety of opportunities, both within the general education classroom and throughout the school. Besides interaction in a classroom setting, ongoing inclusion occurs in the halls, on the playground, in the cafeteria, and at school assemblies.

Stainback, Stainback, and Ayres (1996) also reported that general education teachers who have the opportunity for interaction with children with mental retardation are not fearful of or intimidated by their presence in the school building. Special schools generally offer little, if any, opportunity for interaction with normal peers and deprive the child of valuable learning and socialization experiences. Special schools cannot be financially or ideologically justified. Public school administrators must now plan to include children with retardation in existing general education schools and classes.

What do you think? To give your opinion, go to Chapter 10 of the companion website (www.ablongman.com/hardman8e) and click on Debate Forum.

# FOCUS REVIEW

**FOCUS 1** Identify the major *Essay Questions* components of the AAMR definition of mental retardation.

- Significant limitations in intellectual abilities.
- Significant limitations in adaptive behavior as expressed in conceptual, social, and practical adaptive skills.
- Disability originates before the age of 18
- The severity of the condition is tempered by each individual's participation, interactions, and social roles within the community; their overall physical and mental health; and the environmental context.

**FOCUS 2** Identify four approaches to classifying people with mental retardation.

- Severity of the condition may be described in terms of mild, moderate, severe, and profound mental retardation.
- Classification based on educability expectations designates children as educable or trainable.
- Medical descriptors classify mental retardation on the basis of the origin of the condition (e.g., infection, intoxication, trauma, chromosomal abnormality).
- Classification based on the type and extent of support needed categorizes people with mental retardation in terms of whether they need intermittent, limited, extensive, or pervasive support in order to function in natural settings.

**FOCUS 3** What is the prevalence of mental retardation?

- Over 600,000 students between the ages of 6 and 21 are labeled as having mental retardation

and are receiving service under IDEA. Approximately 11% of all students with disabilities between the ages of 6 and 21 have mental retardation.

- The National Health Survey–Disability Supplement found that people with mental retardation constitute 0.83% of the total population, or 2 million people.
- The President's Committee on Mental Retardation (2000) estimated that between 6.2 and 7.5 million Americans of all ages, or 3% of the general population, experience mental retardation. These figures are considerably higher than the 2 million people reported in the National Health Survey.

**FOCUS 4** Identify the intellectual skills, self-regulation skills, and adaptive skills characteristics of individuals with mental retardation.

- Intellectual characteristics may include learning and memory deficiencies, difficulties in establishing learning sets, and inefficient rehearsal strategies.
- Self-regulation characteristics include difficulty in mediating or regulating behavior.
- Adaptive skills characteristics may include difficulties in coping with the demands of the environment, in developing interpersonal relationships, in developing language skills, and in taking care of personal needs.

**FOCUS 5** Identify the academic, motivational, speech and language, and physical characteristics of children with mental retardation.

- Children with mental retardation exhibit significant deficits

in the areas of reading and mathematics.

- Children with mild mental retardation have poor reading comprehension, compared to their same-age peers.
- Children with mental retardation may be able to learn basic computations but are unlikely to apply concepts appropriately in a problem-solving situation.
- Motivational difficulties may reflect learned helplessness: "No matter what I do, I will not succeed."
- The most common speech difficulties involve articulation problems, voice problems, and stuttering.
- Language differences are generally associated with delays in language development rather than with bizarre use of language.
- Physical differences generally are not evident for individuals with mild mental retardation, because such retardation is usually not associated with genetic factors.
- The more severe the mental retardation, the greater the probability of genetic causation and compounding physiological problems.

**FOCUS 6** Discuss the causes of mental retardation.

- Mental retardation is the result of multiple factors, some known, many unknown. The cause of mental retardation is generally not known for the individual with mild retardation.
- Causes associated with moderate to profound mental retardation include sociocultural influences, biomedical factors, behavioral factors, and unknown prenatal influences.

**FOCUS 7** Why are early intervention services for children with mental retardation so important?

• Early intervention services are needed to provide a stimulating environment for the child to enhance growth and development.
• Early intervention programs focus on the development of communication skills, social interaction, and readiness for formal instruction.

**FOCUS 8** Identify five skill areas that should be addressed in programs for elementary school-age children with mental retardation.

• Motor skills
• Self-help skills
• Social skills
• Communication skills
• Academic skills

**FOCUS 9** Identify four educational goals for adolescents with mental retardation.

• To increase the individual's personal independence
• To enhance opportunities for participation in the local community
• To prepare for employment

• To facilitate a successful transition to the adult years

**FOCUS 10** Why is the inclusion of students with mental retardation in general education settings important to an appropriate educational experience?

• Regardless of the severity of their condition, students with mental retardation benefit from placement in general education environments where opportunities for inclusion with peers without disabilities are systematically planned and implemented.

## FURTHER READINGS

Beirne-Smith, Ittenbach, R. F., & Patton, J. R. (2002). *Mental Retardation* (6th ed.). Upper Saddle River, NJ: Merrill.

*Provides an overview of the basic concepts; biology, psychology, and sociology of mental retardation; intervention issues; and family considerations.*

Drew, C. J., & Hardman, M. L. (2004). *Mental Retardation: A lifespan approach to people with intellectual disabilities* (8th ed.). Columbus, OH: Merrill.

*Provides an interdisciplinary introduction to mental retardation, with an emphasis on stages of human development and the lifespan. Includes chapters on family and social issues, early development, education, and multicultural issues.*

Shriver, M. (2001). *What's Wrong with Timmy?* New York: Little, Brown.

*Uses storytelling to provide answers to children's questions about mental retardation. Maria Shriver tells the story of 8-year-old Kate, who, while at the park with her mother, notices Timmy, a boy who looks and behaves differently from the other children she knows. Kate wonders whether there is something "wrong" with Timmy, but when her mother introduces her to Timmy, the seeds of friendship are planted.*

Trainer, M., & Featherstone, H. (2003). *Differences in Common: Straight talk on Mental Retardation, Down Syndrome, and Your Life.* Bethesda, MD: Woodbine House.

*A collection of almost 50 essays that span more than 20 years of a mother's experience with Down syndrome. A wide variety of issues are explored, including family adjustment, public attitudes, inclusion, and independence.*

## WEB RESOURCES

### American Association on Mental Retardation

www.aamr.org

This is the oldest and largest interdisciplinary organization of professionals (and others) concerned about mental retardation and related disabilities. This website contains AAMR publications, products, and information on the definition of mental retardation.

### The ARC

www.thearc.org

The ARC is a national organization of and for people with mental retardation and related developmental disabilities and their families. This website provides information on promoting and improving supports and services for people with mental retardation and their families, as well as research and resources on the prevention of mental retardation in infants and young children.

**National Down Syndrome Society**

www.ndss.org

The National Down Syndrome Society (NDSS) was established to ensure that people with Down syndrome have the opportunity to achieve their full potential in community life. After the U.S. government, it is the largest supporter of Down syndrome research in the country. This website is a resource for research, educational opportunities, health issues, and life planning. An advocacy center provides up-to-date information on policy issues and national legislation.

## BUILDING YOUR PORTFOLIO

If you are thinking about a career in special education, you should know that many states use national standards developed by the Council for Exceptional Children (CEC) to assess a teacher candidate's knowledge and skills for working with students with disabilities. See a complete listing of the ten CEC Content Standards on the inside front cover of this text.

### CEC Content Standards Addressed in Chapter 10

1. Foundations
2. Development and Characteristics of Learners
3. Individual Learning Differences
5. Learning Environments and Social Interactions
7. Instructional Planning
8. Assessment

### Assess Your Knowledge of the CEC Standards Addressed in Chapter 10

Some states require that teacher candidates develop a portfolio of products that demonstrate mastery of the CEC content standards. To assist in the development of products for this portfolio, you may wish to complete the following activities.

- Complete a written test of the chapter's content.

  *If your instructor requires a written test of your content knowledge for this chapter, keep a copy for your portfo-*lio. *A practice test on the information covered in this chapter is available through the companion website (www.ablongman.com/hardman8e) and the Student Study Guide.*

- Respond to Application Questions for the Case Study, "Including Scott."

  *Review the Case Study and respond in writing to the application questions. Keep a copy of the case study and your written response for your portfolio.*

- Complete the "Take a Stand" activity for the Debate Forum "Can Special Schools for Students with Mental Retardation Be Justified?"

  *Read the Debate Forum in this chapter and then visit our companion website to complete the activity "Take a Stand." Keep a copy of this activity for your portfolio.*

- Participate in a Community Service Learning Activity.

  *Community service is a valuable way to enhance your learning experience. Visit our companion website for suggested community service learning activities that correspond to the information presented in this chapter. Develop a reflective journal of the service learning experience for your portfolio.*

## THEMES OF THE TIMES

Expand your knowledge of the concepts discussed in this chapter by reading current and historical articles from the *New York Times* by visiting the "Themes of the Times" section of the companion website: **www.ablongman.com/hardman8e.**

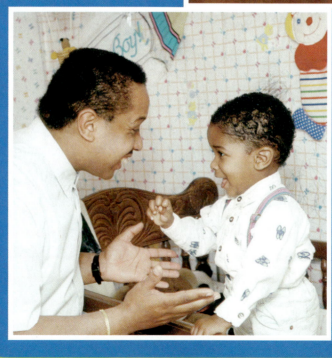

CHAPTER

11

# Communication Disorders

## Disabilities in Communication Not Uncommon

Nearly 19% of the children (6–21 years old) with disabilities who were served under federal law during 2000–2001 had speech or language difficulties. (U.S. Department of Education, 2003)

## Technology Helps Her Expression

"It's her self-expression, her ability to express her feelings and goals. Just being understood makes her feel valued. . . . That's the purpose of technology—to not hold people back." (Norma Velez, speaking about her daughter's voice machine, as quoted by Horiuchi, 1999)

## Free Speech: Help for Stuttering

A story about Dr. Joe Kalinowsky on *Good Morning America* captures the embarrassment and feelings that often accompany stuttering. "'And I prayed every night' Kalinowsky said. 'Take off an arm. Take off my arm, God. 'Cause I know kids will tease me for not having an arm. But if I can talk the same as every other kid, that'll be OK.'" (abcNEWS.com, Good Morning America, December 27, 2002)

## Twelve Months or So

Parents can become overly concerned about the development of their baby's language skills if they interpret the age expectations too rigidly. Dr. Caroline Bowen, a certified speech pathologist, reminds parents that "children vary quite considerably with regard to the rate at which they reach the various speech and language 'milestones.' There is no need to put out an SOS for a speech pathologist if your child does not do the things . . . at precisely the ages stated! When you see language ages and stages and read an age like '12 months,' say to yourself, '12 months or so.'" (Bowen, 2002)

**FOCUS**

**PREVIEW:** To preview the central concepts of this chapter, read the focus questions located in the margins. Using these questions as a guide, ask yourself what you already know and what you want to learn.

# Meghan

given her the opportunity to be a typical sixth grader.

When Meghan was born, we knew she had cerebral palsy. We saw that she had a projected motor delay and cognitive delay, but how much was uncertain. As parents, we wanted a language-based environment, not a life skills environment, for Meghan. We wanted her to have a childhood where her strengths were recognized and her hopes for learning encouraged. Meghan may never tell us on demand the 26 letters of the alphabet, a readiness requirement in the developmental center program, but she was able to return to an inclusive fourth grade community, where she learned the history of California. She knew the people who built the railroad and could tell us this through an adapted curriculum and picture cues, and she was accurate.

Meghan is apraxic. It is hard for her to come up with words—it is hard for her to retrieve them and it is hard for her to summon the motor skills to utter them. But she is driven to talk and to get her messages out. We use many forms of communica-

tion with her: verbal modeling, singing because it builds vocabulary (music uses another part of the brain), sign language for a visual way to focus, and a Dynavox. The Dynavox is touch-activated and creates verbal speech. We can program information on its screen to increase practical language skills as well as link up with the curriculum she is being taught in school.

Meghan just completed an oral presentation on the Alaskan oil spill. We created a page on the Dynavox with picture cues that had verbal messages sequencing the key topics of her report.

One of Meghan's friends helped her program "I'm having a bad hair day" into her Dynavox diary. She uses sassy sixth grade language now, and we think of it as an increase in language skills! We can be the great Mom, Dad, and teachers in her life, but it is her peers who are the most valuable resources, for they see Meghan as a person first and her disability second. They will make the difference in her tomorrows, for they pay attention to what they have in common, not to what makes them different.

Meghan is 12 years old. She is a respected member of her sixth-grade class in a school that has become a powerful inclusive community for her. People are drawn to Meghan because of her courage, her humor, and her belief in living for her dreams.

Meghan has a strong circle of friends who pay attention to who she is as a person and know how to be with her and share in many different mutual experiences. Meghan enjoys skiing, playing tennis, swimming, music, and movies. Meghan's friends call her on the phone and talk to her—even if she chooses only to listen. If they could just see her smile over the telephone! She goes to birthday parties and has slumber parties. Her friends have

---

We communicate many times each day. We order food in a restaurant, thank a friend for doing a favor, ask a question in class, call for help in an emergency, follow instructions regarding the assembly of a piece of furniture, or give directions to someone who is lost. Our lives revolve around communication in many crucial ways. Despite its importance and constant presence in our lives, we seldom think much about communication unless we have a problem with it. Communication is also one of the most complicated processes people undertake. Speech and language are two highly interrelated components of communication. Problems in either can significantly affect a person's daily life. Because of their complexity, determining the cause of a problem in these areas is often perplexing.

Communication is the exchange of ideas, opinions, or facts between senders and receivers. It requires that a sender (an individual or group) compose and transmit a message and that a receiver decode and understand the message (Bernstein, 2002). The sender and receiver are therefore partners in the communication process.

Although related, speech and language are not the same thing. Speech is the audible representation of language. It is one means of expressing language but not the only means. Language represents the message contained in speech. It is possible to have language without speech, such as sign language used by people who are deaf, and speech without language, such as the speech of birds that are trained to talk. Communication is the broader concept. Language is a part of communication. Speech is often thought of as a part of language, although language may exist without speech. Figure 11.1 illustrates the interrelationship of speech, language, and communication.

**FOCUS**
**1**

Identify four ways in which speech, language, and communication are interrelated.

# The Structure of Language

Language consists of several major components, including phonology, syntax, morphology, semantics, and pragmatics. Phonology is the system of speech sounds that an individual utters—that is, rules regarding how sounds can be used and combined (Nicolosi, Harryman, & Krescheck, 2003; Owens, Metz, & Haas, 2002). For example, the word *cat* has three phonemes, C-A-T. Syntax involves the rules governing sentence structure, the way sequences of words are combined into phrases and sentences. For example, the sentence *Will you help Janice?* changes in meaning when the order of the words is changed to *You will help Janice.* Morphology is concerned with the form and internal structure of words—that is, the transformations of words in terms of areas such as tense (for example, present to past tense) and number (singular to plural), and so on. When we add an *s* to *cat*, we have produced the plural form, *cats*, with two morphemes, or units of meaning: the concept of cat and the concept of plural. Such transformations involve prefixes, suffixes, and inflections (Feldman, Barac-Cikoja, & Kostic, 2002; Szagun, 2000). Grammar is constituted from a combination of syntax and morphology. Semantics represents the understanding of language, the component most directly concerned with meaning. Semantics addresses whether the speaker's intended message is conveyed by the words and their combinations in an age-appropriate manner. It involves the meaning of a word to an individual, which may be unique in each of our personal mental dictionaries (e.g., the meaning of the adjective *nice* in the phrase *nice house*).

**Pragmatics** is a component of language that is receiving increased attention in recent literature (e.g., Verhoeven & Vermeer, 2002; Vigil, 2002). It represents the "rules that govern the reason(s) for communicating (called communicative functions or intentions) as well as the rules that govern the choice of codes to be used when communicating" (Bernstein, 2002, p. 9). Pragmatics represents the rules governing the use of language and can be exemplified in the different ways a teacher talks when providing direct instruction, making a point in a faculty meeting, or chatting at a party. Pragmatics includes processes such as turn taking and initiating, maintaining, and ending a conversation. Figure 11.2 illustrates how the various components constitute language.

### FIGURE 11.1

**A Conceptual Model of Communication, Language, and Speech**

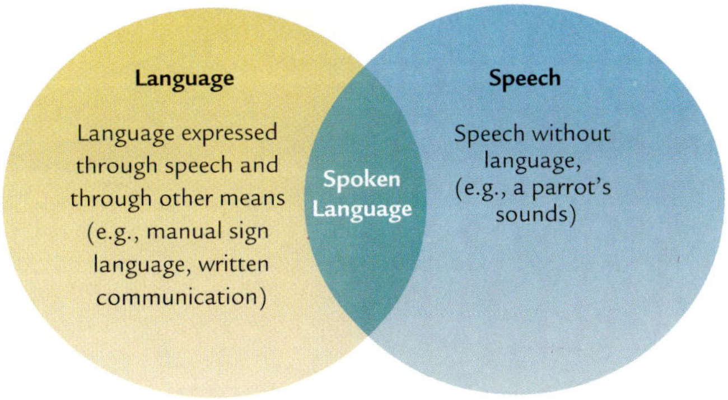

**Language**

Language expressed through speech and through other means (e.g., manual sign language, written communication)

**Spoken Language**

**Speech**

Speech without language, (e.g., a parrot's sounds)

Language can exist without speech (left), and not all speech constitutes language (right), but spoken language (center) is one outcome of typical human development. Communication is the broad umbrella concept that includes speech and language. Although communication *can* be achieved without these components, it is greatly enhanced by them.

# Language Development

In a vast percentage of cases, children develop language in a normal fashion, without significant delays or disruptions to the process. It is important to understand this typical developmental process as we examine and describe language characteristics that differ from the norm and interfere with the effectiveness of communication.

The development of language is a complex process. It is also one of the most fascinating to observe, as parents of infants know well. Young children normally advance through several stages in acquiring language, from a preverbal stage to the use of words in sentences. An infant's initial verbal output is primarily

**Pragmatics**

A component of language that represents the rules that govern the reason(s) for communicating.

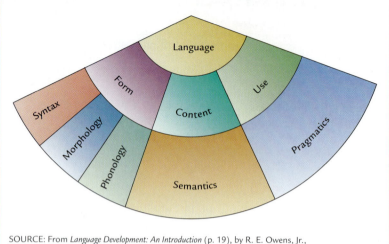

## FIGURE 11.2

### Components in the Structure of Language

Language

Form

Use

Syntax

Content

Morphology

Phonology

Pragmatics

Semantics

SOURCE: From *Language Development: An Introduction* (p. 19), by R. E. Owens, Jr., 2001 (5th ed.). Boston: Allyn and Bacon.

limited to crying and hence is usually associated with discomfort (e.g., from hunger, pain, or being soiled or wet). Before long (around 2 months), babies begin to coo as well as cry, verbally expressing reactions to pleasure as well as discomfort. At about 3 to 6 months of age, they begin to babble, which involves making some consonant and vowel sounds. At this point, babies often make sounds repeatedly when they are alone, seemingly experimenting with their sound making and not necessarily trying to communicate with anyone (Puckett, 2001). They may also babble when their parents or others are with them, playing or otherwise handling them.

A baby's first word is a momentous, long-anticipated event. In fact, eager parents often interpret as "words" sounds that stretch the imagination of more objective observers and probably have no meaning to the child. What usually happens is that the baby begins to string together sounds that occasionally resemble words. To the parents' delight, these sounds frequently include utterances such as "Da-Da" and "Ma-Ma," which, of course, are echoed, repeated, and reinforced greatly by the parents. As the baby actually begins to listen to the speech of adults, exchanges, or "conversations," seem to occur, where the youngster responds by saying "Da-Da" when a parent says that sound. Although this type of interchange sounds like a conversation, the child's vocal productions may be understood only by those close to him or her (e.g., parents or siblings); people other than immediate family members may not be able to interpret their meaning at all. The baby also begins to use different tones and vocal intensity, which makes his or her vocalization vaguely resemble adult speech. The interactions between babies and their parents can do much to enhance babies' developing language at this time. Parents often provide a great deal of reinforcement, such as praise in excited tones, or hugs, for word approximations. They also provide stimulus sounds and words for the baby to mimic, giving the youngster considerable directed practice.

The timing of a baby's actual first word is open to interpretation, although it usually happens between 9 and 14 months. These words often involve echoing (repeating what has been heard) or mimicking responses based on verbalizations by those around the baby. At first the words may have little or no meaning, although

*Within a broad range of 4 to 8 years of age, children with normal language development can correctly articulate most speech sounds in context.*

they soon become attached to people or objects in the child's immediate environment, such as Daddy, Mommy, or milk. Before long these words begin to have more perceptible intent, as the child uses them for requests and as a means of pleasing parents. Strings of two and three words that resemble sentences typically begin between 18 and 24 months of age. At this stage, meaning is usually unmistakable because the child can clearly indicate that he or she wants something. The child uses fairly accurate syntax, with word order generally consisting of subject-verb-object.

Most children with normally developing language are able to use all the basic syntactical structures by 3 to 4 years of age. By 5 years, they have progressed to using six-word sentences, on the average. A child who is developing language at a normal pace articulates nearly all speech sounds correctly and in context somewhere between 4 and 8 years of age. These illustrations are couched in terms of when children produce language—that is, in terms of expressive language development. However, some observations suggest that a child's receptive skills precede his or her ability to express language. Thus children are able to understand a great deal more than they can express. Most children show some understanding of language as early as 6 to 9 months, often responding first to commands such as "no-no" and their names (Owens, 2001; Puckett, 2001).

Variable age ranges are used for each milestone in outlining normal language development, some with rather broad approximations. Several factors contribute to this variability. For one thing, even children who are developing normally exhibit substantial differences in their rates of development. Some variations are due to a child's general health and vitality, others to inheritance, and still others to environmental influences, such as the amount and type of interaction with parents and siblings (Molfese & Molfese, 2002; Shames, 2001). Note also that age ranges become more variable in more advanced stages of development (e.g., 3 to 6 months for babbling; 18 to 24 months for two- and three-word strings). These advanced developments are also more complex, some involving subtleties that are not as singularly obvious as, say, the first "Da-Da." Therefore, observation of when they first occur is perhaps less accurate. Table 11.1 summarizes general milestones of normal language and prelanguage development.

Considerable variability also occurs with abnormal language and speaking ability. In some cases, the same factors that contribute to variability in normal language are considered disorders if they result in extreme performance deviations. In other cases, the definitions differ and characteristics vary among people—the same variability we have encountered with other disorders.

## TABLE 11.1

### Normal Language and Prelanguage Development

| AGE | BEHAVIOR |
| --- | --- |
| Birth | Crying and making other physiological sounds |
| 1 to 2 months | Cooing as well as crying |
| 3 to 6 months | Babbling as well as cooing |
| 9 to 14 months | Speaking first words as well as babbling |
| 18 to 24 months | Speaking first sentences as well as words |
| 3 to 4 years | Using all basic syntactical structures |
| 4 to 8 years | Articulating correctly all speech sounds in context |

SOURCE: Reprinted with permission of Merrill, an imprint of Macmillan Publishing Company, from *Mental Retardation: A Life Cycle Approach*, Eighth Ed. by Clifford J. Drew and Michael L. Hardman. Copyright 2004 by Macmillan Publishing Company.

# Language Disorders

History has witnessed language in many different forms. Some early Native Americans communicated using systems of clucking or clicking sounds made with the tongue and teeth. Such sounds were also used in combination with hand signs and spoken language that often differed greatly between tribes. Such differing language systems have been described extensively in a variety of historical documents and continue to be of interest (e.g., Bartens, 2000).

Current definitions of language reflect the breadth necessary to encompass diverse communication systems. For the most part, these definitions refer to the systems of rules and symbols that people use to communicate, including matters of phonology, syntax, morphology, and semantics (Den-Dikken, 2000; Fodor & Inoue, 2000). In these definitions of language, considerable attention is given to meaning and understanding. For example, Bernstein (2002) defined language as encompassing the "complex rules that govern sounds, words, sentences, meaning, and use. These rules underlie an individual's ability to understand language (language comprehension) and his or her ability to formulate language (language production)" (p. 5).

Speech disorders include problems related to verbal production—that is, vocal expression. Language disorders represent serious difficulties in the ability to understand or express ideas in the communication system being used. The distinction between speech disorders and language disorders is like the difference between the sound of a word and the meaning of a word. As we examine language disorders, we will discuss both difficulties in expressing meaning and difficulties in receiving it. Table 11.2 lists a number of behaviors that might emerge if a child has a language disorder.

## Definition

**FOCUS 2**

Identify how language delay and language disorder are different.

A serious disruption of the language acquisition process may result in language disorders. Such irregular developments may involve comprehension (understanding) or expression in written or spoken language (Bernstein, 2002; Nicolosi et al., 2003). Such malfunctions may occur in one or more of the components of language. Because language is one of the most complex sets of behaviors exhibited by humans, language disorders are complex and present perplexing assessment problems. Language involves memory, learning, message reception and processing, and expressive skills. An individual with a language disorder may have deficits in any of these areas, and it may be difficult to identify the nature of the problem (Doehring, 2002; Johnson & Slomka, 2000). In addition, language problems may arise in the form of language delays.

Language delay occurs when the normal rate of developmental progress is interrupted but the systematic sequence of development remains essentially intact. For youngsters with a language delay, the development follows a normal pattern or course of growth but is substantially slower than in most children of the same age; in other words, children with delays use the language rules typical of a younger child. The term *language disorder* differs in that it refers to circumstances when language acquisition is not systematic and/or sequential; children with language disorders do not acquire rule-governed linguistic behavior in a sequential progression. The term *language disorder* is used in a general sense to refer to several types of behaviors. Where evidence suggests that delay may be a major contributor, we discuss it as such.

## Classification

The terminology applied to the processes involved in language, and to disorders in those processes, varies widely. In many cases, language disorders are classified according to their causes, which may be known or only suspected (Owens et al., 2002;

TABLE 11.2

## Behaviors Resulting in Teacher Referral of Children with Possible Language Impairments

The following behaviors may indicate that a child in your classroom has a language impairment that is in need of clinical intervention. Please check the appropriate items.

_____ Child mispronounces sounds and words.

_____ Child omits word endings, such as plural -s and past tense -ed.

_____ Child omits small unemphasized words, such as auxiliary verbs or prepositions.

_____ Child uses an immature vocabulary, overuses empty words, such as one and thing, or seems to have difficulty recalling or finding the right word.

_____ Child has difficulty comprehending new words and concepts.

_____ Child's sentence structure seems immature or overreliant on forms, such as subject-verb-object. It's unoriginal, dull.

_____ Child's question and/or negative sentence style is immature.

_____ Child has difficulty with one of the following:

| | | |
|---|---|---|
| _____ Verb tensing | _____ Articles | _____ Auxiliary verbs |
| _____ Pronouns | _____ Irreg. verbs | _____ Prepositions |
| _____ Word order | _____ Irreg. plurals | _____ Conjunctions |

_____ Child has difficulty relating sequential events.

_____ Child has difficulty following directions.

_____ Child's questions often inaccurate or vague.

_____ Child's questions often poorly formed.

_____ Child has difficulty answering questions.

_____ Child's comments often off topic or inappropriate for the conversation.

_____ There are long pauses between a remark and the child's reply or between successive remarks by the child. It's as if the child is searching for a response or is confused.

_____ Child appears to be attending to communication but remembers little of what is said.

_____ Child has difficulty using language socially for the following purposes:

| | | |
|---|---|---|
| _____ Request needs | _____ Pretend/imagine | _____ Protest |
| _____ Greet | _____ Request information | _____ Gain attention |
| _____ Respond/reply | _____ Share ideas, feelings | _____ Clarify |
| _____ Relate events | _____ Entertain | _____ Reason |

_____ Child has difficulty interpreting the following:

| | | |
|---|---|---|
| _____ Figurative language | _____ Humor | _____ Gestures |
| | _____ Emotions | _____ Body language |

_____ Child does not alter production for different audiences and locations.

_____ Child does not seem to consider the effect of language on the listener.

_____ Child often has verbal misunderstandings with others.

_____ Child has difficulty with reading and writing.

_____ Child's language skills seem to be much lower than other areas, such as mechanical, artistic, or social skills.

SOURCE: From R. E. Owens, _Language Disorders: A Functional Approach to Assessment and Intervention_ (2nd ed., p. 392). Copyright 1995, All rights reserved. Reprinted by permission of Allyn and Bacon.

Segalowitz, 2000). In other cases, specific labels, such as _aphasia_, tend to be employed. One fruitful approach is to view language disorders in terms of receptive and expressive problems (Mildenberger, Noterdaeme, Sitter, & Amorosa, 2001; Toppelberg & Shapiro, 2000). We examine both of these categories, as well as aphasia, a problem that may occur in both children and adults.

**RECEPTIVE LANGUAGE DISORDERS.** People with **receptive language disorders** have difficulty comprehending what others say. In many cases, receptive language problems in children are noticed when they do not follow an adult's instructions. These children may seem inattentive, as though they do not listen to directions, or

**Receptive language disorders**

Difficulties in comprehending what others say.

they may be very slow to respond. Individuals with receptive language disorders have great difficulty understanding other people's messages and may process only part (or none) of what is being said to them (Nicolosi et al., 2003; Owens et al., 2002). They have a problem in language processing, which is basically half of language (the other part being language production). Language processing is essentially listening to and interpreting spoken language.

Some of this behavior is reminiscent of the discussion in Chapter 7 on learning disabilities. It is not uncommon for receptive language problems to appear in students with learning disabilities (Johnson & Slomka, 2000; Lerner, 2003). Such language deficits contribute significantly to academic performance problems and difficulties in social interactions for these students. Receptive language disorders appear as high-risk indicators of other disabilities and may frequently remain undiagnosed because they are not as evident as problems in language production (Toppelberg & Shapiro, 2000).

**EXPRESSIVE LANGUAGE DISORDERS.** Individuals with **expressive language disorders** have difficulty in language production, or formulating and using spoken or written language. Those with expressive language disorders may have limited vocabularies and use the same array of words regardless of the situation. Expressive language disorders may appear as immature speech, often resulting in interaction difficulties (Vicari et al., 2000). People with expressive disorders also use hand signals and facial expressions to communicate.

**APHASIA.**   **Aphasia** involves a loss of the ability to speak or comprehend because of an injury or developmental abnormality in the brain. Aphasia most often affects those in whom a specific brain injury has resulted in impairment of language comprehension, formulation, and use. Thus definitions of aphasia commonly link the disorder to brain injury, either through mechanical accidents or other damage, such as that caused by a stroke. Over the years, many types of aphasia and/or conditions associated with aphasia have been identified (Basso, 2003; Spreen, 2002). Aphasic language disturbances have also been classified in terms of receptive and expressive problems.

Aphasia may be found both during childhood and in the adult years. The term *developmental aphasia* has been widely used for children, despite the long-standing association of aphasia with neurological damage. Children with aphasia often begin to use words at age 2 or later and to use phrases at age 4. The link between aphasia and neurological abnormalities in children has been of continuing interest to researchers, and some evidence has suggested a connection. In many cases of aphasia in children, however, objective evidence of neurological dysfunction has been difficult to acquire.

Adult aphasia typically is linked to accidents or injuries likely to occur during this part of the lifespan, such as gunshot wounds, motorcycle and auto accidents, and strokes. For this group, it is clear why terms such as *acquired language disorder* emerge: These disorders are typically acquired through specific injury. Current research suggests that different symptoms result from damage to different parts of the brain (e.g., Bates et al., 2001; Nakada, Fujii, Yoneoka, & Kwee, 2001). Those with injury to the front part of the brain often can comprehend better than they can speak; they also have considerable difficulty finding words, have poor articulation with labored and slow speech, omit small words such as *of* and *the*, and generally have reduced verbal production. Individuals with aphasia resulting from injury to the back part of the brain seem to have more fluent speech, but it lacks content. Speech may also be characterized by use of an unnecessarily large number of words to express an idea or use of unusual or meaningless terms. The speech of these individuals appears to reflect impaired comprehension (Basso, 2003).

## Causation

Pinpointing the causes of different language disorders can be difficult. We do not know precisely how normal language acquisition occurs or how malfunctions influence language disorders. We do know that certain sensory and other physiological

**Expressive language disorders**

Difficulties in producing language.

**Aphasia**

An acquired language disorder that is caused by brain damage and characterized by complete or partial impairment of language comprehension, formulation, and use.

systems must be intact and developing normally for language processes to develop normally. For example, if vision or hearing is seriously impaired, a language deficit may result (House & Davidson, 2000; Shriberg, Tomblin, & McSweeny, 1999). Likewise, serious brain damage might inhibit normal language functioning. Learning must also progress in a systematic, sequential fashion for language to develop appropriately. For example, children must attend to communication before they can mimic it or attach meaning to it. Language learning is like other learning: It must be stimulated and reinforced to be acquired and mastered (Bernstein & Levey, 2002).

Many physiological problems may cause language difficulties. Neurological damage that may affect language functioning can occur prenatally, during birth, or anytime throughout life (Indefre et al., 2000; Molfese & Molfese, 2000). For example, language problems can clearly result from oxygen deprivation before or during birth (e.g., Drew & Hardman, 2004). Likewise, a serious accident later in life can disrupt a person's language skills. Furthermore, serious emotional disorders may be accompanied by language disturbances if an individual's perception of the world is substantially distorted (Prizant, Wetherby, & Roberts, 2000).

Language disorders may also occur if learning opportunities are seriously deficient or are otherwise disrupted. As with speech, children may not learn language if the environment is not conducive to such learning (Chapman, 2000). Modeling in the home may be so infrequent that a child cannot learn language in a normal fashion. This might be the case in a family where no speaking occurs because the parents have hearing impairments, even when the children have normal hearing. Such circumstances are rare, but when they do occur, a language delay is likely to result. The parents cannot model language for their children, nor can they respond to and reinforce such behavior.

Remember that learning outcomes are highly variable. In situations that seem normal, we may find a child with serious language difficulty. In circumstances that seem lacking, we may find a child whose language facility is normal. The Snapshot presents an example involving four brothers with normal hearing who were born to and raised by parents who both had severe hearing impairments and no spoken language facility. They have distinguished themselves in various ways, from earning Ph.D.s and M.D.s (one even holds both degrees) to becoming a millionaire through patented inventions. The Snapshot represents a rare set of circumstances, but it is a good illustration of how variable and poorly understood language learning is.

Distinctions between speech problems and language problems are blurred because they overlap as much as the two functions of speech and language overlap. Receptive and expressive language disorders are as intertwined as speech and language. When an individual does not express language well, does he or she have a receptive problem or an expressive problem? These disorders cannot be clearly separated, nor can their causes be clearly divided into categories.

## Intervention

Any treatment for a language disorder must take into account the nature of the problem and the manner in which an individual is affected. It is also important to consider cultural and linguistic background as an intervention is being planned (Toppelberg & Shapiro, 2000). Intervention is an individualized undertaking, just as it is with other types of disorders (Krueger, Krueger, Hugo, & Campbell, 2001; Swenson, 2000). Some causes are rather easily identified and may or may not be remedied by mechanical or medical intervention. Other types of treatment basically involve instruction or language training.

**INDIVIDUALIZED LANGUAGE PLANS.**  A number of integrated steps are involved in effective language training. They include identification, assessment, development of instructional objectives, development of a language intervention program, implementation of the intervention program, reassessment of the child, and reteaching, if necessary. These steps are similar to the general stages of specialized educational interventions that are outlined in IDEA. Specific programs of intervention may also involve other activities aimed at individualized intervention (see, for example, Fey,

**FOCUS 3**

Identify three factors that are thought to cause language disorders.

**FOCUS 4**

Describe how treatment approaches for language disorders generally differ for children and for adults.

LANGUAGE DISORDERS

## Cy

### Language Differences: We Didn't Know They were Different

My name is Cy, and I am one of the four brothers mentioned. Both of my parents were deaf from a very early age; they never learned to speak. When you ask me how we learned speech, I can't really answer, knowing what I now know about how important those very early years are in this area. When we were really young, we didn't even know they were deaf or different (except for Dad's active sense of humor). Naturally, we didn't talk; we just signed. We lived way out in the country and didn't have other playmates. Grandma and Grandpa lived close by, and I spent a lot of time with them. That is when I began to know something was different. We probably began learning to talk there.

When we were about ready to start school, we moved into town. My first memory related to school is sitting in a sandbox, I guess on the playground. We had some troubles in school, but they were fairly minor as I recall. I couldn't talk or pronounce words very well. I was tested on an IQ test in the third grade and they said I had an IQ of 67. Both Mom and Dad worked, so we were all sort of out on our own with friends, which probably helped language, but now I wonder why those kids didn't stay away from us because we were a bit different. Probably the saving grace is that all four of us seem to have pretty well developed social intelligence or skills. We did get in some fights with kids, and people sometimes called us the "dummys' kids." I would guess that all four of us pretty much caught up with our peers by the eighth grade. One thing is for certain: I would not trade those parents for any others in the world. Whatever they did, they certainly did right.

Cy, Ph.D.

---

1999; Gillon, 2002). Teams of professionals must collaborate, and often others, such as parents, are involved (Battle, 2002; Tiegerman-Farber, 2002; Weiss, 2002). Such collaboration among professionals reflects the federal law and also one of our important recurring themes in this book.

Programs of language training are tailored to an individual's strengths and limitations. In fact, current terminology labels them *individualized language plans* (ILPs), similar in concept to the individualized education plans (IEPs) mandated by IDEA (Nelson, 2002). These intervention plans include several components:

- Long-range goals (annual)
- Short-range and specific behavioral objectives
- A statement of the resources to be used in achieving the objectives
- A description of evaluation methods
- Program beginning and ending dates
- Evaluation of the individual's generalization of skills.

For young children, interventions often focus on beginning language stimulation. Treatment is intended to mirror the conditions under which children normally learn language, but the conditions may be intensified and taught more systematically.

Many different approaches have been used to remediate aphasia, although consistent and verifiable results have been slow to emerge. Intervention typically involves the development of an individual's profile of strengths, limitations, age, and developmental level, monolingual or bilingual background, and literacy, as well as considerations regarding temperament that may affect therapy (LaPointe, 2001; Simmons-Mackie, & Damico, 2001; Worrall, McCooey, Davidson, Larkins, & Hickson, 2002). From such a profile, an individualized treatment plan can be designed.

Several questions immediately arise, including what to teach or remediate first and whether teaching should focus on an individual's strong or weak areas. These questions have been raised from time to time with respect to many disorders. Teaching exclusively to a child's weak areas may result in more failure than is either necessary or helpful to his or her overall progress. That is, the child experiences so little success and receives so little reinforcement that he or she may become discouraged about the whole process. Good clinical judgment needs to be exercised in deciding how to divide one's attention between the aphasic child's

# COMPUTERS: A LANGUAGE TUTORIAL PROGRAM

Computer technology has made inroads in many areas of human disability in the past few years and will become increasingly important in the future. Language disability intervention is one area where technology is being used with increasing frequency. Advances in both hardware and software have already affected language training and have great potential for future development.

First Words is a language tutorial program that may have a number of applications for teaching those who are developing or reacquiring language functions. This program uses graphic presentations combined with synthesized speech to teach high-frequency nouns and test a student's acquisition of them. The student is presented with two pictures of an object and asked to decide which one represents the word being taught. Students can select an answer using a computer keyboard or a special selection switch or by touching the object on the screen. First Words is a relatively inexpensive program, costing about $200. The voice synthesizer and the touch screen options must be added to the basic package, but they may be essential to effective intervention, depending on the student's capability.

---

strengths and weaknesses. Intervention programs include the collaborative participation of parents and other family members, as well as any other professionals who may be involved with the overall treatment of the youngster (Nelson, 2002; Tiegerman-Farber, 2002; Weiss, 2002).

The perspective for remediation of adults with aphasia begins from a point different from that for children, in that it involves relearning or reacquiring language function. Views regarding treatment have varied over the years. Early approaches included the expectation that adults with aphasia would exhibit spontaneous recovery. This approach has largely been replaced by the view that patients are more likely to progress if direct therapeutic instruction is implemented.

Strength and limitations must both receive attention when an individualized remediation program is being planned. However, development of an aphasic adult's profile of strengths and deficits may involve some areas different from those that apply to children. For example, social, linguistic, and vocational readjustments are three broad areas that need attention for most adults with aphasia. Furthermore, the notion of readjustment differs substantially from initial skill acquisition. Language

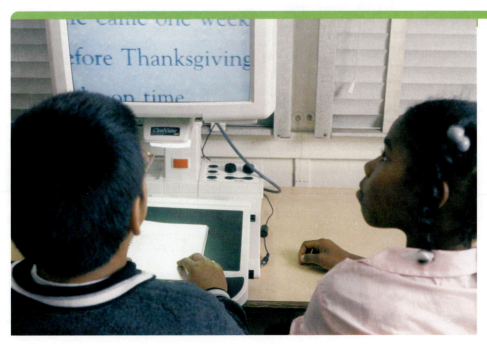

*This student uses a computer that prints in large type that he can easily read. An individual using a computer to communicate probably has a severe physical or cognitive disability that affects communication.*

learning treatment (relearning) is often employed in a way that focuses on the individual's needs and is practical in terms of service delivery (Hopper, Holland, & Rewega, 2002; Simmons-Mackie & Damico, 2001). Some individuals with aphasia are effectively treated in group settings, and for others individual therapy works well (e.g., Hickin, Best, Herbert, Howard, & Osborne, 2002; Van-Slyke, 2002). Advances in technology are continually being integrated into diagnosis and treatment (Beveridge & Crerar, 2002; Laganaro, & Venet, 2001; Linebarger, Schwartz, & Kohn, 2001); see the nearby Assistive Technology.

An individualized treatment plan for adults with aphasia also involves evaluation, profile development, and teaching/therapy in specific areas within each of the broad domains (Worrall et al., 2002). Such training should begin as soon as possible, depending on the person's condition. Some spontaneous recovery may occur during the first 6 months after an incident resulting in aphasia, but waiting beyond 2 months to begin treatment may seriously delay whatever degree of recovery is possible.

**AUGMENTATIVE COMMUNICATION.** Some individuals require intervention via means of communication other than oral language. In some cases, the person may be incapable of speaking because of a severe physical or cognitive disability, so a nonspeech means of communication must be designed and implemented. Known variably as assistive, alternative, and **augmentative communication**, these strategies may involve a variety of approaches, some employing new technological developments. Augmentative communication strategies have received increasing attention in the past few years, partly because of the rapid development of technology and partly because of coverage in the popular press. Applications include a range of circumstances and disability conditions, such as mental retardation, autism, and multiple disabilities that are often in the severe functioning range

**Augmentative communication**

Forms of communication that employ nonspeech alternatives.

## Assistive Technology

## ASSISTIVE DEVICES HELP TO LEVEL THE PLAYING FIELD

Using a pink cap rigged with a long gold stick and pencil eraser, 11-year-old Marisa Velez punches a few buttons on a computerized box.

"Hello, my name is Marisa Velez," the box says in a computerized voice, customized to sound like a girl. "This device lets me speak like anyone else."

For Marisa, who was born with quadriplegia cerebral palsy, the Liberator and other devices in her home and school are the key to a productive life.

Such assistive technology usually is associated with devices that help people with disability, but it also includes commonplace items such as glasses, hearing aids, and canes.

Assistive technology has enabled Marisa to attend regular classes at Westvale Elementary School like any other student. She uses a motorized wheelchair to get around the building and a computer touch-screen to

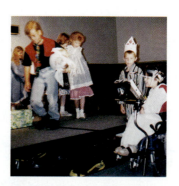

*Marisa uses a Liberator voice machine to talk, a computer touch-screen to write, and a motorized wheelchair. All these devices enable her to participate in a school play.*

write papers. She also can use the Liberator voice machine, which has a built-in printer, to complete assignments and quizzes.

"It's her self-expression, her ability to express her feelings and goals. Just being understood makes her feel valued," said Marisa's mother, Norma Velez. "That's the purpose of technology—to not hold people back." . . .

Norma Velez had to scream and shout to get her insurance to pay for Marisa's Liberator.

"Marisa was the first individual our [insurance] company provided a speech device for," she said. "At first, they said it was not a medical necessity. But the object is to not give up. If she is ill and cannot communicate what is wrong, of course that is a medical necessity."

SOURCE: Adapted from "Assistive Devices Help to Level Playing Field: Machines Can Be Key to Productive Life and Individual Self-Esteem," by V. Horiuchi, 1999, *Salt Lake Tribune*, April 10, p. D8.

(Petersen, Reichle, & Johnston, 2000; Sutton, Soto, & Blockberger, 2002). These strategies must also be individualized to meet the specific needs of those being treated and to take into account their strengths and limitations in operating the technology. Augmentative communication strategies are providing therapists with important new alternatives for intervention with individuals who have language disorders. Research results suggest that carefully chosen techniques and devices can be quite effective (e.g., Beck, Fritz, Keller, & Dennis, 2000; Wolpaw, Birbaumer, McFarland, Pfurtscheller, & Vaughan, 2002). Two examples of specific devices are communication boards with graphics or symbols and electronic appliances that simulate speech sounds. Other approaches include systems of manual communication (e.g., gestures, signs, etc.) that do not depend on mechanical or electronic aids.

# Speech Disorders

Speech disorders involve deviations of sufficient magnitude to interfere with communication. Such speaking patterns are so divergent from what is normal and expected that they draw attention to the speaking act, thereby distracting the hearer's attention from the meaning of the message being sent. Such deviant speaking behavior can negatively affect the listener, the speaker, or both.

Speech is extremely important in contemporary society. Speaking ability can influence a person's success or failure in personal/social and professional arenas. Most people are about average in terms of their speaking ability, and they may envy those who are unusually articulate and pity those who have a difficult time with speech. What is it like to have a serious deficit in speaking ability? Certainly, it is different for each individual, depending on the circumstances in which he or she operates and the severity of the deficit. The Case Study on Ricky illustrates the very personal nature of communication and speech disorders and the social/interpersonal impact.

They often carry strong emotional reactions to their speech that may significantly alter their behavior. Speech is so critical to functioning in society that such disorders often have a significant impact on affected individuals. It is not difficult to imagine the impact that stuttering, for example, may have in classroom settings or in social encounters. Children may be ridiculed by peers, begin to feel inadequate, and suffer emotional stress. And that stress may continue into adulthood, limiting these individuals' social lives and influencing their vocational choices.

There are many different speech disorders and many theoretical perspectives on causes and treatment. Volumes much longer than this book have focused solely on the topic. In this section, we will discuss fluency disorders, delayed speech, articulation disorders, and voice disorders.

## Fluency Disorders

In normal speech we are accustomed to a reasonably smooth flow of words and sentences. For the most part, it has a rhythm and timing that is steady, regular, and rapid. Most of us also have times when we pause to think about what we are saying, either because we have made a mistake or want mentally to edit what we are about to say. However, these interruptions are not frequent and do not constitute a disturbance in the ongoing flow of our speaking. In general, our speech is considered fluent with respect to speed and continuity.

Fluency of speech is a significant problem for people with a fluency disorder. Their speech is characterized by repeated interruptions, hesitations, or repetitions that seriously interfere with the flow of communication. Some people have a fluency disorder known as cluttered speech, or **cluttering**, which is characterized by speech that is overly rapid, disorganized, and occasionally filled with unnecessary words.

**Cluttering**

A speech disorder characterized by excessively rapid, disorganized speaking, often including words or phrases unrelated to the topic.

# RICKY

The following is a statement by Ricky Creech, a person with a serious communication disorder due to cerebral palsy. Ricky communicates by using a computer-controlled electronic augmentative communication device. He provides some insights into assumptions people make about individuals who cannot communicate. This is a portion of a presentation made at the National Institutes of Health.

There is a great need for educating the public on how to treat physically limited people. People are still under the misconception that somehow the ability to speak, hear, see, feel, smell, and reason are tied together. That is, if a person loses one, he has lost the others.

The number one question people ask my parents is "Can he hear?" When I reply that I can, they bend down where their lips are not two feet away from my eyes and say very loudly, "How—are—you? Do—you—like—that—talking—machine?" Now, I don't mind when that person is a pretty, young girl. But when it is an older or married woman, it is a little embarrassing. When the person is a man, I'm tempted to say something not very nice. . . .

I would make a great spy. When I am around, people just keep talking—because I can't speak, they think I can't hear or understand what is being said. I have listened to more private conversations than there are on the Watergate tapes. It is a good thing that I am not a blackmailer. If people knew that I hear and understand everything they say, some would die of embarrassment.

There is another conclusion which people make when first seeing me, which I don't kid about; I don't find it a bit humorous. That is, that I am mentally retarded.

The idea that if a person can't speak, something must be wrong with his mind is the prevalent belief in every class, among the educated as well as the not-so-educated. I have a very good friend who is a nuclear scientist, the most intelligent person I have ever known, but he admitted that when he first saw me, his first conclusion was that I was mentally retarded. This was in spite of my parents' assertions that I was not.

However, this man had a special quality—when he was wrong he could admit it with his mind and his heart—most people can't do both. There are people who know me who know with their minds that I am not mentally retarded, but they treat me as a child because in their hearts they have not really accepted that I have the mentality of an adult. I am an adult and I want to be treated as an adult. I have a tremendous amount of respect for anyone who does.

## APPLICATION

1. Have you ever made the same error that the nuclear scientist made in the case study? Explain what you felt and how you acted.

2. Having read Ricky Creech's description, how would you react now?

3. As a professional, how would you explain Ricky's communication disorder to people so they would understand his abilities?

SOURCE: From "Consumers Speak Out on the Life of the Nonspeaker," by R. Creech and J. Viggiano, 1981, *ASHA*, 23, pp. 550–552. Reprinted by permission of the American Speech-Language-Hearing Association.

---

Stuttering is by far the best-known type of fluency disorder and has fascinated researchers for years.

**STUTTERING.** **Stuttering** occurs when the flow of speech is abnormally interrupted by repetitions, blocking, or prolongations of sounds, syllables, words, or phrases (Perino, Famularo, & Tarroni, 2000). Although it is a familiar concept to most people, stuttering occurs rather infrequently, in between 1% and 5% of the general population, and has one of the lowest prevalence rates among all speech disorders (e.g., Jones, Gebski, Onslow, & Packman, 2002; Mansson, 2000). For example, articulation disorders (e.g., omitting, adding, or distorting certain sounds) occur in about 2% of 6- and 7-year-old children in the United States (American Psychiatric Association, 2000).

Laypeople's high awareness of stuttering partly comes from the nature of the behavior involved. Such interruptions in speech flow are very evident to both speaker and listener, are perhaps more disruptive to communication than any other type of speech disorder, and often affect interpersonal relationships. Furthermore, listeners often grow uncomfortable and may try to assist the stuttering speaker, providing missing or incomplete words (Davis, Howell, & Cooke, 2002; Dorsey & Guenther, 2000; Gabel, Colcord, & Petrosino, 2002). The speaker's discomfort may be magnified by physical movements, gestures, or facial distortions that often accompany stuttering.

Parents often become concerned about stuttering as their children learn to talk. Apprehension is usually unnecessary, however, since most children exhibit some

## Stuttering

A speech disorder that occurs when the flow of speech is abnormally interrupted by repetitions, blocking, or prolongations of sounds, syllables, words, or phrases.

normal nonfluencies that diminish and cease with maturation. However, these normal nonfluencies have historically played a role in some theories about the causes of stuttering.

**Causation of Stuttering.**   Current thinking suggests that stuttering may have a variety of causes (e.g., Bloodstein, 2001; Sommer, Koch, Paulus, Weiller, & Buechel, 2002; Treon, 2002), and most behavioral scientists have abandoned the search for a single cause. Theories regarding causes follow three basic perspectives, regarding stuttering as a symptom of some emotional disturbance, as a result of biological makeup or some neurological problem, or as a learned behavior.

Some investigations of emotional problems have explored psychosocial factors emerging from the parent-child interaction, although this work is somewhat fragmentary. The emotional component has been included in many descriptions of contributors to stuttering, including speculation that stuttering may be caused by an individual's capacity being exceeded by demands. Such theories, however, often consider a person's cognitive, linguistic, and motor capacities as other contributors. Research on the relationship of stuttering to emotion continues only sporadically (Dmitrieva & Gel'man, 2001; Ying, Baokun, & Minggao, 2001). Many professionals have become less interested in emotional theories of the causation of stuttering. Investigation of this perspective is difficult because of problems with research methodology (e.g., Doehring, 2002).

Investigators continue to explore biological causation in a number of different areas. Limited evidence indicates that the brains or neurological structures of some who stutter may be organized or function differently than in people without fluency disorders, although the nature of such differences remains unclear (De-Nil & Kroll, 2001 Forster & Webster, 2001; Sommer et al., 2002). Some research also suggests that individuals who stutter use different sections of the brain to process information than do their counterparts with fluent speech. A few authors suggest that people who stutter may have differences in brain-hemisphere function. For example, the hemispheres of the brain may compete with each other in information processing (e.g., Foundas, Bollich, Corey, Hurley, & Heilman, 2001). Some researchers also suggest that nervous system damage, such as from an injury, can result in stuttering. Other theories imply that a variety of problems may disrupt the person's precise timing ability, which is an important element in speech production (Ingham, 2001; Sommer

FOCUS
5

Identify three factors that are thought to cause stuttering.

*The way in which parents speak greatly affects their child's speech patterns.*

et al., 2002). There is also speculation that control mechanisms for speech production may be unsynchronized in people who stutter or may produce an elevated activity of the muscles involved in speech production.

It has long been theorized that stuttering is learned behavior. According to this perspective, learned stuttering emerges from the normal nonfluency evident in early speech development. Language develops rapidly from 2 to 5 years of age, and stuttering often emerges in that general timeframe as well—between 3 and 5 years of age (e.g., Bernstein & Levey, 2002; Mansson, 2000). From a learning causation point of view, a typical child may become a stuttering child if considerable attention is focused on normal disfluencies at that stage of development. The disfluency of early stuttering may be further magnified by negative feelings about the self, as well as by anxiety (e.g., Dmitrieva & Gel'man, 2001; Vanryckeghem, Hylebos, Brutten, & Peleman, 2001; Whaley & Golden, 2000). Interest in this theory persists, although, like others, it has its critics (e.g., Ratner, 2000).

Theories about the causes of stuttering have included consideration of heredity (Felsenfeld et al., 2000; Bloodstein, 2001). Some evidence suggests that stuttering may be gender-related, because males who stutter outnumber females about 4 to 1, although this hypothesis remains speculative. Heredity has also been of interest because of the high incidence of stuttering and other speech disorders within certain families as well as in twins (Goetestam, 2001). However, it is very hard to separate hereditary from environmental influences—a problem that has long plagued research in human development and behavior disorders (Drew & Hardman, 2004; Lytton & Gallagher, 2002).

Causation has been an especially elusive and perplexing matter for workers in speech pathology. Some recent literature has raised questions about definitions, assessment, and some of the theoretical logic about stuttering (e.g., Craig, 2002; Dayalu, Kalinowski, & Saltuklaroglu, 2002; Pesak & Opavsky, 2000). Researchers and clinicians continue their search for a cause, in the hope of identifying more effective treatment and prevention measures.

**Intervention.**   Many approaches have been used to treat stuttering over the years, with mixed results. Interventions such as modeling, self-monitoring, counseling, and the involvement of support group assistance have been all studied and shown to be somewhat useful for children who stutter (e.g., Bray & Kehle, 2001; DiLollo, Neimeyer, & Manning, 2002; Yaruss et al., 2002). Some research on medication treatment has shown improvements, although pharmacological intervention has not been widely employed (Lavid, Franklin, & Maguire, 1999; Maguire et al., 1999). Hypnosis has been used to treat some cases of stuttering, but its success has been limited. Speech rhythm has been the focus of some therapy, as has developing the naturalness of speaking patterns (Ingham, Sato, Finn, & Belknap, 2001). Relaxation therapy and biofeedback have also been used, since tenseness is often observed in people who stutter (Gilman & Yaruss, 2000). In all the techniques noted, outcomes are mixed, and people who stutter are likely to try several approaches (Craig, 2002; Dayalu et al., 2002). The inability of any one treatment or cluster of treatments consistently to help people who stutter demonstrates the ongoing need for research in this area. There is also need for research on the most effective timing of intervention (e.g., Harris, Onslow, Packman, Harrison, & Menzies, 2002; Onslow, Menzies, & Packman, 2001). Early intervention has long been popular in many areas of exceptionality, although it carries a risk associated with labeling—that is, there is concern that a child may become what he or she is labeled.

For several years, treatment models have increasingly focused on direct behavioral therapy—that is, attempting to teach children who stutter to use fluent speech patterns (e.g., Bray & Kehle, 2001; Onslow, Menzies, & Packman, 2001). In some cases, children are taught to monitor and manage their stuttering by speaking more slowly or rhythmically. Using this model, they are also taught to reward themselves for increasing periods of fluency. Some behavioral therapies include information regarding physical factors (e.g., regulating breathing) and direct instruction about correct speaking behaviors. The overall therapy combines several dimensions, such as an interview regarding the inconvenience of stuttering, behavior modification training, and follow-up. Because stuttering is a complex problem, effective interventions are likely to be complicated.

**DELAYED SPEECH.**    **Delayed speech** is a deficit in communication ability in which the individual speaks like a much younger person. From a developmental point of view, this problem involves a delayed beginning of speech and language development. Delayed speech may occur for many reasons and take various forms. Assessment and treatment differ accordingly (Noell, VanDerHeyden, Gatti, & Whitmarsh, 2001; Stoel-Gammon, 2001).

Delayed speech is often associated with other maturational delays. It may be associated with a hearing impairment, mental retardation, emotional disturbance, or brain injury (e.g., Drew & Hardman, 2004).

Young children can typically communicate at least to some degree, before they learn verbal behaviors. They use gestures, gazing or eye contact, facial expressions, other physical movements, and nonspeech vocalizations, such as grunts or squeals. This early development illustrates the relationship among communication, language, and speech. Children with delayed speech often have few or no verbalizations that can be interpreted as conventional speech. Some communicate solely through physical gestures. Others may use a combination of gestures and vocal sounds that are not even close approximations of words. Still others may speak, but in a very limited manner, perhaps using single words (typically nouns without auxiliary words, like *ball* instead of *my ball*) or primitive sentences that are short or incomplete (e.g., *get ball* rather than *would you get the ball*) (Cheng, 2000). Such communication is normal for infants and very young children, but not for children who are well beyond the age when most are speaking in at least a partially fluent fashion (Delgado et al., 2002; Windfuhr, Faragher, & Conti-Ramsden, 2002).

The differences between stuttering and delayed speech are obvious, but the distinction between delayed speech and articulation disorders is less clear (Stoel-Gammon, 2001; Yavas, 2002). In fact, children with delayed speech usually make many articulation errors in their speaking patterns. However, their major problems lie in grammatical and vocabulary deficits, which are more matters of developmental delay. The current prevalence of delayed speech is not clear, and government

**FOCUS 6**

Identify two ways in which learning theory and home environments are related to delayed speech.

**Delayed speech**

A deficit in speaking proficiency whereby the individual performs like someone much younger.

*Preschool teachers should use all occasions possible to increase the vocabulary of a child with delayed speech. This child may be more comfortable using a puppet to interact with his teacher or other children.*

estimates do not even regularly provide data on the provision of services for delayed speech (U.S. Department of Education, 2003). Such problems, along with definitional differences among studies, have led many to place little confidence in existing prevalence figures.

**Causation of Delayed Speech.**    Because delayed speech can take a variety of forms, the causes of these problems also vary greatly. Several types of environmental deprivation contribute to delayed speech. For example, partial or complete hearing loss may seriously limit an individual's sensory experience and hence cause serious delays in speech development (e.g., Radziewicz & Antonellis, 2002; Szagun, 2002). For those with normal hearing, the broader environment may also contribute to delayed speech (e.g., Bernstein & Levey, 2002; Burgess, Hecht, & Lonigan, 2002). For example, in some children's homes there is minimal conversation, little chance for the child to speak and thus little opportunity to learn speech. Other problems, such as cerebral palsy and emotional disturbance, may also contribute to delayed speech.

Negativism may be one cause of delayed speech. Negativism involves a conflict between parents' expectations and a child's ability to perform, and such a conflict often occurs as children develop speech. Considerable pressure is placed on children during the period when they normally develop their speaking skills: to go to bed when told, to control urination and defecation properly, and to learn appropriate eating skills, among other things. The demands are great, and they may exceed a child's performance ability. Children react in many ways when more is demanded than they are able to produce. They may refuse. They may simply not talk, seeming to withdraw from family interactions. In normal development, children occasionally refuse to follow the directions of adults. One very effective refusal is silence, to which the parents' reprisal options are few and may be ineffective. (As a parent, it is relatively simple to punish refusal to go to bed or to clean one's room, but it is a different matter when parents encounter the refusal to talk. It is not easy to force a child to talk through conventional punishment techniques.) Viewing negativism from another angle, children may be punished for talking in other situations. Parents may be irritated by a child's attempt to communicate. A child may speak too loudly or at inappropriate times, such as when adults are reading, watching television, resting, or talking with other adults (even more rules to learn at such a tender age). Delayed speech may occur in extreme cases of prolonged negativism related to talking (Chapman, 2000).

Such unpleasant environments may raise concerns about the amount of love and caring in such a situation and the role that emotional health plays in learning to speak (e.g., Cohen, 2002; Molfese & Molfese, 2002). But delayed speech can also occur in families that exhibit great love and caring. In some environments, a child may have little need to learn speech. Most parents are concerned about satisfying their child's needs or desires. However, carrying this ambition to the extreme, a "superparent" may anticipate the child's wants (e.g., toys, water, or food) and provide them even before the child makes a verbal request. Such children may only gesture and their parents immediately respond, thereby rewarding gestures and not promoting the development of speech skills. Learning to speak is much more complex and demanding than making simple movements or facial grimaces. If gesturing is rewarded, speaking is less likely to be learned properly.

**Intervention.**    Treatment approaches for delayed speech are as varied as its causes. Whatever the cause, an effective treatment should teach the child appropriate speaking proficiency for his or her age level. In some cases, matters other than just defective learning, such as hearing impairments, must be considered in the treatment procedures (Radziewicz & Antonellis, 2002). Such cases may involve surgery and prosthetic appliances like hearing aids, as well as specially designed instructional techniques aimed at teaching speech.

Treatment is likely to focus on the basic principles of learned behavior if defective learning is the primary cause of delayed speech. In this situation, the stimulus and reinforcement patterns that are contributing to delayed speech must be changed so that appropriate speaking behaviors can be learned. Although the process sounds simple, learning language is very complex, and the identification and control of such contingencies are quite complicated (Johnson & Slomka, 2000; Taatgen & Anderson, 2002). Some success has been achieved through direct instruction, as well as through other procedures aimed at increasing spontaneous speech. Such instruction emphasizes positive reinforcement of speaking to shape the child's behavior in the direction of more normal speech. Other interventions involve collaborative efforts between speech clinicians, teachers, and parents (Nelson, 2002; Tiegerman-Farber, 2002; Weiss, 2002), focusing on modifying not only the child's speech but also the family environment that contributed to the problem. Because different elements cause the delay in each case, therapies must be individually tailored.

**ARTICULATION DISORDERS.**    Articulation disorders represent the largest category of all speech problems, which are termed *phonological disorders* in DSM-IV (American Psychiatric Association, 2000; Fox & Dodd, 2001). For most people with this type of difficulty, the label **functional articulation disorders** is used. This term refers to articulation problems that are not due to structural physiological defects, such as cleft palate and neurological problems, but are likely to have resulted from environmental or psychological influences.

Articulation disorders are characterized by abnormal production of speech sounds, resulting in the inaccurate or otherwise inappropriate execution of speaking. This category of problems often includes omissions, substitutions, additions, and distortions of certain sounds (Gibbon & Wood, 2002; Owens et al., 2002). Omissions most frequently involve dropping consonants from the ends of words (e.g., *los* for *lost*), although omissions may occur in any position in a word. Substitutions frequently include saying *w* for *r* (e.g., *wight* for *right*), *w* for *l* (e.g., *fowo* for *follow*), and *th* for *s* (e.g., *thtop* for *stop*, *thoup* for *soup*). Articulation errors may also involve transitional lisps, where a *th* sound precedes or follows an *s* (e.g., *sthoup* or *yeths* for *soup* or *yes*).

Articulation disorders are a rather prevalent type of speech problem. Research suggests that most problems encountered by speech clinicians involve articulation disorders (e.g., American Psychiatric Association, 2000; Fox & Dodd, 2001). Although the vast majority of these difficulties are functional, some articulation problems may be attributed to physiological abnormalities.

**Causation of Articulation Disorders.**    Articulation disorders develop for many reasons. Some are caused by physical malformations, such as abnormal mouth, jaw, or teeth structures, and others result from nerve injury or brain damage (e.g., Bressmann & Sader, 2001; Ishii, Tamaoka, & Shoji, 2001). Functional articulation disorders are often seen as caused by defective learning of the speaking act. However, such categories of causation overlap in practice, and even the line between functional and structural is indistinct. Furthermore, function and structure, though often related, are not perfectly correlated: Some people with physical malformations that "should" result in articulation problems do not have such problems, and vice versa.

Despite this qualifying note, we will examine the causes of articulation performance deficits in terms of two general categories: those due to physical oral malformations and those that are clearly functional because there is no physical deformity. These distinctions remain useful for instructional purposes, since it is the unusual individual who overcomes a physical abnormality and articulates satisfactorily.

In addition to physical abnormalities of the oral cavity, other types of physical defects, such as an abnormal or absent larynx, can affect articulation performance. Many different physical structures influence speech formulation, and all must be synchronized with learned muscle and tissue movements, auditory feedback, and a multitude of other factors. These coordinated functions are almost never perfect, but for most people they occur in a remarkably successful manner. Oral structure malformations alter the manner in which coordinated movements must take place and sometimes make normal or accurate production of sounds extremely difficult, if not impossible.

FOCUS
7

Identify two reasons why some professionals are reluctant to treat functional articulation disorders in young schoolchildren.

**Functional articulation disorders**

Articulation problems that are not due to structural defects or neurological problems but are likely to have resulted from environmental or psychological influences.

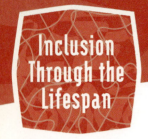

**Inclusion Through the Lifespan**

## PEOPLE WITH COMMUNICATION DISORDERS

### Tips for the Family

- Model speech and language to your infant by talking to him or her in normal tones from a very early age, even though he or she may not yet be intentionally communicating directly with you.
- Respond to babbling and other noises the young child makes with conversation, reinforcing early verbal output.
- Do not overreact if your child is not developing speech at the same rate as someone else's infant; great variation is found between children.
- If you are concerned about your child's speech development, have his or her hearing tested to determine whether that source of stimulation is normal.
- Observe other areas of development to assure yourself that your child is progressing within the broad boundaries of normal variation.
- If you are seeking day care or a preschool program, search carefully for one that will provide a rich, systematic communication environment.

### Tips for the Preschool Teacher

- Encourage parental involvement in all dimensions of the program, including systematic speech and language stimulation at home.
- Consider all situations and events as opportunities to teach speech and language, perhaps focusing initially on concrete objects and later moving to the more abstract, depending on the individual child's functioning level.
- Ask "wh" questions, such as *what, who, when,* and *where,* giving the child many opportunities to practice speaking as well as thinking.
- Practice with the child the use of the prepositions *in, on, out,* and so forth.
- Use all occasions possible to increase the child's vocabulary.

### Tips for Preschool Personnel

- Communicate with the young child. Consider involvement in either direct or indirect communication instruction.

### Tips for Neighbors and Friends

- Interact with young children with communication disorders as you would with any others, speaking to them and directly modeling appropriate communication.
- Intervene if you encounter other children ridiculing the speech and language of these youngsters; encourage sensitivity to individual differences among your own and other neighborhood children.

### Tips for the Family

- Stay involved in your child's educational program through active participation with the school.
- Work in collaboration with the child's teacher on speaking practice, blending it naturally into family and individual activities.
- Communicate naturally with the child; avoid "talking down" and thereby modeling the use of "simpler language."

### Tips for the General Education Classroom Teacher

- Continue promoting parents' involvement in their child's intervention program in whatever manner they can participate.
- Encourage the child with communication disorders to talk about events and things in his or her environment and to describe experiences in as much detail as possible.
- Use all situations possible to provide practice for the child's development of speech and language skills.
- Promote the enhancement of vocabulary for the child in a broad array of topic areas.

### Tips for School Personnel

- Promote an environment where all who are available and in contact with the child are involved in communication instruction, if not directly then indirectly through interaction and modeling.
- Begin encouraging student involvement in a wide array of activities that can also be used to promote speech and language development.

### Tips for Neighbors and Friends

- Interact with children with communication disorders normally; do not focus on the speaking difficulties that may be evident.
- As a neighbor or friend, provide support for the child's parents, who may be struggling with difficult feelings about their child's communication skills.

## SECONDARY/TRANSITION YEARS

### Tips for the Family

- Children who still exhibit communication problems at this level are likely to perform on a lower level, suggesting that communication may focus on functional matters such as grooming, feeding, and so on.
- For some children, communication may involve limited verbalization; consider other means of interacting.
- Interact with your child as much and as normally as possible.

### Tips for the General Education Classroom Teacher

- Embed communication instruction in the context of functional areas (e.g., social interactions, requests for assistance, choice making).
- Consider adding augmented communication devices or procedures to the student's curriculum.

### Tips for School Personnel

- Develop school activities that will encourage use of a broad variety of skill levels in speaking (i.e., not just the debate club).
- Promote school activities that permit participation through communication modes other than speaking (being careful to ensure that these efforts are consistent with therapy goals).

### Tips for Neighbors and Friends

- To the degree that you are comfortable doing so, interact with children using alternative communication approaches (e.g., signs, gesturing, pantomiming).

## ADULT YEARS

### Tips for the Family

- Interact with the adult who has a communication disorder on a level that is functionally appropriate for his or her developmental level. Some adults with communication disorders, the problem may be compounded by other disorders, such as mental retardation. For others, the communication disorder is an inconvenience rather than another disability.

### Tips for Therapists or Other Professionals

- Recognize the maturity level of the person with whom you are working. Do not assume you know the interests or inclinations of a younger client simply because the individual has a communication difficulty.
- Be aware of the lifestyle context of the adult when suggesting augmentative devices. Some techniques may not serve well a person who is employed or otherwise engaged in adult activities.

### Tips for Neighbors and Friends

- Communicate in as normal a fashion as possible, given the severity and type of disorder. If the person uses alternative communication methods, consider learning about them to the degree that you feel comfortable.

One faulty oral formation recognized by most people is the cleft palate, often referred to by speech pathologists as clefts of the lip or palate or both. The **cleft palate** is a gap in the soft palate and roof of the mouth, sometimes extending through the upper lip. The roof of the mouth serves an important function in accurate sound production. A cleft palate reduces the division between the nasal and mouth cavities, influencing the movement of air that is so important to articulation performance. Children with clefts often encounter substantial difficulties in articulation (Bressmann & Sader, 2001; Wermke, Hauser, Komposch, & Stellzig, 2002). Clefts are congenital defects that occur in about 1 of every 700 births and may take any of several forms (e.g., Benson, Gross, & Kellum, 1999; Cochrane & Slade, 1999). Figure 11.3 shows a normal palate in part (a) and unilateral and bilateral cleft palates in parts (b) and (c), respectively; it is easy to see how articulation would be impaired. These problems are caused by developmental difficulties *in utero* and are often corrected by surgery.

Articulation performance is also significantly influenced by a person's dental structure. Because the tongue and lips work together with the teeth to form many sounds, dental abnormalities may result in serious articulation disorders. Some dental malformations are side effects of cleft palates, as shown in parts (b) and (c) of Figure 11.3, but other dental deformities not associated with clefts also cause articulation difficulties.

The natural meshing of the teeth in the upper and lower jaws is important to speech production. The general term used for the closure and fitting together of dental structures is **occlusion**, or dental occlusion. When the fit is abnormal, the condition is known as **malocclusion**. Occlusion involves several factors, including the biting height of the teeth when the jaws are closed, the alignment of teeth in the upper and lower jaws, the nature of curves in upper and lower jaws, and teeth positioning. A normal adult occlusion is illustrated in part (a) of Figure 11.4. The upper teeth normally extend slightly beyond those of the lower jaw, and the bite overlap of those on the bottom is about one third for the front teeth (incisors) when the jaw is closed.

Occlusion abnormalities take many forms, although we will discuss only two here. When the overbite of the top teeth is unusually large, the normal difference between the lower and upper dental structures is exaggerated. Such conditions may be due to the positioning of the upper and lower jaws, as illustrated in part (b) of Figure 11.4. In other cases nearly the opposite occurs, as illustrated in part (c) of Figure 11.4, forming another kind of jaw misalignment. Both exaggerated overbites and underbites may be the result of abnormal teeth positioning or angles, as well as of jaw misalignment. All can result in articulation difficulties.

We turn now to functional articulation disorders. Many such disorders are thought to be due to faulty language learning. The sources of defective speech learning are frequently unknown or difficult to identify precisely (Robinson & Robb, 2002; Silli-

**Cleft palate**

A gap in the soft palate and roof of the mouth, sometimes extending through the upper lip.

**Occlusion**

The closing and fitting together of dental structures.

**Malocclusion**

An abnormal fit between the upper and lower dental structures.

**Normal and Cleft Palate Configurations**

(a) Normal palate configuration     (b) Unilateral cleft palate     (c) Bilateral cleft palate     (d) Repaired cleft palate

## FIGURE 11.4

### Normal and Abnormal Dental Occlusions

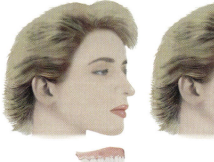
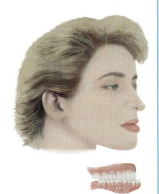

(a) Normal dental occlusion    (b) Overbite malocclusion    (c) Underbite malocclusion

man & Diehl, 2002). Like other articulation problems, those of a functional nature have numerous specific causes. For example, interactions between children and their adult caretakers (parents and others) tend to make a considerable contribution to language acquisition (Bernstein & Levey, 2002; Gelfand & Drew, 2003). In some cases, the existing stimulus and reinforcement patterns may not support accurate articulation. For example, parents may be inconsistent in encouraging and prompting accurate articulation. Parents tend to be very busy. Routinely urging their children to speak properly may not be high on their list of priorities. However, such encouragement is important, particularly if misarticulation begins to emerge as a problem.

Also, adults may unthinkingly view some normal inaccuracies of speech in young children as cute or amusing. "Baby talk," for example, may be reinforced in a powerful manner by parents asking the young child to say a particular word in the presence of grandparents or other guests and rewarding him or her with laughter and hugs and kisses. Such potent rewards can result in misarticulations that linger long beyond the time when normal maturation would diminish or eliminate them. Related defective learning may come from modeling. Parents (or other adults) may model and thus reinforce articulation disorders when they imitate the baby talk of young children or substantially change their manner of speaking in what has been called "parentese" (Owens, 2001). If parents, grandparents, or friends realized the potential results of such behavior, they would probably alter the nature of their verbal interchanges with young children. Modeling is a potent tool in shaping learned behavior. Although the negative influence of baby talk between parents and children has been questioned, modeling and imitation are used in interventions and are thought to influence natural verbal development (Chapman, 2000).

**Intervention.**   Many types of treatment exist for articulation disorders. Clearly, the treatment for disorders due to physical abnormalities differs from that for disorders that are functional. In many cases, however, treatment may include a combination of procedures. The treatment of articulation disorders has also been somewhat controversial, partly because of the large number that are functional in nature. A predictable developmental progression occurs in a substantial number of functional articulation disorders. In such cases, articulation problems diminish and may even cease to exist as the child matures. For instance, the *r, s,* and *th* problems disappear for many children after the age of 5. Thus many school administrators are reluctant to treat functional articulation disorders in younger students. In other words, if a significant proportion of articulation disorders is likely to be corrected as the child continues to develop, why expend precious resources on early treatment? This logic has a certain appeal, particularly in times when there is a shortage of educational resources and their use is constantly questioned (See the nearby Debate Forum). However, this argument must be applied with considerable caution. In general, improvement of articulation performance continues until a child is about 9 or 10 years old. If articulation problems persist beyond this age, they are unlikely to improve without intense intervention. Furthermore, the longer such problems are allowed to continue, the more difficult treatment will become and the less likely it is to be successful. Although some suggest that the impact of articulation difficulties is ultimately minimal, others believe that affected individuals may still have residual indications of the disorder many years later (e.g., Johnson & Slomka, 2000; Molfese & Molfese, 2000).

Deciding whether to treat articulation problems in young children is not easy, and interventions can be quite complex. One option is to combine articulation training with other instruction for all very young children. This approach may serve as an interim measure for those who have continuing problems, facilitate the development of articulation for others, and not overly tax school resources. It does, however, require some training for teachers of young children.

Considerable progress has been made over the years in various types of surgical repair for cleft palates. Current research addresses a number of related matters, such as complex patient assessment before and after intervention (D'Antonio, Scherer, Miller, Kalbfleisch, & Bartley, 2001; Hattee, Farrow, Harland, Sommerlad, & Walsh, 2001; Wermke et al., 2002). The surgical procedures may be intricate because of the dramatic nature of the structural defect. Some such interventions include Teflon implants in the hard portion of the palate, as well as stretching and stitching together of the fleshy tissue. As Figure 11.3 suggests, surgery is often required for the upper lip and nose structures, and corrective dental work may be undertaken as well. It may also be necessary to train or retrain the individual in articulation and to assess his or her emotional status insofar as it is related to appearance or speech skills, depending on the child's age at the time of surgery (Bressmann & Sader, 2001; Cochran & Slade, 1999). A child's continued development may introduce new problems later; for example, the physical growth of the jaw or mouth may create difficulties for someone who underwent surgery at a very young age. Although early correction has resulted in successful healing and speech for a very high percentage of treated cases, the permanence of such results is uncertain in light of later growth spurts.

Treatment of cleft palate may involve the use of prosthetic appliances as well. For example, a prosthesis that basically serves as the upper palate or at least covers the fissures may be employed. Such an appliance may be attached to the teeth to hold it in position; it resembles the palate portion of artificial dentures.

Dental malformations other than those associated with clefts can also be corrected. Surgery can alter jaw structure and alignment. In some cases, orthodontic treatment may involve the repositioning of teeth through extractions and the use of

**Reflect on This**

## TIMOTHY

### I Think I Talk Okay, Don' You?

My name is Timothy. I am almost 7½ years old. Mondays after school, I go to the university where I meet "wif a lady who help me talk betto. It was my teacha's idea 'cause she said I don' say "l" and "r" good an some othos too. I kinda like it [coming here] but I think I talk okay, don' you? I can say "l" good now all the time and "r" when I reeeally think about it. I have lots of friends, fow, no—five. I don' talk to them about comin' hea, guess I'm jus not in the mood. Hey, you witing this down, is that good? You know the caw got hit by a semi this mowning and the doow hanle came off. I'm a little dizzy 'cause we wecked."

Timothy, age 7½

# TO TREAT OR NOT TO TREAT?

Articulation problems represent about 80% of all speech disorders encountered by speech clinicians, making this type of difficulty the most prevalent of all communication disorders. It is also well known that young children normally make a number of articulation errors during the process of maturation as they are learning to talk. A substantial portion do not conquer all the rules of language and produce all the speech sounds correctly until they are 8 or 9 years old, yet they eventually develop normal speech and articulate properly. In lay terminology, they seem to "grow out of" early articulation problems. Because of this maturation outcome and the prevalence of articulation problems, serious questions are asked regarding treatment in the early years.

## POINT

Some school administrators are reluctant to treat young children who display articulation errors because the resources of school districts are in very short supply and budgets are extremely tight. If a substantial proportion of young children's articulation problems will correct themselves through maturation, then shouldn't the precious resources of school districts be directed to other, more pressing problems? Articulation problems should not be treated unless they persist beyond the age of 10 or 11.

## COUNTERPOINT

Although articulation does improve with maturation, delaying intervention is a mistake. The longer such problems persist, the more difficult treatment will be. Even the claim of financial savings is an invalid one. If all articulation difficulties are allowed to continue, those children who do not outgrow such problems will be more difficult to treat later, requiring more intense and expensive intervention than they would have needed if treated early. Early intervention for articulation problems is vitally important.

What do you think? To give your opinion, go to Chapter 11 of the companion website **(www.ablongman.com/hardman8e)** and click on Debate Forum.

braces. Prosthetic appliances, such as full or partial artificial dentures, may also be used. As in other types of problems, the articulation patient who has orthodontic treatment often requires speech therapy to learn proper speech performance.

Treatment of functional articulation disorders often focuses on relearning the speaking act; in some cases, muscle control and usage are the focus. Specific causes of defective learning are difficult to identify precisely, but the basic assumption in such cases is that an inappropriate stimulus and reinforcement situation was present in the environment during speech development (e.g., inappropriate early modeling, defective hearing) (Anderson, 2002; Huttunen, 2001). Accordingly treatment includes an attempt to correct that set of circumstances so that accurate articulation can be learned. Several behavior modification procedures have been employed successfully in treating functional articulation disorders. In all cases, treatment techniques are difficult to implement because interventions must teach proper articulation, must be tailored to the individual case, and must promote the generalization of the new learning to a variety of word configurations and diverse environments beyond the treatment setting (Anderson, 2002; Dehaney, 2000; Williams, 2000). Further research on the treatment of articulation disorders is seriously needed, particularly in view of its prevalence. Moreover, some call for improving the quality of measurement and research methods employed in this and other areas of communication disorders (Johnson & Slomka, 2000).

It should also be noted that differences in language and dialect can create some interesting issues regarding treatment. When a child's first language is other than English or involves an ethnic dialect, that youngster may demonstrate a distinctiveness of articulation that makes his or her speech different and perhaps hard to understand (Battle, 2002; Koch, Gross, & Kolts, 2001; Ohama, Gotay, Pagano, Boles, & Craven, 2000). Does this circumstance require an intervention similar to that applied for articulation disorders? Such a question involves cultural, social, and political implications far beyond those typically considered by professionals working with speech disorders.

**VOICE DISORDERS.** Voice disorders involve unusual or abnormal acoustical qualities in the sounds made when a person speaks. All voices differ significantly in pitch, loudness, and other features from the voices of others of the same gender, cultural group, and age. However, voice disorders involve acoustical qualities that are so different that they are noticeable and may divert a listener's attention from the content of a message.

Relatively little attention has been paid to voice disorders in the research literature, for several reasons. First, the determination of voice normalcy involves a great deal of subjective judgment. Moreover, what is normal varies considerably with the circumstances (e.g., football games, barroom conversation, or seminar discussion) and with geographical location (e.g., the West, a rural area, New England, the Deep South). Another factor that complicates analysis of voice disorders is related to the acceptable ranges of normal voice. Most individuals' voices fall within acceptable tolerance ranges. Children with voice disorders are often not referred for help, and their problems are persistent when not treated (Case, 2002; Ramig, 2000; Rubin, Sataloff, & Korovin, 2002).

Children with voice disorders often speak with an unusual nasality, hoarseness, or breathiness. Nasality involves either too little resonance from the nasal passages (**hyponasality** or **denasality**), which dulls the resonance of consonants and sounds as though the child has a continual cold or stuffy nose, or too much sound coming through the nose (**hypernasality**), which causes a twang in the speech. People with voice disorders of hoarseness have a constant husky sound to their speech, as though they had strained their voices by yelling. Breathiness is a voice disorder with very low volume, like a whisper; it sounds as though not enough air is flowing through the vocal cords. Other voice disorders include overly loud or soft speaking and pitch abnormalities (e.g., monotone speech).

Like so many speech problems, the nature of voice disorders varies greatly. Our description provides considerable latitude, but it also outlines the general parameters of voice disorders often dismissed in the literature: pitch, loudness, and quality. An individual with a voice disorder may exhibit problems with one or more of these factors, and they may significantly interfere with communication (i.e., the listener will focus on the sound rather than the message) (Fawcus, 2000; Hall, Oyer, & Haas, 2001).

**Causation of Voice Disorders.** An appropriate voice pitch is efficient and is suited to the situation and the speech content, as well as to the speaker's laryngeal structure. Correct voice pitch permits inflection without voice breaks or excessive strain. Appropriate pitch varies as emotion and meaning change and should not distract attention from the message. The acoustical characteristics of voice quality include factors such as degree of nasality, breathy speech, and hoarse-sounding speech. As for the other parameters of voice, determination of appropriate loudness is subjective. The normal voice is not habitually characterized by excessive loudness or unusual softness. A normal level of loudness depends greatly on circumstances.

Pitch disorders take several forms. The person's voice may have an abnormally high or low pitch, may be characterized by pitch breaks or a restricted pitch range, or may be monotonal or monopitched. Many individuals experience pitch breaks as they progress through adolescence. Although more commonly associated with young males, pitch breaks also occur in females. Such pitch breaks are a normal part of development, but if they persist much beyond adolescence, they may signal laryngeal difficulties. Abnormally high- or low-pitched voices may signal a variety of problems. They may be learned through imitation, as when a young boy attempts to sound like his older brother or father. They may also be learned from certain circumstances, as when an individual placed in a position of authority believes a lower voice pitch is necessary to evoke the image of power. Organic conditions, such as a hormone imbalance, may also result in abnormally high- or low-pitched voices.

**Voice Disorder**

A condition in which an individual habitually speaks with a voice that differs in pitch, loudness, or quality from the voices of others of the same sex and age in a particular cultural group.

**Hyponasality**

A voice resonance disorder whereby too little air passes through the nasal cavity; also known as denasality.

**Denasality**

A voice resonance problem that occurs when too little air passes through the nasal cavity; also known as hyponasality.

**Hypernasality**

A voice resonance disorder that occurs when excessive air passes through the nasal cavity, often resulting in an unpleasant twanging sound.

Voice disorders involving volume also have varied causes. Voices that are excessively loud or soft may be learned through imitation, perceptions and characteristics of the environment, and even aging (Fawcus, 2000; Rubin et al., 2002; Vilkman, 2000). An example is mimicking the soft speaking of a female movie star. Other cases of abnormal vocal intensity occur because an individual has not learned to monitor loudness. Organic

Factors in voice disorders that interfere with communication are pitch, loudness, and quality. A voice disorder exists when these factors, singly or in combination, cause the listener to focus on the sounds being made rather than the message to be communicated.

problems may also be the culprit. For example, abnormally low vocal intensity may result from problems such as paralysis of vocal cords, laryngeal trauma (e.g., larynx surgery for cancer, damage through accident or disease), and pulmonary diseases such as asthma or emphysema (e.g., Benninger, 2002; Gray & Thibeault, 2002; Weitzel, 2000). Excessively loud speech may occur as a result of organic problems such as hearing impairments and brain damage.

Voice disorders related to the quality of speech include production deviances such as those of abnormal nasality. Hypernasality occurs essentially because the soft palate does not move upward and back to close off the airstream through the nose properly. Such conditions can be due to improper tissue movement in the speech mechanism, or they may result from organic defects such as an imperfectly repaired cleft palate (Benninger, 2002; McCrory, 2001). Excessive hypernasality may also be learned, as in the case of country music or certain rural dialects. Hyponasality or denasality is the type of voice quality experienced during a severe head cold or hay fever. In some cases, however, denasality is the result of learning or abnormal physical structures, rather than these more common problems.

**Intervention.**   The approach to treatment for a voice disorder depends on its cause. In cases where abnormal tissue development and/or dental structures result in unusual voice production, surgical intervention may be necessary. Surgery may also be part of the intervention plan if removal of the larynx is required. Such an intervention will also involve relearning communication through alternative mechanisms, including prostheses, and learning communication techniques to replace laryngeal verbalizations (Benninger, 2002; Case, 2002; McCrory, 2001). In some situations, treatment may include direct instruction to enhance the affected individual's learning or relearning of acceptable voice production. Such interventions entail counseling about the effects of unusual voice sounds on others and behavior modification procedures aimed at retraining the person's speaking. These efforts are more difficult if the behavior has been long-standing and is well ingrained.

Voice disorders are seldom the focus of referral and treatment in the United States. However, some researchers have argued that voice disorders should be treated more aggressively, even to the point of imposing legislative guidelines for workplace conditions (e.g. train conductors, Wall Street, etc.) affecting vocal stress (Vilkman, 2000). One important element in planning interventions for voice disorders is clear and open communication with the person seeking treatment. It is important to avoid setting unrealistic expectations about outcomes and to remember that those being treated are the ultimate arbiters of that treatment's success.

## Prevalence

We have already noted the difficulties involved in estimating the prevalence of other disorders: Many arise from differences in definitions and data collection procedures. The field of speech disorders is also vulnerable to these problems, so prevalence estimates vary considerably. The most typical prevalence figures cited for speech disorders indicate that between 7% and 10% of the population is affected. Nearly 19% of all children (ages 6 to 21) who were served in programs for those with disabilities were categorized as having speech or language impairments in 2000–2001 (U.S. Department of Education, 2003). These figures do not deviate greatly from other estimates over the years, although some data have suggested substantial geographical differences (e.g., significantly higher percentages in some areas of California than in parts of the Midwest). These figures themselves present a problem when we consider the 12% ceiling for services to *all* students with disabilities, as specified in the Individuals with Disabilities Education Act (IDEA). Obviously, individuals with speech disorders of a mild nature cannot be eligible for federally funded services. However, the 24th Annual Report to Congress on the Implementation of IDEA cited speech or language impairments as the second most frequently occurring disability (next to learning disabilities) to receive special services during the 2000–2001 school year (U.S. Department of Education, 2003).

The frequency with which speech problems occur diminishes in the population as age increases. Speech disorders are identified in about 12% to 15% of children in kindergarten through grade 4. For children in grades 5 through 8, the figure declines to about 4% to 5%. The 5% rate remains somewhat constant after grade 8 unless treatment intervenes. Thus age and development diminish speech disorders considerably, though more so with certain types of problems (e.g., articulation difficulties) than with others.

# FOCUS REVIEW

**FOCUS 1** Identify four ways in which speech, language, and communication are interrelated.

- Both speech and language form part, but not all, of communication.
- Some components of communication involve language but not speech.
- Some speech does not involve language.
- The development of communication, that of language, and that of speech overlap to some degree.

**FOCUS 2** Identify how language delay and language disorder are different.

- In language delay, the sequence of development is intact, but the rate is interrupted.
- In language disorder, the sequence of development is interrupted.

**FOCUS 3** Identify three factors that are thought to cause language disorders.

- Defective or deficient sensory systems
- Neurological damage occurring through physical trauma or accident
- Deficient or disrupted learning opportunities during language development

**FOCUS 4** Describe how treatment approaches for language disorders generally differ for children and for adults.

- Treatment for children generally addresses initial acquisition or learning of language.
- Treatment for adults involves relearning or reacquiring language function.

**FOCUS 5** Identify three factors that are thought to cause stuttering.

- Learned behavior, emotional problems, and neurological problems can contribute to stuttering.
- Some research has suggested that brain organization differs in people who stutter.

- People who stutter may learn their speech patterns as an outgrowth of the normal nonfluency evident when speech development first occurs.

**FOCUS 6** Identify two ways in which learning theory and home environments are related to delayed speech.

- The home environment may provide little opportunity to learn speech.
- The home environment may interfere with speech development, as when speaking is punished.

**FOCUS 7** Identify two reasons why some professionals are reluctant to treat functional articulation disorders in young schoolchildren.

- Many articulation problems evident in young children are developmental in nature, so speech may improve "naturally" with age.
- Articulation problems are quite frequent among young children, and treatment resources are limited.

## FURTHER READINGS

Beckoff, M., & Allen, C. (Eds.) (2002). *The Cognitive Animal: Empirical and Theoretical Perspectives on Animal Cognition.* Cambridge, MA: M.I.T. Press.

*Many scientists have asserted that cognition and language distinguish humans from other animals. This volume examines animal cognition and language in animals ranging from dolphins to chimpanzees.*

Case, J. L. (2002). *Clinical Management of Voice Disorders.* Austin: PRO-Ed.

*This volume examines the most commonly used approaches to assessing and treating voice disorders. Both medical procedures and instrumentation are discussed, and a wide array of voice function problems are covered.*

Nelson, C. A., & Luciana, M. (2001). *Handbook of Developmental Cognitive Neuroscience.* Cambridge, MA: M.I.T. Press.

*This volume includes original discussions on basic aspects of neural development, sensory and sensorimotor systems, language, cognition, and emotion. It examines how the human brain remains malleable and plastic throughout much of the lifespan, placing communication in the context of developmental science.*

Wetherby, A. M., & Prizant, B. M. (Eds.) (2000). *Autism Spectrum Disorders: A Transactional Developmental Perspective.* Baltimore: Paul H. Brookes.

*This is volume 9 in a series (Communication and Language Intervention) that provides comprehensive reviews of the research literature in communication and language. It examines issues related to augmentative and alternative communication and literacy for children with autism spectrum disorders.*

# WEB RESOURCES

### Baby BumbleBee

www.babybumblebee.com/learningdifferences.htm

This commercial website provides a wide array of products for parents of children with language delays and challenges. These include language stimulation techniques that can be used in conjunction with interventions and therapies recommended by professionals.

### The Nemours Foundation

kidshealth.org/teen/diseases_conditions/sight/speech_disorders.html

This website covers a number of issues related to teens' health. It seeks to communicate directly with teens who may have articulation disorders or other language challenges. Other topics that are addressed include food and fitness, drugs and alcohol, and sexual health.

### AllRefer.com

health.allrefer.com/health/speech-disorders-info.html

This website covers a variety of health conditions and prominently features speech disorders, including articulation, disfluency, and voice disorders. The site targets the general public and includes information on symptoms, prevention, diagnosis, and links.

### Gus Communications

gusinc.com

This website is a commercial website offering many different assistive technology products for a variety of conditions that result in language and communication disorders. Software is available for assisting people with aphasia, ALS (Lou Gehrig's disease), stroke, and other conditions.

# BUILDING YOUR PORTFOLIO

If you are thinking about a career in special education, you should know that many states use national standards developed by the Council for Exceptional Children (CEC) to assess a teacher candidate's knowledge and skills for working with students with disabilities. See a complete listing of the ten CEC Content Standards on the inside front cover of this text.

### CEC Content Standards Addressed in Chapter 11

1. Foundations
2. Development and Characteristics of Learners
3. Individual Learning Differences
4. Instructional Strategies
5. Learning Environments and Social Interactions
7. Instructional Planning

### Assess Your Knowledge of the CEC Standards Addressed in Chapter 11

Some states require that teacher candidates develop a portfolio of products that demonstrate mastery of the CEC content standards. To assist in the development of products for this portfolio, you may wish to complete the following activities.

• Complete a written test of the chapter's content.

*If your instructor requires a written test of your content knowledge for this chapter, keep a copy for your portfolio. A practice test on the information covered in this chapter is available through the companion website (www.ablongman.com/hardman8e) and the Student Study Guide.*

- Respond to Application Questions for the Case Study "Ricky."

  *Review the Case Study and respond in writing to the application questions. Keep a copy of the case study and your written response for your portfolio.*

- Complete the "Take a Stand" activity for the Debate Forum "To Treat or Not to Treat?"

  *Read the Debate Forum in this chapter and then visit our companion website to complete the activity "Take a Stand." Keep a copy of this activity for your portfolio.*

- Participate in a Community Service Learning Activity.

  *Community service is a valuable way to enhance your learning experience. Visit our companion website for suggested community service learning activities that correspond to the information presented in this chapter. Develop a reflective journal of the service learning experience for your portfolio.*

## THEMES OF THE TIMES

Expand your knowledge of the concepts discussed in this chapter by reading current and historical articles from the *New York Times* by visiting the "Themes of the Times" section of the companion website: **www.ablongman.com/hardman8e.**

# Severe and Multiple Disabilities

## Everyone Has the Right to Live in the Community

All people, as human beings, are inherently valuable.

All people can grow and develop.

All people are entitled to conditions that foster their development.

Such conditions are optimally provided in community settings.

Therefore, in fulfillment of fundamental human rights and in securing optimum developmental opportunities, all people, regardless of the severity of their disabilities, are entitled to community living. (Center on Human Policy, 2000, p. 19)

## Yvonne Belongs with Us!

"Yvonne belongs with us!" we firmly told the psychiatrist when he insisted that we place our 2-year-old daughter in an institution. To us, Yvonne's sudden regression meant that she needed us more than ever—we could not abandon her, we could not reject her. At first we struggled on our own; there were no community supports. Then, together with other parents, we advocated for appropriate supports in the community for children who were labeled "severely mentally handicapped." We believed that Yvonne, and children like her, had a right to live at home, had a right to go to school, and had a right to participate in the life of the community. Our vision was shared and supported by some service providers, but other professionals opposed our view and worked against us. (Penner, 2003)

## What Should I Do To Make Inclusion Work for the Whole Class?

For as long as she can remember, Mrs. Brown has been told that she and other general education teachers were not appropriately trained or qualified to teach students with a wide range of disabilities. She was told, "That's why we have special education classes and schools where students with special educational needs can get the specialized instruction they need." . . . Recently, people started talking about educating students with more significant disabilities in the general education classroom; they referred to it as "inclusive education." Mrs. Brown felt that she had never excluded children before because of their disabilities but, rather, was trying to help them by sending them to a place that would better meet their needs. Now, she was about to have a student with more significant disabilities in her class. She wondered how this would work and what she should do to make sure it worked for her whole class. (Giangreco & Doyle, 2000, pp. 51-52)

**FOCUS**

**PREVIEW:** To preview the central concepts of this chapter, read the focus questions located in the margins. Using these questions as a guide, ask yourself what you already know and what you want to learn.

# Sarina

Sarina never had the opportunity to go to preschool and didn't begin her formal education in the public schools until the age of 6. She is now 15 years old and goes to Eastmont Junior High—her neighborhood school. Sarina does not verbally speak, walk, hear, or see. Professionals have used several labels to describe her, including *severely disabled, severely multiply handicapped, deaf-blind,* and *profoundly mentally retarded.* Her teenage classmates at Eastmont call her Sarina.

Throughout the day, Sarina has a support team of administrators, teachers, paraprofessionals, and peers who work together to meet her instructional, physical, and medical needs. And she has many, many needs. Sarina requires some level of support in everything she does, ranging from eating and taking care of personal hygiene to communicating with others. In the last few years, she has learned to express herself through the use of assistive technology. Sarina has a personal communication board with picture symbols that keeps her in constant contact with teachers, friends, and family. Through the use of an electronic wheelchair and her ability to use various switches, Sarina is able to maneuver her way through just about any obstacle in her environment. She is also learning to feed herself independently.

Sarina lives at home with her family, including three older brothers. Her parents, siblings, and grandparents are very supportive, always looking for ways to help facilitate Sarina's participation in school, family, and community activities. What she loves to do most is go shopping with her mom at the local mall, eat with friends at a fast-food restaurant, relax on the lawn in the neighborhood park, and play miniature golf at Mulligan's Pitch and Putt.

Sarina, in the opening Snapshot, is a person with **severe and multiple disabilities**. In one way or another, she will require services and support in nearly every facet of her life. Some people with severe disabilities have significant intellectual, learning, and behavioral differences; others are physically disabled with vision and hearing loss. Most have significant, multiple disabilities. Sarina has multiple needs, one of which is communication. Yet although she is unable to communicate verbally, she is able to express herself through the use of an assistive communication device, a language board. Sarina's case reminds us that in many circumstances, a disability may be described as severe, but through today's technology and our understanding of how to adapt the environment, the impact on the person may be diminished.

# Definitions

The needs of people with severe and multiple disabilities cannot be met by one profession but must be addressed by the fields of education, medicine, psychology, and social services. Since these individuals present such diverse characteristics and require the attention of several professionals, it is not surprising that numerous definitions have been used to describe them.

## Historical Descriptions of Severe Disabilities

Throughout history, the terminology associated with severe disabilities has communicated a sense of hopelessness and despair. The condition was often described as "extremely debilitating," "inflexibly incapacitating," or "uncompromisingly crippling." Abt Associates (1974) described individuals with severe handicaps as unable "to attend to even the most pronounced social stimuli, including failure to respond to invitations from peers or adults, or loss of contact with reality" (p. v). The definition went on to use terms such as *self-mutilation* (e.g., head banging, body scratching, and hair pulling), *ritualistic behaviors* (e.g., rocking and pacing), and *self-stimulation* (e.g., masturbation, stroking, and patting). The Abt definition focused almost exclusively on the individual's deficits and negative behavioral characteristics.

In 1976 Justen proposed a definition that moved away from negative terminology to descriptions of the individual's developmental characteristics. "The 'severely handicapped' refers to those individuals . . . who are functioning at a general devel-

**Severe and multiple disabilities**

A cross-classification of disabilities that involves significant physical, sensory, intellectual, and/or social-interpersonal performance differences. The need for extensive services and supports is evident in all environmental settings.

opment level of half or less than the level which would be expected on the basis of chronological age and who manifest learning and/or behavior problems of such magnitude and significance that they require extensive structure in learning situations" (p. 5).

Whereas Justen emphasized a discrepancy between normal and atypical development, Sailor and Haring (1977) proposed a definition that was oriented to the educational needs of each individual:

> A child should be assigned to a program for the severely/multiply handicapped according to whether the primary service needs of the child are basic or academic. . . . If the diagnosis and assessment process determines that a child with multiple handicaps needs academic instruction, the child should not be referred to the severely handicapped program. If the child's service need is basic skill development, the referral to the severely/multiply handicapped program is appropriate. (p. 68)

In 1991 Snell further elaborated on the importance of defining severe disabilities on the basis of educational need, suggesting that the emphasis be on supporting the individual in inclusive classroom settings. The Association for Severe Handicaps (Meyer, Peck, & Brown, 1991), while agreeing in principle with Snell, proposed a definition that focused on inclusion in all natural settings: family, community, and school.

## The TASH Definition of Severe Disabilities

TASH, an international association of people with disabilities, their family members, other advocates, and professionals, developed the following definition of severe disabilities:

> These people include individuals of all ages who require extensive ongoing support in more than one major life activity in order to participate in integrated community settings and to enjoy a quality of life that is available to citizens with fewer or no disabilities. Support may be required for life activities such as mobility, communication, self-care, and learning as necessary for independent living, employment, and self-sufficiency. (TASH, 2000)

The TASH definition focused on the relationship of the individual with the environment (adaptive fit), the need to include people of all ages, and "extensive ongoing support" in life activities. The adaptive fit between the person and the environment is a two-way street. First, it is important to determine the capability of the individual to cope with the requirements of family, school, and community environments. Second, how do these various environments recognize and accommodate the needs of the person with severe disabilities? The adaptive fit of the individual with the environment is a dynamic process requiring continuous adjustment that fosters a mutually supportive coexistence. The TASH definition suggests that an adaptive fit can be created only when there is extensive ongoing support (formal and/or natural) for each person as he or she moves through various life activities: engaging in social interactions, taking care of personal needs, and making choices about lifestyle, work, and movement from place to place.

## The IDEA Definitions of Severe and Multiple Disabilities

The Individuals with Disabilities Education Act (IDEA) does not include the term *severe disabilities* as one of the categorical definitions of disability identified in federal regulation. Individuals with severe disabilities may be subsumed under any one of IDEA's categories, such as mental retardation, autism, serious emotional disturbance, speech and language impairments, and so on. (These disability conditions are discussed in other chapters of this text.) IDEA does, however, describe *students with severe disabilities* and their need for intensive instructional services.

**FOCUS 1**

What are the three components of TASH's definition of severe disabilities?

**FOCUS 2**

Define the terms *multiple disabilities* and *deaf-blindness* as described in IDEA.

"Children with severe disabilities" refers to children with disabilities who, because of the intensity of their physical, mental, or emotional problems, need highly specialized education, social, psychological, and medical services in order to maximize their full potential for useful and meaningful participation in society and for self-fulfillment. (IDEA, 34 C.F.R. 300 [315.4[d]]1977)

Although *severe disabilities* is not a category within IDEA, *multiple disabilities* and *deaf-blindness* are categories in federal regulation.

**MULTIPLE DISABILITIES.**   *Multiple disabilities*, as defined in IDEA federal regulations, means concomitant impairments (such as mental retardation–blindness, mental retardation–orthopedic impairment, etc.), the combination of which causes such severe educational needs that the individual cannot be accommodated in special education programs designed solely for one of the impairments. The term does not include deaf-blindness [34 C.F.R. 300.7(c) (7) (1999)].

This definition includes multiple conditions that can occur in any of several combinations. One such combination is described by the term *dual diagnosis*. **Dual diagnosis** involves persons who have serious emotional disturbance or present challenging behaviors in conjunction with severe mental retardation. Estimates of the percentage of people with mental retardation who also have serious challenging behaviors vary, ranging from 5% to 15% of those living in the community to a much higher percentage for people living in institutions (Beirne-Smith, Ittenbach, & Patton, 2002; Griffiths, Nugent, & Gardner, 1998). Why do people with mental retardation and other developmental disabilities often have higher rates of challenging behaviors? Griffiths et al. (1998) indicated that "it is important to understand that the challenging behaviors are not a fundamental characteristic of developmental disabilities" (p. 3). These authors further suggested that the increase is related to various risk factors. People with developmental disabilities have

- an increased prevalence of neurological, sensory, and physical abnormalities.
- lifestyles that frequently are characterized by restrictiveness, prejudice, limited personal independence, restricted personal control, paucity of mentally healthy experiences, and victimization.
- skill deficits in critical functional areas. These skill deficits make it more difficult to appropriately deal with stresses in life.
- atypical learning histories. Often, positive behaviors have not been acknowledged, and negative and disruptive behaviors have attracted excessive attention. (Griffiths et al., pp. 3–4)

For more insight into the life of a person with multiple disabilities, see the nearby Reflect on This, "Mat's Story."

**DEAF-BLINDNESS.**   For some multiple disabilities, mental retardation may not be a primary symptom. One such condition is deaf-blindness. The concomitant vision and hearing difficulties (sometimes referred

**Dual diagnosis**

Identification of both serious emotional problems and mental retardation in the same individual.

*Students with deaf-blindness require extensive support to meet their educational needs, particularly in the area of communication.*

## MAT'S STORY: JOINING THE COMMUNITY

Mat is a 23-year-old man with autism and mental retardation. He lives in a home with one roommate and holds two jobs. One job involves cleaning at a local bar and restaurant for an hour each morning. The second job is delivering a weekly advertiser to 170 homes in his neighborhood. In addition to working in the community, Mat goes shopping, takes walks around a nearby lake, goes to the movies, attends concerts and special events, and eats at a fast-food restaurant where he uses a wallet-sized communication picture board to order his meal, independently.

Mat hasn't always been so well integrated into his local community. In the past he engaged in a number of challenging behaviors, including removing pictures from the wall, taking down drapes and ripping them, dismantling his bed, tearing his clothing, breaking windows, smearing his bowel movements on objects, urinating on his clothing, hurting others, stripping naked, and other disruptive behaviors. For almost an entire year, Mat refused to wear clothing and spent most of his time wrapped in a blanket. He would often cover his head with the blanket and lie on the couch for hours. He frequently stripped in community settings, on those few occasions when staff were able to coax him to go out. After this had continued for months, the assistance of a behavioral analyst was sought. An analysis of the function that the behaviors served revealed that Mat's stripping and subsequent refusal to wear clothing were the result of his attempt to exert control over his environment, primarily to escape or avoid undesirable events. For this reason, the behavior analyst suggested not focusing directly on the issue of wearing clothing but, rather, addressing the development of a communication system for Mat.

Mat was reported to know over 200 signs; however, he was rarely observed to use the signs spontaneously. When he did sign, others in his environment were unable to interpret his signing. Consequently, the behavior analyst and a consultant in augmentative and alternative communication suggested that a communication system using pictures or symbols be implemented to supplement his existing system.

The support program that was developed for Mat had two main components. The first was to enhance his communication and choice-making skills, and the second was to provide opportunities for him to participate in activities that were motivating and required him to wear clothing. To address communication and choice-making skills, several photographs were taken of people Mat knew and had worked with, activities he liked or was required to engage in (e.g. watching MTV, going to McDonald's, shaving, taking a shower, etc.), and a variety of objects (e.g. lotion, pop, cookies, etc.). Then, a minimum of four times each hour, Mat was presented with a choice. Mat would then pick one of the pictures, and staff would help him complete whatever activity he had chosen. Soon he had over 130 photographs in his communication system. The photographs were mounted on hooks in the hallway of the house where he lived, ensuring his easy access to them. Over time, staff reported that Mat began spontaneously using some of the pictures to request items. He would, for example, bring staff the photo of a Diet Pepsi to request a Diet Pepsi. Thus the communication enhanced his ability to make his wants and needs known as well as helping him understand choices presented to him.

While Mat's communication system was being developed, staff were also trying to indirectly address his refusal to wear clothes by capitalizing on the fact that he seemed to genuinely like going out into the community. Staff would periodically encourage Mat to dress. On those occasions when he did dress, he was then able to participate in a community activity that was reinforcing for him. The length of these outings was gradually increased.

SOURCE: From *A Little Help from My Friends* (pp. 14–15), by A. Hewitt & S. O'Nell, 2003, Washington, DC: President's Committee on Mental Retardation. Available: www.acf.dhhs.gov/programs/pcmr/help4.pdf  Retrieved June 10, 2003. Adapted from "Joining the Community," by L. Piche, P. Krage, & C. Wiczek, 1991, *IMPACT, 4*(1), pp. 3, 18.

to as **dual sensory impairments**) exhibited by people with **deaf-blindness** result in severe communication deficits as well as developmental and educational difficulties that require extensive support across several professional disciplines. IDEA defines deaf-blindness as

> concomitant hearing and visual impairments, the combination of which causes such severe communication and other developmental and educational needs that they cannot be accommodated in special education programs solely for children with deafness or children with blindness. [34 C.F.R. 300.7(c) (2) (1999)].

The impact of both vision and hearing loss on the educational needs of the student is a matter of debate among professionals. One view of deaf-blindness is that individuals have such severe mental retardation that both vision and hearing are also affected. Another view is that they have average intelligence and lost their hearing and sight after they acquired language. Intellectual functioning for persons with deaf-blindness may range from normal or gifted to severe mental retardation. All people with deaf-blindness experience challenges in learning to communicate, access information, and comfortably move through their environment. These

**Dual sensory impairments**

A condition characterized by both vision and hearing sensory impairments. This condition can result in severe communication problems as well as developmental and educational difficulties that require extensive support across several professional disciplines.

**Deaf-blindness**

A disorder involving simultaneous vision and hearing impairments.

individuals may also have physical and behavioral disabilities. However, the specific needs of each person will vary enormously according to age, onset, and type of deaf-blindness (Deafblind International, 2003).

**FOCUS 3**

Identify the estimated prevalence and causes of severe and multiple disabilities.

# Prevalence

People with severe and multiple disabilities constitute a very small percentage of the general population. Even if we consider the multitude of conditions, prevalence is no more than 0.1% to 1.0%. Approximately 4 out of every 1,000 persons have severe disabilities where the primary symptom is mental retardation. The U.S. Department of Education (2002) estimated that about 122,559 students between the ages of 6 and 21 were served in the public schools under the label *multiple disabilities.* These students account for 2% of the 6.4 million students considered eligible for services under IDEA. The Department of Education also reported that 1,320 students between the ages of 6 and 21 were labeled deaf-blind. These students account for 0.0002% of the students with disabilities served under IDEA. Overall, about 14,000 individuals in the United States are identified as deaf-blind.

# Causation

Multiple disabilities result from multiple causes. For the vast majority of people with severe and multiple disabilities, the differences are evident at birth. Severe disabilities may be the result of genetic or metabolic disorders, including chromosomal abnormalities, phenylketonuria, and Rh incompatibility. (See Chapter 10 for more in-depth information on these disorders.) Most identifiable causes of severe mental retardation and related developmental disabilities are genetic in origin (The ARC, 2003). Other causes include prenatal conditions: poor maternal health during pregnancy, drug abuse, infectious diseases (e.g., HIV), radiation exposure, venereal disease, and advanced maternal age. Severe and multiple disabilities can also result from incidents or conditions that occur later in life, such as poisoning, accidents, malnutrition, physical and emotional neglect, and disease.

**FOCUS 4**

What are the characteristics of persons with severe and multiple disabilities?

# Characteristics

The multitude of characteristics exhibited by people with severe and multiple disabilities is mirrored by the numerous definitions associated with these conditions. A close analysis of these definitions reveals a consistent focus on people whose life needs cannot be met without substantial support from others, including family, friends, and society. With this support, however, people with severe and multiple disabilities have a much greater probability of escaping the stereotype that depicts them as totally dependent consumers of societal resources. People with severe disabilities can become contributing members of families and communities.

School-age students with severe and multiple disabilities may be characterized according to their instructional needs. Sailor, Gee, and Karasoff (2000) suggested that professionals concentrate more on "the way in which special education services are defined and implemented in inclusive educational settings" (p. 11) and less on general, often stereotyped population characteristics. For Sarina in the opening Snapshot, this would mean concentrating on educational outcomes that will reduce her dependence on others in her environment and create opportunities to enhance her participation at home, at school, and in the community. Instruction would be developed with these outcomes in mind, rather than on the basis of a set of general characteristics associated with the label *severely disabled.* Table 12.1 describes desired outcomes for students with severe disabilities when they attend inclusive school settings.

**TABLE 12.1**

**Desired Outcomes for Students with Disabilities
in Inclusive Settings**

- SKILLS. Inclusive classrooms appear to offer students with disabilities the opportunity to learn more useful and age-appropriate functional academic, social, motor, and communication skills and to generalize them to a variety of settings.
- MEMBERSHIP. Inclusive schools present more and more varied occasions to join peer groups and experience affiliation with classmates during and after school hours than do noninclusive schools.
- RELATIONSHIPS. Inclusive schools provide the context for one or more ongoing, familiar, social interactions with other individuals (disabled and nondisabled) that may take on various patterns, including play and companionship, helper, helpee, reciprocal peer, and adversarial.

SOURCE: Snell & Brown, 2000, pp. 115–116.

## Intelligence and Academic Achievement

Most people with severe and multiple disabilities have mental retardation as a primary condition, so their learning and memory capabilities are diminished. The greater the mental retardation, the more difficulty the individual will have in learning, retaining, and applying information. People with severe and multiple disabilities will require specialized and intensive instruction in order to acquire and use new skills across a number of settings.

Given the diminished intellectual capability of many people with severe and multiple disabilities, academic learning is often a low instructional priority. The vast majority of students with severe disabilities are unable to learn from basic academic programs in reading, writing, and mathematics. Instruction in functional skills is the most effective approach to academic learning. Basic academic subjects are taught in the context of daily living. For example, functional reading focuses on those words that facilitate a child's access to the environment (*restroom, danger, exit,* etc.). Development of functional math skills entails creating strategies for telling time or using money effectively as a consumer. A more in-depth discussion on teaching functional skills to students with severe disabilities is presented later in this chapter.

## Adaptive Skills

The learning of **adaptive skills** is critical to success in natural settings. These skills involve both personal independence and social interaction. Personal independence skills range from taking care of one's basic needs—eating, dressing, and hygiene—to living on one's own in the community (getting and keeping a job, managing money, and finding ways to get around in the environment). Social interaction skills involve being able to communicate one's needs and preferences, as well as listening to others and responding appropriately. People with severe and multiple disabilities often do not have age-appropriate adaptive skills and need ongoing services and supports to facilitate learning and application in this area. We do know that when given the opportunity to learn adaptive skills through participation in inclusive settings with peers without disabilities, children with severe disabilities have a higher probability of maintaining and meaningfully applying this learning over time (Sailor et al., 2000; Snell & Brown, 2000; Westling & Fox, 2000).

## Speech and Language

People with severe and multiple disabilities generally have significant deficits and delays in speech and language skills, ranging from articulation and fluency disorders to an absence of any expressive oral language (Westling & Fox, 2000). Speech and language deficits and delays are positively correlated with the severity of mental retardation (Tager-Flusberg & Sullivan, 1998). As is true for adaptive skill learning, people with severe and multiple disabilities will acquire and use appropriate speech and

**Adaptive skills**

Conceptual, social, and practical skills that facilitate an individual's functioning in community, family, and school settings.

language if these skills are taught and applied in natural settings. Functional communication systems (such as signing, picture cards, communication boards, and gesturing) are also an integral part of instruction. Regardless of the communication system(s) used to teach speech and language skills, they must be applied across multiple settings. For example, if picture cards are used in the classroom, they must also be a part of the communication system used at home and in other environments.

## Physical and Health

People with severe and multiple disabilities have significant physical and health care needs. For instance, these individuals have a higher incidence than others of congenital heart disease, **epilepsy,** respiratory problems, diabetes, and metabolic disorders. They also exhibit poor muscle tone and often have conditions such as **spasticity, athetosis,** and **hypotonia**. Such conditions require that professionals in the schools and other service agencies know how to administer medications, **catheterization, gastronomy tube feeding**, and **respiratory ventilation** (Ault, Rues, Graff, & Holvoet, 2000).

## Vision and Hearing

Although the prevalence of vision and hearing loss is not well documented among people with severe disabilities, Sobsey and Wolf-Schein (1996) suggest that sensory impairments do occur more frequently in people with severe disabilities than in the general population. Some individuals, particularly those described as deaf-blind, have significant vision and hearing disorders that require services and supports beyond those needed for a person with blindness or deafness.

# Educational Supports and Services

The axiom "the earlier, the better" is certainly applicable to educational services and supports for children with severe and multiple disabilities. These services and supports must begin at birth and continue throughout the lifespan.

## Assessment

**IDENTIFYING THE DISABILITY.** Traditionally, there has been a heavy reliance on standardized measurements, particularly the IQ test, in identifying people with severe and multiple disabilities, particularly when the primary condition is mental retardation (see Chapter 10). Some professionals (Brown & Snell, 2000; Silberman & Brown, 1998) have suggested that standardized tests, particularly the IQ test, do not provide useful information in either diagnosing the disability or providing instruction to individuals with severe disabilities. Others (Wehman & Parent, 1997) believe that IQ tests may be appropriate for diagnosis but provide no "meaningful information for making curriculum decisions such as what to teach and how to teach it" (p. 158).

**ASSESSING FOR INSTRUCTION.** Assessments that focus on valued skills to promote independence and quality of life in natural settings are referred to as functional, ecological, or **authentic assessments** (Horner, Albin, Sprague, & Todd, 2000; Siegel-Causey & Allinder, 1998). As described in the TASH definition of severe disabilities, these assessments are concerned with the match between the needs of the individual and the demands of the environment (adaptive fit). The purpose of the assessment is to determine what supports are necessary to achieve the intended outcomes of access and participation in natural settings. Skills are never taught in isolation from actual performance demands. Additionally, the individual does not "get ready" to participate in the community through a sequence of readiness stages, as in the developmental model, but instead learns and uses skills in the setting where the behavior is expected to occur.

**Epilepsy**

A condition that produces brief disturbances in the normal electrical functions of the brain, affecting a person's consciousness, bodily movements, or sensations and resulting in seizures.

**Spasticity**

A condition that involves involuntary contractions of various muscle groups.

**Athetosis**

A condition characterized by constant, contorted twisting motions in the wrists and fingers.

**Hypotonia**

Poor muscle tone.

**Catheterization**

The process of introducing a hollow tube (catheter) into a body cavity to drain fluid, such as introducing a tube into an individual's bladder to drain urine.

**Gastronomy tube feeding**

The process of feeding the individual through a rubber tube that is inserted into the stomach.

**Respiratory ventilation**

Use of a mechanical aid (ventilator) to supply oxygen to an individual with respiratory problems.

**Authentic assessments**

An alternative to the standardized tests traditionally used to measure student progress. Assessment is based on student progress in meaningful learning activities.

**SCHOOL ACCOUNTABILITY.** During the past decade, there has been an increasing emphasis on holding schools more accountable for student learning and progress. States are setting educational standards and then assessing how students progress toward the intended goals. A major challenge for education is to demonstrate accountability for the learning outcomes of *all* students, including those with the most significant disabilities. Ford, Davern, and Schnorr (2001) suggest that

**FOCUS 5**

Identify three types of educational assessments for students with severe and multiple disabilities.

> Regardless of one's perspective on the wisdom and implications of this [accountability] movement, it promises to have a significant effect on curricular guidance and foci for students with [severe] disabilities. . . . A major question facing educators and parents is how can those concerned with the education of students with significant disabilities ensure a continued and focused emphasis on full membership and meaningful outcomes during this era? (p. 215)

IDEA and No Child Left Behind (NCLB) require that schools include students with disabilities in statewide or districtwide assessments of achievement or provide a statement of why that assessment is not appropriate for the child. Both laws also require that individual modifications in the administration of statewide or districtwide assessments be provided as appropriate, in order to enable the child to participate. Examples of student accommodations include large-print text, testing in a separate setting, and extended time. Ysseldyke, Olsen, and Thurlow (2003) estimate that about 85% of students with disabilities have mild or moderate disabilities and can take state or district assessments, either with or without accommodations. For many students with severe disabilities, these assessments are inappropriate, and such students are excluded from taking them. Schools are still accountable, however, for the progress of these students. IDEA and NCLB mandated that states conduct **alternate assessments** to ensure that all students are included in the state's accountability system. Quenemoen and Thurlow (2003) identified five characteristics of good alternate assessments:

- There has been careful stakeholder and policymaker development and definition of desired student outcomes for the population, reflecting the best understanding of research and practice.
- Assessment methods have been carefully developed, tested, and refined.
- Professionally accepted standards are used to score evidence (e.g., adequate training, dual-scoring third-party tie breakers, reliability tests and rechecks of scorer competence).
- An accepted standards-setting process has been used so that results can be included in reporting and accountability.
- The assessment process is continuously reviewed and improved.

Alternate assessment systems should include, as critical criteria, the extent to which the system provides the needed supports and adaptations and trains the student to use them. Alternate assessments may involve either normative or absolute performance standards (Ysseldyke & Olsen, 2003). If a normative assessment is used, then a student's performance is compared to that of peers (other students of comparable age or ability participating in the alternate assessment). If an absolute standard is used, then a student's performance is compared against a set criterion. For example, the student is able to cross the street when the "walk" sign is flashing 100% of the time without assistance. (See nearby Reflect on This, "Alternate Assessment Strategies")

# The Early Childhood Years

Effective early intervention services that start when the child is born are critical to the prevention and amelioration of social, medical, and educational problems that can occur throughout the life of the individual (Guralnick, 2001; Ramey & Ramey, 1999). During the early childhood years, services and supports are concentrated on two age groups: infants and toddlers, and preschool-age children.

**Alternate assessments**

Assessments mandated in IDEA and NCLB for students who are unable to participate in required state- or districtwide assessments. Such assessments ensure that all students, regardless of the severity of their disabilities, are included in the state's accountability system.

## ALTERNATE ASSESSMENT STRATEGIES

### What is an alternate assessment?

An alternate assessment is different from the assessment given to most students. It is best viewed as a process for collecting information about what a student knows and can do. Generally, when we think of assessment, we think of a test. This is because most statewide assessments consist of taking a test, although some states are also using a portfolio approach that allows for collecting samples of student work. The majority of students participate by taking the tests, some by using accommodations. Some students, however, are unable to take the test even with accommodations or modifications. For these students, there must be an alternative way of determining their learning progress.

### What are some data collection strategies that can be used in an alternate assessment system?

- Observing the child in the course of the school day over a specified period of time
- Interviewing parents or family members about what the child does outside of school
- Asking the child to perform a specific activity or task and noting the level of performance
- Administering a commercially developed assessment instrument (e.g., Brigance) and comparing the results with a set of state-established standards
- Reviewing records that have been developed over a designated period of time

SOURCE: Adapted from *Alternate Assessment: Questions and Answers. IDEA practices* by C. Massanari, 2003. Available: http://www.ideapractices.org/resources/detail.php?id=2009   Retrieved June 18, 2003.

## Services and Supports for Infants and Toddlers

Effective programs for infants and toddlers with severe and multiple disabilities are both child- and family-centered. A child-centered approach is focused on identifying and meeting individual needs. Services begin with infant stimulation programs intended to elicit sensory, cognitive, and physical responses in newborns that will connect them with their environment. As the child develops, health care, physical therapy, occupational therapy, and speech and language services may become integral components of a child-centered program.

Family-centered early intervention is characterized by a holistic approach that involves the child as a member of the family unit. The needs, structure, and preferences of the family drive the delivery of services and supports (Ramey & Ramey, 1999). The overall purpose of family-centered intervention is initially to enable family members to cope with the birth of a child with a severe disability. Soon the goal expands to empowering them to grow together and support one another. Berry and Hardman (1998) suggested that family-centered approaches build on and increase family strengths, address the needs of every family member, and support mutually enjoyable family relationships. Supports for families may include parent-training programs, counseling, and **respite care**.

### Respite care

Assistance provided by individuals outside of the immediate family so that parents and other children within the family can spend time away from the child with a disability for a recreational event or a vacation. Some states provide funding for this kind of care.

*Effective programs for infants and toddlers with severe and multiple disabilities are both child- and family-centered. Therapists work closely with the infant and the family to promote early learning and development.*

### Services and Supports for Preschool-Age Children

Preschool programs for young children with severe and multiple disabilities continue the emphasis on family involvement while extending the life space of the child to a school setting. McDonnell, Hardman, and McDonnell (2003) suggest four goals for preschool programs serving children with severe disabilities:

FOCUS 6

Identify the features of effective services and supports for children with severe and multiple disabilities during the early childhood years.

1. Maximize the child's development in a variety of important developmental areas. These include social communication, motor skills, cognitive skills, preacademic skills, self-care, play, and personal management.

2. Develop the child's social interaction and classroom participation skills. Focus on developing peer relationships and teaching the child to follow adults' directions, respond to classroom routines, and become self-directed (complete classroom activities without constant adult supervision).

3. Increase community participation through support to family members and other caregivers. Work to identify alternative caregivers so that the family has a broader base of support and more flexibility to pursue other interests. Help the family to identify activities within the neighborhood that their preschooler would enjoy, in order to give the child opportunities to interact with same-age peers. Activities may involve swimming or dancing lessons, joining a soccer team, attending a house of worship, and so on.

4. Prepare the child for inclusive school placements, and provide support for the transition to elementary school. The transition out of preschool will be facilitated if educators from the receiving elementary school work collaboratively with family and preschool personnel.

To meet these goals, Grenot-Scheyer, Schwartz, and Meyer (1997) proposed that preschool programs for children with severe disabilities blend the principles and elements of developmentally appropriate practices (DAP), multicultural education, and special education. DAP was developed by the National Association for the Education of Young Children as an alternative to an academic curriculum for preschoolers. It emphasizes age-appropriate child exploration and play activities that are consistent with individual needs (see Chapter 3). Multicultural education emphasizes acceptance of people from different cultural and ethnic backgrounds within and across the preschool curriculum. Successful culturally inclusive programs blend principles and practices that guide special education, inclusive education, and multicultural education (Grenot-Scheyer et al., 1997). Special education focuses on assessing individual needs, providing intensive instruction, and teaching explicit skills within the context of an individualized education program (IEP). The combination of

*Culturally inclusive preschool programs blend the principles and practices that guide special education, inclusive education, and multicultural education.*

DAP, multicultural education, and special education work together to provide a quality experience for preschool-age children with severe disabilities.

FOCUS 7

Identify the features of effective services and supports for children with severe and multiple disabilities during the elementary school years.

# The Elementary School Years

Historically, services and supports for students with severe and multiple disabilities have been geared to protection and care. The objective was to protect the individual from society—and society from the individual. This philosophy resulted in programs that isolated the individual and offered physical care rather than preparation for life in a heterogeneous world. Today, educators working in tandem with parents are concentrating their efforts on preparing students with severe and multiple disabilities to participate actively in the life of the family, school, and community. Given this emphasis on lifelong learning and on living in natural settings, educators have identified several features that characterize quality programs for elementary-age students with severe and multiple disabilities:

- Self-determination—student preferences and needs are taken into account in developing educational objectives.
- The school values and supports parental involvement.
- Instruction focuses on frequently used functional skills related to everyday life activities.
- Assistive technology and augmentative communication are available to maintain or increase the functional capabilities of the student with severe and multiple disabilities.

## Self-Determination

People with severe and multiple disabilities, like everyone else, must be in a position to make their own life choices as much as possible. School programs that promote self-determination enhance each student's opportunity to become more independent in the life of the family and in the larger community setting. Giving students with severe disabilities the opportunity to communicate their needs and preferences enhances autonomy, problem-solving skills, adaptability, and self-efficacy expectations (Agran & Wehmeyer, 1999; Bremer, Kachgal, & Schoeller, 2003; Whitney-Thomas, Shaw, Honey, & Butterworth, 1998).

## Parental Involvement

Schools are more successful in meeting the needs of students when they establish positive relationships with the family (Fuller & Olsen, 1998). The important role that parents play during the early childhood years must continue and be supported during elementary school. Parents who actively participate in their child's educational program exert more influence on the development and implementation of instruction that is consistent with individual needs and preferences. Parental involvement can be a powerful predictor of postschool adjustment for students with severe and multiple disabilities. A strong home–school partnership requires that parents and educators

- acknowledge and respect each other's differences in values and culture.
- listen openly and attentively to each other's concerns.
- value varying opinions and ideas.
- discuss issues openly and in an atmosphere of trust.
- share in the responsibility and consequences of making a decision. (Berry & Hardman, 1998)

## Teaching Functional Skills

Effective educational programs focus on the functional skills necessary for students with severe and multiple disabilities to live successfully in the natural settings of family, school, and community. A functional skill is one that will have frequent and meaningful use across multiple environments. Instruction should involve the following elements:

- Many different people

- A variety of settings within the community

- Varied materials that will interest the learner and match performance demands.

If the student with severe disabilities is to learn how to cross a street safely, shop in a grocery store, play a video game, or eat in a local restaurant, the necessary skills should be taught in the actual setting where the skill is to be performed. It should not be assumed that a skill learned in a classroom will transfer to a setting outside the school. Instruction in a more natural environment can ensure that the skill will be useful and will persist over time.

As suggested by Drew and Hardman (2004), a functional approach teaches academic skills in the context of environmental cues. The learning of new skills is always paired directly with environmental stimuli. Snell and Brown (2000) stressed that the teacher must use instructional materials that are real and meaningful to the student. Traditional materials (such as workbooks, basal readers, flash cards, and so on) do not work for students with severe disabilities. Students must be taught using *real objects in real situations* in the home or community setting. For example, when teaching the word *exit*, pair it with an actual exit sign in a movie theater. When teaching the word *stop*, pair it with a stop sign on a street corner.

## Assistive Technology and Augmentative Communication

Assistive technology is any item, piece of equipment, or product system that can be used to increase, maintain, or improve the functional capabilities of students with disabilities (The Technology-Related Assistance for Individuals with Disabilities Act, PL 100-407, [20 U.S.C. Sec. 140(25)]). An assistive technology service "directly assists an individual with a disability in the selection, acquisition, or use of an assistive technology device" [20 U.S.C. Sec 140(26)]. Wehman (1997) identified several categories of assistive technology:

- Mobility (wheelchairs, lifts, adaptive driving controls, scooters, laser canes)

- Seating and positioning (assistance in choosing and using a wheelchair)

- Computers (environmental control units, word processors, software, keyboards)

- Toys and games (software and switch-operated toys)

- Activities of daily living (feeders, lifts, memory books, watch alarms)

- Communication (touch talkers, reading systems, and talking keyboards. (p. 475)

Students with severe and multiple disabilities can benefit from any one or more of these assistive devices or activities.

*When teaching functional skills, teachers should use materials that interest the learner and have meaning within the school and community setting.*

**FOCUS 8**

Describe four outcomes that are important in planning for the transition from school to adult life for adolescents with severe and multiple disabilities.

**FOCUS 9**

Describe four features that characterize successful inclusive education for students with severe and multiple disabilities.

**Augmentative communication**

Communication systems that involve adapting existing vocal or gestural abilities into meaningful communication; teaching manual signing, static symbols, or icons; and using manual or electronic communication devices.

**Blissymbols**

A system developed by C. K. Bliss that ties a specific symbol to a word. There are four types of Blissymbols: pictographic, ideographic, relational, and abstract.

For students with severe disabilities who are unable to use speech and need an additional communication mode, augmentative communication is nearly always an integral component of their individualized education program. **Augmentative communication** involves adapting existing vocal or gestural abilities into meaningful communication; teaching manual signing (such as American Sign Language), static symbols, or icons (such as **Blissymbols**); and using manual or electronic communication devices (such as electric communication boards, picture cues, or synthetic speech) (Westling & Fox, 2000). For more insight into the use of assistive technology for a student with severe disabilities in an inclusive educational setting, see the nearby Assistive Technology, "Meet Joey."

## The Adolescent Years

Societal perceptions about the capabilities of people with severe and multiple disabilities have been significantly altered over the past several years. Until very recently, the potential of these individuals to learn, live, and work in community settings was significantly underestimated. People with severe and multiple disabilities can become active participants in the lives of their community and family. This realization has prompted professionals and parents to seek significant changes in the ways that schools prepare students for the transition into adult life.

In a review of the research on successful community living for people with severe disabilities, McDonnell, Mathot-Buckner, and Ferguson (1996) have pointed out four outcomes that are important in planning for the transition to adult life:

- Establish a network of friends and acquaintances.
- Develop the ability to use community resources on a regular basis.
- Secure a paid job that supports the use of community resources and interaction with peers.
- Establish independence and autonomy in making lifestyle choices. (p. 9)

## Inclusive Education

Many professionals argue that the provision of services and supports in an inclusive educational setting is a critical factor in delivering a quality program for students with severe and multiple disabilities (Giangreco & Doyle, 2000; Sailor et al., 2000; Sax, Fisher, & Pumpian, 1999). Effective educational programs include regular opportunities for interaction between students with severe disabilities and peers without disabilities. Frequent and age-appropriate interactions between students with disabilities and their peers without disabilities can enhance opportunities for successful participation in the community during the adult years. Social interaction can be enhanced by creating opportunities for these students to associate both during and after the school day. Successful inclusion efforts are characterized by the following features:

- Placement of students with severe and multiple disabilities in the general education schools and classes they would attend if they didn't have disabilities
- Systematic organization of opportunities for interaction between students with severe and multiple disabilities and students without disabilities, in order to broaden the horizons of *all* students
- Specific instruction in valued postschool outcomes that will increase the competence of students with severe and multiple disabilities in the natural settings of family, school, and community.

For more insight into importance of friendships for students with severe disabilities, see the nearby Case Study, "The Beginning of a New Circle of Friends."

## MEET JOEY

Identified as having cerebral palsy and also as being "deaf-blind with cognitive disabilities," Joey spent the first four years of his school career in a special day class, where he spent a great deal of time lying in a beanbag chair. He had no consistent method of communication other than screaming and crying, which he used when staff attempted to engage him in an activity. Even the peer helpers from general education classes avoided contact with Joey. The majority of interactions that students or staff had with Joey were to provide personal care services, such as feeding and changing his diaper. About the time that Joey turned 8, his life changed significantly as assistive technology was introduced into his range of supports and services.

Four years ago, when he was 8 years old and still attending a special day class, Joey began to learn about cause and effect through the use of a set of adapted switches connected to a Bart Simpson toy. The standard remote control switch for the toy featured one button to move Bart forward and a second to move him backward. The remote control was rewired so that Joey could hit either a large plate for forward motion or a large pillow switch to reverse the movement. Due to Joey's limited vision, the toy was placed on a table so that, at the very least, he could feel the vibration of the toy moving across the table's surface. As soon as Joey became engaged in the activity, exciting things happened. First, he clearly began to follow the movement of Bart's yellow head as it moved across his field of vision. Second, peers in the room saw this activity as a way to interact with Joey. Finally, as his peers helped him to press the switches, Joey began to associate the operation of the switch with the movement of the toy. As a result, his peers began to consider many more activities in which Joey could participate. The classroom teacher set up a variety of appliances that could be switch-controlled so that Joey could practice throughout the day. It became obvious that Joey could perform these same activities in general education classes.

Over the next couple of years, Joey began spending more time in general education classes where he participated in activities instead of simply observing them. He became more proficient at switch use and was able to operate a number of individualized devices. One device was used for climate control. Because the school operated on a year-round schedule, the children had to acclimate to warm classrooms. Some teachers permitted students to take turns "misting" the classroom. Joey participated by using a switch-operated spray bottle that was modified from a sports bottle. While a classmate pointed the sprayer in different directions, Joey operated the water flow. Other adaptations included a Plexiglas display board

that was used for communication and a variety of appliances that he controlled with his switches.

By the time Joey entered fifth grade, he made the transition from being a "visitor from Room #5" to being a full-time member of the class. New situations required new adaptations. Joey's classmates had been responsible for raising Joey's hand to summon the teacher, but they felt that Joey needed his own method. A "low-tech" light switch was mounted on Joey's laptray so that he could attract the teacher's attention. His ability to use a switch increased so that he could use several of them, coded with Picture Communication Symbols to operate a Speakeasy communication device with messages recorded by a student whom he chose. He used another switch to turn on a tape recorder to play the same book on tape that the other students were reading during "silent reading" time. Consistent use of switches helped to increase his motivation and dexterity for accessing the computer through the Ke:nx program. These abilities would be essential for participating at his neighborhood middle school.

Joey's seating and positioning needs were adjusted, including time scheduled to be out of his wheelchair and sitting at a desk. His therapy needs were met during the regular physical education periods, as coordinated by his teacher, with consultative support from the school district's physical therapist and adaptive physical education specialist. The special education teacher worked closely with the fifth-grade teacher to adapt the curriculum and make accommodations as necessary. Joey's classmates were an invaluable source of creativity who thought of innovative strategies to increase Joey's participation. As they became more familiar with Joey and the way in which he responded, they were key players in identifying new goals based on their keen insights and perceptions of Joey's needs and desires. The entire range of services and supports that were listed on his IEP were designed and implemented through effective collaboration of all of the professionals involved. People learned to perform their roles in new settings and under different circumstances. By the end of the school year, everyone agreed that Joey had surpassed all earlier expectations. Eventually it was determined that Joey no longer required services from the vision and hearing specialists, as he was obviously using both of these sensory modes adequately in all of his daily activities. His transition plan for moving to the middle school included a discussion of scheduling him into classes where he would remain with a number of his fifth grade classmates. The possibilities for Joey are endless, and as luck would have it, his new school is a technology magnet a perfect place for him to continue to build his skills in using all kinds of technology.

SOURCE: Adapted from *Assistive Technology and Inclusion*. Issue Brief (pp. 1–5) by C. Sax, I. Pumpian, & D. Fisher, 1997. Pittsburgh, PA: Consortium on Inclusive Schooling Practices, Allegheny University of the Health Sciences. Reprinted with permission.

One of the most important characteristics of the postschool environments in which students ultimately must function is frequent interaction with people without disabilities. Consequently, it is logical to plan educational programs that duplicate this feature of the environment and actively build skills required for successful inclusion.

As students with severe and multiple disabilities are included in general education schools and classrooms, it is important to find ways to encourage social

## THE BEGINNING OF A NEW CIRCLE OF FRIENDS

Both Joanne and Jennifer are new students with disabilities in the fifth grade homeroom. It is mid-afternoon of their first day at the new school—and time for recess. The special education aide has a break now, so Tom and Maria, two students without disabilities, volunteer to help Jennifer outside to the playground. Halfway down the hall, Jennifer begins to wheel her chair—slowly, but by herself. Tom lights up. "Hey, I didn't know that you could do that. Why didn't you tell me before?"

Jennifer first smiles and then lets out a full laugh. The two other fifth graders join in. They continue slowly outside, where Tom leaves to play softball. Joanne, the other new student, has been invited to join an impromptu soccer game, serving, because of her height, as goalie. Maria, not wanting to leave Jennifer simply sitting by herself during recess, asks, "Do you want to play jump rope?"

Again, Jennifer smiles, and looks toward the group of girls next to the building who have already begun to play jump rope. Maria understands and helps Jennifer over a curb, as the two girls move on to the game. Once there, Maria asks, "Do you know how to twirl?"

Jennifer shakes her head, "no." So Maria places the end of the rope in her hand and holding says, "Okay, hold it like this, and go round this way." She guides her movements with her hand.

Soon Jennifer gets the hang of it, and Maria is able to let go. It's her turn to jump, so she leaves Jennifer's side, and begins her routine. She is able to jump longer than any of the other girls. As she spins around to complete a maneuver, she faces Jennifer as she jumps. Seeing her twirl, Maria sticks out her tongue, and both girls laugh. Unfortunately, the twirling stops, ending Maria's turn. It doesn't really matter, because a new game will start tomorrow, and Maria usually wins anyway.

In a moment Ms. Nelson calls to the students to return to class, and Maria and Jennifer come in together. As they enter the room, Ms. Nelson asks the classmates to take out their library books and use the remaining time to read silently. Marsha, who had been playing soccer with Joanne, asks her teacher if she could lend her one of her books to read. Ms. Nelson approves, and the girls go to the reading corner of the room to choose among Marsha's three books.

### APPLICATION

1. Could this experience have occurred in a special school or if Jennifer had spent her entire day in a special education self-contained classroom?

2. What can be done to ensure that this relationship continues outside of school?

3. Why is being a "member" of the homeroom so important to establishing friendships for children with severe disabilities?

SOURCE: Adapted from *Introduction to Persons with Moderate and Severe Disabilities* (p. 194, 2nd ed.), by J. McDonnell, M. Hardman, & A. P. McDonnell, 2003, Boston: Allyn and Bacon, p. 297.

interactions between these students and students who are not disabled. Planned opportunities for interaction may include the use of in-class peer supports (tutors, circles of friends) as well as access to everyday school activities such as assemblies, recess, lunch, and field trips. For more tips on supporting people with disabilities in natural settings, see the Inclusion Through the Lifespan on page 352.

**FOCUS 10**

Describe four bioethical dilemmas that affect people with severe disabilities and their families.

**Bioethics**

The study of ethics in medicine.

# Severe Disabilities and Biomedical Dilemmas

Rapid advances in medical technology have resulted in the survival of an increasing number of infants with severe and multiple disabilities. Today, many such infants who would have died at birth only five to ten years ago now live well into their adult years. However, this decrease in infant mortality and increase in lifespan have raised a number of serious ethical issues regarding decisions about the prevention of severe disabilities and about the care and selective nontreatment of infants with such disabilities. In recent years, there has been an increasing awareness of and interest in **bioethics,** particularly as it is related to serious illness and severe disabilities. Bioethical issues include concerns about the purpose and use of genetic engineering, screening for genetic diseases, abortion, and the withholding of life-sustaining medical treatment. A number of questions have been raised by both professionals and parents. When do individual rights begin? Who should live, and who should die? What is personhood? Who defines quality of life? What are the rights of the person with severe disabilities vis-à-vis the obligations of society? Who shall make the difficult decisions?

## Genetic Engineering

The purpose of genetic engineering is to conquer disease. Through the identification of a faulty gene that causes a disease, such as cystic fibrosis, scientists are able to prevent its future occurrence and to treat those who have the condition. In 1990 the United States and the United Kingdom joined together with more than 3,000 research scientists in the **Human Genome Project.** The project has several goals:

- Identify the 80,000 genes in human DNA.
- Determine the sequences of the 3 billion chemical base pairs that make up human DNA.
- Store this information in databases.
- Develop tools for data analysis.
- Address the ethical, legal, and social issues that may arise from the project. (U.S. Department of Energy, 2003)

In June 2000, scientists from the Human Genome Project and scientists from a private company, Celera Genomics of Rockville, Maryland, announced that they had successfully completed the first phase of the research. They had sequenced 99% of the human genome and had assembled more than 1 billion letters of genetic code. The next step, which may be the most challenging and controversial, is interpreting what all the codes mean.

The work of scientists in unlocking the secrets of the genetic code has attracted the attention of professionals and parents concerned about the rights of people with severe and multiple disabilities. Although genetic engineering may be seen as holding considerable promise for reducing human suffering, it can also be viewed as a means of enhancing or "perfecting" human beings. Because the vast majority of people with severe and multiple disabilities have genetic disorders (e.g., fragile X syndrome or Down syndrome), they are greatly affected by this debate. The ARC of the United States (a national organization of and for people with mental retardation and related developmental disabilities and their families) points out that people with severe disabilities have been subjected to a long history of discrimination. Thus it is important that the complex ethical issues surrounding the work of the Human Genome Project receive widespread public attention. The ARC (2003) has raised numerous questions in the area of genetic engineering that have yet to be answered:

Should therapies for genetic conditions causing mental retardation [severe disabilities] even be considered?

**Human Genome Project**

Project developed by the United States and the United Kingdom to identify the 80,000 genes in human DNA; to determine the sequences of the 3 billion chemical base pairs that make up human DNA; to store this information in databases; to develop tools for data analysis; and to address the ethical, legal, and social issues that may arise from the project.

*Although genetic engineering holds considerable promise for reducing human suffering, many ethical questions are yet to be answered.*

SEVERE DISABILITIES AND BIOMEDICAL DILEMMAS

**Inclusion Through the Lifespan**

## PEOPLE WITH SEVERE AND MULTIPLE DISABILITIES

### EARLY CHILDHOOD YEARS

#### Tips for the Family

- During the infant and toddler years, seek out family-oriented programs that focus on communication and the building of positive relationships among all individual members.
- Seek supports and services for your preschool-age child that promote communication and play activities with same-age peers without disabilities.
- Seek opportunities for friendships to develop between your child and children without disabilities in family and neighborhood settings.
- Use the individualized family service plan (IFSP) and the individualized education plan (IEP) as a means to establish goals that develop your child's social interaction and classroom participation skills.

#### Tips for the General Education Preschool Teacher

- Establish a classroom environment that promotes and supports diversity.
- Use a child-centered approach to instruction that acknowledges and values every child's strengths, preferences, and individual needs.
- Ignore whatever labels have been used to describe the child with severe and multiple disabilities. There is no relationship between the label and the instruction needed by the child to succeed in natural settings.
- Create opportunities for ongoing communication and play activities among children with severe disabilities and their same-age peers without disabilities. Nurture interactive peer relationships across a variety of instructional areas and settings.

#### Tips for Preschool Personnel

- Support the inclusion of young children with severe and multiple disabilities in all preschool classrooms and programs.
- Always refer to children by name, not by label. If you must label, use child-first language—"children with severe disabilities."
- Communicate genuine respect and support for all teachers, staff, and volunteers who look for ways to include children with severe disabilities in preschool classrooms and schoolwide activities.
- Welcome families into the preschool programs. Listen to what parents have to say about the importance of, or concerns about, including their child in school programs and activities. Create opportunities for parents to become involved in their child's program through volunteering, school governance, and so on.

#### Tips for Neighbors and Friends

- First and foremost, see the child with severe disabilities as an individual who has needs, preferences, strengths, and weaknesses. Avoid the pitfalls of stereotyping and "self-fulfilling prophecies."
- Support opportunities for your children and those of friends and neighbors to interact and play with a child with severe and multiple disabilities.
- Help children without disabilities build friendships rather than caregiving roles with children who have severe and multiple disabilities.
- Provide a supportive community environment for the family of a young child with severe and multiple disabilities. Encourage the family, including the child, to participate in neighborhood activities.

### ELEMENTARY YEARS

#### Tips for the Family

- Actively participate in the development of your son's or daughter's IEP. Write down the priorities and educational goals that you see as important to allow your child to participate in the natural settings of home, school, and community.
- Follow up at home on activities that the school suggests are important to help your child generalize skills learned at school to other natural settings.
- Actively participate as a volunteer in the school, whether it be in your child's classroom or in another situation. Show your appreciation and support for administrators teachers, and staff who openly value and support the inclusion of your child in the school and classroom.
- Continually communicate with administrators and teachers how important it is to include children with severe disabilities in classroom and schoolwide activities (such as riding on the same school bus, going to recess and lunch at the same time, and participating in schoolwide assemblies).

#### Tips for the General Education Classroom Teacher

- See children with severe and multiple disabilities as individuals, not labels. Focus on their similarities with other children, rather than on their differences.
- Openly value and support diversity in your classroom. Set individualized goals and objectives for all children.
- Develop a classroom environment and instructional program that recognizes multiple needs and abilities.
- Become part of a team that works together to meet the needs of all children in your classroom. View the special education teacher as a resource who can assist you in developing an effective instructional program for the child with severe and multiple disabilities.

#### Tips for School Personnel

- Communicate that diversity is a strength in your school. Openly value diversity by providing the resources necessary for teachers to work with students who have a range of needs and come from heterogeneous backgrounds.
- Integrate school resources as well as children. Develop schoolwide teacher-assistance or teacher-support teams that use a collaborative ethic to meet the needs of every student.
- Support general and special education teachers in the development of peer-partner and support networks for students with severe and multiple disabilities.
- Include all students in the programs and activities of the school.

#### Tips for Neighbors and Friends

- Openly communicate to school personnel, friends, and neighbors your support of families who are seeking to have their child with severe and multiple disabilities be a part of an inclusive school setting.
- Communicate to your children and those of friends and neighbors the value of inclusion. Demonstrate this value by creating opportunities for children with severe disabilities and their families to play an active role in the life of the community.

## SECONDARY AND TRANSITION YEARS

### Tips for the Family

- Seek opportunities for students from your son's or daughter's high school to visit your home. Help arrange get-togethers or parties involving students from the neighborhood or school.
- Communicate to the school what you see as priorities for your son or daughter in the transition from school to adult life. Suggest goals and objectives that promote and support social interaction and community-based activities with nondisabled peers. Work with the school to translate your goals into an individualized transition plan (ITP).

### Tips for the General Education Classroom Teacher

- Become part of a school-wide team that works together to meet the needs of all students in high school. Value the role of the special educator as teacher, collaborator, and consultant who can serve as a valuable resource in planning for the instructional needs of students with severe disabilities. Collaborate with special education teachers and other specialists to adapt subject matter in your classroom (e.g., science, math, or physical education) to the individual needs of students with severe and multiple disabilities.
- Communicate the importance of students with severe disabilities being included in school programs and activities. Although their goals and activities may differ from those of other students, with support they will benefit from working with you and other students in the class.
- Support the student with severe disabilities becoming involved in extracurricular high school activities. If you are the faculty sponsor of a club or organization, explore whether this student is interested and how he or she could get involved.

### Tips for School Personnel

- Advocate for parents of high-school-age students with severe and multiple disabilities to participate in the activities and governance of the school.
- Support parental involvement in the transition planning process during the high school years by listening to parents.
- Support high school special education or vocational teachers seeking to develop community-based instruction programs that focus on students learning and applying skills in actual community settings (e.g., grocery stores, malls, theaters, parks, work sites).

### Tips for Neighbors, Friends, and Potential Employers

- Work with the family and school personnel to create opportunities for students with severe and multiple disabilities to participate in community activities (such as going to the movies, "hanging out" with nondisabled peers in the neighborhood mall, and going to high school sporting events) as often as possible.
- As a potential employer, work with the high school to locate and establish community-based employment training sites for students with severe and multiple disabilities.

## ADULT YEARS

### Tips for the Family

- Develop an understanding of life after school for your son or daughter during the adult years. What are the formal (government-funded, parent organizations) and informal supports (family and friends) available in your community? What are the characteristics of adult service programs? Explore adult support systems in the local community in the areas of supported living, employment, and recreation and leisure.

### Tips for Neighbors, Friends, and Potential Employers

- Become part of the community support network for the individual with severe and multiple disabilities. Be alert to ways in which this individual can become and remain actively involved in community employment, neighborhood recreational activities, and functions at a local house of worship.
- As potential employers in the community, seek information on employment of people with severe and multiple disabilities. Find out about programs (such as supported employment) that focus on establishing work for people with severe disabilities while meeting your needs as an employer.

## DISABILITIES MAY KEEP BRIAN CORTEZ FROM HEART TRANSPLANT

**M**oving a step to his right, Brian Cortez dribbles the basketball and arcs a 15-foot shot that sails through the curbside hoop. He flashes a smile, and his fingers move quickly to sign his pleasure to his friends.

It is a happy moment in the troubled times of Cortez, 20. In a life filled with challenges, he is facing perhaps his most difficult.

Cortez is developmentally disabled, is almost deaf, and has lived in poverty since birth. Four years ago he was diagnosed with mild mental illness. Now his heart is sick and eventually will fail without a transplant.

Yet his limited mental abilities may disqualify him from the procedure. University of Washington physicians have said in an initial evaluation that they don't think Cortez, who lives in an adult home, can follow a strict medication regimen or articulate any problems after a transplant. A scarcity of donor hearts nationwide makes patients like Cortez less able to compete for a spot on the waiting list.

Advocates for Cortez—his teacher, his mother, adult-home caregivers, and case workers—disagree. They say University of Washington physicians and a social worker did not speak in depth with key people in the young man's support network. If they had, they would have learned that Cortez takes medications when asked, is aware of his physical condition, and can tell caregivers how he feels.

"They didn't have a true picture of his ability to deal with things," said Ted Karanson, deaf-education teacher at North Thurston High School, where Cortez was a student until his heart problems became worse this winter. "Brian deserves a chance at a transplant like anyone else."

Cortez's situation reflects the consequences of a national shortage of vital organs for transplantation. About 800 people a year die while waiting for heart transplants. More than 5,000 patients nationwide die while waiting for other organs.

The government-contracted agency that allocates organs nationally—the United Network for Organ Sharing—has an elaborate system to channel organs to patients who have the best chance of benefiting. And the law of supply and demand applies: Scarce organs go to those with the best chance of surviving an operation and caring for themselves afterward.

Laurence O'Connell, president of the Park Ridge Center, a Chicago bioethics institute, said the University of Washington is using a widely accepted standard, and the decision couldn't be more difficult:

"To offer the organ to this young man will almost certainly mean another patient will die," O'Connell said.

Brian Cortez's life began with a difficult birth, when his brain was briefly deprived of oxygen. Months later, he was diagnosed with severe hearing loss, impaired mental development, poor fine-motor control, and a faulty heart valve. At age 16, he began occasionally hearing voices. He banged his head against his locker and mumbled threats at other students at North Thurston High School. He was diagnosed with a "thought disorder" and was prescribed medication that silences the voices most of the time. Through it all, Cortez has been undiscouraged and has struggled to learn, Karanson said. He has friends from school, reads the newspaper to keep up with the Seattle Sonics and Mariners, and has firm opinions about current affairs. He expresses himself through signing, speaking, and writing. Last year he worked two days a week for a landscape nursery as part of his school's job-training program.

With a successful transplant, "He could work a job, part time if not full time," said Lisa Flatt, a sign-language interpreter for the North Thurston School District. "He could do something repetitious—landscaping, assembly-line work, working in a mail room. . . . He would be really good at it." Cortez's medical record shows he was given test after test during his two-week stay at the University of Washington hospital. Communication was poor, his mother said, because he did not understand the hospital's sign-language interpreter. The tests and treatment frightened and angered him.

At one point he was restrained in bed because he was spitting at and biting nurses. He wet his bed and hoarded food. He was given heavy doses of anti-psychotic medications to calm him. In the end, doctors wrote in his record: "It was thought during his admission that, due to his developmental delay and inability to understand and comply with instructions, the patient

Is there positive value in [human] diversity? How can we avoid stigmatizing those living with a genetic condition while trying to eliminate the condition in others? Are some conditions so destructive to the individual that if a therapy is possible should it be undertaken? Should parents include their newborn child in experimental gene therapy research? (pp. 1–2)

## Genetic Screening and Counseling

Genetic screening is a search for genes in the human body that are predisposed to disease, are already diseased, or may lead to disease in future generations of the same family. Genetic screening has become widespread throughout the world but is not without controversy and potential for abuse. The Human Genome Project has raised several ethical questions regarding genetic screening. As the

was not a candidate for heart transplant. . . . Due to his mental and psychiatric condition, he is not a candidate for heart transplant and should be medically managed with medications as best as possible." David Smith, an Olympia physician who has seen Cortez in recent months, said he doesn't think doctors at the University of Washington or elsewhere exclude patients from scarce resources because they are disabled. Rather, they consider whether the patient's quality of life would improve with surgery and whether the patient can do his part to make it successful. Arthur Caplan, director of the University of Pennsylvania Center for Bioethics, said that the University of Washington's selection standard is appropriate. But he said it is essential that a patient's support system be considered when evaluating the chances of success.

### POINT

Brian Cortez is clearly a qualified candidate for a heart transplant and should immediately be placed on the waiting list. His support network of family and caregivers have made a strong case that Brian is able to follow a strict medication regimen and communicate any problems he is having following the transplant. His disabilities should not in any way be a factor in the decision. Brian clearly qualifies on the basis of medical need. With reasonable accommodations and his strong family and caregivers support network, there is no reason to believe that Brian's chances for survival from the transplant would be less than anyone else's.

### COUNTERPOINT

The primary issue here is a scarcity of organs that requires that difficult life-and-death decisions be made on the basis of who has the best chance of benefitting from the operation. To give to one person, means that another person must die. As suggested by Brian's behavior during his hospital stay, he has poor communication even with an interpreter; is easily upset by tests and medical treatment; and requires heavy doses of medication to calm him down. Clearly, his developmental disabilities make it difficult for him to understand the critical instructions necessary for him to meet the required medical regimen following the heart transplant. Brian's condition is better managed by medications and not a risky operation and difficult recovery that are beyond his abilities to cope with over the long run.

**Update: Doctors at the University of Washington Medical Center eventually changed their position regarding Brian Cortez's qualifications for a heart transplant. Under threat of a lawsuit from Brian's mother and his special education teacher, doctors at the Medical Center completed a successful heart transplant on Brian in September 2001.**

What do you think? To give your opinion, go to Chapter 12 of the companion website at **(www.ablongman.com/hardman8e)**, and click on Debate Forum.

SOURCE: From "Disabilities May Keep Man from Transplant," by W. King, 2000, *Salt Lake Tribune*, May 2, pp. A1, A7.

availability of genetic information increases, how will society make sure that insurers, employers, courts, schools, adoption agencies, law enforcement, and the military use it in a fair and equitable manner and do not discriminate against certain groups of people? What psychological impact and stigmatization related to an individual's genetic differences might result? How does the information affect society's perceptions of that individual (New Goals for the U.S. Human Genome Project, 1998)?

The next step following genetic screening is counseling for family members to ensure that they understand the results and implications of the screening. The concerns surrounding genetic counseling focus on the neutrality of the counselor. The role of the genetic counselor is to supply information, not to act as a "moral adviser" or psychotherapist for the family. Drew and Hardman (2004) noted that genetic counselors may find it difficult to maintain their neutrality when they have strong personal feelings about what should be done. However, counselors must remain neutral and must not steer family members toward what the counselor might regard as the "right" decision about, say, future pregnancies or ongoing treatment of a condition.

## Selective Abortion and Withholding Medical Treatment

Perhaps no other issue polarizes society so much as the unborn child's right to life versus a woman's right to choose. Rapidly advancing medical technology makes the issue of abortion even more complex. A number of chromosomal and metabolic disorders that may result in severe and multiple disabilities can now be identified *in utero*. Thus parents and physicians are placed in the untenable position of deciding whether to abort a fetus diagnosed with severe anomalies. On one side are those who argue that the quality of life for the child born with severe disabilities may be so diminished that, if given the choice, the individual would choose not to live under such circumstances. Additionally, the family may not be able to cope with a child who is severely disabled. On the other side are those who point out that no one has the right to decide for someone else whether life is "worth living." Major strides in education, medical care, technology, and social inclusion have enhanced quality of life for people with severe disabilities.

Controversy also surrounds the denying of medical treatment to a person with a disability (Drew & Hardman, 2004). Applying one standard for a person without disabilities and another for a person with a severe disability has raised some difficult issues in the medical field. For more insight into these controversial issues, see the Debate Forum on page 354.

Several national organizations The ARC—A National Organization on Mental Retardation, the American Association on Mental Retardation) have strongly opposed the withholding of medical treatment when the decision is based on the individual's having disabilities. These organizations hold that everyone is entitled to the right to life and that society has an obligation to protect people from the ignorance and prejudices that may be associated with disability.

# FOCUS REVIEW

**FOCUS 1** What are the three components of TASH's definition of severe disabilities?

- The relationship of the individual with the environment (adaptive fit)
- The inclusion of people of all ages
- The necessity of extensive ongoing support in life activities

**FOCUS 2** Define the terms *multiple disabilities* and *deaf-blindness* as described in IDEA.

- *Multiple disabilities* refers to concomitant impairments (such as mental retardation–orthopedic

impairments, etc.). The combination causes educational challenges so severe that they cannot be accommodated in special education programs designed solely for one impairment. One such combination is "dual diagnosis," a condition characterized by serious emotional disturbance (challenging behaviors) in conjunction with severe mental retardation.

- *Deaf-blindness* involves concomitant hearing and visual impairments. The combination causes communication and other developmental and edu-

cational challenges so severe that they cannot be accommodated in special education programs designed solely for children who are deaf or for children who are blind.

**FOCUS 3** Identify the estimated prevalence and causes of severe and multiple disabilities.

- Prevalence estimates generally range from 0.1% to 1% of the general population.
- Students with multiple disabilities accounted for about 2% of the 5.5 million students with disabilities served in the public

schools. Approximately 0.0002% of students with disabilities were labeled *deaf-blind*.

- Many possible causes of severe and multiple disabilities exist. Most severe and multiple disabilities are evident at birth. Birth defects may be the result of genetic or metabolic problems. Most identifiable causes of severe mental retardation and related developmental disabilities are genetic in origin. Factors associated with poisoning, accidents, malnutrition, physical and emotional neglect, and disease are also known causes.

**FOCUS 4** What are the characteristics of persons with severe and multiple disabilities?

- Mental retardation is often a primary condition.
- Most such children will not benefit from basic academic instruction in literacy and mathematics. Instruction in functional academics is the most effective approach to learning academic skills.
- People with severe and multiple disabilities often do not have age-appropriate adaptive skills and need ongoing services and supports to facilitate learning in this area.
- Significant speech and language deficits and delays are a primary characteristic.
- Physical and health needs are common, involving conditions such as congenital heart disease, epilepsy, respiratory problems, spasticity, athetosis, and hypotonia. Vision and hearing loss are also common.

**FOCUS 5** Identify three types of educational assessments for students with severe and multiple disabilities.

- Traditionally, there has been a heavy reliance on standardized

measurements, particularly the IQ test, in identifying people with severe and multiple disabilities.

- Assessments that focus on valued skills to promote independence and quality of life in natural settings are referred to as *functional, ecological*, or *authentic assessments*.
- Schools must include students with disabilities in statewide or districtwide assessments of achievement or provide a statement of why that assessment is not appropriate for the child. For many students with severe disabilities, these assessments are inappropriate. Alternative assessments are conducted instead.

**FOCUS 6** Identify the features of effective services and supports for children with severe and multiple disabilities during the early childhood years.

- Services and supports must begin at birth.
- Programs for infants and toddlers are both child- and family-centered.
- The goals for preschool programs are to maximize development across several developmental areas, to develop social interaction and classroom participation skills, to increase community participation through support to family and caregivers, and to prepare the child for inclusive school placement.
- Effective and inclusive preschool programs have a holistic view of the child, see the classroom as community of learners, base the program on a collaborative ethic, use authentic assessment, create a heterogeneous environment, make available a range of individualized supports and services, engage educators in

reflective teaching, and emphasize multiple ways of teaching and learning.

**FOCUS 7** Identify the features of effective services and supports for children with severe and multiple disabilities during the elementary school years.

- Self-determination—student preferences and needs are taken into account in developing educational objectives.
- The school values and supports parental involvement.
- Instruction focuses on frequently used functional skills related to everyday life activities.
- Assistive technology and augmentive communication are available to maintain or increase the functional capabilities of the student with severe and multiple disabilities.

**FOCUS 8** Describe four outcomes that are important in planning for the transition from school to adult life for adolescents with severe and multiple disabilities.

- Establishing a network of friends and acquaintances
- Developing the ability to use community resources on a regular basis
- Securing a paid job that supports the use of community resources and interaction with peers
- Establishing independence and autonomy in making lifestyle choices

**FOCUS 9** Describe four features that characterize successful inclusive education for students with severe and multiple disabilities.

- Placement of students with severe and multiple disabilities in the general education schools and classes that they would attend if they didn't have disabilities

- Systematic organization of opportunities for interaction between students with severe and multiple disabilities and students without disabilities
- Specific instruction to increase the competence of students with severe and multiple disabilities in interacting with students without disabilities
- Highly trained teachers competent in the instructional and assistive technology needed to facilitate social interaction between students with and without disabilities

**FOCUS 10** Describe four bioethical dilemmas that can affect people with severe disabilities and their families.

- Genetic engineering may be used to conquer disease or as a means to enhance or "perfect" human beings.
- Genetic screening may be effective in preventing disease but could also be used by insurance companies, employers, courts, schools, adoption agencies, law enforcement, and the military to discriminate against people with severe disabilities.

- Genetic counselors can provide important information to families, but they may also abandon neutrality and impose their own personal beliefs about what the family should do.
- Selective abortion and options for the withholding of medical treatment may allow parents to make the very personal decision about whether the quality of life for their unborn child might be so diminished that life would not be worth living. However, it can also be argued that no one has the right to make that decision on behalf of someone else.

## FURTHER READINGS

Downing, J. E., & Siegel, E. (2000). *Teaching Communication Skills to Students with Severe Disabilities.* Baltimore: Paul H. Brookes.

*Provides strategies for teaching communication skills to students with severe disabilities in inclusive school and community settings. Topics include assessing the student's communication ability, analyzing the environment, and alternative and augmentative communication techniques.*

McDonnell, J., Hardman, M., & McDonnell, A. P. (2003). *Introduction to Persons with Moderate and Severe Disabilities* (2nd ed.). Boston: Allyn and Bacon.

*Addresses the challenges that people with severe disabilities face in becoming full members of society. Using a lifespan*

*approach, this book provides information on promising practices for services and programs from birth through the adult years.*

M. E. Snell & F. Brown (Eds.), (2000). *Instruction of Students with Severe Disabilities* (5th ed.). Upper Saddle River, NJ: Merrill.

*Provides teaching methods for work with students who have severe disabilities, including students with autism and functional skill needs. Topics include inclusive education, assessment, positive behavior support, health care, basic self-help skills, peer relationships, communication, and transition from school to adult life.*

## WEB RESOURCES

### TASH

**www.TASH.org**

TASH is an international advocacy association of people with disabilities, their family members, other advocates, and people who work in the disability field. This website contains lists of TASH publications, reviews of products, legislative updates, and conference information.

### Human Genome Project

**www.ornl.gov/TechResources/Human_Genome/home.html**

This website provides up-to-date information on what's new in human genome research, frequently asked questions about genetic engineering and research, and discussions of ethical, legal, and social issues.

### National Information Clearinghouse on Children Who Are Deaf-Blind

**www.tr.wou.edu/dblink/index2.htm**

This federally funded information and referral service (DB-LINK) identifies, coordinates, and disseminates information related to children and youth who are deaf-blind (ages birth to 21 years). Four organizations have pooled their expertise into a consortium-based clearinghouse. This collaborative effort utilizes the expertise and resources of the American Association of the Deaf-Blind, the Helen Keller National Center, the Perkins School for the Blind, and Teaching Research at Western Oregon University.

# BUILDING YOUR PORTFOLIO

If you are thinking about a career in special education, you should know that many states use national standards developed by the Council for Exceptional Children (CEC) to assess a teacher candidate's knowledge and skills for working with students with disabilities. See a complete listing of the ten CEC Content Standards on the inside front cover of this text.

## CEC Content Standards Addressed in Chapter 12

1. Foundations
2. Development and Characteristics of Learners
3. Individual Learning Differences
4. Instructional Strategies
5. Learning Environments and Social Interactions
7. Instructional Planning
9. Professional and Ethical Practice

## Assess Your Knowledge of the CEC Standards Addressed in Chapter 12

Some states require that teacher candidates develop a portfolio of products that demonstrate mastery of the CEC content standards. To assist in the development of products for this portfolio, you may wish to complete the following activities.

- Complete a written test of the chapter's content.

*If your instructor requires a written test of your content knowledge for this chapter, keep a copy for your portfolio. A practice test on the information covered in this chapter is available through the companion website (www.ablongman.com/hardman8e) and the Student Study Guide.*

- Respond to the application questions for the Case Study "The Beginning of a Circle of Friends."

*Review the Case Study and respond in writing to the application questions. Keep a copy of the Case Study and your written response for your portfolio.*

- Complete the "Take a Stand" activity for the Debate Forum "Disabilities May Keep Brian Cortez from Heart Transplant."

*Read the Debate Forum in this chapter and then visit our companion website to complete the activity "Take a Stand." Keep a copy of this activity for your portfolio.*

- Participate in a community service learning activity.

*Community service is a valuable way to enhance your learning experience. Visit our companion website for suggested community service learning activities that correspond to the information presented in this chapter. Develop a reflective journal of the service learning experience for your portfolio.*

# THEMES OF THE TIMES

The New York Times
nytimes.com

Expand your knowledge of the concepts discussed in this chapter by reading current and historical articles from the *New York Times* by visiting the "Themes of the Times" section of the companion website: **www.ablongman.com/hardman8e.**

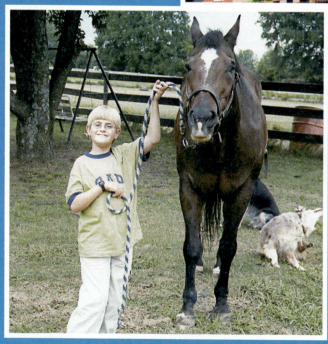

# Autism

### Some Assert Vaccines Cause Autism

Some parents of children with autism have filed lawsuits against selected drug makers claiming that certain vaccines caused their children to develop the condition. While scientific evidence for this assertion is not clear, it is obviously a sensitive and emotional issue with many parents. (CBS News, January 11, 2003)

### I'll Miss Him

"Knowing Chris; he does not speak. He throws his food. When unrestrained, he often bangs his knee against his forehead. When he leaves, not only will I miss him; a small part of my personality will be gone too. . . . Next week, after two years here, Chris will be moved to another institution, one with better access to medical crisis intervention." (Whitaker, 2000, p. Z12)

### Going to Camp

If you're looking for a camp to accommodate a child with special needs, the search is getting easier. There are a growing number of camps that work with [children with special needs]. Programs like those at Bradford Woods in Indiana work with children [with physical and mental disabilities]. These camps provide kids living with conditions like . . . autism . . . the opportunity to meet and bond with others who share similar experiences. (ABCNEWS.com, 2000, pp. 1–2)

### Horses Work "Small Wonders"

Lisa Gatti's company uses horses as a therapeutic tool for a variety of children with disabilities, including autism. She believes that riding horses enhances self-esteem and helps teach discipline as well as enhancing muscle tone. Many parents support such claims, believing that there have been substantial benefits from their children's participation. (CBS News, February 19, 2003)

**FOCUS**

**PREVIEW:** To preview the central concepts of this chapter, read the focus questions located in the margins. Using these questions as a guide, ask yourself what you already know and what you want to learn.

361

## Josh

**J**osh is in a general education class at his elementary school. His friend Marshall, who has learning disabilities, is a close friend to Josh. Marshall says, "Josh likes to dribble the basketball. Other people help Josh, but I help him a lot, too."

When Josh was born, his parents thought he was deaf, but tests showed he could hear. At age 30 months, Josh was diagnosed with autism. His parents couldn't afford a specialized clinic or treatment facility and felt at a loss for what to do. They visited a school with a separate unit for chil-

dren with autism, mental retardation, and other disabilities. During the visit, Josh mingled with other children and mimicked their behavior—shouts, some violent movements. Josh's parents decided not to place Josh in that school.

Josh entered a general education class. The special education teacher at the school was concerned at first because Josh would bite his nails and scratch his legs. He wasn't interacting with the other students. Gradually, he started to talk and interact with the other students. His special education teacher says, "I think this wouldn't have happened if he were only interacting with other autistic children."

Josh's dad feels strongly about including students with disabilities in the general education classroom: "When wheelchairs come in (to school) in the morning and the Down syndrome (students) come in in the morning, and Josh comes in in the

morning, they are the students. They are not the special education students. It's a long process and it's just becoming comfortable."

## Billy

Billy is a blue-eyed, blond little boy of striking beauty; he is almost too perfect physically. His parents first became aware that Billy was different and had special problems when he was 5 years old but had not yet begun to talk. Some of his other behaviors also bothered Billy's parents a great deal. Billy didn't seem to play like other children. He would rock for long periods of time in his crib, and he had little interest in toys. At best, Billy would just spin the wheels of his trucks and stare as they turned. Most disturbing to Billy's parents

## FOCUS
### 1

Identify four areas of functional challenge often found in children with autism.

Federal law first recognized autism as a disability category in the Individuals with Disabilities Education Act of 1990 (IDEA). Although only recently acknowledged in federal law, autism began to appear in the research literature in the first half of the 20th century and is thought to have been described as early as the early 1800s (Siegert & Ward, 2002). *Autism* is taken from the Greek *autos,* meaning "self," to reflect the extreme sense of isolation and detachment from the world around them that characterizes individuals with autism.

Autism symptoms tend to emerge very early in a child's life. Most cases become evident before the age of 2½, and few are diagnosed after the age of 5. Autism is one of the most seriously disruptive of all childhood disabilities. It is characterized by combinations of varying degrees of deficiencies in language, interpersonal skills, emotional or affective behavior, and intellectual functioning (Bauminger, 2002; van der Geest, Kemner, Camfferman, Verbaten, & van Engeland, 2002). It is a disability that impairs the normal development of many areas of functioning.

Autism has received significant attention in the past several years from both researchers and the public media. Consider the words of Rick Whitaker in the chapter opening, which portray his son Chris both through the challenging behaviors he exhibits and also through the personal fingerprint he leaves on at least one individual who knows him. Although some of the more public portrayals of autism are perhaps not typical of the condition, they educate and capture the interest of a considerable segment of the lay public.

## Definition

IDEA employs the following definition of autism:

Autism means a developmental disability significantly affecting verbal and nonverbal communication and social interaction, generally evident before age 3,

was the fact that he showed little affection. Billy was not a warm baby. When his mother picked him up to cuddle, Billy would start to cry and arch his back until he was put back in his crib. Billy treated other children and adults as objects of no consequence in his life. He didn't care about people; he would rather be left alone.

Since Billy's behavior was recognized as different from normal, other changes have occurred. Billy developed language very slowly and in a strange way. His language is what specialists call "echolalic" in nature. When asked a question, Billy simply responds by echoing the question. Billy also has a great deal of trouble using pronouns and prepositions correctly when trying to talk. He will commonly reverse pronouns and refer to himself as "you" or refer to another person as "I." The correct use of prepositions also causes Billy a great deal of difficulty. Up or down, on or under, and a yes-or-no answer to a question are very confusing concepts for Billy. He simply answers yes or no at random. When viewed as a whole, Billy's language is not just delayed; it is also dis-

turbed in some fundamental way. He simply does not learn. Over and over he makes the same language mistakes.

Aside from Billy's atypical language development, he now spends a great deal of time in repetitive, non-goal-oriented behavior called *self-stimulatory* or *stereotypic* behavior. He has progressed from simple rocking and spinning the wheels on his toys to flapping his hands and twirling in circles until he falls from dizziness. If made to stop this behavior, Billy will throw ferocious temper tantrums that include screaming, biting, and often head banging. This self-destructive behavior is very disconcerting because, in his tantrums, Billy not only breaks things but hurts himself as well.

Billy also has a tremendous need to protect himself against any sort of change, including changes in his daily routine or his physical environment. Billy's mother recently rearranged the furniture in the living room while he was napping. When Billy awoke and entered the rearranged room, he immediately started to cry and whine;

then he had a tantrum until the furniture was returned to its original position. Changes in his daily schedule also produce near-panic reactions that end up in tantrums. It seems as though Billy has memorized his environment and daily schedule, and any change inflicts fear of the unknown. Adjustment and relearning are very difficult for him. Billy's behavior cripples his family as well as himself. The furniture arrangement episode is only one of many incidents in which Billy requires his parents' constant attention. If left alone for even short periods of time, Billy can hurt himself or break something. After claiming all the attention his parents and older brother can give, Billy returns little. He is not affectionate and will not even look his brother in the eye, nor does he seek his mother's affection. Billy suffers from a rare childhood developmental disorder known as infantile autism.

SOURCE: Adapted from *Understanding Child Behavior Disorders* (2nd ed., p. 288), by D. M. Gelfand, W. R. Jenson, and C. J. Drew, 1988, New York: Holt, Rinehart and Winston.

that adversely affects educational performance. Characteristics of autism include irregularities and impairments in communication, engagement in repetitive activities and stereotyped movements, resistance to environmental change or change in daily routines, and unusual responses to sensory experiences. (American Psychiatric Association, 2000; Burkhardt & Bucci, 2001; van der Geest et al., 2002)

The IDEA definition refers to the appearance of deviations from normal development before 3 years of age, because the symptoms of **autism** tend to emerge during the early years. The definition does not intend, however, to preclude a diagnosis of autism if a child develops symptoms after age 3. Federal regulations also note that a diagnosis of autism should not be used in cases where children show characteristics of serious emotional disturbance, which is addressed elsewhere in the law. Such attention to autism is relatively recent. The 1991–1992 school year was the first during which data were collected on the number of children identified as having autism and served in the public schools (U.S. Department of Education, 2003).

Definitional statements provide a partial picture of autism, although most professionals are reluctant to make broad generalizations about people with autism. People with autism are certainly not all alike, and it is more accurate to speak of characteristics than to characterize. Although autism has historically been assumed to imply a seriously reduced level of functioning, a broad range of capacity, from severe to mild impairments, occurs. Acknowledgment of this has led to use of the concept of **autism spectrum disorders**, which includes a range of functioning in the multiple skill areas of communication and language, intelligence, and social interaction (Gelfand & Drew, 2003; Zelazo, Jacques, Burack, & Frye, 2002). In some cases debate has arisen about what represents functional variations within the same disability and what constitutes a separate disorder. One example of this is found with **Asperger syndrome**, or Asperger disorder, is a condition that shares certain unusual social interactions and behaviors with autism, but typically it includes no general language delay. The Snapshot on Joseph illustrates some unusual

**Autism**

A childhood disorder with onset prior to 36 months of age. It is characterized by extreme withdrawal, self-stimulation, intellectual deficits, and language disorders.

**Autism spectrum disorders**

A term that reflects the range of functioning found, among those who exhibit symptoms of autism, in the multiple skill areas of communication and language, intelligence, and social interaction.

**Asperger syndrome**

A condition that shares certain unusual social interactions and behaviors with autism but typically includes no general language delay.

behaviors, but the characteristics seem different from traditional descriptions of children with autism. Some researchers argue that Asperger disorder is distinct; others contend it is a higher-functioning version of autism spectrum disorders (Mayes, Calhoun, & Crites, 2001; Ozonoff & Griffith, 2000; Volkmar & Klin, 2001). Although this argument continues unresolved, the notion of a spectrum of disability severity allows students and parents to receive service (Baron-Cohen, 2002; Ozonoff, Dawson, & McPartland, 2002). The diagnostic criteria outlined for autism and for Asperger's disorder by the American Psychiatric Association are shown in Table 13.1. This side-by-side summary illustrates some of the similarities and differences.

## Prevalence

FOCUS 2

What is the general prevalence estimated for autism?

Compared to other conditions, autism is relatively rare. The American Psychiatric Association estimated that the prevalence is about 5 cases per 10,000 (APA, 2000). Although this has been a commonly accepted prevalence range, some research suggests prevalence rates of about 60 per 10,000 (Gillberg, 2002; Scott, Baron-Cohen, Bolton, & Brayne, 2002). It is not clear whether these higher figures should include the complete autism spectrum. It is also not clear whether the apparent change is due to definitional changes or to a genuine increase in incidence remain unclear (Scott et al., 2002; Wing & Potter, 2002). The wide variation in prevalence may diminish over time as greater consensus about what constitutes autism is achieved. Gender differences are evident in autism; males outnumber females substantially. Estimates of these prevalence differences vary from around 4 to 1 to as high as 8 to 1 (Baker, 2002; Scott et al., 2002).

## Characteristics

FOCUS 3

Identify six characteristics of children with autism.

Unusual behaviors often appear very early in the lives of children with autism. They may, for example, exhibit significant impairment in interpersonal interaction as babies. Parents often report that these babies may be particularly unresponsive to physical contact or affection (Gray & Tonge, 2001; Yirmiya, Shaked, & Erel, 2001; Ratey

## SNAPSHOT

### Joseph: A Boy with Asperger Syndrome

Joseph always seemed like a brilliant child. He began talking before his first birthday, much earlier than his older sister and brother. He expressed himself in an adult-like way and was always very polite. When his mother offered to buy him a treat at the movies, for example, Joseph said, "No thank you, M&Ms are not my preferred mode of snacking." He showed a very early interest in letters and by 18 months could recite the whole alphabet. He taught himself to read before his third birthday. Joseph wasn't much interested in typical toys, like balls and bicycles, preferring instead what his proud parents considered "grown-up" pursuits, like geography and science. Starting at age 2, he spent many hours lying on the living room floor, looking at maps in the family's world atlas. By age 5, he could name anywhere in the world, given a description of its geographical location ("What is the northernmost city in Brazil?"). Just as his parents suspected, Joseph *is* brilliant. He also has Asperger syndrome.

SOURCE: *A Parent's Guide to Asperger Syndrome and High-Functioning Autism: How to Meet the Challenges and Help Your Child Thrive* (p. 3), by S. Ozonoff, G. Dawson, & J. McPartland, 2002, New York: Guilford.

TABLE 13.1

## Diagnostic Criteria for Autism and Asperger Disorder

| AUTISM | ASPERGER DISORDER | CRITERIA |
|--------|-------------------|----------|
| | | **SOCIAL INTERACTION** |
| * | * | Qualitative impairment in social interaction manifested by: |
| X | X | • marked impairment in using multiple nonverbal behaviors such as eye-to-eye gaze, facial expressions, body postures, and gestures to regulate social interaction |
| X | X | • failure to develop peer relationships appropriate to developmental level |
| X | X | • lack of spontaneous seeking to share enjoyment, interests, or achievements with others |
| X | X | • lack of social or emotional reciprocity |
| ** | | Delay or abnormal functioning with onset prior to age 3: |
| X | | • social interaction |
| X | | • language used in social communication |
| X | | • symbolic or imaginative play |
| | X | The disturbance causes significant impairment in social, occupational, or other important functioning |
| | | **STEREOTYPED BEHAVIOR PATTERNS** |
| ** | ** | Restricted repetitive and stereotyped behavior patterns, interests, and activities manifested by: |
| X | X | • preoccupation with one or more stereotyped, restricted interest patterns, abnormal in either intensity or focus |
| X | X | • inflexible adherence to specific, nonfunctional rituals |
| X | X | • stereotyped, repetitive motor mannerisms (e.g., hand flapping or twisting, whole body movements) |
| X | X | • persistent preoccupation with parts of objects |
| | | **LANGUAGE/COMMUNICATION** |
| ** | | Qualitative impairment in communication as manifested by: |
| X | | • delay or total lack of spoken language development (not accompanied by alternative communication modes) |
| X | | • marked impairment in initiating or sustaining conversations by those with adequate speech |
| X | | • stereotyped and repetitive use of language or idiosyncratic language |
| X | | • lack of varied, spontaneous play or social imitative play at appropriate developmental level |
| | X | No clinically significant general delay in language (i.e., single words used by age 2, phrases by age 3) |
| | | **COGNITION** |
| | X | No significant delay in cognitive development or age-appropriate self-help skills, adaptive behavior (other than social interaction), and curiosity about the environment |
| | | **EXCLUSIONS** |
| X | | Disturbance not better accounted for by Rett's or childhood disintegrative disorder |
| | X | Criteria are not met for another specific pervasive developmental disorder or schizophrenia |

NOTE: A diagnosis of autism requires six (or more) identified behaviors from the social interaction, stereotyped behavior, and language/communication areas, with at least two from social interaction and one each from stereotyped behavior and language/communication.
*Requires at least two of these symptoms
**Requires at least one of these symptoms

SOURCE: American Psychiatric Association (2000), pp. 75, 84. Reprinted with permission from the *Diagnostic and Statistical Manual of Mental Disorders*, 4th ed., Text Revision. © 2000 APA.
SOURCE: Quoted in *Understanding Child Behavior Disorders* (p. 293), by D. M. Gelfand & C. J. Drew, 2003 (4th ed.), Belmont, CA: Wadsworth.

This young girl loves the activity but has difficulty forming a personal attachment with the adult right behind her.

et al., 2000). It is not unusual for parents to note that their infants become rigid when picked up, that they are "not cuddly," and that they avoid eye contact, averting their gaze rather than looking directly at another person. Such behavior may continue in older children. In some cases, children with autism rely heavily on peripheral vision rather than direct, face-to-face visual contact.

Children with autism are frequently described in terms of social impairments, social unresponsiveness, extreme difficulty relating to others, and difficulty understanding or expressing emotion (Bauminger, 2002; Howlin, 2002). Often, these children seem to prefer interacting with inanimate objects, forming attachments to such objects rather than to people. They appear to be insensitive to the feelings of others and in many cases treat other people as objects, even physically pushing or pulling others around to suit their needs. Clearly, children with autism interact with their environment in ways that are not typical, as though they have difficulty making sense of the world around them.

## Impaired or Delayed Language

Children with autism often exhibit impaired or delayed language development (Bishop & Norbury, 2002; Dawson et al., 2002). Approximately half do not develop speech, and those who do often engage in strange language and speaking behavior, such as **echolalia** (speaking only to repeat what has been said to them) (Rappaport, 2001; Wahlberg, 2001). In many cases, children with autism who speak reproduce parts of conversations that they have heard. But they do so in a very mechanical fashion, with no sign that they attach meaning to what was said. This echolalic behavior is sometimes misinterpreted as an indicator of high intellectual abilities. Children with autism who develop language often have a limited speaking repertoire, exhibit an uneven level of development between language skill areas, and fail to use pronouns in speech directed at other people (Tager-Flusberg, 2003; Tiegerman-Farber, 2002). These children seem to differ from their peers in failing to grasp grammatical complexity and making little use of semantics in sentence structure (e.g., Amorosa & Noterdaeme, 2002; Carpenter, Pennington, & Rogers, 2002; Norbury & Bishop, 2002). Additionally, the tonal quality of their speech is often unusual or flat, and in some cases, their speech appears to serve the purpose of self-stimulation rather than communication. Further investigation of language development in children with autism is needed, as are stronger and novel research methodologies (Keen, Woodyatt, & Sigafoos, 2002; Tager-Flusberg, 2000; Wahlberg, 2001).

**Echolalia**

A meaningless repetition or imitation of words that have been spoken.

## Self-Stimulation

Although not always present, behavior of a self-stimulatory nature is often associated with autism. Children with autism often engage in physical forms of **self-stimulation**, such as flicking their hands in front of their faces repeatedly (Shu, Lung, Tien, & Chen, 2001; Smith, Lovaas, & Lovaas, 2002). They also tend to manipulate objects in a repetitive fashion suggestive of self-stimulation. Behavior such as spinning objects, rocking, or hand flapping may continue for hours. Some behaviors that seem to start as self-stimulation may worsen or take different forms and create the potential for injury to the child. Examples include face slapping, biting, and head banging (e.g., McCracken et al., 2002). Behavior that becomes self-injurious is more often found in low-functioning children with autism and can understandably cause concern and stress for parents and others around them.

## Resistance to Change in Routine

Intense resistance to change, or rigidity, is often mentioned in discussions of children with autism. Familiar routines—during meals or at bedtime, for example—are obsessively important to them, and any deviation from the set pattern may upset them greatly. Youngsters who are affected in this manner may insist on a particular furniture arrangement or on a particular food for a given meal (for example, a specific cereal for breakfast). They may even wash themselves in a particular pattern, in a manner reminiscent of obsessive-compulsive or repetitive behaviors (Baker, 2000; Shu et al., 2001). Often, items must be arranged in a symmetrical fashion to seem proper to the child with autism. There have also been reports relating the rigidity or perseveration of those with autism to obsessive behaviors, including self-mutilation (Rapin, 2002; Verri, Uggetti, Valler, Ceroni, & Federico, 2000).

Such obsessive, ritualistic behaviors create numerous problems, as one might expect, particularly if an effort is made to integrate the child into daily life. For example, most people pay little attention to the exact route they take when driving to the grocery store or to the precise pattern of moving through the store once they arrive. For parents who try to take their child with autism along, however, minor deviations may cause a serious crisis. Transitions from one activity to another may also present challenges for these children in both school and home activities. Research is beginning to address such matters and has revealed that structured verbal and visual cues facilitating communication and may smooth transitions from one activity to another (Bondy & Frost, 2002; Schmidt, Alper, Raschke, & Ryndak, 2000).

## Intelligence

Most children with autism exhibit a lower intellectual functioning than other children; about 75% have measured IQs below 70 (Kauffman, 2001; Mastropieri & Scruggs, 2000; Wahlberg, 2001). The verbal and reasoning skills required in intelligence testing pose particular difficulty for these children. It has long been thought that they have a tendency to imitate what they hear, as evidenced by their echolalic speech. However, more recent thinking suggests that this is more appropriately seen as one or more specific deficits in information processing or cognition (Blair, Frith, Smith, Abell, & Cipolotti, 2002; Scheuffgen, Happe, Anderson, & Frith, 2000).

Intellectual ability varies among children with autism, and high-functioning individuals may test at a normal or near-normal level. High-functioning individuals may have rather substantial vocabularies, but they do not always understand the appropriate use of terms that they can spell and define (Iwanaga, Kawasaki, & Tsuchida, 2000; Scheuffgen et al., 2000). In some cases, very high-functioning people with autism appear to use language quite well, although there may still be clues that something is different. Such is the case with the description of Mike FitzPatrick in the nearby Reflect on This.

Approximately 10% to 15% of those with autism exhibit what are known as splinter skills—areas of ability in which levels of performance are unexpectedly high

**Self-stimulation**

Repetitive behavior that has no apparent purpose other than providing the person with some type of stimulation.

## A SIMPLE MAN: AUTISTIC MAN WRONGLY ACCUSED OF ROBBERY

Mike FitzPatrick has autism . . . but he has managed to meet the challenges of life. He holds down a job as a night janitor in his hometown of Syracuse, New York. He drives a car and does his own shopping.

But, incredibly, this gentle, simple man was charged with the brazen daylight robbery of a bank.

Police looking into the April 15, 1999, robbery of the Ontario National Bank in Clifton Springs, New York, zeroed in on FitzPatrick, 48, as the chief suspect. . . . He had visited the town on vacation in late April. Authorities thought his behavior suspicious and came to believe he was casing yet another bank to rob.

Police interrogated FitzPatrick after picking him up at his job one night. He told the police he had robbed the bank. "Mike tries to please people," explains Anne FitzPatrick, Mike's mother. "He thought in his mind if he told them what they wanted to hear, they'd let him go. He didn't know that would complicate things."

FitzPatrick's confession did complicate things. He was charged with bank robbery and faced 25 years in prison if convicted.

But the real bank robber came forward and told authorities he had robbed the Ontario National Bank on April 15. David Harrington was already in jail, awaiting trial for other bank robberies. He was outraged that an autistic man should be charged for a crime he did not commit. Harrington, 30, confessed to the robbery, giving authorities details only the robber could have known.

Charges against FitzPatrick were finally dropped. . . . He's back at his job as a night janitor. He says he's grateful to Harrington, the man who admitted robbing the bank, for clearing his name. Harrington is still awaiting trial.

SOURCE: From "A Simple Man: Autistic Man Wrongly Accused of Robbery," by J. Siceloff, December 13, 1999. Available: ABCNEWS.com.

---

compared to those of other domains of functioning. For instance, a student with autism may perform unusually well at memory tasks or drawing but have serious deficiencies in language skills and abstract reasoning (Hermelin, 2001). For parents of such students, these splinter skills create enormous confusion. Although most parents realize very early that their child with autism has exceptionalities, they also hope that he or she is healthy. These hopes may be fueled by the child's demonstration of unusual skills. In some cases, the parents may believe that whatever is wrong is their fault, as portrayed in the Snapshot about Steven. A great deal about autism remains unknown. For example, are the narrow islands of high performance (savant-like) portrayed in the movie *Rain Man* simply extremes of splinter skills? Can splinter skills be

## SNAPSHOT

# Steven

### Reflections of a Parent

Steven was 2 ½ years old when our daughter, Katherine, was born. This was the time when I seriously began to search for help. I knew something was wrong shortly after Steve's birth, but when I tried to describe the problem, no one seemed to understand what I was saying. In spite of chronic ear infections, Steve looked very healthy. He was slow in developing language, but that could easily

be attributed to his ear trouble. Since he was our first baby, I thought that maybe we just weren't very good parents.

When he was 2 ½, we enrolled Steven in a diagnostic nursery school. He did not seem to understand us when we spoke. I wondered whether he was retarded or had some other developmental problem. The nursery school gave us their opinion when he was 4. They said Steve seemed to

have normal intelligence, but he perseverated, was behind socially, and did not seem to process verbs. The school said he had some signs of autism and some signs of a learning disability.

When Steve was 4 ½, he did some amazing things. He began to talk, read, write, and play the piano. I was taking beginning adult piano lessons at the time, and Steve could play everything I did. In fact, he could play any song he heard and even

**Reflect on This**

## EXTRAORDINARY TALENTS OF INDIVIDUALS WITH AUTISM

One of the many mysteries surrounding the phenomenon of autism is the extraordinary talents and abilities demonstrated by some individuals. . . . In the past, such individuals were referred to as *idiot savants*. *Idiot* is an antiquated term for someone with mental retardation, and *savant* means "knower" in French. Some professionals now prefer the term *savant syndrome* to describe a condition in which persons with serious mental limitations demonstrate spectacular "islands of brilliance in a sea of mental disability."

Given the scope of talents in the human repertoire, these "islands" are confined to a narrow range of abilities: a flair for music or visual arts, mathematical aptitude, mechanical wizardry, or mnemonic skills such as calendar calculation (being able to report instantly on what day of the week a particular date will fall in a given year, past or future). The trait that binds these unique abilities is superior memory skills that are idiosyncratic, emotionless, and enigmatic. Indeed, savants often seem to accomplish feats of brilliance as if by rote. No emotion shades their performance.

How are savants able to do what they do? No conclusive findings exist, but theories abound. For example, one theory has it that the sensory deprivation and social isolation experienced by many individuals with autism causes them to be bored and thus they adopt trivial preoccupations. Another theory is that autism is associated with deficits in the left hemisphere of the brain, which governs the use of language and other logical, conceptual, and abstract skills. Savants' skills are usually associated with right-brain functions—spatial perception, visualization, mechanical dexterity, and movement—suggesting that the right hemisphere is dominant.

Clearly, much remains unknown about both autism and savant syndrome. Certainly, little is understood about how they exist in the same person. Increased understanding [may in time] benefit those who struggle with autism.

SOURCE: Reprinted by permission of Omni, copyright 1989, Omni Publications International, Ltd.

---

effectively exploited in a functional way to facilitate school or work activity? Some preliminary evidence suggests it is possible, and research in this fascinating area continues (e.g., O'Connor, Cowan, & Samella, 2000; Pring & Hermelin, 2002).

## Learning Characteristics

The learning characteristics of children with autism are frequently different from those of their normally developing peers and may present significant educational challenges. Some characteristics described earlier are prominent in this respect. For

added chords with his left hand. Relatives and friends began to tell us that he was a genius and that this accounted for his odd behavior. I really wanted to believe this genius theory.

I enrolled Steven in a public kindergarten at age 5. This teacher had another theory about Steve's strange behavior. She believed that we were not firm enough with him. She also sent the social worker to our home to see what we were doing with him.

I often wondered if we were just very poor parents. I certainly had enough people tell us so!

Whenever I went to anyone for help, I was likely to begin crying. Then the doctor or whoever would start to watch my behavior closely. I could just see each of them forming a theory in his or her mind: The child is okay, but the mother is a mess. I wondered if I was a very cold mother. Maybe I was subtly rejecting my son. Then again, maybe it was his father. My mother always said he didn't spend enough time with Steve.

I didn't understand when the psychiatrist told me Steve had a *pervasive developmental disorder*. I began to get the picture when the other terms

were used. I had heard of autism before. Something was terribly wrong, but it had a physical basis. It was not my fault at all. This was a relief but also a tremendous blow. It has really helped to have a name for the problem. We used to wonder whether Steve was lying awake nights, dreaming up new ways to get our attention. We lived from crisis to crisis. We would finally handle one problem, only to have a new one develop in its place. Steve still does unusual things, but it doesn't send us into a panic anymore.

*—Sheri*, Steve's Mother

CHARACTERISTICS

example, students who resist change may perseverate on a specific item to be learned and encounter cognitive shifting difficulties in turning their attention to the next topic or problem in an instructional sequence (Liss et al., 2001; Shu et al., 2001). Because of problems understanding social cues and relating to people, students with autism may experience difficulty interacting with teachers and other students in a school setting (Bauminger, 2002; Howlin, 2002; Ochs, Kremer-Sadlik, Solomon, & Sirota, 2001).

The abilities of children with autism frequently develop unevenly, both within and among skill areas. These children may or may not generalize already-learned skills to other settings or topics (O'Neill & Sweetland-Baker, 2001; Plaisted, 2001). They are often impulsive and inconsistent in their responses, which is a matter that teachers may have to address. Children with autism frequently have difficulty with information processing and abstract ideas, and they may focus on one or more select stimuli while failing to understand the general concept (Matthews, Shute, & Rees, 2001).

Some children with autism possess certain qualities that can be viewed as educational strengths or at least can be focused on for instructional purposes. For example, although generalizations about these youngsters are difficult to make, individuals with autism are sometimes noted as enjoying routine, which is consistent with their desire to maintain sameness. If a child shows this tendency, teachers can draw on it when practice or drill is warranted in learning a skill. In certain cases, splinter skills may be capitalized on for positive, productive purposes. Additionally, some individuals with autism seem to have relatively strong, specific long-term memory skills, particularly for factual information like names, numbers, and dates (Pring & Hermelin, 2002). For these students, once they have learned a piece of information, they may not forget it. Their long-term memory skills may equal those of their normally developing peers.

Generalizations regarding children with autism are difficult to make. Despite the many stereotypes about these individuals, they are highly variable. Learning characteristics—both limitations and strengths—must be individually assessed and considered in educational programming. Challenging behavior patterns found in children with autism often cause a variety of difficulties. Restricted behavioral repertoires, communication limitations, stereotypic self-stimulation, resistance to change, and unusual responses to their environment pose problems and may limit inclusion options for some individuals with autism (Schreibman & Anderson, 2001). Some evidence also suggests that the success of inclusion depends heavily on general education classmates, because inclusion is a social process as much as an academic one (Dow & Mehring, 2001; Ochs, Kremer-Sadlik, Solomon, & Sirota, 2001; Westling & Fox, 2000). Continued research is essential if these individuals are to achieve maximum inclusion in the community.

# Causation

**FOCUS 4**

Identify the two broad theoretical views regarding the causes of autism.

Historically, two broad theories about the causes of autism have been most prominent: psychodynamic and biological theories. The **psychodynamic perspective** has implicated family interactions as causal factors in autism. Theorists who subscribe to this view have speculated that the child withdraws from rejection and erects defenses against psychological pain. In so doing, he or she retreats to an inner world and essentially does not interact with the outside environment that involves people. Psychodynamic theories have largely fallen out of favor, because research results have failed to support this position. However, some literature continues to explore this theoretical area by examining topics such as fears and the newborn's anxieties and by searching for the meaning of the child's autism symptoms. Other authors discuss psychodynamic theories as one facet of a balanced presentation of theories about autism (Urwin, 2002; Wenar & Kerig, 2000).

Biological causation in a variety of forms predominates the current research on autism, particularly genetics (Berney, 2000; Cuccaro et al., 2003; Gallagher et al., 2003). For instance, damage to the chromosome structure in a condition known as **fragile X syndrome** emerged in the late 1960s as a potential cause of autism. Researchers found that this condition appeared in a certain percentage of males with autism (e.g., Howlin, 2002; Veenstra-Vanderweele & Cook, 2003; Wassink, Piven, & Patil, 2001). Work on this genetic linkage continues, although it appears that fragile X is simply associated with autism rather than being a major cause (Hatton & Bailey, 2001).

Research has established genetic causation in autism, but it has not provided a clear and complete explanation of how causation occurs (e.g., Cuccaro et al., 2003; Gallagher et al., 2003; Minshew, 2000). One problem in developing a body of genetic information arises from the relative infrequency with which autism appears in the population at large. Although some research on twins has suggested a genetic link, additional evidence is clearly needed (Andres; 2002; Boelte, Feineis-Matthews, & Poustka, 2001).

Abnormal development received attention recently as a cause of autism—along with other investigations of neurological problems, such as brain cell differences, absence of specialization in the brain hemispheres, arrested neurological development, and neurological chemical imbalances (Marazziti, 2002; Pierce & Courchesne, 2002; Rapin, 2000). Major advances in technology have made possible research that once could be conducted only through autopsy, if at all. For example, some people with autism appear to have an abnormality in a portion of the brain. One abnormal area, known as the **vermis** and located in the cerebellum (see Figure 13.1), may be related to the cognitive malfunctions found in autism (Anderson, 2001; Simon, 2000). Further research is needed to confirm this.

Neurological damage to the central nervous system may be caused by a number of problems during prenatal development and early infancy. Maternal infections, alcohol abuse, and other problems during pregnancy have great potential of damaging the developing fetus and have been associated with autism and other disabilities involving the central nervous system (Manning, Baron-Cohen, Wheelwright, & Sanders, 2001; Howard, Williams, Port, & Lepper, 2001; Wilkerson, Volpe, Dean, & Titus, 2002). In particular, viral infections such as rubella have been implicated, although a great deal of research is still needed to explore this area. Problems during the birth process are known causes of neurological injuries in babies, such as unusual hemorrhaging, difficult deliveries, and anoxia (Drew & Hardman, 2004; Wenar

**Psychodynamic perspective**

An approach to psychological disorders that views unconscious conflicts and anxieties as the cause of such disorders.

**Fragile X syndrome**

A condition involving damage to the chromosome structure, which appears as a breaking or splitting at the end of the X chromosome. This condition is found in some males with autism.

**Vermis**

A portion of the cerebellum that appears to be underdeveloped in children with autism.

FIGURE 13.1

**Cerebellum and Vermis**

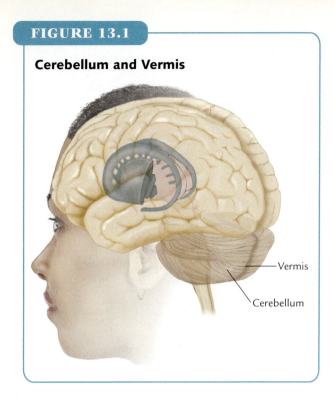

Vermis

Cerebellum

& Kerig, 2000; Wilkerson et al., 2002). Children with autism seem to have more frequent histories of delivery problems than do children without disabilities. Despite the multitude of potential neurological causes, however, no single type of trauma has been consistently identified (Berney, 2000).

Clearly, causes of autism remain unsolved puzzles in the face of ongoing research and widespread interest in the condition. Accumulated evidence has strongly implicated biological factors. Some biological malfunctions may be related to environmental influences, although evidence is only suggestive at this point (Bowers, 2002; Wing & Potter, 2002). Many current researchers have viewed autism as a behavioral syndrome with multiple biological causes (Mueller & Courchesne, 2000; Akshoomoff, Pierce, & Courchesne, 2002; Wilkerson et al., 2002). To date, researchers have not identified any single specific factor that causes autism. Rather, autism appears to be an assortment of symptoms instead of a specific disease, which is why it is often called a syndrome. As with many areas of disability, an understanding of causation is important as we attempt to improve treatment. Research continues to unravel the sources of this perplexing disability, and improved research methodology is vital for further progress in the investigation of autism (e.g., Menn & Bernstein-Ratner, 2000; Tager-Flusberg, 2000).

FOCUS 5

Identify four major approaches to the treatment of autism.

# Interventions

Attempts to identify causes of autism have gone hand in hand with efforts to discover effective treatments. Different approaches have been used as interventions with autism. Some have been based on theories of causation, others have focused on specific observable behaviors, and some appear to be rather trendy and controversial (e.g., Duchan, Calculator, Sonnenmeier, Diehl, & Cumley, 2001; Mostert, 2001; Romanczyk, Arnstein, Soorya, & Gillis, 2003). Significant progress has been made in successful interventions for people with autism, although investigators continually emphasize the importance of further systematic research on the effectiveness of various treatment strategies.

## Educational Interventions

The characteristics of autism and the severity of specific problem areas vary significantly from individual to individual. Consequently, a wide variety of instructional options are required for the effective education of these children. These alternatives range from specialized individual programs to integrated placement with support services. The unusual maladaptive behaviors mentioned earlier have led to the emergence of stereotypes about youngsters with autism and to undue segregation. However, the current literature has emphasized integration for educational purposes to the greatest degree possible, with educational placement and instructional programming dependent on the student's age and functioning level (Panerai, Ferrante, & Zingale, 2002; Schreibman & Anderson, 2001). In most cases, the ultimate goal is to prepare individuals with autism to live in their home community and in the least restrictive setting that is appropriate. The research literature also supports early interventions as an important element in promoting growth for children with autism (Green, Brennan, & Fein, 2002; Smith, Groen, & Wynn, 2000, 2001). Under IDEA, students with autism are entitled to a free appropriate education in the least restrictive environment possible.

Children with autism should have an individualized education program (IEP), including statements of short- and long-term goals (Koegel, Koegel, Frea, & Fredeen, 2001). For most students with autism, it is vital that the IEP have a central component of functional communication and social skills and that it focus on individual strengths and skills required for maximum independence. Functional skills and knowledge will vary among individuals. For some children, functional instruction will mean heavy use of language training, augmentative communication, and social, self-help, and self-protection skills (Chandler, Christie, Newson, & Prevezer,

The IEP of a child with autism should focus on developing functional communication skills and social skills.

2002; Goldstein, 2002 Charlop-Christy, Carpenter, Le, LeBlanc, & Kellet, 2002). For others, functional instruction will focus on what may be traditional academic subjects, as well as on some not always included in general education curricula, such as sexual awareness, sexual behavior, and sex education; other topics may be those of special concern to the children's parents (Cafiero, 2001, 2002; U.S. Department of Education, 2003). Educational interventions for children with autism and other disabilities are also beginning to include greater use of technology enhancements in the teaching process (Mirenda, 2001; Parsons & Mitchell, 2002; Roblyer & Edwards, 2000). Additional research on the effectiveness of such applications is essential, particularly because research on technology applications is still maturing.

Creative, innovative, and positive teachers are particularly important in providing effective education for students with autism (e.g., Dow & Mehring, 2001; Moyes, 2003). As noted earlier, these children present some unique challenges for instruction. Some seemingly insignificant actions by teachers can create great difficulties for students who have autism—difficulties that can easily be avoided if teachers are informed. For example, many high-functioning individuals with autism who have language skills interpret speech literally, so it is important to avoid using slang, idioms, and sarcasm. The individual with autism might take such phrases literally and learn something very different from what was being taught.

Parental participation in preparing children with autism for school and other aspects of life can be of great assistance (Beatson & Prelock, 2002; Perry, 2001; U.S. Department of Education, 2003). Such preparation can include objectives such as instilling a positive attitude in the child, helping him or her with scheduling, and teaching him or her how to find the way around in school. Also helpful is identifying a "safe" place and a "safe" person to seek out should the child become confused or encounter a particularly upsetting event. The accompanying Case Study illustrates parental involvement as we revisit Billy, the boy we met in the chapter-opening Snapshot.

## Psychological and Medical Interventions

Interventions based on the psychodynamic theory of causation historically focused on repairing emotional damage and resolving inner conflict. This approach is aimed at remedying the presumably faulty relationship between the child with

## Case Study

## BILLY

What happens to a boy like Billy, who was discussed in the chapter-opening snapshot? His parents are exhausted from years of caring for their son, who seems oblivious to their efforts. Placing him in the state hospital would be an easy answer, but Billy's parents sense that this would be disastrous for his development and later adjustment. If admitted to the state hospital, he could spend the rest of his life there.

This family was lucky. When Billy was ready to start school, the school district and the local mental health center arranged to place him in a special classroom within a regular public school. The classroom was well staffed, so that he had individual instruction and treatment from a teacher who was trained to manage children with behavior disorders. Billy's disruptive self-stimulation and tantrums were decreased through the use of time-out procedures (seclusion for short periods of time). Intense language training was implemented, and slowly he has learned more appropriate language. His echolalia has begun to disappear. When his appropriate behavior becomes stabilized in the classroom, he will begin an academic program and learn reading and writing.

There have also been changes for Billy's family. The mental health center offered a series of child management classes that taught the family, in-

cluding Billy's brother, how to handle his disruptive behavior. The classes also gave Billy's family a chance to see that other families had similar problems with their children who had disturbances. When the course was officially finished, the parents decided to continue meeting and planning for their children. The group members supported one another in times of need and worked actively to keep their children out of large institutions.

Although Billy is now making progress both behaviorally and academically, he will probably always have autism and be in need of special help. But great things are beginning to happen. The other day, just before the bus came to get Billy, he hugged his mother and kissed her good-bye for the first time.

### APPLICATION

1. What impact do you think Billy's parents had on his ultimate prognosis as a child with autism?

2. How might the outcome have been different if they had placed him in the state hospital?

3. Is it realistic for his mother to expect him to "grow out" of his autistic behaviors?

SOURCE: Adapted from *Understanding Child Behavior Disorders* (2nd ed., p. 312) by D. M. Gelfand, W. R. Jenson, and C. J. Drew, 1988, New York: Holt, Rinehart and Winston.

autism and his or her parents, which, it is assumed, often involved parental rejection or absence and resulted in withdrawal by the child (e.g., Korbivcher, 2001; Minazio, 2002). This treatment model has been criticized because there is little solid empirical evidence to support its effectiveness. The internal psychological nature of problems, as seen by this approach, makes evaluating it very difficult.

Various medical treatments have also been used for children with autism. Some early medical therapies (for example, electroconvulsive shock and psychosurgery) have been discredited for use in children with autism because these treatments appeared to have questionable results and harmful side effects. Likewise, certain medications used in the past (such as D-lysergic acid, more commonly known as LSD) were of doubtful therapeutic value and were very controversial. Other medications used for people with autism have often included antipsychotic drugs, anticonvulsants, and serotonin and dopamine (Malone, Maislin, Choudhury, Gifford, & Delaney, 2002; Schopler, Yirmiya, Shulman, & Marcus, 2001; Strauss, Unis, Cowan, Dawson, & Dager, 2002). Specific symptoms tend to be addressed with specific medication, such as obsessive-compulsive behaviors with clomipramine (e.g., King, Fay, & Wheildon, 2002; Sloman, Konstantareas, & Remington, 2002). Other antipsychotic drugs seem to help reduce some of the unusual speech patterns and self-injurious behaviors, particularly with older patients. Decreases in self-injury and social withdrawal have also been evident in some research on responses to other drugs (Gobbi & Pulvirenti, 2001; Luiselli, Blew, & Thibadeau, 2001; Volkmar, 2001). However, other research on drug therapy has shown mixed results or no improvement in the condition (Kemner et al., 2002).

Generally, medication has shown some promise in the treatment of autism. There appears to be potential for improvement, but such treatment should be used thoughtfully in conjunction with a multicomponent, comprehensive treatment plan (Johnson, 2002; Luiselli et al., 2001; Schopler et al., 2001). The tips found in this chapter's Inclusion Through the Lifespan illustrate how varied and complicated the overall environment is in terms of the various influences on an individual with autism. Most authorities agree that autism represents such a heterogeneous set of symptoms that no single treatment will effectively treat all children with the condition (e.g., Pelios & Lund, 2001).

## Behavioral Interventions

Interventions using behavioral treatment for children with autism are undertaken without concern for the underlying cause(s) of the disability. This approach focuses on enhancing appropriate behaviors and reducing inappropriate or maladaptive behaviors (Kauffman, 2001; Kimball, 2002). Behavior management for individuals with autism requires a statement of precise operational definition, careful observation, and recording of data on behaviors viewed as appropriate and as inappropriate. Accurate and reliable data collection is a cornerstone of behavioral intervention, a process greatly enhanced by new technology (see the Assistive Technology).

Behavioral interventions may focus on conduct such as self-stimulation, tantrum episodes, or self-inflicted injury. Behavioral therapy has substantially reduced or eliminated these problem behaviors in many cases (Britton, Carr, Landaburu, & Romick, 2002; Koegel et al., 2001; Westling & Fox, 2000). Behavioral treatment has also been effective in remediating deficiencies in fundamental social skills and language development, as well as in facilitating community integration for children with autism (Bauminger, 2002; Lovaas, 2003; Rapin, 2002). Furthermore, parental involvement in behavioral treatment has shown promising results. Research has demonstrated that certain students with autism can be effectively taught to employ self-directed behavior management, which further enhances efficiency (Erba, 2000; Ozonoff et al., 2002; Shabani, Wilder, & Flood, 2001). However, finding reinforcements to use in behavioral treatments is sometimes difficult, as suggested in the Debate Forum.

**Assistive Technology**

## COLLECTING DATA: THE VIDEX TIMEWAND

Most of us are familiar with the bar-code scanners used at checkout stands in many stores. The clerk passes the code symbol over a scanner, the price is instantly entered into the cash register, and a record of the sale is made for inventory control. This same technology is now being applied to coding and recording data on behavioral observations.

Known as the *Videx TimeWand*, this device simplifies reliable data collection for behavioral interventions with a variety of conditions, such as autism. Appropriate and inappropriate behaviors are defined very specifically, and then each is given a code, which is translated into a bar-code symbol much like we see at the market. These bar codes are then placed on an observation sheet to be used by the observer. The observer also carries a small, portable bar-code reader with a wand that is passed over the relevant code symbol when that particular behavior is observed. Data on behavioral occurrences are recorded as well as clock-time stamped to indicate when the behavior occurred. These data are stored electronically (the unit will hold up to 16,000 characters of information) and transferred to a portable computer at the end of an observation session, for analysis and graphing.

Use of the TimeWand reduces the strain on therapists who were previously required to physically write down behavioral codes while attempting to continue observation. Use of this technology thereby improves the accuracy of data collection and also expedites data processing and translation into treatment action. Information regarding this automated data collection method is available from Walter Nelson and Gordon Defalco at the Fircrest School in Seattle, Washington, or from Richard Saunders at the Parson Research Center, University of Kansas.

Inclusion
Through the
Lifespan

## PEOPLE WITH AUTISM

### Tips for the Family

- Seek out and read information regarding autism, and become knowledgeable about the disability in all areas possible. Be an active partner in the treatment of your child; take parent training classes (e.g., behavior management workshops).
- When working with the child with autism, concentrate on one behavior at a time as the target for change; emphasize work on the positive, increasing appropriate behavior rather than focusing solely on inappropriate behavior.
- Involve all family members in learning about your child's disability.
- Protect your own health by obtaining respite care when you need a rest or a break. You may need to devise a family schedule that allows adequate time for ongoing sleep and respite. Plan ahead for respite; otherwise, when you need it most, you will be too exhausted to find it.
- Help prepare your child for school by instilling a positive attitude about it, helping him or her with the idea of a school schedule and how to find a "safe" place and a "safe" person at school.

### Tips for the Preschool Teacher

- Depending on the child's level of functioning, you may have to use physical cues or clear visual modeling to persuade him or her to do something; children with autism may not respond to social cues.
- Pair physical cues with verbal cues to begin teaching verbal compliance.
- Limit instruction to one thing at a time; focus on what is concrete rather than abstract.
- Avoid verbal overload by using short, directive sentences.

### Tips for Preschool Personnel

- Encourage the development of programs where older children model good behavior and interact intensely with children with autism.
- Promote ongoing relationships between the preschool and medical personnel who can provide advice and assistance for children with autism.
- Promote the initiation of parent-school relationships to assist both parents and preschool personnel in working together.
- Promote the appropriate involvement of nonteaching staff through workshops that provide information and awareness. Consistent interaction and expectations are important.

### Tips for Neighbors and Friends

- Be supportive of the parents and siblings of a child with autism. They may be under a high level of stress and need moral support.
- Be positive with the parents. They may receive information that places blame on them, which should not be magnified by their friends.
- Offer parents a respite to the degree that you're comfortable; you may give them a short but important time away to go to the store.

### Tips for the Family

- Be active in community efforts for children with autism; join local or national parent groups.
- Consistently follow through with the basic principles of your child's treatment program at home. This may mean taking more workshops or training on various topics.
- Siblings of children with autism may find it difficult to understand the level of attention afforded to the sibling with autism. Siblings and parents need support and information.
- Continue family involvement; be sensitive to the feelings of siblings who may be feeling left out or embarrassed by the child with autism.
- It may be necessary to take safety precautions in the home (e.g., installing locks on all doors).

### Tips for the General Education Classroom Teacher

- Help with organizational strategies, assisting the student with autism with matters that are difficult for him or her (e.g., remembering how to use an eraser).
- Avoid abstract ideas unless they are necessary in instruction. Be as concrete as possible.
- Communicate with specific directions or questions, not vague or open-ended statements.
- If the child becomes upset he or she may need to change activities or go to a place in the room that is "safe" for a period of time.
- Use rules and schedules that are written with accompanying pictures so students clearly understand what is expected of them.
- Begin preparing the child with autism for a more variable environment by programming and teaching adaption to changes in routine. Involve the child in planning for the changes, mapping out what they might be.

### Tips for School Personnel

- Promote an all-school environment where children model appropriate behavior and receive reinforcement for it.
- Develop peer assistance programs, where older students can help tutor and model appropriate behavior for children with autism.
- Encourage the development of strong, ongoing, school-parent relationship and support groups working together to meet the child's needs. Consistent expectations are important.
- Do not depend on the child with autism to take messages home to parents for any reason except trying out

this skill for him or her to learn; communication is a major problem, and even a note may be lost.

## Tips for Neighbors and Friends

- As possible, ignore trivial disruptions or misbehaviors; focus on positive behaviors.
- Don't take misbehaviors personally; the child is not trying to make your life difficult or to manipulate you.
- Avoid using nicknames or cute names such as "buddy" or "pal."
- Avoid sarcasm and idiomatic expressions, such as "beating around the bush." These children may not understand and may interpret what you say literally.

## SECONDARY AND TRANSITION YEARS

### Tips for the Family

- Be alert to developmental and behavioral changes as the child grows older, watching for any changing effects of a medication.
- Continue as an active partner in your child's educational and treatment program, planning for the transition to adulthood.
- Begin acquainting yourself with the adult services that will be available when your child leaves school. If he or she functions at a high level, consider or plan for adult living out of the family home.

### Tips for the General Education Classroom Teacher

- Gradually increase the level of abstraction in teaching, remaining aware of the individual limitations the child with autism has.
- Continue preparing the student for an increasingly variable environment through instruction and example.
- Focus increasingly on matters of vital importance to the student as he or she matures (e.g., social awareness and interpersonal issues between the sexes).
- Teach the student with an eye toward postschool community participation, including matters such as navigating the community physically, activities, and employment. Teach the student about interacting with police in the community, since they require responses different from those appropriate for other strangers.*

### Tips for School Personnel

- To the degree possible for children with autism, promote involvement in social activities and clubs that enhance interpersonal interaction.
- Encourage the development of functional academic programs for students with autism that are combined with transition planning and programs.
- Promote a continuing working relationship with school staff and other agency personnel who might be involved in the student's overall treatment program (e.g., health care providers, social service agencies, and others).
- Work with other agencies that may encounter the child in the community (e.g., law enforcement). Provide workshops, if possible, to inform officers regarding behavioral characteristics of people with autism.

*The authors appreciate Cathy Pratt's review of and contribution to this material (1994).

## Tips for Neighbors and Friends

- Encourage a positive understanding of people with autism among other neighbors and friends who may be in contact with the child; help them to provide environmentally appropriate interaction.
- Promote the positive understanding of people with autism by community agencies that may encounter these individuals at this stage of life (e.g., law enforcement officials, fire department personnel).
- Support the parents as they consider the issues of adulthood for their child. Topics such as guardianship and community living may be difficult for parents to discuss.

## ADULT YEARS

### Tips for the Family

- Continue to be alert for behavioral or developmental changes that may occur as the individual matures. Continued biological maturation may require medication adjustments.
- Continue to seek out adult services that are available to individuals with disabilities.
- Seek legal advice regarding plans for the future when you are no longer able to care for the family member with autism. Plan for financial arrangements and other needs that are appropriate, such as naming an advocate. Backup plans should be made; do not always count on the youngster's siblings. Consider guardianship by other persons or agencies.

Tips for Therapists or Other Professionals

- Remain cognizant of the maturity level of the individual with whom you are working. Despite the presence of autism, some individuals have mature interests and inclinations. Do not treat the person as a child.
- Promote collaboration between appropriate adult service agencies to provide the most comprehensive services.

### Tips for Neighbors and Friends

- Encourage a positive understanding of people with autism by other neighbors and friends who may be in contact with the adult who has autism.
- Promote the positive understanding of people with autism by community agencies that may encounter these individuals at this stage of life (e.g., law enforcement officials, fire department personnel).
- Support the family members as they consider the issues of adulthood for the individual. Topics such as guardianship and community living may be difficult for parents and siblings to discuss.

SOURCE: A portion of this material is adapted from *High-Functioning Individuals with Autism: Advice and Information for Parents and Others Who Care*, by S. J. Moreno and A. M. Donellan, 1991, Crown Point, IN: Maap Services.

# SELF-STIMULATION AS A REINFORCER?

**R**einforcers as behavioral treatments are sometimes difficult to find for some children who have autism. Teachers must often take what the client gives them to work with and remain flexible in designing an intervention program.

Many individuals with autism do not respond to the same types of rewards that others do, and social rewards may not provide reinforcement or have any effect at all on these youngsters, at least in the initial stages of a treatment program. Research has also shown that, in some cases, tangible reinforcers may produce desired results, but they often seem to lose their power for individuals with autism. Given these circumstances, some researchers have suggested that self-stimulation, which appears to be a powerful and durable reinforcer, should be used to assist in teaching appropriate behavior. Self-stimulation is very different for each child and may involve manipulation of items such as coins, keys, and twigs.

## POINT

Because reinforcers are often difficult to identify for children with autism, it is important to use whatever is available and practical in teaching these youngsters. Self-stimulation has been recognized as providing strong reinforcement for those who engage in it. Although typically viewed as an inappropriate behavior, self-stimulation may be very useful in teaching the beginning phases of more adaptive behavior and other skill acquisition. For some children with autism, it may be the most efficient reinforcer available, so why not use it, at least initially?

## COUNTERPOINT

Using inappropriate behavior as a reinforcer carries with it certain serious problems and in fact may be unethical. The use of self-stimulation as a reinforcer may cause an increase in this behavior, making it an even more pronounced part of the child's inappropriate demeanor. Should this occur, it may make self-stimulation more difficult to eliminate later.

What do you think? To give your opinion, go to Chapter 13 of the companion website (www.ablongman.com/hardman8e) and click on Debate Forum.

It is important to emphasize that behavioral therapy does not claim to cure autism. The procedures involved are very specific in focusing on limited behavioral areas that need attention. This approach seems effective for many children with autism, prompting decreases in problem behaviors and potential improvement of survival skills (e.g., Gerdtz, 2000; Lovaas, 2003). Such gains constitute a significant step toward normalization for both the children and their families.

In the early 1990s, autism literature gave some attention to a treatment being used in Australia that specifically focused on communication problems for people with autism. Known as facilitative communication, this procedure emphasizes the use of typing as a means of communicating. A therapist-facilitator provides physical support by touching and putting light pressure on the student's arm or shoulder and provides interpersonal support via positive attitudes and interactions. Facilitative communication as a treatment for autism has been sufficiently controversial to prompt a number of special programs on national television news shows, featuring both proponents and critics. Although advocates of this treatment are emphatic in their support, other researchers are unable to obtain results that support its effectiveness, which of course raises serious questions about its soundness (Duchan et al., 2001; Emerson, Grayson, & Griffiths, 2001; Mostert, 2001). Because of the facilitator's participation through touching the arm of the person, some question whether the person with autism or the facilitator is

communicating. Although some interest persists, little empirical evidence supports the effectiveness of facilitated communication with individuals who have autism (Mostert, 2001).

# Impact on the Family

The arrival or diagnosis of a child with autism presents a significant challenge to parents and other family members (Gray, 2002; Tommasone & Tommasone, 2000). Parents usually have to turn to multiple sources for assistance and information, and relations between professionals and parents are not simple or easy (Freedman & Boyer, 2000). Groups such as the Autism Society of America can provide a great deal of help and support from a perspective not available elsewhere. Parents may find that they have to become aggressive and vocal in their search for services from various agencies (Freedman & Boyer, 2000; Symon, 2001 Choutka, 1999). They must also be conscious of their own health and vitality, since their ability to cope will be significantly affected if they neglect their personal well-being. They are likely to need respite time and care from a number of sources—from the family as a whole and from outside agencies. Perhaps most difficult is realizing that there are no clear-cut answers to many of the questions they have. Intervention to help different families and family members needs to be tailored to the specific circumstances and individuals involved.

The impact of a child with autism on his or her family members is enormous (Yazbak, 2002; Olsson & Hwang, 2001; Weiss, 2002). Living with such a child is exhausting and presents many challenges, including strained relationships, vastly and permanently increased financial burdens, social isolation, grief, and considerable physical and emotional fatigue (Boyd, 2002; Powers, 2000). The youngster with autism may sleep only a few hours each night and spend many waking hours engaged in self-abusive or disruptive behavior. It is easy to see how parents may feel as though they are in a marathon, 24 hours a day, 7 days per week, with no respite. Not only is the family routine interrupted, but the constant demands are physically and emotionally draining, resulting in a number of problems for family members (such as high stress levels and depression) and in some affective disorders among mothers (Boyd, 2002; Olsson & Hwang, 2001; Weiss, 2002). And, as we have noted, the situation may be especially confusing for family members if the child with autism also has savant-like skills in some areas.

*Temple Grandin, an assistant professor of animal science at Colorado State University, is a high-functioning person with autism. In addition to writing several hundred papers on autism, she has revolutionized the treatment of animals and barn design for animals that are being raised for consumption.*

Siblings of children with autism may experience a number of problems, particularly during the early years. They may have difficulty understanding their parents' distress regarding their brother or sister and the level of attention afforded this child, and they may manifest stress or some depression (Bauminger & Yirmiya, 2001; Ozonoff et al., 2002). Siblings may also have difficulty accepting the emotional detachment of the youngster, who may seem not to care for them at all. Like the siblings of children with other disabilities, brothers and sisters of a child with autism may be embarrassed and reluctant to bring friends home. However, if they can become informed and move beyond the social embarrassment, siblings can be a significant resource in assisting parents. Some recent research suggests fairly positive adjustment among siblings of children with autism (Kaminsky & Dewey, 2002).

# FOCUS REVIEW

**FOCUS 1** Identify four areas of functional challenge often found in children with autism.

- Language
- Interpersonal skills
- Emotional or affective behaviors
- Intellectual functioning

**FOCUS 2** What is the general prevalence estimated for autism?

- Approximately 5 cases per 10,000

**FOCUS 3** Identify six characteristics of children with autism.

- As infants, they are often unresponsive to physical contact or affection from their parents, and later they have extreme difficulty relating to other people.
- Most have impaired or delayed language skills, and about half do not develop speech at all.
- Those who have speech often engage in echolalia and other inappropriate behavior.
- They frequently engage in self-stimulatory behavior.
- Changes in their routine are met with intense resistance.
- Most have a reduced level of intellectual functioning.

**FOCUS 4** Identify the two broad theoretical views regarding the causes of autism.

- The psychoanalytic view places a great deal of emphasis on the interaction between the family and the child.
- The biological view attributes autism to neurological damage and/or to genetics.

**FOCUS 5** Identify four major approaches to the treatment of autism.

- Psychoanalytic-based therapy focuses on repairing the emotional damage presumed to have resulted from faulty family relationships.
- Medically based treatment often involves the use of medication.
- Behavioral interventions focus on enhancing specific appropriate behaviors or on reducing inappropriate behaviors.
- Educational interventions employ the full range of educational placements.

## FURTHER READINGS

Jackson, L. (2002). *Freaks, Geeks and Asperger Syndrome: A User Guide to Adolescence.* Philadelphia, PA: Jessica Kingsley Publishers.

*Luke Jackson has a number of challenges in his life, including having Asperger syndrome, one brother with ADHD, and another with autism. This is a delightful story that provides personal views of the world through the lens of a 13-year-old with high-functioning autism. If you think the teen years are a challenge, try seeing them through Luke's eyes.*

Karasik, P., & Karasik, J. (2003). *The Ride Together: A Brother and Sister's Memoir of Autism in the Family.* New York: Atria Books.

*This volume presents siblings' perspective on growing up with a brother who has autism. Paul and Judy (a cartoonist and book editor, respectively) provide a rarely found insight into their lives with brother David. This book also illustrates the changes in treatment approaches from the 1950s to the early 21st century.*

Prince-Hughes, D. (Ed.) (2002). *Aquamarine Blue 5: Personal Stories of College Students with Autism.* Athens, GA: Swallow Press.

*This volume includes the personal experiences of 12 people who encountered the challenges of autism or autism spectrum disorders for years without an explanation of what their diagnosis was. The title comes from one of these contributors who perceives numbers in color; her favorite is "5," which she sees as aquamarine. A nice resource for seeing the personal side of autism.*

## WEB RESOURCES

### Future Horizons, Inc.

www.futurehorizons-autism.com

This website features products, publications, and resources to people interacting with children and adolescents with autism. In many cases the resources will be of interest to family members who find themselves in ongoing and close relationships with such youngsters. Resources provided include conference information, magazines, and medical resources.

### Autism Society of America

www.autism-society.org

This website provides opportunities for people who want to expand their network of resources related to autism. It provides a vehicle for joining ASA, as well as information about legislation and legal cases related to autism. ASA uses this website to encourage participation by people who have a relationship with someone who has autism or have a professional interest in autism.

### The Autism Web

www.autismweb.com

This website is aimed at parents of children with autism and related pervasive developmental disorders. Clearly intended to enhance networking and provide support, this site includes community-based resources, information on conferences, and message boards to promote communication.

### Autism Resources

www.autism-resources.com

This website provides information and links related to autism and Asperger syndrome. A simple and straightforward resource site offering a broad array of information.

## BUILDING YOUR PORTFOLIO

If you are thinking about a career in special education, you should know that many states use national standards developed by the Council for Exceptional Children (CEC) to assess a teacher candidate's knowledge and skills for working with students with disabilities. See a complete listing of the ten CEC Content Standards on the inside front cover of this text.

### CEC Content Standards Addressed in Chapter 13

1. Foundations
2. Development and Characteristics of Learners
3. Individual Learning Differences
4. Instructional Strategies
5. Learning Environments and Social Interactions
7. Instructional Planning

### Assess Your Knowledge of the CEC Standards Addressed in Chapter 13

Some states require that teacher candidates develop a portfolio of products that demonstrate mastery of the CEC content standards. To assist in the development of products for this portfolio, you may wish to complete the following activities.

• Complete a written test of the chapter's content.

*If your instructor requires a written test of your content knowledge for this chapter, keep a copy for your portfolio. A practice test on the information covered in this chapter is available through the companion website (www.ablongman.com/hardman8e) and the Student Study Guide.*

• Respond to the application questions for the Case Study "Billy."

*Review the Case Study and respond in writing to the application questions. Keep a copy of the Case Study and your written response for your portfolio.*

• Complete the "Take a Stand" Activity for the Debate Forum "Self-Stimulation as a Reinforcer?"

*Read the Debate Forum in this chapter and then visit our companion website to complete the activity "Take a Stand." Keep a copy of this activity for your portfolio.*

• Participate in a community service learning activity.

*Community service is a valuable way to enhance your learning experience. Visit our companion website for suggested community service learning activities that correspond to the information presented in this chapter. Develop a reflective journal of the service learning experience for your portfolio.*

## THEMES OF THE TIMES

The New York Times
nytimes.com
expect the world®

Expand your knowledge of the concepts discussed in this chapter by reading current and historical articles from the *New York Times* by visiting the "Themes of the Times" section of the companion website: **www.ablongman.com/hardman8e.**

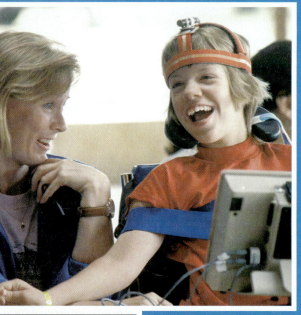

# Traumatic and Acquired Brain Injury

## TO BEGIN WITH ...

### An Astounding Figure

ATLANTA (CNN)—An estimated 5.3 million Americans, a little more than 2% of the U.S. population, currently live with disabilities from traumatic brain injuries, according to a new report by the Centers for Disease Control and Prevention (CDC).

### Yes, I Can

Many times in my life I've heard the familiar phrase "You can't do that," but it never had such an impact on me as when I heard it after learning I had a brain injury as a result of a car accident. Prior to my injury, if someone said I wouldn't be able to do something or that a job was too big for me to handle, I became so determined that I would end up succeeding. After sustaining my brain injury, my world became very different. My work life, where I had been very confident and successful, suddenly seemed complicated and overwhelming. People were talking to me and I couldn't understand what they were saying. I couldn't remember the names of co-workers I had known for years. I spent my days confused and trapped inside my head. It even seemed difficult to walk and breathe. Doctors explained that I wouldn't be able to hold down a full-time job, I wouldn't be able to learn anything new, I couldn't ski down my favorite mountain or live in "mainstream society." In short, I wasn't going to be able to live the way I had prior to the accident.

Well, seven years later I'm holding down a full-time job and have taken on more responsibility. I continue to learn and I've skied down my favorite mountain in Colorado—not like I used to, but I was still able to stand on top of the mountain and see the view I dreamed about seeing again. (Jones, 2003, p. 1)

### Head Injury Perceptions

I received a head injury from a rolling rock at night while fighting a forest fire. The fact that the fire loosened up and caused the rock to roll down the steep hill and hit me was my only instance of bad luck. It was life-saving lucky that I had a hard hat on and that my co-workers were highly skilled in first aid. After being hit by the rock, I was knocked down the hill about fifty feet, and my co-workers checked me and immediately administered cardiopulmonary resuscitation (CPR) until my pulse and breathing resumed. After the accident, I was in a comatose condition for one month and remained hospitalized for three months with outpatient assistance for three+ years. . . .

There are also a lot of things in life I realize that I took, and most other people take, for granted. Many aspects of memory recall, you take for granted. For example, when leaving a department store, you subconsciously recall where and how you entered as you backtrack to leave. Where you parked your car in the parking lot when you arrived, you subconsciously recall as you leave. I must now *consciously* imprint items such as this so I can increase my odds of efficiently getting out and finding the car. . . . It also is very frustrating with a reduced ability to recognize names with faces. They may "look" familiar, but I can't remember their names. This is something that is probably easy to relate to; however, the occurrence of it for me is very frequent. (Becker, 2003, p. 1)

**FOCUS**

**PREVIEW:** To preview the central concepts of this chapter, read the focus questions located in the margins. Using these questions as a guide, ask yourself what you already know and what you want to learn.

# Ashley

Ashley was a very normal child, inquisitive and active. One of her great pleasures was having her picture taken at the local mall. She also loved to run and to blow bubbles. Her favorite activity was visiting the local pet and fish store. There she would move from aquarium to aquarium, pointing with great delight at her favorite fish. Her vocalizations were exuberant and elaborate, even though they were not well understood. Nevertheless, it was clear that she delighted in seeing the fish and being with her mom in the store.

When Ashley was about 18 months old, her life changed in a matter of seconds. She and her mother had just attended a family party. On the way home, Ashley's mom decided to visit a friend and just say hi. After leaving the friend's home, they approached an intersection with the usual stoplight. The light was red and they stopped. Their car's left signal lights indicated their intention to turn, and they waited for traffic opposite them to clear. Ashley was comfortably placed in her car seat. As soon as the oncoming traffic cleared, they appropriately began the left turn.

Her mother relates the remainder of the story as follows: "As I looked out the left side, I saw this van coming toward us. I don't remember him hitting us. We know he did. Then the next thing I remember is being in the emergency room and thinking that everything was okay. If I'm fine, I knew Ashley was on the other side of the car in her car seat, in the back, strapped in, and I figured if I was okay, she was."

Several days passed before Ashley's mom was able to see her. "I went down and saw her a couple of days later. I was released from the hospital and that was the first time I was able to see her. And it was kind of hard to go down there and see your child hooked up to all these machines and just not move, just lie there."

Ashley spent the next 24 days in the intensive care unit (ICU) at Primary Children's Medical Center. She was then moved to a rehabilitation unit where she spent the next 4 months.

"During the time in rehab she went in and out of surgery. She had two internal shunts and two external shunt surgeries to relieve the pressure that had built up inside her head from the accident. When we brought her home, she couldn't see. She was diagnosed cortically blind. She couldn't talk. It was just as if she was a newborn child. She had just barely learned to hold her head up before we left Primary, so it was like having this 30-pound newborn. One thing we missed the most was her smile. It's so nice to see it back."

---

Children, youth, or adults who have experienced traumatic brain injuries are affected in many ways (Jay, 2000; Williams & Stillman, 2000). Memory loss, concentration problems, slowed information processing, seizures, vision problems, severe headaches—any and all of these problems may be present in individuals who have suffered severe head trauma. Think what it might be like to lose your sense of taste, to be able to think of things to say but not be able to actually speak them, and to know what it is like to throw a ball but not be able to release the ball from your hand. The challenges associated with traumatic brain injury (TBI) can be formidable.

## Definition

**Traumatic brain injury (TBI)** occurs when there is a blow to the head or when the head slams against a stationary object. Such injuries happen, for example, in car accidents when the head hits the windshield and in bicycle accidents when the head hits the ground. The injury may occur in one of two ways:

A closed-head injury occurs when the moving head is rapidly stopped, as when hitting a windshield, or when it is hit by a blunt object causing the brain to smash into the hard bony surface inside the skull. Closed-head injury may also occur without direct external trauma to the head if the brain undergoes a rapid forward or backward movement, such as when a person experiences whiplash. (Family Caregiver Alliance Clearing Houses, 2003, p. 1)

The trauma caused by the rapid acceleration or deceleration of the brain may cause the tearing of important nerve fibers in the brain, the bruising of brain itself as it undergoes the impact with the skull, brain stem injuries, and brain swelling (see

**FOCUS**
**1**

Identify three key elements of traumatic brain injury.

**Traumatic brain injury (TBI)**

Direct injury to the brain, such as tearing of nerve fibers, bruising of the brain tissue against the skull, brain stem trauma, and swelling.

nearby Reflect on This). Two types of brain damage, primary and secondary, are described by medical professionals. *Primary damage* is a direct outcome of the initial impact to the brain. *Secondary damage* develops over time as the brain responds to the initial trauma. For instance, an adolescent who is hit accidentally with a baseball bat may develop a hematoma—an area of internal bleeding within the brain. This may be the primary damage. However, with the passage of time, the brain's response to the initial injury may be pervasive swelling, which may cause additional insult to the brain.

In the school context, the Individuals with Disabilities Act (IDEA) defines traumatic brain injury as

> an acquired injury to the brain caused by an external force, resulting in total or partial functional disability or psychosocial impairment, or both, that adversely affects a student's educational performance. The term applies to open and closed head injuries resulting in impairments in one or more areas, such as cognition, language, memory, attention, reasoning, abstract thinking, judgment, problem-solving, sensory, perceptual, and motor abilities; psychosocial behavior, physical functions, information processing, and speech. The term does not apply to brain injuries that are congenital or degenerative or brain injuries induced by birth trauma. (*Federal Register*, *57*, 189, pp. 44, 802)

Another term, **acquired brain injury (ABI)**,

> refers to both traumatic brain injuries, such as open or closed head injuries, and nontraumatic brain injuries, such as strokes and other vascular accidents, infectious diseases (e.g., encephalitis, meningitis), anoxic injuries (e.g., hanging, near-drowning, choking, anesthetic accidents, severe blood loss), metabolic disorders (e.g., insulin shock, liver and kidney disease), and toxic products taken into the body through inhalation or ingestion. The term does not refer to brain injuries that are congenital or brain injuries induced by birth trauma. (Savage & Wolcott, 1994a, pp. 3–4)

These traumatic and acquired brain injuries result in disabilities that may adversely affect individuals' information processing, social behaviors, memory capacities, reasoning and thinking, speech and language skills, and sensory and motor abilities (Murdoch & Theodoros, 2001; Pierangelo & Giuliani, 2001; Thompson & Kerns, 2000).

**Acquired brain injury (ABI)**

Injury that may result from TBI or from strokes and other vascular accidents, infectious diseases, anoxic injuries (hanging, near drowning), anesthetic accidents, severe blood loss, metabolic disorders, and ingestion of toxic products.

**Reflect on This**

## KIDS' CORNER

When a child's brain is injured, it does not heal like a broken bone, torn muscle, or skin. Unlike broken bones that mend, or cut or scraped skin that grows again, the brain cannot repair itself. It cannot grow new brain cells, called neurons, once they are damaged.

Traumatic brain injury is the most frequent cause of disability and death among children and adolescents in the United States.

Each year, more than 1 million children sustain brain injuries, ranging from mild to severe trauma. Annually, more than 30,000 children have permanent disabilities as a result of brain injury.

Of all pediatric injury cases in the United States, about one-third are related to brain injury, according to the National Pediatric Trauma Registry. (Brain Injury Association, Inc., 2000c, p. 1)

Prevention is the only cure for brain injury. (Brain Injury Association, Inc., 2000b, p. 1)

SOURCE: Adapted from "Kids' Corner" by the Brain Injury Association, Inc. 2000. Available: www.biausa.org/Firearmsfs.htm and www.biausa.org/children.htm

# Prevalence

The statistics associated with traumatic brain injury are sobering. According to the most recent data from the Centers for Disease Control and Injury Prevention, it is now estimated that 5.3 million children and adults in the United States are living with the consequences of sustaining a traumatic brain injury. This number equals nearly 2% of the general population (Brain Injury Association, 2003). Traumatic brain injury is the leading cause of acquired disability in the United States (Cronin, 2000). "More than 100,000 children and youth between the ages of birth and 21 are hospitalized each year for brain injuries" (Pierangelo & Giuliani, 2001, p. 97). Of all the head injuries that occur, 40% involve children. About 2% to 5% of the children and youth who experience TBI develop severe neurologic complications, others develop lasting behavior problems, and over one-third experience life-long disabilities (Pierangelo & Giuliani, 2001). Most of these injuries could be prevented with proper use of seat belts, child restraints, helmets, and other preventive measures.

The incidence of TBI peaks during three specific age periods. Children below 5 years of age, individuals between 15 and 24 years of age, and individuals over 70 years of age are more likely to experience head injuries. The peaking of injuries between the ages of 15 and 24 is attributable to several factors, including increased participation in contact sports, greater access to and use of automobiles, more frequent use of racing and mountain bikes, and injuries sustained from firearms. The number of head injuries in males exceeds that in females. As a rule, males are two to three times more likely to sustain serious head injuries, particularly during the adolescent years.

The rate of mortality for TBI is 30 per 100,000. Fifty percent of those who die as a result of their injuries do so within the first two hours following the accident or insult to the brain. Obviously, medical care at the scene of the accident is crucial. Emergency treatment in the field and in the hospital can make a big difference in survival rates of injured individuals. Nevertheless, many die as a result of severe head injuries.

# Characteristics

Individuals with traumatic or acquired brain injury present a variety of challenges to families and professionals. The injuries may affect every aspect of an individual's life (see Table 14.1 for effects on children) (Bowe, 2000; Wood & McMillan, 2001). The re-

**FOCUS 2**

Identify four general characteristics of individuals with traumatic or acquired brain injuries.

*Most of the head injuries five million children experience annually could be prevented with the proper use of preventative aids such as helmets, seat belts, and child restraints.*

**TABLE 14.1**

## Characteristics of Children with Traumatic Brain Injury

**MEDICAL/NEUROLOGICAL SYMPTOMS**

- Sensory deficits affecting vision, hearing, taste, smell or touch
- Decreased motor coordination
- Difficulty breathing
- Dizziness
- Headache
- Impaired balance
- Loss of intellectual capabilities
- Partial to full paralysis
- Poor eye–hand coordination
- Reduced body strength
- Seizure activity (possibly frequent)
- Sleep disorders
- Speech problems (e.g., stuttering, slurring)

**COGNITIVE SYMPTOMS**

- Decreased attention
- Decreased organizational skills
- Decreased problem-solving ability
- Difficulties keeping up at school
- Difficulty with abstract reasoning
- Integration problems (e.g., sensory, thought)
- Poor organizational skills
- Memory deficits
- Perceptual problems
- Poor concentration
- Poor judgment
- Rigidity of thought

- Slowed information processing
- Poor short- and long-term memory
- Word-finding difficulty

**BEHAVIORAL/EMOTIONAL SYMPTOMS**

- Aggressive behavior
- Denial of deficits
- Depression
- Difficulty accepting and responding to change
- Loss of reduction of inhibitions
- Distractibility
- Feelings of worthlessness
- Flat affect (expressionless, lacking emotion)
- Low frustration level
- Unnecessary or disproportionate guilt
- Helplessness
- Impulsivity
- Inappropriate crying or laughing
- Irritability

**SOCIAL SKILLS DEVELOPMENT**

- Difficulties maintaining relationships with family members and others
- Inability to restrict socially inappropriate behaviors (e.g., disrobing in public)
- Inappropriate responses to the environment (e.g., overreactions to light or sound)
- Insensitivity to others' feelings
- Limited initiation of social interactions
- Social isolation

SOURCE: Adapted from *What Every Teacher Should Know About Students with Special Needs: Promoting Success in the Classroom* pp. 98–100, by R. Pierangelo and G. A. Guiliani (2001), Champaign, IL: Research Press.

sulting disabilities also have a profound effect on the individual's family (Semrud-Clikeman, 2001). Often the injuries radically change the individual's capacities for learning (Thompson & Kerns, 2000).

Generally, the individual will need services and supports in four areas: cognition, speech and language, social and behavioral skills, and physical functioning (Keyser-Marcus, Briel, Sherron-Targett, Yasuda, Johnson, & Wehman, 2002). Cognitive problems have an impact on thinking and perception. For example, people who have sustained a brain injury may be unable to remember or retrieve newly learned information. They may be unable to attend or concentrate for appropriate periods of time. Another serious problem is inability to adjust or respond flexibly to changes in home or school environments (Pierangelo & Giuliani, 2001).

A person with TBI may also struggle with speech, producing unintelligible sounds or indistinguishable words (Semrud-Clikeman, 2001). Speech may be slurred and labored. The individual may know what he or she wants to say but be unable to express it. Professionals use the term **aphasia** to describe this condition. **Expressive aphasia** is an inability to express one's own thoughts and desires. Language problems may also be evident. For example, a school-age student may be unable to retrieve a desired word or expression, particularly during a "high-demand"

**Aphasia**

An acquired language disorder that is caused by brain damage and is characterized by complete or partial impairment of language comprehension, formulation, and use.

**Expressive aphasia**

An inability to express one's own thoughts and desires verbally.

instructional setting or during an anxiety-producing social situation. Given their difficulties with word retrieval, individuals with TBI may reduce their overall speech output or use repetitive expressions or word substitutions. Many children with brain injuries express great frustration at knowing an answer to a question but being unable to retrieve it when called on by teachers. (See Chapter 11 for additional information on expressive aphasia.)

Social and behavioral problems may present the most challenging aspects of TBI and ABI. For many individuals, the injury produces significant changes in their personalities, their temperaments, their dispositions toward certain activities, and their behaviors (Semrud-Clikeman, 2001). These social and behavioral problems may worsen over time, depending on the nature of the injury, the preinjury adjustment of the individual and family, the person's age at time of the injury, and the treatment provided immediately after the injury. Behavior effects include increased irritability and emotionality, compromised motivation and judgment, an inability to restrict socially inappropriate behaviors, insensitivity to others, and low thresholds for frustration and inconvenience (Alderman, 2001; Hibbard, Gordon, & Kothera, 2000; Tucker, 2001; Wood & McMillan, 2001).

Neuromotor and physical disabilities are also characteristic of individuals with brain injuries. Neuromotor problems may be exhibited through poor eye–hand coordination. For example, an adolescent may be able to pick up a ball but be unable to throw it to someone else. In addition, there may be impaired balance, an inability to walk unassisted, significantly reduced stamina, or paralysis. Impaired vision and hearing may also be present. The array and extent of the challenges faced by individuals with brain injuries and their families can be overwhelming and disheartening. However, with appropriate support and coordinated, interdisciplinary treatment, the individual and family can move forward with their lives and develop effective coping skills (Pierangelo & Giuliani, 2001).

FOCUS
3

Identify the most common causes of brain injury in children, youth, and adults.

# Causation

What most frequently causes brain injury varies with age and developmental status. The highest incidence of injury in all age groups is automobile-related accidents. For small children, the most common cause is a fall from a short distance. Such children may fall from a tree, playground equipment, their parent's arms, or furniture. Another major cause of injury in young children is physical abuse (Horton & Cruise, 2001). These injuries generally come from the shaking or striking of infants, which may cause sheering of brain matter or severe bleeding. Common causes of head injuries in older children include falls from playground swings or climbers, bicycles, or trees; blows to the head from baseball bats, balls, or other sports equipment; gunshot wounds, and pedestrian accidents.

The first signs of brain injury often manifest themselves in coma. The severity and nature of complications and the eventual outcomes of the trauma are a function of the location and degree of the injury to the brain (see Table 14.2). Jennett and Teasdale (1974) developed a scale to assess the potential impact of head injuries in children and to predict their eventual functioning (see Table 14.3). Scores of 3 to 5 generally indicate poor outcomes in children over time.

The number of children and others who experience serious head trauma would be significantly reduced if seat belts and other child restraint devices were consistently used. Further reductions in such injuries would be achieved by significantly decreasing accidents due to driving under the influence of alcohol and other mind-altering substances (Bowe, 2000).

Programs directed at reducing the number of individuals who drive while under the influence of alcohol or other substances should be vigorously supported. Likewise, children (and everyone else) should wear helmets when bicycling and should obey safety rules that reduce the probability of serious accidents. (See Reflect on This, "You Really Want to Ride a Bicycle?" on page 392.)

## FIREARMS: SHOULDN'T WE PROTECT OUR CHILDREN AND YOUTH?

Hundreds of brain injuries could be avoided if parents limited children's access to firearms.

### SCOPE OF THE PROBLEM

In 1992, firearms surpassed motor vehicles as the number one cause of brain injury fatalities in the United States.

It is estimated that every two hours in the United States, someone's child is killed with a loaded gun. Firearm violence is a uniquely American problem, with a rate 90 times greater than that of any similar country.

It is estimated that half of all American households have firearms.

Every day, 14 American children under the age of 20 are killed and many more are wounded by guns.

It costs more than $14,000 to treat each child wounded by gunfire—enough to pay for a full year at a private college.

### FIREARM USAGE

Although firearms are often kept in the home for protection, they are rarely used for this purpose. Of 198 cases of home

Lisa Kreutz, one of the Columbine High School seniors wounded in the shooting attack at the school, receives her diploma at commencement ceremonies with her mother and father. Two students of the class of 1999 were killed in the shootings, and three were injured.

invasion crimes, only three victims (1.5%) used a gun for self-defense.

The risk of suicide is five times greater if there is a gun in the home, and the risk of domestic homicide is three times greater.

Most children who kill themselves or other children unintentionally while playing with a gun found it in their home or the home of a family member or friend.

News reports state that nearly 90% of accidental shootings involving children are linked to easy-to-find, loaded handguns in the home.

Over half of all handgun owners keep their guns loaded at least some of the time, and over half do not keep their guns locked up.

An estimated 30% of all unintentional shootings could be prevented by the presence of safety features such as trigger locks and loading indicators, but American-made guns are not subject to federal safety standards like other consumer products such as automobiles, aspirin bottles, and children's toys.

### POINT

Gun control of any kind is repugnant to many individuals, particularly those who have strong feelings about the "right to bear arms." These individuals argue that controlling firearms is a violation of their civil rights. Any restriction of access to firearms or control of their use is seen by these individuals as undue government intervention and control.

### COUNTERPOINT

As a society, we can no longer ignore the deaths and injuries to children and youth that are caused by firearms. We ought to treat firearms as we treat cars. Cars must have certain safety devices, or they are not available for purchase or use. Likewise, only those licensed to drive may legally get behind the wheel of a car. These governmental measures are directed at enhancing the safety of citizens. The same measures should apply to firearms. The essential goal is prevention, not control.

What do you think? To give your opinion, go to Chapter 14 of the companion website (www.ablongman.com/hardman8e) and click on Debate Forum.

SOURCE: From *Firearm Safety*, developed by the Brain Injury Association, Inc., 2000b, Alexandria, Virginia

# Educational Supports and Services

Educational supports focus on environmental changes that facilitate daily living and address critical transition issues that arise in preparing the child or youth's return to appropriate school settings (Semrud-Clikeman, 2001). Specific teaching techniques and practices should be informed by current research about learning, the brain, and acquired brain injuries. It is essential that educators and health providers work

| TABLE 14.2 | |
|---|---|

**Descriptors of TBI severity**

| | |
|---|---|
| Minor | No loss of consciousness; head injury not seen by a physician; a minor bump. |
| Mild | Mild or transient loss of consciousness, if any; child may be lethargic and not be able to recall the injury; child may vomit (if more than three times, should be seen by emergency room staff). |
| Moderate | Loss of consciousness is typically less than 5 minutes; on recovery, the child may be able to move spontaneously and purposefully; opens eyes in response to pain. Older children or youth may be combative, telling others to "leave me alone." |
| Severe | Loss of consciousness ranges from 5 to 30 minutes. Surgery may be needed if skull is fractured significantly; neurologic consequences are common. |
| Serious | Loss of consciousness more that 30 minutes, notable neurologic consequences are typical. |

SOURCE: Adapted from *Head Injuries* (p. 225), by J. L. Hill, 1999, Upper Saddle River, NJ: Merrill.

**FOCUS 4**

Describe the focus of educational interventions for individuals with traumatic or acquired brain injuries.

together to blend clinical, educational, and family interventions effectively (Cronin, 2000; Keyser-Marcus, et al., 2002). Unfortunately, many children with brain injuries leave hospitals or rehabilitation settings without adequate preparation for the new environments in which they find themselves. They are not ready to return to school. And many teachers who receive these students are not adequately prepared to respond to their cognitive, academic, and behavioral needs.

Before the child or youth leaves the hospital or rehabilitation facility, several issues and questions need to be addressed by medical, psychological, and educational personnel (see Figure 14.1 on page 396). Pertinent questions include the following:

- How severe was the injury? What is the prognosis for continued recovery?
- What are the major health-related needs of the child? Is an individual health plan needed to establish a protocol for treatment at school?

**Reflect on This**

## YOU REALLY WANT TO RIDE A BICYCLE?

Riding a bicycle can be a lot of fun. Bicycles can be used for transportation, physical fitness, or racing. However, bicycle riding poses many risks and should always be done correctly. Children should never abuse the right to ride a bicycle.

### Crash Statistics

A child is four times more likely to be seriously injured in a bicycle crash than to be kidnapped by a stranger. More kids, ages 5 to 14, go to hospital emergency rooms with injuries related to biking than with any other sport.

Each year, about 567,000 people go to hospital emergency departments with bicycle-related injuries; about 350,000 of those injured are children under 15. Of those children, about 130,000 sustain brain injuries.

Each year, bicycle crashes kill about 900 people; about 200 of those killed are children under age 15. Statistics show that between 70% and 80% of all fatal bicycle crashes involve brain injuries.

Ninety percent of bicycle-related deaths involve collisions with motor vehicles.

### Who, What, When, and Why

The number of people who ride bicycles rose from 66.9 million in 1991 to 80.6 million in 1998.

Distribution of bicycle deaths in 1996: 49% of all deaths occurred between 3 P.M. and 9 P.M.

### Bicycle Helmets

Ninety-six percent of bicyclists killed in 1996 were reportedly not wearing helmets.

Medical research shows that 88% of cyclists' brain injuries can be prevented by a bicycle helmet.

Universal use of helmets could prevent one death every day and one brain injury every four minutes.

SOURCE: From *Bicycle Safety*, developed by the Brain Injury Association, Inc., 2000a, Alexandria, Virginia.

# TABLE 14.3

## Glasgow Coma Scale

| ACTIVITY | SCORE | DESCRIPTION |
|---|---|---|
| **BEST MOTOR RESPONSE** | | |
| Obeys commands | 6 | Follows simple verbal directions |
| Localized pain | 5 | Moves arms and legs to escape painful stimuli |
| Withdrawal from pain | 4 | Normal reflex responses |
| Abnormal flexion | 3 | "Decorticate"—abnormal adduction of shoulder |
| Extensor posturing | 2 | "Decerebrate"—internal rotation of shoulder and pronation of forearm |
| No response | 1 | Limp, without evidence of spinal transection |
| **BEST VERBAL RESPONSE** | | |
| Oriented | 5 | Aware of self, environment, time, and situation |
| Confused | 4 | Attention is adequate and patient is responsive, but responses suggest disorientation and confusion |
| Inappropriate | 3 | Understandable articulation, but speech is used in a nonconversational (exclamatory or swearing manner); conversation is not sustained |
| Incomprehensible | 2 | Verbal response (moaning) but without recognizable words |
| No response | 1 | |
| **EYE OPENING** | | |
| Spontaneous | 4 | Eyes are open; scored without reference to awareness |
| To speech | 3 | Eyes are open to speech or shout without implying a response to a direct command |
| To pain | 2 | Eyes are open with painful stimulus to limbs or chest. |
| None | 1 | No eye opening, not attributable to swelling |

SOURCE: Adapted from "Assessment of Coma and Impaired Consciousness," by B. Jennett & G. Teasdale, 1974, *Lancet*, 2, pp. 81–84.

- Are seizures or other neurologic problems likely? What changes in behavior indicate that a physician should be contacted?

- Are activity restrictions needed to ensure safety and well-being?

- What medications are prescribed? Do they have side effects? Do they need to be administered at school?

- What is the impact of the brain injury on the child's ability to learn new information in verbal and visual-spatial modalities? Are problems with new learning due primarily to deficits in attention, comprehension, memory, response, speed of processing, or reasoning?

- In what areas (e.g., language arts, mathematics, science) is the child most likely to experience success?

- What content area may prove difficult or overwhelming for the learner? What modifications, if any, would facilitate the child's performance in those areas (reading partners, cooperative learning activities, peer tutoring, ... calculators)? (Farmer, Clippard, Luehr-Wiemann, Wright, & Owings, 1997, pp. 40–41, 43, 49)

These questions provide valuable information for school personnel and others who must plan for and implement the youngster's reentry into school. Generally, a

## Inclusion Through the Lifespan

**PEOPLE WITH TRAUMATIC AND ACQUIRED BRAIN INJURY**

### Tips for the Family

- Become fully informed about your child's condition.
- Become familiar with special services available in your school and with health care systems.
- Develop positive relationships with care providers.
- Seek out appropriate assistance through advocacy and support groups.
- Pursue family or individual counseling for persistent relationship-centered problems.
- Develop sensible routines and schedules for the child.
- Communicate with siblings, friends, and relatives; help them become informed about the injury and their role in the treatment process.

### Tips for the Preschool Teacher

- Communicate with parents, special education personnel, and health care providers to develop appropriate expectations, management, and instruction.
- Interact frequently with parents, special education personnel, and health care providers.
- Watch for abrupt changes in the child's behavior. If they occur, notify parents and other professionals immediately.
- Involve socially sophisticated peers and other older children in working with the preschooler with TBI.
- Become familiar with events that "set the child off."
- Use management procedures that promote appropriate independence and foster learning.

### Tips for Preschool Personnel

- Participate in orientation and team meetings with the preschool teacher.
- Develop an understanding of the child and the condition.
- Communicate frequently with the preschool teacher and parents about concerns and promising developments.
- Employ the same management strategies used by the parents and preschool teacher.
- Be patient with the rate of progress behaviorally, socially, and academically.
- Help other children understand the child.

### Tips for Neighbors and Friends

- Offer to become educated about the condition and its impact on the child.
- Become familiar with recommended management procedures for directing the child.
- Inform your own children about the dynamics of the condition; help them understand how to react and respond to variations in behavior.
- Involve the child in appropriate family activities.

### Tips for the Family

- Remember that the transition back to the school and family environment requires explicit planning and preparation.
- Prepare siblings, peers, and neighbors for the child's return to the home and community.
- Learn about and use management procedures that promote the child's well-being.
- Carefully plan with school personnel the child's reentry into school.

### Tips for the General Education Classroom Teacher

- Become fully familiar with the child's condition.
- Communicate with medical and other personnel about expectations, management strategies, and approaches for dealing with persistant problems.
- Use appropriate routines and schedules to foster learning and good behavior.
- Help other children understand how they can contribute to the child's growth and healing within the classroom setting.
- Let peers and older youngsters work with the student on academic and social tasks.
- Do not be reluctant to communicate with other professionals and parents when problems arise.
- Remember that teamwork among caring professionals and parents is essential to the child's success.

### Tips for School Personnel

- Become informed; seek to understand the unique characteristics of TBI.
- Behave as though the child were your own.
- Seek to understand and use instructional and management approaches that are well suited to the child.
- Use the expertise that is present in the school and school system; collaborate with other specialists.

### Tips for Neighbors and Friends

- Adopt an inclusive attitude about family and neighborhood events; invite the child or youth to join in family-centered activities, picnics, appropriate recreational and sports activities, and holiday events.
- Learn how to respond effectively and confidently to the common problems that the child or youth may present.
- Communicate concerns and problems immediately in a compassionate fashion.

## SECONDARY AND TRANSITION YEARS

### Tips for the Family

- Prepare and plan for the secondary, transitional, and adult years.
- Work closely with school and adult services personnel in developing a transition plan.
- Develop a thoughtful and comprehensive transition plan that includes education, employment, housing, and use of leisure time.
- Become aware of all the services and resources that are available through state and national funding.
- Begin to develop plans for the individual's care and support over the lifespan.

### Tips for the General Education Classroom Teacher

- Be sure that appropriate steps have been taken to prepare the youth to return to school and related activities.
- Realize that there will be significant changes in the youth's functioning—academically, socially, and behaviorally.
- Work closely with members of the multidisciplinary team in developing appropriate schooling and employment experiences.
- Report any changes in behavior immediately to parents and other specialists within the school.

### Tips for School Personnel

- Determine what environmental changes need to be made.
- Employ teaching procedures that best fit the youth's current cognitive status and academic functioning.
- Consider having the youth gradually phased into a complete school day.
- Be prepared for anger, depression, and rebellion.
- Focus on the youth's current strengths.
- Help the youth develop appropriate compensatory skills.

### Tips for Neighbors, Friends, and Potential Employers

- Remember that the injury will significantly alter the youth's personality and functioning in many areas.
- Involve the youth in appropriate family, neighborhood, and community activities, particularly youth activities and parties.
- Use successful management procedures employed in the home and school settings.
- Become informed about the youth's capacities and interests.
- Work with vocational and special education personnel in providing employment explorations and part-time employment.

## ADULT YEARS

### Tips for the Family

- Begin developing appropriate independence skills throughout the school years.
- Determine early what steps can be taken to prepare the youth for meaningful part-time or full-time employment.
- Become thoroughly familiar with postsecondary education opportunities and adult services for individuals with disabilities.
- Explore various living and housing options early in the youth's secondary school years.
- Provide opportunities for the young adult to experience different kinds of living arrangements.

### Tips for Neighbors, Friends, and Employers

- Keep up a spirit of neighborliness.
- Create opportunities for the adult to be involved in age-relevant activities, including movies, sports events, going out to dinner, and so on.
- Work closely with educational and adult support services personnel in creating employment opportunities, monitoring performance on the job, and making appropriate adjustments.

## FIGURE 14.1

### Suggested School Reintegration Checklist

Student: _____     School/Grade: _____

Date of Injury: _____     Parent Name: _____     Phone #: _____

**1. IMMEDIATELY FOLLOWING INJURY**

A school representative will be assigned to the case by an administrator. The school representative will:

Contact parent(s) to:
- inquire about their child's condition
- obtain release for hospital contact (get release to and from school)

Contact the child's case manager at the hospital to:
- inform them of the school's concern

Meet with the child's classroom teacher(s) to:
- inform them of the child's condition
- obtain/review current educational records

**2. AFTER STUDENT'S CONDITION HAS STABILIZED**

The school representative will:

Arrange a meeting with the hospital care manager to:
- obtain information regarding the child's condition
- determine if/when to send schoolwork

**3. PRIOR TO DISCHARGE**

The school representative will:

Visit with student and rehabilitation staff

Obtain copies of hospital evaluations (psychological, educational, physical therapy/occupational therapy, speech)

Conduct in-service in school to:
- provide specific information about the school's condition
- provide more general information about TBI
- discuss potential modifications (ramp, wheelchair, lighting)

**4. IMMEDIATELY AFTER HOSPITAL DISCHARGE**

A school representative will:

Contact parent(s) to:
- determine if the child will be getting post-acute rehabilitation care
- set a tentative date for return to school if no further rehabilitation is being provided

Follow up with a hospital case manager to:
- get update on discharge condition/special needs (i.e., tracheotomy, ambulation)

Establish a TBI team and designate a case manager (if different from representative) to:
- develop a tentative plan for school reentry (consider need for environmental modifications, special education, 504, and related services)

**5. ARRIVAL AT SCHOOL**

The team will:
- assign further personnel to conduct initial evaluation and give feedback to teachers and parents
- further modify classroom environment to meet student's needs

**6. AFTER FIRST WEEKS AT SCHOOL**

The team will:
- reassess the student's needs and modify educational plan accordingly
- maintain contact with parents and teachers

SOURCE: From *Children and Adolescents with Traumatic Brain Injury: Reintegration Challenges in Educational Settings* (p. 202), by E. Clark, 1997, Austin, TX: Pro-Ed, Inc. Reprinted with permission.

liaison or case manager works with other medical and health personnel to make certain that the child or youth is safe and sufficiently healthy to leave the health care facility. The transition liaison also ensures that parents and teachers are adequately prepared to receive and care for the child (Klomes, 2000).

Students with traumatic or acquired brain injuries may return to one of several school placements, depending on their needs. Appropriate teaching activities include establishing high expectations, reducing stimuli and conditions that elicit challenging behaviors, using appropriate reductive techniques for stopping or significantly reducing aggressive or noncompliant behaviors, eliminating rewards for negative or problematic behaviors, providing precise feedback, giving students strategies for organizing information, and providing many opportunities for practice.

Educational services must be tailored to a student's specific needs. Effort should be directed at improving students' general behaviors, such as problem solving, planning, and developing insight. Teaching may also focus on appropriate social behaviors (performing in stressful situations, improving initiative taking, working with others, etc.), expressive and receptive language skills (word retrieval, event description, understanding instructions, reading nonverbal cues, etc.), and writing skills (sentence development, legibility, etc.) (see Table 14.4).

Some individuals with TBI are greatly assisted by software programs that allow them to operate computers with speech sounds and commands to produce letters, graphic materials, presentations, and spreadsheets.

The initial individualized education programs (IEPs) for students with brain injuries should be written for short periods of time, perhaps six to eight weeks. Moreover, these IEPs should be reviewed often to make adjustments based on the progress and growth of students. Often, students improve dramatically in the first year following their injuries. Children and youth with TBI generally experience the most gains in the first year following the injury, with little progress made thereafter. Flexibility and responsiveness on the part of teachers and other support staff are essential to the well-being of students with traumatic and acquired brain injuries.

For students who want to move on to postsecondary education, interdisciplinary team members may contribute significantly to the transition process. Critical factors include the physical accessibility of the campus, living arrangements, support for academic achievement, social and personal support systems, and career/vocational training and placement.

For students who might find it difficult to continue their schooling after high school, transition planning for employment is essential. Prior to leaving high school, these students with TBI should have skills associated with filling out job applications, interviewing for jobs, and participating in supervised work experiences. State vocational agencies also play key roles in assisting young people with TBI following high school. They provide services related to aptitude assessment, training opportunities after high school, and trial job placements (Fraser & Clemmons, 2000).

Collaboration and cooperation are the key factors in achieving success with individuals who have traumatic and acquired brain injuries. A great deal can be accomplished when families, students, and care providers come together, engage in appropriate planning, and work collaboratively (Wehman, 2001).

# Medical and Psychological Services

New medical technologies have revolutionized diagnostic and treatment procedures for traumatic and acquired brain injuries. In previous decades, the vast majority of these individuals died within a short time of their accidents. With the development

TABLE 14.4

## Representative Strategies for Developing Cognitive-Communicative Skills

| IMPAIRMENT | CLASSROOM BEHAVIORS | SKILLS AND TEACHING STRATEGIES |
|---|---|---|
| **GENERAL BEHAVIORS** | | |
| Decreased judgment | Is impulsive | Establish a system of verbal or nonverbal signals to cue the student to alter behavior (e.g., call the student's name, touch the student, use a written sign or hand signal). |
| Poor problem-solving skills | Does not carefully think through solutions to situations | To help develop problem-solving skills, ask questions designed to help the student identify the problem. Plan and organize implementation of a solution together. |
| **SOCIAL BEHAVIORS** | | |
| Subtle noncompliance with classroom rules and activities | Is withdrawn and unwilling to participate in group activities (e.g., work on a science project, small-group discussion)<br><br>Refuses to recite in class even when called upon | Help the student strengthen his or her self-concept. Begin to elicit responses from the student during individual activities and seat work when you can be assured that the student can answer correctly; gradually request occasional responses in front of the student's friends, then in small groups; repeat until the student feels comfortable participating in a large group. |
| Rudeness, silliness, immaturity | Makes nasty or inappropriate comments to fellow students and teachers<br><br>Laughs aloud during serious discussions or quiet seat work | Help the student develop better judgment by presenting "what if" situations and choices. Discuss the student's responses together.<br><br>Give the student opportunities to verbally express judgment and decision making regarding appropriate behavior as well as opportunities to role-play such behaviors. |
| **EXPRESSIVE LANGUAGE** | | |
| Tangential (rambling) communication | Tends to ramble without acknowledging the listener's interest or attention<br><br>May discuss the appropriate topic but not focus on the key concept (e.g., when asked to name the major food groups, the student might begin a discussion about growing crops) | When the student begins to digress from the topic, either provide a nonverbal cue or stop the student from continuing in front of classmates.<br><br>Teach the student to recognize nonverbal behaviors indicating lack of interest or desire to make a comment. (Work with this skill during private conversations with the student.)<br><br>Teach about the beginning, middle, and ending of stories.<br><br>Stop the student's response and restate the original question, focusing the student's attention on the key issues. |
| Word retrieval errors | Answers using many vague terms ("this," "that," "those things," "whatchamacallits")<br><br>Has difficulty providing answers in fill-in-the-blank tests | To improve word recall, teach the student to use association skills and to give definitions of words he or she cannot recall.<br><br>Teach memory strategies (rehearsal, association, visualization, etc.). |
| **RECEPTIVE LANGAUGE** | | |
| Inability to determine salient features of questions asked, information presented, or assignments read | Completes the wrong assignment (e.g., teacher requested that the class complete problems 9–12; this student completed problems 1–12) | Encourage the student to write assignments in a daily log. |
| Inability to read nonverbal cues | Is unaware that the teacher or other classmates do not want to be bothered while they are working. | To raise social awareness, use preestablished nonverbal cues to alert the student that the behavior is inappropriate. Explain what was wrong with the behavior and what would have been appropriate. |
| **WRITTEN LANGUAGE** | | |
| Simplistic sentence structure and syntactic disorganization | Uses sentences and chooses topics that are simplistic compared with expectations for age and grade; writes themes that are short and dry | Provide the student with worksheets that focus on vocabulary, grammar, and proofreading skills. |
| Decreased speed and accuracy; poor legibility | Is slower on timed tests than classmates | Accept that the student will take longer to complete assignments; reduce and alter the requirements. |

SOURCE: From "Creating an Effective Classroom Environment," by J. L. Blosser and R. DePomei in *Educational Dimensions of Acquired Brain Injury,* edited by R. C. Savage and G. F. Wolcott, 1994, pp. 413–451. Austin, TX: Pro-Ed, Inc. Reprinted by permission.

## F.T.

**F.T.** is a 15-year-old . . . boy with a history of a TBI 5 years ago. He was referred for a neuropsychological assessment by his school district because educators were unsure of how to manage F.T.'s academic and behavior problems. F.T. had recently entered their school district as a ninth grader, and he was failing all of his classes except for a D- in science and a B+ in physical education. He had particular problems with written expression, with following oral and written directions, and with identifying the main idea in materials presented to him. Teachers were also concerned about his short attention span, staring spells, and poor work completion. F.T. had received special education services under a diagnosis of learning disabilities in his previous school district. This consisted of 1 hour per day of resource room assistance to help him organize his assignments and complete his homework. Since he entered the new school, F.T.'s attendance has been adequate, and teachers perceived him as a friendly, outgoing young man. However, they were considering a secondary educational diagnosis of behavior disorder because of the disruption caused by his impulsive and off-task behaviors.

F.T. sustained a severe TBI in an amusement park accident at the age of 10 years. He experienced full cardiopulmonary arrest at the scene of the accident and remained in a coma for 3 days. His initial Glasgow Coma Scale score was 6. A computerized tomography (CT scan) of the brain showed a large left tempoparietal contusion, but he had no other significant injuries. Upon transfer to acute rehabilitation 15 days postinjury, F.T. displayed a dense right-side hemiparesis and could not talk, but he could follow simple one-step commands. During rehabilitation, he showed a rapid recovery of physical mobility, self-care skills, and basic language functioning. His attention span was extremely short, his short-term memory was poor, and he was impulsive and noncompliant in therapies.

Behaviorally, F.T. was perceived somewhat differently by his teachers and parents. The teachers and his father reported clinically significant problems with attention/concentration, work production, and noncompliance. In addition to these problems, F.T.'s mother also indicated significant concerns about social withdrawal; aggressive behaviors (arguing, fighting, mood swings, temper tantrums); and delinquent behaviors (associating with bad companions, stealing, swearing, and truancy). On a behavioral self-report measure, F.T. [exhibited] mild . . . problems with daydreaming and arguing, suggesting a lack of insight and self-awareness.

F.T. certainly had multiple risk factors that could lead to a poor long-term outcome. He experienced a severe head injury with persistent cognitive and behavioral sequelae that interfered with his ability to keep up with same-age peers, as indicated by neuropsychological testing and by the decline in his IQ scores over time. Prior to his TBI, he had experienced academic problems that were probably associated with his history of physical and sexual abuse. His home environment was chaotic, and litigation over the TBI fueled family conflict and divisions. His single mother had multiple stressors, including the injury of two of her children and severe financial problems, and she did not exhibit strong behavioral management or limit-setting skills. F.T.'s recovery from TBI was affected by frequent family moves and inconsistent (and sometimes inadequate) educational services as a consequence of educators' inexperience and limited educational resources.

### APPLICATION

1. What steps should be taken by medical and educational personnel in responding to F.T. and his particular needs?

2. What ongoing information should be delivered by the mother that would be helpful to F.T.'s teachers?

3. What ongoing information should be delivered by his teachers that would be helpful to F.T.'s mother?

4. How should other agencies and care providers in the community be involved with F.T. and his family?

SOURCE: From "Epilogue: An Ecological Systems Approach to Childhood Traumatic Injury," by J. E. Farmer. In *Childhood Traumatic Brain Injury: Diagnosis, Assessment, and Intervention*, edited by E. E. Bigler, E. Clark, & J. E. Farmer, 1997, pp. 177–190. Austin, TX: Pro-Ed, Inc.

---

of **computerized tomography (CT)** scans, intracranial pressure monitors, **magnetic resonance imaging (MRI)**, and the capacity to control bleeding and brain swelling, many individuals with traumatic brain injury survive. Also, CT scans of individuals without brain injuries now provide physicians and other health care providers with essential, normative information about the extent of the injury to the brain to compare with the uninjured brains of other individuals of the same age and gender.

Head injuries may be described in terms of the nature of the injury. Injuries include concussions, contusions, skull fractures, and epidural and subdural hemorrhages.

- *Concussions.* The most common effects of closed-head injuries, **concussions** occur most frequently in children and adolescents through contact sports such

**Computerized tomography (CT)**

An x-ray imaging technique by which computers create cross-sectional images of specific body areas or organs.

**Magnetic resonance imaging (MRI)**

A magnetic imaging technique by which computers create cross-sectional images of specific body areas or organs.

## Concussion

A jarring injury of the brain resulting in disturbance of cerebral function.

## Contusion

Extensive damage to the brain resulting in intense stupor. This condition is often derived from brutal shaking, violent blows, or other serious impacts to the head.

## Skull fracture

A break, crack, or split of the skull resulting from a violent blow or other serious impact to the head.

## Epidural hematoma

The collecting of blood between the skull and the covering of the brain, which puts pressure on vital brain structures.

## Subdural hematoma

The collecting of blood between the covering of the brain and the brain itself, resulting in pressure on vital brain structures.

as football, hockey, and martial arts. Children who display weakness on one side of the body or a dilated pupil may have a concussion and should be examined immediately by a physician.

- *Contusions.* This kind of injury is characterized by extensive damage to the brain, including laceration of the brain, bleeding, swelling, and bruising. The resulting effect of a **contusion** is intense stupor or coma. Individuals with contusions should be hospitalized immediately.

- *Skull fractures.* The consequences of **skull fractures** depend on the location, nature, and seriousness of the fracture. Unfortunately, some fractures are not easily detectable through radiologic examination. Injuries to the lower back part of the head are particularly troublesome and difficult to detect. These basilar skull fractures may set the stage for serious infections of the central nervous system. Immediate medical care is essential for skull fractures to determine the extent of the damage and to develop appropriate interventions.

- *Epidural and subdural hemorrhages.* Hemorrhaging or bleeding is the central feature of epidural and subdural hematomas. Hematomas are collections of blood, usually clotted. An **epidural hematoma** is caused by damage to an artery (a thick-walled blood vessel carrying blood from the heart) between the brain and the skull (see Figure 14.2). If this injury is not treated promptly and appropriately, the affected individual will die. A **subdural hematoma** is caused by damage to tiny veins that draw blood from the outer layer of the brain (cerebral cortex) to the heart. The aggregation of blood between the brain and its outer covering (dura) produces pressure that adversely affects the brain and its functioning (see Figure 14.3). If the subdural bleeding is left untreated, the result can be death.

Medical treatment of traumatic and acquired brain injury proceeds in stages. At the onset of the injury, medical personnel focus on maintaining the child's life, treat-

---

## FIGURE 14.2

### An Epidural Hematoma

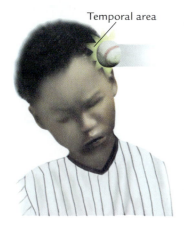

(a) A forceful injury occurs in the temporal area of the brain.

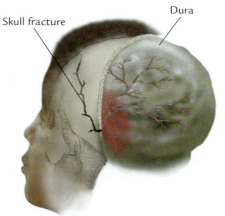

(b) The injury may result in a fractured skull, causing bleeding in the middle meningeal artery. Blood collects between the skull and the dura, a rough membrane covering the brain.

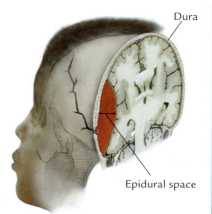

(c) As the blood collects, pressure builds on vital structures within the brain.

SOURCE: Adapted from "Common Neurological Disorders in Children," by Robert H. A. Haslam (p. 330) in R. H. A. Haslam & P. J. Valletutti (eds.), *Medical Problems in the Classroom.* Copyright 1996, Austin, TX: Pro-Ed, Inc. Reprinted by permission.

FIGURE 14.3

**A Subdural Hematoma**

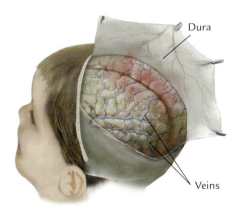

Dura

Veins

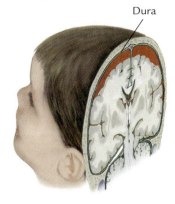

Dura

(a) Violently shaking or hitting a child may cause damage to the cerebral cortex.

(b) Trauma to the brain results in the rupturing of small veins.

(c) Blood gathers between the dura and the brain, resulting in pressure on vital brain structures.

SOURCE: Adapted from "Common Neurological Disorders in Children," by Robert H. A. Haslam (p. 332) in R. H. A. Haslam & P. J. Valletutti (eds.), *Medical Problems in the Classroom.* Copyright 1996, Austin, TX: Pro-Ed, Inc. Reprinted by permission.

ing the swelling and bleeding, minimizing complications, reducing the level of coma, and completing the initial neurologic examination. This stage of treatment is often characterized by strained interactions between physicians and parents. Many physicians are unable to respond satisfactorily to the overwhelming psychological needs of parents and family members because of the complex medical demands presented by the injured child. Other trained personnel—including social workers, psychologists, and clergy—should address the parents' and family's needs.

If the child remains in a coma, physical or occupational therapists may use special stimulation techniques to reduce the depth of the coma. If the child becomes agitated by stimuli in the hospital unit, such as visitors' conversations, noises produced by housecleaning staff, obtrusive light, or touching, steps may be taken to control or reduce the problem. As the injured individual comes out of the coma, orienting him or her to the environment becomes a priority. This may include explaining where the patient is located, introducing care providers, indicating where loved ones are, sharing what has happened since the injury, and responding to the individual's other

*The medical and psychological services available to Russian skater Elena Berezhnaya enabled her to successfully return to skating after receiving a traumatic head injury in practice. After months of care and rehabilitation, she and her partner were bronze medal winners in the XVIII Winter Olympics.*

FOCUS

5

Identify four common types of head injuries.

## Assistive Technology

### SOUNDS LIKE *STAR TREK!*

Dragon Naturally Speaking® is an award-winning piece of speech recognition software. Computers loaded with this software understand speech and voiced commands. An individual who does not have the dexterity, strength, or control to use a keyboard or mouse may now enter computer commands and other information by speaking into a microphone. Users may dictate letters, create visuals, develop presentations, complete spreadsheets, and even navigate the Internet!

### FOCUS 6

Describe five important elements of medical treatment for individuals with traumatic or acquired brain injuries.

questions. Many persons who have been injured do not remember the accident or the medical interventions administered.

The next stage of treatment helps the person relearn and perform preinjury skills and behaviors. This treatment may take time and considerable effort. Children are prepared gradually for return to their homes and appropriate school environments. Their families prepare as well, receiving ongoing support and counseling. Additionally, arrangements are also made for appropriate speech/language, physical, and occupational therapies and for any specialized teaching necessary.

Many individuals return to their homes, schools, or employment settings as vastly different people. These differences often take the shape of unpredictable or extreme expression of emotion. Furthermore, these individuals may have trouble recognizing and accepting their postinjury challenges and deficits (Bowe, 2000). The last stages of intervention focus on providing counseling and therapy to help the individual cope with the injury and its residual effects; help the family maintain the gains that have been achieved; terminating specific head injury services; and referring the person to community agencies, educational programs, and vocational rehabilitation for additional services as needed (Wehman, 2001).

# FOCUS REVIEW

**FOCUS 1**   Identify three key elements of traumatic brain injury.

- The brain is damaged by external forces that cause tearing, bruising, or swelling.
- Both primary and secondary injuries dramatically influence the individual's functioning in several areas, including psychosocial behavior, speech and language, cognitive performance, vision and hearing, and motor abilities.
- The brain injury often results in permanent disabilities.

**FOCUS 2**   Identify four general characteristics of individuals with traumatic or acquired brain injuries.

- Individuals with traumatic or acquired brain injuries often exhibit cognitive deficits, including problems with memory, concentration, attention, and problem solving.
- Speech and language problems are frequently evident, including word retrieval problems, slurred or unintelligible speech, and aphasia.
- These individuals may also present social and behavioral problems, including increased irritability, inability to suppress or manage socially inappropriate behaviors, low thresholds for frustration, and insensitivity to others.
- Neuromotor and physical problems may also be present, including impairments in eye–hand coordination, vision and hearing deficits, and paralysis.

**FOCUS 3**   Identify the most common causes of brain injury in children, youth, and adults.

- The most common causes of brain injury in young children are falls, neglect, and physical abuse.
- For children in the elementary grades, the most common causes are falls, pedestrian or bicycle accidents involving a motor vehicle, and sports.
- For high school students and adults, the most common causes are motor vehicle accidents and sports-related injuries.

**FOCUS 4**   Describe the focus of educational interventions for individuals with traumatic or acquired brain injuries.

- Educational interventions are directed at improving the general behaviors of the individual, including problem solving, planning, and developing insight; at building appropriate social behaviors such as working with others, suppressing inappropriate behaviors, and using appropriate etiquette; at developing expressive and receptive language skills, such as retrieving words, describing events, and understanding instructions; and at developing writing skills.
- Other academic skills relevant to the students' needs and developmental level of functioning are also taught.
- Transition planning for postsecondary education and training is also essential to the well-being of the individual with traumatic or acquired brain injury.

**FOCUS 5**   Identify four common types of head injuries.

- Common head injuries include concussions, contusions, skull fractures, and epidural and subdural hemorrhages.

**FOCUS 6**   Describe five important elements of medical treatment for individuals with traumatic or acquired brain injuries.

- The first stage of treatment is directed at preserving the individual's life, addressing swelling and bleeding, and minimizing complications.
- Once the individual regains consciousness or can benefit from more active therapies, the relearning of preinjury skills begins.
- The last stage focuses on preparing the individual to return to home, school, or work settings and on readying the individual to work with other health care and training providers.
- The last stage is also characterized by the provision of psychological services directed at helping individuals and their families cope with the injuries and their effects.
- Throughout all the stages of treatment, interdisciplinary collaboration and cooperation are essential to the individual's success.

## FURTHER READINGS

Pierangelo, R., & Giuliani, G. A. (2001). *What Every Teacher Should Know About Students with Special Needs: Promoting Success in the Classroom.* Champaign, IL: Research Press.

*This book is an easy-to-read primer about a variety of disabilities. Its quick tours help readers understand definitions, characteristics, educational implications, and classroom management strategies for working with children and youth with disabilities.*

Schoenbrodt, L. (2001). *Children with Traumatic Brain Injury.* Bethesda, MD: Woodbine House.

*This is a timely book for parents whose children have experienced traumatic injuries. It addresses pertinent questions that parents and others have about medical care, education, child management, speech and language development, and legal issues.*

Semrud-Clikeman, M. (2001). *Traumatic Brain Injury in Children and Adolescents: Assessment and Intervention.* New York: Guilford.

*This book is designed for educators, school psychologists, and other professionals who are interested in children and adolescents with traumatic brain injury. It provides basic information about neuroanatomy, family variables affecting recovery, assessment, and classroom interventions.*

Wehman, P. (2001). *Life Beyond the Classroom: Transition Strategies for Young People with Disabilities* (3rd ed.). Baltimore: Paul H. Brookes.

*This book highlights the strategies one might apply in transitioning a student with traumatic brain injuries and other disabilities to school settings or other environments following various treatment phases. It also discusses the various strategies one might use in helping young people with disabilities enter the work force.*

Wood, R. L., McMillan, T. M. (Eds.) (2001). *Neurobehavioural Disability and Social Handicap Following Traumatic Brain Injury.* Philadelphia: Psychology Press.

*This book explores the nature and impact of traumatic brain injuries, the role of families, assessment, rehabilitation, and the management of challenging behaviors. It is designed for medical and health care clinicians and professionals who work with individuals with traumatic brain injuries.*

## WEB RESOURCES

### Brain Injury Association of America

www.biausa.org

This website is a comprehensive source of information for individuals and families who are interested in learning more about brain injuries. The association consists of a national network of more than 40 state organizations that work together for the benefit of individuals who have brain injuries.

### ABLEDATA

www.abledata.com

This website is a premier source for information about assistive technology for children, youth, and adults. It is sponsored by the National Institute on Disability and Rehabilitation Research, U.S. Department of Education. The website describes a vast array of software and assistive devices that are useful to individuals with disabilities.

### Family Caregiver Alliance

www.caregiver.org

The Family Caregiver Alliance was founded in 1977 as a not-for-profit organization that focuses on helping families provide long-term care, at home, to individuals with disabilities and other challenging conditions. This website provides helpful information about caring for loved ones with Alzheimer's disease, stroke, traumatic brain injuries, and other debilitating cognitive disorders.

### National Institute of Disability Management and Research

www.nidmar.ca

The National Institute of Disability Management and Research, a Canadian organization, focuses on workplace reintegration. The institute seeks to help workers return to meaningful employment through training and education.

### Brain Injury Association of Kentucky

www.braincenter.org

This affiliate of the Brain Injury Association of America is a state-based organization that provides information about advocacy, treatment, research, and services for individuals with traumatic brain injury.

## BUILDING YOUR PORTFOLIO

If you are thinking about a career in special education, you should know that many states use national standards developed by the Council for Exceptional Children (CEC) to assess a teacher candidate's knowledge and skills for working with students with disabilities. See a complete listing of the ten CEC Content Standards on the inside front cover of this text.

### CEC Content Standards Addressed in Chapter 14

1. Foundations
2. Development and Characteristics of Learners
3. Individual Learning Differences
5. Learning Environments and Social Interactions
7. Instructional Planning
8. Assessment

### Assess Your Knowledge of the CEC Standards Addressed in Chapter 14

Some states require that teacher candidates develop a portfolio of products that demonstrate mastery of the CEC content standards. To assist in the development of products for this portfolio, you may wish to complete the following activities.

- Complete a written test of the chapter's content.

  *If your instructor requires a written test of your content knowledge for this chapter, keep a copy for your portfolio. A practice test on the information covered in this chapter is available through the companion website (www.ablongman.com.hardman8e) and the Student Study Guide.*

- Respond to the application questions for the Case Study "F. T."

  *Review the Case Study and respond in writing to the application questions. Keep a copy of the Case Study and your written response for your portfolio.*

- Complete the "Take a Stand" activity for the Debate Forum: "Firearms: Shouldn't We Protect Our Children and Youth?"

  *Read the Debate Forum in this chapter and then visit our companion website to complete the activity "Take a Stand." Keep a copy of this activity for your portfolio.*

- Participate in a community service learning activity.

  *Community service learning is a valuable way to enhance your learning experience. Visit our companion website for suggested community service learning activities that correspond to the information presented in this chapter. Develop a reflective journal of the service learning experience for your portfolio.*

## THEMES OF THE TIMES

Expand your knowledge of the concepts discussed in this chapter by reading current and historical articles from the *New York Times* by visiting the "Themes of the Times" section of the companion website: **www.ablongman.com/hardman8e.**

# Hearing Loss

### Quick Facts

Nearly 11 million people in the United States (6% of the population) have a significant irreversible hearing loss. Of those with a hearing loss, about 1 million are deaf. American Sign Language is the third most used language in the United States after English and Spanish. The first and oldest American school for the deaf was founded in 1817 in Hartford, Connecticut. Today, there are nearly 71,000 special education students between the ages of 6 and 21 with hearing impairments in America's schools. Gallaudet University in Washington, D.C., the world's only university in which all programs and services are specifically designed to accommodate deaf and hard of hearing students, has nearly 2,000 enrolled students. Gallaudet was founded in 1864 by an act of Congress, and its charter was signed by President Abraham Lincoln. (Deaf World Web, 2000; U.S. Department of Education, 2002)

### Strike Three . . . Y'er Out!!

Oblivious to jeering or cheering fans and focused on the slight movement of the ball to the left or right, Peter Rozynski finds solace behind the home plate where he calls balls and strikes as he sees them. Rozynski, an umpire [who is deaf], officiates high school softball games in New Jersey. He graduated from the New Jersey School for the Deaf in West Trenton, New Jersey, in 1970. He played junior varsity and varsity baseball at the New Jersey School for the Deaf where he was a student. Rozynski has been an umpire since 1988. Rozynski said of being an umpire, "The proper handling of any softball game demands me to hustle at all times. In addition, three factors are essential to my success: judgment, mechanics and techniques, and knowledge of the rules." There have been a few controversial calls, and Rozynski has had to tell coaches to put the call behind them and move on. (Feldman, 2003)

### Ted Nugent: No Trouble Being Heard, Just Trouble Hearing

No one has ever accused guitar showman and outdoor enthusiast Ted Nugent of being the strong silent type. The Motor City Madman is famous for his loud mouth and even louder concerts. But you might be surprised to learn that while the 51-year-old Nugent has no trouble being heard, he does have trouble hearing. "My left ear is only there for aesthetic purposes. It just balances my head so I don't fall over," jokes Nugent. "I've played over 5,000 concerts and have subjected myself via my cravings to massive sonic punishment. My left ear is beat to hell." . . . While Nugent's rock 'n' roll profession has certainly contributed to the decline of his aural capacity, a new study by the University of Wisconsin in Madison reveals that his passion for firearms may have been equally injurious. [The study found that people who engage in target shooting had a 57% higher risk for high-frequency hearing loss than those who did not shoot guns.] (Morgan & Shoop, 2000)

**FOCUS**

**PREVIEW:** To preview the central concepts of this chapter, read the focus questions located in the margins. Using these questions as a guide, ask yourself what you already know and what you want to learn.

# Tamika

Tamika Catchings is the all-star forward for the W.N.B.A.'s Indiana Fever.... She proudly admits to being an organization freak—in high school she would plan her outfits a month in advance. [Tamika] speaks with a slight speech impediment, as if she hadn't quite come out from under a shot of Novocain. She was born with fairly severe hearing loss in both ears, so she cannot hear certain tones, pitches, or sounds, like "ch" and "th," even in her own voice, an impairment that for years she tried, quite successfully, to hide from anyone outside her family. In third grade, fed up with the abuse from classmates, she tossed her hearing aids into a field and refused to wear new ones.

[Tamika's] hearing problem forced her to learn to read lips, which has left her with the habit of looking intently at anyone who is speaking to her (except while driving). For a professional athlete who was a four-time all-American in both high school and college, she can be surprisingly deferential. When Van Chancellor, the coach of the United States national women's basketball team, chewed out Catchings in practice by informing her that great players have to get back on defense, Catchings wrote him a letter thanking him for thinking of her as a great player.

Almost every program in the country recruited her, and Catchings wrote thank-you notes to each of] the 200 schools that contacted her. ("For me not to say anything would have been selfish," she says.) But she had wanted to go to [the University of Tennessee since eighth grade, when she caught a glimpse of the Lady Vols coach, Pat Summitt, on TV. Summitt is perhaps the one on-court presence in basketball who is more intense than [Tamika]— she has been known to dent her rings by pounding her hands on the hardwood during a particularly trying game. She also demands that her players buy daily planners and schedule their days in minute increments.

[Tamika] had a rough start in Knoxville. "When I would say anything to her in practice, it would break her heart," Summitt recalls. Soon, however, Catchings bloomed under Summitt's exacting system. She already possessed a remarkably well-rounded game—she once rang up a quintuple double in high school—but Summitt required Catchings to learn to play at more than one speed. "We had to slow her down," Summitt says.

Summitt also discovered that her star freshman wasn't comprehending much of what she was being told, especially in loud arenas when she was standing behind the coach. (As they returned to the court after a time-out, [Tamika] would ask a teammate to repeat what Summitt had said.) Summitt asked Catchings to start using a hearing aid. The difference on-court was minimal—"Everything was just magnified," [Tamika] says—but those around her noticed an immediate change in her confidence and ability to communicate. "It made a huge difference," Harvey Catchings says. For the first time in 10 years, she could hear herself speak clearly.

SOURCE: From "Elevated: Tamika Catchings Will Not Let Her Niceness, or Her Deafness, Prevent Her from Becoming the Best Player in the W.N.B.A.," by M. Adams, *New York Times Magazine*, May 25, 2003, pp. 26–29. Copyright 2003, Mark Adams. Reprinted by permission.

Although Tamika from the opening Snapshot is unable to hear many sounds, her life is one of independence, success, and fulfillment. For Tamika, and for many people who are deaf or hard of hearing, the obstacles presented by the loss of hearing are not insurmountable.

In a world often controlled by sound and spoken language, the ability to hear and speak can be an important link in the development of human communication. Children who can hear learn to talk by listening to those around them. Everyday communication systems depend on sound. What would it be like to live in a world that is silent? People talk, but you hear nothing. The television and movie screens are lit up with moving pictures, but you can't hear and thereby understand what is going on. You see your friends enjoying their favorite music, but much of that experience has no meaning to you. A fire engine's siren wails as it moves through traffic, but you are oblivious to its warning. To people with hearing, the thought of such a world can be very frightening. To those without hearing, it is quite simply their world—a place that can be very lonely, frustrating, and downright discriminatory one day, and in the next bring joy, fulfillment, and a life of endless possibilities that is no different from those experienced by "hearing people." The National Academy on an Aging Society (2003) indicated that in comparison to those with "normal" hearing, people with a hearing loss are less likely to participate in social activities; are less satisfied with their life; express greater dissatisfaction with their friendships, family life, health, and financial situation; are less healthy; and are underemployed.

People with a hearing loss are able to learn about the world around them in any number of ways, such as lipreading, gestures, pictures, and writing. Some are able to use their residual hearing with the assistance of a hearing aid. For others, a hearing aid doesn't help because it only makes distorted sounds louder. To express themselves, some people prefer to use their voices; others prefer to use a visual sign language. Most people with a hearing loss use a combination of speech and signing.

People with a hearing loss, such as Tamika from our opening snapshot, may seek and find success in the hearing world. Others seek to be part of a Deaf community or Deaf culture to share a common language (American Sign Language) and customs. In a Deaf culture, those within the community share heritages and traditions. People often marry others who are deaf from within the community. They also have a shared literature and participate in the Deaf community's political, business, arts, and sports programs. People in the Deaf community do not see the loss of hearing as a disability. From their perspective, being deaf is not an impairment and should not be looked upon as a pathology or disease that requires treatment.

# The Hearing Process

**Audition** is the act or sense of hearing. The auditory process involves the transmission of sound to a receiver via the vibration of an object or medium. The process originates with a vibrator—such as a string, reed, membrane, or column of air—that causes displacement of air particles. To become sound, a vibration must have a medium to carry it. Air is the most common carrier, but vibrations can also be carried by metal, water, and other substances. The displacement of air particles by the vibrator produces a pattern of circular waves that move away from the source.

This movement, which is referred to as a sound wave, can be illustrated by imagining the ripples that result when a pebble is dropped in a pool of water. Sound waves are patterns of pressure that alternately push together and pull apart in a spherical expansion. Sound waves are carried through a medium (such as air) to a receiver. The human ear is one of the most sensitive receivers there is. It can be activated by incredibly small amounts of pressure and is able to distinguish more than half a million different sounds. The ear is the mechanism through which sound is collected, processed, and transmitted to a specific area in the brain that decodes the sensations into meaningful language. The anatomy of the hearing mechanism is discussed in terms of the outer ear, middle ear, and inner ear. These structures are illustrated in Figure 15.1.

## The Outer Ear

The outer ear consists of a cartilage structure on the side of the head called the auricle, or pinna, and an outer ear canal referred to as the meatus. The only outwardly visible part of the ear, the auricle, is attached to the skull by three ligaments. Its purpose is to collect sound waves and funnel them into the meatus. The meatus secretes a wax called cerumen, which protects the inner structures of the ear by trapping foreign materials and lubricating the canal and eardrum. The eardrum, or tympanic membrane, is located at the inner end of the canal between the outer and middle ear. The concave membrane is positioned in such a manner that, when struck by sound waves, it can vibrate freely.

## The Middle Ear

The inner surface of the eardrum is located in the air-filled cavity of the middle ear. This surface consists of three small bones that form the **ossicular chain**: the malleus, incus, and stapes, which are often referred to as the hammer, anvil, and stirrup because of similarities in shape to these common objects. The three bones transmit the vibrations from the external ear through the cavity of the middle ear to the inner ear.

**FOCUS 1**

Describe how sound is transmitted through the human ear.

**Audition**

The act or sense of hearing.

**Ossicular chain**

The three small bones, the malleus, incus, and stapes (or hammer, anvil, and stirrup), that transmit vibrations through the middle-ear cavity to the inner ear.

FIGURE 15.1

**Structure of the Ear**

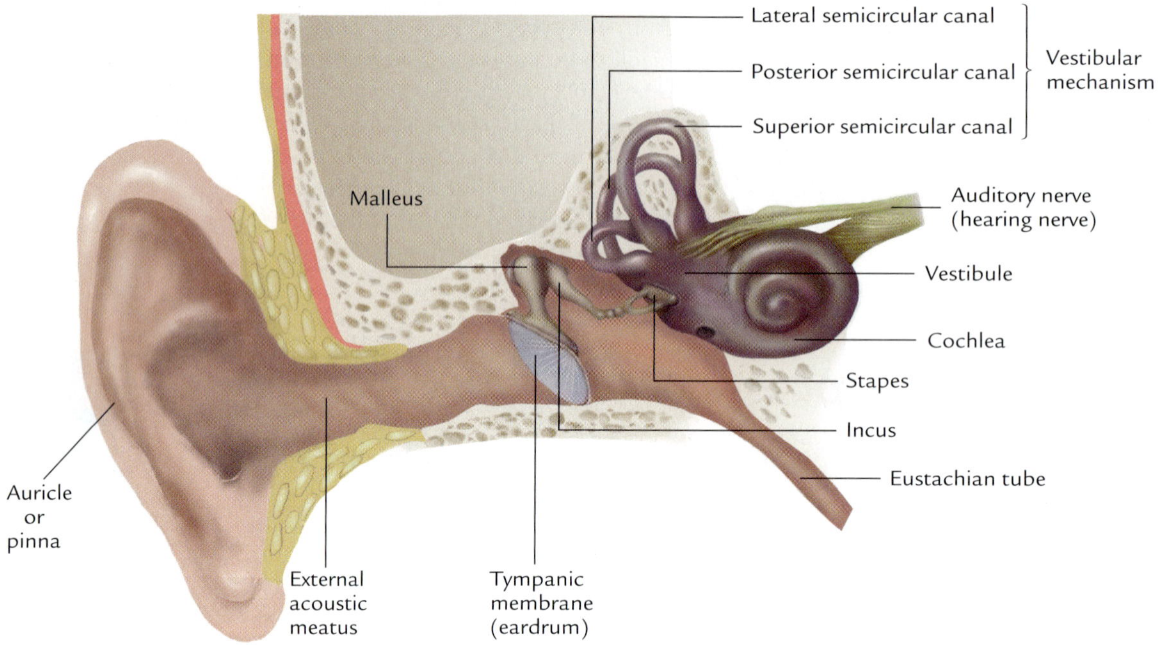

The **eustachian tube**, which extends from the throat to the middle-ear cavity, equalizes the air pressure on the eardrum with that of the outside by controlling the flow of air into the middle-ear cavity. Although air conduction is the primary avenue through which sound reaches the inner ear, conduction can also occur through the bones of the skull. The patterns of displacement produced in the inner ear are similar in both kinds of conduction.

### The Inner Ear

The inner ear consists of a multitude of intricate passageways. The cochlea lies horizontally in front of the vestibule (a central cavity where sound enters directly from the middle ear); here it can be activated by movement in the ossicular chain. The cochlea is filled with fluid similar in composition to cerebral spinal fluid. The cochlea contains highly specialized cells that translate vibrations into nerve impulses that are sent directly to the brain.

The other major structure within the inner ear is the **vestibular mechanism**, containing the semicircular canals that control balance. The semicircular canals have enlarged portions at one end and are filled with fluid that responds to head movement. The vestibular mechanism integrates sensory input passing to the brain and helps the body maintain equilibrium. Motion and gravity are detected through this mechanism, allowing the individual to differentiate between sensory input associated with body movement and input coming from the external environment. Whenever the basic functions of the vestibular mechanism or any of the structures in the external, middle, and inner ear are interrupted, hearing loss may occur.

## Definitions and Classification

Two terms, *deaf* and *hard of hearing* (or *partial hearing*), are commonly used to describe the severity of a person's hearing loss. *Deaf* is often overused and misunder-

**Eustachian tube**

A structure that extends from the throat to the middle-ear cavity and controls air flow into the cavity.

**Vestibular mechanism**

A structure in the inner ear containing three semicircular canals filled with fluid. It is sensitive to movement and assists the body in maintaining equilibrium.

stood and is commonly applied to describe a wide variety of hearing loss. However, as discussed in this section, the term should be used in a more precise fashion.

## Definitions

Deafness and hearing loss may be defined according to the degree of hearing impairment, which is determined by assessing a person's sensitivity to loudness (sound intensity) and pitch (sound frequency). The unit used to measure sound intensity is the decibel (dB); the range of human hearing is approximately 0 to 130 dB. Sounds louder than 130 dB (such as those made by jet aircraft at 140 dB) are extremely painful to the ear. Conversational speech registers at 40 to 60 dB, loud thunder at about 120 dB, and a rock concert at about 110 dB.

The frequency of sound is determined by measuring the number of cycles that vibrating molecules complete per second. The unit used to express cycles per second is the **hertz (Hz)**. The higher the frequency, the higher the hertz. The human ear can hear sounds ranging from 20 to approximately 15,000 Hz. The pitch of speech sounds ranges from 300 to 4,000 Hz, whereas the pitches of the sounds that can be made on a piano keyboard range from 27.5 to 4,186 Hz. Although the human ear can hear sounds at the 15,000-Hz level, the vast majority of sounds in our environment range from 300 to 4,000 Hz.

**DEAF AND HARD OF HEARING.**   Deafness means hearing loss in the extreme—the loss of 90 dB or greater. Even with the use of hearing aids or other forms of amplification, for people who are deaf the primary means for developing language and communication is through the visual channel. **Deafness**, as defined by the Individuals with Disabilities Education Act (IDEA), means "a hearing impairment which is so severe that the child is impaired in processing linguistic information through hearing, with or without amplification, which adversely affects educational performance" (IDEA, 34 C.F.R. 300.7).

A person who is deaf is most often described as someone who cannot hear sound. Consequently, the individual is unable to understand human speech. Many people who are deaf have enough residual hearing to recognize sound at certain frequencies, but they still may be unable to determine its meaning.

For persons defined as **hard of hearing**, audition is deficient but remains somewhat functional. Individuals who are hard of hearing have enough residual hearing that, with the use of a hearing aid, they are able to process human speech auditorily.

The distinction between being deaf and being hard of hearing, assessed on the basis of the functional use of residual hearing, is not as clear as many traditional definitions imply. New breakthroughs in the development of hearing aids, as well as improved diagnostic procedures, have enabled many children labeled as deaf to use their hearing functionally under limited circumstances.

Two other factors involved in the assessment of hearing loss are the age of the individual at onset and the anatomical site of the loss.

**AGE OF ONSET.**   Hearing loss may be present at birth (congenital) or acquired at any time during life. **Prelingual loss** occurs prior to the age of 2, or before speech development. **Postlingual loss** occurs at any age following speech acquisition. In nine out of ten children, deafness occurs at birth or prior to the child's learning to speak. The distinction between a congenital and an acquired hearing loss is important. The age of onset will be a critical variable in determining the type and extent of interventions necessary to minimize the effect of the individual's disability. This is particularly true in relation to speech and language development. A person who is born with hearing loss has significantly more challenges, particularly in the areas of communication and social adaptation (Chouard, 1997; Magnuson, 2000).

**ANATOMICAL SITE OF THE HEARING LOSS.**   The two primary types of hearing loss, in terms of anatomical location, are peripheral problems and central auditory problems. There are three types of peripheral hearing loss: conductive,

**FOCUS 2**

Distinguish between the terms *deaf* and *hard of hearing*.

**FOCUS 3**

Why is it important to consider age of onset and anatomical site when defining a hearing loss?

**Hertz (Hz)**

A unit used to measure the frequency of sound in terms of the number of cycles that vibrating molecules complete per second.

**Deafness**

A hearing loss greater than 90 dB. Individuals who are deaf have vision as their primary input and cannot understand speech through the ear. As defined by IDEA, deafness means a hearing impairment so severe that the child is impaired in procesing linguistic information through hearing, which adversely affects educational performance.

**Hard of hearing**

A term used to describe individuals with a sense of hearing that is deficient but somewhat functional.

**Prelingual loss**

Hearing impairments occurring prior to the age of 2, or before speech development.

**Postlingual loss**

Hearing impairments occurring at any age following speech development.

sensorineural, and mixed. A **conductive hearing loss** results from poor conduction of sound along the passages leading to the sense organ (inner ear). The loss may result from a blockage in the external canal, as well as from an obstruction interfering with the movement of the eardrum or ossicle. The overall effect is a reduction or loss of loudness. A conductive loss can be offset by amplification (hearing aids) and medical intervention. Surgery has proved to be effective in reducing or even restoring a conductive loss.

A **sensorineural hearing loss** is a result of an abnormal sense organ and a damaged auditory nerve. A sensorineural loss may distort sound, affecting the clarity of human speech, and cannot presently be treated adequately through medical intervention. A sensorineural loss is generally more severe than a conductive loss and is permanent. Losses of greater than 70 dB are usually sensorineural and involve severe damage to the inner ear. One common way to determine whether a loss is conductive or sensorineural is to administer an air and bone conduction test. An individual with a conductive loss would be unable to hear a vibrating tuning fork held close to the ear, because of blocked air passages to the inner ear, but might be able to hear the same fork applied to the skull as well as someone with normal hearing would. An individual with a sensorineural loss would not be able to hear the vibrating fork, regardless of its placement. This test is not always accurate, however, and must therefore be used with caution. **Mixed hearing loss**, a combination of conductive and sensorineural problems, can also be assessed through the use of an air and bone conduction test. In the case of a mixed loss, abnormalities are evident in both tests.

Although most hearing losses, such as conductive and sensorineural problems, are peripheral, some occur where there is no measurable peripheral loss. This type of loss, referred to as a **central auditory disorder**, occurs when there is a dysfunction in the cerebral cortex. The cerebral cortex, the outer layer of gray matter of the brain, governs thought, reasoning, memory, sensation, and voluntary movement. Consequently, a central auditory problem is not a loss in the ability to hear sound but, rather, a disorder of symbolic processes, including auditory perception, discrimination, comprehension of sound, and language development (expressive and receptive).

## Classification

Hearing loss may be classified in terms of the severity of the condition. Table 15.1 illustrates a symptom severity classification system and presents information about a child's ability to understand speech patterns at the various severity levels.

Classification systems based solely on a person's degree of hearing loss should be used with great caution when determining appropriate services and supports. These systems do not reflect the person's capabilities, background, or experience; they merely suggest parameters for measuring a physical defect in auditory function. As a young child, for example, Tamika from the opening Snapshot was diagnosed as having a hearing loss in both ears, yet throughout her life she adjusted to both school and community experiences. She went on to college and is now pursuing a successful career as a professional basketball player in the W.N.B.A. Clearly, many factors beyond the severity of the hearing loss affect the individual's potential. General intelligence, emotional stability, scope and quality of early education and training, the family environment, and the occurrence of other disabilities must also be considered.

# Prevalence

Hearing loss gets worse over time and increases dramatically with age. Estimates of hearing loss in the United States range as high as 28 million people. Of these 28 million, approximately 11 million people have significant irreversible hearing loss, and

**FOCUS 4**

What are the estimated prevalence and causes of hearing loss?

**Conductive hearing loss**

A hearing loss resulting from poor conduction of sound along the passages leading to the sense organ.

**Sensorineural hearing loss**

A hearing loss resulting from an abnormal sense organ (inner ear) and a damaged auditory nerve.

**Mixed hearing loss**

A hearing loss resulting from a combination of conductive and sensorineural problems.

**Central Auditory Disorder**

A hearing loss that occurs in the cerebral cortex of the brain.

TABLE 15.1

## Classification of Hearing Loss

| HEARING LOSS IN DECIBELS (DB) | CLASSIFICATION | EFFECT ON ABILITY TO UNDERSTAND SPEECH |
|---|---|---|
| 0–15 | Normal hearing | None |
| 15–25 | Slight hearing loss | Minimal difficulty with soft speech |
| 25–40 | Mild hearing loss | Difficulty with soft speech |
| 40–55 | Moderate hearing loss | Frequent difficulty with normal speech |
| 56–70 | Moderate to severe hearing loss | Occassional difficulty with loud speech |
| 71–90 | Severe hearing loss | Frequent difficulty with loud speech |
| >91 | Profound hearing loss | Near total or total loss of hearing |

1 million are deaf. Only 5% of people with hearing loss are under the age of 17. Nearly 43% are over the age of 65, a figure that assumes great significance when we consider that only 12% of the general population is over 65 (Deaf World Web, 2000; National Academy on an Aging Society, 2003). Men are more likely than women to have a hearing loss; Caucasians are overrepresented among people with a hearing loss; and prevalence of hearing loss decreases as family income and education increase (National Academy on an Aging Society, 2003).

The U.S. Department of Education (2002) indicated that 70,767 students defined as having a hearing impairment between the ages of 6 and 21 were receiving special education services in U.S. schools in 2000–2001. These students account for approximately .11% of all school-age students. It is important to note that these figures represent only those students who receive special services; a number of students with hearing loss who could benefit from additional services do not receive them. Of the students with a hearing loss who were receiving special education, 40% were being served in general education classrooms for at least 80% of the school day. This is nearly double the number of students in these classrooms a decade ago. Another 44% spent at least a part of their day in a general education classroom; 7% attended separate public or private day schools for students with a hearing loss; and 8.6% were in public or private residential living facilities (U.S. Department of Education, 2002).

# Causation

A number of congenital (existing at birth) or acquired factors may result in a hearing loss. Approximately one in a thousand children is born deaf because of factors associated with heredity, maternal rubella (German measles), or drugs taken during pregnancy. Substance abuse, disease, and constantly being subjected to loud noises are all causes of hearing loss. Loss of hearing is also a normal part of the aging process; it begins as early as the teen years, when we lose some of the high-frequency hearing we had in childhood.

## Congenital Factors

**HEREDITY.** Although more than 200 types of deafness have been related to hereditary factors, the cause of 33% of prelingual hearing loss remains unknown (Center for Assessment and Demograhic Studies, 2002). One of the most common diseases affecting the sense of hearing is **otosclerosis**. The cause of this disease is unknown, but it is generally believed to be hereditary and is manifested most often in early adulthood. About 10% of adults have otosclerosis. It can be passed from one generation to the next but may not manifest itself for several generations.

### Otosclerosis

A disease of the ear characterized by destruction of the capsular bone in the middle ear and the growth of a web-like bone that attaches to the stapes. The stapes is restricted and unable to function properly.

The disease is characterized by destruction of the capsular bone in the middle ear and by the growth of web-like bone that attaches to the stapes, rendering it unable to function properly. Hearing loss results in about 15% of all cases of otosclerosis and at twice the rate for females as for males. Victims of otosclerosis suffer from high-pitched throbbing or ringing sounds known as **tinnitus**, a condition associated with disease of the inner ear. There is no specific treatment or medication that will improve the hearing in people with otosclerosis. Surgery (stapedectomy) may be recommended when the stapes (stirrup) bone is involved.

**PRENATAL DISEASE.** Several conditions, though not inherited, can result in sensorineural loss. The major cause of congenital deafness is infection; rubella, cytomegalovirus (CMV), and toxoplasmosis are the most common in this regard. The rubella epidemic of 1963–1965 dramatically increased the incidence of deafness in the United States. During the 1960s, approximately 10% of all congenital deafness was associated with women contracting rubella during pregnancy. For about 40% of the individuals who are deaf, the cause is rubella. About 50% of all children with rubella acquire a severe hearing loss. Most hearing losses caused by rubella are sensorineural, although a small percentage may be mixed. In addition to hearing loss, children who have had rubella sometimes acquire heart disease (50%), cataracts or glaucoma (40%), and mental retardation (40%). Since the advent of the rubella vaccine, the elimination of this disease has become a nationwide campaign, and the incidence of rubella has decreased dramatically.

**Congenital cytomegalovirus (CMV)** is a viral infection that spreads through close contact with another person who is shedding the virus in body secretions. It is also spread by blood transfusions and from a mother to her newborn infant. CMV is the most frequently occurring virus among newborns, about 40,000 of whom contract the disease each year. CMV disease is characterized by jaundice, microcephaly, hemolytic anemia, mental retardation, hepatosplenomegaly (enlargement of the liver and spleen), and hearing loss. Although no vaccine is currently available to treat CMV, some preventive measures can be taken, such as ensuring safe blood transfusions and good hygiene and avoiding contact with persons who have the virus (Pediatric Bulletin, 2000). CMV is detectable *in utero* through amniocentesis.

**Congenital toxoplasmosis infection** is characterized by jaundice and anemia, but frequently the disease also results in central nervous system disorders (e.g., seizures, hydrocephalus, microcephaly). Approximately 15% of infants born with this disease are deaf.

Other factors associated with congenital sensorineural hearing loss include maternal Rh-factor incompatibility and the use of ototoxic drugs. Maternal Rh-factor incompatibility does not generally affect a firstborn child, but as antibodies are produced during subsequent pregnancies, multiple problems can result, including deafness. Fortunately, deafness as a result of Rh-factor problems is no longer common. Since the advent of an anti-Rh gamma globulin (RhoGAM) in 1968, the incidence of Rh-factor incompatibility has significantly decreased. When this substance is injected into the mother within the first 72 hours after the birth of the first child, she does not produce antibodies that harm future unborn infants.

Ototoxic drugs are so labeled because of their harmful effects on the sense of hearing. If taken during pregnancy, these drugs can result in a serious hearing loss in the infant. Congenital sensorineural loss can also be caused by congenital syphilis, maternal chicken pox, anoxia, and birth trauma.

A condition known as **atresia** is a major cause of congenital conductive hearing loss. Congenital aural atresia results when the external auditory canal is either malformed or completely absent at birth. A congenital malformation may lead to an accumulation of cerumen, which is a wax that hardens and blocks incoming sound waves from being transmitted to the middle ear.

**Tinnitus**

High-pitched throbbing or ringing sounds in the ear, associated with disease of the inner ear.

**Congenital cytomegalovirus (CMV)**

A viral infection that spreads through close contact with another person who is shedding the virus in body secretions.

**Congenital toxoplasmosis infection**

An infection that is characterized by jaundice and anemia and frequently also results in central nervous system disorders.

**Atresia**

The absence of a normal opening or cavity.

## Acquired Factors

**POSTNATAL DISEASE.**   One of the most common causes of hearing loss in the post-natal period is infection. Postnatal infections—such as measles, mumps, influenza, typhoid fever, and scarlet fever—are all associated with hearing loss. Meningitis, an inflammation of the membranes that cover the brain and spinal cord, is a cause of severe hearing loss in school-age children. Sight loss, paralysis, and brain damage are further complications of this disease. The incidence of meningitis has declined, however, with the development of antibiotics and chemotherapy.

Another problem that may result from postnatal infection is known as **otitis media**, an inflammation of the middle ear. This condition, which results from severe colds that spread from the eustachian tube to the middle ear, is the most common cause of conductive hearing loss in younger children. Otitis media ranks second to the common cold as the health problem most often seen in preschool children. Three out of every four children have had at least one episode by the time they reach 3 years of age. The disease is difficult to diagnose, especially in infancy, at which time symptoms are often absent. Otitis media has been found to be highly correlated with hearing problems (National Institute on Deafness and Other Communication Disorders, 2000a).

**ENVIRONMENTAL FACTORS.**   Environmental factors—including extreme changes in air pressure caused by explosions, physical abuse of the cranial area, impact from foreign objects during an accident, and loud music—also contribute to acquired hearing loss. Loud noise is rapidly becoming one of the major causes of hearing problems, for about 30 million people are subjected to dangerous levels of noise in everyday life (National Institute on Deafness and Other Communication Disorders, 2000a). All of us are exposed to hazardous noise, such as the sound of jet engines and loud music, more often than ever before. With the increasing use of headphones, such as those on portable compact disc or DVD players, many people (particularly adolescents) are subjected to damaging noise levels. Occupational noise (e.g., from jackhammers, tractors, and sirens) is now the leading cause of sensorineural hearing loss. Other factors associated with acquired hearing loss include degenerative processes in the ear that may be caused by aging, cerebral hemorrhages, allergies, and intercranial tumors.

**Otitis media**

An inflammation of the middle ear.

*Loud noise is a leading cause of hearing problems. Adolescents are subjected to damaging noise levels when headphones on CD or DVD players are turned up too high.*

**FOCUS 5**

Describe the basic intelligence, speech and language skills, educational achievement, and social development associated with people who are deaf or hard of hearing.

# Characteristics

The effects of hearing loss on the learning or social adjustment of individuals range from the far-reaching, as in the case of prelingual sensorineural deafness, to the quite minimal, as in the case of a mild postlingual conductive loss. Fortunately, prevention, early detection, and intervention have recently been emphasized, resulting in a much improved prognosis for individuals who are deaf or hard of hearing.

## Intelligence

Research on the intellectual characteristics of children with hearing loss has suggested that the distribution of IQ scores for these individuals is similar to that of hearing children (Moores, 2001; Schirmer, 2000). Findings suggested that intellectual development for people with hearing loss is more a function of language development than of cognitive ability. Any difficulties in performance appear to be closely associated with speaking, reading, and writing the English language but are not related to level of intelligence. For example, children who use sign language have to divide their attention between the signs and the instructional materials. Although the child may seem to be learning more slowly, the reality may be that the child simply needs more time to process the information.

## Speech and English Language Skills

Speech and English language skills are the areas of development most severely affected for those with a hearing loss, particularly for children who are born deaf. These children develop speech at a slower pace than their peers with normal hearing, and thus they are at greater risk for emotional difficulties and isolation from peers and family (Kaland & Salvatore, 2003). The effects of a hearing loss on English language development vary considerably. For children with mild and moderate hearing losses, the effect may be minimal. Even for individuals born with moderate losses, effective communication skills are possible because the voiced sounds of conversational speech remain audible. Although individuals with moderate losses cannot hear unvoiced sounds and distant speech, English language delays can be prevented if the hearing loss is diagnosed and treated early (Schirmer, 2000). The majority of people with hearing loss are able to use speech as the primary mode for English language acquisition.

For the person who is congenitally deaf, most loud speech is inaudible, even with the use of the most sophisticated hearing aids. These people are unable to receive information through speech unless they have learned to lip-read. Sounds produced by the person who is deaf may be extremely difficult to understand. Children who are deaf exhibit significant problems in articulation, voice quality, and tone discrimination. Even as early as 8 months of age, babies who are deaf appear to babble less than babies who can hear. One way to help these babies develop language is to provide early and extensive training in English language production and comprehension. Another approach is to teach them sign language long before they learn to speak. (See the nearby Reflect on This, "A New Language for Baby.")

## Educational Achievement

The educational achievement of students with a hearing loss may be significantly delayed, compared to that of students who can hear. Students who are deaf or have a partial hearing loss have considerable difficulty succeeding in an educational system that depends primarily on the spoken word and written language to transmit knowledge. Low achievement is characteristic of students who are deaf (Kuntze, 1998; Schirmer, 2000); they average three to four years below their age-appropriate grade levels. Reading is the academic area most negatively affected for students with a

## A NEW LANGUAGE FOR BABY

Languishing in front of the tube, watching a gripping episode of *Teletubbies*, a baby of 10 months waves down Mom and signals for a bottle of the good stuff. No crying, no fuss. He just moves his hands in a pantomime of milking a cow—the international sign for *milk*. Mom smiles, signs back her agreement, and fetches Junior's bottle. No, this is not science fiction, but a portrayal of what's now possible at a U.S. university research facility where babies as young as 9 months old are taught sign language, long before they can speak. In a pilot program at Ohio State University, infants and their teachers learned to use a number of specific signs from American Sign Language to communicate with each other. Researcher Kimberlee Whaley says parents, when they think about it, won't be surprised to hear that children can communicate physically, before they can do so verbally. "Think of an infant raising his or her hands up in the air," says Ms. Whaley. "What does the baby want? To be picked up, and we all recognize that."

What we didn't recognize is that kids also have the cognitive ability, and the motor skills, to sign for simple words, such as *eat, more, stop,* and *share.*

It's almost spooky to think that babies who aren't even walking yet are capable of basic understanding and communication. That's not the half of it, says Dr. Whaley. She says it's not unusual for babies to teach the signs to adults who have forgotten them. It happened to Dr. Whaley when one baby girl indignantly reminded the researcher of the sign for *juice.* "I felt about two inches tall," said Dr. Whaley, an associate professor of human development and family science.

The sign language, she says, has allowed for much more effective communication between teachers and infants. "It is so much easier for our teachers to work with 12-month-olds who can sign that they want their bottle, rather than just cry and have us try to figure out what they want. This is a great way for infants to express their needs before they can verbalize them."

It's interesting, too, that some babies will grunt to be noticed and then use sign language to get more specific about what they want to say, she says.

The researchers are embarking on a larger, two-year study and hope to answer questions raised by the early study: How early can babies learn sign language? And is there a gender difference? Girls appear to learn or use sign language more easily. Dr. Whaley thinks children of 6 or 7 months, who are able to sit up on their own, will learn basic signs.

But what about at night? What happens to a hungry or wet baby when Mom and Dad are asleep? "They revert to crying," Dr. Whaley says.

SOURCE: From "A New Language for Baby," by S. McKeen, *The Ottawa Citizen,* February 26, 1999. Available: www.deafworldweb.org/pub/b/baby.news99.html

---

hearing loss. Any hearing loss, whether mild or profound, appears to have detrimental effects on reading performance (Gallaudet Research Institute, 2000; Kuntz, 1998). Students who are deaf obtain their highest achievement scores in reading during the first three years of school, but by third grade, reading performance is surpassed by both arithmetic and spelling performance. By the time students who are deaf reach adolescence (age 13), their reading performance is equivalent to that of about a third grade child with normal hearing (Gallaudet Research Institute, 2000).

To counteract the difficulty with conventional reading materials, specialized instructional programs have been developed for students with a hearing loss (McAnally, Rose, & Quigley, 1999). One such program is the Reading Milestones series (Quigley & King, 1985), which uses content that focuses on the interests and experiences of children with a hearing loss, while incorporating linguistic controls: careful pacing of new vocabulary, clear identification of syntactic structures, and movement from simple to complex in introducing new concepts (e.g., idioms, inferences). For two nearly decades, Reading Milestones has been the most widely used reading program for students who are deaf.

### Social Development

A hearing loss modifies a person's capacity to receive and process auditory stimuli. People who are deaf or have a partial hearing loss receive a reduced amount of auditory information. That information is also distorted, compared to the auditory input received by those with normal hearing. Thus the perceptions of auditory information by people with a hearing loss, particularly those who are deaf,

When 20-year-old Terence Parkin arrived at the Sydney 2000 Olympic Games, his goal was to make his mark for South Africa and show the world what people who are deaf can accomplish. Terence, who was born with a severe hearing disability and uses sign language to communicate with his coach, achieved his goal by swimming to a silver medal in the 200-meter breaststroke. "I think it will confirm that deaf people can do things," he said afterwards. . . . "Other people will hopefully think now that we're just like other people. The only thing deaf people can't do is hear."

differ from those of people who can hear. Ultimately, this difference in perception has a direct effect on each individual's social adjustment to the hearing world.

**ADJUSTMENT TO THE HEARING WORLD.** Reviews of the literature on social and psychological development in children who are deaf have suggested that their development differs from that of children who can hear (Easterbrooks, 1999; Kaland & Salvatore, 2003). Different or delayed language acquisition may lead to more limited opportunities for social interaction. Children who are deaf may have more adjustment challenges when attempting to communicate with children who can hear. However, they appear to be more secure when conversing with peers who have a hearing loss (Hilburn, Marini, & Slate, 1997).

**THE DEAF CULTURE.** Some people who are deaf do not consider social isolation from the hearing world an adjustment problem. On the contrary, it is a natural state of being, where people are bonded together by a common language, customs, and heritage. People in the **Deaf culture** seek each other out for social interaction and emotional support. The language of the culture is sign language, where communication is through hand signs, body language, and facial expressions. Sign language is not one universal language. American Sign Language (ASL) is different from Russian Sign Language (RSL), which is different from French Sign Language (FSL), and so on. ASL is not a form of English or any other language. It has its own grammatical structure, which must be mastered in the same way as the grammar of any other language. (American Sign Language is discussed in more depth later in this chapter.)

In addition to a common language, the Deaf culture has it own unique set of interactive customs. For example, people value physical contact with one another even more than in a hearing community. It is common to see visual and animated expressions of affection, such as hugs and handshakes both in greetings and departures. Regardless of the topic, discussions are frank, and there is no hesitation in getting to the point. Gatherings within the Deaf culture may last longer because people like to linger. This may be particularly true at a dinner, where it is perfectly okay to sign (talk) with your mouth full. It will obviously take longer to eat, because it is difficult to sign and hold a knife and fork at the same time.

Within the Deaf community, the social identity of being a deaf person is highly valued, and there is a fierce internal loyalty. Everyone is expected to support activities within the Deaf culture, be they related to sports, arts and literature, or politics. The internal cohesion among the community's members includes a strong expectation that people will marry within the group. In fact, nine out ten people in the Deaf culture marry others within the same community. This loyalty is so strong that deaf parents may hope for a deaf child in order to pass on the heritage and tradition of the Deaf culture to their offspring. Hearing people may be welcomed within the Deaf community, but they are seldom accepted as full members. (See the Debate Forum, "Living in a Deaf Culture.")

**Deaf culture**

A culture wherein people who are deaf become bonded together by a common language (sign language) and by shared customs and heritage. People in the Deaf culture seek each other out for social interaction and emotional support.

## LIVING IN A DEAF CULTURE

**D**eaf culture: a cultural group comprising persons who share similar and positive attitudes toward deafness. The "core Deaf culture" consists of those persons who have a hearing loss and who share a common language, values, and experiences and a common way of interacting with each other. The broader Deaf community is made up of individuals (both deaf and hearing) who have positive, accepting attitudes toward deafness which can be seen in their linguistic, social, and political behaviors. People in a Deaf culture seek each other out for social interaction and emotional support.

The inability to hear and understand speech may lead an individual to seek community ties and social relationships primarily with other individuals who are deaf. These individuals may choose to isolate themselves from hearing peers and to live, learn, work, and play in a social subculture known as "a Deaf culture or Deaf community."

### POINT

The Deaf culture is a necessary and important component of life for many people who are deaf. The person who is deaf has a great deal of difficulty adjusting to life in a hearing world. Through the Deaf culture, he or she can find other individuals with similar problems, common interests, a common language (American Sign Language), and a common heritage and culture. Membership in the Deaf culture is an achieved status that must be earned by the individual who is deaf. The individual must demonstrate a strong identification with the Deaf world, understand and share experiences that come with being deaf, and be willing to participate actively in the Deaf community's educational, cultural, and political activities. The Deaf culture gives such persons a positive identity that can't be found among their hearing peers.

### COUNTERPOINT

Participation in the Deaf culture only serves to isolate people who are deaf from those who hear. A separate subculture unnecessarily accentuates the differences between people who can and who cannot hear. The life of the person who is deaf need not be different from that of anyone else. Children who are deaf can be integrated into general education schools and classrooms. People who are deaf can live side by side with their hearing peers in local communities, sharing common bonds and interests. There is no reason why they can't participate together in the arts, enjoy sports, and share leisure and recreational interests. Membership in the Deaf culture will only further reinforce the idea that people who have disabilities should both grow up and live in a culture away from those who do not. The majority of people who are deaf do not seek membership in the Deaf culture. These people are concerned that the existence of such a community makes it all the more difficult for them to assimilate into society at large.

What do you think? To give your opinion, go to Chapter 15 of the companion website **(www.ablongman.com/hardman8e)** and click on Debate Forum.

# Educational Services and Supports

In the United States, educational programs for children who are deaf or hard of hearing emerged in the early 19th century. The residential school for the deaf was the primary model for delivery of educational services; it was a live-in facility where students were segregated from the family environment. In the latter half of the 19th century, day schools were established in which students lived with their families while receiving an education in a special school exclusively for deaf students. As the century drew to a close, some public schools established, within general education schools, special classes for children with a hearing loss.

The residential school continued to be a model for educational services well into the 20th century. However, with the introduction of electrical amplification, advances in medical treatment, and improved educational technology, more options became available within the public schools. Today, educational programs for students who are deaf or hard of hearing range from the residential school to inclusive education in a general education classroom with support services. For a more in-depth look at the importance of educational supports for students with hearing loss placed in general education settings, see the Case Study on Mario and Samantha.

Research strongly indicates that children with a hearing loss must receive early intervention as soon as possible if they are to learn the language skills necessary for reading and other academic subjects (Calderon & Naidu, 2000). There is little disagreement that the education of the child with a hearing loss must begin at the time of the diagnosis. Educational goals for students with a hearing loss are comparable to goals for students who can hear. The student with a hearing loss brings many of the same strengths and weaknesses to the classroom as the hearing student. Adjustment to learning experiences is often comparable for both groups, as well. Students with a hearing loss, however, face the formidable problems associated with being unable to communicate effectively with teachers and students who can hear. For more information on interacting with people who have a hearing loss, see Inclusion Through the Lifespan.)

## Teaching Communication Skills

Four approaches are commonly used in teaching communication skills to students with a hearing loss: auditory, oral, manual, and total communication. There is a long history of controversy over which approach is the most appropriate. However, no sin-

**FOCUS 6**

Identify four approaches to teaching communication skills to persons with a hearing loss.

**Case Study**

# MARIO AND SAMANTHA

### MARIO

It's a Monday in May, near the end of the school year. The classroom door is open, and the hearing students are pouring in, greeting their friends and talking excitedly about their weekend experiences. Mario, who is deaf, slips in silently, sits down alone, and buries his head in a book as he waits for class to begin. He cannot hear the buzz of activity and conversation around him. He was not a part of the weekend activities. No one speaks to him. He looks up as a girl he likes comes up the row to her seat and drops her books down on the desk. He ventures to speak softly to her, not noticing that she is already talking and joking with a guy across the room. Mario finally captures her glance and asks his question, but the girl doesn't understand what he says. (His speech is slightly impaired, and the room is noisy.) After two more repetitions of "How was your weekend?" he is rewarded with a perfunctory "Oh, fine!" before she turns around and gets wrapped up in a detailed, secret exchange with her best girlfriend, who sits right behind her. They giggle and talk, glancing up once in a while to catch the eye of the boy across the room. Mario rearranges the papers on his desk.

Finally, the teacher begins to lecture, and the lively conversational exchanges become subdued. The hearing students settle into pseudo-attentive postures, reverting to subtle, subversive communications with those around them. Mario, in his front row, corner seat, turns his eyes on the interpreter. He keeps his focus there, working to grasp visually what the other students are effortlessly half-listening to. The teacher questions a student in the back of the room. Her hearing friends whisper help. Their

encouragement boosts her confidence and she boldly answers the teacher. Satisfied, the teacher moves on to question someone else. The first student joins those whispering to the boy who's now on the spot. He picks up the quiet cues and impresses the instructor with his evident mastery of the subject. A peer support system of companionable cooperation helps keep everyone afloat.

However, only those with sensitive hearing and social support can tap into this interwoven network of surreptitious assistance. When a pointed question is directed to Mario, he is on his own. No student schemes bring him into the "we" of class camaraderie. Instead, when he speaks, the students suddenly stop talking and stare. But he is oblivious to the awkward silence in the room. He is verbally stumbling, searching for an answer that will pacify the teacher yet not be too specific. He strains to minimize the risk of opening himself up for embarrassment of saying something that misses the mark entirely. While he is still speaking, the bell rings and the other students pack up and start moving out the back door. Mario, his eyes on the teacher, doesn't notice the interpreter's signal that the bell has already sounded. The teacher smiles uncomfortably and cuts him off to give last-minute instructions as the students pour out the door.[1]

### SAMANTHA

It is a crisp autumn morning, the kind that some people breathe in deeply as they look forward to the challenges of the day. School has begun an hour ago. Mrs. Jones's algebra class is examining some equations. Puzzled by Mrs. Jones's explanation, Samantha raises her hand and questions her

gle method or collection of methods can meet the individual needs of all children with a hearing loss. Our intent is not to enter into the controversy regarding these approaches but to present a brief description of each approach.

**THE AUDITORY APPROACH.** The auditory approach emphasizes the use of amplified sound and residual hearing to develop oral communication skills. The auditory channel is considered the primary avenue for language development, regardless of the severity or type of hearing loss. The basic principles of the auditory approach are as follows:

- Detecting hearing impairment as early as possible through screening programs, ideally in the newborn nursery and throughout childhood.

- Pursuing prompt and vigorous medical and audiologic management, including selection, modification, and maintenance of appropriate hearing aids, cochlear implants, or other sensory aids.

- Guiding, counseling, and supporting parents and caregivers as the primary models for spoken language through listening, and helping them understand the impact of deafness and impaired hearing on the entire family.

- Helping children integrate listening into their development of communication and social skills.

- Supporting children's auditory–verbal development through one-to-one teaching.

teacher about an equation. While Samantha signs her question, Mrs. Jones watches Samantha (pleased that she understands much of what Samantha is signing) and listens to Samantha's interpreter. Several of Samantha's classmates watch her signing, nodding in agreement that the explanation was not clear. Later, as the students work some math problems, Samantha and a hearing friend exchange suggestions through signs. As Samantha and her classmates leave for their next class, Mrs. Jones calls out to the class and signs to Samantha, "Have a nice day."

Samantha and two of her hearing friends hurry to their next class. On the way, they animatedly sign to each other about the upcoming school dance. Samantha's planning to go with one of her friends from the inclusive education program, Jason, who is deaf. As they reach their next class, they meet Mike and Ernestine, two other students in the inclusive program who are deaf. Samantha and her two friends greet Mike and Ernestine and they enter the class together. During the civics class the students and teachers have a lively exchange about the responsibility of citizens when faced with a law they feel is immoral. (Occasionally the teacher reminds the students not to interrupt one another or talk too fast, so that all of the students, deaf and hearing, can catch what is being said.) Samantha, Mike, and Ernestine join in through sign language, and several of the hearing students sign as they speak. An interpreter speaks and signs as needed.

After civics, Samantha and Ernestine head to an English class and Mike to a physical education class. The English class is taught by Mr. Roberts, a deaf education teacher in the inclusive program. Being deaf, Mr. Roberts signs gracefully and eloquently. The class is alive as they discuss poetry by hearing and deaf poets. Tony, Margaret, and Lee, three hearing students, are in the class with Samantha and her deaf classmates. They will attend for two weeks as the class discusses and dramatizes poetry. Mr. Roberts uses his voice to help them understand, though they sign quite well. At the end of the two weeks, the class will dramatize and sign several poems for other deaf and hearing students.[2]

## APPLICATION

1. Compare and contrast the social and educational isolation of Mario in a general education setting with the inclusive nature of Samantha's school experiences.

2. Are the two case studies of Mario and Samantha representative of your experiences with students who are deaf in general education classroom settings? Why or why not?

3. How is a school like Samantha's organized? What is needed to support and include students who are deaf in the social and academic life of the school?

[1]SOURCE: Adapted from "Alone in the Crowd," by C. Wixtrom, 1988, *The Deaf American, 38* (12), pp. 14–15.
[2]SOURCE: Adapted from "The Challenges of Educating Together Deaf and Hearing Youth: Making Mainstreaming Work," by P. C. Higgins, 1990, Springfield, IL: Charles C Thomas.

**Inclusion Through the Lifespan**

# PEOPLE WITH HEARING LOSS

### Tips for the Family

- Promote family learning about diversity in all people in the context of understanding the child with a hearing loss.
- Keep informed about organizations and civic groups that can provide support to the young child with a hearing loss and also to the family.
- Get in touch with your local health, social services, and education agencies about infant, toddler, and preschool programs for children with a hearing loss. Become familiar with the individualized family service plan (IFSP) and how it can serve as a planning tool to support the inclusion of your child in early intervention programs.
- Focus on the development of communication for your child. Work with professionals to determine what mode of communication (oral, manual, and/or total communication) will be most effective in developing early language skills.
- Label stimuli (e.g., objects and people) both visually and verbally as often as possible to provide the child with multiple sources of input.

### Tips for the Preschool Teacher

- Language deficits are a fundamental problem for young children with a hearing loss. Focus on developing some form of expressive and receptive communication in the classroom as early as possible. Help young children with a hearing loss to understand words that are abstract, have multiple meanings, and are part of idiomatic expressions (e.g., *run down the street* versus *run for president*).
- Help hearing classmates interact with the child with a hearing loss. Help hearing children be both verbal and visual with the student who is deaf or hard of hearing. If the child with a hearing loss doesn't respond to sound, have the hearing children learn to stand in the line of sight. Teach them to gain the attention of the child with a hearing loss without physical prompting.
- Work closely with parents so that early communication and skill development for the young child with a hearing loss is consistent across school and home environments.
- Become very familiar with acoustical devices (e.g., hearing aids) that may be used by the young child with a hearing loss. Make sure that these devices are worn properly and work in the classroom environment.

### Tips for Preschool Personnel

- Support the inclusion of young children with a hearing loss in your classrooms and programs.
- Support teachers, staff, and volunteers as they attempt to create successful experiences for the young child with a hearing loss in the preschool setting.
- Work very closely with families to keep them informed and active members of the school community.

### Tips for Neighbors and Friends

- Work with the family of a young child with a hearing loss to seek opportunities for interactions with hearing children in neighborhood play settings.
- Focus on the capabilities of the young child with a hearing loss, rather than on the disabilities. Understand how the child communicates: orally? manually? or both? If the child uses sign language, take the time to learn fundamental signs that will enhance your communication with him or her.

### Tips for the Family

- Learn about your rights as parents of a child with a hearing loss. Actively participate in the development of your child's individualized education program (IEP). Through active participation, fight for goals on the IEP that will focus on your child's developing social interaction and communication skills in natural settings.
- Participate in as many school functions for parents as is reasonable (e.g., PTA, parent advisory groups, volunteering) to connect your family to the school.
- Seek information on in-school and extracurricular activities available that will enhance opportunities for your child to interact with hearing peers.
- Keep the school informed about the medical needs of your child. If he or she needs or uses acoustical devices to enhance hearing capability, help school personnel understand how these devices work.

### Tips for the General Education Classroom Teacher

- Outline schoolwork (e.g., the schedule for the day) on paper or the blackboard so the student with a hearing loss can see it.
- As much as possible, require classroom work to be answered in complete sentences to provide the necessary practice.
- Remember that students with hearing loss don't always know how words fit together to make understandable sentences. Help them develop skills by always writing in complete sentences.
- Have the student with a hearing loss sit where he or she can see the rest of the class as easily as possible. Choose a buddy to sit nearby and keep him or her aware of what is going on.
- When lecturing, have the student with a hearing loss sit as close to you as possible.
- Don't be surprised to see gaps in learning. Demonstrations of disappointment or shock will make the student feel he or she is at fault.
- Be sure to help the student with a hearing loss know what is going on at all times (e.g., pass on announcements made over the intercom).
- Always give short, concise instructions and then make sure the student with a hearing loss understood them by having him or her repeat the information before performing the task.
- Type scripts (or outlines of scripts) for movies and videotapes used in class. Let the student read the script for the movie.
- When working with an interpreter, remember to:
  — Introduce the interpreter to the class at the beginning of the year, and explain his or her role.

— Always speak directly to the student, not to the interpreter.

— Pause when necessary to allow the interpreter to catch up, since he or she may often be a few words behind.

— Face the class when speaking. (When using a blackboard, write on the board first, then turn to face the class to speak.)

— Include students who are deaf in class activities and encourage these students to participate in answering questions.

### Tips for School Personnel

- Integrate school resources as well as children. Wherever possible, help general education classroom teachers access the human and material resources necessary to meet the needs of students with a hearing loss. For example:

  — *The audiologist.* Keep in close contact with this professional, and seek advice on the student's hearing and the acoustical devices being used.

  — *The special education teacher trained in hearing loss.* This professional is necessary both as a teacher of students with a hearing loss and as a consultant to general educators. Activities can range from working on the development of effective communication skills to dealing with behavioral difficulties. The general education teacher may even decide to work with the special education teacher on learning sign language, if appropriate.

  — *Speech and language specialists.* Many students with a hearing loss will need help with speech acquisition and application in the school setting.

- Assist general and special education teachers to develop peer partner and support networks for students with a hearing loss. Peer partners may help by serving as tutors or just by reviewing for tests and class assignments.

- Work to help the student with a hearing loss strive for independence. Assistance from peers is sometimes helpful, but it should never reach the point where other students are doing work for the student with a hearing loss.

Tips for Neighbors and Friends

- Help families with a child who is deaf or hard of hearing to be an integral part of neighborhood and friendship networks. Seek ways to include the family and the child in neighborhood activities (e.g., outings, barbecues, outdoor yard and street cleanups, crime watches).

## SECONDARY AND TRANSITION YEARS

### Tips for the Family

- Become familiar with adult services systems (e.g., rehabilitation services, Social Security, health care) while your son or daughter is still in high school. Understand the type of vocational or employment training that he or she will need prior to graduation.

- Create opportunities out of school for your son or daughter to participate in activities with same-age hearing peers.

### Tips for the General Education Classroom Teacher

- Collaborate with specialists in hearing loss and other school personnel to help students adapt to subject matter in your classroom (e.g., science, math, physical education).

- Become aware of the needs of and resources available for students with a hearing loss in your classroom. Facilitate student learning by establishing peer support systems (e.g., note takers) to help students with a hearing loss be successful.

- Use diagrams, graphs, and visual representations whenever possible when presenting new concepts.

- Help the student with a hearing loss become involved in extracurricular high school activities. If you are the faculty sponsor of a club or organization, explore whether the student is interested and how he or she could get involved.

### Tips for School Personnel

- Encourage parents of high-school-age students with a hearing loss to participate in school activities (such as committees, PTA).

- Parents will be more active when school personnel have general and positive contact with the family.

### Tips for Neighbors, Friends, and Potential Employers

- Work with family and school personnel to create opportunities for students with a hearing loss to participate in community activities as much as possible with individuals who are deaf or hard of hearing, as well as with those who are not.

- As a potential employer for people with a hearing loss, work with the high school and vocational rehabilitation counselors to locate and establish employment training sites.

## ADULT YEARS

### Tips for the Family

- Become aware of the supports and services available for your son or daughter in the local community in which they will live as adults. What formal supports are available in the community through government-funded programs or advocacy organizations for people with a hearing loss? through informal supports (family and friends)?

- Explore adult services in the local community in the areas of postsecondary education, employment, and recreation.

### Tips for Neighbors, Friends, and Potential Employers

- Seek ways to become part of a community support network for individuals with a hearing loss. Be alert to ways in which these individuals can become and remain actively involved in community employment, neighborhood recreational activities, and local church functions.

- As potential employers in the community, seek out information on employment of people with a hearing loss. Find out about programs that focus on establishing employment opportunities for people with a hearing loss, while meeting your needs as an employer.

- Helping children monitor their own voices and the voices of others in order to enhance the intelligibility of their spoken language.

- Using developmental patterns of listening, language, speech, and cognition to stimulate natural communication.

- Continually assessing and evaluating children's development in the above areas and, through diagnostic intervention, modifying the program when needed.

- Providing support services to facilitate children's educational and social inclusion in regular [general] education classes. (Auditory–Verbal International, 2000)

The auditory approach uses a variety of electroacoustic devices to enhance residual hearing, such as binaural hearing aids, acoustically tuned earmolds, and FM units. FM units employ a behind-the-ear hearing aid connected to a high-powered frequency-modulated radio-frequency (FM-RF) system. These units use a one-way wireless system on radio-frequency bands. The student wears a receiver unit about the size of a deck of cards, and a wireless microphone-transmitter-antenna unit is worn by the teacher. One advantage of using an FM-RF system is that the teacher can be connected to several students at a time.

**THE ORAL APPROACH.** The oral approach to teaching communication skills also emphasizes the use of amplified sound and residual hearing to develop oral language. This approach stresses the need for persons with a hearing loss to function in the hearing world. Individuals are encouraged to speak and be spoken to. In addition to electroacoustic amplification, the teacher may employ speechreading, reading and writing, and motokinesthetic speech training (feeling an individual's face and reproducing breath and voice patterns). **Speechreading** is the process of understanding another person's speech by watching lip movement and facial and body gestures. This skill is difficult to master, especially for the person who has been deaf from an early age and thus never acquired speech. Problems with speechreading include the fact that many sounds are not distinguishable on the lips and that the reader must attend carefully to every word spoken—a difficult task for preschool and primary-age children. Additionally, the speechreader must be able to see the speaker's mouth at all times.

Auditory–Verbal International (2000), a major international organization whose principal objective is to promote listening and speaking as a way of life for children who are deaf or hard of hearing, maintains that there is compelling evidence for the auditory and oral approach to teaching communication skills:

- The majority of children with hearing loss have useful residual hearing.

- When properly aided, children with hearing loss can detect most, if not all, of the speech spectrum.

- Once residual hearing is accessed through amplification technology, a child will have the opportunity to develop language in a natural way through the auditory modality.

- In order for the child to benefit from the "critical periods" of neurologic and linguistic development, appropriate amplification and medical technology and stimulation of hearing must occur as early as possible.

- If hearing is not accessed during the years critical to language learning, a child's ability to use acoustic input meaningfully will deteriorate as a consequence of physiological (retrograde deterioration of auditory pathways) and psychosocial (attention, practice, learning) factors.

- Current information about normal language development provides the framework and justification for the structure of auditory–verbal practice. That is, infants, toddlers, and children learn language most efficiently through consistent and continual meaningful interactions in a supportive environment with significant caretakers.

**Speechreading**

The process of understanding another person's speech by watching lip movement and facial and body gestures.

- As verbal language develops through the auditory input of information, reading skills can also develop.

- Parents in auditory–verbal programs do not have to learn sign language or cued speech. More than 90% of parents of children with hearing loss have normal hearing.

- Studies show that over 90% of parents with normal hearing do not learn sign language beyond a basic preschool level of competence.

If a severe or profound hearing loss automatically made an individual neurologically and functionally "different" from people with normal hearing, then the auditory–verbal philosophy would not be tenable. The fact is, however, that outcome studies show that individuals who have, since early childhood, been taught through the active use of amplified residual hearing are indeed independent, speaking, and contributing members of mainstream society.

**THE MANUAL APPROACH.** The manual approach to teaching communication skills stresses the use of signs in teaching children who are deaf to communicate. The use of signs is based on the premise that many such children are unable to develop oral language and consequently must have some other means of communication. Manual communication systems are divided into two main categories: sign languages and sign systems.

A **sign language** is a systematic and complex combination of hand movements that communicate whole words and complete thoughts rather than the individual letters of the alphabet. One of the most common sign languages is **American Sign Language (ASL)**, with a vocabulary of more than 6,000 signs. Examples of ASL signs from different regional areas in the United States are shown in Figure 15.2. ASL is

## FIGURE 15.2

### Examples of "Faint" Expressed in American Sign Language

Faint: My mother fainted from the ammonia fumes.

Alabama, Hawaii

Arkansas, Florida, Maine, Kentucky, Louisiana, Virginia, North Carolina, South Carolina

California, Illinois, Utah

Colorado, Texas (1 of 2)

Massachusetts

Michigan, Ohio

SOURCE: Reprinted by permission of the publisher, from E. Shroyer and S. Shroyer, *Signs Across America*, (1984): 79-80. Washington, DC: Gallaudet University Press. Copyright © 1984 by Gallaudet University.

**Sign language**

A systematic and complex combination of hand movements that communicate whole words and complete thoughts rather than individual letters. An example is the American Sign Language (ASL).

**American sign language (ASL)**

A type of sign language commonly used by people with hearing impairments. ASL signs represent concepts rather than single words.

currently the most widely used sign language among many adults who are deaf because it is easy to master and has historically been the preferred mode of communication. It is a language, but it is not English. Its signs represent concepts rather than single words. The use of ASL in a school setting has been strongly recommended by some advocates for people who are deaf, because it is considered their natural language (Lane, Hoffmeister, & Bahan, 1996).

**Sign systems** differ from sign languages in that they attempt to create visual equivalents of oral language through manual gestures. With finger spelling, a form of manual communication that incorporates all 26 letters of the English alphabet, each letter is signed independently on one hand to form words. Figure 15.3 shows the manual alphabet. In recent years, finger spelling has become a supplement to ASL. It is common to see a person who is deaf using finger spelling when there is no ASL sign for a word. The four sign systems used in the United States are Seeing Essential English, Signing Exact English, Linguistics of Visual English, and Signed English.

### FIGURE 15.3

**The American Manual Alphabet**

The manual alphabet as the receiver sees it:

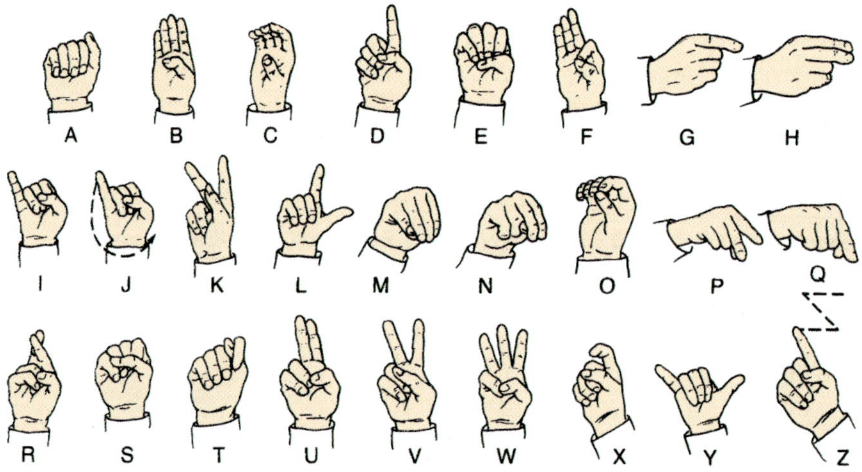

The manual alphabet as the sender sees it:

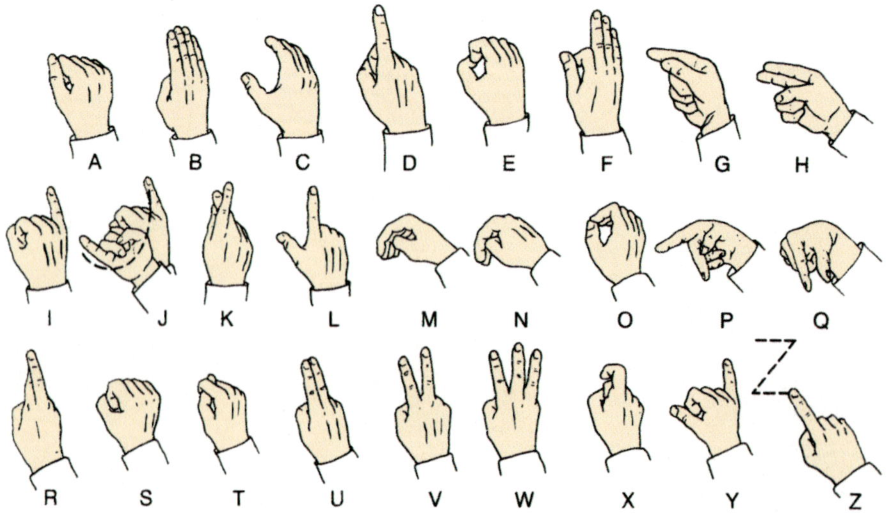

**Sign systems**

Systems of communication that create visual equivalents of oral language through manual gestures. For example, finger spelling incorporates all 26 letters of the English alphabet, and each letter is signed independently on one hand to form words.

There is a continuing debate regarding the use of ASL and signing English systems in providing academic instruction to students who are deaf. Should ASL or English be the primary language for instruction? Those who advocate a **bicultural–bilingual approach** believe that ASL should be the primary language and English the second language. As the primary language, ASL would then serve as the foundation for the learning of English. The rationale for ASL as the primary language emerges from the values held dear by the Deaf community: Children who are deaf must learn academic content in the language of their culture, their natural language. The primary language for children who are deaf is visual, not verbal. Children who are deaf should be considered bilingual students, not students with disabilities. As is true in bilingual education programs for students with differing language backgrounds, debate also arises about whether ASL should be taught first, and then English, or the two languages should be taught simultaneously. One side emphasizes the importance of the child first acquiring the natural language (ASL). The other side stresses the need to expose the child to both ASL and English simultaneously and as early as possible. There is little research to support either position. What is available (Prinz et al., 1996; Strong & Prinz, 1997) suggests that exposure to ASL at an early age enhances English skills.

**TOTAL COMMUNICATION.**   Total communication has roots traceable to the 16th century. Over the past four centuries, many professionals advocated an instructional system that employed every method possible to teach communication skills: oral, auditory, manual, and written. This approach was known as the combined system or the simultaneous method. The methodology of the early combined system was imprecise; essentially, any recognized approach to teaching communication was used as long as it included a manual component. The concept of total communication differs from the older combined system in that it is not used only when the oral method fails or when critical learning periods have long since passed. In fact, total communication is not a system at all, but a philosophy.

The philosophy of **total communication** holds that the simultaneous presentation of signs and speech will enhance each person's opportunity to understand and use both systems more effectively. Total communication programs use residual hearing, amplification, speechreading, speech training, reading, and writing in combination with manual systems. A method that may be used as an aid to total communication but is not a necessary component of the approach is cued speech.

**Bicultural–bilingual approach**

Instructional approach advocating ASL as the primary language and English as the second language for students who are deaf. ASL would thus serve as the foundation for learning English.

**Total communication**

The philosophy that people with hearing impairments learn to communicate best though simultaneous presentation of manual and oral techniques.

*This teacher embraces the philosophy of total communication. Students use residual hearing, amplification, and speech reading in combination with sign language.*

## FOCUS 7

Describe the uses of closed-caption television, computers, and the Internet for people with a hearing loss.

**Cued speech** facilitates the development of oral communication by combining eight different hand signals in four different locations near the person's chin. The hand signals provide information concerning sounds that are not identifiable by speechreading. The result is that an individual has access to all sounds in the English language through either the lips or the hands.

## Assistive Technology

Educational and leisure opportunities for people with a hearing loss have been greatly expanded through technological advances such as closed-caption television, computers, the Internet and telecommunication devices (see Figure 15.4). In this section, we examine 21st-century technology for persons with a hearing loss.

**CLOSED CAPTIONING.** **Closed-caption television** translates dialogue from a television program into printed words (captions or subtitles). These captions are then converted to electronic codes that can be inserted into the television picture on sets specially adapted with decoding devices. The process is called the line-21 system because the caption is inserted into blank line 21 of the picture.

Captioning is not a new idea. In fact, it was first used on motion picture film in 1958. Most libraries in the United States distribute captioned films for individuals with a hearing loss. Available nationwide only since 1980, closed captioning on television has experienced steady growth over the past 20 years. In its first year of operation, national closed-caption programming was available about 30 hours per week. By 1987, more than 200 hours per week of national programming were captioned in a wide range of topics, from news and information to entertainment and commercials. By 1993, all major broadcast networks were captioning 100% of their prime-time broadcasts, national news, and children's programming. Subsequent to passage

---

### FIGURE 15.4

### Milestones in Technology for the Deaf

| **1892** | **1964** | **1972** | **1985** |
|---|---|---|---|
| The first electrical hearing aid, which weighs several pounds, is invented. | The teletypewriter, or TTY, which enables deaf people to call each other and type conversations, is invented by Robert Weitbrecht, who is deaf. | The first television show featuring captioning—Julia Child's *The French Chef*—is broadcast on PBS. | The FDA approves cochlear implants. |

### 1990s and Beyond

| | | | |
|---|---|---|---|
| All new televisions 13 inches or larger sold in the U.S. are required by the FCC to have decoding chips, which allow deaf people to view programs with captions. | New vibrating pagers are developed that provide deaf people with easy, on-the-go communication. | Computer technology—including laptops, e-mail and the Internet—gives deaf people a level playing field with the hearing world in job opportunities and social communication. | Advances include real-time captioning (spoken words typed simultaneously on a screen); video-relay interpreting (deaf and hearing people speak via a remote video interpreter); and signing avatars (onscreen figures who sign words spoken into a microphone). |

SOURCE: "They're Breaking the Sound Barrier," by L. A. Walker, *Parade Magazine*, May 13, 2001, p. 4.

---

**Cued speech**

A technique that facilitates the development of oral communication by combining eight different hand signals, in four different locations near the person's chin, to provide additional information concerning sounds that is not identifiable via speechreading.

**Closed-caption television**

Process by which people with hearing impairments are provided translated dialogue, in the form of subtitles, from television programs.

of the Television Decoder Circuitry Act of 1993, the numbers of viewers watching caption expanded even more dramatically. This act required that all television sets sold in the United States that are 13 inches or larger be equipped with a decoder that allows captions to be placed anywhere on the television screen. This prevents captions from interfering with on-screen titles or other information displayed on the TV broadcast. In 1997, the U.S. Congress passed the Telecommunications Act, which required virtually all new television programming to be captioned by January 2006. Although Congress provided for some exemptions to this requirement (e.g., non-English programming, commercials and public service announcements, and late-night programs), the clear intent of the law was to continue expanding access to television for millions of people who are deaf.

There is the mistaken belief that the Americans with Disabilities Act (ADA) mandates captioning for television and movies. In fact, the ADA requires captioning only on government-funded television public service announcements. Federal law does not extend beyond television because the Federal Communications Commission has jurisdiction only over the airwaves. There is no law covering the captioning of movies in theaters or videotapes (Robson, 2000).

**COMPUTERS AND THE INTERNET.** Personal computers offer an exciting dimension to information access for persons with a hearing loss. The computer places the person in an interactive setting with the subject matter. It is a powerful motivator. Most people find computers fun and interesting to work with on a variety of tasks. Furthermore, computer-assisted instruction can be individualized so that students can gain independence by working at their own pace and level.

Computer programs are now used for instructional support in a variety of academic subject areas, from reading and writing to learning basic sign language. Software is now available that will display a person's speech in visual form on the screen to assist in the development of articulation skills. Another innovative computer system is called C-print, developed by the National Technical Institute for the Deaf. Using a laptop computer equipped with a computer shorthand system and commercially available software packages, C-print provides real-time translations of the spoken word. A trained operator listens to speech and then types special codes representing words into the computer. These codes are transcribed into words that are shown almost simultaneously on a screen sitting atop an overhead projector. A printout of the transcription can be obtained as well. C-print is a great boon to students with a hearing loss as they attend college classes or oral lectures; they typically find note taking an extremely difficult activity, even when an oral interpreter is available (Northeast Technical Assistance Center, 2000).

The interactive videodisc is another important innovation in computer-assisted instruction. The videodisc, a record-like platter, is placed in a videodisc player that is connected to a microcomputer and television monitor. The laser-driven disc is interactive, and the individual can move through instruction at his or her own pace. Instant repetitions of subject matter are available to the learner at the touch of a button.

Perhaps the most important advance in technology for people with a hearing loss is access to information via the Internet. Whether it be e-mail, interactive chatrooms, or the infinite number of websites, the World Wide Web offers people with a hearing loss access to all kinds of visual information through the quickest and most convenient means possible. Websites, such as Deaf Resources (www.deafresources.com) and the American Sign Language Browser (commtechlab.msu.edu/sites/aslweb/) are just two of many websites designed specifically for people who are deaf. For more in-depth information on the way assistive technology is opening up employment opportunities, entertainment, and communication for people who are deaf, see the Assistive Technology feature, "They're Breaking the Sound Barrier." Additional information on web resources is available at the end of this chapter.

**TELECOMMUNICATION DEVICES.** A major advance in communication technology for people with a hearing loss is the telecommunication device. One such device is the **text telephone (TT)**. TTs send, receive, and print messages through thou-

**Text telephone (TT)**

Telephones that send, receive, and print messages through thousands of stations across the United States.

## THEY'RE BREAKING THE SOUND BARRIER

arvin Herbold of Gaithersburg, Maryland, wanted a job in the computer game industry after college, so he e-mailed a résumé to Bethesda Softworks. The company asked him to write a simple computer program depicting a 3-D cube. Herbold went further. His 3-D program showed an entire chessboard and pieces. Impressed, Bethesda sent back an e-mail asking him to come for an interview. Herbold e-mailed to let the interviewer know he was deaf.

"Not a problem," was the reply.

After the interview, he was hired on the spot. "They were far more interested in what I could do," says Herbold, now 26, "than [in] any disabilities I may have had."

As recently as a decade ago, things were far more difficult for deaf people looking for employment. Few dared apply for white-collar jobs, unless they were in the "deaf job ghetto"—a handful of lowly government positions—or teaching deaf children.

Today, not only is technology opening up employment opportunities, it also has changed the ways deaf people socialize, receive entertainment, communicate with the hearing world and plan their futures.

I've seen it firsthand, in my own family. My mother and father are deaf, as were my aunt and uncle, and I signed even before I spoke. Not long ago, I went to a senior citizens' luncheon for deaf people in Indianapolis. As hands flew, I noticed something quite surprising about the conversations I was seeing among my parents' friends. These older people were wired! "Did you get my e-mail?" "When I was surfing the Web, I found a great new site. . . ." This was not the deaf world I knew growing up.

I was aware of these changes as I talked with some of the men and women who are using technology in their day-to-day lives. As a reporter, I have never used so many different methods for conducting interviews. Naturally, I communicated using American Sign Language. But I also used e-mail, faxes, and telephones with text. At times, I spoke by phone with a deaf person at the other end who used a sign-language interpreter to receive my words but was speaking for himself. During one conversation, the other person used an amplifying device hooked into a cochlear implant (a device that places electrodes directly into the cochlea, where sound waves are absorbed and interpreted by the auditory nerve).

[People who are deaf] now are able to be more plugged in to politics and other events than ever before. When I was home recently, I noticed my mother and father constantly zipping over to the computer to check the news. Not only did they receive regular updates on the happenings in the deaf world around the country, but there also were local deaf news bulletins being placed constantly. I asked my dad how technology had affected him. "My English has improved," he said. With e-mails and faxes, I write and keep in touch with deaf people much more." And then he smiled. "My life is better than before."

SOURCE: From "They're Breaking the Sound Barrier," by L. A. Walker, *Parade Magazine*, May 13, 2001, pp. 4–5.

---

sands of stations across the United States. People with a hearing loss can now dial an 800 number to set up conference calls, make appointments, or order merchandise or fast food. Anyone who wants to speak with a person using a TT can do so through the use of a standard telephone.

The teletypewriter and printer (TTY) is another effective use of technology for people who are deaf. It enables them to communicate by phone via a typewriter that converts typed letters into electric signals through a modem. These signals are sent through the phone lines and then translated into typed messages and printed on a typewriter connected to a phone on the other end. Computer software is now available that can turn a personal computer into a TTY.

## Medical and Social Services

In this new century, advances in medicine and social services are opening up opportunities never thought possible for people with a hearing loss. Medical services play a major role in the prevention, early detection, and remediation of a hearing loss. Community services and supports are helping to reduce the social isolation of people who are deaf or have a partial hearing loss. Societal perspectives on people with a hearing loss are changing dramatically, as evidenced in the life of Tamika Catchings in the opening Snapshot and that of Marvin Herbold from the nearby Assistive Technology.

## Medical Services

Several specialists are integrally involved in medical assessment and intervention, including the geneticist, the pediatrician, the family practitioner, the otologist, the neurosurgeon, and the audiologist.

**THE GENETICIST.**    Prevention of a hearing loss is a primary concern of the genetics specialist. A significant number of hearing losses are inherited or occur during prenatal, perinatal, and postnatal development. Consequently, the genetics specialist plays an important role in preventing disabilities through family counseling and prenatal screening.

**THE PEDIATRICIAN AND FAMILY PRACTITIONER.**    Early detection of a hearing loss can prevent or at least minimize the impact of the disability on the overall development of an individual. Generally, it is the responsibility of the pediatrician or family practitioner to recognize a problem and refer the family to an appropriate hearing specialist. These responsibilities require that the physician be familiar with family history and conduct a thorough physical examination of the child. The physician or nurse practitioner must be alert to any symptoms (e.g., delayed language development) that indicate potential sensory loss. (For more information on the importance of screening for hearing loss in young children, see the nearby Reflect on This, "The Cries Grow Louder: Check Newborns' Hearing.")

**THE OTOLOGIST.**    The **otologist** is a medical specialist who is most concerned with the hearing organ and its diseases. Otology is a component of the larger specialty of diseases of the ear, nose, and throat. Like the pediatrician, the otologist screens for potential hearing problems, but the process is much more specialized and exhaustive. The otologist also conducts an extensive physical examination of the ear to identify syndromes that are associated with conductive or sensorineural loss. This information, in conjunction with family history, provides data used in determining what medical treatment is appropriate.

Treatment may involve medical therapy or surgical intervention. Common therapeutic procedures include monitoring aural hygiene (keeping the external ear free from wax), blowing out the ear (a process to remove mucus blocking the eustachian tube), and administering antibiotics to treat infections. Surgical techniques may involve the cosmetic and functional restructuring of congenital malformations such as a deformed external ear or closed external canal (atresia). Fenestration is the surgical creation of a new opening in the labyrinth of the ear to restore hearing. A stapedectomy is a surgical process conducted under a microscope whereby a fixed stapes is replaced with a prosthetic device capable of vibrating, thus permitting the transmission of sound waves. A myringoplasty is the surgical reconstruction of a perforated tympanic membrane (eardrum).

Another widely used surgical procedure involves a **cochlear implant.** This electronic device is surgically placed under the skin behind the ear. It consists of four parts: (1) a microphone for picking up sound; (2) a speech processor to select and arrange sounds picked up by the microphone; (3) a transmitter and receiver/stimulator to receive signals from the speech processor and convert them into electric impulses; and (4) electrodes to collect the impulses from the stimulator and send them to the brain. The implant does not restore or amplify hearing. Instead, it provides people who are deaf or profoundly hard of hearing with a useful "sense" of sound in the world around them. The implant overcomes "nerve deafness" (the blocking of sounds from reaching the auditory nerve) by getting around damage to the tiny hair cells in the inner ear and directly stimulating the auditory nerve. An implant electronically finds useful or meaningful sounds, such as speech, and then sends these sounds to the auditory nerve.

Cochlear implants are becoming more widely used with both adults and children. More than 25,000 people worldwide (50% children and 50% adults) have had

**FOCUS 8**

Why is the early detection of hearing loss so important?

**FOCUS 9**

Distinguish between an otologist and an audiologist.

**Otologist**

A medical specialist involved in the study of the ear and its diseases.

**Cochlear implant**

A surgical procedure that implants an electronic device under the skin behind the ear. The implant overcomes "nerve deafness" by getting around damage to the cells in the inner ear and directly stimulating the auditory nerve.

**Reflect on This**

## THE CRIES GROW LOUDER: CHECK NEWBORNS' HEARING

Some deaf babies are lucky enough to be born in a hospital where inexpensive hearing tests are performed on all newborns. Those babies are leaving the hospital on a road toward hearing and developing normal language skills.

But because the tests are so rarely administered, an estimated 30 U.S. newborns a day go home with significant hearing impairment, and it will take an average of 2 ½ years for their disability to be discovered. By then, the children's brains will have developed largely without the influence of words.

This disparity reflects the sporadic way in which new technologies are being introduced across the United States.

The technologies are simple tests that expose an infant to clicking noises and register the responses in either the child's ear or the brain. Both are used widely and cost less than $50 a child.

Since the National Institutes of Health recommended in 1993 that all babies undergo such testing within the first three months of life, about 20 states have passed laws encouraging the tests; 12 of those demand that babies be tested. Federal legislation is being considered that would make it a national requirement.

One of every 300 newborns has some hearing loss. Half of those children have moderate to severe hearing loss in both ears.

Through traditional screening methods and limited mandatory testing of all babies, only about 19% of newborns have their hearing checked, but traditional screening methods have had major limitations.

A complex brain scan that showed some hearing loss was expensive and applied only to babies known to be at high risk of hearing loss—some premature babies and those born after problems during pregnancy.

More commonly, doctors could do little but expose babies to a loud noise and try to judge by the reaction whether the child could hear.

But at least half of all babies born with hearing loss are not considered at high risk.

"We knew by following that protocol we would miss 50% of the babies with hearing loss," says Gilbert Herer, chairman of the hearing and speech department at Children's National Medical Center in Silver Spring, Mary-land. "I never thought I would see the day when I had the technology to identify hearing loss during the newborn period."

Sometimes the problem is easy to fix. Some babies are born with "gunk" in the ear that is removed surgically. Other times, the hearing is permanently damaged because the tiny "hairs" deep inside the ear that transmit sound signals to the brain don't work properly.

But today's high-tech hearing aids and cochlear implants allow babies whose hearing loss is identified early to grow up tuned in to the world around them. One hearing aid has a radio that allows parents or teachers to wear a microphone that transmits their voices directly to the ear. The mother washing dishes can chatter as the child plays nearby, teaching the baby language.

"The brain is developing so rapidly during this time," Herer says, "If you don't stimulate the auditory system, these neural tracks and neural clusters don't develop to support what we as human beings use all the time."

### Early Signs of Ear Trouble

If the baby doesn't have the following behavior, a doctor should be consulted.

**Birth to 3 months:**

- Reacts to sounds
- Is soothed by your voice
- Turns head to you when you speak
- Is awakened by loud voices and sounds
- Smiles when spoken to
- Seems to know your voice and quiets down if crying

**3 to 6 months:**

- Looks upward or turns toward a new sound
- Responds to "no" and to changes in tone of voice
- Imitates his/her own voice
- Enjoys rattles and other toys that make sound
- Begins to repeat sounds (such as *ooh, aah* and *ba-ba*)
- Becomes scared by a loud voice

SOURCE: From "The Cries Grow Louder: Check Newborns' Hearing," by R. Davis, *USA Today*, May 24, 1999, p. 10D.

the surgery (National Institute on Deafness and Other Communication Disorders, 2000b). Some adults who were deafened in their later years reported useful hearing following the implant, and others still needed speechreading to understand the spoken word. Most children receive the implants between the ages of 2 and 6 years. Some disagreement exists about which age is optimal for the surgery, but it appears that the earlier, the better. The Cochlear Implants Association (2000) suggests that children from 18 months to 17 years of age are appropriate candidates for an implant if they have profound hearing loss in both ears, little or no useful benefit from hearing aids, and no medical contraindications and if both child and family have high motivation and appropriate expectations. The association also recommends that after surgery, the child be placed in an educational program that emphasizes the development of auditory skills. Similar criteria are suggested for adults, with the additional caveat that the person must have a strong desire to be part of the hearing world.

The existing research suggests that cochlear implants enhance the learning of speech, language, and social skills, particularly for young children. However, there are still issues to be addressed, such as understanding the risk of possible damage to an ear that has some residual hearing, as well as the risk of infection from the implant (McKinley & Warren, 2000). Some people who are deaf view cochlear implants as a direct attack on the values and heritage of the Deaf culture; others view the implants as a medical miracle.

> There are many deaf and hard-of-hearing people who are against the use of implants with children; and there are many who support [their] use with children. There are people who are opposed to use of implants in anyone at any age; and there are people who don't care if a deaf or hard-of-hearing adult makes a personal decision to be implanted. Cochlear implants have been controversial in our [Deaf] community because some people feel that the implants are being used in an attempt to eradicate our community; but the medical community and the parents seem to see implants as a miraculous way to conquer deafness and keep their implanted children in the mainstream society on a permanent basis. (National Association of the Deaf, 2000)

**THE AUDIOLOGIST.**     The degree of hearing loss, measured in decibels and hertz, is determined by an audiologist via a process known as audiometric evaluation. The listener receives tones that are relatively free of external noise (pure-tone audiometry) or receives spoken words, in which speech perception is measured (speech audiometry). An **audiometer** detects the person's response to sound stimuli, and a record (**audiogram**) obtained from the audiometer graphs the individual's threshold for hearing at various sound frequencies.

Whereas an otologist presents a biological perspective on hearing loss, an **audiologist** emphasizes the functional impact of losing one's hearing. The audiologist first screens the individual for a hearing loss, and then determines both the nature and the severity of the condition. Social, educational, and vocational implications of the hearing loss are next discussed and explored. Although audiologists are not specifically trained in the field of medicine, these professionals interact constantly with otologists to provide a comprehensive assessment of hearing.

Working together, audiologists and otologists provide assistance in the selection and use of hearing aids. At one time or another, most people with a hearing loss wear hearing aids. Hearing aids amplify sound, but they do not correct hearing. Hearing aids have been used for centuries. Early acoustic aids included cupping one's hand behind the ear, as well as the ear trumpet. Modern electroacoustic aids do not depend on the loudness of the human voice to amplify sound but, rather, utilize batteries to increase volume. Electroacoustic aids come in three main types: body-worn aids, behind-the-ear aids, and in-the-ear aids. Which hearing aid is best for a particular person depends on the degree of hearing loss, the age of the individual, and the physical condition of the individual.

Body-worn hearing aids are typically worn on the chest, using a harness to secure the unit. The hearing aid is connected by a wire to a transducer, which is worn at ear level and delivers a signal to the ear via an earmold. Body-worn aids are becoming less common because of the disadvantages of their being chest-mounted, the location of the microphone, and inadequate high-frequency response. The behind-the-ear aid (also referred to as an ear-level aid) is a common electroacoustic device for children with a hearing loss. All components of the behind-the-ear aid are fitted in one case behind the outer ear. The case then connects to an earmold that delivers the signal directly to the ear. In addition to their portability, behind-the-ear aids have the advantage of producing the greatest amount of electroacoustic flexibility (amount of amplification across all frequencies). The primary disadvantage is problems with acoustic feedback. The behind-the-ear aid may be used with an FM-RF system, as

**Audiometer**

An electronic device used to detect a person's response to sound stimuli.

**Audiogram**

A record, obtained from an audiometer, of an individual's response to sound stimuli.

**Audiologist**

A specialist in the assessment of a person's hearing ability.

discussed earlier in this chapter. These aids may be fitted monaurally (on one ear) or binaurally (on both ears).

The in-the-ear aid fits within the ear canal. All major components (microphone, amplifier, transducer, and battery) are housed in a single case that has been custom-made for the individual user. The advantage of the in-the-ear aid is the close positioning of the microphone to the natural reception of auditory signals in the ear canal. In-the-ear aids are recommended for individuals with mild hearing losses who do not need frequent changes in earmolds. Thus these aids are not usually recommended for young children.

Although the quality of commercially available aids has improved dramatically in recent years, they do have distinct limitations. They do make sounds louder, but they do not necessarily make them more clear and distinct. An aid's effectiveness depends on wearability and each person's communication skills.

The stimulation of residual hearing through a hearing aid enables most people with a hearing loss to function as hard of hearing. However, the use of a hearing aid must be implemented as early as possible, before sensory deprivation takes its toll on the child. It is the audiologist's responsibility to weigh all the factors involved (e.g., convenience, size, weight) in the selection and use of an aid for the individual. The individual should then be directed to a reputable dealer in hearing aids.

## Social Services

The social consequences of being deaf or hard of hearing are highly correlated with the severity of the loss. For the individual who is deaf, social inclusion may be extremely difficult because societal views of deafness have reinforced social isolation. The belief that such people are incompetent has been predominant from the time of the early Hebrews and Romans, who deprived them of their civil rights, to 20th-century America, where, in some areas, it is still difficult for adults who are deaf to obtain driver's licenses or adequate insurance coverage or to be gainfully employed. The people who have the greatest difficulty are those born with congenital deafness. The inability to hear and understand speech has often isolated these people from those who can hear. For example, people who are deaf tend to marry other people who are deaf.

Some individuals who are deaf are actively involved in organizations and communities specifically intended to meet their needs. The National Association for the Deaf (NAD) was organized in 1880. The philosophy of NAD is that every person who

**FOCUS**
**10**

Identify factors that may affect the social inclusion of people who are deaf in the hearing world.

*In the past, an inability to hear often isolated these children from their hearing peers. Today, about 8 out of 10 students with a hearing loss are educated in the general education classroom for at least part of the school day.*

is deaf has the same rights as those in the hearing world—the right to life, liberty, and the pursuit of happiness. NAD emphasizes that the exercise of these rights must be to the satisfaction of those who are deaf—not to the satisfaction of their teachers and parents who do not have the condition. NAD serves individuals who are deaf in many capacities. Among its contributions, NAD publishes books on deafness, sponsors cultural activities, and lobbies throughout the United States for legislation promoting the rights of people who are deaf.

Another prominent organization is the Alexander Graham Bell Association for the Deaf, which advocates the inclusion of persons with a hearing loss in the social mainstream. The major thrust of this approach is the improvement of proficiency in speech communications. As a clearinghouse for information for people who are deaf and their advocates, the association publishes widely in the areas of parent counseling, teaching methodology, speechreading, and auditory training. In addition, it sponsors national and regional conferences that focus on a variety of issues pertinent to the social adjustment of people who are deaf.

# FOCUS REVIEW

**FOCUS 1** Describe how sound is transmitted through the human ear.

- A vibrator—such as a string, reed, or column of air—causes displacement of air particles.
- Vibrations are carried by air, metal, water, or other substances.
- Sound waves are displaced air particles that produce a pattern of circular waves that move away from the source to a receiver.
- The human ear collects, processes, and transmits sounds to the brain, where they are decoded into meaningful language.

**FOCUS 2** Distinguish between the terms *deaf* and *hard of hearing*.

- A person who is deaf typically has profound or total loss of auditory sensitivity and very little, if any, auditory perception.
- For the person who is deaf, the primary means of information input is through vision; speech received through the ears is not understood.
- A person who is hard-of-hearing (partially hearing) generally has residual hearing through the use of a hearing aid, which is sufficient to process language through the ear successfully.

**FOCUS 3** Why is it important to consider age of onset and anatomical site when defining a hearing loss?

- Age of onset is critical in determining the type and extent of intervention necessary to minimize the effect of the hearing loss.

- Three types of peripheral hearing loss are associated with anatomical site: conductive, sensorineural, and mixed.
- Central auditory hearing loss occurs when there is a dysfunction in the cerebral cortex (outer layer of gray matter in the brain).

**FOCUS 4** What are the estimated prevalence and causes of hearing loss?

- It has been extremely difficult to determine the prevalence of hearing loss. Estimates of hearing loss in the United States go as high as 28 million people; approximately 11 million people have significant irreversible hearing loss, and 1 million are deaf.
- Nearly 71,000 students between the ages of 6 and 21 have a hearing impairment and are receiving special education services in U.S. schools. These students account for approximately 1.5% of school-age students identified as having a disability.
- Although more than 200 types of deafness have been related to hereditary factors, the cause of 50% of all hearing loss remains unknown.
- A common hereditary disorder is otosclerosis (bone destruction in the middle ear).
- Nonhereditary hearing problems evident at birth may be associated with maternal health problems: infections (e.g., rubella), anemia, jaundice, central nervous system disorders, the use of drugs, sexually transmitted disease, chicken pox, anoxia, and birth trauma.

- Acquired hearing losses are associated with postnatal infections, such as measles, mumps, influenza, typhoid fever, and scarlet fever.
- Environmental factors associated with hearing loss include extreme changes in air pressure caused by explosions, head trauma, foreign objects in the ear, and loud noise. Loud noise is rapidly becoming one of the major causes of hearing problems.

**FOCUS 5** Describe the basic intelligence, speech and language skills, educational achievement, and social development associated with people who are deaf or hard of hearing.

- Intellectual development for people with hearing loss is more a function of language development than cognitive ability. Any difficulties in performance appear to be closely associated with speaking, reading, and writing the English language, but are not related to level of intelligence.
- Speech and English language skills are the areas of development most severely affected for those with a hearing loss. The effects of a hearing loss on English language development vary considerably.
- Most people with a hearing loss are able to use speech as the primary mode for language acquisition. People who are congenitally deaf are unable to receive information through the speech process unless they have learned to speechread.
- Reading is the academic area most negatively affected for students with a hearing loss.

- The social and psychological development in children with a hearing loss is different in comparison to children who can hear. Different or delayed language acquisition may lead to more limited opportunities for social interaction. Children who are deaf may have more adjustment challenges when attempting to communicate with children who can hear, but appear to be more secure when conversing with children who are also deaf. For some people who are deaf, social isolation from the hearing world is not considered an adjustment problem. It is a natural state of being where people are bonded together by a common language, customs, and heritage.

**FOCUS 6**   Identify four approaches to teaching communication skills to persons with a hearing loss.

- The auditory approach to communication emphasizes the use of amplified sound and residual hearing to develop oral communication skills.
- The oral approach to communication emphasizes the use of amplified sound and residual hearing but may also employ speechreading, reading and writing, and motokinesthetic speech training.
- The manual approach stresses the use of signs in teaching children who are deaf to communicate.

- Total communication employs the use of residual hearing, amplification, speechreading, speech training, reading, and writing in combination with manual systems to teach communication skills to children with a hearing loss.

**FOCUS 7**   Describe the uses of closed-caption television, computers, and the Internet for people with a hearing loss.

- Closed-caption television translates dialogue from a television program into captions (subtitles) that are broadcast on the television screen. Closed-caption television provides the person with a hearing loss greater access to information and entertainment.
- Computers place people with a hearing loss in interactive settings with access to vast amounts of information. Computer programs are now available for instructional support in a variety of academic subject areas, from reading and writing to learning basic sign language. Certain software can display a person's speech in visual form on the screen to assist in the development of articulation skills.
- E-mail, interactive chatrooms, and the infinite number of web sites provide people with a hearing loss access to many kinds of visual information.
- TT systems provide efficient ways for people who are deaf to

communicate over long distances. TTY devices allow people who are deaf to use a personal computer or typewriter, modem, and printer to communicate over the phone.

**FOCUS 8**   Why is the early detection of hearing loss so important?

- Early detection of hearing loss can prevent or minimize the impact of the disability on the overall development of an individual.

**FOCUS 9**   Distinguish between an otologist and an audiologist.

- An otologist is a medical specialist who is concerned with the hearing organ and its diseases.
- An audiologist is concerned with the measurement of hearing loss and its sociological and educational impact on an individual.
- Both the audiologist and otologist assist in the process of selecting and using a hearing aid.

**FOCUS 10**   Identify factors that may affect the social inclusion of people who are deaf in the hearing world.

- The inability to hear and understand speech has isolated some people who are deaf from those without hearing loss.
- Societal views of deafness may reinforce isolation.

## FURTHER READINGS

Candlish, P. M. (1996). *Not Deaf Enough: Raising a Child Who Is Hard of Hearing with Hugs and Humor.* Washington, DC: Alexander Graham Bell Association for the Deaf and Hard-of-Hearing.

*Written by the mother of a child with hearing loss, this book is a reflection of a family's experiences in raising a child with a hearing loss while working with (and sometimes against) professionals in human services.*

Grayson, G. (2003). *Talking with Your Hands, Listening with Your Eyes: A Complete Photographic Guide to American Sign Language.* New York: Square One Publishers.

*This book is designed to make it easier to understand, duplicate, and remember the vocabulary of American Sign Language. It covers more than 900 signs that represent*
*nearly 1,800 words and phrases, with signs grouped by topic, e.g., common and polite phrases; mealtime and food; school and education; careers, jobs and the workplace; and the body and health. Photos of professional signers demonstrating the sign formation accompany a discussion of each sign.*

Matlin, M. (2002). *Deaf Child Crossing.* New York: Simon and Schuster.

*Academy award-winning actor and producer Marlee Matlin writes about a topic she knows very well—the difficulties of growing up deaf. The book chronicles the relationship between Megan, a child who is deaf and Cindy, her hearing friend. Together, they forge an unlikely friendship that is tested when the two decide to attend summer camp together and meet up with another child who is deaf.*

## WEB RESOURCES

**The Alexander Graham Bell Association for the Deaf and Hard of Hearing**

www.agbell.org

This website offers information on a wide range of programs and services for parents of children with hearing loss, educators, adults with hearing loss, and hearing health professionals. The website has links on updated news and information, advocacy for people with a hearing loss, and publications and products.

**The American Speech-Hearing-Language Association (ASHA)**

www.asha.org

ASHA is the professional, scientific, and credentialing association for more than 100,000 speech-language
pathologists; audiologists; and speech, language, and hearing scientists in the United States and internationally. The ASHA website provides information and resources on speech-language pathology and audiology for family members, practitioners, researchers, and the general public.

**The National Association of the Deaf (NAD)**

www.nad.org

This website provides information on programs and publications focused on advocacy; the deaf community and deaf culture; policy and research on deafness; and public awareness.

## BUILDING YOUR PORTFOLIO

If you are thinking about a career in special education, you should know that many states use national standards developed by the Council for Exceptional Children (CEC) to assess a teacher candidate's knowledge and skills for working with students with disabilities. See a complete listing of the ten CEC Content Standards on the inside front cover of this text.

### CEC Content Standards Addressed in Chapter 15

1. Foundations
2. Development and Characteristics of Learners
3. Individual Learning Differences
4. Instructional Strategies
5. Learning Environments and Social Interactions
7. Instructional Planning

### Assess Your Knowledge of the CEC Standards Addressed in Chapter 15

Some states require that teacher candidates develop a portfolio of products that demonstrate mastery of the CEC content standards. To assist in the development of products for this portfolio, you may wish to complete the following activities.

- Complete a written test of the chapter's content.

  *If your instructor requires a written test of your content knowledge for this chapter, keep a copy for your portfolio. A practice test on the information covered in this chapter is available through the companion website (www.ablongman.com/hardman8e) and the Student Study Guide.*

- Respond to the application questions for the Case Study "Mario and Samantha."

  *Review the Case Study and respond in writing to the application questions. Keep a copy of the Case Study and your written response for your portfolio.*

- Complete the "Take a Stand" activity for the Debate Forum "Living in a Deaf Culture."

  *Read the Debate Forum in this chapter and then visit our companion website to complete the activity "Take a Stand." Keep a copy of this activity for your portfolio.*

- Participate in a community service learning activity.

  *Community service is a valuable way to enhance your learning experience. Visit our companion website for suggested community service learning activities that correspond to the information presented in this chapter. Develop a reflective journal of the service learning experience for your portfolio.*

## THEMES OF THE TIMES

Expand your knowledge of the concepts discussed in this chapter by reading current and historical articles from the *New York Times* by visiting the "Themes of the Times" section of the companion website: **www.ablongman.com/hardman8e.**

# Vision Loss

### Like a Seeing Eye Dog That Reads and Talks

Print-to-speech reading machines for [people who are] blind are now very small, inexpensive, palm-sized devices that can read books (those that still exist in paper form) and other printed documents, and other real-world text such as signs and displays. These reading systems are equally adept at reading the trillions of electronic documents that are instantly available from the ubiquitous wireless worldwide network. After decades of ineffective attempts, useful navigation devices have been introduced that can assist [people who are] blind in avoiding physical obstacles in their path and finding their way around, using global positioning system (GPS) technology. A [person who is] blind can interact with her personal reading-navigation systems through two-way voice communication, kind of like a Seeing Eye dog that reads and talks. (Kurzweil, 2000)

### That All May Read

Braille readers can now read their books on the Internet, thanks to a historic technological breakthrough by The Library of Congress called Web-Braille. Readers now have access to [more than 3,000] electronic braille books placed on the Internet for the use of eligible braille readers by the Library's National Library Service for the Blind and Physically Handicapped (NLS). Each year many hundreds of new titles will be added. As a result of new computer technology, braille readers may now access Web-Braille digital braille book files with a computer and a refreshable braille display (electronic device that raises or lowers an array of pins to create a line of braille characters) or a braille embosser. About 40 new titles per month are released in braille and immediately available online to users. The Library of Congress also produces braille versions of many national magazines and is now exploring the feasibility of adding these magazines to Web-Braille for its users. (Library of Congress, 2003)

### Millions Have Impaired Eyesight

From a practical point of view, if you can't count the fingers held up by someone ten feet away in broad daylight, you're blind. At least one million in [the United States] are legally blind, and 75,000 new cases develop every year. However, millions more, while not legally blind, have seriously impaired eyesight that, for example, prevents them from reading a newspaper even with glasses. (Rosenfeld, 2001, p. 12)

**FOCUS**

**PREVIEW:** To preview the central concepts of this chapter, read the focus questions located in the margins. Using these questions as a guide, ask yourself what you already know and what you want to learn.

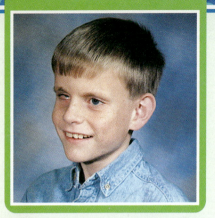

## John

**B**orn prematurely and weighing only 1 pound 13 ounces, John is a child with vision loss. Now 9 years old, John lives with his parents and brother Michael, none of whom have any visual problems. John loves technology and has a CB radio, several TVs, a computer, and a tape recorder. He doesn't care for outdoor activities and isn't into sports. He uses braille to read and has a cane to help him find his way through the world.

John: "I really like to be blind, it's a whole lot of fun. The reason I like to be blind is because I can learn my way around real fast and I have a real fast thinking memory. I can hear things that some people can't hear and smell. Actually, my sense of hearing is the best. . . . I have a CB radio that [I] talk to different people on and sometimes I can talk to people in different places around the world."

John's parents: "John can do anything he wants to do if he puts his mind to it. He's smart enough, he loves all kinds of radio communications. He talks about being on the radio, on TV, and there's no reason why he can't do that as long as he studies hard in school."

Michael: "I didn't want a blind brother."

John: "Sometimes my brother gets along good and sometimes he comes here in my room and under my desk there's a little power switch that controls all my TVs, scanner, CB, and tape recorder.

He'll flip that then he'll laugh about it, run and go somewhere and I'll have to turn it back on, lock my door, and go tell Mom. So that's how he handles it and she puts him in time out."

John's third-grade teacher: "John is very well adjusted. He has a wonderful, delightful personality. He's intelligent. We were a little worried about his braille until this year. Probably because of his prematurity, [he has] a little trouble with the tactual. Of course, braille is all tactual. . . . But he's pulling out of that and that was his last problem with education. He's very bright. He could do many things. He loves computers."

John: "I'd like to be a few different things, and I'll tell you a few of them. I'd like to be a newscaster, an astronaut, or something down at NASA and a dispatcher. So that's three of the things out of a whole million or thousand things I'd like to be."

---

Through the visual process, we observe the world around us and develop an appreciation for and a greater understanding of the physical environment. Vision is one of our most important means of acquiring and assimilating knowledge, but we often take it for granted. From the moment we wake up in the morning, our dependence on sight is obvious. We rely on our eyes to guide us around our surroundings, to inform us through the written word, and to give us pleasure and relaxation.

What if this precious sight was lost or impaired? How would our perceptions of the world change? Losing sight is one of our greatest fears—a fear that is often exacerbated by the misconception that people with vision loss are helpless and unable to lead satisfying or productive lives. It is not uncommon for people with sight to have little understanding of those with vision loss. People who are sighted may believe that most adults who are blind are likely to be socioeconomically and culturally deprived. Children who have sight may believe that their peers who are blind are incapable of learning many basic skills, such as telling time and using a computer or of enjoying leisure and recreational activities such as swimming and watching television. Historically, some religions have even promoted the belief that blindness is a punishment for sins.

As the opening Snapshot about John strongly suggests, these negative perceptions of people with vision loss are often inaccurate. John is an active child who has not allowed his vision loss to keep him from the activities that he values. To understand more clearly the nature of vision loss within the context of normal sight, we begin our discussion with an overview of the visual process. Because vision is fundamentally the act of seeing with the eye, we first review the physical components of the visual system.

## The Visual Process

The physical components of the visual system include the eye, the **visual cortex** in the brain, and the **optic nerve**, which connects the eye to the visual cortex. The basic anatomy of the human eye is illustrated in Figure 16.1. The **cornea** is the ex-

**FOCUS 1**

Why is it important to understand the visual process as well as to know the physical components of the eye?

**Visual cortex**

The visual center of the brain, located in the occipital lobe.

**Optic nerve**

The nerve that connects the eye to the visual center of the brain.

**Cornea**

The external covering of the eye.

ternal covering of the eye, and it bends, or refracts, light rays. These light rays pass through the **pupil**, which is an opening in the iris. The pupil dilates or constricts to control the amount of light entering the eye. The **iris**, the colored portion of the eye, consists of membranous tissue and muscles whose function is to adjust the size of the pupil. The **lens**, like the cornea, bends light rays so that they strike the retina directly. And like a camera lens, the lens of the eye reverses the images. The **retina** consists of light-sensitive cells that transmit the image to the brain by means of the optic nerve. Images from the retina remain upside down until they are flipped over in the visual cortex occipital lobe of the brain.

The visual process is a much more complex phenomenon than suggested by a description of the physical components involved. This crucial link to the physical world helps us to gain information beyond the range of our other senses and also helps us to integrate the information we have acquired primarily through hearing, touch, smell, and taste. For example, our sense of touch can tell us that what we are feeling is furry, soft, and warm, but only our eyes can tell us that it is a brown rabbit with a white tail and pink eyes. Our nose may perceive something with yeast and spices cooking, but only our eyes can confirm that it is a large pepperoni pizza with

**Pupil**

The expandable opening in the iris that dilates or constricts to control the amount of light entering the eye.

**Iris**

The colored portion of the eye whose function is to adjust the size of the pupil.

**Lens**

The clear structure of the eye that bends light rays so that they strike the retina directly.

**Retina**

A structure consisting of light-sensitive cells in the interior of the eye that transmit images to the brain via the optic nerve.

## FIGURE 16.1

### The Parts of the Human Eye

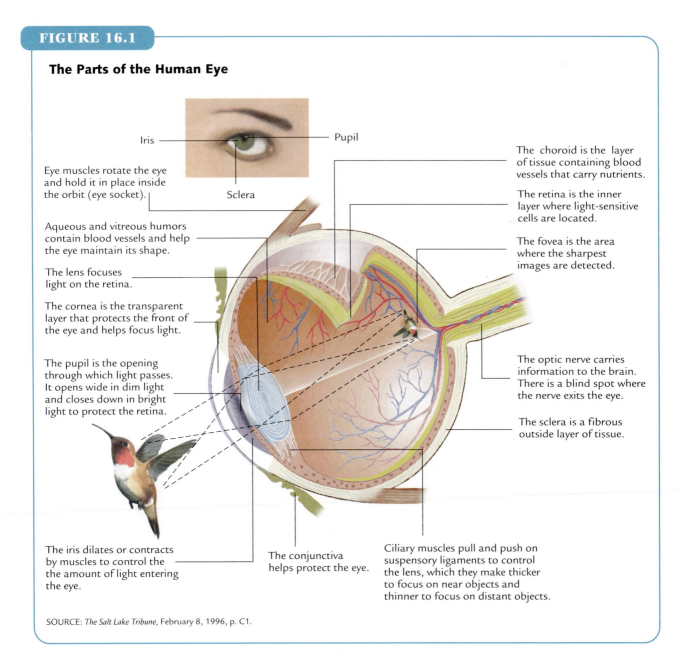

Iris

Pupil

Eye muscles rotate the eye and hold it in place inside the orbit (eye socket).

Sclera

The choroid is the layer of tissue containing blood vessels that carry nutrients.

The retina is the inner layer where light-sensitive cells are located.

Aqueous and vitreous humors contain blood vessels and help the eye maintain its shape.

The fovea is the area where the sharpest images are detected.

The lens focuses light on the retina.

The cornea is the transparent layer that protects the front of the eye and helps focus light.

The pupil is the opening through which light passes. It opens wide in dim light and closes down in bright light to protect the retina.

The optic nerve carries information to the brain. There is a blind spot where the nerve exits the eye.

The sclera is a fibrous outside layer of tissue.

The iris dilates or contracts by muscles to control the the amount of light entering the eye.

The conjunctiva helps protect the eye.

Ciliary muscles pull and push on suspensory ligaments to control the lens, which they make thicker to focus on near objects and thinner to focus on distant objects.

SOURCE: *The Salt Lake Tribune*, February 8, 1996, p. C1.

bubbling mozzarella and green peppers. Our hearing can tell us that a friend sounds angry and upset, but only our vision can perceive the scowl, clenched jaw, and stiff posture. The way we perceive visual stimuli shapes our interactions with and reactions to the environment, while providing a foundation for the development of a more complex learning structure.

**FOCUS**

**2**

Distinguish between the terms *blind* and *partially sighted*.

# Definitions and Classification

The term *vision loss* encompasses people with a wide range of conditions, including those who have never experienced sight, those who had normal vision prior to becoming partially or totally blind, those who experience a gradual or sudden loss of acuity across their field of vision, and those with a restricted field of vision.

## Definitions

A variety of terms are used to define vision loss, and this has created some confusion among professionals in various fields of study. The rationale for the development of multiple definitions is directly related to their intended use. For example, eligibility for income-tax exemptions or special assistance from the American Printing House for the Blind requires that individuals with vision loss qualify under one of two general subcategories: blind or partially sighted (low vision).

**BLINDNESS.** The term *blindness* has many meanings. In fact, there are over 150 citations for *blind* in an unabridged dictionary. **Legal blindness**, as defined by the Social Security Administration (2003), means that vision cannot be corrected to better than 20/200 in the better eye or that the visual field is 20 degrees or less, even with a corrective lens. Many people who meet the legal definition of blindness still have some sight and may be able to read large print and get around without support (e.g., a guide dog or cane). As we have noted, the definition of legal blindness takes into account both acuity and field of vision (Corn & Koenig, 1996).

**Visual acuity** is most often determined by asking the individual to read letters or numbers on a chart using the **Snellen Test** or via an index that refers to the distance from which an object can be recognized. The person with normal eyesight is defined as having 20/20 vision. However, if an individual is able to read at 20 feet what a person with normal vision can read at 200 feet, then his or her visual acuity would be described as 20/200. Most people who are legally blind have some light perception; only about 20% are totally without sight.

A person is also considered blind if his or her field of vision is limited at its widest angle to 20 degrees or less (see Figure 16.2). A restricted field is also referred to as **tunnel vision** (or as pinhole vision or tubular vision). A restricted field of vision severely limits a person's ability to participate in athletics, read, or drive a car.

Blindness can also be characterized as an educational disability. Educational definitions of blindness focus primarily on students' ability to use vision as an avenue for learning. Children who are unable to use their sight and must rely on other senses, such as hearing and touch, are described as functionally blind. Functional blindness, in its simplest form, may be defined in terms of whether vision is used as a primary channel of learning. Regardless of the definition used, the purpose of labeling a child as functionally blind is to ensure that he or she receives an appropriate instructional program. This program must assist the student who is blind in utilizing other senses as a means to succeed in a classroom setting and in the future as an independent and productive adult.

**PARTIAL SIGHT (LOW VISION).** People with partial sight or low vision have a visual acuity greater than 20/200 but not greater than 20/70 in the best eye after correction. The field of education also distinguishes between being blind and being partially sighted when determining the level and extent of additional support ser-

**Legal blindness**

Visual acuity of 20/200 or worse in the best eye with correction, as measured on the Snellen test, or a visual field of 20% or less.

**Visual Acuity**

Sharpness or clearness of vision.

**Snellen Test**

A test of visual acuity.

**Tunnel Vision**

A field of vision that is 20 degrees or less at its widest angle.

## FIGURE 16.2

**The Field of Vision**

(a) 180°
Normal field of vision is about 180°.

(b) 20°
A person with a field of vision of 20° or less is considered blind.

FOCUS 3

What are the distinctive features of refractive eye problems, muscle disorders of the eye, and receptive eye problems?

vices required by a student. The term **partially sighted** describes students who are able to use vision as a primary source of learning.

A vision specialist often works with students with vision loss to help them make the best possible use of remaining sight. This includes elimination of unnecessary glare in the work area, removal of obstacles that could impede mobility, use of large-print books, and use of special lighting to enhance visual opportunities. Although children with low vision often use printed materials and special lighting in learning activities, some use **braille** because they can see only shadows and limited movement. These children need to use tactile or other sensory channels to gain the greatest possible benefit from learning opportunities (Bishop, 1996a).

Two distinct perspectives have evolved about individuals who are partially sighted and their use of residual vision. The first suggests that such individuals should make maximal use of their functional residual vision through magnification, illumination, and specialized teaching aids (e.g., large-print books and posters), as well as any exercises that will increase the efficiency of their remaining vision. This position is contrary to the more traditional philosophy of sight conservation, or sight saving, which advocates restricted use of the eye. It was once believed that students with vision loss could keep what sight they had much longer if it was used sparingly. However, extended reliance on residual vision, in conjunction with visual stimulation training, now appears actually to improve a person's ability to use sight as an avenue for learning.

### Classification

Vision loss may be classified in terms of the anatomical site of the problem. Anatomical disorders include impairment of the refractive structures of the eye, muscle anomalies in the visual system, and problems of the receptive structures of the eye.

**REFRACTIVE EYE PROBLEMS.** **Refractive problems**, the most common type of vision loss, occur when the refractive structures of the eye (the cornea and lens) fail to focus light rays properly on the retina. The four types of refractive problems are hyperopia, or farsightedness; myopia, or nearsightedness; astigmatism, or blurred vision; and cataracts.

**Hyperopia** occurs when the eyeball is excessively short from front to back (has a flat corneal structure), forcing light rays to focus behind the retina. The person with hyperopia can clearly visualize objects at a distance but cannot see them at close range. This individual may require convex lenses so that light rays will focus on the retina.

**Myopia** occurs when the eyeball is excessively long (has increased curvature of the corneal surface), forcing light rays to focus in front of the retina. The person with

**Partially sighted**

Having visual acuity greater than 20/200 but not greater than 20/70 in the better eye after correction.

**Braille**

A system of writing used by many people who are blind. It involves combinations of six raised dots punched into paper, which can be read with the fingertips.

**Refractive problems**

Visual disorders that occur when the refractive structures of the eye fail to focus light rays properly on the retina.

**Hyperopia**

Farsightedness; a refractive problem wherein the eyeball is excessively short, focusing light rays behind the retina.

**Myopia**

Nearsightedness; a refractive problem wherein the eyeball is excessively long, focusing light in front of the retina.

## Astigmatism

A refractive eye problem that occurs when the surface of the cornea is uneven or structurally defective, preventing light rays from converging at one point.

## Cataract

A clouding of the eye lens, which becomes opaque, resulting in visual problems.

## Nystagmus

Uncontrolled rapid eye movements.

## Strabismus

Crossed eyes (internal) or eyes that look outward (external).

## Esotropia

A form of strabismus that causes the eyes to be pulled inward toward the nose.

## Exotropia

A form of strabismus in which the eyes are pulled outward toward the ears.

## Amblyopia

Loss of vision that may occur when the muscles of the eyes are unable to pull equally.

## Optic atrophy

A degenerative disease caused by deteriorating nerve fibers connecting the retina to the brain.

## Retinitis pigmentosa

A hereditary condition that results from a break in the choroid and is associated with progressive loss of vision

myopia can view objects at close range clearly but cannot see them well at a distance (e.g., 100 feet). Eyeglasses may be necessary to help the individual focus on distant objects. Figure 16.3 illustrates the myopic and hyperopic eyeballs and compares them to the normal human eye.

**Astigmatism** occurs when the curvature or surface of the cornea is uneven, preventing light rays from converging at one point. The rays of light are refracted in different directions, producing unclear, distorted visual images. Astigmatism may occur independently of or in conjunction with myopia or hyperopia.

**Cataracts** occur when the lens becomes opaque, resulting in severely distorted vision or total blindness. Surgical treatment for cataracts (such as lens implants) has advanced rapidly in recent years and can restore most of the vision that was lost.

**MUSCLE DISORDERS.** Muscular defects of the visual system occur when one or more of the major muscles within the eye are weakened in function, resulting in a loss of control and an inability to maintain tension. People with muscle disorders cannot focus on a given object for even short periods of time. The three types of muscle disorders are nystagmus (uncontrolled rapid eye movement), strabismus (crossed eyes), and amblyopia (an eye that appears normal but does not function properly). **Nystagmus** is a continuous, involuntary, rapid movement of the eyeballs in either a circular or a side-to-side pattern. **Strabismus** occurs when the muscles of the eyes are unable to pull equally, thus preventing the eyes from focusing together on the same object. Internal strabismus (**esotropia**) occurs when the eyes are pulled inward toward the nose; external strabismus (**exotropia**) occurs when the eyes are pulled out toward the ears. The eyes may also shift on a vertical plane (up or down), but this condition is rare. Strabismus can be corrected through surgical intervention. Persons with strabismus often experience a phenomenon known as double vision, because the deviating eye results in two very different pictures coming to the brain. To correct the double vision and reduce visual confusion, the brain attempts to suppress the image in one eye, and the unused eye loses its ability to see. This condition, known as **amblyopia**, can also be corrected by surgery or by forcing the affected eye into focus by covering the unaffected eye with a patch.

**RECEPTIVE EYE PROBLEMS.** Disorders associated with the receptive structures of the eye occur when there is a degeneration of or damage to the retina and the optic nerve. These disorders include optic atrophy, retinitis pigmentosa, retinal detachment, retinopathy of prematurity (ROP), and glaucoma. **Optic atrophy** is a degenerative disease that results from the deterioration of nerve fibers connecting the retina to the brain. **Retinitis pigmentosa**, the most common hereditary condition associated with loss of vision, appears initially as night blindness and gradually results in degeneration of the retina. Eventually, it causes total blindness.

---

### FIGURE 16.3

**Normal, Myopic, and Hyperopic Eyeballs**

The image is focused on the retina upside down, but the brain immediately reverses it.

40 ft

In normal vision, an image is focused on the retina.

In nearsightedness, (myopia), the image is focused in front of the retina.

In farsightedness, (hyperopia), the image is focused behind the retina.

(a) Normal      (b) Myopic      (c) Hyperopic

**Retinal detachment** occurs when the retina separates from the choroid and the sclera. This detachment may result from disorders such as glaucoma, retinal degeneration, or extreme myopia. It can also be caused by trauma to the eye, such as a boxer's receiving a hard right hook to the face.

**Retinopathy of prematurity (ROP)**, formerly known as retrolental fibroplasia, is one of the most devastating eye disorders in young children. It occurs when too much oxygen is administered to premature infants, resulting in the formation of scar tissue behind the lens of the eye, which prevents light rays from reaching the retina. ROP gained attention in the early 1940s, with the advent of improved incubators for premature infants. These incubators substantially improved the concentration of oxygen available to the infant but resulted in a drastic increase in the number of children with vision loss. The disorder has also been associated with neurological, speech, and behavior problems in children and adolescents. Now that a relationship has been established between increased oxygen levels and blindness, premature infants can be protected by carefully controlling the amount of oxygen received in the early months of life.

**FOCUS 4**

What are the estimated prevalence and causes of vision loss?

# Prevalence

The prevalence of vision loss is often difficult to determine. For example, although about 20% of children and adults in the United States have some vision loss, most of these conditions can be corrected to a level where they do not interfere with everyday tasks (e.g., reading, driving a car). Approximately 1 in 3,000 American children is considered legally blind (Batshaw, 2003), and 3% of the total population (9 million people) have a significant vision loss that will require some type of specialized services and supports. About 5% of American children (approximately 1.2 million) have a serious eye disorder (KidSource, 2003). This figure increases to 20% for people over the age of 65. If cataracts are included, nearly 50% of people over 65 have a significant vision loss. The U.S. Department of Education (2002) reports that 25,975 school-age children with vision loss between the ages of 6 and 21 received specialized services in U.S. public schools in the 2000–2001 school year.

# Causation

## Genetic Disorders

A number of genetic conditions can result in vision loss:

- **Albinism** (resulting in **photophobia** due to lack of pigmentation in eyes, skin, and hair)
- Retinitis pigmentosa (degeneration of the retina)
- **Retinoblastoma** (malignant tumor in the retina)
- Optic atrophy (loss of function of optic nerve fibers)
- Cataracts (opaque lens resulting in severely distorted vision)
- Severe myopia associated with retinal detachment
- Lesions of the cornea
- Abnormalities of the iris
- **Microphthalmia** (abnormally small eyeball)
- **Hydrocephalus** (excess cerebrospinal fluid in the brain), leading to optic atrophy
- **Anophthalmia** (absence of the eyeball),
- **Glaucoma** or **buphthalmos** (abnormal distention and enlargement of the eyeball)

**Retinal detachment**

A condition that occurs when the retina is separated from the choroid and sclera.

**Retinopathy of prematurity**

An eye disorder that results when too much oxygen is administered to premature infants.

**Albinism**

Lack of pigmentation in eyes, skin, and hair.

**Photophobia**

An intolerance to light.

**Retinoblastoma**

A malignant tumor in the retina.

**Microphthalmia**

An abnormally small eyeball.

**Hydrocephalus**

Condition resulting in excess cerebrospinal fluid in the brain.

**Anophthalmia**

Absence of the eyeball.

**Glaucoma**

A disorder of the eye, which is characterized by high pressure inside the eyeball.

**Buphthalmos**

An abnormal distention and enlargement of the eyeball.

Glaucoma results from increased pressure within the eye, which damages the optic nerve if left untreated. It is responsible for about 4% of all blindness in children (Batshaw, 2003). The incidence of glaucoma is highest in persons over the age of 40 who have a family history of the disease. Glaucoma is treatable, either through surgery to drain fluids from the eye or through the use of medicated eye drops to reduce pressure.

### Acquired Disorders

Acquired disorders can occur prior to, during, or after birth. Several factors present prior to birth, such as radiation or the introduction of drugs into the fetal system, may result in vision loss. A major cause of blindness in the fetus is infection, which may be due to diseases such as rubella and syphilis. Other diseases that can result in blindness include influenza, mumps, and measles.

The leading cause of acquired blindness in children worldwide is vitamin A deficiency (**xerophthalmia**). Approximately 70% of the 500,000 children who become blind each year do so because of xerophthalmia (World Health Organization, 2003).

Another cause of acquired blindness is retinopathy of prematurity. As noted earlier, ROP results from the administering of oxygen over prolonged periods of time to low-birthweight infants. Almost 80% of preschool-age blind children lost their sight as a result of ROP during the peak years of the disease (1940s through 1960s).

Vision loss after birth may be due to several factors. Trauma, infections, inflammations, and tumors are all related to loss of sight. **Cortical visual impairment (CVI)** is a leading cause of acquired blindness. CVI, which involves damage to the occipital lobes and/or the visual pathways to the brain, can result from severe trauma, asphyxia, seizures, infections of the central nervous system, drugs, poisons, or other neurological conditions. Most children with CVI have residual vision.

The most common cause of preventable blindness is **trachoma**. This infectious disease affects more than 150 million people worldwide. Trachoma is associated with the living standards and hygiene within a community (such as lack of water and unsanitary conditions). The World Health Organization cautions that although the incidence of trachoma has been reduced worldwide, it remains a serious health risk to millions of people in underserved rural areas (World Health Organization, 2003).

The most common vision problems in adults, particularly those over the age of 60, are caused by **macular degeneration**. This condition is the result of a breakdown of the tissues in the macula (a small area in the middle of the retina). Macular degeneration affects more than 165,000 people annually, and each year 16,000 go blind as a result of the disease. Nearly two million Americans have impaired vision as a consequence macular degeneration. With macular degeneration, central vision becomes distorted and blurry. The individual also has considerable difficulty differentiating colors (Rosenfeld, 2001). New advances in the treatment of macular degeneration include laser surgery and drug therapy.

# Characteristics

A vision loss present at birth will have a more significant effect on individual development than one that occurs later in life. Useful visual imagery may disappear if sight is lost prior to the age of 5. If sight is lost after the age of 5, it is possible for the person to retain some visual memories for years to come, which will help the person better understand newly learned concepts. Total blindness that occurs prior to age 5 has the greatest negative influence on overall functioning. However, many people who are blind from birth or early childhood are able to function at a level comparable to that of sighted persons of equal ability.

**Xerophthalmia**

A condition caused by vitamin A deficiency that can lead to blindness.

**Cortical visual impairment (CVI)**

A leading cause of acquired blindness, which involves damage to the occipital lobes and/or the visual pathways to the brain. CVI can result from severe trauma, asphyxia, seizures, infections of the central nervous system, drugs, poisons, or various neurological conditions.

**Trachoma**

A slowly progressing, infectious bacterial disease associated with poor living standards and inadequate hygiene.

**Macular degeneration**

An age-related condition in which the macula (tissues within the retina) break down, resulting in distorted and blurred central vision.

## Intelligence

Children with vision loss sometimes base their perceptions of the world on input from senses other than vision. This is particularly true of the child who is congenitally blind, whose learning experiences are significantly restricted by the lack of vision. Consequently, everyday learning opportunities that people with sight take for granted, such as reading the morning newspaper or watching television news coverage, may be substantially altered.

Reviews of the literature on intellectual development suggest that children with vision loss differ from children with sight in some areas of intelligence, ranging from understanding of spatial concepts to general knowledge of the world (Batshaw, 2003; Kingsley, 1997). However, comparing the performances of individuals with and without sight may not be appropriate if those with sight have an advantage. The only valid way to compare the intellectual capabilities of these children must be based on tasks in which vision loss does not interfere with performance.

## Speech and Language Skills

For children with sight, speech and language development occurs primarily through the integration of visual experiences and the symbols of the spoken word. Depending on the degree of loss, children with vision loss are at a distinct disadvantage in developing speech and language skills because they are unable to associate words with objects visually. Because of this, such children must rely on hearing or touch for input, and their speech may develop at a slower rate. Once these children have learned speech, however, it is typically fluent.

Preschool-age and school-age children with vision loss may develop a phenomenon known as **verbalisms**, or the excessive use of speech, in which individuals may use words that have little meaning to them (e.g., "Crusaders are people of a religious sex" or "Lead us not into Penn Station"). Silberman and Sowell (1998) maintain that children with visual impairments have particular difficulties in expressing themselves verbally because of their "incomplete awareness of all the details of an experience" (p. 163). These authors suggested that these children have a restricted oral vocabulary, compared to that of sighted peers, because they lack the visual input necessary for them to piece together all of the information available in a given experience.

## Academic Achievement

The academic achievement of students with vision loss may be significantly delayed relative to that of students with sight. In fact, the academic achievement of these students often resembles that of children with learning disabilities (Bishop, 1996b). Numerous variables influence academic achievement for students with vision loss. In the area of written language, these students may have more difficulty writing a composition because they lack the opportunity to read newspapers and magazines. Decoding in the area of reading may be delayed because students with visual impairments often use braille or large-print books as the media to decode. Decoding is a much slower process when one is using these two media. Reading comprehension is also affected because it depends so much on the experiences of the reader. Once again, the experience of students with visual impairments may be limited in comparison to students with sight, and therefore these children don't bring as much information to the reading task (Silberman & Sowell, 1998).

Other possible reasons for delays in academic achievement range from excessive school absences due to the need for eye surgery or treatment to years of failure in programs that did not meet each student's specialized needs.

On the average, children with vision loss may lag 2 years behind sighted children in grade level. Thus most direct comparisons of students with vision loss to those with sight would indicate significantly delayed academic growth. However, this phenomenon may have resulted from children with vision loss having entered school at

**FOCUS 5**

Describe how a vision loss can affect intelligence, speech and language skills, educational achievement, social development, physical orientation and mobility, and perceptual-motor development.

**Verbalisms**

Excessive use of speech (wordiness) in which individuals use words that have little meaning to them.

a later age, from frequent absence due to medical problems, or from lack of appropriate school resources and facilities.

## Social Development

The ability of children with vision loss to adapt to the social environment depends on a number of factors both hereditary and experiential. It is true that each of us experiences the world in his or her own way, but common bonds provide a foundation on which to build perceptions of the world around us. One such bond is vision. Without vision, perceptions about ourselves and those around us can be drastically different.

For the person with vision loss, these differences in perception may produce some social-emotional challenges. For example, Crocker and Orr (1996) found that although preschool-age children with significant vision loss were capable of interacting with same-age peers without disabilities, there were some differences between the two groups of children. Children with vision loss were less likely to initiate a social interaction and had fewer opportunities to socialize with other children. These authors pointed out that the success of an inclusive preschool depends on the "presence of specialized programs [supports] to encourage and reinforce interactions between children with visual impairments and their peers with full sight" (p. 461).

People with vision loss are unable to imitate the physical mannerisms of others and therefore do not develop one very important component of social communication: body language. Because the subtleties of nonverbal communication can significantly alter the intended meaning of spoken words, a person's inability to learn and use visual cues (e.g., facial expressions, hand gestures) has profound consequences for interpersonal interactions. The person with vision loss can neither see the visual cues that accompany the messages received from others nor sense the messages that he or she may be conveying through body language.

Differences between people with a vision loss and those who are sighted may also result from the exclusion of the person with a vision loss from social activities that are integrally related to the use of sight (e.g., sports, movies). People with vision loss are often excluded from such activities without a second thought, simply because they cannot see. This reinforces the mistaken notion that they do not want to participate and would not enjoy these activities. Social skills can be learned and effectively used by people with vision loss. Excluding them from social experiences more often stems from negative public attitudes than from the individuals' lack of social adjustment skills. For more in-depth information about social development and people with a vision loss, see the nearby Reflect on This, "Losing Sight: Reflection on a Friend Who Is Blind."

## Orientation and Mobility

A unique limitation facing people with vision loss is the basic problem of getting from place to place. Such individuals may be unable to orient themselves to other people or objects in the environment simply because they cannot see them, and therefore they will not understand their own relative position in space. Consequently, they may be unable to move in the right direction and may fear getting injured, so they may attempt to restrict their movements in order to protect themselves. In addition, parents and professionals may contribute to such fears by overprotecting the person who

*Young children with a vision loss often have limited opportunities to socially interact with peers who are not disabled, and they are less likely to initiate social contact.*

## LOSING SIGHT: REFLECTION ON A FRIEND WHO IS BLIND

Twelve years ago, at the birthday party of a friend, was the first time I met somebody my own age who had a disability. He was tall for his age, thin, and wore eyeglasses, just like I did. It was this commonality that initially attracted me to him, since I didn't know very many kindergartners who wore glasses. I had begun wearing glasses to correct a case of strabismus at age 2 and was able to see perfectly when I put them on. However, I was not aware of the fact that his glasses did very little to sharpen his vision and that he was legally blind.

On the last day of second grade, at the unofficial annual picnic at Westland Hills Park, we became good friends. As we moved from the swings to the jungle gym to the sprinklers, I realized how much we truly had in common. We enjoyed the same things: Legos, swimming, and being Cub Scouts.

Throughout third grade, we spent nearly every weekend together. During this time, though I had been informed of his disability, I never made any differentiation between his abilities or personality and my own. Although I often helped to direct him when he didn't seem to quite have his bearings, I never doubted that his capabilities were similar to my own.

After that year, we were not assigned the same teachers for fourth grade, and unfortunately, we drifted apart. As we finished elementary school and I watched him from a greater distance, his disability somehow became more apparent to me. When other kids asked me if I knew him, I would think of him as the boy who couldn't see well, or the one in the class who had to read large-type books. Why was I doing this? In part, it may have been because I was forced to look at his situation with less subjectivity. Perhaps it was because I began to recognize there were a few things he couldn't do as well as others. Most of all, I believe that my feel-

ings came from the fact that society emphasizes disabilities as a difference between human beings.

While it is necessary to be aware of others' disabilities, they should not be the distinguishing factor between two people. As we continued through middle school, I realized that losing contact often causes one to lose sight of somebody's true personality and the characteristics that make the person who he or she is. However, I would eventually notice his maturity, perseverance, and determination in all areas of his life, qualities which have led him to develop into a young man I truly admire.

During my junior year, we were placed in the same aquatics class. I discovered our interests now differed, but that we had both pursued and achieved a number of personal goals. The last time we spoke, at his parents' New Year's party, I was inspired by the amount of things he had accomplished in the past year. He had become manager of the school store and had won Albany High School's only gold medal in the regional DECA business competition. He got a job at Eastern Mountain Sports. Over the summer, he had participated in a rigorous mountain climbing and hiking trip in the Adirondacks, not for a second letting his disability get in the way of doing something he loved.

I thought back to that first day at the park, when I had worried that his sight might cause him to fall and hurt himself. Now, he had pushed himself to do something considered difficult for anybody. This inspirational individual has never allowed his disability to become his most prominent quality, and consequently, he has encouraged me to view disabilities in the same way. I feel that he has served as an example to society, showing that disabilities do not dictate an individual's personality or quality of life.

—Nathaniel Lewis, Albany High School, New York

SOURCE: From "Losing Sight," by N. Lewis, Summer 1999, *Newsletter of the New York State Commission on Quality of Care*, p. 76. Available: *http://www.cqc.state.ny.us/76nlewis.htm*

---

has vision loss from the everyday risks of life. Shielding the individual in this way will hinder her or his acquisition of independent mobility skills and may promote lifelong overdependence on caregivers.

Vision loss can affect fine motor coordination and undermine the ability to manipulate objects. Poor eye–hand coordination interferes with learning how to use tools related to job skills and daily living skills (e.g., eating utensils, a toothbrush, a screwdriver). Prevention or remediation of fine motor problems may require training in the use of visual aid magnifiers and improvement of basic fine motor skills. This training must begin early and focus directly on experiences that will enhance opportunities for independent living.

### Perceptual-Motor Development

Perceptual-motor development is essential to locomotion skills, but it is also important in the development of cognition, language, socialization, and personality. Most children with vision loss appear to have perceptual discrimination abilities (e.g., discriminating texture, weight, and sound) comparable to those of children with

Author and mountaineer Erik Weihenmayer didn't let blindness interfere with his life's passion to scale some of the world's highest mountains.

sight (Bishop, 1996b). However, children with vision loss do not perform as well on more complex tasks of perception, including form identification, spatial relations, and perceptual-motor integration (Bouchard & Tetreault, 2000; Stone, 1997).

A popular misconception regarding the perceptual abilities of persons with vision loss is that because of their diminished sight, they will develop greater capacity in other sensory areas. For example, people who are blind are often assumed to be able to hear or smell some things that people with normal vision cannot perceive. This notion has never been empirically validated.

# Educational Supports and Services

**FOCUS 6**

What is a functional approach to assessment for students with a vision loss?

## Assessment

In addition to assessing the cognitive ability, academic achievement, language skills, motor performance, and social-emotional functioning of a student with a vision loss, an IEP team must also focus on how the student utilizes any remaining vision (visual efficiency) in conjunction with other senses. The Visual Efficient Scale (see Barraga and Erin, 2001), assesses the overall visual functioning of the individual to determine how he or she uses sight to acquire information. As suggested by Bishop (1996a), "When a child still has some useful vision, it should be utilized; it cannot be 'conserved' by not using it, as was once thought; it must be practiced to reach maximum efficiency" (p. 92).

A functional approach to assessment focuses on an individual's visual capacity, attention, and processing. Visual capacity includes both acuity and field of vision but also encompasses the response of the individual to visual information. The assessment of visual attention involves observing the individual's sensitivity to visual stimuli (alertness), ability to use vision to select information from a variety of sources, attention to a visual stimulus, and ability to process visual information. Assessment of visual-processing determines which, if any, of the components of normal visual functioning are impaired.

**FOCUS 7**

Describe two content areas that should be included in educational programs for students with vision loss.

## Mobility Training and Daily Living Skills

The educational needs of students with vision loss are comparable to those of their sighted counterparts. In addition, many instructional methods currently used with students who are sighted are appropriate for students with vision loss. However, educators must be aware that certain content areas that are not usually necessary for sighted students are essential to the success of students with vision loss in a classroom situation. These areas include mobility and orientation training, as well as acquisition of daily living skills.

The ability to move safely, efficiently, and independently through the environment enhances the individual's opportunities to learn more about the world and thus be less dependent on others. Lack of mobility restricts individuals with vision loss in nearly every aspect of educational life. Such students may be unable to orient themselves to physical structures in the classroom (e.g., desks, chairs, and aisles), hallways, rest rooms, library, or cafeteria. Whereas a person with sight can automatically establish a relative position in space, the individual with vision loss must be taught some means of compensating for a lack of visual input. This may be accomplished in a number of ways. It is important that students with vision loss not only learn the physical structure of their school but also develop specific techniques to orient themselves to unfamiliar surroundings.

*This talking ATM machine allows people with a vision loss to conveniently access their bank account and complete a transaction.*

These orientation techniques involve using the other senses. For example, the senses of touch and hearing can help identify cues that indicate where the bathroom is in the school. Although it is not true that people who are blind have superior hearing, they may learn to use their hearing more effectively by focusing on subtle auditory cues that often go unnoticed. The efficient use of hearing, in conjunction with the other senses (including any remaining vision), is the key to independent travel for people with vision loss.

Independent travel with a sighted companion but without the use of a cane, guide dog, or electronic device is the most common form of travel for young school-age children. The major challenges for children with low vision in moving independently and safely through their environment include

- Adjusting to glare
- Adapting to lighting changes
- Negotiating drop-offs (stairs and curbs)
- Negotiating street crossings
- Negotiating changes in terrain
- Walking through crowded areas
- Bumping into objects and obstacles
- Walking in inclement weather
- Seeing details (street names and house numbers) during travel (Smith & Geruschat, 1996, pp. 307–308)

With the increasing emphasis on instructing young children in orientation at an earlier age, use of the long cane (Kiddy Cane) for young children has become more common. As these children grow older, they may be instructed in the use of a Mowat Sensor. The **Mowat Sensor**, approximately the size of a flashlight, is a hand-held ultrasound travel aid that uses high-frequency sound to detect objects. Vibration frequency increases as objects become closer; the sensor vibrates at different rates to warn of obstacles in front of the individual. The device ignores everything but the closest object within the beam.

**Mowat Sensor**

A handheld travel aid, approximately the size of a flashlight, used by people who are blind. It serves as an alternative to a cane for finding obstacles in the person's pathway.

*Guide dogs and electronic mobility devices (such as this global positioning device) help people who are blind to move safely, efficiently, and independently through their environment.*

Guide dogs or electronic mobility devices may be appropriate for the adolescent or adult, because the need to travel independently significantly increases with age. A variety of electronic mobility devices are currently being used for everything from enhancing hearing efficiency to detecting obstacles.

The **laser cane** converts infrared light into sound as light beams strike objects in the path of the person who is blind. It uses a range-finding technique with a semiconductor laser and a position-sensitive device (PSD). Proximity to an obstacle is signaled by vibration at different levels of frequency.

The **Sonicguide**, or Sonic Pathfinder, which is worn on the head, emits ultrasound and converts the reflections of sound from objects into audible noise in such a way that the individual can learn about the structure of the objects. For example, loudness indicates size: The louder the noise, the larger the object. To use the Sonicguide effectively, the person with low vision should have mobility skills. It is designed for outdoor use in conjunction with a cane, a guide dog, or residual vision.

The acquisition of daily living skills is another content area important to success in the classroom and to overall independence. Most people take for granted such routine activities as eating, dressing, bathing, and toileting. A person with sight learns very early in life the tasks associated with perceptual-motor development, including grasping, lifting, balancing, pouring, and manipulating objects. These daily living tasks become more complex during the school years as a child learns personal hygiene, grooming, and social etiquette. Eventually, people with sight acquire many complex daily living skills that later contribute to their independence as adults. Money management, grocery shopping, doing laundry, cooking, cleaning, household repairs, sewing, mowing the lawn, and gardening are all daily tasks associated with adult life and are learned from experiences that are not usually a part of an individual's formal educational program.

For children with vision loss, however, routine daily living skills are not easily learned through everyday experiences. Family and friends must encourage and support these children as they develop life skills and must not overprotect them from everyday challenges and risks.

## Instructional Content

Mobility training and daily living skills are components of an educational program that must also include an academic curriculum. Koenig and Rex (1996, p. 285) suggested that teachers of students with low vision focus on several core areas:

- Ensuring that students develop a solid experiential and conceptual basis for literacy
- Structuring early literacy experiences in the home so as not to rely solely on incidental experiences
- Teaching the effective use of visual skills in authentic contexts, such as efficient scanning to locate words in a dictionary or to interpret a map
- Teaching students to interpret pictures of increasing complexity
- Teaching students to use optical and nonoptical low-vision devices
- Providing practice to build automatic skills in the use of low-vision devices

**Laser cane**

A mobility device for people who are blind. It converts infrared light into sound as light beams strike objects.

**Sonicguide**

An electronic mobility device for people who are blind, which is worn on the head, emits ultrasound, and converts reflections of objects into audible noise.

- Providing targeted instruction to increase fluency and stamina in reading

- Teaching functional applications of reading and writing skills if they have not already been taught in the classroom

- Arranging the physical environment to maximize the visual learning of young students and increase their comfort

- Helping the student assume responsibility for gaining access to print

- Teaching keyboarding and computer word-processing skills if these skills are not part of the early regular curriculum

- Teaching a variety of literacy tools for gaining access to print independently, such as using a monocular (magnified eye glass) to take notes from a chalkboard.

Particular emphasis must be placed on developing receptive and expressive language skills. Students with vision loss must learn to listen in order to understand the auditory world more clearly. Finely tuned receptive skills contribute to the development of expressive language, which enables these students to describe their perceptions of the world orally. Koenig and Rex suggested using a language experience approach (LEA) to develop language skills and prepare students for reading. The LEA involves several steps, as described in Table 16.1.

Oral expression can be expanded to include handwriting as a means of communication. The acquisition of social and instructional language skills opens the door to many areas, including reading and mathematics. Reading can greatly expand the knowledge base for children with vision loss. For people who are partially sighted, various optical aids are available: video systems that magnify print, handheld magnifiers, magnifiers attached to eyeglasses, and other telescopic aids. Another way to facilitate reading for partially sighted students is the use of large-print books, which are generally available through the American Printing House for the Blind and the Library of Congress in several print sizes. Other factors that must be considered in teaching reading to students who are partially sighted include adequate illumination and the reduction of glare. Advance organizers prepare students by previewing the instructional approach and materials to be used in a lesson. These organizers essentially identify the topics or tasks to be learned, give the student an organizational framework, indicate the concepts to be introduced, list new vocabulary, and state the intended outcomes for the student.

## TABLE 16.1

### General Steps in the Language Experience Approach

1. Arrange an experience for the student, or use a naturally occurring one.

2. Have the student tell a story about the experience. Write down the story as the student tells it and watches.

3. Read the story back to the student immediately, pointing to each word.

4. Continue to reread the story with the student over several days or weeks. The student will systematically read more and more of the story independently.

5. Structure appropriate activities around the story, such as the following:

   - *Word recognition* (for example, place selected words from the story on note cards and review them with the student; have the student find the words in the story)

   - *Phonics* (for instance, identify a recurring consonant or vowel sound from the story, make up other words that start with the identified sound, and read words with the identified sound)

   - *Comprehension* (for example, make up a title for the story that expresses its main idea; suggest titles that may be too broad or too narrow for the story)

   - *Art activities* (for instance, draw pictures or create other works of art that depict the experiences in the story)

SOURCE: From "Instruction of Literacy Skills to Children and Youth with Low Vision," by A. J. Koenig and E. J. Rex. In *Foundations of Low Vision: Clinical and Functional Perspectives*, edited by the American Foundation for the Blind Press, 1996, p. 292, New York: Author.

Abstract mathematical concepts may be difficult for students who are blind. These students will probably require additional practice as they learn to master symbols, number facts, and higher-level calculations. As concepts become more complex, additional aids may be necessary to facilitate learning. Specially designed talking microcomputers, calculators, rulers, and compasses, as well as the Crammer abacus, have been developed to assist students in this area.

## Communication Media

For students who are partially sighted, their limited vision remains a means of obtaining information. The use of optical aids in conjunction with auditory and tactile stimuli allows these individuals an integrated sensory approach to learning. However, this approach is not possible for students who are blind. Because they do not have access to visual stimuli, they may have to compensate through the use of tactile and auditory media. Through these media, children who are blind develop an understanding of themselves and the world around them. One facet of this development process is the acquisition of language, and one facet of language acquisition is learning to read.

For the student who is blind, the tactile sense can open up the symbolic world of reading. The most widely used tactile medium for teaching reading is the braille system. This system, which originated with the work of Louis Braille in 1829, is a code that utilizes a six-dot cell to form 63 different alphabetical, numerical, and grammatical characters. To become a proficient braille reader, a person must learn 263 different configurations, including letters of the alphabet, punctuation marks, short-form words, and contractions. Braille is not a tactile reproduction of the standard English alphabet but a separate code for reading and writing.

Braille is composed of from one to six raised dots depicted in a cell or space that contains room for two vertical rows of three dots each. On the left the dots are numbered 1, 2, and 3 from top to bottom; on the right the dots are numbered 4, 5, and 6 (see Figure 16.4). This makes it easy to describe braille characters. For example, a is dot 1, p is dots 1, 2, 3, and 4, and h is dots 1, 2, and 5. . . .

In braille any letter becomes a capital by putting dot 6 in front of it. For example, if a is dot 1, A is dot 6 followed by dot 1 and if p is dots 1, 2, 3, and 4, P is dot 6 followed by dots 1, 2, 3, and 4. This sure is easier than print, which requires different configurations for more than half of the capital letters. If h is dots 1, 2, and 5, what is H?

Research has shown that the fastest braille readers use two hands. Using two hands also seems to make it easier for beginning braille readers to stay on the line. Do you think this might have something to do with two points constituting a line, as my geometry teacher used to tell us? (Pester, 2003).

Braille is used by about 1 out of every 10 students who are blind and is considered by many to be an efficient means of teaching reading and writing. The American Printing House for the Blind produces about 28 million pages in English braille each year (Pester, 2003). Critics of the system argue that most readers who use braille are much slower than those who read from print and that braille materials are bulky and tedious. It can be argued, however, that without braille, people who are blind would be much less independent. Some people who are unable to read braille (such as people with diabetes who have decreased tactile sensitivity) are more dependent on sight readers and recordings. Simple tasks—such as labeling cans, boxes, or cartons in a bathroom or kitchen—become nearly impossible to complete.

Braille writing is accomplished through the use of a slate and stylus. Using this procedure, a student writes a mirror image of the reading code, moving from right to left. The writing process may be facilitated by using a braille writer, a hand-operated machine with six keys that correspond to each dot in the braille cell.

Certain innovations for braille readers reduce some of the problems associated with the medium. The Mountbatten Brailler is electronic, thus making it easier to operate

**FOCUS 8**

How can communication media facilitate learning for people with vision loss?

**FIGURE 16.4**

**Braille Bits**

● 1    ● 4

● 2    ● 5

● 3    ● 6

than a manual unit. It weighs about 15 pounds and can be hooked up to a computer keyboard attachment to input information.

The Braille 'n Speak is a pocket-size battery-powered braille note taker with keyboard for data entry and with voice output. The device can translate braille into synthesized speech or print. Files may be printed in formatted text to a printer designed to enable users to input information through a braille keyboard. The Braille 'n Speak has accessories for entering or reading text for a host computer, for reading computer disks, and for sending or receiving a fax.

The Braille 'n Speak translates braille into synthesized speech and is so portable it can be carried anywhere.

In regard to educational programs for students who are blind, the U.S. Congress responded to concerns that services for these students were not addressing their unique educational and learning needs, particularly their needs for instruction in reading, writing, and composition. In IDEA, Congress mandated that schools make provision for instruction in braille and for the use of braille unless the IEP team determines that such instruction and use are not appropriate to the needs of the student (U.S. Department of Education, 2000).

One tactile device that does not use the braille system is the Optacon Scanner. This machine exposes printed material to a camera and then reproduces it on a fingerpad, using a series of vibrating pins that are tactile reproductions of the printed material. This device was developed by J. C. Bliss and has been available commercially since 1971; thousands of Optacons are currently in use worldwide. Although the Optacon greatly expands access to the printed word, it has drawbacks as well. It requires tactile sensitivity, so reading remains a slow, laborious process. Additionally, considerable training is necessary for the individual to become a skilled user. These drawbacks, along with the development of reading machines, have resulted in the declining use and production of the Optacon Scanner.

Many of the newer communication systems do not make use of the tactile sense because it is not functional for all people who are blind (many, including some elderly people, do not have tactile sensitivity). Such individuals must rely solely on the auditory sense to acquire information. Specialized auditory media for people who are blind are becoming increasingly available. One example is the reading machine, hailed as a major breakthrough in technology for persons with a vision loss. Reading machines convert printed matter into synthetic speech at a rate of 1 to 2.5 pages per minute. They can also convert print into braille. The costs associated with reading machines have decreased substantially in the past few years, and most can be purchased with computer accessories for about $1,000. Several advocacy organizations for those with blindness and many banks throughout America currently provide low-interest loans for people with vision loss so that they can purchase the device. The first reading machines were invented by Ray Kurzweil in the 1970s, culminating in the L&H Kurzweil 1000 Reading System in 1998. For more information on Kurzweil Reading Machines, see Assistive Technology, "The Magic Machines of Ray Kurzweil."

Other auditory aids that assist people who are blind include microcomputers with voice output, talking calculators, talking-book machines, compact disc players, and audiotape recorders. For example, the Note Teller is a small, compact machine that can identify denominations of U.S. currency. It "speaks" via a voice synthesizer that communicates in either English or Spanish.

## Assistive Technology

### THE MAGIC MACHINES OF RAY KURZWEIL

In the late 1960s, Ray Kurzweil walked on stage, played a composition on an old upright piano, and then whispered to *I've Got a Secret* host Steve Allen, "I built my own computer." "Well that's impressive," Steve Allen replied, "but what does that have to do with the piece you just played?" Ray then whispered the rest of his secret: "The computer composed the piece I just played." . . . Ray programmed his computer to analyze the patterns in musical compositions by famous composers and then compose original new melodies in a similar style. For the project, Ray won First Prize in the International Science Fair. From there, he went on to become one of the world's leading inventors, developing Kurzweil Computer Products and Optical Character Recognition (OCR)—teaching a computer to identify printed or typed characters regardless of type style and print quality.

At first, this new technology was a solution in search of a problem. Then a chance plane flight sitting next to a man who was blind convinced Ray that the most exciting application of this new technology would be to create a machine that could read printed and typed documents out loud,

thereby overcoming the reading disability of people who were visually impaired. This goal introduced new hurdles. Because there were no readily available scanners or speech synthesizers in the 1970s, Ray and his colleagues developed the first full text-to-speech synthesizer and combined these technologies into the first print-to-speech reading machine for people who are blind. Ray, along with the National Federation of the Blind, announced the Kurzweil Reading Machine at a press conference covered by all of the networks and leading print publications. Walter Cronkite used it to deliver his signature sign-off, "And that's the way it was, January 13, 1976." Stevie Wonder happened to catch Ray demonstrating the Kurzweil Reading Machine on the *Today Show* and dropped by Kurzweil Computer Products to pick up the first production unit. This was the beginning of a long-term friendship between the inventor and the musical star, which led to Ray Kurzweil's subsequent innovations in computer-based music.

Today, the L&H Kurzweil Reading Systems are used by people with visual impairments around the world.

SOURCE: Adapted from *A Brief Biography of Ray Kurzweil*, by Kurzweil Technologies, 2003, Burlington, MA. Lernout & Hauspie. Available: www.kurzweiltech.com/raybio.htm. Retrieved June 12, 2003.

Communication media that facilitate participation of people with vision loss in the community include specialized library and newspaper services that offer books in large print, on cassette, and in braille. The *New York Times*, for example, publishes a weekly special edition with type three times the size of its regular type. The sale of large-print books has increased during the past ten years, and many have also become available through the Internet or on computer disk (electronic books).

Responding to a human voice, devices known as **personal digital assistants (PDAs)** can look up a telephone number and dial it. Using a synthesized voice, some PDAs can read a newspaper delivered over telephone lines, balance a checkbook, turn home appliances on and off, and maintain a daily appointment book.

**Closed-circuit television (CCTV)** systems are another means of enlarging the print from books and other written documents. CCTV systems were initially explored in the 1950s. Their design became more practical in the 1970s, and they are now in wider use than ever before. The components of the CCTV systems include a small television camera with variable zoom lens and focusing capacity, a TV monitor, and a sliding platform table for the printed materials. An individual sits in front of the television monitor to view printed material that can be enhanced to up to 60 times its original size through the use of the TV camera and zoom lens. Some CCTVs are also available with split-screen capability to allow near and distant objects to be viewed together. These machines can accept input directly from a computer as well as printed material.

**Personal Digital Assistants (PDAs)**

Handheld computer device that can be programmed to perform multiple functions, such as dialing a telephone, reading a newspaper, or maintaining a daily calendar or address book.

**Closed-circuit television (CCTV)**

A TV system that includes a small television camera with zoom lens, TV monitor, and sliding platform table, which allows an individual with vision loss to view printed material enlarged up to 60 times its original size.

# Educating Students with Vision Loss in the Least Restrictive Environment

Historically, education for students with vision loss—specifically, blindness—was provided through specialized residential facilities. These segregated centers have traditionally been referred to as asylums, institutions, or schools. One of the first such facilities in the United States was the New England Asylum for the Blind, later renamed the Perkins School. This facility opened its doors in 1832 and was one of several eastern U.S. schools that used treatment models borrowed from well-established European institutions. For the most part, the early U.S. institutions operated as closed schools, where a person who was blind would live and learn in an environment that was essentially separate from the outside world. The objective was to get the person who was blind "ready for the outside world," even though this approach provided little real exposure to it.

More recently, some residential schools have advocated an open system of intervention. These programs are based on the philosophy that children who are blind should have every opportunity to gain the same experiences that would be available if they were growing up in their own communities.

Both open and closed residential facilities exist today as alternative intervention modes, but they are no longer the primary social or educational systems available to people who are blind. Like John in the chapter-opening Snapshot, the vast majority of people who are blind or partially sighted now live at home, attend local public schools, and interact within the community. For more information on tips for including people with vision loss in family, school, and community, see the nearby Inclusion Through the Lifespan.

Educational programs for students with vision loss are based on the principle of flexible placement. Thus a wide variety of services are available to these students, ranging from placement in general education classes, with little or no assistance from specialists, to separate residential schools. Between these two levels of service, the public schools generally offer several alternative classroom structures, including the use of consulting teachers, resource rooms, part-time special classes, or full-time special classes. Placement of a student in one of these programs depends on the extent to which the loss of vision affects his or her overall educational achievement. Many students with vision loss are able to function successfully within inclusive educational programs if the learning environment is adapted to meet their needs. Such is the case for Michael in the Case Study on page 462. Michael has been going to school with other students without disabilities since the fifth grade. Now in high school, he has a strong peer support group and access to the assistive technology needed to ensure his success in general education classes.

Some organizations advocating for students who are blind strongly support the concept of flexible placements. The American Foundation for the Blind (2000) recommends an entire spectrum of alternative placements, emphasizing that students who are visually impaired are most likely to succeed in educational systems where a full array of programs and services are provided by qualified staff to address each student's unique educational needs. (See the Debate Forum: "General Education Schools versus Special Schools: Where Should Students Who Are Blind Be Educated?" on page 463.)

Whether the student is to be included in the general education classroom or taught in a special class, a vision specialist must be available, either to support the general education classroom teacher or to provide direct instruction to the student. A vision specialist has received concentrated training in the education of students with vision loss. This specialist and the rest of the educational support team have knowledge of appropriate educational assessment techniques, specialized curriculum materials and teaching approaches, and the use of various communication media. Specialized instruction for students who have vision loss may involve major modifications in curricula, including the teaching of concepts that children who are sighted learn incidentally (e.g., walking down the street, moving from one room to the next in the school building, getting meals in the cafeteria, and using public transportation).

FOCUS 9

What educational placements are available to students with vision loss?

# Medical and Social Services

Medical services for vision loss include initial screenings based on visual acuity; preventive measures that include genetic screening, appropriate prenatal care, and early developmental assessments; and treatment ranging from optical aids to surgery. Some people with vision loss may have social adjustment difficulties,

## PEOPLE WITH VISION LOSS

### EARLY CHILDHOOD YEARS

#### Tips for the Family

- Assist your child with vision loss in learning how to get around in the home environment. Then give him or her the freedom to move freely about.
- Help your child become oriented to the environment by removing all unnecessary obstacles around the home (e.g., shoes left on the floor, partially opened doors, a vacuum cleaner left out). Keep him or her informed of any changes in room arrangements.
- Instruction in special mobility techniques should begin as early as possible with the young child who has vision loss.
- Keep informed about organizations and civic groups that can provide support to the child and the family.
- Get in touch with your local health, social services, and education agencies about infant, toddler, and preschool programs for children with vision loss. Become familiar with the individualized family service plan (IFSP) and how it can serve as a planning tool to include your child in early intervention programs.

#### Tips for the Preschool Teacher

- Mobility is a fundamental part of early intervention programs for children with vision loss. Help them learn to explore the environment in the classroom, school, and local neighborhood.
- Work with the child on developing a sense of touch and using hearing to acquire information. The young child may also need assistance in learning to smile and make eye contact.
- Work closely with the family to develop orientation and mobility strategies that can be learned and applied in both home and school settings.
- Help sighted children in the classroom interact with the young child with vision loss by teaching them to speak directly to him or her in a normal tone of voice so as not to raise the noise level.
- Become very familiar with both tactile (e.g., braille) and auditory aids (e.g., personal readers) that may be used by the young child to acquire information.

#### Tips for Preschool Personnel

- Support the inclusion of young children with vision loss in your classrooms and programs.
- Support teachers, staff, and volunteers as they attempt to create successful experiences for the young child with vision loss in the preschool setting.
- Work very closely with families to keep them informed and active members of the school community.

#### Tips for Neighbors and Friends

- Never assume that because a young child has a vision loss, he or she cannot or should not participate in family and neighborhood activities that are associated with sight (e.g., board games, sports, hide-and-seek).
- Work with the young child's family to seek opportunities for interaction with sighted children in neighborhood play settings.

### ELEMENTARY YEARS

#### Tips for the Family

- Learn about the programs and services available during the school years for your child with vision loss. Actively participate in the development of your child's individualized education program (IEP).
- Participate in as many school functions for parents as is reasonable to connect your family to the school (e.g., PTA, parent advisory groups, volunteering).
- Seek information on in-school and extracurricular activities that will enhance opportunities for your child to interact with sighted peers.
- Keep the school informed about the medical needs of your child.
- If your child needs or uses specialized mobility devices to enhance access to the environment, help school personnel to understand how these devices work.

#### Tips for the General Education Classroom Teacher

- Remove obstacles in the classroom that may interfere with the mobility of students with vision loss, from small things like litter on the floor to desks that are blocking aisles.
- The child with vision loss should also sit as close as possible to visual objects associated with instruction (e.g., blackboard, video monitor, or classroom bulletin board).
- Be consistent in where you place classroom materials so that the child with vision loss can locate them independently.
- When providing instruction, always try to stand away from the windows. It is very difficult for a person with vision loss to look directly into a light source.
- Work closely with a vision specialist to determine any specialized mobility or lighting needs for the student with vision loss (e.g., special desk lamp, cassette recorder, large-print books, personal reader).
- Help the student gain confidence in you by letting him or her know where you are in the classroom. It is especially helpful to let the student know when you are planning to leave the classroom.

#### Tips for School Personnel

- Integrate school resources as well as children. Wherever possible, help general education classroom teachers access the human and material resources necessary to meet the needs of students with vision loss. For example:
  - *A vision specialist.* A professional trained in the education of students with vision loss can serve as an effective consultant to you and the children in several areas (e.g., mobility training, use of special equipment, communication media, instructional strategies).
  - *An ophthalmologist.* Students with a vision loss often have associated medical problems. It is helpful for the teacher to understand any related medical needs that can affect the child's educational experience.

— *Peer buddy and support systems.* Peer support can be an effective tool for learning in a classroom setting. Peer buddy systems can be established in the school to help the child with initial mobility needs and/or to provide any tutoring that would help him or her succeed in the general education classroom.

- Support keeping the school as barrier-free as possible; this includes providing adequate lighting in classrooms and hallways.
- It is critical that children with vision loss have access to appropriate reading materials (e.g., braille books, large-print books, cassette recordings of books) in the school library and media center.

### Tips for Neighbors and Friends

- Help the family of a child who is visually impaired be an integral part of the neighborhood and friendship networks. Seek ways to include the family and child wherever possible in neighborhood activities.

## SECONDARY AND TRANSITION YEARS

### Tips for the Family

- Become familiar with the adult services system (e.g., rehabilitation services, Social Security, health care) while your son or daughter is still in high school. Understand the type of vocational or employment training that he or she will need prior to graduation.
- Find out the school's view on what it should do to assist students with vision loss in making the transition from school to adult life.
- Create opportunities for your son or daughter to participate in out-of-school activities with same-age sighted peers.

### Tips for the General Education Classroom Teacher

- Help students with vision loss to adapt to subject matter in your classroom while you adapt the classroom to meet their needs (e.g., in terms of seating, oral instruction, mobility, large-print or braille textbooks).
- Access to auditory devices (e.g., cassette recorders for lectures) can facilitate students' learning.
- Support the student with vision loss in becoming involved in extracurricular activities. If you are the faculty sponsor of a club or organization, explore whether the student is interested and how he or she could get involved.

### Tips for School Personnel

- Encourage parents of students with vision loss to participate actively in school activities (e.g., parent/ teacher groups and advisory committees).
- Maintain positive and ongoing contact with the family.

### Tips for Neighbors, Friends, and Potential Employers

- Seek ways of becoming part of a community support network for individuals with a vision loss. Be alert to ways in which individuals can become and remain actively involved in community employment, neighborhood recreational activities, and local church functions.
- As potential employers in the local community, seek information on employment of people with a vision loss.

## ADULT YEARS

### Tips for the Family

- Become aware of the support and services available for your son and daughter in the local community in which she or he will live as an adult. Identify the government-supported programs available to assist people with vision loss in the areas of postsecondary education opportunities, employment, and recreation/leisure. Identify informal supports, such as family and friends, to assist your son or daughter.

### Tips for Neighbors, Friends, and Potential Employers

- Work with the person who has vision loss and the family to become part of a community support network for individuals with vision loss. Help the individual with vision loss to become and remain involved in community employment, neighborhood recreational activities, and local church functions.
- As an employer in the community, seek out information on the employment of people with vision loss. Find out about the programs that focus on establishing employment opportunities for people with a vision loss, while meeting your needs as an employer.

# MICHAEL

Clasping a cane in his right hand and a book bag in his left, Michael Harris is darting though Kearns High School on his way to his next class. Peer tutor Rebecca Hale is helping this student, who is blind, negotiate the crowd.

"Hi, Mike!" blurt passers-by.

Suddenly, in a rich baritone voice, Michael belts out the first chorus of "I'll Be Home for Christmas."

No one marvels. The voice is familiar and pleasant. Frequently, the 17-year-old stays after school, where he sits cross-legged, propped against a locker, and sings. He even takes requests.

"The most important thing is these kids are just like any other kids," says Deanne Graves, teacher for those with visual impairments in Granite School District. "They have ups and downs. We need to treat them just like everybody else. Just because they have a disability does not mean they cannot aspire to whatever they want."

Michael has been part of the inclusion movement since he was a fifth-grader at Western Hills Elementary. He prefers it to his time at the Utah Schools for the Deaf and the Blind.

"One of the things I like about mainstreaming [is that there are kids from my neighborhood]. When I went to the School for the Blind, there were kids from all over the valley," he says. "So basically there was nobody from my neighborhood."

During his third-period college prep English course, the class is reading *Cyrano de Bergerac* aloud. Since Michael has fallen slightly behind, he sits outside the room with his tutor, Rebecca, listening to *Cyrano* on tape.

Unexpectedly, the fire alarm sounds. It is a routine fire drill. Rebecca, who gets school credit for helping Michael, leads him out of the building in the mass student exodus.

About three minutes later, Michael is swarmed by a crowd as they listen to his jokes.

"What do you call twins before they are born?" he asks. "Womb mates." The crowd laughs; Michael loves it.

## APPLICATION

1. Are Michael's experiences similar to or different from those of other students with vision loss that you have known in high school?

2. Describe any accommodations or supports that Michael is probably receiving that help him function so well in a general education classroom.

SOURCE: Adapted from *Disabled Students Making It in the Mainstream*, by S. A. Autman (October 31, 1994), *Salt Lake Tribune*, pp. B1, B2. Reprinted by permission of S. A. Autman and the *Salt Lake Tribune*.

---

## FOCUS 10

What steps can be taken to prevent and medically treat vision loss?

including lack of self-esteem and general feelings of inferiority. To minimize these problems, social services should be made available as early as possible in the person's life.

## Medical Services

Initial screenings for vision loss are usually based on the individual's visual acuity. Visual acuity may be measured via the Snellen test, developed in 1862 by Dutch ophthalmologist Herman Snellen. This visual screening test is used primarily to measure central distance vision. The subject stands 20 feet from a letter chart, or E-chart (the standard eye test chart), and reads each symbol, beginning with the top row. The different sizes of the letters or symbols in each row represent what a person with normal vision would see at the various distances. As indicated earlier in this chapter, a person's visual acuity is then expressed in terms of an index that reflects the distance at which an object can be recognized. A person with normal eyesight is defined as having 20/20 vision.

Since the Snellen test measures only visual acuity, it must be used primarily as an initial screening device and supplemented by more in-depth assessments, such as a thorough ophthalmological examination. Parents, physicians, school nurses, and educators must also carefully observe the child's behavior, and a complete history of possible symptoms of a vision loss should be documented. These observable symptoms fall into three categories: appearance, behavior, and complaints. Table 16.2 describes some warning signs of vision loss. The existence of symptoms does not necessarily mean a person has a significant vision loss, but it does indicate that an appropriate specialist should be consulted for further examination.

## GENERAL EDUCATION SCHOOLS VERSUS SPECIAL SCHOOLS

### Where Should Students Who Are Blind Be Educated?

In 1900, the first class for students who were blind opened in the Chicago public schools. Prior to this, such children were educated in state residential schools, where they lived away from their families. Until 1950, the ratio of students attending schools for the blind to those in general education public schools was about 10 to 1. In that year, however, the incidence of children with retrolental fibroplasia (now known as retinopathy of prematurity) in-creased, resulting in significant numbers of children who were blind attending public schools. By 1960, more children with blindness were being educated with their nondisabled peers in general education public schools than in schools for the blind. Nonetheless, the issue of what is the most appropriate educational environment for children who are blind continues to be debated internationally.

### POINT

Children who are blind should be educated in public schools and classrooms alongside their seeing peers. Inclusion enables children who are blind to remain at home with their families and live in a local neighborhood, which is just as important for these children as it is for their sighted friends. It also gives children who are blind greater opportunities for appropriate modeling of acceptable behaviors.

Schools for children who are blind have endeavored over the years to offer the best education possible, one intended to be equivalent to that offered to children who can see. However, these schools cannot duplicate the experiences of living at home and being part of the local community. Although it can be argued that the special school is geared entirely to the needs of the child who is blind, there is much more to education than a segregated educational environment can provide. During the growing years, the child must be directly involved in the seeing world in order to have the opportunity to adjust and become a part of society.

### COUNTERPOINT

The special school for children who are blind provides a complete education that is oriented entirely to the unique needs of these individuals. The teachers in these schools have years of experience in working exclusively with children who are blind and are well aware of what educational experiences are needed to help them reach their fullest potential. Additionally, special schools are equipped with a multitude of educational resources developed for children who are blind. General education schools and classrooms cannot offer the intensive, individualized programs in areas such as music, physical education, and arts and crafts that are available through schools for the blind. The strength of the special school is that it is entirely geared to the specialized needs of the child who is blind. Thus, it can more effectively teach him or her the skills necessary to adapt to life experiences.

What do you think? To give your opinion, go to Chapter 16 of the companion website (www.ablongman.com/hardman8e) and click on Debate Forum.

**PREVENTION.**    Prevention of vision loss is one of the major goals of the field of medicine. Because some causes of blindness are hereditary, it is important for the family to be aware of genetic services. One purpose of genetic screening is to identify those who are planning to have a family and who may possess certain detrimental genotypes (such as albinism or retinoblastoma) that can be passed on to their descendants. Screening may also be conducted after conception to determine whether the fetus possesses any genetic abnormalities. Following screening, a genetic counselor informs the parents of the test results so that the family can make an informed decision about conceiving a child or carrying a fetus to term.

Adequate prenatal care is another means of preventing problems. Parents must be made aware of the potential hazards associated with poor nutritional habits, the use of drugs, and exposure to radiation (e.g., x-rays) during pregnancy. One example of preventive care during this period is the use of antibiotics to treat various infections (e.g., influenza, measles, syphilis), thus reducing the risk of infection to the unborn fetus.

TABLE 16.2

## Warning Signs of Visual Problems

| PHYSICAL SYMPTOMS | OBSERVABLE BEHAVIOR | COMPLAINTS |
|---|---|---|
| Eyes are crossed. | Blinks constantly | Frequent dizziness |
| Eyes are not functioning in unison. | Trips or stumbles frequently | Frequent headaches |
| Eyelids are swollen and crusted, with red rims. | Covers one eye when reading | Pain in the eyes |
| Eyes are overly sensitive to light. | Holds reading material either very close or very far away | Itching or burning of the eyes or eyelids |
| Sties occur frequently. | Distorts the face or frowns when concentrating on something in the distance | Double vision |
| Eyes are frequently bloodshot. | Walks cautiously | |
| Pupils are of different sizes. | Fails to see objects that are to one side or the other | |
| Eyes are constantly in motion. | | |

Developmental screening is also a widely recognized means of prevention. (It was through early developmental screening that a medical specialist confirmed that John, in the chapter-opening Snapshot, had a serious vision loss and would require the assistance of a trained vision specialist.) Early screening of developmental problems enables the family physician to analyze several treatment alternatives and, when necessary, to refer the child to an appropriate specialist for a more thorough evaluation of developmental delays.

This screening—which also includes examination of hearing, speech, motor development, and psychological development—includes attention to vision as well. Early screening involves conducting a medical examination at birth and obtaining a complete family medical history. The eyes should be carefully examined for any abnormalities, such as infection or trauma.

At 6 weeks of age, visual screening forms part of another general developmental assessment. This examination should include input from the parents on how their child is responding (e.g., smiling and looking at objects or faces). The physician should check eye movement and search for infection, crusting on the eyes, or **epiphora** (an overflow of tears resulting from obstruction of the lacrimal ducts).

The next examination should occur at about 6 months of age. A defensive blink should be present at this age, and eye movement should be full and coordinated. If any imbalance in eye movements is noted, a more thorough examination should be conducted. Family history is extremely important, since in many cases there is a familial pattern of vision problems.

Between the ages of 1 and 5, visual evaluation should be conducted at regular intervals, especially just before the child enters school. Visual problems must not go undetected as children attempt to cope with the new and complex demands of the educational environment.

**TREATMENT.** In addition to medicine's emphasis on prevention of vision loss, significant strides have been made in the treatment of these problems. The nature of medical in-

**Epiphora**

An overflow of tears resulting from obstruction of the lacrimal ducts of the eye.

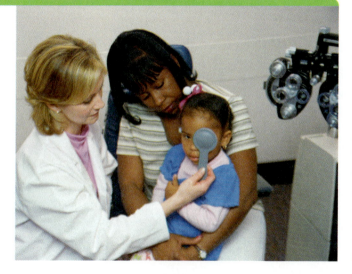

Early developmental screening for eye infection, trauma, and other abnormalities is widely recognized as an effective means to prevent future vision loss.

terventions depends on the type and severity of the loss. For people who are partially sighted, use of an optical aid can vastly improve access to the visual world. Most of these aids take the form of corrective glasses or contact lenses, which are designed to magnify the image on the retina. Some aids magnify the retinal image within the eye, and others clarify it. Appropriate use of optical aids, in conjunction with regular medical examinations, not only helps correct existing visual problems but also may prevent further deterioration of vision.

Surgery, muscle exercises, and drug therapy have also played important roles in treating persons with vision loss. Treatment may range from complex laser surgical procedures and corneal transplants to the process known as atropinization. **Atropinization** is a treatment for cataracts that involves washing out the eye with the alkaloid drug atropine, which permanently dilates the pupil.

## Social Services

Social services can begin with infant stimulation programs and counseling for the family. As the child grows older, group counseling can help him or her cope with feelings concerning blindness and provide guidance in the area of human sexuality (limited vision may distort perception of the physical body). Counseling eventually focuses on marriage, family, and adult relationships. For the adult with vision loss, special guidance may be necessary in preparation for employment and independent living.

Mobility of the person with vision loss can be enhanced in large cities by the use of audible traffic signals (ATS) at crosswalks. The *walk* and *don't walk* signals are indicated by auditory cues, such as actual verbal messages (e.g., "Please do not cross yet"), different bird chirps for each signal, or a sonalert buzzer. ATS is somewhat controversial among people who are blind and among professionals in the field. Those who do not support the use of ATS have two basic concerns: (1) The devices promote negative public attitudes, indicating a presumption that such assistance is necessary for a person who is blind to be mobile; and (2) By masking traffic noise, the devices may actually contribute to unsafe conditions for the person who is blind.

Restaurant menus, elevator floor buttons, and signs in buildings (such as rest rooms) can be produced in braille. Telephone credit cards, personal checks, ATM cards, special mailing tubes, and panels for household appliances are also available in braille. Access to community services is greatly enhanced when synthesized speech is used in devices for purchasing subway and rail tickets or obtaining money from automatic teller machines.

FOCUS
11

Why is the availability of appropriate social services important for people with vision loss?

**Atropinization**

Treatment for cataracts that involves washing the eye with atropine, permanently dilating the pupil.

# FOCUS REVIEW

**FOCUS 1** Why is it important to understand the visual process as well as to know the physical components of the eye?

- The visual process is an important link to the physical world, helping people to gain information beyond that provided by the other senses and also helping to integrate the information acquired primarily through sound, touch, smell, and taste.
- Our interactions with the environment are shaped by the way we perceive visual stimuli.

**FOCUS 2** Distinguish between the terms *blind* and *partially sighted*.

- Legal blindness is visual acuity of 20/200 or worse in the best eye after correction, or a field of vision of 20% or less.
- Educational definitions of blindness focus primarily on the student's inability to use vision functionally as an avenue for learning.
- A person who is partially sighted has a visual acuity greater than 20/200 but not greater than 20/70 in the best eye after correction.
- A person who is partially sighted can still use vision as a primary means of learning.

**FOCUS 3** What are the distinctive features of refractive eye problems, muscle disorders of the eye, and receptive eye problems?

- Refractive eye problems occur when the refractive structures of the eye (cornea and lens) fail to focus light rays properly on the retina. Refractive problems include hyperopia (farsightedness), myopia (nearsighted-

ness), astigmatism (blurred vision), and cataracts.
- Muscle disorders occur when the major muscles within the eye are inadequately developed or atrophic, resulting in a loss of control and an inability to maintain tension. Muscle disorders include nystagmus (uncontrolled rapid eye movement), strabismus (crossed eyes), and amblyopia (loss of vision due to muscle imbalance).
- Receptive eye problems occur when the receptive structures of the eye (retina and optic nerve) degenerate or become damaged. Receptive eye problems include optic atrophy, retinitis pigmentosa, retinal detachment, retinopathy of prematurity (ROP), and glaucoma.

**FOCUS 4** What are the estimated prevalence and causes of vision loss?

- Approximately 20% of all children and adults have some vision loss; 3% (9 million people) have a significant vision loss.
- Fifty percent of people over the age of 65 experience a significant loss of vision (includes cataracts).
- Over 26,000 students have visual impairments and receive specialized services in U.S. public schools.
- Genetic conditions that can result in vision loss include albinism, retinitis pigmentosa, retinoblastoma, optic atrophy, cataracts, severe myopia associated with retinal detachment, lesions of the cornea, abnormalities of the iris, microphthalmia, hydrocephalus, anophthalmia, and glaucoma.
- Acquired disorders that can lead to vision loss prior to birth

include radiation, the introduction of drugs into the fetal system, and infections. Vision loss after birth may be due to several factors, including trauma, infections, inflammations, and tumors.
- The leading cause of acquired blindness in children worldwide is vitamin A deficiency (xerophthalmia). Cortical visual impairment (CVI) is also a leading cause of acquired blindness.

**FOCUS 5** Describe how a vision loss can affect intelligence, speech and language skills, educational achievement, social development, physical orientation and mobility, and perceptual-motor development.

- Performance on tests of intelligence may be negatively affected in areas ranging from spatial concepts to general knowledge of the world.
- Children with vision loss are at a distinct disadvantage in developing speech and language skills because they are unable to associate words with objects visually. They cannot learn speech by visual imitation but must rely on hearing or touch for input.
- Students with vision loss have more difficulty organizing their thoughts to write a composition. Decoding for reading is a much slower process with braille or large-print books. Reading comprehension is also affected because it depends so much on the experiences of the reader.
- Other factors that may influence academic achievement include (1) late entry to school; (2) failure in school programs that were inappropriate; (3) loss

of time in school due to illness, treatment, or surgery; (4) lack of opportunity; and (5) slower acquisition of information.

- People with vision loss are unable to imitate the physical mannerisms of sighted peers and thus do not readily develop body language, an important form of social communication. A person with sight may misinterpret what is said by a person with a vision loss because his or her visual cues may not be consistent with the spoken word.
- People with vision loss are often needlessly excluded from social activities that are integrally related to the use of vision.
- Lack of sight may prevent a person from understanding his or her own relative position in space. A vision loss may affect fine motor coordination and interfere with a person's ability to manipulate objects.
- The perceptual discrimination abilities of people with vision loss in the areas of texture, weight, and sound are comparable to those of sighted peers.
- People who are blind do not perform as well as people with sight on complex tasks of perception, including identification of form, spatial relations, and perceptual-motor integration.

**FOCUS 6**   What is a functional approach to assessment for students with a vision loss?

- Assessment focuses specifically on how the student utilizes any remaining vision (visual efficiency) in conjunction with other senses to acquire information.
- A functional approach to assessment goes beyond determining visual acuity and focuses on ca-

pacity, attention, and processing.

**FOCUS 7**   Describe two content areas that should be included in educational programs for students with vision loss.

- Mobility and orientation training. The ability to move safely, efficiently, and independently through the environment enhances the individual's opportunities to learn more about the world and thus be less dependent on others. Lack of mobility restricts individuals with vision loss in nearly every aspect of educational life.
- The acquisition of daily living skills. For children with a vision loss, routine daily living skills are not easily learned through everyday experiences. These children must be encouraged and supported as they develop life skills and should not be overprotected.

**FOCUS 8**   How can communication media facilitate learning for people with vision loss?

- Through communication media such as optical aids, in conjunction with auditory and tactile stimuli, individuals with vision loss can better develop an understanding of themselves and the world around them.
- Tactile media, including the raised-dot braille system and the Optacon Scanner, can greatly enhance the individual's access to information.
- Specialized media—including personal readers, microcomputers with voice output, closed-circuit TV systems, personal digital assistants, talking calculators, talking-book machines, CD players, and audiotape recorders—provide opportunities for people with vision loss

that were not thought possible even a few years ago.

**FOCUS 9**   What educational placements are available to students with vision loss?

- Residential facilities attempt to provide children who are blind with opportunities to have the same kinds of experiences that would be available if they were growing up in their own communities.
- The vast majority of people with vision loss live at home, attend public schools, and interact within their own communities.
- Services available within the public schools range from general education class placement, with little or no assistance, to special day schools.

**FOCUS 10**   What steps can be taken to prevent and medically treat vision loss?

- Vision loss can be prevented through genetic screening and counseling, appropriate prenatal care, and early developmental assessment.
- The development of optical aids, including corrective glasses and contact lenses, has greatly improved access to the sighted world for people with vision loss.
- Medical treatment may range from complex laser surgical procedures and corneal transplants to drug therapy (e.g., atropinization).

**FOCUS 11**   Why is the availability of appropriate social services important for people with vision loss?

- Social services address issues of self-esteem and feelings of inferiority that may stem from having a vision loss.

## FURTHER READINGS

*Future Reflections*

*Future Reflections is a magazine for parents and teachers of children who have a visual impairment. It is published quarterly by the National Organization of Parents of Blind Children, a Division of the National Federation of the Blind (NFB). The magazine focuses on children as they grow from birth through college. Each issue provides resources and information for parents and teachers, as well as a positive philosophy about blindness. Future Reflections also offers access to a national network of parents who have had similar experiences and who can provide information, support, and encouragement.*

**Kuusisto, S. (1998).** *Planet of the Blind.* **Addlestone, England: Delta Publishing.**

*Born with only residual vision in one eye and the other eye unseeing, the author, a gifted poet, was induced by his mother and the ignorance of the society around him to make an elaborate and harrowing attempt to appear sighted. The effort was at times life-threatening (such as his riding a bicycle between the ages of 10 to 30) and at other times profoundly humiliating. Kuusisto's story is of a lifelong struggle that leads to his acceptance of his blindness.*

**Weihenmayer, E. (2001)** *Touch the Top of the World: A Blind Man's Journey to Climb Farther Than the Eye Can See.* **New York: Plume.**

*This moving and adventure-packed autobiography traces the author's adventures through life, which eventually carry him to the summits of some of the world's highest mountains, as well as onto the frequently hazardous slopes of daily life as a person who is blind.*

## WEB RESOURCES

### American Foundation for the Blind

www.afb.org

This foundation—to which Helen Keller devoted her life—focuses on eliminating barriers that prevent Americans who are blind or visually impaired from reaching their potential. This website provides resources on independent living, literacy, employment, and technology for people with visual impairments.

### American Printing House for the Blind

www.aph.org

APH is the world's largest company devoted solely to creating products and services for people who are visually impaired. This website contains accessible publications and products, employment resources, and government links.

### National Federation of the Blind

www.nfb.org

NFB is the largest U.S. membership organization of people who are blind. The purpose of the National Federation of the Blind is to assist people with visual impairments in achieving greater self-confidence and self-respect, and to act as a vehicle for collective self-expression. This website includes information on accessible products and services, assistive technology, training and employment opportunities, and the use of braille.

## BUILDING YOUR PORTFOLIO

If you are thinking about a career in special education, you should know that many states use national standards developed by the Council for Exceptional Children (CEC) to assess a teacher candidate's knowledge and skills for working with students with disabilities. See a complete listing of the ten CEC Content Standards on the inside front cover of this text.

**CEC Content Standards Addressed in Chapter 16**

1. Foundations
2. Development and Characteristics of Learners
3. Individual Learning Differences
4. Instructional Strategies
5. Learning Environments and Social Interactions
7. Instructional Planning

**Assess Your Knowledge of the CEC Standards Addressed in Chapter 16**

Some states require that teacher candidates develop a portfolio of products that demonstrate mastery of the CEC content standards. To assist in the development of products for this portfolio, you may wish to complete the following activities.

- Complete a written test of the chapter's content.

  *If your instructor requires a written test of your content knowledge for this chapter, keep a copy for your portfolio. A practice test on the information covered in this chapter is available through the companion website (www.ablongman.com/hardman8e) and the Student Study Guide.*

- Respond to the application questions for the Case Study "Michael."

  *Review the Case Study and respond in writing to the application questions. Keep a copy of the Case Study and your written response for your portfolio.*

- Complete the "Take a Stand" activity for the Debate Forum "General Education Schools versus Special Schools: Where Should Students Who Are Blind Be Educated?"

  *Read the Debate Forum in this chapter and then visit the companion website to complete the activity "Take a Stand." Keep a copy of this activity for your portfolio.*

- Participate in a community service learning activity.

  *Community service learning is a valuable way to enhance your learning experience. Visit our companion website for suggested community service learning activities that correspond to the information presented in this chapter. Develop a reflective journal of the service learning experience for your portfolio.*

## THEMES OF THE TIMES

The New York Times
nytimes.com
expect the world*

Expand your knowledge of the concepts discussed in this chapter by reading current and historical articles from the *New York Times* by visiting the "Themes of the Times" section of the companion website: **www.ablongman.com/hardman8e.**

# Physical Disabilities and Health Disorders

### Superman's Super Recovery

Though he may not be able to leap tall buildings in a single bound quite yet, paralyzed Superman star Christopher Reeve may be making some miraculous strides toward recovery.

The actor, who was paralyzed in a near-fatal horseback riding accident in 1995, said he has regained some movement and can feel mild sensations in his arms and legs. A spokesperson for the superstar become medical activist said that after an intense treatment program, Reeve can now move his right wrist, the fingers of his left hand, and his feet and can feel the sensations of hot and cold. She says there is even a possibility he may walk again. . . .

The former man in blue has been working diligently toward recovery for the past three years with Dr. John McDonald, medical director of the Spinal Cord Injury Program at Washington University School of Medicine in St. Louis. The program, which tentatively seems like a success, involves an intensive combination of electrical muscle stimulation and repetitive motion exercises.

The renowned specialist told *People* that the strides Reeve has taken do indeed border on superhero status. He said the actor has made unprecedented progress with the "activity-based" treatment and might one day fulfill his dreams of stepping out of his wheelchair. (Keller, 2002, p. 1)

### Too Many!

- Persons under age 25 accounted for 15% of all suicides in 2000.

- For young people 15–24 years old, suicide is the third leading cause of death, behind unintentional injury and homicide. In 1999, more teenagers and young adults died from suicide than from cancer, heart disease, AIDS, birth defects, stroke, and chronic lung disease combined.

- Among persons aged 15–19 years, firearm-related suicides accounted for more than 60% of the increase in the overall rate of suicide from 1980 to 1997.

- The risk for suicide among young people is greatest among young white males; however, from 1980 through 1995, suicide rates increased most rapidly among young black males. Although suicide among young children is a rare event, the dramatic increase in the rate among persons aged 10–14 years underscores the urgent need for intensifying efforts to prevent suicide among persons in this age group. (National Center for Injury Prevention and Control, 2003, p.2)

### 1500 Children Every Day

- More than 1500 children become infected with HIV every day. The vast majority (more than 90%) acquire the infection from their mother.

- In 2001, more than 2.6 million pregnant women had HIV infection, and more than half a million transmitted the virus to their infants.

- Since the beginning of the pandemic, of the over 5 million infants who have been infected with HIV, 90% were born in Africa. However, the number of cases in Central Asia, Eastern Europe, India, and South-East Asia is rising.

- Access to highly active antiretroviral therapy (HAART) in industrialized countries is making HIV infection in children a chronic illness associated with a prolonged lifespan and a better quality of life. While access to HAART in developing countries is improving, many infected children will not receive therapy, even as prices continue to come down.

- The most effective way to reduce the number of children who become infected with HIV is to prevent HIV infection in parents-to-be and to prevent unplanned pregnancies in HIV-infected women. Among pregnant women already infected with HIV, antiretroviral prevention treatment, including treatment for their own illness, if indicated, safe delivery practices and safe infant-feeding options to reduce the risk of mother-to-child transmission of HIV should be provided (UNAIDS Best Practices Collection, 2003, p. 2).

**FOCUS**

**PREVIEW:** To preview the central concepts of this chapter, read the focus questions located in the margins. Using these questions as a guide, ask yourself what you already know and what you want to learn.

## Linda

I just turned 21. I never thought I would actually reach the official age of adulthood, but it has come and gone; and I am, at least according to law, a little more responsible for my behavior. Actually, I've been responsible for a lot of my behavior since I was a young child. For reasons that I don't completely understand, I've always had a personal resilience that helped me deal with the challenges that have been an integral part of my life.

My mother, who is an exquisitely beautiful woman, was very excited about my birth. I was her first child. The expectations she had for me were wonderful. But within moments of my delivery, it was discovered that I had a serious birth defect known as spina bifida. This discovery altered many of my mom's expectations for me. Although my parents didn't know a great deal about spina bifida at the time, they shortly became specialists.

Their major concern at the time of my birth was not my physical appearance, even though the sac on my spine was quite gross, but the prevention of infection, my intellectual capacity, and the degree of paralysis.

The sac and related nerve tissue were surgically cared for very early in my life through several operations. Fortunately, the infection that was an ever-present threat during the first days and months of my existence was successfully prevented. Because of the location of the sac with neural tissue, I'm paralyzed from the waist down. I walk with the aid of crutches now.

As for my intellectual capacity, I've just completed my second year of college. I'm not an academic superstar, but I do hold my own in my major, which is fashion merchandising.

To be frank with you, my greatest challenge hasn't been my paralysis per se, but my lack of bowel control. I'd love to have the facility that most normal people have, but I don't. I'm working on my attitude about this particular problem. I'm not nearly as sensitive about it as I once was.

---

**Physical disabilities**

Disabilities that can affect a person's ability to move about, use the arms and legs, and/or breathe independently.

**Other health impaired**

A category of disability under the Individuals with Disabilities Education Act that includes students with limited strength as a consequence of health problems.

**Health disorders**

Disabling conditions characterized by limited stamina, vitality, or alertness due to chronic or acute health problems.

**Medically fragile**

A disability category that includes people who are at risk for medical emergencies and often depend on technological support, such as a ventilator or nutritional supplements, to sustain health or even life.

**Technologically dependent**

A disability category that includes people who require some technological assistance to breathe, to pass urine, or to meet other essential health needs while participating in home, school, or community activities.

Physical disabilities can affect a person's ability to move about, to use arms and legs effectively, to swallow food, and/or to breathe independently. They may also affect other primary functions, such as vision, cognition, speech, language, hearing, and bowel control (Nickel & Desch, 2000). The Individuals with Disabilities Education Act (IDEA) uses the term *orthopedically impaired* to describe students with **physical disabilities** and the term **other health impaired** to describe students with health disorders.

As described in IDEA, **health disorders** cause individuals to have "limited strength, vitality, or alertness, due to chronic or acute health problems such as a heart condition, tuberculosis, rheumatic fever, nephritis, asthma, sickle cell anemia, hemophilia, epilepsy, lead poisoning, leukemia, or diabetes which adversely affect . . . educational performance" (23 Code of Federal Regulations, Section 300.5 [7]). For example, children and youth with sickle cell anemia often experience periods of persistent pain in their arms, legs, abdomen, or back that frequently interfere with their school performance and also prevent them from participating in activities that are important to their social and emotional well-being.

In recent years, new subgroups have emerged within the health disorders area. They are often referred to as **medically fragile** and/or **technologically dependent** (Katsiyannis & Yell, 2000; Ueda & Caulfield, 2001). These individuals are at risk for medical emergencies and often require specialized support in the form of ventilators or nutritional supplements. Often children or youth who are medically fragile have progressive diseases such as cancer or AIDS. Other children have episodic conditions that lessen their attentiveness, stamina, or energy. Sickle cell anemia is a good example of a condition that is episodic in nature.

Individuals who benefit from various kinds of technology use devices such as ventilators for breathing, urinary catheters and colostomy bags for bowel and bladder care, tracheotomy tubes for supplying oxygen-enriched air to congested lungs, or suctioning equipment for the removal of mucus from airways. Some of these devices will be discussed in greater detail later in the chapter.

Physical disabilities and health disorders also affect how individuals with various conditions or diseases view themselves and how they are seen by others—parents, brothers and sisters, peers, teachers, neighbors, and employers. The impact of these disabilities is also felt on a number of social, educational, and psychological fronts. For example, children and youth who must spend significant periods of time away from their homes, neighborhoods, or schools for medical care or support may have limited opportunities to develop friendships with neighborhood and school peers, to attend special social events, and to develop essential social skills. The degree to which individuals with physical disabilities and health disorders participate in their neighborhoods and communities is directly related to the quality and timeliness of treatment received from various professionals; the nurturing and encouragement provided by parents, siblings, and teachers; and the support and acceptance offered by neighbors and other community members (Katsiyannis & Yell, 2000).

Individuals with physical and health disorders often require highly specialized interventions to realize their maximum potential. Moreover, the range of medical services, educational placements, and therapies is extremely diverse and highly specific to the person and his or her needs. Students with physical disabilities and health disorders may be served in general education, special education, hospital, home, or residential settings.

# PHYSICAL DISABILITIES

The discussion of physical disabilities will be limited to a representative sample of physically disabling conditions: cerebral palsy, spina bifida, spinal cord injuries, and muscular dystrophy. We will present pertinent information about definitions, prevalence, causation, and interventions.

# Cerebral Palsy

## Definition and Concepts

**Cerebral palsy (CP)** represents a group of chronic conditions that affect muscle coordination and body movement. It is a neuromuscular disorder caused by damage to one or more specific areas of the brain, usually occurring during fetal development; before, during, or shortly following birth; or during infancy (Mecham, 2002). *Cerebral* refers to the brain, *palsy* to muscle weakness and poor control. Secondary conditions can develop with CP, which may improve, worsen, or remain the same. Although CP is not "curable," carefully targeted interventions and therapies may improve an individual's functioning (United Cerebral Palsy, 2003). There are three primary types of CP: spastic—stiff and difficult movement; athetoid—involuntary and uncontrolled movement; and ataxic—disturbed depth perception and very poor sense of balance.

CP is a complicated and perplexing condition. Individuals with CP are likely to have mild to severe problems in nonmotor areas of functioning, including hearing impairments, speech and language disorders, intellectual deficits, visual impairments, and general perceptual problems. Because of the multifaceted nature of this condition, many individuals with CP are considered persons with multiple disabilities. Thus CP cannot be characterized by any set of homogeneous symptoms; it is a condition in which a variety of problems may be present in differing degrees of severity (Mecham, 2002).

## Prevalence and Causation

In the United States, 500,000 children and adults present one or more of the features of CP (United Cerebral Palsy, 2003). The prevalence of CP "is approximately 6 infants in every 1,000 live births" (Mecham, 2002, p. 6). These figures fluctuate as a function of several variables. For example, some infants born with severe forms of CP do not survive, and the birth prevalence rate does not include these children who die. Other children may be diagnosed with CP several months or years after birth.

**FOCUS 1**

Identify the disabilities that may accompany cerebral palsy.

**Cerebral palsy (CP)**

A neurological disorder characterized by motor problems, general physical weakness, lack of coordination, and perceptual difficulties.

The causes of CP are varied (see Table 17.1). Any condition that can adversely affect the brain can cause CP. Chronic diseases, insufficient oxygen to the brain, premature birth, maternal infection, birth trauma, blood incompatibility, fetal infection, and postbirth infection may all be sources of this neurological-motor disorder (Pellegrino, 2001; United Cerebral Palsy, 2003).

## Interventions

Rather than treating CP, professionals and parents work at managing the condition and its various manifestations (Mecham, 2002). It is essential that the management and interventions begin as early as the CP is diagnosed. The interventions center on the

---

### TABLE 17.1

### Factors Influencing the Occurrence of Cerebral Palsy

| PERIOD OF TIME | FACTORS |
| --- | --- |
| Preconception (parental background) | • Biological aging (parent or parents over age 35)<br>• Biological immaturity (very young parent or parents)<br>• Environmental toxins<br>• Genetic background and genetic disorders<br>• Malnutrition<br>• Radiation damage |
| First trimester of pregnancy (0 to 3 months) | *Early weeks:*<br>• Nutrition: malnutrition, vitamin deficiencies, amino acid intolerance<br>• Toxins: alcohol, drugs, poisons, toxins from smoking<br>*Late weeks:*<br>• Maternal disease: thyrotoxicosis (abrupt oversecretion of thyroid hormone, resulting in elevated heart rate and potential coma), genetic disorders<br>• Nutrition: malnutrition, amino acid intolerance |
| Second trimester of pregnancy (3+ to 6 months) | *Early weeks:*<br>• Infection: CM (cytomegalo) virus, rubella, HIV, syphilis, chicken pox, uterine infection<br>*Late weeks:*<br>• Placental abnormalities, vascular blockages, fetal malnutrition, chronic hypoxia, growth factor deficiencies |
| Third trimester of pregnancy (6+ to 9 months) | *Early weeks:*<br>• Prematurity and low birthweight<br>• Blood factors: Rh incompatibility, jaundice<br>• Cytokines: neurological tissue destruction<br>• Inflammation and infection of the uterine lining<br>*Late weeks:*<br>• Prematurity and low birthweight<br>• Hypoxia: insufficient blood flow to the placenta, perinatal hypoxia<br>• Infection: listeria, meningitis, streptococcus group B (bacterial infection), septicemia (bacteria growing in the bloodstream), inflammation and infection of the uterine lining |
| Perinatal period and infancy (first 2 postnatal years) | • Endocrine: hypoglycemia, hypothyroidism<br>• Hypoxia: perinatal hypoxia, respiratory distress syndrome<br>• Infection: meningitis, encephalitis<br>• Multiple births: death of a twin or triplet<br>• Stroke: hemorrhagic or embolic stroke<br>• Trauma: abuse, accidents |

SOURCE: Adapted from "Cerebral Palsy: Contributing Risk Factors and Causes," Research Fact Sheets; September 1995; by United Cerebral Palsy Research and Education Foundation, Copyright 1995. Reprinted by permission.

---

child's movement, social and emotional development, learning, speech, and hearing (Pellegrino, 2001 & 2002; United Cerebral Palsy, 2003).

Effective interventions for the various forms of CP are based on accurate and continuous assessments. Motor deficits and other challenges associated with CP are not unchanging but evolve over time. Continuous assessment allows care providers to adjust treatment programs and select placement options in accordance with the emerging needs of the child or youth.

Treatment of CP is a multifaceted process that involves many medical and human service specialties aggregated in interdisciplinary and transdisciplinary teams (United Cerebral Palsy, 2003). These teams, composed of medical experts, physical and occupational therapists, teachers, social workers, volunteers, and family members join together to help children, youth, and adults with CP realize their full potential.

*Many children with cerebral palsy benefit from the care provided by a physical therapist.*

The thrust of management efforts depends on the nature of the problems and strengths presented by the individual child or youth. Generally, interventions are directed at preventing additional physical deformities; developing useful posture and movements; providing appropriate orthopedic surgery when needed to lengthen heel cords, hamstrings, or tendons; dealing with feeding and swallowing problems; securing suitable augmentative communication and other assistive devices; prescribing appropriate medications (muscle relaxants); and developing mobility and independence. Because of the multifaceted nature of CP, other specialists may also be involved, including ophthalmologists, audiologists, speech and language clinicians, and vocational and rehabilitation specialists (Pellegrino, 2001 & 2002).

Physical and occupational therapists play very significant roles in the lives of children and youth with CP (Bowe, 2000). These individuals provide essentially three types of crucial services: assessments to detect deformities and deficits in movement quality; program planning such as assisting with the writing of IEPs, selection of adaptive equipment and assistive devices, and development of home programs for parents and other family members; and delivery of therapy services. School-centered services may include indirect treatment provided in the form of consultation, inservice training, and informal monitoring of student performance; direct service through regular treatment sessions in out-of-class settings; and in-class or multisite service delivery to students in general education classrooms, on playgrounds, in their homes, or at other community sites (Pellegrino, 2001 & 2002).

Recent developments in augmentative communication and computer-centered technologies have had a tremendous impact on children, youth, and adults with CP and other conditions that impair speech and language production. Many augmentative communication devices are electronic or computer-based. The Touch Talker and the Light Talker provide children and youth with symbols or icons that, when pressed or activated with an optical pointer in certain sequences, produce audio output such as "I'd like a Quarter Pounder with fries and a large Coke, please." "I need to go to the bathroom." "Do you know what we are having for lunch?" Selecting augmentative communication devices for a child or youth is a team effort. Teachers,

## LIVING WITH CEREBRAL PALSY

I do not know many scientific facts about CP (cerebral palsy), but I do know how it has affected my life. This is what I want to share with you. I hope it will help you to better understand people with CP.

When I was young, having cerebral palsy was never an issue in our home. I was treated no differently than my brothers or sisters. However, things changed when I started school. The first few years of school were great, to the best of my recollection. I was probably in the third or fourth grade when I became aware that children, in their innocence, can be cruel. I wore a brace on my leg and was faced with much teasing and ridicule. This caused me to become shy and introverted. I did not easily make friends and still don't!

My grandfather liked to take walks on sunny afternoons, so one day I went with him and was having a very pleasant time until we saw someone walking toward us. My grandpa made me change sides so that it would be harder to see that his granddaughter had cerebral palsy. That was a very hurtful thing to learn. I realized that he was ashamed of me.

People should be judged by their hearts and not by their looks. I have learned to judge myself harshly and I strive for perfection in all I attempt to do. Needless to say, I constantly fail miserably! It is easier not to try than to fail.

I need to learn to like me even with all my many imperfections. I need to learn that it is okay that not everyone I meet will like me.

### APPLICATION

1. Given what you have learned about children and youth with disabilities and their families, how would you as a teacher help your students without disabilities treat children with disabilities well? How do we help children look beyond outward appearances?

2. How would you help your grandparents respond well to a new grandchild with a challenging disability?

3. How would you help a child with a disability deal with the teasing that is often inflicted by other children? How do we help children with disabilities become resilient and appropriately optimistic?

SOURCE: Adapted from "Living with cerebral palsy," Author, 2000. Available at http://www.geocities.com/Athens/Ithaca/2418/cp.html

parents, speech and language specialists, physical and occupational therapists, and rehabilitation engineers play important roles in providing essential information (Bowe, 2000).

As persons with CP move into adulthood, they may require various kinds of support, including continuing therapy, personal assistance services, independent living services, vocational training, and counseling. These kinds of support help individuals with CP realize their full potential in employment, relationships with others, and participation in their own neighborhoods and communities (United Cerebral Palsy, 2003).

# Spina Bifida

## Definitions and Concepts

**Spina bifida**

A developmental defect of the spinal column.

The most frequently occurring permanently disabling birth defect is **spina bifida** (Spina Bifida Association of America, 1999). It is characterized by an abnormal opening in the spinal column. It originates in the first days of pregnancy, often before a mother even knows that she is expecting a child. Through the process of cell division and differentiation, a neural tube forms in the developing fetus. At about 26–27 days, this neural tube fails to completely close, for reasons not wholly understood. This failure results in various forms of spina bifida, frequently involving some paralysis of various portions of the body, depending on the location of the opening (Liptak, 2002). It may or may not influence intellectual functioning. Spina bifida is usually classified as either spina bifida occulta or spina bifida cystica.

**Spina bifida occulta** is a very mild condition in which a small slit is present in one or more of the vertebral structures. Most people with spina bifida occulta are are unaware of its presence unless they have had a spinal x-ray for diagnosis of some other condition. Spina bifida occulta has little, if any, impact on a developing infant.

**Spina bifida cystica** is a malformation of the spinal column in which a tumor-like sac herniates through an opening or cleft on the infant's back (see Figure 17.1). Spina bifida cystica exists in many forms; however, two prominent forms will receive attention in this discussion: spina bifida meningocele and **spina bifida my-elomeningocele**. In spina bifida meningocele, the sac contains spinal fluid but no nerve tissue. In the myelomeningocele type, the sac contains nerve tissue.

Spina bifida myelomeningocele is the most serious form of spina bifida. It generally results in weakness or paralysis in the legs and lower body, an inability to control the bladder or bowel voluntarily, and the presence of other orthopedic problems (club feet, dislocated hip, etc.). There are two types of myelomeningocele. In one the tumor-like sac is open, revealing the neural tissue, and in the other the sac is closed or covered with a combination of skin and membrane.

Children with spina bifida occulta exhibit the normal range of intelligence. Most children with myelomeningocele also have normal IQs. For children whose learning capacity is normal or above average, no special educational programming is required.

## Prevalence and Causation

Prevalence figures for spina bifida, both myelomeningocele and meningocele, vary. Spina bifida affects about 1 out of every 1,000 newborns in the United States (Spina Bifida Association of America, 2003).

FOCUS

**2**

What is spina bifida myelomeningocele?

**Spina bifida occulta**

A very mild form of spina bifida in which an oblique slit is present in one or several of the vertebral structures.

**Spina bifida cystica**

A malformation of the spinal column in which a tumor-like sac is produced on the infant's back.

**Spina bifida myelomeningocele**

A type of spina bifida cystica in which the characteristic tumor-like sac contains both spinal fluid and nerve tissue.

## FIGURE 17.1

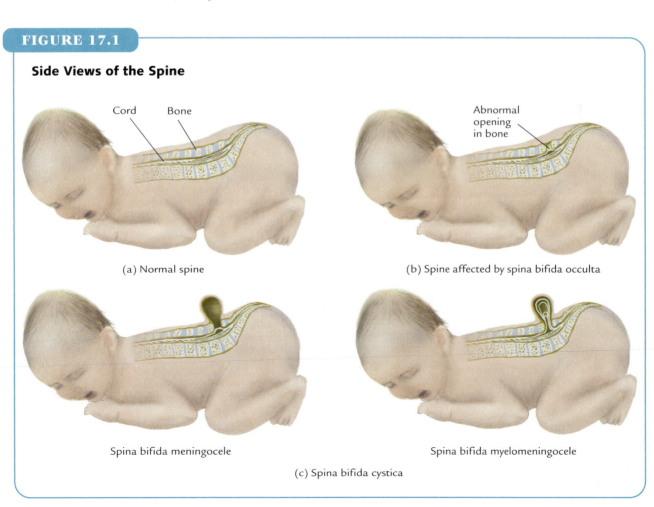

**Side Views of the Spine**

(a) Normal spine

(b) Spine affected by spina bifida occulta

Spina bifida meningocele

Spina bifida myelomeningocele

(c) Spina bifida cystica

The exact cause of spina bifida is unknown, although there is a slight tendency for the condition to run in families. In fact, myelomeningocele appears to be transmitted genetically, probably as a function of certain prenatal factors interacting with genetic predispositions. It is also possible that certain harmful agents taken by the mother prior to or at the time of conception, or during the first few days of pregnancy, are responsible for the defect.

**Teratogens** that may induce malformations in the spine include radiation, maternal hyperthermia (high fever), and excess glucose. Other causative factors include congenital rubella and chromosome abnormalities.

Folic acid deficiencies have been implicated strongly in the causation of spina bifida (Spina Bifida Association of America, 2003). Pregnant mothers should take particular care to augment their diets with 0.4 mg of folic acid each day. Folic acid is a common water-soluble B vitamin. Intake of this vitamin reduces the probability of neural tube defects in developing infants.

### Interventions

Several tests are now available to identify babies with myelomeningocele before they are born. One such test involves analysis of the mother's blood for the presence of a specific fetal protein (alfa-fetoprotein, AFT). This protein leaks from the developing child's spine into the amniotic fluid of the uterus and subsequently enters the mother's bloodstream. If blood tests prove positive for this AFT, ultrasonic scanning of the fetus may be performed to confirm the diagnosis.

Confirmation of the myelomeningocele creates intense feelings in parents. If the diagnosis is early in the child's intrauterine development, parents are faced with the decision of continuing or discontinuing the pregnancy (Bell & Stoneman, 2000; Roberts, Stoygh, & Parrish, 2002) or subjecting the emerging fetus to intrauterine surgery (Bruner, Richards, Tulipan, & Arney, 1999). If parents decide to continue the pregnancy, they have time to process their intense feelings and to prepare for the child's surgery, birth, and care. If the decision is to discontinue the pregnancy, they must deal with the feelings produced by this action as well (Bell & Stoneman, 2000; Roberts, Stoygh, & Parrish, 2002). If the condition is discovered at the time of the child's birth, it also produces powerful and penetrating feelings, the first of which is generally shock. All members of the health team (physicians, nurses, social workers,

**Teratogens**

Substances or conditions that cause malformations.

## FETUS UNDERGOES SURGERY INSIDE THE WOMB AT 21 WEEKS

Julie Armas, a 27-year-old obstetrics nurse, found out that she was carrying a fetus with spina bifida at 14 weeks gestation. In many cases where spina bifida is detected prenatally, parents opt for abortion (there are no accurate numbers on precisely how often this happens). Julie, however, refused to accept abortion as a "solution" for the child that she and her husband had already decided to name Samuel Alexander.

Scouring the Internet for information, the Armas family discovered that a brand new surgery is being carried out on spina-bifida-affected fetuses at Vanderbilt University in Nashville, Tennessee (Fetal Diagnosis and Treatment at Vanderbilt University Medical Center). Julie was put in touch with Dr. Joseph Bruner. Although the surgery is still very new, it gives hope for preventing or lessening the brain and spinal cord damage associated with spina bifida.

The surgery involved removing Julie's uterus by C-section, gently placing the uterus on Julie's belly, and then making a tiny incision through which Dr. Bruner operated on the fetus. After the incision was opened, Samuel reached out to grab Dr. Bruner's finger. An hour later, the surgery was over.

Samuel has since arrived without any major neural complications, although he has some stiffness in his legs. He is already bringing his parents a lot of happiness and joy.

SOURCE: Adapted from "Fetus Undergoes Surgery Inside the Womb at 21 Weeks," (2003). Webring. Retrieved on May 30, 2003 from http://www.pagerealm.com/handhope/

etc.), as well as other persons (religious advisers, siblings, parents, and close friends), help the parents cope with the feelings they experience and the decisions that must be made.

Immediate action is often called for when the child with myelomeningocele is born, depending on the nature of the lesion, its position on the spine, and the presence of other, related conditions. Decisions regarding medical interventions are extremely difficult to make, for they often entail problems and issues that are not easily or quickly resolved. For example, in 80% of children with myelomeningocele, a portion of the spinal cord is exposed, placing them at great risk for developing bacterial meningitis, which has a mortality rate of over 50%.

The decision to undertake surgery is often made quickly if the tissue sac is located very low on the infant's back. The purpose of the surgery is to close the spinal opening and lessen the potential for infection. Another condition that often accompanies myelomeningocele is hydrocephalus, a condition characterized by excessive accumulation of cerebral fluid within the brain. More than 25% of children with myelomeningocele exhibit this condition at birth. Moreover, 80% to 90% of all children with myelomeningocele develop it after they are born. Surgery may also be performed for this condition in the first days of life. The operation includes inserting a small, soft plastic tube between the ventricles of the brain and connecting this tube with an absorption site in the abdomen. The excessive spinal fluid is diverted from the ventricles of the brain to a thin layer of tissue, the peritoneum, which lines the abdominal cavity (see Figure 17.2).

Children with spina bifida myelomeningocele may have little if any voluntary bowel or bladder control. This condition is directly attributable to the paralysis caused by malformation of the spinal cord and removal of the herniated sac containing nerve tissues. However, children as young as 4 years old can be taught effective procedures to manage bladder problems. As they mature, they can develop effective regimens and procedures for bowel management.

Physical therapists play a critical role in helping children as they learn to cope with the paralysis caused by myelomeningocele. Paralysis obviously limits the children's exploratory activities so critical to later learning and perceptual-motor performance. With this in mind, many such children are fitted with modified skateboards, which allow them to explore their surroundings. Utilizing the strength in their arms and hands, they may become quite adept at exploring their home environments. Gradually, they move to leg braces, crutches, a wheelchair, or a combination of the three. Some children are ambulatory and do not require the use of a wheelchair.

Education programs for students with serious forms of spina bifida vary according to the needs of each student. The vast majority of students with myelomeningocele are served in general education settings. School personnel can contribute to the well-being of these students in several ways: making sure that physical layouts permit students to move effectively with their crutches or wheelchairs through classrooms and other settings; supporting students' efforts in using various bladder and bowel management procedures and ensuring appropriate privacy in using them; requiring these students to be as responsible as anyone else in the class for customary assignments; involving them fully in field trips, physical education, and other school-related activities; and communicating regularly with parents. Additionally, if the student has a shunt, teachers should be alert to signs of its malfunctioning, including irritability, neck pain, headache, vomiting, reduced alertness, and decline in

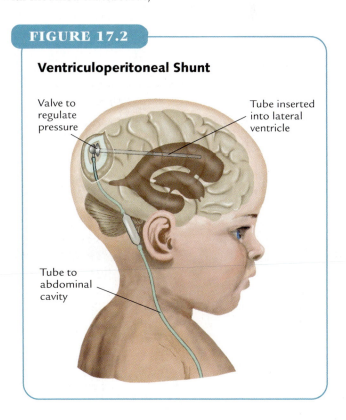

**FIGURE 17.2**

**Ventriculoperitoneal Shunt**

Valve to regulate pressure

Tube inserted into lateral ventricle

Tube to abdominal cavity

SPINA BIFIDA    479

school performance. As with all physical disabilities, collaboration and cooperation among all caregivers are critical to the well-being of each child or youth.

# Spinal Cord Injury

## Definitions and Concepts

When the spinal cord is traumatized or severed, **spinal cord injury (SCI)** occurs. Trauma can result through extreme extension or flexing from a fall, an automobile accident, or a sports injury. The cord can also be severed through the same types of accidents, although such occurrences are extremely rare. Usually in such cases, the cord is bruised or otherwise injured, after which swelling and (within hours) bleeding often occur. Gradually, a self-destructive process ensues, in which the affected area slowly deteriorates and the damage becomes irreversible (Cockrell, 2000; Spinal Cord Injury Resource Center, 2003).

The overall impact of injury on an individual depends on the site and nature of the insult. If the injury occurs in the neck or upper back, the resulting paralysis and effects are usually quite extensive. If the injury occurs in the lower back, paralysis is confined to the lower extremities. Like individuals with spina bifida, those who sustain injuries in an SCI may experience loss of voluntary bowel and bladder function. For a brief review of the topographical descriptions of paralytic conditions, see Table 17.2.

Spinal cord injuries rarely occur without individuals sustaining other serious damage to their bodies. Accompanying injuries may include head trauma, fractures of some portion of the trunk, and significant chest injuries (Bowe, 2000).

The physical characteristics of spinal cord injuries are similar to those of spina bifida myelomeningocele except there is no tendency for the development of hydrocephalus. The terms used to describe the impact of spinal cord injuries are as follows: **paraplegia**, **quadriplegia**, and **hemiplegia**. Note, however, that these terms are global descriptions of functioning and are not precise enough to convey accurately an individual's actual level of motor functioning.

## Prevalence and Causation

About 450,000 individuals live with SCI in the United States. Every year there are some 10,000 new cases of SCI (National Spinal Cord Injury Statistical Center, 2003). From 85% to 90% of patients treated for spinal cord injuries are young men between the ages of 16 and 30 (Spinal Cord Injury Resource Center, 2003). The incidence of spinal cord injuries increases during the summer months. These injuries generally occur in the early hours of the morning. Causes include motor vehicle accidents

---

**Spinal cord injury (SCI)**

An injury in which the spinal cord is traumatized or transected.

**Paraplegia**

Paralysis that involves the legs only.

**Quadriplegia**

A condition characterized by paralysis of all four extremities and usually the trunk.

**Hemiplegia**

Paralysis that involves one side of the body.

---

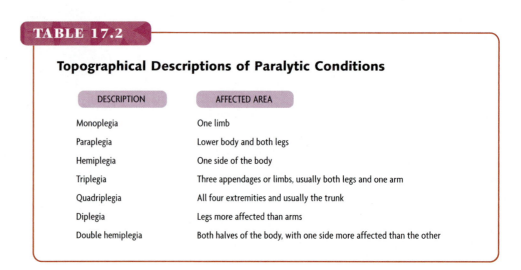

**TABLE 17.2**

### Topographical Descriptions of Paralytic Conditions

| DESCRIPTION | AFFECTED AREA |
| --- | --- |
| Monoplegia | One limb |
| Paraplegia | Lower body and both legs |
| Hemiplegia | One side of the body |
| Triplegia | Three appendages or limbs, usually both legs and one arm |
| Quadriplegia | All four extremities and usually the trunk |
| Diplegia | Legs more affected than arms |
| Double hemiplegia | Both halves of the body, with one side more affected than the other |

## FISHING MADE EASIER FOR ALL OF US

Electric Fishing Reel Systems, Inc. has created an electric, battery-powered drive for fishing reels. Now, most anyone can pull in a fish, even a big one. As the company says, "Whether it's Alaskan Halibut or a string of Snapper in the Florida Keys, Elec-Tra-Mate® takes the work out of bringing them up." Individuals with disabilities who may not be able to use their hands and arms to reel in a fish need only have the capacity to activate an on or off switch. This switch [can be activated] in many ways; thus almost anyone who wants to catch a fish may do so.

The prototype drive was first produced in 1970. Now the company offers seventeen different models designed exclusively for nineteen different Penn® Reels, ranging from small, lightweight models to large, big-game reels. The Elec-Tra-Mate® drives operate on a 12-volt auto or marine battery. A push-button switch or optional toggle switch on the Elec-Tra-Mate® operates the drive system. The company also produces a waterproof remote switch.

SOURCE: Electric Fishing Reel Systems, Inc., Greensboro, North Carolina, 2003.

---

(38.5%); violence, primarily gunshot wounds (24.5%); and falls (21.8%) (Spinal Cord Injury Resource Center, 2003). Twenty-five percent of the injuries are alcohol-related. Only 7.2% of the injuries are caused by sporting activities (Spinal Cord Injury Information Network, 2003).

### Interventions

The immediate care rendered to a person with SCI is crucial. The impact of the injury can be magnified if proper procedures are not employed soon after the accident or onset of the condition.

The first phase of treatment provided by a hospital is the management of shock. Quickly thereafter, the individual is immobilized to prevent movement and possible further damage. As a rule, surgical procedures are not undertaken immediately. The major goal of medical treatment at this point is to stabilize the spine, manage swelling, and prevent further complications. Pharmacological interventions are critical during this phase of treatment. Recent studies support the use of high and frequent doses of methylprednisolone. This medication often reduces the severity of the injury, improves the functional outcome for the affected individual, and reduces secondary damage (Cockrell, 2000). Catheterization may be employed to control urine flow, and steps may be taken to reduce swelling and bleeding at the injury site. Traction may be used to stabilize certain portions of the spinal column and cord.

**FOCUS 3**

Identify specific treatments for individuals with spinal cord injuries.

*John Gilpatrick is seen with his guide dog Ice at his Hanover, Massachusetts home. Gilpatrick, a former hockey player, suffered a spinal injury in 1996 after crashing into a goalpost; he is now able to walk again.*

Medical treatment of spinal cord injuries is lengthy and often tedious. Once physicians have successfully stabilized the spine and treated other medical conditions, the rehabilitation process promptly begins. The individual is taught to use new muscle combinations and to take advantage of any and all residual muscle strength. He or she is also taught to use orthopedic equipment, such as handsplints, braces, reachers, headsticks (for typing), and plateguards. Together with an orthopedic specialist, occupational and physical therapists become responsible for the physical reeducation and training process.

Psychiatric and other support personnel are also engaged in rehabilitation activities. Psychological adjustment to SCI and its impact on the individual's functioning can take a great deal of time. The goal of all treatment is to help the injured person become as independent as possible.

As the individual masters necessary self-care skills, other educational and career objectives can be pursued with the assistance of the rehabilitation team. The members of this team change constantly with the skills and needs of the individual.

Education for individuals with spinal cord injuries is similar to that for uninjured children or adults. Teachers must be aware, however, that some individuals with spinal cord injuries will be unable to feel pressure and pain in the lower extremities, so pressure sores and skin breakdown may occur in response to prolonged sitting. Opportunities for repositioning and movement will help prevent these problems. Parents and teachers should be aware of signs of depression that may accompany reentry into school. (See the nearby Reflect on This.)

**Reflect on This**

## GENE THERAPY: A MEDICAL REVOLUTION

Recently scientists completed the mapping of the entire human genome, effectively decoding the entire human genetic script. It's not hard to grasp the significance of this accomplishment. According to Mayo Clinic Women's HealthSource, doctors believe they can use this information to treat known genetic disorders, as well as major killers such as cancer, heart disease, and AIDS.

Single genetic defects are known to be responsible for more than 4,000 diseases, including sickle cell anemia, hemophilia, and Huntington's disease. Researchers now hope to understand how different genes interact to influence diseases like diabetes and stroke.

If doctors can understand the relationships between genes and diseases, they may be able to develop more accurate methods of diagnosis and treatment. The most promising application for treatment is gene therapy—a way of supplying cells with healthy copies of genes to treat, cure, or even prevent disease.

Other applications for gene-based medicine include

• *Replacing damaged, defective, or missing genes.* For example, in cystic

fibrosis, a single missing gene causes the buildup of thick mucus in the lungs. Replacing this gene could reverse the mucus problem.

• *Pharmacological gene therapy*—that is, injecting a gene into cells so that the body can make a protein that's missing or produced in too little quantity. This may be useful for some types of anemia, where certain proteins must be repeatedly injected to stimulate the production of red blood cells.

• *Killing cells.* Injecting an appropriate gene into cells so that they produce a protein that kills cells or causes them to be susceptible to drugs. This could be applied to cancer treatment.

The road to successful gene therapy will be a long one, and many eagerly awaited advances will not occur until years in the future. Finding effective ways to deliver genes to targeted cells is also a major hurdle to overcome. But researchers are optimistic, and it is almost certain that the genetic revolution will result in cures for and prevention of many medical problems.

SOURCE: Adapted from Mayo Clinic (2003). *"Gene therapy: A medical revolution."* Retrieved June 5, 2003 from http://www.mayoclinic.org/news2000-rst/719.html

## A REVOLUTIONARY NEW WHEELCHAIR

We have the know-how to fly to the moon, but most people who can't walk still get around with what's essentially 200-year-old technology: the wheelchair. One inventor has decided it's time to get wheelchair riders rolling into the 21st century. He says his machine can take you just about anywhere you want to go. He's been keeping his top-secret invention under wraps until now.

Wheelchairs can get you around, but they don't get close enough to the places disabled people might like to go. You've heard the expression "confined to a wheelchair"? Well, actually, if you think about it, it's the wheelchairs that are confined to the relatively few smooth, easy-rolling places in the world. But what if somebody came up with a device that, as they say, could go where no wheelchairs have gone before?

It would take someone on a mission. Someone with the money and genius and time to put into the project. It would take someone like Dean Kamen. He's one of this nation's most prestigious inventors. He's a sort of Thomas Edison in the medical world.

Kamen thought about this old problem in a revolutionary new way. What if instead of getting a chair that could go upstairs, you could make a machine that could stand up and balance the way humans do? "Your mother remembers your first steps. It's a big deal that humans walk erect," says Kamen. "It's difficult to do. But once we've learned to do it, we're capable of dealing with curbs and a world with stairs."

Kamen and his engineers came up with a two-wheeled balancing prototype that worked and became a top-secret patented invention crammed full of sophisticated gyroscopes, electric motors, and computers.

*What is this extraordinary machine capable of doing?*
It can climb stairs, roll through sand, and even raise its height to reach the top of shelves. What's exciting about this device is not the technology, it's the choices: The user can go from point A to point B anyway you want. And this isn't some exotic experiment on a device that no one is ever going to see. The builders of this machine intend it to be used out in the world, and soon.

Since a wheelchair is a medical device, it has to be tested by the Food and Drug Administration. It's more like a drug than like a bicycle or a lawnmower. With the idea that virtually any failure could be catastrophic, Kamen's engineers have rocked, rolled, bounced, drowned, and pounded their new machine. Can Dean Kamen's new device change the world? Nobody knows until the FDA approves it for use outside of the lab and beyond the inventor's own property. But one thing is certain: The emotional impact can already be felt.

Brace yourself for the price: Dean Kamen's invention will cost about $20,000 when it becomes available to the public. But because it could spare users the expense of customizing homes with ramps and wider doorways, and mechanical lifts in cars, the money spent could be offset in money saved.

SOURCE: From "Research and New Updates: A Revolutionary New Wheelchair on the Horizon," by the Spinal Cord Injury Research Center, 2000. [Online] Available: http://www.spinalinjury.net/html/wheelchair.html And from "A Revolutionary New Wheelchair on the Horizon," by MSNBC, 1999 (June). [Online] Available: http://www.msnbc.com/news/285231.asp

# Muscular Dystrophy

## Definitions and Concepts

The term **muscular dystrophy** refers to a group of genetic diseases marked by progressive weakness and degeneration of the skeletal, or voluntary, muscles, which control movement. The muscles of the heart and some other involuntary muscles are also affected in some forms of muscular dystrophy, and a few forms involve other organs as well (Leet, Dormans, & Tosi, 2002). Muscular dystrophy is a progressive disorder that may affect the muscles of the hips, legs, shoulders, and arms, progressively causing these individuals to lose their ability to walk and to use their arms and hands effectively. The loss of ability is attributable to fatty tissue that gradually replaces muscle tissue. Heart muscle may also be affected, resulting in symptoms of heart failure. There are actually nine different types of muscular dystrophy. The seriousness of the various dystrophies is influenced by heredity, age of onset, the

**Muscular dystrophy**

A group of inherited, chronic disorders that are characterized by gradual wasting and weakening of the voluntary skeletal muscles.

**FOCUS 4**

Describe the
physical limitations
associated with
muscular dystrophy.

physical location and nature of onset, and the rate at which the condition progresses (Leet, Dormans, & Tosi, 2002).

Duchenne-type muscular dystrophy (DMD) is the most common form of childhood muscular dystrophy. DMD generally manifests itself between the ages of 2 and 6. Early in the second decade of life, individuals with DMD use wheelchairs to move from place to place. By the end of the second decade of life, or early in the third, young adults with DMD die from respiratory insufficiency or cardiac failure (Muscular Dystrophy Association, 2000).

DMD is first evidenced in the pelvic girdle, although it sometimes begins in the shoulder girdle muscles. With the passage of time, individuals begin to experience a loss of respiratory function and are unable to cough up secretions that may result in pneumonia. Also, severe spinal curvature develops over time with wheelchair use, although this curvature may be prevented with spinal fusion. (See Assistive Technology on page 483.)

## Prevalence and Causation

"Flaws in muscle protein genes cause muscular dystrophies. Each cell in our bodies contains tens of thousands of genes. Each gene is a string of the chemical DNA and is the 'code' for a protein. (Another way to think of a gene is that it is the 'instructions' or 'recipe' for a protein.) If the recipe for a protein is wrong, the protein is made wrong or in the wrong amount or sometimes not at all" (Muscular Dystrophy Association, 2000, p. 2). The missing or diminished ingredient is dystrophin, an essential and critical component of healthy muscle fibers (Bushby & Anderson, 2001; Leet, Dormans, & Tosi, 2002).

About 200,000 people are affected by muscular dystrophies and related disorders. About 1 in every 3,000 to 3,500 males is affected by DMD. Mothers who are carriers transmit this condition to 50% of their male offspring. One-third of the cases of DMD arise by mutation in families with no history of the disease (Muscular Dystrophy Association, 2000).

Molecular genetics has contributed greatly to our understanding of neuromuscular diseases and their causes. In some cases, the specific genetic locus of the dystrophy can be identified. Such is the case with DMD, which is tied to a sex-linked recessive gene. Additionally, the biochemical defects associated with various dystrophies can now be recognized.

## Interventions

There is no known cure for muscular dystrophy. The focus of treatment is maintaining or improving the individual's functioning and preserving his or her ambulatory independence for as long as possible. The first phases of maintenance and prevention are handled by a physical therapist, who works to prevent or correct contractures (a permanent shortening and thickening of muscle fibers). As the condition becomes more serious, treatment generally includes prescribing supportive devices, such as walkers, braces, nightsplints, surgical corsets, and hospital beds. Eventually, the person with muscular dystrophy will need to use a wheelchair.

The terminal nature of DMD poses challenging problems to affected individuals, their families, and caregivers. Fortunately, significant progress has been made in helping individuals with terminal illnesses deal with death. Programs developed for families who have a terminally ill child, youth, or adult serve several purposes. They give children with terminal illnesses opportunities to ask questions about death, to express their concerns, and to work through their feelings.

Programs for parents are designed to help them understand their children's conceptions about death, to suggest ways in which the parents might respond to certain questions or concerns, and to outline the steps they might take in successfully preparing for and responding to the child's death and related events. One such program is Compassionate Friends. This organization, which is composed of parents who have lost children to death, provides sensitive support and resources to other parents who have lost a child to injury or disease.

At this juncture, you may want to examine Inclusion Through the Lifespan. It offers valuable suggestions for interacting with young children, school-age children, youth, and adults with physical and health disorders.

# HEALTH DISORDERS

**Health disorders** affect children, youth, and adults in a variety of ways. For example, a child with juvenile diabetes who has engaged in a vigorous game of volleyball with classmates may need to drink a little fruit juice or soda pop just before or after the activity to regulate blood sugar levels. An adult with diabetes may need to follow a special diet and regularly receive appropriate doses of insulin. By way of review, IDEA describes persons with health disorders as individuals with "limited strength, vitality, or alertness, due to chronic or acute health problems such as a heart condition, tuberculosis, rheumatic fever, nephritis, asthma, sickle cell anemia, hemophilia, epilepsy, lead poisoning, leukemia, or diabetes which adversely affect . . . educational performance" (23 Code of Federal Regulations, Section 300.5 [7]).

Acquired immune deficiency syndrome (AIDS), seizure disorders (epilepsy), diabetes, cystic fibrosis (CF), and sickle cell anemia (SCA) will be reviewed in some depth in this section.

# Human Immunodeficiency Virus (HIV) and Acquired Immune Deficiency Syndrome (AIDS)

## Definitions and Concepts

"Acquired immunodeficiency syndrome (AIDS) is the symptomatic clinical manifestation of impaired cellular immunity due to infection with the human immunodeficiency virus type 1 (HIV-1)" (Nickel, 2000a, p. 392) AIDS in children and youth is defined by the following characteristics: (1) the presence of the **human immunodeficiency virus (HIV)**, a virus that attacks certain white blood cells within the body, and/or the presence of antibodies to HIV in the blood or tissues as well as (2) recurrent bacterial diseases (Nickel, 2000a).

The first reports regarding some of the features of AIDS, received by the Centers for Disease Control in the spring of 1981, dealt exclusively with young men who had a rare form of pneumonia. Simultaneously, the Centers for Disease Control received reports of an increased incidence of a rare skin tumor, Kaposi's sarcoma. Individuals who had developed these conditions were homosexual men in their 30s and 40s. Many died or were severely debilitated within 12 months of diagnosis.

Prior to the spring of 1981, primary-care physicians in New York, San Francisco, and other large cities had seen many cases of swollen lymph nodes in homosexual men. Many of these individuals exhibited this condition for months or even years after their initial diagnosis without suffering serious side effects. However, those who developed **opportunistic infections** often experienced severe side effects or even death. Eventually, these opportunistic infections were linked to a breakdown in the functioning of the **immune system**. People affected with these infections exhibit pronounced depletions of a particular subset of white blood cells, T lymphocytes.

**Health disorders**

Disabling conditions characterized by limited stamina, vitality, or alertness due to chronic or acute health problems.

**Human immunodeficiency virus (HIV)**

A virus that reduces immune system function and has been linked to AIDS.

**Opportunistic infection**

An infection caused by germs that are not usually capable of causing infection in healthy people but can do so given certain changes in the immune system (opportunity).

**Immune system**

The normally functioning system within a person's body that protects it from disease.

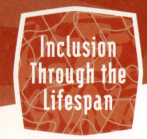

**Inclusion Through the Lifespan**

# PEOPLE WITH PHYSICAL DISABILITIES AND HEALTH DISORDERS

### Tips for the Family

- Work closely with medical personnel to lessen the overall impact of the disorder over time. This may include using prophylactic medications, monitoring the impact of certain medications, asking for reading materials, following dietary routines, communicating honest concerns, and asking questions about instructions not well understood.
- Give the child who has physical or health disabilities opportunities to freely explore his or her environment to the maximum degree possible. This may require some adaptations or specialized equipment (e.g., custom-made wheelchairs, prosthetic devices)
- Involve the child with other children as time and energy permit. Only children can teach one another certain things. This may include inviting one or several children to your home for informal play activities, celebration of social events, and other age-appropriate activities.
- Join advocacy and support groups that provide the information and assistance you need.

### Tips for the Preschool Teacher

- Be sure that the physical environment in the classroom lends itself to the needs of children who may have physical or health disorders (e.g., aisles in the classroom are sufficiently large for free movement in a wheelchair). Like any other children, these children benefit from moving around and fully exploring every inch of every environment. Also, it readies them in a gradual way to become appropriately independent.
- Become aware of specific needs of the child by consulting with parents. For example, the child may need to refrain from highly physical activities.

### Tips for Preschool Personnel

- Be sure that other key personnel in the school who interact directly with the child are informed of his or her needs.
- Orient all the children in your classroom to the needs of the child with physical or health disabilities. This could be done by you, the parents or siblings, or other educational personnel in the school. Remember, your behavior toward the child will say more than words will ever convey.
- Be sure that arrangements have been made for emergency situations. For example, some peers may know exactly what to do if a fellow class member begins to have a seizure. Additionally, classmates should know how they may be helpful in directing and assisting the child during a fire drill or other emergency procedure.

### Tips for Neighbors and Friends

- Involve the child with physical or health disabilities and his or her family in holiday gatherings. Be sensitive to dietary regimens, opportunities for repositioning, and alternative means for communicating.
- Become aware of the things that you may need to do. For example, you may need to learn what to do if a child with insulin-dependent diabetes shows signs of glucose buildup.

### Tips for the Family

- Maintain a healthy and ongoing relationship with the care providers who are part of your child's life. Acknowledge their efforts and reinforce behaviors and actions that are particularly helpful to you and your child.
- Continue to be involved with advocacy and support groups.
- Stay informed by subscribing to newsletters that are produced and disseminated by advocacy organizations.
- Develop and maintain good relationships with the people who teach and serve your child within the school setting.

### Tips for the General Education School Teacher

- Be informed and willing to learn about the unique needs of the child with physical or health disorders in your classroom. For example, schedule a conference with the child's parents before the year begins to talk about medications, prosthetic devices, levels of desired physical activities, and so on.
- Inform the other children in the class. Help them become aware of their crucial role in contributing to the well-being of the child with physical or health disorders.
- Use socially competent and mature peers to assist you (e.g., providing tutoring, physical assistance, social support in recess activities).
- Be sure that plans have been made and practiced for dealing with emergency situations (e.g., some children may need to be carried out of a building or room).
- If the child's condition is progressive and life-threatening, begin to discuss the ramifications of death and loss. Many excellent books about this topic are available for children.

### Tips for School Personnel

- Be sure that all key personnel in the school setting who interact with the child on a regular basis are informed about treatment regimens, dietary requirements, and signs of potentially problematic conditions such as fevers and irritability.
- Meet periodically as professionals to deal with emergent problems, brainstorm for solutions, and identify suitable actions.
- Children can be involved periodically in brainstorming activities that focus on involving the child with physical or health disorders to the maximum degree possible.
- Institute cross-age tutoring and support. When possible, have the child with a physical or health condition become a tutor.

### Tips for Neighbors and Friends

- Involve the child with physical or health disorders in your family activities.
- Provide parents with some respite care. They will appreciate the time to themselves.
- Be informed! Be aware of the needs of the child by regularly talking to his or her parents. They will sincerely appreciate your concern.

## SECONDARY AND TRANSITION YEARS

### Tips for the Family

- Remember that for some individuals with physical or health disabilities, the secondary or young adult years may be the most trying, particularly if the conditions are progressive in nature.
- Begin planning early in the secondary school years for the youth's transition from the public school to the adult world. Incorporate goals related to independent living in the IEP.
- Be sure that you are well informed about the adult services offered in your community and state.

### Tips for the General Education School Teacher

- Continue to be aware of the potential needs for accommodation and adjustment.
- Treat the individual as an adult.
- Realize that the youth's studies may be interrupted from time to time with medical treatments or other important health care services.

### Tips for School Personnel

- Acknowledge individuals by name, become familiar with their interests and hobbies, joke with them occasionally, and involve them in meaningful activities such as fund raisers, community service projects, and decorating for various school events.
- Provide opportunities for all students to receive recognition and be involved in school-related activities.
- Realize that peer assistance and tutoring may be particularly helpful to certain students. Social involvement outside the school setting should be encouraged (e.g., going to movies, attending concerts).
- Use members of teacher assistance teams to help with unique problems that surface from time to time. For example, you may want to talk with special educators about management ideas that may improve a given child's behavior in your classroom.

### Tips for Neighbors, Friends, and Potential Employers

- Continue to be involved in the individual's life.
- Be aware of assistance that you might provide in the event of a youth's gradual deterioration or death.
- Involve the individual in age-appropriate activities (e.g., cookouts, video nights, or community events).
- Encourage your own teens to volunteer as peer tutors or job coaches.
- If you are an employer, provide opportunities for job sampling, on-the-job training, or actual employment.

## ADULT YEARS

### Tips for the Family

- Make provisions for independent living away from home. Work with adult service personnel and advocacy organizations in lining up appropriate housing and related support services.
- Provide support for appropriate employment opportunities.
- Work closely with local and state adult services personnel. Know what your rights are and how you can qualify your son or daughter for educational or other support services.

### Tips for Neighbors, Friends, and Employers

- Provide appropriate accommodations for leisure and work activities.
- Adopt an adult for regular recreational and social activities.
- Provide regular opportunities for recognition and informative feedback. When persons with disabilities are hired, be sure that they regularly receive specific information about their work performance. Feedback may include candid comments about their punctuality, rate of work completion, and social interaction with others. Withholding information, not making reasonable adjustments, and not expecting these individuals to be responsible for their behaviors are great disservices to them.

## AIDS AND THE PUBLIC SCHOOLS

**G**uillermo is a first-grader. Unless you knew him well, you would assume that he was a very normal kid. He likes cold drinks and pizza and watches cartoons every Saturday morning.

In school, he performs reasonably well. He's not an academic superstar, but he is learning to read and write quite well. His teacher likes him and says that he is quite sociable for his age and size. Guillermo is a little on the small side, but he doesn't let that get in the way of his enjoying most things in life.

Since his foster parents have had him, he has been quite happy. The crying and whining that characterized his first weeks in their home have disappeared. He is now pretty much a part of the family.

His older foster brother, John, likes him a lot. John and Guillermo spend a good deal of time together. They are about 16 months apart in age. John is a second-grader and a mighty good one at that. He has always excelled in school, and he loves to help Guillermo when he can.

Guillermo, from day one of his placement, has been ill regularly. He has one infection after another. Of course, his foster parents knew that this would be the case, since Guillermo has AIDS. His biological mother could not care for him, as she was a drug addict and has AIDS herself.

Keeping a secret is sometimes very hard, and such was the case for John. From the very beginning of Guillermo's placement in his home, John knew that there was something special about him. His parents have talked to him about Guillermo and his condition. It was a family decision to have Guillermo live in their home. John is often scared, not for himself but for Guillermo. He wonders how long he will be able to play with his young friend and constant companion. Also, it is often hard to keep the family secret about Guillermo.

Guillermo attends the neighborhood school. Those who are aware of his condition are his classmates, their parents, his teacher, the principal, the school board members, and, of course, John. Just about everyone kept the secret at first, and Guillermo was well received by the overwhelming majority of his classmates. He played with them, enjoyed stories with them, and had a good wrestle now and then with some of the boys in his class.

Over time, other parents and students learned about Guillermo's condition, and a big uproar ensued about his being in school. The PTA was divided. The principal was in favor of Guillermo's continued attendance, but a few vocal parents circulated a petition calling for Guillermo be taught by a teacher for the homebound.

### POINT

Given our current knowledge about the ways in which AIDS is spread in adults and children, there is no reason to remove Guillermo from his neighborhood school. His behavior and physical condition do not place other children at risk for acquiring the HIV virus or developing AIDS.

### COUNTERPOINT

With the limited knowledge we have about AIDS and its transmission, we should not let children with AIDS or the HIV virus attend neighborhood schools. We should wait until we know a great deal more about the disease. The potential risks for other children are too great.

What do you think? To give your opinion, go to Chapter 17 of the companion website (www.ablongman.com.hardman8e) and click on Debate Forum.

White blood cells fight infections; without sufficient numbers and kinds of them, the body is defenseless. Individuals with this condition become subject to a wide range of opportunistic infections and tumors affecting the gastrointestinal system, central nervous system, and skin.

Individuals with AIDS move through a series of disease stages (Pavia, 2001). The first stage is the exposure stage, or the period during which the transmission of the HIV occurs. Young people may be infected with HIV but may not yet exhibit the life-threatening conditions associated with AIDS. The second stage is characterized by the production of antibodies in infected individuals. These antibodies appear about 2 to 12 weeks after the initial transmission of the virus. About 30% of individuals experience flu-like symptoms for a few days to several weeks. During stage three, the immune system declines, and the virus begins to destroy cells of the immune system. However, many individuals with HIV are asymptomatic during this stage. This asymptomatic phase may continue for 3 to 10 years. About half of all individuals with HIV develop AIDS within 10 years. For children, the onset of AIDS ranges from 1 to 3 years. At stage four, individuals begin to manifest symptoms of a damaged immune system, including weight loss, fatigue, skin rashes, and night sweats. In more severe cases, opportunistic diseases appear in individuals with AIDS. At stage five, recurrent and chronic diseases begin to take their toll on individuals. Gradually, the immune system fails and death occurs.

Researchers have identified several patterns of disease development in HIV-infected children. The mean age of onset in exposed children is about 4.1 years. About 33% of exposed children remain AIDS-free until up to 13 years of age (Nickel, 2000b). Often the most serious symptoms do not appear until these children enter school or begin their adolescent years.

## Prevalence and Causation

AIDS is the leading cause of death in many developing countries. Three million people died of AIDS in the year 2000, and more than 36 million individuals were living with HIV or AIDS. Of that number, two-thirds lived in sub-Saharan Africa. Of that 36 million, 1.4 million were children under age 15 (Spiegel & Bonwit, 2002).

The Centers for Disease Control and Prevention (CDC) estimate that 650,000 to 900,000 individuals in the United States are HIV-infected, of whom more than 200,000 are not aware of their infection (National Institute of Allergy and Infectious Diseases, 2000d). In the United States, the average prevalence rate for AIDS cases is 19.9 per 100,000 individuals. About 8,600 children under age 13 in the United States have been diagnosed with AIDS. About 420,000 individuals die of AIDS each year in the United States; about 5,000 of these are children or youth less than 15 years of age. Half of all of the new HIV infections involve young people between the ages of 13 and 24 (American Academy of Pediatrics, 2001a).

The cause of AIDS is the human immunodeficiency virus (HIV). This virus is passed from one person to another through sexual contact that includes the exchange of bodily fluids, usually semen or vaginal secretions; blood exchange through injection drug use (IDU); and transfusions, perinatal contact, and breast milk (Nickel, 2000a).

Sixty percent of adolescents develop AIDS through sexual activity or intravenous drug use. Adolescent males acquire the HIV infection primarily through homosexual activity. Adolescent females generally acquire the infection through heterosexual activity and intravenous drug use.

Many children with AIDS do not grow normally, do not make appropriate weight gains, are slow to achieve important motor milestones (crawling, walking, etc.), and evidence neurological damage. As the HIV turns into AIDS, these children are attacked by life-threatening opportunistic infections. Also, many of the children, as indicated earlier, develop more serious neurological problems associated with mental retardation, cerebral palsy, seizure disorders, and autism (National Institute for Allergy and Infectious Diseases, 2000a).

## Interventions

To date, there is no known cure for AIDS. The best cure for AIDS in children and youth is prevention. Treatment is generally provided by an interdisciplinary team composed of medical, educational, and health care professionals (Spiegel & Bonwit, 2002).

Much progress has been made in testing new antiretroviral therapies to combat AIDS and in developing agents to treat opportunistic infections (Pavia, 2001). Nevertheless, there is still much work to be done to find satisfactory drugs and related therapies for HIV infections and AIDS. Despite this progress, 10% to 15% of infected children develop AIDS in the first months of life and die shortly thereafter, and another 15% to 20% develop AIDS following the infancy period. Sixty-five percent to 75% of children who test positive for HIV thrive.

Early diagnosis of infants with HIV is crucial. Early antiviral therapy and prophylactic treatment of opportunistic diseases can contribute significantly to the infected child's well-being and prognosis over time (Jankelevich, 2001; Pavia, 2001). The fre-

**FOCUS 5**

What steps should be taken to help infants and children with AIDS?

HIV AND AIDS    489

quency and nature of treatment depend on the age of onset and the age at which the child develops the first opportunistic infection.

Providing appropriate interventions for infants with AIDS can be challenging. These infants, like infants without AIDS, are totally dependent on others for their care (National Pediatric & Family HIV Resource Center, 2001). Many mothers who pass the AIDS virus on to their children are not adequately prepared to care effectively for their infants. Typically, these mothers come from impoverished environments with little access to health care and other appropriate support services. Additionally, these mothers are often intravenous drug users and thus are not reliable caregivers.

However, recent research gives us all cause for hope. "Control of maternal disease [HIV-1] during pregnancy not only results in improved maternal health and survival, it also serves to protect the fetus from infection by its mother" (Beckerman, 2001, p. 12).

Treating adolescents with HIV and AIDS can be very challenging. For example, compliance with medical regimens for all age groups is difficult. However, for those who are HIV-positive and have no obvious symptoms, keeping regular medical appointments and taking antiviral medications are not only highly problematic but also constant reminders of an impending fatal disease. Youth with HIV and AIDS need to learn how to make medical regimens a regular part of their lives to maintain good health and longevity. They also need assistance in dealing with the psychological reactions of anxiety and depression that often accompany the discovery of HIV infection. Finally, they and others benefit significantly from instruction directed at helping them to understand AIDS, to make wise decisions about their sexual behavior, to use assertiveness skills, and to communicate effectively with others (National Institute of Allergy and Infectious Disease, 2000a).

Neither students with AIDS nor their parents are compelled by law to disclose their HIV medical status to school personnel. Nevertheless, the parents or students may share this information with a limited number of school-based personnel, including the school nurse, the principal, and the primary teacher. This information should be treated with the utmost confidentiality. Students with HIV who are on strict medical regimens will need time to take their medications. Missing a dosage could seriously jeopardize a student's health. Fatigue is a common occurrence in these students. Ample opportunities should be available for rejuvenation and respite from demanding physical activities (Depaepe, Garrison-Kane, & Doelling, 2002).

# Seizure Disorders (Epilepsy)

## Definitions and Concepts

**Epilepsy**

A condition that from time to time produces brief disturbances in the normal electrical functions of the brain, affecting a person's consciousness, bodily movements, or sensations. The intensity and length of these effects depend on the severity of the seizure.

A neurological condition, "**epilepsy** from time to time produces brief disturbances in the normal electrical functions of the brain. Normal brain function is made possible by millions of tiny electrical charges passing between nerve cells in the brain to all parts of the body. When someone has epilepsy [or a seizure disorder], this normal pattern may be interrupted by intermittent bursts of electrical energy that are much more intense than usual. They may affect a person's consciousness, bodily move-

## Assistive Technology

## THE FIRST NEW, FDA-APPROVED APPROACH TO TREATING EPILEPSY IN 100 YEARS

Vagus nerve stimulation (VNS) with the Cyberonics NeuroCybernetic Prosthesis (NCP) system is the first new approach to the treatment of epilepsy in over 100 years. After 15 years of research and clinical studies, VNS was approved on July 16, 1997, as an add-on therapy in reducing the frequency of seizures in adults and adolescents over 12 years of age with partial onset seizures that are refractory to antiepileptic medications. To date, over 8,000 patients of all ages with a variety of seizure types have been treated by physicians at over 350 centers in the United States and Europe.

VNS sends signals from the vagus nerve in the neck to the brain. The device is implanted in the chest and neck. The implant procedure does not involve the brain.

VNS consists of electrical signals that are applied to the vagus nerve in the neck for transmission to the brain. *Vagus* means "wanderer" in Greek. The vagus nerve is appropriately named, considering that it averages 22 inches in length in adults and wanders throughout the upper body. The vagus nerve has proved to be a good way to communicate with the brain because there are few if any pain fibers in the vagus nerve. Over 80% of the electrical signals applied to the vagus nerve in the neck are sent upwards to the brain. The stimulation lead may be attached to the vagus nerve in a surgical procedure that does not involve the brain and is not brain surgery.

SOURCE: From "The First New, FDA-Approved Approach to Treating Epilepsy in 100 Years," by Cyberonics, 2000, pp. 1–2. [Online] Available: http://www.cyberonics.com/pat_guide.htm

---

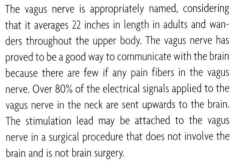

ments, or sensations for a short time" (Epilepsy Foundation of America, 2000a, p. 1). A **seizure** is a cluster of behaviors that occur in response to abnormal neurochemical activity in the brain. It typically alters the individual's level of consciousness and simultaneously results in certain characteristic motor patterns (Weinstein, 2002).

Several classification schemes have been employed to describe the various types of seizure disorders. We will briefly discuss two types of seizures: tonic/clonic and absence.

Generalized **tonic/clonic seizures**, formerly called *grand mal seizures*, affect the entire brain. The **tonic phase** of these seizures is characterized by a stiffening of the body, the **clonic phase** by repeated muscle contractions and relaxations. Tonic/clonic seizures are often preceded by a warning signal known as an **aura**, in which the individual senses a unique sound, odor, or physical sensation just prior to the onset of the seizure. In some instances, the seizure is also signaled by a cry or similar sound. The tonic phase of the seizure begins with a loss of consciousness, after which the individual falls to the ground. Initially, the trunk and head become rigid during the tonic phase. The clonic phase follows and consists of involuntary muscle contractions (violent shaking) of the extremities. Irregular breathing, blueness in the lips and face, increased salivation, loss of bladder and bowel control, and perspiration may occur.

The nature, scope, frequency, and duration of tonic/clonic seizures vary greatly from person to person. Such seizures may last as long as 20 minutes or less than 1 minute. One of the most dangerous aspects of tonic/clonic seizures is potential injury from falling and striking objects in the environment (see Figure 17.3).

A period of sleepiness and confusion usually follows a tonic/clonic seizure. The individual may exhibit drowsiness, nausea, headache, or a combination of these symptoms. Such symptoms should be treated with appropriate rest, medication, or other therapeutic remedies. The characteristics and aftereffects of seizures vary in many ways and should be treated with this in mind.

**Absence seizures**, formerly identified as *petit mal seizures*, are characterized by brief periods (moments or seconds) of inattention that may be accompanied by rapid eye blinking and head twitching. During these seizures, the brain ceases to function

**Seizure**

A cluster of behaviors (altered consciousness, characteristic motor patterns, etc.) that occurs in response to abnormal neurochemical activity in the brain.

**Tonic/clonic seizures**

Seizures in which the entire brain is affected. These seizures are characterized by stiffening of the body, followed by a phase of rapid muscle contractions (extreme shaking).

**Tonic phase**

The phase of a seizure in which the entire body becomes rigid and stiff.

**Clonic phase**

The phase of a seizure in which the muscles of the body contract and relax in rapid succession.

**Aura**

A sensation that is experienced just before a seizure and that the person is able to remember.

**Absence seizures**

Seizures characterized by brief lapses of consciousness, usually lasting no more than ten seconds. Eye blinking and twitching of the mouth may accompany these seizures.

FIGURE 17.3

**First Aid for Seizures**

1. Cushion the head.

2. Loosen tight necktie or collar.

3. Turn on side.

4. Put nothing in the mouth.

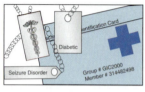

5. Look for identification.

6. Don't hold the person down.

7. Seizure ends.

8. Offer help

SOURCE: Adapted from *Information and Education: First Aid for Seizures* (p. 1), by the Epilepsy Foundation of America, 2000b. (online) Available: http://www. efa.org/education/firstaid/chart/html

as it normally would. The individual's consciousness is altered in an almost imperceptible manner. People with this type of seizure disorder may experience these seizures as often as 100 times a day. Such inattentive behavior may be viewed as daydreaming by a teacher or work supervisor, but the episode is really due to a momentary burst of abnormal brain activity that the individual cannot control. The lapses in attention caused by this form of epilepsy can greatly hamper the individual's ability to respond properly to or profit from a teacher's presentation or a supervisor's instruction. Treatment and control of absence seizures are generally achieved through prescribed medication.

## Prevalence and Causation

Prevalence figures for seizure disorders vary, in part because of the social stigma associated with them. About 2,500,000 people in the United States evidence some form of seizure disorders. Of this number, 30% are children. Also, a large number of adults and children have seizure disorders that remain undiscovered and untreated (Epilepsy Foundation of America, 2000a). Seizure disorders or epilepsies occur in about 1% of the population by age 20 (Bailet & Turk, 1997).

The causes of seizure disorders are many, including perinatal factors, tumors of the brain, complications of head trauma, infections of the central nervous system, vascular diseases, alcoholism, infection, maternal injury or infection, and genetic factors (Manford, 2003). Also, some seizures are caused by ingestion of street drugs, toxic chemicals, and poisons. Nevertheless, no explicit cause can be found in seven out of ten individuals with seizure disorders.

Researchers are endeavoring to determine what specific biophysical features give rise to seizures. If they can discover the underlying parameters, they may be able to prevent seizures from occurring. This could be done through molecular genetic techniques (Milton & Jung, 2003).

## Interventions

The treatment of seizure disorders begins with a careful medical investigation in which the physician develops a thorough health history of the individual and completes an in-depth physical examination. Moreover, it is essential that the physician receive a thorough description of the actual seizure itself. These preliminary treatment steps may be followed by other diagnostic procedures, including blood tests, video capturing of seizure episodes, CT scans or MRIs, and spinal fluid taps to determine whether the individual has meningitis. EEGs (electroencephalograms) may also be performed to confirm the physician's clinical impressions (Manford, 2003). The electroencephalogram is a test to detect abnormalities in the electrical activity of the brain. However, it should be noted that many seizure disorders are not detectable through electroencephalographic measures.

Many types of seizures can be treated successfully with precise drug management. Significant headway has been made with the discovery of effective drugs, particularly for children with tonic/clonic and absence seizures. Anticonvulsant drugs must be chosen very carefully, however. The potential risk and benefit of each medication must be balanced. Once a drug has been prescribed, families should be educated in its use, in the importance of noting any side effects, and in the need for consistent administration. Maintaining a regular medication regimen can be very challenging for children and their parents. In some instances, medication may be discontinued after several years of seizure-free behavior. This is particularly true for those young children who do not have some form of underlying brain pathology (Manford, 2003).

Other treatments for seizure disorders include surgery, stress management, and diet modifications. The goal of surgery is to remove the precise part of the brain that is damaged and is causing the seizures. Surgery is considered for those individuals with uncontrollable seizures, essentially those who have not responded to anticonvulsant medications. Using a variety of sophisticated scanning procedures, physicians attempt to isolate the damaged area of the brain that corresponds with the seizure activity. The outcomes of surgery for children and youth with well-defined foci of seizure activity are excellent (Epilepsy Foundation of America, 2000b). Obviously, the surgery must be done with great care. Brain tissue, once removed, is gone forever, and the function that the tissue performed is eliminated or only marginally restored. Unfortunately, only 1% of seizures disorders are treatable through surgery (Manford, 2003).

Stress management is designed to increase the child or youth's general functioning. Because seizures are often associated with illnesses, inadequate rest, and other stressors, parents and other care providers work at helping children, youth, and adults understand the importance of attending consistently to their medication routines, developing emotional resilience, and maintaining healthful patterns of behavior.

Diet modifications are designed to alter the way the body uses energy from food. Typically, our bodies convert the carbohydrates we consume into glucose (sugar). Several types of seizures can be controlled by instituting a ketogenic diet. This diet focuses on consuming fats rather than carbohydrates. Instead of producing glucose, individuals on this diet produce ketones, a special kind of molecule. This change in food consumption causes alterations in the metabolism of the brain that normally uses sugars to "fire" its functions. For reasons that are not completely understood, the brain is less receptive to certain kinds of seizures under this diet. However, the diet is extraordinarily difficult to maintain on a long-term basis and is now rarely used or recommended (Smith & Wallace, 2001).

Individuals with seizure disorders need calm and supportive responses from others. The treatment efforts of various professionals and family members must be carefully orchestrated to provide these individuals with opportunities to use their abilities and talents. Educators should be aware of the basic fundamentals of seizure disorders and their management. They should also be aware of their critical role in observing seizures that may occur at school. The astute observations of a teacher may be invaluable to a health care team that is developing appropriate medical interventions for the child or youth.

**FOCUS 6**

Describe the immediate treatment for a person who is experiencing a tonic/clonic seizure.

**FOCUS**
**7**

Identify three problems that individuals with diabetes may eventually experience.

# Diabetes

## Definitions and Concepts

The term **diabetes mellitus** refers to a developmental or hereditary disorder characterized by inadequate secretion or use of **insulin**, a substance that is produced by the pancreas and used to process carbohydrates. There are two types of diabetes mellitus: insulin-dependent diabetes mellitus (IDDM), commonly known as Type I or juvenile onset diabetes, and non-insulin-dependent diabetes mellitus (NIDDM), referred to as Type II or adult onset diabetes (American Diabetes Association, 2003a & b).

Glucose—a sugar, one of the end products of digesting carbohydrates—is used by the body for energy. Some glucose is used quickly, whereas some is stored in the liver and muscles for later use. However, muscle and liver cells cannot absorb and store the energy released by glucose without insulin, a hormone produced by the pancreas that converts glucose into energy that body cells use to perform their various functions. Without insulin, glucose accumulates in the blood, causing a condition known as hyperglycemia. Left untreated, this condition can cause serious, immediate problems for people with IDDM, leading to loss of consciousness or to a diabetic coma (American Diabetes Association, 2003b).

Typical symptoms associated with glucose buildup in the blood are extreme hunger, thirst, and frequent urination. Although progress has been made in regulating insulin levels, the prevention and treatment of the complications that accompany diabetes, which include blindness, cardiovascular disease, and kidney disease—still pose tremendous challenges for health care specialists (American Diabetes Association, 2003a; Depaepe et al., 2002).

IDDM, or juvenile onset diabetes, is particularly troublesome. Compared to the adult form, this disease tends to be more severe and progresses more quickly (Levetan, 2001). Generally, the symptoms are easily recognized. The child develops an unusual thirst for water and other liquids. His or her appetite also increases substantially, but listlessness and fatigue occur despite increased food and liquid intake.

NIDDM is the most common form of diabetes and is often associated with obesity in individuals over age 40. Individuals with this form of diabetes are at less risk for diabetic comas, and most individuals can manage the disorder through exercise and dietary restrictions. If these actions fail, insulin therapy may be necessary.

## Prevalence and Causation

It is estimated that a little more than 6% (17 million) of the U.S. population has diabetes. The prevalence rate for children with insulin-dependent diabetes (those who

**Diabetes mellitus**

A disease characterized by inadequate use of insulin, resulting in disordered metabolism of carbohydrates, fats, and proteins.

**Insulin**

A substance secreted by the pancreas that functions to process carbohydrates, enabling glucose to enter the body's cells.

Assistive Technology

## NO MORE SHOTS!

Canadian researchers . . . have developed a cell transplant technique that eliminates the need for insulin injections in the treatment of diabetes. The development is so striking that the *New England Journal of Medicine* released the University of Alberta study almost two months early and put it up on its website.

Scientists injected pancreas cells near the liver of eight diabetes patients. The cells took up residence in the liver and began producing the long-lost insulin that controls blood sugar levels.

If the results are confirmed in a larger study and if doctors can find a better source for the cells, which must now be harvested from cadavers, it could mean the end of insulin-dependent diabetes.

The long-term safety and effectiveness of the technique must still be established. In addition, the recipients must now take a combination of three drugs designed to prevent the body from rejecting the transplanted cells. Those drugs increase the risk of cancer and infection.

SOURCE: Adapted from "Diabetes Cure," by CBS News, June 6, 2000, pp. 1–2.

must administer insulin) is approximately 1 per 400 children. About 6 million people have diabetes and are unaware that they have the disease (American Diabetes Association, 2003a).

The causes of diabetes remain obscure, although considerable research has been conducted on the biochemical mechanisms responsible for it. Diabetes develops gradually in individuals. Individuals with Type I diabetes have a genetic predisposition to the disease. A youngster's environment and heredity interact in determining the severity and the long-term nature of the condition. However, even in identical twins, when one twin develops Type I diabetes, the other twin is affected only 25% to 50% of the time. There must be an environmental trigger that activates the onset of the disease. Some researchers believe that trigger to be a particular virus, Coxsackie B. Progressively, the body's immune system is affected, and the destruction of beta cells occurs. These are the cells in the pancreas that produce and regulate insulin production. Without insulin, the child develops the classic symptoms of Type I diabetes: excessive thirst, urination, and hunger, along with weight loss, fatigue, blurred vision, and high blood sugar levels.

## Interventions

Medical treatment centers on the regular administration of insulin, which is essential for children and youth with juvenile diabetes. Several exciting advances have been made in recent years in the monitoring of blood sugar levels and the delivery of insulin to people with diabetes (MiniMed, 2000a). Recent success with pancreas transplants has virtually eliminated the disease for some individuals. Also, significant progress is being made in the development of the bioartificial pancreas and gene therapy.

Solid headway has been made in transplanting insulin-producing islet cells to individuals with Type I diabetes. However, this approach is complicated by shortages in available, whole pancreases and by the rejection of these new cells in recipients. Other sources of pancreatic tissue are present in fetal tissue. This controversial approach makes use of tissues derived from aborted fetuses. Also, animal islet cells are currently being investigated, particularly islet cells derived from pigs, whose insulin differs by only one molecule from that of humans. However, transplantation of these cells poses similar rejection problems for recipients (American Diabetes Association, 2003a) (see the nearby Assistive Technology).

Hybrid technologies are also being pursued (National Diabetes Clearinghouse, 2003). Perhaps the most promising is the production of artificial beta cells that could be used in an artificial pancreas. This approach entails inserting, into naturally occurring cells, new genes that would produce insulin and be sensitive to the rise and fall of blood glucose (Children with Diabetes, 2000).

Maintaining normal levels of glucose is now achieved in many instances with an insulin infusion pump, which is worn by persons with diabetes and powered by small batteries. The infusion pump operates continuously and delivers the dose of insulin determined by

*Diabetes affects 1 in every 600 children.*

the physician and the patient. This form of treatment is effective only when used in combination with carefully followed diet and exercise programs. These pumps, if carefully monitored and operated, contribute greatly to "controlling" diabetes, thus reducing or slowing the onset and risks for eye disease, nerve damage, and kidney disease (MiniMed, 2000b, p. 1).

Juvenile diabetes is a lifelong condition that can have a pronounced effect on the child in a number of areas. Complications for children with long-standing diabetes include blindness, heart attacks, and kidney problems. Many of these problems can be delayed or prevented by maintaining adequate blood sugar levels with appropriate food intake, exercise, and insulin injections.

# Cystic Fibrosis

### Definitions and Concepts

**Cystic fibrosis (CF)** is an inherited, systemic, generalized disease that begins at conception. CF is a disorder of the secretion glands, which produce abnormal amounts of mucus, sweat, and saliva. Three major organ systems are affected: the lungs, pancreas, and sweat glands. The glue-like mucus in the lungs obstructs their functioning and increases the likelihood of infection, gradually destroying the lungs after repeated infections (Cystic Fibrosis Foundation, 2003). As lung deterioration occurs, the heart is burdened, and heart failure may result. The pancreas is affected in a similar fashion when excessive amounts of mucus prevent critical digestive enzymes from reaching the small intestine. Without these enzymes, proteins and fats consumed by the individual with CF are lost in frequent, greasy, flatulent stools.

### Prevalence and Causation

Cystic fibrosis is primarily a Caucasian phenomenon. It affects 30,000 children and adults in the United States (Cystic Fibrosis Foundation, 2003). CF is virtually absent in Japan and China. Males and females appear to be affected in about equal numbers. CF manifests itself in slightly more than 3 infants in every 10,000 live births (Bowe, 2000).

CF is a genetically transmitted disease. A child must inherit a defective copy of the CF gene from each parent to develop the disease. The gene for the CF transfer regulator (CFTR) is very large, and some 2,000 mutations have already been identified with the disease. CFTR, a protein, produces improper transportation of sodium and salt (chloride) within cells that line organs such as the lungs and pancreas. CFTR prevents chloride from exiting these cells. This blockage affects a broad range of organs and systems in the body, including reproductive organs in men and women, the lungs, sweat glands, and the digestive system (Cystic Fibrosis Foundation, 2003).

### Interventions

The prognosis for an individual with CF depends on a number of factors. The two most critical are early diagnosis of the condition and the quality of care provided after diagnosis. If the diagnosis occurs late, irreversible damage may be present. With early diagnosis and appropriate medical care, most individuals with CF can achieve weight and growth gains similar to those of their normal peers. Early diagnosis and improved treatment strategies have lengthened the average lifespan of children with CF; more than half now live beyond the age of 31.

The best and most comprehensive treatment is provided through CF centers located throughout the United States. These centers provide experienced medical and support staff (respiratory care personnel, social workers, dieticians, genetic counselors, and psychologists). Moreover, they maintain diagnostic laboratories especially equipped to perform pulmonary function testing and sweat testing. Sweat of children

**FOCUS 8**

Identify present and future interventions for the treatment of children and youth with cystic fibrosis.

**Cystic fibrosis (CF)**

A hereditary disease that usually appears during early childhood. This generalized disorder of the exocrine glands is characterized by respiratory problems and excessive loss of salt in perspiration.

with CF has abnormal concentrations of sodium or chloride; in fact, sweat tests provide the definitive data for a diagnosis of CF in infants and young children (Cystic Fibrosis Foundation, 2003).

Interventions for CF are varied and complex, and treatment continues throughout the person's lifetime. Consistent and appropriate application of the medical, social, educational, and psychological components of treatment enable these individuals to live longer and with less discomfort and fewer complications than in years past.

Treatment of CF is designed to achieve a number of goals. The first is to diagnose the condition before any severe symptoms are exhibited. Other goals include control of chest infection, maintenance of adequate nutrition, education of the child and family regarding the condition, and provision of a suitable education for the child.

Management of respiratory disease caused by CF is critical. If respiratory insufficiency can be prevented or minimized, the individual's life will be greatly enhanced and prolonged. Antibiotic drugs, postural drainage (chest physical therapy), and medicated vapors play important roles in the medical management of CF.

Diet management is also essential for the child with CF. Generally, the child with this condition requires more caloric intake than his or her normal peers. The diet should be high in protein and should be adjusted if the child fails to grow and/or make appropriate weight gains. Individuals with CF benefit significantly from the use of replacement enzymes that assist with food absorption. Also, the intake of vitamins is very important to individuals with digestive system problems.

The major social and psychological problems of children with CF are directly related to chronic coughing, small stature, offensive stools, gas, delayed onset of puberty and secondary sex characteristics, and unsatisfying social relationships. Also, these children and youth may spend significant amounts of time away from school settings. Thus teachers, counselors, and other support personnel play essential roles in helping these students feel at home in school, make up past-due work, and form friendships. Moreover, support groups play important roles in helping students with CF understand themselves and their disease and develop personal resilience and ongoing friendships.

Emerging and exciting interventions for CF are being explored, including gene therapy, lung transplants, mucus-thinning drugs, and the use of high doses of ibuprofen with young children. Gene therapy is particularly promising, because it addresses the root cause of CF (Cystic Fibrosis Foundation, 2003).

Development of new drugs has improved treatment for many individuals with CF. One such antibiotic is Pulmozyme. It has proved effective in reducing respiratory infections and in improving lung functioning in individuals with CF. On the horizon are new antibiotics such as TOBI™ (tobramycin solution for inhalation) and IB 367. These promising compounds and others yet to be developed should help physicians and individuals with CF more effectively manage chronic lung infections and related conditions.

# Sickle Cell Anemia

## Definitions and Concepts

**Sickle cell anemia** (SCA) is an inherited disorder that profoundly affects the structure and functioning of red blood cells. The hemoglobin molecule in the red blood cells of individuals with SCA is abnormal in that it is vulnerable to structural collapse when the blood-oxygen level is significantly diminished. As the blood-oxygen level declines, these blood cells become distorted and form bizarre shapes. This process, which is known as sickling, distorts the normal donut-like shapes of cells into shapes like microscopic sickle blades. Obstructions in the vessels of affected individuals can lead to stroke and to damage of other organs in the body (Depaepe, Garrison-Kane, & Doelling, 2002; Sickle Cell Information Center, 2003).

**FOCUS 9**

Describe the impact on body tissues of the sickling of red blood cells.

**Sickle cell anemia (SCA)**

An inherited disease that has a profound effect on the structure and functioning of red blood cells.

People affected by sickle cell anemia experience unrelenting **anemia**. In some cases it is tolerated well; in others the condition is quite debilitating. Another aspect of SCA involves frequent infections and periodic vascular blockages, which occur as sickled cells block microvascular channels. These blockages can often cause severe and chronic pain in the extremities, abdomen, or back. In addition, the disease may affect any organ system of the body. SCA also has a significant negative effect on the physical growth and development of infants and children (Sickle Cell Information Center, 2003; Mayo Clinic, 2003b).

### Prevalence and Causation

Approximately 1 in 500 African American infants has SCA (National Center for Biotechnology Information, 2003). Moreover, about 7% to 10% of African Americans carry the sickle cell gene. Sickle cell disease is most prevalent in areas of the world in which malaria is widespread. Individuals from the Mediterranean basin—from Greece, Italy, and Sardinia—may carry the mutant gene for SCA, as may individuals from India and the Arabian Peninsula.

Sickle cell anemia is caused by various combinations of genes (Mayo Clinic, 2001a). A child who receives a mutant S-hemoglobin gene from each parent exhibits SCA to one degree or another. The disease usually announces itself at 6 months of age and persists throughout the individual's lifetime.

### Interventions

A number of treatments may be employed to deal with the problems caused by sickle cell anemia, but the first step is early diagnosis. Babies—particularly infants who are at risk for this disease—should be screened at birth. Early diagnosis lays the groundwork for the prophylactic use of antibiotics to prevent infections in the first 5 years of life. This treatment, coupled with appropriate immunizations and nutrition, prevents further complications of the disease. Moreover, these treatments significantly reduce the death rate associated with SCA (Mayo Clinic, 2001b).

Children, youth, and adults usually learn to adapt to their anemia and lead relatively normal lives. When their lives are interrupted by crises, a variety of treatment approaches can be used. For children, comprehensive and timely care is crucial. For example, children with SCA who develop fevers should be treated aggressively. In fact, parents of these children may be taught how to palpate the spleen and recognize early signs of potentially serious problems. Hydration is also an important component of treatment. Lastly, pain management may be addressed with narcotic and nonnarcotic drugs (Mayo Clinic, 2001b).

Several factors predispose individuals to SCA crises: dehydration from fever, reduced liquid intake, and hypoxia (a result of breathing air that is poor in oxygen content). Stress, fatigue, and exposure to cold temperatures should be avoided by those who have a history of SCA crises.

Treatment of crises is generally directed at keeping the individual warm, increasing liquid intake, ensuring good blood oxygenation, and administering medication for infection. Assistance can also be provided during crisis periods by partial-exchange blood transfusions with fresh, normal red cells. Transfusions may also be necessary for individuals with SCA who are preparing for surgery or are pregnant (Depaepe, Garrison-Kane, & Doelling, 2002).

# SOCIAL AND HEALTH-RELATED PROBLEMS

**Anemia**

A condition in which the blood is deficient in red blood cells.

This section reviews child abuse and neglect, adolescent pregnancy, suicide among youth, and maternal drug and alcohol abuse. Although these conditions are not typically thought of as physical disabilities and health disorders, they influence significant numbers of families and place children and youth at risk for problems in their schools and communities.

# Child Abuse and Neglect

## Definitions and Concepts

Child abuse and neglect have been defined by both state and federal legislation. Each state is responsible for defining child abuse in conformance with the standards set by Child Abuse and Prevention Treatment Act (CAPTA) (U.S. Code: 42 USC 5101 et seq; 42 USC 5116 et seq). Most definitions include these descriptions:

Neglect is failure to provide for a child's basic needs. Neglect may be

- Physical (e.g., lack of appropriate supervision or failure to provide necessary food, shelter, or medical care).

- Educational (e.g., failure to educate a child or attend to special education needs).

- Emotional (e.g., inattention to a child's emotional needs or exposure to domestic violence).

These situations do not always mean that a child is neglected. Sometimes cultural values, the standards of care in the community, and poverty are contributing factors, indicating that the family is in need of information or assistance. When a family fails to use information and resources, and the child's needs continue to be unmet, then further intervention on the part of child welfare professionals may be required.

- Physical abuse is physical injury (ranging from minor bruises to severe fractures or death) as a result of punching, beating, kicking, biting, shaking, throwing, stabbing, choking, hitting (with a hand, stick, strap, or other object), burning, or otherwise harming a child. Such injury is considered abuse regardless of whether the caretaker intended to hurt the child.

- Sexual abuse includes activities by a parent or caretaker such as fondling a child's genitals, penetration, incest, rape, sodomy, indecent exposure, and commercial exploitation through prostitution or the production of pornographic materials.

- Emotional abuse is any pattern of behavior that impairs a child's emotional development or sense of self-worth. This may include constant criticism, threats, or rejection, as well as withholding love, support, or guidance. (Caliber, 2003b, p.1)

**Child abuse** and **child neglect** can be regarded as maladaptive means of coping by parents. Abusive parents and caregivers are confronted with personal and family challenges that influence their responses to children. Some parents are able to cope with these challenges with adaptive behaviors that help their children; other parents, unfortunately, respond with maladaptive, harmful behaviors (Crosson-Tower, 2002; Horton & Cruise, 2001).

Numerous factors contribute to the neglect of children. Many parents living in poverty cannot provide the shelter, food, clothing, and health care required for the well-being of their children. Often the stress experienced by these parents is overwhelming, and few resources are available in the way of support systems and services to help them. Other parents who neglect their children simply do not understand their children's behaviors and their own important role in caring for them. Moreover, many parents who neglect their children have very serious problems themselves, including substance abuse and serious psychiatric problems (Crosson-Tower, 2002).

Child neglect results when parents abandon their children or fail to care for them in healthy ways. In short, children who are not adequately cared for are considered

**Child abuse**

Nonaccidental sexual, physical, and/or psychological trauma and/or injury inflicted on a child.

**Child neglect**

A lack of interaction with a child on the part of other family members, which deprives that youngster of vital opportunities for development.

neglected. These children are often malnourished, infrequently bathed or changed, left without suitable supervision, and rarely held or appropriately stimulated.

Neglect is evidenced in many ways. Some of these children are grossly underweight for their age. They often fail to thrive and yet display no medical problems. Some may exhibit persistent and severe diaper rashes because of inconsistent care.

Physical abuse of children generally results in serious physical harm or injury to the affected child and sometimes even death (National Clearinghouse on Child Abuse and Neglect Information, 2000). Abusive parents often exhibit inconsistent childrearing practices. Furthermore, their child management approaches are often hostile and aggressive. These parents may also experience stress-eliciting problems arising from unemployment, youthful parenthood, limited income, and other related factors.

Another form of child mistreatment is **sexual abuse**—incest, assault, or sexual exploitation (Horton & Cruise, 1997). "Sexual abuse involves any sexual activity with a child where consent is not or cannot be given" (Berliner & Elliott, 1996, p. 51). Girls are at greater risk for sexual abuse than boys. And children and youth with disabilities are 1.75 times more likely than children without disabilities to be sexually abused (U.S. Department of Health and Human Services, 2003a).

Behavioral indicators of sexual abuse include anxiety, depression, age-inappropriate knowledge about sex, running away from home, suicide attempts, substance abuse problems, and fantasies with sexual connotations. However, many children who have been sexually abused show no signs. Manifestations of their maltreatment may not surface until the adult years and are often reflected in problems with interpersonal relationships, (Horton & Cruise, 2001).

Emotional abuse or psychological maltreatment is often the result of behaviors related to rejecting, terrorizing, isolating, and exploiting. Outcomes of this kind of abuse are many and varied. Children who have been severely ignored are often lethargic and apathetic. Often they are developmentally delayed in physical development, language acquisition, and cognitive development.

## Prevalence and Causation

Establishing accurate and precise prevalence estimates for child abuse is very difficult. In addition to the problem of underreporting, much of the difficulty is attributable to the lack of consistent criteria for child abuse and to the sundry reporting procedures used in various states. Annually, about 900,000 children experience child abuse or neglect. Recent studies suggest that the prevalence for child abuse and neglect is about 12.2 cases per 1,000 children (U.S. Department of Health and Human Services, 2003b). More than half of these children experienced neglect, and 19% suffered physical abuse. Almost 10% of the children were sexually abused. Twenty-seven percent were victims of other forms of abuse (Caliber, 2003a). The age group that experienced the highest rates of abuse was the 0–3 age group (National Clearinghouse on Child Abuse and Neglect Information, 2003).

Several factors may cause a parent or caregiver to be abusive. These include crises caused by unemployment, poverty, unwanted pregnancy, serious health problems, substance abuse, high levels of mobility, isolation from natural and community support networks, marital problems, death of a significant other, inadequate intellectual and moral development, and economic difficulties (Crosson-Tower, 2002). Other potential factors include the withdrawal of spousal support, having a child at a very young age, having a particularly challenging infant (one with severe disabilities), and caring for a nonbiologically related child (Sullivan, 2000). Several personality traits often characterize abusive parents: poor impulse control, deficits in role-taking and empathy, and low self-esteem (Baumrind, 1995).

Research suggests that parents who were abused as children are at risk of engaging in child abuse themselves. However, most children who were abused do not grow up to be abusive parents.

**FOCUS 10**

Identify five factors that may contribute to child abuse and neglect.

**Sexual abuse**

A form of mistreatment involving sexual misconduct such as incest, assault, or sexual exploitation.

Child abuse and neglect occur among all ethnic groups and at all socioeconomic levels (Horton & Cruise, 2001; U.S. Department of Health and Human Services, 2003b) . Thus all educators of children and youth must be aware of its existence and willing to address it. State laws designate educators and other professionals who work with children (e.g., health care providers, police officers, social workers, clergy) as mandated reporters, which means they have a legal responsibility to report suspected abuse or neglect to their administrators and/or appropriate law enforcement or child protection agencies (National Clearing House on Child Abuse and Neglect Information, 2003). Laws vary from state to state; educators must become familiar with the definition of abuse used in their jurisdiction, as well as with their responsibilities in reporting.

Clearly, reporting child abuse or neglect is a serious undertaking; however, the responsibility need not be intimidating. Although the reporter should have ample reason to suspect that abuse or neglect has occurred, he or she is not responsible for proving that it has. Moreover, laws often protect individuals who report abuse and neglect by ensuring some level of confidentiality. The reporter's primary consideration should be the welfare of the child (Crosson-Tower, 2002).

## Interventions

Treatment of child abuse and neglect is a multifaceted process. The entire family must be involved. The first goal is to treat the abused or neglected child for any serious injuries and simultaneously prevent further harm or neglect. Hospitalization may be necessary to deal with immediate physical injuries or other complications, and during this time, the child protection and treatment team, in conjunction with the family, develops a comprehensive treatment plan. Once the child's immediate medical needs have been met, a variety of treatment options may be employed: individual play therapy, therapeutic playschool, regular preschool, foster care, residential care, hospitalization, and/or group treatment.

Prevention and treatment programs for parents and families of abused and neglected children are directed at helping parents and other family members function more appropriately in responding to their children's needs as well as their own (U.S. Department of Health and Human Services, 2003a). These programs focus on behaviors and skills such as personal impulse control, alternative methods of disciplining, and anger management. Neglectful parents may receive one-on-one assistance with practical child care tasks such as feeding and diapering an infant, managing a challenging 2-year-old, and effectively dealing with various kinds of crying. Ways may be found to help parents provide adequate and nutritious food, suitable clothing, regular medical and dental care, and appropriate housing. Reviews of treatment programs for abusive and neglecting families suggest that these programs achieve mixed results and are generally ineffective. Some are effective in producing the desired changes, however, particularly with parents who have been involved in child neglect. The most effective approaches seem to be directed at the children themselves.

Some programs are directed at reducing economic and emotional stress by supplying affordable day care, helping parents become employable and employed, or providing opportunities for additional education and training. Also, collaboration among service providers is beginning to emerge. Such collaboration makes it possible for families to receive services that are tailored to their specific strengths and needs (U.S. Department of Health and Human Services, 2003a).

Interventions for children and youth who are abused are directed at the effects of the maltreatment. In some instances, the child or youth may receive treatment for depression, anxiety, stress, or even rage. Other children may need assistance with anger control or assertiveness training. Any number of problems or symptoms may surface as a result of abuse, including sleeping disorders, regression in toileting and language development for young children, insomnia, eating disorders, and ulcers. Early and ongoing treatment for these problems and symptoms is essential for children and youth who have experienced abuse and neglect. These interventions are best delivered by an array of educational and health care professionals (Horton & Cruise, 2001).

# Adolescent Pregnancy

**FOCUS**

**11**

Identify factors that may contribute to the increased prevalence of adolescent pregnancy.

## Definitions and Concepts

Adolescent pregnancy is the outcome of conception in girls 19 years old or younger. The impact of adolescent pregnancy is highly variable, depending on age, class, and race. More than 80% of the pregnancies that occur during the adolescent years are unwanted. Of these, the vast majority of adolescent mothers remain unmarried, leave school, and experience severe financial problems; many become reliant on welfare . Moreover, very few negotiate the challenges associated with adolescent pregnancy to complete their schooling and eventually enter the work force without being dependent on welfare services (American Academy of Pediatrics, 2001b).

Teens undergo a number of developmental changes during adolescence: construction of an identity, development of personal relationships and responsibilities, gradual preparation for vocational or professional work through education, independence from their parents, and various adjustments to a complex society. Many—if not all—of these developmental changes are significantly affected by pregnancy.

The risks and consequences associated with adolescent pregnancy are substantial, particularly if the young mother is 15 years of age or younger. Children born to these mothers experience higher rates of infant mortality, birth defects, mental retardation, central nervous system problems, and intelligence deficits (American Academy of Pediatrics, 2001b; The National Campaign to Prevent Teen Pregnancy, 2003). Additionally, the fathers of adolescent mothers' babies are not generally adolescents themselves. They are men beyond their teen years. These dads are often fathers in absentia; few truly assume the role of parent or even partial provider (American Academy of Pediatrics, 2001b). Seventy percent of the births to adolescent women occur out of wedlock. It is the adolescent mother and her immediate family who shoulder the burdens of caring for and supporting the child. Four out of five adolescent mothers are on government welfare within a year of the birth of their first child (Resource Center for Adolescent Pregnancy Prevention, 2003).

## Prevalence and Causation

The birthrate for adolescent females 15–19 years of age is about 50 births per 1,000 teenagers. The United States has the highest rate of teen pregnancies among developed nations. The prevalence of adolescent pregnancy is staggering. About 1 million girls become pregnant each year in the United States. By age 16, one of every three girls has had sex. By age 18, two out of three boys have had sex (American Academy of Pediatrics, 2001b; The National Campaign to Prevent Teen Pregnancy, 2003)

Adolescent girls become pregnant for a number of varied and complex reasons. Contributing factors include lack of knowledge about conception and sexuality, lack of access to or misuse of contraceptives,

*The United States has the highest rate of teen pregnancies among developed nations. About one million teenagers become pregnant each year in the United States. Of these, about one in ten is a deliberate choice.*

desire to escape family control, alcohol consumption, need to be more adult, aspirations to have someone to love, means of gaining attention and care, and inability to make sound decisions. Societal factors also play a role in the increased number of adolescents who become pregnant: greater permissiveness and freedom, social pressure from peers, and continual exposure to sexuality through the media.

## Interventions

The goals of treatment for the pregnant adolescent are varied. The first goal is to help the prospective mother cope with the discovery that she is pregnant. What emerges from this discovery is a crisis—for her, for the father, and for the families of both individuals, although responses vary among various ethnic and socioeconomic groups. Some adolescents may respond with denial, disbelief, bitterness, disillusionment, or a variety of other feelings. Parents often react to the announcement with anger, then shame and guilt.

Treatment during this period focuses on reducing interpersonal and intrapersonal strain and tension. A wise counselor involves the family in crisis intervention, which is achieved through careful mediation and problem solving. For many adolescents, this period involves some very intense decision making: Should I keep the baby? Should I have the baby and then put it up for adoption? Should I have an abortion? Should I get married? If the adolescent chooses to have the baby, nutritional support for the developing infant, quality prenatal and perinatal care, training for eventual child care, education, and instruction in employment skills become the focus of the intervention efforts. Additionally, young expectant mothers are provided assistance for managing smoking, alcohol consumption, and other drug use or abuse as appropriate (American Academy of Pediatrics, 2001b).

Treatment models for adolescent mothers vary. Some are school-based. Others are multidisciplinary, focusing on medical care, psychological support, and life skills support. These programs are often delivered through medical centers or in ambulatory clinic settings where regular visits take place. Both the young mother and the young infant receive care simultaneously. All of the programs focus on strengthening parenting skills, building parent-child relationships, and the enhancing the mothers' personal functioning. These programs provide for prenatal and well-baby care, vocational training, and family-planning education. Also, every effort is made to help young mothers stay in school and to continue or conclude their secondary education (American Academy of Pediatrics, 2001b).

Unfortunately, many services rendered to pregnant adolescents fade after delivery of the child. One of the major hazards for these mothers is becoming pregnant again. Steps should be taken to help young mothers explore options and approaches that significantly reduce the potential for repeated pregnancies and other, related challenges. Problems do not cease with delivery; the development of functional life skills for independent living is a long-term educational and rehabilitation process.

# Suicide in Youth

## Definitions and Concepts

**Suicide** is the third leading cause of death in young people (Natinoal Center for Health Statistics, 2003). Suicide among the young is generally a premeditated act that culminates in the taking of one's life. Several other terms have been developed to describe suicide. *Completed suicide* is death caused by a set of acts meant to end life. *Attempted suicide* consists of self-harm behaviors that could end in death. *Suicidal ideation* is the thoughts one has about suicide and the frequency of these thoughts during a set period of time (Goldston, 2000).

Suicide is a means of satisfying needs, alleviating pain, dealing with depression, and coping with the challenges and stressors inherent in being a youth in today's society (American Academy of Pediatrics, 2003). "Over 50% of suicides occur in young

**Suicide**

The taking of one's own life.

people who are sad, despairing, or depressed; another 20% are described as angry, with the suicidal attempt occurring rather impulsively (see Table 17.3). Substance abuse is implicated in at least 20% of the suicides" (Clark, 1997, p. 197).

## Prevalence and Causation

The prevalence of suicide among young people ages 15–19 is 8.2 per 100,000. The prevalence rate for children 14 years old and younger is 1.5 per 100,000 (National Institute of Mental Health, 2003b). Many professionals believe that these figures rep-

**TABLE 17.3**

### Common Warning Signs of Suicidal Behavior

| WARNING SIGNS | DISCUSSION |
|---|---|
| Suicide notes | Suicide notes are a very real sign of danger and should always be taken seriously. |
| Direct and indirect suicide threats | Most individuals give clues that they have suicidal thoughts. Clues include direct ("I have a plan to kill myself") and indirect threats ("I might as well be dead"). |
| Making final arrangements | Making funeral arrangements, writing a will, paying debts, saying good-bye, and the like could be signs that a youth is suicidal. |
| Giving away prized possessions | In effect, the youth is executing a will. |
| Talking about death | This could be a sign that the youth is exploring death as a solution to problems. |
| Reading or writing and/or creating artwork about death | Sometimes warnings include writing death poems or filling sheets of paper with macabre drawings. |
| Hopelessness or helplessness | A youth who feels there is no hope that problems will improve and who feels helpless to change things may consider suicide. |
| Social withdrawal and isolation | These behaviors may be a sign of depression and may be a precursor of suicide. |
| Loss of involvement in interests and activities | A youth who is considering suicide may see no purpose in continuing previously important interests and activities. |
| Increased risk taking | Youths who choose high-risk sports, daredevil hobbies, and other unnecessarily dangerous activities may be suicidal. |
| Heavy use of alcohol and drugs | Substance abusers have a six times greater risk for suicide than the general population. |
| Abrupt changes in appearance | Youths who no longer care about their appearance may be suicidal. |
| Sudden weight or appetite change | These changes may be a sign of depression, which can increase the risk of suicide. |
| Sudden changes in personality or attitude | The shy youth who suddenly becomes a thrill seeker or the outgoing person who becomes withdrawn and unfriendly may be giving signals that something is seriously wrong. |
| Inability to concentrate or think rationally | This inability may be a sign of depression or other mental illness and may increase the risk of suicide. |
| Sudden unexpected happiness | Sudden happiness, especially following prolonged depression, may indicate that the person is profoundly relieved after having made a decision to commit suicide. |
| Sleeplessness or sleepiness | This behavior may be a sign of depression and may increase the risk of suicide. |
| Increased irritability or crying easily | Depressed, stressed, and potentially suicidal youths demonstrate wide mood swings and unexpected displays of emotion. |
| Low self-esteem | Youths with low self-esteem may consider suicide. |
| Abrupt changes in attendance | Remain alert to excessive absenteeism in a student with a good attendance record, particularly when the change is sudden. |
| Dwindling academic performance | Question unexpected and sudden decrease in performance. |
| Failure to complete assignments | Sudden failure is often seen in the depressed and suicidal. |
| Lack of interest and withdrawal | One of the first signs of potentially suicidal youth is withdrawal, disengagement, and apathy. A sudden lack of interest in extracurricular activities may be seen. |
| Changed relationships | Abrupt changes in social relationships may offer evidence of personal despair. |
| Despairing attitude | Students may make comments about being unhappy, feeling like a failure, not caring about the future, or even not caring about living or dying. |

SOURCE: Adapted from *California's Helper's Handbook for Suicide Intervention*, by R. F. Ramsay, B. L. Tanney, R. J. Tierney, & W. A. Lang, 1990, Sacramento, CA: State Department of Mental Health.

resent only a small portion of the actual number of youth suicides, particularly if one considers the number of youth whose deaths are described as accidental. Far more young males than females commit suicide; the ratio is 5:1 (National Institute of Mental Health, 2003b). However, females are three times more likely to attempt suicide. In contrast to males, females use far less violent and lethal means.

The causes of suicide are multidimensional. Suicide is best viewed as a collection of interacting risk factors, including psychopathological (mental or addictive disorders), biological, familial (family history of suicide, parental separation, etc.), and situational factors (available firearms in the home, interpersonal loss or conflict with a boyfriend or girlfriend, etc.). For example, some studies suggest that alterations in brain chemistry place some youth at risk for suicide (Goldsmith, Pellmar, Kleinman, & Bunney, 2002). Personal factors associated with suicide include clinical depression, hopelessness, impulsivity, and other psychiatric conditions. In fact, many clinicians believe that depression is the most powerful discriminant for suicidal behavior (American Academy of Pediatrics, 2003).

Families of suicidal youth may present several problems. These include family violence, rejection, indifference, a lack of warmth or connectedness with their children, extreme rigidity or chaos, severe marital discord, and parental death or suicide (Borowsky, Ireland, & Resnick, 2001). "Having a first degree relative who completed suicide increases an individual's risk of suicide six-fold" (Goldsmith, Pellmar, Kleinman, & Bunney, 2002, p. 3).

Peers strongly influence the views that adolescents have about themselves and how they behave. The youth who feels rejected or isolated is at risk for suicide. This is also true of youth whose romantic relationships are problematic or highly unstable. Another factor related to suicide in youth is sexual identity. Youth who struggle with their sexual identity and experience extreme peer rejection are vulnerable to suicide (American Academy of Pediatrics, 2003).

Generally, suicide is the culmination of serious, numerous, and long-standing problems. As a child moves into adolescence, these problems often become more serious. Findings from psychological autopsy studies suggest that 93% to 95% of adults who die by suicide met objective criteria for a mental disorder in the weeks preceding their deaths, most commonly major depression, substance abuse, and schizophrenia. Similar studies have been conducted with populations of youth. Findings suggest that drug abuse is the most common problem encountered, followed closely by depression.

## Interventions

Treatment of suicidal youth is directed at protecting them from further harm, decreasing acute suicidal tendencies, addressing suicide risk factors, and treating mental disorders or other contributing conditions, such as drug or alcohol abuse (National Institute for Mental Health, 2003a). Interventions are also aimed at enhancing factors that protect against suicidal tendencies and decrease vulnerability to repeated suicidal behavior. These interventions may include "sterilizing" the home of pills, guns, knives, razor blades, and other dangerous items. Driving restrictions may also be imposed as one of the interventions. Moreover, school counseling personnel may initiate a no-suicide contract in which the youth commits herself or himself to certain positive actions and coping strategies, particularly in situations that might evoke suicidal thoughts. These contracts may cover one day or several days. Counseling personnel may provide key phone numbers for obtaining assistance or support. Such contracts are recommended for students whose risk for suicidal behaviors is low.

Hospitalization may be the first step for youth who attempt suicide. Any physical injuries or complications that the youth may have suffered are addressed first. Then a variety of professionals, together with parents, begin the planning process and implementation of treatment. Therapies directed at decreasing the problems manifested by suicide attempters include individual, peer group, family, and drug therapies (Goldsmith et al., 2002).

**FOCUS 12**

Identify the major causes of youth suicide.

Multiple levels and kinds of prevention may be implemented for youth who are suicidal. For example, crisis intervention is directed at moving youth away from imminent suicide and making referrals for appropriate treatment. In contrast, prevention programs are designed to provide early intervention, assist children and youth in developing coping skills, teach them how to manage stress, and provide counseling and other therapeutic services for children and adolescents throughout their school years.

Prevention is in many ways a community endeavor, aimed at developing a network of social connections that give adolescents meaningful experiences with peers and other individuals. These connections may avert problems associated with loneliness, hopelessness, and alienation.

FOCUS
13

Identify the potential effects of maternal substance abuse on the developing child.

# Maternal Drug and Alcohol Abuse

## Definitions and Concepts

Expectant mothers who use illegal drugs or alcohol place their children and themselves at risk for a variety of serious medical, psychological, and health-related problems (American College of Obstetricians and Gynecologists, 2002; March of Dimes Birth Defects Foundation 2003; Nickel, 2000a). Substance-exposed infants are affected in several ways. These infants often of low birth weight, exhibit tremors, problems sleeping and eating, impaired cognitive development, learning problems, delayed expressive language, impeded motor development, and behavior problems (National Institute on Drug Abuse, 2001a, 2001b, & 2002).

Drug abuse in parents produces other problems that affect young children. Caring for infants and young children requires a great deal of selflessness and patience. If the children's parents are primarily concerned about obtaining and using drugs, they are not able to provide the nurturing, stimulation, and care essential for normal development and attachment.

## Prevalence and Causation

The actual prevalence of infants directly affected by substance abuse is difficult to determine. Many expectant mothers are reluctant to reveal their abuse for fear that they will be prosecuted for child maltreatment. Some 5% to 15% of all newborns are exposed prenatally to illegal drugs and/or alcohol (Nickel, 2000a). Furthermore, about three million infants are prenatally affected by maternal alcohol consumption. Fetal alcohol syndrome (FAS) affects about 0.5 to 2 infants per 1,000 births in the United States. If we include FAS, alcohol-related neurodevelopmental disorder (ARND), and alcohol-related birth defects (ARBD), the rate jumps to 10 infants per 1,000 births (National Institute on Alcohol Abuse and Alcoholism, 2003). FAS is the leading known cause of mental retardation.

Maternal drug abuse and alcohol abuse affect infants in several ways (March of Dimes, 2003a). For example, cocaine is readily available, easily ingested, and highly addictive. In fact, it is the drug of choice for many substance abusers. Because of the low molecular weight of cocaine, it readily crosses the placenta to the developing fetus or child. Cocaine easily passes through the blood–brain barrier, thereby altering the chemistry and functioning of the emerging infant's brain. Cocaine may also be passed from the mother to the child through her breast milk. The regular presence of cocaine in the developing fetus or child affects its development and functioning in a variety of detrimental ways (see Figure 17.4). Each drug (marijuana, heroin, LSD, ecstasy, amphetamines, etc.) creates its own havoc within the mother and the developing infant (American College of Obstetricians and Gynecologists, 2003; National Institutes of Health., 2003; Nickel, 2000a).

FIGURE 17.4

**The Effects of Maternal Cocaine Use on Mothers and Fetuses/Babies**

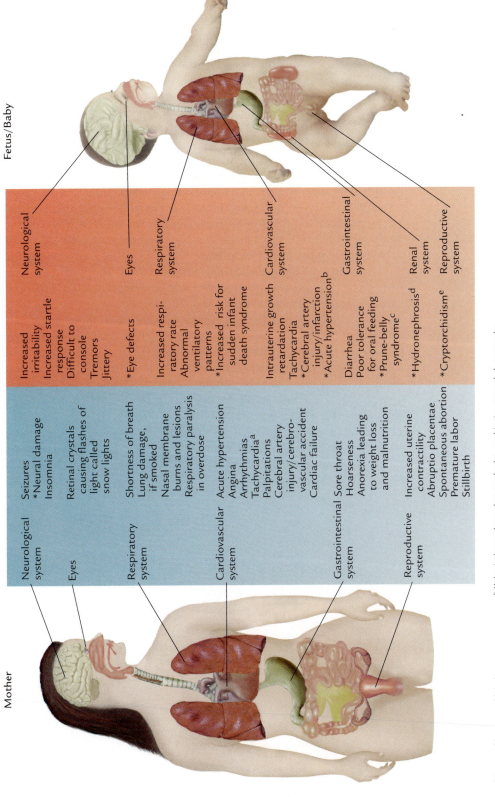

Mother

Fetus/Baby

Neurological system — Seizures / *Neural damage / Insomnia — Increased irritability / Increased startle response / Difficult to console / Tremors / Jittery — Neurological system

Eyes — Retinal crystals causing flashes of light called snow lights — *Eye defects — Eyes

Respiratory system — Shortness of breath / Lung damage, if smoked / Nasal membrane burns and lesions / Respiratory paralysis in overdose — Increased respiratory rate / Abnormal ventilatory patterns — Respiratory system

Cardiovascular system — Acute hypertension / Angina / Arrhythmias / Tachycardia[a] / Palpitations / Cerebral artery injury/cerebrovascular accident / Cardiac failure — *Increased risk for sudden infant death syndrome / Intrauterine growth retardation / Tachycardia / *Cerebral artery injury/infarction / *Acute hypertension[b] — Cardiovascular system

Gastrointestinal system — Sore throat / Hoarseness / Anorexia leading to weight loss and malnutrition — Diarrhea / Poor tolerance for oral feeding / Prune-belly syndrome[c] — Gastrointestinal system

*Hydronephrosis[d] — Renal system

Reproductive system — Increased uterine contractility / Abruptio placentae / Spontaneous abortion / Premature labor / Stillbirth — *Cryptorchidism[e] — Reproductive system

* Suspected but not established
[a] Abnormally high heart rate
[b] An episode of dangerously high blood pressure
[c] Abdominal musculature does not develop, resulting in a stomach that protrudes
[d] Swollen kidney(s)
[e] Testicles remain in the abdominal cavity

SOURCE: From "The Dangers of Prenatal Cocaine Use," by J. Smith, 1988, *American Journal of Maternal Child Nursing*, 13(3), p. 175. Copyright 1988 by *American Journal of Maternal Child Nursing*.

## Interventions

Implementing interventions for mothers and their babies who have been exposed to drugs is a challenging and complex process, particularly if the mother is addicted (Nickel, 2000a). Mothers with histories of serious drug abuse may need as much treatment as their affected infants. Often, in fact, mothers need more assistance. Think for a moment about being a pediatrician or family physician faced with deciding whether to release an infant who is at risk and needs sophisticated care to a mother burdened with drug abuse. What action would you take?

Some infants are initially placed with grandparents or other caregivers until their mothers are capable of caring for them. Others are placed with relatives, foster parents, or respite care providers. Some are eventually adopted (National Resource Center for Respite and Crisis Care, 2003; Nickel, 2000a).

Educationally oriented treatments for preschoolers affected by substance abuse focus on designing well-structured learning environments, creating small classes (eight children per teacher), and providing developmentally appropriate learning environments that are child-sized, visually interesting, and suitably stimulating. These environments also provide learning activities that are experiential rather than paper-and-pencil tasks. Programs for school-age children are beginning to emerge as practitioners and researchers learn more about the effects of substance abuse on the development and performance of young children. Many of these children benefit from early, comprehensive intervention services delivered by special education, medical, and psychological specialists (Nickel, 2000a).

Comprehensive models of treatment for drug-abusing women and their children are emerging. As we have noted, these models include intake screening and comprehensive health assessment; medical interventions for mothers, their children, and other family members; early intervention services for drug-exposed infants and toddlers; home-based support; counseling for HIV and AIDS; linkages to other service providers for outreach, residential, and outpatient services; substance abuse and psychological counseling; parenting education; health education; life skills education; training and remediation services; child care services; transportation support; housing assistance; and continuing care after intensive therapies and interventions have been applied (National Institute on Drug Abuse, 2003; Office of National Drug Control Policy, 2003).

# FOCUS REVIEW

**FOCUS 1**  Identify the disabilities that may accompany cerebral palsy.

- Often, individuals with cerebral palsy have several disabilities, including hearing impairments, speech and language disorders, intellectual deficits, visual impairments, and general perceptual problems.

**FOCUS 2**  What is spina bifida myelomeningocele?

- Spina bifida myelomeningocele is a type of spina bifida cystica that announces itself in the form of a tumor-like sac, on the back of the infant, that contains both spinal fluid and nerve tissue.
- Spina bifida myelomeningocele is also the most serious variety of spina bifida in that it generally includes paralysis or partial paralysis of certain body areas, causing lack of bowel and bladder control.

**FOCUS 3**  Identify specific treatments for individuals with spinal cord injuries.

- The first step is immediate pharmacological interventions with high and frequent doses of methylprednisolone. These doses reduce the severity of the injury and improve the functional outcome over time.
- Stabilization of the spine is critical to the overall outcome of the injury.
- Once the spine has been stabilized, the rehabilitation process begins. Physical therapy helps the affected individual make full use of any residual muscle strength.
- The individual is taught to use orthopedic devices, such as handsplints, braces, reachers, headsticks, and other augmentative devices.
- Psychological adjustment is aided by psychiatric and psychological personnel.
- Rehabilitation specialists assist in retraining or reeducating the individual; they may also help the individual secure employment.
- Some individuals will need part-time or full-time attendant care for assistance with daily activities (e.g., bathing, dressing, and shopping).

**FOCUS 4**  Describe the physical limitations associated with muscular dystrophy.

- Individuals with muscular dystrophy progressively lose their ability to walk and to use their arms and hands effectively, because fatty tissue begins to replace muscle tissue.

**FOCUS 5**  What steps should be taken to help infants and children with AIDS?

- Infants and children should be provided with the most effective medical care available, particularly medications to control opportunistic infections.
- Children with AIDS should attend school unless they exhibit behaviors that are dangerous to others or are at risk for developing infectious diseases that would exacerbate their condition.

**FOCUS 6**  Describe the immediate treatment for a person who is experiencing a tonic/clonic seizure.

- Cushion the head.
- Loosen any tight necktie or collar.
- Turn the person on his or her side.
- Put nothing in the mouth of the individual.
- Look for identification.
- Don't hold the person down.
- As seizure ends, offer help.

**FOCUS 7**  Identify three problems that individuals with diabetes may eventually experience.

- Structural abnormalities that occur over time may result in blindness, cardiovascular disease, and kidney disease.

**FOCUS 8**  Identify present and future interventions for the treatment of children and youth with cystic fibrosis.

- Drug therapy for prevention and treatment of chest infections
- Diet management, use of replacement enzymes for food absorption, and vitamin intake
- Family education regarding the condition
- Chest physiotherapy and postural drainage
- Inhalation therapy
- Psychological and psychiatric counseling
- Use of mucus-thinning drugs, gene therapy, and lung or lung/heart transplant

**FOCUS 9**  Describe the impact on body tissues of the sickling of red blood cells.

- Because sickled cells are more rigid than normal cells, they frequently block microvascular channels. The blockage of channels reduces or terminates circulation in these areas, and tissues in need of blood nutrients and oxygen die.

**FOCUS 10**  Identify five factors that may contribute to child abuse and neglect.

- Unemployment, poverty, and substance abuse
- Isolation from natural and community support networks
- Marital/relationship problems
- Having a particularly challenging, needy, or demanding infant
- Poor impulse control

# CHAPTER 17

**FOCUS 11**  Identify factors that may contribute to the increased prevalence of adolescent pregnancy.

- General factors include a lack of knowledge about conception and sexuality, a desire to escape family control, an attempt to be more adult, a desire to have someone to love, a need for attention and love, and an inability to make sound decisions.
- Societal factors include greater sexual permissiveness and freedom, social pressure from peers, and continual exposure to sexuality through the media.

**FOCUS 12**  Identify the major causes of youth suicide.

- The causes of suicide are multidimensional. They involve biological, personal, family, peer, and community factors.
- Alterations in brain chemistry put some individuals at risk for suicide.
- Often, clinical depression or other psychiatric conditions precede suicide.
- Other causative factors include extreme peer rejection, problems with sexual identity, and substance abuse.

**FOCUS 13**  Identify the potential effects of maternal substance abuse on the developing child.

- The effects include low birthweight, sleeping and eating disorders, heightened sensitivity, and challenging temperaments.
- Children exposed to cocaine are at greater risk for neurological problems, eye defects, respiratory problems, cardiovascular complications, and other health problems.

## FURTHER READINGS

Batshaw, M. L. (2001). *When Your Child Has a Disability.* Baltimore, MD: Paul H. Brooks.

*This is a carefully crafted sourcebook for parents and others who are interested in caring for children with disabilities. Dr. Batshaw and other contributors address topics that are of real interest to parents, including "Making the Most of Doctor Visits," "Why My Child?", "Commonly Used Medicines," and "What About Our Next Child?"*

Bryan, J. (2000). *Living with Diabetes.* Austin, TX: Raintree Steck-Vaughn Publishers.

*This children's book presents information about the symptoms, treatment, and course of juvenile diabetes. It also offers interesting information about recommended diets, monitoring devices, and family relationships.*

Carter, A. R. (2000). *Stretching Ourselves: Kids with Cerebral Palsy.* Morton Grove, IL: Albert Whitman.

*This wonderful picture book is designed for children. It portrays a young girl named Emily and other children as they experience various aspects of their lives in school, with friends, and with care providers.*

Harris, J. (2001). *Sickle Cell Disease.* Brookfield, CT: Twenty-First Century Books.

*This very readable book about sickle cell anemia answers many questions about the ways in which the disease is inherited, how and why episodic crises occur, and what treatments are commonly used.*

Reeve, Christopher. (2003). *Nothing Is Impossible: Reflections on a New Life.* Waterville, ME: Thorndike Press.

*The title of this book says it all. Christopher Reeve talks to all of us about humor, the mind-body connection, parenting, religion, advocacy, recovery, faith, and hope. Wonderful photos, taken by his son Matthew, are included.*

Rhema, Dan. (2001). *The Day the Animals Lost Their True Colors.* Louisville, KY: Brain Injury Association of Kentucky Press.

*A wonderful picture book for children and the young at heart. Author Dan Rhema contracted break bone fever, also known as Dengue fever. Because of his near-death experience with this fever, he created a book for children about animals who experienced profound changes much like those encountered by individuals who have sustained traumatic brain or spinal cord injuries.*

## WEB RESOURCES

**Epilepsy Foundation**

www.epilepsyfoundation.org

This website is a great source of information about services and programs for individuals with epilepsy or seizure disorders. If you are interested in the latest research, legislation, or medical treatment for individuals with epilepsy, you should examine this website in some depth.

### Link for Life

www.diabetes.org/main/info/LinkForLifeAd/chooser.htm

This terrific site offers an entertaining and informative multimedia presentation on diabetes. It is sponsored by the drug company GlaxoSmithKline.

### Spinal Cord Injury Peer Information Library on Technology

www.scipilot.com/_g/home_g/index.shtml

This is an astounding website for individuals who are interested in seeing real stories about individuals who have used assistive technologies to vastly improve their lives. Available on the site are actual video clips in which individuals with spinal cord injuries relate their experiences in using a wide array of technologies both high-tech and homemade.

### American Foundation for Suicide Prevention

www.afsp.org/education/recommendations/6/index.html

The "Talk to the Experts" page is part of a valuable website for reporters and others who are writing art-icles about suicide. One may contact a psychiatrist who specializes in suicide prevention and the treatment of depression.

### National Campaign to Prevent Teen Pregnancy

www.teenpregnancy.org

This website provides concerned parents and teens with information about preventing teen pregnancy, research related to adolescent pregnancy, and national media events.

### Too Young to Die

www.deepelm.com/tytd/tytd.html

Created by Deep Elm Records and its artists, this website provides songs and other educational materials for youth and others who are interested in preventing suicide. Each of the featured songs was carefully selected for lyrics that promote faith, hope, and perseverance. These songs reinforce the idea that youth who experience loneliness, doubt, and depression are not alone.

## BUILDING YOUR PORTFOLIO

If you are thinking about a career in special education, you should know that many states use national standards developed by the Council for Exceptional Children (CEC) to assess a teacher candidate's knowledge and skills for working with students with disabilities. See a complete listing of the ten CEC Content Standards on the inside front cover of this text.

### CEC Content Standards Addressed in Chapter 17

1. Foundations
2. Development and Characteristics of Learners
3. Individual Learning Differences
5. Learning Environments and Social Interactions

### Assess Your Knowledge of the CEC Standards Addressed in Chapter 17

Some states require that teacher candidates develop a portfolio of products that demonstrate mastery of the CEC content standards. To assist in the development of products for this portfolio, you may wish to complete the following activities.

- Complete a written test of the chapter's content.

  *If your instructor requires a written test of your content knowledge for this chapter, keep a copy for your port-*folio. *A practice test on the information covered in this chapter is available through the companion website (www.ablongman.com/hardman8e) and the Student Study Guide.*

- Respond to the application questions for the Case Study "Living with Cerebral Palsy."

  *Review the Case Study and respond in writing to the application questions. Keep a copy of the case study and your written response for your portfolio.*

- Complete the "Take a Stand" activity for the Debate Forum "AIDS and the Public Schools".

  *Read the Debate Forum in this chapter and then visit our companion website to complete the activity "Take a Stand." Keep a copy of this activity for your portfolio.*

- Participate in a community service learning activity.

  *Community service is a valuable way to enhance your learning experience. Visit our companion website for suggested community service learning activities that correspond to the information presented in this chapter. Develop a reflective journal of the service learning experience for your portfolio.*

## THEMES OF THE TIMES

Expand your knowledge of the concepts discussed in this chapter by reading current and historical articles from the *New York Times* by visiting the "Themes of the Times" section of the companion website: **www.ablongman.com/hardman8e.**

# Gifted, Creative, and Talented

## TO BEGIN WITH...

### Is your sibling gifted?

If your answers to the following questions are preponderantly yes, you may have a sibling who is gifted.

- Does your sibling constantly drive you crazy with questions?
- Does your sibling remember things that you would prefer to forget?
- Does your sibling like to be challenged with new ideas?
- Does your sibling have a vocabulary larger than life?
- Is your sibling aware of situations and does he or she have questions about things that are difficult, if not impossible, to answer?
- Does your sibling prefer the company of adults or older children [to that of same-age] peers?
- Does your sibling have a zany sense of humor?
- Does your sibling like to take control and organize tasks, and/or seek to tell you and others how to get the tasks done?
- Does your sibling push the limits, refuse to take no for an answer, and act like a junior lawyer at age four?
- Does your sibling have a wide range of interests or one consuming area of interest? (Walker, 2002, p. 1)

### Are we squandering a precious resource?

- The United States is squandering one of its most precious resources—the gifts and talents of many of its students.
- These youngsters are not challenged to do their best work. They perform poorly in comparison with top students in other countries.
- America relies on its top-performing students to provide leadership in science, math, writing, politics, dance, art, business, history, health, and other human pursuits.
- Most gifted and talented students spend their school days without attention to their special learning needs; teachers make few if any provisions for gifted students.
- In elementary school, gifted students already have mastered 35 to 50 percent of the curriculum to be offered before they begin the school year. (Davis & Rimm, 2004, p.9)

### Is giftedness more than potential, more than IQ?

At the most basic level, all theories of intelligence [or giftedness] are about values. Before the process of identifying, measuring, and evaluating can begin, every theory of intelligence [or giftedness] must put forth a list of what qualities it feels represent the best indicators of intelligence. . . . [It] is the individual's intelligent performance over time and in diverse circumstances that is held up as being of import. From this perspective one sees that ability alone will not suffice as an indicator of intelligence [or giftedness]. (Ritchhart, 2001, p. 149)

**FOCUS**

**PREVIEW:** To preview the central concepts of this chapter, read the focus questions located in the margins. Using these questions as a guide, ask yourself what you already know and what you want to learn.

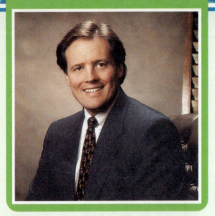

## Dwight

Dwight spends most of his time in a variety of creative business endeavors. For nearly 18 years he served as a senior executive and board member of a publicly traded communications firm that specialized in the delivery of business information via satellite, FM wireless, cable, and Internet technologies. Dwight has been a pioneer in developing and utilizing these technologies for videoconferencing, data transfer, and advertising in businesses throughout North America.

Dwight is an exceptionally talented musician, composer, and arranger, aided in part by a rare phenomenon known as "perfect pitch." He began his professional career performing with the New Christy Minstrels, based in Los Angeles. He soon became their musical director and continued to arrange music for the group long after he left their performing ranks. Subsequently, Dwight was hired by the Osmond family. During several years of association there, he became responsible for the music coordination and contracting of numerous projects, including the *Danny & Marie Show* for ABC television as well as several other network specials and syndicated programs. Dwight's musical arrangements have been played on *The Tonight Show, The Bob Hope 80th Anniversary Special, The Suzanne Sommers Special*, and numerous other national programs. His vocal talent has been heard in commercials and on national television, including work for ABC television and the Disney Channel.

When he was a youngster, Dwight's siblings and classmates referred to him as "the little professor" or "Doc." Throughout his school years, Dwight easily mastered the content in his classes, from science to math to creative writing. His interests were broad, including four stints as a student body or class officer. He finished high school with scholarship offers from several colleges and universities, as well as recognition by the local newspaper as one of the top three scholars statewide in his field.

The terms *gifted, creative*, and *talented* are associated with individuals who have extraordinary abilities in one or more areas of performance. In many cases we admire such individuals, and occasionally we are a little envious of their talents. Their ease in mastering diverse and difficult concepts is impressive. Because of their unusual abilities and skills, educators and policy makers frequently assume that these individuals will reach their full potential without any specialized programs or assistance.

For many years, behavioral scientists described children with exceptionally high intelligence as being **gifted**. Only recently have researchers and practitioners included the adjectives **creative** and **talented** in their descriptions, to suggest domains of performance other than those measured by traditional intelligence tests. Not all individuals who get high scores on intelligence tests are creative (Gallagher, 2003). Capacities associated with creativity include *elaboration* (the ability to embellish or enrich an idea), *transformation* (the ability to construct new meanings or change an idea into something new and novel), and *visualization* (the capacity to manipulate ideas or images mentally). Individuals who are talented display extraordinary skills in mathematics, sports, music, or other performance areas. Dwight is one of those individuals who is gifted, creative, *and* talented (see the chapter-opening Snapshot). Not only did he excel in intellectual (traditional academic) endeavors, but he also exhibited tremendous prowess with regard to producing and performing music. Certainly, the behaviors and traits associated with these terms interact with one another to produce the various constellations of giftedness. Some individuals soar to exceptional heights in the talent domain, others achieve in intellectual areas, and still others excel in creative endeavors. A select few exhibit remarkable achievement across several domains.

## Historical Background

Definitions that describe the unusually able in terms of intelligence quotients and creativity measures are recent phenomena. Not until the beginning of the twentieth century was there a suitable method for quantifying or measuring the human at-

### Gifted, creative, and talented

Terms applied to people with extraordinary abilities, and capable of superior performance, in one or more areas.

### Mental age

A concept used in psychological assessment that arrives at the general mental ability of a child or youth by matching the tasks the child is able to perform to a scale of typical performance of children at various stages.

tribute of intelligence. The breakthrough occurred in Europe when Alfred Binet, a French psychologist, constructed the first developmental assessment scale for children in the early 1900s. This scale was created by observing children at various ages to identify specific tasks that ordinary children were able to perform at each age. These tasks were then sequenced according to age-appropriate levels. Children who could perform tasks well above that which was normal for their chronological age were identified as being developmentally advanced.

Binet and Simon (1905, 1908) developed the notion of **mental age**. The mental age of a child was derived by matching the tasks (memory, vocabulary, mathematical, and comprehension, etc.) that the child was able to perform according to the age scale (which gave the typical performance of children at various stages). Although this scale was initially developed and used to identify children with mental retardation in the Parisian schools, it eventually became an important means for identifying those who had higher than average mental ages, as well.

Lewis M. Terman, an American educator and psychologist, expanded the concepts and procedures developed by Binet. He was convinced that Binet and Simon had hit on an approach that would be useful for measuring intellectual abilities in all children. This belief prompted him to revise the Binet instrument, adding greater breadth to the scale. In 1916, Terman published the **Stanford-Binet Intelligence Scale** in conjunction with Stanford University. During this period, Terman introduced the term **intelligence quotient**, or **IQ**. The IQ score was obtained by dividing a child's mental age by his or her chronological age and multiplying that figure by 100 (MA/CA × 100 = IQ). For example, a child with a mental age of 12 and a chronological age of 8 would have an IQ of 150 (12/8 × 100 = 150).

Gradually, more researchers became interested in studying the nature and assessment of intelligence. They tended to view intelligence as an underlying ability or capacity that expressed itself in a variety of ways. The unitary IQ scores that were derived from the Stanford-Binet tests were representative of and contributed to this notion.

**FOCUS 1**

Briefly describe several historical developments directly related to the measurement of various types of giftedness.

**Stanford-Binet Intelligence Scale**

A standardized individual intelligence test, originally known as the Binet-Simon Scales, which was revised and standardized by Lewis Terman at Stanford University.

**Intelligence Quotient (IQ)**

A score obtained from an intelligence test that provides a measure of mental ability in relation to age.

## SNAPSHOT

# Eduardo

Eduardo and his family are recent immigrants to the United States. At age 10, he has become quite adept at speaking English. His primary language is Spanish. He is the oldest of seven children.

Eduardo's father is a supervisor on a large farm in southern California. With a lot of effort, he developed sufficient English skills to be of great value to farm owners who now employ him full-time. They have hired him to work directly with migrant workers who regularly assist with the harvest of various kinds of produce and fruit. He is also skilled mechanically and, in the off-season, repairs equipment and farm machinery.

Eduardo's schooling was quite irregular until the past two years. Prior to having a stable residence, he traveled with his family up and down the West Coast of the United States, like many migrant families.

Eduardo's schoolmates really enjoy him. He has lots of friends and is invited frequently to birthday parties and social events. He seems to have a real knack for making friends, and adults like him.

Eduardo's parents view him as especially alert and bright. He seems to be interested in many topics and is rarely bored. At the moment, he is intrigued with tractors. His mother indicates that he always "questioned her to death." Moreover, he

seems to be capable of easily entertaining himself. Recently, he spent an entire afternoon looking through a farm magazine and drawing farm equipment that caught his attention.

Since the beginning of this school year, Eduardo has made phenomenal gains in reading, math, and English. In fact, he has become an avid reader of both Spanish and English books that are available at his school. Although it has been difficult to assess his innate ability, he appears to be a child of some promise, intellectually and socially. However, his parents are worried about providing him with the resources he will need to utilize his curiosity and ability fully. They are also concerned about his late start with consistent schooling.

Lewis Terman developed the term intelligence quotient, or IQ

Over time, however, other researchers came to believe that intellect was represented by a variety of distinct capacities and abilities (Cattell, 1971; Guilford, 1959). This line of thinking suggested that each distinct, intellectual capacity could be identified and assessed. Several mental abilities were investigated, including memory capacity, divergent thinking, vocabulary usage, and reasoning ability (see Figure 18.1). Gradually, use of the multiple-ability approach outgrew that of the unitary-intelligence notion. Its proponents were convinced that the universe of intellectual functions was extensive and that the intelligence assessment instruments utilized at that time measured a very small portion of an individual's true intellectual capacities.

One of the key contributors to the multidimensional theory of intelligence was J. P. Guilford (1950, 1959). He saw intelligence as a diverse range of intellectual and creative abilities. Guilford's work led many researchers to view intelligence as more than a broad, unitary ability and to focus their scientific efforts on the emerging field of creativity and its various subcomponents, such as divergent thinking, problem solving, and decision making. Gradually, tests or measures of creativity were developed, using the constructs drawn from models created by Guilford and others.

In summary, conceptions of giftedness during the early 1920s were closely tied to the score that an individual obtained on an intelligence test. Thus a single score—one's IQ—was the index by which one was identified as being gifted. Commencing with the work of Guilford (1950, 1959) and Torrance (1961, 1965, 1968), notions regarding giftedness were greatly expanded. *Giftedness* began to be used to refer not only to those with high IQs but also to those who demonstrated high aptitude on creativity measures such as Torrance Tests of Creative Thinking (Torrance, 1966), PRIDE (Preschool and Primary Interest Descriptor; Rimm, 1982), Sternberg Triarchic Abili-

## FIGURE 18.1

### Guilford's Structure of the Intellect Model

Each little cube represents a unique combination of one kind of operation, one kind of content, and one kind of product—and hence a distinctly different intellectual ability or function.

**Operations**

Cognition
Memory
Divergent production
Convergent production
Evaluation

**Products**

Units
Classes
Relations
Systems
Transformations
Implications

**Contents**

Visual
Symbolic
Semantic
Behavioral

SOURCE: From *Way Beyond the IQ: Guide to Improving Intelligence and Creativity* (p. 151), by J. P. Guilford, 1977, Buffalo, NY: Creative Education Foundation. Copyright 1977 by Creative Education Foundation. Reprinted by permission.

ties Test (Sternberg, 1993), and GIFT (Gift Inventory for Finding Talent; Rimm & Davis, 1983). More recently, the term *talented* has been added to the descriptors associated with giftedness. As a result, individuals who demonstrate remarkable skills in the visual or performing arts or who excel in other areas of performance may be designated as gifted. Figure 18.2 reveals how our perspectives on giftedness have changed over time with the acceptance of new, multifaceted definitions of giftedness.

Currently, there is no federal mandate in the United States requiring educational services for students identified as gifted, as is the case with other exceptional conditions. Some federal funding is provided through the Jacob K. Javits Gifted and Talented Students Act as a part of the No Child Left Behind legislation (O'Connell, 2003).

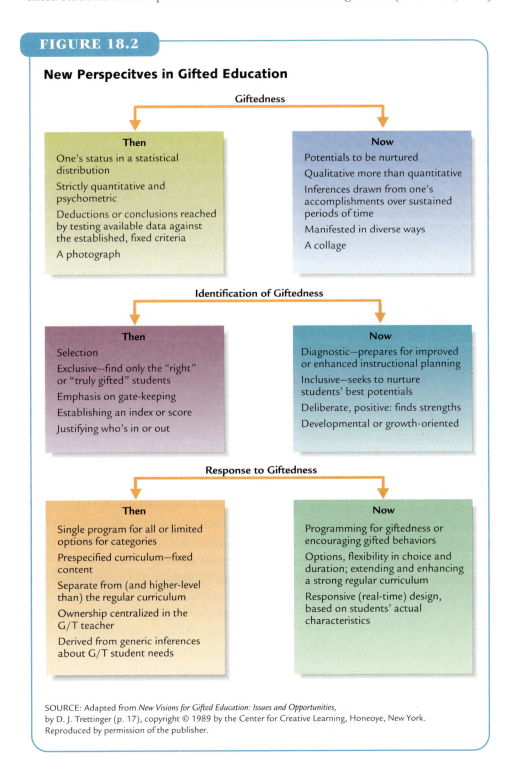

**FIGURE 18.2**

### New Perspecitves in Gifted Education

**Giftedness**

| Then | Now |
|---|---|
| One's status in a statistical distribution | Potentials to be nurtured |
| Strictly quantitative and psychometric | Qualitative more than quantitative |
| Deductions or conclusions reached by testing available data against the established, fixed criteria | Inferences drawn from one's accomplishments over sustained periods of time |
| A photograph | Manifested in diverse ways |
| | A collage |

**Identification of Giftedness**

| Then | Now |
|---|---|
| Selection | Diagnostic—prepares for improved or enhanced instructional planning |
| Exclusive—find only the "right" or "truly gifted" students | Inclusive—seeks to nurture students' best potentials |
| Emphasis on gate-keeping | Deliberate, positive: finds strengths |
| Establishing an index or score | Developmental or growth-oriented |
| Justifying who's in or out | |

**Response to Giftedness**

| Then | Now |
|---|---|
| Single program for all or limited options for categories | Programming for giftedness or encouraging gifted behaviors |
| Prespecified curriculum—fixed content | Options, flexibility in choice and duration; extending and enhancing a strong regular curriculum |
| Separate from (and higher-level than) the regular curriculum | Responsive (real-time) design, based on students' actual characteristics |
| Ownership centralized in the G/T teacher | |
| Derived from generic inferences about G/T student needs | |

SOURCE: Adapted from *New Visions for Gifted Education: Issues and Opportunities,* by D. J. Trettinger (p. 17), copyright © 1989 by the Center for Creative Learning, Honeoye, New York. Reproduced by permission of the publisher.

This act supports a national research center, demonstration programs, and activities for leadership personnel throughout the United States. The actual funding of services for individuals who are gifted is a state-by-state, local challenge, so there is tremendous variability in the quality and types of programs offered to students (Davis & Rimm, 2004).

In coming years, we will probably see *talent development* replace gifted education as the guiding concept. This description suggests a kind of programming that is directed at all students, not just those identified as gifted (Davis & Rimm, 2004). A "benefit [of this kind of programming] is that the talent development orientation eliminates the awkwardness of the words *gifted* and, by exclusion, *not gifted*" (Davis & Rimm, 2004, p. 28).

# Definitions and Concepts

Capturing the essence of any human condition in a definition can be very perplexing. This is certainly the case in defining the human attributes, abilities, and potentialities that constitute giftedness.

Definitions of giftedness serve several important purposes. For example, definitions may have a profound influence on the number and kinds of students ultimately selected in a school system, on the types of instruments and selection procedures used, on the scores students must obtain in order to qualify for specialized instruction, on the amount of funding required to provide services, and on the types of training individuals need to teach students who are gifted and talented. Thus definitions are important from both practical and theoretical perspectives (Davis & Rimm, 2004).

Definitions of giftedness have been influenced by a variety of innovative and knowledgeable individuals (Cattell, 1971; Gardner, 1983; Guilford, 1959; Piirto, 1999; Ramos-Ford & Gardner, 1997; Renzulli & Reis, 2003; Sternberg, 1997; Torrance, 1966). As you will soon discover, there is no universally accepted definition of giftedness (Davis & Rimm, 2004).

The Javits Gifted and Talented Education Act of 1988 (P.L. 100-297) defined giftedness as follows:

> Children and youth with outstanding talent perform or show the potential for performing at remarkably high levels of accomplishment when compared with others of their age, experience, or environment. These children and youth exhibit high performance capability in intellectual, creative, and/or artistic areas, possess an unusual leadership capacity, or excel in specific academic fields. They require services or activities not ordinarily provided by the schools. Outstanding talents are present in children and youth from all cultural groups, across all economic strata, and in all areas of human endeavor (U.S. Department of Education, 1993, p. 3).

This federal definition helped school personnel achieve several important objectives. These include identifying a variety of students across disciplines with diverse talents, using many different kinds of assessment measures to identify gifted students, providing students of all backgrounds with equal access to opportunities to develop their potential, identifying capacities not readily apparent in some students, and taking into account students' drives and passions for achievement in various areas.

New ways to conceive of giftedness and intelligence have recently emerged from theoretical and research literature (Ramos-Ford & Gardner, 1997; Sternberg, 1997). One of the new approaches to intelligence is Sternberg's triarchic theory of human intelligence (Sternberg, 1997), according to which intellectual performance is divided into three parts: analytic, synthetic, and practical. Analytic intelligence is exhibited by people who perform well on aptitude and intelligence tests. Individuals

**FOCUS 2**

Identify six major components of definitions that have been developed to describe giftedness.

with synthetic giftedness are unconventional thinkers who are creative, intuitive, and insightful. People with practical intelligence are extraordinarily adept in dealing with problems of everyday life and those that arise in their work environments.

Another conceptualization of giftedness or talent development has been proposed by Gagné, (1999a). It centers on catalysts that have both positive and negative impacts (see Figure 18.3). These catalysts (intrapersonal and environmental) shape and influence developmental processes that give rise to talents. It is clear from this conceptualization of giftedness that the emergence of talents depends on environmental, motivational, and interpersonal factors (Piirto, 1999).

Gagné, has also recommended the reexamination of IQ thresholds by which giftedness would be defined; the development of subcategories of talents, such as musical improvisation, mechanical prowess, and social precocity; and acknowledgment of talents in nontraditional areas of performance, including cooking, building, and farming (Piirto, 1999). These recommendations would democratize the field of gifted education, giving many more children and youth opportunities for talent development (Gagné, 1999b).

Another view of giftedness has been developed by Ramos-Ford and Gardner (1997). They have defined intelligence or giftedness as "an ability or set of abilities that permit an individual to solve problems or fashion products that are of consequence in a particular cultural setting" (Ramos-Ford & Gardner, 1991, p. 56). This

## FIGURE 18.3

### Catalysts for the Development of Gifts and Talents

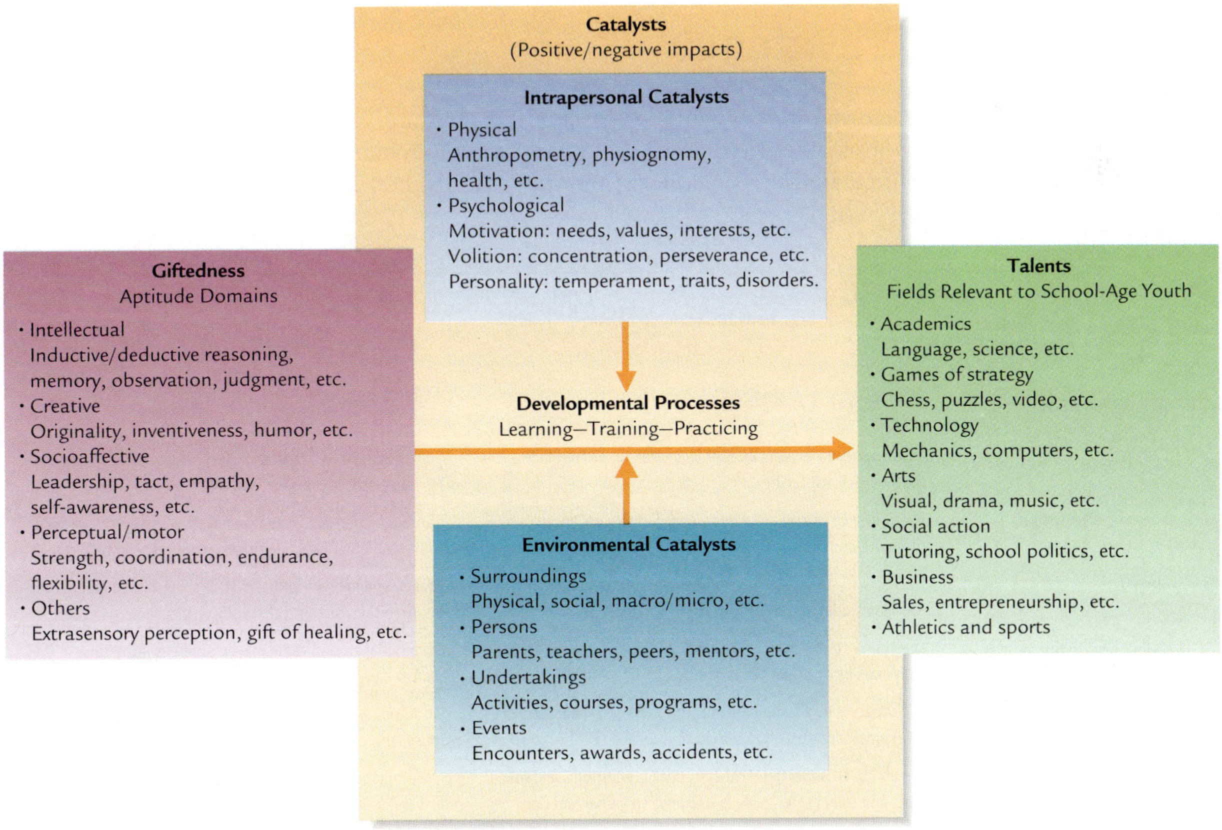

**Catalysts**
(Positive/negative impacts)

**Intrapersonal Catalysts**
- Physical
  Anthropometry, physiognomy, health, etc.
- Psychological
  Motivation: needs, values, interests, etc.
  Volition: concentration, perseverance, etc.
  Personality: temperament, traits, disorders.

**Giftedness**
Aptitude Domains
- Intellectual
  Inductive/deductive reasoning, memory, observation, judgment, etc.
- Creative
  Originality, inventiveness, humor, etc.
- Socioaffective
  Leadership, tact, empathy, self-awareness, etc.
- Perceptual/motor
  Strength, coordination, endurance, flexibility, etc.
- Others
  Extrasensory perception, gift of healing, etc.

**Developmental Processes**
Learning—Training—Practicing

**Talents**
Fields Relevant to School-Age Youth
- Academics
  Language, science, etc.
- Games of strategy
  Chess, puzzles, video, etc.
- Technology
  Mechanics, computers, etc.
- Arts
  Visual, drama, music, etc.
- Social action
  Tutoring, school politics, etc.
- Business
  Sales, entrepreneurship, etc.
- Athletics and sports

**Environmental Catalysts**
- Surroundings
  Physical, social, macro/micro, etc.
- Persons
  Parents, teachers, peers, mentors, etc.
- Undertakings
  Activities, courses, programs, etc.
- Events
  Encounters, awards, accidents, etc.

SOURCE: From "Is There Any Light at the End of the Tunnel?" by F. Gagné, 1999, *Journal of the Education of the Gifted, 22* (2), pp. 191-234.

perspective on giftedness is referred to as the theory of multiple intelligences. Intelligence is assumed to manifest itself in linguistic, logical-mathematical, spatial, musical, bodily-kinesthetic, interpersonal, and intrapersonal behaviors. Table 18.1 provide brief definition of each of these behaviors, as well as the child and adult roles associated with each type of intelligence.

More recently, Piirto has constructed a pyramid of talent development (see Figure 18.4). She defines the gifted as

> those individuals who by way of learning characteristics such as superior memory, observational powers, curiosity, creativity, and the ability to learn school-related subject matters rapidly and accurately with a minimum drill and repetition, have a right to an education that is differentiated according to their needs. These children become apparent early and should be served through their educational lives, from preschool through college (Piirto, 1999, p. 28).

These and other definitions of giftedness have moved from unitary measures of IQ to multiple measures of creativity, problem-solving ability, talent, and intelligence. However, despite the movement away from IQ scores and other changes in definitions of giftedness, critics argue that many if not most local, district, and state definitions are elitist in nature and favor the "affluent" and "privileged" (Borland, 2003; Ford, 2003).

The definitions of giftedness are diverse. Each of the definitions we have examined reveals the difficulty associated with defining the nature of giftedness. In a multicultural, pluralistic society, such as that of the United States, different abilities and capacities are encouraged and valued by different parents and teachers. Also, definitions of giftedness are often a function of educational, societal, and political priorities at a particular time and place (Gottfredson, 2003).

# Prevalence

Determining the number of children who are gifted is a challenging matter. The complexity of the task is directly related to problems inherent in determining who is gifted and what constitutes giftedness (Gallagher, 2003). The numerous definitions of

## TABLE 18.1

### The Seven Intelligences

| INTELLIGENCE | BRIEF DESCRIPTION | RELATED CHILD AND ADULT ROLES |
|---|---|---|
| Linguistic | The capacity to express oneself in spoken or written language with great facility | Superb storyteller, creative writer, or inventive speaker: Novelist, lyricist, lawyer |
| Logical-mathematical | The ability to reason inductively and deductively and to complete complex computations | Thorough counter, calculator, notation maker, or symbol user: Mathematician, physicist, computer scientist |
| Spatial | The capacity to create, manipulate, and represent spatial configurations | Creative builder, sculptor, artist, or skilled assembler of models: Architect, talented chess player, mechanic, navigator |
| Bodily-kinesthetic | The ability to perform various complex tasks or activities with one's body or part of the body | Skilled playground game player, emerging athlete or dancer: Surgeon, dancer, professional athlete |
| Musical | The capacity to discriminate musical pitches, to hear musical themes, and to sense rhythm, timbre, and texture | Good singer, creator of original songs or musical pieces: Musician, composer, director |
| Interpersonal | The ability to understand others' actions, emotions, and intents and to act effectively in response to verbal and nonverbal behaviors of others | Child organizer or orchestrator, child leader, or a very social child: Teacher, therapist, political social leader |
| Intrapersonal | The capacity to understand well and respond to one's own thoughts, desires, feelings, and emotions | A sensitive child, a resilient child, or an optimistic child: Social worker, therapist, counselor, hospice worker |

FIGURE 18.4

## The Piirto Pyramid of Talent Development

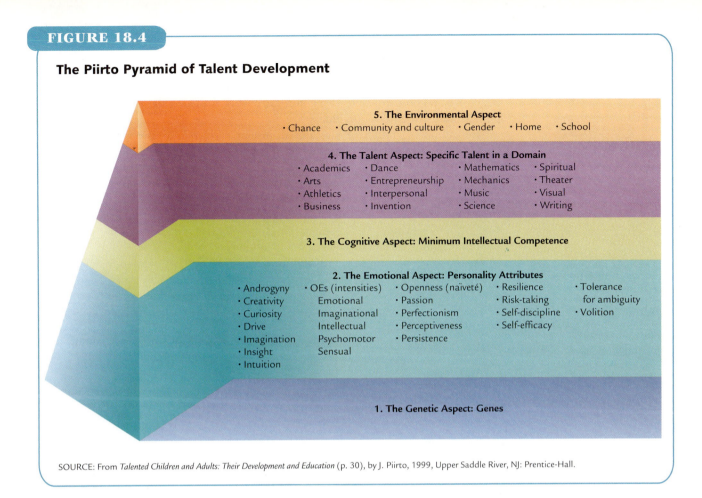

**5. The Environmental Aspect**
• Chance   • Community and culture   • Gender   • Home   • School

**4. The Talent Aspect: Specific Talent in a Domain**
| | | | |
|---|---|---|---|
| • Academics | • Dance | • Mathematics | • Spiritual |
| • Arts | • Entrepreneurship | • Mechanics | • Theater |
| • Athletics | • Interpersonal | • Music | • Visual |
| • Business | • Invention | • Science | • Writing |

**3. The Cognitive Aspect: Minimum Intellectual Competence**

**2. The Emotional Aspect: Personality Attributes**
| | | | | |
|---|---|---|---|---|
| • Androgyny | • OEs (intensities) | • Openness (naïveté) | • Resilience | • Tolerance |
| • Creativity | Emotional | • Passion | • Risk-taking | for ambiguity |
| • Curiosity | Imaginational | • Perfectionism | • Self-discipline | • Volition |
| • Drive | Intellectual | • Perceptiveness | • Self-efficacy | |
| • Imagination | Psychomotor | • Persistence | | |
| • Insight | Sensual | | | |
| • Intuition | | | | |

**1. The Genetic Aspect: Genes**

SOURCE: From *Talented Children and Adults: Their Development and Education* (p. 30), by J. Piirto, 1999, Upper Saddle River, NJ: Prentice-Hall.

giftedness range from quite restrictive (in terms of the number of children to whom they apply) to very inclusive and broad. Consequently, the prevalence estimates are highly variable.

Prevalence figures compiled before the 1950s were primarily limited to the intellectually gifted: those identified for the most part by intelligence tests. At that time, 2% to 3% of the general population was considered gifted. During the 1950s, when professionals in the field advocated an expanded view of giftedness (Conant, 1959; DeHann & Havighurst, 1957), the prevalence figures suggested for program planning were substantially affected. Terms such as *academically talented* were used to refer to the upper 15% to 20% of the general school population.

Thus prevalence estimates have fluctuated, depending on the views of policy makers, researchers, and professionals during past decades. Currently, 3% to 25% of the students in the school population may be identified as gifted, depending on the regulations from state to state and the types of programs offered (Davis & Rimm, 2004).

# Characteristics

Accurately identifying the characteristics of gifted people is an enormous task (Piirto, 1999). Many characteristics attributed to those who are gifted have been generated by different types of studies (MacKinnon, 1962; Terman, 1925). Gradually, what emerged from these studies were stereotypical views of giftedness.

For example, shortly after the publication of the Stanford-Binet Intelligence Scale, Terman (1925) received funding to begin his intriguing "genetic studies of genius." Terman's initial group of subjects included more than 1,500 students, drawn from

**FOCUS 3**

Identify four problems inherent in accurately describing the characteristics of individuals who are gifted.

both elementary and secondary classroom settings, who had obtained IQ scores at or above 140 on the Stanford-Binet. In conjunction with other associates, he investigated their physical characteristics, personality attributes, psychological and marital adjustment, educational attainment, and career achievement at the average ages of 20, 35, and so on (see Table 18.2). Terman's work provided the impetus for the systematic study of gifted individuals.

Unfortunately, much of the initial research related to the characteristics of giftedness was conducted with restricted population samples. Generally, the studies did not include adequate samples of females or individuals from various ethnic and cultural groups; nor did early researchers carefully control for factors directly related to socioeconomic status. Therefore, the characteristics generated from these studies were not representative of gifted individuals as a whole but, rather, reflected the characteristics of gifted individuals from advantaged environments.

Given the present multifaceted definitions of giftedness and emerging views of intelligence (Davis & Rimm, 2004), we must conclude that gifted people are members of a heterogeneous population. Consequently, research findings of the past must be interpreted with great caution as practitioners assess a particular youth's behavior, attributes, and talents.

Gifted students, who are intellectually able, demonstrate one resounding trait— "they are developmentally advanced in language and thought" (Davis & Rimm, 2004, p. 35). Many learn to speak and read very early. Their mental ages, as revealed in intelligence tests, far exceed their chronological ages. Moreover, their innate curiosity and capacity for asking questions can drive some parents and even teachers to the

*Children with gifts and talents come from every ethnic, cultural, and socioeconomic background. While some individuals achieve in intellectual endeavors, others excel through the arts.*

## TABLE 18.2

### Terman's Findings in the Study of People Who Are Gifted

| DOMAINS | DIFFERENTIATING CHARACTERISTICS |
|---|---|
| Physical characteristics | • Robust and in good health<br>• Above average in physical stature |
| Personality attributes and aesthetic psychological adjustment | • Above average in willpower, popularity, perseverance, emotional maturity, aesthetic perceptivity, and moral reasoning<br>• Keen sense of humor and high levels of self-confidence<br>• Equal to peers in marital adjustment<br>• Well adjusted as adults; few problems with substance abuse, suicide, and mental health |
| Educational attainment | • Generally read before school entrance<br>• Frequently promoted<br>• Excelled in reading and mathematical reasoning<br>• Consistently scored in the top 10% on achievement tests |
| Career achievement | • Mates primarily involved in professional and managerial positions<br>• Women primarily teachers or homemakers (probably due to cultural expectations at the time)<br>• By age 40 had completed 67 books, 1,400 scientific and professional papers, 700 short stories, and a variety of other creative and scholarly works<br>• Adult achievers came primarily from encouraging home environments |

brink of exhaustion and desperation. These students can be unusually tenacious in pursuing ideas, concerns, and questions. They may also have interests that would be characteristic of older children and/or adults.

Generally, gifted student are well adjusted and socially adept. There are, of course, exceptions. One of the more interesting attributes of gifted children and youth is their penchant for "emotional excitability" and "high sensitivity" (Rimm & Davis, 2004, p. 37). In this regard, their reactions can be more intense—that is, they may feel more joy and also experience greater sadness than age mates. Table 18.3 lists characteristics often evident in gifted students.

Students who are described as creative share a number of salient personality attributes. They often exhibit high energy and high motivation to succeed or perform. They have a real zest for pursuing tasks and seeking solutions to problems that they encounter. Furthermore, they also have a proclivity for risk taking. They love to try new activities, to experiment with new behaviors, and to consider new ways of processing problems or creating things (artistic, mechanical, etc.) Table 18.4 lists characteristics often evident in students described as creative.

No student who is identified as gifted will exhibit all of the characteristics cited in this section. However, parents, teachers, coaches, and mentors have an opportunity, as well as an obligation, to encourage these traits or to foster their emergence.

# Origins of Giftedness

Scientists have long been interested in identifying the origins of intelligence. Conclusions have varied greatly. For years, many scientists adhered to a hereditary explanation of intelligence: that people inherit their intellectual capacity at conception. Thus intelligence was viewed as an innate capacity that remained relatively fixed during an individual's lifetime. The prevailing belief then was that little could be done to enhance intellectual ability.

During the 1920s and 1930s, scientists such as John Watson began to explore the

**FOCUS**

**4**

Identify three factors that appear to contribute significantly to the emergence of various forms of giftedness.

## TABLE 18.3

### Characteristics of Students Who Are Gifted

| POSITIVE CHARACTERISTICS | | NEGATIVE CHARACTERISTICS |
|---|---|---|
| Unusual alertness in infancy and later | Wide interests, interested in new topics | Uneven mental development |
| Early and rapid learning | High curiosity, explores how and why | Interpersonal difficulties, often due to intellectual differences |
| Rapid language development as a child | Multiple capabilities (multipotentiality) | Underachievement, especially in uninteresting areas |
| Superior language ability—verbally fluent, large vocabulary, complex grammar | High care ambitions (desire to be helpful to others) | Nonconformity, sometimes in disturbing directions |
| Enjoyment of learning | Overexcitability | Perfectionism, which can be extreme |
| Academic superiority, large knowledge base, sought out as a resource | Emotional intensity and sensitivity | Excessive self-criticism |
| Superior analytic ability | High alertness and attention | Self-doubt, poor self-image |
| Keen observation | High intellectual and physical activity level | Variable frustration and anger |
| Efficient, high-capacity memory | High motivation, concentrates, perseveres, persists, task-oriented | Depression |
| Superior reasoning, problem solving | Active—shares information, directs, leads, offers help, eager to be involved | |
| Thinking that is abstract, complex, logical, insightful | Strong empathy, moral thinking, sense of justice, honesty, intellectual honesty | |
| Insightful, sees "big picture," recognizes patterns, connects topics | Aware of social issues | |
| Manipulates symbol systems | High concentration, long attention span | |
| Uses high-level thinking skills, efficient strategies | Strong internal control | |
| Extrapolates knowledge to new situations, goes beyond what is taught | Independent, self-directed, works alone | |
| Expanded awareness, greater self-awareness | Inquisitive, asks questions | |
| Greater metacognition (understanding own thinking) | Excellent sense of humor | |
| Advanced interests | Imaginative, creative, solves problems | |
| Needs for logic and accuracy | Preference for novelty | |
| | Reflectiveness | |
| | Good self-concept | |

SOURCE: Adapted from Rimm & Davis 2004, p. 33.

new notion of behavioral psychology, or behaviorism. Like other behaviorists who followed him. Watson believed that the environment played an important role in the development of intelligence as well as personality traits. Initially, Watson largely discounted the role of heredity and its importance in intellectual development. Later, however, he moderated his views, moving somewhat toward a theoretical perspective in which both heredity and environment contributed to an individual's intellectual ability.

During the 1930s, many investigators sought to determine the relative influence of heredity and environment on intellectual development. Some proponents of genetics asserted that as much as 70% to 80% of an individual's capacity is determined by heredity and the remainder by environmental influences. Environmentalists believed otherwise. The controversy over the relative contributions of heredity and environment to intelligence (known as the **nature versus nurture** controversy) is likely to continue for some time, in part because of the complexity and breadth of the issues involved (Plomin & Price, 2003). However, important progress has been made in teasing apart the genetic and environmental contributors to high intelligence. "For example, developmental genetic research indicates that the heritability of intelligence increases with age, and that genetic factors contribute to age-to-age change, especially during the transition to middle childhood" (Plomin & Price, 2003,

**Nature versus nurture**

Controversy concerning how much of a person's ability is related to sociocultural influences (nurture) and how much to genetic factors (nature).

## TABLE 18.4

### Characteristics of Students Who Are Creative

| POSITIVE TRAITS | APPROXIMATE SYNONYMS |
| --- | --- |
| Original | Imaginative, resourceful, flexible, unconventional, thinks metaphorically, challenges assumptions, irritated and bored by the obvious, avoids perceptual set, asks "what if?" |
| Aware of creativeness | Creativity-conscious, values originality, values own creativity |
| Independent | Self-confident, individualistic, nonconforming, sets own rules, unconcerned with impressing others, resists societal demands |
| Risk-taking | Not afraid to be different or to try something new, willing to cope with hostility, willing to cope with failure |
| Motivated | Energetic, adventurous, sensation-seeking, enthusiastic, excitable, spontaneous, impulsive, intrinsically motivated, perseveres, works beyond assigned tasks |
| Curious | Questions norms and assumptions, experiments, inquisitive, wide interests, is a problem-finder, asks "why?" |
| Sense of humor | Playful, plays with ideas, child-like freshness in thinking |
| Attracted to complexity | Attracted to novelty, asymmetry, the mysterious, theoretical and abstract problems; is a complex person; tolerant of ambiguity, disorder, incongruity |
| Artistic | Artistic and aesthetic interests, attracted to beauty and order |
| Open-minded | Receptive to new ideas, other viewpoints, new experiences, and growth; liberal, altruistic |
| Needs alone time | Reflective, introspective, internally preoccupied, sensitive, may be withdrawn, likes to work alone |
| Intuitive | Perceptive, sees relationships, finds order in chaos, uses all senses in observing |
| Intelligent | Verbally fluent, articulate, logical, good decision maker, detects gaps in knowledge, visualizes |

SOURCE: Adapted from Davis & Rimm, 2004, p. 42.

p. 121). Stated in another fashion, as gifted children age and move to adulthood, they "actively select, modify, and even create environments conducive to the development of genetic proclivities" (Plomin & Price, 2003, p. 118).

For example, studies of identical twins raised in different environments suggest that 44% to 72% of their intelligence (general cognitive ability) is inherited. With regard to environmental factors, we are just beginning to understand the dynamic relationships between nature and nurture. Again, "bright children select and are selected by peers and educational programs that foster their abilities. They read and think more. This is the profound meaning of finding genetic influences on measures of the environment. Genes contribute to the experience itself" (Plomin & Price, 2003, p. 120). Plomin and Price (2003) captured it best when they said, "it may well be more appropriate to think about [general cognitive ability] as an appetite rather than an aptitude" (p. 121). This appetite allows gifted children and youth to profit more fully from environmental influences over their lifetimes.

Thus far, we have focused on the origins of intelligence rather than on giftedness per se. Many of the theories about the emergence or essence of giftedness have been derived from the study of general intelligence. Few authors have focused directly on the origins of giftedness. Moreover, the ongoing changes in the definitions of giftedness have further complicated the precise investigation of its origins.

Recently, Tannenbaum (2003) proposed the "Star Model" (see Figure 18.5) for explaining the causes and antecedents of giftedness. It is composed of five elements, each of which contributes to gifted behavior. These elements are superior general intellect, distinctive special aptitudes, nonintellective factors, environmental supports, and chance. Associated with each are the descriptors *dynamic* and *static*. The static dimension includes factors that remain relatively constant or unchanged, such as the child or youth's race and economic status. The dynamic dimension includes factors that are fluid and responsive to contextual or environmental changes or interventions.

**FIGURE 18.5**

**The Star Model: Psychosocial Factors Accounting for Gifted Achievements**

General Ability

Special Aptitude

Chance

Environmental Supports

Nonintellective Requisites

DYNAMIC · STATIC · DYNAMIC · STATIC · STATIC · DYNAMIC · STATIC · DYNAMIC · STATIC · DYNAMIC

SOURCE: "Nature and Nurture of Giftedness," by A. J. Tannebaum, 2003, in *Handbook on Gifted Education*, edited by N. Colangelo and G. A. Davis (p. 47). Boston, MA: Allyn and Bacon.

The abilities associated with superior intelligence are generally factors assessed through intelligence tests (verbal, spatial, and memory capacity). Special abilities are those found, for example, in child prodigies who show [or manifest] extraordinary musical, mathematical, or other emerging talents. Nonintellective factors are a wide-ranging set of attributes, including, believe it or not, psychopathology and perfectionism: Many gifted artists and writers show clear signs of pathological deviance or emotional distress. Other, more positive factors associated with this element include motivation, self-concept, and resilience. The influence of environmental support is obvious. "Giftedness requires [a] social context that enables it to mature. . . . Human potential needs nurturance, urgings, encouragement, and even pressures from a world that cares" (Tannenbaum, 2003, p. 54). Last is the element of chance. Often, external factors that coincide with one's preparation and talent development contribute to one's eventual imminence or greatness. All of these factors come together in a unique fashion to produce various kinds of giftedness.

FOCUS 5

Indicate the range of assessment devices used to identify the various types of giftedness.

# Assessment

The focus of assessment procedures for identifying potential giftedness is beginning to change. Elitist definitions and exclusive approaches are being replaced with more defensible, inclusive methods of assessment (Davis & Rimm, 2004; Richert, 2003). Tests for identifying persons with potential for gifted performance are being more

carefully selected; that is, tests are being used with the children for whom they were designed. Children who were once excluded from programs for the gifted because of formal or standard cut-off scores that favored particular groups of students are now being included as candidates (Richert, 2003). Multiple sources of information are now collected and reviewed in determining who is potentially gifted (Davis & Rimm, 2004; Richert, 2003). Ideally, the identification process is now directed at identifying needs and potentials rather than merely labeling individuals as gifted.

Several approaches have also been developed to identify children who are disadvantaged and also gifted. Some theorists and practitioners have argued for the adoption of a contextual paradigm or approach. Rather than using information derived solely from typical intelligence tests or other talent assessments, this approach relies on divergent views of giftedness as valued and determined by community members, parents, grandparents, and competent informants (Davis & Rimm, 2004). Similar approaches focus on nontraditional measures of giftedness. These approaches use multiple criteria, broader ranges of scores for inclusion in special programs, peer nomination, assessments by persons other than educational personnel, and information provided by adaptive behavior assessments. Furthermore, these approaches seek to understand students' motivations, interests, capacity for communication, reasoning abilities, imagination, and humor (Davis & Rimm, 2004; Richert, 2003). For example, if 60% of students in a given school population come from a certain cultural minority group and only 2% are identified as gifted via traditional measures, the screening committee may want to reexamine and adjust its identification procedures.

Elementary and secondary students who are gifted are identified in a variety of ways. The first step is generally screening. During this phase, teachers, psychologists, and other school personnel attempt to select all students who are potentially gifted. A number of procedures are employed in the screening process. Historically, information obtained from group intelligence tests and teacher nominations has been used to select the initial pool of students. However, many other measures and data collection techniques have been instituted since the approach to assessment of giftedness changed from one-dimensional to multidimensional (Davis & Rimm, 2004; Richert, 2003). These techniques may include developmental inventories, parent and peer nominations, achievement tests, creativity tests, motivation assessments, teacher nominations, and evaluations of student projects.

Many districts use Renzulli's talent pool strategy, which is an integral part of the Schoolwide Enrichment Model. This model has several advantages, including liberal percentages of students who may qualify and participate; a focus on continuous identification of students, not a one-time assessment; and access for children and youth whose talents may not be readily recognized or assessed (Renzulli & Reis, 2003).

## Teacher Nomination

Teacher nomination has been an integral part of many screening approaches. This approach is fraught with problems, however. Teachers often favor children who are cooperative, well-mannered, and task-oriented. Bright underachievers and those who are bright and disruptive may be overlooked. Also, many teachers are unfamiliar with the general traits, behaviors, and dispositions that underlie giftedness.

Fortunately, some of these problems have been addressed. Several scales, approaches, and guidelines are now available to aid teachers and others responsible for making nominations (Davis & Rimm, 2004; Renzulli & Reis, 2003). Teachers who have a thorough understanding of the various kinds of giftedness are in a much better position to provide good information in the screening and selection process.

## Intelligence and Achievement Tests

Intelligence testing continues to be a major source of information for screening and identifying general ability or intellectual giftedness in children and adolescents. These tests must be carefully selected. For example, some intelligence tests have low ceilings; that is, they do not allow the participating child or youth to demonstrate his or her full potential. The same is true of some group-administered intelligence tests. They are not designed to identify students who may have exceptionally high intellectual ability.

One advantage of intelligence testing is that it often identifies underachievers. Intelligence test scores often reveal students who have wonderful intellectual capacity that has gone unrecognized because of their poor school performance.

A serious limitation associated with intelligence tests emerges when they are administered to individuals with cultural differences. Very few intelligence tests can adequately assess the abilities of children and adolescents who are substantially different from the core culture for whom the tests were designed. However, some progress is being made in helping educators identify gifted children who are members of minority groups, underachievers, or at risk (Ford 2003; Richert, 2003).

Similar problems are inherent in achievement tests, which, like intelligence tests, are not generally designed to measure the true achievement of children who are academically gifted. Such individuals are often prevented from demonstrating their unusual prowess because of the restricted range of the test items. These **ceiling effects** prevent children who are gifted from demonstrating their achievement at higher levels. However, achievement tests do play a very useful role in identifying students with specific academic talents (Davis & Rimm, 2004).

## Creativity Tests

Tests for creativity serve several purposes. Often they help the teacher or practitioner discover capacity that may not be evident in normal classroom interactions and performances. Also, these tests are useful in confirming attributes related to creativity. However, we must realize that creativity tests are difficult to construct. The degree to which they actually measure creativity is always called into question. Because of the nature of creativity and the many forms in which it can be expressed, developing tests to assess its presence and magnitude is a formidable task (Davis & Rimm, 2004). In spite of these challenges, a number of creativity tests have been formulated (Rimm, 1982; Rimm & Davis, 1983; Torrance, 1966; Williams, 1980). Two main types of creativity tests are presently in use: (1) tests designed to assess divergent thinking and (2) inventories that provide information about students' personal-

**Ceiling effects**

A restricted range of test questions or problems that does not permit academically gifted students to demonstrate their true capacity or achievement.

ities and biographical traits. Several prominent researchers have suggested the use of multiple measures of creativity to substantiate prowess in this area of performance (Davis & Rimm, 2004). A typical question on a test of divergent thinking might read, "What would happen if your eyes could be adjusted to see things as small as germs?"

Once the screening steps have been completed, the actual identification and selection of students begins. During this phase, each of the previously screened students is carefully evaluated again, using more individualized procedures and assessment tools. Ideally, these techniques should be closely related to the definition of giftedness used by the district and to the program envisioned or offered to students.

Davis and Rimm (2004) have developed a series of recommendations and statements that summarize this section on assessment and identification (see Table 18.5). If these recommendations are carefully followed, more appropriate and equitable decisions will be made in identifying and serving children and youth who are gifted or potentially gifted.

# Services and Supports

## Early Childhood

Parents can promote the early learning and development of their children in a number of ways (Jackson, 2003; Jin & Feldhusen, 2000). During the first 18 months of life, 90% of all social interactions with children take place during such activities as feeding, bathing, changing diapers, and dressing. Parents who are interested in advancing their child's mental and social development use these occasions for talking to him or her; providing varied sensory experiences such as bare-skin cuddling, tickling, and smiling; and conveying a sense of trust. Early, concentrated, language-centered involvement with young children gives rise to solid cognitive, social, and linguistic skills.

As children progress through the infancy, toddler, and preschool periods, the experiences provided become more varied and uniquely suited to the child's emerging interests. Language and cognitive development are encouraged by means of stories that are read and told. Children are also urged to make up their own stories. Brief periods are reserved for discussions or spontaneous conversations that arise from events that have momentarily captured their attention. Requests for help in saying or printing a word are promptly fulfilled. Thus many children who are gifted learn to read before they enter kindergarten or first grade (Davis & Rimm, 2004; Jackson, 2003).

---

**TABLE 18.5**

### Current Thinking and Recommendations for Identifying Gifted Students

- Adopt a clearly defined but broadened conception of giftedness.
- Avoid using a single cut-off score.
- Use multiple alternative criteria—not multiple required hurdles—from several different sources.
- Use separate instruments or procedures for different areas of giftedness; be sure that tests (including ratings and nominations) are reliable and valid.
- Include authentic assessment (e.g., portfolios, examples of work) and performance-based procedures (e.g., evaluation tasks that elicit problem solving and creativity).
- Be aware that giftedness may appear in different forms in different cultural or socioeconomic groups.
- Repeat assessments over time to identify additional gifted students.
- Use identification data to enhance your understanding of students.

SOURCE: Adapted from "Identifying Gifted and Talented Students" in Davis & Rimm, 2004, p. 81.

*Parents can promote early learning and development in the young child by providing a variety of sensory experiences and encouraging creativity.*

During the school years, parents continue to encourage their children's development by providing opportunities that correspond to their children's strengths and interests. The simple identification games played during the preschool period become more complex. Discussions frequently take place with peers and other interesting adults in addition to parents. The nature of the discussions and the types of questions asked become more sophisticated. Parents help their children move to higher levels of learning by asking questions that involve analysis (comparing and contrasting ideas), synthesis (integrating and combining ideas into new and novel forms), and evaluation (judging and disputing books, newspaper articles, etc.). Parents can also help by (1) furnishing books and reading materials on a broad range of topics; (2) providing appropriate equipment as various interests surface (e.g., microscopes, telescopes, chemistry sets); (3) encouraging regular trips to the public library and other resource centers; (4) providing opportunities for participation in cultural events, lectures, and exhibits; (5) encouraging participation in extracurricular and community activities outside the home; and (6) fostering relationships with potential mentors and other resource people in the community.

**PRESCHOOL PROGRAMS.** A variety of preschool programs have been developed for young children who are gifted. Some children are involved in traditional programs, which focus on activities and curricula devoted primarily to the development of academic skills. Many of the traditional programs emphasize affective and social development, as well. The entry criteria for these programs are varied, but the primary considerations are usually the child's IQ and social maturity. Moreover, the child must be generally skilled in following directions, attending to tasks of some duration, and controlling impulsive behavior.

Creativity programs are designed to help children develop their natural endowments in a number of artistic and creative domains. Another purpose of such programs is to help the children discover their own areas of promise. Children in these programs are also prepared for eventual involvement in traditional academic areas of schooling.

## Childhood and Adolescence

Giftedness in elementary and secondary students may be nurtured in a variety of ways. A number of service delivery systems and approaches are used in responding to the needs of students who are gifted. The nurturing process has often been referred to as **differentiated education**—that is, an education uniquely and predominantly suited to the natural abilities and interests of individuals who are gifted (Gagn,, 2003: Karnes & Bean, 2001). Generally, programs for the gifted are targeted at delivering content more rapidly, delivering more content, examining content in greater depth, pursuing highly specialized content, and/or dealing with more complex and higher levels of subject matter.

**INSTRUCTIONAL APPROACHES.** Instructional approaches are selected on the basis of a variety of factors. First, the school system must determine what types of giftedness it is capable of serving. It must also establish identification criteria and

**Differentiated education**

Instruction and learning activities that are uniquely and predominantly suited to the capacities and interests of gifted students.

## Case Study

# IS CALVIN GIFTED?

What follows is a series of cartoon strips from *Calvin and Hobbes*. They depict in part the relationship Calvin has with his dad.

## APPLICATION

1. Is Calvin gifted, creative, and talented? Provide a rationale for your answer.

2. If Calvin's dad asked you how to handle Calvin's "giftedness," what recommendations would you make? Give a rationale for your answers.

3. If Calvin's dad were enrolled in your parenting class and asked for your counsel as the group leader, what would you recommend?

SERVICES AND SUPPORTS

**Inclusion Through the Lifespan**

## PEOPLE WHO ARE GIFTED, CREATIVE, AND TALENTED

### Tips for the Family

- Realize that giftedness is evidenced in many ways (e.g., concentration, memory, pleasure in learning, sense of humor, social knowledge, task orientation, ability to follow and lead, capacity and desire to compete, information capacity).
- Provide toys for children who are gifted that may be used for a variety of activities.
- Take trips to museums, exhibits, fairs, and other places of interest.
- Provide an environment that is appropriately challenging.
- Supply proper visual, auditory, verbal, and kinesthetic stimulation.
- Talk to the child in ways that foster give-and-take conversation.
- Begin to expose the child to picture books and ask him or her to find certain objects or animals or respond to age-appropriate questions.
- Avoid unnecessary restrictions.
- Provide play materials that are developmentally appropriate and may be a little challenging.

### Tips for the Preschool Teacher

- Look for ways in which various talents and skills may be expressed (e.g., cognitive, artistic, leadership, socialization, motor ability, memory, special knowledge, imagination).
- Provide opportunities for the child who is gifted to express these talents.
- Capitalize on the child's curiosity. Develop learning activities related to his or her passions.
- Allow the child to experiment with all the elements of language—even written language—as he or she is ready.

### Tips for Preschool Personnel

- Remember that conversation is critical to the child's development. Do not be reluctant to spend a great deal of time asking the child questions as he or she engages in various activities.
- Become a specialist in looking for gifts and talents across a variety of domains (e.g., artistic, social, cognitive).
- Allow for rapid mastery of concepts, and then allow the child to move on to other more challenging activities rather than holding him or her back.

### Tips for Neighbors and Friends

- Recognize that people have a variety of gifts and talents that can be encouraged.
- Provide preschool opportunities for all children who are potentially gifted to have the necessary environmental ingredients to use their talents or gifts fully.
- Enjoy and sometimes endure the neighborhood child who has chosen your home as his or her lab for various experiments in cooking, painting, and building.

### Tips for the Family

- Maintain the search for individual gifts and talents; some qualities may not be evident until the child is older.
- Provide out-of-school experiences that foster talent or skill development (e.g., artistic, physical, academic, leadership).
- Enroll the child who is gifted in summer programs that are offered by universities or colleges.
- Monitor the child's school environment to be sure that adequate steps are being taken to respond to his or her unique skills.
- Join an advocacy group for parents in your community or state.
- Subscribe to child publications that are related to your child's current interests.
- Encourage your child's friendships and associations with other people who have like interests and aptitudes.

### Tips for the General Education School Teacher

- Provide opportunities for enrichment as well as acceleration.
- Allow students who are gifted to pursue individual projects that require sophisticated forms of thinking or production.
- Become involved in professional organizations that provide assistance to teachers of students who are gifted.
- Take a course that specifically addresses the instructional strategies that might be used with children who are gifted.
- Encourage children to become active participants in various events that emphasize particular skill or knowledge areas (e.g., science fairs, music competitions).

### Tips for School Personnel

- Develop clubs and programs that allow children who are gifted to pursue their talents.
- Create award programs that encourage talent development across a variety of domains.
- Involve community members in offering enrichment and acceleration activities (e.g., artists, engineers, writers).
- Foster the use of inclusive procedures for identifying students who are potentially gifted from groups that are culturally diverse, disadvantaged, or have disabilities.

### Tips for Neighbors and Friends

- Contribute to organizations that foster talent development.
- Volunteer to serve as judges for competitive events.
- Be willing to share your talents with young, emergent scholars, musicians, athletes, and artists.
- Become a mentor for someone in your community.

## SECONDARY AND TRANSITION YEARS

### Tips for the Family

- Continue to provide sources of support for talent development outside of the home.
- Regularly counsel your child about courses that he or she will take.
- Provide access to tools (e.g., computers, video cameras) and resources (e.g., specialists, coaches, mentors) that contribute to the child's performance.
- Expect variations in performance from time to time.
- Provide opportunities for relaxation and rest from demanding schedules.
- Continue to encourage involvement with peers who have similar interests and aptitudes.

### Tips for the General Education School Teacher

- Provide a range of activities for students with varying abilities.
- Provide opportunities for students who are gifted to deal with real problems or develop actual products.
- Give opportunities for genuine enrichment activities, not just more work.
- Remember that giftedness manifests itself in many ways. Determine how various types of giftedness may be expressed in your content domain.
- Help to eliminate the conflicting and confusing signals about career choices and fields of study that are often given to young women who are gifted.

### Tips for School Personnel

- Provide, to the degree possible, a variety of curriculum options, activities, clubs, and the like.
- Acknowledge excellence in a variety of performance areas (e.g., leadership, visual and performing arts, academics).
- Continue to use inclusive procedures in identifying individuals who are potentially gifted and talented.
- Encourage participation in competitive activities in which students are able to use their gifts and talents (e.g., science fairs, debate tournaments, music competitions).

### Tips for Neighbors, Friends, and Potential Employers

- Provide opportunities for students to "shadow" talented professionals.
- Volunteer as a professional to work directly with students who are gifted in pursuing a real problem or producing an actual product.
- Become a mentor for a student who is interested in what you do professionally.
- Support the funding of programs for students who are gifted and talented and who come from disadvantaged environments.
- Provide summer internships for students who have a particular interest in your profession.
- Serve as an adviser for a high school club or other organization that gives students additional opportunities to pursue talent areas.

## ADULT YEARS

### Tips for the Family

- Continue to nurture appropriate interdependence and independence.
- Assist with the provision of specialized assistance.
- Celebrate the accomplishments and provide support for challenges.
- Let go.

### Tips for Educational Personnel

- Exhibit behaviors associated with effective mentoring.
- Provide meaningful ways to deal with pressure.
- Allow the individuals to be themselves.
- Provide adequate time for discussion and interaction.
- Be aware of other demands in the individuals' lives.

### Tips for Potential Employers

- Establish appropriately high expectations.
- Provide opportunities for diversion and fun.
- Be sensitive to changing interests and needs.
- Allow employees to be involved with young gifted students on a volunteer basis.

measures that enable it to select qualified students fairly. For example, if the system is primarily interested in enhancing creativity, measures and indices of creativity should be utilized. If the focus of the program is accelerating math achievement and understanding, instruments that measure mathematical aptitude and achievement should be employed. Second, the school system must select the organizational structures through which children who are gifted are to receive their differentiated education (Karnes & Bean, 2001; Schiever & Maker, 2003). Third, school personnel must select the instructional approaches to be utilized within each program setting. Fourth, school personnel must select continuous evaluation procedures and techniques that help them assess the overall effectiveness of the program. Data generated from such evaluation can serve as a catalyst for making appropriate changes (Davis & Rimm, 2004).

**SERVICE DELIVERY SYSTEMS.** Once the types of giftedness to be emphasized have been selected and appropriate identification procedures have been established, planning must be directed at selecting suitable service delivery systems. Organizational structures for students who are gifted are similar to those found in other areas of special education. Clark (1997) described several options that have been used to develop services for students who are gifted (see Figure 18.6). Each of the learning environments in the model has advantages and disadvantages. For example, students who are enrolled in general education classrooms and are given opportunities to spend time in seminars, resource rooms, special classes, and other novel learning environments profit from these experiences because they are allowed to work at their own levels of ability. Furthermore, such pull-out activities provide a means for students to interact with one another and to pursue interests to which the usual school curriculum offers little access. However, the disadvantages of such a program are numerous. The major part of the instructional week is spent doing things that may not be appropriate for students who are gifted, given their abilities and interests. Also, when they return to general education classes, they are frequently required to make up missed assignments.

Another example of Clark's alternatives for elementary, middle, and high schools is assignment to a special class, supplemented with opportunities for course work integrated with regular classes. This approach has many advantages. Students have the best of both worlds, academically and socially. Directed independent studies, seminars, mentorships, and cooperative studies are possible through this arrangement. Students who are gifted are able to interact in an intensive fashion with other able students, as well as with regular students in their integrated classes. This program also has disadvantages, however. A special class requires a well-prepared teacher, and many school systems simply do not have sufficient funds to hire a specialist in gifted education. Without a skilled teacher, the special class instruction or other specialized learning activities may just be more of the general education curriculum.

Implementing service delivery and designing curricula for gifted students are significant but rewarding challenges. They demand the availability of sufficient financial and human resources, flexibility in determining student placement and progress, and a climate of excellence characterized by high standards and significant student engagement in learning activities. Optimally, delivery systems should facilitate the achievement of specific curricular goals and should correspond with the types of giftedness being nurtured.

## FIGURE 18.6

### Clark's Continuum Model for Ability Grouping

General education classroom

General education class with cluster

General education class with pull-out

General education class with cluster and pull-out

Individualized classroom

Individualized classroom with cluster

Individualized classroom with pull-out

Individualized classroom with cluster and pull-out

Special class with some integrated classes

Special class

Special school

SOURCE: From *Growing Up Gifted*, 5th ed., by Barbara Clark, Copyright © 1979. Adapted by permission of Prentice-Hall, Inc., Upper Saddle River, NJ.

Conditions and strategies associated with successful classrooms and programs for gifted students include teachers who have advanced preparation and knowledge specifically related to gifted education, who relish change, and who enjoy working collaboratively with other professionals. Furthermore, these teachers believe in differentiated instruction, have access to a variety of strategies for delivering this kind of instruction, and have a disposition for leadership and some autonomy in fulfilling their teaching responsibilities.

**ACCELERATION.** Traditionally, programs for students who are gifted emphasize the practices of **acceleration** and enrichment (Schiever & Maker, 2003). Acceleration enables gifted students to progress rapidly and learn at a rate commensurate with their abilities. Early entrance to kindergarten or college, part-time grade acceleration, and grade skipping are all examples of acceleration. In the past, grade skipping was a common administrative approach to meeting the needs of high-ability learners. But this practice has declined because some individuals believe that grade skipping may increase the likelihood of a student's becoming socially maladjusted. Others believe that accelerated students experience significant gaps in learning because of grade skipping. Acceleration is generally limited to two years in the typical elementary school program. In any case, acceleration unfortunately does not provide gifted students with a differentiated curriculum suited to their specific needs (Schiever & Maker, 2003).

Another practice related to grade skipping is telescoped or condensed schooling, which enables students to progress through the content of several grades in a significantly reduced time. An allied practice is allowing students to progress rapidly through a particular course or content offering. Acceleration of this nature provides students with the sequential, basic learning at a pace commensurate with their abilities. School programs that are ungraded are particularly suitable for telescoping.

**FOCUS 6**

Identify eight strategies that are utilized to foster the development of children and adolescents who are gifted.

**Acceleration**

A process whereby students are allowed to achieve at a rate that is consistent with their capacity.

**Reflect on This**

## DR. KAMEN, INVENTOR EXTRAORDINAIRE

Kamen's life, unlike his inventions, isn't enigmatic. The 49-year-old inventor actually courts attention, holding lavish parties for famous and powerful people, all the while pushing the idea that inventors will become the superstars of the 21st century.

He nurtures this belief by operating a not-for-profit venture called U.S. First (For *I*nspiration and *R*ecognition of *S*cience and *T*echnology), which encourages children and teens to follow an engineering or scientific career path.

"Our culture celebrates one thing: sports heroes," he said in a recent *Wired* magazine article, "You have teenagers thinking they're going to make millions as NBA stars when that's not realistic for even 1% of them. Becoming a scientist or an engineer is."

Kamen's own childhood was filled with scientific achievements and inventions. He's a self-taught physicist whose aptitude for entrepreneurism was earning him $60,000 a year before he even graduated from high school. One of his biggest jobs as a teenager was to automate the ball drop for New York's Times Square New Year's Eve celebrations.

One of his first highly successful inventions in the 1970s was inspired by his brother, who was a medical student at the time. Kamen invented the first portable infusion pump to assist in the reliable, scheduled delivery of drugs to hospital patients.

Another of his famous and lucrative creations was a dialysis machine the size of a phone book, invented in the mid-1990s. Up to this point, all dialysis machines had been very large, and patients had to travel to them in the hospital. Kamen's invention made it possible for patients to have home care, freeing up hospital resources.

"I don't work on a project unless I believe that it will dramatically improve life for a bunch of people," Kamen told NBC news last year.

Kamen thrives on publicity. He's frequently in the company of powerful and famous people, including former president Bill Clinton, to whom he recently showed one of his latest inventions.

His goal? To have every student in the United States enrolled in U.S. FIRST.

SOURCE: Adapted from BeatnikPad, Sympatico Articles, 2003, retrieved 27 June 2003 from http://www.beatnikpad.com/writing/archives/000156.php

*Accelerated programs allow students to achieve at a rate consonant with their capabilities, often by skipping a grade. Enrichment experiences broaden the student's knowledge through the curriculum by providing courses in areas such as music appreciation, foreign language, or mythology.*

Regardless of their chronological ages, students may progress through a learning or curriculum sequence that is not constricted by artificial grade boundaries.

Other forms of condensed programming found at the high school level include earning credit through examination, enrolling in extra courses for early graduation, reducing or eliminating certain course work, enrolling in intensive summer programs, and taking approved university courses while completing high school requirements. Many of these options enable students to enter college early or begin bachelor's

## Debate Forum

## WHAT WOULD YOU DO WITH JANE?

**M**any children who are gifted are prevented from accelerating their growth and learning for fear that they will be hurt emotionally and socially.

Parents' comments such as these are common: She's so young. Won't she miss a great deal if she doesn't go through the fourth and fifth grades? What about her friends? Who will her friends be if she goes to college at such a young age? Will she have the social skills to interact with kids who are much older? If she skips these two grades, won't there be gaps in her learning and social development?

On the other hand, the nature of the questions or comments by parents about acceleration may also be positive: She is young in years only! She will adjust extremely well. Maybe she is emotionally mature enough to handle this type of acceleration. The increased opportunities provided through university training will give her greater chances to develop her talents and capacities. Perhaps the older students with whom she will interact are better suited to her intellectual and social needs.

Consider Jane, a child who is gifted. In third grade, she thrived in school, and just about everything associated with her schooling at that time was positive. Her teacher was responsive and allowed her and others to explore well beyond the usual "read-the-text-then-respond-to-the-ditto-sheet" routine. Much self-pacing was possible, and materials galore were presented for both independent studies and queries.

In the fourth and fifth grades, however, things began to change radically. Jane's teachers were simply unable to provide enough interesting and challenging work for her. It was during the latter part of the fourth grade that she began to view herself as different. Not only did she know, but her classmates knew, that learning came exceptionally easily to her. At this same time, Jane was beginning to change dramatically in her cognitive capacity. Unfortunately, her

teachers persisted in unnecessary drills and other mundane assignments, and Jane gradually became bored and lapsed into a type of passive learning. Rather than attacking assignments with vigor, she performed them carelessly, often making many stupid errors. Gradually, what emerged was a child who was very unhappy in school. School had been the most interesting place for her to be before she entered fourth grade. Then it became a source of pain and boredom.

Jane's parents decided that they needed to know more about her capacities and talents. Although it was expensive and quite time-consuming, they visited a nearby university center for psychological services. Jane was tested, and the results were very revealing. For the first time, Jane's parents had some objective information about her capacities. She was in fact an unusually bright and talented young lady. Jane's parents then began to consider the educational alternatives available to her.

The counselor who provided the interpretation of the results at the university center strongly recommended that Jane be advanced to the seventh grade in a school that provided services to students who were talented and gifted. This meant that Jane would skip one year of elementary school and have an opportunity to move very rapidly through her junior and senior high school studies. Furthermore, she might be able to enter the university well in advance of her peers.

Jane's parents knew that her performance had diminished significantly in the last year. Moreover, her attitude and disposition about school seem to be worsening. What would you do as her parents? What factors would you consider important in making the decision? Or is the decision Jane's and hers alone?

programs with other advanced students. Dwight, the talented musician and broadcasting entrepreneur described in the chapter-opening Snapshot, was able to earn college credit before his actual enrollment in a university. Many students who are gifted are ready for college-level course work at age 14, 15, or 16. Some students of unusually high abilities are prepared for college-level experiences prior to age 14.

Again, research on acceleration and its impact reveals that carefully selected students profit greatly from such experiences (Assouline, 2003; Kulik, 2003; Shiever & Maker, 2003). Studies suggest that these accelerated students are well adjusted emotionally and socially, have positive self-concepts, and are on average not as troublesome as same age peers (Gallagher, 2003). This is also true of gifted students who enter college earlier than peers. They perform well academically and benefit from the experiences associated with their university studies. Unfortunately, reform movements that stress equity have often reduced the number of specialized classes and experiences available for gifted students (Gallagher, 2003; Gottfredson, 2003).

**ENRICHMENT.** **Enrichment**, like acceleration, is possible in curricular as well as service delivery systems (Schiever & Maker, 2003). Enrichment experiences extend or broaden a person's knowledge. Music appreciation, foreign languages, and mythology are enrichment courses that are added to a student's curriculum and are usually

**Enrichment**

Educational experiences for gifted students that enhance their thinking skills and extend their knowledge in various areas.

## POINT

Jane should be allowed to accelerate her educational pace. Moving to the seventh grade will benefit her greatly, intellectually and socially. Most girls develop more rapidly physically and socially than boys do. Skipping one grade will not hinder her social development at all. In fact, she will benefit from the interactions that she will have with other able students, some of whom will also have skipped a grade or two. Additionally, the research regarding the impact of accelerating students is positive, particularly if the students are carefully selected. Jane has been carefully evaluated and deserves to have the opportunity to be excited about learning and achieving again.

## COUNTERPOINT

There are some inherent risks in having Jane skip her sixth grade experience and move on to the seventh grade. Jane is neither socially nor emotionally prepared to deal with the junior high environment. She may be very able intellectually, and her achievement may be superior, but this is not the time to move her into junior high. Socially, she is still quite awkward for her age. This awkwardness would be intensified in the junior high setting. Acceleration for Jane should be considered later on, when she has matured more socially.

She should be able to receive the acceleration that she needs in her present elementary school. Certainly, other able students in her school would benefit from joining together for various activities and learning experiences. The acceleration should take place in her own school, with other students who are gifted and of her own age. Maybe all Jane needs is some time to attend a class or two elsewhere. Using this approach, she could benefit from involvement with her same-age peers and still receive the stimulation that she so desperately needs. Allowing her to skip a grade now would hurt her emotionally and socially in the long run.

What do you think? To give your opinion, go to Chapter 18 of the companion website **(www.ablongman.com/hardman8e)** and click on Debate Forum.

not any more difficult than other classes in which the student is involved. Other examples of enrichment involve experiences in which the student develops sophisticated thinking skills (i.e., synthesis, analysis, interpretation, and evaluation) or has opportunities to master advanced concepts in a particular subject area. Some forms of enrichment are actually types of acceleration. A student whose enrichment involves fully pursuing mathematical concepts that are well beyond his or her present grade level is experiencing a form of acceleration. Obviously, the two approaches are interrelated (Schiever & Maker, 2003).

Enrichment is the most common administrative approach to serving students who are gifted. It is also the most abused approach in that it is often applied in name only and in a sporadic fashion, without well-delineated objectives or rationale. There are also other problems with the enrichment approach. It is often implemented superficially, as a token response to the demands of parents of children who are gifted. Enrichment activities are viewed by some professionals as periods devoted to educational trivia or to instruction heavy in student assignments but light in content. Quality enrichment programs are characterized by carefully selected activities, modules, or units; challenging but not overwhelming assignments; and evaluations that are rigorous yet fair. Additionally, good enrichment programs focus on thoughtful and careful plans for student learning and on learning activities that stress higher-order thinking and application skills (Schiever & Maker, 2003).

Enrichment may include such activities as exploring exciting topics not normally pursued in the general curriculum, group-centered activities that focus on cognitive or affective skills and/or processes, and small-group investigations of actual, real-life problems (Renzulli & Reis, 2003). The keys to these endeavors are high student interest, excellent teaching, and superb mentoring (Feldhusen, 1998a & 1998b).

There is a paucity of systematic experimental research on enrichment programs (Schiever & Maker, 2003). Despite many of the limitations of current and past research, evidence supports the effectiveness of enrichment, particularly when it is delivered to specific ability groups and when the content and rigor of the curriculum coincide with the abilities of the targeted students (Schiever & Maker, 2003).

Enrichment activities do not appear to detract from the success that students experience on regularly administered achievement tests. Sociometric data on students who are pulled out of general education classrooms for enrichment activities are also positive. Students do not appear to suffer socially from involvement in enrichment programs that take place outside their general education classrooms. Acceleration and enrichment are essentially complementary parts of curricular and service delivery systems (Schriever & Maker, 2003).

**SPECIAL PROGRAMS AND SCHOOLS.** Programs designed to nurture the talents of individuals in nonacademic areas, such as the visual and performing arts, have grown rapidly in recent years (Clasen & Clasen, 2003; Feldhusen, 2003; Kolloff, 2003; Olszewski-Kubilius, 2003; Winner & Martino, 2003). Students involved in these programs frequently spend half their school day working in academic subjects and the other half in arts studies. Often the arts instruction is provided by an independent institution, but some school systems maintain their own separate schools. Most programs provide training in the visual and performing arts, but a few emphasize instruction in creative writing, motion picture and television production, and photography.

So-called governor's schools (distinctive summer programs generally held at university sites), talent identification programs, and specialized residential or high schools in various states also provide valuable opportunities for students who are talented and academically gifted (Davis & Rimm, 2004). Competitively selected students are provided with curricular experiences that are closely tailored to their individual aptitudes and interests. Faculties for these schools are meticulously selected for competence in various areas and for their ability to stimulate and motivate students. However, these schools and special programs are few and serve only a small number of the students who would profit from them.

**CAREER EDUCATION.** Career education, career guidance, and counseling are essential components of a comprehensive program for students who are gifted (Colangelo, 2003). Ultimately, career education activities and counseling are designed to help students make educational, occupational, and personal decisions. Because of their multipotentiality (their capacity for doing so many things well), it is frequently difficult for gifted students to make educational and career choices.

Differentiated learning experiences give elementary and middle school students opportunities to investigate and explore. Many of these investigations and explorations are career-related and designed to help students understand what it might be like to be a zoologist, neurosurgeon, or film maker. Students also become familiar with the training and effort necessary for work in these fields. For gifted students in the elementary grades, these explorations often take place on Saturdays. They help such students understand themselves, their talents, and the preparations needed for entry into specific fields of study.

In group meetings, gifted students and talented professionals may discuss the factors that influenced a scientist or group of researchers to pursue a given problem or conduct experiments that led to important discoveries or products. As students mature both cognitively and physically, the scope of their career education activities becomes more sophisticated and varied.

**MENTORING.** Some students are provided opportunities to work directly with research scientists, artists, musicians, or other professionals. Students may spend as many as three or four hours a day, two days a week, in laboratory facilities, mentored by the scientists and professionals with whom they work (Clasen & Clasen, 2003). Other students rely on intensive workshops or summer programs in which they are exposed to specialized careers through internships and individually tailored instruction (Olszewski-Kubilius, 2003).

The benefits of mentoring to gifted students are numerous. Students have sophisticated learning experiences that are highly motivating and stimulating. They gain invaluable opportunities to explore careers and to confirm their commitment to certain areas of study or reexamine their interests. Mentoring experiences may affirm potential in underachieving students or students with disabilities—potential that was not being tapped through conventional means. Mentoring may also promote the development of self-reliance, specific interpersonal skills, and life-long, productive friendships. As Clasen and Clasen (2003) indicated, "mentorships may mean the difference between a dream withered and a dream realized" (p. 265).

**CAREER CHOICES AND CHALLENGES.** Career interests, values, and dispositions appear to crystallize early in gifted students. In fact, their interests are neither broader nor more restricted than those of their classmates. Many gifted students know quite early what paths they will follow in postsecondary schooling. These paths often lead to careers in engineering, health professions, and physical sciences.

Counseling programs are particularly helpful to adolescents who are gifted. Often they know more about their academic content than they know about themselves (Colangelo, 2003). As gifted students come to understand themselves, their capacities, and their interests more fully, they will make better choices in selecting courses of study and professional careers.

Family counseling may also be helpful to parents and other family members. Problems caused by excessive or inappropriate parental expectations may need to be addressed in a family context. Counselors and therapists may help parents develop realistic expectations consistent with their child's abilities, aspirations, and true interests (Colangelo, 2003). As with other exceptionalities, counseling services are best provided through interdisciplinary efforts.

**PROBLEMS AND CHALLENGES OF GIFTEDNESS.** Students who are gifted must cope with a number of problems. One problem is the expectations they have of themselves and those that have been explicitly and implicitly imposed by parents, teachers, and others. Students who are gifted frequently feel an inordinate amount of

**FOCUS**

**7**

What are some of the social-emotional needs of students who are gifted?

pressure to achieve high grades or to select particular professions. They often feel obligated or duty-bound to achieve excellence in every area, a syndrome called perfectionism (Colangelo & Davis, 2003). Sadly, such pressure can foster a kind of conformity and prevent students from selecting avenues of endeavor that truly fit them and reflect their personal interests.

Van Tassel-Baska (1989) identified several social-emotional needs that differentiate students who are gifted from their same-age peers:

- Understanding how they are different from and how they are similar to their peers.
- Appreciating and valuing their own uniqueness as well as that of others.
- Understanding and developing relationship skills.
- Developing and valuing their high-level sensitivity.
- Gaining a realistic understanding of their own abilities and talents.
- Identifying ways of nurturing and developing their own abilities and talents.
- Adequately distinguishing between the pursuit of excellence and the pursuit of perfection.
- Developing behaviors associated with negotiation and compromise.

Students who are gifted need ongoing and continual access to adult role models who have interests and abilities that parallel theirs; the importance of these role models cannot be overstated (Clasen & Clasen, 2003). Role models are particularly important for gifted students who grow up and receive their schooling in rural and remote areas. Such students often complete their public schooling without the benefit of having a mentor or professional person with whom they can talk or discuss various educational and career-related issues. Some students who live in rural or remote communities now have access to mentoring at a distance through telementoring or the Internet. Examples of this form of mentoring include the National Mentoring Partnership, sponsored by the U.S. Department of Education; the SET (Study of Exceptional Talent) Mentor Program Center for Talented Youth, sponsored by John Hopkins University; and the Hewlett Packard Email Mentor Program (Clasen & Clasen, 2003).

# Historically Neglected Groups

## Females

Gifted females face several problems, particularly during the middle school years. During this time period, their confidence may wane. It may be eclipsed by uncertainty and diminished expectations for success. These girls begin to discount their intelligence and related abilities in an effort to enhance their chances for social acceptance and minimize their risk of social isolation.

The number of girls identified as gifted appears to decline with age. Olshen (1987) referred to this decline as the disappearance of giftedness in girls. This phenomenon is surprising when we realize that girls tend to walk and talk earlier than their male counterparts; that girls, as a group, read earlier; that girls score higher than boys on IQ tests during the preschool years; and that the grade-point averages of girls during the elementary years are higher than those of boys (Kerr & Nicpon, 2003).

Just exactly what happens to girls? Is the decline in the number of girls identified as gifted related to their socialization? Does some innate physiological or biological mechanism account for this decline? Why do some gifted females fail to realize their potential? To what extent do value conflicts about women's roles contribute to mixed achievement in gifted women? The answers to these and other important questions are gradually emerging (Kerr & Nicpon, 2003).

One of the explanations given for this decline is the gender role socialization that girls receive. Behaviors associated with competitiveness, risk taking, and independence are not generally encouraged in girls. Behaviors that are generally fostered in girls include dependence, cooperation, and nurturing. The elimination of independent behaviors in girls is viewed by Silverman (1986) as being the most damaging aspect of their socialization. More recent research suggests that girls who develop social self-esteem, "the belief that one has the ability to act effectively and to make decisions independently," are more likely to realize their potential (Davis & Rimm, 2004). Without independence, the development of high levels of creativity, achievement, and leadership are severely limited. Overcoming the impact of sociocultural influences requires carefully applied

*People with gifts and talents often have a variety of interests. Marjorie Scardino is Chief Executive Officer of Pearson plc, one of the world's largest media/education conglomerates. She is also a rodeo barrel racer, prairie populist, attorney, and First Amendment Scholar as well as a former reporter and publisher of the Pulitzer-prize winning Georgia Weekly. Ms. Scardino is pictured here with Sir Dennis Stevenson, Chairman of Pearson.*

**Reflect on This**

## OLIVIA, I DON'T WANT HER

During the years of beatings by her mother, years of being whipped with an extension cord, smacked in the mouth with a telephone, pounded against a wall, punched in the lip, dragged by the hair through the hallway, tossed in the shower, and scalded with hot water, school was Olivia's salvation. The only kind words she heard, the only love she felt, the only compliments she received, were from her teachers. At home, no matter how she was tormented, no matter how long she cried, when the beatings were over, she always read her assignments and prepared for her tests.

But one afternoon after school, when her mother left for work, Olivia decided to run away instead. She ripped out of the Yellow Pages the shelter listings for abused children and battered women. She stuffed them in her back pocket and filled a duffle bag with clothes. Then, as an afterthought, she grabbed her mother's black leather jacket.

A few months later a court hearing was held to determine Olivia's fate. She felt as if she were in a fog as the judge and social workers discussed her case. She remembers only the end of the hearing, when the judge told her mother that if she wanted the opportunity to regain custody of her daughter, she would have to undergo psychological testing, individual counseling, and family counseling. Olivia's mother told the judge, "She's the crazy one. Not me." The last words Olivia remembers her mother saying were "I don't want her!"

When Olivia was about to start high school, a compassionate group-home administrator gave her a pamphlet that listed the magnet schools in the Los Angeles school district. These schools were for students who had an interest in a particular field of study, or who had a talent for music or art, or who were classified as gifted because of their high IQ or standardized test scores. Olivia studied the pamphlet and discovered that one of the two high schools in the city for gifted students was located at Crenshaw High School, only a few miles from her South-Central group home.

One afternoon she took the bus from her junior high school to Crenshaw and talked to several administrators. They told Olivia that her IQ and her standardized test scores—which were in the top 5th percentile of the nation—were well above the minimum requirement. She enrolled in the gifted magnet program in the ninth grade.

The gifted magnet program was a refuge for Olivia, and she immediately felt comfortable in it. She met many other students who, like her, had wretched childhoods yet had managed to stay focused on school and retain a love of learning. Olivia thrived in the program, and at the end of her first year, she was one of only two ninth graders who received all A's in their academic subjects. Her home life remained chaotic, but school, once again, was her escape, her respite from the loneliness of having no family, the rootlessness of having no home. Olivia enjoyed the courses in the gifted program and the challenging class discussions. But most of all she appreciated the interest and concern of her teachers, the camaraderie among her classmates. This, she felt, was the family she never had.

SOURCE: From *And Still We Rise* (pp. 9–13), by M. Corwin, 2000, New York: Morrow.

FOCUS
8

Identify four
challenges that
females face in
dealing with
their giftedness.

interventions, counseling, and heightened levels of awareness (Davis & Rimm, 2004; Kerr & Nicpon, 2003; Maltby & Devlin, 2000).

Females who are gifted and talented experience additional problems, (Davis & Rimm, 2004), including fear of appearing "unfeminine" or unattractive when competing with males, competition between marital and career aspirations, stress induced by traditional cultural and societal expectations, and self-imposed and/or culturally imposed restrictions related to educational and occupational choices. Although many of these problems are far from being resolved at this point, some progress is being made. Women in greater numbers are choosing to enter professions traditionally pursued by men (Davis & Rimm, 2004; Kerr & Nicpon, 2003).

Fortunately, multiple role assignments are emerging in many families, wherein the tasks traditionally performed by mothers are shared by all members of the family or are completed by someone outside the family. Cultural expectations are changing, and as a result, options for women who are gifted are rapidly expanding (Davis & Rimm, 2004; Kerr & Nicpon, 2003).

## Persons with Disabilities

For some time, intellectual giftedness has been largely associated with high IQs and high scores on aptitude tests. These tests, by their very nature and structure, measure a limited range of mental abilities. Because of such limitations, they have not been particularly helpful in identifying persons with disabilities who are intellectually or otherwise gifted. However, persons with disabilities such as cerebral palsy, learning disabilities, and other disabling conditions can be gifted (Davis & Rimm, 2004; Hua, 2002). Helen Keller, Vincent van Gogh, and Ludwig van Beethoven are prime examples of individuals with disabilities who were also gifted. Some theorists and practitioners suggest that as many as 2% of individuals with disabilities are gifted. Fortunately, we have begun to look for various kinds of giftedness in children with disabilities.

In this context, the gifted disabled are individuals with exceptional ability or potential and who achieve high performance despite such disabilities as hearing, speech, orthopedic, or emotional impairments, learning disabilities, or health problems, either singly or in combination (Davis & Rimm, 2004). Although many challenges are still associated with identifying individuals with disabilities who are gifted, much progress has been made.

Unfortunately, the giftedness of children with disabilities is often invisible to parents and teachers. Factors critical to the recognition of giftedness include environments that elicit signs of mental giftedness and availability of information about the individual's performance gathered from many sources. With regard to these eliciting environments, it is important that the child be given opportunities to perform tasks on which his or her disabling condition is no impediment. Also, if and when tests of mental ability are used, they must be appropriately adapted, both in administration and scoring (Davis & Rimm, 2004). Furthermore, the identification screening should occur at regular intervals. Some children with disabilities change dramatically with appropriate instruction and related assistive technologies. The developmental delays present in children with disabilities and the disabilities themselves pose the greatest challenges to identification efforts (Davis & Rimm, 2004).

Itzhak Perlman is one of the most gifted violinists of our time. Performing here with the University of Southern Mississippi Symphony Orchestra, he has been a friend and mentor to countless numbers of young musicians. He was struck with polio at the age of four and has been a tireless advocate for the rights of persons with disabilities throughout his life.

## ENCOURAGING GIFTEDNESS IN GIRLS

### Suggestions for the Family

Hold high expectations for daughters.

Do not purchase gender-role-stereotyped toys.

Avoid overprotectiveness.

Encourage high levels of activity.

Allow girls to get dirty.

Instill beliefs in their capabilities.

Support their interests.

Identify them as gifted during their preschool years.

Find for them playmates who are gifted to identify with and emulate.

Foster interests in mathematics outside of school.

Consider early entrance and other opportunities to accelerate.

Encourage enrollment in mathematics courses.

Introduce them to professional women in many occupations.

Encourage their mothers to acknowledge their own giftedness.

Encourage their mothers to work at least part-time outside the home.

Encourage fathers to spend time alone with daughters in so-called masculine activities.

Share household duties equally between the parents.

Assign chores to siblings on a nonsexist basis.

Discourage the use of sexist language or teasing in the home.

Monitor television programs for sexist stereotypes, and discuss these with children of both genders.

Encourage siblings to treat each other equitably, rather than according to the traditional gender role stereotypes they may see outside the home.

### Suggestions for Teachers and Counselors

Believe in girls' logicomathematical abilities, and provide many opportunities for them to practice mathematical reasoning within other subject areas.

Accelerate girls through the science and mathematics curriculum whenever possible.

Have special clubs in mathematics for girls who are high-achieving.

Design coeducational career development classes in which both girls and boys learn about career potentialities for women.

Expose boys and girls to role models of women in various careers.

Discuss nontraditional careers for women, including salaries for men and women and schooling requirements.

Help girls set long-term goals.

Discuss underachievement among females who are gifted and ask how they can combat it in themselves and others.

Have girls read biographies of famous women.

Arrange opportunities for girls to "shadow" a female professional for a few days to see what her work entails.

Discourage sexist remarks and attitudes in the classroom.

Boycott sexist classroom materials, and write to the publishers for their immediate correction.

Discuss sexist messages in the media.

Advocate special classes and after-school enrichment opportunities for students who are gifted.

Form support groups for girls with similar interests.

SOURCE: From "What Happens to the Gifted Girl?" by L. K. Silverman. In *Critical Issues in Gifted Education, Vol. 1: Defensible Programs for the Gifted*, edited by C. J. Maker, 1986, pp. 43–89. Austin, TX: Pro-Ed. (Copyright owned by author.) Adapted by permission.

---

Differential education for children with disabilities who are gifted is still in its infancy. A great deal of progress has been made, particularly in the adaptive uses of computers and related technologies, but much remains to be done. Additionally, a great deal is still unknown about the service delivery systems and materials that are best suited for these individuals. One of the best things that parents and teachers can do for children and youth with disabilities who are gifted is to foster self-confidence and independence. Unfortunately, the need for one-to-one instruction frequently gives rise to dependence and undermines self-confidence (Davis & Rimm, 2004).

## Children from Diverse Cultural Backgrounds and Children of Poverty

Very rarely are culturally diverse and economically disadvantaged youth identified as gifted (Davis & Rimm, 2004). These youth are dramatically underrepresented in programs for the gifted and talented (Esquivel & Houtz, 2000). Ford (2003) has suggested that this underrepresentation is a function of several factors: excessive reliance on testing and test scores that may not accurately capture potential, IQ-based

Identify eight essential elements of programs for gifted children who come from diverse backgrounds and who may live in poverty.

definitions of giftedness, identification based on achievement test scores, and polices and practices that are exclusive rather than inclusive. As suggested at the beginning of this chapter, we are now focusing more on inclusive practices in identifying giftedness and are paying more attention to talent development.

Identification procedures often fail to identify children as being gifted when they come from minority groups or disadvantaged environments (Esquivel & Houtz, 2000). However, many practitioners are now using multiple criteria to reveal potential giftedness in children who are poor or from diverse cultural backgrounds (Davis & Rimm, 2004). Past research conducted by VanTassel-Baska and Chepko-Sade (1986) has suggested that as many as 15% of the gifted population may be children with disadvantages.

Effective instructional programs for children and adolescents who are disadvantaged and gifted have several key components. First and foremost, the teachers in these programs are well trained in adapting and differentiating instruction for these students. They understand learning styles, how to build and capitalize on students'

## SNAPSHOT

## Sadikifu

Sadi's mother, Thelma, who was one week shy of her 41st birthday when her only child was born, considers her son a gift from Allah. He was unexpected and unplanned. Thelma and Sadi's father, who never married, became Muslims in the 1970s, and they gave their son an Islamic name—Sadikifu—which means "truthful and honest."

Because Thelma never had been around children, and Sadi was her only child, she talked to him like a peer. That is one reason, she believes, why he is so bright and articulate. In the third grade he was classified as gifted by the school district when he scored in the 95th percentile on a national achievement test. In the fourth grade he won an oratorical contest, sponsored by a local bank, for a speech on homelessness. Thelma still proudly displays the trophy—next to a picture of Elijah Muhammad—in her small, immaculate two-bedroom apartment (p. 32).

Sadi, unfortunately, went the wrong way. In the ninth grade, he enrolled in Crenshaw's gifted program, but after only two months of high school he was thrown out for instigating a fight between his tagging crew and a rival set. Although his mother was livid, Sadi's expulsion probably saved his life because the next afternoon his best friend was shot to death by a rival tagging crew called "Nothin' But Trouble." Sadi always spent

every day after school with his friend, whose street name was Chaos. Sadi knew that if he had not been stuck all afternoon enrolling in his new high school, he would have been walking down Vermont Avenue with Chaos. He probably would have been killed, too (pp. 33–34).

On Sadi's first day of school he discovered he was the only black student in his gifted classes. When students passed out worksheets, they skipped him. When he asked for the assignments, the students invariably said, "I thought you were here for detention."

Although he was now attending a suburban high school far from South-Central, at night and on week-ends he was immersed in the gang life. He had graduated from his tagging crew to the Front Hood 60s and was known by his street name—Little Cloudy. And even though he had been arrested several times, three of his homies had recently been killed in drive-bys, and about ten were in jail, he kept gangbanging.

One weekday afternoon, when school was canceled because of an earthquake, he and two other 60s were walking down Western Avenue, on their way to buy some Thunderbird at a liquor store near 69th Street. They spotted a teenager across the street whom they did not recognize. Sadi and his two homies threw up the hand sign for the Front Hood 60s. The gangbanger across the

street threw up the sign for the Eight-Tray Gangsters, a bitter rival of the 60s. One of Sadi's homies pulled out a semiautomatic .380-caliber pistol and fired at the Eight-Tray. Then everyone sprinted for cover. Two LAPD officers in a patrol car heard the shots, pulled up, and grabbed Sadi and another 60. The shooter and the Eight-Tray, who had not been hit, escaped.

Sadi and his homie were handcuffed, arrested, and taken to the 77th Street Division station. They were questioned by detectives, who then dabbed their hands with a sticky aluminum tab that tests for gunshot residue. When the test came back negative and a witness told detectives that neither of them was the shooter, they were released. But the incident precipitated an epiphany for Sadi.

Seeing the flash of the gun, just inches away, marked a turning point for him. It inalterably changed the course of his life. In an instant, he realized how transitory life was, how transitory *his* life was. How all his decisions were wrong. How he was destined to die in a drive-by or languish in prison. He realized that maybe his mother had been right about school. Maybe his intelligence was, as his mother told him, a gift from Allah (pp. 34–35).

SOURCE: From *And Still We Rise* (pp. 32–35), by M. Corwin, 2000, New York: Morrow.

interests, and how to maximize students' affective, cognitive, and ethical capacities. In addition to providing the typical curricular options for enrichment, acceleration, and talent development, the best programs for these children and youth include additional elements: (1) embrace and celebrate ethnic diversity, (2) provide extracurricular cultural enrichment, (3) address differences in learning style, (4) provide counseling, (5) foster parent support groups, and (6) give these children and youth access to significant models (Davis and Rimm, 2004).

There is general agreement that programs for these children should begin early and should be tailored to the needs and interests of each identified child. They should focus on individual potentialities rather than deficits and should help parents understand their roles in fostering giftedness and talent development. Often, the emphasis in the early years is on reading instruction, language development, and foundation skills. Other key components include experiential education that provides children with many opportunities for hands-on learning, activities that foster self-expression, plentiful use of mentors and role models who represent the child's cultural or ethnic group, involvement of the community, and counseling throughout the school years that gives serious consideration to the cultural values of the family and the child who is gifted. Finally, the programs are enhanced by a team approach in which mentors, parents, teachers, and other community members work together to meet the needs of these very special children.

## FOCUS REVIEW

**FOCUS 1:** Briefly describe several historical developments directly related to the measurement of various types of giftedness.

- Alfred Binet developed the first developmental scale for children during the early 1900s. Gradually, there emerged the notion of mental age—that is, a representation of what the child was capable of doing compared with age-specific developmental tasks.
- Lewis M. Terman translated the Binet scale and made modifications suitable for children in the United States.
- Gradually, the intelligence quotient, or IQ, became the gauge for determining giftedness.
- Intelligence was long viewed as a unitary structure or underlying ability. But this view gradually changed, and researchers began to believe that intelligence was represented in a

variety of distinct capacities and abilities.
- J. P. Guilford and other social scientists began to develop a multidimensional theory of intelligence, which prompted researchers to develop models and assessment devices for examining creativity.
- Programs were gradually developed to foster and develop creativity in young people.
- More recently, V. Ramos-Ford and H. Gardner developed the theory of multiple intelligences, which manifest themselves in linguistic, logical-mathematical, spatial, musical, bodily-kinesthetic, interpersonal, and intrapersonal behaviors.

**FOCUS 2** Identify six major components of definitions that have been developed to describe giftedness.

- Children and adolescents who are gifted perform or show potential for performing at remarkably high levels

when compared with others of their age, experience, or environment.
- Children who are gifted exhibit high performance capability in intellectual, creative, and/or artistic areas.
- Such children may possess unusual leadership capacity or excel in specific academic fields.
- Gifted children become extraordinarily proficient performers or creative producers, excelling in a wide range of potential activities from cooking to musical improvisation.
- Gifted children have the capacity over time to solve challenging problems and to create products valued and needed by a culture.
- Such children and adolescents need well-designed environments and opportunities to realize their full intellectual and creative potential.

**FOCUS 3** Identify four problems inherent in accurately

describing the characteristics of individuals who are gifted.

- Individuals who are gifted vary significantly on a variety of characteristics; they are not a homogeneous group.
- Because research on the characteristics of people who are gifted has been conducted with different population groups, the characteristics that have surfaced tend to represent the population studied rather than the gifted population as a whole.
- Many early studies of individuals who are gifted led to a stereotypical view of giftedness.
- Historically, studies on the characteristics of individuals who are gifted have not included adequate samples of females, minority or ethnic groups, or the poor.

**FOCUS 4** Identify three factors that appear to contribute significantly to the emergence of various forms of giftedness.

- Genetic endowment certainly contributes to giftedness.
- Environmental stimulation provided by parents, teachers, coaches, tutors, and others contributes significantly to the emergence of giftedness.
- The interaction of innate abilities with environmental influences and encouragement fosters the development and expression of giftedness.

**FOCUS 5** Indicate the range of assessment devices used to identify the various types of giftedness.

- Developmental checklists and scales
- Parent and teacher inventories
- Intelligence and achievement tests
- Creativity tests
- Other diverse observational information provided by parents,

grandparents, and other knowledgeable informants

**FOCUS 6** Identify eight strategies that are utilized to foster the development of children and adolescents who are gifted.

- Environmental stimulation provided by parents from infancy through adolescence.
- Differentiated education and specialized service delivery systems that provide enrichment activities and/or possibilities for acceleration. Examples include early entrance to kindergarten or school; grade skipping; early admission to college; honors programs at the high school and college levels; specialized schools in the performing and visual arts, math, and science; mentor programs with university professors and other talented individuals; and specialized counseling services.

**FOCUS 7** What are some of the social-emotional needs of students who are gifted?

- Understanding, appreciating, and valuing their own uniqueness as well as that of others
- Understanding the importance and the development of relationship skills
- Expanding and valuing their high-level sensitivity
- Gaining a realistic understanding of their own abilities and talents
- Identifying ways of nurturing and developing their own abilities and talents
- Adequately distinguishing between the pursuit of excellence and the pursuit of perfection
- Developing the behaviors associated with negotiation and compromise

**FOCUS 8** Identify four challenges that females face in dealing with their giftedness.

- Fear of appearing "unfeminine"

or unattractive when competing with males
- Competition between marital and career aspirations
- Stress induced by traditional cultural and societal expectations
- Self-imposed and/or culturally imposed restrictions related to educational and occupational choices

**FOCUS 9** Identify eight important elements of programs for gifted children who come from diverse backgrounds and who may live in poverty.

- The programs are staffed with skilled and competent teachers and other support personnel.
- The staff members work as a team.
- Teachers and others responsible for shaping the learning experience understand learning styles, students' interests, and how to build students' affective, cognitive, and ethical capacities.
- The programs maintain and encourage ethnic diversity, provide extracurricular cultural enrichment, offer counseling, foster parent support groups, and give children and youth access to significant models.
- The programs focus on students' strengths, not on their deficits.
- The programs help parents understand their key role in developing their children's talents and giftedness.
- The programs provide many opportunities for hands-on learning, activities that foster self-expression, and generous use of mentors and role models from the child's cultural or ethnic group.
- The programs are characterized by a team approach involving parents, teachers, mentors, and other family members.

## FURTHER READINGS

Castellano, J. A. (2002). *Reaching New Horizons.* Boston, MA: Allyn and Bacon.

*This book is particularly useful for educators and others interested in gifted students who are linguistically and culturally diverse. It is packed with information about the complexities and opportunities associated with educating these students.*

Colangelo, N., & Davis, G. A. (2003). *Handbook on Gifted Education.* Boston, MA: Allyn and Bacon.

*This graduate-level text explores the many and varied aspects of the education of gifted people. The contributing authors are all respected and eminently qualified scholars.*

Freeman, J. (2001). *Gifted Children Grown Up.* London: David Fulton Publishers.

*The book is the culmination of studies of gifted individuals over time (27 years). It is full of insights about their experiences with parents, teachers, and schooling and other aspects of their lives.*

Rogers, K.B. (2002). *Re-Forming Gifted Education: Matching the Program to the Child.* Scottsdale, AZ: Great Potential Press.

*This author carefully addresses issues related to planning and providing educational experiences tailored to the gifted child. The book is replete with valuable resources for teachers and parents.*

## WEB RESOURCES

### National Research Center on the Gifted and Talented

www.gifted.uconn.edu/nrcgt.html

This center is funded by the Jacob K. Javits Gifted and Talented Students Education Act. It represents a national array of researchers, practitioners, policymakers, and other individuals who are interested in promoting the development of gifted young people from preschool through postsecondary levels. Its website is loaded with resources for parents, teachers, and professionals interested in gifted education.

### Center for Talented Youth at John Hopkins University

www.jhu.edu/gifted/

This website describes the programs and opportunities offered through the center, which identifies academically talented students in grades 2 through 8 and provides distinctive educational programs through their first and second years of high school. This identification takes place through a talent search in which students are sought out because of their high national test scores in mathematics. The center also sponsors summer programs and conferences tailored to the special interests of gifted students.

### National Association for Gifted Children

www.nagc.org

This nonprofit organization is composed of parents, teachers, educators, and other professionals. It promotes programs, polices, and legislation that benefit gifted children and youth. This website provides valuable information for individuals who are interested in promoting educational and other support services for children and youth who are gifted, talented, or creative.

### Duke University Talent Identification Program

www.tip.duke.edu/

This website provides information for educational leaders who are interested in identifying and providing innovative programs for gifted children and youth. The site also offers valuable information about developing model programs for academically able children and youth.

### Center for Gifted Education Policy

www.apa.org/ed/cgep.html

This website promotes public awareness of gifted children and youth. It also provides crucial information about research and innovative programs for gifted children and youth. The website focuses on programs and initiatives for all kinds of giftedness, including academics, sports, and the performing arts.

## BUILDING YOUR PORTFOLIO

If you are thinking about a career in special education, you should know that many states use national standards developed by the Council for Exceptional Children (CEC) to assess a teacher candidate's knowledge and skills for working with students with disabilities. See a complete listing of the ten CEC Content Standards on the inside front cover of this text.

### CEC Content Standards Addressed in Chapter 18

1. Foundations
2. Development and Characteristics of Learners
3. Individual Learning Differences
5. Learning Environments and Social Interactions
7. Instructional Planning
8. Assessment

### Assess Your Knowledge of the CEC Standards Addressed in Chapter 18

Some states require that teacher candidates develop a portfolio of products that demonstrate mastery of the CEC content standards. To assist in the development of products for this portfolio, you may wish to complete the following activities.

• Complete a written test of the chapter's content.

*If your instructor requires a written test of your content knowledge for this chapter, keep a copy for your portfo-*

*lio. A practice test on the information covered in this chapter is available through the companion website (www.ablongman.com/hardman8e) and the Student Study Guide.*

• Respond to the application questions for the Case Study "Is Calvin Gifted?"

*Review the Case Study and respond in writing to the application questions. Keep a copy of the Case Study and your written response for your portfolio.*

• Complete the "Take a Stand" activity for the Debate Forum "What Would You Do with Jane?"

*Read the Debate Forum in this chapter and then visit the companion website to complete the activity "Take a Stand." Keep a copy of this activity for your portfolio.*

• Participate in a Community Service Learning Activity.

*Community service is a valuable way to enhance your learning experience. Visit our companion website for suggested community service learning activities that correspond to the information presented in this chapter. Develop a reflective journal of the service learning experience for your portfolio.*

## THEMES OF THE TIMES

Expand your knowledge of the concepts discussed in this chapter by reading current and historical articles from the *New York Times* by visiting the "Themes of the Times" section of the companion website: **www.ablongman.com/hardman8e.**

# Appendix: What Every Teacher Should Know About IDEA 2004

## Myrna Mandlawitz

MRM Associates, Legislative and Consulting Services

## Abbreviations Key

**AYP:** adequate yearly progress

**FAPE:** free appropriate public education

**HOUSSE:** High Objective Uniform State Standard of Education

**IAES:** interim alternative educational setting

**IDEA:** Individuals with Disabilities Education Act

**IEP:** individualized education program

**IFSP:** individualized family service plan

**LEA:** local educational agency (local school district)

**LRE:** least restrictive environment

**NCLB:** No Child Left Behind Act of 2001

**NIMAC:** National Instructional Materials Access Center

**NIMAS:** National Instructional Materials Accessibility Standard

**SEA:** State educational agency

**"Secretary":** United States Secretary of Education

## Table of Contents

# PART A: General Provisions

## Section 602: Definitions

Several new definitions have been added to the IDEA, reflecting the continuing evolution of the law and the desire to align the IDEA with the No Child Left Behind Act of 2001 (NCLB).

| IDEA '97 (P.L. 105-17) | IDEA '04 (P.L. 108-446) |
|---|---|
| *Sec. 602(1). "Assistive Technology Device."* Any item, equipment, or product used to increase, maintain, or improve functional capabilities. | *Sec. 602(1)(B). "Assistive Technology Device."* Adds that term does not include surgically implanted medical device or replacement of such a device. |

**"Assistive Technology Device."** This exception arose in part from a concern, heightened by several due process hearings, that school districts might be held responsible for provision of cochlear implants for children with hearing impairments.

| IDEA '97 (P.L. 105-17) | IDEA '04 (P.L. 108-446) |
|---|---|
| *Sec. 602. "Core Academic Subjects."* No comparable language in IDEA '97. | *Sec. 602(4). "Core Academic Subjects."* Adds NCLB definition (Sec. 9101) "Core Academic Subjects" are English, reading and language arts, mathematics, science, foreign languages, civics and government, economics, arts, history, and geography. |
| *Sec. 602. "Highly Qualified."* No comparable language in IDEA '97. | *Sec. 602(10). "Highly Qualified."*<br>1. Requirements for All Special Education Teachers:<br>  a. All special education teachers come under NCLB definition (Sec. 9101); *PLUS, special education teachers must*<br>  b. Have State special education certification OR have passed State licensing exam AND have license to teach special education;<br>  c. Have not had certification or licensure waived on emergency, temporary, or provisional basis; AND<br>  d. Have at least a bachelor's degree.<br>2. Special Education Teachers Teaching Students under Alternate Achievement Standards:<br>  Used for teachers teaching core academic subjects *only* to children assessed against alternate standards, as established under NCLB regulations.<br>  a. Must EITHER meet NCLB Highly Qualified requirements (Sec. 9101) for any teacher new or not new to the profession, OR<br>  b. Meet NCLB requirements for elementary teachers or middle or high school teachers with subject knowledge appropriate to the level of instruction being provided.<br>3. Special Education Teachers Teaching Multiple Subjects:<br>  Applicable to those teaching two or more core academic subjects *only* to children with disabilities.<br>  a. Must EITHER meet NCLB highly qualified requirements for any teacher new or not new to the profession; OR<br>  b. If not a new teacher, must demonstrate competence in all subjects taught, as under NCLB, which may include "high objective uniform State standard of evaluation" (HOUSSE) covering multiple subjects; OR<br>  c. If a new teacher who is highly qualified in math, language arts, or science, must demonstrate competence in other core subjects taught, as under NCLB, which may include a HOUSSE, *not later than 2 years after being hired.* |

4. This definition does not create a right of action by a single student or a class of students for failure of the teacher to be highly qualified.

5. Teachers deemed highly qualified under this provision are considered highly qualified for purposes of NCLB.

------------------------------------------------------------------------

**"Highly Qualified."** The addition of this definition to the IDEA is very significant. The NCLB definition of "highly qualified" refers to "any public elementary or secondary school teacher" and requires those teachers to meet this standard by the close of school year 2005–2006. Considerable debate has occurred since the passage of NCLB on whether special education teachers, who are not specifically mentioned in NCLB, were also required to meet the "highly qualified" provisions of that law. The debate was particularly intense because NCLB requires that new teachers teaching multiple core subjects, as defined in NCLB and now in the IDEA, have an academic major or advanced degree, or pass a competency exam in each subject area taught. Teachers not new to the profession under NCLB may demonstrate competency based on a "high objective uniform State standard of evaluation" (HOUSSE), which may involve multiple measures of teacher competency as established by the individual State.

Because middle or high school special education teachers working in a resource capacity provide assistance to students in the full range of academic subject areas, the standard for new teachers would have proven particularly difficult for most special education teachers to meet. Therefore, the IDEA allows special educators teaching multiple core subjects to (a) meet either the NCLB requirements for teachers new or not new to the profession; (b) meet the HOUSSE option; or, (c) for teachers already deemed highly qualified in math, language arts, or science, establish competence not later than two years after being hired in any other core areas taught.

According to the conference report accompanying the IDEA amendments (H. Rep. No. 108-77, Nov. 17, 2004, p. 171), special education teachers providing only consultative services to general education teachers should be considered "highly qualified" if they meet the requirements for "all special education teachers," as outlined above (Sec. 602(10)(a)). Consultative services do not include direct instruction in core academic subjects, but may include adjustments to the learning environment, modification of instructional methods, and curriculum adaptations.

---

*Sec. 602. "Homeless Children."* No comparable language in IDEA '97.

*Sec. 602(11). "Homeless Children."* Adds definition from McKinney-Vento Homeless Assistance Act (Sec. 725): Children who don't have a regular, adequate nighttime residence, including children (a) sharing others' housing due to loss of housing, economic hardship, or similar reason; living in motels, hotels, trailer parks, or campgrounds due to lack of alternative adequate accommodations; living in emergency or transitional shelters; abandoned in hospitals; or awaiting foster care placement; (b) whose primary nighttime residence is a public or private place not designed for or ordinarily used for regular sleeping accommodation; (c) living in cars, public spaces, abandoned buildings, substandard housing, bus or train stations, or similar settings; and, (d) who are migratory youth living in circumstances described in (a)–(c).

---

*Sec. 602. "Limited English Proficient."* No comparable language in IDEA '97.

*Sec. 602(18). "Limited English Proficient."* Adds definition from NCLB (Sec. 9101): An individual, aged 3–21, enrolled or preparing to enroll in an elementary or secondary school,

1. (a) who wasn't born in the U.S. or whose native language isn't English; (b) who is a Native American or Alaska Native, or native resident of the outlying areas and comes from an environment where a language other than English has significantly impacted level of English language proficiency; or (c) ho is migratory, with a native language other than English, from an environment where a language other than English is dominant; and

2. whose difficulties in speaking, reading, writing, or understanding English may be sufficient to deny the child (a) ability to meet proficient level of achievement on State

|  |  |
|---|---|
|  | assessments; (b) ability to successfully achieve in class where instruction is in English; or (c) opportunity to participate fully in society. |
| *Sec. 602. "Ward of the State."* No comparable language in IDEA '97. | *Sec. 602(36). "Ward of the State."* Adds new definition: A child who, as determined by State of residence, is a foster child, ward of the State, or in custody of a public child welfare agency. Does not include foster children whose foster parents meet IDEA "parent" definition. |

**"Homeless Children," "Limited English Proficient," and "Ward of the State."** These additions clarify that every child who is a "child with a disability" under the law must be provided special education and related services and receive the protections of the IDEA, regardless of socioeconomic, language, or other differences. While the spirit and intent of the law has always been that all children with disabilities needing special education and related services are located and served, the law has never specified these categories of children.

|  |  |
|---|---|
| *Sec. 602(19). "Parent."* Includes legal guardians and surrogate parents. | *Sec. 602(23). "Parent."* Adds "natural, adoptive, or foster parent"; guardian (but not the State if child is a ward of the State); or a person acting in place of a natural or adoptive parent with whom the child lives or who is legally responsible for the child. |
| *Sec. 602(22). "Related Services."* Transportation, and developmental, corrective, and supportive services. A number of specific services are mentioned, but the list is not intended to be exclusive. | *Sec. 602(26). "Related Services."* Adds "school nurse services" and "interpreting services." |
| *Sec. 602(30). "Transition Services."* Services designed to promote movement from school to postschool activities based on students' needs and taking into account preferences and interests. | *Sec. 602(34). "Transition Services."* Adds that services must be focused on improving academic and functional achievement, and that the student's strengths must also be taken into account. |
| *Sec. 602. "Universal Design."* No comparable language in IDEA '97. | *Sec. 602(35). "Universal Design."* Adds definition from the Assistive Technology Act of 1998 (Sec. 3): "A concept or philosophy for designing and delivering products and services that are usable by people with the widest possible range of functional capabilities, which include products and services that are directly usable (without requiring assistive technologies) and products and services that are made usable with assistive technologies." |

**"Universal Design."** With few exceptions, children with disabilities are expected to meet the same high academic standards as children without disabilities using the general education curriculum. The dearth of instructional materials and assessment tools that are accessible, valid, and appropriate for use with children with a broad range of disabilities has made this goal more difficult. The concept of universal design is incorporated throughout the amendments to the law. The law allows States to use federal funds to support technology with universal design principles, requires that States and school districts develop and administer assessments, to the extent feasible, using these principles; and, directs research toward incorporating universal design into the development of standards, assessments, curricula, and instructional methods.

## Sections 607–609: Requirements for Prescribing Regulations; State Administration; Paperwork Reduction

| IDEA '97 (P.L. 105-17) | IDEA '04 (P.L. 108-446) |
|---|---|
| **Sec. 607. Requirements for Prescribing Regulations.** Public shall have at least 90 days to comment on proposed regulations. Regulations may not be implemented in any way that lessens protections of the law. | **Sec. 607. Requirements for Prescribing Regulations.** Public comment period is changed to not less than 75 days. Regulations are limited only to those necessary to ensure compliance with requirements of the law. |
| **Sec. 608. State Administration.** No comparable language in IDEA '97. | **608. State Administration.** States must notify LEAs and the Secretary in writing of any State rules, regulations, or policies not required by federal law or regulation. States must minimize the number of such rules, regulations, or policies, and those that are issued must be designed to enable students to meet academic achievement standards. |
| **Sec. 609. Paperwork Reduction.** No comparable language in IDEA '97. | **Sec. 609. Paperwork Reduction.** Authorizes a 15-State pilot program authorizing waivers of Part B statutory or regulatory requirements to reduce "excessive paperwork and non-instructional time burdens" that do not improve students' educational or functional results. Requirements pertaining to civil rights or procedural safeguards may not be waived, and waivers may not affect the right to a free appropriate public education (FAPE). The Secretary will include information in an annual report to Congress on the effectiveness of waivers, including recommendations for broader implementation of waivers. |

# PART B: Assistance for Education of All Children with Disabilities

## Section 611: Allotment and Use of Funds; Authorization of Appropriations

| IDEA '97 (P.L. 105-17) | IDEA '04 (P.L. 108-446) |
|---|---|
| **Sec. 611. Technical Assistance.** No comparable language in IDEA '97. | **Sec. 611(c). Technical Assistance.** Secretary may reserve not more than $1/2$ of 1% of Part B funds for technical assistance to States under the monitoring and enforcement section (Sec. 616). |
| **Sec. 611(f). State-Level Activities.** IDEA '97 provides a list of required activities paid out of State activity funds from which States may choose. | **Sec. 611(e)(2)(B). Required Activities; (C). Authorized Activities.** States, as in IDEA '97, are required to use reserved funds for monitoring, enforcement, and complaint investigation, and to implement mediation. The law now includes a list of discretionary uses for State activity funds. These activities include: reducing paperwork; assisting LEAs to provide positive behavioral supports and interventions, and appropriate mental health services; improving classroom use of technology; developing transition programs, alternative programs for expelled students, and appropriate accommodations and alternate assessments; and, providing technical assistance to schools identified for improvement under NCLB. |

*Sec. 611. Local Educational Agency Risk Pool.* No comparable language in IDEA '97.

*Sec. 611(e)(3). Local Educational Agency Risk Pool.* States may opt to reserve annually 10% of funds reserved for State-level activities to establish a high-cost fund and to support innovative ways of cost sharing.

1. The State must develop a plan that
   a. includes a definition of a "high-need child with a disability," addresses the financial impact on LEAs' budgets, and ensures that the cost of ahigh-need child exceeds three times the State's average per pupil expenditure;
   b. establishes eligibility criteria for LEA participation, accounting for number and percentage of high-need children served; and,
   c. develops mechanism and schedule for annual distribution of funds.

2. Costs associated with high-need children are only those incurred in the provision of direct special education and related services. Funds may not be used for legal fees or costs otherwise paid by Medicaid.

3. This provision does not limit or condition the right to FAPE or to authorize an SEA or LEA to limit the amount spent on a child's education.

4. For States having existing pools, those funds may be used if the current program meets eligibility criteria developed under this provision.

---

*Sec. 611. Flexibility in Using Funds for Part C.* No comparable language in IDEA '97.

*Sec. 611(e)(7). Flexibility in Using Funds for Part C.* States eligible to receive preschool grants (Sec. 619) may develop and implement a policy, with the Part C lead agency, to provide Part C services to children who were previously served in that program and are now eligible for preschool services, until the children are eligible for kindergarten.

---

**Flexibility in Using Funds for Part C.**  The details of this program are found in Part C, Sec. 635(c). The Part C program, which serves infants and toddlers with disabilities ages birth through 2, and the Section 619 Preschool program, which serves children ages 3 through 5, operate under significantly different rules and regulations. The State designates a lead agency, not necessarily the State education agency, that is responsible for implementation of Part C. Services to the child and the family are delivered in the "natural environment," most often the home or childcare setting, by a variety of providers under an Individualized Family Service Plan (IFSP), and the lead agency may require that parents pay for certain services based on a sliding fee scale.

The Preschool program operates under the same rules and regulations as the Part B program serving students ages 5–21. Children receive a free appropriate public education (FAPE), based on an Individualized Education Program (IEP), provided in the least restrictive environment, which may be a public preschool program if available or a private program paid for by the school district.

Under this new provision, parents must receive an explanation of the differences between Part C and the Preschool program, including possible costs to the family. Parents would then have the option to keep their child in Part C or move him or her to the Preschool program.

---

*Sec. 611(j). Authorization of Appropriations.* For the purposes of carrying out Part B, serving children with disabilities ages 3–21, except for Sec. 619 (Preschool Grants), Congress authorizes such sums as may be necessary.

*Sec. 611(i). Authorization of Appropriations.* The law includes specific appropriations levels for federal Fiscal Years 2005–2011 and provides "such sums as may be necessary" for Fiscal Year 2012 and beyond.

---

**Authorization of Appropriations.**  Since its original enactment in 1975, federal aid to States for students with disabilities has been based on the number of students receiving services adjusted by a uniform percentage of the national average per pupil expenditure. The law states that the adjustment should be 40% of the per pupil expenditure; however, the current percentage paid to States by the federal government is slightly less than half that amount. Debate has also focused on whether or not the appropriations for IDEA should be mandatory, i.e., an entitlement program, or discretionary, in which congressional appropriations committees decide annually what, if any, increase in funding to provide. The new provision provides appropriations targets to reach the 40% "full funding" amount by 2011, but leaves discretion for reaching these targets to the annual congressional appropriations process.

## Section 612: State Eligibility

| IDEA '97 (P.L. 105-17) | IDEA '04 (P.L. 108-446) |
|---|---|
| **Sec. 612. State Flexibility.** No comparable language in IDEA '97. | **Sec. 612(a)(1)(C). State Flexibility.** States having a policy allowing Part C services for preschool-aged children (see Sec. 611(e)(7)) are not required to provide a free appropriate public education (FAPE) to children choosing to continue in Part C. |
| **Sec. 612(a)(3). Child Find.** States are required to identify, locate, and evaluate all children with disabilities, including private school students, regardless of the severity of their disabilities, who are in need of special education and related services. The law does not require that children be classified by disability, as long as they meet the definition of "child with a disability" (Sec. 602(3)). | **Sec. 612(a)(3). Child Find.** Adds that "homeless children" and "wards of the State" who may be children with disabilities in need of special education and related services must also be identified, located, and evaluated. |
| **Sec. 612(a)(10). Children in Private Schools.** Children enrolled by their parents in private schools are eligible for special education and related services. The amount spent for those services shall be equal to a proportionate amount of federal funds available under Part B. Services may be provided on premises of private and parochial schools. The LEA is not required to reimburse costs for parentally placed students, unless a court or hearing officer determines that the LEA did not provide FAPE to the student. | **Sec. 612(a)(10). Children in Private Schools.** Additions include:<br><br>1. State and local funds may supplement, but not supplant, the proportionate amount of federal funds that must be spent.<br><br>2. LEA must report to the State the number of children evaluated, determined eligible, and served under this provision.<br><br>3. Child find process must ensure equitable participation of parentally placed private school children and an accurate count of those children.<br><br>4. Costs of child find and evaluations may not be counted in determining whether the LEA has met its obligation under this provision.<br><br>5. The LEA must consult with representatives of the private school and the parents regarding the following: Child find and equitable participation; determination of proportionate amount of federal funds; how, when, and by whom services will be provided; and, provision of a written explanation of why the LEA chooses not to provide services to a child.<br><br>6. Private school may submit State complaint alleging that LEA did not engage in meaningful consultation or consider private school's views. |
| **Sec. 612(a)(13). Comprehensive System of Personnel Development.** State is required to develop a system to ensure an adequate supply of qualified special and regular education teachers and related services personnel to meet the State's needs. | **Comprehensive System of Personnel Development:** *was eliminated.* The State Personnel Development Grants (Part D, Subpart 1) incorporates much of what was previously included in this section. |

### Sec. 612(a)(15). Personnel Standards.

1. States must establish and maintain standards to ensure that personnel are appropriately and adequately prepared and trained. Standards must be consistent with any State-approved or recognized certification or licensure or other comparable requirements.

2. To the extent those standards are not based on the highest State requirements applicable to a specific profession or discipline, the State is taking steps to retrain or hire personnel that meet the highest requirements.

3. State standards shall allow appropriately trained and supervised paraprofessionals and assistants to assist in provision of services.

4. States may require LEAs to make ongoing good faith efforts to recruit and hire appropriately and adequately trained personnel, including where there are shortages, individuals who will meet the highest standard within three years.

### Sec. 612(a)(14). Personnel Qualifications. Throughout the law, the word *standards* has been replaced by the word *qualifications* in regard to personnel issues. The "highest requirement" language has been eliminated. Other changes include:

1. Qualifications established for related services personnel must ensure that those individuals meet any State-approved or State-recognized certification, licensure, registration, or other comparable requirements. Licensure or certification may not have been waived on an emergency, temporary, or provisional basis.

2. Special education teachers must be highly qualified by the NCLB deadline (not later than the end of the 2005–06 school year).

3. Language regarding three-year waiver to meet highest standard has been eliminated. Instead, the State must adopt a policy that requires LEAs to take "measurable steps to recruit, hire, train, and retain highly qualified personnel."

4. This provision does not create a right of action for the failure of a staff person to be highly qualified. However, parents may file a State complaint about staff qualifications.

---

**Personnel Qualifications.** In the conference report, the Conference Committee states its intention that SEAs establish "rigorous qualifications" (p. 192) for related services personnel. The Committee felt that SEAs needed greater flexibility and should consult with other State agencies, LEAs, and the professional organizations representing the service providers in establishing these standards.

---

### Sec. 612(a)(16). Performance Goals and Indicators. States must establish performance goals consistent with standards for students without disabilities. States must have performance indicators to assess progress toward meeting performance goals that, at a minimum, address performance on assessments and dropout and graduation rates.

### Sec. 612(a)(15). Performance Goals and Indictors. Additions include:

1. Performance goals must be the same as the State's definition of adequate yearly progress, including the State's objectives for progress by children with disabilities, as required under NCLB.

2. States report annually on progress toward meeting goals, which may include elements of the reports required under NCLB.

---

**Performance Goals and Indicators.** Performance goals for students with disabilities must conform to the State's definition of "adequate yearly progress" (AYP) under NCLB. AYP is a measure established by each State to demonstrate students' progress in meeting proficiency on assessments keyed to the State's academic achievement standards. Students with disabilities constitute a specific subgroup under NCLB, and data on those students' progress must be disaggregated and publicly reported.

---

### Sec. 612(a)(17). Participation in Assessments. Children with disabilities will be included in general State- and district-wide assessments, with appropriate accommodations.

1. State or LEA, as appropriate, develops guidelines for participation and develops and conducts alternate assessments.

2. State must report, with the same frequency as for children without disabilities, on the number of children with disabilities taking regular and alternate assessments and on the performance on those assessments.

### Sec. 612(a)(16) Participation in Assessments. Adds the following:

1. *All* children with disabilities participate in *all* assessments, with accommodations and alternate assessments as indicated on the IEP.

2. State, or, for district-wide assessments, the LEA guidelines must provide for alternate assessments aligned with the State's academic content and achievement standards. If the State has adopted alternate achievement standards, students working under those standards are assessed on those standards.

3. State must report on the number of students provided accommodations on regular assessments, the number taking alternate assessments based on alternate standards, and a comparison of performance of students with disabilities with all students, including students with disabilities, on those assessments.

4. State or LEA must, to the extent feasible, use universal design principles in developing and administering any assessments.

**Participation in Assessments.** Under NCLB, States may develop alternate achievement standards for students with significant cognitive disabilities, as defined by each State, as indicated on their IEPs. Students whose instruction is based on alternate achievement standards will take alternate assessments keyed to those standards. There is no limit on the number of students who may take alternate assessments based on alternate standards; however, a cap of up to 1% of those scores may be used in the AYP calculation.

| | |
|---|---|
| *Sec. 612(a)(21). State Advisory Panel.* State establishes advisory panel for purpose of providing policy guidance on special education and related services. Panel advises on unmet needs, evaluations, data reporting, and coordinating services and provides comments on proposed rules and regulations. | *Sec. 612(a)(21). State Advisory Panel.* The following new members have been added: an official responsible for carrying out the McKinney-Vento Homeless Assistance Act and a representative of the State child welfare agency responsible for foster care. |
| *Sec. 612(a)(22). Suspension and Expulsion Rates.* State examines data for significant discrepancies in rates of long-term suspensions and expulsions among LEAs in the State and compared to rates for students without disabilities. | *Sec. 612(a)(22). Suspension and Expulsion Rates.* Data must now be disaggregated by race and ethnicity. |
| *Sec. 612. Access to Instructional Materials.* No comparable language in IDEA '97. | *Sec. 612(a)(23). Access to Instructional Materials.* <br><br> 1. States must adopt the National Instructional Materials Accessibility Standard (NIMAS) to provide instructional materials to blind persons or those with disabilities in relation to print. <br><br> 2. States do not have to coordinate with the National Instructional Materials Access Center (NIMAC), but must assure that they will provide materials to blind or print-disabled individuals in a timely manner. <br><br> 3. If State coordinates with NIMAC, no later than two years after enactment of IDEA '04 the State must contract with publishers to provide electronic files of print instructional materials to NIMAC using the NIMAS or must buy materials in specialized formats. |
| *Sec. 612. Overidentification and Disproportionality.* No comparable language in IDEA '97. | *Sec. 612(a)(24). Overidentification and Disproportionality.* State adopts policies and procedures designed to prevent inappropriate identification or disproportionate representation by race and ethnicity of children as children with disabilities. |
| *Sec. 612. Prohibition on Mandatory Medication.* No comparable language in IDEA '97. | *Sec. 612(a)(25). Prohibition on Mandatory Medication.* <br><br> 1. State shall prohibit State and local education agency personnel from requiring a child to obtain a prescription for medications covered by the Controlled Substances Act as a condition of school attendance or receiving an evaluation or services. |

2. This provision shall not create a prohibition against teachers or other school personnel consulting or sharing classroom observations with parents regarding academic and functional performance, behavior, or the need for an evaluation for special education and related services.

## Section 613: Local Educational Agency Eligibility

***Sec. 613(a)(2)(C). Treatment of Federal Funds in Certain Fiscal Years.*** In any year in which the federal appropriation for Part B exceeds $4.1 billion, the LEA may treat as local funds up to 20% of federal funds it receives that exceed the amount received in the previous fiscal year.

***Sec. 613(a)(2)(C). Adjustment to Local Fiscal Effort in Certain Fiscal Years.*** The provision is changed as follows:

1. In any year in which the LEA's federal allocation exceeds the previous year's amount, the LEA may reduce its level of expenditures by not more than 50% of the amount of excess.

2. If the LEA chooses to reduce its level of expenditure, it must use an amount equal to the reduction for activities authorized under NCLB.

3. Funds spent by the LEA on "early intervening" (Sec. 613(f)) shall count toward the maximum amount the LEA may reduce.

***Sec. 613(a)(4). Permissive Use of Funds.*** LEA may use funds for services and aids that also benefit nondisabled students and for a coordinated service system.

***Sec. 613(a)(4). Permissive Use of Funds.*** Deletes Coordinated Services System, and adds the following permitted uses of funds:

1. Develop and implement coordinated, early intervention educational services system (Sec. 613(f));

2. Establish and implement cost- or risk-sharing funds, consortia, or cooperatives for high-cost special education and related services (Sec. 611(e)(3));

3. Purchase technology for record-keeping, data collection, and other case management activities.

***Sec. 613. Purchase of Instructional Materials.*** No comparable language in IDEA '97.

***Sec. 613(a)(6). Purchase of Instructional Materials.*** No later than two years after enactment of IDEA '04, LEAs opting to coordinate with NIMAC shall acquire materials in the same manner and under the same conditions as the State (Sec. 612(a)(23)).

***Sec. 613. Records Regarding Migratory Children with Disabilities.*** No comparable language in IDEA '97.

***Sec. 613(a)(9). Records Regarding Migratory Children with Disabilities.*** LEA works with the Secretary under NCLB (Sec. 1308) to provide among States an electronic exchange of health and educational information on migratory children.

***Sec. 613(f). Coordinated Services System.*** LEAs may use up to 5% of federal funds annually to implement a system to improve results for all children, including children with disabilities. Activities allowed under this provision include developing strategies that promote accountability for results, service coordination and case management, developing interagency financing strategies, and interagency personnel development for personnel working on coordinated services.

***Coordinated Services System.*** *Was eliminated.*

| | |
|---|---|
| **Sec. 613. Early Intervening Services.** No comparable language in IDEA '97. | **Sec. 613(f). Early Intervening Services.**<br><br>1. An LEA may use up to 15% of its federal allotment annually, in combination with other funds, to develop and implement coordinated early intervention services for students, grades K–12 (focusing on K–3), who have not been identified as needing special education and related services, but who need extra academic and behavioral support to succeed in the general education environment.<br><br>2. Activities may include professional development to deliver scientifically based academic and behavioral interventions, and provision of educational and behavioral evaluations, services, and supports.<br><br>3. This provision neither limits nor creates a right to FAPE.<br><br>4. LEA will report annually to the State on the number of students served for two years under this provision, and the number who subsequently receive special education and related services.<br><br>5. These funds may be used for services aligned with NCLB, if funds are used to supplement and not supplant NCLB funds. |

**Early Intervening Services.** This provision specifically targets at-risk general education students and has generated some controversy, since IDEA funds will be used for students who are not identified as needing special education and related services. A number of school districts already use systems whereby struggling students receive classroom interventions of varying levels of intensity over a period of time. If students are not successful after a series of these interventions, they may be referred for evaluation for special education and related services.

LEAs are required to report on students served in this program for two years to determine if this program reduces the number of referrals for special education and related services. The two-year period applies to the two years after the child has received these services. (Conf. Report, p. 199.)

| | |
|---|---|
| **Sec. 613(g). School-Based Improvement Plan.** LEAs may use federal funds to permit schools to implement school-based improvement plans to improve educational and transitional results for children with and without disabilities. | **School-Based Improvement Plan.** *Was eliminated.* |
| **Sec. 613. State Agency Flexibility.** No comparable language in IDEA '97. | **Sec. 613(j). State Agency Flexibility.**<br><br>1. In any year in which the State's Part B allotment exceeds the amount received the previous year, and, if the State in school year 2003–04 or any subsequent school year pays or reimburses all LEAs for 100% of the nonfederal share of special education and related services, the SEA may reduce the level of expenditures from State sources by not more than 50% of the amount of excess.<br><br>2. If the Secretary determines that the State cannot meet the requirements of the law and needs assistance or intervention under Sec. 616, the Secretary shall prohibit the State from using this authority.<br><br>3. If the State uses this authority, the SEA shall use funds from State sources in an amount equal to the reduction to support activities authorized under NCLB or to support need-based or teacher higher education programs. |

# Section 614: Evaluations, Eligibility Determinations, Individualized Education Programs, and Educational Placements

### IDEA '97 (P.L. 105-17)

***Sec. 614(a). Initial Evaluation and Reevaluation.***

1. Initial Evaluation:
   a. SEA or LEA shall conduct an initial evaluation to determine eligibility for services and educational needs.
   b. LEA must obtain parents' informed consent before conducting evaluation, and consent shall not be construed as consent for placement.
   c. If parents refuse consent, LEA may pursue evaluation through mediation and due process procedures.

2. Reevaluation:
   a. LEA shall conduct reevaluation if conditions warrant or if parents or child's teacher requests such, but at least once every 3 years.
   b. Parents' informed consent should be secured prior to reevaluation; however, informed consent is not necessary if the LEA can demonstrate that reasonable measures were taken to obtain consent and parents did not respond.

### IDEA '04 (P.L. 108-446)

***Sec. 614(a)(1)(B). Request for Initial Evaluation.*** Changes include:

1. Initial Evaluation:
   a. Either parents or the SEA, other state agency or LEA may request an initial evaluation.
   b. Eligibility determination must be made within 60 days of receiving parental consent for evaluation, or, if the State has an established time frame for evaluation, that time frame may be used.
   c. The time frame does not apply
      if (1) the child enrolls after the relevant time frame has begun and before the eligibility determination is made by the child's previous LEA, but only if the new LEA is making sufficient progress to ensure prompt completion of the evaluation, and the parent and the new LEA agree to a specific time for completion of the evaluation.
      (2) the parent repeatedly fails or refuses to produce the child for evaluation.

2. Parental Consent for Services:
   a. Agency responsible for providing FAPE shall seek to obtain parents' informed consent before providing special education and related services.
   b. If parents refuse to provide consent for services, LEA shall not provide services by utilizing the due process procedures
   c. LEA shall not be considered to be in violation of the requirement to provide FAPE if parents refuse to consent or refuse to respond to request for consent, nor shall LEA be required to convene an IEP meeting or develop an IEP.
   d. Consent for Wards of State:
      (1) If the child is a ward of the State and not residing with parents, agency shall make reasonable efforts to obtain parents' informed consent for initial evaluation.
      (2) Agency shall not be required to obtain parents' informed consent for initial evaluation if, despite reasonable efforts, agency cannot find the parent, parents' rights have been terminated, or the right to make educational decisions has been assigned by a court to another individual.

3. Screening of a student by a teacher or specialist to determine instructional strategies shall not be considered evaluation for eligibility for special education and related services.

4. Reevaluation:
   a. LEA shall ensure reevaluation if it determines that educational or related needs, including improved academic and functional performance, warrant.
   b. Reevaluation shall occur not more often than once a year, unless parent and LEA agree otherwise, but should occur at least once every three years, unless parent and LEA agree that reevaluation is not necessary.

**Initial Evaluation and Reevaluation.** The law clarifies that both parents and agency personnel may request an initial evaluation and establishes a time frame within which the evaluation must be completed. The law also prohibits school districts from providing services without parental consent. In the past, school districts could use the due process procedures to provide services even without parental consent, but the new provisions bar districts from using those procedures for this purpose.

## IDEA '97 (P.L. 105-17)

### Sec. 614(b). Evaluation Procedures.

1. LEA shall provide notice to parents describing any evaluation procedures to be conducted.

2. LEA shall use a variety of assessment tools, including information provided by parents; shall not use any single procedure to make determination of eligibility; and, shall use technically sound instruments to assess cognitive, behavioral, physical, and developmental factors.

3. Other requirements
   a. Evaluation materials must be selected and administered so as not to be racially or culturally discriminatory.
   b. Tests must be administered in the child's native language or other mode of communication, unless not feasible to do so.
   c. Child must be assessed in all areas of suspected disability.
   d. Assessments must provide information to determine educational needs.

4. A team of qualified professionals and the parents will determine if the child meets eligibility requirements.

5. Eligibility cannot be determined based on lack of reading or math instruction or based on limited English proficiency.

6. If an IEP team determines that no additional data are needed to determine continued eligibility, LEA must notify parents of that determination and of the parents' right to request an assessment, and shall not be required to conduct an assessment unless parents so request.

7. LEA shall evaluate the child before determining that the child is no longer a child with a disability.

## IDEA '04 (P.L. 108-446)

### Sec. 614(b). Evaluation Procedures. Changes and additions include:

1. Conduct of Evaluation:
   a. Assessments must be provided and administered in "the language and form most likely to yield accurate information on what the child knows and can do academically, developmentally, and functionally. . . ."
   b. Assessments of a child who transfers to another school district during the school year are coordinated between prior and subsequent schools for expeditious completion of evaluation.
   c. Child will not be determined a "child with a disability" if the determining factor is "lack of appropriate instruction in reading, including in the essential components of reading instruction" (as defined in NCLB, Sec. 1208(3)).

2. Specific Learning Disabilities:
   a. When determining if a child has a specific learning disability, the "LEA shall not be required to take into consideration whether [the] child has a severe discrepancy between achievement and intellectual ability in oral expression, listening comprehension, written expression, basic reading skill, reading comprehension, mathematical calculation, or mathematical reasoning."
   b. In making this determination, LEA may use "a process that determines if the child responds to scientific, research-based intervention" as a part of the regular special education evaluation procedures.

3. Evaluation before change in eligibility:
   a. Evaluation is not required before eligibility is terminated due to graduation with a regular diploma or to exceeding the age requirement for provision of FAPE under State law.
   b. For a child whose eligibility ends due to graduation with regular diploma or exceeding the age requirement, the LEA shall provide a summary of the child's academic achievement and functional performance, including recommendations on how to assist the child in meeting postsecondary goals.

**Evaluation Procedures/Specific Learning Disabilities.** The IQ-discrepancy model has always been quite controversial, particularly in recent years, since over 50% of all students with disabilities receiving services under the IDEA are identified as having specific learning disabilities. The model uses a severe discrepancy between the student's intellectual ability, as measured by an IQ test, and actual achievement and performance as the primary indicator of a learning disability.

The controversy has arisen for several reasons. First, despite the fact that the law has never required the use of an IQ-discrepancy model and, in fact, requires the use of a variety of assessment tools and strategies to make a determination of eligibility under any disability category, some school districts have adopted this model as the sole criterion for determining specific learning disabilities. Second, a broad range of researchers and advocates believe that using this model as the sole criterion has resulted in over- and misidentification of learning disabilities and does not account for other possible factors resulting in academic failure, such as poor instruction or lack of appropriate interventions.

These provisions clarify that school districts do not have to find a severe discrepancy between ability and achievement to determine a child eligible for special education and related services under the category of specific learning disabilities. In addition, the law allows school districts to try research-based interventions in the general education setting as part of the evaluation process. If these interventions result in academic improvement, school personnel should consider whether or not the child has a true learning disability or his or her academic difficulties are due to lack of proper instruction or other factors.

## IDEA '97 (P.L. 105-17)

### Sec. 614(d)(1)(A). Individualized Education Programs.
The Individualized Education Program (IEP) includes statements of:

1. Present levels of educational performance, including how the disability affects involvement and progress in the general curriculum, or for preschoolers, how disability affects participation in appropriate activities.
2. Annual goals and short-term objectives.
3. Special education and related services and supplementary aids and services needed to advance toward annual goals and to be involved and make progress in the general curriculum.
4. The extent to which the child will not participate in the regular classroom.
5. Modifications needed to participate in assessments, and if an assessment is not appropriate, how the child will be assessed.
6. Frequency and location of services and modifications.
7. Transition service needs, beginning at age 14, and, at age 16, transition services, including interagency responsibilities.
8. Information regarding transfer of rights at the age of majority.
9. How child's progress will be measured and how parents will be informed.

## IDEA '04 (P.L. 108-446)

### Sec. 614(d)(1)(A). Individualized Education Programs.
**Deleted**

1. **Benchmark**s or short-term objectives: Retained only for children who take alternate assessments aligned to alternate achievement standards.
2. Transition requirement at age 14.

**Added**

IEP must include a statement, beginning not later than the first IEP in effect when the student is 16 and updated annually, of "appropriate measurable postsecondary goals based on age appropriate transition assessments related to training, education, employment, and where appropriate, independent skills." Will also include transition services, including courses, needed to assist in reaching goals, contained previously in the age-14-transition requirement.

---

### Sec. 614(d). IEP Team Attendance; IEP Team Transition; Meetings. No comparable language in IDEA '97.

### Sec. 614(d)(1)(C), (D); 614(3)(D)–(F). IEP Team Attendance, IEP Team Transition; Meetings.

1. IEP team attendance:
   a. A team member is not required to attend a meeting if parents and LEA agree that the member's attendance is not necessary because the member's curriculum area or related service will not be discussed.
   b. Member may be excused from attendance when his or her curriculum area or related service is being discussed if parents and LEA consent, and member submits written input to parents and team before the meeting.
   c. Parents' agreement and consent under these sections must be in writing.

2. IEP team transition:
   For child previously served under Part C, at parents' request, Part C service coordinator or other Part C representatives shall be invited to the initial IEP meeting to assist in the smooth transition of services.

3. Meetings:
   a. Parents and LEA may agree not to convene an IEP meeting to make changes that are needed after the annual IEP meeting, but instead may develop a written document to amend or modify the current IEP.

| IDEA '97 (P.L. 105-17) | IDEA '04 (P.L. 108-446) |
|---|---|

b. LEA shall encourage consolidation of reevaluation and other IEP meetings.

c. Changes to the IEP may be made either by the entire team, or by amending rather than redrafting the entire IEP. Parents may request a revised copy with amendments incorporated.

d. For IEP and placement meetings and administrative matters under the Procedural Safeguards section (sec. 615), parents and LEA may agree to use alternative means of meeting participation, e.g., video-conferences or conference calls.

---

**IEP Team Transition.** Allowing parents to have a Part C representative at an initial IEP meeting may provide a smoother transition for children moving into the Preschool program. The Part C and Preschool programs differ in the types of services provided, as well as duration, frequency, and location of services. Program representatives should help parents understand these changes as an IEP is developed.

---

**Sec. 614(d). Program for Children Who Transfer School Districts.** No comparable language in IDEA '97.

**Sec. 614(d)(2)(C). Program for Children Who Transfer School Districts.**

1. Transfer within the same State:
If a child with an IEP in effect transfers to another school district within the State during the school year, the new LEA shall provide FAPE, including services comparable to the previous IEP, in consultation with parents, until new LEA adopts the previous IEP or develops and implements a new IEP.

2. Transfer outside State:
If a child with an IEP in effect transfers to a school in another state during the school year, the new LEA shall provide FAPE, including services comparable to the previous IEP, in consultation with parents, until new LEA conducts an evaluation, if deemed necessary, and develops a new IEP.

3. Transmittal of Records:
Child's new school shall take reasonable steps to promptly obtain records, including the IEP and other documents relating to the provision of special education and related services. The previous school shall take reasonable steps to respond promptly to such request.

---

**Sec. 614(d). Multiyear IEP Demonstration.** No comparable language in IDEA '97.

**Sec. 614(d)(5). Multiyear IEP Demonstration.**

1. Authorizes 15-State pilot program for an optional multi-year (not to exceed three years) IEP. Secretary will report to Congress within two years on effectiveness of the pilot and provide any recommendations for broader implementation.

2. Program must be optional to parents, and parents must provide informed consent before multiyear IEP is developed.

3. The IEP must include:
a. Measurable goals to enable the child to make progress in the general education curriculum and meet other needs that coincide with natural transition points (preschool to elementary; elementary to middle; middle to secondary; secondary to postsecondary, but in no case longer than three years); and,

|  |  |

**IDEA '04 (P.L. 108-446)**

b. Measurable annual goals for determining progress toward meeting academic goals.

4. Program must include process for review and revision of IEPs, including:
   a. Review at natural transition points;
   b. In years other than natural transition points, an annual review to determine current levels of progress and whether goals are being met, and a requirement to amend IEP, as appropriate, to allow continued progress toward goals;
   c. Requirement, if team determines that child isn't making sufficient progress toward meeting goals, that LEA ensures a more thorough review of the IEP within 30 days; and,
   d. At parents' request, requirement that the team conduct a review of the IEP rather than or subsequent to an annual review.

**Multiyear IEP.** This pilot program attempts to address excessive paperwork burdens by streamlining the number of IEP meetings and revisions to the document. Districts and parents will most likely find that a multiyear IEP is more appropriate for children with mild to moderate disabilities, rather than those who receive multiple services that may require more frequent review of the IEP.

## Section 615: Procedural Safeguards and Discipline Provisions

**IDEA '97 (P.L. 105-17)**

*Sec. 615(b). Procedural Safeguards — Types of Procedures.* The law requires the following:

1. Opportunity for parents to examine all records; to participate in meetings regarding identification, evaluation, and placement, and provision of FAPE; and, to have an independent evaluation;
2. Protection of child's rights when LEA, after reasonable efforts, cannot locate parents;
3. Written prior notice to parents when LEA proposes to initiate or change or refuses to initiate or change identification, evaluation, or placement, or provision of FAPE;
4. Assurance that written prior notice fully informs parents, in native language unless not feasible, of all safeguards;
5. Opportunity for parents to present complaints;
6. Opportunity for mediation;
7. Provision of notice regarding a complaint to the SEA or LEA by parents or their attorney that includes (a) child's name, address, and school, (b) description of and facts related to the problem, and (c) proposed resolution to the problem; and,
8. Development of model form by SEA to assist parents in filing complaints.

**IDEA '04 (P.L. 108-446)**

*Sec. 615(b). Types of Procedures.* Changes and additions include:

1. Regarding surrogates making educational decisions:
   a. In the case of a ward of the State, judge overseeing child's care may appoint a surrogate.
   b. LEA appoints a surrogate for unaccompanied homeless youth.
   c. State shall make reasonable efforts to ensure appointment of surrogate within 30 days after determination of need.
2. "Any party" may present a complaint that alleges a violation occurring not more than two years before the party knew or should have known about the alleged action that is the basis of the complaint. If there is already a State time limitation for presenting complaints, that time line may be used.
3. State must establish procedures that require either a party or that party's attorney to provide *due process complaint notice* (See Sec. 615(c)(2) below) to the other party and forward a copy of the notice to the SEA. Notice must include (a) child's name, address, and school the child attends; (b) for homeless child, available contact information and school the child attends; (c) description of and facts related to the problem; and (d) proposed resolution. May not have a due process hearing until the party or party's attorney files the due process complaint notice.
4. State must develop model due process complaint notice.

**Types of Procedures.** The law now establishes that both parents and local school districts may file complaints. The IDEA '97 regulations stated that "a parent or a public agency may initiate a hearing" (34 CFR Sec. 300.507); however, the statutory language was not as clear. Also, the law includes a statute of limitations for filing complaints. The previous law did not limit the amount of time that could elapse between the alleged violation and bringing a complaint. This sometimes resulted in complaints being raised that allegedly occurred a number of years earlier, making fact-finding more difficult and possibly resulting in orders for compensatory education long after the violation had been cured or the student had exited the school system. The statute of limitations may also serve to reduce the number of hearings and to encourage attempts to resolve complaints outside the hearing process through mediation or other alternative dispute resolution mechanisms.

# IDEA '97 (P.L. 105-17)

### Sec. 615(c), (d). Content of Prior Written Notice; Procedural Safeguards Notice.

1. Prior written notice must include (a) the action proposed or refused by the LEA; (b) why the LEA proposed or refused to take action; (c) other actions considered and why rejected; and (d) other relevant factors. It must also include a statement that includes (a) that the parents have protections under the law's procedural safeguards, (b) how a copy may be obtained, and (c) sources where parents may obtain assistance to understand these protections.

2. Procedural Safeguards Notice:
   a. Must be given to parents at least at initial referral for evaluation, at each notification of an IEP meeting and reevaluation, and when complaints are filed.
   b. Notice must include a full explanation of the procedural safeguards, written in family's native language, if feasible, and in easily understandable language.
   c. Notice covers regulations related to independent evaluation; prior written notice; parental consent; access to educational records; opportunity to present complaints; child's placement during due process proceedings; procedures for a child in an interim alternative educational setting; requirements for placement of the child by parents in a private school at public expense; mediation; due process hearings; appeals; civil actions; and, attorneys' fees.

# IDEA '04 (P.L. 108-446)

### Sec. 615(c), (d). Notification Requirements; Procedural Safeguards Notice.

1. No changes in Prior Written Notice requirements.

2. Due Process Complaint Notice (new notice requirement):
   a. Notice is deemed sufficient unless receiving party gives written notification to the hearing officer (within 15 days of receiving complaint) and the other party that the receiving party believes the notice hasn't met the requirements of Sec. 615(b).
   (1) Within five days of receipt of notification, hearing officer must make a determination as to whether the notice meets requirements.
   (2) A party may amend a complaint notice only if (a) the other party gives written consent to an amendment and has an opportunity to resolve the complaint through the "resolution session" (Sec. 615(f)); or, (b) the hearing officer grants permission no later than five days before due process hearing occurs.
   b. LEA's response to complaint:
   (1) If LEA hasn't sent prior written notice to parents on a subject in the complaint notice, LEA must, within ten days of receiving the complaint, send a response to parents that includes (a) why the LEA proposed or refused to take action raised in the complaint; (b) other options that were considered and why they were rejected; each evaluation procedure, assessment, record or records used by the agency as basis for action; and (c) other relevant factors.
   (2) LEA's response does not preclude it from asserting that parents' due process complaint notice was insufficient.
   c. Other party's response: Noncomplaining party must, within ten days of receiving complaint, send response that specifically addresses issues raised.
   d. Parents are not precluded from filing a separate due process complaint on issues separate from the complaint already filed.

3. Procedural Safeguards Notice:
   a. Notice shall be given to parents only once a year, except that it shall also be given at (1) initial referral or parental request for evaluation; (2) first filing of a complaint; and, (3) parents' request.
   b. LEA may put notice on web site.
   c. Notice requirements are same as IDEA '97, except that they must include regulations related to time line for filing and LEA's opportunity to resolve complaints, and time line for filing civil actions.

| IDEA '97 (P.L. 105-17) | IDEA '04 (P.L. 108-446) |
|---|---|

<table>
<tr><td></td><td>4. Parents may opt to receive notices by email, if that option is available.</td></tr>
</table>

| | |
|---|---|
| **Sec. 615(e). Mediation.** | **Sec. 615(e). Mediation.** Procedures are the same, with the following addition: If a resolution is reached through the mediation, the parties shall execute a "legally binding agreement" signed by parents and an authorized agency representative. Agreement is enforceable in State court or U.S. district court. |
| 1. Mediation must be voluntary; may not be used to deny or delay parents' right to a hearing or other rights under the law; must be conducted by qualified impartial mediator from the State's list; and agreement must be in writing. | |
| 2. LEA or SEA may have procedures to require parents who do not choose mediation to meet with a disinterested party to urge its use and explain the benefits of mediation. | |
| 3. Mediation discussions are confidential and may not be used in subsequent hearings or civil proceedings. | |

| | |
|---|---|
| **Sec. 615(f). Impartial Due Process Hearings.** | **Sec. 615(f). Impartial Due Process Hearing.** |
| 1. Whenever a complaint is received, parents shall have the opportunity for a hearing. | 1. Resolution Session:<br>Before opportunity for a hearing and within 15 days of receiving notice of a complaint, LEA shall convene a meeting with parents and relevant members of the IEP team with specific knowledge of the facts of the complaint. During this meeting, parents discuss the issues in the complaint, and the LEA has an opportunity to resolve those issues. |
| 2. SEA or LEA personnel involved in the child's education shall not conduct the hearing. | a. Parents and LEA may agree in writing to waive this meeting or to use the mediation process. |
| 3. At least five business days before a hearing, each party must disclose all evaluations and recommendations that each intends to use at the hearing. Failure to disclose may result in a bar to introduction at the hearing without the other party's consent. | b. Meeting must include LEA representative with decision-making authority, and it may not include LEA's attorney, unless parents bring an attorney. |
| | c. If LEA hasn't resolved the complaint to parents' satisfaction within 30 days of receipt of complaint, a hearing may occur and all applicable time lines for a hearing will begin to run. |
| | d. If resolution is reached, parties shall execute a legally binding agreement signed by the parents and authorized agency representative, which is enforceable in State court or U.S. district court. Either party may void the agreement within three business days of agreement's execution. |
| | 2. Limitations on Hearing: |
| | a. A hearing officer (1) shall not be an SEA or LEA employee involved in the child's education or care; (2) shall not have professional interest that would conflict with objectivity; (3) shall have knowledge and understanding of the law and regulations and legal interpretations; and (4) shall have the ability to conduct hearings under standard legal practice. |
| | b. Party requesting a hearing shall not be allowed to raise issues at hearing not previously raised in the due process complaint notice. |
| | c. Parent or LEA shall request hearing within two years of when the party "knew or should have known about the alleged action" on which the complaint is based.<br>(1) If State has a time limitation for requesting hearing, that time line is used.<br>(2) Time line does not apply to parents if they were prevented from requesting a hearing due to (a) specific misrepresentations by the LEA that it had resolved the issue in the complaint; or (b) LEA withheld information that it was required to divulge. |

3. Hearing officer decisions:
   a. Such decisions must be made on substantive grounds based on a determination of whether child received FAPE.
   b. Where procedural violations are alleged, hearing officer may find that child did not receive FAPE only if procedural "inadequacies"(1) impeded child's right to FAPE; (2) "significantly impeded" parents' opportunity to participate in decision-making process regarding provision of FAPE; or, (3) caused deprivation of educational benefits.
   (3) Hearing officer is not precluded from ordering LEA to comply with procedural requirements.
   (4) This section shall not be construed to affect parents' right to file a complaint with the SEA.

---

**Impartial Due Process Hearing.** The resolution session is an attempt to reduce the number of due process hearings and to encourage less adversarial means of dispute resolution. Hearing officer requirements have been moved from the regulations to statute.

This section also clarifies that complaints based solely on procedural violations will be successful only if those violations are significant. This addition addresses a continuing concern that the IDEA has focused too much on process and not enough on improving educational outcomes for students with disabilities. Requiring that the basis of complaints be on substantive rather than procedural grounds reinforces the focus on results.

---

*Sec. 615(i). Administrative Procedures.*

1. Civil Action: Any party aggrieved by a hearing officer's decision or by a civil action, or who does not have a right to an administrative appeal shall have the right to bring a civil action.

2. Attorneys' Fees: The court, in its discretion, may award reasonable attorneys' fees to parents who are the prevailing party.

*Sec. 615(i). Administrative Procedures.* Changes and additions include:

1. Civil Action: A party bringing a civil action shall have 90 days from the date of the hearing officer's decision to bring an action, or, if the State has an explicit time line, shall follow the State law time line.

2. Attorneys' Fees:
   a. In addition to award of fees to parents, court may award fees to:
   (1) Prevailing SEA or LEA against parents' attorney (a) who files complaint or other cause of action that is frivolous, unreasonable, or without foundation; or, (b) who continues to litigate after litigation clearly became frivolous, unreasonable, or without foundation.
   (2) Prevailing SEA or LEA against parents' attorney *or against parent* if complaint or subsequent cause of action was presented for "any improper purpose," e.g., to harass, cause unnecessary delay, or needlessly increase cost of litigation.
   b. Attorneys' fees are not available for prehearing "resolution session."
   c. Fees may be reduced if parent *or parents' attorney* unreasonably protracted final resolution of controversy.

---

**Administrative Procedures.** This section includes another new time line. Also, it provides for attorneys' fees under certain circumstances to a school district that is a prevailing party. Award of attorneys' fees to the school district under the stated circumstances comports with provisions under other civil rights laws.

## Sec. 615(k). Placement in Alternative Educational Setting.

1. School personnel may order a change in placement to an appropriate interim alternative educational setting (IAES), another setting, or suspension for not more than ten school days, and to an IAES for not more than 45 days for violations involving weapons or drugs.

2. LEA must conduct a functional behavioral assessment and develop a behavioral intervention plan or review an existing plan not later than 10 days after disciplinary action is taken.

3. Hearing officers may order change in placement to IAES for not more than 45 days if they decide that keeping the student in the current placement is substantially likely to result in injury to the child or others. That decision is based on determination of appropriateness of placement, whether the LEA made reasonable efforts to minimize harm in the placement, and whether the IAES meets legal requirements of this section.

4. IAES must be a setting where the child can continue to participate in the general curriculum and receive IEP services and services to address the behavior.

5. Manifestation Determination: The IEP team must determine whether there is a connection between the disability and the behavior. It may determine that behavior was not a manifestation of the disability only if the team considers all relevant information and determines that (a) placement and IEP were appropriate, (b) disability did not impair child's ability to understand impact and consequences of behavior, and (c) disability did not impair ability to control the behavior.
   a. If behavior is not a manifestation of the disability, the child may be disciplined under a general conduct code.
   b. If parents disagree with manifestation determination, they may request and will receive an expedited hearing.

6. For a child in IAES, that placement is where the child remains, for the allowable time of 45 days, during a hearing. School personnel may decide that it is too dangerous to return child to original placement at the end of the 45-day period and may request an expedited hearing to maintain the child in the IAES until a decision is reached.

7. Children not yet determined to be eligible for special education and related services that violate the conduct code may assert protections of IDEA if LEA had "knowledge" that child was "child with a disability" before the incident occurred.

8. Agency may report crime to appropriate authorities and must ensure that special education and disciplinary records are transmitted to authorities.

## Sec. 615(k). Placement in Alternative Educational Setting.
Changes and additions include:

1. Authority of School Personnel:
   a. Personnel may consider unique circumstances on case-by-case basis when deciding whether to order change in placement for violation of student conduct code.
   b. May remove child who *violates student conduct code* from current placement to IAES, another setting, or suspension for not more than ten schooldays to the extent that such alternatives are applied to a child without disabilities.
   c. If they seek to order change in placement exceeding ten schooldays and behavior is *not* a manifestation of the disability, they may apply same disciplinary action applicable to children without disabilities "in the same manner and for the same duration," although it may be in an IAES.
   d. Continuation of Services: Whether or not behavior is a manifestation of disability, a child removed from current placement shall continue to receive educational services enabling progress toward IEP goals and participation in general education curriculum, and shall receive, as appropriate, a functional behavioral assessment and behavioral intervention services and modifications.
   e. Manifestation Determination:
      (1) Except for short-term removals, within ten schooldays of decision to change placement, LEA, parents, and relevant IEP team members (as determined by LEA and parents) shall review all relevant information (including IEP, teacher observations, and relevant information provided by parents) to determine if:
         (a) the conduct was "caused by, or had a direct and substantial relationship to" child's disability; or,
         (b) the conduct was a "direct result of LEA's failure to implement the IEP."
      (2) If either instance above applies, the conduct is a manifestation of the disability, and the IEP team shall:
         (a) conduct a functional behavioral assessment, if one was not done prior to the incident, and implement a behavioral intervention plan or review previous plan for modification, as needed; and,
         (b) except when violations involve weapons, drugs, or serious bodily injury, return child to previous placement, unless parents and LEA agree to a change in placement as part of modification of behavioral intervention plan.
   f. Special Circumstances: Child may be removed to IAES for not more than 45 days, *without regard to whether or not behavior is a manifestation of the disability,* for violations involving weapons, drugs, or infliction of serious bodily injury.

2. Appeal:
   a. Either parents or LEA may request an appeal. SEA or LEA must arrange for an expedited hearing, which must occur within 20 schooldays of date the hearing is requested and must result in a decision within ten schooldays after hearing.

b. During appeal, child remains in IAES pending decision or until expiration of time period allowed for students without disabilities, whichever occurs first, unless parents and LEA agree otherwise.

c. In reaching a decision, the hearing officer may order a change in placement to (1) placement from which child was removed or (2) an IAES for not more than 45 schooldays if he or she determines that there is substantial likelihood in current placement of injury to child or others.

3. Protections for Children Not Yet Eligible for IDEA Services: This section is basically the same as IDEA '97, with the following changes:

a. LEA is deemed to have knowledge that the child is a child with a disability if (1) parents expressed concern in writing to *supervisory or administrative* personnel or *a teacher of the child* that child needs services; or, (2) teacher or other LEA personnel expressed "specific concerns about a pattern of behavior . . . directly" to the special education director or other "supervisory" personnel.

b. LEA is not deemed to have knowledge if parent has not allowed an evaluation or has refused services, or child has been evaluated and was determined not to be eligible.

**Placement in Alternative Educational Setting.** Prior to IDEA '97, the law did not mention disciplinary actions. These provisions were, in large measure, a result of serious discussion regarding whether or not schools employ a dual system of discipline. Once it was apparent that discipline provisions would become part of the law, advocates focused on how imposing disciplinary measures would be balanced with addressing behaviors that might arise as a manifestation of the child's disability. The concern about a dual disciplinary system carried over into the discussions of the 2004 amendments, resulting in a broader use of general disciplinary measures and explicit language allowing students with disabilities to be removed for any violation of the student conduct code. For infractions resulting in 45-day removals for students with disabilities, including the addition of "serious bodily injury," removals may now extend beyond the 45-day period if longer removals are applicable to students without disabilities. The caveat remains that students with disabilities removed for longer than ten schooldays in a school year must receive educational services and behavioral interventions. In fact, a number of States have now passed laws that require continuation of services for all students removed for disciplinary action. These legislative actions bolster the view of some researchers that suspension and expulsion do little to improve behavior and may, in fact, leave students who act out due to academic failure even farther behind.

The manifestation determination has been considerably streamlined to ease and improve implementation. School administrators expressed frustration that the determination required considerable staff time and almost always resulted in finding some connection between the behavior and the disability. The provision now requires that the conduct was "caused by, or had a direct and substantial relationship to, the child's disability." Previously the law specifically addressed only what the school district must do when the behavior was not a manifestation of the disability. Now the law addresses what actions will be taken if the behavior is or is not a manifestation. Students may be removed to an interim alternative educational setting without a manifestation determination when the violation involves weapons, drugs, or serious bodily injury.

The House bill had eliminated the functional behavioral assessment, which was retained in the final legislation. The functional behavioral assessment involves a review of how the child functions across settings—school, home, community—and is used to develop a plan that addresses the underlying cause of the behavior.

# Section 616: Monitoring, Technical Assistance, and Enforcement

| IDEA '97 (P.L. 105-17) | IDEA '04 (P.L. 108-446) |
|---|---|

**Sec. 616. *Monitoring, Technical Assistance, and Enforcement.*** No comparable language in IDEA '97.

**Sec. 616. *Monitoring, Technical Assistance, and Enforcement.***

1. Federal and State Monitoring:
   a. Secretary shall (1) monitor implementation of law through oversight of general supervisory responsibility and the State performance plan (see below), and (2) require States to monitor LEAs.
   b. Primary focus of monitoring shall be on improving "educational results and functional outcomes for all children with disabilities."
   c. Monitoring priorities will be (1) provision of FAPE in least restrictive environment (LRE), (2) State's general supervisory authority, and (3) disproportionate representation of ethnic and racial minorities resulting in inappropriate identification.

2. State Performance Plans:
   States must have a performance plan to evaluate implementation efforts and describe how implementation will be improved. Secretary approves plans, and State reviews them at least once every six years.
   a. State establishes "measurable and rigorous targets" for indicators under priority areas, collects data on priorities, and reports annually to Secretary.
   b. States use targets to analyze and report annually to the public on LEAs' performance and to the Secretary on State's performance.
   c. Secretary annually reviews performance plan and determines if the State meets the law's requirements or needs assistance to implement the law.

3. Enforcement:
   a. "Needs Assistance": If, for two consecutive years, Secretary determines that State needs assistance in implementing the law, Secretary shall do one or more of the following: (1) advise State of technical assistance sources; (2) direct use of State-level funds to where assistance is needed; or, (3) identify State as high-risk grantee and impose conditions on grant.
   b. "Needs Intervention": If, for three or more consecutive years, Secretary determines that State needs intervention, he or she may take any of the actions described in (a) and shall do one or more of the following: (1) require corrective action or improvement plan if problem is correctable in one year; (2) require compliance agreement if it is not correctable in one year; (3) for each year of determination, withhold not less than 20% or more than 50% of State's funds until problems are corrected; (4) seek to recover funds; (5) withhold some or all of payments; or, (6) refer State for appropriate enforcement, including to the Department of Justice.
   c. "Needs Substantial Intervention": Secretary shall do one or more of the following: (1) recover funds; (2) withhold some or all of payments; (3) refer to U.S.

| IDEA '97 (P.L. 105-17) | IDEA '04 (P.L. 108-446) |
|---|---|
| | Department of Education Inspector General; or, (4) refer for appropriate enforcement, including to the Department of Justice. |
| | d. Opportunity for Hearing: Before withholding funds, Secretary must provide notice and opportunity for hearing. Pending outcome of hearing, payments and/or authority to obligate funds may be suspended. |
| | e. Secretary reports to Congress within 30 days of action taken. |
| | 4. State Enforcement: If State finds that LEA is not meeting requirements, State shall prohibit LEA from reducing maintenance of effort for any year. |
| | 5. Data Capacity: Secretary shall review States' data collection and analysis capacity and provide technical assistance as needed to improve capacity. |

**Monitoring, Technical Assistance, and Enforcement.** The previous law stated that, when a State had not substantially complied with the requirements of the law, the Secretary could withhold payments or refer the matter for appropriate action, including to the Department of Justice. The new law directs federal and State monitoring to focus more heavily on improving educational results than it had in the past, at which time the emphasis had been mainly on process; law also provides for a series of sanctions for several levels of noncompliance.

## Sections 617 and 618: Administration; Program Information

| IDEA '97 (P.L. 105-17) | IDEA '04 (P.L. 108-446) |
|---|---|
| **Sec. 617. Administration.** Secretary shall:<br><br>1. Provide technical assistance to States to implement the law.<br><br>2. Issue regulations only to the extent necessary to ensure compliance.<br><br>3. Assure confidentiality of personally identifiable information. | **Sec. 617. Administration.** Provisions on regulations have been deleted from this section. Additions include:<br><br>1. Federal government cannot "mandate, direct, or control" specific instructional content, academic standards and assessments, curriculum, or program of instruction of any SEA, LEA, or individual school.<br><br>2. Secretary will provide model forms for IEP, IFSP, and procedural safeguards and prior written notices. |
| **Sec. 618. Program Information.** States submit data annually, by race, ethnicity, and disability on<br><br>1. Number of infants and toddlers (by race/ethnicity only) and children receiving FAPE or early intervention services.<br><br>2. Number of children participating in regular education, in separate classes, schools, or facilities, or in residential facilities.<br><br>3. Number of students, ages 14–21, who stopped receiving services and why, and ages birth to 2 (by race/ethnicity) who stopped early intervention services.<br><br>4. Number of students removed to interim alternative educational settings and subject to long-term suspensions and expulsions, and the acts causing removals.<br><br>5. Number of infants and toddlers (by race/ethnicity) at risk of substantial developmental delay and receiving early intervention services.<br><br>6. Significant discrepancies in rate of long-term suspensions and expulsions among LEAs in a State or compared to rates for nondisabled students. | **Sec. 618. Program Information.** Data will be collected by both number and percentage of students and by race, ethnicity, limited English proficiency, gender, and disability categories.<br><br>1. New data collections include such data as:<br>   a. Incidence and duration of disciplinary actions, including suspensions of one day or more.<br>   b. Comparison of students with and without disabilities removed to alternative settings or expelled.<br>   c. Number of (1) due process complaints filed and hearings conducted; (b) hearings requested under discipline provisions and resulting changes in placement; and, (c) mediations held and settlements reached<br><br>2. Secretary may provide technical assistance to States on data collection and reporting.<br><br>3. LEAs with policies resulting in significant disproportionality must reserve maximum amount allowed (Sec. 613(f)) for early intervening services, particularly to serve students in groups significantly overidentified. |

## Section 619: Preschool Grants

### IDEA '97 (P.L. 105-17)

**Sec. 619. Preschool Grants.**

1. Grants are provided to States under this section to serve children with disabilities, ages 3 through 5, and, at the State's discretion, 2-year-olds turning 3 during the school year. States receiving grants must provide FAPE to children served.

2. States shall use funds reserved for State-level activities for support services, direct services, a coordinated services system, and meeting State performance goals.

3. Part C does not apply to any children receiving FAPE under this section.

### IDEA '04 (P.L. 108-446)

**Sec. 619. Preschool Grants.** State reserve funds may be used for two new activities:

1. Provision of Part C early intervention services to children eligible for preschool who previously received Part C services, until they enter or are eligible for kindergarten; or,

2. At a State's discretion, to continue service coordination or case management for families receiving services under Part C.

## PART C: Infants and Toddlers with Disabilities

### IDEA '97 (P.L. 105-17)

**Secs. 631–644.**

1. Grants are provided to assist states to establish and maintain a coordinated, multidisciplinary, interagency system of early intervention services for infants and toddlers with disabilities and their families.

2. The Statewide system (Sec. 635) must include the following components, among others:
   a. Definition of "developmental delay."
   b. Policy ensuring services are available to all eligible infants and toddlers and their families, including Indian children residing on reservations.
   c. Comprehensive multidisciplinary evaluation of each child and identification of the family's needs in assisting in child's development.
   d. Individualized family service plan, including service coordination, for each eligible child and family.
   e. Child-find system, including referral system.
   f. Public awareness program focusing on early identification.
   g. State interagency coordinating council.
   h. Systems of personnel development and personnel standards.
   i. Policy ensuring that services are provided, to the maximum extent appropriate, in the natural environment.

2. States must submit a grant application (Sec. 637) containing, among other items:
   a. Designation of lead agency responsible for administration.
   b. If State provides services to at-risk infants and toddlers, description of those services.
   c. Policies and procedures to ensure smooth transitions from Part C to preschool or other appropriate services.

### IDEA '04 (P.L. 108-446)

**Sec. 635. Requirements for Statewide System.** Additions to the system include:

1. Services are based, *to the extent practicable, on scientifically based research* and available to infants/ toddlers with disabilities, including *homeless children.*

2. Child find includes "rigorous standards" of identification to reduce need for future services.

3. Public awareness targets parents of premature infants or those with other physical risk factors associated with learning or developmental problems.

4. Training is provided for personnel in the social and emotional development of young children.

**Sec. 635. Flexibility to Serve 3-Year-Olds Until Elementary School.**
SEA and Part C lead agency may develop a joint system allowing Part C children eligible for Preschool services to continue in Part C until they enter or are eligible for kindergarten.

1. System must ensure:
   a. Annual notice to parents of right to receive B or C services with an explanation of program differences, including possible costs to parents for Part C services.
   b. Services, including an educational component promoting school readiness and incorporating preliteracy, language, and numeracy skills.
   c. Child may receive FAPE under Part B, if parents so choose.
   d. IFSP services continue while eligibility determination is made.
   e. Informed written consent before child turns 3 is required for continuation of Part C services.
   f. In substantiated cases of trauma due to exposure to family violence, evaluation referral for Part C is made.

# IDEA '97 (P.L. 105-17)

3. States must provide procedural safeguards to families, similar to Part B procedures.

4. Secretary establishes the Federal Interagency Coordinating Council to minimize duplication of programs and activities across federal, State, and local agencies, ensure effective coordination of federal early intervention and preschool services across agencies, identify gaps in programs and services, and identify barriers to interagency cooperation.

# IDEA '04 (P.L. 108-446)

2. State reports on number/percentage of children eligible for Preschool but continuing under Part C.

3. State is not required to provide FAPE for preschool-aged children served under Part C.

**Sec. 637. State Application and Assurances.** Application includes description of (a) policies requiring referral for children involved in substantiated cases of neglect/abuse or affected by substance abuse; and, (b) efforts to promote collaboration among Early Head Start, early education and child care programs, and Part C.

Added:

**Sec. 640(b): Obligations Related to and Methods of Ensuring Services.** Basically the same as Part B, Sec. 612(a)(12) establishing financial responsibility for services through interagency agreements.

**Sec. 641. State Interagency Coordinating Council (SICC).** (*NOTE:* Federal Interagency Coordinating Council was eliminated.) New SICC members include representatives of the Medicaid program, education programs for homeless children, and agencies responsible for foster care and for children's mental health.

**Sec. 643(e). Reservation for State Incentive Grants.** In any year when the federal appropriation for Part C exceeds $460 million, the Secretary shall reserve 15% of the increase for State grants for flexibility provisions (see Sec. 635 above).

# PART D: National Activities to Improve Education of Children with Disabilities

Part D programs provide support for the Part B and Part C grant programs through research, professional development, and technical assistance. These programs have been reorganized in P.L. 108-446, although most of the same functions and activities remain. There are new focuses on coordinating grants with requirements under the No Child Left Behind Act and ensuring that academic achievement of students with disabilities improves as a result of these grants. Other major themes include ensuring that programs and services are based on scientifically based research, and also ensuring appropriate training for both general and special education personnel, including related services personnel and administrators, to meet the needs of students with disabilities. Several new sections in Part D are highlighted below.

## Subpart 1: State Personnel Development Grants

# IDEA '97 (P.L. 105-17)

**Subpart 1. State Program Improvement Grants.**
Competitive grants awarded to States to reform and improve educational, early intervention, and transition systems to improve student results. Required that at least 75% of funds be used to ensure sufficient numbers of personnel.

# IDEA '04 (P.L. 108-446)

**Subpart 1. State Personnel Development Grants.**

1. In any year when appropriation for this section is less than $100 million, competitive grants will be awarded, with priority to States with greatest personnel shortages or that demonstrate greatest difficulty in meeting "Personnel Qualifications" requirements (see Sec. 612(a)(14)).

2. In years in which the appropriation equals or exceeds $100 million, formula grants will be awarded to all States.

3. Requires a State Personnel Development Plan, and not less than 90% of the grant must be used for professional development.

# Subpart 2: Personnel Preparation, Technical Assistance, Model Demonstration Projects, and Dissemination of Information

| IDEA '97 (P.L. 105-17) | IDEA '04 (P.L. 108-446) |
|---|---|
| **Subpart 2. Sec. 664(c). Accountability for Students Held to Alternative Achievement Standards.** No comparable language in IDEA '97. | **Subpart 2. Sec. 664(c). Accountability for Students Held to Alternative Achievement Standards.** National studies to examine criteria States use in determining eligibility for alternate assessments, validity and reliability of instruments and procedures, alignment with State content standards, and use and effectiveness in appropriately measuring progress and outcomes specific to individualized instructional need. |
| **Subpart 2. Sec. 665. Interim Alternative Educational Settings, Behavioral Supports, and Systemic School Interventions.** No comparable language in IDEA '97. | **Subpart 2. Sec. 665. Interim Alternative Educational Settings, Behavioral Supports, and Systemic School Interventions.** Grants awarded to support safe learning environments that foster academic achievement by improving quality of interim settings and providing increased behavioral supports and systemic interventions. Funds may support activities such as training for staff on identification and preferral and referral procedures, and on positive behavioral supports and interventions and classroom management; stronger links between school-based and community mental health services; and use of behavioral specialists and related services personnel to implement behavioral supports. Funds may also be used to improve interim alternative educational settings by improving staff training, providing referrals for counseling services, increasing the use of instructional technology, and promoting interagency coordination of service delivery. |
| **Subpart 2. Sec. 682. Parent Training and Information Centers.** Grants to parent organizations to support centers that provide training and information to parents, particularly to underserved parents and parents of children inappropriately identified, and to assist parents to understand their rights under the law. | **Subpart 2. Sec. 682. Parent Training and Information Centers.** Has become Subpart 3. Sec. 671. Parent Training and Information Centers. |

# Subpart 3: Supports to Improve Results for Children with Disabilities

| IDEA '97 (P.L. 105-17) | IDEA '04 (P.L. 108-446) |
|---|---|
| | **Subpart 3. Sec. 671. Parent Training and Information Centers.** New required activities include:<br><br>1. Providing training and information to parents to enable their children to meet "developmental and functional goals" and challenging academic achievement goals and be prepared for independent living.<br><br>2. Providing training and information meeting needs of low-income parents and parents of limited English proficient children.<br><br>3. Helping parents participate in school activities that benefit their children.<br><br>4. Helping parents understand, prepare for, and participate in "resolution sessions" (Sec. 615(f)(1)(B)). |

| IDEA '97 (P.L. 105-17) | IDEA '04 (P.L. 108-446) |
|---|---|
| **Subpart 3. Sec. 674(e). National Instructional Materials Access Center.** No comparable language in IDEA '97. | **Subpart 3. Sec. 674(e). National Instructional Materials Access Center.** Secretary establishes and supports NIMAC to receive and maintain a catalog of print instructional materials prepared in the National Instructional Materials Accessibility Standard, to provide access to these materials, and to adopt procedures to protect against copyright infringement. |

# TITLE II: National Center for Special Education Research

| IDEA '97 (P.L. 105-17) | IDEA '04 (P.L. 108-446) |
|---|---|
| **National Center for Special Education Research.** No comparable language in IDEA '97. | 1. Title II establishes the National Center for Special Education Research.<br><br>2. The Center will carry out research activities that are consistent with its mission to:<br>a. Sponsor research to expand knowledge and understanding of the needs of infants, toddlers, and children with disabilities in order to improve developmental, educational, and transitional results.<br>b. Sponsor research to improve services under the law in order to improve:<br>(1) academic achievement, functional outcomes, and educational results.<br>(2) developmental outcomes for infants and toddlers with disabilities.<br>c. Evaluate implementation and effectiveness of the IDEA.<br><br>3. Commissioner of Special Education Research will direct the Center and will propose a research plan to the Director of the Institute, developed in collaboration with the Assistant Secretary of Education for Special Education and Rehabilitative Services, that (a) is consistent with the priorities and mission of the Institute and the Center; (b) is consistent with purposes of the IDEA; (c) has appropriate balance across all age ranges and types of disabilities; and (d) provides for objective research and uses measurable indicators to assess progress and results. |

----

**National Center for Special Education Research.** Title II amends the Education Sciences Reform Act of 2002 (20 U.S.C. 9501 et. seq.) and becomes Part E of that Act. The Education Sciences Reform Act established the Institute, which replaces the Office of Educational Research and Information (OERI) as the main research branch of the U.S. Department of Education. Special education research previously was not housed under OERI, but will now become a part of the larger Department of Education research function.

# TITLE III, Sec. 302: Effective Dates

♦ Parts A, B, C, and Subpart 1 of Part D take effect on July 1, 2005.

♦ The requirements of Sec. 602(10) "Highly Qualified" provisions took effect on the date of enactment.

♦ Subparts 2, 3, and 4 of Part D took effect on the date of enactment.

♦ Title II, "National Center on Special Education Research," took effect on the date of enactment; Sec. 201(a)(2), which deals with development of the research plan, takes effect on October 1, 2005.

# References

## CHAPTER 1

*Air Carrier Access Act,* 49 U.S. 1374 (2001 as amended).

*Americans with Disabilities Act,* 42 USC 12101. (1990).

Baron, R. A., & Byrne, D. (2003). *Social psychology: Understanding human interaction* (10th ed.). Boston: Allyn and Bacon.

Blatt, B., & Kaplan, F. (1974). *Christmas in purgatory: A photographic essay on mental retardation.* Syracuse, NY: Human Policy Press.

Braddock, D., & Parish, S. L. (2002). An institutional history of disability. In D. Braddock (Ed.), *Disability at the dawn of the 21st century and the state of the states* (pp. 1–61). Washington, DC: American Association on Mental Retardation.

Carlson, N. R., & Buskist, W. (1997). *Psychology: The science of behavior* (5th ed.). Boston: Allyn and Bacon.

*Civil Rights Act of 1964,* 42 USC 2000a et seq (1964).

Cook, B. G. (2001). A comparison of teachers' attitudes toward their included students with mild and severe disabilities. *Journal of Special Education, 34*(4), 203–213.

Dajini, K. F. (2001, January). What's in a name: Terms used to refer to people with disabilities. *Disabilities Studies Quarterly, 21*(3), 196–209.

Dole, R. (1995, April 14). Franklin Delano Roosevelt: A disability hero. *Polio survivor's page* [Online]. Available: http://www.eskimo.com/~dempt/fdr.htm

Drew, C. J., & Hardman, M. L. (2004). *Mental retardation: A lifespan approach to people with intellectual disabilities* (8th ed.). Columbus, OH: Merrill.

Forts, A. (1998, October). *Status and effects of labeling: An interview with Alan Robichaud. TASH Newsletter,* 13.

Fox-Grage, W., Folkemer, D., Straw, T., & Hansen, A. (2002). *The States' response to the Olmstead decision: A work in progress.* Washington, DC: National Conference of State Legislatures.

Gustavsson, A. (1999). Integration in the changing Scandinavian welfare states. In H. Daniels & P. Garner (Eds.), *Inclusive education: World yearbook of education, 1999* (pp. 92–98). London: Kogan Page.

Hastings, R. P., & Remington, B. (1993). Connotations of labels for mental handicap and challenging behavior: A review and research evaluation. *Mental Handicap Research, 6,* 237–249.

Hastings, R. P., Songua-Barke, E. J. S., & Remington, B. (1993). An analysis of labels for people with learning disabilities. *British Journal of Clinical Psychology, 32,* 463–465.

James, W. (1890). *Principles of psychology.* New York: Henry Holt.

Joseph P. Kennedy, Jr. Foundation, The. (no date). *Opening doors for you.* Washington, DC: Author.

Kammeyer, K. C. W., Ritzer, G., & Yetman, N. T. (1997). *Sociology: Experiencing changing societies* (7th ed). Boston: Allyn and Bacon.

Kauffman, J. M. (1998). Commentary: Today's special education and its messages for tomorrow. *Journal of Special Education, 32*(3), 127–137.

Kliewer, C., & Biklen, D. (1996). Labeling: Who wants to be retarded.? In W. Stainback & S. Stainback (Eds.), *Controversial issues confronting special educa-tion: Divergent perspectives* (pp. 83–95). Boston: Allyn and Bacon.

Lapadat, J. C. (1998). Implicit theories and stigmatizing labels. *Journal of College Reading and Learning, 29*(1), 73–81.

*L.C. & E.W. vs. Olmstead,* 98-536 S. Ct. (1999).

Lipsky, D. K., & Gartner, A. (1999). Inclusive education: A requirement of a democratic society. In H. Daniels & P. Garner (Eds.), *Inclusive education: World yearbook of education, 1999* (pp. 12–23). London: Kogan Page.

National Council on Disability. (1996). *Achieving independence: The challenge for the 21st century.* Washington, DC: Author.

National Council on Disability (2000, January). *From privileges to rights: People labeled with psychiatric disabilities speak for themselves.* Washington, DC: Author.

N.O.D./Harris, L., & Associates (1995). *National Organization on Disability/Harris Survey of Americans with Disability.* New York: Author.

N.O.D./Harris, L., & Associates (1999). *National Organization on Disability/Harris Survey of Americans with Disability.* New York: Author.

N.O.D./Harris, L., & Associates (2000). *National Organization on Disability/Harris Survey of Americans with Disability.* New York: Author.

N.O.D./Harris, L., & Associates. (2002). *National Organization on Disability/Harris Survey of Americans with Disability.* New York: Author.

Parish, S. L. (2002). Forces shaping developmental disabilities services in the states: A comparative study. In D. Braddock (Ed.), *Disability at the dawn of the 21st century and the state of the states* (pp. 353–475). Washington, DC: American Association on Mental Retardation.

Paul, P. V. (1998, November/December). Radical heart, moderate mind: A perspective on inclusion. *TASH Newsletter,* 16–18.

Persaud, N. (2000). *Labeling: Its effects on labeled students.* International Special Education Congress 2000: Including the Excluded. Manchester, England: University of Manchester School of Education in association with Manchester Metropolitan University.

Rosenhan, D. I. (1973). On being sane in insane places. *Science, 179,* 250–258

United States Department of Justice. (2003). A resort community improves access to city programs and services for residents and vacationers [Online]. Available: http://www.usdoj.gov/crt/ada/fernstor.htm. Retrieved February 18, 2003.

Watson, J. B., & Rayner, R. (1920). Conditioned emotional reactions. *Journal of Experimental Psychology, 3,* 1–14.

Wolfensberger, W. (1975). *The origin and nature of our institutional models.* Syracuse, NY: Human Policy Press.

## CHAPTER 2

Billingsley, F. F., Liberty, K. A., & White, O. R. (1994). The chronology of instruction. In E. C. Cipani & F. Spooner (Eds.), *Curricular and instructional approaches for persons with severe disabilities* (pp. 81–116). Boston: Allyn and Bacon.

Bogdan, W. K. (2000). Celebrating our diversity in the new millennium: An opportunity for success. *Teaching Exceptional Children, 32*(3), 4–5.

Bradley, D. F., & King-Sears, M. E. (1997). The change process: Change for people and schools. In D. F. Bradley, M. E. King-Sears, & D. Tessier-Switlick (Eds.), *Teaching students in inclusive settings: From theory to practice* (pp. 56–82). Boston: Allyn and Bacon.

*Brown v. Topeka, Kansas, Board of Education,* 347 U.S. 483 (1954).

Cassidy, V. M., & Stanton, J. E. (1959). *An investigation of factors involved in the educational placement of mentally retarded children: A study of differences between children in special and regular classes in Ohio.* (U.S. Office of Education Cooperative Research Program, Project No. 043). Columbus: Ohio State University.

Children's Defense Fund. (1999). *Moments in America for children.* Washington, DC: Author.

Children's Defense Fund. (2003). The state of America's children yearbook . Washington, DC: Author.

*Education for All Handicapped Children Act,* 20 U.S.C. § 1400 (1975).

Eggen, P., & Kauchak, D. (2001). *Educational psychology: Windows on classrooms* (5th ed.). Upper Saddle River, NJ: Merrill/Prentice-Hall.

Elbaum, B. E., Vaughn, S., Hughes, M., & Moody, S. W. (2000). How effective are one-to-one tutoring programs in reading for elementary students at risk for reading failure? *Journal of Educational Psychology, 92*(4), 605–619.

Erickson, R.N. (1998). *Special education in an era of school reform: Accountability, standards, and assessment.* Washington, DC: The Federal Resource Center.

Erickson, R. N., Thurlow, M. L., & Thor, K. (1995). *1994 state special education outcomes.* Minneapolis: University of Minnesota, National Center on Educational Outcomes.

Friend, M. P., & Bursuck, W. D. (2001). *Including students with special needs: A practical guide for classroom teachers* (3rd ed.). Boston: Allyn and Bacon.

Hahne, K. (2000). One parent's struggle with inclusion. In S. E. Wade (Ed.), *Inclusive education: A casebook and readings for prospective and practicing teachers.* London: Lawrence Erlbaum.

Hardman, M. L., McDonnell, J., & Welch, M. (1998). *Preparing special education teachers in an era of school reform.* Washington, DC: The Federal Resource Center, Academy for Educational Development.

Hartwig, E. P., & Ruesch, G. M. (2000). Disciplining students in special education. *The Journal of Special Education, 33*(4), 240–247.

Hehir, T. (2002). IDEA 2002 Reauthorization: An opportunity to improve educational results for students with disabilities. *A timely IDEA: Rethnking federal education programs for children with disabilities.* Washington, DC: Center on Educational Policy.

*Hendrick Hudson District Board of Education v. Rowley,* 458 U.S. 176 (1982).

Hocutt, A.M. (1996). Effectiveness of special education: Is placement the critical factor? In The Center for the Future of Children, *Special education for students with disabilities* (pp. 77–102). Los Angeles, CA: The Center for the Future of Children.

*Individuals with Disabilities Education Act* (IDEA) (Public Law 105-17). C.F.R. 300 (1997).

IDEA, 20 U.S.C. 1412, (1990).

Jarrow, J. (1999, Spring). Understanding the law to give students with disabilities full potential. *Opportunity Outlook: The Journal of the Council for Opportunity in Education,* 1–5.

Johnson, G. O. (1961). *A comparative study of the personal and social adjustment of mentally handicapped children placed in special classes with mentally handicapped children who remain in regular classes.* Syracuse, NY: Syracuse University Research Institute, Office of Research in Special Education and Rehabilitation.

Johnson, G. O. (1962). Special education for the mentally handicapped—A paradox. *Exceptional Children, 29,* 62–69.

Johnson, J., Duffett, A., Farkas, S., & Wilson, L. (2002). *When it's your own child: A report on special education from the families who use it.* Baltimore, MD: The Annie E. Casey Foundation.

Jordan, A. M., & deCharms, R. (1959). Personal-social traits of mentally handicapped children. In T. G. Thurstone (Ed.), *An evaluation of educating mentally handicapped children in special classes and regular classes.* Chapel Hill: School of Education, University of North Carolina.

Lyon, G. R. (1996). Learning disabilities. In The Center for the Future of Children, *Special education for students with disabilities* (pp. 54–76). Los Angeles, CA: The Center for the Future of Children.

Manning, M. L., & Baruth, L. G. (1995). *Students at risk.* Boston: Allyn and Bacon.

McLaughlin, M. (1998). *Special education in an era of school reform: An overview.* Washington, DC: The Federal Resource Center.

McLaughlin, M. (2002). Issues for consideration in the re-authorization of Part B of the Individuals with Disabilities Education Act. *A timely IDEA: Rethinking federal education programs for children with disabilities.* Washington, DC: Center on Educational Policy.

McLaughlin, M. J., Fuchs, L., & Hardman, M. (1999). Individual rights to education and students with disabilities: Some lessons from U.S. policy. In H. Daniels and P. Garner (Eds.), *Inclusive education: World yearbook of education 1999* (pp. 24–35). London: Kogan Page.

Metropolitan Life/Louis Harris & Associates, Inc. (1996, April). *The Metropolitan Life Survey of the American Teacher,* 1984–1995. New York: Author.

*Mills v. District of Columbia Board of Education,* 348 F. Supp. 866 (D.D.C. 1972).

Montgomery, A., & Rossi, R. (1994, January). *Educational reforms and students at risk: A review of the current state of the art.* Washington, DC: U.S. Department of Education: Office of Educational Research and Improvement.

National Center for Education Statistics. (1998). *Violence and discipline problems in U.S. public schools: 1996–1997.* Washington, DC: U.S. Department of Education.

National Center for Education Statistics. (2002). *Indicators of school crime and safety.* Washington, DC: Author.

National Council on Disability. (2000). *Back to school on civil rights.* Washington, DC: Author.

National Information Center for Children and Youth with Disabilities. (2003). *Office of Special Education Programs IDEA 97 Training Package.* Washington, DC: Author [Online]. Available: http://www.nichcy.org/Trainpkg/trainpkg.htm. Retrieved February 25, 2003.

National Research Council. (1997). *Educating one and all: Students with disabilities and standards-based reform.* Washington, DC: National Academy Press.

Nevin, A. (1998). Curricular and instructional adaptations for including students with severe disabilities in cooperative groups. In J. Putam (Ed.), *Cooperative learning and strategies for inclusion* (2nd ed.) (pp. 49–65). Baltimore, MD: Paul H. Brookes.

O'Connor, R. (2000). Increasing the intensity of intervention in kindergarten and first grade. *Learning Disabilities Research and Practice, 15,* 43–54.

*Pennsylvania Association for Retarded Citizens v. Commonwealth of Pennsylvania,* 334 F. Supp. 1257 (E.D.Pa. 1971).

Peterson, M. (2000). *Key elements of whole schooling.* Detroit, MI: Renaissance Community Press, Wayne State University.

Peterson, J. M., & Hittie, M. M. (2003). *Inclusive teaching: Creating effective schools for all learners.* Boston: Allyn and Bacon.

Powell, T. H., & Graham, P. L. (1996). Parent–professional participation. In *Improving the implementation of the Individuals with Disabilities Education Act: Making schools work for all of America's children.* (Supplement, pp. 603–628). Washington, DC: National Council on Disability.

President's Commission on Excellence in Special Education. (2002). *A new era: Revitalizing special education for children and their families.* Washington, DC: Education Publications Center, U.S. Department of Education.

Tarver, S. (1996). Direct instruction. In W. Stainback & S. Stainback (Eds.), *Controversial issues confronting special education: Divergent perspectives* (2nd ed., pp. 143–152). Boston: Allyn and Bacon.

Torgesen, J. K. (1996, January). *The prevention and remediation of reading disabilities.* John F. Kennedy Center Distinguished Lecture Series. Nashville, TN: Vanderbilt University.

Thurstone, T. G. (1959). *An evaluation of educating mentally handicapped children in special classes and regular classes* (U.S. Office of Education, Cooperative Research Project No. OE-SAE 6452). Chapel Hill: University of North Carolina.

U.S. Department of Education. (2002). *To assure the free appro-*

priate public education of all children with disabilities, *Twenty-fourth annual report to Congress on the implementation of the Individuals with Disabilities Education Act.* Washington, DC: U.S. Government Printing Office.

U.S. Department of Education. (2003). *Introduction to No Child Left Behind* [Online]. Available: http://www.nclb.gov/next/overview/index.html. Retrieved March 1, 2003.

Vaughn, S., Bos, C. S., & Schumm, J. S. (2003). *Teaching exceptional, diverse, and at-risk students.* Boston: Allyn and Bacon.

Wood, J. W. (1997). Adapting instruction to accommodate students in inclusive settings (3rd ed.). Upper Saddle River, NJ: Prentice-Hall.

## CHAPTER 3

Ainscow, M. (1999). Understanding the development of inclusive schools. *Studies in inclusive education series.* London: Falmer Press.

Als, H., & Gilkerson, L. (1995). Developmentally supportive care in the neonatal intensive care unit. *Zero to Three, 15*(6), 1–10.

Berry, J., & Hardman, M. L. (1998). *Lifespan perspectives on family and disability.* Boston: Allyn and Bacon.

Bloom, B. S. (1964). *Stability and change in human characteristics.* New York: Wiley.

Bruder, M. B. (2001). Inclusion of infants and toddlers: Outcomes and ecology. In M. J. Guralnick (Ed.), *Early childhood inclusion: Focus on change* (pp. 203–228). Baltimore, MD: Paul H. Brookes.

Burchinal, M. R., Campbell, F. A., Bryant, D. M., Wasik, B. H., & Ramey, C. T. (1997). Early intervention and mediating processes in cognitive performance of children of low-income African-American families. *Child Development, 68*, 935–954.

Carnine, D. (2000). *Why education experts resist effective practices (And what it would take to make education more like medicine).* Washington, DC: Fordham Foundation.

Center for Applied Special Technology. (1999). *Summary of universal design concepts* [Online]. Available: http://www.cast.org/concepts/concepts_summary.htm

Council for Exceptional Children. (1999). Special education works. *Today, 6*(2), p. 1, 5.

Davis, M. D., Kilgo, J. L., & Gamel-McCormick, M. (1998). *Young children with special needs.* Boston: Allyn and Bacon.

Devore, S., & Hanley-Maxwell, C. (2000). "I wanted to see if we could make it work." Perspectives on inclusive childcare. *Exceptional Children, 66*(2), 241–255.

Drew, C. J., & Hardman, M. L. (2004). *Mental retardation: A lifespan approach to people with intellectual disabilities* (8th ed.). Upper Saddle River, NJ: Prentice-Hall.

Dunn, L. M. (1968). Special education for the mildly retarded: Is much of it justifiable? *Exceptional Children, 35*, 229–237.

Dupre, A. P. (1997). Disability and the public schools: The case against "inclusion." *Washington Law Review, 72*, 775–858.

Edyburn, D. L., (2003). *What every teacher should know about assistive technology.* Boston: Allyn and Bacon.

Eggen, P., & Kauchak, D. (2001). *Educational psychology: Windows on classrooms* (5th ed.). Upper Saddle River, NJ: Merrill/Prentice-Hall.

Fox, N., & Ysseldyke, J. E. (1997). Implementing inclusion at the middle school level: Lessons from a negative example. *Exceptional Children, 64*, 81–98.

Friend, M. P. & Bursuck, W. D. (2002). *Including students with special needs: A practical guide for classroom teachers* (3rd ed.). Boston: Allyn and Bacon.

Friend, M. P., & Cook, L. (2003). *Interactions: Collaboration skills for school professionals.* Boston: Allyn and Bacon.

Gee, K. (1996). Least restrictive environment: Elementary and middle school. In The National Council on Disability, *Improving the implementation of the Individuals with Disabilities Education Act: Making schools work for all children* (Supplement) (395–425). Washington, DC: The National Council on Disability.

Giangreco, M. F. (1997). *Quick guides to inclusion: Ideas for educating students with disabilities.* Baltimore, MD: Paul H. Brookes.

Gillies, R. M., & Ashman, A. F. (2000). The effects of cooperative learning on students with learning difficulties in the lower elementary school. *Journal of Special Education, 34*, 19–27.

Graves, D. K., & Bradley, D. F. (1997) Establishing the classroom as a community. In D.

F. Bradley, M. E. King-Sears, & D. Tessier-Switlick (Eds.), *Teaching students in inclusive settings: From theory to practice* (pp. 365–383). Boston: Allyn and Bacon.

Guralnick, M. J. (1997). Second-generation research in the field of early intervention. In M. J. Guralnick (Ed.), *The effectiveness of early intervention* (pp. 3–22). Baltimore, MD: Paul H. Brookes.

Guralnick, M. J. (1998). Effectiveness of early intervention for vulnerable children: A developmental perspective. *American Journal of Mental Retardation, 102*(4), 319–345.

Guralnick, M. J. (2001). A framework for change in early childhood inclusion. In M. J. Guralnick (Ed.), *Early childhood inclusion: Focus on change* (pp. 3–35). Baltimore, MD: Paul H. Brookes.

Harden, T. (2003, April 13). The disabilities you can see may be easier to deal with than the ones you can't. *New York Times*, Education Life, Section 4a, 25–26.

Hobbs, T. (1997). *Planning for inclusion: A comparison of individual and cooperative procedures.* Unpublished doctoral dissertation, Florida State University, Tallahassee.

Hocutt, A. M. (1996) Effectiveness of special education: Is placement the critical factor? In The Center for the Future of Children, *Special education for students with disabilities* (pp. 77–102). Los Angeles, CA: The Center for the Future of Children.

Horner, R. H., Albin, R. W., Sprague, J. R., & Todd, A. W. (2000). Positive behavior support. In M. E. Snell & F. Brown (Eds.), *Instruction of students with severe disabilities* (pp. 207–243). Upper Saddle River, NJ: Merrill Publishing.

Howell, K.W., & Nolet, V. (2000). *Curriculum-based evaluation.* Stamford, CT: Wadsworth.

Huefner, D. S. (2000). The risks and opportunities of the IEP requirements under IDEA 97. *The Journal of Special Education, 33*(4), 195–204.

Hunt, J. M. (1961). *Intelligence and experience.* New York: Ronald Press.

IDEA (Public Law 105-17), C.F.R. 300 (1997).

Johnson, J., & Duffett, A. (2002). *When it's your own child: A report on special education and the families who use it.* New York: The Public Agenda.

Kavale, K. A., & Forness, S. R. (2000). History, rhetoric, and reality. *Remedial and Special Education, 21*(5), 279–296.

Kauffman, J. M., & Hallahan, D. P. (1997). A diversity of restrictive environments: Placement as a problem of social ecology. In J. W. Lloyd, E. J. Kameenui, & D. Chard (Eds.), *Issues in educating students with disabilities* (pp. 325–342). Hillsdale, NJ: Erlbaum.

King-Sears, M. E., Burges, M., & Lawson, T. L. (1999 Sept./Oct.). Applying curriculum-based assessment in inclusive settings. *Teaching Exceptional Children*, 30–38.

Landers, M. F. & Weaver, M. F. (1997). *Inclusive education: A process, not a placement.* Swampscott, MA: Watersun Publishing.

Liaw, F., & Brooks-Gunn, J. (1994). Cumulative familial risks and low-birthweight children's cognitive and behavioral development. *Journal of Clinical Child Psychology, 23*(4), 360–372.

Lipsky, D. K., & Gartner, A. (1999). Inclusive education: A requirement of a democratic society. In H. Daniels & P. Garner (Eds.), *Inclusive education: World yearbook of education, 1999* (pp. 12–23). London: Kogan Page.

Maheady, L., Harper, G. F., & Mallette, B. (2001). Peer-mediated instruction and interventions and students with disabilities. *Remedial and Special Education, 22*(1), 4–14.

McDonnell, J., Hardman, M., & McDonnell, A. P. (2003). *Introduction to persons with moderate and severe disabilities* (p. 299). Boston: Allyn and Bacon.

McLean, M. E., Wolery, M., & Bailey, D. B. (1996). *Assessing infants and preschoolers with special needs.* Upper Saddle River, NJ: Prentice-Hall.

Meyer, L. H. (2001). The impact of inclusion on children's lives: Multiple outcomes, and friendship in particular. *International Journal of Disability, Development, and Education, 48*(1), 9–31.

Mills, P. E., Cole, K. N., Jenkins, J. R., & Dale, P. S. (1998). Effects of differing levels of inclusion on preschoolers with disabilities. *Exceptional Children, 65*, 79–90.

National Association for the Education of Young Children. (1997). *NAEYC position statement* [Online]. Available: http://www.naeyc.org/public_affairs/pubaff_index.htm

National Association of School Psychologists. (2003). *Position statement on inclusive programs for students with disabilities.*[Online]. Available: http://www.nasponline.org/information/pospaper_ipsd.html. Retrieved March 20, 2003.

National Institute for Urban School Improvement. (2003). *Improving education: The promise of inclusive schooling.* Denver, CO: Author.

National Research Council. (1997). *Educating one and all: Students with disabilities and standards-based reform.* Washington, DC: National Academy Press.

Odom, S. L., & Bailey, D. B. (2001). Inclusive preschool programs: Classroom eclogy and child outcomes. In M. J. Guralnick (Ed.), *Early childhood inclusion: Focus on change* (pp. 253–276). Baltimore, MD: Paul H. Brookes.

Orelove, F. P., & Sobsey, D. (1996). *Educating children with multiple disabilities: A transdisciplinary approach* (3rd ed.). Baltimore, MD: Paul H. Brookes.

Paul, P. V. (1998, Nov./Dec.). Radical heart, moderate mind. *TASH Newsletter,* 16–19.

Peterson, J. M., & Hittie, M. M. (2003). *Inclusive teaching: Creating effective schools for all learners.* Boston: Allyn and Bacon.

Piaget, J. (1970). Piaget's theory. In P. H. Mussen (Ed.), *Carmichael's manual of child psychology* (3rd ed., Vol. 1). New York: Wiley.

Putnam, J. (1998a). The process of cooperative learning. In J. Putnam (Ed.), *Cooperative learning and strategies for inclusion* (2nd ed., pp. 17–47). Baltimore, MD: Paul H. Brookes.

Putnam, J. (1998b). The movement toward teaching and learning in inclusive classrooms. In J. Putnam (Ed.), *Cooperative learning and strategies for inclusion* (2nd ed., pp. 1–16). Baltimore, MD: Paul H. Brookes.

Ramey, C. T., & Ramey, S. L. (1999). *Right from birth.* New York: Goddard Press.

Resources for Young Children and Families. (2000). *The individualized family service plan.* Colorado Springs, CO: Author [Online]. Available: http://www.rycf.org/ifsp.html

Rose, D. H., & Meyer, A. (2002). *Teaching every student in the digital age: Universal design for learning.* Alexandria, VA: Association for Supervision and Development.

Rous, B., & Hallam, M. A. (1998). Easing the transition to kindergarten: Assessment of social, behavioral and functional skills in young children with disabilities. *Young Exceptional Children, 1*(4), 17–26.

Sailor, W., Gee, K., & Karasoff, P. (2000). Inclusion and school restructuring. In M. Snell & F. Brown (Eds.), *Instruction of students with severe disabilities* (5th ed., pp. 1–30). Columbus, OH: Charles Merrill.

Sainato, D. M., & Morrison, R. S. (2001). Transition to inclusive environments for young children with disabilities. In M. J. Guralnick (Ed.), *Early childhood inclusion: Focus on change* (pp. 293–306). Baltimore, MD: Paul H. Brookes.

Schwartz, I. S., Billingsley, F. F., & McBride, B. M. (1998, Winter). Including preschool children with autism in inclusive preschools: Strategies that work. *Young Exceptional Children,* 19–26.

Schwartz, I. S., & Meyer, L. H. (1997, April). Blending best practices for young children: Inclusive early childhood programs. *TASH Newsletter,* 8–10.

Scruggs, T. E., & Mastropieri, M. A. (1996). Teacher perceptions of mainstreaming/inclusion, 1958–1995: A research synthesis. *Exceptional Children, 63*(1), 59–74.

Smith, C. R. (1998). *Learning disabilities: The interaction of learner, task, and setting* (4th ed.). Boston: Allyn and Bacon.

Stainback, S., Stainback, W., & Ayres, B. (1996). Schools as inclusive communities. In W. Stainback & S. Stainback (Eds.), *Controversial issues confronting special education: Divergent perspectives* (pp. 31–43). Boston: Allyn and Bacon.

Stein, M., Carnine, D., & Dixon, R. (1998). Direct instruction: Integrating curriculum design and effective teaching practices. *Intervention in School and Clinic, 33*(4), 227–234.

*Technology-Related Assistance for Individuals with Disabilities Act,* USC 2201-2217 (1998).

Tomlinson, C. A. (1995). *How to differentiate instruction in mixed ability classrooms* [Online]. Available: http://www.ascd.org/readingroom/books/tomlin95book.html. Retrieved April 23, 2003.

Udell, T., Peters, J., Templeman, T. P. (1998 Jan./Feb.). Inclusive early childhood programs. *Teaching Exceptional Children,* 44–49.

United Nations Educational, Scientific, and Cultural Organization. (2003). *The Salmanca statement and framework for action on special needs education.* [Online]. Available: http://www.unesco.org/education/educprog/sne/files_pdf/framew_e.pdf. Retrieved May 7, 2003.

U.S. Department of Health and Human Services. (2003). *Head Start: Promoting early childhood development..* Washington, DC: Administration on Families and Children [Online]. Available: http://www.hhs.gov/news/press/2002pres/headstart.html. Retrieved June 1, 2003.

Vaughn, S., Bos, C. S., & Schumm, J. S. (2003). *Teaching exceptional, diverse, and at-risk students.* Boston: Allyn and Bacon.

Vaughn, S., Moody, S., & Schumm, J. S. (1998). Broken promises: Reading instruction in the resource room. *Exceptional Children, 64,* 211–225.

Wade, S. E., & Zone, J. (2000). Creating inclusive classrooms: An overview. In S. E. Wade (Ed.), *Inclusive education: A casebook and readings for prospective and practicing teachers.* (pp. 1–27). Mahwah, NJ: Lawrence Erlbaum.

Wagner, M., & Blackorby, J. (1996). Transition from high school to work or college: How special education students fare. In The Center for the Future of Children, *Special education for students with disabilities* (pp. 103–120). Los Angeles, CA: The Center for the Future of Children.

White, B. L. (1975). *The first three years of life.* Englewood Cliffs, NJ: Prentice-Hall.

Young, M. E. (1996). *Early child development: Investing in the future.* Washington, DC: The World Bank.

## CHAPTER 4

Abery, B. (1994). Self-determination: It's not just for adults. *IMPACT, 6*(4), 2. (ERIC Document Reproduction Service No. ED 368 109)

Agran, M., & Wehmeyer, M. (1999). *Innovations: Teaching problem solving to students with mental retardation.* Washington, DC: American Association on Mental Retardation.

Alberto, P. A., Taber, T., Brozovic, S. A., & Elliot, N. E. (1997). Continuing issues of collaborative transition planning in the secondary schools. *Journal of Vocational Rehabilitation, 8,* 197–204.

Benjamin, C. (1996). *Problem solving in school.* Upper Saddle River, NJ: Globe Fearon Educational Publisher.

Berry, J., & Hardman, M. L. (1998). *Lifespan perspectives on family and disability.* Boston: Allyn and Bacon.

Braddock, D. (1999). Aging and developmental disabilities: Demographic and policy issues affecting American families. *Mental Retardation, 37,* 155–161.

Braddock, D., Hemp, R., Rizzolo, M. C., Parish, S., & Pomeranz, A. (2002). The state of the state in developmental disabilities. In D. Braddock (Ed.), *Disability at the dawn of the 21st century and the state of the states* (pp. 83–130). Washington, DC: American Association on Mental Retardation.

Bremer, C. D., Kachgal, M., & Schoeller, K. (2003, April). Self-determination: Supporting successful transition. *Research to Practice Brief of the National Center on Secondary Education and Transition, 2*(1), 1–5.

Browder, D., & Bambara, L. M. (2000). Home and community. In M. E. Snell & F. Brown (Eds.), *Instruction of students with severe disabilities* (pp. 543–589). Upper Saddle River, NJ: Merrill Publishing.

Browder, D., & Snell, M. E. (2000). Teaching functional academics. In M. E. Snell & F. Brown (Eds.), *Instruction of students with severe disabilities* (pp. 493–542). Upper Saddle River, NJ: Merrill Publishing.

Chadsey-Rusch, H., & Heal, L. W. (1998). Building consensus from transition experts on social integration outcomes and interventions. *Exceptional Children, 62*(2), 165–187.

deFur, S. (1999). *Transition planning: A team effort.* Washington, DC: The National Information Center for Children and Youth with Disabilities.

deFur, S. (2000). Designing individualized education (IEP) transition plans. *ERIC Digest (EDO-EC-00-7).* Reston, VA: Council for Exceptional Children/ERIC Clearinghouse on Disabilities and Gifted Education.

Drew, C. J., & Hardman, M. L. (2004). *A Lifespan Approach to People with Intellectual Disabilities.* (8th ed.). Upper Saddle River, NJ: Merrill Publishing.

Fennick, E. (2001, July/August). Co-teaching: An inclusive curriculum for transition. *Teaching Exceptional Children,* 60–66.

Ferguson, P. M., & Ferguson, D. L. (2000). The promise of adulthood. In M. E. Snell & F.

Brown (Eds.), *Instruction of students with severe disabilities* (pp. 629–656). Upper Saddle River, NJ: Merrill Publishing.

Field, S., & Hoffman, A. (1999). The importance of family involvement for promoting self-determination in adolescents with autism and other developmental disabilities. *Focus on Autism and Other Developmental Disabilities, 14*(1), 36–41.

Freedman, R. I., Krauss, M. W., & Seltzer, M. (1997). Aging parents' residential plans for adult children with mental retardation. *Mental Retardation, 35*(2), 114–123.

Friend, M. P. & Bursuck, W. D. (2002). *Including students with special needs: A practical guide for classroom teachers* (3rd ed.). Boston: Allyn and Bacon.

Gartin, B. C., Rumrill, P., & Serebreni, R. (1996). The higher education transition model: Guidelines for facilitating college transition among college-bound students with disabilities. *Teaching Exceptional Children, 29*(1), 30–33.

Getzel, E. E., & Gugerty, J. J. (2001). Applications for youth with learning disabilities. In P. Wehman (Ed.), *Life beyond the classroom: Transition strategies for young people with disabilities* (3rd ed., pp. 371–398). Baltimore, MD: Paul H. Brookes.

Griffiths, D. L., & Unger, D. G. (1994, April). Views about planning for the future among parents and siblings of adults with mental retardation. *Family Relations, 43,* 221–227.

Hasazi, S. B., Furney, K. S., & Destefano, L. (1999). Implementing the IDEA transition initiatives. *Exceptional Children, 65*(4), 555–566.

Heller, T. (2000, Winter). Aging family caregivers: Needs and policy concerns. *Family Support Policy Brief #3, National Center for Family Support,* 1–15.

*Individuals with Disabilities Education Act* (IDEA) (Public Law 105–17), C.F.R. 300 (1997).

Krauss, M. W., Seltzer, M. M., Gordon, R., & Friedman, D. H. (1996, April). Binding ties: The roles of adult siblings of persons with mental retardation. *Mental Retardation, 34*(2), 83–93.

Mank, D., Cioffi, A., & Yovanoff, P. (1998). Employment outcomes for people with severe disabilities: Opportunities for improvement. *Mental Retardation, 36,* 205–216.

McDonnell, J. M., Hardman, M. L., & McDonnell, A. P. (2003). *Introduction to persons with moderate and severe disabilities.*

Boston: Allyn and Bacon.

McDonnell, J., Mathot-Buckner, C., & Ferguson, B. (1996). *Transition programs for students with moderate/severe disabilities.* Pacific Grove, CA: Brooks/Cole.

Moon, M. S., & Inge, K. (2000). Vocational preparation and transition. In M. E. Snell & F. Brown (Eds.), *Instruction of students with severe disabilities* (pp. 591–628). Upper Saddle River, NJ: Merrill Publishing.

Morgan, R. L., Ellerd, D. A., Jensen, K., & Taylor, M. J. (2000). A survey of community placements: Where are youth and adults with disabilities working? *Career Development for Exceptional Individuals, 23,* 73–86.

Morgan, R. L., Ellerd, D. A., Gerity, B. P., & Blair, R. J. (2000). That's the job I want: How technology helps young people in transition. *Teaching Exceptional Children, 32*(4), 44–49.

National Research Council. (1997). *Educating one and all: Students with disabilities and standards-based reform.* Washington, DC: National Academy Press.

N.O.D & Harris, L., & Associates. (2000). *National Organization on Disability/Harris Survey of Americans with Disabilities.* New York: Author.

Prouty, R. W., Smith, G., & Lakin, K. C. (2001, June). *Residential services for persons with developmental disabilities: Status and trends through 2000.* Minneapolis: University of Minnesota, College of Education and Human Development, Institute on Community Integration, Research and Training Center on Community Living.

Ryan, D. J. (2000). *Job search handbook for people with disabilities.* Indianapolis, Indiana: Jist Publishing.

Seltzer, M. M., & Krauss, M. W. (1994). Aging parents with resident adult children: The impact of lifelong caregiving. In M. M. Seltzer, M. W. Krauss, & M. P. Janicki (Eds.), *Life course perspectives on adulthood and old age* (pp. 3–18). Washington, DC: The American Association on Mental Retardation.

Siegel-Causey, E., McMorris, C., McGowen, S., & Sands-Buss, S. (1998, Sept./Oct.). In junior high you take earth science. *Teaching Exceptional Students, 31*(1), 66–72.

Thomas, S. B. (2000). College students and disability law. *The Journal of Special Education, 33*(4), 248–257.

Tymchuk, A. J., Lakin, K. C., & Luckasson, R. (2001). Life at the margins: Intellectual, demographic, economic, and social circumstances of adults with mild cognitive limitations. In A. J. Tymchuk, K. C. Lakin, & R. Luckasson (Eds.), *The forgotten generation: The status and challenges of adults with mild cognitive limitations* (pp. 21–38). Baltimore, MD: Paul H. Brookes.

University of Illinois at Chicago National Research and Training Center. (2003). *Self-determination framework for people with psychiatric disabilities.* Chicago, IL: Author [Online]. http://www.psych.uic.edu/UICNRTC/sdframework.pdf. Retrieved May 20, 2003.

U.S. Department of Education. (2002) To assure the free appropriate public education of all children with disabilities, *Twenty-fourth annual report to Congress on the implementation of the Individuals with Disabilities Education Act.* Washington, DC: U.S. Government Printing Office.

Wagner, M., & Blackorby, J. (1996). Transition from high school to work or college: How special education students fare. In The Center for the Future of Children, *Special education for students with disabilities,* (pp. 103–120). Los Angeles, CA: The Center for the Future of Children.

Wehman, P. (2001). *Life beyond the classroom: Transition strategies for young people with disabilities* (3rd ed.). Baltimore, MD: Paul H. Brookes.

Wehman, P., Everson, J. M., & Reid, D. H. (2001). Beyond programs and placements: Using person-centered practices to individualize the transition process and outcomes. In P. Wehman (Ed.), *Life beyond the classroom: Transition strategies for young people with disabilities* (3rd ed., pp. 91–126). Baltimore, MD: Paul H. Brookes.

Wehmeyer, M. (2001) Self-determination and transition. In P. Wehman (Ed.), *Life beyond the classroom: Transition strategies for young people with disabilities* (3rd ed., pp. 35–60). Baltimore, MD: Paul H. Brookes.

## CHAPTER 5

Abernathy, T. J., Webster, G., & Vermeulen, M. (2002). Relationship between poverty and health among adolescents. *Adolescence, 37*(145), 55–68.

Alexander, K. L, Entwisle, D. R., & Kabbani, N. S. (2001). The dropout process in life course perspective: Early risk factors at home and school. *Teachers College Record, 103,* 760–822.

Baca, L. M., & Cervantes, H. T. (1998). *The bilingual special education interface* (3rd ed.). Columbus, OH: Merrill/Macmillan.

Bailey, D. B., Jr. (2001). Evaluating parent involvement and family support in early intervention and preschool programs. *Journal of Early Intervention, 24,* 1–14.

Banks, J. A. (2002). *An introduction to multicultural education* (3rd ed.). Boston: Allyn and Bacon.

Banks, J. A. (2003). Multicultural education: Characteristics and goals. In J. A. Banks and C. A. M. Banks (Eds.), *Multicultural education: Issues and perspectives, Update* (4th ed., pp. 3–30). New York: Wiley.

Barnett, W. S., & Camilli, G. (2002). Compensatory preschool education, cognitive development, and "race." In J. M. Fish (Ed.), *Race and intelligence: Separating science from myth* (pp. 369–406). Mahwah, NJ: Lawrence Erlbaum.

Battin-Pearson, S., Newcomb, M. D., Abbott, R. D., Hill, K. G., Catalano, R. F., & Hawkins, J. D. (2000). Predictors of early high school dropout: A test of five theories. *Journal of Educational Psychology, 92,* 568–582.

Battle, D. E. (2002). Language and communication disorders in culturally and linguistically diverse children. In D. K. Bernstein & E. Tiegerman-Farber (Eds.), *Language and communication disorders in children* (5th ed., pp. 354–386). Boston: Allyn and Bacon.

Becker, B. E., & Luthar, S. S. (2002). Social-emotional factors affecting achievement outcomes among disadvantaged students: Closing the achievement gap. *Educational Psychologist, 37,* 197–214.

Beekmans, R., Eyckmans, J., Janssens, V., Dufranne, M., & Van de Velde, H. (2001). Examining the Yes/No vocabulary test: Some methodological issues in theory and practice. *Language Testing, 18,* 236–274.

Bondurant-Utz, J. A. (2002). *The practical guide to assessing infants and preschoolers with special needs.* Columbus, OH: Merrill/Prentice-Hall.

Bond, M. H. (2002). Reclaiming the individual from Hofstede's ecological analysis—A 20-year odyssey: Comment on

Oyserman et al. *Psychological Bulletin, 128,* 73–77.

Boudah, D. J., Lenz, B. K., Bulgren, J. A., Schumaker, J. B., & Deshler, D. D. (2000). Don't water down! Enhance content learning through the unit organizer routine. *Teaching Exceptional Children, 33*(3), 48–56.

Buckner, J. C., Bassuk, E. L., & Weinreb, L. F. (2002). Predictors of academic achievement among homeless and low-income housed children. *Journal of School Psychology, 39,* 45–69.

Capage, L. C., Bennett, G. M., & McNeil, C. B. (2001). A comparison between African American and Caucasian children referred for treatment of disruptive behavior disorders. *Child and Family Behavior Therapy, 23,* 1–14.

Causey, V. E., Thomas, C. D., & Armento, B. J. (2000). Culture diversity is basically a foreign term to me: The challenges of diversity for preservice teacher education. *Teaching and Teacher Education, 16,* 33–45.

Chiappe, P., Siegel, L. S, & Gottardo, A. (2002). Reading-related skills of kindergartners from diverse linguistic backgrounds. *Applied Psycholinguistics, 23,* 95–116

Choi, Y., & Harachi, T. W. (2002). The cross-cultural equivalence of the Suinn-Lew Asian Self-Identity Acculturation Scale among Vietnamese and Cambodian Americans. *Journal of Social Work Research and Evaluation, 3,* 5–17.

Collier, C. (1998). Including bilingual exceptional children in the general education classroom. In L. M. Baca & H. T. Cervantes (Eds.), *The bilingual special education interface* (3rd ed., pp. 290–325). Columbus, OH: Merrill/Macmillan.

Cohen, G. L., & Steele, C. M. (2002). A barrier of mistrust: How negative stereotypes affect cross-race mentoring. In J. Aronson (Ed.), *Improving academic achievement: Impact of psychological factors on education* (pp. 303–327). San Diego, CA: Academic Press.

Cohen, M. N. (2002). An Anthropologist looks at "race" and IQ testing. In J. M. Fish (Ed.), *Race and intelligence: separating from myth* (pp. 201–223). Mahwah, NJ: Erlbaum.

Conlon, E., Devaraj, S, & Matta, K. F. (2001). The relationship between initial quality perceptions and maintenance behavior: The case of the automotive industry. *Management Science, 47,* 1191–1202.

Coutinho, M. J., & Oswald, D. P. (2000). Disproportionate representation in special education: A synthesis and recommendations. *Journal of Child and Family Studies, 9*(2), 135–156.

Craig, H. K., & Washington, J. A. (2000). An assessment battery for identifying language impairments in African American children. *Journal of Speech, Language, and Hearing Research, 43,* 366–379.

Craig, S., Hull, K., Haggart, A. G., & Perez-Selles, M. (2000). Promoting cultural competence through teacher assistance teams. *Teaching Exceptional Children, 32*(3), 6–12.

Dana, R. H. (2000). *Handbook of cross-cultural and multicultural personality assessment.* Mahwah, NJ: Lawrence Erlbaum.

Dancy, J., Jr., & Ralston, P. A. (2002). Health promotion and Black elders: Subgroups of greatest need. *Research on Aging, 24*(2), 218–242.

De Valenzuela, J. S., & Cervantes, H. (1998). Issues and theoretical considerations in the assessment of bilingual children. In L. M. Baca & H. T. Cervantes (Eds.), *The bilingual special education interface* (3rd ed., pp. 144–166). Columbus, OH: Merrill/Macmillan.

*Diana v. State Board of Education* (1970, 1973). C-70, 37 RFP (N.D. Cal., 1970, 1973).

Dika, S. L., & Singh, K. (2002). Applications of social capital in educational literature: A critical synthesis. *Review of Educational Research, 72,* 31–60.

Dong, Y. R. (2002). Integrating language and content: How three biology teachers work with non-English-speaking students. *International Journal of Bilingual Education and Bilingualism, 5,* 40–57.

Drew, C. J., & Hardman, M. L. (2004). *Mental retardation: A lifespan approach to people with intellectual disabilities* (8th ed.). Columbus, OH: Merrill.

Edwards, J. C. (2001). Self-fulfilling prophecy and escalating commitment: Fuel for the Waco fire. *Journal of Applied Behavioral Science, 37,* 343–360.

Elfenbein, H. A. & Ambady, N. (2002). Is there an in-group advantage in emotion recognition? *Psychological Bulletin, 128,* 243–249.

Ewart, C. K., & Suchday, S. (2002). Discovering how urban poverty and violence affect health: Development and validation of a neighborhood stress index. *Health Psychology, 21,* 254–262.

Fernandez, R. C. (2000). No hablo ingles: Bilingualism and multiculturalism in preschool settings. *Early Childhood Education Journal, 27*(3), 159–163.

Fiske, A. P. (2002). Using individualism and collectivism to compare cultures—A critique of the validity and measurement of the constructs: Comment on Oyserman et al. *Psychological Bulletin, 128,* 78–88.

Franklin, W. (2000). Students at promise and resilient: A historical look at risk. In M. G. Sanders (Ed.), *Schooling students placed at risk: Research, policy, and practice in the education of poor and minority adolescents* (pp. 3–16). Mahwah, NJ: Lawrence Erlbaum.

Gallo, L. C., & Matthews, K. A. (2003). Understanding the association between socioeconomic status and physical health: Do negative emotions play a role? *Psychological Bulletin, 129,* 10–51.

Gelfand, D. M., & Drew, C. J. (2003). *Understanding child behavior disorders* (4th ed.). Belmont, CA: Wadsworth.

Gollnick, D. M., & Chinn, P. C. (2002). *Multicultural education in a pluralistic society* (6th ed.). Columbus, OH: Merrill.

Gordijn, E. H., Koomen, W., & Stapel, D. A. (2002). Level of prejudice in relation to knowledge of cultural stereotypes. *Journal of Experimental Social Psychology, 37,* 150–157.

Grant, C. A., & Gomez, M. L. (2001). *Campus and classroom: Making schooling multicultural* (2nd ed.). Columbus: Merrill/Prentice-Hall.

Grant, C. A., & Sleeter, C. E. (2003). Race, class, gender, and disability in the classroom. In J. A. Banks and C. A. M. Banks (Eds.), *Multicultural education: Issues and perspectives, Update* (4th ed., pp. 59–81). New York: Wiley.

Grossman, H. (2002). *Ending discrimination in special education* (2nd ed.). Springfield, IL: Charles C Thomas.

Guadarrama, I. (2000). The empowering role of service learning in preparation of teachers. In C. R. O'Grady (Ed.), *Integrating service learning and multicultural education in colleges and universities* (pp. 227–243). Mahwah, NJ: Lawrence Erlbaum.

Halfon, N., & McLearn, K. T. (2002). Families with children under 3: What we know and implications for results and policy. In N. Halfon and K. T. McLearn (Eds.), *Child rearing in America: Challenges facing parents with young children* (pp. 367–412). New York: Cambridge University Press.

Harrison-Hale, A. O. (2002). Conflict resolution styles among African American children and youth. In H. P. McAdoo (Ed.), *Black children: Social, educational, and parental environments* (2nd ed., pp 193–206). Thousand Oaks, CA: Sage.

Hendrick, J. (2001). *The whole child: Developmental education for the early years* (7th ed.). Columbus: Merrill/Prentice-Hall.

Heredia, R. R., & Altarriba, J. (2002). *Bilingual sentence processing.* San Diego, CA: Elsevier Science.

Hernandez, H. (2001). *Multicultural education: A teacher's guide to linking context, process, and content* (2nd ed.). Columbus: Merrill/Prentice-Hall.

Holzer, C. E., & Copeland, S. (2000). Race, ethnicity, and the epidemiology of mental disorders in adults. In I. Cuellar and F. A. Paniagua (Eds). *Handbook of multicultural mental health* (pp. 341–357). San Diego, CA: Academic Press.

Hout, M. (2002). Test scores, education, and poverty. In J. M. Fish (Ed.), *Race and intelligence: Separating science from myth* (pp. 329–354). Mahwah, NJ: Lawrence Erlbaum.

Husaini, B. A., Sherkat, D. E., Levine, R., Bragg, R., Holzer, C., Anderson, K., Cain, V., & Moten, C (2002). Race, gender, and health care service utilization and costs among medicare elderly with psychiatric diagnoses. *Journal of Aging and Health, 14,* 79–95.

Jones, L., & Menchetti, B. M. (2001). Identification of variables contributing to definitions of mild and moderate mental retardation in Florida. *Journal of Black Studies, 31*(5), 619–634.

Lam, S., Yim, P., & Lam, T. (2002). Transforming school culture: Can true collaboration be initiated? *Educational Research, 44,* 181–195.

*Larry P. v. Riles.* (1972). C-71-2270 US.C, 343 F. Supp. 1306 (N.D. Cal. 1972).

*Larry P. v. Riles.* (1979). 343 F. Supp. 1306, 502 F. 2d 963 (N.D. Cal. 1979).

*Lau v. Nichols.* (1974). 414, U.S., 563–572 (1974, January 21).

Law, J., Lindsay, G., Peacey, N., Gascoigne, M., Soloff, N., Radford, J., & Band, S. (2002). Consultation as a model for providing speech and language therapy in schools: A panacea or one step too far? *Child Language Teaching and Therapy, 18*(2), 145–163.

Li, S. C. (2003). Biocultural orchestration of developmental plasticity across levels: The interplay of biology and culture in shaping the mind and behavior across the life span. *Psychological Bulletin, 129,* 171–194.

Linn, R. L. (2002). Constructs and values in standards-based assessment. In H. I. Braun and D. N. Jackson, (Eds.), *The role of constructs in psychological and educational measurement* (pp. 231–254). Mahwah, NJ: Lawrence Erlbaum.

Linn, R. L., & Gronlund, N. E. (2000). *Measurement and assessment in teaching* (8th ed.). Columbus, OH: Merrill/Prentice-Hall.

Littlewood, R. (2001). "Case definition and culture: Are people all the same?": Comment. *British Journal of Psychiatry, 179,* 460.

Locke, D. C. (1995). Counseling interventions with African American youth. In C. C. Lee (Ed.), *Counseling for diversity* (pp. 21–40). Boston: Allyn and Bacon.

Lopez, G. R. (2001). The value of hard work: Lessons on parent involvement from an (im)migrant household. *Harvard Educational Review, 71*(3), 416–437.

Manly, J. J., & Jacobs, D. M. (2002). Future directions in neuropsychological assessment with African Americans. In F. R. Ferraro (Ed.), *Minority and cross-cultural aspects of neuropsychological assessment. Studies on neuropsychology, development, and cognition* (pp. 79–96). Bristol, PA: Swets & Zeitlinger.

Matsumoto, D. (2002). Methodological requirements to test a possible in-group advantage in judging emotions across cultures: Comments on Elfenbein and Ambady (2002) and evidence. *Psychological Bulletin, 128,* 236–242.

McConnell, S. R. (2001). Parent involvement and family support: Where do we want to go, and how will we know we are headed there? *Journal of Early Intervention, 24,* 15–18.

McKinnon, J. (2001). The black population: 2000. U.S. Census Bureau, U.S. Department of Commerce, C2KBR/01-5.

McKinnon, J. (2003). The black population in the United States: March 2002. U. S. Census Bureau, U.S. Department of Commerce, P20–541.

Merrell, K. W. (2002). *Behavioral, social, and emotional assessment of children and adolescents* (2nd ed.). Mahwah, NJ: Lawrence Erlbaum.

Meyer, L. H., Bevan-Brown, J., Harry, B., & Sapon-Shevin, M. (2003). School inclusion and multicultural issues in special education. In J. A. Banks and C. A. M. Banks (Eds.), *Multicultural education: Issues and perspectives, Update* (4th ed., pp. 327–352). New York: Wiley.

Mirel, J. (2002). Civic education and changing definitions of American identity, 1900–1950. *Educational Review, 54,* 143–152.

Mitchell, A. (2000). Historical trends in federal education policies that target students placed at risk. In M. G. Sanders (Ed.), *Schooling students placed at risk: Research, policy, and practice in the education of poor and minority adolescents* (pp. 17–35). Mahwah, NJ: Lawrence Erlbaum.

Morrison, G. S. (2001). *Early childhood education today* (8th ed.). Columbus, OH: Merrill/Prentice-Hall.

Mueller, J. A., & Pope, R. L. (2001). The relationship between multicultural competence and White racial consciousness among student affairs practitioners. *Journal of College Student Development, 42,* 133–144.

Nakagawa, K., Stafford, M. E., Fisher, T. A., & Matthews, L. (2002). The "city migrant" dilemma: Building community at high-mobility urban schools. *Urban Education, 37,* 96–125.

O'Connor, C. (2002). Black women beating the odds from one generation to the next: How the changing dynamics of constraint and opportunity affect the process of educational resilience. *American Educational Research Journal, 39,* 855–903.

Oyserman, D., Coon, H. M., & Kemmelmeier, M. (2002). Rethinking individualism and collectivism: Evaluation of theoretical assumptions and metaanalyses. *Psychological Bulletin, 128,* 3–72.

Pawlik, K., Zhang, H., Vrignaud, P., Roussalov, V., & Fernandez-Ballesteros, R. (2000). Psychological assessment and testing. In K. Pawlik and M.

R. Rosenzweig (Eds.), *International handbook of psychology* (pp. 365–406). London: Sage Publications.

Pierangelo, R., & Giuliani, G. A. (2002). Why your students do what they do and what to do when they do it: A practical guide for understanding classroom behavior (Grades 6–12). *Adolescence, 37,* 657.

Pena, E., Iglesias, A., & Lidz, C. S. (2001). Reducing test bias through dynamic assessment of children's word learning ability. *American Journal of Speech Language Pathology, 10*(2), 138–154.

Proctor, B. D. (1998). Poverty. Population Profile of the United States: 1997. (pp. 40–41). *U.S. Bureau of the Census, Current Population Reports,* Series P23–194. Washington, DC: U.S. Government Printing Office.

Puckett, M. (2001). *The young child: Development from pre-birth through age 8* (3rd ed.). Columbus, OH: Merrill/Prentice-Hall.

Reynolds, D. W. (2001). Language in the balance: Lexical repetition as a function of topic, cultural background, and writing development. *Language Learning, 51,* 437–476.

Rueda De Leon, I. C. (2001). Predictors of perceptions about negative cultural stereotypes in Mexican Americans. *Dissertation Abstracts International: Section B: The Sciences and Engineering, 62,* (2-B), 1098.

Sanders, M. G. (2000). *Schooling students placed at risk: Research, policy, and practice in the education of poor and minority adolescents.* Mahwah, NJ: Lawrence Erlbaum.

Santos, R. M., Fowler, S. A., Corso, R. M., & Bruns, D. A. (2000). Acceptance, acknowledgment, and adaptability: Selecting culturally and linguistically appropriate early childhood materials. *Teaching Exceptional Children, 33*(3), 14–22.

Scheffner-Hammer, C, Pennock-Roman, M., Rzasa, S., & Tomblin, J. B. (2002). An analysis of the Test of Language Development—Primary for item bias. *American Journal of Speech Language Pathology, 11,* 274–284.

Schwartz, I. S., & Rodriguez, P. B. (2001). A few issues to consider: The who, what, and where of family support. *Journal of Early Intervention, 24,* 19–21.

Seccombe, K. (2002). "Beating the odds" versus "changing the odds": Poverty, resilience, and family policy. *Journal of Marriage and Family, 64*(2): 384–394.

Seidl, B., & Friend, G. (2002). Learning authority at the door: Equal-status community-based experiences and the preparation of teachers for diverse classrooms. *Teaching and Teacher Education, 18,* 421–433.

Sheldon, S. B. (2002). Parents' social networks and beliefs as predictors of parent involvement. *Elementary School Journal, 102*(4), 301–316.

Spinelli, C. (2002). *Classroom assessment for students with special needs in inclusive settings.* Columbus, OH: Merrill/Prentice-Hall.

Taylor, S. V. (2000). Multicultural is who we are: Literature as a reflection of ourselves. *Teaching Exceptional Children, 33*(3), 24–29.

Teresi, J. A., Holmes, D., Ramirez, M., Gurland, B. J., & Lantigua, R. (2001). Performance of cognitive tests among different racial/ethnic and education groups: Findings of differential item functioning and possible item bias. *Journal of Mental Health and Aging, 7*(1), 79–89.

Tighe, E. A. (2001). The multiple relationships between health and environment risk factors and school performance: A longitudinal investigation of urban elementary students. *Dissertation Abstracts International Section B: The Sciences and Engineering, 62*(2-B), 1011.

Torres, J. B. (2002). Creating a Latino/Hispanic alliance: Eliminating barriers to coalition building. *Journal of Human Behavior in the Social Environment, 5*(3–4): 189–213.

Trawick-Smith, J. (2000). *Early childhood development: A multicultural perspective* (2nd ed.). Columbus, OH: Merrill/Prentice-Hall.

Twenge, J. M., & Crocker, J. (2002). Race and self-esteem revisited: Reply to Hafdahl and Gray-Little (2002). *Psychological Bulletin, 128,* 417–420.

Ukrainetz, T. A., Harpell, S., Walsh, C., & Coyle, C. (2000). A preliminary investigation of dynamic assessment with Native American kindergartners. *Language, Speech, and Hearing Services in Schools, 31*(2), 142–154.

U.S. Bureau of the Census. (1998). Population Profile of the United States: 1997. *U.S. Bureau of the Census, Current Population Reports,* Series

P23–194. U.S. Washington, DC: Government Printing Office.

U.S. Bureau of the Census. (2000). *Poverty in the United States: 2000.* [Online]. www.census.gov/dmd.

*U.S. News & World Report,* "Separate and unequal." December 13, 1993, pp. 46–60.

Venn, J. J. (2000). *Assessing children with special needs* (2nd ed.). Columbus, OH: Merrill/Prentice-Hall.

Willingham, W. W. (2002). Seeking fair alternatives in construct design. In H. I. Braun and D. N. Jackson (Eds), *The role of constructs in psychological and educational measurement* (pp. 231–254). Mahwah, NJ: Lawrence Erlbaum.

Zapata, J. T. (1995). Counseling Hispanic children and youth. In C. C. Lee (Ed.), *Counseling for Diversity* (pp. 85–108). Boston: Allyn and Bacon.

Zigler, E. F., Finn-Stevenson, M., & Hall, N. W. (2002). *The first three years and beyond: Brain development and social policy.* New Haven, CT: Yale University Press.

## CHAPTER 6

Adams, J. F. (2001). Impact of parent training on family functioning. *Child and Family Behavior Therapy, 23,* 29–42.

Affleck, G., & Tennen, H. (1993). Cognitive adaptation to adversity: Insights from parents of medically fragile infants. In A. P. Turnbull, J. M. Patterson, S. K. Behr, D. L. Murphy, D. L. Marguis, & M. J. Blue-Banning (Eds.), *Cognitive coping, families, and disability* (pp. 135–150). Baltimore, MD: Paul H. Brookes.

Amlund, J. T., & Kardash, C. M. (1994). Group approaches to consultation and advocacy. In S. K. Alper, P. J. Schloss, & C. N. Schloss (Eds.), *Families of students with disabilities* (pp. 181–204). Boston: Allyn and Bacon.

Anton, G. (2002). Back toward normal: How our family recovered after Alison was born. *The Exceptional Parent, 32,* 28–32.

Baxter, C., Cummins, R. A., & Yiolitis, L. (2000). Parental stress attributed to family members with and without disability: A longitudinal study. *Journal of Intellectual & Developmental Disability, 25,* 105–118.

Beach Center on Families and Disability. (1998a). *Dads feel left out* [Online]. Available:

http://www.lsi.ukans.edu/beach/dis2.htm

Beach Center on Families and Disability. (1998b). *Family stories: Gathering for the future* [Online]. Available: http://www.lsi.ukans.edu/beach/htmlsfam2.htm

Beach Center on Families and Disability. (1998c). *How to: Better cope with a family member's disability* [Online]. Available: http://www.1si.edu/beach/html/c1.htm

Beach Center on Families and Disability. (1998d). *How to: Deal with the news that your baby needs special care* [Online]. Available: http://www.lsi.ukans.edu/beach/html/c7.htm

Beach Center on Families and Disability. (1998e). *How to: Honor cultural diversity* [Online]. Available: http://www.lsi.ukans.edu/beach/html/m1.htm

Beach Center on Families and Disability. (1998f). *How to: Renew family energy through respite care* [Online]. Available: http://www.lsi.ukans.edu/beach/html/fs6.htm

Beach Center on Families and Disabilities. (1998g). *Quality indicators for exemplary family empowerment* [Online]. Available: http://www.1si.ukans.edu/beach/html/x5.htm

Beach Center on Families and Disability. (1998h). *Quality indicators of exemplary family-centered programs* [Online]. Available: http://www.lsi.ukans.edu/beach/html/f19.htm

Beach Center on Families and Disability. (1998i). *Research brief: Effectiveness of parent to parent support* [Online]. Available: http://www.lsi.ukans.edu/beach/html/12p.htm.

Beach Center on Families and Disability. (1998j). *What you should know about American Indians and disability* [Online]. Available: http://www.lsi.ukans.edu/beach/html/m6.htm.

Bell, M. L., & Smith, B. R. (1996). Grandparents as primary caregivers: Lessons in love. *Teaching Exceptional Children, 28,* 18–19.

Berry, J., & Hardman, M. L. (1998). *Lifespan perspectives on family and disability.* Boston: Allyn and Bacon.

Blacher, J. (1984). Sequential stages of parental adjustment to the birth of a child with handicaps: Fact or artifact? *Mental Retardation, 22*(2), 55–68.

Blacher, J. (2002). The mystery of family research: Parents magically change from invisible to prominent. *Exceptional Parent, 32,* 46–48.

Blaska, J. K. (1998). *Cyclical grieving: Reoccurring emotions experienced by parents who have children with disabilities.* Minneapolis, MN: EDRS Price.

Bruder, M. B. (2000). Family-centered early intervention: Clarifying our values for the new millenium. *Topics In Early Childhood Special Education, 20,* 105–115, 122.

Cantu, C. (2002). Early intervention services: A family-professional partnership. *Exceptional Parent, 32*(12), 47–50.

Carpenter, B. (2000). Sustaining the family: Meeting the needs of families of children with disabilities. *British Journal of Special Education, 27,* 135–144.

Chan, J. B., & Sigafoos, J. (2000). A review of child and family characteristics related to the use of respite care in developmental disability services. *Child and Youth Care Forum, 29,* 27–37.

Correa, V. I., & Jones, H. (2000). Multicultural issues related to families of children with disabilities. In M. J. Fine & R. L. Simpson (Eds.), *Collaboration with parents and families of children with exceptionalities* (2nd ed., pp. 133–154). Austin, TX: PRO-ED.

Cuskelly, M., Chant, D., & Hayes, A. (1998). Behavior problems in the siblings of children with Down syndrome: Associations with family responsibilities and stress. *International Journal of Disability, Development, and Education, 45*(3), 295–311.

Danseco, E. R. (1997, March). Parental beliefs on childhood disability: Insights on culture, child development and intervention. *International Journal of Disability, Development, and Education, 44,* 41–52.

Darley, S., Porter, J., Werner, J., & Eberly, S. (2002). Families tell us what makes families strong. *Exceptional Parent, 32,* 34–36.

Derer, K. R., & D'Alonzo, B. J. (2000). When help is helpful: Parent and helper perspectives. *Preventing School Failure, 44,* 73–80.

Devore, S., & Hanley-Maxwell, C. (2000). "I wanted to see if we could make it work:" Perspectives on inclusive childcare. *Exceptional Children, 66,* 241–255.

Dollahite, D. C. (2001, August). Beloved children, faithful fathers: Caring for children with

special needs. *Marriage and Families,* 16–21

Dunst, C. J. (2002). Family-centered practices: Birth through high school. *Journal of Special Education, 36,* 139–147.

Epstein, S. H., & Bessel, A. G. (2002). A parent's determination and a pre-K dream realized. *The Exceptional Parent, 32,* 56–60.

Ferguson, P. M. (2002). A place in the family: An historical interpretation of research on parental reactions to having a child with a disability. *Journal of Special Education, 36,* 124–130.

Fine, M. J., & Nissenbaum, M. S. (2000). The child with disabilities and the family: Implications for professionals. In M. J. Fine, & R. L. Simpson (Eds.), *Collaboration with parents and families of children with exceptionalities* (2nd ed., pp. 3–26). Austin, TX: PRO-ED.

Fine, M. J., & Simpson, R. L. (2000). *Collaboration with parents and families of children with exceptionalities* (2nd ed.). Austin, TX: PRO-ED.

Fischer, S. (2003). Fathers are caregivers too! [Online]. Available: http://www.fathersnetwork.org/572.html

Fish, M. C. (2000). Children with special needs in nontraditional families. In M. J. Fine, & R. L. Simpson (Eds.). *Collaboration with parents and families of children with exceptionalities* (2nd ed., pp. 49–68). Austin, TX: PRO-ED.

Fox, L., & Dunlap, G. (2002). Family-centered practices in positive behavior support. *Beyond Behavior,* 24–26.

Fox, L., Vaughn, B. J., Wyatte, M. L., & Dunlap, G. (2002). "We can't expect other people to understand": Family perspectives on problem behavior. *Exceptional Children, 68,* 437–450.

Frankland, H. C., Edmonson, H., & Turnbull, A. P. (2001). Positive behavioral support: Family, school, and community partnerships. *Beyond Behavior,* 7–9.

Friend, M., & Cook, L. (2003). *Interactions: Collaboration skills for school professionals* (4th ed.). Boston: Allyn and Bacon.

Frost, J. (2002). Sarah syndrome: A mother's view of having a child with no diagnosis. *Exceptional Parent, 32,* 70–71.

Fuller, M. L., & Olsen, G. (1998). *Home-school relations: Working successfully with parents and families.* Boston: Allyn and Bacon.

Geisthardt, C. L., Brotherson, M. J., & Cook, C. C. (2002).

Friendships of children with disabilities in the home environment. *Education and Training in Mental Retardation and Developmental Disabilities, 37,* 235–252.

Gray, D. E. (2002). Ten years on: A longitudinal study of families of children with autism. *Journal of Intellectual and Developmental Disability, 27,* 215–222.

Harland, P., Cuskelly, M. (2000). The responsibilities of adult siblings of adults with dual sensory impairments. *International Journal of Disability Development and Education, 47,* 293–307.

Harmon, D. (1999). The do's and don'ts planning for your grandchild with special needs. *Exceptional Parent, 29* (12), 74–75.

Hastings, R. P., Taunt, H. M. (2002). Positive perceptions in families of children with developmental disabilities. *American Journal on Mental Retardation, 107,* 116–27.

Hauser-Cram, P., Warfield, M. E., Shonkoff, J. P., Krauss, M. W. (2001). Children with disabilities: A longitudinal study of child development and parent well-being. *Monographs of the Society for Reasearch in Child Development, 66,* 1–114.

Herbert, M. J., Klemm, D. & Schimanski, C. (1999). Giving the gift of support: From parent to parent. *Exceptional Parent, 29*(8), 58–62.

Howie, D. (1999). Models and morals: Meanings underpinning the scientific study of special educational needs. *International Journal of Disability, Development, and Education, 46*(1), 9–24.

Johnson, C. (2000). What do families need? *Journal of Positive Behavior Interventions, 2,* 115–117.

Kellegrew, D. H. (2000). Constructing daily routines: A qualitative examination of mothers with young children with disabilities. *American Journal of Occupational Therapy, 54,* 252–259.

Kolb, S. M., & Hanley-Maxwell, C. (2003). Critical social skills for adolescents with high incidence disabilities: Parental perspectives. *Council for Exceptional Children, 69,* 163–179.

Kroth, R. L., & Edge, D. (1997). *Strategies for communicating with parents and families of exceptional children.* Denver, CO: Love.

Lake, J. F., & Billingsley, B. S. (2000). An analysis of factors that contribute to

parent–school conflict in special education. *Remedial and Special Education, 21,* 240–251.

Lamb, M. E., & Meyer, D. J. (1991). Fathers of children with special needs. In M. Seligman (Ed.), *The family with a handicapped child* (2nd ed., pp. 151–180). Boston: Allyn and Bacon.

Lambie, R. (2000a). *Family systems within educational contexts: Understanding at-risk and special needs students* (2nd ed.). Denver: Love Publishing Company.

Lambie, R. (2000b). Working with families of at-risk and special needs students: A systems change model. *Focus on Exceptional Children, 32,* 1–23.

Larson, E. A. (2000). The orchestration of occupation: The dance of mothers. *American Journal of Occupational Therapy, 54,* 269–280.

Last, E. C. (2001). I have learned. . . . In S. D. Klein & K. Schive (Eds.), *You will dream new dreams* (pp. 56–60). New York: Kensington Books.

Lee, A. L., Strauss, L., Wittman, P., Jackson, B., & Carstens, A. (2001). The effects of chronic illness on roles and emotions of caregivers. *Occupational Therapy in Health Care, 14,* 47–60.

Levinson, E. M., McKee, L., & Dematteo, F. J. (2000). The exceptional child grows up: Transition from school to adult life. In M. J. Fine & R. L. Simpson (Eds.), *Collaboration with parents and families of children with exceptionalities* (2nd ed., pp. 409–436). Austin, TX: PRO-ED.

Linan-Thompson, S., & Jean, R. E. (1997). Completing the parent participation puzzle: Accepting diversity. *Teaching Exceptional Children, 30* (Nov./Dec.), 46–50.

Lobato, D. J., Faust, D., & Spirito, A. (1988). Examining the effects of chronic disease and disability on children's sibling relationships. *Journal of Pediatric Psychology, 13,* 389–407.

Lucyshyn, J. M., Blumberg, E. R., & Kayser, A. T. (2000). Improving the quality of support to families of children with severe behavior problems in the first decade of the new millennium. *Journal of Positive Behavior Interventions, 2,* 113–115.

Masson, E. J., Kruse, L. A., Farabaugh, A., Gershberg, R., and Kohler, M. S. (2000). Children with exceptionalities: Opportunities for collaboration between family and

school. In M. J. Fine & R. L. Simpson (Eds.), *Collaboration with parents and families of children with exceptionalities* (2nd ed., pp. 69–88). Austin, TX: PRO-ED.

McHugh, M. (1999). *Special siblings.* New York: Hyperion.

McKay, M. M. (2000). What we can do to increase involvement of urban children and families in mental health services and prevention programs. *Report on Emotional and Behavioral Disorders in Youth, 1,* 11–12, 20.

McPhee, N. (1982). A very special magic: A grandparent's delight. *Exceptional Parent, 12*(3), 13–16.

Meyer, D. J. (1995). *Uncommon fathers: Reflections on raising a child with a disability.* Bethesda, MD: Woodbine House.

Meyers, D. (1997). *Views from our shoes: Growing up with a brother or sister with special needs.* Bethesda, MD: Woodbine House.

Muscott, H. S. (2002). Exceptional partnerships: Listening to the voices of families. *Preventing School Failure, 46,* 66–69.

Nassar-Mcmillan, S., & Algozzine, B. (2001). Improving outcomes and future practices: Family-centered programs and services. In D. J. O'Shea, L. J. O'Shea, B. Algozzine, & D. Hammitte (Eds.), *Families and teachers of individuals with disabilities: Collaborative orientations and responsive practices* (pp. 273–292). Boston: Allyn & Bacon.

O'-Shea, D. J., O'Shea, L. J., Algozzine, B., Hammitte, D. (2001). Families and teachers of individuals with disabilities: *Collaborative orientations and responsive practices.* Boston: Allyn & Bacon.

Overton, J. (2000). Letter to my son. *Focus on Autism and Other Developmental Disabilities, 15,* 221–223.

Parent Project for Muscular Dystrophy Research. (2000). *Band-aids and blackboards: Brothers and sisters have something to say: Love me, love me not* [Online]. Available: http://www.parentdmd.org/frame20.htm

Park, J., Turnbull, A. P., & Turnbull, H. R., III (2002). Impacts of poverty on quality of life in families of children with disabilities. *Exceptional Children, 68,* 151–170.

Peterson, S. M. P., Derby, K. M., Berg, W. K., & Horner, R. H. (2002). Collaboration with families in the functional behavior assessment of and in-

tervention for severe behavior problems. *Education and Treatment of Children, 25,* 5–25.

Pipp-Siegel, S., Sedey, A. L., & Yoshinaga-Itano, C. (2002). Predictors of parental stress in mothers of young children with hearing loss. *Journal of Deaf Studies and Deaf Education, 7,* 1–17.

Powell-Smith, K. A., & Stollar, S. A. (1997). Families of children with disabilities. In G. G. Bear, K. M. Minke, & A. Thomas (Eds.), *Children's needs II: Development, problems, and alternatives* (pp. 667–680). Bethesda, MD: National Association of School Psychologists.

Rivers, K. O. (2000). Working with caregivers of infants and toddlers with special needs from culturally and linguistically diverse backgrounds. *Infant Toddler Intervention: The Transdisciplinary Journal, 10,* 61–72.

Sandler, A. G., Warren, S. H., & Raver, S. A. (1995). Grandparents as a source of support for parents of children with disabilities: A brief report. *Mental Retardation, 33* (August), 248–250.

Santarelli, G., Koegel, R. L., Casas, J. M., & Koegel, L. K. (2001). Culturally diverse families participating in behavior therapy parent education programs for children with developmental disabilities. *Journal of Positive Behavior Interventions, 3,* 120–123.

Scherman, A., Gardner, J. E., & Brown, P. (1995). Grandparents' adjustment to grandchildren with disabilities. *Educational Gerontology, 21* (April/May), 261–273.

Seligman, M. (1991). Siblings of disabled brothers and sisters. In M. Seligman (Ed.), *The family with a handicapped child* (2nd ed., pp. 181–202). Boston: Allyn and Bacon.

Seligman, M., & Darling, R. B. (1989). *Ordinary families, special children.* New York: Guilford.

Shelden, M. L., & Rush, D. D. (2001). The ten myths about providing early intervention services in natural environments. *Infants and Young Children, 14,* 1–13.

Simmerman, S., Blacher, J., & Baker, B. L. (2001). Fathers' and mothers' perceptions of father involvement in families with young children with a disability. *Journal of Intellectual and Developmental Disability, 26,* 325–338.

Simpson, R. L., & Zurkowski, J. K. (2000). Parent and

professional collaborative relationships in an era of change. In M. J. Fine, & R. L. Simpson (Eds.), *Collaboration with parents and families of children with exceptionalities* (2nd ed., pp. 89–102). Austin, TX: PRO-ED.

Skinner, D., Bailey, D. B, Correa, V., & Rodriguez, P. (1999). Narrating self and disability: Latino mothers' construction of identities vis-à-vis their child with special needs. *Exceptional Children, 65*(4), 481–495.

Stebelton, M. (2001). Learning to cope. In S. D. Klein & K. Schive (Eds.), *You will dream new dreams* (pp. 73–74). New York, NY: Kensington Books.

Taylor, J. M., & Baglin, C. A. (2000). Families of young children with disabilities: Perceptions in the early childhood special education literature. *Infant Toddler Intervention. The Transdisciplinary Journal, 10,* 239–257.

Turbiville, V. (1997). *Literature review: Fathers, their children, and disability.* Lawrence, KS: The Beach Center on Families and Disability, The University of Kansas.

Turbiville, V. P., & Marquis, J. G. (2001). Father participation in early education programs. *Topics in Early Childhood Special Education, 21,* 223–231.

Turnbull, A. P., & Turnbull, H. R., III. (1993). Participatory research on cognitive coping: From concepts to research planning. In A. P. Turnbull, J. M. Patterson, S. K. Behr, D. L. Murphy, D. L. Marquis, & M. J. Blue-Banning (Eds.), *Cognitive coping, families, and disability* (pp. 1–14). Baltimore, MD: Paul H. Brookes.

Turnbull, A., & Turnbull, H. R., III. (1997). *Families, professionals, and exceptionality: A special partnership.* Upper Saddle River, NJ: Merrill/Prentice-Hall.

Turnbull, A. P., & Turnbull, H. R. (2002). From the old to the new paradigm of disabilities and families: Research to enhance family quality and life outcomes. In J. L. Paul, C. D. Lavely, A. Cranston-Gingras, & E. L. Taylor (Eds.), *Rethinking professional issues in special education.* Westport, Connecticut.

Turner, M. H. (2000). The developmental nature of parent–child relationships: The impact of disabilities. In M. J. Fine & R. L. Simpson (Eds.), *Collaboration with parents and families of children*

*with exceptionalities* (2nd ed., pp. 103–130). Austin, TX: PRO-ED.

Tynan, W. D., & Wornian, K. (2002). Parent management training: Efficacy, effectiveness, and barriers to implementation. *Report on Emotional and Behavioral Disorders in Youth, 2,* 57–58, 71–72.

Vacca, J., & Feinberg, E. (2000). Why can't families be more like us?: Henry Higgins confronts Eliza Doolittle in the world of early intervention. *Infants and Young Children, 13,* 40–48.

Ward, M. J., Cronin, K. B., Renfro, P. D., Lowman, D. K., & Cooper, P. D. (2000). Oral motor feeding in the neonatal intensive care unit: Exploring perceptions of parents and occupational therapists. *Occupational Therapy in Health Care, 12,* 19–37.

West, E. (1981). My child is blind—thoughts on family life. *Exceptional Parent, 1*(1), S9–S12.

Willoughby, J. C., & Glidden, L. M. (1995). Father helping out: Shared child care and marital satisfaction of parents and children with disabilities. *American Journal on Mental Retardation, 99*(4), 399–406.

Worthington, J., Hernandez, M., Friedman, B., & Uzzell, D. (2001). Systems of care: Promising practices in children's mental health, 2001 Series, Vol. 11. Washington DC: Center for Effective Collaboration and Practice, American Institutes for Research.

Young, D. M., & Roopnarine, J. L. (1994). Fathers' childcare involvement with children with and without disabilities. *Topic in Early Childhood Special Education, 14* (Winter), 488–502.

Zhang, C., & Bennett, T. (2001). Multicultural views of disability: Implications for early intervention professionals. *Infant Toddler Intervention: The Transdisciplinary Journal, 11,* 143–154.

## CHAPTER 7

Airasian, P. W. (2002). *Educational Research: Competencies for analysis and application* (7th ed.). Upper Saddle River, NJ: Prentice-Hall.

Alarcon, M., Knopik, V. S., & DeFries, J. C. (2000). Covariation of mathematics achievement and general cognitive ability in twins. *Journal of School Psychology, 38,* 63–77.

American Psychiatric Association. (2000). *Diagnostic and statistical manual of mental disorders* (4th ed.–text revision). Washington, DC: Author.

Apel, K. (2001). Developing evidence-based practices and research collaborations in school settings. *Language, Speech, and Hearing Services in Schools, 32*(3), 196–197.

Bauer, A. M., & Brown, G. M. (2001). *Adolescents and inclusion: Transforming secondary schools.* Baltimore, MD: Paul H. Brookes.

Baum, S. M., & Olenchak, F. R. (2002). The alphabet children: GT, ADHD, and more. *Exceptionality, 10*(2), 77–91.

Bayliss, D. M., & Roodenrys, S. (2000). Executive processing and attention deficit hyperactivity disorder: An application of the supervisory attentional system. *Developmental Neuropsychology, 17*(2), 161–180.

Bender, W. N. (2001). *Learning disabilities: Characteristics, identification, and teaching strategies* (4th ed.). Boston: Allyn and Bacon.

Bender, W. N. (2002). *Differentiating instruction for students with learning disabilities: Best teaching practices for general and special educators.* Thousand Oaks, CA: Corwin Press.

Bimmel, P. (2001). Effects of reading strategy instruction in secondary education—A review of intervention studies. *Educational Studies in Language and Literature, 1*(3), 273–298.

Bishop, A., & Jones, P. (2002). Promoting inclusive practice in primary initial teacher training: Influencing hearts as well as minds. *Support for Learning, 17*(2), 58–63.

Bitter, G. G., & Pierson, M. E. (2002). *Using technology in the classroom* (5th ed.). Boston: Allyn and Bacon.

Blum, R. W., Kelly, A., & Ireland, M. (2001). Health-risk behaviors and protective factors among adolescents with mobility impairments and learning and emotional disabilities. *Journal of Adolescent Health, 28,* 481–490.

Bradshaw, Y. M. (2001). Case studies of postsecondary college students with learning disabilities. *Dissertation Abstracts International Section A: Humanities and Social Sciences, 62*(2-A), 469.

Bredberg, E. A., & Siegel, L. S. (2001). Learning disability and behavior therapy: A review of practice and a view to the future. *Behavior Therapy, 32,* 651–666.

Brook, U., Watemberg, N., & Geva, D. (2000). Attitude and knowledge of attention deficit hyperactivity disorder and learning disability among high school teachers. *Patient Education and Counseling, 40,* 247–252.

Calhoon, J. A. (2001). Factors affecting the reading of rimes in words and nonwords in beginning readers with cognitive disabilities and typically developing readers: Explorations in similarity and difference in word recognition cue use. *Journal of Autism and Developmental Disorders, 31,* 491–504.

Carnine, D. (2000). *Why education experts resist effective practices (And what it would take to make education more like medicine).* Washington, DC: Thomas B. Fordham Foundation.

Cawley, J., Parmar, R., Foley, T. E., Salmon, S., & Roy, S. (2001). Arithmetic performance of students: Implications for standards and programming. *Exceptional Children, 67,* 311–328.

Cirino, P. T., Morris, M. K., & Morris, R. D. (2002). Neuropsychological concomitants of calculation skills in college students referred for learning difficulties. *Developmental Neuropsychology, 21*(2), 201–218.

Collis, B., & Pals, N. (2000). A model for predicting an individual's use of a telematics application for a learning-related purpose. *International Journal of Educational Telecommunications, 6,* 63–103.

Conner, D., Ferri, B., Sollis, S., Valle, J., & Vopitta, D. (2002). Mediating discourses of disabilities: Teachers with LD revising the script. Paper presented at the Annual Meeting of the American Educational Research Association, New Orleans, Louisiana.

Cooper, S. A., & Bailey, N. M. (2001). Psychiatric disorders amongst adults with learning disabilities: Prevalence and relationship to ability level. *Irish Journal of Psychological Medicine, 18*(2), 45–53.

Cosden, M., Brown, C., & Elliott, K. (2002). Development of self-understanding and self-esteem in children and adults with learning disabilities. In B. Y. L. Wong and M. L. Donahue (Eds.), *The social dimensions of learning disabilities: Essays in honor of Tanis Bryan.* (pp. 33–51). Mahwah, NJ: Lawrence Erlbaum.

Coyne, M. D., Kame'enui, E. J., & Simmons, D. C. (2001). Prevention and intervention in beginning reading: Two complex systems. *Learning Disabilities Research and Practice, 16*(2), 62–73.

Crawford, L., Tindal, G., & Stieber, S. (2001). Using oral reading rate to predict student performance on statewide achievement tests. *Educational Assessment, 7,* 303–323.

Cummings, E. M., Davies, P., & Campbell, S. (2002). *Developmental psychopathology and family processes, theory, research, and clinical implications.* New York: Guilford.

Cummings, R., Maddux, C. D., & Casey, J. (2000). Individualized transition planning for students with learning disabilities. *Career Development Quarterly, 49,* 60–72.

Dettmer, P. A., Thurston, L. P., & Dyck, N. J. (2002). *Consultation, collaboration, and teamwork for students with special needs* (4th ed.). Boston: Allyn and Bacon.

DiCecco, V. M., & Gleason, M. M. (2002). Using graphic organizers to attain relational knowledge from expository text. *Journal of Learning Disabilities, 35,* 306–320.

Division of Learning Disabilities (1999). *Current Practice Alerts,* (Issue 2), Council for Exceptional Children.

Doyle, A. E., Faraone, S. V., DuPre, E. P., & Biederman, J. (2001). Separating attention deficit hyperactivity disorder and learning disabilities in girls: A familial risk analysis. *American Journal of Psychiatry, 158,* 1666–1672.

Drew, C. J., & Hardman, M. L. (2004). *Mental retardation: A life-cycle approach to people with intellectual disabilities* (8th ed.). Columbus, OH: Merrill.

Dupuy, C. A. (2001). The role of working memory and transcription automaticity in written language among adolescents with learning disabilities: A comparison of production by hand and by computer. *Dissertation Abstracts International Section A: Humanities and Social Sciences, 62*(4-A), 1375.

Erden, G., & Yalin, A. (2001). Patterns of Visual Aural Digit Span Test (VADS) at children with learning disabilities. *Turk Psikoloji Dergisi, 16*(48), 71–86.

Ernsbarger, S. C. (2002). Simple, affordable, and effective strategies for prompting reading behavior. *Reading and Writing Quarterly: Overcoming Learning Difficulties, 18,* 279–284.

Esser, M. M. S. (2002). The effects of metacognitive strategy training and attribution retraining on reading comprehension in African-American students with learning disabilities. *Dissertation Abstracts International, Section A: Humanities and Social Sciences, 62*(7-A), 2340.

Faraone, S. V., Biederman, J., Monuteaux, M. C., Doyle, A. E., & Seidman, L. J. (2001). A psychometric measure of learning disability predicts educational failure four years later in boys with attention-deficit/hyperactivity disorder. *Journal of Attention Disorders, 4*(4), 220–230.

Flanagan, D. P., Bernier, J., Keiser, S., & Ortiz, S. O. (2003). *Diagnosis of learning disability in adulthood.* Boston: Allyn and Bacon.

Fletcher, J. M., Lyon, G. R., Barnes, M., Stuebing, K. K., Francis, D. J., Olson, R. K., Shaywitz, S. E., & Shaywitz, B. A. (2001). Classification of learning disabilities: An evidence-based evaluation. Paper presented at the Learning Disabilities Summit: Building a Foundation for the Future. Washington, DC: August 27–28, 2001.

Forness, S. R., & Kavale, K. A. (2001). ADHD and a return to the medical model of special education. *Education and Treatment of Children, 24*(3), 224–247.

Frank, Y. (2000) Learning disabilities: Classification, clinical features and treatment. In K. J. Palmer (Ed.), *Topics in paediatric psychiatry* (pp. 107–120). Kwai Chung, Hong Kong: Adis International Publications.

Fuchs, D., Fuchs, L. S., Mathes, P. G., Lipsey, M. W., & Roberts, P. H. (2001). Is "learning disabilities" just a fancy term for low achievement?: A meta-analysis of reading differences between low achievers with and without the label. Paper presented at the Learning Disabilities Summit: Building a Foundation for the Future. Washington, DC: August 27–28, 2001.

Fuchs, D., Fuchs, L. S., Thompson, A., Otaiba, S. A., Yen, L., Yang, N. J., Braun, M., & O'Connor, R. E. (2001). Is reading important in reading-readiness programs? A randomized field trial with teachers as program implementers. *Journal of Educational Psychology, 93,* 251–267.

Fuchs, L. S., Fuchs, D., Eaton, S. B., Hamlett, C. L., & Karns, K. M. (2000). Supplemental teacher judgments of mathematics test accommodations with objective data sources. *School Psychology Review, 29,* 65–85.

Fuchs, L. S., Fuchs, D., Hamlett, C. L., & Appleton, A. C. (2002). Explicitly teaching for transfer: Effects on the mathematical problem-solving performance of students with mathematics disabilities. *Learning Disabilities Research and Practice, 17,* 90–106.

Gangadharan, S., Bretherton, K., & Johnson, B. (2001). Pattern of referral to a child learning disability service. *British Journal of Developmental Disabilities, 47*(93, Pt. 2), 99–104.

Geary, D. C., & Hoard, M. K. (2001). Numerical and arithmetical deficits in learning-disabled children: Relation to dyscalculia and dyslexia. *Aphasiology, 15,* 635–647.

Gelfand, D. M., & Drew, C. J. (2003). *Understanding child behavior disorders* (4th ed.). Belmont, CA: Wadsworth.

Gersten, R., Fuchs, L. S., Williams, J. P., & Baker, S. (2001). Teaching reading comprehension strategies to students with learning disabilities: A review of research. *Review of Educational Research, 71,* 279–320.

Gettinger, M., & Koscik, R. (2001). Psychological services for children with learning disabilities. In J. N. Hughes and A. M. La Greca (Eds.), *Handbook of psychological services for children and adolescents* (pp. 421–435). London: Oxford University Press.

Gettinger, M., & Seibert, J. K. (2002). Contributions of study skills to academic competence. *School Psychology Review, 31,* 350–365.

Gonzalez, J. E. J. (2002). Reading disabilities in a language with transparent orthography. In E. Witruk and A. D. Friederici (Eds.), *Basic functions of language, reading and reading disability. Neuropsychology and cognition,* Vol. 20 (pp. 251–264). Dordrecht, Netherlands: Kluwer Academic Publishers.

Gosling, V., & Cotterill, L. (2000). An employment project as a route to social inclusion for people with learning difficulties? *Disability and Society, 15,* 1001–1018.

Graham, S., Harris, K. R., & Larsen, L. (2001). Prevention and intervention of writing difficulties for students with learning disabilities. *Learning Disabilities Research and Practice, 16*(2), 74–84.

Grant, K. E., Compas, B. E., Stuhlmacher, A. F., Thurm, A. E., McMahon, S. D., & Halpert, J. A. (2003). Stressors and child and adolescent psychopathology: Moving from markers to mechanisms of risk. *Psychological Bulletin, 129,* 447–466.

Gregg, N., Coleman, C., Stennett, R. B., & Davis, M. (2002). Discourse complexity of college writers with and without disabilities: A multidimensional analysis. *Journal of Learning Disabilities, 35,* 23–38, 56.

Gresham, F. M., Sugai, G., & Horner, R. H. (2001). Interpreting outcomes of social skills training for students with high-incidence disabilities. *Exceptional Children, 67,* 331–344.

Grigorenko, E. L., & Lockery, D. (2002). Smart is as stupid does: Exploring bases of erroneous reasoning of smart people regarding learning and other disabilities. In R. J. Sternberg (Ed.), *Why smart people can be so stupid* (pp. 159–186). New Haven, CT: Yale University Press.

Gronlund, N. E. (2000). *How to write and use instructional objectives* (6th ed.). Columbus, OH: Merrill/Prentice-Hall.

Gronlund, N. E. (2003). *Assessment of student achievement* (7th ed.). Boston: Allyn and Bacon.

Gutstein, S. E., & Sheely, R. K. (2002). *Relationship development intervention with young children: Social and emotional development activities for Asperger Syndrome, autism, PPD and NLD.* London, England: Jessica Kingsley Publishers.

Hallahan, D. P. (2002). *Identification of learning disabilities: Research to policy.* Mahwah, NJ: Lawrence Erlbaum.

Hamilton, J. (2001). Evidence-based medicine. *Journal of the American Academy of Child and Adolescent Psychiatry, 40,* 617–618.

Hartman-Hall, H. M., & Haaga, D. A. F. (2002). College students' willingness to seek help for their learning disabilities. *Learning Disability Quarterly, 25,* 263–276.

Heiman, T. (2002). Parents of children with disabilities: Resilience, coping, and future expectations. *Journal of*

*Developmental and Physical Disabilities, 14*(2), 159–171.

Henry, L. A. (2001). How does the severity of a learning disability affect working memory performance? *Memory, 9*(4–6), 233–247.

Hutchinson, N. L., Freeman, J. G., & Bell, K. S. (2002). Children and adolescents with learning disabilities: Case studies of social relations in inclusive classrooms. In B. Y. L. Wong and M. L. Donahue (Eds.), *The social dimensions of learning disabilities: Essays in honor of Tanis Bryan* (pp. 189–214). Mahwah, NJ: Lawrence Erlbaum.

Jefferson-Wilson, P. (2000). Community college students with learning disabilities: Percept of emotional self-efficacy. *Dissertation Abstracts International Section A: Humanities and Social Sciences, 60*(10-A), 3611.

Johnson, C. R., & Slomka, G. (2000). Learning, motor, and communication disorders. In M. Hersen and R. T. Ammerman (Eds.), *Advanced abnormal child psychology* (2nd ed., pp. 371–385). Mahwah, NJ: Lawrence Erlbaum.

Jordon, N. C., Kaplan, D., & Hanich, L. B. (2002). Achievement growth in children with learning difficulties in mathematics: Findings of a two-year longitudinal study. *Journal of Educational Psychology, 94,* 586–597.

Joseph, L. M., & Hunter, A. D. (2001). Differential application of a cue card strategy for solving fraction problems: Exploring instructional utility of the Cognitive Assessment System. *Child Study Journal, 31,* 123–136.

Kamhi, A. G., & Catts, H. W. (2002). The language basis of reading: Implications for classification and treatment of children with reading disabilities. In K. G. Bulter and E. R. Silliman (Eds.), *Speaking, reading, and writing in children with language learning disabilities: New paradigms in research and practice* (pp. 45–72). Mahwah, NJ: Lawrence Erlbaum.

Kaukiainen, A., Salmivalli, C., Lagerspetz, K., Tamminen, M., Vauras, M., Maeki, H., & Poskiparta, E. (2002). Learning difficulties, social intelligence and self-concept: Connections to bully–victim problems. *Scandinavian Journal of Psychology, 43,* 269–278.

Kavale, K. A. (2001). Discrepancy models in the identification of learning disability. Paper presented at the Learning Disabilities Summit: Building a Foundation for the Future. Washington, DC: August 27–28, 2001.

Kennedy, C. H., & Fisher, D. (2001). *Inclusive middle schools.* Baltimore: Paul H. Brookes.

Kerr, G. R. D. (2001). Assessing the needs of learning disabled young people with additional disabilities: Implications for planning adult services. *Journal of Learning Disabilities, 5,* 157–174.

Kirk, S. A. (1963). Behavioral diagnosis and remediation of learning disabilities. *Proceedings: Conference on exploration into the problems of the perceptually handicapped* (Vol. 1). First Annual Meeting, Chicago.

Klassen, R. (2002). A question of calibration: A review of the self-efficacy beliefs of students with learning disabilities. *Learning Disability Quarterly, 25*(2), 88–102.

Klinger, J. K., & Vaughn, S. (2002). The changing roles and responsibilities of an LD specialist. *Learning Disability Quarterly, 25,* 19–31.

Kujala, T. (2002). The mismatch negativity as an index of auditory dysfunction in dyslexia. In E. Witruk and A. D. Friederici (Eds.), *Basic functions of language, reading and reading disability. Neuropsychology and cognition, 20,* (pp. 359–368). Dordrecht, Netherlands: Kluwer Academic Publishers.

Lardieri, L. A., Blacher, J., & Swanson, H. L. (2000). Sibling relationships and parent stress in families of children with and without learning disabilities. *Learning Disability Quarterly, 23,* 105–116.

Larsen, S. (1978). Learning disabilities and the professional educator. *Learning Disability Quarterly, 1*(1), 5–12.

Lerner, J. (2003). Learning disabilities: Theories, diagnosis, and teaching strategies (9th ed.). Boston: Houghton Mifflin.

Lichtenberger, E. O. (2001). The Kaufman tests—K-ABC and KAIT. In A. S. Kaufman and N. L. Kaufman (Eds.), *Specific learning disabilities and difficulties in children and adolescents: Psychological assessment and evaluation* (pp. 97–140). New York: Cambridge University Press.

Linn, R. L., & Gronlund, N. E. (2001). *Measurement and assessment in teaching* (8th ed.). Columbus, OH: Merrill/Prentice-Hall.

Lovett, M. W., Lacerenza, L., & Borden, S. L. (2000). Putting struggling readers on the PHAST track: A program to integrate phonological and strategy-based remedial reading instruction and maximize outcomes. *Journal of Learning Disabilities, 33,* 458–476.

Lovett, M. W., Lacerenza, L., Borden, S. L., Frijters, J. C., Steinbach, K. A., & DePalma, M. (2000). Components of effective remediation for developmental reading disabilities: Combining phonological and strategy-based instruction to improve outcomes. *Journal of Educational Psychology, 92,* 263–283.

MacArthur, C. A. (2000). New tools for writing: Assistive technology for students with writing difficulties. *Topics in Language Disorders, 20*(4), 85–100.

Martin, A., Scahill, L., Klin, A., & Volkmar, F. R. (1999). Higher-functioning pervasive developmental disorders: Rates and patterns of psychotropic drug use. *Journal of the American Academy of Child and Adolescent Psychiatry, 38,* 923–931.

Mastropieri, M. A., & Scruggs, T. E. (2000). *The inclusive classroom: Strategies for effective instruction.* Columbus, OH: Merrill/Prentice-Hall.

Mati-Zissi, H., & Zafiropoulou, M. (2001). Drawing performance in prediction of special learning difficulties of kindergarten children. *Perceptual and Motor Skills, 92*(3, Pt. 2), 1154–1166.

Mayes, S. D., Calhoun, S. L., & Crowell, E. W. (2000). Learning disabilities and ADHD: Overlapping spectrum disorders. *Journal of Learning Disabilities, 33,* 417–424.

Mazza, D. B. (2002). Developing services for learning disabled students at a postsecondary institution. *Dissertation Abstracts International Section A: Humanities and Social Sciences. 62*(7-A), 2360.

Mazzocco, M. M. M. (2001). Math learning disability and math LD subtypes: Evidence from studies of Turner syndrome, fragile X syndrome, and neurofibromatosis type 1. *Journal of Learning Disabilities, 34,* 520–533.

McCurdy, A. E. (2001). Differences in neuropsychological performance among traumatic brain-injured and learning-disabled adults. *Dissertation Abstracts International Section B: The Sciences and Engineering, 61*(12-B), 6753.

McDonough-Ryan, P., DelBello, M., Shear, P. K., Ris, M. D., Soutullo, C., & Strakowski, S. M. (2002). Academic and cognitive abilities in children of parents with bipolar disorder: A test of the nonverbal learning disability model. *Journal of Clinical and Experimental Neuropsychology, 24,* 280–285.

Merrell, K. W. (2002). *Behavioral, social, and emotional assessment of children and adolescents* (2nd ed.). Mahwah, NJ: Lawrence Erlbaum.

Miao, Y., Darch, C., & Rabren, K. (2002). Use of precorrection strategies to enhance reading performance of students with learning and behavior problems. *Journal of Instructional Psychology, 29,* 162–174.

Molina, B. S. G., & Pelham, W. E. (2001). Substance use, substance abuse, and LD among adolescents with a childhood history of ADHD. *Journal of Learning Disabilities, 34,* 333–342.

Moore, D. (2001). Friend or foe? A selective review of the literature concerning abuse of adults with learning disability by those employed to care for them. *Journal of Learning Disabilities, 5,* 245–258.

Morgan, C. N., Roy, M., Nasr, A., Chance, P., Hand, M., Mlele, T., & Roy, A. (2002). A community survey establishing the prevalence rate of autistic disorder in adults with learning disability. *Psychiatric Bulletin, 26*(4), 127–130.

Muir, W. J. (2000). Genetics advances and learning disability. *British Journal of Psychiatry, 176,* 12–19.

Nadeau, K. G., & Quinn, P. O. (2002). An overview of coexisting conditions for women with AD/HD. In K. G. Nadeau and P. O. Quinn (Eds.), *Understanding women with AD/HD* (pp. 152–176). Silver Spring, MD: Advantage Books.

Naglieri, J. A., & Johnson, D. (2000). Effectiveness of a cognitive strategy intervention in improving arithmetic computation based on the PASS theory. *Journal of Learning Disabilities, 33,* 591–597.

Naik, B. I., Gangadharan, S., & Alexander, R. T. (2002). Personality disorders in learning disability: The clinical experience. *British Journal of Developmental Disabilities, 48*(95, Pt. 2), 95–100.

National Joint Committee on Learning Disabilities. (1998). Operationalizing the NJCLD definition of learning disabilities for ongoing assessment in schools. *Learning Disability Quarterly, 24,* 186–193.

National Research Center on Learning Disabilities (2002).

Finding common ground: Consensus statements. NRCLD *Information Digest 2* [Online]. www.nrcld.org.

Nitko, A. J. (2001). *Educational assessment of students* (3rd ed.). Columbus, OH: Merrill/Prentice-Hall.

Oosterhof, A. (2001). *Classroom application of educational measurement* (3rd ed.). Columbus, OH: Merrill/Prentice-Hall.

Osman, B. B. (2000). Learning disabilities and the risk of psychiatric disorders in children and adolescents. In L. L. Greenhill (Ed.), *Learning disabilities: Implications for psychiatric treatment. Review of psychiatry series,* (Vol. 19, no. 5, pp. 33–57). Washington, DC: American Psychiatric Publishing.

Parette, H. P., & Anderson, C. L. (2001). Family and related service partnerships in home computer decision-making. *Special Services in the Schools,17*(1–2), 97–113.

Pavri, S., & Monda-Amaya, L. (2001). Social support in inclusive schools: Student and teacher perspectives. *Exceptional Children, 67,* 391–411.

Pelham, W. E., Hoza, B., Pillow, D. R., Gnagy, E. M., Kipp, H. L., Greiner, A. R., Waschbusch, D. A., Trane, S. T., Greenhouse, J., Wolfson, L., & Fitzpatrick, E. (2002). Effects of methyphenidate and expectancy on children with ADHD: Behavior, academic performance, and attributions in a summer treatment program and regular classroom settings. *Journal of Consulting and Clinical Psychology, 70,* 320–335.

Picton, T. A., & Karki, C. (2002). Referral patterns of children to a psychiatric learning disability service. *British Journal of Developmental Disabilities, 48*(94, Pt. 1), 53–59.

Pozzi, M. E. (2000). Ritalin for whom? Understanding the need for Ritalin in psychodynamic counselling with families of under-5s. *Journal of Child Psychotherapy, 26*(1), 25–43.

Pretorius, E., Naude, H., & Becker, J. (2002). Can excess bilirubin levels cause learning difficulties? *Early Child Development and Care, 172,* 391–404.

Prochnow, J. E., Kearney, A. C., & Carroll-Lind, J. (2000). Successful inclusion: What do teachers say they need? *New Zealand Journal of Educational Studies, 35*(2), 157–177.

Putnam, S. C. (2001). *Nature's Ritalin for the marathon mind:*

*Nurturing your ADHD child with exercise.* Hinesburg, VT: Upper Access.

Rapport, M. D., & Moffitt, C. (2002). Attention deficit/hyperactivity disorder and methylphenidate. A review of height/weight, cardiovascular and somatic complaint side effects. *Clinical Psychology Review, 22,* 1107–1131.

Rath, K. A., & Royer, J. M. (2002). The nature and effectiveness of learning disability services for college students. *Educational Psychology Review, 14,* 353–381.

Reiff, H. B., Hatzes, N. M., Bramel, M. H., & Gibbon, T. (2001). The relation of LD and gender with emotional intelligence in college students. *Journal of Learning Disabilities, 34,* 66–78.

Richman, L. C., & Wood, K. M. (2002). Learning disability subtypes: Classification of high functioning hyperlexia. *Brain and Language, 82,* 10–21.

Riikonen, R., Salonen, I., & Verho, S. (1999). Brain perfusion SPECT and MRI in foetal alcohol syndrome. *Developmental Medicine and Child Neurology, 41,* 652–659.

Roderiques, A. B. (2002). A comparison of ability–achievement discrepancy models for identifying learning disabilities. *Dissertation Abstracts International Section A: Humanities and Social Sciences, 62*(8-A), 2683.

Salkind, N. J. (2002). *Exploring research* (5th ed.). Upper Saddle River, NJ: Prentice-Hall.

Schmidt, R. J., Rozendal, M. S., & Greenman, G. G. (2002). Reading instruction in the inclusion classroom: Research-based practices. *Remedial and Special Education, 23*(3), 130–140.

Scott, C. M. (2000). Principles and methods of spelling instruction: Applications for poor spellers. *Topics in Language Disorders, 20*(3), 66–82.

Shapiro, B. K. (2001). Learning disabilities. In M. L. Batshaw, (Ed.), *When your child has a disability: The complete sourcebook of daily and medical care* (rev. ed., pp. 373–387). Baltimore, MD: Paul H. Brookes.

Shapiro, J. (2002). Back to school for women with AD/HD. In K. G. Nadeau and P. O. Quinn (Eds.), *Understanding women with AD/HD* (pp. 373–391). Silver Spring, MD: Advantage Books.

Shaywitz, B. A., Shaywitz, S. E., Pugh, K. R., Mencl, W. E., Fulbright, R. K., Skudlarkski, P.,

Constable, R. T., Marchione, K. E., Fletcher, J. M., Lyon, G. R., & Gore, J. C. (2002). Disruption of posterior brain systems for reading in children with developmental dyslexia. *Biological Psychiatry, 52*(2), 101–110.

Simner, M. L., & Eidlitz, M. R. (2000). Towards an empirical definition of developmental dysgraphia: Preliminary findings. *Canadian Journal of School Psychology, 16*(1), 103–110.

Smith, C. R. (2000). *Learning disabilities: The interaction of learner, task, and setting* (5th ed.). Boston: Allyn and Bacon.

Smith, S. W., & Travis, P. C. (2001). Conducting social competence research considering conceptual frameworks. *Behavioral Disorders, 26,* 360–369.

Snider, V. E., Frankenberger, W., & Aspenson, M. R. (2000). The relationship between learning disabilities and attention deficit hyperactivity disorder: A national survey. *Developmental Disabilities Bulletin, 28,* 18–38.

Stacey, W. (2001). The stress of progression from school to work for adolescents with learning disabilities . . . What about life progress? *Work: Journal of Prevention, Assessment and Rehabilitation, 17*(3), 175–182.

Stanton-Chapman, T. L., Chapman, D. A., & Scott, K. G. (2001). Identification of early risk factors for learning disabilities. *Journal of Early Intervention, 24*(3), 193–206.

Stein, M. A., & Batshaw, M. L. (2001). Attention-deficit/hyperactivity disorder. In M. L. Batshaw (Ed.), *When your child has a disability: The complete sourcebook of daily and medical care* (rev. ed., pp. 355–371). Baltimore, MD: Paul H. Brookes.

Stone, C. A., & May, A. L. (2002). The accuracy of academic self-evaluations in adolescents with learning disabilities. *Journal of Learning Disabilities, 35,* 370–383.

Stuebing, K. K., Fletcher, J. M., LeDoux, J. M., Lyon, G. R., Shaywitz, S. E., & Shaywitz, B. A. (2002). Validity of IQ-discrepancy classifications of reading disabilities: A meta-analysis. *American Educational Research Journal, 39,* 469–518.

Summers, N., & Jenkins, C. (2001). Enabling practice: An investigation into the support of families with children with learning disabilities. *Journal of Learning Disabilities, 5,* 57–67.

Svetaz, M. V., Ireland, M., & Blum, R. (2000). Adolescents with learning disabilities: Risk and protective factors associated with emotional well-being: Findings from the National Longitudinal Study of Adolescent Health. *Journal of Adolescent Health, 27,* 340–348.

Swanson, H. L., & Hoskyn, M. (2001). Instructing adolescents with learning disabilities: A component and composite analysis. *Learning Disabilities Research and Practice, 16*(2), 109–119.

Taylor, H. G., Anselmo, M., Foreman, A. L., Schatschneider, C., & Angelopoulos, J. (2000). Utility of kindergarten teacher judgments in identifying early learning problems. *Journal of Learning Disabilities, 33,* 200–210.

Taylor, L. K., Alber, S. R., & Walker, D. W. (2002). The comparative effects of a modified self-questioning strategy and story mapping on the reading comprehension of elementary students with learning disabilities. *Journal of Behavioral Educatoin, 11*(2) 69–87.

Taylor, R. (2000). *Assessment of exceptional students: Educational and psychological procedures* (5th ed.). Boston: Allyn and Bacon.

Torgeson, J. K. (2001). Empirical and theoretical support for direct diagnosis of learning disabilities by assessment of intrinsic processing weaknesses. Paper presented at the Learning Disabilities Summit: Building a Foundation for the Future. Washington, DC: August 27–28, 2001.

Torgerson, C. J., & Elbourne, D. (2002). A systematic review and meta-analysis of the effectiveness of information and communication technology (ICT) on the teaching of spelling. *Journal of Research in Reading, 25,* 129–143.

Troia, G. A., & Graham, S. (2002). The effectiveness of a highly explicit, teacher-directed strategy instruction routine: Changing the writing performance of students with learning disabilities. *Journal of Learning Disabilities, 35*(4), 290–305.

Trusdell, M. L., & Horowitz, I. W. (2002). *Understanding learning disabilities: A parent guide and workbook* (3rd ed.). Timonium, MD: York Press.

Ungerleider, D., & Maslow, P. (2001). Association of educational therapists: Position paper on the SAT. *Journal of*

*Learning Disabilities, 34,* 311–314.

U.S. Department of Education, Office of Special Education Programs. (2002). *Twenty-fourth annual report to Congress on the implementation of the Individuals with Disabilities Education Act.* Washington, DC: Author.

Vaid, J., Singh, M., Sakhuja, T., & Gupta, G. C. (2002). Stroke direction asymmetry in figure drawing: Influence of handedness and reading/writing habits. *Brain and Cognition, 48*(2–3), 597–602.

Vallecorsa, A. L., deBettencourt, L., & Zigmond, N. (2000). *Students with mild disabilities in general education settings: A guide for special educators.* Columbus, OH: Merrill/Prentice-Hall.

Van den Broeck, W. (2002). "Will the real discrepant learning disability please stand up?" Reply. *Journal of Learning Disabilities, 35,* 209–213.

Van-Noord, R. G., & Prevatt, F. F. (2002). Rater agreement on IQ and achievement tests effect on evaluations of learning disabilities. *Journal of School Psychology, 40*(2), 167–176.

Vaughn, S., Elbaum, B., & Boardman, A. G. (2001). The social functioning of students with learning disabilities: Implications for inclusion. *Exceptionality, 9,* 47–66.

Vaughn, S., Gersten, R., & Chard, D. J. (2000). The underlying message in LD intervention research: Findings from research syntheses. *Exceptional Children, 67,* 99–114.

Vaughn, S., Levy, S., Coleman, M., & Bos, C. S. (2002). Reading instruction for students with LD and EBD: A synthesis of observation studies. *Journal of Special Education, 36,* 2–13.

Watkins, M. W., & Kush, J. C. (2002). Confirmatory factor analysis of the WISC-III for students with learning disabilities. *Journal of Psychoeducational Assessment, 20,* 4–19.

Watkins, M. W., Kush, J. C., & Schaefer, B. A. (2002). Diagnostic utility of the Learning Disability Index. *Journal of Learning Disabilities, 35,* 98–103.

Watkins, M. W., & Worrell, F. C. (2000). Diagnostic utility of the number of WISC-III subtests deviating from mean performance among students with learning disabilities. *Psychology in the Schools, 37,* 303–309.

Weinberg, N. Z. (2001). Risk factors for adolescent substance abuse. *Journal of Learning Disabilities, 34,* 343–351.

Welch, M. W., & Jensen, J. (1991). Write, P.L.E.A.S.E.: A video-assisted strategic intervention to improve written expression of inefficient learners. *Journal of Remedial and Special Education, 12,* 37–47.

Welch, M., & Sheridan, S. M. (1995). *Educational partnerships: An ecological approach to serving students at risk.* San Francisco, CA: Harcourt.

Wenar, C., & Kerig, P. (2000). *Developmental psychopathology: From infancy through adolescence* (4th ed.). New York: McGraw-Hill.

Westby, C. (2002). Beyond decoding: Critical and dynamic literacy for students with dyslexia, language learning disabilities (LLD), or attention-deficit/hyperactivity disorder (ADHD). In K. G. Bulter and E. R. Silliman (Eds.), *Speaking, reading, and writing in children with language learning disabilities: New paradigms in research and practice* (pp. 73–107). Mahwah, NJ: Lawrence Erlbaum.

Whittel, B., & Ramcharan, P. (2000). The trouble with kids: An account of problems experienced with local children by people with learning disabilities. *British Journal of Learning Disabilities, 28,* 21–24.

Willcutt, E. G., Pennington, B. F., & DeFries, J. C. (2000). Etiology of inattention and hyperactivity/impulsivity in a community sample of twins with learning difficulties. *Journal of Abnormal Child Psychology, 28,* 149–159.

Willner, P., Jones, J., Tams, R., & Green, G. (2002). A randomized controlled trial of the efficacy of a cognitive-behavioural anger management group for clients with learning disabilities. *Journal of Applied Research in Intellectual Disabilities, 15,* 224–235.

Willson, V. L., & Reynolds, C. R. (2002). "Misconceptions in Van den Broeck's representation of misconceptions about learning disability research." Comment. *Journal of Learning Disabilities, 35,* 205–208.

Woltz, D. J. (2003). Implicit cognitive processes as aptitudes for learning. *Educational Psychologist, 38,* 95–104.

Woodward, J., & Morocco, C. C. (2002). Introduction to the special issue. *Learning Disabilities Research and Practice, 17*(3), 141–143.

Youngstrom, N. (1991). Most child clinicians support prescribing. *APA Monitor, 22*(3), 21.

Zuriff, G. E. (2000). Extra examination time for students with learning disabilities: An examination of the maximum potential thesis. *Applied Measurement in Education, 13,* 99–117.

## CHAPTER 8

Abikoff, H. (2001). Tailored psychosocial treatments for ADHD: The search for a good fit. *Journal of Community Psychology, 30,* 122–125.

Achenbach, T. M. (1991). *Manual for the Teacher's Report Form and 1991 Profile.* Burlington, VT: University of Vermont, Department of Psychiatry.

Achenbach, T. M. (1992). *Manual for the Child Behavior Checklist/2-3 and 1992 Profile.* Burlington, VT: University of Vermont, Department of Psychiatry.

American Academy of Pediatrics (2000). Diagnosis and evaluation of the child with attention-deficit/hyperactivity disorder (AC0002). *Pediatrics, 105,* 1158–1170.

American Psychiatric Association. (2000). *Diagnostic and statistical manual of mental disorders* (4th ed.–text revision). Washington, DC: Author.

Anastopoulos, A. D., Klinger, E. E., & Temple, E. P. (2001). Treating children and adolescents with attention-deficit/hyperactivity disorder. In J. N. Hughes, N. Jan, and A. M. La Greca (Eds.), *Handbook of psychological services for children and adolescents* (pp. 245–266). London: Oxford University Press.

Bank, C. (2000). Coping with attention deficit disorder. *MSNBC report by Philadelphia, PA Channel 10, NBC, February 1* [Online]. www.msnbc.com/local/ WCAU/245787.asp

Barbosa, J., Tannock, R., & Manassis, K. (2002). Measuring anxiety: Parent–child reporting differences in clinical samples. *Depression and Anxiety, 15*(2), 61–65.

Barkley, R. A., Edwards, G., Laneri, M., Fletcher, K., & Metevia, L. (2001). Executive functioning, temporal discounting, and sense of time in adolescents with attention deficit hyperactivity disorder (ADHD) and oppositional defiant disorder (ODD). *Journal of Abnormal Child Psychology, 29,* 541–556.

Barkley, R. A., Fischer, M., Smallish, L., & Fletcher, K. (2002). The persistence of attention-deficit/hyperactivity disorder into young adulthood as a function of reporting source and definition of disorder. *Journal of Abnormal Psychology, 111,* 279–289.

Baum, S. M., & Olenchak, F. R. (2002). The alphabet children: GT, ADHD, and more. *Exceptionality, 10*(2), 77–91.

Bender, W. N. (2001). *Learning disabilities: Characteristics, identification, and teaching strategies* (4th ed.). Boston: Allyn and Bacon.

Bhaumik, S., Brandford, D., Naik, B. I., & Biswas, A. B. (2000). A retrospective audit of selective serotonin re-uptake inhibitors (fluoxetine and paroxetine) for the treatment of depressive episodes in adults with learning disabilities. *British Journal of Developmental Disabilities, 46*(91, Pt. 2), 131–139.

Biederman, J., Mick, E., & Faraone, S. V. (2000). Age-dependent decline of symptoms of attention deficit hyperactivity disorder: Impact of remission definition and symptom type. *American Journal of Psychiatry, 157,* 816–818.

Bradley, J. D. D., & Golden, C. J. (2001). Biological contributions to the presentation and understanding of attention-deficit/hyperactivity disorder: A review. *Clinical Psychology Review, 21,* 907–929.

Bradshaw, J. L. (2001). *Developmental disorders of the frontostriatal system: Neuropsychological, neuropsychiatric and evolutionary perspectives.* Philadelphia, PA: Psychology Press.

Brand, N., Geenen, R., Oudenhoven, M., Lindeborn, B., van-der-Ree, A., Cohen-Kettenis, P., & Buitelaar, J. K. (2002). Brief report: Cognitive functioning in children with Tourette's syndrome with and without comorbid ADHD. *Journal of Pediatric Psychology, 27,* 203–208.

Brook, U., Watemberg, N., & Geva, D. (2000). Attitude and knowledge of attention deficit hyperactivity disorder and learning disability among high school teachers. *Patient Education and Counseling, 40,* 247–252.

Burns, G. L., & Walsh, J. A. (2002). The influence of ADHD-hyperactivity/impulsivity symptoms on the development of oppositional defiant disorder symptoms in a 2-year longitudinal study. *Journal of Abnormal Child Psychology, 30,* 245–256.

Cains, R. A. (2000). Children diagnosed ADHD: Factors to guide intervention. *Educational Psychology in Practice, 16,* 59–180.

Casey, B. J. (2001). Disruption of inhibitory control in developmental disorders: A mechanistic model of implicated frontostriatal circuitry. In J. L. McClelland and R. S. Siegler (Eds.), *Mechanisms of cognitive development: Behavioral and neural perspectives. Carnegie Mellon symposia on cognition* (pp. 327–349). Mahwah, NJ: Lawrence Erlbaum.

Chi, T. C., & Hinshaw, S. P. (2002). Mother–child relationships of children with ADHD: The role of maternal depressive symptoms and depression-related distortions. *Journal of Abnormal Child Psychology, 30,* 387–400.

Connor, D. F. (2002). Preschool attention deficit hyperactivity disorder: A review of prevalence, diagnosis, neurobiology, and stimulant treatment. *Journal of Developmental and Behavioral Pediatrics, 23*(Supplement 1), S1–S9.

Crystal, D. S., Ostrander, R., Chen, R., & August, G. J. (2001). Multimethod assessment of psychopathology among DSM-IV subtypes of children with attention-deficit/hyperactivity disorder: Self-, parent, and teacher reports. *Journal of Abnormal Child Psychology, 29*(3), 189–205.

Davies, S., & Witte, R. (2000). Self-management and peer-monitoring within a group contingency to decrease uncontrolled verbalizations of children with attention-deficit/hyperactivity disorder. *Psychology in the Schools, 37,* 135–147.

De-La-Paz, S. (2001). Teaching writing to students with attention deficit disorders and specific language impairment. *Journal of Educational Research, 95,* 37–47.

Demaray, M. K., & Elliot, S. N. (2001). Perceived social support by children with characteristics of attention-deficit/hyperactivity disorder. *School Psychology Quarterly, 16,* 68–90.

Dendy, C. A. Z. (2000). Teaching teens with ADD and ADHD: A quick reference guide for teachers and parents. Bethesda, MD: Woodbine House.

Drew, C. J., & Hardman, M. L. (2004). *Mental retardation: A lifespan approach to people with intellectual disabilities* (8th ed.). Columbus, OH: Merrill.

Eshleman, A. S. (1999). Relationship between perinatal complications and attention deficit hyperactivity disorder and other behavioral characteristics. *Dissertation Abstracts International Section A: Hu-*

manities and Social Sciences, 59(10-A), 3836.

Evans, S. W., Pelham, W. E., Smith, B. H., Bukstein, O., Gnagy, E. M., Greiner, A. R., Altenderfer, L., & Baron M. C. (2001). Dose–response effects of methylphenidate on ecologically valid measures of academic performance and classroom behavior in adolescents with ADHD. *Experimental and Clinical Psychopharmacology, 9,* 163–175.

Faraone, S. V. (2000). Attention deficit hyperactivity disorder in adults: Implications for theories of diagnosis. *Current Directions in Psychological Science, 9,* 33–36.

Forbes, G. B. (2001). A comparison of the Conners' Parent & Teacher Rating Scales, the ADD-H Comprehensive Teacher's Rating Scale, and the Child Behavior Checklist in the clinical diagnosis of ADHD. *Journal of Attention Disorders, 5*(1), 25–40.

Forness, S. R., & Kavale, K. A. (2001). ADHD and a return to the medical model of special education. *Education and Treatment of Children, 24*(3), 224–247.

Fredericksen, K. A., Cutting, L. E., Kates, W. R., Mostofsky, S. H., Singer, H. S., Cooper, K. L., Lanham, D. C., Denckla, M. B., & Kaufmann, W. E. (2002). Disproportionate increases of white matter in right frontal lobe in Tourette syndrome. *Neurology, 58,* 85–89.

Frick, P. J., Silverthorn, P., & Evans, C. S. (1994). Assessment of childhood anxiety using structured interviews: Patterns of agreement among informants and association with maternal anxiety. *Psychological Assessment, 6,* 372–379.

Gelfand, D. M., & Drew, C. J. (2003). *Understanding child behavior disorders* (4th ed.). Belmont, CA: Wadsworth.

Greenberg, M. T., Speltz, M. L., DeKlyen, M., & Jones, K. (2001) Correlates of clinic referral for early conduct problems: Variable- and person-oriented approaches. *Development and Psychopathology, 13,* 255–276.

Greene, R. W., Biederman, J., Faraone, S. V., Monuteaux, M. C., Mick, E., DuPre, E. P., Fine, C. S., & Goring, J. G. (2001). Social impairment in girls with ADHD: Patterns, gender comparisons, and correlates. *Journal of the American Academy of Child and Adolescent Psychiatry, 40,* 704–710.

Gresham, F. M., Lane, K. L., & Lambros, K. M. (2001). Comorbidity of conduct problems and ADHD: Identification of "fledgling psychopaths." In H. M. Walker and M. H. Epstein (Eds.), *Making schools safer and violence free: Critical issues, solutions, and recommended practices* (pp. 17–27). Austin, TX: PRO-ED.

Handen, B. L., Feldman, H. M., Lurier, A., & Murray, P. J. H. (1999). Efficacy of methylphenidate among preschool children with developmental disabilities and ADHD. *Journal of the American Academy of Child and Adolescent Psychiatry, 38,* 805–812.

Hankin, C. S., Wright, A., & Gephart, H. (2001). The burden of attention-deficit/hyperactivity disorder. *Drug Benefit Trends, 13*(4), 7BH–13BH.

Hepperlen, T. M., Clay, D. L., Henly, G. A., & Barke, C. R. (2002). Measuring teacher attitudes and expectations toward students with ADHD: Development of the Test of Knowledge About ADHD (KADD). *Journal of Attention Disorders, 5*(3), 133–142.

Hirshfeld-Becker, D. R., Biederman, J., Faraone, S. V., Violette, H., Wrightsman, J., & Rosenbaum, J. F. (2002). Temperamental correlates of disruptive behavior disorders in young children: Preliminary findings. *Biological Psychiatry, 51,* 563–574.

Jackson, D. A. (2002). The negative halo effect of oppositional defiant behaviors on teacher ratings of ADHD: Impact of child gender. *Dissertation Abstracts International Section B: The Sciences and Engineering, 62*(9-B), 4221.

Jensen, P. S., & Members of the MTA Cooperative Group. (2002). ADHD comorbidity findings from the MTA Study: New diagnostic subtypes and their optimal treatments. In J. E. Helzer and J. J. Hudziak (Eds.), *Defining psychopathology in the 21st century: DSM-V and beyond* (pp. 169–192). Washington, DC: American Psychiatric Publishing.

Jerome, L, & Segal, A. (2001). Benefit of long-term stimulants on driving in adults with ADHD. *Journal of Nervous and Mental Disease, 189,* 63–64.

Johnson, D. E., Epstein, J. N., Waid, L. R., Latham, P. K., Voronin, K. E., & Anton, R. F. (2001). Neuropsychological performance deficits in adults with attention-deficit/hyperactivity disorder. *Archives of*

Clinical Neuropsychology, 16, 587–604.

Johnson, J. H., & Reader, S. K. (2002). Assessing stress in families of children with ADHD: Preliminary development of the Disruptive Behavior Stress Inventory (DBSI). *Journal of Clinical Psychology in Medical Settings, 9,* 51–62.

Kamphaus, R. W., & Frick, P. J. (1996). *Clinical assessment of child and adolescent personality and behavior.* Needham Heights, MA: Allyn and Bacon, p. 131.

Kelly, K. M. (2001). An assessment of the peer relationships of elementary school children diagnosed with attention deficit hyperactivity disorder. *Dissertation Abstracts International Section A: Humanities and Social Sciences, 62*(4-A), 1324.

Kim, B. N., Lee, J. S., Shin, M. S., Cho, S. C., & Lee, D. S. (2002). Regional cerebral perfusion abnormalities in attention deficit/hyperactivity disorder: Statistical parametric mapping analysis. *European Archives of Psychiatry and Clinical Neuroscience, 252*(5), 219–225.

Klein, D. A. (2002). The relationship between elementary school teachers' understanding of attention deficit-hyperactivity disorder and teaching stress. *Dissertation Abstracts International Section A: Humanities and Social Sciences, 62*(8-A), 2682.

Klingberg, T., Forssberg, H., & Westerberg, H. (2002). Training of working memory in children with ADHD. *Journal of Clinical and Experimental Neuropsychology, 24,* 781–791.

Klorman, R. (2000). Psychophysiological research on childhood psychopathology. In M. Hersen and R. T. Ammerman (Eds.), *Advanced abnormal child psychology* (2nd ed., pp. 57–80). Mahwah, NJ: Lawrence Erlbaum.

Knapp, S. E., & Jongsma, A. E., Jr. (2002). *The school counseling and school social work treatment planner.* New York: Wiley.

Kollins, S. H., MacDonald, E. K., & Rush, C. R. (2001). Assessing the abuse potential of methylphenidate in nonhuman and human subjects: A review. *Pharmacology, Biochemistry and Behavior, 68,* 611–627.

Krane, E., & Tannock, R. (2001). WISC-III third factor indexes learning problems but not attention deficit/hyperactivity disorder. *Journal of Attention Disorders, 5*(2), 69–78.

Kube, D. A., Petersen, M. C., & Palmer, F. B. (2002). Attention deficit hyperactivity disorder: Comorbidity and medication use. *Clinical Pediatrics, 41,* 461–469.

Kutcher, S. (2002). *Practical child and adolescent psychopharmacology.* New York: Cambridge University Press.

Livni, E. (2000). Misdiagnosing misbehavior?: First Lady calls for a closer look at psychotropics for kids. ABC News, March 20.

Lohman, M. C. (2002). Cultivating problem-solving skills through problem-based approaches to professional development. *Human Resource Development Quarterly, 13,* 243–261.

Martin, N., Scourfield, J., & McGuffin, P. (2002). Observer effects and heritability of childhood attention-deficit/hyperactivity disorder symptoms. *British Journal of Psychiatry, 180,* 260–265.

Matazow, G. S., & Kamphaus, R. W. (2001). Behavior Assessment System for Children (BASC): Toward accurate diagnosis and effective treatment. In J. J. W. Andrews and D. H. Saklofske (Eds.), *Handbook of psychoeducational assessment: Ability, achievement, and behavior in children. A volume in the educational psychology series* (pp. 257–288). San Diego, CA: Academic.

Matthews, D. D. (2002). *Attention deficit disorder sourcebook.* Detroit: Omnigraphics.

Mayes, S. D., Calhoun, S. L., & Crowell, E. W. (2000). Learning disabilities and ADHD: Overlapping spectrum disorders. *Journal of Learning Disabilities, 33,* 417–424.

McGoey, K. E., Eckert, T. L., & DuPaul, G. J. (2002). Early intervention for preschool-age children with ADHD: A literature review. *Journal of Emotional and Behavioral Disorders, 10,* 14–28.

Merrell, K. W. (2002). *Behavioral, social, and emotional assessment of children and adolescents* (2nd ed.). Mahwah, NJ: Lawrence Erlbaum.

Mick, E., Biederman, J., Prince, J., Fischer, M. J., & Faraone, S. V. (2002). Impact of low birth weight on attention-deficit/hyperactivity disorder. *Journal of Developmental and Behavioral Pediatrics, 23,* 16–22.

Molina, B. S. G., Smith, B. H., & Pelham, W. E. (2001). Factor structure and criterion validity of secondary school teacher ratings of ADHD and ODD. *Journal of Abnormal Child Psychology, 29,* 71–82.

Mrug, S., Hoza, B., & Gerdes, A. C. (2001). Children with attention-deficit/hyperactivity disorder: Peer relationships and peer-oriented interventions. In D. W. Nangle and C. A. Erdley (Eds.), *The role of friendship in psychological adjustment. New directions for child and adolescent development* (pp. 51–77). San Francisco, CA: Jossey-Bass/Pfeiffer.

MTA Cooperative Group. (1999a). A 14-month randomized clinical trial of treatment strategies for attention-deficit/hyperactivity disorder. *Archives of General Psychiatry, 56,* 1073–1086.

MTA Cooperative Group. (1999b). Moderators and mediators of treatment response for children with attention-deficit/hyperactivity disorder: The multimodal treatment study of children with attention-deficit/hyperactivity disorder. *Archives of General Psychiatry, 56,* 1088–1096.

Nadder, T. S., Silberg, J. L., Rutter, M., Maes, H. H., & Eaves, L. J. (2001). Comparison of multiple measures of ADHD symptomatology: A multivariate genetic analysis. *Journal of Child Psychology and Psychiatry and Allied Disciplines, 42,* 475–486.

Nadeau, K. G., & Quinn, P. O. (2002). An overview of coexisting conditions for women with AD/HD. In K. G. Nadeau and P. O. Quinn (Eds.), *Understanding women with AD/HD* (pp. 152–176). Silver Spring, MD: Advantage Books.

Naik, B. I., Gangadharan, S., & Alexander, R. T. (2002). Personality disorders in learning disability: The clinical experience. *British Journal of Developmental Disabilities, 48*(95, Pt. 2), 95–100.

National Institutes of Health (1998). Diagnosis and treatment of attention deficit hyperactivity disorder. *NIH Consensus Statement Online, 16*(2), Nov. 16–18, 1–37.

Neef, N. A., Bicard, D. F., & Endo, S. (2001). Assessment of impulsivity and the development of self-control in students with attention deficit hyperactivity disorder. *Journal of Applied Behavior Analysis, 34,* 397–408.

Niederhofer, H., Hackenberg, B., Lanzendorfer, K., Staffen, W., & Mair, A. (2002). Family coherence and ADHD. *Psychological Reports, 91,* 123–126.

Nigg, J. T., John, O. P., Blaskey, L. G., Huang-Pollock, C. L., Willicut, E. G., Hinshaw, S. P., & Pennington, B. (2002). Big Five dimensions and ADHD symptoms: Links between personality traits and clinical symptoms. *Journal of Personality and Social Psychology, 83,* 451–469.

Nolan, E. E., Gadow, K. D., & Sprafkin, J. (2001). Teacher reports of DSM-IV ADHD, ADD, and CD symptoms in schoolchildren. *Journal of the American Academy of Child and Adolescent Psychiatry, 40,* 241–249.

Nolan, M., & Carr, A. (2000). Attention deficit hyperactivity disorder. In A. Carr (Ed.), *What works with children and adolescents?: A critical review of psychological interventions with children, adolescents and their families* (pp. 65–101). Florence, KY: Taylor & Francis/Routledge.

Northup, J., Gulley, V., Edwards, S., & Fountain, L. (2001). The effects of methylphenidate in the classroom: What dosage, for which children, for what problems? *School Psychology Quarterly, 16,* 303–323.

Oades, R. D. (2002). Dopamine may be "hyper" with respect to noradrenaline metabolism, but "hypo" with respect to serotonin metabolism in children with attention-deficit hyperactivity disorder. *Behavioural Brain Research, 130*(1–2), 97–102.

O'Donnell, J. P., McCann, K. K., & Pluth, S. (2001). Assessing adult ADHD using a self-report symptom checklist. *Psychological Reports, 88,* 871–881.

Paoni, M. F. (2001). The synthesis of a social information processing model of attention-deficit/hyperactivity disorder and social competence intervention. *Dissertation Abstracts International Section B: The Sciences and Engineering, 61*(11-B), 6144.

Paule, M. G., Rowland, A. S., Ferguson, S. A., Chelonis, J. J., Tannock, R., Swanson, J. M., & Castellanos, F. X. (2000). Attention deficit/hyperactivity disorder: Characteristics, interventions, and models. *Neurotoxicology and Teratology, 22,* 631–651.

Pelham, W. E., Hoza, B., Pillow, D. R., Gnagy, E. M., Kipp, H. L., Greiner, A. R., Waschbusch, D. A., Trane, S. T., Greenhouse, J., Wolfson, L., & Fitzpatrick, E. (2002). Effects of methyphenidate and expectancy on children with ADHD: Behavior, academic performance, and attributions in a summer treatment program and regular classroom settings. *Journal of Consulting and Clinical Psychology, 70,* 320–335.

Phillips, P. L., Greenson, J. N., Collett, B. R., & Gimpel, G. A. (2002). Assessing ADHD symptoms in preschool children: Use of the ADHD symptoms rating scale. *Early Education and Development, 13,* 283–299.

Pisecco, S., Wristers, K., Swank, P., Silva, P. A., & Baker, D. B. (2001). The effect of academic self-concept on ADHD and antisocial behaviors in early adolescence. *Journal of Learning Disabilities, 34,* 450–461.

Radford, P. M., & Ervin, R. A. (2002). Employing descriptive functional assessment methods to assess low-rate, high-intensity behaviors: A case example. *Journal of Positive Behavior Interventions, 4*(3), 146–155.

Rapport, M. D. (2001). Attention-deficit/hyperactivity disorder. In M. Hersen and V. B. Van Has ' (Eds.), *Advanced abnorm psychology* (2nd ed., pp. 191–208). Dordrecht, Netherlands: Kluwer Academic Publishers.

Rasmussen, K., Almvik, R., & Levander, S. (2001). Performance and strategy indices of neuropsychological tests: Relations with personality, criminality and violence. *Journal of Forensic Neuropsychology, 2*(2), 29–43.

Ravenel, S. D. (2002). A new behavioral approach for ADD/ADHD and behavioral management without medication. *Ethical Human Sciences and Services, 4*(2), 93–106.

Richardson, W. (2000). Criminal behavior fueled by attention deficit hyperactivity disorder and addiction. In D. H. Fishbein (Ed.), *The science, treatment, and prevention of antisocial behaviors: Application to the criminal justice system* (pp. 18–1 to 18–15). Kingston, NJ: Civic Research Institute.

Rhee, S. H., Waldman, I. D., Hay, D. A., & Levy, F. (2001). Aetiology of the sex difference in the prevalence of DSM-III-R ADHD: A comparison of two models. In F. Levy and D. A. Hay (Eds.), *Attention, genes, and ADHD* (pp. 139–156). New York: Brunner-Routledge.

Robison, L. M., Skaer, T. L., Sclar, D. A., & Galin, R. S. (2002). Is attention deficit hyperactivity disorder increasing among girls in the US? Trends in diagnosis and the prescribing of stimulants. *CNS Drugs, 16*(2), 129–137.

Rosston, K. F., & Buckingham, P. (2001). An interactive group-based curriculum to increase mental health awareness and empathy in juvenile delinquents. In G. Landsberg and A. Smiley (Eds.), *Forensic mental health: Working with offenders with mental illness* (pp. 35–1 to 35–9). Kingston, NJ: Civic Research Institute.

Rowland, A. S., Lesesne, C. A., & Abramowitz, A. J. (2002). The epidemiology of attention-deficit/hyperactivity disorder (ADHD): A public health view. *Mental Retardation and Developmental Disabilities Research Reviews, 8*(3), 162–170.

Rucklidge, J. J., & Tannock, R. (2002). Neuropsychological profiles of adolescents with ADHD: Effects of reading difficulties and gender. *Journal of Child Psychology and Psychiatry and Allied Disciplines, 43,* 988–1003.

Samuelsson, S., Finnstroem, O., Leijon, I., & Mard, S. (2000). Phonological and surface profiles of reading difficulties among very low birth weight children: Converging evidence for the developmental lag hypothesis. *Scientific Studies of Reading, 4*(3), 197–217.

Sarampote, C. S., Efron, L. A., Robb, A. S., Pearl, P. L., & Stein, M. A. (2002). Can stimulant rebound mimic pediatric bipolar disorder? *Journal of Child and Adolescent Psychopharmacology, 12,* 63–67.

Sealover, I. E. (2002). Counselor intervention using visual learning strategies for adolescent attention deficit disorder. *Dissertation Abstracts International Section A: Humanities and Social Sciences, 62*(12-A), 4076.

Schloesser, C., Kovacs, A., & Ferrero, F. (2002). Outcome of ADHD syndrome in adulthood: Epidemiological and clinical aspects. *Schweizer Archiv fuer Neurologie und Psychiatrie, 153,* 29–36.

Shaffer, D., Fisher, P., Lucas, C. P., Dulcan, M. K., & Schwab-Stone, M. E. (2000). NIMH Diagnostic Interview Schedule for Children, Version IV (NIMH DISC-IV): Description, differences from previous versions, and reliability of some common diagnoses. *Journal of the American Academy of Child and Adolescent Psychiatry, 39,* 28–38.

Shaw, B. M. (2000). College adjustment, social skills, and self-esteem in students with attention deficit hyperactivity disorder. *Dissertation Abstracts International Section A: Humanities and Social Sciences, 60*(12-A), 4322.

Solanto, M. V. (2001). Attention-deficit/hyperactivity disorder: Clinical features. In M. V. Solanto and A. F. T. Arnsten (Eds.), Stimulant drugs and ADHD: *Basic and clinical neuroscience* (pp. 3–30). London: Oxford University Press.

Solanto, M. V., Arnsten, A. F. T., & Castellanos, F. X. (2001). *Stimulant drugs and ADHD: Basic and clinical neuroscience.* London: Oxford University Press.

Sonuga-Barke, E. J. S., Dalen, L., Daley, D., & Remington, B. (2002). Are planning, working memory, and inhibition associated with individual differences in preschool ADHD symptoms? *Developmental Neuropsychology, 21,* 255–272.

Sprich, S., Biederman, J., Crawford, M. H., Mundy, E., & Faraone, S. V. (2000). Adoptive and biological families of children and adolescents with ADHD. *Journal of the American Academy of Child and Adolescent Psychiatry, 39,* 1432–1437.

Stefanatos, G. A., & Wasserstein, J. (2001). Attention deficit/hyperactivity disorder as a right hemisphere syndrome: Selective literature review and detailed neuropsychological case studies. In J. Wasserstein and L. E. Wolf (Eds.), *Adult attention deficit disorder: Brain mechanisms and life outcomes* (pp. 172–195). New York: New York Academy of Sciences.

Stevens, J., Quittner, A. L., Zuckerman, J. B., & Moore, S. (2002). Behavioral inhibition, self-regulation of motivation, and working memory in children with attention deficit hyperactivity disorder. *Developmental Neuropsychology, 21*(2), 11–140.

Sullivan, M. A., & Rudnik-Levin, F. (2001). Attention deficit/hyperactivity disorder and substance abuse: Diagnostic and therapeutic considerations. In J. Wasserstein and L. Wolf (Eds.), *Adult attention deficit disorder: Brain mechanisms and life outcomes.* (pp. 251–270). New York: New York Academy of Sciences.

Swanson, J. M., Arnold, L. E., Vitiello, B., Abikoff, H. B., Wells, K. C., Pelham, W. E., March, J. S., Hinshaw, S. P., Hoza, B.,

Epstein, J. N., Elliot, G. R., Greenhill, L. L., Hechtman, L., Jensen, P. S., Kraemer, H. C., Kotkin, R., Molina, B., Newcorn, J. H., Owens, E. B., Severe, J., Hoagwood, K., Simpson, S., Wigal, T., & Hanley, T. (2002). Response to commentary on the Multimodal Treatment Study of ADHD (MTA): Mining the meaning of the MTA. *Journal of Abnormal Child Psychology, 30,* 327–332.

Tervo, R. C., Azuma, S., Fogas, B., & Fiechtner, H. (2002). Children with ADHD and motor dysfunction compared with children with ADHD only. *Developmental Medicine and Child Neurology, 44,* 383–390.

Theriault, S. W., & Holmberg, D. (2001). Impulsive, but violent? Are components of the attention deficit-hyperactivity syndrome associated with aggression in relationships? *Violence Against Women, 7,* 1464–1489.

Trawick-Smith, J. (2000). *Early childhood development: A multicultural perspective* (2nd ed.). Columbus, OH: Merrill/Prentice-Hall.

U.S. Department of Education, Office of Special Education Programs. (2002). *Twenty-fourth annual report to Congress on the implementation of the Individuals with Disabilities Education Act.* Washington, DC: Author.

Venn, J. J. (2000). *Assessing students with special needs* (2nd ed.). Columbus, OH: Merrill/Prentice-Hall.

Volpe, R. J., & DuPaul, G. J. (2001). Assessment with brief behavior rating scales. In J. J. W. Andrews and D. H. Saklofske (Eds.), *Handbook of psychoeducational assessment: Ability, achievement, and behavior in children. A volume in the educational psychology series* (pp. 357–387). San Diego, CA: Academic Press.

Waldman, I. D., Rhee, S. H., Levy, F., & Hay, D. A. (2001). Causes of the overlap among symptoms of ADHD, oppositional defiant disorder, and conduct disorder. In F. Levy and D. A. Hay (Eds.), *Attention, genes, and ADHD* (pp. 115–138). New York: Brunner-Routledge.

Wasserstein, J., Wolf, L. E., & LeFever, F. F. (2001). *Adult attention deficit disorder: Brain mechanisms and life outcomes.* New York: New York Academy of Sciences.

Weiss, M., Hechtman, L. T., & Weiss, G. (1999). *ADHD in*

adulthood: A guide to current theory, diagnosis, and treatment.* Baltimore, MD: Johns Hopkins University Press.

Whalen, C. K., Jamner, L., Henker, B., Delfino, R. J., & Lozano, J. M. (2002). The ADHD spectrum and everyday life: Experience sampling of adolescent moods, activities, smoking, and drinking. *Child Development, 73,* 209–227.

Wigg, K., Zai, G., Schachar, R., Tannock, R., Roberts, W., Malone, M., Kennedy, J. L., & Barr, C. L. ( 2002). Attention deficit hyperactivity disorder and the gene for dopamine beta-hydroxylase. *American Journal of Psychiatry, 159,* 1046–1048.

Wilens, T. E., & Spencer, T. J. (2000). The stimulants revisited. *Child and Adolescent Psychiatric Clinics of North America, 9,* 573–603.

Yeschin, N. J. (2000). A new understanding of attention deficit hyperactivity disorder: Alternate concepts and interventions. *Child and Adolescent Social Work Journal, 17,* 227–245.

Zimmermann, S. H. (1999). Portrait of success: A situational analysis case study of students challenged by attention-deficit/hyperactivity disorder. *Dissertation Abstracts International Section A: Humanities and Social Sciences, 59*(7–A), 2368.

## CHAPTER 9

Achenbach, T. M. (1966). The classification of children's psychiatric symptoms: A factor analytic study. *Psychological Monographs: General and Applied, 615,* 1–37.

Achenbach, T. M. (1991a). *Manual for the Child Behavior Checklist/4–18 and 1991 Profile.* Burlington, VT: University of Vermont, Department of Psychiatry.

Achenbach, T. M. (1991b). *Manual for the Teacher's Report Form and 1991 Profile.* Burlington, VT: University of Vermont, Department of Psychiatry.

Algozzine, B., & White, R. (2002). Preventing problem behaviors using schoolwide discipline. In B. Algozzine, & P. Kay (Eds.), *Preventing problem behaviors* (pp. 85–103). Thousand Oaks, CA: Corwin Press.

American Psychiatric Association. Diagnostic and statistical manual of mental disorders (4th ed.–text revision).

Washington, DC, American Psychiatric Association, 2002.

Bavolek, S. J. (2000, November) The nurturing parenting programs. *Juvenile Justice Bulletin*, pp. 1–11.

Becky. (2000). Violent 4 year old/telling lies, The Behavior Home Page, Kentucky Department of Education. Retrieved March 28, 2003 from http://ebd.coe.uky.edu/Interaction$/behavior/behavior2/181517606/0?id=MAJFC

Benner, G. J., Nelson, J. R., & Epstein, M. H. (2002). Language skills of children with EBD: A literature review. *Journal of Emotional and Behavioral Disorders, 10,* 43–59.

Bower, E. M. (1959). The emotionally handicapped child and the school. *Exceptional Children, 26,* 6–11.

Braaten, S. (1998). *Behavioral objective sequence.* Champaign, IL: Research Press.

Braaten, S., Kauffman, J. M., Braaten, B., Polsgrove, L., & Nelson, C. M. (1988). The regular education initiative: Patent medicine for behavioral disorders. *Exceptional Children, 55*(1), 21–27.

Brandenburg, N. A., Friedman, R. M., & Silver, S. E. (1990). The epidemiology of childhood psychiatric disorders: Recent prevalence findings and methodologic issues. *Journal of the American Academy of Child and Adolescent Psychiatry, 29,* 76–83.

Brown, R. T., & Sawyer, M. G. (1998). *Medication for school-age children: Effects on learning and behavior.* New York: Guilford, 1998.

Bullis, M. (2001). Job placement and support considerations in transition programs for adolescents with emotional disabilities. In L. M. Bullock & R. A. Gable (Eds.), *Addressing the social, academic, and behavioral needs of students with challenging behavior in inclusive and alternative settings* (pp. 31–36). Las Vegas, NV: Council for Children with Behavioral Disorders.

Bullis, M., Yovanoff, P., Mueller, G., & Havel, E. (2002). Life on the "outs"—Examination of the facility-to-community transition of incarcerated youth. *Exceptional Children, 69,* 7–22.

Bullock, L. M., & Gable, R. A. (1994). *Monograph on inclusion: Ensuring appropriate services to children and youth with emotional and behavioral disorders.* Reston, VA: Council for Exceptional Children.

Bullock, L. M., & Gable, R. A. (Eds.). (2000). *Positive academic and behavioral supports: Creating safe, effective, and nurturing schools for all students.* Norfolk, VA: Council for Children with Behavioral Disorders.

Burchard, J. D., & Clark, R. T. (1990). The role of individualized care in a service delivery system for children and adolescents with severely maladjusted behavior. *Journal of Mental Health Administration, 17*(1), 48–60.

Burrell, S., & Warboys, L. (2000, July). Special education and the juvenile justice system. *Juvenile Justice Bulletin,* 1–15.

Campbell, S. B. (1995). Behavior problems in preschool children: A review of recent research. *Journal of Child Psychology and Psychiatry, 36*(1), 113–149.

Cassidy, E., James, A., & Wiggs, L. (2001). The prevalence of psychiatric disorder in children attending a school for pupils with emotional and behavioral difficulties. *British Journal of Special Education, 28,* 167–173.

Center for Effective Collaboration and Practice. (1999). *Executive summary. Volume 3: The role of education in the system of care; Effectively serving children with emotional or behavioral disorders* [Online]. Available: http://cecp.air.org/promising practices/documents.htm#3

Cheney, D., & Barringer, C. (1999). A trandisciplinary model for students' social and emotional development: Creating a context for inclusion. In J. R. Scotti & L. H. Meyer (Eds.), *Behavioral intervention: Principles, models, and practices* (pp. 149–174). Baltimore, MD: Paul H. Brookes.

Coleman, M. C., & Webber, J. (2002). *Emotional and behavioral disorders: Theory and practice.* Boston: Allyn and Bacon.

Cosmos, C. (2002, Sept./Oct.). Children behaving badly—helping students with emotional disorders. *Today,* 1.

Council for Children with Behavior Disorders. (1987). Position paper on definition and identification of students with behavior disorders. *Behavioral Disorders, 13*(1), 9–19.

Council for Children with Behavior Disorders. (1989). *A new proposed definition and terminology to replace "serious emotional disturbance" in Education of the Handicapped Act.* Reston, VA: Author.

Council for Children with Behavior Disorders. (1990). *Position paper on the exclusion of children with conduct disorders and behavior disorders.* Reston, VA: Author.

Council for Exceptional Children. (1991). *Report of the CEC advocacy and governmental relations committee regarding the new proposed U.S. federal definition of serious emotional disturbance.* Reston, VA: Author.

Crosson-Tower, C. (2002). *When children are abused: An educator's guide to intervention.* Boston: Allyn and Bacon.

Duchnowski, A. J., & Friedman, R. M. (1990). Children's mental health: Challenges for the nineties. *Journal of Mental Health Administration, 17* (1), 3–12.

Eber, L., Sugai, G., Smith, C., & Scott, T. (2002). Wraparound and positive behavioral interventions and supports in the schools. *Journal of Emotional and Behavioral Disorders, 10,* 171–180.

Eddy, J. M., Reid, J. B., & Fetrow, R. A. (2000). An elementary school–based prevention program targeting modifiable antecedents of youth delinquency and violence: Linking the interests of families and teachers (LIFT). *Journal of Emotional and Behavioral Disorders, 8,* 165–176.

Epstein, M. H. (1998). Using strength-based assessment in programs for children with emotional and behavioral disorders. *Beyond Behavior, 9* (2), 25–27.

Epstein, M. H., & Sharma, J. M. (1997). *Behavior and Emotional Rating Scale.* Austin, TX: PRO-ED.

Erickson, M. (1998). *Behavior disorders of children and adolescents.* Upper Saddle River, NJ: Prentice-Hall.

Esbensen, F-A. (2000, September). Preventing adolescent gang involvement. *Juvenile Justice Bulletin,* 1–11.

Fishbein, D. H. (2000). *The science, treatment, and prevention of antisocial behaviors: Application to the criminal justice system.* Kingston, NJ: Civic Research Institute.

Forness, S. R. (1996). Schoolchildren with emotional or behavioral disorders: Perspectives on definition, diagnosis, and treatment. In B. Brooks & D. Sabatino (Eds.), *Personal perspectives on emotional disturbance/behavioral disorders* (pp. 84–95). Austin, TX: PRO-ED.

Forness, S. R., & Kavale, K. A. (2000). Emotional or behavior disorders: Background and current status of the E/BD terminology and definition. *Behavior Disorders, 24,* 264–269.

Forness, S. R., & Kavale, K. A. (2001). ADHD and a return to the medical model of special education. *Education and Treatment of Children, 24,* 224–247.

Forness, S. R., & Knitzer, J. K. (1990). *A new proposed definition and terminology to replace "serious emotional disturbance" in the Education of the Handicapped Act.* Alexandria, VA: National Mental Health Association.

Fox, L., Dunlap, G., & Cushing, L. (2002). Early intervention, positive behavior support, and transition to school. *Journal of Emotional and Behavioral Disorders, 10,* 149–157.

Fuchs, D., & Fuchs, L. S. (1994). Inclusive schools movement and the radicalization of special education reform. *Exceptional Children, 60*(4), 294–309.

Gibb, G. S., Allred, K. W., Ingram, C. F., Young, J. R., & Egan, M. W. (1999). Lessons learned from the inclusion of students with emotional and behavioral disorders in one junior high. *Behavioral Disorders, 24*(2), 122–136.

Greenberg, M. T., Domitrovich, C., & Bumbarger, B. (2001, March). The prevention of mental disorders in school-aged children: Current state of the field. Retrieved April 22, 2003, from *Prevention & Treatment.*

Henry, D. B., Tolan, P. H., & Gorman-Smith, D. (2001). Longitudinal family and peer group effects on violence and nonviolent delinquency. *Journal of Clinical Child Pshychology, 30,* 172–186.

Hernandez, M., Gomez, A., Lipien, L., Greenbaum, P. E., Armstrong, K. H., & Gonzalez, P. (2001). Use of the system-of-care practice review in the national evaluation: Evaluating the fidelity of practice to system-of-care principles. *Journal of Emotional and Behavioral Disorders, 9,* 43–52.

Horton, C. B., & Cruise, T. K. (2001). *Child abuse and neglect: The school's response.* New York: Guilford.

Howell, J. C., & Lynch, J. P. (2000, August). Youth gangs in schools. *Juvenile Justice Bulletin,* 1–7.

Huefner, D. S. (2000). Getting comfortable with special education law: A framework for working with children with disabilities. Norwood,

MA: Christopher-Gordon Publishers.

Ialongo, N., Poduska, J., Werthamer, L., & Kellam, S. (2001). The distal impact of two first-grade preventive interventions on conduct problems and disorder in early adolescence. *Journal of Emotional and Behavioral Disorders, 9*, 146–160.

Kauffman, J. M. (1997). Characteristics of emotional and behavioral disorders of children and youth. Upper Saddle River, NJ: Prentice-Hall.

Kauffman, J. M., & Lloyd, J. W. (1995). A sense of place: The importance of placement issues in contemporary special education. In J. M. Kauffman, J. W. Lloyd, D. P. Hallahan, & T. A. Astuto (Eds.), *Issues in educational placement: Students with emotional and behavioral disorders* (pp. 3–19). Hillsdale, NJ: Erlbaum.

Kauffman, J. M., & Smucker, K. (1995). The legacies of placement: A brief history of placement options and issues with commentary on their evolution. In J. M. Kauffman, J. W. Lloyd, D. P. Hallahan, & T. A. Astuto (Eds.*), Issues in educational placement: Students with emotional and behavioral disorders* (pp. 21–44). Hillsdale, NJ: Erlbaum.

Kauffman, J. M., Bantz, J., & McCullough, J. (2002). Separate and better: A special public school class for students with emotional and behavioral disorders. *Exceptionality, 10*, 149–170.

Kavale, K. A., & Forness, S. R. (2000). History, rhetoric, and reality: Analysis of the inclusion debate. *Remedial and Special Education, 21*, 279–296.

Kay, P., Fitzgerald, M., & McConaughy, S. H. (2002). Building effective parent–teacher partnerships. In B. Algozzine & P. Kay (Eds.), *Preventing problem behaviors* (pp. 104–125). Thousand Oaks: Corwin Press.

Kea, C. D., Cartledge, G., & Bowman, L. J. (2002). Interventions for African American learners with behavioral problems. In F. E. Obiakor & B. A. Ford (Eds.), *Creating successful learning environments for African American learners with exceptionalities* (pp. 79–94). Thousand Oaks, CA: Corwin Press.

Keenan, S. M. (1997). Program elements that support teachers and students with learning and behavior problems. In P. Zionts (Ed.), *Inclusion strategies for students with learning and behavior problems* (pp. 117–138). Austin, TX: PRO-ED.

Kendziora, K., Bruns, E., Osher, D., Pacchiano, D., & Mejia, B. (2001). *Systems of care: Promising practices in children's mental health,* 2001 series, vol. I. Washington, DC: Center for Effective Collaboration and Practice, American Institutes for Research.

Kennedy, C. H., Long, T., Jolivette, K., Cox, J., Tang, J., & Thompson, T. (2001). Facilitating general education participation for students with behavior problems by linking positive behavior supports and person-centered planning. *Journal of Emotional and Behavioral Disorders, 9*, 161–171.

Knitzer, J. (1982). *Unclaimed children: The failure of public responsibility to children and adolescents in need of mental health services.* Washington, DC: Children's Defense Fund.

Knitzer, J., Steinberg, Z., & Fleisch, B. (1990). *At the schoolhouse door: An examination of programs and policies for children with behavioral and emotional problems.* New York: Bank Street College of Education.

Koyanagi, C., & Feres-Merchant, D. (2000). For the long haul: Maintaining systems of care beyond the federal investment. *Systems of care: Promising practices in children's mental health,* 2000 series, vol. III. Washington, DC: Center for Effective Collaboration and Practice, American Institutes for Research.

Koyangi, C., & Gaines, S. (1993). *All systems failure: An examination of the results of neglecting the needs of children with serious emotional disturbance.* Washington, DC: National Mental Health Association.

Kutash, K., Duchnowski, A. J., Sumi, W. C., Rudo, Z., & Harris, K. M. (2002). A school, family, and community collaborative program for children who have emotional disturbances. *Journal of Emotional and Behavioral Disorders, 10*, 99–107.

Lewis, T. J., Chard, D., & Scott, T. M. (1994). Full inclusion and the education of children and youth with behavioral disorders. *Behavioral Disorders, 19*(4), 277–293.

Lyons, J. S. (1997). *Child and adolescent strengths assessment.* Chicago, IL: Northwest University, Department of Psychiatry and Behavioral Sciences.

MacMillan, D. L., Gresham, F. M., & Forness, S. R. (1996). Full inclusion: An empirical perspective. *Behavioral Disorders, 21*(2), 145–159.

McEvoy, A., & Welker, R. (2000). Antisocial behavior, academic failure, and school climate: A critical review. *Journal of Emotional and Behavioral Disorders, 8*, 130–140.

Morse, W. C., Cutler, R. L., & Fink, A. H. (1964). *Public school classes for emotionally handicapped: A research analysis.* Washington, DC: Council for Exceptional Children.

National Information Center for Children and Youth with Disabilities. (1999). *Interventions for chronic behavior problems.* Washington, DC: National Information Center for Children and Youth with Disabilities.

Nelson, J. R., Roberts, M. L., & Smith, D. J. (1998). *Conducting functional behavioral assessments: A practical guide.* Longmont, CO: Sopris West.

Newcomer, P. L. (2003). *Understanding and teaching emotionally disturbed children and adolescents* (3rd ed.). Austin: PRO-ED.

Novotney, L. C., Mertinko, E., Lange, J., & Baker, T. K. (2000, September) Juvenile mentoring program: A progress review. *Juvenile Justice Bulletin*, 1–7.

Osher, D., & Hanley, T. V. (1996). Implications of the national agenda to improve results for children and youth with or at risk of serious emotional disturbance. In R. J. Illback & C. M. Nelson (Eds.), *Emerging school-based approaches for children with emotional and behavioral problems: Research and practice in service integration* (pp. 7–36). Binghamton, NY: The Haworth Press.

Osher, D., Osher, T., & Smith, C. (1994). Toward a national perspective in emotional and behavioral disorders: A developmental perspective. *Beyond Behavior, 6*(1), 6–17.

Patterson, G. R., DeBaryshe, B. D., & Ramsey, E. (1989). A developmental perspective on antisocial behavior. *American Psychologist, 44*(2), 329–355.

Peacock Hill Working Group. (1990). *Problems and promises in special education and related services for children and youth with emotional and behavioral disorders.* Charlottesville, VA: Author.

Peterson, N. L. (1987). *Early intervention for handicapped and at-risk children: An introduction to early childhood special education.* Denver, CO: Love.

Place, M., Wilson, J., Martin, E., & Hulsmeier, J. (1999). Attention deficit disorder as a factor in the origin of behavioural disturbance in schools. *British Journal of Special Education, 26*, 158–163.

Praisner, Cindy L. (2003). Attitudes of elementary school principals toward the inclusion of students with disabilities. *Council for Exceptional Children, 69*, 135–145.

Quay, H. C. (1975). Classification in the treatment of delinquency and antisocial behavior. In N. Hobbs (Ed.), *Issues in the classification of children* (vol. 1, pp. 377–392). San Francisco, CA: Jossey-Bass.

Quay, H. C. (1979). Classification. In H. C. Quay & J. S. Werry (Eds.), *Psychopathological disorders of childhood* (2nd ed., pp. 1–41). New York: Wiley.

Rosenberg, M. S., Wilson, R., Maheady, L., & Sindelar, P. T. (2004). *Educating students with behavior disorders* (3rd ed.). Boston: Allyn and Bacon.

Ruehl, M. E. (1998). Educatiing the child with severe behavioral problems: Entitlement, empiricism, and ethics. *Behavioral Disorders, 23*(3), 184–192.

Sachs, J. (1999). The hidden conspiracy in our nation's schools. *Behavioral Disorders, 25*, 80–82.

Sachs, J. J., & Cheney, D. (2000). What do the members of the Council for Children with Behavioral Disorders say about inclusion? *Beyond Behavior, 10*, 18–23.

Sampers, J., Anderson, K. G., Hartung, C. M., & Scambler, D. J. (2001). Parent training programs for young children with behavior problems. *Infant Toddler Intervention: The Transdisciplinary Journal, 11*, 91–110.

Seifert, Kathryn (2000). Juvenile violence: An overview of risk factors and programs. *Reaching Today's Youth, 4*, 60–71.

Serna, L., Nielsen, E., Lambros, K., & Forness, S. (2000). Primary prevention with children at risk for emotional and behavioral disorders: Data on a universal intervention for Head Start classrooms. *Behavioral Disorders, 26*, 70–84.

Shapiro, E. S., Miller, D. N., Sawka, K., Gardill, M. C., & Handler, M. W. (1999). Facilitating the inclusion of students with EBD into general education classrooms. *Journal of Emotional and Behavioral Disorders, 7*(2), 83–93, 127.

Shores, R. E., & Wehby, J. H. (1999). Analyzing the

classroom social behavior of students with EBD.

Simpson, J. S., Jivanjee, P., Koroloff, N., Doerfler, A., & Garcia, M. (2001). Promising practices in early childhood mental health. *Systems of care: Promising practices in children's mental health, 2001 series, vol. III.* Washington, DC: Center for Effective Collaboration and Practice, American Institutes for Research.

Snell, M. W. (1990). Schools are for all kids: The importance of integration for students with severe disabilities and their peers. In J. W. Lloyd, A. C. Repp, & N. N. Singh (Eds.), *The regular education initiative: Alternative perspectives on concepts, issues, and models* (pp. 133–148). Sycamore, IL: Sycamore Publishing Company.

Stainback, S. B. (2000). The inclusion movement: A goal for restructuring special education. In M. A. Winzer & K. Mazurek (Eds.), *Special education in the 21st century: Issues of inclusion and reform* (pp. 27–40). Washington, DC: Gallaudet University Press.

Stainback, W., & Stainback, S. (1990). *Supportive networks for inclusive schooling.* Baltimore, MD: Paul H. Brookes.

Stainback, W., & Stainback, S. (1992). *Curriculum considerations in inclusive classrooms: Facilitating learning for all students.* Baltimore, MD: Paul H. Brookes.

Stephens, S. A., & Lakin, K. C. (1995). Where students with emotional or behavioral disorders go to school. In J. M. Kauffman, J. W. Lloyd, D. P. Hallahan, & T. A. Astuto (Eds.), *Issues in educational placement: Students with emotional and behavioral disorders* (pp. 47–74). Hillsdale, NJ: Erlbaum.

Stroul, B. A., & Friedman, R. M. (1986). *A system of care for severely emotionally disturbed children and youth.* Washington, DC: Georgetown University.

Terrasi, S., Sennett, K. H., & Macklin, T. O. (1999). Comparing learning styles for students with conduct and emotional problems. *Psychology in the Schools, 36*(2), 159–166.

U.S. Department of Education. (1998). *To assure the free appropriate public education of all children with disabilities: Twentieth annual report to Congress on the implementation of the Individuals with Disabilities Act.*

Washington, DC: U.S. Government Printing Office.

U.S. Department of Education (1999). *To assure the free appropriate public education of all children with disabilities: Twenty-first annual report to Congress on the implementation of the Individuals with Disabilities Act.* Washington, DC: U.S. Government Printing Office.

U.S. Department of Education. (2000). *Twenty-second annual report to Congress on implementation of the Individuals with Disabilities Education Act.* Washington, DC: U.S. Government Printing Office.

U.S. Department of Education. (2002). *To assure the free appropriate public education of all children with disabilities: Twenty-fourth annual report to Congress on the implementation of the Individuals with Disabilities Education Act.* Washington, DC: U.S. Government Printing Office.

Umansky, W., & Hooper, S. R. (Eds.). (1998). *Young children with special needs* (3rd ed.). Upper Saddle River, NJ: Merrill.

Venn, J. J. (2000). *Assessing students with special needs* (2nd ed.). Upper Saddle River, New Jersey: Merrill.

Von Isser, A., Quay, H. C., & Love, C. T. (1980). Interrelationships among three measures of deviant behavior. *Exceptional Children, 46*(4), 272–276.

Wagner, M., Newman, L., DeAmico, R., Jay, E. D., Bulter-Nalin, P., Marder, C., & Cox, R. (1991). *Youth with disabilities: How are they doing? The first comprehensive report from the national longitudinal study of special education students.* Menlo Park, CA: SRI International.

Walker, H. M., & Severson, H. H. (1992). Systematic screening for behavior disorders. Longmont, CO: Sopris West.

Webster-Stratton, C. (2000, June) The incredible years training series. *Juvenile Justice Bulletin,* pp. 1–23.

Webster-Stratton, C., & Reid, M. J. (2002). An integrated approach to prevention and management of aggressive behavior problems in preschool and elementary grade students: Schools and parents collaboration. In K. L. Lane, F. M. Gresham, & T. E. O'Shaughnessy, (Eds.), *Interventions for children with or at risk for emotional and behavioral disorders* (pp. 261–278). Boston: Allyn and Bacon.

Wicks-Nelson, R., & Israel, A. C. (2003). *Behavior disorders of childhood* (5th ed.). Upper Saddle River, NJ: Prentice-Hall.

Wilde, J. (2002). *Anger management in schools: Alternatives to student violence* (2nd ed.). Lanham, MD: The Scarecrow Press.

Winzer, M. A., & Mazurek, K. (Eds.). (2000). *Special education in the 21st century: Issues of inclusion and reform.* Washington, DC: Gallaudet University Press.

Winzer, M. A. (2000). The inclusion movement: Review and reflections on reform in special education. In M. A. Winzer & K. Mazurek (Eds.). *Special education in the 21st century: Issues of inclusion and reform* (pp. 5–26). Washington, DC: Gallaudet University Press.

Witt, J. C., Daly, E. M., & Noell, G. (2000). Functional assessments: A step-by-step guide to solving academic and behavior problems. Longmont, CO: Sopris West.

Woodruff, D. W., Osher, D., Hoffman, C. C., Gruner, A., King, M. A., Snow, S. T., & McIntire, J. C. (1999). The role of education in a system of care: Effectively serving children with emotional or behavioral disorders. *Systems of care: Promising practices in children's mental health, 1998 series, vol. III.* Washington, DC: Center for Effective Collaboration and Practice, American Institutes for Research.

Worthington, J., Hernandez, M., Friedman, B., & Uzzell, D. (2001). *Systems of care: Promising practices in children's mental health, 2001 series, vol. II.* Washington, DC: Center for Effective Collaboration and Practice, American Institutes for Research.

Yell, M. L. (1995). *Clyde K. & Sheila K. v. Puyallup School District:* The courts, inclusion, and students with behavior disorders. *Behavior Disorders, 20*(3), 179–189.

Yell, M. L. (1998). *The law and special education.* Upper Saddle River, NJ: Merrill.

## CHAPTER 10

AAMR Ad Hoc Committee on Terminology and Classification. (2002). *Mental retardation: Definition, classification, and systems of support* (10th ed.). Washington, DC: American Association on Mental Retardation.

Agran, M., & Hughes, C. (1997). Problem solving. In M. Agran (Ed.), *Student-directed learning: Teaching self-determination skills* (pp. 171–198). Pacific Grove, CA: Brooks/Cole.

Agran, M., & Wehmeyer, M. (1999). *Innovations: Teaching problem solving to students with mental retardation.* Washington, DC: American Association on Mental Retardation.

Beirne-Smith, M., Ittenbach, R. F., & Patton, J. R. (2002). *Mental retardation* (6th ed.). Upper Saddle River, NJ: Merrill.

Benjamin, C. (1996). *Problem solving in school.* Upper Saddle River, NJ: Globe Fearon Educational Publisher.

Bergen, A. E., & Mosley, J. L. (1994). Attention and attention shift efficiency in individuals with and without mental retardation. *American Journal on Mental Retardation, 98*(6), 732–743.

Berry, J., & Hardman, M. L. (1998). *Lifespan perspectives on the family and disability.* Boston: Allyn and Bacon.

Bonn, H., & Bonn, B. (2000a). In the best interests of the child. In S. E. Wade (Ed.), *Inclusive education: A casebook and readings for prospective and practicing teachers* (pp. 173–180). Mahwah, NJ: Lawrence Erlbaum.

Bonn, H., & Bonn, B (2000b). Part B of the case: "In the best interests of the child." In S. E. Wade (Ed.), *Preparing teachers for inclusive education* (pp. 209–211). Mahwah, NJ: Lawrence Erlbaum.

Browder, D. M., & Snell, M. E. (2000). Teaching functional academics. In M. E. Snell & F. Brown (Eds.), *Instruction of students with severe disabilities* (pp. 493–542). Upper Saddle River, NJ: Merrill.

Centers for Disease Control (2003). *Women and smoking: A report of the surgeon general: Tobacco use and reproductive outcomes fact sheet* [Online]. Available: http://thearc.org/faqs/Hiv.html. Retrieved May 29, 2003.

Children's Defense Fund (2003). *The state of America's children yearbook.* Washington, DC: Author.

Cipani, E., & Spooner, F. (1994). *Curricular and instructional approaches for persons with severe disabilities.* Boston: Allyn and Bacon.

Corum, S. (2003, May 18). Life is short. *Washington Post,* Section D, 1.

Dever, R. B., & Knapczyk, D. R. (1997). *Teaching persons with* mental retardation. Madison, WI: Brown and Benchmark.

Drew, C. J., & Hardman, M. L. (2004). Mental retardation: A lifespan approach to people with intellectual disabilities (8th ed.). Columbus, OH: Merrill.

Gresham, F. P., & MacMillan, D. L. (1997). Social competence and affective characteristics of students with mild disabilities. Review of Educational Research, 67(4), 377–415.

Guralnick, M. J. (2001). A framework for change in early childhood inclusion. In M. J. Guralnick (Ed.), Early childhood inclusion: Focus on change (pp. 3–35). Baltimore, MD: Paul H. Brookes.

Guy, B., Scott, J. R., Hasazi, S., & Patten, A. (no date). Stories of work. Unpublished manuscript. Burlington, VT: University of Vermont.

Henry, L. A., & Gudjonsson, G. H. (1999). Eyewitness memory and suggestibility in children with mental retardation. American Journal of Mental Retardation, 104(6), 491–508.

Horvat M. (2000). Physical activity of children with and without mental retardation in inclusive recess settings. Education and Training in Mental Retardation, 35 (2), 160–167.

Hughes, C. (1992). Teaching self-instruction utilizing multiple exemplars to produce generalized problem solving among individuals with severe mental retardation. American Journal on Mental Retardation, 97(3), 302–314.

Jay, A. S., Grote, I., & Baer, D. M. (1999). Teaching participants with developmental disabilities to comply with self-instructions. American Journal on Mental Retardation, 104(6), 509–522.

Kaiser, A. P. (2000). Teaching functional communication skills. In M. E. Snell & F. Brown (Eds.), Instruction of persons with severe disabilities (5th ed., pp. 453–492). Columbus, OH: Merrill.

Katims, D. S. (1996). The emergence of literacy in elementary students with mild retardation. Focus on Autism and Other Developmental Disabilities, 11, 147–157.

Katims, D. S. (2000). Literacy instruction for people with mental retardation: Historical highlights and contemporary analysis. Education and Training in Mental Retardation and Developmental Disabilities, 35(1), 3–15.

Kowalski, J. T. (2003). HIV AIDS and Mental Retardation. Silver Spring, MD: The ARC—A National Organization on Mental Retardation [Online]. Available: http://thearc.org/faqs/Hiv.html. Retrieved May 29, 2003.

Mithaug, D. E., Wehmeyer, M. L., Agran, M., Martin, J. E., & Palmer, S. (1998). The self-determined learning model of instruction: Engaging students to solve their learning problems. In M. L. Wehmeyer & D. J. Sands (Eds.), Making it happen: Student involvement in education planning, decision making, and instruction (pp. 299–328). Baltimore, MD: Paul H. Brookes.

Morgan, R. L., Ellerd, D. A., Gerity, B. P., & Blair, R. J. (2000). "That's the job I want." How technology helps young people in transition. Teaching Exceptional Children, 32(4), 44–49

National Down Syndrome Society (2000). Down syndrome: Myths and truths. New York: Author. [Online]. Available: http://www.ndss.org/aboutds/aboutds.html#Down

National Organization on Fetal Alcohol Syndrome (2000). What is fetal alcohol syndrome. [Online]. Available: http://www.nofas.org/stats.htm

Nirje, B. (1970). The normalization principle and its human management implications. Journal of Mental Subnormality, 16, 62–70.

Otley, K. (2000). The keys are mine. In T. Fields & C. Lakin (Eds.), Consumer-controlled housing (p. 24). Minneapolis, MN: ARC-Minneota and the Institute on Community Integration.

President's Committee on Mental Retardation. (2000). Mission [Online]. Available: http://www.acf.dhhs.gov/programs/pcmr/mission.htm

Ramey, C. T., & Ramey, S. L. (1999). Right from birth. New York: Goddard Press.

Reiff, H. B., Ginsberg, R., & Gerber, P. J. (1997). Exceeding expectations: Successful adults with learning disabilities. Austin, TX: PRO-ED.

Research and Training Center on Community Living. (1999, January). 1994 National Health Interview Survey: Disability Supplement. MR/DD Data Brief, 1(1), 1–7.

Siperstein, G. N., & Leffert, J. S. (1997). Comparison of socially accepted and rejected children with mental retardation. Mental Retardation, 101(4), 339–351.

Sternberg, R. J. (2001). Successful intelligence: Understanding what Spearman had rather than what he studied. In J. M. Collis & S. Messick (Eds.), Intelligience and personality: Bridging the gap in theory and measurement (pp. 347–373). Mahwah, NJ: Lawrence Erlbaum.

Sternberg, R. J. (2002). Successful intelligence: A new approach to leadership. In R. E., Riggio, S. E. Murphy, & F. J. Pirozzolo (Eds.). Multiple intelligences and leadership (pp. 9–28). Mahwah, NJ: Lawrence Erlbaum.

Tager-Flusberg, H., & Sullivan, K. (1998). Early language development in children with mental retardation. In J. A. Burack, R. M. Hodapp, & E. Zigler (Eds.), Handbook of mental retardation and development (pp. 208–239). New York: Cambridge University Press.

The Arc (2000). Genetic issues in mental retardation. Silver Spring, MD: Author [Online]. Available: http://TheArc.org/depts/gbr01.html

Turner, L., Dofny, E., & Dutka, S. (1994). Effective strategy and attribution training on strategy maintenance and transfer. American Journal on Mental Retardation, 98(4), 445–454.

U.S. Census Bureau. (2000). Projections of the total resident population by five-year age groups and sex, with special age categories: Middle series 2025-2045. Washington, DC: U.S. Census Bureau, Populations Projections Program, Population Division.

U.S. Department of Education (2002). To assure the free appropriate public education of all children with disabilities: Twenty-fourth annual report to Congress on the implementation of the Individuals with Disabilities Education Act. Washington, DC: U.S. Government Printing Office.

Warren, S. F. (2002, May/June). Mental retardation: Curse, characteristic, or coin of the realm? AAMR News and Notes, 1, 10–11.

Warren, S. F., & Yoder, P. J. (1997). Communication, language, and mental retardation. In W. E. MacLean (Ed.), Ellis' handbook of mental deficiency, psychological theory, and research (pp. 379–403). Mahwah, NJ: Lawrence Erlbaum.

Wehman, P. (2001). Life beyond the classroom: Transition strategies for young people with disabilities (3rd ed.). Baltimore, MD: Paul H. Brookes.

Wehmeyer, M. L., & Kelchner, K. (1995). Interpersonal cognitive problem-solving skills of individuals with mental retardation. Education and Training in Mental Retardation and Developmental Disabilities, 29, 265–278.

Westling, D., & Fox, L. (2000). Teaching students with severe disabilities. Upper Saddle River, NJ: Merrill.

Young, M. E. (1996). Early child development: Investing in the future. Washington, DC: The World Bank.

## CHAPTER 11

American Psychiatric Association. (2000). Diagnostic and statistical manual of mental disorders (4th ed.–text revision). Washington, DC: Author.

Anderson, R. T. (2002). Onset clusters and the sonority sequencing principle in Spanish: A treatment efficacy study. In F. Windsor, L. M. Kelly, and N. Hewlett (Eds.), Investigations in clinical phonetics and linguistics (pp. 213–224). Mahwah, NJ: Lawrence Erlbaum.

Bartens, A. (2000). Ideophones and sound symbolism in Atlantic creoles. Helsinki, Finland: Academia Scientiarum Fennica.

Basso, A. (2003). Aphasia and its therapy. New York: Oxford University Press.

Bates, E., Reilly, J., Wulfeck, B., Dronkers, N., Opie, M., Fenson, J., Kriz, S., Jeffries, R., Miller, L., & Herbst, K. (2001). Differential effects of unilateral lesions on language production in children and adults. Brain and Language, 79, 223–265.

Battle, D. E. (2002). Language and communication disorders in culturally and linguistically diverse children. In D. K. Bernstein & E. Tiegerman-Farber (Eds.), Language and communication disorders in children (5th ed., pp. 354–386). Boston: Allyn and Bacon.

Beck, A. R., Fritz, H., Keller, A., & Dennis, M. (2000). Attitudes of school-aged children toward peers who use augmentative and alternative communication. AAC: Augmentative and Alternative Communication, 16, 13–26.

Benninger, M. S. (2002). Benign disorders of the voice.

Alexandria, VA: American Academy of Otolaryngology–Head & Neck Surgery Foundation.

Benson, B. A., Gross, A. M., & Kellum, G. (1999). The siblings of children with craniofacial anomalies. *Children's Health Care, 28,* 51–68.

Bernstein, D. K. (2002). The nature of language and its disorders. In D. K. Bernstein and E. Tiegerman-Farber (Eds.), *Language and communication disorders in children* (5th ed., pp. 2–26). Boston: Allyn and Bacon.

Bernstein, D. K., & Levey, S. (2002). Language development: A review. In D. K. Bernstein and E. Tiegerman-Farber (Eds.), *Language and communication disorders in children* (5th ed., pp. 27–94). Boston: Allyn and Bacon.

Beveridge, M. A., & Crerar, M. A. (2002). Remediation of asyntactic sentence comprehension using a multimedia microworld. *Brain and Language, 82,* 243–295.

Bloodstein, O. (2001). Incipient and developed stuttering as two distinct disorders: Resolving a dilemma. *Journal of Fluency Disorders, 26,* 67–73.

Bowen, C. (2002). Speech and language development in infants and young children [Online]. www.members.tripod.com/Caroline_Bowen/devel1.htm. Retrieved September 6, 2002.

Bray, M. A., & Kehle, T. J. (2001). Long-term follow-up of self-modeling as an intervention for stuttering. *School Psychology Review, 30,* 135–141.

Bressmann, T., & Sader, R. (2001). Speech rate in cleft lip and palate speakers with compensatory articulation. *Clinical Linguistics and Phonetics, 15*(1–2), 129–132.

Burgess, S. R., Hecht, S. A., & Lonigan, C. J. (2002). Relations of the home literacy environment (HLE) to the development of reading-related abilities: A one-year longitudinal study. *Reading Research Quarterly, 37,* 408–426.

Case, J. L. (2002). *Clinical management of voice disorders* (4th ed.). Austin, TX: PRO-ED.

Chapman, R. S. (2000). Children's language learning: An interactionist perspective. *Journal of Child Psychology and Psychiatry and Allied Disciplines, 41,* 33–54.

Cheng, L. R. L. (2000). Children of yesterday, today and tomorrow: Global implications for child language. *Folia Phoniatrica et Logopaedica, 52*(1–3), 39–47.

Cochrane, V. M., & Slade, P. (1999). Appraisal and coping in adults with cleft lip: Associations with well-being and social anxiety. *British Journal of Medical Psychology, 72*(4), 485–503.

Cohen, N. J. (2002). Developmental language disorders. In P. Howlin and O. Udwin (Eds.), *Outcomes in neurodevelopmental and genetic disorders: Cambridge child and adolescent psychiatry* (pp. 26–55). New York: Cambridge University Press.

Craig, A. R. (2002). Fluency outcomes following treatment for those who stutter. *Perceptual and Motor Skills, 94*(3, Pt. 1), 772–774.

D'Antonio, L. L., Scherer, N. J., Miller, L. L., Kalbfleisch, J. H., & Bartley, J. A. (2001). Analysis of speech characteristics in children with velocardiofacial syndrome (VCFS) and children with phenotypic overlap without VCFS. *Cleft Palate Craniofacial Journal, 38,* 455–467.

Davis, S., Howell, P., & Cooke, F. (2002). Sociodynamic relationships between children who stutter and their non-stuttering classmates. *Journal of Child Psychology and Psychiatry and Allied Disciplines, 43,* 939–947.

Dayalu, V. N., Kalinowski, J., & Saltuklaroglu, T. (2002). Active inhibition of stuttering results in pseudofluency: A reply to Craig. *Perceptual and Motor Skills, 94*(3, Pt. 1), 1050–1052.

Dehaney, R. (2000). Literacy hour and the literal thinker: The inclusion of children with semantic-pragmatic language difficulties in the literacy hour. *Support for Learning, 15,* 36–40.

Delgado, C. E. F., Mundy, P., Crowson, M., Markus, J., Yale, M., & Schwartz, H. (2002). Responding to joint attention and language development: A comparison of target locations. *Journal of Speech, Language, and Hearing Research, 45,* 715–719.

Den-Dikken, M. (2000). The syntax of features. *Journal of Psycholinguistic Research, 29,* 5–23.

De-Nil, L. F., & Kroll, R. M. (2001). Searching for the neural basis of stuttering treatment outcome: Recent neuroimaging studies. *Clinical Linguistics and Phonetics, 15*(1–2), 163–168.

DiLollo, A., Neimeyer, R. A., & Manning, W. H. (2002). A personal construct psychology view of relapse: Indications for a narrative therapy component to stuttering treatment. *Journal of Fluency Disorders, 27,* 19–42.

Dmitrieva, E. S., & Gel'man, V. Y. (2001). Perception of the emotional speech component by stuttering children associated with noise: Communication II. Analysis of the temporal characteristics of the recognition of different emotions. *Human Physiology, 27,* 36–41.

Doehring, D. G. (2002). *Research strategies in human communication disorders* (3rd ed.). Austin, TX: PRO-ED.

Dorsey, M., & Guenther, R. K. (2000). Attitudes of professors and students toward college students who stutter. *Journal of Fluency Disorders, 25,* 77–83.

Drew, C. J., & Hardman, M. L. (2004). *Mental retardation: A lifespan approach to people with intellectual disabilities* (8th ed.). Columbus, OH: Merrill.

Fawcus, M. (2000). The causes and classification of voice disorders. In M. Freeman and M. Fawcus (Eds.), *Voice disorders and their management* (3rd ed., pp. 47–68). London: Whurr Publishers, Ltd.

Feldman, L. B., Barac-Cikoja, D., & Kostic, A. (2002). Semantic aspects of morphological processing: Transparency effects in Serbian. *Memory and Cognition, 30,* 629–636.

Felsenfeld, S., Kirk, K. M., Zhu, G., Statham, D. J., Neale, M. C., & Martin, N. G. (2000). A study of the genetic and environmental etiology of stuttering in a selected twin sample. *Behavior Genetics, 30,* 359–366.

Fodor, J. D., & Inoue, A. (2000). Syntactic features in reanalysis: Positive and negative symptoms. *Journal of Psycholinguistic Research, 29,* 25–36.

Forster, D. C., & Webster, W. G. (2001). Speech-motor control and interhemispheric relations in recovered and persistent stuttering. *Developmental Neuropsychology, 19,* 125–145.

Foundas, A. L., Bollich, A. M., Corey, D. M., Hurley, M., & Heilman, K. M. (2001). Anomalous anatomy of speech-language areas in adults with persistent developmental stuttering. *Neurology, 57,* 207–215.

Fox, A. V., & Dodd, B. (2001). Phonologically disordered German-speaking children. *American Journal of Speech Language Pathology, 10,* 291–303.

Gabel, R. M., Colcord, R. D., & Petrosino, L. (2002). Self-reported anxiety of adults who do and do not stutter. *Perceptual and Motor Skills, 94*(3, Pt. 1), 775–784.

Gelfand, D. M., & Drew, C. J. (2003). *Understanding child behavior disorders* (4th ed.). Belmont, CA: Wadsworth.

Gibbon, F. E., & Wood, S. E. (2002). Articulatory drift in the speech of children with articulation and phonological disorders. *Perceptual and Motor Skills, 95,* 295–307.

Gilman, M., & Yaruss, J. S. (2000). Stuttering and relaxation: Applications for somatic education in stuttering treatment. *Journal of Fluency Disorders, 25,* 59–76.

Goetestam, K. O. (2001). Handedness and creativity in a sample of homosexual men. *Perceptual and Motor Skills, 92*(3, Pt. 2), 1069–1074.

Gray, S. D., & Thibeault, S. L. (2002). Diversity in voice characteristics—Interaction between genes and environment, use of microarray analysis. *Journal of Communication Disorders, 35,* 347–354.

Hall, B. J., Oyer, H. J., & Haas, W. H. (2001). *Speech, language, and hearing disorders: A guide for the teacher* (3rd ed.). Boston: Allyn and Bacon.

Harris, V., Onslow, M., Packman, A., Harrison, E., & Menzies, R. (2002). An experimental investigation of the impact of the Lidcombe Program on early stuttering. *Journal of Fluency Disorders, 27*(3), 203–214.

Hattee, C., Farrow, K., Harland, K., Sommerlad, B., & Walsh, M. (2001). Are we ready to predict speech development from babble in cleft lip and palate children? *International Journal of Language and Communication Disorders, 36*(Supplement), 115–120.

Hickin, J., Best, W., Herbert, R., Howard, D., & Osborne, F. (2002). Phonological therapy for word-finding difficulties: A reevaluation. *Aphasiology, 16,* 981–999.

Hopper, T., Holland, A., & Rewega, M. (2002). Conversational coaching: Treatment outcomes and future directions. *Aphasiology, 16,* 745–761.

Horiuchi, V. (1999). Assistive devices help to level playing field: Machines can be key to productive life and individual self-esteem. *Salt Lake Tribune,* April 10, 1999, D8.

House, S. S., & Davidson, R. C. (2000). Increasing language

development through orientation and mobility instruction. *RE:view, 31*(4), 149–153.

Huttunen, K. H. (2001). Phonological development in 4–6-year-old moderately hearing impaired children. *Scandinavian Audiology, 30*(Supplement 53), 79–82.

Indefre, P., Levelt, W. J. M., Norris, D., et al. (2000). Language. In M. S. Gazzaniga (Ed.), *The new cognitive neurosciences* (2nd ed., pp. 845–958). Cambridge, MA: The MIT Press.

Ingham, R. J. (2001). Brain imaging studies of developmental stuttering. *Journal of Communication Disorders, 34,* 493–516.

Ingham, R. J., Sato, W., Finn, P., & Belknap, H. (2001). The modification of speech naturalness during rhythmic stimulation treatment of stuttering. *Journal of Speech, Language, and Hearing Research, 44,* 841–852.

Ishii, K., Tamaoka, A., & Shoji, S. (2001). A case of the primary focal lingual dystonia induced by speaking. *European Journal of Neurology, 8,* 507.

Johnson, C. R., & Slomka, G. (2000). Learning, motor, and communication disorders. In M. Hersen & R. T. Ammerman, (Eds.), *Advanced abnormal child psychology* (2nd ed., pp. 371–385). Mahwah, NJ: Lawrence Erlbaum.

Jones, M., Gebski, V., Onslow, M., & Packman, A. (2002). Statistical power in stuttering research: A tutorial. *Journal of Speech, Language, and Hearing Research, 45,* 243–255.

Koch, L. M., Goss, A. M., & Kolts, R. (2001). Attitudes toward Black English and code switching. *Journal of Black Psychology, 27,* 29–42.

Krueger, R. J., Krueger, J. J., Hugo, R., & Campbell, N. G. (2001). Relationship patterns between central auditory processing disorders and language disorders, learning disabilities, and sensory integration dysfunction. *Communication Disorders Quarterly, 22*(2), 87–98.

Kumin, L. (2002). Maximizing speech and language in children and adolescents with Down syndrome. In W. I. Cohen and L. Nadel (Eds.), *Down syndrome: Visions for the 21st century* (pp. 407–419). New York: Wiley-Liss.

Laganaro, M., & Venet, M. O. (2001). Acquired alexia in multilingual aphasia and computer-assisted treatment in both languages: Issues of

generalisation and transfer. *Folia Phoniatrica et Logopaedica, 53*(3), 135–144.

LaPointe, L. L. (2001). Darley and the psychosocial side. *Aphasiology, 15,* 249–260.

Lavid, N., Franklin, D. L., & Maguire, G. A. (1999). Management of child and adolescent stuttering with olanzapine: Three case reports. *Annals of Clinical Psychiatry, 11*(4), 233–236.

Lederer, S. H. (2001). Efficacy of parent–child language group intervention for late-talking toddlers. *Infant Toddler Intervention, 11*(3–4), 223–235.

Lerner, J. (2003). Learning disabilities: Theories, diagnosis, and teaching strategies (9th ed.). Boston: Houghton Mifflin.

Linebarger, M. L., Schwartz, M. F., & Kohn, S. E. (2001). Computer-based training of language production: An exploratory study. *Neuropsychological Rehabilitation, 11,* 57–96.

Lytton, H., & Gallagher, L. (2002). Parenting twins and the genetics of parenting. In M. H. Bornstein (Ed.), *Handbook of parenting: Vol. 1: Children and parenting* (2nd ed., pp. 227–253). Mahwah, NJ: Lawrence Erlbaum.

Maguire, G. A., Gottschalk, L. A., Riley, G. D., Franklin, D. L., Bechtel, R. J., & Ashurst, J. (1999). Stuttering: Neuropsychiatric features measured by content analysis of speech and the effect of risperidone on stuttering severity. *Comprehensive Psychiatry, 40*(4), 308–314.

Mansson, H. (2000). Childhood stuttering: Incidence and development. *Journal of Fluency Disorders, 25,* 47–57.

McCrory, E. (2001). Voice therapy outcomes in vocal fold nodules: A retrospective audit. *International Journal of Language and Communication Disorders, 36*(Supplement), 19–24.

Mildenberger, K., Noterdaeme, M., Sitter, S., & Amorosa, H. (2001). Behavioural problems in children with specific and pervasive developmental disorders, evaluated with the psychopathological documentation (AMDP). *Praxis der Kinderpsychologie und Kinderpsychiatrie, 50,* 649–663.

Molfese, D. L., & Molfese, V. J. (2000). The continuum of language development during infancy and early childhood. In C. Rovee-Collier & L. P. Lipsitt (Eds.), *Progress in infancy research* (vol. 1, pp. 251–287).

Mahwah, NJ: Lawrence Erlbaum.

Molfese, V. J., & Molfese, D. L. (2002). Environmental and social influences on reading skills as indexed by brain and behavioral responses. *Annals of Dyslexia, 52,* 121–137.

Nakada, T., Fujii, Y., Yoneoka, Y., & Kwee, I. L. (2001). Planum temporale: Where spoken and written language meet. *European Neurology, 46,* 121–125.

Nelson, N. W. (2002). Language intervention in school settings. In D. K. Bernstein and E. Tiegerman-Farber (Eds.), *Language and communication disorders in children* (5th ed., pp. 315–353). Boston: Allyn and Bacon.

Nicolosi, L., Harryman, E., & Kresheck, J. (2003). *Terminology of communication disorders, speech, language and hearing* (5th ed.). Philadelphia, PA: Lippincott Williams & Wilkins.

Noell, G. H., VanDerHeyden, A. M., Gatti, S. L., & Whitmarsh, E. L. (2001). Functional assessment of the effects of escape and attention on students' compliance during instruction. *School Psychology Quarterly, 16,* 253–269.

Ohama, M. L. F., Gotay, C. C., Pagano, I. S., Boles, L., & Craven, D. D. (2000). Evaluations of Hawaii Creole English and standard English. *Journal of Language and Social Psychology, 19,* 357–377.

Onslow, M., Menzies, R. G., & Packman, A. (2001). An operant intervention for early stuttering: The development of the Lidcombe program. *Behavior Modification, 25,* 116–139.

Owens, R. E., Jr. (1995). *Language disorders: A functional approach to assessment and intervention* (2nd ed.). Needham Heights, MA: Allyn and Bacon.

Owens, R. E., Jr. (2001). *Language development: An introduction* (5th ed.). Boston: Allyn and Bacon.

Owens, R. E., Metz, D. E., & Haas, A. (2002). *Introduction to communication disorders: A lifespan approach* (2nd ed.). Boston: Allyn and Bacon.

Perino, M., Famularo, G., & Tarroni, P. (2000). Acquired transient stuttering during a migraine attack. *Headache, 40,* 170–172.

Pesak, J., & Opavsky, J. (2000). Decreased serum copper level in developmental stutterers. *European Journal of Neurology, 7,* 748.

Petersen, K., Reichle, J., & Johnston, S. S. (2000). Examining preschoolers' performance in linear and row-column scanning techniques. *AAC: Augmentative and Alternative Communication, 16,* 27–36.

Prizant, B. M., Wetherby, A. M., & Roberts, J. E. (2000). Communication problems. In C. H. Zeanah, Jr. (Ed.), *Handbook of infant mental health* (2nd ed., pp. 282–297). New York: Guilford.

Puckett, M. (2001). *The young child: Development from pre-birth through age 8* (3rd ed.). Columbus, OH: Merrill/Prentice-Hall.

Radziewicz, C., & Antonellis, S. (2002). Considerations and implications for habilitation of hearing impaired children. In D. K. Bernstein and E. Tiegerman-Farber (Eds.), *Language and communication disorders in children* (5th ed., pp. 565–598). Boston: Allyn and Bacon.

Ramig, L. O. (2000). Voice problems of speakers with dysarthria. In M. Freeman and M. Fawcus (Eds.), *Voice disorders and their management* (3rd ed., pp. 156–171). London: Whurr Publishers.

Ratner, N. B. (2000). Elicited imitation and other methods for the analysis of trade-offs between speech and language skills in children. In L. Menn and N. B. Ratner (Eds.), *Methods for studying language production* (pp. 291–311). Mahwah, NJ: Lawrence Erlbaum.

Robinson, N. B., & Robb, M. P. (2002). Early communication assessment and intervention: A dynamic process. In D. K. Bernstein and E. Tiegerman-Farber (Eds.), *Language and communication disorders in children* (5th ed., pp. 155–196). Needham Heights, MA: Allyn and Bacon.

Rubin, J. S., Sataloff, R. T., & Korovin, G. S. (2002). *Diagnosis and treatment of voice disorders* (2nd ed.). San Diego, CA: Singular Publishing Group.

Segalowitz, S. J. (2000). Predicting child language impairment from too many variables: Overinterpreting stepwise discriminant function analysis. *Brain and Language, 71,* 337–343.

Shames, G. H. (2001). *Human communication disorders* (6th ed.). Boston: Allyn and Bacon.

Shriberg, L. D., Tomblin, J. B., & McSweeny, J. L. (1999). Prevalence of speech delay in

6-year old children and co-morbidity with language impairment. *Journal of Speech, Language, and Hearing Research, 42,* 1461–1481.

Silliman, E. R., & Diehl, S. F. (2002). Assessing children with language disorders. In D. K. Bernstein and E. Tiegerman-Farber (Eds.), *Language and communication disorders in children* (5th ed., pp. 181–255). Boston: Allyn and Bacon.

Simmons-Mackie, N., & Damico, J. S. (2001). Intervention outcomes: A clinical application of qualitative methods. *Topics in Language Disorders, 22,* 21–36.

Sommer, M., Koch, M. A., Paulus, W., Weiller, C., & Buechel, C. (2002). Disconnection of speech-relevant brain areas in persistent developmental stuttering. *Lancet, 360,* 380–383.

Spreen, O. (2002). *Assessment of aphasia.* New York: Oxford University Press.

Stoel-Gammon, C. (2001). Transcribing the speech of young children. *Topics in Language Disorders, 21*(4), 12–21.

Sutton, A., Soto, G., & Blockberger, S. (2002). Grammatical issues in graphic symbol communication. *AAC: Augmentative and Alternative Communication, 18*(3), 192–204.

Swenson, N. C. (2000). Comparing traditional and collaborative settings for language intervention. *Communication Disorders Quarterly, 22,* 12–18.

Szagun, G. (2000). The acquisition of grammatical and lexical structures in children with cochlear implants: A developmental psycholinguistic approach. *Audiology and Neuro-Otology, 5,* 39–47.

Szagun, G. (2002). Learning the h(e)ard way: The acquisition of grammar in young German-speaking children with cochlear implants and with normal hearing. In F. Windsor, L. M. Kelly, and N. Hewlett (Eds.), *Investigations in clinical phonetics and linguistics* (pp. 131–144). Mahwah, NJ: Lawrence Erlbaum.

Taatgen, N. A., & Anderson, J. R. (2002). Why do children learn to say "broke"? A model of learning the past without feedback. *Cognition, 86,* 123–155.

Tiegerman-Farber, E. (2002). Interactive teaming: The changing role of the speech-language pathologist. In D. K. Bernstein & E. Tiegerman-Farber (Eds.), *Language and communication dis-*

*orders in children* (5th ed., pp. 96–125). Boston: Allyn and Bacon.

Toppelberg, C. O., & Shapiro, T. (2000). Language disorders: A 10-year research update review. *Journal of the American Academy of Child and Adolescent Psychiatry, 39*(2), 143–152.

Treon, M. (2002). A proposed etiologic psychopathology and neurolinguipathology based linguistic and paralinguistic processing deficit syndrome in stuttering. *Psychology and Education: An Interdisciplinary Journal, 39*(3–4), 42–60.

U.S. Department of Education. (2002). *Twenty-fourth annual report to Congress on the implementation of the Individuals with Disabilities Education Act.* Washington, DC: Author.

Vanryckeghem, M., Hylebos, C., Brutten, G. J., & Peleman, M. (2001). The relationship between communication attitude and emotion of children who stutter. *Journal of Fluency Disorders, 26,* 1–15.

Van-Slyke, P. A. (2002). Classroom instruction for children with Landau-Kleffner syndrome. *Child Language Teaching and Therapy, 18,* 23–42.

Verhoeven, L., & Vermeer, A. (2002) Communicative competence and personality dimensions in first and second language learners. *Applied Psycholinguistics, 23,* 361–374.

Vicari, S., Albertoni, A., Chilosi, A. M., Cipriani, P., Cioni, G., & Bates, E. (2000). Plasticity and reorganization during language development in children with early brain injury. *Cortex, 36,* 31–46.

Vigil, D. C. (2002). Cultural variations in attention regulation: A comparative analysis of British and Chinese populations. *International Journal of Language and Communication Disorders, 37,* 433–458.

Vilkman, E. (2000). Voice problems at work: A challenge for occupational safety and health arrangement. *Folia Phoniatrica et Logopaedica, 52,* 120–125.

Weiss, A. L. (2002). Planning language intervention for young children. In D. K. Bernstein & E. Tiegerman-Farber (Eds.), *Language and communication disorders in children* (5th ed., pp. 256–314). Boston: Allyn and Bacon.

Weitzel, A. (2000). Overcoming loss of voice. In D. O. Braithwaite & T. L. Thompson (Eds.), *Handbook of communication and people with disabilities: Research and application*

(pp. 451–466). Mahwah, NJ: Lawrence Erlbaum.

Wermke, K., Hauser, C., Komposch, G., & Stellzig, A. (2002). Spectral analysis of prespeech sounds (spontaneous cries) in infants with unilateral cleft lip and palate (UCLP): A pilot study. *Cleft Palate Craniofacial Journal, 39,* 285–294.

Whaley, B. B., & Golden, M. A. (2000). Communicating with persons who stutter: Perceptions and strategies. In D. O. Braithwaite and T. L. Thompson (Eds.), *Handbook of communication and people with disabilities: Research and application* (pp. 423–438). Mahwah, NJ: Lawrence Erlbaum.

Wilkins, M., & Ertmer, D. J. (2002). Introducing young children who are deaf or hard of hearing to spoken language: Child's voice, an oral school. *Language, Speech, and Hearing Services in Schools, 33*(3), 196–204.

Williams, A. L. (2000). Multiple oppositions: Theoretical foundations for an alternative contrastive intervention approach. *American Journal of Speech Language Pathology, 9,* 282–288.

Windfuhr, K. L., Faragher, B., & Conti-Ramsden, G. (2002). Lexical learning skills in young children with specific language impairment. *International Journal of Language and Communication Disorders, 37,* 415–432.

Wolpaw, J. R., Birbaumer, N., McFarland, D. J., Pfurtscheller, G., & Vaughan, T. M. (2002). Brain-computer interfaces for communication and control. *Clinical Neurophysiology, 113,* 767–791.

Worrall, L., McCooey, R., Davidson, B., Larkins, B., & Hickson, L. (2002). The validity of functional assessments of communication and the Activity/Participation components of the ICIDH-2: Do they reflect what really happens in real-life? *Journal of Communication Disorders, 35*(2), 107–137.

Yaruss, J. S., Quesal, R. W., Reeves, L., Molt, L. F., Kluetz, B., Caruso, A. J., McClure, J., & Lewis, F. (2002). Speech treatment and support group experiences of people who participate in the National Stuttering Association. *Journal of Fluency Disorders, 27*(2), 115–134.

Yavas, M. (2002). Voice onset time patterns in bilingual phonological development. In F. Windsor, L. M. Kelly, and N.

Hewlett (Eds.), *Investigations in clinical phonetics and linguistics* (pp. 341–349). Mahwah, NJ: Lawrence Erlbaum.

Ying, L., Baokun, D., & Minggao, L. (2001). Personality trait and affective symptom of stuttering. *Chinese Mental Health Journal, 15*(4), 217–219.

## CHAPTER 12

Abt Associates (1974). *Assessments of selected resources for severely handicapped children and youth. Vol I: A state-of-the-art paper.* Cambridge, MA: Author (ERIC Document Reproduction Service No. ED 134 614).

Agran, M., & Wehmeyer, M. (1999). *Innovations: Teaching problem solving to students with mental retardation.* Washington, DC: American Association on Mental Retardation.

Ault, M. M., Rues, J. P., Graff, J. C., & Holvoet, J. F. (2000). Special health care procedures. In M. Snell & F. Brown (Eds.), *Instruction of students with severe disabilities* (pp. 245–290). Columbus, OH: Merrill.

Beirne-Smith, M., Ittenbach, R. F., & Patton, J. R. (2002). *Mental retardation* (6th ed.). Upper Saddle River, NJ: Merrill.

Berry, J., & Hardman, M. L. (1998). *Lifespan perspectives on family and disability.* Boston: Allyn and Bacon.

Bremer, C. D., Kachgal, M., & Schoeller, K. (2003, April). Self-determination: Supporting successful transition. *Research to Practice Brief of the National Center on Secondary Education and Transition, 2*(1), 1–5.

Brown, F., & Snell, M. (2000). Meaningful assessment. In M. E. Snell & F. Brown (Eds.), *Instruction of students with severe disabilities* (pp. 67–114). Upper Saddle River, NJ: Merrill.

Center on Human Policy (2000, June/July). The community imperative. *TASH Newsletter, 26,* 18-19.

Deafblind International (2003). *What is deafblindness?* [Online]. Available: http://www.deafblindinternational.org/whatisdb/whatisdb.htm. Retrieved June 7, 2003.

Drew, C. J., & Hardman, M. L. (2004). *Mental retardation: A lifespan approach to people with intellectual disabilities* (8th ed.). Columbus, OH: Merrill.

Ford, A., Davern, L., & Schnorr, R. (2001, July/August). Learners with significant disabilities: Curricular relevance in an era of standards-based reform. *Remedial and Special Education, 22*(4), 214–222.

Fuller, M. L., & Olsen, G. (1998) *Home–school relations.* Boston: Allyn and Bacon.

Giangreco, M. F., & Doyle, M. B. (2000). *Curricular and instructional considerations for teaching students with disabilities in general education classrooms.* In S. E. Wade (Ed.), *Inclusive education: A casebook and readings for prospective and practicing teachers* (pp. 51–70). Mahwah, NJ: Lawrence Erlbaum.

Grenot-Scheyer, M., Schwartz, I. S., & Meyer, L. H. (1997, April). Blending best practices for young children: Inclusive early childhood programs. *TASH Newsletter,* 8–11.

Griffiths, D. M., Nugent, J. A., & Gardner, W. I. (1998). Introduction. In D. M. Griffiths, W. I. Gardner, & J. A. Nugent (Eds.), *Behavioral supports: Individual centered interventions* (pp. 1–5). Kingston, NY: NADD Press.

Guralnick, M. J. (2001). A framework for change in early childhood inclusion. In M. J. Guralnick (Ed.), *Early childhood inclusion: Focus on change* (pp. 3–35). Baltimore, MD: Paul H. Brookes.

Hewitt, A., & O'Nell, S. (2003). *A little help from my friends.* Washington, DC: President's Committee on Mental Retardation [Online]. Available: http://www.acf.dhhs.gov/programs/pcmr/help4.pdf. Retrieved June 10, 2003.

Horner, R. H., Albin, R. W., Sprague, J. R., & Todd, A. W. (2000). Positive behavior support. In M. E. Snell & F. Brown (Eds.), *Instruction of students with severe disabilities* (pp. 207–243). Upper Saddle River, NJ: Merrill.

Justen, J. (1976). Who are the severely handicapped? A problem in definition. *AAESPH Review, 1*(5), 1–11.

King, W. (2000, May 2). Disabilities may keep man from transplant. *Salt Lake Tribune,* A1, A7.

Massanari, C. (2003). *Alternate assessment: Questions and answers. IDEA practices.* [Online]. Available: http://www.ideapractices.org/resources/detail.php?id=2009. Retrieved June 18, 2003.

McDonnell, J., Hardman, M., & McDonnell, A. P. (2003). *Introduction to persons with moderate and severe disabilities* (2nd ed.). Boston: Allyn and Bacon.

McDonnell, J., Mathot-Buckner, C., & Ferguson, B. (1996).

*Transition programs for students with moderate/severe disabilities.* Pacific Grove, CA: Brooks/Cole.

Meyer, L. H., Peck, C. A., & Brown, L. (1991). Definitions and diagnosis. In L. H. Meyer, C. A. Peck, & L. Brown (Eds.), *Critical issues in the lives of people with disabilities* (p. 17). Baltimore, MD: Paul H. Brookes.

New Goals for the U.S. Human Genome Project: 1998–2003. (1998). *Science, 282,* 682–689.

Penner, I. (2003). *The right to belong: The story of Yvonne.* [Online]. Available: http://www3.nb.sympatico.ca/ipenner/. Retrieved May 7, 2003.

Quenemoen, R., & Thurlow, M. (2003). *NCEO policy directions: Including alternate assessment results in accountability decisions.* [Online]. Available: http://education.umn.edu/nceo/OnlinePubs/Policy13.htm. Retrieved June 10, 2003.

Ramey, C. T., & Ramey, S. L. (1999). *Right from birth.* New York: Goddard Press.

Sailor, W., Gee, K., & Karasoff, P. (2000). Inclusion and school restructuring. In M. Snell & F. Brown (Eds.), *Instruction of students with severe disabilities* (5th ed., pp. 1–30). Columbus, OH: Merrill.

Sailor, W., & Haring, N. (1977). Some current directions in the education of the severely/multiply handicapped. *AAESPH Review, 2,* 67–86.

Sax, C., Fisher, D., & Pumpian, I. (1999). We didn't always learn what we were taught: Inclusion does work. In D. Fisher, C. Sax, & I. Pumpian (Eds.), *Inclusive high schools* (pp. 5–26). Baltimore, MD: Paul H. Brookes.

Sax, C., Pumpian, I., & Fisher, D. (1997, March). *Assistive technology and inclusion.* San Diego, CA: Interwork Institute, Consortium on Inclusive Schooling Practices, San Diego State University.

Siegel-Causey, E., & Allinder, R. M. (1998). Using alternate assessment for students with severe disabilities: Alignment with best practices. *Education and Training in Mental Retardation and Developmental Disabilities, 33*(2), 168–178.

Silberman, R. K., & Brown, F. (1998). Alternative approaches to assessing students who have visual impairments with other disabilities in classroom and community environments. In S. Z. Sacks & R. K. Silberman (Eds.), *Educating*

*students who have visual impairments with other disabilities* (pp. 73–98). Baltimore, MD: Paul H. Brookes.

Snell, M. E. (1991). Schools are for all kids: The importance of integration for students with severe disabilities and their peers. In J. Lloyd, N. N. Singh, & A. C. Repp (Eds.), *The regular education initiative: Alternative perspectives on concepts, issues, and models* (pp. 133–148). Sycamore, IL: Sycamore.

Snell, M. E., & Brown, F. (2000). Development and implementation of educational programs. In M. E. Snell & F. Brown (Eds.), *Instruction of students with severe disabilities* (5th ed.), pp. 115–172. Upper Saddle River, NJ: Merrill.

Sobsey, D., & Wolf-Schein, E. G. (1996). Children with sensory impairments. In F. P. Orelove & D. Sobsey (Eds.), *Educating children with multiple disabilities: A transdisciplinary approach* (3rd ed., pp. 411–450). Baltimore, MD: Paul H. Brookes.

Tager-Flusberg, H., & Sullivan, K. (1998). Early language development in children with mental retardation. In J. A. Burack, R. M. Hodapp, & E. Zigler (Eds.), *Handbook of mental retardation and development* (pp. 208–239). New York: Cambridge University Press.

TASH (2000). *TASH Resolution on the People for Whom TASH Advocates.* Baltimore: Author. (Definition was originally adopted April 1975; Revised December 1985 and March 2000.) [Online]. Available: http://www.tash.org/resolutions/R21PEOPL.html

The ARC (2003). *Genetic issues in mental retardation* [Online]. Silver Spring, MD: Author [Online]. Available: http://TheArc.org/depts/gbr01.html. Retrieved April 24, 2003

U.S. Department of Education (2002). To assure the free appropriate public education of all children with disabilities. *Twenty-fourth annual report to Congress on the implementation of the Individuals with Disabilities Education Act.* Washington, DC: U.S. Government Printing Office.

U.S. Department of Energy (2003). *Human Genome Project information* [Online]. Available: http://www.ornl.gov/hgmis/. Retrieved June 12, 2003.

Wehman, P. (1997). Traumatic brain injury. In P. Wehman (Ed.), *Exceptional individuals*

*in school, community, and work* (pp. 451–485). Austin, TX: PRO-ED.

Wehman, P., & Parent, W. (1997). Severe mental retardation. In P. Wehman (Ed.), *Exceptional individuals in school, community, and work* (pp. 145–173). Austin, TX: PRO-ED.

Westling, D., & Fox, L. (2000). *Teaching students with severe disabilities.* Upper Saddle River, NJ: Merrill. When genetic testing says no. *Time* (1999, January 11), *153*(1). [Online]. Available: http://www.time.com/time/magazine/articles/0,3266,17683-3,00.html. Retrieved October 3, 1999.

Whitney-Thomas, J., Shaw, D., Honey, K., & Butterworth, J. (1998). Building a future: A study of student participation in person-centered planning. *Journal of the Association for Persons with Severe Handicaps, 23*(2), 119–133.

Ysseldyke, J. E., & Olsen, K. (2003). *Putting alternate assessments into practice: What to measure and possible sources of data. NCEO Synthesis Report 28.* Minneapolis: The National Center on Educational Outcomes, University of Minnesota. [Online]. Available: http://education.umn.edu/NCEO/OnlinePubs/Synthesis28.htm. Retrieved January 15, 2000.

Ysseldyke, J. E., Olsen, K., & Thurlow, M. (2003). *Issues and considerations in alternate assessments. NCEO Synthesis Report 27.* Minneapolis: The National Center on Educational Outcomes, University of Minnesota. [Online]. Available: http://education.umn.edu/NCEO/OnlinePubs/Synthesis27.htm. Retrieved June 3, 2003.

## CHAPTER 13

ABCNEWS.com. (2000). Summer camps your kids will love. *Camping it up: A quick guide for parents on choosing the right camps for your kids.* April 9, 1–2.

Akshoomoff, N., Pierce, K., & Courchesne, E. (2002). The neurobiological basis of autism from a developmental perspective. *Development and Psychopathology, 14,* 613–634.

American Psychiatric Association. (2000). Diagnostic and statistical manual of mental disorders (DSM-IV-TR) (4th ed.—text revision). Washington, DC: Author.

Amorosa, H., & Noterdaeme, M. (2002). Early childhood autism: Age at onset and early regression. *Zeitschrift fuer Kinder und Jugendpsychiatrie und Psychotherapie, 30*(3), 211–220.

Anderson, C. M. (2001). The integrative role of the cerebellar vermis in cognition and emotion. *Consciousness and Emotion, 2,* 284–299.

Andres, C. (2002). Molecular genetics and animal models in autistic disorder. *Brain Research Bulletin, 57,* 109–119.

Baker, H. C. (2002). A comparison study of autism spectrum disorder referrals, 1997 and 1989. *Journal of Autism and Developmental Disorders, 32*(2), 121–125.

Baker, M. J. (2000). Incorporating the thematic ritualistic behavior of children with autism into games: Increasing social play interactions with siblings. *Journal of Positive Behavior Interactions, 2*(2), 66–84.

Baron-Cohen, S. (2002). Is Asperger syndrome necessarily viewed as a disability? *Focus on Autism and Other Developmental Disabilities, 17*(3), 186–191.

Bauminger, N. (2002). The facilitation of social-emotional understanding and social interaction in high-functioning children with autism: Intervention outcomes. *Journal of Autism and Developmental Disorders, 32,* 283–298.

Bauminger, N., & Yirmiya, N. (2001). The functioning and well-being of siblings of children with autism: Behavioral-genetic and familial contributions. In J. A. Burack and T. Charman (Eds.). *The development of autism: Perspectives from theory and research* (pp. 61–80). Mahwah, NJ: Lawrence Erlbaum.

Beatson, J. E., & Prelock, P. A. (2002). The Vermont Rural Autism Project: Sharing experiences, shifting attitudes. *Focus on Autism and Other Developmental Disabilities, 17,* 48–54.

Berney, T. P. (2000). Autism—an evolving concept. *British Journal of Psychiatry, 176,* 20–25.

Bishop, D. V. M., & Norbury, C. F. (2002). Exploring the borderlands of autistic disorder and specific language impairment: A study using standardised diagnostic instruments. *Journal of Child Psychology and Psychiatry and Allied Disciplines, 43,* 917–929.

Blair, R. J. R., Frith, U., Smith, N., Abell, F., & Cipolotti, L. (2002). Fractionation of visual memory: Agency detection and its impairment in autism. *Neuropsychologia, 40,* 108–118.

Boelte, S., Feineis-Matthews, S., & Poustka, F. (2001). The neuropsychology of autism. *Zeitschrift fuer Neuropsychologie, 12,* 221–231.

Bondy, A., & Frost, L. (2002). *A picture's worth: PECS and other visual communication strategies in autism.* Bethesda, MD: Woodbine House.

Bowers, L. (2002). An audit of referrals of children with autistic spectrum disorder to the dietetic service. *Journal of Human Nutrition and Dietetics, 15,* 141–144.

Boyd, B. A. (2002). Examining the relationship between stress and lack of social support in mothers of children with autism. *Focus on Autism and Other Developmental Disabilities, 17,* 208–215.

Britton, L. N., Carr, J. E., Landaburu, H. J. & Romick, K. S. (2002). The efficacy of noncontingent reinforcement as treatment for automatically reinforced stereotypy. *Behavioral Interventions, 17*(2), 93–103.

Burkhardt, S., & Bucci, M. E. (2001). Counseling issues for parents of children with autistic spectrum disorders. In T. Wahlberk and F. Obiakor (Eds.), *Autistic spectrum disorders: Educational and clinical interventions. Advances in special education* (Vol. 14, pp. 211–233). Oxford: Elsevier Science.

Cafiero, J. M. (2001). The effect of an augmentative communication intervention on the communication, behavior, and academic program of an adolescent with autism. *Focus on Autism and Other Developmental Disabilities, 16*(3), 179–189.

Cafiero, J. M. (2002). "The effect of an augmentative communication intervention on the communication, behavior, and academic program of an adolescent with autism": Erratum. *Focus on Autism and Other Developmental Disabilities, 17*(3), 137.

Carpenter, M., Pennington, B. E., & Rogers, S. J. (2002). Interrelations among social-cognitive skills in young children with autism. *Journal of Autism and Developmental Disorders, 32*(2): 91–106.

CBSNEWS.com (2003). Scrapping late favors in homeland law. January 11.

CBSNEWS.com (2003). Using horses for "small wonders". February 19.

Chandler, S., Christie, P., Newson, E., & Prevezer, W. (2002). Developing a diagnostic and intervention package for 2- to 3-year-olds with autism: Outcomes of the Frameworks for Communication approach. *Autism, 6,* 47–69.

Choutka, C. M. (1999). Experiencing the reality of service delivery: One parent's perspective. *Journal of the Association for Persons with Severe Handicaps, 24,* 213–217.

Charlop-Christy, M. H., Carpenter, M., Le, L., LeBlanc, L. A., & Kellet, K. (2002). Using the picture exchange communication system (PECS) with children with autism: Assessment of PECS acquisition, speech, social-communicative behavior, and problem behavior. *Journal of Applied Behavior Analysis, 35,* 213–231.

Cuccaro, M. L., Shao, Y., Bass, M. P., Abramson, R. K., Ravan, S. A., Wright, H. H., Wolpert, C. M., Donnelly, S. L., & Pericak-Vance, M. A. (2003). Behavioral comparisons in autistic individuals from multiplex and singleton families. *Journal of Autism and Developmental Disorders, 33,* 87–91.

Dawson, G., Webb, S., Schellenberg, G. D., Dager, S., Friedman, S., Aylward, E., & Richards, T. (2002). Defining the broader phenotype of autism: Genetic, brain, and behavioral perspectives. *Development and Psychopathology, 14,* 581–611.

Dow, M. J., & Mehring, T. A. (2001). Inservice training for educators of individuals with autism. In T. Wahlberg and F. Obiakor (Eds.), *Autistic spectrum disorders: Educational and clinical interventions. Advances in special education* (Vol. 14, pp. 89–107). Oxford: Elsevier Science.

Drew, C. J., & Hardman, M. L. (2004). *Mental retardation: A lifespan approach to people with intellectual disabilities* (8th ed.). Columbus, OH: Merrill.

Duchan, J. F., Calculator, S., Sonnenmeier, R., Diehl, S., & Cumley, G. D. (2001). A framework for managing controversial practices. *Language, Speech, and Hearing Services in Schools, 32,* 133–141.

Emerson, A., Grayson, A., & Griffiths, A. (2001). Can't or won't? Evidence relating to authorship in facilitated communication. *International Journal of Language and Communication Disorders, 36*(Supplement), 98–103.

Erba, H. W. (2000). Early intervention programs for children with autism: Conceptual frameworks for implementation. *American Journal of Orthopsychiatry, 70,* 82–94.

Freedman, R. I., & Boyer, N. C. (2000). The power to choose: Supports for families caring for individuals with developmental disabilities. *Health and Social Work, 25,* 59–68.

Gallagher, L., Becker, K., Kearney, G., Dunlop, A., Stallings, R., Green, A., Fitzgerald, M., & Gill, M. (2003). A case of autism associated with del(2)(q32.1q32.2) or (q32.2q32.3). *Journal of Autism and Developmental Disorders, 33,* 105–108.

Gelfand, D. M., & Drew, C. J. (2003). *Understanding child behavior disorders* (4th ed.). Belmont, CA: Wadsworth.

Gerdtz, J. (2000). Evaluating behavioral treatment of disruptive classroom behaviors of an adolescent with autism. *Research on Social Work Practice, 10,* 98–110.

Gillberg, C. (2002). *A guide to Asperger syndrome.* New York: Cambridge University Press.

Gobbi, G., & Pulvirenti, L. (2001). Long-term treatment with clozapine in an adult with autistic disorder accompanied by aggressive behavior. *Journal of Psychiatry and Neuroscience, 26,* 340–341.

Goldstein, H. (2002). Communication intervention for children with autism: A review of treatment efficacy. *Journal of Autism and Developmental Disorders, 32,* 373–396.

Gray, D. E. (2002). Ten years on: A longitudinal study of families of children with autism. *Journal of Intellectual and Developmental Disability, 27,* 215–222.

Gray, K. M., & Tonge, B. J. (2001). Are there early features of autism in infants and preschool children? *Journal of Paediatrics and Child Health, 37,* 221–226.

Green, G., Brennan, L. C., & Fein, D. (2002). Intensive behavioral treatment for a toddler at high risk for autism. *Behavior Modification, 26,* 69–102.

Hatton, D. D., & Bailey, D. B., Jr. (2001). Fragile X syndrome and autism. In E. Schopler and N. Yirmia (Eds.), *The research basis for autism intervention* (pp. 75–89). New York: Kluwer Academic/Plenum.

Heaton, P., Pring, L., & Hermelin, B. (1999). A pseudo-savant: A case of exceptional musical splinter skills. *Neurocase: Case Studies in Neuropsychology,*

Neuropsychiatry, and Behavioural Neurology, 5, 503–509.

Hermelin, B. (2001). *Bright splinters of the mind: A personal story of research with autistic savants.* London: Jessica Kingsley Publishers.

Howard, V. F., Williams, B. F., Port, P. D., & Lepper, C. (2001). *Very young children with special needs: A formative approach for the twenty-first century* (2nd ed.). Columbus, OH: Merrill/Prentice-Hall.

Howlin, P. (2002). Autistic disorders. In P. Howlin and O. Udwin (Eds.), *Outcomes in neurodevelopmental and genetic disorders: Cambridge child and adolescent psychiatry* (pp. 136–168). New York: Cambridge University Press.

Iwanaga, R., Kawasaki, C., & Tsuchida, R. (2000). Brief report: Comparison of sensorymotor and cognitive function between autism and Asperger syndrome in preschool children. *Journal of Autism and Developmental Disorders, 30*(2), 169–174.

Johnson, C. R. (2002). Mental retardation. In M. Hersen (Ed.), *Clinical behavior therapy: Adults and children* (pp. 420–433). New York: Wiley.

Kaminsky, L., & Dewey, D. (2002). Psychosocial adjustment in siblings of children with autism. *Journal of Child Psychology and Psychiatry and Allied Disciplines, 43*, 225–232.

Kauffman, J. (2001). *Characteristics of emotional and behavioral disorders of children and youth* (7th ed.). Columbus, OH: Merrill/Prentice-Hall.

Keen, D., Woodyatt, G., & Sigafoos, J. (2002).Verifying teacher perceptions of the potential communicative acts of children with autism. *Communication Disorders Quarterly, 23*(3), 133–142.

Kemner, C., Willemsen-Swinkels, S. H. N., de-Jonge, M., Tuynman-Qua, H., & van-Engeland, H. (2002). Open-label study of olanzapine in children with pervasive developmental disorder. *Journal of Clinical Psychopharmacology, 22*, 455–460.

Kimball, J. W. (2002). Behavior analytic instruction for children with autism: Philosophy matters. *Focus on Autism and Other Developmental Disabilities, 17*(2), 66–75.

King, R., Fay, G., & Wheildon, H. (2002). Re: Clomipramine vs. haloperidol in the treatment of autistic disorder: A double-blind, placebo, crossover study. *Journal of Clinical Psychopharmacology, 22*, 525–526.

Koegel, L. K., Koegel, R. L., Frea, W. D., & Fredeen, R. M. (2001). Identifying early intervention targets for children with autism in inclusive school settings. *Behavior Modification, 25*, 745–761.

Korbivcher, C. F. (2001). The autistic states and the theory of transformations: The autistic transformations: A proposition. *Revista Brasileira de Psicanalise, 35*, 935–958.

Liss, M., Fein, D., Allen, D., Dunn, M., Feinstein, C., Morris, R., Waterhouse, L., & Rapin, I. (2001). Executive functioning in high-functioning children with autism. *Journal of Child Psychology and Psychiatry and Allied Disciplines, 42*, 261–270.

Lovaas, O. I. (2003). *Teaching individuals with developmental delays: Basic intervention techniques.* Austin, TX: PRO-ED.

Luiselli, J. K., Blew, P., & Thibadeau, S. (2001). Therapeutic effects and long-term efficacy of antidepressant medication for persons with developmental disabilities: Behavioral assessment in two cases of treatment-resistant aggression and self-injury. *Behavior Modification, 25*, 62–78.

Luiselli, J. K., Campbell, S., Cannon, B., DiPietro, E., Ellis, J. T., Taras, M., & Lifter, K. (2001). Assessment instruments used in the education and treatment of persons with autism: Brief report of a survey of national service centers. *Research in Developmental Disabilities, 22*, 389–398.

Malone, R. P., Maislin, G., Choudhury, M. S., Gifford, C., & Delaney, M. A. (2002). Risperidone treatment in children and adolescents with autism: Short- and long-term safety and effectiveness. *Journal of the American Academy of Child and Adolescent Psychiatry, 41*(2), 140–147.

Manning, J. T., Baron-Cohen, S., Wheelwright, S., & Sanders, G. (2001). The 2nd to 4th digit ratio and autism. *Developmental Medicine and Child Neurology, 43*, 160–164.

Marazziti, D. (2002). A further support to the hypothesis of a link between serotonin, autism and the cerebellum. *Biological Psychiatry, 52*, 143.

Mastropieri, M. A., & Scruggs, T. E. (2000). *The inclusive classroom: Strategies for effective instruction.* Upper Saddle River, NJ: Prentice-Hall.

Matthews, B., Shute, R., & Rees, R. (2001). An analysis of stimulus overselectivity in adults with autism. *Journal of Intellectual and Developmental Disability, 26*, 161–176.

Mayes, S. D., Calhoun, S. L., & Crites, D. L. (2001). Does DSM-IV Asperger's disorder exist? *Journal of Abnormal Child Psychology, 29*, 263–271.

McCracken, J. T., McGough, J., Shah, B., Cronin, P., Hong, D., Aman, M. G., Arnold, L. E., Lindsay, R., Nash, P., Hollway, J., McDougle, C. J., Posey, D., Swiezy, N., Kohn, A., Scahill, L., Martin, A., Koenig, K., Volkmar, F., Carroll, D., Lancor, A., Tierney, E., Ghuman, J., Gonzalez, N. M., Grados, M., Vitiello, B., Ritz, L., Davies, M., Robinson, J., & McMahon, D. (2002). Risperidone in children with autism and serious behavioral problems. *New England Journal of Medicine, 347*(5), 314–321.

Menn, L., & Bernstein-Ratner, N. (2000). *Methods for studying language production.* Mahwah, NJ: Lawrence Erlbaum.

Minazio, N. (2002). Autistic states: Are these a figure of defeat of the psyche? *Revue Française de Psychanalyse, 66*, 1771–1778.

Minshew, N. (2000). Autism's home in the brain: Reply. *Neurology, 54*, 269.

Mirenda, P. (2001). Autism, augmentative communication, and assistive technology: What do we really know? *Focus on Autism and Other Developmental Disabilities, 16*(3), 141–151.

Mostert, M. P. (2001). Facilitated communication since 1995: A review of published studies. *Journal of Autism and Developmental Disorders, 31*, 287–313.

Moyes, R. (2003). Incorporating social goals in the classroom—A guide for teachers and parents of children with high functioning autism and Asperger syndrome. *British Journal of Educational Psychology, 73*, 138–139.

Mueller, R. A., & Courchesne, E. (2000). Autism's home in the brain: Reply. *Neurology, 54*, 270.

Norbury, C. F., & Bishop, D. V. M. (2002). Inferential processing and story recall in children with communication problems: A comparison of specific language impairment, pragmatic language impairment and high-functioning autism. *International Journal of Language and Communication Disorders, 37*, 227–251.

Ochs, E., Kremer-Sadlik, T., Solomon, O., & Sirota, K. G. (2001). Inclusion as social practice: Views of children with autism. *Social Development, 10*, 399–419.

O'Connor, N., Cowan, R., & Samella, K. (2000). Calendrical calculation and intelligence. *Intelligence, 28*, 31–48.

Olsson, M. B., & Hwang, C. P. (2001). Depression in mothers and fathers of children with intellectual disability. *Journal of Intellectual Disability Research, 45*, 535–543.

O'Neill, R. E., & Sweetland-Baker, M. (2001). Brief report: An assessment of stimulus generalization and contingency effects in functional communication training with two students with autism. *Journal of Autism and Developmental Disorders, 31*, 235–240.

Ozonoff, S., Dawson, G., & McPartland, J. (2002). *A parent's guide to Asperger syndrome and high-functioning autism: How to meet the challenges and help your child thrive.* New York: Guilford Press.

Ozonoff, S., & Griffith, E. M. (2000). Neuropsychological function and the external validity of Asperger syndrome. In A. Klin, F. R. Volkmar, & S. S. Sparrow (Eds.), *Asperger syndrome* (pp. 72–96). New York: Guilford Press.

Panerai, S., Ferrante, L., & Zingale, M. (2002). Benefits of the Treatment and Education of Autistic and Communication Handicapped Children (TEACCH) programme as compared with a non-specific approach. *Journal of Intellectual Disability Research, 46*, 318–327.

Parsons, S., & Mitchell, P. (2002). The potential of virtual reality in social skills training for people with autistic spectrum disorders. *Journal of Intellectual Disability Research, 46*, 430–443.

Pelios, L. V., & Lund, S. K. (2001). A selective overview of issues on classification, causation, and early intensive behavioral intervention for autism. *Behavior Modification, 25*, 678–697.

Perry, L. (2001). Never, ever give up. In C. Maurice and G. Green (Eds.). *Making a difference: Behavioral intervention for autism.* (pp. 195–208). Austin, TX: PRO-ED.

Pierce, K., & Courchesne, E. (2002). "A further support to the hypothesis of a link between serotonin, autism and the cerebellum": Reply. *Biological Psychiatry, 52*, 143.

Plaisted, K. C. (2001). Reduced generalization in autism: An alternative to weak central coherence. In J. A. Burack and T. Charman (Eds.), *The development of autism: Perspectives from theory and research* (pp. 149–169). Mahwah, NJ: Lawrence Erlbaum.

Powers, M. D. (2000). Children with autism and their families. In M. D. Powers (Ed.), Children with autism: *A parents' guide* (2nd ed., pp. 119–153). Bethesda, MD: Woodbine House.

Pring, L., & Hermelin, B. (2002). Numbers and letters: Exploring an autistic savant's unpractised ability. *Neurocase, 8,* 330–337.

Rapin, I. (2000). "Autism's home in the brain": Reply. *Neurology, 54,* 269.

Rapin, I. (2002). The autistic-spectrum disorders. *New England Journal of Medicine, 347*(5), 302–303.

Rappaport, M. F. (2001). Notes from the speech pathologist's office. In C. Maurice and G. Green (Eds.), *Making a difference: Behavioral intervention for autism.* (pp. 163–181). Austin, TX: PRO-ED.

Ratey, J. J., Dymek, M. P. Fein, D., Joy, S., Green, L. A., & Waterhouse, L. (2000). Neurodevelopmental disorders. In B. S. Fogel & R. B. Schiffer, (Eds.), *Synopsis of neuropsychiatry* (pp. 245–271). Philadelphia, PA: Lippincott-Raven Publishers.

Roblyer, M. D., & Edwards, J. (2000). *Integrating educational technology into teaching* (2nd ed.). Columbus, OH: Merrill/Prentice-Hall.

Romanczyk, R. G., Arnstein, L., Soorya, L. V., & Gillis, J. (2003). The myriad of controversial treatments for autism: A critical evaluation of efficacy. In S. O. Lilienfeld and S. J. Lynn (Eds.), *Science and pseudoscience in clinical psychology* (pp. 363–395). New York: Guilford.

Sacks, O. (1993). A neurologist's notebook: An anthropologist on Mars. *The New Yorker,* December 27, 1993/January 3, 1994, 106–125.

Scheuffgen, K., Happe, F., Anderson, M., & Frith, U. (2000) High "intelligence," low "IQ"? Speed of processing and measured IQ in children with autism. *Development and Psychopathology, 12,* 83–90.

Schmidt, J., Alper, S., Raschke, D., & Ryndak, D. (2000). Effects of using a photographic cuing package during routine school transitions with a child who has autism. *Mental Retardation, 38,* 131–137.

Schopler, E., Yirmiya, N., Shulman, C., & Marcus, L. M. (2001). *The research basis for autism intervention.* New York: Kluwer Academic/Plenum.

Schreibman, L., & Anderson, A. (2001). Focus on integration: The future of the behavioral treatment of autism. *Behavior Therapy, 32,* 619–632.

Scott, F. J., Baron-Cohen, S., Bolton, P., & Brayne, C. (2002). Brief report: Prevalence of autism spectrum conditions in children aged 5–11 years in Cambridgeshire, UK. *Autism, 6,* 231–237.

Shabani, D. B., Wilder, D. A., & Flood, W. A. (2001). Reducing stereotypic behavior through discrimination training, differential reinforcement of other behavior, and self-monitoring. *Behavioral Interventions, 16,* 279–286.

Shu, B. C., Lung, F. W., Tien, A. Y., & Chen, B. C. (2001). Executive function deficits in nonretarded autistic children. *Autism, 5,* 165–174.

Siceloff, J. (1999). A simple man: Autistic man wrongly accused of robbery. December 13, ABCNEWS.com.

Siegert, R. J., & Ward, T. (2002). Clinical psychology and evolutionary psychology: Toward a dialogue. *Review of General Psychology, 6,* 235–259.

Simon, N. (2000). Autism's home in the brain. *Neurology, 24,* 269.

Sloman, L., Konstantareas, M., & Remington, G. (2002). "Re: Clomipramine vs. haloperidol in the treatment of autistic disorder: A double-blind, placebo, crossover study." Reply to Dr. King and associates. *Journal of Clinical Psychopharmacology, 22,* 526.

Smith, T., Groen, A. D., & Wynn, J. W. (2000). Randomized trial of intensive early intervention for children with pervasive developmental disorder. *American Journal on Mental Retardation, 105,* 269–285.

Smith, T., Groen, A. D., & Wynn, J. W. (2001). "Randomized trial of intensive early intervention for children with pervasive developmental disorder." Errata. *American Journal on Mental Retardation, 106,* 208.

Smith, T., Lovaas, N. W., & Lovaas, O. I. (2002). Behaviors of children with high-functioning autism when paired with typically developing versus delayed peers: A preliminary study. *Behavioral Interventions, 17*(3), 129–143.

Strauss, W. L., Unis, A. S., Cowan, C., Dawson, G., & Dager, S. R. (2002). Fluorine magnetic res-

onance spectroscopy measurement of brain fluvoxamine and fluoxetine in pediatric patients treated for pervasive developmental disorders. *American Journal of Psychiatry, 159,* 755–760.

Symon, J. B. (2001). Parent education for autism: Issues in providing services at a distance. *Journal of Positive Behavior Interventions, 3*(3), 160–174.

Tager-Flusberg, H. (2000). The challenge of studying language development in children with autism. In L. Menn & N. Bernstein Ratner (Eds.), Methods for studying language production (pp. 313–332). Mahwah, NJ: Lawrence Erlbaum.

Tager-Flusberg, H. (2003). Language impairment in children with complex neurodevelopmental disorders: The case of autism. In Y. Levy and J. Schaeffer (Eds.), *Language competence across populations: Toward a definition of specific language impairment* (pp. 297–321). Mahwah, NJ: Lawrence Erlbaum.

Tiegerman-Farber, E. (2002). Autism spectrum disorders: Learning to communicate. In D. K. Bernstein and E. Tiegerman-Farber (Eds.), *Language and communication disorders in children* (5th ed., pp. 510–564). Boston: Allyn and Bacon.

Tommasone, L., & Tommasone, J. (2000). Adjusting to your child's diagnosis. In M. D. Powers (Ed.), *Children with autism: A parents' guide* (2nd ed., pp. 45–65). Bethesda, MD: Woodbine House.

Urwin, C. (2002). A psychoanalytic approach to language delay: When autistic isn't necessarily autism. *Journal of Child Psychotherapy, 28,* 73–93.

U.S. Department of Education, Office of Special Education Programs. (2002). *Twenty-fourth annual report to Congress on the implementation of the Individuals with Disabilities Education Act.* Washington, DC: Author.

Van der Geest, J. N., Kemner, C., Camfferman, G., Verbaten, M. N., & van Engeland, H. (2002). Looking at images with human figures: Comparison between autistic and normal children. *Journal of Autism and Developmental Disorders, 32,* 69–75.

Veenstra-Vanderweele, J., & Cook, E. H., Jr. (2003). Genetics of childhood disorders:

XLVI. Autism, part 5: Genetics of autism. *Journal of the American Academy of Child and Adolescent Psychiatry, 42,* 116–118.

Verri, A., Uggetti, C., Vallero, E., Ceroni, M., & Federico, A. (2000). Oral self-mutilation in a patient with rhombencephalosynapsys. *Journal of Intellectual Disability Research, 44,* 86–90.

Volkmar, F. R. (2001). Pharmacological interventions in autism: Theoretical and practical issues. *Journal of Community Psychology, 30,* 80–87.

Volkmar, F. R., & Klin, A. (2001). Asperger's disorder and higher functioning autism: Same or different? In L. M. Glidden (Ed.). *International review of research in mental retardation: Autism* (vol. 23, pp. 83–110).

Wahlberg, T. (2001). Language development and text comprehension in individuals with autism. In T. Wahlberg and F. Obiakor (Eds.), *Autistic spectrum disorders: Educational and clinical interventions. Advances in special education* (vol. 14, pp. 133–150). Oxford: Elsevier Science.

Wassink, T. H., Piven, J., & Patil, S. R. (2001). Chromosomal abnormalities in a clinic sample of individuals with autistic disorder. *Psychiatric Genetics, 11*(2), 57–63.

Weiss, M. J. (2002). Hardiness and social support as predictors of stress in mothers of typical children, children with autism, and children with mental retardation. *Autism, 6,* 115–130.

Wenar, C., & Kerig, P. (2000). Developmental psychopathology: From infancy through adolescence (4th ed.). New York: McGraw-Hill.

Westling, D. L., & Fox, L. (2000). Teaching students with severe disabilities (2nd ed.). Columbus, OH: Merrill/Prentice-Hall.

Whitaker, R. (2000). Knowing Chris. *Washington Post,* March 21, Z12.

Wilkerson, D. S., Volpe, A. G., Dean, R., & Titus, J. B. (2002). Perinatal complications as predictors of infantile autism. *International Journal of Neuroscience, 112,* 1085–1098.

Williams, D. (1992). *Nobody nowhere: The extraordinary autobiography of an autistic.* New York: Avon Books.

Wing, L., & Potter, D. (2002). The epidemiology of autistic spectrum disorders: Is prevalence rising? *Mental Retardation and*

Developmental Disabilities Research Reviews, 8(3), 151–161.

Yazbak, K. (2002). Connections: The new autism: One family's perspective. Clinical Child Psychology and Psychiatry, 7, 505–517.

Yirmiya, N., Shaked, M., & Erel, O. (2001). Comparison of siblings of individuals with autism and siblings of individuals with other diagnoses: An empirical summary. In E. Schopler, and Yirmiya (Eds.), The research basis for autism intervention (pp. 59–73). New York: Kluwer Academic/ Plenum.

Zelazo, P. D., Jacques, S., Burack, J. A., & Frye, D. (2002). The relation between theory of mind and rule use: Evidence from persons with autism-spectrum disorders. Infant and Child Development, 11, 171–195.

## CHAPTER 14

Alderman, N. (2001). Managing challenging behavior. In R. L. Wood & T. M. McMillan (Eds.), Neurobehavioral disability and social handicap following traumatic injury (pp. 175–208). East Sussex, England: Psychology Press.

Becker, A. (2003). Head injury perceptions [Online]. Retrieved May 17, 2003, from http:// www.biausa.org/Pages/ Personal%20Stories.html# survival

Blosser, J. L., & DePompei, R. (1994). Creating an effective classroom environment. In R. C. Savage & G. F. Wolcott (Eds.), Educational dimensions of acquired brain injury (pp. 413–451). Austin, TX: PRO-ED.

Bowe, F. (2000). Physical, sensory, and health disabilities. Upper Saddle River, NJ: Merrill.

Brain Injury Association of America. (2003). TBI incidence [Online]. Retrieved May 23, 2003, from http://www.biausa.org

Brain Injury Association. (2000a). Bicycle safety [Online]. http://www.biausa.org/ Bicyclefs.htm

Brain Injury Association. (2000b). Firearm safety [Online]. http://www.biausa.org/ Firearmsfs.htm

Brain Injury Association. (2000c). Kids corner [Online]. http://www.biausa.org/ children.htm

Clark, E. (1997). Children and adolescents with traumatic brain injury: Reintegration challenges in educational set-

tings. In E. D. Bigler, E. Clark, & J. E. Farmer (Eds.), Childhood traumatic brain injury: Diagnosis, assessment, and intervention (pp. 191–211). Austin, TX: PRO-ED.

Cronin, A. F. (2000). Traumatic brain injury in children: Issues in community function. The American Journal of Occupational Therapy, 55(4), 377–384.

Family Caregiver Alliance Clearinghouse. (2003). Definition [Online]. Retrieved May 17, 2003, from http://www. caregiver.org/factsheets/ diagnoses/head_injury.html

Farmer, J. (1997). Epilogue: An ecological systems approach to childhood traumatic brain injury. In E. D. Bigler, E. Clark, & J. E. Farmer (Eds.), Childhood traumatic brain injury: Diagnosis, assessment, and intervention (pp. 261–276). Austin, TX: PRO-ED.

Farmer, J. E., Clippard, D. S., Luehr-Wiemann, Y., Wright, E., & Owings, S. (1997). Assessing children with traumatic brain injury during rehabilitation: Promoting school and community reentry. In E. D. Bigler, E. Clark, & J. E. Farmer (Eds.), Childhood traumatic brain injury: Diagnosis, assessment, and intervention (pp. 33–62). Austin, TX: PRO-ED.

Federal Register, Vol. 57, No. 189, pp. 44, 802.

Fraser, R. T., & Clemmons, D. C. (Eds.). (2000). Traumatic brain injury rehabilitation: Practical vocational, neuropsychological, and psychotherapy interventions. Boca Raton, FL: CRC Press.

Hibbard, M. R., Gordon, W. A., & Kothera, L. M. (2000). Traumatic brain injury. In F. M. Dattilio & A. Freeman (Eds.), Cognitive-behavioral strategies in crisis intervention. New York: Guilford Press.

Hill, J. L. (1999). Meeting the needs of students with special physical and health care needs. Upper Saddle River, NJ: Merrill.

Horton, C. B., & Cruise, T. K. (2001). Child abuse and neglect: The school's response. New York: Guilford.

Jay, G. W. (2000). Minor traumatic brain injury handbook: Diagnosis and treatment. Boca Raton: CRC Press.

Jennett, B., & Teasdale, G. (1974). Assessment of coma and impaired consciousness. Lancet, 2, 81–84.

Jones, D. ( 2003). Yes, I can [Online]. Retrieved May 17, 2003, from http://www.biausa.org/

Pages/Personal%20Stories. html#yes

Keyser-Marcus, L., Briel, L., Sherron-Targett, P., Yasuda, S., Johnson, S., & Wehman, P. (2002). Enhancing the schooling of students with traumatic brain injury. Teaching Exceptional Children, 34, 62–67.

Klomes, J. M. (2000). The school reentry process for students with traumatic brain injury. Advances in Special Education, 13, 199–216.

Murdoch, B. E., & Theodoros, D. G. (2001). Traumatic brain injury: Associated speech, language and swallowing disorders. San Diego: Singular Thomson Learning.

Pierangelo, R., & Giuliani, G. A. (2001). What every teacher should know about students with special needs: Promoting success in the classroom. Champaign, IL: Research Press.

Savage, R. C., & Wolcott, G. F. (Eds.). (1994a). Educational dimensions of acquired brain injury. Austin, TX: PRO-ED.

Savage, R. C., & Wolcott, G. F. (1994b). Overview of acquired brain injury. In R. C. Savage & G. F. Wolcott (Eds.), Educational dimensions of acquired brain injury (pp. 3–12). Austin, TX: PRO-ED.

Schoenbrodt, L. (Ed.). (2001). Children with traumatic brain injury. Bethesda, MD: Woodbine House.

Semrud-Clikeman, M. (2001). Traumatic brain injury in children and adolescents: Assessment and intervention. New York: Guilford.

Thomson, J. B., & Kerns, K. A. (2000). Mild traumatic brain injury in children. In S. A. Raskin & C. A. Mateer (Eds.), Neuropsychological management of mild traumatic brain injury. New York: Oxford University Press.

Wehman, P. (2001). Life beyond the classroom: Transition strategies for young people with disabilities (3rd ed.). Baltimore, MD: Paul H. Brooks.

Williams, S., & Stillman, M. (2000). Pediatric traumatic brain injury. In B. H. Woo & S. Nesathurai (Eds.), The rehabilitation of people with traumatic brain injury (pp. 199–122). Malden, MA: Boston Medical Center.

Wood, R. L., & McMillan, T. M. (Eds.). (2001). Neurobehavioral disability and social handicap following traumatic brain injury. Philadelphia: Psychology Press.

## CHAPTER 15

Adams, M. (2003, May 25). Elevated: Tamika Catchings will not let her niceness, or her deafness, prevent her from becoming the best player in the W.N.B.A. New York Times Magazine, 26–29.

Auditory-Verbal International (2000). Principles of auditory-verbal practice [Online]. Available: http://deafness. miningco.com/health/ deafness/gi/dynamic/offsite. htm?site=http://www. auditory%2Dverbal.org/

Calderon, R., & Naidu S. (2000). Further support for the benefits of early identification and intervention for children with hearing loss. The Volta Review, 100(5), 53–84.

Center for Assessment and Demographic Studies. (2002). 2001-2202 Annual survey of deaf and hard of hearing children and youth. Washington, DC: Gallaudet University.

Chouard, C. H. (1997). Cochlear implants in deaf children— Medical and social problems today and, perhaps, tomorrow. Audiologia Newsletter, 3, 26–29.

Cochlear Implants Association. (2000). What is a cochlear implant? [Online]. Available: http://www.cici.org/english/ englinks.htm

Davis, R. (1999, May 24). The cries grow louder: Check newborns' hearing. USA Today, 10D.

Deaf World Web. (2000). Deaf America Web [Online]. Available: http://deafworldweb. org/int/us/

Easterbrooks, S. (1999). Improving practices for students with hearing impairments. Exceptional Children, 65, 537–554.

Feldman, S. (2003). Strike y'er out [Online]. Silver Spring, MD: National Association for the Deaf. Available: http:// www.nad.org/infocenter/ newsroom/nadnews/ rozynski.html. Retrieved July 6, 2003.

Gallaudet Research Institute. (2000). Literacy and Deaf students [Online]. Washington, DC: Author. Available: http://gri.gallaudet.edu/ Assessment/literacy. html

Hillburn, S., Marini, I., & Slate, J. R. (1997). Self-esteem among deaf versus hearing children with deaf versus hearing parents. JADARA, 30(2–3), 9–12.

Kaland, M., & Salvatore, K. (2003). Psychology of hearing loss [Online]. Available:

http://professional.asha.org/news/020319d.cfm. Retrieved July 1, 2003.

Kuntz, M. (1998). Literacy and deaf children: The language question. *Topics in Language Disorders, 18*(4), 1–15.

Lane, H., Hoffmeister, R., & Bahan, B. (1996). *A journey into the deaf world.* San Diego, CA: Dawn Sign Press.

Magnuson, M. (2000) Infants with congenital deafness: On the importance of early sign language acquisition. *American Annals of the Deaf, 145*(1), 6–14.

McAnally, P. L., Rose, S., & Quigley, S. P. (1999). *Reading practices with deaf children.* Austin, TX: PRO-ED.

McKeen, S. (1999, February 26). A new language for baby. *The Ottowa Citizen* [Online]. Available: http://www.deafworldweb.org/pub/b/baby.news99.html

McKinley, A. M., & Warren, S. F. (2000). The effectiveness of cochlear implants for children with prelingual deafness. *Journal of Early Intervention, 23,* 252–263.

Melich, M. (1996, October 14). Now hear this. *Salt Lake Tribune,* c1, c8.

Moores, D. F. (2001). *Educating the deaf: Psychology, principles and practices* (5th ed.). Boston: Houghton Mifflin.

Morgan, J., & Shoop, S. A. (2000, May 19). Rocker sounds off about hearing loss. *USA Today* [Online]. Available: http://www.usatoday.com/life/health/doctor/lhdoc155.htm

National Academy on an Aging Society. (2003). *Hearing loss: A growing problem that affects quality of life, 2,* 1–6. [Online]. Available: http://www.agingsociety.org/hearing.pdf. Retrieved July 2, 2003.

National Association of the Deaf. (2000). *I have heard that deaf people are against technology. Is that true?* Silver Spring, MD: Author. [Online]. Available: http://www.nad.org/infocenter/infotogo/tech/against.html

National Institute on Deafness and Other Communication Disorders. (2000a). Otitis media. *Health information: Hearing and balance* [Online]. Available: http://www.nih.gov/nidcd/health/pubs_hb/otitism.htm#effects

National Institute on Deafness and Other Communication Disorders. (2000b). Cochlear implants. *Health information: Hearing and balance* [Online]. Available: http://www.nih.

gov/nidcd/health/pubs_hb/coch.htm

Northeast Technical Assistance Center. (2000). *C-Print: A computer aided speech to print transition system* [Online]. Rochester, NY: Author available: http://netac.rit.edu/c-print.html

Pediatric Bulletin. (2000). *Congenital Cyomegalovirus Infection and Disease* [Online]. Available: http://home.coqui.net/myrna/cmv.htm

Prinz, P. M., Strong, M., Kuntze, M., Vincent, M., Firedman, J., Moyers, P., & Helman, E. (1996). A path to literacy through ASL and English for Deaf children. In C. E. Johnson & J. H. V. Gilbert (Eds.), *Children's language* (pp. 235–251). Mahwah, NJ: Erlbaum.

Quigley, S. P., & King, C. (Eds.). (1985). *Reading milestones.* Beaverton, OR: Dormac.

Robson, G. (2000, January). Captioning and the law. *Journal of Court Reporting* [Online]. Available: http://www.robson.org/gary/writing/jcr-captionlaw.html

Schirmer, B. R. (2000). *Language and literacy development in children who are deaf* (2nd ed.). Boston: Allyn and Bacon.

Strong, M., & Prinz, P. M. (1997). A study of the relationship between American Sign Language and English literacy. *Journal of Deaf Studies and Deaf Education, 122,* 37–46.

U.S. Department of Education. (2002). To assure the free appropriate public education of all children with disabilities. *Twenty-fourth annual report to Congress on the implementation of the Individuals with Disabilities Education Act.* Washington, DC: U.S. Government Printing Office.

Walker, L. A. (2001, May 13). They're breaking the sound barrier. *Parade Magazine,* 4–5.

Wixtrom, C. (1988, Summer). Alone in the crowd. *Deaf American, 38*(12), 14–15.

## CHAPTER 16

American Foundation for the Blind. (2000). *Educating students with visual impairments for inclusion in society: A paper on the inclusion of students with visual impairments* [Online]. Louisville, KY: Author. Available: http://www.afb.org/education/jltlipaper.html

Autman, S. A. (1994, October 31). Disabled students making it in the mainstream. *Salt Lake Tribune,* B1, B2.

Barraga, N. C., & Erin, J. N. (2001).*Visual handicaps and learning* (4th ed.). Austin, TX: PRO-ED.

Batsashaw, M. L. (2003). *Children with disabilities* (5th ed.). Baltimore, MD: Paul H. Brookes.

Bishop. V. E. (1996a). *Teaching visually impaired children* (2nd ed.). Springfield, IL: Charles C Thomas.

Bishop. V. E. (1996b). Causes and functional implications of visual impairment. *In Foundations of low vision: Clinical and functional perspectives* (pp. 86–114). New York: American Foundation for the Blind Press.

Bouchard, D., & Tetreault, S. (2000). The motor development of sighted children and children with moderate low vision aged 8–13. *Journal of Visual Impairments and Blindness, 94,* 564–573.

Corn, A. L., & Koenig, A. J. (1996). Perspectives on low vision. In *Foundations of low vision: Clinical and functional perspectives* (pp. 1–21). New York: American Foundation for the Blind Press.

Crocker, A. D., & Orr, R. R. (1996) Social behaviors of children with visual impairments enrolled in preschool programs. *Exceptional Children, 62*(5), 451–462.

KidSource. (2003). *Undetected vision disorders are blinding children: Earlier testing needed to preserve good eyesight* [Online]. Available: http://www.kidsource.com/kidsource/content/news/vision.html. Retrieved July 14, 2003

Kingsley, M. (1997). The effect of a vsiual loss. In H. Mason & S. McCall (Eds.), *Visual impairment: Access to education for children and young people* (pp. 23–29). London: Fulton.

Koenig, A. J., & Rex, E. J. (1996). Selection of learning and literacy media for children and youths with low vision. In *Foundations of low vision: Clinical and functional perspectives* (pp. 280–305). New York: American Foundation for the Blind Press.

Kurzweil, R. (2000). *The age of spiritual machines.* New York: Penguin Putnam. [Online]. Available: http://www.penguinputnam.com/kurzweil/excerpts/exmain.htm. Retrieved September 2, 2000.

Kurzweil Technologies. (2003). *A brief biography of Ray Kurzweil.* Burlington, Mass: Lernout & Hauspie. [Online]. Available: http://www.

kurzweiltech.com/raybio.htm. Retrieved June 12, 2003.

Lewis, N. (1999, Summer). Losing sight. Newsletter of the New York State Commission on Quality of Care, 76 [Online]. Available: http://www.cqc.state.ny.us/76nlewis.htm

Library of Congress. (2003). *That all may read.* National Library Service for the Blind and Physically Handicapped (NLS). [Online]. Available: http://www.loc.gov/nls/nls-wb.html. Retrieved July 11, 2003.

Pester, P. (2003). *Braille bits.* Louisville, KY: American Printing House for the Blind [Online]. Available: http://www.aph.org/edresearch/bits898.htm. Retrieved July 15, 2003.

Rosenfeld, I. (2001, July 8). When you can't see what's in front of you. *Parade Magazine,* 12–13.

Silberman, R. K., & Sowell, V. (1998). Educating students who have visual impairments with learning disabilities. In S. Z. Sacks & R. K. Silberman (Eds.), *Educating students who have visual impairments with other disabilities* (161–185). Baltimore, MD: Paul H. Brookes.

Smith, A. J., & Geruschat, D. R. (1996). Orientation and mobility for children and adults with low vision. In *Foundations of low vision: Clinical and functional perspectives* (pp. 306–321). New York: American Foundation for the Blind Press.

Social Security Administration. (2003). *Disability planner: Special rules for people who are blind.* Washington, DC: Author. [Online]. Available: http://www.ssa.gov/dibplan/dqualify8.htm. Retrieved July 21, 2003.

Stone, J. (1997). The preschool child. In H. Mason & S. McCall (Eds.), *Visual impairment: Access to eduation for children and young people* (pp. 87–96). London: Fulton.

U.S. Department of Education. (2000, June). *Educating Blind and Visually Impaired Students: Policy Guidance.* Washington, DC: Office of Special Education and Rehabilitative Services, 65 FR 36586.

U.S. Department of Education. (2002). To assure the free appropriate public education of all children with disabilities. *Twenty-fourth annual report to Congress on the implementation of the Individuals with Disabili-

*ties Education Act.* Washington, DC: U.S. Government Printing Office.

World Health Organization. (2003). *PBL activities: The World Health Organization program for the prevention of blindness* [Online]. Available: http://www.who.int/pbd/pbl/act.htm#vitamin_A_def. Retrieved June 30, 2003.

Zimmerman, G. J. (1996). Optics and low vision devices. In *Foundations of low vision: Clinical and functional perspectives* (pp. 115–142). New York: American Foundation for the Blind Press.

## CHAPTER 17

American Academy of Pediatrics. (2001a). Adolescent and human immunodeficiency virus infection: The role of the pediatrician in prevention and intervention. *Pediatrics, 107*(1), 1–5.

American Academy of Pediatrics. (2001b). Care of adolescent parents and their children. (RE0020). *Pediatrics, 107*(2), 429–434.

American Academy of Pediatrics. (2003). News release: AAP updates policy on adolescent suicide [Online]. Retrieved June 6, 2003 from http://www.aap.org/advocacy/archives/aprsui.htm

American College of Obstetricians and Gynecologists. (2002). *Illegal drugs and pregnancy* [Online]. Retrieved October 27, 2003 from http//www.medem.com/MedLB/article_detaillb.cfm?article_ID=ZZZN0X8997C&sub_cat=2005

American College of Obstetricians and Gynecologists. (2003). *Illegal drugs and pregnancy* [Online]. Retrieved June 6, 2003 from http://www.medem.com/MedLB/article_detaillb.cfm?article_ID=AAANOX8997C&sub_cat=2005

American Diabetes Association. (2003a). Basic diabetes information [Online]. Retrieved May 31, 2003 from http://www.diabetes.org/main/application/commercewf?origin=*.jsp&event=link(B)

American Diabetes Association. (2003b). National diabetes fact sheet [Online]. Retrieved May 31, 2003 from http://www.diabetes.org/main/info/facts/facts_natl.jsp

American Diabetes Association. (2003c). *Type I diabetes* [Online]. Retrieved May 31, 2003

from http://www.diabetes.org/main/application/commercewf?origin=*.jsp&event=link(C)

Bailet, L. L., & Turk, W. R. (1997). Epilepsy. In G. G. Bear, K. M. Minke, & A. Thomas (Eds.), *Children's needs II: Development, problems, and alternatives* (pp. 801–813). Bethesda, MD: National Association of School Psychologists.

Batshaw, M. L. (2001). *When your child has a disability.* Baltimore, MD: Paul H. Brookes.

Baumrind, D. (1995). *Child maltreatment and optimal caregiving in social contexts.* New York: Garland.

Beckerman, K. P. (2001, June). *Reproductive care, maternal health, and prevention of pediatric AIDS.* HIV InSite Knowledge Base Chapter. [Online]. Retrieved May 24, 2003 from http://hivinsite.ucsf.edu/InSite?page=kb-beckerman

Bell, M., & Stoneman, Z. (2000). Reactions to prenatal testing: Reflection of religiosity and attitudes toward abortion and people with disabilities. *American Journal on Mental Retardation, 105*(1), 1–13.

Berliner, L., & Elliott, D. M. (1996). Sexual abuse of children. In J. Briere, L. Berliner, J. A. Bulkley, C. Jenny, & T. Reid (Eds.), *The APSAC handbook on child maltreatment* (pp. 51–71). Thousand Oaks, CA: Sage.

Borowsky, W. I., Ireland, M., & Resnick, M. D. (2001). Adolescent suicide attempts: Risks and protectors. *Pediatrics, 107*(3), 485–493.

Bowe, F. (2000). *Physical, sensory, and health disabilities.* Upper Saddle River, NJ: Merrill.

Brassard, M. R. (1997). Psychological and physical abuse. In G. G. Bear, K. M. Minke, & A. Thomas (Eds.), *Children's needs II: Development, problems, and alternatives* (pp. 707–718). Bethesda, MD: National Association of School Psychologists.

Bruner, J. P., Richards, W. O., Tulipan, N.B., & Arney, T. L. (1999). Endoscopic coverage of fetal myelomeningocele in utero. *American Journal of Obstetrics & Gynecology, Part 1, 180*(1), 153–158.

Bushby, K. M., & Anderson, L. V. B. (2001). *Muscular dystrophy: Methods and protocols.* Totowas, NJ: Humana Press.

Caliber. (2003a). *Child abuse and neglect: The national scope of the problem* [Online]. Retrieved June 5, 2003 from http://www.calib.com/

nccanch/prevention/overview/problem.pdf

Caliber. (2003b). *What is child abuse?* [Online]. Retrieved June 5, 2003 from http://www.calib.com/nccanch/prevention/overview/child.pdf

Carter, A. R. (2000). *Stretching ourselves: Kids with cerebral palsy.* Morton Grove, IL: Albert Whitman.

Children with Diabetes. (2000). *Islet cell transplantation: Working toward a cure* [Online]. Available: http://www.childrenwithdiabetes.com/d_0n_701.htm

Clark, R. B. (1997). Suicide in children and adolescents. In W. W. Hay, Jr., J. R. Groothuis, A. R. Hayward, & M. J. Levin (Eds.), *Current pediatric diagnosis and treatment* (pp. 197–198). Norwalk, CT: Appleton & Lange.

Cockrell, Janice L. (2000). Spinal cord injury. In R. E. Nickel & L. W. Desch, (Eds.), *The physician's guide to caring for children with disabilities and chronic conditions* (pp. 545–578). Baltimore, MD: Paul H. Brookes.

Crosson-Tower, C. (2002). *When children are abused: An educator's guide to intervention.* Boston: Allyn and Bacon.

Cybertronics. (2000). *Patient's guide to VNS: The first new, FDA-approved approach to treating epilepsy in 100 years* [Online]. Available: http://www.cyberonics.com/pat_guide.htm

Cystic Fibrosis Foundation. (2000a). *Facts about cystic fibrosis* [Online]. Available: http://www.cff.org/facts.htm

Cystic Fibrosis Foundation. (2000b). *Gene therapy and cystic fibrosis* [Online]. Available: http://www.cff.org/publications03.htm

Cystic Fibrosis Foundation. (2003). *What is CF?* [Online]. Retrieved May 31, 2003 from http://www.cff.org/about_cf/what_is_cf.cfm?CFID=1007391&CFTOKEN=22213501

DePaepe, P., Garrison-Kane, L., & Doelling, J. (2002). Supporting students with health needs in schools: An overview of selected health conditions. *Focus on Exceptional Children, 35*(1), 1–24.

Epilepsy Foundation of America. (2000a). *Information and education: First aid for seizures* [Online]. Available: http://www.efa.org/education/firstaid/poster.html

Epilepsy Foundation of America. (2000b). *Information and edu-*

*cation: Seizure recognition + first aid.* [Online]. Available: http://www.efa.org/education/firstaid/chart.html

Goldsmith, S. K., Pellmar, T. C., Kleinman, A. M., & Bunney, W. E. (2002). *Reducing suicide: A national imperative.* Washington, DC: The National Academies Press.

Goldston, D. B. (2000). Assessment of suicidal behaviors and risk among children and adolescents. Technical report submitted to the National Institute of Mental Health (NIMH) under Contract No. 263-MD-909995.

Harris, J. (2001). *Sickle cell disease.* Brookfield, CT: Twenty-First Century Books.

Horton, C. B., & Cruise, T. K. (1997). Child sexual abuse. In G. G. Bear, K. M. Minke, & A. Thomas (Eds.), *Children's needs II: Development, problems, and alternatives* (pp. 719–727). Bethesda, MD: National Association of School Psychologists.

Horton, C. B., & Cruise, T. K. (2001). *Child abuse and neglect: The school's response.* New York: Guilford.

Jankelevich, S. (2001, February). *Serious bacterial infections in children with HIV.* HIV InSite Knowledge Base Chapter. [Online]. Retrieved May 24, 2003 from http://hivinsite.ucsf.edu/InSite.jsp?page=kb-05&doc=kb-05-01-01-01

Katsiyannis, A., & Yell, M. L. (2000). The Supreme Court and School Health Services: *Cedar Rapids v. Garret F. Exceptional Children, 66*(3), 317–326.

Keller, J. (2002, September). *Reeve's super recovery.* Eonline, September 11, 2002, p.1. Retrieved May 24, 2003 from http://www.eonline.com/News/Items/0,1,10515,00.html

Leet, A. I., Dormans, J. P., & Tosi, L. L. (2002). Muscles, bones, and nerves: The body's framework. In M. L. Batshaw (Ed.), *Children with disabilities* (5th ed., pp. 263–284). Baltimore, MD: Paul H. Brookes.

Levetan, C. (2001). Into the mouths of babes. The diabetes epidemic in children. *Clinical Diabetes, 19*(3), 102–104.

Liptak, Gregory S. (2002). Neural tube defects. In M. L. Batshaw (Ed.), *Children with disabilities* (5th ed.). Baltimore, MD: Paul H. Brookes.

Manford, M. (2003). *Practical guide to epilepsy.* Burlington, MA: Butterworth Heinemann.

March of Dimes. (2003). *Quick reference and fact sheets: Cocaine use during pregnancy* [Online]. Retrieved June 6, 2003 from http://www.marchofdimes.com/professionals/681_1169.asp

March of Dimes Birth Defects Foundation. (2003). *Drinking alcohol during pregnancy* [Online]. Retrieved October 27, 2003 from http://www.marchofdimes.com/search/MsmGo.exe?grab_id=98429942&extra_arg=&page_id=1039&host_id=1&query=Alcohol+Abuse&hiword=ALCOHOL+ABUSE+

Mayo Clinic. (2001a). *Sickle cell anemia: Causes* [Online]. Retrieved May 31, 2003 from http://www.mayoclinic.com/invoke.cfm?objectid=193554B1-F187-461C-9041DDD189B031A6&section=3

Mayo Clinic. (2001b). *Sickle cell anemia: Treatment* [Online]. Retrieved May 31, 2003 from http://www.mayoclinic.com/invoke.cfm?objectid=193554B1-F187-461C-9041DDD189B031A6&section=7

Mayo Clinic. (2003a). *Gene therapy: A medical revolution* [Online]. Retrieved June 5, 2003 from http://www.mayoclinic.org/news2000-rst/719.html

Mayo Clinic. (2003b). *Sickle cell anemia: Signs and symptoms: Overview* [Online]. Retrieved June 5, 2003 from http://www.mayoclinic.com/invoke.cfm?objectid=193554B1-F187-461C-9041DDD189B031A6&section=2

Mecham, M. J. (2002). *Cerebral palsy* (3rd ed.). Austin, TX: PRO-ED.

Milton, J., & Jung, P. (Eds.). (2003). *Epilepsy as a dynamic disease.* New York: Springer-Verlag.

MiniMed. (2000a). *Why good control is important* [Online]. Available: http://www.minimed.com/files/gd_cntrl.htm

MiniMed. (2000b). *Pump therapy: Why pump therapy?* [Online]. Available: http://www.minimed.com/files/whypi.htm

Muscular Dystrophy Association. (2000). *Facts about muscular dystrophy: Most frequently asked questions about muscular dystrophy, Part I* [Online]. Available: http://www.mdausa.org/publications/fa-md-qa.html

National Center for Biotechnology Information. (2003). *Genes and diseases: Blood and lymph diseases: Sickle cell anemia* [Online]. Retrieved June 5, 2003 from http://www.ncbi.nlm.nih.gov/books/bv.fcgi?call=bv.View.ShowSection&rid=gnd.section.98

National Center for Health Statistics. (2003). *Suicide* [Online]. Retrieved June 6, 2003 from http://www.cdc/gov/nchs.fastats/sucide.html

National Center for Injury Prevention and Control. (2003). *Suicide in the United States.* Atlanta, GA: Department of Health and Human Services.

National Clearing House on Child Abuse and Neglect Information. (2000). *What is child maltreatment?* [Online]. Available: http://www.calib.com/nccanch/index.htm

National Clearing House on Child Abuse and Neglect Information. (2003). *Mandatory reporters of child abuse and neglect* [Online]. Retrieved June 5, 2003 from http://www.calib.com/nccanch/statutes/define.cfm

National Diabetes Clearinghouse. (2003). *What is the status of diabetes research?* [Online]. Retrieved May 31, 2003 from http://www.niddk.nih.gov/health/diabetes/pubs/dmover/dmover.htm#status

National Institute of Allergy and Infectious Diseases. (2000a). *Fact sheet: HIV/AIDS statistics* [Online]. Available: http://www.niaid.nih.gov/factsheets/aidsstat.htm

National Institute of Allergy and Infectious Diseases. (2000b). *Fact sheet: HIV infection and adolescents* [Online]. Available: http://www.niaid.nih.gov/factsheets/hivadolescent.htm

National Institute of Allergy and Infectious Diseases. (2000c). *Fact sheet: How HIV causes AIDS* [Online]. Available: http://www.niaid.nih.gov/factsheets/howhiv.htm

National of Institute of Allergy and Infectious Diseases. (2000d). *Pediatric AIDS* [Online]. Available: http://www..niaid.nih.gov/factsheets/pedaids.htm

National Institute on Alcohol Abuse and Alcoholism. (2003). *Estimating the prevalence of fetal alcohol syndrome: A summary* [Online]. Retrieved June 7, 2003 from http://www.niaaa.nih.gov/publications/arh25-3/159-167.htm

National Institute on Drug Abuse. (2001a). *Consequences of prenatal drug exposure: Research findings (from 9/01)* [Online]. Retrieved June 6, 2003 from http://www.nida.nih.gov/ICAW/prenatal/Prenatalfindings901.html

National Institute on Drug Abuse. (2001b). *Consequences of prenatal drug exposure: Research findings (from 5/01)* [Online]. Retrieved June 7, 2003 from http://www.drugabuse.gov/ICAW/prenatal/PrenatalFindings.html

National Institute on Drug Abuse. (2002). *Consequences of prenatal drug exposure: Research findings (from 5/02)* [Online]. Retrieved June 7, 2003 from http://www.drugabuse.gov/ICAW/prenatal/PrenatalFindings502.html

National Institute on Drug Abuse. (2003). *Principles of drug addiction treatment: A research based guide* [Online]. Retrieved June 6, 2003 from http://www.nida.nih.gov/PODAT/PODAT10.html#Matrix

National Institute of Mental Health. (2003a). *In harm's way: Suicide in America* [Online]. Retrieved June 6, 2003 from http://www.himh.nih.gov/publicat/haraway.cfm

National Institute of Mental Health. (2003b). *Suicide facts* [Online]. Retrieved June 6, 2003 from http://www.nimh.nih.gov/research/suifact.cfm

National Institutes of Health. (2003). NIH news release: *Significant deficits in mental skills observed in toddlers exposed to cocaine before birth* [Online]. Retrieved June 6, 2003 from http://www.nih.gov/news/pr/apr2002/nida19.htm

National Pediatric & Family HIV Resource Center. (2001). *Working with parents in HIV-affected families: A guide for providers.* Newark, NJ: Author.

National Resource Center for Respites and Crisis Care Services. (2003). *Fact sheet Number 49: Children prenatal drug and/or alcohol exposure* [Online]. Retrieved June 7, 2003 from http://www.archrespite.org/archfs49.htm

Nickel, R. E. (2000a). Human immunodeficiency virus infection. In R. E. Nickel & L. W. Desch, (Eds.), *The physician's guide to caring for children with disabilites and chronic conditions* (pp. 391–424). Baltimore, MD: Paul H. Brookes.

Nickel, R. E. (2000b). Prenatal drug exposure. In R. E. Nickel & L. W. Desch (Eds.), *The physician's guide to caring for children with disabilities and chronic conditions* (pp. 357–389). Baltimore, MD: Paul H. Brookes.

Nickel, R. E., & Desch, L. W. (Eds.), (2000). *The physician's guide to caring for children with disabilities and chronic conditions.* Baltimore, MD: Paul H. Brookes.

Office of the National Drug Control Policy. (2003). *Types of treatment* [Online]. Retrieved June 6, 2003 from http://www.whitehousedrugpolicy.gov/treat/treatment.html

Pavia, A. T. (2001, July). *Primary care of infants and children with HIV. HIV InSite Knowledge Base Chapter.* [Online]. Retrieved May 24, 2003 from http://hivinsite.ucsf.edu/InSite.jsp?doc=kb-03-01-14

Pellegrino, L. (2001). Cerebral palsy. In M. L. Batshaw (Ed.), *When your child as a disability* (pp. 275–287). Baltimore, MD: Paul H. Brookes.

Pellegrino, L. (2002). Cerebral palsy. In M. L. Batshaw (Ed.), *Children with disabilities* (pp. 443–466). Baltimore, MD: Paul H. Brookes.

Resource Center for Adolescent Pregnancy Prevention. (2003). *Current research: Journal summary December 2002/January 2003: Mothers' influence on teen sex: Connections that promote postponing sexual intercourse* [Online]. Retrieved June 5, 2003 from http://www.etr.org/recapp/research/journal200212.htm

Roberts, C. D., Stough, L. M., & Parrish, L. H. (2002). The role of genetic counseling in the elective termination of pregnancies involving fetuses with disabilities. *The Journal of Special Education, 36*(1), 48–55.

Sickle Cell Information Center. (2003). *What is sickle cell anemia?* [Online]. Retrieved May 31, 2003 from http://www.scinfo.org/sicklept.htm

Smith, P. E. M., & Wallace, S. J. (2001). *Clinician's guide to epilepsy.* New York: Oxford University Press.

Spiegel, H. M. L., & Bonwit, A. M. (2002). HIV infection in children. In M. L. Batshaw (Ed.), *Children with disabilities* (5th ed.). Baltimore, MD: Paul H. Brookes.

Spina Bifida Association of America. (2003). *Facts about spina bifida* [Online]. Retrieved May 31, 2003 from http://www.sbaa.org/html/sbaa_facts.html

Spinal Cord Injury Information Network. (2003). *Facts and figures at a glance* [Online]. Retrieved May 31, 2003 from http://www.spinalcord.uab.edu/show.asp?durki=21446

Spinal Cord Injury Resource Center. (2003). *Some questions and answers* [Online]. Retrieved

May 31, 2003 from http://www.spinalinjury.net/html/_spinal_cord_101.html

Sullivan, P. M. (2000). *Violence and abuse against children with disabilities*. Omaha, NE: Center for Abused Children with Disabilities, Boys Town National Research Hospital.

The National Campaign to Prevent Teen Pregnancy. (2003). *General facts and stats* [Online]. Retrieved June 5, 2003 from http://www.teenpregnancy.org/resources/data/genlfact.asp

U.S. Department of Health and Human Services. (2003a). *In Focus: The risk and prevention of maltreatment of children with disabilities* (2/01) [Online]. Retrieved June 5, 2003 from http://www.calib.com/nccanch/prevention/publications/risk.cfm#scope

U.S. Department of Health and Human Services, Administration on Children, Youth and Families. (2003b). *12 Years of reporting child maltreatment* (2001). Washington, DC: U.S. Government Printing Office.

U.S. Department of Health and Human Services. (2003c). *Who are the children affected by abuse and neglect?* [Online]. Retrieved June 5, 2003 from http://www.calib.com/nccanch/prevention/overview/problem.pdf

Ueda, D., & Caulfield, R. (2001). Management of medically fragile infants. *Early Childhood Education Journal, 28,* 247–249.

UNAIDS. (2002, September). *Paediatric HIV Infection and AIDS: UNAIDS points of view*. Joint United Nations Programmr on HIV/AIDS [Online]. Retrieved May 24, 2003 from http://www.unaids.org/publications/documents/children/JC750-Paediatric-PoV_en.pdf

United Cerebral Palsy. (2003). *Cerebral palsy–Facts and figures* [Online]. Retrieved May 30, 2003 from http://www.ucpa.org/ucp_generaldoc.cfm/1/9/37/37-37/447

Weinstein, S. (2002). Epilepsy. In M. L. Batshaw (Ed.), *Children with disabilities* (5th ed., pp. 493–523). Baltimore, MD: Paul H. Brookes.

## CHAPTER 18

Assouline, S. G. (2003). Psychological and educational assessment of gifted children. In N. Colagnelo & G. A. Davis (Eds.), *Handbook of gifted education* (pp. 124–145). Boston: Pearson Education.

Binet, A., & Simon, T. (1905). Méthodes nouvelles pour le diagnostique du mivea intellectual des anomaux. *L'Année Psychologique, 11,* 196–198.

Binet, A., & Simon, T. (1908). Le dévelopment de l'intelligence chez les enfants. *L'Année Psychologique, 14,* 1–94.

Borland, J. H. (2003). Evaluating gifted programs: A broader perspective. In N. Colagnelo & G. A. Davis (Eds.), *Handbook of gifted education* (pp. 293–307). Boston: Pearson Education.

Cattell, R. B. (1971). *Abilities: Their structure, growth, and action*. Boston: Houghton Mifflin.

Clark, B. (1997). *Growing up gifted* (5th ed.). Columbus, OH: Merrill.

Clasen. D. R., Clasen. R. E. (2003). Mentoring the gifted and talented. In N. Colagnelo & G. A. Davis (Eds.), *Handbook of Gifted Education* (3rd ed., pp. 254–267). Boston: Pearson Education.

Colagnelo, N. (2003). Counseling gifted students. In N. Colagnelo & G. A. Davis (Eds.), *Handbook of gifted education* (3rd ed., pp. 373–387). Boston: Pearson Education.

Colagnelo, N., & Davis, G. A. (2003). *Handbook of gifted education* (3rd ed.). Boston: Allyn and Bacon.

Conant, J. B. (1959). *The American high school today*. New York: McGraw-Hill.

Davis, G. A., & Rimm, S. B. (2004). *Education of the gifted and talented* (5th ed.). San Francisco: Allyn and Bacon.

DeHann, R., & Havighurst, R. J. (1957). *Educating gifted children*. Chicago, IL: University of Chicago Press.

Esquivel, G. B., & Houtz, J. C. (Eds.). (2000). *Creativity and giftedness in culturally diverse students*. Cresskill, NJ: Hampton Press.

Feldhusen, J. F. (1998a). Programs and services at the elementary level. In J. Van Tassel-Baska (Ed.), *Excellence in educating gifted and talented learners* (3rd ed., pp. 211–223). Denver: Love.

Feldhusen, J. F. (1998b). Programs and services at the elementary level. In J. Van Tassel-Baska (Ed.), *Excellence in educating gifted and talented learners* (3rd ed., pp. 235–240). Denver: Love.

Feldhusen, J. F. (1998c). Programs and services at the secondary level. In J. VanTassel-Baska (Ed.), *Excellence in educating gifted and talented learners* (3rd ed., pp. 229–237). Denver: Love.

Feldhusen, J. F. (2003). Talented youth at the secondary level. In N. Colagnelo & G. A. Davis (Eds.), *Handbook of gifted education* (3rd ed., pp. 229–237). Boston: Pearson Education.

Ford, D. Y. (2003). Equity and excellence: Culturally diverse students in gifted education. In N. Colagnelo & G. A. Davis (Eds.), *Handbook of gifted education* (3rd ed., pp. 506–520). Boston: Pearson Education.

Gagné, F. (1999a). Is there any light at the end of the tunnel? *Journal for the Education of the Gifted, 22*(2), 191–234.

Gagné, F. (1999b). My convictions about the nature of abilities, gifts, and talents. *Journal for the Education of the Gifted, 22*(2), 109–136.

Gagné, F. (2003). Transforming gifts into talents: The DMGT as a developmental theory. In N. Colagnelo & G. A. Davis (Eds.), *Handbook of gifted education* (3rd ed., pp. 60–74). Boston: Pearson Education.

Gallagher, J. J. (2003). Issues and challenges in the education of gifted students. In N. Colagnelo & G. A. Davis (Eds.), *Handbook of gifted education* (3rd ed., pp.11–23). Boston: Pearson Education.

Gardner, H. (1983). *Frames of mind: The theory of multiple intelligences*. New York: Basic Books.

Gottfredson, L. S. (2003). The science and politics of intelligence in gifted education. In N. Colagnelo & G. A. Davis (Eds.), *Handbook of gifted education* (3rd ed., pp. 24–40). Boston: Pearson Education.

Guilford, J. P. (1950). Creativity. *American Psychologist, 5,* 444–454.

Guilford, J. P. (1959). Three faces of intellect. *American Psychologist, 14,* 469–479.

Hua, C. B. (2002). Career self-efficacy of the student who is gifted/learning disabled: A case study. *Journal for the Education of the Gifted, 25*(4), 375–404.

Jackson, N. E. (2003). Young gifted children. In N. Colagnelo & G. A. Davis (Eds.), *Handbook of gifted education* (3rd ed., pp. 470–482). Boston: Pearson Education.

Jin, S., & Feldhusen, J. F. (2000). Parent identification of the talents of gifted students. *Gifted Education International, 14,* 230–236.

Karnes, F. A., & Bean, S. M. (Eds.). (2001). *Methods and materials for teaching the gifted*. Waco, TX: Prufrock Press.

Kerr, B. A., & Nicpon, M. F. (2003). Gender and giftedness. In N. Colagnelo & G. A Davis (Eds.), *Handbook of gifted education* (3rd ed., pp. 493–505). Boston: Allyn and Bacon.

Kolloff, P. B. (2003). State-supported residential high school. In N. Colagnelo & G. A. Davis (Eds.), *Handbook of gifted education* (3rd ed., pp. 238–246). Boston: Pearson Education.

Kulik, J. A. (2003). Grouping and tracking. In N. Colagnelo & G. A. Davis (Eds.), *Handbook of gifted education* (3rd ed., pp. 268–281). Boston: Pearson Education.

MacKinnon, D. W. (1962). The nature and nurture of creative talent. *American Psychologist, 17*(7), 484–495.

Maltby, F., & Devlin, M. (2000). Breaking through the glass ceiling without bruising: The breakthrough programme for high ability girls. *Gifted Education International, 14,* 112–124.

O'Connell, P. (2003). Federal involvement in gifted and talented education. In N. Colagnelo & G. A. Davis (Eds.), *Handbook of Gifted Education* (3rd ed., pp. 604–608). Boston: Pearson Education.

Olshen, S. R. (1987). The disappearance of giftedness in girls: An intervention strategy. *Roeper-Review. 9*(4), 251–254.

Olszewski-Kubilius, P. (2003). Special summer and Saturday programs for gifted students. In N. Colagnelo & G. A. Davis (Eds.), *Handbook of gifted education* (3rd ed., pp. 219–228). Boston: Pearson Education.

Piirto, J. (1999). *Talented children and adults: Their development and education*. Upper Saddle River, NJ: Prentice-Hall.

Plomin, R., & Price, T. S. (2003). The relationship between genetics and intelligence. In N. Colagnelo & G. A. Davis (Eds.), *Handbook of gifted education* (3rd ed., pp. 113–123). Boston: Pearson Education.

Ramos-Ford, V., & Gardner, H. (1991). Giftedness from a multiple intelligences perspective. In N. Colagnelo & G. A. Davis (Eds.), *Handbook of gifted education* (pp. 55–64). Boston: Allyn and Bacon.

Ramos-Ford, V., & Gardner, H. (1997). Giftedness from a

multiple intelligences perspective. In N. Colangelo & G. A. Davis (Eds.), *Handbook of gifted education* (2nd ed., pp. 54–66). Boston: Allyn and Bacon.

Renzulli, J. S., & Reis, S. M. (2003). The schoolwide enrichment model: Developing creative and productive giftedness. In N. Colangelo & G. A. Davis (Eds.), *Handbook of gifted dducation* (3rd ed., pp. 184–203). Boston: Pearson Education.

Richert, E. S. (2003). Excellence with justice in identification and programming. In N. Colangelo & G. A. Davis (Eds.), *Handbook of gifted education* (3rd ed., pp. 146–161). Boston: Pearson Education.

Rimm, S. B. (1982). *PRIDE: Preschool and primary interest descriptor*. Watertown, WI: Educational Assessment Service.

Rimm, S. B., & Davis, G. A. (1983, September/October). Identifying creativity, Part II. *G/C/T,* 19–23.

Ritchhart, R. (2001). From IQ to IC: A dispositional view of intelligence. *Roeper Review, 23,* 143–150.

Schiever, S. W., & Maker, C. J. (2003). New directions in enrichment and acceleration. In N. Colangelo & G. A. Davis (Eds.), *Handbook of gifted education* (3rd ed., pp. 163–173). Boston: Pearson Education.

Silverman, L. K. (1986). What happens to the gifted girl? In C. J. Maker (Ed.), *Critical issues in gifted education: Defensible programs for the gifted,* Vol. 1 (pp. 43–89). Austin, TX: PRO-ED.

Sternberg, R. J. (1993). Sternberg triarchic abilities test. Unpublished test.

Sternberg, R. J. (1997). A triarchic view of giftedness: Theory and practice. In N. Colangelo & G. A Davis (Eds.), *Handbook of gifted education* (2nd ed., pp. 43–53). Boston: Allyn and Bacon.

Tannenbaum, A. J. (2003). Nature and nurture of giftedness. In N. Colangelo & G. A Davis (Eds.), *Handbook of gifted education* (3rd ed., pp. 45–59). Boston: Allyn and Bacon.

Terman, L. M. (1925). *Genetic studies of genius*: Vol. 1. *Mental and physical traits of a thousand gifted children.* Stanford, CA: Stanford University Press.

Torrance, E. P. (1961). Problems of highly creative children. *Gifted Child Quarterly, 5,* 31–34.

Torrance, E. P. (1965). *Gifted children in the classroom.* New York: Macmillan.

Torrance, E. P. (1966). *Torrance tests of creative thinking.* Bensenville, IL: Scholastic Testing Service.

Torrance, E. P. (1968). Finding hidden talent among disadvantaged children. *Gifted and Talented Quarterly, 12,* 131–137.

U.S. Department of Education. (1993). *National excellence: A case for developing America's talent.* Washington, DC: Office of Education Research and Improvement, U.S. Department of Education.

VanTassel-Baska, J. (1989). Counseling the gifted. In J. Feldhusen, J. VanTassel-Baska, & K. Seeley (Eds.), *Excellence in educating the gifted.* Denver, CO: Love.

VanTassel-Baska, J., & Chepko-Sade, D. (1986). *An incidence study of disadvantaged gifted students in the Midwest.* Evanston, IL: Center for Talent Development, Northwestern University.

Walker, S. (2002). *The survival guide for parents of gifted kids.* Minneapolis: Free Spirit Publishing.

Williams, F. E. (1980). *Creativity assessment packet.* East Aurora, NY: DOK.

Winner, E., Martino, G. (2003). Artistic giftedness. In N. Colangelo & G. A. Davis (Eds.), *Handbook of gifted education* (pp.335–349). Boston: Pearson Education.

# Author Index

Gillon, 312
Gilman, M., 318
Gimpel, G.A., 213
Ginsberg, R., 296
Giuliana, 122
Giuliani, G.A., 387–390
Gleason, M.M., 192
Glidden, L.M., 146
Gnagy, E.M., 202, 203, 221
Gobbi, G., 374
Goetestam, K.O., 318
Goetz, L., 298
Golden, C.J., 219
Golden, M.A., 318
Goldsmith, S.K., 505
Goldstein, H., 373
Goldston, D.B., 503
Gollnick, D.M., 116, 118
Gomez, A., 252
Gomez, M.L., 116
Gonzalez, J.E.J., 175
Gonzalez, N.M., 367
Gonzalez, P., 252
Gordijn, 116
Gordon, R., 109
Gordon, W.A., 390
Gore, J.C., 182
Goring, J.G., 218
Gosling, V., 198
Gotay, C.C., 327
Gottardo, A., 120
Gottfredson, L.S., 520, 537
Gottschalk, L.A., 318
Grados, M., 367
Graham, P.L., 33
Graham, S., 176, 177, 187
Grant, C.A., 116, 118, 125
Grant, K.E., 202
Graves, D.K., 67
Gray, D.E., 138, 140, 141, 150, 379
Gray, K.M., 364
Gray, S.D., 329
Grayson, A., 378
Green, A., 371
Green, G., 193, 372
Green, L.A., 364–366
Greenbaum, P.E., 252
Greenberg, M.T., 211, 252, 254
Greene, R.W., 218
Greenhill, L.L., 220, 224
Greenhouse, J., 202, 203, 221
Greenman, G.G., 175, 190, 191, 193, 201
Greenson, J.N., 213
Gregg, N., 175, 181
Greiner, A.R., 202, 203, 221
Grenot-Scheyer, M., 345
Gresham, F.M., 186, 187, 190, 209, 262, 264
Gresham, F.P., 280
Griffith, E.M., 364
Griffiths, A., 378
Griffiths, D.L., 109
Griffiths, D.M., 338
Grigorenko, E.L., 168
Groen, A.D., 372
Gronlund, N.E., 121, 122, 184, 187
Gross, A.M., 324, 327
Grossman, H., 118, 121
Gruner, A., 261
Guadarrama, 124
Gudjonsson, G.H., 280
Guenther, R.K., 316
Gugerty, J.J., 100
Guilford, J.P., 516, 518
Gulley, V., 221

Gupta, G.C., 177
Guralnick, M.J., 67, 69, 289, 343
Gurland, B.J., 122
Gustavsson, A., 9
Gutstein, S.E., 196

Haaga, D.A.F., 198
Haas, A., 305, 308, 310, 321
Haas, W.H., 328
Hackenberg, B., 217
Haggart, A.G., 126, 131
Hahne, K., 26
Halfon, N., 119
Hall, B.J., 328
Hall, N.W., 119
Hallahan, D.P., 61, 166
Hallam, M.A., 76
Halpert, J.A., 202
Hamilton, J., 202
Hamlett, C.L., 174, 178
Hand, M., 173
Handen, B.L., 222
Handler, M.W., 265
Hanich, L.B., 175
Hankin, C.S., 214
Hanley, T., 220, 224
Hanley-Maxwell, C., 75, 153, 154
Hansen, A., 13, 139
Happe, F., 367
Harachi, T.W., 120, 123
Harden, T., 63
Hardman, M.L., 18, 44, 60, 64, 66, 67, 69, 70, 71, 75, 76, 93, 95, 97, 102, 104, 118, 124, 125, 128, 130, 131, 150, 151, 182, 185, 202, 220, 224, 278, 281, 282, 283, 296, 307, 311, 318, 319, 344, 345, 347, 350, 355, 356, 371
Haring, N., 337
Harland, K., 326
Harland, P., 149, 150
Harmon, D., 160
Harpell, S., 123
Harper, G.F., 66
Harris, 16
Harris, K.R., 187
Harris, V., 318
Harrison, E., 318
Harrison-Hale, A.O., 113, 118
Harry, B., 117
Harryman, E., 305, 308, 310
Hartman-Hall, H.M., 198
Hartung, C.M., 241
Hartwig, E.P., 52
Hasazi, S.B., 93
Haslam, R.H.A., 400, 401
Hastings, R.P., 9, 138
Hattee, C., 326
Hatton, D.D., 371
Hatzes, N.M., 198
Hauser, C., 324, 326
Hauser-Cram, P., 138, 139, 148, 149, 153
Havel, E., 262
Havighurst, R.J., 521
Hawkins, J.D., 118
Hay, D.A., 220
Hayes, A., 138, 150
Heal, L.W., 93
Hecht, S.A., 320
Hechtman, L.T., 220, 224, 225
Hehir, T., 47
Heilman, K.M., 317
Heiman, T., 187

Heller, T., 105
Helman, E., 427
Hemp, R., 107, 108
Hendrick, J., 126, 131
Henker, B., 225
Henly, G.A., 215
Henry, L.A., 170, 173, 180, 280
Hepperlen, T.M., 215
Herbert, M.J., 158
Herbert, R., 314
Herbst, K., 310
Heredia, R.R., 120
Hermelin, B., 368, 369, 370
Hernandez, H., 123
Hernandez, M., 156–157, 157, 252, 258
Hewitt, A., 339
Hibbard, M.R., 390
Hickin, J., 314
Hickson, L., 312, 314
Hilburn, 418
Hill, J.L., 392
Hill, K.G., 118
Hinshaw, S.P., 209, 220, 224, 225
Hirshfeld-Becker, D.R., 218
Hitchcock, C., 83
Hittie, M.M., 44, 45, 59, 60, 63, 81
Hoagwood, K., 220, 224
Hoard, M.K., 177
Hobbs, T., 80
Hocutt, A.M., 44
Hoffman, C.C., 261
Hoffmeister, R., 426
Holland, A., 314
Hollmann, F.W., 120
Hollway, J., 367
Holmberg, D., 211, 222
Holmes, D., 122
Holzer, C.E., 118
Honey, K., 346
Hong, D., 367
Hooper, S.R., 253
Hopper, T., 314
Horiuchi, V., 303, 314
Horner, R.H., 73, 157, 186, 187, 190, 342
Horowitz, I.W., 198
Horton, C.B., 390, 499, 500, 501, 502
Horvat, M., 282
Hoskyn, M., 195
House, S.S., 311
Hout, M., 119, 128
Houtz, J.C., 543, 544
Howard, D., 314
Howard, V.F., 371
Howell, J.C., 242, 262, 263
Howell, K.W., 83
Howell, P., 316
Howie, D., 139
Howlin, P., 366, 370, 371
Hoza, B., 202, 203, 218, 220, 221, 224
Hua, C.B., 542
Huang-Pollock, C.L., 225
Huefner, D.S., 79
Hughes, C., 280
Hughes, M., 44
Hugo, R., 311
Hull, K., 126, 131
Hulsmeier, J., 242
Hunt, J.M., 67
Hunt, P., 298
Hunter, A.D., 187
Hurley, M., 317
Husaini, B.A., 118

Hutchinson, N.L., 182
Huttunen, K.H., 327
Hwang, C.P., 379
Hylebos, C., 318

Ialongo, N., 242
Indefre, P., 311
Inge, K., 104
Ingham, R.J., 317, 318
Ingram, C.F., 265
Inoue, A., 308
Ireland, M., 194, 198, 505
Ishii, K., 321
Israel, A.C., 242, 259–260
Ittenbach, R.F., 280, 281, 282, 284, 294, 338
Iwanaga, R., 367

Jackson, B., 139, 140, 141, 142, 159
Jackson, D.A., 211
Jackson, N.E., 529
Jackson, R., 83
Jacobs, D.M., 122
Jacques, S., 363
James, A., 241
Jameson, E.J., 157
Jamner, L., 225
Jankelevich, S., 489
Janssens, V., 120, 122, 123
Jarrow, J., 48
Jay, G.W., 386
Jean, R.E., 144
Jefferson-Wilson, P., 186
Jeffries, R., 310
Jenkins, C., 187
Jenkins, J.R., 59, 60
Jennett, B., 390, 393
Jensen, J., 196
Jensen, K., 108
Jensen, P.S., 220, 221, 224
Jenson, W.R., 208, 210, 363, 374
Jerome, L., 221
Jin, S., 529
Jivanjee, P., 253
John, O.P., 225
Johnson, B., 170
Johnson, C., 149, 155
Johnson, C.R., 180, 183, 308, 310, 321, 326, 327, 375
Johnson, D., 178
Johnson, D.E., 225
Johnson, G.O., 27
Johnson, J., 33, 60
Johnson, J.H., 214
Johnson, S., 389, 392
Johnston, S.S., 315
Jolivette, K., 254
Jones, D., 385
Jones, H., 159
Jones, J., 193
Jones, K., 211
Jones, L., 118, 121
Jones, M., 316
Jones, P., 201
Jongsma, A.E., Jr., 219
Jordan, A.M., 27
Jordon, N.C., 175
Joseph, L.M., 187
Joy, S., 364–366
Jung, P., 492
Justen, J., 336–337

Kabbani, N.S., 118
Kachgal, M., 101, 346
Kaiser, A.P., 282

Valle, 201
Vallecorsa, A.L., 187
Vallero, E., 367
Van Den Broeck, W., 171
Van Der Geest, J.N., 362, 363
VanDerHeyden, A.M., 319
Vander-Ree, A., 209
Van De Velde, H., 120, 122, 123
Van Engeland, H., 362, 363, 374
Van-Noord, R.G., 178, 179, 185
Vanryckeghem, M., 318
Van-Slyke, P.A., 314
Van Tassel-Baska, J., 540, 544
Vaughan, T.M., 315
Vaughn, B.J., 139, 152, 155, 156, 253
Vaughn, S., 44, 45, 60, 66, 67, 175, 182, 187, 194, 195, 201, 202
Vauras, M., 179, 182, 194, 195, 202
Veenstra-Vanderweele, J., 371
Venet, M.O., 314
Venn, J.J., 121, 213, 251
Verbaten, M.N., 362, 363
Verho, S., 183
Verhoeven, L., 305
Vermeer, A., 305
Vermeulen, M., 128
Verri, A., 367
Vicari, S., 310
Viggiano, J., 316
Vigil, D.C., 305
Vilkman, E., 329
Vincent, M., 427
Vioilette, H., 218
Vitiello, B., 220, 224, 367
Volkmar, F.R., 202, 364, 367, 374
Volpe, A.G., 371, 372
Volpe, R.J., 215
Von Isser, A., 236
Vopitta, 201
Voronin, K.E., 225
Vrignaud, P., 122

Wade, S.E., 62, 63
Wagner, M., 60, 93
Wahlberg, T., 366, 367
Waid, L.R., 225
Waldman, I.D., 220
Walker, D.W., 175, 195, 196
Walker, L.A., 430
Walker, S., 513
Wallace, S.J., 493
Walsh, C., 123
Walsh, J.A., 209

Walsh, M., 326
Warboys, L., 242, 261
Ward, 159
Ward, T., 362
Warfield, M.E., 138, 139, 148, 149, 153
Warren, S.F., 273, 282, 433
Warren, S.H., 152
Waschbusch, D.A., 202, 203, 221
Washington, J.A., 120
Wasik, B.H., 67
Wasserstein, J., 219, 225
Wassink, T.H., 371
Watemberg, N., 181, 216
Waterhouse, L., 364–366, 370
Watkins, M.W., 178, 179, 186
Watson, J.B., 20
Weaver, M.F., 62
Webb, S., 366
Webber, J., 234, 235, 236, 240, 241, 264
Webster, G., 128
Webster, W.G., 317
Webster-Stratton, C., 253
Wehby, J.H., 258, 261
Wehman, P., 93, 96, 98, 100, 296, 342, 347, 389, 392, 397–398, 402
Wehmeyer, M., 99, 102, 280, 290, 346
Weiller, C., 317, 317–318
Weinburg, 183
Weinreb, L.F., 118, 128, 130
Weinstein, S., 491
Weiss, A.L., 312, 313, 321
Weiss, G., 225
Weiss, M., 225
Weiss, M.J., 379
Weitzel, A., 329
Welch, M., 44, 192, 196
Welker, R., 241
Wells, K.C., 220, 224
Wenar, C., 198, 371, 371–372
Wermke, K., 324, 326
Werner, J., 149, 150, 152
Werthamer, L., 242
West, E., 141
Westby, C., 173, 181, 182
Westerberg, H., 219
Westling, D.L., 280, 282, 291, 341, 348, 371, 375
Wetherby, A.M., 311
Whalen, C.K., 225
Whaley, B.B., 318
Wheelwright, S., 371
Wheildon, H., 374

Whitaker, R., 361
White, B.L., 67
White, O.R., 44, 45
White, R., 231
Whitmarsh, E.L., 319
Whitney-Thomas, J., 346
Whittel, B., 196–197
Wicks-Nelson, R., 242, 259–260
Wigal, T., 220, 224
Wigg, K., 220
Wiggs, L., 241
Wilbers, J.S., 74
Wilde, J., 262
Wilder, D.A., 375
Wilkerson, D.S., 371, 372
Willcutt, E.G., 183
Willemsen-Swinkels, S.H.N., 374
Williams, A.L., 327
Williams, B.F., 371
Williams, F.E., 528
Williams, J.P., 191
Williams, S., 386
Willicut, E.G., 225
Willingham, W.W., 122
Willner, P., 193
Willoughby, J.C., 146
Willson, V.L., 171
Wilson, J., 242
Wilson, L., 33
Wilson, R., 240, 241, 242, 250
Windfuhr, K.L., 319
Wing, L., 364, 372
Winner, E., 538
Winzer, M.A., 263, 264
Witt, J.C., 248
Witte, R., 219
Wittman, P., 139, 140, 141, 142, 159
Wixtrom, C., 421
Wolcott, G.F., 387, 398
Wolery, M., 73, 74
Wolf, L.E., 225
Wolfensberger, W., 10
Wolf-Schein, E.G., 342
Wolfson, L., 202, 203, 221
Wolpaw, J.R., 315
Wolpert, C.M., 371
Woltz, D.J., 179, 196
Wood, J.W., 46
Wood, K.M., 170, 171, 173
Wood, R.L., 388, 390
Wood, S.E., 321
Woodruff, D.W., 261
Woodward, J., 166
Woodyatt, G., 366

World Health Organization, 448
Wornian, K., 158, 159
Worrall, L., 312, 314
Worrell, F.C., 179
Worthington, J., 156–157, 157, 252, 258
Wright, A., 214
Wright, E., 393
Wright, H.H., 371
Wrightsman, J., 218
Wristers, K., 219
Wulfeck, B., 310
Wyatte, M.L., 139, 152, 155, 156, 253
Wynn, J.W., 372

Yale, M., 319
Yalin, A., 181
Yang, N.J., 175
Yaruss, J.S., 318
Yasuda, S., 389, 392
Yavas, M., 319
Yazbak, K., 379
Yell, M.L., 264, 472, 473
Yen, L., 175
Yeschin, N.J., 218
Yetman, N.T., 7, 21
Yim, P., 125
Ying, L., 317
Yiolitis, L., 141
Yirmiya, N., 364, 374, 375, 380
Yoder, P.J., 282
Yoneoka, Y., 310
Yoshinaga-Itano, C., 138
Young, D.M., 148
Young, M.E., 69, 265, 289
Yovanoff, P., 108, 262
Ysseldyke, J.E., 59, 60, 343

Zafiropoulou, M., 187, 191
Zai, G., 220
Zapata, J.T., 115
Zelazo, P.D., 363
Zhang, C., 139, 144, 157, 159
Zhang, H., 122
Zhu, G., 318
Zigler, E.F., 119
Zigmond, N., 187
Zimmermann, S.H., 219
Zingale, M., 372
Zone, J., 62, 63
Zuckerman, J.B., 217, 219
Zuriff, G.E., 199
Zurkowski, J.K., 155

# Subject Index

Page numbers in **bold** indicate definitions; page numbers followed by *f* or *t* indicate figures or tables, respectively

Delinquency
  emotional/behavioral disorders and, 242
  gang membership, 261–262, 263t
  labeling and, 244
Denasality, **328**, 329
Dental abnormalities
  articulation disorders and, 324, 325f
  correction of, 326–327
Depression
  over birth of child with disability, 139, 140f
  emotional/behavioral disorders and, 242
  suicide and, 503, 505
Deprivation, sibling's feelings of, 151
Development
  assessing, 74
  teaching to enhance, 73
Developmental aphasia, 310
Developmental approach, 45
  to labeling, 6–7
Developmental delays, mental retardation
    and, 273
Developmental disabilities, **276**, 338. *See also*
    Mental retardation
Developmental disorders, pervasive, 237
Developmentally appropriate practices (DAP),
    **73**–74, 345
Developmentally supportive care, **69**–70
Developmental milestones approach, 289
Developmental reading programs, 191, 193
Developmental screening, 464
Deviance, historical perspective on, 9–10
Deviant, **20**–21
Diabetes mellitus, 244, **494**–496
  causation, 495
  definitions and concepts, 494
  insulin-dependent or juvenile onset, 493,
    494, 495, 496
  interventions, 495–496
    cell transplant treatment, 494
  noninsulin-dependent or adult onset, 493,
    494
  prevalence, 494
Diabetic coma, 494
Diagnosis, dual, **338**
*Diagnostic and Statistical Manual of Mental Dis-
    orders*, 169, 210, 212t
  categories and subcategories of, 237–240
Diagnostic Interview Schedule for Children
    (DISC-2.3), 216
Diagnostic-prescriptive reading programs,
    192–193
Diamond Ranch Academy website, 229
*Diana v. California State Board of Education*
    (1970), 29t, 121–122
Diet management
  for cystic fibrosis, 497
  metabolic disorders and, **285**
  for seizure disorders, 493
Differences, labeling, 5–9. *See also* Exception-
    ality, understanding
Differential association, 245
Differentiated education, **530**, 534, 535, 539
Differentiated instruction. *See* Multilevel in-
    struction
Dillon, James, 254
Diploma, high school, 101–102, 103
Direct instruction, **82**, **294**
  for the learning disabled, 165
  for voice disorders, 329
Disabilities, **5**. *See also specific disabilities*
  definition of, 11–12, 48
  famous people with, 8
  giftedness and, 542–543
  multidisciplinary perspectives on, 17–21
    medical model, 17–19

psychological perspective on, 19–20
sociological perspective on, 20–21
special education eligibility, 30–31, 49t
DISC-2.3, ADHD assessment using, 216
Discipline, 51, 52
  emotional/behavioral disorders and,
    245
  zero-tolerance principle and, 48–51
Discrepancy approaches to classification of
    learning disabilities, 170, 171
Discrimination. *See also* Americans with Dis-
    abilities Act (1990)
  history of, 9–10
  labeling and, 6
  legislating against, 11–13
  special education as tool of, 117, 119
Disease model, of exceptionality. *See* Medical
    model, of people with disabilities
Disney, Walt, 8
Disorder(s), **5**. *See also specific disorders*
Disruptive disorders, 237
Divergent thinking, test of, 528, 529
Diversity. *See also* Cultural diversity; Multicul-
    tural education
  appreciation of, 3
  designing for, 81–82
  growing student, 77, 78
  inclusion and, 62
  language, 29t, 122–123, 130, 131
DMD. *See* Duchenne-type muscular dystrophy
    (DMD)
Dole, Robert, 4
Down syndrome, **139**, 142, 143, 160, 235, 271,
    295. *See also* Mental retardation
  characteristic features, 284
  chromosomal abnormality and, 284–285
  educating child with, 26
  myths and truths about, 286
  physical health and, 283
Dragon Naturally Speaking (software), 402
Dropout rates, 60
  emotional/behavioral disorders and, 243
  income and, 118–119
  among minorities, 118
Drug therapy. *See* Medications
Drug use/abuse. *See* Substance abuse
DSM-IV. *See Diagnostic and Statistical Manual
    of Mental Disorders*
Dual diagnosis, **338**
Dual sensory impairments, **339**
Duchenne-type muscular dystrophy (DMD),
    484
Due process, in education, 33, 49t
Duke University Talent Identification Program
    website, 548
Dyadic relationships, **145**
Dynavox, 304
Dyslexia, 167, 176, 197
Dystrophin, 484

Ear, anatomy of, 409–410, 410f
Eardrum, 409
Early adulthood, 92
Early childhood. *See also* Infant(s) and tod-
    dlers; Preschool children
  ADHD in, 226
  autism in, 376
  communication disorders in, 322
  emotional/behavioral disorders in, 252–254,
    256
  family-centered support in, 153
  giftedness in, 529–530, 532
  hearing loss in, 422
  learning disabilities in, 188
  mental retardation in, 289, 292

physical disabilities and health disorders in,
    486
severe and multiple disabilities in, 343, 352
transition from preschool to elementary
    school, 76–77
traumatic and acquired brain injury in, 394
vision loss in, 460
Early intervention, **67**, 69–72, 318
  autism and, 372
  effective, 69–72
  effects on poor children, 119
  eligibility for, 69
  for emotional/behavioral disorders, 258
  family-centered, 71, 344
    parent training, 158–159
  for hearing loss, 420
  individualized, intensive, and comprehen-
    sive services, 71–72
  for mental retardation, 289
  under Part C of IDEA, 69
  service delivery, 69–71
  for severe and multiple disabilities, 344
  for stuttering, 318
  timing of, 69
Eating disorders, 238
E/BD. *See* Emotional and behavioral disorders
    (E/BD)
Echolalia, **282**, 363, **366**
Ecocultural, **139**
Ecological approach, to abnormal behavior, **20**
Econpresis, 238
Edison, Thomas, 7, 200
Educability expectations in mental retarda-
    tion, 277
Education, 25–55. S̶ *̶iso* Inclusion; Multicul-
    tural educati̶ ̶; Special education
  access to, 25, 26
  approaches to, 115–117
  changes in, 26–28
  cultural pluralism and role of, 115–117
  current trends in, 43–52
  differentiated, **530**, 534, 535, 539
  gap in, 94
  legal precedents in, 28–29t
  purposes of general, 115–117
Educational achievement. *See* Academic
    achievement
Educational Amendments Acts (1974), 29t
Educational collaboration. *See* Collaboration
The Education for All Handicapped Children
    Act, **28**–30
Education of the Handicapped Act (1975),
    29–30, 29t
  amendments (1986), 29t, 30, 68
EEGs (electroencephalograms), 492
Einstein, Albert, 8, 173f, 200
Elaboration, 514
Elective mutism, 239
Elec-Tra-Mate®, 481
Electroacoustic aids, 433–434
Electroencephalogram, 492
Electronic Magazine of Multicultural Educa-
    tion website, 134
Electronic mobility devices, 454
Elementary school, 77–85
  ADHD in, 221–224, 226
  autism in, 376
  building general education/special educa-
    tion partnership, 77–81
  communication disorders in, 322
  effective practices in inclusive programs,
    81–85
  emotional/behavioral disorders in, 254–260
  family-centered support in, 153–154
  giftedness in, 530–540

hearing loss in, 422–423
learning disabilities in, 187–194
mental retardation in, 289–294
parental involvement in, 346
physical disabilities and health disorders in, 486
severe and multiple disabilities and, 346–348, 352
transition from preschool to, 76–77
traumatic and acquired brain injury in, 394
vision loss in, 460
Eligibility
for early intervention, 69
for special education, 30–31, 37t, 38, 49t
Elimination disorders, 239
Emotion
learning disabilities and, 182
stuttering and, 317
Emotional abuse, 499, 500
Emotional and behavioral disorders (E/BD), 231–269
ADHD and, 209
assessment, 246–252
factors, 247–248
screening, prereferral interventions, and referral, 246–247
techniques, 249–252, 249t, 250t, 251t
causation, 243–246
behavioral approach, 244
biophysical approach, 243–244
phenomenological approach, 244
psychoanalytic approach, 244
sociological-ecological approach, 244–245
characteristics of, 241–243
classification of, 235–240
clinically derived classification systems, 237–240
statistically derived classification systems, 236–237
definitions, 232–235
Council for Exceptional Children (CEC) definition, 234–235
IDEA definition, 233–234
normal behavior, identifying, 235
factors influencing types of behaviors, 235
inclusion and, 256–257, 262–265
interventions, 252–265
adolescent years, 261–262
early childhood years, 252–254
elementary school years, 254–260
family-centered, 252, 253–254, 253t
inclusive education, 262–265
language disturbances and, 311
learning disabilities and, 178–179
prevalence, 240–241
promising practices for, 265–266
Emotional disorders, 232. See also Emotional and behavioral disorders (E/BD)
Emotional disorganization, 142
Employment, 16
ADA and, 12–13, 15
ADHD and, 227
case study of, 17
competitive, 107–108
Down syndrome and, 286
emotional and behavioral disorders and, 243, 257
giftedness and, 533
government-funded programs and, 107–108
hearing loss and, 423, 430
learning disabilities and, 198
mental retardation and, 293, 295–297, 295f
physical disabilities and health disorders and, 487
severe and multiple disabilities and, 353

supported, **108**, **295**–296
transition from school to, 95–96, 97f, 98, 102–104, 195f, 198, 295–297
traumatic brain injury and, 395, 397
vision loss and, 461
Employment rates, 93, 94, 243
Encephalitis, **288**
Endometriosis, 233
English language
hearing loss and development of, 416
manual alphabet, 426f
signed systems, **426**, 427
English-only education, 121
Enrichment, **537**–538
Entertainment/going out, 94
Enuresis, 238
Environment
ADHD and, 219–220
delayed speech and, 320
emotional/behavioral disorders and, 245
giftedness and, 524–526, 526f, 542
hearing loss and, 415
impoverished, effects of, 127–129
intelligence and, 523–526
language disorders and, 311
learning disabilities and, 183
mental retardation and, 276
nature versus nurture and, **18**, **284**, **524**
Environmental bias, 9
Environmental cues for functional skills, 347
Epicanthal folds, 284
Epidural hematoma, **400**, 400f
Epilepsy, **342**, **490**–493, 494. See also Seizure disorders
Epilepsy Foundation of America website, 510
Epiphora, **464**
Esotropia, **446**
Ethic(s)
bioethics, **350**–356
collaborative, 63
Eustachian tube, **410**
Evaluations under IDEA and Section 504/ADA, 49t. See also Assessment
Exceptional, **5**, 9
Exceptionality, understanding, 3–23. See also Americans with Disabilities Act (1990)
describing people with differences, 5–9
inclusion and, 9–10
multidisciplinary perspectives on, 17–21
medical model, 17–19
psychological, 19–20
sociological, 20–21
terminology, 18f
Exclusion, labeling and, 6
Exclusion approach to classification of learning disabilities, 170
Executive function, **209**
Exotropia, **446**
Expectations
educability, in mental retardation, 277
parental, 97
Explicit skills, teaching of, 45–46
Exploration of possibilities, encouraging, 101t
Expressive aphasia, **389**
Expressive language
traumatic brain injury and, 397, 398t
vision loss and, 455
Expressive language disorders, **310**
Extended family, **151**–152
support in adulthood from, 109
Extensive supports, 278
Externalizing disorders, 236
Eye. See also Vision loss
muscle disorders, 446

parts of, 443, 443f
receptive problems, 446–447
refractive problems, **445**–446
visual process and, 442–444

Facilitative communication, 378
Faculty in higher education, advocate on, 199
Falls, traumatic brain injury and, 390
Families and Advocates Partnership for Education (FAPE) website, 163
Family(ies), 137–163
ADHD and, 226–227
adolescent pregnancy and, 503
attitude toward exceptionality, 124, 125
autism and, 376–377, 379–380
characteristics and interactions, 144–145
child abuse intervention and, 501
communication disorders and, 322–323
emotional/behavioral disorders and, 245, 256–257
extended, 109, **151**–152
genetic counseling for, 355–356
giftedness and, 532–533, 543
hearing loss and, 422–423
historical perspective on, 9–10
home communication for culturally diverse students, 132t
individualized family service plan (IFSP), **30**, **69**, 70t, 158, 253
learning disabilities and, 188–189
medical model and, 18
mental retardation and, 292–293
migrant, 129–130
parent-child relationships, 147–149
father-child, 148–149
mother-child, 147–148
physical disabilities and health disorders and, 486–487
power structure, 145
reactions to birth of exceptional child, 137, 138, 139–143
reciprocal relationship with, establishing, 74
severe and multiple disabilities and, 352–353
sibling relationships, 149–151
as social/ecological system, 138–139
spousal relationships, 145–147
suicide in youth and, 505
support in adulthood from, 108–109
transition planning for adult life and, 95
traumatic and acquired brain injury and, 394–395
types of, 145
understanding child in context of, 124
vision loss and, 460–461
Family Caregiver Alliance website, 404
Family-centered services and programs, 152–160
collaboration with professionals, 155–157
early intervention, 71, 158–159, 344
emotional/behavioral disorders and, 252, 253–254, 253t
giftedness and, 539, 543
goals, 158
individualized family service plan, **30**, **69**, 70t, 158, 253
life cycle of family and, 153
strengthening supports, 158
training for parents, professionals, and families, 158–160
Family interest and concerns, IFSP, 70
Family liaisons or advocates, 258–259
Family practitioner, hearing loss diagnosis and, 431

accommodations on SAT, 165
achievement discrepancy, 178
ADHD and, 209
in adolescents, 189, 194–200
alcohol abuse and, 198
assessment of, 183–187
causation, 182–183
characteristics, 173–182
classifications, 170–171
cognition and information processing and, 179–180
definitions, **166**, 167–170
direct instruction and, 165
in elementary school years, 187–194
gender and, 165
hyperactivity and, 181
inclusion and, 188–189, 190, 201
intelligence and, 178–179, 185–186
intraindividual variability, 179
as label, 9
learning characteristics and, 180–181
in mathematics, 177–178, 190–191
medical services and, 202–203
prevalence of, 171f–173
in reading, 175, 191–193
receptive language problems and, 310
screening for, 185
services and supports for, 187
social and emotional characteristics, 182
in writing and spelling, 176–177f
Learning Disabilities Association, 10n
   website, 205
Learning Disabilities Council website, 204
Learning disorders, 169. *See also* Learning disabilities
Learning sets, establishing, 280
Learning strategies approach, 196
   for ADHD, 225
Least restrictive environment, 30, **34**, 35f, 58
   for culturally diverse students, 126–127
   determining, 37t, 39
   vision loss and, 458–459
Legal blindness, **444**
Lens, **443**
LEP. *See* Limited English proficiency (LEP)
Leveling effect of general education, 117
Levitz, Mitchell, 143
L&H Kurzweill 1000 Reading System, 457, 458
Liasons, family, 258–259
Liberator voice machine, 314
Light Talker, 475
Limited English proficiency (LEP), 120, 123, 251. *See also* Language diversity
Limited supports, 278
Linguistic intelligence, 520t
Link for Life website, 511
Lithium carbonate, 222t
Local education agency (LEA), 30, 38
Locke, John, 18
Logical-mathematical intelligence, 520t
Loneliness, sibling's feelings of, 150
Low birthweight, **287**
Low vision, 444–445
LRE. *See* Least restrictive environment

Mcdonald, John, 471
Macular degeneration, **448**
Magnetic resonance imaging (MRI), **399**
Maindumping, 59
Mainstreaming, 58–**59**. *See also* Inclusion
   bilingual-bicultural inclusion models, 128f
Malaria, sickle cell anemia and, 498
Malocclusion, **324**
Managed care, 156–157
Manual alphabet, 426f

Manual approach to teaching communication skills, 425–427
Marriage. *See also* Family(ies)
   Down syndrome and, 286
   spousal relationships, 145–147
Marriage laws, 9
Martin, Casey, 14
Maternal drug and alcohol abuse, 287, 506–508
   definitions and concepts, 506
   effects of, 507f
      fetal alcohol syndrome, **287**, 288, 506
   interventions, 508
   prevalence and causation, 506
Maternal infections
   autism and, 371
   hearing loss and, 414
   HIV, 489
   mental retardation and, **287**–288
   vision loss and, 448
Mathematics
   functional math program, 281, 294
   learning disabilities in, 177–178, 190–191
   mental retardation and, 281, 294
   universal design curriculum applied to, 82t
   vision loss and, 456
Mathematics assessment instruments, 186–187
Maturational delay, learning disabilities and, 183
Maturation philosophy, 289
Mauer, Harriet, 255
MD. *See* Muscular dystrophy
Measurement. *See* Assessment
Measurement bias, **122**
Meatus, 409
Media, children with disabilities in, 143
Mediation, in education, 33
Medicaid, **106**–107
Medical classification system for mental retardation, 277
Medical history/developmental information, IFSP, 70
Medically fragile, **472**
Medical model, of people with disabilities, **17**–19
Medical services, 18–19
   for ADHD, 213, 214
   for autism, 374–375
   for hearing loss, 430–434
   for learning disabilities, 202–203
   for traumatic brain injury, 397–402
   for vision loss, 459, 462–465
Medical technology, bioethics and, **350**–356
Medical treatments, withholding, 356
Medicare, **107**
Medications
   for ADHD, 221–222, 225
      concerns over, 221–222, 223, 224
      Ritalin, 202, 207, 221–222, 223, 225
   for autism, 374–375
   for cystic fibrosis, 497
   for emotional/behavioral disorders, 260
   for learning disabilities, 202–203
   for seizure disorders, 493
   side effects and uses, 221, 222t
   for stuttering, 318
Memory
   autism and, 369, 370
   learning disabilities and, 179–180
   mental retardation and, 279–280
   savant syndrome and, 369
Meningitis, 415
Mental age, **514**
Mental health, retardation and, 276

Mental health care, trading custody of children for, 254–255
Mental hospitals, 9, 10
Mental retardation, **5**, 9, 138, 271–301
   autism and, 339
   causation, 283–288
      behavioral factors, **287**–288
      biomedical factors, **284**–286
      sociocultural influences, 284
      unknown prenatal influences, 288
   with challenging behaviors, 338
   characteristics of, 279–283
      academic achievement, 281, 294
      learning and memory, 279–280
      motivation, 281–282t
      physical development, 282–283t
      self-regulation, 280–281
      speech and language, 282, 283t
   classification of, 276–278
      based on needed support, 277–278
      by educability expectations, 277
      by medical descriptors, 277
      by severity of condition, 276–277
   cultural differences in view of, 125
   cultural-familial retardation, **284**
   definition, 274–276
   distinctions between learning disabilities and, 179
   educational services and supports, 288–297
      early childhood years, 289
      elementary school years, 289–294
      transition from school to adult life, 293, 294–297
   evolving terminology, 273–274
   fathers of children with, 148
   fetal alcohol syndrome and, 506
   inclusion and, 292–293, 295, 297–298
   prevalence of, 278–279f
   severe and multiple disabilities and, 341
Mentoring of gifted students, 539, 540
Metabolic disorders, **285**, 340
Metacognition, 196, 280
Methylphenidate (Ritalin), 202, 207, 221–222, 223, 225
Methylprednisolone, 481
Microphthalmia, **447**
Middle ear, 409–410
Migrant families, children in, 129–130
Mild mental retardation, 273
*Mills* v. *District of Columbia Board of Education* (1972), 28, 29t
Minimal brain dysfunction, 167
Minorities, cultural and ethnic. *See* Cultural diversity
Mirror writing, **176**
Misdiagnosis, 119
Mitochondrial cytopathy, 156
Mixed hearing loss, **412**
Mobility, vision loss and, 450–451, 465
Mobility of migrant families, effect of, 129–130
Mobility training, 452–454
Modeling, of language and speech, 311, 325
Moderate mental retardation, 272–273
Morphology, 305
Mothers. *See also* Maternal drug and alcohol abuse; Maternal infections; Parent(s)
   adolescent, 502–503, 502f
   mother-child relationships, 147–148
   overprotectiveness of, 145, 148
   spousal relationship, 145–146
   trauma and strain experienced by, 144
Motivation, mental retardation and, 281–282t
Motor skills, mental retardation and, 290
Mountbatten Brailler, 456–457

child abuse and neglect, 127, 245, **499**–501
collaboration with professionals, 64, 155–157
from different cultures, involvement of, 124–125
drug abuse by, 287, 506–508
hearing impaired, language learning in children with, 311, 312
IEP and, 38–39
informed consent of, 37–38
language and speech development and, 306, 311, 320, 325
muscular dystrophy and, 485
reaction to birth of child with disability, 137, 138, 139–143, 140*f*
role as team member, 65
safeguards and involvement, in education, 31, 32–33, 49*t*
severe and multiple disabilities and, 346
sibling relationships and attitude/behavior of, 149
support groups for, 10
support of adult children, 108
trading custody for care of children, 254–255
training for, 158–159
transition process and, 96–97
Parent-child interaction, stuttering and, 317*f*
Parent-child relationships, 147–149
factors influencing, 147
father-child relationships, 148–149
mother-child relationships, 147–148
Parenting Stress Index, 215
Parent notification, 35–36, 37
content of notice, 36–37
Parent's Place website, 229
Parent-teacher conferences, 247
Parent-to-parent programs, 158
Parkin, Terence, 418*f*
Part C in 1997 IDEA amendments, 68–69
early intervention under, 69
purposes, 68
services provided, 69*t*
Partial inclusion, **59**
Partially sighted, 444–**445**
Pathological, 17
Pathology, **17**
Patient, 17
Patient's disease, 17
Patton, George S., Jr., 8
PBS. *See* Positive behavioral support (PBS)
Pediatrician, hearing loss diagnosis and, 431
Peer-mediated instruction, **67**
Peers, suicide in youth and, 505
Peer support, 66–67
Peer tutoring, **67**
*Pennsylvania Association for Retarded Citizens* v. *Commonwealth of Pennsylvania*, 28, 29*t*
Perception difficulties, learning disabilities and, 180–181
Perceptual disorders, 167
Perceptual-motor development, vision loss and, 451–452
Perceptual-motor theories of learning disabilities, 169
Perfectionism, 540
Peripheral hearing loss, 411–412
Perkins School, 459
Perlman, Itzhak, 542*f*
Personal digital assistants (PDAs), 250, **458**
Personal independence. *See* Independence
Person-centered approach to transition planning, 97
Pervasive developmental disorders, 237
Pervasive supports, 278

Petit mal seizures. *See* Absence seizures
Pharmacological control. *See* Medications
Pharmacological gene therapy, 482
Phenomenological approach, 244
Phenylalanine, 285
Phenylketonuria (PKU), **285**
Phonological disorders. *See* Articulation problems
Phonology, 305
Photophobia, **447**
Physical abuse, 499, 500
Physical development, mental retardation and, 282–283*t*
Physical disabilities, **472**, 473–485. *See also specific disabilities*
cerebral palsy, 68, 304, 314, 316, 349, **473**–476
inclusion and, 486–487
muscular dystrophy, **483**–485
spina bifida, **139**, 472, **476**–480
spinal cord injury, **480**–482
traumatic brain injury and, 390
Physical health. *See* Health
Physical therapists, **19**, 475*f*, 479
Physician(s). *See also* Medical services
learning disabilities and, 202–203
parental collaboration with, 155
support and care, in disabilities, 19
training for, 19
Pica, 238
Pinel, Philippe, 18
Pitch disorders, 328
PKU. *See* Phenylketonuria (PKU)
Place value in arithmetic, problems with, 178
Play therapy, 244
Pluralism, cultural, 115–117, **116**
Point systems, 259, 260*f*
Population growth, by race and Hispanic origin, 119–120*f*
Positive attitude, 199
Positive behavioral support (PBS), 156, 251–252, 259
Postlingual loss, **411**
Postnatal brain disease, 286
Postsecondary education, 93. *See also* College
traumatic brain injury and, 397
Poverty, 113, 138
child abuse and neglect and, 499, 500
conditions associated with, 127–129*f*
dropout rates and family, 118–119
emotional/behavioral disorders and, 245
giftedness and, 543–545
of migrant families, 129–130
Power structure, family, 145
Practical intelligence, 519
Pragmatics, **305**
Pregnancy. *See also* Prenatal period, disabilities caused during
adolescent, 502–503, 502*f*
health risks and poverty during, 127–128
HIV transmitted during, 471
infection and intoxication during, 287
substance abuse during, 287, 506–508
Prelingual loss, **411**, 413
Prematurity, 147–148, **287**
retinopathy of, **447**, 448, 463
Prenatal period, disabilities caused during
ADHD, 219–220
autism, 371
cerebral palsy, 474*t*
hearing loss, 414
mental retardation, 287, 288
preventive care for, 463
severe and multiple disabilities, 340
vision loss, 448
Prereferral intervention, **35**–36, 247, 251

Preschool children, 30. *See also* Early childhood
autism in, 376
communication disorders in, 322
gifted programs for, 530, 532
hearing loss in, 422
legal precedents affecting, 28, 29*t*, 68
maternal substance abuse and, 508
mental retardation and, 289, 292
otitis media in, 415
physical disabilities and health disorders and, 486
services for, 72–76
Head Start, **76**, **289**
IEP, 73
indicators of quality, 75, 76*t*
severe and multiple disabilities in, 344–346, 352
developmentally appropriate practices for, 345
program goals for, 345
transition to elementary school from, 76–77
traumatic and acquired brain injury and, 394
vision loss in, 460
Preschool services, 72–76
effective practices, 73–76
Head Start, **76**, **289**
IEP, 73
inclusive program, indicators of quality of, 75, 76*t*
Preschool transition plan, IFSP, 70, 77
Pressure
on gifted students, 539–540
siblings' perceived, 151
Prevention
of AIDS, 489, 490*f*
of child abuse and neglect, 501
of emotional/behavioral disorders, 252–253
schoolwide, 252, 258
of suicide, 506
of vision loss, 463–464
PRIDE (Preschool and Primary Interest Descriptor), 516
Primary brain damage, 387
*Principles of Psychology, The* (James), 19
Print-to-speech reading machines, 441
Problem solving, encouraging, 101*t*
Professional Golf Association (PGA) tour, ADA applied to, 14
Professionals. *See also* Teacher(s)
inclusion and. *See* Inclusion
parental collaboration with, 155–157
training for, 123–124, 159
Profound retardation, 273
Prosthesis for cleft palate, 326
Psychoanalytic approach, 244
Psychodynamic perspective, **371**
autism in, 371, 373–374
Psychological adjustment to spinal cord injuries, 482
Psychological perspective on people with disabilities, 19–20
Psychological services, traumatic brain injury and, 401, 402
Psychostimulants, ADHD intervention using (Ritalin), 202, 207, 221–222, 223, 224, 225
Psychotic disorders/psychosis, **20**
Public accommodations, 13
Public transportation, 13, 94
Pull-out program, 59, 61, **127**, 128*f*, 534
Pulmozyme, 497
Pupil (eye), **443**
Putamen, 221

Quadriplegia, **480**
Quality of inclusive preschool classroom, indicators of, 75, 76*t*

Race/ethnicity, population growth by, 119–120*f. See also* Cultural diversity; Multicultural education
Ransom Program, 192
Rappo, Peter D., 157
Reactive attachment disorder, 239
Reading
    decoding in, 449
    diagnostic-prescriptive programs, 192–193
    direct instruction in, **294**
    explicit teaching of, 45
    functional, 281, 294, 341
    functional life skills approach to, 46
    hearing loss and, 416–417
    learning disabilities and, 175, 191–193
    mental retardation and, 281, 294
    vision loss and, 449, 455, 456–457
    whole-language instruction, 192
Reading machine, 457, 458
Reading Milestones series, 417
Reading tests, 186
Realization stage, 142
Reasonable accommodations, **13**, 15, 48, 199, 200
Receptive eye problems, 446–447
Receptive language
    traumatic brain injury and, 397, 398*t*
    vision loss and, 455
Receptive language disorders, **309**–310
Reciprocal relationships with families, establishing, 74
Recreation opportunities, 16
Reeve, Christopher, 471
Referral
    for ADHD assessment, 214
    of culturally diverse students, 132*t*
    for emotional/behavioral disorders, 247
    initiating, 35–38
    for preschool services, 72
Reflective teaching, 76*t*
Reform
    current wave of, 77–78
    school, 46–48, 119
Refractive problems, **445**–446
Regular education initiative (REI), **64**
Rehabilitation
    for spinal cord injuries, 482
    vocational, 95–96, **108**
Reinforcement
    self-stimulation as reinforcer, 378
    token systems of, 194, 259
Related services, **30**
Related-services specialist, 65
Relaxation therapy, 318
Religion, 20
Research
    comorbidity, 173–174
    on learning disabilities, problems with, 170
    subtype, 173–174
Resentment of siblings, 150–151
Residential living, federal government support for, 107
Residential schools, 419–420, 459, 463
Residual vision, extended reliance on, 445
Resistance to change, autism and, 367
Resourcefulness, attitude of, 199
Resource room, 35*f*
Resource room teacher, 65
Respect, 3
Respiratory disease management, cystic fibrosis and, 497
Respiratory ventilation, 342

Respite care, **146**, 152, **344**
Responsibility, sharing, 64–66
Restoration/maintenance model of bilingual-bicultural inclusion, 128*f*
Retina, **443**
Retinal detachment, **447**
Retinitis pigmentosa, **446**, 447
Retinoblastoma, **447**
Retinopathy of prematurity (ROP), **447**, 448, 463
Retrolental fibroplasia, 447
Rh-factor incompatibility, 287, 414
Rhogam (anti-Rh gamma globulin), 287, 414
Rights, 3
    civil, 10, 11
    to education, 28–29*t*
Risk taking, promoting reasonable, 101*t*
Ritalin, 202, 207, 221–222, 223, 224, 225
Ritualistic behaviors, 336, 367
Rockefeller, Nelson, 8, 200
Role models for gifted students, need for, 540
Roosevelt, Franklin Delano, 4–5
ROP. *See* Retinopathy of prematurity (ROP)
Rozynski, Peter, 407
Rubella, **287**, 414, 478
Rumination disorder, 238

Safer, Morley, 50–51
Safe schools, 48–52
Safety skills, 100–101
Sample, normative, 274
SAT, learning disability accommodations on, 165
Satisfaction with life, 94
Savant syndrome, 369
SCA. *See* Sickle cell anemia (SCA)
Scardino, Marjorie, 541*f*
Schimmer, Raymond, 254
Schizophrenia, 244
School administrator, 65
School-based case management, 258
School-based interventions for ADHD, 223–224, 225
School personnel, inclusion and. *See* Inclusion
School psychologist, 65
School reform, 46–48, 119
    inclusive education and, 47
Schools
    accountability of, 46–48, 343
    safe, 48–52
School Situations Questionnaire (SSQ), 214
School-to-Work Opportunities Act, 95, 96
Schoolwide assistance teams (SWATs), 64–**65**
Schoolwide Enrichment Model, 528
Schoolwide prevention, 252, 258
Schoolwide support system, 63
SCI. *See* Spinal cord injury (SCI)
Screening, **185**
    developmental, 464
    for emotional/behavioral disorders, 246–247
    genetic, 354–356, 463
    for giftedness, 527–529
    for vision loss, 462, 464
Seat belts, use of, 390
Secondary brain damage, 387
Secondary education
    for adolescents with learning disabilities, 194–197
Secondary school. *See also* Adolescent(s)
    ADHD in, 227
    autism in, 377
    communication disorders in, 323
    emotional/behavioral disorders in, 257, 261–262
    family-centered support in, 154–155
    giftedness in, 530–540

    hearing loss in, 423
    learning disabilities in, 189, 194–200
    mental retardation in, 293, 294–297
    physical disabilities and health disorders in, 487
    role in preparing students for adult life, 98–104. *See also* Transition services
    severe and multiple disabilities in, 348, 353
    traumatic and acquired brain injury in, 395
    vision loss in, 461
Secretion glands, disorder of, 496
Section 504, **11**, 29*t*
    comparison with IDEA, 49*t*
    definition of disability, 11–12
    enforcement, 49*t*
    students with disabilities and, 48, 49*t*
Sedatives, 222*t*
Segregation
    in education, 27
    history of, 9–10
Seizure, **491**
    absence, **491**
    first aid for, 492*f*
    tonic/clonic, **491**
Seizure disorders, 490–493
    causation, 492
    definitions and concepts, 490–491
    interventions, 492–493, 494
    prevalence, 492
Selective abortion, 356
Selective attention, **180**
Self-advocacy, promoting, 101*t*
Self-determination, **46**, 99–100, 101*t*, 346
Self-directed involvement in learning, 192
Self-esteem, 101*t*, 127
Self-fulfilling prophecy, 131
Self-help skills, mental retardation and, 290
Self-identity, understanding disabilities and, 101*t*
Self-labeling, 7
Self-mutilation, 336
Self-regulation, **280**
    ADHD and, 216–217, 218, 221
    mental retardation and, 280–281
Self-stimulation, 336, **367**, 378
Semantics, 305
Semicircular canals, 410
Semi-independent apartment or home, **107**
Senses, vision loss and use of other, 453
Sensorineural hearing loss, **412**
Sensory impairments, dual, **339**. *See also* Hearing loss; Vision loss
Separation anxiety disorder, 239
Services, organization to improve, 10
*Sesame Street* (TV), 143
SET (Study of Exceptional Talent) Mentor Program Center for Talented Youth, 540
Severe and multiple disabilities, 335–359
    biomedical dilemmas and, 350–356
        genetic engineering, 351–354, 351*f*
        genetic screening and counseling, 354–356, 463
        selective abortion, 356
        withholding medical treatment, 356
    causation, 340
    characteristics, 340–342
    definitions, **336**–340
        historical descriptions, 336–337
        IDEA, 337–340
        TASH, 337
    desired outcomes in inclusive settings, 341*t*
    educational supports and services, 342–350
        adolescent years, 348
        assessment, 342–343
        early childhood years, 343–346
        elementary school years, 346–348

college and, 91, 92, 93, 95, 98, 99t, 105, 198–200
communication disorders in, 323
emotional/behavioral disorders and, 257
giftedness and, 533
hearing loss and, 423
learning disabilities and, 189, 197–200
mental retardation and, 293, 294–297
parent and student involvement in, 96–97
physical disabilities and health disorders in, 487
secondary school's role in, 98–104
severe and multiple disabilities and, 348, 353
traumatic and acquired brain injury in, 395, 396
vision loss and, 461
Transportation, 13, 94
Trauma
birth, 288, 311, 371–372
mental retardation from, 288
spinal cord injury and, 480
Traumatic brain injury, 29t, 30, **31**, 385–406
causation, 390–391
characteristics, 388–390, 389t
definition, **386**–387
descriptors of severity, 392t
educational supports and services, 391–397
developing cognitive-communicative skills, 398t
issues and questions to address, 392–393
suggested school reintegration checklist, 396f
inclusion and, 394–395
medical and psychological services, 397–402
types of head injuries, 399–400
prevalence, 387, 388
Travel aids, visual loss and, 453–454
Treatment. See Interventions; *specific disabilities*
Trephining, 20
Triarchic theory of human intelligence, 518–519
Trisomy 21, **284**–285
Troubled Teen Advisor website, 229
Tuberous sclerosis, **286**
Tunnel vision, **444**
Tutoring
cross-age, **67**
peer, **67**
Twin studies, 183
Tympanic membrane, 409
Type I/II diabetes. See Diabetes mellitus

Undersocialized aggression, 242
United Cerebral Palsy Organization (UCP), 10
United Nations Salamanca Statement, 57

United Network for Organ Sharing, 354
United States, population growth by ethnic background in, 119–120f
U.S. Department of Education, National Longitudinal Transition Study, 93
U.S. Department of Justice, 13
U.S. FIRST (For Inspiration and Recognition of Science and Technology), 535
U.S. Supreme Court, 13
Universal design for learning (UDL), **82,** 83t
Universal health care, debate over, 255

Vaccine(s)
autism and, 361
rubella, 414
Vagus nerve stimulation (VNS), 494
Ventriculoperitoneal shunt, 479f
Verbalisms, **449**
Vermis, **371**, 372f
Vestibular mechanism, **410**
Videx Timewand, 375
Vinson, Ann, 50–51
Violence
firearm, 48, 391
gang membership and, 262
safe schools legislation and, 48–52
Vision
field of, 444, 445f
low, 444–445
tunnel, **444**
Vision loss, 441–469
age of onset and, 448
causation, 447–448
acquired disorders, 448
genetic disorders, 447–448
characteristics, 448–452
classification, 445–447
muscle disorders, 446
receptive eye problems, 446–447
refractive problems, **445**–446
deaf-blindness, 338–340, 338f, **339**
definitions, 444–445
educational supports and services, 452–459
assessment, 452
communication media, 456–458
instructional content, 454–456
in least restrictive environment, 458–459
mobility training and daily living skills, 452–454
inclusion and, 460–461
medical services, 459, 462–465
negative perceptions of people with, 442
prevalence, 447
severe and multiple disabilities and, 342
social services, 462, 465
warning signs of, 464t
Vision specialist, 459
Visual acuity, **444**, 462

Visual attention, 452
Visual capacity, 452
Visual cortex, **442**
Visual discrimination, **180**–181
Visual Efficient Scale, 452
Visualization, 514
Visual perception problems, 180–181
Visual process, 442–444
Visual-processing, assessment of, 452
Visual screening, 464
Vitamin A deficiency (xerophthalmia), 448
VNS. See Vagus nerve stimulation (VNS)
Vocational rehabilitation, 95–96, **108**
Vocational Rehabilitation Act, 11, 95–96. See also Section 504
Voice disorders, **328**–329, 329f
Voice problems, **282**
Volume, voice disorders involving, 329
Voting, 94

Watson, John, 19–20, 523
Weapons, student discipline for carrying, 51
Web-Braille, 441
Web resources, 22, 54–55, 88, 111, 134, 162–163, 204–205, 229, 268, 300, 332, 359, 382, 404, 429, 438, 468, 510–511, 548
Weihenmayer, Erik, 452f
Wheelchairs, 483
Whetstone, David, 50–51
Whole-language strategies, 192
Wild boy of Aveyon, 18
Williams syndrome, **285**
Wilson, Woodrow, 200
Word knowledge and word recognition, 175
Work experience program, 102
Work Incentives Improvement Act, 95, 96, 106
Wraparound approach (WRAP), 252, 258–259, **261,** 262
WRITE, P.L.E.A.S.E. learning strategy, 196
Writing
braille, 456
learning disabilities and, 176–177f
mirror, **176**
software for, 191
traumatic brain injury and, 397, 398t
vision loss and, 449
Wundt, Wilhelm, 19

Xerophthalmia, **448**

Young adults. See Adolescent(s); Adulthood; Transition to adult life, planning for

Zeltwanger, Tracy, 254
Zero-exclusion principle, **30**, 50–51, 108
Zero-tolerance, **48**–50
debate over, 50–51

# PHOTO CREDITS

## CHAPTER ONE
Page 2: (top) Richard Hutchings/PhotoEdit; (middle) Journal Courier/The Image Works; (bottom) Getty Images, Inc.–Taxi; p. 4: Margaret Suckley/Franklin D. Roosevelt Library; p. 6: Chuck Savage/Corbis/Bettmann; p. 8: (top row, left) Topham/The Image Works; (top row, center and right) Corbis/Bettmann; (middle row, left and center) AP/Wide World Photos; (middle row, right) Corbis/Bettmann; (bottom row, left) Corbis/Bettmann; (bottom row, center) Stephane Cardinale/Corbi/Sygma; (bottom row, right) AP/Wide World Photos; p. 12 (top) Jose Carrillo/PhotoEdit; (bottom) James Shaffer/PhotoEdit; p. 14: Corbis/Bettmann; p. 16: Ariel Skelley/Corbis/Bettmann; p. 19 Rob Lewine/Corbis/Bettmann.

## CHAPTER TWO
Page 24: (top and middle) Getty Images, Inc.–Taxi; (bottom) Will Hart; p. 31: Charles Gupton/Corbis/Bettmann; p. 32: Laura Dwight Photograhy; p. 38: Elizabeth Crews Photography; p. 47: AP/Wide World Photos; p. 50: Phil Mislinski/Getty Images, Inc.–Liason.

## CHAPTER THREE
Pge 56: (top) Michael Newman/PhotoEdit; (middle) Will Hart; (bottom) Laura Dwight/Corbis/Bettmann; p. 62: Michael Newman/PhotoEdit; p. 64: David Mager/Pearson Learning; p. 67: Ariel Skelley/Corbis Stock Market; p. 68: Ray Chernush/Getty Images Inc.–ImageBank; p. 69: Jonathan Nourok/PhotoEdit; p. 75: AP/Wide World Photos; p. 79: Tom Lindfors Photography; p. 83: Courtesy of Recording for the Blind and Dyslexic, Princeton, NJ.

## CHAPTER FOUR
Page 90: (top) Steven Rubin/The Image Works; (middle) Bob Rowan/Corbis/Bettmann; (bottom) Roy Morsch/Corbis/Bettmann; p. 98: Phil Martin/PhotoEdit; p. 102: Jose Luis Pelaez, Inc./Corbis/Bettmann; p. 108: Michael Newman/PhotoEdit.

## CHAPTER FIVE
Page 112: (top) Ed Bock/Corbis/Bettmann; (middle) Chuck Savage/Corbis/Bettmann; (bottom) Tom Stewart/Corbis/Bettmann; p. 114: EyeWire Collection/Getty Images–Photodisc; p. 116: David Young–Wolff/PhotoEdit; p. 118: Will Hart/Photo Edit; p. 123: Bob Daemmrich/The Image Works; p. 125: Jose Luis Pelaez, Inc./Corbis/Bettmann; p. 127: Elizabeth Crews Photography.

## CHAPTER SIX
Page 136: (top) George Shelley/Corbis/Bettmann; (middle) Michael Newman/PhotoEdit; (bottom) Comstock Royalty Free Division; p. 139: Spencer Grant/PhotoEdit; p. 143: (top and bottom) Courtesy of Emily Kingsley; p. 146: Rick Gomez/Corbis/Bettmann; p. 148: Laura Dwight/PhotoEdit; p. 149: Ron Chapple/Getty Images, Inc.–Taxi; p. 150: Cathy Melloan Resources/PhotoEdit; p. 151: Bob Daemmrich/Stock Boston; p. 152: Getty Images, Inc.–Photodisc; p. 153: Peter Byron/PhotoEdit; p. 159: A. Ramey/PhotoEdit.

## CHAPTER SEVEN
Page 164: (top) Bill Stanton/Rainbow; (middle) Jose Luis Pelaez/Corbis/Bettmann; (bottom) Creatas; p. 166: SW Productions/Getty Images, Inc.–Photodisc; p. 173: Science Photo Library/Photo Researchers, Inc.; p. 174: Mug Shots/Corbis/Bettmann; p. 179: Brian Smith, Photographer; pp. 184, 195: Will Hart.

## CHAPTER EIGHT
Page 206: (top) Creatas; (middle and bottom) Getty Images, Inc.–Photodisc; p. 208: Getty Images, Inc.–Stone Allstock; p. 217: (top) Michael Malyszko/Getty Images, Inc.–Taxi; (bottom) GeoStock/Getty Images, Inc.–Taxi; p. 218: Chip Henderson/Getty Images, Inc.–Stone Allstock.

## CHAPTER NINE
Page 230: (top) Tony Freeman/PhotoEdit; (middle) Creatas; (bottom) Getty Images, Inc.–Photodisc; p. 236: Maggie Leonard/Rainbow; p. 239: Express Newspapers/Getty Images, Inc.–Liaison; p. 240: Robert Harbison; p. 261: Tom Lindfors Photography.

## CHAPTER TEN
Page 270: (top) Dan McCoy/Rainbow; (middle) Stephen McBrady/PhotoEdit; (bottom) James Shaffer/PhotoEdit; p. 275: James Shaffer/PhotoEdit; p. 278: Richard Hutchings/PhotoEdit; p. 281: Stephen McBrady/PhotoEdit; p. 285: Lynn Johnson/Black Star; p. 288: George Steinmetz/San Francisco AIDS Foundation; p. 290: Dan McCoy/Rainbow; p. 295: Bob Rowan/Corbis/Bettmann.

## CHAPTER ELEVEN
Page 302: (top) Robin L. Sachs/PhotoEdit; (middle) Jose Luis Pelaez/Corbis/Bettmann; (bottom) Robert Brenner/PhotoEdit; p. 306: Tom Prettyman/PhotoEdit; p. 313: Michael Newman/PhotoEdit; p. 314: Courtesy of Norma Velez; p. 317: Robert Brenner/PhotoEdit; p. 319: Tom Lindfors Photography; p. 329: Mary Kate Denny/PhotoEdit.

## CHAPTER TWELVE
Page 334: (top) Cindy Charles/PhotoEdit; (middle) Dennis MacDonald/PhotoEdit; (bottom) AP/Wide World Photos; p. 338: Robin Sachs/PhotoEdit; p. 344: Eric Fowke/PhotoEdit; p. 345: David Young–Wolff/PhotoEdit; p. 347: Michael Newman/PhotoEdit; p. 351: Getty Images, Inc.–Taxi.

## CHAPTER THIRTEEN
Page 360: (top) Bill Aron/PhotoEdit; (middle and bottom) AP/Wide World Photos; p. 366: Jonathan Nourok/PhotoEdit; p. 370: Paul Conlin/PhotoEdit; pp 373, 379: Brian Smith, Photographer; p. 380: Michael Schwartz/Getty Images, Inc.–Liason.

## CHAPTER FOURTEEN
Page 384: (top) Myrleen Ferguson/PhotoEdit; (middle) Bob Daemmrich/Stock Boston; (bottom) AP/Wide World Photos; p. 388: Myrleen Ferguson/PhotoEdit; p. 391: Rick Wilking/Getty Images Inc.–Hulton Archive Photos; p. 397: Richard T. Nowitz/Corbis/Bettmann; p. 401: AP/Wide World Photos.

## CHAPTER FIFTEEN
Page 406: (top) Michael Newman/PhotoEdit; (middle) Getty Images, Inc.–Stone Allstock; (bottom) David Young–Wolff/PhotoEdit; p. 408: AP/Wide World Photos; p. 415: Larry Williams/Corbis/Bettmann; p. 418: AP/Wide World Photos; p. 427: Will Hart; p. 434: David Young–Wolff/PhotoEdit.

## CHAPTER SIXTEEN
Page 440: (top) Syracuse Newspapers/Chien Yi Hung/The Image Works; (middle) David Young–Wolff/PhotoEdit; (bottom) Robin Sachs/PhotoEdit; p. 450: David Young–Wolff/PhotoEdit; p. 452: Didrik Johnck/Corbis/Sygma; p. 453: David Young–Wolff/PhotoEdit; p. 454: Hank Morgan/Rainbow; p. 457: Robin Sachs/PhotoEdit; p. 464: Corbis Royalty Free.

## CHAPTER SEVENTEEN
Page 470: (top) Joshua Kristal/NEWSCOM; (middle) David Young–Wolff/PhotoEdit; (bottom) Tony Freeman/PhotoEdit; p. 475: Tom Stewart/Corbis/Bettmann; p. 481: Michael Fein/*The Boston Herald;* p. 483: (both) DEKA Research; p. 490: Will Hart; p. 495: Tony Freeman/PhotoEdit; p. 502: Michael Newman/PhotoEdit.

## CHAPTER EIGHTEEN
Page 512: (top) Corbis Royalty Free; (middle) Laura Dwight/PhotoEdit; (bottom) Tony Freeman/PhotoEdit; p. 516: Archives of the History of American Psychology; p. 522: (left and top right) David Young–Wolff/PhotoEdit; (bottom right) Li–Hua Lan/The Syracuse Newspapers/The Image Works; p. 527: Vladimir Sichov/SIPA Press; p. 530: Robert Ginn/PhotoEdit; p. 535: Rick Friedman/Corbis/Bettmann; p. 536: Rex Perry/AP/Wide World Photos; p. 541: Jillian Edelstein/Corbis/SABA Press Photos, Inc.; p. 542: David Budny/AP/Wide World Photos.

For #9 &10

See P 12,13,15